B 23

D0888681

袖珍漢英詞典

CHINESE - ENGLISH
POCKET DICTIONARY

吳景榮　沈壽源　黃鍾青　秦亞青　金莉　編

商務印書館

商務袖珍漢英詞典

編　　纂 ……	吳景榮　　沈壽源　　黃鐘青
	秦亞青　　金莉
顧　　問 ……	熊德輗
責任編輯 ……	劉秀英
出　　版 ……	商務印書館（香港）有限公司
	香港鰂魚涌芬尼街2號D僑英大廈
	中國對外翻譯出版公司
	北京西城區太平橋大街四號
排　　版 ……	外文出版社電腦照排室
印　　刷 ……	美雅印刷製本有限公司
	九龍官塘榮業街6號海濱工業大廈4樓A
版　　次 ……	1997年4月第1版
	1997年9月第2次印刷

© 1994　1997　商務印書館（香港）有限公司

ISBN 962 07 0166 6 （精裝本）

ISBN 962 07 0199 2 （平裝本）

Printed in Hong Kong

目　錄 (Contents)

編 者 的 話

　　本詞典是一本簡明實用的漢英對照雙語工具書，主要供外國讀者學習查檢中文和中國讀者學習查檢英文用，也是從事中英文雙語翻譯的必備工具書。全書共收單字條目 4,800 餘條，多字條目 24,000 餘條。所收條目包括字、詞、詞組、熟語、成語，並注重收錄新詞、新義和縮略語。除一般語匯外，還收了一些常用的文言詞語和專門術語。義項中附必要的例句或例語，力求新穎，同時還用英語加注必要的用法說明，不僅考慮到漢語讀者學習和使用英語的需要，而且也適合外國讀者學習和使用漢語的需要。

　　本詞典承何大基、關夏亭、陳抗諸人提供可貴意見、審閱修改，謹在此一併鳴謝。

EDITORS' NOTE

This dictionary is a concise and practical bilingual tool designed as an easy reference for the foreign reader learning Chinese and the Chinese reader learning English. It is also a handy tool for the Chinese-English translator.

Between the covers of this dictionary are collected over 4,800 single-character and 24,000 multiple-character entries, which encompass not only words and compound words but also idioms and set phrases. Special attention has been given to including new terms, new meanings and acronyms. Apart from everyday words and expressions, the dictionary also contains common classical Chinese expressions and scientific terms. Illustrative phrases and sentences, often samples of the latest development in meaning and usage, are provided wherever necessary and explanatory notes on usage are given in English in an effort to cater for the needs of both Chinese readers in learning and writing English and English readers who learn Chinese for practical use.

The compilers owe their sincere gratitude to Mr. He Daji and Ms. Guan Xiating of the China Translation and Publishing Corporation for their helpful comments on the manuscript and meticulous reading of the proof.

用 法 説 明

一、條目

1. 本詞典所收單字條目使用大字體，按部首排列。同部首的按筆畫數多少爲序，少的在前，多的在後。同筆畫數的按起筆筆形、(點)—(橫)∣(直)丿(撇)爲序，依次排列。起筆筆形相同的，按第二筆筆形排列，以下類推。一字多音的按音序分列。

2. 多字條目使用較小字體，外加魚尾括號，按第一個字分別列於單字條目之下。單字條目下所列的多字條目不止一條的，按第二字的筆畫數多少排列，少的在前，多的在後。

二、注音

1. 條目均用漢語拼音字母注音。

2. 輕聲字不標調號。

3. 兒化音在基本形式後面加"r"。

4. 多字條目的注音中，音節界限有可能混淆時加隔音號"'"，如：【昏暗】hūn'àn。

5. 專有名詞和姓氏的注音，第一個字母大寫。

三、釋義

1. 條目在注音後面用圓括號注明詞類，不同詞類用羅馬數字分開，分別釋義。

2. 多義詞條用 ❶ ❷ 等分列義項。

3. 修辭略語和學科略語均放在尖括號内。

4. 關於條目語法特徵的説明放在方括號内。

　　5.無對應英語的漢語特有名詞用斜體漢語拼音(不加調號)對譯。

　　6.必要時在釋義後舉例,例子放在冒號的後面。

四、爲了便利讀者使用,本詞典在前面提供部首檢字表、漢語拼音檢字表及略語表。本詞典的後面附有漢語拼音方案,漢語拼音聲母韵母和國際音標對照表,中國歷史年代簡表,中國各省、自治區、直轄市的名稱、簡稱及其人民政府所在地表,中國十二生肖表和國際時間計算表。

Guide to the Use of the Dictionary

I. Entries

1. The single-character entries are in larger type and are arranged to the order of radicals. Characters with the same radical are listed in the order of strokes, with more strokes coming after less strokes. Characters with the same number of strokes are listed according to the first stroke in the order of ﹑,—, ｜ and ﹁. Characters with the same first stroke are listed according to the second stroke, and the rest is arranged on the analogy of this. A polyphonic character is listed separately in the order of the tone.

2. Multiple-character entries are given in smaller type with the black brackets and arranged under their respective single-character entries. More than one multiple-character entries under a single-character entry are listed according to the number of strokes of the second character with less strokes coming before more strokes.

II. Phonetics

1. The Mandarin (standard Chinese) pronunciation of each entry is indicated in symbols of the Chinese phonetic alphabet (*pinyin*), usually with the tone marked.

2. No tonal mark is used for the light tone.

3. The retroflexion of an end vowel is indicated by the addition of "r" to the phonetic form of the character.

4. An apostrophe is used, where necessary, to indicate the

syllabic division in the phonetic transcription of a multiple-character entry, e.g., 【昏暗】hūn'àn.

5. The first letter of the phonetic transcription is capitalized in the case of a proper noun or family name.

Ⅲ. Definitions

1. The part of speech of an entry is indicated in round parentheses following the transcription. If the entry can be classified under more than one part of speech, they are labelled separately after Roman numerals and defined separately.

2. If an entry has two or more different meanings, they are listed separately and introduced by white Arabic numerals in black circles: ❶ ❷ ⋯

3. Abbreviations for style distinction and for special fields of work are provided in angle brackets.

4. Explanatory notes on grammatical features are given in square brackets.

5. Special Chinese terms with no English equivalents are transliterated in *pinyin* (without tonal indications) in italics.

6. Where necessary, an illustrative example is offered following the definition and introduced by a colon.

Ⅳ. For the benefit of the user, a radical index, a Chinece phonetic alphabet index and a list of abbreviations used in the dictionary are provided preceding the body of the dictionary. Appendices include a) the scheme for the Chinese phonetic alphabet; b) the consonants and vowels of the Chinese phonetic alphabet and their corresponding international phonetic symbols; c) a brief Chinese chronology; d) names and abbreviations of China's provinces, autonomous regions and municipalities directly under the central government and their seats of the people's government; e) the Chinese zodiac; and f) an international time calculator.

部首檢字表

(一) 部首目錄

西	783	青	828	飛	844	鬯	860	黃	867	鼻	871
釆	787	非	830	食	845	鬼	860	黍	868	齊	871
里	787	**九畫**		首	848	**十一畫**		黑	868	**十五畫**	
八畫		面	830	香	849	魚	861	**十三畫**		齒	872
金	790	革	832	**十畫**		鳥	863	黽	870	**十六畫以上**	
長	800	韋	833	馬	850	鹵	865	鼎	870	龍	872
門	801	韭	833	骨	855	鹿	865	鼓	870	龜	873
阜	809	音	833	高	856	麥	866	鼠	871		
隸	818	頁	834	髟	858	麻	866	**十四畫**			
隹	818	風	842	鬥	859	**十二畫**					
雨	823										

(二)　檢字表

一部		丘	23	**丿部**		**乙部**		**二部**		亨	38
		五畫以上				乙	30	二	34	亭	38
一	1	丞	23	**一至三畫**		九	30	于	34	京	38
一至二畫		並	24	乃	28	也	30	亓井	34	亳	38
丁	7	**丨部**		久	28	乞	30	五	34	亮	38
七	7			之	28	乳	30	互	35		
三	7	丫	24	**四至五畫**		乾	31	亞	35	**人部**	
下	8	丰	24	乏	28	亂	32	些	35		
丈	11	中	24	乎	29					人	38
上	11		26	乍	29	**亅部**		**亠部**		**二畫**	
三至四畫		串	26	丟	29					仄	41
丏	14	**丶部**		乒	29	了	32	亡	35	以	41
不	14			乓	29	予	33	亢	36	今	42
丑	22	丸	26	**七畫以上**		事	33	交	36	介	42
丙	22	丹	26	乖	29					仁	42
世	23	主	26	乘	29					什	43
且	23									仆	43
										仇	43

悅	294	慨	299	憂	304	懸	308	扃	314	折	323
悖	294	惻	299	慼	305	懺	309	扈	314		324
悚	294	惺	299	慰	305	懾	309	扉	314	扳	324
悟	294	愕	299	慮	305	懼	309			抓	324
悄	294	愣	299	慾	305	戀	309	**手部**		承	325
悍	294	愠	299	慫	305					**五畫**	
悔	295	復	299			**十二畫**		手	314	拌	325
悛	295	惶	299	**十二畫**		**戈部**		才	316	拉	325
患	295	惱	300	憧	305			**一至三畫**			326
悉	295	慈	300	憐	305	戈	309	扎	316	挂	326
悠	295	惹	300	憎	305	**二至四畫**		打	316	抨	326
您	295	想	300	憤	306	戊	309	扔	318	抹	326
		感	301	憫	306	戎	309	扒	318	拒	326
八畫		愚	301	憬	306	成	309	扛	318	拔	326
惋	295	愛	301	憒	306	戒	310	扣	318	拓	327
悴	295	愈	301	憔	306	我	311	扦	318	抵	327
惦	295	愁	302	憑	306	或	311	托	318	拂	327
情	295			憨	306	**七畫以上**				披	327
悵	296	**十畫**		憩	306	戚	311	**四畫**		招	327
惜	296	慌	302	憊	306	戟	311	抖	319	押	328
悼	296	慄	302			戝	311	抗	319	抻	328
惆	296	慎	303	**十三畫**		截	311	扶	319	抽	328
惕	296	慍	303	憶	306	戮	311	技	320	拐	329
悸	296	愴	303	憧	306	戰	311	找	320	拈	329
惘	296	愧	303	憾	306	戲	312	抵	320	拙	329
惟	296	態	303	懈	306	戴	312	抒	320	拇	329
悲	297			懊	306	戳	312	抉	320	拎	329
惠	297	**十一畫**		應	306			扭	320	拖	329
惡	297	慷	303			**戶部**		把	321	拆	330
	298	慚	303	懇	307			抄	321	抱	330
惑	298	慳	303			**戶部**		扯	321	拘	330
悶	298	慢	304	**十四畫**		戶	313	批	322	拍	331
		慣	304	**以上**		房	313	扮	322	抵	331
九畫		慘	304	懦	307	戾	313	抛	322	拆	331
意	298	慶	304	懲	308	所	313	投	322	拗	332
惇	299	慧	304	懷	308	扁	314	抑	323	拜	332
愜	299	慕	304	懶	308	扇	314				
惰	299			懵	308						

溺	475	澈	482	潰	486	炳	489	煦	499	爐	503
滑	475	澇	482	濾	486	炯	489	煞	499	爆	503
溫	476	潔	482	濺	486	炸	489	**十畫**		爍	503
滔	476	澆	482	澤	486	炮	489	熔	499	爐	503
溪	476	澎	482	瀏	486	炭	489	煽	499	爛	503
滄	476	潭	482	**十六畫**		**六畫**		熒	499		
準	476	潮	482	**以上**		烤	489	熘	499	**爪部**	
溜	477	潸	483	瀚	486	烘	489	熄	499		
溴	477	潜	483	瀝	486	烙	490	熙	499	爪	504
滕	477	潤	483	瀕	486	烈	490	熏	499	爭	504
十一畫		澗	483	瀟	486	烏	490	熊	499	爬	504
演	477	潺	483	瀾	486	**七畫**		**十一畫**		爲	504
滴	477	澄	483	灌	487	烹	490	熟	499		505
滸	478	潑	484	瀰	487	烯	490	熵	500	爵	505
漉	478	潰	484	灘	487	焊	490	熬	500		
滾	478	潘	484	灣	487	烽	490	熱	500	**父部**	
滬	478	澤	484	**十三畫**		**八畫**		熨	501		
漾	478	澱	484	**火部**		焙	491	**十二畫**		父	505
潰	478	澡	484			焰	491	燙	501	爸	505
漸	478	澤	484	火	487	煮	491	熾	501	爹	505
漱	478	濃	484	**二至三畫**		焚	491	燉	501	爺	505
漂	478	濁	484	灰	488	無	491	燧	502		
漢	478	激	484	灼	488	然	496	燒	502	**爻部**	
滿	479	澳	485	灸	488	焦	496	燎	502		
漚	480	**十四畫**		災	488	**九畫**		燜	502	爽	506
滯	480	濱	485	**四畫**		煎	496	燈	502	爾	506
漆	480	濠	485	炕	488	煸	496	燃	502		
漲	480	濟	485	炎	488	煉	496	燕	502	**爿部**	
漏	481	濤	485	炔	488	煙	496	**十三畫**			
漠	481	濫	485	炒	488	煤	497	營	502	牀	506
漫	481	澀	485	炊	488	煳	497	燦	503	牆	506
漁	481	濕	486	炙	488	煩	497	燥	503		
滌	482	濛	486	**五畫**		煨	498	燭	503	**片部**	
滲	482	**十五畫**		炫	488	煌	498	燴	503		
漿	482	瀉	486	炬	489	煥	498	**十四畫**			
十二畫						照	498	**以上**			

腴 644
脾 644

九畫

腰 644
腱 644
腿 644
腸 644
腮 644
腥 644
腭 644
腳 644
腫 645
腹 645
腺 645
腦 645

十畫

膏 645
膂 645
膀 645
膊 646
膈 646

十一畫

膚 646
膘 646
膜 646
膝 646
膠 646
腔 646

十二畫

膳 646
膩 646
膨 646

十三畫

膺 646
臀 646
臂 647

臆 647
臃 647
膿 647
臊 647
臉 647
膾 647
膽 647

**十四畫
以上**

臍 647
臘 648
臟 648

臣部

臣 648
臥 648
臧 648
臨 648

自部

自 649
臭 651

至部

至 652
致 652
臺 652
臻 653

臼部

臼 653
臾 653
舂 653
與 653
舅 653
興 654
舉 654
舊 655

舌部

舌 655
舍 655
舐 655
舒 656
舔 656
舖 656

舛部

舜 656
舞 656

舟部

舟 656

三至五畫

舢 656
舫 656
航 656
般 657

舵 657
舷 657
舸 657
船 657
舶 657

七畫以上

艄 657
艇 657
艘 657
艙 657
艦 657

艮部

良 658
艱 658

色部

色 658
659
艷 659

艸部

二至三畫

艾 659
芒 659
芋 659
芍 659

四畫

芳 659
芯 659
芙 659
芫 659
芸 659
芽 659
芭 659
芮 659
芬 660
芥 660
花 660
芹 661
芻 661

五畫

范 661
苧 661
茉 661
苣 661
苛 661
苯 661
苦 661
若 662
茂 662
茅 662
茄 662
苫 663
苜 663
苗 663
英 663
茁 663
苞 663
苟 663
苔 664

六畫

茫 664
茭 664
荒 664
荆 664
茸 664
茜 664
茬 664
荔 664
草 664
茵 665
茴 665
茶 665
荀 665
荏 665

七畫

莘 665
莢 665
莖 666
莫 666
莧 666
莊 666
莠 666
莓 666
荷、 666
莜 667

八畫

萍 667
菠 667
菩 667
菁 667
華 667
菱 667
著 667
萁 667
萊 667
萘 667
萌 667
菌 667

	668	蒼	673	齊	676	虞	680	蛛	682	**十一畫**	
菲	668	蒯	673	藉	676	虜	680	**七畫**		蟄	683
菜	668	蓬	673	藍	676	虧	680	蜇	682	蟑	684
萎	668	蓓	673	藏	676			蜃	682	蟀	684
菊	668	蒐	674	薩	676	**虫部**		蛻	682	蟎	684
萄	668	**十一畫**		貌	676			蜈	682	螳	684
菇	668	蔗	674	**十五畫**		**二至三畫**		蜊	682	螻	684
九畫		蔦	674	藩	676	虱	681	蜉	682	螺	684
落	668	蔚	674	藕	676	虹	681	蛾	682	蟈	684
蒂	669	蔭	674	藝	676	虹	681	蜂	682	蟋	684
菫	669	蔓	674	藤	677	虼	681	蜀	682	**十二畫**	
葫	669	蔑	674	藥	677	**四畫**		**八畫**		蟯	684
葉	669	蔣	674	**十六畫**		蚤	681	蜜	682	蟬	684
葬	670	蔡	674	藻	677	蚊	681	蜿	682	蟲	684
葦	670	**十二畫**		藹	677	蚜	681	蜣	682	蟠	684
葵	670	蕩	674	蘑	677	蚋	681	蜻	682	**十三畫**	
萬	670	蕊	674	蘆	677	蚍	681	蜥	682	蟻	684
萼	671	蕨	674	蘋	677	蚌	681	蜘	682	蠅	684
蒿	671	蕁	674	蘇	677	**五畫**		蜚	682	蠍	684
葛	671	蔬	674	蘊	677	蛋	681	蝕	683	蟾	684
董	671	蔽	674	**十七畫**		蛇	681	**九畫**		蟹	684
葡	671	蕉	674	**以上**		蛀	681	蝙	683	**十四畫**	
蔥	671	蕎	675	蘭	678	蚶	681	蝴	683	蠻	684
葆	671	蕉	675	蘸	678	蛆	681	蝶	683	蠐	684
十畫		**十三畫**		蘿	678	蚰	681	蝦	683	蠑	684
蒲	671	薄	675			蚱	681	蝎	683	蠕	685
蔆	671	薪	675	**虍部**		蚯	681	蝸	683	**十五畫**	
蓑	672	薦	675			**六畫**		蝮	683	**以上**	
蒺	672	薔	675	虎	678	蛟	681	蝌	683	蠹	685
蓆	672	薑	675	虐	678	蛙	681	蝗	683	蠟	685
蓄	672	薔	675	虔	678	蛭	681	**十畫**		蠢	685
蒙	672	薯	675	虛	678	蛐	681	螢	683	蠶	685
蒜	673	薈	676	處	679	蛔	681	融	683	蠻	685
蓮	673	薛	676	號	679	蛤	681	螃	683	蠷	685
蓋	673	**十四畫**			680		682	螞	683	蠼	685
蒸	673										

閣	807	除	812	**佳部**		需	826	**面部**	**音部**
闊	808	**八畫**				震	826		
闌	808	陪	813	**二至五畫**		霄	826	面	830	音	833
十畫以上		陳	813	隻	818	霆	826	靦	832	韻	834
闕	808	陸	813	雀	818	霉	826			響	834
闖	808	陵	813	雅	819	霎	826	**革部**		
闔	808	陰	814	雁	819	霖	826			**頁部**
闐	808	陲	814	雄	819	霏	827	革	832	
關	808	陶	814	集	819	霍	827	**四至六畫**		頁	834
闡	808	陷	814	雍	820	霓	827	靶	832	**二至四畫**
闢	809	**九畫**		雎	820	**九畫以上**		靴	832	頂	834
		隊	815	雋	820	霜	827	靳	832	頃	835
阜部		隋	815	**六畫以上**		霞	827	鞏	832	項	835
		陽	815	雌	820	霧	827	鞍	832	順	835
阜	809	階	815	雕	820	霸	827	鞋	832	須	836
三至四畫		隆	815	雖	820	霹	827	**七畫以上**		頑	836
阡	809	隍	815	雜	820	露	827	鞘	832	頓	836
防	809	**十畫以上**		雛	821	靄	828	鞠	832	預	836
阱	809	隘	815	雙	821	靈	828	鞣	833	頌	837
阮	809	隔	816	離	821			鞦	833	頒	837
五至六畫		隕	816	難	822	**青部**		鞭	833	頗	837
陀	809	隗	816	雞	823					領	837
阿	810	障	816			青	828	**韋部**		**五至七畫**
阻	810	隙	816	**雨部**		靖	829			頤	837
附	810	際	816			靚	829	韋	833	頜	837
陋	811	隧	816	雨	823	靛	829	韌	833	頰	838
陌	811	隨	816	**三至五畫**		靜	829	韓	833	頷	838
限	811	險	817	雪	823			韜	833	頭	838
降	811	隱	818	雲	823	**非部**				頹	839
七畫		隴	818	電	824			**韭部**		頸	839
院	812			雷	825	非	830			頻	839
陣	812	**隶部**		零	825	靠	830	韭	833	頰	839
陡	812			雹	826	靡	830			頰	839
陜	812	隸	818	**六至八畫**						**八至十畫**
陛	812									

顴 840
額 840
顏 840
趣 840
顎 840
頦 840
顛 840
願 841

十二畫以上

顧 841
顥 841
顫 841
顰 842
顳 842
顴 842
顙 842
顱 842

風部

風 842
颭 844
颮 844
颶 844
飄 844
颼 844

飛部

飛 844

食部

食 845

二至五畫

飢 845
飭 845
飲 845
飯 845
飼 846
飾 846
飽 846
飴 846

六至七畫

養 846
餃 847
餅 847
餌 847
餐 847
餞 847
餘 847
餓 848

八至九畫

館 848
餞 848
餛 848
餚 848
餡 848
餿 848

十畫以上

饉 848
饉 848
饅 848
饒 848
饋 848
饑 848
饞 848

首部

首 848

香部

香 849
馥 850

馬部

馬 850

二至四畫

馮 851
馭 851
馱 851
馳 851
馴 851
駁 851

五至七畫

駝 852
駐 852
駛 852
駒 852
駙 852
駕 852
駭 852
駱 852
騁 852
駿 852

八至十一畫

騎 852

騙 853
驃 853
騷 853
騰 853
驅 853
驟 853
驀 853

十二畫以上

驍 853
驕 853
驛 854
駿 854
驚 854
驟 855
驢 855
驤 855

骨部

骨 855
骯 855
骷 855
骸 855
骼 855
骾 855
髀 855
髑 856
髏 856
體 856

高部

高 856

八至十一畫

彭部

髮 858
髯 858
髻 858
髭 858
鬃 858
鬍 858
鬆 858
鬚 859
鬢 859
鬢 859

鬥部

鬧 859
鬩 859
鬮 860

鬯部

鬱 860

鬼部

鬼 860
魂 861
魁 861
魄 861
魅 861
魏 861
魍 861
魔 861

魚部

魚 861

四至六畫

魷 862
魯 862
鮮 862
鮁 862
鮎 862
鮑 862
鮊 862
鮮 862
鮭 862

七至九畫

鯊 862
鯽 862
鯉 862
鯨 862
鯖 862
鯢 862
鯤 862
鰈 862
鰓 863

十至十一畫

鰟 863
鰱 863
鰭 863
鰣 863
鰷 863
鱈 863
鱗 863

漢語拼音檢字表

		癌	538			槾	696	
		壋	544	**àn**		**ào**		**bà**
A				岸	253			壩 194
		ǎi		按	332	傲	71	把 321
ā		噯 171		暗	392	坳	183	爸 505
		矮 560		案	412	奧	209	罷 621
啊 162		藹 677		黯	870	懊	332	耙 631
腌 644		靄 828				拗	332	霸 827
阿 810		**ài**		**āng**		澳	485	鮁 862
á		唉 160		骯	855			**ba**
啊 162		嗳 171		**áng**		**B**		吧 149
ǎ		嫒 220		昂	386			**bāi**
啊 162		愛 301		**àng**		**bā**		掰 347
à		暖 395		盎	546	八	85	**bái**
啊 162		礙 566		**āo**		叭	141	白 541
a		艾 659		凹	96	吧	149	**bǎi**
啊 162		隘 815		熬	500	巴	258	佰 56
āi		**ān**		**áo**		扒	318	捭 346
		安 225		嗷	168	捌	337	擺 362
哀 155		庵 268		敖	370	疤	535	柏 411
哎 156		氨 444		熬	500	笆	585	百 542
唉 160		諳 719		翱	626	芭	659	**bài**
埃 184		鞍 832		遨	776	**bá**		拜 332
挨 338		鵪 864		鏖	797	拔	326	敗 371
		ǎn		**ǎo**		跋	743	稗 575
ái		俺 63		媪	219	**bǎ**		
呆 148		銨 792		襖		把	321	**bǎng**
挨 339				靿	832	靶	832	榜 421

bān		**bàn**	
扳	324	伴	48
搬	353	半	124
斑	377	扮	322
瘢	518	拌	325
癍	538	瓣	523
斑	538	絆	603
般	657	辦	756
頒	837		
bǎn		**bāng**	
坂	182	幫	262
板	409	梆	416
版	507	邦	781

绑 608	暴 394	锛 795	妣 214	编 612	**biào**
膀 645	爆 503	**běn**	彼 278	編 683	鳔 863
bàng	豹 728	本 404	比 440	边 780	**biē**
傍 70	鉋 792	畚 531	秕 573	鞭 833	憋 306
棒 417	鲍 862	苯 661	笔 586	鯿 862	瘪 539
磅 564	**bēi**	**bèn**	鄙 783	**biǎn**	鳖 863
蚌 681	卑 126	奔 207	**bì**	匾 122	**bié**
谤 720	悲 297	笨 585	哔 169	扁 314	别 103
镑 796	杯 408	**bēng**	壁 192	褊 695	蹩 746
bāo	碑 564	嘣 169	婢 218	贬 729	**biě**
剥 109	背 639	崩 254	币 262	**biàn**	瘪 539
包 119	**běi**	绷 615	庇 267	便 57	**biè**
孢 222	北 121	**béng**	弊 271	卞 127	别 104
炮 489	**bèi**	甭 528	弼 274	弁 271	**bīn**
胞 640	倍 62	**běng**	必 286	忭 288	傧 75
苞 663	备 70	绷 615	復 299	辨 618	彬 277
褒 695	悖 294	**bèng**	敝 373	变 724	滨 485
鲍 872	惫 306	泵 459	毙 375	辨 756	濒 486
báo	焙 491	绷 615	愍 441	辩 757	缤 618
薄 675	背 639	蹦 746	滗 484	遍 770	宾 733
雹 826	蓓 673	迸 760	壁 522	**biāo**	**bìn**
bǎo	被 696	**bī**	毕 531	彪 277	摈 360
保 59	褙 696	逼 771	碧 564	标 422	殡 438
堡 189	贝 728	**bí**	秘 573	膘 646	鬓 859
宝 237	辈 752	荸 665	笓 591	镖 798	**bīng**
葆 671	钡 794	鼻 871	臂 647	鑣 799	兵 87
饱 846	**bei**	**bǐ**	蓖 674	飙 844	冰 92
鸨 864	呗 159	匕 121	蔽 674	**biǎo**	槟 428
bào	**bēn**		裨 695	婊 218	
报 187	奔 207		辟 755	表 690	
抱 330	贲 731		避 778	裱 695	
			闭 803	镖 794	
			陛 812		
			biān		
			编 496		

bǐng		cā		càn		cén		杈 407
	薄 675							杈 689
丙 22	鈹 792	嚓 171	燦 503	岑 252		詫 710
屏 249	駁 851	擦 361	粲 595			chāi
柄 410	bǒ		cāi	cāng		céng	
炳 489	簸 592	猜 513		層 250	差 257
稟 569	跛 743		cái	倉 62	曾 397	拆 331
秉 572		才 316	滄 476		釵 791
餅 847	bò	材 407	艙 657	cèng	
	擘 360	纔 619	蒼 673	蹭 746	chái
bìng	簸 593	裁 692			柴 415
並 24	薄 675	財 729	cáng	chā	豺 728
併 54			藏 676	叉 133	
病 535	bo	cǎi		喳 165	chān
	膊 646	彩 277	cāo	差 257	攙 363
bō		採 344	操 359	插 350	
剝 109	bǔ	睬 557	糙 597	杈 407	chán
撥 356	卜 127	踩 745			嬋 219
播 358	哺 158		cáo	chá	孱 223
波 456	堡 189	cài	嘈 168	叉 133	潺 483
玻 518	捕 336	菜 668	曹 397	察 235	禪 570
菠 667	補 693	蔡 674	槽 422	搽 351	蟬 618
鉢 792				查 411	蟾 684
	bù	cān	cǎo	楂 420	蟾 684
bó	不 14		草 664	碴 564	讒 725
伯 52	佈 49	cān		茬 664	饞 848
勃 114	埠 185	參 132	cè	茶 665	
博 127	布 259	餐 847	側 69		chǎn
帛 260	怖 289		冊 90	chǎ	產 526
搏 351	步 434	cán	廁 223	叉 133	諂 718
泊 458	簿 592	慚 303	惻 299		鏟 797
渤 472	部 782	殘 437	測 474	chà	闡 808
箔 589		蠶 685	策 586	剎 108	
脖 643	C			姹 216	chàn
膊 646		cǎn	cēn	岔 252	懺 309
舶 657		慘 304	參 133	差 257	顫 841

chāng

娼 218
昌 385
猖 514

cháng

償 76
賞 168
場 188
嫦 219
常 260
腸 644
長 800

chǎng

場 188
廠 270
敞 373
氅 443

chàng

倡 64
唱 162
悵 296
暢 393

chāo

剿 111
吵 149
抄 321
綽 610
超 741
鈔 791

cháo

嘲 170
巢 255
晁 390
朝 402
潮 482

chǎo

吵 149
炒 488

chē

車 748

chě

扯 322

chè

徹 283
掣 346
撤 355
澈 482

chēn

嗔 167
抻 328

chén

塵 190
忱 288
晨 390
橙 426
沉 450
臣 648
辰 757
陳 813

chèn

稱 576
櫬 697
趁 741

chēng

撐 357
瞠 558
稱 576
蟶 684
鐺 799

chéng

丞 23
乘 29
呈 149
城 183
懲 308
成 309
承 325
橙 426
澄 483
盛 546
程 575
誠 711

chěng

逞 767
騁 852

chèng

秤 574

chī

吃 144
嗤 167
痴 537
笞 586

chí

匙 121
弛 273
持 333
池 449
踟 745
遲 777
馳 851

chǐ

侈 56
尺 247
恥 293
褫 696
齒 872

chì

叱 141
敕 371
斥 378
熾 501
翅 626
赤 738
飭 845

chōng

充 77
仲 288
憧 305
沖 452
舂 653
衝 688

chóng

崇 253
种 573
蟲 684
重 788

chǒng

寵 237

chòng

衝 689

chōu

抽 328

chóu

仇 43
惆 296
愁 302
疇 534
稠 575
籌 593
綢 611
躊 746
酬 785

chǒu

丑 22
醜 786

chòu

臭 651

chū

出 96
初 102
齣 872

chú

廚 269
櫥 428
鋤 661
鉏 794
除 812
雛 821

chǔ

儲 75
楚 420
礎 566
處 679

chù

怵 289
畜 530
矗 558
絀 604
處 679
觸 704
黜 869

chuāi

揣 349

chuǎi

揣 349

chuài

踹 746

chuān

川 255
穿 579

chuán			
傳	71	搥	345
椽	420	槌	420
船	657	錘	795
		陲	814

chuán

傳 71
椽 420
船 657

chuǎn

喘 166
舛 656

chuàn

串 26
釧 791

chuāng

創 110
瘡 538
窗 581

chuáng

幢 262
牀 506

chuǎng

闖 808

chuàng

創 110
愴 303

chuī

吹 150
炊 488

chuí

垂 183

搥 345
槌 420
錘 795
陲 814

chūn

春 387
椿 420

chún

脣 158
淳 466
純 601
醇 786

chǔn

蠢 685

chuō

戳 312

chuò

啜 162
綽 610
輟 752

cī

呲 157
疵 536

cí

慈 300
瓷 523
磁 564
祠 568
詞 709

辭 756
雌 820

cǐ

此 433

cì

伺 50
刺 105
次 429
賜 735

cōng

從 281
忽 291
樅 424
聰 634
蔥 671

cóng

叢 137
從 281
淙 466

còu

湊 472

cū

粗 594

cú

徂 279
殂 437

cù

促 60

猝 513
簇 591
蹴 746
醋 786

cuān

汆 448
躥 747
鑹 799

cuàn

竄 582
篡 591

cuī

催 73
崔 254
摧 355

cuì

啐 161
悴 295
淬 467
瘁 537
粹 595
翠 626
脆 641

cūn

村 407

cún

存 221

cǔn

忖 287

---

cùn

寸 237

cuō

搓 347
撮 357
磋 564
蹉 745

cuó

嵯 254

cuò

挫 338
措 342
錯 794

D

dā

嗒 167
搭 351
答 587
耷 632

dá

怛 290
打 316
查 454
答 588
達 771

dǎ

打 316

---

dà

大 198

dāi

呆 148
待 279

dǎi

傣 70
歹 436
逮 768

dài

代 44
大 201
岱 253
帶 260
待 279
怠 292
戴 312
殆 437
袋 692
貸 732
逮 768

dān

丹 26
單 165
擔 360
殫 438
眈 552
耽 632

dǎn

撣 357

膽 647	蹈 746	**dī**	**diān**	弔 273	訂 706
dàn	**dào**	低 52	巔 254	掉 343	釘 791
但 50	倒 64	堤 188	掂 341	調 718	錠 794
彈 275	到 106	提 347	滇 475	釣 791	**diū**
擔 360	悼 296	滴 477	癲 539	**diē**	丟 29
旦 383	盜 546	**dí**	顛 840	爹 505	**dōng**
氮 446	稻 577	嘀 168	**diǎn**	跌 743	冬 92
淡 468	道 771	嫡 219	典 89	**dié**	東 407
蛋 681	**dé**	敵 373	碘 564	喋 165	**dǒng**
誕 715	得 280	滌 482	踮 745	堞 188	懂 306
dāng	德 283	狄 511	點 869	牒 507	董 671
當 532	**de**	的 544	**diàn**	疊 534	**dòng**
襠 696	地 180	笛 586	佃 50	碟 564	侗 56
鐺 799	得 281	羅 598	墊 190	蝶 683	凍 94
dǎng	的 543	迪 759	奠 208	諜 719	動 116
擋 359	**děi**	**dǐ**	店 267	迭 759	恫 293
黨 869	得 281	底 267	惦 295	鰈 862	棟 418
dàng	**dēng**	抵 331	殿 439	**dīng**	洞 460
檔 427	燈 502	砥 562	淀 466	丁 7	**dōu**
當 533	登 539	詆 710	澱 484	叮 140	兜 81
蕩 674	**děng**	邸 781	玷 518	疔 535	都 782
dāo	戥 311	**dì**	電 824	町 549	**dǒu**
刀 99	等 586	地 180	錠 829	酊 783	抖 319
叨 141	**dèng**	帝 260	**diāo**	釘 791	斗 377
dǎo	凳 96	弟 273	凋 95	**dǐng**	陡 812
倒 63	澄 483	的 544	刁 99	頂 834	**dòu**
導 241	瞪 558	第 586	叼 141	鼎 870	痘 536
島 253	磴 566	締 612	碉 564	**dìng**	豆 726
搗 353	鄧 783	蒂 669	貂 728	定 227	逗 763
禱 571		諦 719	雕 820	碇 563	
		遞 775	**diào**	腚 643	
			吊 144		

鬥	859			掇	342	訛	708	耳	632	**fán**
dū		**duàn**		裰	695	額	840	餌	847	
		斷	379			鵝	864			凡 95
嘟	168	段	438	**duó**				**èr**		樊 424
督	556	緞	614	奪	209	**ě**				煩 497
都	782	鍛	796	度	268	噁	170	二	34	蹯 566
				踱	745			貳	731	繁 614
dú		**duī**				**è**				
毒	440	堆	185	**duǒ**		厄	130	**F**		**fǎn**
瀆	486			垛	184	呃	149			反 133
犢	511	**duì**		朵	406	噩	170	**fā**		返 759
獨	514	兌	80	躲	748	惡	297			
讀	724	對	240			愕	299	發	539	**fàn**
髑	856	隊	815	**duò**		扼	320			梵 416
黷	870			剁	106	腭	644	**fá**		泛 452
		dūn		垛	184	萼	671	乏	28	犯 511
dǔ		噸	170	墮	191	軛	749	伐	46	範 591
堵	185	墩	191	惰	299	遏	774	筏	588	范 661
睹	556	敦	372	舵	657	鄂	782	罰	621	販 730
篤	591	蹲	746	跺	744	顎	848	閥	807	飯 845
肚	638			馱	851	餓	848			
賭	735	**dǔn**				鱷	863	**fǎ**		**fāng**
		盹	552	**E**		鶚	864	法	454	妨 213
dù								砝	561	方 380
妒	214	**dùn**		**ē**		**ēn**				芳 659
度	267	囤	175			恩	294	**fà**		
杜	407	燉	501	婀	218			琺	518	**fáng**
渡	472	盾	554	屙	250	**èn**		髮	858	坊 181
肚	638	遁	774	阿	810	摁	352			妨 213
蠹	685	鈍	791					**fān**		房 313
鍍	796	頓	836	**é**		**ér**		帆	259	防 809
				俄	62	兒	81	幡	382	
duān		**duō**		娥	217	而	630	番	532	**fǎng**
端	584	咄	152	峨	253			翻	627	仿 45
duǎn		哆	157	蛾	682	**ěr**		藩	676	紡 601
短	559	多	196			爾	506			舫 656

訪	707	吩	149	**fěng**		輻	752

G

肝	638

fàng

氛	444
紛	602
芬	660

gǎn

放	368

諷	720

fèng

gā

感	301
擀	359
敢	371
桿	416
橄	424
稈	575
趕	742

fēi

酚	784

俸	62
奉	206
縫	614
鳳	864

咖	152
嘎	169
夾	205
旮	384
胳	641

fén

妃	211
扉	314
緋	611
菲	668
霏	682
非	830
飛	844

墳	191
焚	491

fó

佛	49

gàn

fěn

幹	265
紺	603
贛	737

gāi

粉	594

fǒu

該	710

fèn

否	148

gǎi

féi

份	46
分	102
奮	209
憤	305
糞	598

fū

改	367

gāng

肥	638
腓	644

夫	203
孵	223
敷	374
膚	646
麩	866

gài

剛	108
岡	253
綱	611
缸	619
肛	638
鋼	795

丐	14
概	420
溉	474
蓋	673
鈣	791

fěi

匪	122
斐	377
翡	626
菲	668
誹	717

fēng

丰	24
封	237
峰	253
楓	420
烽	490
瘋	538
蜂	682
豐	726
鋒	794
風	842

fú

伏	46
俘	61
輻	261
扶	319
拂	327
服	401
浮	464
福	570
符	586
芙	659
蜉	682

gān

gǎng

崗	254
港	473

乾	31
坩	183
尷	247
干	262
杆	407
柑	410
泔	455
甘	523
矸	561
竿	585

gàng

槓	421

fèi

吠	149
廢	269
沸	455
狒	512
痱	537
肺	638
費	731

gāo

皋	557
篙	591
糕	597
羔	623

fēn

féng

縫	614
逢	768
馮	851

副	110
富	218
復	233
復	282
服	401
父	505
縛	614
腹	645
蝮	683
複	696
覆	698
訃	706
負	728
賦	735
赴	739
阜	809
附	810
馥	850
駙	852

fù

分	100

fèng

俯	62
府	267
撫	358
斧	378
甫	528
脯	643
腐	643
輔	751
釜	791

fǔ

付	44
傅	70

膏	645	饹	855	宮	231	購	736	痼	537	**guǎn**	
高	856			工	255			顧	841	管	589
gǎo		**gě**		弓	272	**gū**				館	848
搞	350	舸	657	恭	293	估	48	**guā**		**guàn**	
稿	576	葛	671	攻	367	咕	152	刮	106		
縞	614	**gè**		躬	748	呱	153	呱	153	冠	91
鎬	797	個	64	龔	873	姑	215	瓜	522	慣	304
gào		各	147	**gǒng**		孤	222	**guǎ**		摜	355
告	151	虼	681	拱	333	沽	455	剐	110	灌	487
膏	645	**gěi**		汞	450	菇	589	寡	234	盥	548
郜	782	給	607	鞏	832	菰	668	**guà**		罐	620
gē		**gēn**		**gòng**		粘	750			觀	702
仡	45	根	414	供	56	辜	755	卦	128	貫	730
割	110	跟	743	共	87	骨	855	掛	341	鸛	865
咯	157	**gěng**		貢	729	**gú**		褂	695	**guāng**	
哥	158	更	396	**gōu**		骨	855	**guǎi**		光	78
戈	309	羹	625	佝	52	**gǔ**		乖	29	**guǎng**	
擱	361	耕	631	勾	119	古	138	摑	355	廣	269
歌	431	**gěng**		溝	475	汩	452	**guǎi**		獷	515
疙	535	哽	158	篝	591	穀	576	拐	329	**guàng**	
胳	642	梗	416	鉤	791	股	639	**guài**		逛	768
鴿	864	耿	632	**góu**		臌	647	怪	289	**guī**	
gé		**gèng**		狗	512	蠱	685	**guān**		圭	180
嗝	167	更	396	苟	663	谷	726	倌	62	歸	435
擱	361			**gòu**		買	733	冠	91	瑰	522
格	415			勾	119	骨	855	官	228	皈	483
胳	642	**gōng**		垢	184	鵠	864	棺	417	硅	563
膈	646	供	55	夠	198	鼓	870	觀	702	規	700
蛤	681	公	85	媾	219	**gù**		關	808	閨	807
閣	807	功	112	構	421	僱	74			鮭	862
隔	816			詬	712	固	175			鰈	863
革	832					故	369			龜	873
						梏	416				

擊 360	級 602	覬 702	架 412	健 67	講 720
機 426	脊 641	計 705	稼 576	劍 112	
激 484	蒺 672	記 706	駕 852	建 271	**jiàng**
犄 510	輯 753	際 816		毽 443	匠 122
璣 522	集 819	驥 855	**jiān**	漸 478	將 239
畸 533		髻 858	兼 89	澗 483	強 274
稽 577	**jǐ**	鯽 862	堅 185	濺 486	漿 482
箕 589	己 258		奸 210	箭 590	犟 511
緝 613	幾 266	**jiā**	尖 244	腱 644	絳 607
績 613	戟 311	伽 50	煎 496	艦 657	虹 681
羇 622	擠 361	佳 54	犍 510	薦 787	醬 787
肌 637	濟 485	加 113	監 547	見 699	降 811
譏 722	紀 599	嘉 168	箋 590	諫 719	
迹 760	給 607	夾 205	緘 613	賤 735	**jiāo**
飢 848	脊 641	家 230	肩 638	踐 745	交 36
饑 848	麂 866	枷 410	艱 658	鍵 796	嬌 219
鷄 864		浹 463	間 806	鑒 799	教 370
齎 872	**jì**	痂 536		間 807	椒 419
	伎 45	茄 662	**jiǎn**	餞 848	澆 482
jí	冀 89		儉 75		焦 496
亟 35	劑 112	**jiá**	剪 109	**jiāng**	礁 566
即 129	妓 214	夾 206	揀 347	僵 75	膠 646
及 134	季 222	莢 666	撿 360	姜 216	茭 664
吉 142	寄 232	頰 839	柬 410	將 239	蕉 675
嫉 218	寂 233		檢 427	江 449	蛟 681
岌 252	忌 287	**jiǎ**	減 473	漿 533	郊 782
急 291	悸 296	假 68	臉 558	疆 533	驕 853
棘 417	技 320	岬 253	簡 592	繮 617	
極 418	既 382	甲 528	繭 617	薑 675	**jiáo**
楫 438	曁 393	買 733	蠒 617	豇 726	嚼 172
殛 438	濟 485	鉀 792	蹇 746		
汲 449	祭 569		鹼 865	**jiǎng**	**jiǎo**
疾 536	紀 599	**jià**		奬 209	佼 54
瘠 538	繫 617	假 69	**jiàn**	槳 424	僥 74
籍 593	繼 618	價 75	件 46	耩 632	剿 111
	齊 676	嫁 218		蔣 674	攪 364

涓 464	**juě**	**kāi**	**kàng**	**kě**	**kōu**
鐫 799	蹶 746	揩 349	亢 36	可 139	摳 354
		開 803	伉 45	渴 474	瞘 557
juǎn	**juè**		抗 319		
卷 130	倔 64	**kǎi**	炕 488	**kè**	**kǒu**
捲 341		凱 96		克 80	口 137
	jūn	慨 299	**kǎo**	刻 105	
juàn	君 148	楷 420	拷 333	剋 108	**kòu**
倦 62	均 182	鎧 797	烤 489	可 140	叩 141
卷 130	菌 667		考 629	嗑 167	寇 232
圈 176	軍 749	**kān**		客 229	扣 318
眷 555	鈞 791	刊 102	**kào**	恪 293	
絹 609	龜 873	勘 115	犒 511	課 717	**kū**
雋 820		堪 188	銬 792		哭 159
	jùn	戡 311	靠 830	**kěn**	枯 410
juē	俊 62	看 553		啃 162	窟 581
撅 356	峻 253	龕 873	**kē**	墾 192	骷 855
	浚 466		坷 183	懇 307	
jué	竣 584	**kǎn**	柯 410	肯 638	**kǔ**
倔 64	菌 668	侃 56	棵 419		苦 661
厥 131	郡 781	坎 182	疴 535	**kēng**	
噘 172	駿 852	檻 428	瞌 557	吭 148	**kù**
崛 253		砍 561	磕 565	坑 181	庫 268
抉 320			科 573	鏗 798	褲 696
掘 342	**K**	**kàn**	窠 581		酷 785
攫 364		看 553	苛 661	**kōng**	
橛 426	**kā**	瞰 557	蝌 683	空 578	**kuā**
決 451	咖 152		頦 838		誇 711
爵 505	喀 165	**kāng**	顆 840	**kǒng**	
絕 606		康 268		孔 220	**kuǎ**
蕨 674	**kǎ**	慷 303	**ké**	恐 293	垮 183
覺 702	卡 127	糠 597	咳 156		
角 703	咔 152		殼 439	**kòng**	**kuà**
訣 707	喀 157	**káng**		控 339	挎 334
蹶 746		扛 318		空 579	胯 641

跨	743	**kuī**		**kuò**		**lài**		**lǎng**	
kuǎi		巋	254	廓	269	癩	539	朗	401
剐	673	盔	546	括	336	睞	557	**làng**	
kuài		窺	582	擴	362	籟	593	浪	463
儈	75	刳	680	闊	808	賴	736	**lāo**	
塊	190	**kuí**		**L**		**lán**		撈	356
快	288	奎	207			嵐	254	**láo**	
會	399	睽	557			攔	363	勞	117
筷	588	葵	670	**lā**		欄	428	嘮	169
膾	647	逵	768	垃	183	瀾	486	牢	508
kuǎn		隗	816	拉	325	籃	593	癆	538
寬	236	魁	861	邋	780	藍	676	**lǎo**	
kuǎn		**kuǐ**		**lá**		蘭	678	佬	55
款	430	傀	71	拉	326	襤	696	姥	217
kuāng		**kuì**		**lǎ**		斕	725	老	627
哐	156	匱	123	喇	165	闌	808	**lào**	
框	414	愧	303	**là**		**lǎn**		澇	482
筐	586	憒	306	剌	108	懶	308	烙	490
诓	710	潰	484	臘	648	攬	364	絡	607
kuáng		饋	848	落	668	纜	619	落	668
狂	511	**kūn**		蠟	685	覽	702	酪	785
誑	715	坤	183	辣	755	**làn**		**lè**	
kuàng		昆	385	**la**		濫	485	勒	115
況	93	**kǔn**		啦	161	爛	503	樂	424
曠	395	捆	338	**lái**		**láng**		**le**	
框	414	**kùn**		來	52	廊	268	了	32
眶	555	困	175	萊	667	榔	419	**lēi**	
礦	566	睏	556			狼	512	勒	115
壙	783					琅	519		
						郎	781		
						鋃	793		

擂　359

léi
擂　359
累　602
雷　825

lěi
壘　193
磊　565
累　602
蕾　675

lèi
擂　359
淚　467
累　603
肋　637
類　840

lei
嘞　169

léng
棱　418

lěng
冷　93

lèng
愣　299

lī
哩　159

lí
梨　416

犁	510	礫	567	遼	777
狸	513	礰	567	**liǎo**		鱗	597

犁　510
狸　513
籬　594
羅　621
釐　790
離　821
黎　868

lǐ
俚　59
李　407
理　520
禮　571
裏　693
里　787
鯉　794
鯉　862

lì
例　56
傈　70
儷　76
利　104
力　112
勵　118
屬　132
吏　142
慄　302
庚　313
曆　395
栗　413
櫟　428
櫪　428
歷　435
瀝　486
痢　537

礫　567
礰　567

liáng
立　582
笠　585
粒　594
荔　664
莅　671
酈　783
隸　818
麗　866

liǎ
俪　63

lián
廉　269
憐　305
連　475
廉　592
聯　635
連　673
連　763
鐮　798
鏈　863

liǎn
斂　375
臉　647

liàn
戀　309
殮　438
煉　496
練　613
鏈　797

liáng
梁　415
涼　466
樑　595
糧　598
良　658
量　789

liǎng
兩　84

liàng
亮　38
晾　391
涼　466
諒　716
踉　745
輛　752
量　789
靚　829

liāo
撩　356

liáo
僚　74
嘹　170
寥　234
寮　236
撩　356
燎　502
療　514
療　538
繚　617
聊　632

遼　777

liǎo
了　32
瞭　558
釕　791

liào
廖　269
撂　355
料　377
瞭　558
釕　791
窖　148
賃　733

liě
咧　156

liè
冽　94
列　102
劣　114
洌　459
烈　490
獵　515
裂　692
趔　742

līn
拎　329

lín
嶙　254
林　408
淋　470
磷　566

鱗　597
臨　648
遴　777
鄰　783
霖　826
鱗　863

lǐn
凜　95
檁　427

lìn
吝　148
賃　733

líng
伶　50
凌　94
囹　176
玲　518
綾　610
羚　624
翎　626
聆　632
菱　667
鈴　792
陵　813
零　825
靈　828
齡　872

lǐng
令　43
嶺　254
領　837

lìng
令　43
另　141

liū
溜　477
熘　499

liú
劉　112
榴　422
流　462
瀏　486
琉　519
留　530
瘤　538
硫　563
餾　797

liǔ
柳　411
綹　611

liù
六　85
溜　477
碌　775
遛　775
鎦　797
陸　813
餾　848

lóng
嚨　171
籠　593

聾 636	蘆 677	縷 615	**lùn**	鰻 848
隆 815	顱 842	膂 645	論 717	鰻 863
龍 872	鱸 863	鋁 794		
			má	**mǎn**
lǒng	**lǔ**	**lǜ**	麻 866	滿 479
壟 193	擄 359	律 279		蟎 684
攏 363	櫓 428	慮 305	**mǎ**	
籠 593	虜 680	氯 446	嗎 167	**màn**
隴 818	鑥 799	濾 486	瑪 522	幔 261
	魯 862	率 516	碼 565	慢 303
lòng	鹵 865	綠 611	螞 683	曼 397
弄 271			馬 850	漫 481
	lù	**luán**		蔓 674
lōu	戮 311	攣 224	**mà**	縵 722
摟 355	漉 478	孿 254	罵 621	鏝 798
	碌 564	巒 364	螞 683	
lóu	祿 570			**máng**
嘍 169	綠 611	**luǎn**	**ma**	忙 287
婁 217	路 744	卵 129	嗎 167	盲 549
樓 424	轆 753		嘛 168	芒 659
螻 684	錄 796	**luàn**		茫 664
	陸 813	亂 32	**mái**	
lǒu	露 827		埋 184	**mǎng**
摟 355	鹿 865	**lüè**		莽 665
簍 591		掠 340	**mǎi**	蟒 684
	lǘ	略 532	買 732	
lòu	驢 855			**māo**
漏 481		**lūn**	**mài**	貓 728
鏤 798	**lǚ**	掄 345	脈 642	
陋 811	侶 61		賣 734	**máo**
露 827	呂 151	**lún**	邁 778	毛 441
	屢 250	倫 65	麥 866	氂 443
lú	履 250	淪 471		矛 558
廬 270	捋 338	綸 611	**mán**	茅 662
爐 503	旅 381	輪 752	埋 184	貓 728
盧 548			瞞 557	錨 796

M

mā
媽 219　抹 326　摩 353

luō
羅 622

luó
籮 594　羅 622　蘿 678　螺 684　邏 780　鑼 853

luǒ
裸 695

luò
摞 355　犖 510　咯 519　絡 607　落 668　駱 852

mán
蠻 685　饅 722

mǎo	寐 234	**mèng**	眠 555	**miè**	**mō**
卯 128	眛 387	夢 198	綿 611	滅 475	摸 354
鉚 792	魅 861	孟 222	**miǎn**	篾 591	**mó**
mào	**mēn**	**mī**	免 80	蔑 674	摩 353
冒 90	悶 298	咪 156	冕 91	**mín**	摹 355
帽 261	**mén**	眯 555	勉 115	民 443	模 423
茂 662	捫 343	**mí**	娩 217	**mǐn**	磨 565
貌 728	鍆 795	彌 276	緬 613	憫 306	膜 646
貿 732	門 801	獼 516	靦 832	抿 327	蘑 677
me	**mèn**	麋 597	**miàn**	敏 372	饃 848
麼 867	悶 298	謎 719	面 830	泯 455	魔 861
méi	燜 502	迷 760	麵 866	皿 545	**mǒ**
媒 218	**men**	醚 786	**miāo**	閩 807	抹 326
枚 409	們 64	麛 866	喵 165	**míng**	**mò**
梅 416	**mēng**	**mǐ**	**miáo**	冥 91	墨 191
沒 453	蒙 672	弭 273	描 347	名 145	寞 234
煤 497	**méng**	眯 555	瞄 557	明 385	抹 326
玫 518	朦 403	米 594	苗 663	盟 547	末 404
眉 552	濛 486	脒 641	**miǎo**	瞑 557	歿 437
莓 666	盟 546	麛 830	淼 471	螟 573	沒 454
酶 785	萌 667	**mì**	渺 474	銘 793	沫 454
鋂 796	蒙 672	冪 92	秒 573	鳴 863	漠 481
霉 826	虻 681	嘧 168	邈 779	**mǐng**	磨 566
měi	**měng**	密 232	**miào**	酩 785	秣 574
每 440	懵 308	泌 454	妙 214	**mìng**	脈 642
美 622	猛 513	秘 574	廟 269	命 153	茉 661
鎂 796	蒙 672	蜜 682	繆 615	**miù**	莫 666
mèi	錳 795	覓 701	**miē**	謬 721	陌 811
妹 215		**mián**	咩 156		驀 853
媚 218		棉 419			默 868
					mōu
					哞 158

móu		ná		náng		ňg		niǎn		顳 842
牟 508		拿 336		囊 172		嗯 167		捻 344		nín
謀 719		鎿 797		nǎng		ǹg		撚 362		您 295
mǒu		nǎ		攮 364		嗯 167		碾 565		níng
某 410		哪 158		náo		nì		niàn		凝 95
mú		nà		撓 356		倪 65		廿 124		寧 234
模 423		呐 149		蟯 684		呢 152		唸 162		擰 360
mǔ		捺 342		nǎo		尼 152		埝 185		檸 428
拇 329		納 601		惱 300		泥 455		念 289		獰 515
母 439		那 781		腦 645		鈮 792		niáng		nǐng
牡 508		鈉 791		nào		霓 827		娘 217		擰 360
畝 529		nǎi		鬧 859		鯢 862		niàng		nìng
mù		乃 28		ne		nǐ		釀 787		寧 234
募 118		奶 210		呢 152		你 50		niǎo		niū
墓 190		氖 444		něi		擬 361		裊 695		妞 214
幕 261		nài		餒 847		nì		鳥 863		niú
慕 304		奈 206		nèi		匿 122		niào		牛 507
暮 394		耐 630		內 82		睨 395		尿 248		niǔ
木 403		萘 667		nèn		泥 456		脲 643		忸 288
沐 451		nān		嫩 219		溺 475		niē		扭 320
牧 508		囡 175		néng		膩 646		捏 337		紐 601
目 548		nán		能 642		逆 761		niè		鈕 791
睦 556		南 127		ńg		niān		嚙 171		niù
穆 577		喃 165		嗯 167		拈 329		孽 224		拗 332
首 663		楠 420				蔫 674		囁 636		nóng
鉬 792		男 529				nián		躡 747		濃 484
		難 822				年 264		鎳 797		膿 647
N		nàn				鮎 862		鑷 799		
		難 823				黏 868				

農	757			爬	504	叛	136	袍	692	抨	326

農　757

nòng

弄　271

nú

奴　210

nǔ

努　114
弩　273

nù

怒　292

nǚ

女　209
釹　791

nuǎn

暖　393

nüè

瘧　538
虐　678

nuó

挪　337

nuò

喏　165
懦　307
糯　598
諾　719
鍩　796

O

ó

哦　159

ò

哦　159

ōu

區　122
歐　431
毆　439
謳　721
鷗　865

ǒu

偶　69
嘔　168
藕　676

òu

慪　303
漚　480

P

pā

啪　162
趴　742

pá

扒　318

爬　504
笆　588
杷　631

pà

帕　259
怕　290

pāi

拍　331

pái

徘　280
排　343
牌　507

pǎi

排　343
迫　759

pài

哌　157
派　461

pān

攀　363
潘　484

pán

盤　548
磐　565
蟠　684
蹒　746

pàn

判　103

叛　136
畔　530
盼　553
襻　697
鎜　793

pāng

乓　29
滂　475
膀　645

páng

彷　278
旁　381
磅　564
膀　645
螃　683
鰟　863
龐　872

pǎng

嗙　167
耪　632

pàng

胖　640

pāo

抛　322
泡　457

páo

刨　105
咆　153
炮　489
袍　512

袍　692

pǎo

跑　743

pào

泡　457
炮　489
疱　536

pēi

呸　152
胚　640

péi

培　184
裴　695
賠　735
陪　813

pèi

佩　56
沛　451
轡　755
配　784

pēn

噴　169

pén

盆　545

pèn

噴　170

pēng

怦　289

抨　326
澎　482
烹　490
砰　561

péng

彭　277
朋　401
棚　419
硼　564
篷　591
膨　646
蓬　673
鵬　864

pěng

捧　341

pèng

碰　563

pī

劈　111
坯　183
批　322
披　327
砒　561
紕　602
霹　827

pí

啤　163
枇　408
毗　441
琵　521
疲　536

皮	544	漂	478	**pìn**		**pōu**		**qī**		麒	866
脾	644	縹	615	牝	508	剖	108	七	7	齊	871
蚍	681	飄	844	聘	633			凄	94	**qǐ**	
pǐ		**piáo**		**pīng**		**pū**		喊	169	乞	30
劈	111	嫖	219	乒	29	仆	43	妻	214	企	45
匹	122	朴	406			噗	170	戚	311	啟	160
擗	359	瓢	523	**píng**		撲	357	期	402	杞	407
痞	537			坪	183	鋪	793	柒	409	綺	610
癖	539	**piǎo**		屏	249			棲	417	豈	726
		漂	478	平	263	**pú**		橙	421	起	739
pì		瞟	557	憑	306	僕	74	槭	423		
僻	75			瓶	523	匍	120	欺	430	**qì**	
媲	219	**piào**		萍	667	璞	522	沏	451	器	170
屁	247	漂	478	薸	677	脯	643	漆	480	契	208
臂	723	票	569	評	709	菩	667	蹊	746	愒	306
闢	809			鮃	862	葡	671			棄	417
		piē		蒲	671			**qí**		氣	444
piān		撇	357			**pǔ**		亓	34	汽	452
偏	66	瞥	558	**pō**		圃	176	其	88	泣	454
片	506			坡	183	普	391	奇	169	砌	561
篇	590	**piě**		泊	458	樸	426	崎	253	訖	707
翩	626	撇	357	潑	483	浦	463	旗	382	迄	758
				頗	837	譜	722	棋	418		
pián		**pīn**				蹼	746	歧	434	**qiā**	
便	58	姘	216	**pó**				琪	521	掐	345
		拼	333	婆	217	**pù**		畦	531		
piǎn						曝	395	祁	567	**qiǎ**	
諞	719	**pín**		**pǒ**		瀑	486	祈	567	卡	128
		貧	730	叵	140	鋪	656	臍	647		
piàn		頻	839	笸	586			其	667	**qià**	
片	506	顰	842					蠐	684	恰	293
騙	853			**pò**		**Q**		顑	837	洽	460
		pǐn		破	562			騎	852	髂	855
piāo		品	156	迫	759			麒	862		
剽	111			魄	861			鰭	863	**qiān**	
										仟	45

千	123	槍	421	蕎	675	親	701	**qìng**	
悭	303	羌	622	**qiǎo**		**qín**		趨	742
扦	318	腔	643					慶	304	軀	748
牽	510	蜣	682	巧	256	勤	118	磬	566	驅	853
簽	593	鏘	798	**qiào**		噙	171	馨	620	麵	866
謙	720	鎗	798			擒	360	親	701	駿	869
遷	777	**qiáng**		俏	59	琴	521	**qióng**		**qú**	
釺	791			峭	253	禽	571				
鉛	792	強	274	撬	358	秦	573	瓊	522	渠	472
阡	809	牆	506	殼	439	芹	661	穹	579	瞿	558
qián		薔	675	竅	582	覃	698	窮	581	蠼	685
		qiǎng		翹	626	**qǐn**		**qiū**		**qǔ**	
前	106			鞘	832						
掮	341	強	275	**qiē**		寢	234	丘	23	取	135
潛	483	搶	352			**qìn**		楸	420	娶	217
蕁	674	羥	625	切	99			秋	573	曲	396
虔	678	襁	696	**qié**		沁	450	蚯	681	苣	661
鉗	791	**qiàng**				**qīng**		邱	781	麴	872
錢	794			茄	663			鞦	833	**qù**	
黔	869	嗆	168	**qiě**		傾	72	**qiú**			
qiǎn		**qiāo**				氫	446			去	132
				且	23	清	468	仇	43	覷	702
淺	470	悄	294	**qiè**		蜻	682	囚	173	趣	742
譴	723	敲	373			輕	751	求	448	**quān**	
遣	775	橇	426	切	99	青	828	泅	457		
qiàn		磽	746	妾	214	**qíng**		犰	511	圈	176
		鍬	796	怯	289			球	519	悛	295
塹	190	**qiáo**		愜	299	情	295	裘	694	**quán**	
嵌	254			挈	332	擎	360	酋	783		
欠	429	僑	74	竊	582	晴	391	**qū**		全	83
歉	431	喬	167	鍥	796	氰	446			拳	332
縴	615	憔	306	**qīn**		**qǐng**		區	122	權	429
茜	644	橋	426					屈	249	泉	459
qiāng		樵	426	侵	58	苘	663	曲	395	痊	536
		瞧	558	欽	430	請	716	祛	567	詮	711
嗆	167	翹	626	衾	691	頃	835	蛆	681	蹎	745

醛	786	髯	858			融	683	**ruǐ**	
顴	842			**rén**		蠑	684		
鬈	858	**rǎn**		人	38			蕊	674
		冉	90	仁	42	**rǒng**		**ruì**	
quǎn		染	409	任	47	冗	91	枘	408
犬	511							瑞	521
		rāng		**rěn**		**róu**		芮	659
quàn		嚷	172	忍	288	揉	347	蚋	681
券	105			荏	665	柔	411	銳	793
勸	119	**ráng**				蹂	746		
		瓤	523	**rèn**		糅	833	**rùn**	
quē				任	47			潤	483
炔	488	**rǎng**		刃	99	**ròu**		閏	803
缺	619	嚷	172	妊	214	肉	637		
		壤	194	紉	599			**ruò**	
qué				認	714	**rú**		偌	66
瘸	538	**ràng**		韌	833	儒	75	弱	273
		讓	725			如	212	箬	591
què				**rēng**		孺	224	若	662
卻	130	**ráo**		扔	318	蠕	685		
確	565	橈	425			銣	793	**S**	
闋	808	饒	848	**réng**					
雀	818			仍	43	**rǔ**		**sā**	
鵲	864	**rǎo**				乳	30		
		擾	362	**rì**		汝	449	仨	44
qún				日	383	辱	757	撒	356
羣	625	**rào**							
裙	694	繞	617	**róng**		**rù**		**sǎ**	
				容	231	入	81	撒	356
R		**rě**		戎	309	褥	696	灑	487
		惹	300	榮	421				
				榕	421	**ruǎn**		**sà**	
rán		**rè**		溶	474	阮	638	卅	124
然	496	熱	500	熔	499	軟	749	脎	641
燃	502			絨	606	阮	809		
				茸	664			**sāo**	

ruǐ		**sāi**		
薩	676			
颯	844			
		噻	170	
sāi		塞	189	
		腮	644	
		鰓	863	
sài				
塞	189			
賽	736			
		sān		
		三	7	
		叁	132	
sǎn				
傘	70			
散	372			
sàn				
散	372			
sāng				
喪	164			
桑	415			
sǎng				
嗓	167			
sàng				
喪	164			
sāo				
搔	351			

纏 617	**shǎ**	閃 802	艄 657	舍 655	笙 586
臁 647	傻 73	陝 812	鞘 832	設 708	聲 634
騷 853	**shà**	**shàn**	**sháo**	赦 738	**shéng**
sǎo	唼 163	善 163	勺 119	麝 866	繩 617
嫂 218	厦 269	單 166	芍 659	**shēn**	**shěng**
掃 342	煞 499	扇 314	**shǎo**	伸 50	省 552
sào	霎 826	擅 358	少 243	參 133	**shèng**
掃 343	**shāi**	疝 535	**shào**	呻 152	剩 110
臊 647	篩 591	繕 617	哨 159	深 467	勝 117
sè	**shǎi**	膳 646	少 244	申 528	盛 546
嗇 167	色 659	苫 663	邵 781	砷 562	聖 633
塞 189	**shài**	訕 707	**shē**	紳 603	**shī**
澀 485	曬 395	贍 737	奢 208	身 747	噓 169
瑟 521	**shān**	騸 853	猞 514	**shén**	失 204
色 658	刪 105	鱔 863	畬 532	什 43	屍 249
銫 793	姍 216	**shāng**	賒 734	神 568	師 260
sēn	山 251	傷 73	**shé**	**shěn**	施 380
森 418	搧 351	商 160	佘 47	嬸 220	濕 486
sēng	杉 407	熵 500	折 323	審 236	獅 514
僧 74	潸 483	**shǎng**	舌 655	沈 450	虱 681
shā	煽 499	晌 390	蛇 681	**shèn**	詩 711
剎 108	珊 518	賞 735	**shě**	慎 303	**shí**
杉 407	羶 625	**shàng**	捨 344	滲 482	什 43
殺 438	舢 656	上 11	**shè**	甚 524	十 123
沙 451	苫 663	尚 245	射 238	腎 643	實 234
煞 499	衫 690	**shāo**	懾 309	脤 682	拾 335
痧 536	釤 791	捎 337	攝 363	**shēng**	時 389
砂 561	**shǎn**	梢 416	涉 464	什 124	石 560
紗 601	睒 556	燒 502	社 567	牲 509	蝕 683
鯊 862		稍 575		性 524	識 722
		筲 589		生 527	食 845

鰣 863	飾 846	孰 223	**shuāi**	稅 575	寺 237
shǐ	**shōu**	熟 499	摔 354	說 712	肆 636
使 55	收 365	秫 574	衰 691	**shǔn**	飼 846
史 142	**shóu**	贖 737	**shuǎi**	吮 151	駟 852
始 216	熟 499	**shǔ**	甩 527	**shùn**	**sōng**
屎 249	**shǒu**	屬 251	**shuài**	瞬 558	松 408
矢 559	守 224	數 374	帥 260	順 835	鬆 858
駛 852	手 314	暑 391	率 516	**shuō**	**sǒng**
shì	首 848	曙 395	**shuān**	說 712	悚 294
世 23	**shòu**	署 620	拴 335	**shuò**	慫 305
事 33	受 136	薯 675	栓 414	數 374	聳 635
仕 44	售 163	蜀 682	閂 802	朔 402	**sòng**
似 46	壽 194	黍 868	**shuàn**	爍 503	宋 227
侍 55	授 344	鼠 871	涮 470	碩 564	訟 707
勢 118	狩 512	**shù**	**shuāng**	**sī**	誦 714
嗜 167	獸 515	墅 191	孀 220	司 140	送 760
噬 171	瘦 538	庶 268	雙 821	嘶 170	頌 837
士 194	**shū**	恕 294	霜 827	廝 269	**sōu**
室 229	叔 135	戍 309	**shuǎng**	思 290	嗖 166
市 258	抒 320	數 374	爽 506	撕 356	搜 350
式 272	書 396	束 406	**shuí**	斯 378	艘 657
恃 292	梳 423	樹 425	誰 718	私 572	餿 848
拭 334	樞 423	漱 478	**shuǐ**	絲 608	**sǒu**
是 387	殊 437	竪 584	水 446	**sǐ**	嗾 168
柿 410	淑 471	術 688	**shuì**	死 436	**sòu**
氏 443	疏 534	述 759	睡 557	**sì**	嗽 168
示 567	舒 656	**shuā**		似 46	**sū**
舐 655	蔬 674	刷 106		伺 50	穌 578
視 700	輸 753	**shuǎ**		四 173	蘇 677
試 710	**shú**	耍 631			
誓 715	塾 190	**shuà**			
逝 765		刷 106			
適 775					
釋 787					

酥	785	熶	502	**tǎ**		**tán**		蟶	684	**téng**	
sú		碎	563			壇	192	鐺	798	滕	477
俗	61	崇	569	塔	189	墰	194	**tǎng**		疼	536
sù		穗	578	獺	516	彈	276	倘	64	藤	677
塑	189	遂	771	**tà**		曇	395	淌	471	臘	721
夙	197	隧	816	拓	327	檀	427	躺	748	騰	853
宿	233	**sūn**		撻	356	潭	482	**tàng**		**tī**	
溯	475	孫	223	榻	421	痰	537	燙	501	剔	109
粟	595	**sǔn**		沓	454	罩	698	趟	742	梯	416
素	600	損	351	踏	745	談	716	**tāo**		踢	745
肅	637	筍	588	**tāi**		譚	722	叨	141	**tí**	
訴	710	**suō**		胎	640	**tǎn**		掏	345	啼	165
速	764	唆	159	**tái**		坦	183	滔	476	提	347
suān		梭	416	擡	361	忐	288	濤	485	蹄	745
酸	785	縮	614	檯	428	毯	443	縧	616	題	840
suàn		蓑	672	臺	652	袒	692	韜	833	**tǐ**	
算	590	**suǒ**		苔	664	**tàn**		**táo**		體	856
蒜	673	所	313	邰	781	嘆	168	桃	415	**tì**	
suī		瑣	522	颱	844	探	340	淘	471	剃	108
尿	248	索	600	**tài**		炭	489	萄	668	嚏	171
雖	820	鎖	797	太	203	碳	564	逃	762	屜	250
suí				態	303	**tāng**		陶	814	惕	296
綏	609	**T**		汰	451	湯	474	**tǎo**		替	397
隋	815			泰	458	蹚	745	討	706	涕	463
隨	816	**tā**		**tān**		**táng**		**tào**		**tiān**	
suǐ		他	44	坍	182	唐	158	套	208	天	201
髓	855	塌	190	攤	363	堂	186	**tè**		添	471
suì		她	212	灘	487	塘	189			**tián**	
歲	434	它	224	癱	539	搪	351	特	509	填	189
		踏	745	貪	730	糖	597				
						膛	646				

恬 293	聽 636	**tōu**	**tuān**	**tuó**	**wǎi**
甜 524		偷 69	湍 474	陀 809	崴 254
田 528	**tíng**			馱 851	
	亭 38	**tóu**	**tuán**	駝 852	**wài**
tiǎn	停 65		團 178	鴕 864	外 195
舔 656	庭 268	投 322	糰 598		
	廷 270	頭 838		**tuǒ**	**wān**
tiāo	霆 826		**tuī**	妥 213	剜 108
挑 335		**tòu**	推 345	橢 426	彎 276
	tǐng	透 768			灣 487
tiáo	挺 338		**tuí**	**tuò**	蜿 682
條 417	艇 657	**tou**	頹 839	唾 163	豌 726
笤 586	鋌 794	頭 839		拓 327	
調 718			**tuǐ**		**wán**
迢 759	**tōng**	**tū**	腿 644	**W**	丸 26
	通 765	凸 96			完 226
tiǎo		禿 572	**tuì**	**wā**	玩 517
挑 335	**tóng**	突 580	蛻 682		纨 600
	佟 52		褪 695	哇 156	頑 836
tiào	同 142	**tú**	退 761	挖 333	
眺 556	彤 277	圖 179		窪 581	**wǎn**
跳 744	桐 414	塗 189	**tūn**	蛙 681	婉 217
	瞳 558	屠 250	吞 148		宛 228
tiē	童 584	徒 280		**wá**	惋 295
帖 259	銅 792	涂 465	**tún**	娃 217	挽 338
貼 731		茶 666	囤 175		晚 390
	tǒng	途 767	屯 251	**wǎ**	皖 544
tiě	捅 351		臀 646	瓦 523	碗 563
帖 259	桶 416	**tǔ**			
鐵 789	筒 587	吐 142	**tuō**	**wà**	**wàn**
	統 605	土 179	托 318	瓦 523	腕 643
tiè			拖 329	襪 696	萬 670
帖 259	**tòng**	**tù**	脫 642		
	痛 537	兔 81		**wāi**	**wāng**
tīng	通 767	吐 142		歪 434	汪 450
廳 270					

wáng

亡　35
王　517

wǎng

往　278
惘　296
枉　408
網　610
罔　620
魍　861

wàng

妄　210
往　278
忘　286
旺　385
望　402

wēi

偎　69
危　129
威　216
巍　254
微　282
煨　498
萎　668
透　769

wéi

唯　163
圍　177
帷　261
惟　296
桅　415
爲　504
維　611
違　772
韋　833

wěi

偉　69
偽　74
唯　163
娓　217
尾　248
猥　514
痿　538
緯　613
萎　668
葦　670
諉　718

wèi

位　48
味　151
喂　165
尉　239
慰　305
未　403
爲　505
畏　529
胃　640
蔚　640
衛　688
謂　720
魏　861

wēn

溫　476
瘟　538

wén

文　375
紋　601
聞　633
蚊　681

wěn

刎　102
吻　150
穩　578
紊　600

wèn

問　161

wēng

嗡　168
翁　626

wèng

甕　523

wō

喔　165
渦　581
窩　671
蝸　683
踒　745

wǒ

我　311

wò

握　347
斡　378
沃　452
臥　648
齷　872

wū

嗚　168
屋　249
巫　257
污　449
烏　490
誣　713
鄔　783
鎢　797

wú

吳　149
梧　416
毋　439
無　491
蕪　674
蜈　682

wǔ

五　34
伍　45
侮　62
午　124
嫵　219
捂　337
武　434
舞　656

wù

兀　77
務　116
勿　119
塢　190
悟　294
惡　298
晤　390
焐　490
物　508
痦　537
誤　715
霧　827

X

xī

吸　150
嘻　169
夕　195
奚　208
嬉　219
希　259
息　294
悉　294
惜　296
昔　384
晰　392
曦　395
析　449
汐　449
溪　476
熄　499
熙　499
犀　510
犧　511
矽　561
硒　563
稀　575
膝　646
蜥　682
蟋　684
西　697
蹊　746
郗　781
錫　795
顧　871

xí

媳　219
席　260
檄　428
習　626
蓆　672
襲　697

xǐ

喜　163
屣　250
徙　280
洗　460
璽　522
銑　793

xì

係　62
戲　312
系　598
細　603
繫　617
隙　816

xiā

呷　152

瞎	557	舷	657	詳	710
蝦	683	賢	734	降	812

xiá ・ 衡 793 ・ 閑 806 ・ 鹹 865

俠	58					曉	395
匣	122			**xiǎng**		**xiào**	
峽	253	**xiǎn**		享	38	嘯	171
暇	393	冼	94	想	300	孝	222
狎	512	洗	461	響	834	效	369
狹	513	險	817			校	413
瑕	521	顯	841	**xiàng**		笑	585
糈	753			像	74	肖	638
遐	772	**xiàn**		向	147		
霞	827	憲	305	巷	258	**xiē**	
黠	869	獻	516	橡	424	些	35
		現	520	相	551	楔	419
xià		綫	610	象	727	歇	430
下	8	縣	614	項	835	蝎	683
嚇	171	羡	624				
夏	195	腺	645	**xiāo**		**xié**	
		莧	666	削	108	偕	67
xiān		限	811	哮	158	協	126
仙	45	陷	814	嚣	172	挾	336
先	79	餡	848	宵	231	携	353
掀	346			消	463	斜	378
氙	444	**xiāng**		瀟	486	脅	641
籼	594	廂	269	硝	563	諧	720
纖	619	湘	473	簫	593	邪	780
鍁	796	相	550	蕭	675	鞋	832
鮮	862	箱	591	逍	767		
		襄	696	銷	793	**xiě**	
xián		鄉	783	霄	826	寫	237
嫌	218	鑲	799	驍	853	血	685
嫻	219	香	849				
弦	273			**xiáo**		**xiè**	
涎	466	**xiáng**		淆	471	卸	130
		翔	626			屑	250
				xiǎo		懈	306
				小	242	械	416

溲	460	行	687
瀉	486	邢	780
蟹	684		
褻	696	**xǐng**	
解	704	擤	361
謝	721	省	552
邂	779	醒	786
xīn		**xìng**	
心	284	姓	215
新	378	幸	265
欣	429	性	290
芯	659	杏	407
薪	675	興	654
辛	755		
鋅	793	**xiōng**	
xín		兄	77
尋	240	兇	78
		凶	96
xìn		匈	120
信	56	洶	461
芯	659	胸	641
釁	787		
		xióng	
xīng		熊	499
惺	299	雄	819
星	388		
猩	514	**xiū**	
腥	644	休	45
興	654	修	61
		羞	623
		饈	848
		xiǔ	
		宿	233
		朽	406

xiù	蓄 672	**xuě**	**yā**	閹 807	燕 502
	酗 784				硯 563
嗅 168		雪 823	丫 24	**yán**	艷 659
溴 477	**xuān**	鱈 863	呀 149	嚴 171	諺 719
秀 572	喧 164		壓 192	妍 214	贋 736
繡 617	宣 228	**xuè**	押 328	嚴 254	釀 787
袖 692	暄 392	血 685	鴉 864	延 270	雁 819
銹 794	軒 749		鴨 864	檐 428	驗 854
		xūn		沿 458	
xū	**xuán**	勛 117	**yá**	炎 488	**yāng**
吁 142	懸 308	熏 499	崖 253	研 561	央 204
嘘 169	旋 382	醺 787	涯 470	筵 589	映 437
墟 190	玄 516		牙 507	芫 659	泱 457
虛 678		**xún**	芽 659	言 707	秧 574
需 826	**xuǎn**	尋 240	蚜 681	顏 840	
須 836	癬 539	巡 255	衙 688	鹽 865	**yáng**
鬚 859	選 777	循 282			佯 54
		旬 384	**yǎ**	**yǎn**	揚 348
xú	**xuàn**	荀 665	啞 161	偃 67	楊 420
徐 280	旋 382	詢 712	雅 819	儼 76	洋 459
	渲 472	馴 851		奄 207	瘍 538
xǔ	炫 488	鱘 863	**yà**	掩 342	羊 622
栩 414	眩 555		亞 35	演 477	陽 815
許 708	絢 607	**xùn**	揠 347	眼 555	
	鏇 798	徇 279	氬 707	衍 688	**yǎng**
xù		殉 437	砑 707	魘 871	仰 47
恤 130	**xuē**	汛 449	軋 748		氧 444
叙 137	削 108	訊 707		**yàn**	癢 539
婿 218	薛 676	訓 707	**yān**	厭 131	養 846
序 267	靴 832	迅 758	咽 157	喑 158	
旭 384		遜 775	嫣 219	嚥 171	**yàng**
煦 499	**xué**		淹 470	堰 188	怏 290
畜 530	噱 170	**Y**	湮 473	宴 231	恙 293
絮 604	學 223		煙 496	沿 458	樣 422
緒 610	穴 578		胭 641	焰 491	漾 478
續 618			醃 786		

yāo		yé		彝	276	翌	626	yìn		映	388
吆	145	揶	347	怡	290	翼	626	印	128	硬	563
夭	203	爺	505	疑	534	肄	637	蔭	674	yō	
妖	214	yě		痍	536	臆	647	飲	845	喲	167
約	599	也	30	移	574	藝	676	卸	862	yo	
腰	644	冶	94	胰	641	裔	693	yīng		喲	167
要	697	野	789	貽	732	詣	711	嬰	220	yōng	
邀	779	yè		遺	777	誼	715	應	306	傭	71
yáo		夜	197	飴	846	議	722	櫻	428	壅	192
姚	217	曳	396	yǐ		譯	723	纓	619	庸	268
徭	283	業	467	乙	30	軼	769	罌	620	擁	358
搖	352	液	467	以	41	逸	769	膺	646	癰	539
瑤	522	腋	643	倚	63	驛	854	英	663	臃	647
窯	582	葉	669	已	258	yīn		鶯	864	雍	820
謠	721	頁	834	椅	418	因	174	鷹	865	鏞	863
遙	775	yī		蟻	684	姻	217	鸚	865	yǒng	
餚	848	一	1	yì		殷	438	yíng		俑	58
yǎo		伊	46	億	74	茵	665	贏	220	勇	115
咬	155	依	54	噫	172	蔭	674	熒	499	咏	151
杳	408	咿	194	屹	252	銦	793	營	502	永	448
窈	580	壹	194	弈	271	陰	814	盈	545	泳	454
舀	653	衣	689	役	278	音	833	縈	663	湧	528
yào		醫	786	意	298	yín		螢	683	甬	528
耀	627	銥	792	憶	306	吟	149	蠅	684	蛹	682
藥	677	yí		抑	323	銀	792	贏	737	踴	746
要	697	儀	74	易	386	齦	872	迎	758	yòng	
鑰	799	咦	156	毅	439	yǐn		yǐng		傭	71
yē		夷	205	溢	475	尹	247	影	277	用	527
噎	169	姨	216	異	531	引	272	穎	577	yōu	
掖	341	宜	228	疫	535	癮	539	yìng		優	76
椰	420			癔	538	隱	818	應	307		
				益	545	飲	845				
				縊	614						
				義	625						

呦 153	**yū**	域 185	圜 178	**yún**	**zāi**
幽 266	淤 467	嫗 219	圓 178	勻 119	栽 412
悠 295	迂 758	寓 234	垣 183	耘 631	災 488
憂 304		尉 239	援 349	芸 659	甾 529
yóu	**yú**	峪 253	源 475	雲 823	**zǎi**
尤 245	于 34	御 282	猿 514	**yǔn**	宰 230
柚 411	余 48	愈 302	緣 614	允 77	崽 254
油 457	俞 56	慾 305	芫 659	殞 438	載 750
游 472	娛 217	欲 430	袁 691	隕 816	**zài**
猶 514	愉 299	浴 465	轅 753	**yùn**	再 90
由 528	愚 301	獄 514	黿 870	孕 221	在 181
疣 535	於 380	玉 517	**yuǎn**	惲 303	載 750
莜 667	榆 420	禦 571	遠 774	慍 303	**zān**
蚰 681	渝 474	籲 594	**yuàn**	暈 393	簪 591
遊 770	漁 481	育 638	怨 292	熨 501	**zán**
郵 782	瑜 522	與 653	院 812	蘊 677	咱 157
鈾 792	盂 545	芋 659	願 841	運 770	**zǎn**
魷 862	腴 644	裕 693	**yuē**	醞 786	攢 364
yǒu	虞 680	譽 724	曰 395	韻 834	**zàn**
友 133	蝓 719	豫 727	約 599		暫 393
有 399	輿 753	遇 774	**yuè**	**Z**	贊 737
莠 666	逾 847	郁 781	岳 253		鑒 797
銪 792	餘 847	預 836	悅 294	**zā**	**zāng**
黝 869	魚 861	馭 851	月 399	匝 152	臧 648
yòu	**yǔ**	鬱 860	樂 424	紮 602	臟 737
又 133	予 33	鷸 865	粵 595	**zá**	髒 855
右 140	宇 224	**yuān**	越 740	砸 561	**zàng**
幼 266	嶼 254	冤 91	躍 747	雜 820	臟 648
柚 411	羽 625	淵 474	鑰 799	**zǎ**	
誘 715	與 653	鴛 864	閱 807	咋 153	
釉 787	語 713	**yuán**	**yūn**		
鼬 871	雨 823	元 77	暈 393		
	yù	原 130			
	喻 166	員 159			

葬 670
藏 676

zāo
糟 597
遭 776

záo
鑿 800

zǎo
早 383
棗 417
澡 484
蚤 681

zào
噪 171
燥 503
皂 543
電 582
躁 746
造 767

zé
則 108
擇 359
澤 484
責 729

zè
仄 41

zéi
賊 733

zén
怎 291

zēng
增 191
憎 305
曾 397

zèng
贈 736

zhā
喳 165
扎 316
查 411
楂 420
渣 473
紮 602

zhá
札 406
炸 489
軋 748
鍘 796
閘 807

zhǎ
拃 330
眨 552

zhà
乍 29
柵 411
榨 421
炸 489

痄 536
蚱 681
詐 710

zhāi
摘 354
齋 872

zhái
宅 225
擇 359
翟 626

zhǎi
窄 580

zhài
債 71
寨 234

zhān
占 128
甑 443
沾 456
瞻 558
粘 594
詹 712
譫 723

zhǎn
展 250
嶄 254
斬 378
盞 546
幝 753

zhàn
佔 50
戰 311
棧 418
湛 473
站 583
綻 610
蘸 678
顫 841

zhāng
張 273
彰 277
樟 422
獐 514
章 583
蟑 684

zhǎng
掌 346
漲 480
長 801

zhàng
丈 11
仗 44
帳 261
杖 407
漲 480
瘴 538
賬 643
脹 735
障 816

zhāo
招 327
昭 388
朝 402
沼 456
着 624

zháo
着 624

zhǎo
找 320
爪 504

zhào
兆 78
召 140
照 498
笊 585
罩 620
筆 637
詔 709
趙 742

zhē
折 324
蜇 682
遮 776

zhé
哲 158
折 324
摺 324
蜇 682
蟄 683
讁 721
輒 751
轍 755

zhě
者 630
褶 696
赭 738
鍺 794

zhè
浙 463
蔗 674
這 763
鷓 865

zhe
着 624

zhēn
偵 69
斟 378
榛 421
珍 518
甄 523
真 554
砧 562
胗 640
臻 653
貞 729
針 790

zhěn
枕 408
疹 536
縝 614
診 709

zhèn
振 336

賑 734	梔 411	桎 414	仲 46	諸 717	**zhuāi**
鎮 797	汁 448	治 458	種 576	豬 727	拽 334
陣 812	知 559	滯 480	衆 686		
震 826	織 617	炙 488	重 788	**zhú**	**zhuān**
	肢 638	痔 536		燭 503	專 238
zhēng	脂 641	痣 536	**zhōu**	竹 585	磚 566
崢 254	蜘 682	秩 574	周 154	逐 765	
征 278	隻 818	稚 575	州 255		**zhuǎn**
徵 283		窒 580	洲 459	**zhǔ**	轉 753
挣 344	**zhí**	緻 614	粥 595	主 26	
正 432	侄 56	置 620	舟 656	囑 173	**zhuàn**
爭 504	值 63	至 652	謅 721	拄 326	傳 72
狰 514	執 184	致 652		煮 491	撰 356
癥 539	指 334	蛭 681	**zhóu**	矚 558	篆 591
睜 557	植 418	製 695	妯 215		賺 736
箏 590	殖 437	誌 713	軸 750	**zhù**	轉 754
蒸 673	直 549	質 735		住 48	
錚 795	職 635	雉 820	**zhǒu**	助 114	**zhuāng**
			帚 259	柱 410	妝 213
zhěng	**zhǐ**	**zhōng**	肘 638	注 454	椿 422
拯 334	址 182	中 24		祝 569	莊 666
整 374	指 334	忠 289	**zhòu**	築 591	裝 694
	旨 384	盅 545	咒 152	苧 661	
zhèng	枳 411	終 604	晝 390	著 667	**zhuàng**
挣 344	止 432	衷 691	皺 545	蛀 681	壯 194
政 369	紙 432	鍾 796	縐 614	註 708	幢 262
正 432	祇 691	鐘 798	驟 855	貯 731	撞 355
症 535	趾 743			鑄 799	狀 511
證 722	酯 785	**zhǒng**	**zhū**	駐 852	
鄭 783		冢 91	侏 56		**zhuī**
	zhì	種 576	朱 406	**zhuā**	椎 419
zhī	制 106	腫 645	株 414	抓 324	追 762
之 28	志 287	踵 746	珠 519		錐 795
指 334	摯 354		硃 563	**zhuǎ**	
支 364	擲 362	**zhòng**	蛛 682	爪 504	**zhuì**
枝 408	智 392	中 26	誅 711		墜 191

缀	610	着	624	恣	293	**zòu**		**zuǎn**		**zuó**
赘	736	苗	663	渍	478	奏	207	纂	618	作	51
zhǔn		酌	784	自	649	揍	347	**zuàn**		昨	389
		镯	799	**zōng**		**zū**		攥	364	琢	521
肫	638	**zī**		宗	227	租	574	钻	800	**zuǒ**	
谆	715			棕	417	**zú**		**zuǐ**		左	256
zhǔn		咨	155	综	610	卒	126	嘴	170	撮	357
		姿	216	踪	745	族	382	**zuì**		**zuò**	
准	95	孜	222	鬃	858	足	742	最	398	作	51
準	476	滋	472	**zǒng**		**zǔ**		罪	621	做	66
zhuō		资	733	总	615	祖	568	醉	786	坐	182
		髭	858	**zòng**		组	603	**zūn**		座	268
卓	126	鲻	862	粽	595	俎	709	尊	240	柞	411
拙	329	**zǐ**		纵	616	阻	810	遵	776	鑿	800
捉	337			**zōu**		**zuān**		鳟	863		
桌	415	仔	45	邹	783	钻	800	**zuō**			
zhuó		姊	216	**zǒu**				作	51		
		子	220	走	738						
啄	162	梓	415								
浊	484	籽	594								
灼	488	紫	604								
琢	521	**zì**									
		字	221								

略　語　表
List of Abbreviations

一、詞類略語 (Abbreviations for Parts of Speech)

（名）　名詞 noun
（動）　動詞 verb
（形）　形容詞 adjective
（副）　副詞 adverb
（介）　介詞 preposition
（代）　代詞 pronoun
（數）　數詞 numeral
（嘆）　感嘆詞 interjection
（量）　量詞 classifier; measure word
（象）　象聲詞 onomatope
（助）　助詞 auxiliary word
（連）　連詞 conjunction

二、修辭略語 (Abbreviations for Style Distinction)

〈敬〉　敬辭 polite expression
〈套〉　套語 polite formula
〈口〉　口語 colloquial expression
〈舊〉　舊時用語 old use
〈成〉　成語 idiom
〈方〉　方言 dialect
〈諷〉　諷刺語 satirical expression
〈謙〉　謙辭 self-depreciatory expression
〈書〉　書面語 literary language
〈貶〉　貶義詞 derogatory expression

〈簡〉　簡稱 abbreviation

〈婉〉　委婉語 euphemism

〈罵〉　罵人用語 abusive language; abuse

三、學科略語 (Abbreviations for Special Fields of Work)

〈測〉　測繪 cartography

〈電〉　電學、電工 electricity; electrical engineering

〈紡〉　紡織 textile industry

〈化〉　化學、化工 chemistry; chemical engineering

〈建〉　建築 architecture

〈經〉　經濟 economics

〈軍〉　軍事 military science

〈邏〉　邏輯學 logic

〈氣〉　氣象學 meteorology

〈攝〉　攝影 photography

〈生化〉　生物化學 biochemistry

〈數〉　數學 mathematics

〈體〉　體育 physical culture

〈外〉　外交 diplomacy

〈微〉　微生物 microbiology

〈物〉　物理學 physics

〈冶〉　冶金 metallurgy

〈印〉　印刷 printing

〈樂〉　音樂 music

〈植〉　植物學 botany

〈地〉　地質學、地理學 geology; geography

〈法〉　法律 law

〈工美〉　工藝美術 industrial art

〈機〉　機械 mechanical engineering

〈交〉　交通運輸 communications and transportations

〈劇〉　戲劇 drama

〈礦〉　礦物、採礦業 mineralogy; mining industry

〈農〉　農業 agriculture

〈商〉　商業 commerce

〈生〉　生物學 biology

〈生理〉　生理學、解剖學 physiology, anatomy

〈水〉　水利 hydraulic engineering

〈天〉　天文學 astronomy

〈無〉　無綫電 radio

〈藥〉　藥物學 pharmaceutics

〈醫〉　醫學 medicine

〈語〉　語言學 linguistics

〈哲〉　哲學 philosophy

〈宗〉　宗教 religion

一 部

一 yī Ⅰ（數）one; a: ～張牀 a bad Ⅱ（形）❶ whole; all: ～屋子的人 a roomful of people ❷ single: 她仍是～人過。She is still single. ❸ same: 兩張畫看上去幾乎完全一樣。The two pictures look very much alike. ❹ every; each: ～天去三次 go there three times a day

【一一】yīyī（副）one by one: ～介紹客人 present the guests one by one

【一二】yī'èr（名）a little; a few; a bit: 略知～ know something about it

【一刀切】yīdāoqiē（動）carry out with rigid uniformity; allow no flexibility

【一刀兩斷】yī dāo liǎng duàn〈成〉cut into two with one stroke; break off relations once and for all

【一下】yīxià（副）❶ once: 嘗～have a taste of ❷ in a short time; suddenly: 天～冷了起來。It suddenly turned cold.

【一口】yīkǒu Ⅰ（形）a mouthful: 喝～水 have a drink of water Ⅱ（副）readily; categorically: ～咬定 obstinately insist

【一口氣】yīkǒuqì（副）at one go; at one stretch: 坐着～讀完這本小說 finish reading this novel at one sitting

【一小撮】yīxiǎocuō（形）a handful of

【一手】yīshǒu Ⅰ（名）❶ skill: 他寫得～好字。He writes in a neat hand. ❷ trick: 這～真卑鄙! What a dirty trick! Ⅱ（副）by oneself; single-handed: ～包辦 run the whole show all by oneself

【一手遮天】yī shǒu zhē tiān〈成〉deceive the public; fool the people

【一月】yīyuè（名）January

【一心】yīxīn（副）❶ wholeheartedly: 爲了教育事業 devote oneself wholeheartedly to education ❷ of one mind

【一心一意】yī xīn yī yì〈成〉heart and soul: ～搞科研 throw oneself heart and soul into scientific research

【一五一十】yī wǔ yī shí〈成〉a detailed account of sth.; in detail: ～地講了事情的經過 give a detailed account of the event

【一元化】yīyuánhuà（形）centralized; unified: ～領導 unified leadership

【一文不名】yī wén bù míng〈成〉be penniless; be broke

【一文不值】yī wén bù zhí〈成〉be entirely worthless

【一毛不拔】yī máo bù bá〈成〉extremely close-fisted; miserly

【一天到晚】yī tiān dào wǎn（副）from morning till night

【一方面】yīfāngmiàn Ⅰ（名）one side; one aspect Ⅱ（連）on the one hand: 他～想更加努力地工作，又～擔心自己虛弱的身體。While he wants to work even harder, he worries about his fragile health.

【一不做，二不休】yī bù zuò, èr bù xiū〈成〉once something is started, it will be pursued to the very end; carry things through regardless of the consequences

【一切】yīqiè〈代〉all; every: ～後果由你負責。You will be held responsible for all the consequences.

【一反常態】yī fǎn cháng tài〈成〉depart from one's usual of doing things; act contrary to one's normal practice

【一日遊】yīrìyóu〈名〉day excursion; day trip; whole-day tour

【一半】yíbàn〈名〉half

【一旦】yīdàn Ⅰ〈副〉in a single day; overnight Ⅱ〈連〉once; now that: 你～有了信心，就可以動手幹。Once you gain confidence, you can go ahead.

【一生】yīshēng〈名〉all one's life; lifetime

【一目十行】yī mù shí háng〈成〉learn ten lines at a glance

【一目了然】yī mù liǎo rán〈成〉can see clearly at a glance

【一丘之貉】yī qiū zhī hè〈成〉jackals from the same lair; birds of a feather

【一句話】yī jù huà〈副〉in a word

【一本正經】yī běn zhèng jīng〈成〉pretend to be serious or in real earnest; strike a serious pose; be sanctimonious

【一本萬利】yī běn wàn lì〈成〉make big profits with a small investment

【一次】yīcì〈副〉once: 我去過～。I've been there once.

【一共】yīgòng〈副〉altogether; in all

【一同】yītóng〈副〉together

【一向】yīxiàng〈副〉❶ always; all along ❷ lately

【一行】yīxíng〈名〉group; party: 總統及其～the president and his party

【一再】yīzài〈副〉again and again; repeatedly: ～聲明 state time and again; make repeated statements

【一早】yīzǎo〈副〉early in the morning

【一年一度】yī nián yī dù〈成〉once a year; annually

【一年四季】yī niánsìjì〈成〉throughout the year

【一年到頭】yī nián dào tóu〈成〉all the year round

【一成不變】yī chéng bù biàn〈成〉remain unchanged for ever; immutable: 沒有～的死規定。There is no hard and fast rule.

【一如既往】yī rú jì wǎng〈副〉as always; as before

【一帆風順】yī fān fēng shùn〈成〉plain sailing: 祝你～wish you every success

【一批】yīpī〈形〉a batch of; a group of

【一身】yīshēn Ⅰ〈副〉❶ all over the body: ～汗 be sweating all over ❷ alone: 獨自～all alone Ⅱ〈量〉suit: ～兩件套西裝 a two-piece suit

【一技之長】yī jì zhī cháng〈名〉particular skill: 人必須有～。A man must acquire a professional skill.

【一把手】yībǎshǒu〈名〉❶ good hand; competent person: 她持家真是～。She's a good housekeeper. ❷ first in command; chief: 學校的～headmaster

【一言不發】yī yán bù fā〈成〉not say a word; remain silent

【一言以蔽之】yī yán yǐ bì zhī〈成〉in a word; in short; in brief

【一言堂】yī yán táng〈成〉one person alone dictates everything

【一言爲定】yī yán wéi dìng〈成〉

【一言難盡】yì yán nán jìn〈成〉cannot tell the story in a few words; it is a long story; it is difficult to say

【一見如故】yí jiàn rú gù〈成〉become close friends at the first meeting; feel like old friends from the start

【一見鍾情】yí jiàn zhōng qíng〈成〉fall in love at first sight

【一系列】yíxìliè〈形〉a series of

【一步登天】yí bù dēng tiān〈成〉reach the top in one giant step; be suddenly promoted to the top leadership

【一併】yíbìng（副）together: 兩個問題要～解決。The two problems will have to be solved at the same time.

【一些】yìxiē（形）some; a few; a little

【一定】yídìng I（形）❶ certain: 在～條件下 under certain circumstances ❷ fixed; regular: ～的複習時間 fixed time for review II（副）surely; certainly; no doubt: 他～會準時到達。He will surely arrive on time. III（動）must: 你～看過這部電影了。You must have seen the film.

【一味】yíwèi（副）blindly; stubbornly: ～批評 criticize endlessly／～堅持 insist doggedly; adhere to

【一直】yìzhí（副）❶ straight: ～往前走 go straight forward ❷ always; all along: 他學習～很用功。He has always been working hard.

【一表人才】yìbiǎo réncái（名）man of handsome appearance

【一念之差】yí niàn zhī chā〈成〉a momentary slip（with terrible consequences）

【一知半解】yì zhī bàn jiě〈成〉have only a smattering; know sth. superficially

【一官半職】yī guān bàn zhí（名）some official post

【一呼百應】yì hū bǎi yìng〈成〉when one calls, many respond; have hundreds at one's beck and call

【一剎那】yíchànà（副）in an instant; in the twinkling of an eye; in no time

【一事無成】yí shì wú chéng〈成〉accomplish nothing

【一往無前】yì wǎng wú qián〈成〉advance fearlessly

【一命嗚呼】yí mìng wūhū（動）die; go west

【一度】yídù（副）once; for a time: 他～教中文。He taught Chinese for a time.

【一律】yílǜ I（形）same: 強求～ impose a rigid uniformly II（副）invariably; without exception

【一面】yímiàn I（名）one side II（副）at the same time; while: ～走，～談 talk while walking

【一面之詞】yímiàn zhī cí（名）one-sided story; oneside of the story; distorted account

【一星半點】yì xīng bàn diǎn〈成〉a tiny bit; an iota

【一哄而起】yì hōng ér qǐ〈成〉plunge precipitatingly into mass action

【一哄而散】yì hōng ér sàn〈成〉break up all at once; disperse in an uproar

【一風吹】yìfēngchuī（動）❶ cancel all things together ❷ cancel indiscriminately

【一派胡言】yípài húyán（名）sheer

nonsense

【一晃】yīhuǎng（動）❶ flash ❷ pass in a flash

【一致】yīzhì（形）unanimous; identical; consistent: ~ 通過 pass unanimously

【一起】yīqǐ（副）❶ at the same place: 站在 ~ stand side by side ❷ altogether: 統統算在 ~，我在那裏住了十年。I lived there off and on for ten years.

【一陣】yīzhèn（量）a burst; a fit: ~ 雷鳴 a clap of thunder/ ~ 大笑 a fit of laughter

【一時】yīshí I（名）a period of time II（副）❶ for the time being; for a while: ~ 無法決定 unable to decide for the time being ❷ now ... now: 她瘋了，~ 哭，~ 笑。She's gone mad, crying one moment and laughing the next.

【一時一刻】yīshí yīkè（副）［usu. used in a negative statement］: for a single moment: 哨兵一也不能放鬆警惕。A sentry mustn't be off his guard for a single moment.

【一般】yībān（形）❶ same: 兩人一大。The two of them are the same age. ❷ general; common: ~ 人 the man in the street/ 很 ~ just so-so ❸ plain: 她長得很 ~。She is quite plain.

【一般化】yībānhuà（名）generalization

【一連】yīlián（副）in succession; on end; without stop: ~ 工作十個小時 work nonstop for ten hours

【一連串】yīliánchuàn（形）a series of: ~ 的挫折 a succession of setbacks

【一氣呵成】yī qì hē chéng〈成〉get sth. done at a stretch

【一針見血】yī zhēn jiàn xiě〈成〉come straight to the point; hit the nail on the head; strike home

【一脈相承】yī mài xiāng chéng〈成〉come from the same origin; follow the same path

【一笑置之】yī xiào zhì zhī〈成〉dismiss with a smile（laugh）; laugh off; parry（a question）with a laugh

【一馬當先】yī mǎ dāng xiān〈成〉gallop at the head; take the lead

【一條心】yītiáoxīn（動）be of one mind; unite as one

【一清二楚】yī qīng èr chǔ（形）abundantly clear; crystal clear

【一清早】yīqīngzǎo（副）early in the morning

【一唱一和】yī chàng yī hè〈成〉echo each other; sing in chorus with one another

【一唱百和】yī chàng bǎi hè〈成〉get numerous favourable responses; receive universal support

【一乾二淨】yī gān èr jìng〈成〉thoroughly

【一貧如洗】yī pín rú xǐ〈成〉in dire poverty; as poor as a church mouse

【一國兩制】yī guó liǎng zhì（名）one nation, two systems

【一望無際】yī wàng wú jì〈成〉be boundless; stretch far and beyond

【一視同仁】yī shì tóng rén〈成〉offer equal treatment to all people; treat all alike without bias

【一敗塗地】yī bài tú dì〈成〉meet one's Waterloo; fail completely; suffer a crushing defeat

【一貫】yīguàn（形）consistent: ~ 立場 consistent stand

【一道】yīdào（副）together: ~ 回家 go home together

【一廂情願】yī xiāng qíng yuàn〈成〉one's own wishful thinking; fond dream

【一等】yīděng〈形〉first-class; first-rate; top-notch

【一統】yītǒng〈動〉unify

【一朝一夕】yī zhāo yī xī〈成〉overnight; in a single day

【一絲一毫】yī sī yī háo〈成〉a tiny bit: 不允許~的馬虎 not tolerate even a tiny careless mistake

【一絲不苟】yī sī bù gǒu〈成〉be meticulously careful; go into every detail; be very careful and serious in work

【一絲不掛】yī sī bù guà〈成〉be stark naked

【一筆勾銷】yī bǐ gōu xiāo〈成〉write off with a stroke of the pen

【一筆抹殺】yī bǐ mǒ shā〈成〉deny categorically; dismiss sth. with a wave of the hand: 不能~ cannot be totally negated

【一勞永逸】yī láo yǒng yì〈成〉settle a matter once and for all; work out a permanent solution to a problem

【一場空】yī chǎng kōng〈成〉end up with nothing; be futile

【一無所有】yī wú suǒ yǒu〈成〉own nothing; be extremely poor

【一無所知】yī wú suǒ zhī〈成〉be utterly ignorant of; be kept in the dark

【一無所獲】yī wú suǒ huò〈成〉make no gains at all

【一無是處】yī wú shì chù〈成〉have not a single merit; be utterly wrong

【一經】yījīng〈副〉once; as soon as: 政策~制定，就應迅速實施。Once a policy is formulated, it should be instantly carried out.

【一路】yīlù Ⅰ〈副〉all the way: ~歌聲不斷 keep singing all the way Ⅱ〈形〉of the same sort; of the same feather: ~人 people of the same kind / 他們是~貨。They are birds of a feather. Ⅲ〈動〉go the same way

【一路平安】yīlù píng'ān Ⅰ〈動〉a pleasant journey Ⅱ〈套〉bon voyage

【一羣】yīqún〈名〉group; crowd: ~流氓 a group of hooligans

【一準】yīzhǔn〈副〉surely; certainly: 他~在辦公室裏。He must be in his office.

【一概】yīgài〈副〉totally; without exception

【一概而論】yī gài ér lùn〈成〉lump together; treat without discrimination

【一鼓作氣】yī gǔ zuò qì〈成〉do sth. at one go; go ahead without let-up

【一意孤行】yī yì gū xíng〈成〉indulge in wilful actions despite repeated warnings; be bent on having one's own way; be self-opinioned

【一會兒】yīhuìr〈副〉❶（for）a while ❷ in a while: 我~就回來。I'll be back in no time.

【一塊兒】yīkuàir〈副〉❶ at the same place: 在～上學 study at the same school ❷ together: 他們～跳舞。They danced together.

【一溜煙】yīliùyān〈副〉swiftly: ~逃跑了 run away swiftly; take to one's heels

【一塌糊塗】yī tā hú tú〈成〉in a muddle; in utter chaos; topsy-turvy

【一落千丈】yī luò qiān zhàng〈成〉suffer a ruinous fall; sustain a sudden decline

【一線】yīxiàn Ⅰ（形）a ray of; a gleam of Ⅱ（名）front line

【一齊】yīqí（副）at the same time; together

【一端】yīduān（名）one end; one respect

【一網打盡】yī wǎng dǎ jìn〈成〉capture all at one swoop; completely wipe out

【一鳴驚人】yī míng jīng rén〈成〉(of an unknown) achieve spectacular success

【一團和氣】yī tuán hé qì〈成〉maintain good relations with people at all cost; be on good terms with everybody

【一團糟】yītuánzāo（名）hopeless mess; utter chaos

【一模一樣】yī mú yī yàng（形）exactly alike; identical; the very image of

【一暴十寒】yī pù shí hán〈成〉work by fits and starts; lack perseverance in one's work

【一輩子】yībèizi（名）all one's life; lifetime

【一箭雙雕】yī jiàn shuāng diāo〈成〉kill two birds with one stone

【一樣】yīyàng（形）same; alike: 他所有的孩子都和他一～誠實。All his children are honest like him.

【一舉】yījǔ（副）at one stroke; at the first try: ～搗毀敵軍總部 smash up the enemy's headquarters instantly

【一舉一動】yī jǔ yī dòng（名）every action; every movement

【一舉兩得】yī jǔ liǎng dé〈成〉kill two birds with one stone; achieve a dual purpose

【一鍋粥】yīguōzhōu（名）mess; disorder: 亂成～ be in a complete mess

【一幫】yìbāng（名）band; gang: ～強盜 a gang of robbers

【一瞥】yīpiē（名）❶ glance ❷ glimpse: 首都～ a glimpse of the capital

【一瞬】yīshùn（副）in no time; in an instant

【一總】yīzǒng（副）❶ altogether; in all: 我們～需要十本書。We need ten copies of the book altogether. ❷ all; entirely: 這～是他的責任。This is entirely his responsibility.

【一點一滴】yīdiǎn yīdī（名）every little bit

【一點兒】yīdiǎnr（副）a bit; a little; somewhat

【一臂之力】yī bì zhī lì〈成〉a helping hand; help

【一邊】yībiān Ⅰ（名）one side: 我們都站在他們～。We are all with him. Ⅱ（副）aside: 把椅子搬到～ move the chair aside Ⅲ（連）while; as: ～唱～跳 sing and dance at the same time

【一邊倒】yībiāndǎo（動）❶ lean to one side; side completely with sb. ❷ overwhelm; predominate

【一竅不通】yī qiào bù tōng〈成〉be stupid and ignorant; be an ignoramus

【一觸即發】yī chù jí fā〈成〉be on the simmer; be explosive: 局勢緊張，～。The situation is tense and explosive.

【一籌莫展】yī chóu mò zhǎn〈成〉fail to find any solution; be at a loss; find oneself helpless

【一覽】yīlǎn（名）general survey

【一覽表】yīlǎnbiǎo〈名〉timetable; schedule

【一體】yītǐ〈名〉❶ integral whole; unity ❷ all; all people concerned

【一攬子】yīlǎnzi〈名〉wholesale; package: ～計劃 package plan/～交易 package deal

丁 dīng Ⅰ〈名〉❶ population; people ❷ man; 園～ gardener ❸ cube: 肉～ meat cubes ❹〈Dīng〉a surname Ⅱ〈數〉fourth

【丁字】dīngzì〈形〉T-shaped: ～尺 T-square

【丁香】dīngxiāng〈名〉❶ lilac ❷ clove: ～油 clove oil

【丁當】dīngdāng〈象〉dingdong: 鐘聲～響。Dingdong goes the bell.

七 qī〈數〉seven: 第～ seventh

【七十二行】qīshí èr háng〈名〉all kinds of occupations; all walks of life

【七上八下】qī shàng bā xià〈成〉be on tenterhooks; be filled with anxiety

【七手八腳】qī shǒu bā jiǎo〈成〉with a lot of people on the scene; each trying to lend a hand; in a bustle

【七月】qīyuè〈名〉July

【七老八十】qī lǎo bā shí〈成〉in one's seventies; of advanced age

【七折八扣】qī zhé bā kòu〈成〉allow or make a big discount on sth.

【七律】qīlǜ〈名〉eight-line Chinese poem with seven characters to a line

【七拼八湊】qī pīn bā còu〈成〉piece together

【七絕】qījué〈名〉four-line Chinese poem with seven characters to a line

【七零八落】qī líng bā luò〈成〉straggling; in great disorder

【七嘴八舌】qī zuǐ bā shé〈成〉with all the people talking at the same time: 引起一場～的議論 raise a babel of argument

【七邊形】qībiānxíng〈名〉heptagon

【七顛八倒】qī diān bā dǎo〈成〉at sixes and sevens

三 sān〈數〉❶ three: 第～ third ❷ several; many: ～令五申 repeated instructions

【三九】sānjiǔ〈名〉third nine-day period after the winter solstice; coldest days of winter

【三十六行】sānshí liù háng〈名〉all trades and professions

【三三兩兩】sān sān liǎng liǎng〈成〉in twos and threes

【三叉神經】sānchā shénjīng〈名〉〈生理〉trigeminal nerve

【三方】sānfāng〈形〉tripartite: ～條約 tripartite treaty

【三月】sānyuè〈名〉March

【三心二意】sān xīn èr yì〈成〉❶ in two minds; undecided ❷ half-hearted

【三天兩頭】sān tiān liǎng tóu〈成〉very often; nearly every day

【三五成羣】sān wǔ chéng qún〈成〉in groups of three or five

【三伏】sānfú〈名〉❶ three ten-day periods after the summer solstice; hottest season ❷ last of these 10-day periods

【三合板】sānhébǎn〈名〉three-ply board; plywood

【三尖瓣】sānjiānbàn〈名〉〈生理〉tricuspid valve

【三角】sānjiǎo〈名〉❶ triangle ❷〈數〉trigonometry

【三角肌】sānjiǎojī〈名〉〈生理〉deltoid muscle

【三角形】sānjiǎoxíng (名)〈數〉triangle

【三角洲】sānjiǎozhōu (名)(river) delta

【三角旗】sānjiǎoqí (名) pennant; pennon

【三角褲】sānjiǎokù (名) panties; briefs

【三位一體】sān wèi yī tǐ (名) ❶〈宗〉the Trinity ❷ trinity; three in one

【三岔路口】sān chà lùkǒu (名) a fork in the road

【三言兩語】sān yán liǎng yǔ (成) (in) a few words; (speak) very briefly

【三弦】sānxián (名)〈樂〉sanxian, a three-stringed plucked instrument

【三長兩短】sān cháng liǎng duǎn (成) unforeseen mishap (usu. referring to death)

【三明治】sānmíngzhì (名) sandwich

【三軍】sānjūn (名) ❶ army ❷ the three armed services

【三重】sānchóng (形) triple; threefold

【三重奏】sānchóngzòu (名)〈樂〉(instrumental) trio

【三重唱】sānchóngchàng (名)〈樂〉(vocal) trio

【三思而行】sān sī ér xíng (成) think twice before you act

【三連冠】sānliánguàn (動) win three championships in succession

【三級跳遠】sānjí tiàoyuǎn (名)〈體〉hop, step, and jump; triple jump

【三彩】sāncǎi (名)〈考古〉three-colour glazed pottery (esp. of the Tang Dynasty)

【三部曲】sānbùqǔ (名) trilogy

【三教九流】sān jiào jiǔ liú (名) ❶ people of different professions and trades ❷ people of all sorts

【三番五次】sān fān wǔ cì (成) time and again; repeatedly

【三極管】sānjíguǎn (名)〈無〉triode

【三棱鏡】sānléngjìng (名)〈物〉(triangular) prism

【三脚架】sānjiǎojià (名) tripod

【三輪車】sānlúnchē (名) tricycle; pedicab; trishaw

【三輪摩托車】sānlún mótuōchē(名) motor tricycle

【三頭六臂】sān tóu liù bì (成) superhuman powers; extraordinary ability

【三聯單】sānliándān (名) triplicate form

【三鮮】sānxiān (名) a Chinese dish composed of any three kinds of delicacies

【三權分立】sān quán fēn lì (名) separation of powers; separation of the legislative, executive and judicial powers of a state

下 xià I (副) ❶ down; downward: 往~看 look downward ❷ below; under: 牀底~ under the bed II (形) ❶lower; inferior: ~脚貨 inferior goods; trash ❷ next; latter: ~學期 next term III (動) ❶ descend; go down; get off: ~自行車 get off a bike ❷ go to: ~鄉 go and work in the country ❸ (of rain, etc.) fall: ~雪了. It's snowing. ❹ issue; deliver: ~指示 give instructions ❺ put in: ~作料 put in some condiments ❻ finish (work, etc.): ~課了. The class is over. ❼ form (an opinion, etc); make out: ~結論 conclude ❽ apply; use: ~著

put chopsticks to food; start eating Ⅳ (助) [used after a verb as a complement] ❶ down: 坐～ sit down ❷ off: 摘～手錶 take off one's watch ❸ [used to indicate completion]: 立～大功 render meritorious services; make great contributions ❹ [used to indicate holding capacity]: 這隻桶裝得～十公斤水。This pail can hold ten kilograms of water. /汽車只能坐～四個人。The car will only seat four. Ⅴ (量) (of action) time: 看一～ have a look

【下工夫】 xiàgōngfu (動) put in a good deal of effort: 狠～學數學 make a painstaking effort to study mathematics

【下凡】 xiàfán (動) (of a god or immortal) come down from the celestial sphere to this mortal human world

【下巴】 xiàba (名) chin

【下手】 xiàshǒu Ⅰ (動) start; set about: 這項工作應從何處～？How should we go about the work? Ⅱ (名) ❶ right-hand seat ❷ 〈口〉assistant; helper

【下文】 xiàwén (名) ❶ what follows (in an article): 這個問題～中再述。This question will be taken up again later (in the book). ❷ outcome; further information: 他退出政界之事全無～。There's no further information about his retiring from politics.

【下午】 xiàwǔ (名) afternoon

【下水】 xiàshuǐ (動) ❶ (of a ship) be launched ❷ do evil: 逼人～ compel sb. to do evil

【下水道】 xiàshuǐdào (名) sewer; drainage

【下不爲例】 xià bù wéi lì 〈成〉 the exception should not be taken as a precedent

【下令】 xiàlìng (動) issue orders; order

【下去】 xiàqù Ⅰ (動) go down Ⅱ (介) [used after a verb as a complement] ❶ down: 石頭滾～了。The stone rolled down. ❷ on: 說～，我聽着呢。Do go on. I'm listening. / 走～ walk on

【下半場】 xiàbànchǎng (名) second half (of a game or show)

【下半旗】 xiàbànqí (動) fly a flag at half-mast

【下列】 xiàliè (形) following; listed below

【下次】 xiàcì (副) next time; next

【下地】 xiàdì (動) ❶ go and work in the fields ❷ (of a patient) get up and move about

【下旬】 xiàxún (名) last ten days of a month

【下沉】 xiàchén (動) sink; submerge

【下車】 xiàchē (動) get off (a bus, train, etc.)

【下身】 xiàshēn (名) ❶ lower part of the body ❷ private parts ❸ trousers

【下放】 xiàfàng (動) ❶ delegate (power) to a lower level: 把權力～到地方 transfer power to local governments ❷ send cadres to work at the grass roots level or to do manual labour

【下來】 xiàlái (介) [used after a verb as a complement] ❶ down: 走～ come down / 坐～ sit down ❷ off: 把大衣脫～ take off the overcoat ❸ [indicating completion]: 整本書

他都讀～了。He has read the book from cover to cover.

【下肢】xiàzhī（名）lower limbs; legs

【下坡路】xiàpōlù（名） down-hill path; path to decline or destruction

【下風】xiàfēng（名）❶ leeward ❷ inferior position: 處於～ be in an inferior position; be at a disadvantage

【下面】xiàmiàn Ⅰ（介）below; under: 桌子～ under the table Ⅱ（形）next; following: ～一個發言者 the next speaker Ⅲ（名）lower levels: 向～傳達這個決定 relay this decision to the lower levels

【下毒手】xiàdúshǒu（動）do sb. in; murder in cold blood

【下降】xiàjiàng（動）descend; fall; go down

【下班】xiàbān（動）come off work; be off duty

【下級】xiàjí（名）❶ lower level ❷ subordinate

【下流】xiàliú（形）obscene; base and mean: 無恥 sordid and shameless

【下馬】xiàmǎ（動）❶ dismount ❷ stop or discontinue (a major project etc.)

【下馬威】xiàmǎwēi（成）❶ show sternness when one assumes office with the intention to inspire awe; start off with a show of one's authority ❷ a head-on blow at the first encounter

【下船】xiàchuán（動）come on shore; disembark

【下蛋】xiàdàn（動）lay eggs

【下崗】xiàgǎng（動）come off sentry duty

【下情】xiàqíng（名）(actual) situation at the grass roots level; feelings of the common people

【下野】xiàyě（動）retire from office

【下筆】xiàbǐ（動）set pen to paper; start writing or painting

【下策】xiàcè（名）bad plan; unsound policy; unwise move

【下場】xiàchǎng（名）end; fate: ～可悲 come to a bad end

【下達】xiàdá（動）convey (to lower levels); assign: ～任務 assign task

【下等】xiàděng（形）inferior; lower

【下款】xiàkuǎn（名）❶donor's name ❷ signature

【下棋】xiàqí（動）play chess

【下游】xiàyóu（名）❶ (of a river) lower reaches ❷ (of a person) at a lower level: 他雖已努力，但仍居～。Hard-working as he is, he is still rated as inferior.

【下腳料】xiàjiǎoliào（名） left-over bits and pieces

【下意識】xiàyìshí（名） subconsciousness

【下落】xiàluò Ⅰ（名）whereabouts: 此人～不明。Nobody knows his whereabouts. Ⅱ（動）drop; go down

【下榻】xiàtà（動）stay; be accommodated: 在國賓館～ stay in the state guesthouse

【下臺】xiàtái（動）❶ leave office: 被迫～ be forced to step down; be compelled to resign ❷ extricate oneself from an embarrassing situation: 他聽到這種批評後覺得難以～。He felt very much embarrassed on hearing this criticism.

【下種】xiàzhǒng（動）sow (seeds)

【下輩】xiàbèi（名）❶ children and grandchildren ❷ next generation in the clan hierarchy

【下層】xiàcéng（名）lower levels;

grass roots: 社會～ the lower strata of society

【下賤】xiàjiàn（形）low; mean

【下鋪】xiàpù（名）lower berth

【下頭】xiàtou Ⅰ（形）〈口〉following Ⅱ（介）below; under Ⅲ（名）lower level

【下聯】xiàlián（名）second line of a couplet

【下顎】xià'è（名）lower jaw

【下屬】xiàshǔ（名）subordinate

丈 zhàng Ⅰ（名）*zhang*, a unit of length = 3.333 metres) Ⅱ（動）measure（land）

【丈人】zhàngren（名）wife's father; father-in-law

【丈夫】zhàngfu（名）husband

【丈母娘】zhàngmǔniáng（名）wife's mother; mother-in-law

【丈量】zhàngliáng（動）measure（land）

上 shàng Ⅰ（形）❶ upper; upward; above: ～齒 upper teeth / 向～的趨勢 an upward tendency ❷ higher; superior: ～層人物 people in high places ❸ first（part）; previous: ～週 last week / ～次 last time Ⅱ（動）❶ go up; mount; get on: ～火車 board a train ❷ appear（in）; be recorded in: ～賬 enter sth. in an account ❸ go to; leave for: ～商店 go shopping ❹ go ahead ❺ supply; serve: ～菜 serve out dishes ❻ apply; paint: ～藥 apply ointment ❼ engage oneself: ～夜班 be on night shift ❽ amount to; add up to: 成千上萬 up to thousands and tens of thousands Ⅲ（副）❶ [used after a verb to indicate fulfilment]: 戴～手套 put on one's gloves / 趕～末班車 catch the last bus ❷ [used together with "來" or "去" to indicate the direction]: 迎～去 go up to sb. ❸ [used after a noun to indicate scope]: within; in: 在報～發表 be published in the press

【上工】shànggōng（動）go to work; start work

【上口】shàngkǒu（動）make smooth reading; be suitable for reading aloud: 這個劇本～。The play reads well.

【上下】shàngxià（名）❶ the leadership and the ordinary people; the old and the young: 舉國～同心協力。The whole nation works in concert. ❷ comparative superiority or advantage: 難分～ hard to say which is superior Ⅱ（副）from top to bottom; up and down: ～打量 look sb. up and down Ⅲ（動）go up and down: 山上修了電纜車，旅遊者～很方便。With the installation of the cable car, tourists can easily go up and down the mountain. Ⅳ（形）about; or so: 五十人～ fifty people or so

【上下文】shàngxiàwén（名）context

【上火】shànghuǒ（動）〈方〉❶ get angry: 他又～了。He flared up again. ❷〈中醫〉suffer internal heat（inflammation, constipation etc.）

【上天】shàngtiān Ⅰ（名）Heaven; God Ⅱ（動）go up into the sky

【上文】shàngwén（名）preceding paragraph（s）

【上午】shàngwǔ（名）morning

【上升】shàngshēng（動）rise; ascend; be in the ascendant

【上水道】shàngshuǐdào（名）〈建〉

watersupply line

【上市】 shàngshì（動）(of vegetables, fruit, etc.) be readily available; be on the market; be in season

【上司】 shàngsi（名）boss; superior

【上去】 shàngqù Ⅰ（動）go up: ～看看他們回來了沒有。Go up and see if they're back. Ⅱ（副）[used after a verb to indicate motion from a lower position to a higher one or to a distance farther away from the speaker]: 把書放回書架～ put the books back on the shelves

【上甲板】 shàng jiǎbǎn（名）upper deck

【上吊】 shàngdiào（動）hang oneself

【上好】 shànghǎo（形）first-rate; superb

【上任】 shàngrèn（動）take up one's post; come to office

【上色】 shàngshǎi（動）apply colour (to a picture; furniture, etc.)

【上刑】 shàngxíng（動）torture

【上旬】 shàngxún（名）first ten days of a month

【上衣】 shàngyī（名）jacket; coat

【上年紀】 shàng niánji（上歲數 shàng suìshu）（動）be advanced in age; be getting on in years

【上車】 shàngchē（動）board; get on a bus (train or other passenger-carrying vehicle): ～地點 pick-up point / ～時間 pick-up time

【上告】 shànggào（動）complain to the higher authorities or appeal to a higher court

【上身】 shàngshēn（名）upper part of the body

【上身兒】 shàngshēnr（名）jacket; shirt; blouse

【上沃爾特】 Shàng Wò'ěrtè（名）the

Upper Volta: ～人 Voltan

【上岸】 shàng'àn（名）disembarkation: ～許可證 overland pass; shore pass / ～遊覽 overland tour; shore excursion

【上官】 Shàngguān（名）a surname

【上空】 shàngkōng（名）sky

【上來】 shànglái Ⅰ（動）come up: 快～吧! 這裏涼快。Come up quickly. It's cool here. Ⅱ（副）❶ [used after a verb to indicate motion from a lower position to a higher one]: 現在就把你的問題提～吧。Raise your questions right now. ❷ [used after a verb to indicate success of action]: 你能説～這首詩的作者嗎? Can you identify the author of the poem?

【上門】 shàngmén（動）❶come or go to see sb.; visit ❷ lock the door; bolt the door

【上述】 shàngshù（形）above-mentioned; aforesaid

【上弦】 shàngxián Ⅰ（名）〈天〉first quarter (of the moon) Ⅱ（動）wind up a watch or clock

【上肢】 shàngzhī（名）upper limbs

【上呼吸道】 shànghūxīdào（名）〈生理〉upper respiratory tract

【上牀】 shàngchuáng（動）go to bed

【上帝】 Shàngdì（名）God

【上風】 shàngfēng（名）superior position; upper hand: 佔～ get the upper hand

【上面】 shàngmiàn Ⅰ（副）above; over; on the surface of: 牆～掛着一幅油畫。An oil painting hangs on the wall. Ⅱ（形）above-mentioned; foregoing: ～提到的那些作家的作品 the works of the aforementioned writers Ⅲ（名）❶ higher authorities: ～發的文件 the document issued by the higher authorities ❷ respect: 她在藝術～造詣很高。She has high artistic attainments.

【上映】shàngyìng（動）show (a film)：電影院今天～什麼？What's on at the cinema today?

【上班】shàngbān（動）go to work; start work

【上凍】shàngdòng（動）freeze

【上級】shàngjí（名）higher level; higher authorities

【上流】shàngliú（名）❶upper reaches (of a river) ❷ upper class

【上馬】shàngmǎ（動）❶ mount a horse ❷ start (a project, etc.)

【上座】shàngzuò（名）seat of honour

【上船】shàngchuán（動）embark; board a ship：～港 port of embarkation

【上訪】shàngfǎng（動）appeal to the higher authorities

【上將】shàngjiàng（名）〈軍〉(U.S. air force) general; (British air force) air chief marshal; (navy) admiral

【上進】shàngjìn（動）make progress

【上報】shàngbào（動）❶appear in a newspaper ❷ report to the leadership

【上策】shàngcè（名）best policy; best solution

【上場】shàngchǎng（動）❶〈劇〉appear on the stage ❷〈體〉enter the court or field; join in a contest

【上等】shàngděng（上品 shàngpǐn）（形）first-class; high-quality

【上鉤】shànggōu（動）take the bait; get hooked

【上街】shàngjiē（動）❶ go out ❷ go shopping

【上稅】shàngshuì（動）pay taxes

【上訴】shàngsù（動）〈法〉appeal (to a higher court)

【上游】shàngyóu（名）❶ upper reaches (of a river) ❷ advanced position

【上當】shàngdàng（動）be taken in; be cheated

【上賓】shàngbīn（名）distinguished guest; guest of honour

【上算】shàngsuàn（形）worthwhile: 不～。It does not pay (to do sth.).

【上臺】shàngtái（動）❶ make one's appearance on a public stage ❷ come to power

【上演】shàngyǎn（動）give a public performance

【上漲】shàngzhǎng（動）rise; go up

【上輩】shàngbèi（名）❶ ancestors ❷ the elder generation of one's family

【上膘】shàngbiāo（動）(of animals) become fat; fatten

【上調】shàngdiào（動）❶ promote sb. to a higher post, particularly from a lower administrative unit to a higher one ❷ transfer goods to the higher administrative unit

【上課】shàngkè（動）❶ have a class; attend a lecture ❷ give a lesson or lecture

【上鋪】shàngpù（名）upper berth

【上頜】shànghé（名）〈生理〉upper jaw; maxilla

【上層】shàngcéng（名）upper stratum

【上層建築】shàngcéng jiànzhù（名）superstructure

【上學】shàngxué（動）go to school; attend school

【上臂】shàngbì（名）upper arm

【上聯】shànglián（名）first line of a couplet

【上聲】shàngshēng（名）〈語〉third tone in modern standard Chinese pronunciation

【上竄下跳】shàng cuàn xià tiào〈成〉dash around on vicious errands

【上顎】shàng'è（名）maxilla（of a mammal）; upper jaw

【上繳】shàngjiǎo（動）hand over to the higher authorities

【上議院】shàngyìyuàn（名）upper house;（of Britain）the House of Lords

【上癮】shàngyǐn（動）be addicted（to alcohol, smoking, drugs, etc.）

丐 gài（名）beggar

不 bù（副）❶［used with a verb, an adjective or an adverb to indicate negation］not: ～高興 displeased; unhappy ❷［used before a noun to form a negative adjective］a lack of; the opposite of: ～名譽 dishonourable ❸［used as a negative answer to a question, whether in the affirmative or negative］no: 你去吧？——，我～去。Are you going? — No, I am not. ／你～去吧？——，我去。Aren't you going? — Yes, I am. ❹〈方〉［used at the end of a statement to turn it into a kind of disjunctive question］: 他現在身體好～? He is in good health now, isn't he? ❺［used between a verb and its complement to indicate impossibility of fulfilment］: 做～完 cannot finish it ❻［used between a pair of repetitive words to indicate indifference, often preceded by 什

麼］: 什麼願意～願意, 反正你要向領導匯報。You will have to report back to the leadership whether you like it or not. ❼［used in conjunction with 就 to indicate an alternative］: 他～在教室就在圖書館。He is either in the classroom or in the library.（Note: When 不 comes before a word with tone 4, it is pronounced in tone 2.）

【不一】bùyī（動）very; differ: 其說～。There are different interpretations.（There are different versions of the story.）

【不力】bùlì（副）ineffectively

【不了】bùliǎo（副）❶［used after a verb］unable to: 受～ cannot stand it ❷［used after a verb + 個］without end: 雪連着好幾天下個～。Snow kept falling for days on end.

【不了了之】bù liǎo liǎo zhī〈成〉bring sth. to an end by giving up halfway; not see a matter through

【不人道】bùréndào（形）inhuman

【不大】bùdà（副）❶ seldom; not often; hardly: 他～講話。He is a man of few words. ❷ not quite; not very: ～可能的事 something improbable

【不已】bùyǐ（副）unceasingly; endlessly

【不凡】bùfán（形）out of the common run: 身手～ have extraordinary skill

【不久】bùjiǔ（副）❶ soon ❷ soon after

【不三不四】bù sān bù sì〈成〉❶ dubious: ～的人 dubious character ❷ nondescript; neither fish nor fowl: 講～的話 make silly remarks; talk nonsense

【不丹】Bùdān（名）Bhutan: ～人 Bhutanese / ～語 Bhutanese (language)

【不比】bùbǐ（动）be unlike; differ from: 這裏的冬天～南方，氣候很冷。Winter here, unlike that in the south, is rather cold.

【不乏】bùfá（动）there is no lack of: ～先例。There is no lack of precedents.

【不分】bùfēn Ⅰ（动）make no distinction between: ～好壞 make no distinction between good and bad Ⅱ（副）regardless of; irrespective of: ～男女老幼 regardless of age or sex

【不止】bùzhǐ（副）❶ more than: ～一次 more than once ❷ incessantly: 流血～ bleed continuously

【不日】bùrì（副）in a few days; one of these days

【不⋯不⋯】bù⋯bù⋯ ❶ [used with two synonyms to make an emphatic negative]: ～屈～撓 unflinching, indomitable ❷ [used with two antonyms to indicate 'neither⋯ nor ⋯']: ～長～短 neither too long nor too short; just the right length ❸ [used with two antonyms of identical structures to indicate that the first is a necessary condition of the second]: ～經一事，～長一智。Experience is the mother of wisdom.

【不及】bùjí（形）❶ inferior to: 他的手藝～他兄弟。He cannot compare with his brother in workmanship. ❷ too late (to do sth.): 躲閃～ too late to dodge

【不及格】bù jígé（动）be disqualified; fail (in schoolwork)

【不中用】bù zhōngyòng（形）useless; good for nothing

【不亢不卑】bù kàng bù bēi〈成〉neither arrogant nor humble; neither pert nor meek

【不切實際】bù qiè shí jì（形）impractical; unrealistic

【不以爲然】bù yǐ wéi rán〈成〉disagree; object to; take exception to

【不必】bùbì（动）need not; not have to: ～說 needless to say; it goes without saying

【不甘】bùgān（不甘心 bù gānxīn）（动）be unreconciled to: ～於自己的失敗 be unwilling to take one's defeat lying down

【不只】bùzhǐ（副）not merely; not only

【不外】bùwài（不外乎 bùwàihu）（副）only; nothing but: 他談的～是工作問題。He is only talking shop.

【不巧】bùqiǎo（副）unluckily; unfortunately

【不平】bùpíng Ⅰ（名）injustice; unfairness Ⅱ（形）❶ uneven; not smooth ❷ resentful; indignant

【不平衡】bù pínghéng Ⅰ（名）imbalance Ⅱ（形）unbalanced; not evenly or fairly arranged

【不可】bùkě（动）❶ must not; cannot: ～抗拒 irresistible ❷ [used after a verb preceded by 非 to indicate one's determination to do sth.]: 非去～ be bent on going

【不可多得】bù kě duō dé〈成〉rare; hard to come by

【不可收拾】bù kě shōu shi〈成〉in a hopeless mess

【不可告人】bù kě gào rén（形）unmentionable; secret; shameful

【不可思議】bù kě sī yì〈成〉incon-

【不可救藥】bù kě jiù yào〈成〉 incurable; incorrigible; beyond hope

【不可開交】bù kě kāi jiāo〈成〉[used after 得 as its complement] be locked in; be tied up with: 吵得 ~ have a terrible row

【不用】bùyòng（動）need not

【不用客氣】bùyòng kèqi（套）❶ [in response to "thank you"] don't mention it ❷ don't stand on ceremony; make yourself at home

【不由自主】bù yóu zì zhǔ〈成〉involuntarily; in spite of oneself

【不由得】bùyóude（動）can't but (do sth.); can't help (doing sth.)

【不正之風】bù zhèng zhī fēng（名）unhealthy tendency

【不打不相識】bù dǎ bù xiāngshí〈成〉out of blows friendship grows; no discord, no concord

【不打自招】bù dǎ zì zhāo〈成〉confess freely of one's own accord

【不出所料】bù chū suǒ liào〈成〉just as expected

【不安】bù'ān（形）❶ unpeaceful; unstable ❷ uneasy; anxious: 志忑 ~ restless ❸ sorry: 老來打攪您，真是～。Sorry to have troubled you time and again.

【不忙】bùmáng（副）no hurry; take one's time

【不合】bùhé（動）❶ be unsuited to: ~ 我的口味 not to my taste ❷ be out of keeping with: ~ 手續 not follow the proper procedures / 他們的意見～。They disagree among themselves.

【不如】bùrú Ⅰ（形）not so good as Ⅱ（動）had better: 你～改天去。It would be better for you to go some other time.

【不行】bùxíng Ⅰ（動）❶ will not do; not be allowed; nothing doing: 我看你的車行嗎？一～，我還沒看完呢。May I read your newspaper? —Nothing doing. I haven't finished it yet. ❷ not work; be no good: 這個主意～。This idea is no good. Ⅱ（形）not good; poor: 他的演技～。His acting is not good. Ⅲ（副）extremely; utterly: 累得～ dog-tired

【不朽】bùxiǔ（形）immortal; imperishable

【不休】bùxiū（副）continuously; endlessly

【不再】bùzài（副）no longer; not any more

【不…而…】bù…ér…［used to indicate a result (after 而) without a direct cause or condition (after 不)］: 不勞而獲 reap where one has not sown

【不同】bùtóng（形）different; unlike

【不同凡響】bù tóng fán xiǎng〈成〉unique; extraordinary

【不成】bùchéng Ⅰ（動）won't do: 這事就算了吧。一那～! Let's give it up. —No, that won't do! Ⅱ（助）［used at the end of a rhetorical question to indicate doubt or challenge, the question being often preceded by 難道 or 莫非］: 難道這就算了？Are we to let the matter drop as it is?

【不成文法】bùchéngwénfǎ（名）〈法〉common law; unwritten law

【不在】bùzài（動）❶ not be in; be out ❷〈婉〉be dead

【不在乎】bù zàihu（動）not mind; not care; not take to heart: ~ 人家說閑話 not mind people gossiping about oneself

【不在意】bù zàiyì（动）❶ not mind ❷ be inattentive; be careless

【不在话下】bù zài huà xià（成）be nothing difficult; be a cinch

【不至于】bùzhìyú（动）will not go so far as to

【不死心】bù sǐxīn（动）will not give up hope

【不自量】bù zìliàng（动）be over-confident; overestimate one's own abilities

【不好过】bù hǎoguò（动）❶ have a tough time ❷ be unwell; be out of sorts

【不好意思】bù hǎoyìsi Ⅰ（形）embarrassed; bashful Ⅱ（动）find sth. embarrassing: ～拒绝 find it embarrassing to decline

【不共戴天】bù gòng dài tiān（成）implacable; irreconcilable: ～的仇敌 sworn enemy

【不妨】bùfáng（动）might as well; there is no harm in: ～再考虑考虑。There is not harm in thinking twice before you decide.

【不利】bùlì（形）❶ adverse; un-favourable: 处于～地位 be at a dis-advantage ❷ unsuccessful: 出师～ lose the first battle; meet with ini-tial setbacks

【不良】bùliáng（形）bad; undesir-able: ～风气 undesirable social trends

【不但】bùdàn（连）[used in conjunc-tion with 而且 (but also)] not only

【不快】bùkuài（形）❶ unhappy; dis-pleased ❷ under the weather

【不免】bùmiǎn（副）inevitably: ～失望 would naturally feel disap-pointed

【不妙】bùmiào（形）(of a turn of events) not nearly good: 情况～。Things are getting tough.

【不忍】bùrěn（动）cannot bear; have not the heart to

【不足】bùzú（形）❶ insufficient; in-adequate: 能源～ short of energy ❷ less than ❸ not worth: ～为奇 (of something) not to be surprised at

【不妥】bùtuǒ（形）improper; inap-propriate

【不见】bùjiàn（动）❶ haven't met (seen): ～不散 will not leave till we meet ❷ be missing

【不见得】bù jiàndé（副）❶ not nec-essarily: ～好到哪里去 not neces-sarily any better ❷ not likely: ～会有用 not likely to be useful

【不含糊】bù hánhu（形）〈口〉❶ un-equivocal; explicit: 在原则问题上～ brook no prevarication in matters of principle ❷ very good: 手艺真～ exquisite workmanship

【不近人情】bù jìn rén qíng（成）un-reasonable; inconsiderate

【不折不扣】bù zhé bù kòu（成）❶ out and out; complete; utter ❷ one hundred per cent; absolutely

【不言而喻】bù yán ér yù（成）self-evident; too obvious to require any explanation

【不求甚解】bù qiú shèn jiě（成）seek no deep understanding

【不明】bùmíng Ⅰ（形）not clear; unidentified: ～飞行物 Unidentified Flying Object (UFO) Ⅱ（动）not know: ～事理 lack common sense; not sensible

【不和】bùhé Ⅰ（动）be on bad terms: 父母～。The parents do not get

along well. Ⅱ (名) discord

【不到】 bùdào (动) ❶ be absent: ～會 not attend the meeting ❷ be below; be under; be less than: ～三十歲 under thirty; in one's late twenties

【不迭】 bùdié (副) ❶ [used after a verb to indicate haste]: 跑～ be kept on the run ❷ [used after a verb to indicate repetition]: 稱謝～ express profuse thanks

【不定】 bùdìng Ⅰ (副) without knowing for certain: ～好不好呢! I am not sure if it is good. Ⅱ (形) ❶ unsteady; restless: 心神～ feel ill at ease ❷ indefinite: ～冠詞 indefinite article

【不法】 bùfǎ (形) illegal; lawless: ～分子 person who defies the law

【不治之症】 bù zhì zhī zhèng (成) fatal disease; incurable disease

【不服】 bùfú (动) ❶ remain unconvinced; refuse to comply: ～氣 not be reconciled to; not take sth. lying down ❷ not be used to: 水土～ not be accustomed to the climate and (or) food of a new place

【不拘】 bùjū (动) ❶ not stick to; not bother about: ～一格 not stick to one type alone ❷ whatever: ～什麼後果我都願承擔。 I'll take any consequences whatever.

【不宜】 bùyí (形) not proper; not advisable: 宜早～遲 must start early rather than late; the sooner the better

【不幸】 bùxìng Ⅰ (名) bad luck; misfortune; narrow escape: 遭受種種～ be afflicted with all kinds of misfortunes Ⅱ (形) unfortunate; unlucky Ⅲ (副) unfortunately; un-

luckily: 他～遇難。 Much to our grief, he was killed in an accident.

【不知】 bùzhī (动) ❶ not know: ～分寸 lack tact ❷ wonder if: ～您是否能幫忙? I wonder if you could help?

【不知不覺】 bù zhī bù jué (成) unwittingly; before one is aware of it

【不知所措】 bù zhī suǒ cuò (成) be at a loss; be at one's wit's end

【不亞於】 bùyàyú (动) be as good as; not be inferior to

【不咎既往】 bù jiù jì wǎng (成) forgive sb. for what he has done in the past; let bygones be bygones

【不受歡迎的人】 bù shòu huānyíng de rén (名) 〈外〉 persona non grata; personae non gratae

【不便】 bùbiàn (形) ❶ inconvenient ❷ inappropriate; unsuitable: 病人～見客。 The patient is not in a proper condition to see visitors. ❸ short of cash: 一時手頭～ be hard up for the moment

【不軌】 bùguǐ (动) act in defiance of the law and discipline; engage in conspiracy

【不是】 bùshì (名) fault; being in the wrong: 這怎麼是我的～? How can you lay the blame at my door?

【不是…就是…】 bùshì… jiùshì… (連) either…or…

【不要】 bùyào (动) ❶ don't (do sth.): ～遲到。 Don't be late. ❷ not want: ～烈性酒 do not care for strong liquor

【不要緊】 bù yào jǐn (成) it does not matter; never mind: 他不在? ～, 你以後告訴他就是了。 So he is not in? No matter. You can tell him later.

【不要臉】bùyàoliǎn(形)〈罵〉shameless; brazen

【不相干】bù xiānggān (形) irrelevant; impertinent: 跟他 ~ have nothing to do with him

【不相上下】bù xiāng shàng xià〈成〉more or less equal; on more or less equal footing

【不客氣】bù kèqi I (形) impolite: ~地說 frankly; to put it bluntly II (動) be rude: 我要(對你)~了。I'm sorry, but I'll have to be rude. III〈套〉❶ [in response to "thank you"] you are welcome; don't mention it ❷ [in response to sb.'s offer]: ~, 我自己來。Please don't bother. I would rather do it myself.

【不怎麼】bù zěnme (副) not very (much): ~高 not very tall

【不怎麼樣】bù zěnmeyàng (形) just so-so; none so good (well)

【不修邊幅】bù xiū biān fú〈成〉down at heel; slovenly

【不省人事】bù xǐng rén shì〈成〉fall unconscious; lose consciousness

【不計】bùjì (動) disregard: ~個人得失 not take personal advantage into acount

【不計名投票】bùjìmíng tóupiào (名) secret ballot

【不計其數】bù jì qí shù〈成〉countless; innumerable

【不料】bùliào (副) unexpectedly

【不時】bùshí (副)❶ every now and then ❷ at any time: ~之需 keep sth. in store for future use

【不通】bùtōng I (形)❶ impassable; blocked up: 下水道~。The sewer is blocked. ❷ [of writings] making no sense; ungrammatical

and unidiomatic: 文理~ illogical and ungrammatical II (副) getting nowhere: 想 ~ not be convinced; feel perplexed

【不容】bùróng (動) not permit; not tolerate: ~侵犯 brook no infringement

【不值】bùzhí (動) not deserve; not be worth: 一錢~ not worth a penny; worthless

【不配】bùpèi (動) be unworthy of; not qualified

【不致】bùzhì (動) be unlikely to cause inconvenience

【不准】bùzhǔn (動) forbid; prohibit: ~吸煙。No smoking.

【不祥】bùxiáng (形) ominous; inauspicious; unlucky: 聽起來有~之感 sound ominous

【不屑】bùxiè (動) disdain; scorn; not condescend to do: ~作答 disdain to reply

【不務正業】bù wù zhèng yè〈成〉neglect one's duties

【不能不】bùnéngbù (動) cannot but

【不倒翁】bùdǎowēng (名) tumbler; roly-poly; political survivor of all upheavals

【不凍港】bùdònggǎng (名) ice-free port; year-round port

【不速之客】bù sù zhī kè〈成〉unexpected guest; gate-crasher

【不倦】bùjuàn (形) tireless

【不倫不類】bù lún bù lèi〈成〉neither fish nor fowl; nondescript; inappropriate

【不符】bùfú (動) not tally with; be inconsistent with: 說話前後~ speak inconsistently

【不理】bùlǐ (動) ignore; neglect: ~他 pay no attention to him

【不够】 bùgòu（形）not enough

【不惜】 bùxī（动）❶ spare: ～力 spare no effort ❷ not scruple to

【不问】 bùwèn Ⅰ（动）ignore; pay no attention to: ～政治 be apolitical; have no interest in politics Ⅱ（副）irrespective of: ～地位高低 irrespective of status

【不许】 bùxǔ（动）forbid; not allow; be impermissible: ～停车。No parking.

【不得】 bùdé（动）must not: ～随地乱扔纸屑杂物。No littering.

【不得】 bude（动）[used after a verb to indicate inappropriateness]: 怪～他。He is not to blame.

【不得了】 bù déliǎo Ⅰ（副）very much; extremely; awfully: 我累得～。I am dog-tired. Ⅱ（叹）good heavens: ～，出事啦！Good heavens! There has been an accident. Ⅲ（形）serious; terrible; disastrous: 有什麽～的事？Is there anything seriously wrong?

【不得人心】 bù dé rén xīn〈成〉be unpopular

【不得已】 bùdéyǐ（动）have no choice but to; be obliged to: ～缒鋌而走险 be driven to take desperate measures

【不得不】 bùdébù（动）have to; cannot but: 天太晚，～告辞了 have to say goodbye as it is getting rather late

【不敢】 bùgǎn（动）dare not; dare to: ～问津 not dare to inquire about（the price of expensive goods）

【不敢当】 bùgǎndāng〈谦〉[used as a polite response to a compliment] I wish I could deserve it

【不动产】 bùdòngchǎn（名）real estate; immovable property

【不动声色】 bù dòng shēng sè（不露声色 bù lù shēng sè）〈成〉remain composed as ever; not bat an eyelid

【不偏不倚】 bù piān bù yǐ〈成〉impartial; unbiased

【不假思索】 bù jiǎ sī suǒ〈成〉(act, respond, etc.) without thinking; readily

【不测】 bùcè Ⅰ（名）accident; eventuality: 险遭～ nearly run into a disaster; escape by the skin of one's teeth Ⅱ（形）unpredictable: 天有～风云 A storm may be brewing in the sky at any moment.（Something unexpected may happen at any-time.）

【不曾】 bùcéng（副）not; never: 说过此话 have never said such words

【不过】 bùguò Ⅰ（副）❶ only; just: 只～是時間問題 merely a matter of time ❷ [used after an adjective to indicate the highest degree] most: 再壞～的片子 worst possible film Ⅱ（连）but; nevertheless: 花很美，～花期太短了。The flowers are beautiful, only they do not last long.

【不堪】 bùkān Ⅰ（动）cannot bear: ～其苦 cannot stand the hardships Ⅱ（副）extremely: 破舊～ in an appallingly dilapidated state

【不單】 bùdān（副）not the only: ～是他。He is not the only one involved.

【不等】 bùděng（形）different; unequal; various; of different quantities

【不然】 bùrán Ⅰ（形）not so: 我意～。I have a different idea. Ⅱ（副）

[used at the beginning of a sentence to indicate disagreement] no Ⅲ (连) or else: 明天我有事，～不以跟你們一道去。I'll be busy tomorrow, otherwise I would go with you.

【不勝】bùshèng Ⅰ(动) ❶ too…to: 一枚舉 be far too numerous to enumerate; be legion ❷ [used between two duplicate verbs to indicate impossibility]: 数～数 too numerous to count Ⅱ (副) very much; deeply: ～欷疚 terribly sorry

【不善】bùshàn (形) ❶ not good at ❷ evil; bad

【不無】bùwú (副) not without: ～可取之處 not without merit

【不結盟】bù jiéméng (形) nonalignment: ～ 運動 nonalignment movement

【不景氣】bù jǐngqì (名) depression; recession

【不痛不癢】bù tòng bù yǎng〈成〉superficial; perfunctory: ～的話 superficial remarks

【不詳】bùxiáng (形) ❶ not in detail ❷ not quite clear: 内容～。Little is known about the content.

【不會】bùhuì (动) ❶ be unable to: 我還～。I have yet to learn. ❷ be not likely to: 他～來的。He is not likely to come. ❸ [used to show displeasure]: 事前他就～打個招呼。He could have forewarned us of it.

【不解】bùjiě Ⅰ(动) not understand: ～之謎 enigma; mystery Ⅱ(形) indestructible: ～之仇 irreconcilable enmity

【不禁】bùjīn (动) can't help: ～大叫起來 can't help screaming

【不遠萬里】bù yuǎn wàn lǐ〈成〉make light of a long journey

【不僅】bùjǐn (副) not just: 這～是猜測。It's not just guesswork. Ⅱ (连) not only: ～跑得快而且跳得高 not only run fast but also jump high

【不像話】bù xiànghuà (形) ❶ ridiculous; unreasonable ❷ outrageous; scandalous: 太～了 simply shocking

【不像樣】bù xiàngyàng (形) unpresentable; improper

【不愧】bùkuì (动) be worthy of

【不當】bùdàng (形) improper; inappropriate: 處罰～ inappropriate punishment

【不義之財】bù yì zhī cái〈成〉ill-gotten wealth

【不算】bùsuàn (动) ❶ not count: 他說的～。What he said does not count. ❷ go back on one's word: 你老是說了～。You never mean what you say.

【不端】bùduān (形) dishonourable; improper

【不對】bùduì Ⅰ(形) ❶ wrong; incorrect ❷ abnormal: 神色～ look queer Ⅱ(名) fault; blame: 是我的～。It's my fault. Ⅲ (副) [used independently to indicate the preceding statement is wrong] no: ～，這不是她的過錯。No, no, it's not her fault.

【不滿】bùmǎn (形) dissatisfied; resentful

【不管】bùguǎn (连) no matter (what, when, etc.): ～三七二十一 recklessly; regardless of the con-

【不管部部長】bùguǎnbù bùzhǎng〈名〉minister without portfolio

【不聞不問】bù wén bù wèn〈成〉not bother to ask or to listen; care nothing about

【不厭其煩】bù yàn qí fán〈成〉take great pains; be very patient

【不論】bùlùn〈連〉no matter (what, who, etc.); irrespective of: ~困難有多大，他都不氣餒。Whatever the difficulties, he never loses heart.

【不熟】bùshú〈形〉❶ (of food) uncooked ❷ unripe ❸ unacquainted; unfamiliar

【不遺餘力】bù yí yú lì〈成〉spare no pains; do one's utmost

【不銹鋼】bùxiùgāng〈名〉stainless steel

【不錯】bù cuò Ⅰ〈形〉right; correct: 假如我記得～的話 if I remember correctly Ⅱ〈副〉[used independently] yes; exactly: ～，我是說過這樣的話。Yes, I did say so.

【不錯】bùcuò〈形〉〈口〉pretty good; not bad: 這裏的景色～! It is quite lovely here!

【不興】bùxīng〈動〉❶ be out of fashion ❷ not be allowed: ～在這裏游泳。Swimming is not allowed here.

【不擇手段】bù zé shǒu duàn〈成〉unscrupulously; by fair means or foul

【不謀而合】bù móu ér hé〈成〉happen to hold identical views

【不懈】bùxiè〈形〉unremitting; persistent

【不學無術】bù xué wú shù〈成〉ignorant and incompetent

【不謝】bùxiè〈動〉〈套〉don't men-

tion it; you are welcome

【不濟】bùjì〈動〉be failing: 體力～cannot go on working on account of failing strength; be physically incapable of going on with the job

【不講情面】bù jiǎng qíng miàn〈副〉regardless of personal feelings; without sparing sb.'s sensibilities

【不簡單】bù jiǎndān〈形〉❶ not simple; complicated ❷ remarkable: 這個表演～。The performance is superb.

【不斷】búduàn〈副〉continuously

【不懷好意】bù huái hǎo yì〈成〉not act with the best of intentions

【不辭而別】bù cí ér bié〈成〉leave without saying goodbye

【不辭勞苦】bù cí láo kǔ〈不辭辛苦 bù cí xīn kǔ〉〈成〉make nothing of hard-ships

【不識時務】bù shí shí wù〈成〉❶ be ignorant of the current trends ❷ have no sense of value

【不顧】búgù〈動〉disregard; ignore; give no thought to: ～情面 without fear of offending sb.'s sensibilities

【不歡而散】bù huān ér sàn〈成〉not part as friends

【不靈】bùlíng〈動〉not work: 刹車～。The break does not work.

丑 chǒu〈名〉❶ clown in Chinese opera ❷ the 2nd of the 12 Earthly Branches

【丑角兒】chǒujuér（丑角 chǒujué）〈名〉clown

丙 bǐng〈名〉❶ the third of the ten Celestial Stems ❷ third ❸ C

【丙級】bǐngjí〈名〉third grade; grade C

【丙種維生素】bǐngzhǒng wéishēngsù

(名) vitamin C

世 shì (名) ❶ lifetime; life: 永～難忘 always bear in mind for the rest of one's life; unforgettable ❷ generation: 生生～～ generation after generation ❸ era; epoch ❹ world: 人一間 this (mortal human) world ❺ 〈地〉 epoch

【世人】shìrén (名) world's people; common people

【世上】shìshàng (副) on earth: ～沒有不變的事物。Everything on earth is subject to change.

【世仇】shìchóu (名) feud between families; blood feud

【世外桃源】shì wài Táo Yuán 〈成〉Land of Peach Blossoms; imaginary land of peace and tranquillity

【世代】shìdài (副) for generations: ～書香 come of an intellectual family background

【世交】shìjiāo (名) ❶ friendship lasting for generations ❷ old family friend

【世事】shìshì (名) affairs of the human world

【世故】shìgù (名) experience in social life; the ways of the world: 不懂人情～ be entirely ignorant of the ways of the world

【世故】shìgu (形) worldly-wise; sophisticated

【世界】shìjiè (名) ❶ world ❷ all the places on earth ❸ sphere of human activity: 科學～ scientific world

【世界語】Shìjièyǔ (名) Esperanto

【世界觀】shìjièguān (名) world outlook

【世紀】shìjì (名) century

【世面】shìmiàn (名) various aspects of society: 沒見過～ have not seen much of the world; be inexperienced

【世俗】shìsú I (名) prevalent custom: ～之見 unenlightened views II (形) non-religious; secular

【世家】shìjiā (名) aristocratic family; noble family

【世道】shìdào (名) the present state of affairs in society

【世傳】shìchuán (形) handed down from generation to generation

【世態】shìtài (名) interpersonal relationships

【世態炎涼】shì tài yán liáng 〈成〉fickleness of human relationships

【世襲】shìxí (形) hereditary

且 qiě I (副) ❶ for the time being: ～住幾日 stay here just for a few days ❷ for a long time: 這雪一下著呢。It will go on snowing for a long time yet. ❸ even: ～不說冬天，那夏八月份都夠冷的。It was cold there even in August, not to mention the winter months. II (連) ❶ while; as: 孩子們～走一唱。The children sang as they walked along. ❷ both … and …: 既深～冷 both deep and cold

【且慢】qiěmàn (動) wait a minute: ～，還有許多手續要辦呢。Wait a minute. There are a lot of formalities to go through yet.

丘 qiū (名) ❶ mound; hillock ❷ (Qiū) a surname

【丘疹】qiūzhěn (名)〈醫〉papule

【丘陵】qiūlíng (名) hills

丞 chéng

【丞相】 chéngxiàng (名) chief minister (in ancient China)

並 bìng Ⅰ (副) ❶ simultaneously; side by side: 不能相提～論 cannot be mentioned in the same breath ❷ [used before a negative for emphasis] (not) at all: 事實～非如此。That is not a fact. Ⅱ (連) [used to join two verbs to indicate simultaneous or consecutive actions] and: 討論～通過提案 discuss and adopt a bill

【並且】 bìngqiě (連) ❶ [used to join two verbs or two verbal phrases to indicate simultaneous or consecutive actions] and; and ... as well ❷ [used as a coordinate in a compound sentence to introduce further information] besides; moreover; in addition

【並存】 bìngcún (動) coexist

【並列】 bìngliè (動) stand side by side; put on a par with: ～第二名 be both runner-ups; tie for second place

【並肩】 bìngjiān (副) shoulder to shoulder; side by side

【並重】 bìngzhòng (動) attach equal importance to; lay equal stress on

【並排】 bìngpái (副) abreast; side by side: ～坐着 sit side by side

【並駕齊驅】 bìng jià qí qū (成) keep pace with each other

【並舉】 bìngjǔ (動) develop or promote simultaneously: 工農業～ develop industry and agriculture simultaneously

丨 部

丫 yā (名) fork: 脚～toes

【丫杈】 yāchà (名) fork; bifurcation

【丫頭】 yātou (名) ❶ girl ❷ slave girl

丰 fēng (名) graceful bearing; charm

【丰姿】 fēngzī (名) fine bearing

中 zhōng Ⅰ (名) ❶ centre; middle: 路～ (in) the middle of the street ❷ (Zhōng) China Ⅱ (介) ❶ in; among; amid: 水～ in the water / 在朋友～ among one's friends ❷ in the process of; during: 治療～的病人 the patient under treatment Ⅲ (形) ❶ middle; mid-: 期～考試 mid-term examination / ～指 middle finger ❷ fit for; good for: ～看 pleasant to the eye ❸ medium: ～型 medium-sized
see also zhòng

【中子】 zhōngzǐ (名) 〈物〉 neutron

【中山裝】 zhōngshānzhuāng (名) Chinese tunic suit

【中文】 zhōngwén (名) Chinese language; Chinese

【中午】 zhōngwǔ (名) noon; midday

【中心】 zhōngxīn (名) centre; heart: 市～ civil centre

【中止】 zhōngzhǐ (動) discontinue; suspend: ～談判立即返國 suspend the negotiations and return home at once

【中央】 zhōngyāng (名) ❶ centre; middle ❷ central authorities: ～機構 central organs

【中世紀】 zhōngshìjì (名) Middle

Ages

【中外】zhōngwài（名）China and foreign countries；home and abroad

【中用】zhōngyòng（動）be of use

【中古】zhōnggǔ（名）medieval age；Middle Ages

【中立】zhōnglì（形）neutral

【中旬】zhōngxún（名）middle ten days of a month

【中伏】zhōngfú（名）second of the three ten-day periods of the hot season

【中式】zhōngshì（名）Chinese style

【中年】zhōngnián（名）middle age

【中性】zhōngxìng（形）neutral

【中雨】zhōngyǔ（名）moderate rain

【中波】zhōngbō（名）〈無〉medium wave

【中和】zhōnghé（名）〈化〉neutralization

【中美洲】Zhōng Měizhōu（名）Central America

【中秋節】Zhōngqiūjié（名）the Mid-autumn Festival；Moon Festival

【中班】zhōngbān（名）❶ middle shift ❷ middle class in a kindergarten

【中草藥】zhōngcǎoyào（名）Chinese herbal medicine

【中級】zhōngjí（形）intermediate；secondary

【中途】zhōngtú（名）midway

【中專】zhōngzhuān（名）special or technical secondary school；polytechnical school

【中庸】zhōngyōng（名）the mean（of the Confucian school）

【中堅】zhōngjiān（名）backbone；mainstay

【中部】zhōngbù（名）central part

【中產階級】zhōngchǎn jiējí（名）middle class

【中國】Zhōngguó（名）China：～人 Chinese

【中國人民政治協商會議】Zhōngguó Rénmín Zhèngzhì Xiéshāng Huìyì（名）the Chinese People's Political Consultative Conference

【中國人民解放軍】Zhōngguó Rénmín Jiěfàngjūn（名）the Chinese People's Liberation Army

【中國共產黨】Zhōngguó Gòngchǎndǎng（名）the Communist Party of China；the Chinese Communist Party

【中間】zhōngjiān Ⅰ（介）among；between：在場的人～，我只認識兩人。Among all those present, I knew only two persons. Ⅱ（名）centre；middle Ⅲ（形）intermediate；middle

【中游】zhōngyóu（名）❶ middle reaches（of a river）❷ state of mediocrity：居～ stay middling

【中程】zhōngchéng（名）intermediate range：～導彈 intermediate-range missile

【中等】zhōngděng（形）❶ average；medium：～身材 of medium height ❷ secondary：～教育 secondary school education

【中隊】zhōngduì（名）〈軍〉squadron

【中華】Zhōnghuá（名）China：～民族 the Chinese nation

【中華人民共和國】Zhōnghuá Rénmín Gònghéguó（名）the People's Republic of China

【中提琴】zhōngtíqín（名）viola

【中飯】zhōngfàn（名）lunch

【中層】zhōngcéng（形）middle-level

【中樞】zhōngshū（名）axis：神經～ nerve centre

【中篇小說】zhōngpiān xiǎoshuō（名）novelette

【中學】zhōngxué（名）secondary school; middle school

【中餐】zhōngcān（名）Chinese food

【中醫】zhōngyī（名）❶ traditional Chinese medical science ❷ doctor of traditional Chinese medicine

【中藥】zhōngyào（名）traditional Chinese medicine

【中斷】zhōngduàn（動）break off; discontinue: 學習 ～ discontinue one's studies

中 zhòng（動）❶ hit; fit exactly: 子彈命～目標。The bullet hit home. ❷ be hit by; be affected by: ～了圈套 fall into a trap/～了一顆子彈 be hit by a bullet
see also zhōng

【中肯】zhòngkěn（形）(of remarks) pertinent; to the point

【中毒】zhòngdú（動）be poisoned

【中風】zhòngfēng（名）apoplexy; stroke

【中計】zhòngjì（動）fall into a trap; be victimized by a scheme

【中暑】zhòngshǔ（動）suffer heat-stroke

【中意】zhòngyì（動）be to one's liking

【中傷】zhòngshāng（動）slander; vilify; libel

【中獎】zhòngjiǎng（動）win a prize in a lottery

串 chuàn Ⅰ（動）❶ string together ❷ conspire: ～供 gang up to make a false confession ❸ go from one place to another: ～門(兒) drop in (for a chat) ❹ act a part (in a play, opera, film, etc.): 客～ be a guest performer Ⅱ（量）string; cluster; bunch: 一～珍珠 a string of pearls

【串通】chuàntōng（動）gang up; conspire: ～一氣 act in cahoots with each other

【串綫】chuànxiàn（動）get the (telephone) lines crossed

【串聯】chuànlián Ⅰ（動）establish contact Ⅱ（名）〈物〉series connection

、部

丸 wán（名）pellet; pill; ball

【丸子】wánzi（名）ball（of minced meat, fish, etc.）: 魚～ fish ball

【丸藥】wányào（名）pill; bolus of Chinese medicine

丹 dān（形）red

【丹心】dānxīn（名）loyal heart; loyalty

【丹田】dāntián（名）pubic region

【丹麥】Dānmài（名）Denmark: ～人 Dane / ～語 Danish（language）

主 zhǔ Ⅰ（名）❶ host ❷ owner; possessor: 業～ proprietor /户～ head of a household ❸ person or party concerned: 失～ owner of the lost property /事～ the victim of a crime ❹〈宗〉God; Lord ❺〈宗〉Allah ❻ view; stand; proposition: 心裏没～ feel at a loss Ⅱ（動）take charge of; head: ～婚 preside over a wedding ceremony Ⅲ（形）main; principal

【主力】zhǔlì（名）main force

【主人】zhǔrén（名）❶ master; owner ❷ host

【主人公】zhǔréngōng（名）hero or heroine（in a literary work）; protagonist

【主子】zhǔzi（名）master; boss

【主心骨】zhǔxīngǔ（名）backbone; pillar

【主犯】zhǔfàn（名）prime culprit; principal criminal

【主句】zhǔjù（語）main clause

【主任】zhǔrèn（名）director; chairman: 系～ dean（head）of a department

【主次】zhǔcì（名）the primary and the secondary: 分清～ differentiate what is primary from what is secondary

【主攻】zhǔgōng（名）main attack

【主見】zhǔjiàn（名）opinion of one's own: 她没有～。She does not hold any definite view on anything.

【主角】zhǔjué（名）main character; protagonist

【主持】zhǔchí（動）❶ manage; preside over: ～家務 manage the household; keep house/ ～會議 chair a meeting ❷ uphold: ～正義 uphold justice

【主食】zhǔshí（名）staple food

【主修】zhǔxiū（動）major; specialize: ～文學 major in literature

【主要】zhǔyào（形）main; principal; chief: ～產品 major products

【主流】zhǔliú（名）❶ main current ❷ main trend

【主席】zhǔxí（名）chairman

【主席臺】zhǔxítái（名）rostrum; platform

【主宰】zhǔzǎi（動）dominate; dictate; control

【主從】zhǔcóng（名）the principal and the subordinate

【主動】zhǔdòng（名）initiative: 採取～ take the initiative

【主動脈】zhǔdòngmài（名）〈生理〉aorta

【主婦】zhǔfù（名）housewife; hostess

【主教】zhǔjiào（名）bishop

【主張】zhǔzhāng I（動）maintain; hold; advocate: ～立即停火 propose an immediate ceasefire II（名）view; opinion; proposition

【主義】zhǔyì（名）doctrine; -ism: 享樂～ hedonism

【主意】zhǔyì（名）idea; plan; decision: 這是誰的～? Whose idea is this?

【主語】zhǔyǔ（名）〈語〉subject

【主演】zhǔyǎn（動）play the leading role（in a film or play）

【主管】zhǔguǎn I（動）be in charge of II（名）person in charge

【主課】zhǔkè（名）main subject

【主導】zhǔdǎo（形）dominant; leading

【主編】zhǔbiān（名）editor in chief

【主謀】zhǔmóu（名）chief instigator

【主辦】zhǔbàn（動）sponsor; be in charge of: 辯論會由學生會～。The debate was sponsored by the Student Union.

【主講】zhǔjiǎng（動）be the speaker

【主題】zhǔtí（名）theme; subject

【主顧】zhǔgù（名）customer; client; patron

【主權】zhǔquán（名）sovereignty

【主體】zhǔtǐ（名）❶ main body; main part ❷〈哲〉subject

【主觀】zhǔguān（形）subjective

丿部

【乃】nǎi Ⅰ（動）〈書〉be: 此～上策。
This is the best solution. Ⅱ（副）
then; only then: 必須勤奮，只有勤
奮～能成功。You must work hard,
and only then can you succeed.

【乃至】nǎizhì（連）and even; as well

【久】jiǔ Ⅰ（副）for long: ～有此意
have long cherished this idea Ⅱ（名）
duration of time: 他搬走了有多～?
How long ago did he move out?

【久久】jiǔjiǔ（副）for a long time: 他
的心情～不能平靜。It was long
before he calmed down.

【久仰】jiǔyǎng〈套〉it's such an honour to make your acquaintance; I've
heard so much about you

【久而久之】jiǔ ér jiǔ zhī〈口〉in
time; as time goes on; with the passage of time

【久別重逢】jiǔ bié chóng féng〈成〉
meet after a long separation

【久留】jiǔliú（動）stay for a long
time; have a prolonged stay

【久違】jiǔwéi〈套〉haven't seen you
for ages

【久遠】jiǔyuǎn（形）age-old: 這個文
件年代～，字迹已不可辨認。The
handwriting is irrecognizable, as
this is an age-old document.

【久經考驗】jiǔ jīng kǎo yàn〈成〉
long-tested

【之】zhī Ⅰ（助）[equivalent to 的]: 三
分～一 one third / 意料～外 be-
yond one's expectations Ⅱ（代）
[used to substitute for a person or
an object]: 敬而遠～ keep sb. at a
respectful distance / 不能等閑視～
should not treat it lightly

【之上】zhī shàng（介）over; above:
價在二十元～ cost over twenty
dollars

【之下】zhī xià（介）under; below:
在他的領導～ under his lead-
ership; led by him

【之内】zhī nèi（介）within: 一小時
～ within an hour / 在能力範圍～
in one's power

【之外】zhī wài（介）beyond; besides;
except: 青山～，還有一條河。Be-
yond the blue hills there is a river. /
除了她～，他在這裏不認識別人。
He knew nobody here except her.

【之乎者也】zhī hū zhě yě（名）a
mixture of archaic and vernacular
expressions in speech or writing: 滿
口～ be full of archaisms inter-
spersed with vernacular terms;
sound highly pedantic

【之前】zhī qián（副）before; ago;
prior to: 很久～ long ago / 她睡覺
～讀了一會兒書。She read for a
while before she went to bed.

【之後】zhī hòu（副）after; later;
then: 兩周～ two weeks later / 我
又去了圖書館。I went to the li-
brary afterwards.

【之間】zhī jiān（介）between: 你我
～ between you and me

【乏】fá（形）❶ lacking: 不～其人 no
lack of such people ❷ tired

【乏味】fáwèi（形）insipid; dull

【乎】hū Ⅰ（助）[used as a particle to
express doubt or conjecture]: 可～?
Is it all right? Ⅱ [suffix of a verb]:

合～真理 stand to reason Ⅲ [suffix of an adjective or an adverb]: 迥～不同 entirely different

乍 zhà (副) ❶ suddenly; abruptly: ～晴～雨。Hardly had it cleared when it began to rain again. ❷ for the first time; just: ～看上去，她很年輕。She looked very young at first sight.

【乍得】Zhàdé (名) Chad: ～人 Chadian

丢 diū (動) ❶ lose ❷ throw; cast: 不要亂～果皮。Don't litter fruit peels all over the place. ❸ put aside; shake off

【丢三落四】diū sān là sì 〈成〉be always losing or mislaying things; be forgetful

【丢卒保車】diū zú bǎo jū 〈成〉sacrifice the pawn to save the rook

【丢掉】diūdiào (動) lose

【丢棄】diūqì (動) lose; abandon

【丢臉】diūliǎn (丢面子 diūmiànzi) (動) lose face

乒 pāng (象) bang: ～～地敲桌子 bang one's fist on the table

乓 pīng (象) crack of a fire arm

【乒乓】pīngpāng Ⅰ (象) rattle Ⅱ (名) table tennis; ping-pong

【乒乓球】pīngpāngqiú (名) ❶ table tennis; ping-pong ❷ table tennis (ping-pong) ball

乖 guāi Ⅰ (動) run counter to; contradict: 於原意相～ go against one's original intention Ⅱ (形) (of a child) well-behaved; obedient

【乖巧】guāiqiǎo (形) ❶ cute; lovely ❷ clever

【乖戾】guāilì (形) (of behaviour, action, language, etc.) perverse

【乖張】guāizhāng (形) odd to the point of absurdity

【乖僻】guāipì (形) eccentric and aloof

【乖謬】guāimiù (形) absurd; preposterous

【乖覺】guāijué (形) clever and resourceful

乘 chéng (動) ❶ take; ride: ～飛機 travel by air (plane) ❷ make use of ❸ multiply: 二～五等於十。Two multiplied by five is ten.

【乘人之危】chéng rén zhī wēi 〈成〉attack sb. when he is in trouble

【乘法】chéngfǎ (名) 〈數〉multiplication

【乘便】chéngbiàn (動) take the opportunity to

【乘客】chéngkè (名) passenger

【乘涼】chéngliáng (動) enjoy the cool

【乘務員】chéngwùyuán (名) attendant (on a train); steward (on a ship); air hostess

【乘虛而入】chéng xū ér rù 〈成〉act when one's opponent is off guard; break through at a weak point

【乘勝】chéngshèng (動) follow up a victory (with further action)

【乘機】chéngjī (動) avail oneself of the opportunity: ～逃走 seize the chance to make one's escape

【乘興】chéngxìng (副) while one is in a cheerful mood: ～而去 go on a trip cheerfully

乙 部

【乙】yǐ (名) second; B

【乙炔】yǐquē (名)〈化〉acetylene; ethyne

【乙烯】yǐxī (名)〈化〉ethylene

【乙等】yǐděng (名) second grade

【乙醇】yǐchún (名)〈化〉ethanol; alcohol

【乙醚】yǐmí (名)〈化〉ether

【九】jiǔ I (数) nine: ～十幾歲的人 nonagenarian II (名) each of the nine nine-day periods following the Winter Solstice: 冷在三～。The coldest days are often in the third nine-day period after the Winter Solstice. III (形) numerous: 三彎～轉 numerous sharp turns

【九九表】jiǔjiǔbiǎo (名)(数) multi-plication table

【九九一】jiǔ jiǔ guī yī (成) in the last analysis; all things considered

【九月】jiǔyuè (名)❶ September ❷ the Ninth Month (of the lunar year)

【九天】jiǔtiān (名)(in Chinese my-thology) the Ninth Heaven; the highest of heavens

【九牛一毛】jiǔ niú yī máo 〈成〉 a drop in the bucket; entirely negligi-ble

【九牛二虎之力】jiǔ niú èr hǔ zhī lì 〈成〉herculean efforts; utmost ef-forts: 費了～ exert tremendous ef-forts

【九死一生】jiǔ sǐ yī shēng 〈成〉 a close shave; escape death by the skin of one's teeth

【九泉】jiǔquán (名) the nether world: 使他在～之下不能瞑目 make him turn in his grave

【九霄雲外】jiǔ xiāo yún wài〈成〉 cast to the winds; too far away to be visible: 一切計劃都抛到～了。All plans were thrown overboard.

【也】yě (副)❶ too; also: 我～在這裏工作。I'm also working here. ❷ [used for emphasis] 我永遠～不會忘記故鄉。Never shall I forget my hometown. ❸ [used to indicate concession]: 費盡力氣～沒有説服他。I tried hard to convince him, but without success. ❹ [used to in-dicate resignation]: 天色已晚，～只好趕緊回去。It's getting late and we'll have to hurry back.

【也門】Yěmén (名) Yemen: ～人 Yemeni; Yemenite

【也許】yěxǔ (副) perhaps; maybe: 天～要下雨。It lool s like rain.

【也罷】yěbà I (副) [used to indicate tolerance or resignation]: 不看～, 那電影没什麼意思。All right, we'll not go to see the film, it isn't much fun. II (連) whether… or…; no matter whether: 你幹～, 不幹～, 都没有什麼關係。It doesn't matter whether you accept the job or turn it down.

【乞】qǐ (動) beg

【乞丐】qǐgài (名) beggar

【乞求】qǐqiú (動) beg for; beseech

【乞討】qǐtǎo (動) go begging

【乞援】qǐyuán (動) ask for assis-tance

【乞憐】qǐlián (動) beg for mercy

【乳】rǔ I (名)❶ breast ❷ milk II

（形）young; newborn: ～燕 young swallow; squab

【乳化】rǔhuà（名）〈化〉emulsification

【乳牛】rǔniú（名）milch cow

【乳白】rǔbái（形）cream-coloured; milk white

【乳汁】rǔzhī（名）milk

【乳名】rǔmíng（名）child's pet name

【乳房】rǔfáng（名）❶ breasts ❷（of a cow, sheep, etc.）udder

【乳凍】rǔdòng（名）junket

【乳脂】rǔzhī（名）butterfat

【乳脂糖】rǔzhītáng（名）toffee; taffy

【乳臭未乾】rǔ xiù wèi gān〈成〉still smell of the baby; be immature and inexperienced

【乳罩】rǔzhào（名）brassiere; bra

【乳酪】rǔlào（名）cheese

【乳腺】rǔxiàn（名）〈生理〉mammary gland

【乳腺炎】rǔxiànyán（名）mastitis

【乳腺癌】rǔxiàn'ái（名）cancer of the breast; mastocarcinoma

【乳酸】rǔsuān（名）lactic acid

【乳製品】rǔzhìpǐn（名）dairy products

【乳齒】rǔchǐ（名）milk tooth; deciduous tooth

【乳膠】rǔjiāo（名）〈化〉emulsion

【乳糖】rǔtáng（名）milk sugar; lactose

【乳頭】rǔtóu（名）nipple; teat

【乳濁液】rǔzhuóyè（名）〈化〉emulsion

【乳糜】rǔmí（名）〈生理〉chyle

乾 gān I（形）❶ dry: ～魚 dried fish ❷ empty; hollow: 外强中～ outwardly strong but inwardly weak

❸ not included in family relationships: ～兒子 adopted son II（副）in vain; fruitlessly: ～看着 look on helplessly III（名）dried food: 葡萄～ raisin

【乾巴】gānba（形）〈口〉dried up

【乾巴巴】gānbābā（形）❶ dry; arid ❷（of language）vapid; dull

【乾冰】gānbīng（名）〈化〉dry ice

【乾貝】gānbèi（名）dried scallop

【乾旱】gānhàn I（形）arid II（名）drought

【乾杯】gānbēi（動）cheers: 爲他的健康～。Let's drink (a toast) to his health.

【乾枯】gānkū（形）withered

【乾洗】gānxǐ（動）dry-clean

【乾淨】gānjìng I（形）clean: ～利落 neat and tidy II（副）completely; totally: 消滅～ completely wipe out

【乾草】gāncǎo（名）hay

【乾脆】gāncuì I（形）clear-cut; straightforward II（副）❶ frankly: ～說 to put it bluntly ❷ simply; just: ～不承認 simply deny everything

【乾涸】gānhé（動）（of riverbed, pond, etc.）dry up; run dry

【乾菜】gāncài（名）dried vegetables

【乾飯】gānfàn（名）cooked rice

【乾酪】gānlào（名）cheese

【乾電池】gāndiànchí（名）dry cell; battery

【乾燥】gānzào（形）❶ dry; arid ❷ uninteresting; insipid

【乾糧】gānliang（名）solid food ration (prepared for a long journey or an expedition)

【乾癟】gānbiě（形）❶ shrivelled ❷（of speech or writing）dull and dry; vapid

亂 luàn I (形) ❶ in disorder; untidy; in a mess: 把事情搞～了 make a mess of the matter ❷ confused; upset: 心慌意～ be seized with anxiety; feel a flutter of panic II (副) at random; carelessly: ～丟煙頭 litter the ground with cigarette ends III (名) confusion; chaos; turbulence

【亂七八糟】luàn qī bā zāo 〈成〉 at sixes and sevens; in great confusion

【亂子】luànzi (名) trouble; mishap

【亂世】luànshì (名) years of turmoil; war years

【亂兵】luànbīng (名) ❶ rebellious troops; rebels ❷ routed troops

【亂來】luànlái (動) act foolishly or recklessly

【亂哄哄】luànhōnghōng (形) noisy; in an uproar: 禮堂裏～。There is such a din in the assembly hall.

【亂砍亂伐】luàn kǎn luàn fá (名) excessive and random lumbering

【亂紛紛】luànfēnfēn (形) disorderly; messy: 心裏～的 feel at a loss

【亂套】luàntào (動) mess things up; upset the whole arrangement

【亂彈琴】luàntánqín (動) talk nonsense; act foolishly or wildly

【亂糟糟】luànzāozāo (形) ❶ chaotic; messy: 屋裏～ a messy room ❷ confused; troubled: 我心裏～的。My mind is in a turmoil.

【亂離】luànlí (動) be torn asunder by war

丿 部

了 le (助) ❶ [used after a verb or adjective to indicate the completion of an action or change]: 孩子長高～。The child has grown taller. / 春天來～。Spring has come. ❷ [used at the end of a sentence or phrase to indicate that a situation that has emerged or is emerging]: 起風～，你得多穿些衣服。It's getting windy, so you'd better put on more clothes. ❸ [used at the end of a sentence to express affirmation]: 他可以不要顧慮～。He should have no misgivings now. ❹ [used as part of an imperative]: 好～, 好～, 別哭～。There, there, don't cry.
see also liǎo

了 liǎo I (動) finish; end: 事情就這麼笑笑～之。The matter was dismissed with a laugh. II (助) [used after a verb to indicate possibility]: 去得(不)～ be able (unable) to go
see also le

【了了】liǎoliǎo (動) know clearly: 我不甚～。I have a very hazy notion of it.

【了不起】liǎobuqǐ (形) outstanding; remarkable

【了不得】liǎobude (副) ❶ exceedingly; terrifically: 快得～ amazingly fast ❷ terribly; seriously: 可～, 房子起火啦! My goodness, the house is on fire!

【了局】liǎojú (名) ❶ end; outcome ❷ solution

【了事】liǎoshì (動) finish: 草草～ hurry through the work

【了卻】liǎoquè (動) make an end of; settle: ～一樁心事 take a load off one's mind

【了得】liǎode (形) [used at the end of a sentence to indicate seriousness]: 他竟敢罵人，那還～! He had the audacity to call you names! How terrible!

【了結】liǎojié (動) resolve; finish: 這事總算～了。The matter is settled at long last.

予 yǔ (動) give: ～以獎勵 award a prize (to sb.)

事 shì Ⅰ (名) ❶ matter; thing: 家庭瑣～ trivial family matters ❷ trouble; mishap: 他出了什麼～了? What happened to him? ❸ job: 辦～認真 do one's work conscientiously ❹ involvement; responsibility: 沒你的～。It has nothing to do with you. Ⅱ (動) be engaged in; deal with: 大～宣揚 give enormous publicity to

【事半功倍】shì bàn gōng bèi〈成〉achieve double results with half the effort; efficient way of doing things

【事件】shìjiàn (名) event; incident; occurrence: 重大歷史～ important historical events

【事在人為】shì zài rén wéi〈成〉human effort is the decisive factor in an undertaking; the success of an undertaking hinges on human effort

【事例】shìlì (名) example; instance

【事事】shìshì (代) everything: 他～不如意。Nothing has gone right with him.

【事物】shìwù (名) thing: 沒有一成不變的～。Nothing is immutable.

【事宜】shìyí (名) [used mostly in formal documents and decrees] matters calling for attention: 有關～relevant matters

【事到臨頭】shì dào lín tóu (副) when things become critical; when one is faced with a crisis

【事迹】shìjì (名) deeds: 生平～story of one's life

【事前】shìqián (事先 shìxiān) (副) beforehand; in advance: 他們～通知他了。They notified him in advance.

【事故】shìgù (名) accident: 交通～traffic accident

【事後】shìhòu (副) afterwards; later; after the event

【事務】shìwù (名) ❶ work done or to be done ❷ general affairs: 忙於～性工作 be busy with routine work

【事倍功半】shì bèi gōng bàn〈成〉achieve only half the result though with redoubled efforts; inefficient way of doing things

【事假】shìjià (名) leave of absence

【事理】shìlǐ (名) reason: 不明～will not listen to reason

【事情】shìqíng (名) matter; thing: 我有很多急待處理的～。I have many urgent matters to attend to.

【事項】shìxiàng (名) item; matter: 出國人員注意～ points for attention for citizens going abroad

【事業】shìyè (名) ❶ undertaking; cause: 衛生～ undertakings in health care ❷ facilities; utilities: 公用～ public utilities

【事與願違】shì yǔ yuàn wéi〈成〉
things turn out contrary to one's
wishes

【事端】shìduān（名）incident; disturbance

【事態】shìtài（名）situation; things:
密切注視～的發展 keep a close
watch on the situation

【事實】shìshí（名）fact; reality: ～
上 in fact; in reality /既成～ accomplished fact; *fait accompli*

【事變】shìbiàn（名）❶ incident;
(usu. of political or military importance): 西安～ the Xi'an Incident
(1936) ❷ exigency: 應付突然～
prepare for any eventuality

二 部

一 èr Ⅰ（數）❶ two ❷ second Ⅱ
（形）different 不～法門 the one
and only way; standard practice

【二心】èrxīn（形）❶ disloyal; un-
faithful ❷ in two minds

【二月】èryuè（名）February

【二百二】èrbǎi'èr（名） mercuro-
chrome

【二百五】èrbǎiwǔ（名） simpleton;
fool

【二重】èrchóng（形）dual

【二重奏】èrchóngzòu（名）〈樂〉in-
strumental duet

【二重唱】èrchóngchàng（名）vocal
duet

【二胡】èrhú（名）*erhu* (a two-
stringed Chinese fiddle)

【二流子】èrliúzi（名）idler; regular
loafer

【二等】èrděng（形）second-class: ～
艙 second-class cabin; tourist class /
～秘書〈外〉Second Secretary

【二話】èrhuà（名）demur: 決没～
raise no objection whatever

于 Yú（名）a surname

亓 Qí（名）a surname

井 jǐng（名）❶ well: 一口～ a well
❷ thing shaped like a well; pit;
shaft: 下～ go down the pit ❸
（Jǐng）a surname

【井下】jǐngxià（副）in the pit; under
the shaft

【井井有條】jǐng jǐng yǒu tiáo〈成〉
orderly; methodical

【井底之蛙】jǐng dǐ zhī wā〈成〉 a
frog at the bottom of a well; a person with a narrow vision

【井然】jǐngrán（形）in good order:
一切 都～有序。Everything is in
proper order.

五 wǔ（數）five

【五一】Wǔ Yī（名）May Day: ～國
際勞動節 May Day; International
Labour Day

【五月】wǔyuè（名）❶ May ❷ fifth
month of the lunar year

【五分制】wǔfēnzhì（名） five-grade
marking system

【五斗櫃】wǔdǒuguì（名） chest of
drawers

【五光十色】wǔguāng shísè（形）❶
resplendent with multifarious colours: ～的寶石 beautiful gems of
various colours ❷ a great variety
of: ～的工藝品 a great variety of
handicrafts

【五更】wǔgēng（副） just before

dawn

【五角星】wǔjiǎoxīng（名） five-pointed star

【五言詩】wǔyánshī（名）poem with five characters to a line

【五金】wǔjīn（名）metals; hardware: ~店 hardware store

【五官】wǔguān（名）❶ five sense organs ❷ features

【五味】wǔwèi（名） all sorts of flavours

【五花八門】wǔ huā bā mén〈成〉a motley of; variegated; manifold; rich in variety

【五指】wǔzhǐ（名）the five fingers: 伸手不見~ be pitch-dark

【五彩】wǔcǎi（形） multi-coloured; variegated: ~繽紛 a riot of colours

【五湖四海】wǔ hú sì hǎi〈成〉all parts of the country

【五綫譜】wǔxiànpǔ（名）〈樂〉staff; stave

【五穀】wǔgǔ（名）food crops; cereals

【五穀豐登】wǔ gǔ fēng dēng〈成〉reap a bumper harvest

【五邊形】wǔbiānxíng（名）pentagon

【五顏六色】wǔ yán liù sè〈成〉a profusion of brilliant hues; colourful

【五臟】wǔzàng（名）the five internal organs（heart, liver; spleen; lungs and kidneys）

【五體投地】wǔ tǐ tóu dì〈成〉kneel at sb.'s feet with admiration; throw oneself at sb.'s feet in veneration

互 hù（副）mutually; each other

【互助】hùzhù（動）help each other

【互利】hùlì（名）mutual benefit

【互相】hùxiāng（副）mutually

【互訪】hùfǎng（動）exchange visits

【互惠】hùhuì（形）mutually beneficial

亞 yà I（形）second; inferior II（Yà）（名）Asia: ~運會 Asian Games

【亞於】yàyú（動）be second to: 他的能力不~你。He is by no means inferior to you in ability.

【亞洲】Yàzhōu（名）Asia: ~人 Asian

【亞軍】yàjūn（名） second place; runner-up: 在錦標賽中獲~ win second place in the tournament

【亞蔴】yàmá（名）flax: ~布 linen

【亞熱帶】yàrèdài（名） subtropical zone; subtropics

吸 jí（副）urgently; anxiously: ~待修理 want repairing badly

些 xiē I（量）some: 好~天 many days /看~書 read some books II（副）a little; a bit: 她病好~了。She feels better. / 今天有~冷。It's a bit cold today.

亠 部

亡 wáng I（動）❶ flee; escape: 流~在外 be in exile ❷ lose ❸ die: 傷~慘重 suffer heavy casualties II（形）deceased: ~友 deceased friend

【亡羊補牢】wáng yáng bǔ láo〈成〉it's not too late to mend the fold after a sheep is lost; take precautions against further losses

【亡命】wángmìng I（動）go into exile II（形）desperate; venturous: ~

徒 reckless person; desperado

【亡國】 wángguó Ⅰ (動) (of a country) be subjugated; be conquered Ⅱ (名) conquered nation; ~奴 person without a country; people of a subjugated nation

【亡魂喪膽】 wáng hún sàng dǎn 〈成〉 frightened to death

亢 kàng Ⅰ (形) ❶ haughty; lordly: 不~不卑 be neither overbearing nor obsequious ❷ excessive; exceeding: ~旱 severe drought Ⅱ (Kàng) (名) a surname

【亢進】 kàngjìn (形) 〈醫〉 hyperfunction

【亢奮】 kàngfèn (形) stimulated; excited

交 jiāo Ⅰ (動) ❶ give; confer; hand over; pay: ~房租 pay rent ❷ reach (a place or a period of): ~午 (at) noontime ❸ intersect; cross: 兩條路在這兒相~。The two roads intersect (cross) each other here. ❹ associate with; get acquainted with: ~友要謹慎 be cautious in making friends ❺ have sex with: 雜~水稻 crossbred rice Ⅱ (名) ❶ juncture; junction: 此地在四縣之~。This district is contiguous with four counties. ❷ friend; friendship; acquaintance ❸ fall; tumble Ⅲ (副) reciprocally; mutually: ~相輝映 enhance each other's splendour

【交叉】 jiāochā (動) ❶ intersect; crisscross ❷ overlap: ~的意見 overlapping views ❸ stagger: ~上課 stagger classes

【交公】 jiāogōng (動) turn over (one's extra earnings, etc.) to the collective or the state

【交互】 jiāohù (副) ❶ reciprocally; mutually: 他們~批改作業。They corrected each other's homework. ❷ alternately: 兩者可以~使用。The two of them may be used alternately.

【交出】 jiāochū (動) give; surrender: ~證件 surrender one's papers; hand over one's credentials

【交代】 jiāodài (動) ❶ hand over; turn over: ~工作 turn over one's work to another ❷ give instructions: 他没~一聲就走了。He left without leaving a message. ❸ explain the situation; state one's views; confess: 坦白~ plead guilty and make confessions

【交付】 jiāofù (動) give; deliver; turn over: ~定金 pay a deposit; make a down payment

【交加】 jiāojiā (動) (of two things) appear simultaneously: 驚喜~ be pleasantly surprised

【交好】 jiāohǎo (動) forge a good relationship (with)

【交往】 jiāowǎng Ⅰ (動) associate with Ⅱ (名) contact: 我跟他們向無~。I have had no contact with them.

【交底】 jiāodǐ (動) tell (sb.) of one's intention; tell (sb.) what it is all about

【交卷】 jiāojuàn (動) ❶ hand in one's exam paper ❷ fufil a task; finish a job: 我已經~了。I am through with the work.

【交易】 jiāoyì (名) deal; transaction; trade: 骯髒~ dirty deal

【交易所】 jiāoyìsuǒ (名) exchange: 證券~ stock exchange

【交易會】jiāoyìhuì（名）trade fair

【交差】jiāochāi（動）report to the authorities concerned on the result of one's mission

【交界】jiāojiè（動）(of territory, field, etc.) border on: 與印度～ border on India／兩國的～綫 the boundary (line) between two countries

【交班】jiāobān（動）hand over one's duties to another

【交納】jiāonà（動）pay what is due to the government or an organization: ～所得稅 pay the income tax

【交配】jiāopèi（交尾 jiāowěi）（動）mate; copulate

【交流】jiāoliú I（動）exchange; interchange: ～工作經驗 exchange work experience II（名）exchange; interflow: 學術～ academic exchange

【交流電】jiāoliúdiàn（名）alternating current

【交涉】jiāoshè（動）make representations; try to resolve a problem by consulting with the other party: 就此事向有關機關～ make representations to the organization concerned about this affair

【交通】jiāotōng（名）traffic; communication: ～擁擠 heavy traffic

【交貨】jiāohuò I（動）deliver goods II（名）delivery (of goods): ～付款 cash on delivery (COD)

【交接】jiāojiē（動）❶ connect: 水天～。The sky and the water seem to merge. ❷ hand over work; take over work: 嚴格遵守一班制度 strictly adhere to the regulations governing the hand-over and take-over procedure ❸ associate: 他～

許多政界名人。He associated with a number of prominent politicians.

【交情】jiāoqíng（名）friendship; acquaintanceship: 他們～不深。They are not on very close terms.

【交椅】jiāoyǐ（名）❶ ancient folding chair ❷ armchair: 坐第一把～ be the first in command; play first fiddle

【交換】jiāohuàn（動）exchange: ～留學生 exchange international students

【交換機】jiāohuànjī（名）〈郵電〉exchange

【交換價值】jiāohuàn jiàzhí（名）〈經〉exchange value

【交集】jiāojí（動）(of feelings) be mixed; intermingle: 百感～ be assailed by a multitude of feelings

【交替】jiāotì I（動）replace; rotate II（副）alternately; in turn

【交遊】jiāoyóu（動）make friends (with); be friends (with): ～甚廣 have a wide circle of acquaintances

【交感神經】jiāogǎn shénjīng（名）〈生理〉sympathetic nerve

【交際】jiāojì（名）social intercourses: 好～ be sociable

【交際舞】jiāojìwǔ（名）ballroom dancing

【交鋒】jiāofēng（動）fight a battle; compete in a game or contest: 北京隊將和上海隊～。The Beijing team will play against the Shanghai team.

【交談】jiāotán（動）talk with; have a conversation with

【交賬】jiāozhàng（動）❶ hand over the accounts ❷ give an account of the task one has undertaken: 我怎麼向他～啊？How am I to account for all this?

【交錯】jiāocuò（動）interlock; inter-wind; crisscross: 全國鐵路縱橫～。Railway lines crisscross the whole country.

【交還】jiāohuán（動）return; restore: 把報紙～原處。Put back the newspapers to where they belong.

【交戰】jiāozhàn（動）fight; join battle; wage war

【交戰狀態】jiāozhàn zhuàngtài（名）state of war

【交頭接耳】jiāo tóu jiē ěr〈成〉whisper to each other; talk in whispers

【交織】jiāozhī（動）form; interweave; intermingle: ～成各種顏色的美麗圖案 form a beautiful multi-coloured pattern

【交響樂】jiāoxiǎngyuè（名）symphony: ～團 philharmonic orchestra

【交驗】jiāoyàn（動）❶ (of product, etc.) deliver for a check (before acceptance by the user) ❷ (of credentials, etc.) present for a check

亨 hēng

【亨通】hēngtōng（形）prosperous; flourishing

享 xiǎng（動）enjoy

【享有】xiǎngyǒu（動）enjoy: ～優先權 have priority/～盛名 enjoy a high reputation

【享年】xiǎngnián〈敬〉die at the age of

【享受】xiǎngshòu Ⅰ（動）enjoy: ～幸福生活 enjoy a happy life Ⅱ（名）enjoyment; treat: 從音樂中得到極大的～ derive immense enjoyment from music

【享福】xiǎngfú（動）live in ease and comfort

【享樂】xiǎnglè（動）seek pleasure; indulge in luxury and extravagance

京 jīng（名）❶ (national) capital ❷ (Jīng) short for Beijing

【京城】jīngchéng（名）capital city

【京胡】jīnghú（名）jinghu, two-stringed bowed instrument used as an accompaniment to Beijing opera

【京韻大鼓】jīngyùn dàgǔ（名）storytelling in Beijing dialect with drum accompaniment

【京劇】jīngjù(京戲 jīngxì)（名）Beijing opera

亭 tíng（名）❶ pavilion ❷ kiosk: 電話～ telephone booth; kiosk

【亭子】tíngzi（名）pavilion; kiosk

【亭子間】tíngzijiān（名）〈方〉garret

亮 liàng Ⅰ（形）❶ bright; luminous: 天剛～。It is dawning. ❷ sonorous Ⅱ（動）❶ be enlightened: 心裏～了 feel enlightened ❷ show; disclose: ～出底牌 show one's hand

【亮光】liàngguāng（名）light

【亮度】liàngdù（名）brightness

【亮相】liàngxiàng（動）❶ strike a pose ❷ elaborate one's views; take a stance

【亮堂】liàngtang（形）❶ bright ❷

【亮晶晶】liàngjīngjīng（形）twinkling; glittering

人 部

人 rén（名）❶ human being; person: 年輕～ young people / 那裏邊

没～。Nobody is in there. ❷ other people: 待～诚恳坦白 be frank and sincere with people ❸ personality; character: 他为～忠厚。He is honest and kind by nature. ❹ everybody; each: ～各有志。Everybody has his own ambition. ❺ manpower; hand: ～浮於事 be overstaffed

【人人】rénrén（名）everybody; everyone

【人丁】réndīng（名） population; number of people in a family

【人力】rénlì（名）manpower; labour power: ～资源 human resources

【人力车】rénlìchē（名）rickshaw

【人大】Réndà（名）〈short for 全國人民代表大會 Quánguó rénmín dàibiǎo dàhuì〉NPC; the National People's Congress

【人工】réngōng Ⅰ（形） man-made; artificial: ～授精 artificial insemination Ⅱ（名）❶ manual work; work done by hand: 这條地毯由～织成。This carpet is handwoven. ❷ man-power; man-day

【人士】rénshì（名）personage; public figure: 戲劇界～ people of theatrical circles

【人才】réncái（名）❶ talented person; qualified personnel ❷ handsome appearance

【人才外流】rén cái wài liú（名）brain drain

【人才辈出】rén cái bèi chū〈成〉talented people are coming forth in great numbers

【人口】rénkǒu（名）❶ population ❷ number of people in a family

【人口普查】rénkǒu pǔchá（名）census

【人口學】rénkǒuxué（名）demography

【人口爆炸】rénkǒu bàozhà （名）population explosion

【人山人海】rén shān rén hǎi〈成〉huge crowds of people

【人之常情】rén zhī cháng qíng〈成〉it's only human; that's the way of the world

【人手】rénshǒu（名） manpower; hand

【人心】rénxīn（名）public feeling: ～所向 the popular sentiment; the will of the people

【人云亦云】rén yún yì yún〈成〉parrot what others have said; me-tooism

【人文科学】rénwén kēxué（名）the humanities

【人生】rénshēng（名）life: ～观 outlook on life

【人民】rénmín（名）the people: 群衆 the masses

【人民公社】rénmín gōngshè （名）people's commune

【人民政府】rénmín zhèngfǔ（名）the People's Government

【人民幣】rénmínbì（名） *Renminbi* (RMB); currency of the PRC

【人世】rénshì（名）the world; this world; the world of the living

【人次】réncì（名）person-time

【人行天橋】rénxíng tiānqiáo （名）overpass; pedestrian bridge

【人行地道】rénxíng dìdào （名）underpass; pedestrian tunnel

【人行道】rénxíngdào （名） pavement; sidewalk

【人行橫道】rénxíng héngdào（名）pedestrian crosswalk; zebra crossing

【人防】rénfáng（名）〈short for 人民

防空 rénmín fángkōng) people's air defence; civil air defence

【人均】rénjūn（形）per capita; per head

【人身】rénshēn（名）person; human body: ～自由 freedom of person

【人命】rénmìng（名）human life

【人事】rénshì（名）❶ personnel affairs: ～局 the personnel bureau ❷ common sense and human relationship ❸ consciousness (of the outside world): ～不知 lose consciousness ❹ human efforts: 盡～ do everything possible (to save a situation)

【人物】rénwù（名）❶ figure; personage: 顯要～ notable (figure) ❷ character (in a literary work): 虛構的～ fictitious character

【人性】rénxìng（名）human nature

【人定勝天】rén dìng shèng tiān〈成〉man is bound to prevail over nature

【人品】rénpǐn（名）moral character

【人家】rénjiā（名）❶ household ❷ family: 小康～ family which is moderately well-off

【人家】rénjia（代）❶ [used to refer to people other than oneself] other people; another: ～都不擔心, 就你擔心。Nobody is worried except you. ❷ [used to refer to a certain person or people]: ～又不想理你, 何必自討沒趣？Why ask for a snub since he does not seem to pay any attention to you? ❸ [used to refer to the speaker himself]: ～的話你總是不聽。You never listen to me.

【人馬】rénmǎ（名）❶ forces; troops ❷ team: 全班～ the entire team

【人們】rénmen（名）people; the public: 善良的～ people of good will; fair-minded people

【人員】rényuán（名）staff; personnel: 管理～ administrative personnel

【人造】rénzào（形）man-made; artificial: ～裘皮 artificial fur / ～衛星 man-made satellite

【人格】réngé（名）character; personality: ～化 personification

【人情】rénqíng（名）❶ norm of human behaviour ❷ favour: 托～ ask a favour of sb. ❸ human relationship: ～世故 the ways of the world / ～味 human touch

【人參】rénshēn（名）ginseng

【人間】rénjiān（名）the world: ～天堂 paradise on earth

【人為】rénwéi（形）man-made; artificial

【人道】réndào（名）humanity; humanism

【人道主義】réndào zhǔyì（名）humanism; humanitarianism

【人羣】rénqún（名）crowd; throng

【人微言輕】rén wēi yán qīng〈成〉words of an insignificant person carry little weight

【人煙】rényān（名）human habitation: 渺無～ uninhabited

【人稱】rénchēng（名）〈語〉person: 第三～ the third person

【人種】rénzhǒng（名）race

【人種學】rénzhǒngxué（名）ethnology

【人際關係】rénjì guānxì（名）interpersonal relationship

【人選】rénxuǎn（名）candidate; person selected for a position

【人影】rényǐng（名）❶ shadow of a person ❷ trace of a person's presence: 一轉眼就不見他～了。He simply vanished in the twinkling of an eye.

【人質】rénzhì（名）hostage

【人緣】rényuán（名）relations with people：～好 get on well with everybody; be popular

【人類】rénlèi（名）mankind; humanity

【人類學】rénlèixué（名）anthropology

【人證】rénzhèng（名）〈法〉testimony of a witness; ～物證 human testimony and material evidence

【人權】rénquán（名）human rights

【人體】réntǐ（名）human body

仄 zè I（形）narrow II（名）〈語〉oblique tones

【仄聲】zèshēng（名）〈語〉oblique tones (in classical Chinese pronunciation)

以 yǐ I（動）use; take：～此爲武器 use this as a weapon II（介）❶ according to; based on：～時間爲序 in order of time ❷ because of：～自己的學術成就而自豪 be proud of one's academic achievement III（連）in order to：～求貫徹 to carry it out

【以一當十】yǐ yī dàng shí〈成〉pit one against ten

【以上】yǐshàng I（介）above; over II（形）previous; above; preceeding：～所說的 the above-mentioned

【以下】yǐxià I（介）below; under：二十歲～ under the age of twenty II（形）following：～所列的書單 the books listed below

【以及】yǐjí（連）as well as; and

【以內】yǐnèi（介）in; within; inside：一年～ within a year

【以外】yǐwài（介）outside; beyond;

besides：八小時～ outside one's working hours/ 地平綫～ beyond the horizon

【以次】yǐcì（副）in proper order

【以色列】Yǐsèliè（名）Israel：～人 Israeli

【以免】yǐmiǎn（連）in order not to; so as to avoid：～耽誤班機 in order not to miss the flight

【以卵投石】yǐ luǎn tóu shí〈成〉throw an egg at a rock; court one's ruin

【以身作則】yǐ shēn zuò zé〈成〉set an example (by one's own action)

【以身殉職】yǐ shēn xùn zhí〈成〉die at one's post; give one's life in the discharge of one's duties

【以防萬一】yǐ fáng wàn yī〈成〉be prepared for any eventuality

【以來】yǐlái（介）since：建校～ since the founding of the university / 三年～ over the past three years

【以往】yǐwǎng（副）before; in the past

【以便】yǐbiàn（連）so that; in order to; so as to：我們一大早動身，～準時到達。We set off early in the morning in order to arrive on time.

【以前】yǐqián（副）ago; before：二百年～ two centuries ago

【以毒攻毒】yǐ dú gōng dú〈成〉combat poison with poison; fight fire with fire

【以怨報德】yǐ yuàn bào dé〈成〉return evil for good; repay kindness with malice

【以後】yǐhòu（副）later; afterwards：我三天～到。I'll be there in three days.

【以致】yǐzhì（連）so that; with the result that：他太粗心，～考試沒

有及格。He was so careless that he failed the examination.

【以逸待勞】yǐ yì dài láo〈成〉wait in readiness for the advance of an exhausted enemy

【以訛傳訛】yǐ é chuán é〈成〉relay wrong messages; snowball a rumour; spread misinformation

【以眼還眼，以牙還牙】yǐ yǎn huán yǎn, yǐ yá huán yá〈成〉eye for eye and tooth for tooth; measure for measure; tit for tat

【以爲】yǐwéi〈動〉think; believe: 我～他會來的。I thought he would come.

【以德報怨】yǐ dé bào yuàn〈成〉return good for evil

【以禮相待】yǐ lǐ xiāng dài〈成〉treat sb. with courtesy

【以權謀私】yǐ quán móu sī〈成〉abuse one's power for personal gain; seek private profit by exploiting one's position and power

今 jīn I〈名〉❶ modern times: 古往～來 in ancient or modern times; throughout the ages ❷ the present time: 當～ nowadays II〈形〉current: ～晨 this morning /～年 current year

【今日】jīnrì〈副〉today: 代表團定於～到達。The delegation arrives today.

【今天】jīntiān〈副〉today

【今生】jīnshēng〈名〉this life

【今世】jīnshì〈名〉❶ this life ❷ present age

【今見】jīn II〈名〉〈口〉today

【今昔】jīnxī〈名〉the present and the past: ～相比，確有重大變化。Comparing the present with the past, we find the changes are significant.

【今後】jīnhòu〈副〉from now on; in the future

【今朝】jīnzhāo〈名〉today; present day

介 jiè I〈動〉be located between; interpose: ～於兩市之間 lie between the two cities II〈名〉❶ armour; shell: ～殼 shell (of oysters, lobsters, etc.) ❷ (Jiè) a surname

【介入】jièrù〈動〉be involved: 這場糾紛 be involved in the dispute

【介紹】jièshào〈動〉❶ introduce ❷ recommend ❸ brief; give information

【介紹信】jièshàoxìn〈名〉letter of introduction; letter of recommendation

【介詞】jiècí〈名〉preposition

【介意】jièyì〈動〉take to heart; mind: 希望你不要～。I hope you won't take it to heart.

仁 rén〈名〉❶ benevolence; humanity ❷ kernel: 杏～ almond

【仁人志士】rénrén zhìshì〈名〉people with moral integrity and noble aspirations

【仁至義盡】rén zhì yì jìn〈成〉reach the limit of one's forbearance; be extremely magnanimous: 爲了避免摩擦，我們已經做到～。We have gone to great lengths to avoid friction.

【仁者見仁，智者見智】rén zhě jiàn rén, zhì zhě jiàn zhì〈成〉when people look at a matter from different angles, they come to different conclusions; opinions vary

【仁政】rénzhèng〈名〉mercy; benevolent government

【仁义】rényì (名) kindheartedness and a sense of justice

【仁爱】rén'ài (名) kindness; kindly disposition

【仁慈】réncí (形) kindhearted; compassionate

什 shén
see also shí

【什么】shénme (代) ❶ [used to indicate interrogation] what; which: 你吃～? What would you like to eat? ❷ [used to indicate sth. indefinite]: 他仿佛想说～. It seemed that he wanted to say something. ❸ [used before 也 or 都 to indicate that there are no exceptions] any: 他～运动也不喜欢. He is not keen on any kind of sport. ❹ [used after a verb to indicate disapproval]: 吹～牛。Stop boasting. ❺ [used to introduce an enumeration]: 他藏书丰富，～小说、诗歌、戏剧，样样都有。He has a rich collection of books, novels, poems, plays and what not.

【什么的】shénmede (代) and so on: 晚上他喜欢读报刊杂志～. In the evenings, he likes to read newspapers; magazines and what not.

什 shí (形) assorted; mixed
see also shén

【什物】shíwù (名) sundry articles for everyday use

【什锦】shíjǐn (形)〈食品〉assorted: ～素 assorted vegetable dish

仆 pū (动) fall down: ～地 fall on the ground / 前～后继。(of fighting) As one falls, another dashes ahead.

仇 chóu (名) ❶ enemy; adversary ❷ hatred; hostility: 与他有～ nurse hatred against him; have scores to settle with him
see also Qiú

【仇人】chóurén (名) (personal) enemy

【仇恨】chóuhèn (名) hatred; enmity

【仇视】chóushì (动) regard with enmity; be hostile to

【仇敌】chóudí (名) enemy; foe

仇 Qiú (名) a surname
see also chóu

仍 réng (副) still; yet: 他～住在那个村子里。He still lives in that village.

【仍然】réngrán (副) still; yet

【仍旧】réngjiù Ⅰ (动) remain the same Ⅱ (副) still; as before: 她看起来～那么年轻。She still looks very young.

令 líng (量) ream: 一～纸 a ream of paper
see also lìng

令 lìng Ⅰ (名) ❶ order; command ❷ season: 冬～ winter Ⅱ (动) make; cause: ～人愤慨 make one furious; fill one with indignation Ⅲ〈敬〉❶ good: ～德 high virtue ❷ your: ～兄 your elder brother
see also líng

【令人发指】lìng rén fà zhǐ〈成〉make one's blood boil

【令行禁止】lìng xíng jìn zhǐ〈成〉strictly carry out laws and decrees; all orders and laws are carried out without exception

【令箭】lìngjiàn (名) arrow-shaped

token of military authority (used in issuing orders in ancient China); imperative order

仨 sā (数)〈口〉three: 咱們～ we three; the three of us

仕 shì (名) ❶〈旧〉official ❷ bodyguard, a piece in Chinese chess
【仕女】shìnǚ (名)〈美术〉traditional Chinese painting of beautiful women
【仕途】shìtú (名)〈旧〉official career

付 fù (动) deliver; pay: ～現款 pay in cash
【付之一炬】fù zhī yī jù〈成〉commit to the flames
【付之一笑】fù zhī yī xiào〈成〉dismiss with a laugh
【付出】fùchū (动) pay: ～生命 sacrifice one's life
【付款】fùkuǎn (动) make payments: 貨到～ cash on delivery (COD)
【付諸東流】fù zhū dōng liú〈成〉be irrevocably lost; all efforts are in vain

代 dài Ⅰ (名) ❶ historical period: 近～ modern times / 唐～ the Tang Dynasty ❷ generation: 老一～ the older generation ❸ (Dài) a surname Ⅱ (动) replace; act for Ⅲ (形) acting: ～總理 acting premier
【代表】dàibiǎo Ⅰ (名) representative; deputy; delegate Ⅱ (形) representative Ⅲ (动) represent; speak or act for
【代表團】dàibiǎotuán (名) delegation
【代理】dàilǐ (动) act for
【代理人】dàilǐrén (名) agent

【代詞】dàicí (名)〈语〉pronoun
【代替】dàitì (动) replace; be in sb.'s stead
【代數】dàishù (名) algebra
【代價】dàijià (名) price; cost
【代辦】dàibàn Ⅰ (动) act on sb.'s behalf Ⅱ (名)〈外〉charge d'affaires
【代謝】dàixiè (名) supersession: 新陳～ metabolism

仗 zhàng Ⅰ (名) battle; war: 打過許多～ fight many battles Ⅱ (动) rely on; depend on: 憑～自己的努力 rely on one's own efforts
【仗勢欺人】zhàng shì qī rén〈成〉bully others by relying on one's position or powerful connections
【仗義執言】zhàng yì zhí yán〈成〉speak out in defence of justice
【仗義疏財】zhàng yì shū cái〈成〉be loyal to one's friends and generous to the needy

他 tā (代) ❶ he; him ❷ [used to denote any person male or famale, when no distinction of sex is required or possible]: 不管是誰, 只要考第一, 這個獎就歸～。This prize will be awarded to whoever comes out first in the examination. ❸ other; another: 挪做～用 be used for other purposes / 流落～鄉 be stranded in a strange land
【他人】tārén (名) others; another person
【他們】tāmen (代) they; them: ～的書
【他殺】tāshā (名)〈法〉homicide
【他國】tāguó (名) other countries; another country
【他媽的】tāmāde〈骂〉Damn (it)!

仔 zǐ（形）(of domestic animals or fowls) young: ～豬 piglet; pigling

【仔细】 zǐxì（形）careful; attentive: ～觀察 carefully observe

仙 xiān（名）immortal

【仙人掌】 xiānrénzhǎng（名）cactus

【仙女】 xiānnǚ（名）fairy (maiden); maid from the celestial sphere

【仙境】 xiānjìng（名）fairyland; wonderland

【仙鶴】 xiānhè（名）red-crowned crane

仡 gē

【仡佬族】 Gēlǎozú（名）the Gelo nationality

仟 qiān（數）[the elaborate form of the numeral 千, used on cheques, banknotes, etc.] thousand

企 qǐ

【企求】 qǐqiú（動）seek; pine (for or after)

【企望】 qǐwàng（動）long for; look forward to

【企業】 qǐyè（名）enterprise; undertaking: ～家 entrepreneur; enterpriser

【企圖】 qǐtú（動）〈貶〉try; attempt

【企鵝】 qǐé（名）penguin

仿 fǎng（動）❶ imitate; copy ❷ resemble

【仿生學】 fǎngshēngxué（名）bionics

【仿佛】 fǎngfú（動）❶ seem; look as if ❷ resemble

【仿效】 fǎngxiào（動）imitate

【仿照】 fǎngzhào（動）follow

【仿製】 fǎngzhì（仿造 fǎngzào）（動）reproduce; imitate: ～品 reproduc-

tion; replica

伉 kàng

【伉儷】 kànglì（名）husband and wife: 結爲～ become husband and wife; get married

伙 huǒ

【伙房】 huǒfáng（名）kitchen of a canteen (at a school, etc.)

伎 jì（名）❶ skill; craft; trick ❷ professional female singer or dancer in ancient China

【伎倆】 jìliǎng（名）〈貶〉trick; wile: 採取卑鄙的～ play dirty tricks

伍 wǔ Ⅰ（數）five [the elaborate form of the numeral 五, used on cheques, banknotes, etc.] Ⅱ（名）❶ army: 退～ retire from the army; be demobilized ❷ company: 與壞人爲～ keep bad company ❸ (Wǔ) a surname

休 xiū Ⅰ（動）❶ rest; break: 全～一月 complete rest for a month ❷ stop; cease: 喋喋不～ talk endlessly Ⅱ（副）never: ～要胡言亂語。Don't talk rubbish.

【休止】 xiūzhǐ（動）stop; cease; end: 無～ endless

【休克】 xiūkè（名）〈醫〉shock

【休眠】 xiūmián（名）dormancy: ～火山 dormant volcano

【休息】 xiūxi Ⅰ（動）rest Ⅱ（名）rest; interval; intermission

【休戚相關】 xiū qī xiāng guān〈成〉be bound together by common interests

【休戚與共】 xiū qī yǔ gòng〈成〉share joys and sorrows; have a common destiny

【休假】xiūjià (动) have a holiday; go on furlough; be on leave: 因病 ~ be on sick leave

【休会】xiūhuì (动) adjourn

【休业】xiūyè (动) suspend business

【休养】xiūyǎng (动) recuperate: ~ 地 health resort/ ~ 所 sanatorium

【休整】xiūzhěng (名) (of troops) rest and reorganization

【休战】xiūzhàn (名) truce; cease-fire

【休学】xiūxué (动) discontinue one's studies for a specified period of time

伐 fá (动) ❶ fell; cut ❷ send an expedition against; attack

【伐木】fámù (动) fell trees: ~ 工 lumberjack

伏 fú Ⅰ (动) ❶ bend over ❷ give up; admit ❸ hide Ⅱ (名) summer; hot season

【伏天】fútiān (名) hottest days in summer

【伏兵】fúbīng (名) soldiers in ambush

【伏法】fúfǎ (动) be executed

【伏帖】fútiē (形) feel comfortable; be at ease

【伏案】fú'àn (动) bend over one's desk

【伏特】fútè (名)〈电〉volt

【伏笔】fúbǐ (名) (in literature) foreshadowing

【伏贴】fútiē (形) docile and obedient

【伏击】fújī (动) ambush

伊 yī

【伊拉克】Yīlākè (名) Iraq: ~ 人 Iraqi

【伊始】yīshǐ (名) beginning

【伊朗】Yīlǎng (名) Iran: ~ 人 Iranian

【伊斯兰教】Yīsīlánjiào (名) Islam: ~ 徒 Moslem

仲 zhòng (形) ❶ middle; intermediate ❷ mid; second: ~ 夏 mid-summer; second month of summer

【仲裁】zhòngcái (动) arbitrate: 在双方之间进行 ~ arbitrate between two parties

似 shì

see also sì

【似的】shìde (助) [used after nouns, pronouns or verbs to indicate likeness]: 他像是着了魔 ~。He looks like a man possessed.

似 sì Ⅰ (形) similar; analogous: 类 ~ 的例子很多。Similar instances are numerous. Ⅱ (动) seem Ⅲ (介) than; surpassing: 一个高一个 ~。One is taller than another.

see also shì

【似乎】sìhu (动) seem; appear: 天 ~ 要下雨。It looks like rain.

【似…非…】sì…fēi… [used to indicate intermediacy in character]: 似蓝非蓝 bluish / 似鱼非鱼 an animal that looks like fish but is not; fishlike animal

【似是而非】sì shì ér fēi〈成〉specious

份 fèn Ⅰ (名) share; part: 分成四 ~ divide it into four parts Ⅱ (量) 一 ~ 报纸 a newspaper

【份子】fènzi (名) one's share for a group present, etc.: 凑 ~ club together to buy a gift

【份额】fèn'é (名) share

件 jiàn Ⅰ (量) [of clothes, events,

etc]：一～ 小事 a small matter; a trifling matter / 兩～ 背心 two vests Ⅱ（名）❶ piece; item; unit: 零～ spare part /事～ incident; event ❷ document; letter: 證～ credential; certificate /急～ urgent document (dispatch) / 信～ mail

任 Rén（名）a surname

see also rèn

任 rèn Ⅰ（動）❶ appoint; designate: 被～爲公司經理 be appointed manager of the company ❷ hold a post; take on a job ❸ permit; allow: ～其自然。Let things take their natural course. Ⅱ（名）official post; office: 在～ during one's tenure of office / 連～ serve a second term Ⅲ（連）no matter (how, what, etc.): ～誰也不準打擾病人。Nobody is allowed to disturb the patient no matter who he is.

see also Rén

【任人唯親】rèn rén wéi qīn〈成〉appoint people by nepotism; practise favouritism

【任人唯賢】rèn rén wéi xián〈成〉appoint people on their merits

【任何】rènhé（代）any; whatever: 你～一天來都行。Come any day you like.

【任免】rènmiǎn Ⅰ（動）appoint and dismiss Ⅱ（名）appointments and dismissals

【任命】rènmìng（動）appoint; designate

【任性】rènxìng（形）wilful; wayward

【任重道遠】rèn zhòng dào yuǎn〈成〉the road is long and the difficulties ahead are numerous

【任務】rènwu（名）assignment; task

【任期】rènqī（名）term; tenure of office

【任勞任怨】rèn láo rèn yuàn〈成〉work tirelessly and without complaining

【任意】rènyì（副）wantonly; at will

【任憑】rènpíng Ⅰ（介）at one's discretion; at will: ～他處理 act at his own discretion Ⅱ（連）no matter (how, what, etc.): ～你怎麼解釋,你還得承擔主要責任。Whatever explanations you may offer, you will have to take the major part of the blame.

【任職】rènzhí（動）hold a post; serve: 他在一家銀行～。He works in a bank.

仰 yǎng（動）❶ turn up one's head: ～起頭 look up ❷ admire: 敬～他的品德 have great respect for his moral integrity ❸ rely on; depend on

【仰人鼻息】yǎng rén bí xī〈成〉take orders from a powerful man and act slavishly

【仰仗】yǎngzhàng（動）rely on; be backed up by

【仰泳】yǎngyǒng（名）backstroke

【仰臥】yǎngwò（動）lie on one's back

【仰望】yǎngwàng（動）❶ look up at: ～星空 look up at the starry skies ❷ look up to; count on: ～得到您的贊同 sincerely expect you to give your blessing

【仰慕】yǎngmù（動）admire; respect: ～他的文才 admire him for his literary talent

佘 Shé（名）a surname

余 Yú（名）a surname

位 wèi Ⅰ（名）❶ place; location; seat ❷ place — occupy a high position; hold high office ❸ throne: 即～ ascend the throne ❹〈数〉place; digit: 四～数 four-digit number Ⅱ（量）〈敬〉(of people) 两～先生 two gentlemen

【位子】wèizi（名）seat; place

【位次】wèicì（名）precedence; seating arrangement

【位次卡】wèicìkǎ（名）place card

【位于】wèiyú（动）be situated: ～中东 be located in the Middle East

【位置】wèizhì（名）place; position; seat

住 zhù（动）❶ live; stay; dwell: ～在郊区 live in the suburbs／赴美途中在东京～了一天 stop over in Tokyo for a day on one's way to the U.S. ❷ stop; cease: 风～了。 The wind has abated. ❸［used after some verbs to indicate a halt or firm hold］: 突然站～ stop short／抓～ catch hold of／禁得～ be able to stand (the test, etc.)

【住口】zhùkǒu（动）shut up; keep one's mouth shut

【住户】zhùhù（名）household

【住手】zhùshǒu（动）stop（doing sth.）

【住宅】zhùzhái（名）residence

【住址】zhùzhǐ（名）address

【住房】zhùfáng（名）housing; lodgings

【住所】zhùsuǒ（名）residence; lodgings

【住持】zhùchí（名）（Buddhist or Taoist）abbot

【住院】zhùyuàn（动）be hospitalized

【住宿】zhùsù（名）accommodation: 安排～ arrange accommodation

【住处】zhùchù（名）residence; lodgings; quarters

伴 bàn Ⅰ（名）companion; partner; mate: 小伙～们 little friends Ⅱ（动）accompany

【伴侣】bànlǚ（名）companion; partner; mate: 终身～ lifelong companion (spouse)

【伴奏】bànzòu Ⅰ（动）accompany; provide a musical accompaniment for Ⅱ（名）(instrumental) accompaniment: 手风琴～ accordion accompaniment

【伴郎】bànláng（名）best man

【伴娘】bànniáng（名）brides-maid

【伴唱】bànchàng（名）vocal accompaniment

【伴随】bànsuí（动）accompany; attend; follow

估 gū

【估计】gūjì（动）estimate; appraise: 过高(低)～ over- (under-)estimate

【估量】gūliàng（动）estimate; calculate

【估价】gūjià（动）❶ make a rough estimate of the price ❷ appraise; evaluate

何 hé Ⅰ（代）［used to denote interrogation］: ～地 where Ⅱ（Hé）（名）a surname

【何不】hébù（副）why not

【何止】hézhǐ（动）far more than expected: 理由～这些! The list of reasons so far advanced is by no means exhaustive!

【何以】héyǐ（副）how; why: 既经

說定，～反悔？ Why all this change since we have clinched the deal?

【何必】hébì (副) [often used in a rhetorical question] why: ～自找麻煩？ Why ask for trouble?

【何去何從】hé qù hé cóng〈成〉 what attitude to take: ～，由你自己選擇。As to what attitude to take on this issue, it is up to you to decide.

【何在】hézài (副) where: 問題～？ What's the cause of the trouble?

【何妨】héfáng (副) why not; might as well: ～摸摸她的底？ Why not sound her out?

【何況】hékuàng (連) even less; let alone

【何足掛齒】hé zú guà chǐ〈成〉 not worth mentioning

【何其】héqí (副) how: ～毒也。 How vicious!

【何苦】hékǔ (副) why bother; why worry about: 打個電話就可以了，～跑一次呢？ Why bother to make a trip when you can make a telephone call?

【何許】héxǔ (形) what kind of: 他～人也？ Who is he?

【何等】héděng (副) [used in exclamations to suggest unusual qualities or circumstances]: 這是～美妙的景色！ What a magnificent view!

【何嘗】hécháng (副) [used to denote mild negation]: 我～不知讀書重要，只是那時讀不起罷了。Not that I didn't know the importance of formal schooling, I just couldn't afford it.

【何謂】héwèi (副)〈書〉 how would you define

佈 bù (動) ❶ make known: 公～

於眾 be announced ❷ spread: 分～ 均匀 distribute evenly ❸ deploy; arrange

【佈防】bùfáng (動) deploy troops on garrison duty; make tactical arrangements for a defence

【佈告】bùgào (名) notice; bulletin: 出～ put up a notice

【佈局】bùjú (名) ❶ layout; overall arrangement (often referring to the composition of a picture or that of a piece of writing) ❷ positioning (the way to make initial moves to occupy strategic positions on the chessboard)

【佈施】bùshī (名)〈宗〉 alms; charity

【佈景】bùjǐng (名) ❶〈劇〉 set; backdrop ❷ composition of a traditional Chinese painting

【佈雷】bùléi (動) mine; lay mines: ～艇 minelayer

【佈置】bùzhì (動) ❶ arrange: ～作業 assign (homework for students) ❷ decorate; fix up

佛 fó (名) ❶ Buddha ❷ Buddhism ❸ statue of Budha

【佛寺】fósì (名) Buddhist temple

【佛門】fómén (名) Buddhism: ～弟子 Buddhists

【佛得角】Fódéjiǎo (名) Cape Verde: ～人 Cape Verdean

【佛教】fójiào (名) Buddhism

【佛堂】fótáng (名) family Buddhist hall

【佛經】fójīng (名) Buddhist Scripture

【佛爺】fóye (名) Buddha

【佛像】fóxiàng (名) statue or image of Buddha

【佛龕】fókān（名）niche for a Buddha statue

伺 cì
see also sì

【伺候】cìhou（動）wait upon: ～病人 attend a patient

伺 sì（動）watch; await
see also cì

【伺機】sìjī（動）bide one's time; wait for one's opportunity

伽 jiā（名）〈物〉gal (a unit of acceleration)

【伽耶琴】jiāyēqín（名）Korean plucked stringed instrument

佔 zhàn（動）❶ occupy; seize: ～座位 occupy a seat ❷ constitute; make up: ～優勢 gain an advantage / 女學生～了一半。The girl students make up half of the total.

【佔先】zhànxiān（動）take precedence; take the lead

【佔有】zhànyǒu（動）❶ own; possess: 非法～土地 take illegal possession of land; squat ❷ occupy; hold

【佔便宜】zhàn piányi（動）gain advantage by unfair means; benefit at others' expense

【佔領】zhànlǐng（動）occupy; seize: ～城市 seize a city

【佔綫】zhànxiàn〈電話〉the line is busy

【佔據】zhànjù（動）occupy; hold: ～重要地位 hold an important position

但 dàn Ⅰ（副）only; merely: ～願 merely hope Ⅱ（連）but; however

【但是】dànshì（連）but; yet; however

【但書】dànshū（名）proviso

伸 shēn（動）stretch; extend: ～出舌頭 put out one's tongue / ～直腿 stretch one's legs

【伸手】shēnshǒu（動）❶ stretch out one's hand ❷ ask for help, etc.: 不要老向父母～要錢。Don't always ask your parents for money.

【伸展】shēnzhǎn（動）extend; stretch: 他的勢力一直～到海外。His influence extends beyond the seas.

【伸張】shēnzhāng（動）uphold; promote: ～正義 uphold justice

【伸腰】shēnyāo（動）straighten one's back; stretch oneself

【伸縮】shēnsuō Ⅰ（動）stretch out and draw back; expand and contract Ⅱ（形）flexible; elastic; adjustable

【伸懶腰】shēn lǎnyāo（動）stretch oneself

佃 diàn（動）rent land

【佃户】diànhù(佃農 diànnóng) tenant farmer

【佃租】diànzū（名）land rent

伶 líng

【伶仃】língdīng（形）lonely; forlorn: 孤苦～ lonely and friendless

【伶俐】línglì（形）clever; adroit: 口齒～ speak fluently

你 nǐ（代）❶ [second person singular] you; your: ～在做什麽? What are you doing? / ～姐姐 your sister ❷ you; one; anyone

【你好】nǐhǎo [used as a greeting] how do you do; how are you; hello; hi

【你死我活】nǐ sǐ wǒ huó〈成〉involving the life and death of the people concerned: ～的鬥爭 a life-and-death struggle

【你們】nǐmen（代）[second person plural] you

作 zuò I（動）[used only in certain compound words and idioms] do: ～孽 do evil II（名）workshop: 洗衣～ laundry
see also zuó; zuò

【作坊】zuōfang（名）workshop

【作弄】zuōnòng（動）make a fool of; play a trick on

【作揖】zuōyī（動）make a bow with hands folded in front

作 zuó
see also zuō; zuò

【作料】zuóliào（名）condiment; seasoning

作 zuò I（動）❶ do; make: ～判斷 pass judgment/ ～操 do exercises ❷ write; compose ❸ 曲 compose music; compose ❸ pretend; affect: 故～不知 pretend ignorance ❹ regard as: 把他～爲榜樣 take sb. as one's example ❺ act as; be: ～顧問 act as consultant II（名）writings; work: 傑～ masterpiece / 原～ original work
see also zuō; zuó

【作文】zuòwén（名）composition; essay

【作用】zuòyòng I（動）affect; act on: 酸～金屬 Acids act on metals. II（名）❶ function; role: 起重要～ play an important role ❷ action; effect: 化學～ chemical action / 鎮靜～ tranquilizing effect

【作怪】zuòguài（動）make trouble;

do mischief: 這全是同行的妒忌心～。It is professional jealousy that has caused all the trouble.

【作者】zuòzhě（名）author; writer

【作物】zuòwù（名）crop: 糧食～ grain crops

【作保】zuòbǎo（動）be sb.'s guarantor; sponsor sb.

【作風】zuòfēng（名）style of work; way of doing things: 官僚主義～ bureaucratic style of work

【作品】zuòpǐn（名）(literary or artistic) work

【作威作福】zuò wēi zuò fú〈成〉play the tyrant; ride roughshod over others

【作家】zuòjiā（名）writer

【作案】zuò'àn（動）commit a crime

【作祟】zuòsuì（動）❶（of a ghost or apparition）haunt a place ❷ cause trouble; make mischief

【作息】zuòxī（名）work and rest: ～時間 daily schedule

【作梗】zuògěng（動）obstruct; impede; crate difficulties

【作陪】zuòpéi（動）be invited along with the guest of honour at a banquet

【作惡】zuò'è（動）do evil

【作爲】zuòwéi I（名）❶ conduct; action: 他的～令人欽佩。His conduct commands admiration. ❷ accomplishment; achievement: 很有～ have accomplished much II（動）use as; regard as: 把它～行動的指南 regard it as a guide to action II（介）as: ～朋友，我會盡力幫助你。As a friend, I'll do my best to help you.

【作業】zuòyè（名）❶ school assignment: 家庭～ homework ❷ work;

task; operation: 機械化採礦 ~ mechanized mining operations

【作對】zuòduì（動）set oneself against; be opposed to

【作嘔】zuòǒu（動）feel sick: 令人 ~ disgusting; nauseating; sickening

【作罷】zuòbà（動）drop; cancel; call off

【作弊】zuòbì（動）practise fraud; cheat: 考試 ~ cheat at the exam

【作廢】zuòfèi（動）become invalid; be made null and void

【作價】zuòjià（動）set a price; assess

【作戰】zuòzhàn（動）fight

【作證】zuòzhèng（動）be a witness in court; testify

【作難】zuònán（動）❶ feel embarrassed ❷ make things difficult for sb.

【作繭自縛】zuò jiǎn zì fù〈成〉be caught in a trap of one's own making

佝 gōu

【佝僂病】gōulóubìng（名）rickets

佟 Tóng（名）a surname

伯 bó（名）❶ father's elder brother: 大 ~ uncle (a polite form of address for an elderly man) ❷ eldest of brothers ❸ earl; count

【伯父】bófù (伯伯 bóbo)（名）uncle; address for any elderly man of one's parent's generation

【伯母】bómǔ（名）aunt (wife of father's elder brother); address for any elderly woman of one's parent's generation

【伯樂】Bólè（名）❶ name of an ancient Chinese horse trainer known for his ability to pick out good

horses ❷ one who has the rare ability to spot talent

【伯爵】bójué（名）earl; count: ~ 夫人 countess

低 dī Ⅰ（形）low: ~ 空 at low altitude Ⅱ（動）lower; droop: ~ 頭 bow one's head

【低三下四】dī sān xià sì〈成〉servile and submissive

【低劣】dīliè（形）inferior; shoddy

【低沉】dīchén（形）❶ (of sky) covered with low-lying clouds ❷ (of voice) deep or low ❸ (of person) in low spirits

【低估】dīgū（動）underestimate

【低級】dījí（形）❶ elementary; simple ❷ vulgar; bad: 迎合 ~ 趣味 cater to low tastes

【低能】dīnéng（形）imbecile; feeble-minded

【低產】dīchǎn（名）low yield

【低溫】dīwēn（名）low temperature

【低廉】dīlián（形）cheap

【低落】dīluò（形）low: 士氣 ~ sagging morale

【低微】dīwēi（形）❶ (of sound) feeble ❷ (of station in society) humble

【低潮】dīcháo（名）low tide

【低調】dīdiào（形）low-key

來 lái Ⅰ（動）❶ come: ~ 訪 come to visit ❷ (of problems, affairs, etc.) crop up; happen ❸ [used to stand for a specific verb] do: 再 ~ 一個! Encore! ❹ [used with "得" or "不" to express possibility or impossibility]: 借得 ~ can be loaned ❺ [used before another verb to indicate future action]: 大家 ~ 幫幫他 的忙。Let's all lend him a helping

hand. ❻ [used after another verb or verbal phrase to indicate what one has come for]: 我們看預展～了。We have come for the preview. Ⅱ (助) ❶ [used before a verb or verbal phrase to indicate purpose] in order to: 我們用什麼道理一説明他？How shall we try to convince him? ❷ [used after numerals in enumerating one's reasons]: (他没去。) 一～他太忙了, 二一路也太遠。(He didn't go.) For one thing, he was too busy. For another, it was such a long distance from here. ❸ [used after a verb to indicate movement in the direction of the speaker]: 請拿張椅子～。Please get me a chair. Ⅲ (形) ❶ next: ～年 next year ❷ (of a person or thing) incoming: ～客 visitor / ～電 incoming telegram Ⅳ (副) ❶ since: 三年～ since three years ago ❷ [used after numerals like 十, 百, 千, etc. to indicate a round number] about: 二十～歲的青年人 a young man some twenty years of age Ⅴ (名) (Lái) a surname

【來不及】lái bu jí〈口〉too late (to do sth.); not much time left: 我們根本～準備。We can't possibly get things ready in time.

【來日方長】lái rì fāng cháng〈成〉you have a bright future ahead of you

【…來…去】…lái…qù [used after each of two identical or synonymous verbs to indicate repetition] again and again: 看來看去不懂 try in vain to grasp the meaning

【來回】láihuí Ⅰ (動) make a round trip: ～票 return ticket / ～票價 return fare Ⅱ (副) to and fro; back and forth

【來到】láidào (動) come; arrive

【來往】láiwǎng (動) come and go: ～行人 passing pedestrians

【來往】láiwang (名) contact; transactions: 同他們已經没什麼～ have hardly anything to do with them

【來勁】láijìn Ⅰ (動)〈方〉be in high spirits: 他越説越～。The more he spoke, the more enthusiastic he became. Ⅱ (形) stimulating; exciting

【來信】láixìn (來函 láihán) Ⅰ (動) send a letter here Ⅱ (名) incoming mail; your letter

【來得及】lái de jí〈口〉there is still time (to do sth.); be able to do sth. in time: 我們馬上出發還～。If we start off right now, we can make it.

【來者】láizhě (助) [used to refer to what has happened]: 你忘了爹怎麼告訴咱們～。You have forgotten what Dad told us.

【來勢】láishì (名) momentum

【來源】láiyuán Ⅰ (名) source; origin: 生活～ means of livelihood Ⅱ (動) originate; derive; spring (from)

【來賓】láibīn (名) guest

【來歷】láilì (名) (of a person or thing) background; origin: ～不明的人 person of dubious background

【來頭】láitou (名) ❶ (of a person) background; backing: 他大有～。He has powerful backing. ❷ (of remarks, words, etc.) cause; motivation ❸ momentum

【來頭兒】láitour (名)〈口〉fun: 打紙牌可有～了。It's great fun playing cards.

【來臨】láilín (動) come; arrive

佼 jiǎo（形）handsome; good-looking

【佼佼者】jiǎojiǎozhě（名）outstanding person

依 yī Ⅰ（动）❶ depend on: 唇齿相～ be mutually dependent ❷ comply with; listen to: 定当～命 will certainly comply with your wishes / 不能～你的办 cannot act the way you want us to Ⅱ（介）according to: ～法办理 handle the matter according to law

【依仗】yīzhàng（动）rely on: ～人民的支持 rely on popular support

【依次】yīcì（副）in proper order; in turn

【依存】yīcún（动）depend upon each other for existence

【依附】yīfù（动）depend on; be attached to; adhere to

【依依不舍】yī yī bù shě〈成〉be reluctant to leave; be unwilling to part

【依从】yīcóng（动）comply with

【依顺】yīshùn（动）be obedient

【依稀】yīxī（副）vaguely; dimly

【依然】yīrán（副）still: ～健康 as healthy as ever

【依然故我】yī rán gù wǒ〈成〉be still one's old self; remain unchanged

【依照】yīzhào（介）according to; in the light of: ～计划行事 do sth. as planned

【依靠】yīkào Ⅰ（动）rely on; depend on: ～自己的努力 rely on one's own effort Ⅱ（名）backing; support

【依据】yījù Ⅰ（名）basis; foundation: 毫无～ groundless Ⅱ（介）according to; judging by: ～宪法 in accordance with the Constitution

【依赖】yīlài（动）rely on; depend on

【依旧】yījiù（副）as before; still: 天冷了，但他一天天游泳。It's getting cold, but he still swims every day as before.

【依恋】yīliàn（动）be reluctant to leave; be attached to: ～故土 feel reluctant to leave one's native land

佯 yáng（动）pretend; feint

【佯死】yángsǐ（名）feint death

【佯攻】yánggōng（名）feint attack

【佯言】yángyán（动）lie

【佯作不知】yáng zuò bù zhī〈成〉pretend to be ignorant

併 bìng（动）combine; merge; integrate: 两家公司合～ merger of the two companies

【併入】bìngrù（动）merge into; amalgamate into; incorporate in

【併吞】bìngtūn（动）annex; swallow up

【併发】bìngfā（动）❶ be complicated by; erupt simultaneously ❷ (of disease) occur concurrently: ～症 complication

佳 jiā（形）excellent; wonderful; fine: 身体欠～ not in very good health

【佳人】jiārén（名）beautiful woman; beauty

【佳作】jiāzuò（名）excellent piece of writing; splendid work (book)

【佳肴】jiāyáo（名）delicacy; delicious dish

【佳音】jiāyīn（名）good news; glad tidings

【佳期】jiāqī（名）wedding day

【佳话】jiāhuà（名）praise-worthy deed or amusing anecdote widely

circulated as a topic for conversation: 此事一時傳爲～。This praise-worthy deed was for a time on everybody's lips.

【佳節】jiājié（名）joyous festival

【佳賓】jiābīn（名）guest of honour

侍 shì（動）wait upon; tend: 服～病人 look after a patient

【侍女】shìnǚ（名）maidservant

【侍奉】shìfèng（動）wait upon; tend on

【侍候】shìhòu（動）wait upon; attend on

【侍從】shìcóng（名）attendant; retinue: ～副官 aide-de-camp（A. D. C.）

【侍衛】shìwèi（名）imperial bodyguard

佬 lǎo（名）〈貶〉guy: 鄉巴～ country cousin; bumpkin

使 shǐ Ⅰ（動）❶ send or tell sb. to do sth. ❷ use; work: 他頭腦很好～。He has got a good brain. ❸ make; let; enable: 這個主意～我們少花了一百萬 yuan．This idea saved us a million yuan. Ⅱ（名）envoy; emissary; messenger: 駐日大～ Ambassador to Japan

【使不得】shǐbude（動）❶ be useless; be no longer serviceable: 這個電視機～了。This TV set no longer works. ❷ be impermissible; be undesirable: 他有心臟病, 過度勞累可～。He shouldn't overexert himself since he has heart trouble.

【使出】shǐchu（動）exert: ～各種手法 play all sorts of tricks

【使用】shǐyòng（動）use; employ

【使命】shǐmìng（名）mission

【使性子】shǐ xìngzi（動）get into a temper

【使者】shǐzhě（名）envoy; emissary

【使勁兒】shǐjìnr（動）exert one's strength

【使得】shǐde（動）❶ be usable: 這架打字機還～。This typewriter is still serviceable. ❷ be feasible; be all right: 你這樣魯莽如何～? How can you be so rash? ❸ make; let: 戰爭～這個國家付出了沉重的代價。The war cost the country dearly.

【使眼色】shǐ yǎnsè（動）throw a sidelong glance; wink

【使喚】shǐhuan（動）❶ order about: 你不能這樣～人。You shouldn't order others about like that. ❷ 〈口〉use: 這把剪子好～。This pair of scissors is pretty handy.

【使節】shǐjié（名）(diplomatic) envoy

【使領館】shǐlǐngguǎn（名）diplomatic and consular missions

【使館】shǐguǎn（名）embassy

【使壞】shǐhuài（動）〈口〉give a piece of bad advice; play a cunning trick

供 gōng（動）supply; provide
see also gòng

【供水】gōngshuǐ（名）water supply

【供不應求】gōng bù yìng qiú〈成〉supply falls short of demand

【供求】gōngqiú（名）supply and demand

【供給】gōngjǐ（動）supply; provide

【供電】gōngdiàn（名）power supply

【供養】gōngyǎng（動）provide for; support: ～父母 provide for one's parents

【供销】gōngxiāo（名）supply and marketing: ~（合作）社 supply and marketing cooperative

【供应】gōngyìng（动）supply: 商品 ~ commodity supply

供 gòng Ⅰ（动）❶ lay（offerings）❷ confess Ⅱ（名）❶ offering ❷ confession: 口~ oral confession　see also gōng

【供奉】gòngfèng（动）enshrine and worship

【供词】gòngcí（名）confession; deposition

【供认】gòngrèn（动）confess

【供养】gòngyǎng（动）make offerings to deity and ancestors

【供职】gòngzhí（动）hold a post

例 lì（名）❶ example; instance: 以這個城市為~ take this city for example ❷ precedent: 有~可循 have an example to follow ❸ rule; regulation: 違~ break a rule ❹ routine

【例子】lìzi（名）example; case

【例外】lìwài（名）exception

【例句】lìjù（名）example sentence

【例如】lìrú（副）for example; for instance

【例行公事】lìxíng gōngshì（名）❶ routine（business）❷ mere formality

【例言】lìyán（名）❶ introductory remarks; guide to the use of a book ❷ example

【例假】lìjià（名）❶ official holiday; statutory holiday ❷〈婉〉（menstrual）period

【例会】lìhuì（名）regular meeting

【例题】lìtí（名）illustrative example

【例证】lìzhèng（名）illustration; instance

佰 bǎi（数）[the elaborate form of the numeral 百, used on cheques, banknotes, etc.] hundred

侄 zhí（名）brother's son; nephew

【侄女】zhínǚ（名）niece

【侄子】zhízi（名）nephew

侗 Dòng

【侗族】Dòngzú（名）the Dong nationality

侃 kǎn

【侃大山】kǎndàshān（动）〈口〉chit-chat; gossip

【侃侃而谈】kǎn kǎn ér tán〈成〉speak with ease and confidence

侏 zhū

【侏儒】zhūrú（名）dwarf; pygmy; midget

侈 chǐ Ⅰ（名）extravagant Ⅱ（动）exaggerate

【侈谈】chǐtán（动）talk in high-sounding terms about sth.

佩 pèi（动）❶ wear; carry ❷ admire

【佩服】pèifú（动）admire

【佩带】pèidài（动）wear; carry: ~武器 bear arms ／ ~勋章 wear a medal

俞 Yú（名）a surname

信 xìn Ⅰ（名）❶ confidence; trust: 取~於民 gain the trust of the people ❷ letter: 推薦~ letter of recommendation ❸ message; word: 捎個~ give sb. a message Ⅱ（动）believe: 他的話我不~。 I don't believe what he said. Ⅲ (形) true

【信口开河】 xìn kǒu kāi hé〈成〉
make unprovoked, irresponsible
comments

【信心】 xìnxīn (名) faith; confidence: 对他的能力我很有～。I
have every confidence in his ability.

【信手拈来】 xìn shǒu niān lái〈成〉
write with fluency

【信用】 xìnyòng (名) ❶ credit: 不
讲～ go back on one's word ❷ (经)
credit: ～社 credit cooperative

【信用卡】 xìnyòngkǎ (名) credit card

【信件】 xìnjiàn (名) mail; letters

【信任】 xìnrèn Ⅰ (动) trust Ⅱ (名)
trust; confidence: 完全～他 have
complete confidence in him

【信仰】 xìnyǎng (名) belief; convic-
tion

【信步】 xìnbù (动) take a stroll

【信奉】 xìnfèng (动) believe in: ～
佛教 believe in Buddhism

【信服】 xìnfú (动) be convinced: 不
能令人～的 unconvincing

【信念】 xìnniàn (名) belief; faith

【信使】 xìnshǐ (名) courier; messenger: 外交～ diplomatic courier

【信物】 xìnwù (名) token; keepsake

【信封】 xìnfēng (名) envelope

【信徒】 xìntú (名) disciple; follower;
believer

【信託】 xìntuō (名) trust: ～公司
trust company

【信息】 xìnxī (名) information; message: ～论 information theory

【信条】 xìntiáo (名) credit

【信访】 xìnfǎng (名) letters and visits from the masses

【信教】 xìnjiào (动) be religious

【信筒】 xìntǒng (名)   pillar-box;
mailbox

【信号】 xìnhào (名) signal

【信义】 xìnyì (名) faith; honesty: 毫
無～的人 faithless person

【信匯】 xìnhuì (名)   mail   transfer
(M/T)

【信箋】 xìnjiān (名) letter-paper

【信誓旦旦】 xìn shì dàn dàn〈成〉
give a solemn pledge

【信箱】 xìnxiāng (名) ❶ pillar-box;
mailbox ❷ letter box ❸ post-office
box (P.O.B.)

【信赖】 xìnlài (动) trust; rely on

【信譽】 xìnyù (名) reputation; credit:
～很高的公司 company with a good
reputation

便

biàn Ⅰ (形) ❶ convenient; expedient; handy: 不～参加 be in no
position to participate ❷ informal;
plain: 家常～饭 homely meal Ⅱ
(名) ❶ convenience ❷ piss; shit:
小～ piss; urine Ⅲ (副) then; in
that case: 如果繼續這樣下雨，～
會出現災情。There is bound to be a
serious flood if it goes on raining like
this. Ⅳ (连) ❶ [used to indicate a
subjunctive concession] even if;
even though: 即～ even if ❷ as
soon as: 他一進門～看見有人坐在
那兒。As soon as he went in, he
saw somebody sitting there.
see also pián

【便士】 biànshì (名) penny

【便中】 biànzhōng (副) at one's convenience; when convenient: ～請回
信。I look forward to hearing from
you at your convenience.

【便池】 biànchí (名) urinal

【便血】 biànxiě (名) have (pass)
blood in one's stool or urine

【便衣】 biànyī (名) ❶ civilian clothes

❷ informal dress ❸ plain-clothes-man: ～警察 plain-clothes police-man

【便利】biànlì Ⅰ (形) convenient Ⅱ (动) facilitate: ～乘客 save trouble for the passengers Ⅲ (名) facility; convenience: 提供～ provide facilities for

【便于】biànyú (动) be convenient for: 这架收音机体积小，～携带。This radio set is handy and easy to carry.

【便服】biànfú (便装 biànzhuāng) (名) ❶ informal (ordinary) dress ❷ civilian dress (as against military uniform)

【便函】biànhán (名) informal letter from an organization

【便宜行事】biàn yí xíng shì〈成〉(authorized to) act at one's discretion or as one sees fit

【便盆】biànpén (名) bedpan; chamber pot

【便秘】biànbì (名)〈医〉constipation

【便宴】biànyàn (名) informal dinner

【便条】biàntiáo (名) ❶ (brief) note; memo ❷ memo sheet; memo slip

【便道】biàndào (名) ❶ shortcut: 抄～回家 go back home by a shortcut ❷ pavement; sidewalk ❸ temporary path; makeshift road

【便饭】biànfàn (名) simple meal; potluck: 随时来我家吃～。Drop in any time for a meal.

【便帽】biànmào (名) cap or hat for ordinary wear

【便当】biàndang (形) ❶ convenient: 如果～的话 if it is convenient ❷ easy: 这事办起来很～。This is easy to handle.

【便笺】biànjiān (名) memo pad; notepaper

【便鞋】biànxié (名) ❶ loafer; slipper ❷ cloth shoe

【便桥】biànqiáo (名) emergency bridge; makeshift bridge

便 pián

see also biàn

【便宜】piányi Ⅰ (形) cheap; inexpensive Ⅱ (名) unfair advantage Ⅲ (动) give somebody advantage: 这下～了你。You have got the best of the bargain.

侠 xiá

【侠客】xiákè (名) chivalrous swordsman

【侠义】xiáyì (名) chivalry

俑 yǒng (名) figurine: 兵马～ terra-cotta warriors and horses

侵 qīn Ⅰ (动) invade; encroach upon Ⅱ (形) approaching: ～晨 at the break of dawn

【侵犯】qīnfàn (动) violate; invade: ～人权 violate human rights / ～别国领土 encroach upon another country's territory

【侵占】qīnzhàn (动) occupy; seize: ～公共财产 expropriate public property

【侵吞】qīntūn (动) ❶ embezzle: ～公款 embezzle public funds ❷ annex: ～别国领土 annex the territory of another country

【侵害】qīnhài (动) encroach upon

【侵略】qīnlüè (名) aggression; invasion: ～行为 act of aggression Ⅱ (动) commit aggression against

【侵蚀】qīnshí (动) erode; corrode

【侵扰】qīnrǎo (动) harass; make frequent raids on: ~边境 harass the frontiers

【侵袭】qīnxí (动) invade and attack

侯 hóu (名) ❶ marquis ❷ nobleman; high official ❸ (Hóu) a surname

【侯爵】hóujué (名) marquis

俏 qiào (形) cute; pretty

【俏皮】qiàopí (形) ❶ lively; witty ❷ cute; nice-looking

【俏皮话】qiàopíhuà (名) witty, humorous or ironical remark

【俏货】qiàohuò (名) goods that are in great demand

【俏丽】qiàolì (形) pretty; good-looking

俚 lǐ (形) vulgar

【俚俗】lǐsú (形) unrefined

【俚语】lǐyǔ (名) slang

保 bǎo I (动) ❶ protect; safeguard ❷ preserve: 明哲～身. Wise men court no trouble. ❸ guarantee; ensure: ～你准时到. You may rest assured that it will arrive in time. ❹ go bail for sb. II (名) guarantor; bail: 铺～ guarantee (for a person) given by a shopkeeper

【保人】bǎoren (名) guarantor

【保不住】bǎo bu zhù (副) probably; quite possibly: ～他们已经走了. They may have left already.

【保加利亚】Bǎojiālìyà (名) Bulgaria: ～人 Bulgarian

【保安】bǎo'ān (动) ensure public security: ～措施 security measures

【保存】bǎocún (动) preserve; keep: ～古迹 preserve historic relics

【保守】bǎoshǒu I (动) guard; keep: 此事必须～秘密. This must be kept secret. II (形) conservative: ～疗法 conservative treatment (in medicine)

【保全】bǎoquán (动) preserve; defend; protect against damage: ～名誉 preserve one's good name

【保全工】bǎoquángōng (名) maintenance worker

【保佑】bǎoyòu (动) bless

【保姆】bǎomǔ (名) ❶ children's nurse ❷ domestic help

【保育】bǎoyù (名) child care

【保育员】bǎoyùyuán (名) nurse; child-care worker

【保持】bǎochí (动) keep; maintain; retain; preserve: ～生态平衡 maintain the cological balance

【保送】bǎosòng (动) send sb. on a training course or study programme; recommend sb. for exemption from the entrance examination to school

【保重】bǎozhòng (动) take care of oneself

【保皇党】bǎohuángdǎng (名) royalists

【保修】bǎoxiū (动) guarantee to keep sth. in good repair: ～半年 six months' guarantee

【保真】bǎozhēn (名) 〈电子〉 fidelity (of audio equipment): 高～ hi-fi

【保留】bǎoliú (动) ❶ retain; keep intact ❷ reserve; keep: 这些座位是给贵宾~的. These seats are reserved for distinguished guests.

【保留剧目】bǎoliú jùmù (名) repertoire (of a theatrical corps)

【保密】bǎomì I (动) keep sth. secret II (形) confidential: ～文件 confidential (classified) documents

【保健】bǎojiàn（名）health care; health protection

【保健站】bǎojiànzhàn（名）health centre; clinic

【保健箱】bǎojiànxiāng（名）medical kit

【保單】bǎodān（名）guaranty; guarantee slip; insurance policy

【保溫】bǎowēn（動）preserve heat; keep warm

【保溫杯】bǎowēnbēi（名）thermos mug（which keeps hot water, tea or milk warm for some time）

【保溫瓶】bǎowēnpíng（名）thermos; thermos flask

【保管】bǎoguǎn I（動）take care of: ～好您的衣物。Keep an eye on your clothes and belongings. II（名）safekeeping III（副）surely; certainly: ～您滿意。I bet you will enjoy it.

【保障】bǎozhàng I（動）safeguard; protect: ～新聞自由 guarantee the freedom of press II（名）guarantee; security: 就業～ security of employment

【保養】bǎoyǎng（動）❶ keep fit; take good care of one's health ❷ maintain; keep in good repair: 公路～ road maintenance

【保價】bǎojià（形）assured: ～證券 guaranteed bond

【保駕】bǎojià（動）（literally）escort the Emperor；[usu. jocular in current usage] escort sb. so as to ensure his safety

【保衛】bǎowèi（動）defend; safeguard; protect: ～工作 security work

【保險】bǎoxiǎn I（名）insurance: ～費 premium II（副）surely: 他～要

生氣。He is sure to get angry.

【保險絲】bǎoxiǎnsī（名）〈電〉fuse

【保險櫃】bǎoxiǎnguì（名）safe

【保鏢】bǎobiāo（名）bodyguard; armed escort（for passenger or cargo）

【保藏】bǎocáng（動）keep in store; preserve

【保證】bǎozhèng I（動）guarantee; ensure; pledge: 這消息～可靠。I can assure you that the information is reliable. II（名）guarantee: 和平的～ guarantee for peace

【保證人】bǎozhèngrén（名）guarantor; warrantor; sponsor

【保證金】bǎozhèngjīn（名）earnest（money）;（cash）deosit; bail

【保證書】bǎozhèngshū（名）written pledge; affidavit

【保釋】bǎoshì（動）bail; bail out; release on bail

【保齡球】bǎolíngqiú（名）bowling

【保護】bǎohù（動）protect; safeguard; defend; preserve: ～國家財產 protect state property

【保護人】bǎohùrén（名）protector; guardian

【保護色】bǎohùsè（名）protective colouration

【保護國】bǎohùguó（名）protectorate

【保護貿易主義】bǎohù màoyì zhǔyì（貿易保護主義 màoyì bǎohù zhǔyì）（名）protectionism

【保護關稅】bǎohù guānshuì（名）protective tariff

促 cù I（形）of short duration: 急～的腳步聲 sound of hurried steps II（動）urge

【促成】cùchéng（動）bring to success

【促使】cùshǐ（动）impel; urge on

【促进】cùjìn（动）promote; accelerate: ～相互了解 promote mutual understanding

【促膝】cùxī（动）sit knee to knee: ～谈心 have a tête-à-tête conversation

侣 lǚ（名）companion; partner

修 xiū（动）❶ repair; fix; mend: ～鞋 mend shoes ❷ build; construct: ～地铁 build an underground railway ❸ trim; prune: ～果树 prune fruit trees ❹ study: 专～美学 major in aesthetics

【修女】xiūnǚ（名）nun; sister

【修士】xiūshì（名）brother; friar

【修正】xiūzhèng（动）revise; correct; amend: ～案 amendment

【修正液】xiūzhèngyè（名）correction fluid

【修行】xiūxíng（动）practise Buddhism or Taoism

【修改】xiūgǎi（动）alter; modify; amend: ～文章 revise an article / ～宪法 amend the constitution

【修长】xiūcháng（形）slender

【修建】xiūjiàn（动）build; construct

【修订】xiūdìng（动）revise; amend: ～计划 revise a plan/～本 revised edition

【修面】xiūmiàn（动）shave

【修配】xiūpèi（动）make repairs and supply replacements

【修剪】xiūjiǎn（动）prune; trim

【修理】xiūlǐ（动）repair; fix

【修复】xiūfù（动）repair; renovate

【修道院】xiūdàoyuàn（名）monastery; convent

【修补】xiūbǔ（动）mend; patch; repair

【修脚师】xiūjiǎoshī（名）pedicurist

【修饰】xiūshì（动）❶ decorate; adorn: ～房间 decorate a room ❷ polish; embellish: ～文章 polish an article ❸ make oneself up

【修业】xiūyè（动）pursue one's studies

【修养】xiūyǎng（名）❶ accomplishment; good taste; training: 有文学～ have a fine literary taste ❷ culture: 学术～ academic training / 很有～的人 a cultured person; a person of cultivated taste

【修整】xiūzhěng（动）repair; prune: ～工具 repair one's tools／～树木 prune trees

【修筑】xiūzhù（动）build: ～机场 build an airfield

【修缮】xiūshàn（动）repair; revamp

【修辞】xiūcí（名）rhetoric

俘 fú Ⅰ（动）capture: 被～ be taken prisoner Ⅱ（名）captive

【俘虏】fúlǔ Ⅰ（动）capture Ⅱ（名）captive; prisoner of war

俗 sú Ⅰ（名）custom; convention: 风～习惯 customs and habits Ⅱ（形）❶ popular; current: 通～歌曲 pop song ❷ coarse; vulgar: 庸～作风 vulgar way of doing things; philistinism ❸ secular; profane

【俗不可耐】sú bù kě nài〈成〉dreadfully vulgar

【俗气】súqì（形）❶ boorish; coarse ❷ vulgar

【俗套】sútào（名）convention; common usage

【俗话】súhuà（俗语 súyǔ）（名）proverb; saying

俄 é（副）soon; suddenly: ～頃 in a moment

【俄語】Éyǔ（名）Russian (language)

【俄羅斯族】Éluósīzú（名）the Eluosi (Russian) nationality

侮 wǔ（動）bully; overbear; insult

【侮辱】wǔrǔ（動）insult; outrage; humiliate

【侮慢】wǔmàn（動）bully and insult: 肆意～ treat with wilful insolence

係 xì（動）❶〈書〉be: 純～謊言 be a fabrication, pure and simple ❷ hinge on: 成功所～ be exactly what success hinges on

【係數】xìshù（名）〈數〉coefficient

俊 jùn Ⅰ（形）handsome; of handsome features Ⅱ（名）talented person

【俊秀】jùnxiù（形）elegant; graceful; delicate

【俊美】jùnměi（形）handsome; good-looking

【俊俏】jùnqiào（形）〈口〉charming; pretty; cute

【俊傑】jùnjié（名）person of no common ability: 識時務者為～。He who understands the times is a hero.

倉 cāng（名）storehouse: 穀～ barn; granary

【倉促】cāngcù（副）in haste; hurriedly: ～作出結論 jump to conclusions; draw a hasty conclusion

【倉皇】cānghuáng（形）in a flurry; in a panic: ～離去 leave in panic

【倉庫】cāngkù（名）storehouse; warehouse

倌 guān（名）herdsman: 豬～ keeper of pigs; swineherd

倍 bèi Ⅰ（名）times; fold: 甲的重量是乙的三～。A is three times as heavy as B. Ⅱ（形）double; twice as much: 加～小心 be doubly careful

【倍數】bèishù（名）〈數〉multiple

【倍增】bèizēng（動）double

俯 fǔ（動）❶ bow ❷ dive

【俯仰】fǔyǎng（名）every single move: ～之間 in the twinkling of an eye

【俯首帖耳】fǔ shǒu tiē ěr〈成〉act with servile obedience

【俯拾即是】fǔ shí jí shì〈成〉can be found everywhere; be available everywhere

【俯視】fǔshì（動）look down

【俯衝】fǔchōng（動）dive

【俯瞰】fǔkàn（動）take a bird's-eye view

倦 juàn（形）❶ tired; fatigued ❷ weary; bored: 孜孜不～ assiduously; tirelessly

俸 fèng（名）salary

借 jiè（動）❶ borrow; loan: ～三本書 borrow three books ❷ lend: ～錢給他 lend him some money ❸ utilize; exploit

【借刀殺人】jiè dāo shā rén〈成〉commit murder with a borrowed dagger; stab sb. with sb. else's knife

【借口】jièkǒu Ⅰ（動）use as an excuse: ～身體欠佳拒絕參加會議 refuse to attend the conference on the pretext of ill health Ⅱ（名）ex-

cuse; pretext; pretence: 拙劣的～
lame excuse

【借以】jièyǐ〈介〉for the purpose of;
so as to: ～説明這個短語的用法
for the purpose of illustrating the
usage of the phrase

【借光】jièguāng〈口〉〈套〉 [used
when one asks another not to stand
in one's way] excuse me

【借助】jièzhù〈介〉with the aid of:
～詞典閲讀本書原文 read the book
in the original with the help of a dictionary

【借故】jiègù〈動〉make an excuse

【借宿】jièsù〈動〉stay overnight at
sb.'s place: 他要在這裏～一晚。
He will put up here for the night.

【借款】jièkuǎn I〈動〉 ❶ borrow
money; ask for a loan ❷ lend money; provide a loan II〈名〉money on
loan; loan

【借調】jièdiào〈動〉(of a person) be
on loan; be dispatched to a post
temporarily: 他在戰時～給另一部
門。He was loaned to another department in the war years.

【借題發揮】jiè tí fā huī〈成〉 seize
an opportunity to put across one's
own ideas quite irrelevant to the occasion

【借鑒】jièjiàn〈動〉draw on sb.'s experience

值 zhí I〈名〉value: 價～(cost)
value ❷〈數〉value: 比～ratio II
〈動〉be worth: 這枝筆～五元。
The pen is worth five *yuan*. ❷
happen to: 正～佳節。It happened
to be a festive occasion. ❸ be on
duty; take one's turn at sth.

【值日】zhírì〈動〉be on duty for the
day

【值班】zhíbān〈動〉be on duty

【值得】zhíde〈動〉be worth; de-
serve: 這本書～讀。The book is
worth reading. / ～大家注意的問
題 problems deserving of public attention

【值勤】zhíqín〈動〉(of an armyman,
policeman, etc.) be on duty

【值錢】zhíqián〈形〉valuable: 這是
仿製品,不值多少錢。This is an
imitation, worth nothing much.

俩 liǎ〈數〉〈口〉two

倚 yǐ〈動〉❶ lean against; rest on:
～在桌旁 lean on the table ❷ rely
on; depend on

【倚仗】yǐzhàng〈動〉rely on

【倚老賣老】yǐ lǎo mài lǎo〈成〉
flaunt one's seniority

【倚重】yǐzhòng〈動〉repose trust in;
count on for support: 今後許多事
都要～您了。We'll count upon you
in many of our future undertakings.

【倚勢欺人】yǐ shì qī rén〈成〉abuse
one's power and bully people

【倚靠】yǐkào〈動〉❶ lean against
❷ rely on

俺 ǎn〈代〉〈方〉❶ we (referring
only to the speakers themselves):
～們 we ❷ I ❸ my; our: ～娘 my
mother

倒 dǎo〈動〉❶ fall; collapse ❷ be
overthrown; go bankrupt ❸
change; shift: ～班 change shifts
see also dào

【倒戈】dǎogē〈動〉 transfer allegiance; change sides in a war

【倒車】dǎochē〈動〉change trains or
buses

【倒閉】dǎobì（動）be out of business; close down

【倒爺】dǎoyé（名）profiteer

【倒塌】dǎotā（動）collapse

【倒賣】dǎomài（動）resell at a profit

【倒霉】dǎoméi（動）have bad luck; be out of luck

倒 dào Ⅰ（動）❶ reverse; invert ❷ pour; ～茶 pour tea ❸ move backward; ～車 back one's car Ⅱ（副）on the contrary; yet
see also dǎo

【倒打一耙】dào dǎ yī pá〈成〉frame the accuser

【倒行逆施】dào xíng nì shī〈成〉go against the trend of history; put the clock back; become reactionary

【倒退】dàotuì（動）move backward; retrogress

【倒叙】dàoxù（名）flashback

【倒彩】dàocǎi（名）hooting noise: 喝～ make catcalls

【倒置】dàozhì（動）reverse; set up side-down: 本末～ put the non-essentials before the essentials

【倒數】dàoshǔ（動）count backward: ～第四行 the fourth line from the bottom

【倒懸】dàoxuán（動）❶ hang by the feet ❷ be in a predicament

倘 tǎng（連）if; supposing

【倘若】tǎngruò（倘使 tǎngshǐ）（連）if; supposing; in case: 你～不信，就親自去看看吧。If you don't believe it, go and see for yourself whether it is not so.

們 men [used after a noun or personal pronoun to indicate a plural number]: 他～ they /老師～ teachers

倔 jué（形）gruff; surly
see also juè

【倔强】juéjiàng（形）headstrong; stubborn

倔 juè（形）gruff; crusty: 脾氣～ be stubborn
see also jué

【倔頭倔腦】juè tóu juè nǎo〈成〉be pigheaded

俱 jù（形）all: 事實～在。The facts are all there.

【俱全】jùquán（形）complete: 一應～。Everything needed is there.

【俱樂部】jùlèbù（名）club

倡 chàng（動）initiate

【倡導】chàngdǎo（動）take the lead; advocate

【倡議】chàngyì Ⅰ（動）propose Ⅱ（名）proposal

個 gè Ⅰ（量）：一～故事 a story /五～孩子 five children Ⅱ（形）individual: 逐～ one by one Ⅲ（名）size; build: 高～子 tall fellow; lanky chap

【個人】gèrén（名）❶ individual (person)：～成見 personnal prejudice ❷ oneself: 以我～的名義 in my own name

【個子】gèzi（名）height; stature; build

【個別】gèbié（形）❶ individual ❷ few; rare: ～情况 rare case

【個兒】gèr Ⅰ（名）height; stature; size Ⅱ（副）one by one

【個性】gèxìng（名）individuality; personality

【個個】gègè（名）each; every one; all

【個體】gètǐ (名) individual

【個體户】gètǐ hù (名) self-employed person; individually operated businessman

【個體經濟】gètǐ jīngjì (名) individual economy

候 hòu Ⅰ (動) wait; await Ⅱ (名) ❶ greetings; regards: 問～ give one's regards ❷ time; season: 季～ season ❸ condition; state

【候車室】hòuchēshì (名) waiting room (at a railway or bus station)

【候鳥】hòuniǎo (名) migratory bird

【候診】hòuzhěn (動) wait one's turn in the outpatient department: ～室 waiting room (in a hospital)

【候補】hòubǔ (形) alternate: 列入～名單 put on the alternate list

【候選人】hòuxuǎnrén (名) candidate

【候機室】hòujīshì (名) waiting room at an airport

倫 lún (名) ❶ rival; equal ❷ human relationships ❸ order; logic

【倫巴】lúnbā (名) rumba

【倫比】lúnbǐ (動) match: 無與～ matchless

【倫次】lúncì (名) [usu. used in the negative] (of speech, or writing) coherence: 語無～ give a disjointed account; make confused statements

【倫理】lúnlǐ (名) ethics; morality: ～學 ethics

倪 Ní (名) a surname

停 tíng (動) ❶ stop; halt: ～電 power cut; power failure ❷ stop over ❸ park; anchor; be in good order: 商議～妥 be agreed upon through negotiation; have reached

agreement

【停工】tínggōng (動) stop work: ～檢修設備 stop work for an overhaul of the equipment

【停火】tínghuǒ (動) cease-fire: 宣布～ declare a cease-fire

【停止】tíngzhǐ (動) stop; halt; call off: ～使用 out of use

【停刊】tíngkān (動) (of a newspaper or periodical) stop (suspend) publication

【停車】tíngchē (動) ❶ (of a vehicle) stop; halt ❷ park: ～標誌 stop sign / ～場 carpark; parking lot / ～費 parking rate / 此處不準～。No parking. ❸ (of a machine) stop working

【停泊】tíngbó (動) anchor

【停放】tíngfàng (動) park: 不準～自行車。No bicycle parking.

【停建緩建】tíngjiàn huǎnjiàn (動) suspend or defer (a construction project)

【停息】tíngxī (動) stop; subside

【停留】tíngliú (動) stop over; remain: 去上海途中在南京～兩天 stop over in Nanjing for a couple of days on one's way to Shanghai

【停産】tíngchǎn (動) stop production

【停當】tíngdang (形) ready; fixed; set

【停頓】tíngdùn (動) ❶ halt; stop; be at a standstill ❷ pause (in speaking)

【停歇】tíngxiē (動) ❶ shut down (a business) ❷ have a break; let up ❸ stop; cease

【停業】tíngyè (動) stop business; shut down a business

【停滯】tíngzhì (動) stagnate; get bogged down: ～不前 be at a standstill

【停靠】tíngkào（动）（of a train）stop;（of a vessel）berth; anchor: ~港 port of call

【停课】tíngkè（动）suspend classes

【停办】tíngbàn（动）close down

【停学】tíngxué（名）drop out of school

【停战】tíngzhàn（名）armistice; truce

【停机坪】tíngjīpíng（名）〈航空〉(parking) apron

【停摆】tíngbǎi（动）stop; cease to work

【停职】tíngzhí（动）be temporarily relieved of one's post

偏 piān Ⅰ（形）❶ inclined to one side: 那幅画向右~了。That painting slants to the right. ❷ partial; biased Ⅱ（副）contrary to what is expected; wifully: 留他吃晚饭, 可他~要回家。I asked him to stay for dinner, but he insisted on going home.

【偏方】piānfāng（名）folk prescription for herbal medicine

【偏心】piānxīn（形）partial

【偏巧】piānqiǎo（副）❶ by chance; by coincidence ❷ contrary to what is expected

【偏向】piānxiàng Ⅰ（动）be biased towards Ⅱ（名）deviation; erroneous tendency

【偏见】piānjiàn（名）prejudice; bias

【偏重】piānzhòng（动）lay undue emphasis upon

【偏差】piānchā（名）deviation; error

【偏旁】piānpáng（名）radical of a Chinese character

【偏袒】piāntǎn（动）be partial to

【偏偏】piānpiān（副）❶ wilfully: 天这么晚了, 他~要出去。He insisted on going out at such a late hour. ❷ opposite to what would be expected or accepted as normal: 我正在散步, 可天~下起雨来。I was taking a walk when it started to rain. ❸［used to single out an exception］他各门功课都考得很好, ~物理不及格。He got good marks in every other subject, but failed in physics.

【偏远】piānyuǎn（形）remote; outlying

【偏爱】piān'ài（动）be partial to; have a preference for: 她~最小的儿子。Her youngest son is her favourite.

【偏废】piānfèi（动）overemphasize one thing at the expense of another

【偏僻】piānpì（形）out-of-the-way; difficult of access

【偏激】piānjī（形）extreme; radical

【偏离】piānlí（动）deviate; stray

【偏听偏信】piān tīng piān xìn（成）hear and believe a one-sided story; be prejudiced

【偏瘫】piāntān（名）half-paralyzed; hemiplegia

偌 ruò（副）such; so

【偌大】ruòdà（形）of such a size: ~一个城市 such a large city

做 zuò（动）❶ do; engage in: ~生意 do business ❷ make; produce; manufacture: ~一件上衣 make a coat ❸ write; compose ❹ be; become: ~母亲 become a mother ❺ be used as: 那间屋子现在～了仓库。That room is now used as a warehouse.

【做人】zuòrén（动）❶ conduct oneself; behave: 他很不会～。He is not versed in the ways of the world. ❷ be an upright person: 重新～ turn over a new leaf

【做人情】zuò rénqíng（动）do sb. a favour

【做文章】zuò wénzhāng（动）❶ write an essay ❷ make an issue of sth.: 大～ make a mountain out of a molehill

【做主】zuòzhǔ（动）❶ decide: 自己～ decide by oneself ❷ back; support

【做伴】zuòbàn（动）keep sb. company

【做作】zuòzuo（形）affected; unnatural

【做法】zuòfǎ（名）way of doing things; practice

【做事】zuòshì（动）❶ handle matters ❷ work; have a job

【做官】zuòguān（动）be an official

【做东】zuòdōng（动）play the host; stand treat

【做客】zuòkè（动）be a guest

【做鬼脸】zuò guǐliǎn（动）make faces; pull a face

【做绝】zuòjué（动）leave oneself no room for retreat

【做媒】zuòméi（动）be a matchmaker; play Cupid

【做贼心虚】zuò zéi xīn xū（成）have a guilty conscience

【做梦】zuòmèng（动）dream; have a dream: 他是白日～。He is daydreaming.

【做寿】zuòshòu（动）celebrate the birthday (usu. of an elderly person)

【做戏】zuòxì（动）❶ act in a play ❷ put on a show

【做声】zuòshēng（动）make a sound: 别～! Be quiet!

【做礼拜】zuò lǐbài（动）go to church (on Sundays)

偕

偕 xié（副）together with; accompanied by

【偕同】xiétóng（动）be accompanied by

【偕行】xiéxíng（动）travel together; accompany

偃

偃 yǎn

【偃旗息鼓】yǎn qí xī gǔ（成）cease fighting; cease criticizing or attacking others

健

健 jiàn Ⅰ（形）healthy; strong; sound Ⅱ（动）❶ make strong: ～身 physical build-up ❷ be good at: ～步 walk briskly

【健全】jiànquán Ⅰ（形）sound; healthy: 身心～ sound in body and mind Ⅱ（动）make sound; strengthen: ～组织 put an organization on a sound basis

【健在】jiànzài（形）(of an old person) still living; going strong

【健壮】jiànzhuàng（形）physically fit

【健忘】jiànwàng（动）be forgetful; have a poor (short) memory

【健身房】jiànshēnfáng（名）gymnasium; gym

【健儿】jiàn'ér（名）❶ soldier ❷ athlete; sportsman

【健旺】jiànwàng（形）full of vim and vigour

【健美】jiànměi（形）physically well-developed

【健美比赛】jiànmeǐ bǐsài（名）body-building contest

【健美体操】jiànmeǐ tǐcāo（名）calisthenics

【健康】jiànkāng Ⅰ（形）healthy: 身体 ~ in good health Ⅱ（副）healthily: ~成长 grow up healthily Ⅲ（名）health: ~状况 state of health / ~证明 health certificate / ~保险 health insurance

【健将】jiànjiàng（名）❶ activist: 女权运动中的 ~ an activist in the feminist movement ❷ grand master: 运动 ~ master sportsman（title for an outstanding athlete in China）

【健谈】jiàntán（动）be a good conversationalist

假

假 jiǎ Ⅰ（形）false; artificial; counterfeit: ~名 pseudonym / ~钞票 forged banknote Ⅱ（动）borrow; make use of: 不 ~思索 without thinking Ⅲ（连）if: ~若 if; supposing

see also jià

【假山】jiǎshān（名）rockery

【假手】jiǎshǒu Ⅰ（动）make use of sb. to achieve one's evil purpose: ~于人 make sb. else do the dirty work Ⅱ（名）artificial hand

【假仁假义】jiǎ rén jiǎ yì〈成〉put on a false appearance of benevolence and righteousness; be hypocritical

【假公济私】jiǎ gōng jì sī〈成〉make use of public business to seek private gain

【假充】jiǎchōng（动）pretend to be; try to pass oneself off as: ~公安人员 pose as a public security officer

【假如】jiǎrú（假若 jiǎruò）（连）if; in the event that

【假托】jiǎtuō（动）❶ use as a pretext; pretend: 他~有约在先，拒绝了邀请。He turned down the invitation on the pretext of a previous engagement. ❷ use the name of others ❸ use as a means

【假扮】jiǎbàn（动）dress oneself up as; pretend to be

【假定】jiǎdìng Ⅰ（动）suppose; presume: ~一切非常顺利 supposing everything goes well Ⅱ（名）hypothesis

【假使】jiǎshǐ（连）if; supposing

【假冒】jiǎmào（动）pass off as: ~海关人员 pose as a customs officer

【假面具】jiǎmiànjù（名）❶ mask ❷ pretense; hypocrisy

【假案】jiǎ'àn（名）frame-up

【假造】jiǎzào（动）forge; fabricate; counterfeit; invent: ~证据 produce false evidence

【假借】jiǎjiè（动）make unwarranted use of: ~名义，招摇撞骗 practise cheating under false pretences

【假设】jiǎshè Ⅰ（动）assume; suppose Ⅱ（名）hypothesis

【假象】jiǎxiàng（名）false impression; semblance; facade: 识破 ~ see through a false appearance

【假惺惺】jiǎxīngxīng（副）hypocritically: ~地笑着 laugh hypocritically

【假话】jiǎhuà（名）lie; false statement: 讲 ~ lie; tell lies

【假想】jiǎxiǎng Ⅰ（名）presumption; conjecture; supposition Ⅱ（形）imaginary; conjectural

【假意】jiǎyì Ⅰ（名）hypocrisy: 虚情 ~ hypocritical show of friendliness or affection Ⅱ（副）deliberately; affectedly: 她~笑着说："我没有意见。" She gave a forced smile and said, "I have no objection."

【假裝】jiǎzhuāng（動）pretend; sham: ～有病 pretend illness

【假慈悲】jiǎcíbēi（動）shed crocodile tears

【假說】jiǎshuō（名）hypothesis

【假髮】jiǎfà（名）wig

【假釋】jiǎshì（動）release on probation; parole

假 jià（名）holiday; vacation; leave; day off: 請病～ ask for sick leave / 請事～ ask for leave of absence on personal grounds

see also jiǎ

【假日】jiàrì（名）holiday; day off

【假條】jiàtiáo（名）❶ application for leave of absence ❷ leave permit: 醫生開的病～ doctor's sick-leave certificate

【假期】jiàqī（名）holidays; vacation

偉 wěi（形）great

【偉人】wěirén（名）great man

【偉大】wěidà（形）great; signal: ～的貢獻 great contribution

【偉業】wěiyè（名）great achievement

偵 zhēn（動）detect; scout; spy

【偵查】zhēnchá（動）〈法〉investigate (a crime)

【偵探】zhēntàn Ⅰ（動）do detective work; spy Ⅱ（名）detective; spy

【偵察】zhēnchá（動）〈軍〉scout; reconnoitre: ～兵 scout

【偵緝】zhēnjī（動）investigate and arrest

【偵聽】zhēntīng（動）〈軍〉intercept or monitor (enemy radio communications)

側 cè Ⅰ（名）side; flank: 街道兩～ on both sides of the street Ⅱ（動）incline; tilt: ～目而視 look askance at

【側泳】cèyǒng（名）(in swimming) sidestroke

【側門】cèmén（名）side door; side entrance

【側面】cèmiàn Ⅰ（名）side; profile Ⅱ（副）sideways; sidewise: 從～打聽 try to find out from indirect sources

【側重】cèzhòng（動）stress; emphasize: ～教育 lay emphasis on education

偶 ǒu Ⅰ（名）❶ image; idol ❷ mate; spouse: 配～ spouse Ⅱ（形）even: ～數 even number Ⅲ（副）by chance; occasionally

【偶合】ǒuhé（名）coincidence

【偶然】ǒurán（形）accidental; fortuitous

【偶像】ǒuxiàng（名）image; idol

【偶爾】ǒu'ěr（副）occasionally; once in a long while

偎 wēi（動）nestle

【偎依】wēiyī（動）nestle up to

偷 tōu Ⅰ（動）❶ steal; commit theft: ～乘 stow away ❷ find (time): 忙裏～閑 find time despite a busy schedule Ⅱ（副）stealthily: ～跑 run away secretly

【偷工減料】tōu gōng jiǎn liào〈成〉do shoddy work and use inferior material; cheat in work and cut down material

【偷生】tōushēng（動）drag out an ignoble existence

【偷空】tōukòng（動）take time off in a busy schedule

【偷眼】tōuyǎn（動）steal a glance

【偷偷】tōutōu（副）stealthily; furtively

【偷偷摸摸】tōutōu mōmō（副）on the sly; stealthily; secretly

【偷税】tōushuì（动）evade tax

【偷摸】tōumō（动）pilfer; do petty thefts; filch

【偷懒】tōulǎn（动）shirk one's duties so as to enjoy leisure and comfort; loaf on one's job

【偷窃】tōuqiè（偷 盗 tōudào）（动）steal; pinch

【偷袭】tōuxí（动）launch a surprise attack; carry out a raid

伞 sǎn（名）❶ umbrella: 折叠～ folding umbrella ❷ sth. shaped like an umbrella: 降落～ parachute

【伞衣】sǎnyī（名）canopy

【伞兵】sǎnbīng（名）paratrooper; parachuter

傍 bàng（动）be close to; be alongside of: 依山～水 nestle at the foot of a hill and by the side of a stream

【傍人门户】bàng rén mén hù〈成〉live off sb.

【傍晚】bàngwǎn Ⅰ（名）dusk; twilight Ⅱ（副）at nightfall; at dusk; towards evening

傣 Dǎi

【傣族】Dǎizú（名）the Dai nationality

傅 fù Ⅰ（名）❶ teacher; instructor: 师～ master (often for passing on one's special skill) ❷（Fù）a surname Ⅱ（动）apply; lay on: ～粉 powder (one's face)

偀 lì

【偀僳族】Lìsùzú（名）the Lisu nationality

备 bèi Ⅰ（动）❶ have; reserve: 具～有利条件 enjoy certain advantages; be provided with certain favourable conditions ❷ prepare; get ready: 萬事俱～。Everything is ready. ❸ prepare against: 以～萬一 prepare against any eventuality ❹ equip: 配～空調器 equip with an air conditioner Ⅱ（名）equipment; installation; facilities: 設～更新 renewal of equipment Ⅲ（副）all; fully: 關懷～至 be extremely solicitous

【備用】bèiyòng（形）alternate; reserve: ～電池 standby battery

【備件】bèijiàn（名）spare part

【備考】bèikǎo（名）(of a book, document, form, table, etc.) appendix or note for reference

【備而不用】bèi ér bù yòng〈成〉keep handy; have in reserve; just in case

【備忘錄】bèiwànglù（名）memorandum; memo

【備取】bèiqǔ（形）on the waiting list (for admission to a school): ～生 student on the substitution list

【備受歡迎】bèi shòu huān yíng（动）enjoy great popularity

【備查】bèichá（副）for reference

【備案】bèi'àn（动）file or register with the authorities; keep on record

【備料】bèiliào（动）❶ (of a workshop) prepare material for processing ❷〈牧〉prepare feed

【備馬】bèimǎ（动）saddle a horse for riding

【備荒】bèihuāng（动）prepare against natural disasters

【備註】bèizhù（名）❶ remarks column in a form ❷ remarks in such a column

【備課】bèikè（動）prepare a lesson

【備戰】bèizhàn（動）prepare for war; be prepared against war

傑 jié Ⅰ（名）person of outstanding talent: 豪～ hero Ⅱ（形）outstanding; remarkable; eminent: ～作 masterpiece

【傑出】jiéchū（形）eminent; prominent: ～才能 eminent ability

傀 kuǐ

【傀儡】kuǐlěi（名）puppet; stooge: ～政權 puppet regime; bogus regime

傭 yōng Ⅰ（動）hire Ⅱ（名）servant: 女～ maidservant; maid see also yòng

傭 yòng（動）commission see also yōng

【傭金】yòngjīn（名）commission; brokerage

債 zhài（名）debt: 還～ pay one's debts / 公～（government）bonds

【債戶】zhàihù（名）debtor

【債主】zhàizhǔ（名）creditor

【債券】zhàiquàn（名）bond; debenture

【債務】zhàiwù（名）debt; liabilities

【債款】zhàikuǎn（名）loan

【債臺高築】zhài tái gāo zhù〈成〉run into huge debt; be saddled with huge debts

【債權】zhàiquán（名）〈法〉creditor's rights

傲 ào（形）proud; haughty; disdainful: 高～ conceited; arrogant

【傲骨】àogǔ（名）undaunted spirit

【傲氣】àoqì（名）arrogant airs; haughtiness: ～十足 downright haughty

【傲視】àoshì（動）treat with disdain

【傲慢】àomàn（形）haughty; arrogant

傳 chuán（動）❶ pass（on）: ～話 pass on a message; leave word ❷ hand down: 祖～秘方 secret recipe handed down from the ancestors ❸ teach; instruct: ～授 impart （knowledge, skill, etc.）❹ spread; disseminate: 不要外～。Do not leak it to outsiders. ❺ transmit: ～電 conduct electricity ❻ convey; express: ～情 make overtures of love ❼ summon: ～被告 summon the defendant ❽ infect see also zhuàn

【傳布】chuánbù（動）spread; disseminate

【傳奇】chuánqí（名）legend: ～式的人物 legendary figure

【傳呼電話】chuánhū diànhuà（名）neighbourhood telephone service; relay telephone call

【傳送帶】chuánsòngdài（名）〈機〉conveyer belt

【傳染】chuánrǎn（動）infect: ～上猩紅熱 be infected with scarlet fever

【傳神】chuánshén Ⅰ（動）catch（capture）the spirit Ⅱ（形）vivid; graphic

【傳家寶】chuánjiābǎo（名）❶ family heirloom ❷ cherished heritage

【傳真】chuánzhēn（名）〈訊〉facsimile; fax

【傳教】chuánjiào（動）preach one's religious faith; do missionary work

【傳票】chuánpiào（名）〈法〉summons; subpoena

【傳單】chuándān（名）leaflet

【傳統】chuántǒng（名）tradition

【傳揚】chuányáng（動）spread far and wide

【傳達】chuándá（動）relay; pass on (information, etc.)

【傳達室】chuándáshì（名）janitor's room; reception office

【傳遞】chuándì（動）pass on; transmit

【傳說】chuánshuō Ⅰ（動）they say: ～銀行要提高利率。They say the bank will raise the interest rate. Ⅱ（名）❶ hearsay; rumour ❷ legend

【傳誦】chuánsòng（動）be widely read; be on everybody's lips

【傳聞】chuánwén（名）hearsay; rumour

【傳播】chuánbō（動）disseminate; popularize; propagate

【傳導】chuándǎo Ⅰ（動）conduct; transmit Ⅱ（名）〈物〉conduction

【傳閱】chuányuè（動）pass round or circulate a notice, document, etc.

【傳聲筒】chuánshēngtǒng（名）❶ megaphone ❷ mouthpiece

傳 zhuàn（名）❶ biography: 自～ autobiography ❷ story about historical events or figures
see also chuán

【傳記】zhuànjì（名）biography

【傳略】zhuànlüè（名）brief biography; life story

僅 jǐn（副）only; alone

【僅僅】jǐnjǐn（副）only; but: 這～是猜想。This is mere speculation.

傾 qīng（動）❶ incline; lean: 塔～向一邊。The tower leans to one side. ❷ collapse; topple ❸ pour out; empty: ～吐衷情 unbosom oneself ❹ exert to the utmost: ～全力支援災區 make every effort to aid the stricken area

【傾心】qīngxīn Ⅰ（動）fall in love: 一見～ love at first sight Ⅱ（副）sincerely: 他們～交談, 互相勉勵。They exchanged views in all sincerity and encouraged each other.

【傾向】qīngxiàng Ⅰ（名）inclination; trend Ⅱ（動）incline to; tend to: 他～於過分樂觀。He tends to be over-optimistic. / 我一另一種觀點。I incline to another point of view.

【傾向性】qīngxiàngxìng（名）❶ tendentiousness ❷ prejudice (in favour of or against)

【傾軋】qīngyà（動）engage in internal strife: 各派互相一, 爭權奪利。The different factions went in for political in-fighting and jockeyed for position.

【傾注】qīngzhù（動）❶ pour into ❷ dedicate to: 把全部心血一到科學研究上 devote oneself heart and soul to scientific research

【傾盆大雨】qīng pén dà yǔ（成）torrential rain; downpour

【傾倒】qīngdǎo（動）❶ topple and fall ❷ greatly admire: 爲她所～ be infatuated with her

【傾倒】qīngdào（動）dump; empty; pour out: 把一肚子苦水都～出來 air all one's grievances

【傾家蕩產】qīng jiā dàng chǎn〈成〉

run through one's family fortune; dissipate one's fortune

【傾巢】 qīngcháo (动)〈贬〉turn out in full force: 敌人～来犯。The enemy launched an attack with all available strength.

【傾斜】 qīngxié (动) be out of the perpendicular

【傾斜度】 qīngxiédù (名) gradient

【傾訴】 qīngsù (动) pour forth; pour out: ～深情 pour out one's profound feelings

【傾慕】 qīngmù (动) adore; worship

【傾銷】 qīngxiāo (动) dump (goods, etc.)

【傾瀉】 qīngxiè (动) pour down (in torrents)

【傾覆】 qīngfù (动) overturn; topple: ～一個軍事獨裁政權 topple a military dictatorship

【傾聽】 qīngtīng (动) listen attentively

催 cuī (动) ❶ urge; hurry: ～他還書 notify him to return books ❷ speed up: ～産 expedite child delivery

【催促】 cuīcù (动) hasten; urge

【催眠】 cuīmián (动) lull; hypnotize

【催眠曲】 cuīmiánqǔ (名) lullaby

【催涙彈】 cuīlèidàn (名) tear-gas grenade

傷 shāng I (名) injury; wound: 槍～ bullet wound / 重～ serious injury II (动) ❶ hurt; injure: 他～了腿。He injured himself in the leg. ❷ feel sad: 哀～ be mournful ❸ damage: 有～名譽 be harmful to one's reputation

【傷口】 shāngkǒu (名) wound; cut

【傷亡】 shāngwáng (名) casualties

【傷心】 shāngxīn (形) sad; broken-hearted

【傷疤】 shāngbā (名) scar

【傷神】 shāngshén (动) ❶ overtax one's nerves ❷ be much grieved

【傷食】 shāng shí (动) get ill from overeating

【傷風】 shāngfēng I (动) catch cold II (名) cold

【傷風敗俗】 shāng fēng bài sú〈成〉be an offence against decency; violate the public code of ethics

【傷害】 shānghài (动) hurt; harm; damage: 我們不能～他的感情。We must not offend his sensibilities.

【傷員】 shāngyuán (名) the wounded

【傷痕】 shānghén (名) scar; bruise

【傷寒】 shānghán (名)〈醫〉typhoid fever; typhoid: 副～ paratyphoid / 斑疹～ typhus

【傷感】 shānggǎn (动) be distressed; be sentimental

【傷勢】 shāngshì (名) condition of a wound

【傷腦筋】 shāngnǎojīn (动) be a headache to sb.: 他這個人真叫人～。He is such a nuisance.

傻 shǎ (形) ❶ foolish; silly ❷ one-track-minded: 別～了,她對你沒有好感。Don't be so silly. She hasn't a soft spot for you.

【傻子】 shǎzi (名) fool; idiot

【傻瓜】 shǎguā (名) fool; blockhead

【傻勁兒】 shǎjìnr (名) ❶ eccentricity: 這人有點～。This chap is a bit of a crank. ❷ sheer physical strain; sheer doggedness

【傻笑】 shǎxiào (动) laugh like an idiot; giggle; titter

【傻眼】 shǎyǎn (动) be dumb-founded; be stupefied

像 xiàng I (名) portrait; picture: 塑～ statue II (動) ❶ be like; resemble: 這孩子～母親。The child takes after her mother. ❷ seem; appear: 他～是心情不好。He seems to be in a bad mood. III (介) such as; like: ～這樣的事不勝枚舉的。Things like this are too numerous to enumerate.

【像章】xiàngzhāng (名) badge with sb.'s likeness on it; badge

【像話】xiànghuà (形) proper; reasonable: 他真不～。He ought to be ashamed of himself.

傀 gù (動) hire; employ

【傀工】gùgōng (名) hired labourer

【傀主】gùzhǔ (名) employer

【傀員】gùyuán (名) employee

【傀農】gùnóng (名) farmhand; farm labourer

【傀傭】gùyōng (動) employ; hire

【傀傭軍】gùyōngjūn (名) mercenary army; mercenaries

僧 sēng (名) Buddhist monk; monk

【僧侶】sēnglǚ (名) monks and priests; clergy

【僧俗】sēngsú (名) monks and laymen; religious and secular people

僥 jiǎo

【僥幸】jiǎoxìng (副) by sheer luck; by chance

僚 liáo (名) ❶ official ❷ colleague

【僚機】liáojī (名) wing plane

僕 pú (名) servant

【僕人】púrén (名) servant

【僕從】púcóng (名) henchman; foot-

man

偽 wěi (形) ❶ false; fake: ～劣商品 fake and shoddy goods ❷ puppet; puppet troops

【偽君子】wěijūnzǐ (名) hypocrite

【偽造】wěizào (動) forge; counterfeit: ～一百圓大鈔 counterfeit 100-*yuan* notes

【偽善】wěishàn (形) hypocritical; pharisaical

【偽裝】wěizhuāng I (動) feign; disguise II (名) disguise; mask; camouflage

【偽幣】wěibì (偽鈔 wěichāo) (名) counterfeit money; forged note

【偽證】wěizhèng (名) 〈法〉perjury: 作～ bear false witness; commit perjury

僑 qiáo I (動) reside abroad II (名) national residing abroad: 歸國華～ returned overseas Chinese

【僑民】qiáomín (名) national residing abroad

【僑居】qiáojū (動) reside abroad

【僑胞】qiáobāo (名) compatriots who do not reside in the country

【僑務】qiáowù (名) affairs concerning nationals living abroad

【僑眷】qiáojuàn (名) relatives of nationals residing abroad

【僑資】qiáozī (名) investment by overseas Chinese

【僑匯】qiáohuì (名) overseas remittance

億 yì (數) a hundred million

儀 yí (名) ❶ appearance; mien ❷ rite; ceremony: 禮～ etiquette ❸ gift; present: 謝～ gift as a token of gratitude ❹ apparatus; instrument: 地磁~ magnetometer

【儀仗隊】 yízhàngduì（名）guard of honour

【儀式】 yíshì（名）rite; ceremony

【儀表】 yíbiǎo（名）❶ appearance; mien; bearing: ~ 非凡 have impressive looks ❷ meter; instrument

【儀容】 yíróng（名）appearance

【儀器】 yíqì（名）apparatus; instrument

僵 jiāng（形）❶ stiff; numb: 凍~ be stiff with cold ❷ difficult to handle: 事情弄~了。Things are at a stalemate.

【僵化】 jiānghuà（動）become ossified: 思想~ ossified thinking

【僵局】 jiāngjú（名）deadlock; stalemate: 我們無法打破~。We can do nothing to break the stalemate.

【僵持】 jiāngchí（動）be locked in a stalemate: 核~ nuclear stalemate

【僵屍】 jiāngshī（名）dead body; corpse

【僵硬】 jiāngyìng（形）❶ difficult to bend or flex; stiff: 他的兩條腿~了。His legs have gone stiff. ❷ inflexible; rigid: 工作方法~ rigid in one's style of work

價 jià（名）❶ price: 跌~ price fall ❷ value; worth ❸〈化〉valence
see also jie

【價目】 jiàmù（名）（marked）price

【價值】 jiàzhí（名）❶ value: ~規律 law of value ❷ worth; value: 很有~的資料 valuable information or data

【價值連城】 jià zhí lián chéng〈成〉be beyond price; invaluable

【價格】 jiàgé（名）price: ~放開 decontrol of fixed state prices; price decontrol / ~ 雙軌制 two-tier price system

【價廉物美】 jià lián wù měi（物美價廉 wù měi jià lián）（成）（of commodity）inexpensive and of good quality

【價錢】 jiàqian（名）price; cost（of commodity or service）; charge: ~很便宜。The price is very reasonable.

價 jie（助）[used as a suffix to certain adverbs for emphasis]: 終日~ 吵吵鬧鬧 make a lot of noise all day long
see also jià

儆 jǐng（動）warn; deter: 以~效尤 so as to deter others from committing the same offence

僻 pì（形）❶ out-of-the-way; remote ❷ eccentric: 孤~ unsociable

【僻靜】 pìjìng（形）secluded

【僻壤】 pìrǎng（名）remote place

儈 kuài（名）middle-man: 市~習氣 philistinism; the air of a knavish broker

儉 jiǎn（形）frugal; economical: 克勤克~ be hard-working and thrifty

【儉省】 jiǎnshěng（形）economical

【儉樸】 jiǎnpǔ（形）simple and plain

儐 bīn

【儐相】 bīnxiàng（名）❶ best man ❷ bridesmaid

儒 rú（名）❶（Rú）Confucianism; Confucianist ❷ scholar

【儒家】 Rújiā（名）the Confucian school

儲
chǔ Ⅰ (動) store up; keep in reserve Ⅱ (Chǔ) (名) a surname

【儲存】chǔcún (動) lay up; put away: ~糧食 store up grain

【儲備】chǔbèi Ⅰ (動) store; lay up Ⅱ (名) reserve: 外匯~ foreign exchange reserve

【儲量】chǔliàng (名) reserve; deposit: 石油~ oil deposit

【儲蓄】chǔxù (動) save; deposit: ~存款 savings deposit

【儲藏】chǔcáng Ⅰ (動) preserve Ⅱ (名) deposit; reserve

優
yōu (形) excellent; fine; outstanding: 擇~錄取 choose the best from among the candidates

【優化組合】yōuhuà zǔhé (名) optimal organization of labour groups

【優生學】yōushēngxué (名) 〈生〉 eugenics

【優先】yōuxiān (動) have priority; take precedence: 在選擇職業上,優秀學生有~權。Outstanding students have priority over others in getting jobs.

【優秀】yōuxiù (形) outstanding

【優良】yōuliáng (形) fine; good

【優美】yōuměi (形) beautiful; exquisite; graceful

【優待】yōudài (動) give preferential treatment to

【優柔寡斷】yōu róu guǎ duàn 〈成〉 irresolute and indecisive; weak and irresolute; shilly-shally

【優厚】yōuhòu (形) (of treatment) liberal; generous: 待遇~ get very good pay with liberal benefits

【優異】yōuyì (形) excellent; remarkable; outstanding

【優等】yōuděng (形) high-grade; first-rate

【優惠】yōuhuì (形) preferential; favourable: ~政策 preferential policies

【優勝】yōushèng (形) superior to others in performance

【優裕】yōuyù (形) affluent; well-to-do: 生活~ be quite well-off

【優越】yōuyuè (形) superior; advantageous: 擺出智力~的架勢 flaunt one's intellectual superiority

【優勢】yōushì (名) superiority; advantage: 在這些方面她有~。She enjoys certain advantages in these respects.

【優質】yōuzhì (名) high quality: ~酒 quality wine

【優選法】yōuxuǎnfǎ (名) optimization

【優點】yōudiǎn (名) merit; strong point; virtue

償
cháng (動) ❶ repay; compensate: 賠~損失 compensate for the loss ❷ have (one's wish) fulfilled

【償付】chángfù (動) pay; repay: 延期~貸款 defer payment of credit

【償命】chángmìng (動) pay the price of one's life for a murder

【償還】chánghuán (動) repay: 如期~ repay in time

【償願】chángyuàn (動) fulfil one's wish; get what one desires

儷
lì (名) pair; couple: 伉~ husband and wife

儼
yǎn

【儼然】yǎnrán (連) as if; just like: 神氣~是個專家 look as if one were an expert; pose as an expert

儿 部

【兀】 wù (形) ❶ towering ❷ bald
【兀立】 wùlì (動) stand upright
【兀鷲】 wùjiù (名) griffon vulture

【元】 yuán I (形) ❶ first; primary: ～年 the first year of an era ❷ chief; principal: ～帥 marshal ❸ component: 單～ unit ❹ basic; fundamental: ～素 element II (量) yuan, the monetary unit of China, equal to 10 jiao or 100 fen III (Yuán) (名) a surname
【元月】 yuányuè (名) the first month of the year, January
【元凶】 yuánxiōng (名) arch-criminal (culprit)
【元旦】 Yuándàn (名) New Year's Day
【元件】 yuánjiàn (名) element; component; part
【元老】 yuánlǎo (名) foundation member (of an organization); senior member; grand old man
【元首】 yuánshǒu (名) head of state
【元音】 yuányīn (名)〈語〉vowel
【元氣】 yuánqì (名) vitality; vigour: 大傷～ greatly undermine a person's constitution or a natoin's vitality
【元宵】 yuánxiāo (名) ❶ Lantern Festival (the night of the 15th of the 1st lunar month) ❷ sweet dumplings (made of glutinous rice flour)
【元勛】 yuánxūn (名) founding father: 開國～ founder of a state

【允】 yǔn I (動) permit; allow: 不～ forbid II (形) proper: 公～ fair and proper
【允許】 yǔnxǔ (動) permit; allow
【允諾】 yǔnnuò (動) promise; consent

【兄】 xiōng (名) elder brother
【兄弟】 xiōngdì I (名) brothers II (形) brotherly; fraternal: ～一般的友誼 fraternal relations
【兄長】 xiōngzhǎng (名) elder brother

【充】 chōng I (形) sufficient; full II (動) ❶ fill; cram: ～電 charge (a battery) ❷ serve as: ～任隊長 serve as a team leader ❸ pass off as; pretend to be: ～行家 pose as an expert
【充分】 chōngfèn I (形) sufficient; ample: ～餘地 enough leeway; ample room II (副) fully: ～發揮 give full play to
【充公】 chōnggōng (動) confiscate
【充斥】 chōngchì (動)〈貶〉glut; flood: ～市場 flood the market
【充耳不聞】 chōng ěr bù wén〈成〉turn a deaf ear to
【充足】 chōngzú (形) adequate; sufficient
【充沛】 chōngpèi (形) full; abundant: 雨水～ abundant rainfall
【充其量】 chōngqíliàng (副) at most; at worst; at best: ～也不過數十人 only dozens of people at most
【充飢】 chōngjī (動) stay one's stomach; appease one's hunger
【充當】 chōngdāng (動) serve as; act as
【充裕】 chōngyù (形) plentiful; am-

ple:經濟～ well-off

【充滿】chōngmǎn（動）be full of; be replete with:～錯誤 teem with errors

【充實】chōngshí I（形）rich; substantial II（動）augment; enlarge; solidify:～論據 reinforce one's argument

【充數】chōngshù（動）pass muster:也許我可以～。Maybe, I can pass muster.

光 guāng I（名）❶ light; ray ❷ honour; glory:增～ add lustre to ❸ scenery:風～ scene; view I（形）❶ smooth; polished; glossy ❷ bare; naked ❸ used up III（副）only; solely; alone:～剩下他一個人了。He was the only one left behind.

【光天化日】guāng tiān huà rì〈成〉broad daylight:～之下 in broad daylight

【光年】guāngnián（名）〈天〉light-year

【光芒】guāngmáng（名）rays of light; beams

【光明】guāngmíng I（名）light II（形）bright:～前景 bright prospect

【光明正大】guāng míng zhèng dà〈成〉honourable and upright

【光明磊落】guāng míng lěi luò〈成〉open and above-board; open-hearted

【光怪陸離】guāng guài lù lí〈成〉outlandish and motley; fantastic; grotesque

【光亮】guāngliàng（形）bright; luminous; shining

【光速】guāngsù（名）〈物〉velocity of light

【光陰】guāngyīn（名）time:～似

箭。Time flies.

【光彩】guāngcǎi（名）❶ brilliance:～奪目 dazzling ❷ honour; glory

【光棍】guānggùn（名）unmarried man; bachelor

【光景】guāngjǐng I（名）conditions; circumstances II（副）about; approximately:約五點鐘～ around five o'clock

【光復】guāngfù（動）recover（lost territory, etc.）

【光滑】guānghuá（形）smooth; glossy

【光榮】guāngróng I（名）honour; glory II（形）glorious

【光線】guāngxiàn（名）light; ray

【光輝】guānghuī I（名）brilliance; radiance; glory II（形）brilliant; glorious

【光學】guāngxué（名）optics:～儀器 optical instrument

【光澤】guāngzé（名）lustre

【光臨】guānglín（動）〈敬〉be present: 敬請～ request your gracious presence

【光纖】guāngxiān（名）optic fibre

兆 zhào I（名）omen; sigh; augury: 吉～ propitious sign II（數）❶ million; mega- ❷ a million millions; billion III（動）portend; presage: 瑞雪～豐年。A timely snow promises a bumper harvest.

【兆周】zhàozhōu（名）〈無〉megacycle

【兆頭】zhàotou（名）omen; sign; augury

兇 xiōng（形）❶ fierce; cruel: 目露～光 have a cruel glitter in one's eyes ❷ terrible; fearful: 火勢～。The fire is raging.

【兇手】xiōngshǒu（名） murderer; assassin

【兇犯】xiōngfàn（名）murderer

【兇狠】xiōnghěn（形）brutal; cruel

【兇相】xiōngxiàng（名） fiendish look; atrocious features

【兇相畢露】xiōng xiàng bì lù〈成〉reveal one's ugly features; bare one's fangs

【兇神惡煞】xiōng shén è shà〈成〉ferocious and savage evildoers

【兇殺】xiōngshā（動）murder; homicide

【兇猛】xiōngměng（形）fiery; violent

【兇惡】xiōng'è（形）devilish; ferocious

【兇殘】xiōngcán（形）cruel; savage

【兇暴】xiōngbào（形） ferocious; brutal

【兇器】xiōngqì（名）tool or weapon used by a criminal

【兇險】xiōngxiǎn（形） dangerous: 局勢～。The situation is very dangerous

先 xiān I（副）first; earlier; before: 讓我～瞧瞧。Let me have a look first. /他比我一起床。He got up earlier than I. II（名）earlier generation; ancestor

【先人】xiānrén（名）ancestor

【先入爲主】xiān rù wéi zhǔ〈成〉be biased by first impressions

【先天】xiāntiān（形）innate; inherent

【先生】xiānsheng（名） ❶ teacher ❷ [polite form of address for a man] mister（Mr.）; gentleman; sir: 主席～ Mr. Chairman

【先兆】xiānzhào（名）omen; portent

【先行】xiānxíng（動）go in front: ～者 forerunner

【先行官】xiānxíngguān（名） commander of an advance unit or vanguard

【先決條件】xiānjué tiáojiàn （名）prerequisite

【先見之明】xiān jiàn zhī míng（名）foresight

【先例】xiānlì（名）precedent

【先知】xiānzhī（名）prophet; person of foresight

【先來後到】xiān lái hòu dào〈成〉make priority arrangements according to order of arrival; order of precedence

【先前】xiānqián（副）before; previously: 他～在這裏工作。He used to work here.

【先後】xiānhòu I（名）priority; order: 處理問題要分～。The problems must be dealt with in order of priority. II（副）successively; one after another: 他們～參觀了五個城市。They visited five cities in succession.

【先烈】xiānliè（名）martyr

【先進】xiānjìn（形）advanced

【先斬後奏】xiān zhǎn hòu zòu〈成〉take action without the prior approval of one's superior

【先發制人】xiān fā zhì rén〈成〉strike first to gain the initiative; seize the initiative by attacking the opponent first

【先遣】xiānqiǎn（動）send in advance: ～隊 advance party

【先輩】xiānbèi（名）senior generation; ancestors; forefathers

【先導】xiāndǎo（名）guide; forerunner

【先鋒】xiānfēng（名）vanguard

【先頭】xiāntóu Ⅰ（副）ahead; in advance Ⅱ（形）一部隊 advance unit

【先聲奪人】xiān shēng duó rén（成）overwhelm one's opponent by a display of strength

【先驅】xiānqū（名）forerunner; pioneer

兑 duì（動）exchange; convert

【兑現】duìxiàn（動）❶ cash (a check) ❷ fulfil; keep one's promise

【兑換】duìhuàn（動）exchange one currency for another

【兑換率】duìhuànlǜ（名）rate of exchange

克 kè Ⅰ（動）❶ be capable of : ～勤～儉 work hard and live a frugal life; be hardworking and thrifty ❷ overcome; restrain: ～己奉公 throw oneself heart and soul into one's work in the interest of the public. ❸ take (a stronghold); subdue Ⅱ（量）gram

【克拉】kèlā（量）carat

【克制】kèzhì（動）exercise restraint

【克服】kèfú（動）❶ overcome; get rid of: ～重重障礙 surmount numerous obstacles/ ～壞習慣 get rid of bad habits ❷〈口〉endure (hardship); put up with (an inconvenient circumstance)

免 miǎn（動）❶ free sb. from; exempt: 這項工作太沒意思，給我～了吧。I wish to be excused from this boring job. ❷ avoid: 以～受罰 avoid punishment ❸ be forbidden: ～開尊口。I beg you to say no more.

【免不了】miǎnbu liǎo（動）be un-

avoidable; be certain to happen: 人～犯錯誤。To err is human.

【免刑】miǎnxíng（動）exempt from penalty

【免役】miǎnyì（動）exempt from service

【免於】miǎnyú（動）exempt from: ～起訴 exempt sb. from prosecution

【免冠】miǎnguān（形）bareheaded: ～照片 a bareheaded photo

【免疫】miǎnyì（名）〈醫〉immunity

【免疫學】miǎnyìxué（名）immunology

【免疫證書】miǎnyì zhèngshū（名）bill of health

【免除】miǎnchú（動）❶ remove; relieve: ～職務 be relieved of one's post ❷ prevent; avert: ～天災人禍 avert both natural and man-made disasters

【免得】miǎnde（連）in order not to; so as to avoid: ～難堪 so as to avoid embarrassment

【免票】miǎnpiào Ⅰ（名）free ticket Ⅱ（形）free of charge

【免費】miǎnfèi（形）free of charge; gratis; complimentary: ～接送客人 free pick-up service/ ～票 free pass

【免稅】miǎnshuì Ⅰ（形）free of charge; tax-free: ～進口貨物 duty-free imports / ～券 tax-exemption slip / ～商品 duty-free shop / ～商品 duty-free goods Ⅱ（動）exempt from taxation

【免罪】miǎnzuì（動）exempt from punishment

【免職】miǎnzhí Ⅰ（動）relieve sb. of his post Ⅱ（名）dismissal from office

【免驗】miǎnyàn（動）exempt from customs examination

兔 tù（名）rabbit; hare: ~子 rabbit; hare

【兔兒爺】tùréye（名）traditional clay toy with a rabbit's head and a human body

【兔崽子】tùzǎizi（名）〈罵〉bastard; brat

兒 ér（名）❶ child ❷ son ❸ youngster

【兒子】érzi（名）son

【兒女】érnǚ（名）❶ sons and daughters ❷ young man and woman: ~情長 be passionately attached to each other

【兒科】érkē（名）paediatrics

【兒孫】érsūn（名）children and grandchildren; posterity

【兒童】értóng（名）child; children: ~心理學 child psychology / ~醫院 children's hospital

【兒媳婦】érxífu（名）daughter-in-law

【兒歌】érgē（名）nursery rhymes

【兒戲】érxì（名）matter of no importance: 視同~ regard (sth. serious) as a trifling matter

兜 dōu Ⅰ（名）pocket; bag Ⅱ（動）❶ wrap up ❷ solicit customers ❸ move around: 説話~圈子 speak in a roundabout way ❹ undertake; bear responsibility

【兜肚】dōudù（兜兜 dōudou）（名）undergarment covering the chest and the belly

【兜風】dōufēng（動）go for a ride

【兜捕】dōubǔ（動）round up; hunt down

【兜售】dōushòu（動）tout for business; hawk

【兜攬】dōulǎn（動）❶ canvass; tout

❷ take on oneself

兢 jīng

【兢兢業業】jīng jīng yè yè〈成〉conscientiously; assiduously

入 部

入 rù Ⅰ（動）❶ enter: 破門而~ break into a house /進~新時代 enter upon a new era ❷ join; become a member of: ~股 become a shareholder Ⅱ（名）income

【入口】rùkǒu Ⅰ（動）enter the mouth Ⅱ（名）entrance; gateway

【入土】rùtǔ（動）be buried

【入手】rùshǒu（動）start with: 從基礎教育~ start with elementary education

【入不敷出】rù bù fū chū〈成〉fail to make both ends meet

【入耳】rù'ěr（形）pleasant to the ear

【入伏】rùfú（動）enter the hottest period of the summer

【入伍】rùwǔ（動）enlist in the armed forces; join the army

【入味】rùwèi（形）❶ engrossing ❷ savoury

【入門】rùmén Ⅰ（動）learn the rudiments of a subject Ⅱ（名）elementary course; primer; ABC: 化學~ the ABC of chemistry

【入迷】rùmí（動）be fascinated; be captivated; be enchanted: 她非凡的表演使他~了 Her superb performance entranced him.

【入侵】rùqīn（動）invade; intrude

【入神】rùshén Ⅰ（動）be entranced; be engrossed: 聽得~ listen spellbound Ⅱ (形) superb; excellent

【入席】 rùxí (动) take one's place (seat) at a banquet, etc.

【入库】 rùkù (动) be put in storage

【入托】 rùtuō (动) (of a child) be sent to a nursery

【入时】 rùshí (形) fashionable; in vogue; modish; à la mode

【入超】 rùchāo (名) unfavourable balance of trade; trade deficit

【入场】 rùchǎng (动) ❶ enter a theatre, cinema, assembly hall, etc.: 免费 ～ admission free ❷ (of athletes) enter the arena

【入场券】 rùchǎngquàn (名) (admission) ticket

【入乡随俗】 rù xiāng suí sú 〈成〉 do in Rome as the Romans do

【入伙】 rùhuǒ (动) ❶ join in a partnership ❷ join a mess ❸ join in a gang

【入境】 rùjìng Ⅰ (动) enter a country Ⅱ (名) entry: ～口岸 port of entry / ～签证 entry visa / ～手续 entry procedure

【入睡】 rùshuì (动) fall asleep

【入狱】 rùyù (动) go to prison; be thrown into prison

【入账】 rùzhàng (动) charge; put into account; enter upon an account

【入选】 rùxuǎn (动) be selected; be chosen

【入学】 rùxué (动) ❶ go to school: ～年龄 school age ❷ enter a school or college

【入殓】 rùliàn (动) encoffin

【入声】 rùshēng (名) 〈语〉 entering tone, one of the four tones in classical Chinese pronunciation

内 nèi (形) inner; inside; internal:

国～税收 internal revenue

【内水】 nèishuǐ (名) ❶ internal waters ❷ water-logging; surface water

【内心】 nèixīn (名) heart; inner being: 人的～活动 one's inmost thoughts

【内分泌】 nèifēnmì (名) 〈生理〉 endocrine; internal secretion

【内兄】 nèixiōng (名) wife's elder brother; brother-in-law

【内衣】 nèiyī (名) underwear; underclothes

【内因】 nèiyīn (名) internal cause

【内在】 nèizài (形) intrinsic; inherent: ～的价值 intrinsic value

【内向】 nèixiàng (形) introvert

【内奸】 nèijiān (名) hidden traitor

【内行】 nèiháng (名) expert; masterhand

【内地】 nèidì (名) inland; hinterland

【内弟】 nèidì (名) wife's younger brother; brother-in-law

【内河】 nèihé (名) inland river: ～航行 inland navigation

【内疚】 nèijiù (名) guilty conscience

【内科】 nèikē (名) (department of) internal medicine: ～医生 physician

【内胎】 nèitāi (名) inner tube of a tyre

【内省】 nèixǐng (名) 〈心〉 introspection

【内政】 nèizhèng (名) internal affairs

【内讧】 nèihòng (名) internal strife

【内务】 nèiwù (名) internal affairs

【内海】 nèihǎi (名) inland sea

【内容】 nèiróng (名) content

【内涵】 nèihán (名) intension; connotation

【内部】 nèibù (名) inside; interior: ～消息 inside information

【内参】nèicān（名）restricted reference material; confidential reference items

【内陆】nèilù（名）inland; interior

【内贸】nèimào（名）(short for 国内贸易 guónèi màoyì) internal trade; domestic trade

【内勤】nèiqín（名）❶ office staff ❷ office work

【内伤】nèishāng（名）〈医〉internal injury

【内乱】nèiluàn（名）internal disturbances or turmoil; civil strife

【内详】nèixiáng（名）name and address of sender enclosed

【内债】nèizhài（名）internal debt

【内蒙】Nèiměng（名）(short for 内蒙古自治区 Nèi Měnggǔ Zìzhìqū) the Nei Monggol（Inner Mongolia）Autonomous Region

【内线】nèixiàn（名）❶ planted agent ❷ inside telephone connections

【内阁】nèigé（名）cabinet

【内幕】nèimù（名）inside story

【内忧外患】nèi yōu wài huàn〈成〉domestic trouble and foreign invasion

【内销】nèixiāo（动）sell on the home market

【内卫】nèiwèi（名）❶ internal security ❷（internal）guards

【内战】nèizhàn（名）civil war

【内燃机】nèiránjī（名）〈机〉internal-combustion engine

【内燃机车】nèirán jīchē（名）diesel locomotive

【内脏】nèizàng（名）internal organs

全 quán Ⅰ（形）❶ complete: 作品～集 sb.'s complete works ❷ whole; entire: ～年 all year Ⅱ（动）

preserve; keep intact: 不能两～ cannot satisfy both parties or claims Ⅲ（副）entirely; completely: ～忘了 be utterly forgotten Ⅳ（名）（Quán）a surname

【全力】quánlì（名）all one's strength: ～以赴 spare no effort; go all out

【全才】quáncái（名）all-round person; person of versatile genius

【全日制】quánrìzhì（名）full-time

【全天候】quántiānhòu（形）all-weather: ～公路 all-weather road

【全心全意】quán xīn quán yì（副）wholeheartedly: 他～地投身工作之中。He threw himself into his work heart and soul.

【全民】quánmín（名）all the people

【全民所有制】quánmín suǒyǒuzhì（名）ownership by the whole people; state-run

【全年】quánnián（形）annual; yearly: ～产量 annual output

【全休】quánxiū（名）complete rest: 大夫说他要～。The doctor says he needs a complete rest.

【全局】quánjú（名）overall situation

【全面】quánmiàn（形）comprehensive; overall: ～解决 overall settlement

【全神贯注】quán shén guàn zhù〈成〉be absorbed in; be preoccupied with; concentrate on

【全能】quánnéng（形）〈体〉all-round: 十项～运动 decathlon

【全速】quánsù（名）full speed; top speed

【全家福】quánjiāfú（名）〈方〉❶ photograph of the whole family ❷ hotch-potch（as a dish）

【全脂奶粉】quánzhī nǎifěn（名）

whole milk powder

【全息照相】quánxī zhàoxiàng（名）hologram

【全息摄影】quánxī shèyǐng（名）holography

【全部】quánbù（形）whole; complete; all

【全盛】quánshèng（形）in full bloom: ～时期 in its heyday; at the zenith of its power

【全国】quánguó Ⅰ（名）whole nation (country) Ⅱ（形）national; nation-wide

【全球】quánqiú（名）the whole world: 誉满～ known throughout the world

【全程】quánchéng（名）entire journey; whole course

【全景】quánjǐng（名）panorama; full view: 京城～ panoramic view of the capital

【全然】quánrán（副）completely; utterly

【全勤】quánqín（名）regular attendance (at work for a period of time, e.g., a month, year): ～奖 bonus for full attendance

【全称】quánchēng（名）full name; name in full

【全貌】quánmào（名）complete picture

【全蚀】quánshí（名）〈天〉total eclipse

【全盘】quánpán（形）overall; comprehensive

【全优】quányōu（形）（of students）excellent in every subject

【全体】quántǐ（名）（of a group of people）all; entire

【全权】quánquán（名）full powers; plenary powers

【全权代表】quánquán dàibiǎo（名）plenipotentiary

两 liǎng Ⅰ（数）❶ two: ～位数字的通货膨胀 two-digit inflation ❷ both; either: ～个词都能用。Either word will do. ❸ a few; a couple of: 喝上～杯 have a couple of drinks Ⅱ（量）liang（a unit of weight = 0.05kg）

【两口子】liǎngkǒuzi（名）married couple; husband and wife

【两小无猜】liǎng xiǎo wú cāi〈成〉（of children particularly between boy and girl）be innocent playmates

【两半】liǎngbàn（名）two halves: 分成～ divide in half

【两可】liǎngkě（动）be all right one way or the other: 今晚我去不去看戏仍是～。I may or may not be going to the theatre tonight.

【两全】liǎngquán（动）be acceptable to both sides; cater to two divergent needs: 事难～ It would be difficult to please both sides.

【两全其美】liǎng quán qí měi〈成〉give satisfaction to both parties

【两回事】liǎnghuíshì（两码事 liǎngmǎshì）（名）a different story; two different things: 这是～。This is a different matter altogether.

【两性】liǎngxìng（名）both sexes

【两便】liǎngbiàn（形）suit the convenience of both sides: 这当然是～。This is of course convenient for both sides.

【两重】liǎngchóng（形）dual; double

【两面三刀】liǎng miàn sān dāo〈成〉double-dealing; double-faced

【两面光】liǎngmiànguāng（动）try to please both sides

【两面派】liǎngmiànpài（名）double-dealer

【两相情愿】liǎng xiāng qíng yuàn〈成〉both parties cherish the same wish; both parties are willing

【两栖】liǎngqī（形）amphibious

【两院制】liǎngyuànzhì（名）bicameralism

【两袖清风】liǎng xiù qīng fēng〈成〉be morally incorruptible as an official

【两败俱伤】liǎng bài jù shāng〈成〉both contending parties suffer; neither side is the victor

【两极】liǎngjí（名）❶ the North and South Poles ❷ two extremes; two direct opposites: ～分化 polarization

【两样】liǎngyàng（形）different

【两头】liǎngtóu（名）both ends; both sides

【两头落空】liǎng tóu luò kōng〈成〉run after two hares and catch neither

【两翼】liǎngyì（名）both wings

【两边】liǎngbiān（名）both sides: 路～both sides of the road／～都同意恢复谈判。Both parties have agreed to resume negotiations.

【两难】liǎngnán（副）in a dilemma: 进退～ be caught between the devil and the deep sea

【两党制】liǎngdǎngzhì（名）bipartisan system

八 部

八 bā（数）eight: ～字還没見一

撇。Nothing tangible is in sight yet.

【八方】bāfāng（副）all around; in all quarters: ～响應 call forth response from all quarters

【八月】bāyuè（名）❶ August ❷ eighth month of the lunar calendar: ～節 the Mid-Autumn Festival (15th day of the 8th lunar month)

【八仙】Bāxiān（名）Eight Immortals (in Chinese legend): ～过海，各顯神通 like the Eight Immortals crossing the sea, each displaying his or her special prowess

【八成】bāchéng（副）❶ eighty per cent ❷〈口〉most probably

【八角】bājiǎo I（名）（植）Chinese star anise II（形）octagonal

【八股】bāgǔ（八 股 文 bāgǔwén）（名）(eight-part) stereotyped writing

【八面玲珑】bā miàn líng lóng〈成〉(of a person) slick

【八寶】bābǎo（名）eight treasures (choice ingredients of certain Chinese dishes): ～菜 eight-treasure pickles

六 liù（数）six

【六月】liùyuè（名）June; the sixth month of the lunar year

【六神無主】liù shén wú zhǔ〈成〉be stupefied; look blank

【六親不認】liù qīn bù rèn〈成〉disown even one's closest relatives and friends

【六邊形】liùbiānxíng（名）hexagon

公 gōng I（形）❶ state-owned; collective; public ❷ fair; just: 秉～而論 to be fair; in fairness to sb. II（名）❶ official business ❷ male (animal): ～牛 bull ❸ father-in-law ❹ duke ❺ (Gōng) a surname

【公尺】gōngchǐ (名) metre (m)

【公分】gōngfēn (名) ❶ centimetre (cm) ❷ gram (g)

【公斤】gōngjīn (名) kilogram (kg)

【公文】gōngwén (名) official document

【公允】gōngyǔn (形) fair and just; even-handed

【公元】gōngyuán (名) the Christian era; A.D.

【公元前】gōngyuánqián (名) B.C.

【公平】gōngpíng (形) fair; just

【公司】gōngsī (名) company; corporation; firm

【公用】gōngyòng (形) for public use: ~事業 public utilities / ~電話亭 telephone booth

【公正】gōngzhèng (形) impartial

【公主】gōngzhǔ (名) princess

【公民】gōngmín (名) citizen

【公民權】gōngmínquán (名) civil rights

【公共】gōnggòng (形) public; common; communal: ~衛生 public health

【公式】gōngshì (名) formula

【公休】gōngxiū (名) public holiday

【公有】gōngyǒu (形) publicly-owned

【公安】gōng'ān (名) public security

【公安局】gōng'ānjú (名) public security bureau

【公佈】gōngbù (動) promulgate; publish

【公告】gōnggào (名) announcement; public notice

【公里】gōnglǐ (名) kilometre (km)

【公社】gōngshè (名) commune

【公函】gōnghán (名) official letter

【公使】gōngshǐ (名)〈外〉minister; envoy: ~館 legation

【公事】gōngshì (名) public affairs; official business

【公物】gōngwù (名) public property

【公制】gōngzhì (名) metric system

【公約】gōngyuē (名) ❶ convention; pact ❷ joint pledge

【公差】gōngchāi (名) official errand: 出~ go on official business

【公案】gōng'àn (名) ❶ complicated legal case ❷ controversial issue

【公害】gōnghài (名) environmental pollution

【公海】gōnghǎi (名) high seas

【公益】gōngyì (名) public welfare

【公務】gōngwù (名) public affairs; public business

【公務員】gōngwùyuán (名) ❶ manual or semi-manual worker in institutions ❷ civil servant: ~制度 civil service system

【公孫】Gōngsūn (名) a surname

【公頃】gōngqǐng (名) hectare (ha)

【公章】gōngzhāng (名) official seal

【公報】gōngbào (名) communiqué; bulletin

【公道】gōngdào I (名) justice II (形) fair; impartial: 辦事~ be fair in handling matters

【公開】gōngkāi I (形) open; overt II (動) make public

【公款】gōngkuǎn (名) public fund

【公然】gōngrán (副) openly; brazenly; unscrupulously

【公訴】gōngsù (名)〈法〉public prosecution

【公寓】gōngyù (名) flat; apartment house

【公眾】gōngzhòng (名) the public

【公费】gōngfèi（形）at public or state expense

【公费医疗】gōngfèi yīliáo（名）free medical care

【公债】gōngzhài（名）(government) bonds

【公园】gōngyuán（名）park

【公路】gōnglù（名）highway; road

【公墓】gōngmù（名）cemetery

【公仆】gōngpú（名）public servant

【公认】gōngrèn（动）be generally recognized; be universally acknowledged

【公演】gōngyǎn（动）give a public performance

【公德】gōngdé（名）social morality

【公敌】gōngdí（名）public enemy

【公论】gōnglùn（名）public opinion

【公审】gōngshěn（名）public trial

【公历】gōnglì（名）Gregorian calendar

【公愤】gōngfèn（名）public indignation

【公爵】gōngjué（名）duke

【公断】gōngduàn（动）❶ arbitrate: ～人 arbitrator ❷ judge impartially

【公粮】gōngliáng（名）agricultural tax paid in grain

【公职】gōngzhí（名）public office; public employment

【公证】gōngzhèng（名）notarization: ～人 notary; notary public

共 gòng I（副）❶ together: ～享 share ❷ altogether; in all: ～三千美元 a total of 3,000 US dollars II（形）common; general: ～通 common to all

【共存】gòngcún（动）coexist

【共同】gòngtóng I（形）common: ～纲领 common programme II（副）together; jointly

【共和】gònghé（名）republic: ～国 republic

【共事】gòngshì（动）work together: ～多年 have worked side by side for years

【共性】gòngxìng（名）general character

【共青团】gòngqīngtuán（名）Communist Youth League

【共计】gòngjì（动）amount to ; add up to

【共振】gòngzhèn（名）〈物〉resonance

【共产主义】gòngchǎn zhǔyì（名）communism

【共产党】gòngchǎndǎng（名）Communist Party: ～员 member of the Communist Party; Communist

【共处】gòngchǔ（动）coexist: 和平～ peaceful coexistence

【共鸣】gòngmíng（名）❶〈物〉resonance ❷ responsive feelings: 引起～ evoke a sympathetic response

兵 bīng（名）❶ soldier; serviceman: 民～ militiaman; militia ❷ troops; armed forces: 按～不动 hold one's troops in readiness but take no action; bide one's time ❸ rank and file: 官～ officers and men ❹ weapons; arms: 动刀～ resort to arms ❺ arm of the services: 步～ infantry ❻ war; military operations ❼ military strategy and tactics ❽ pawn — one of the pieces in Chinese chess

【兵力】bīnglì（名）troops; military strength: 集中（分散）～ concentration (dispersion) of forces

【兵士】bīngshì（名）non-commissioned soldier; private; serviceman

【兵工廠】 bīnggōngchǎng（名）ordnance factory; armoury; arsenal

【兵不血刃】 bīng bù xuè rèn〈成〉(win a battle) without firing a shot

【兵不厭詐】 bīng bù yàn zhà〈成〉there can never be too much deception in war; all is fair in war

【兵役】 bīngyì（名）（compulsory）military service: 服～ enlist in the armed forces

【兵法】 bīngfǎ（名）art of war; military strategy and tactics

【兵馬】 bīngmǎ（名）men and horses; military forces: ～俑 terra cotta warriors and horses buried with the dead; terra cotta army (in Xi'an)

【兵家】 bīngjiā ❶ military strategist in ancient China ❷ military commander: 勝敗乃～常事。Victory or defeat is a common occurrence for a military commander. ❸

【兵書】 bīngshū（名）book on military strategy and tactics

【兵員】 bīngyuán（名）troops; rank-and-file soldiers

【兵強馬壯】 bīng qiáng mǎ zhuàng〈成〉strong soldiers and sturdy horses; well-trained and well-equipped troops

【兵貴神速】 bīng guì shén sù〈成〉speed is vital in war

【兵種】 bīngzhǒng（名）arm of the services: 各軍～ all services and arms

【兵團】 bīngtuán（名）❶ corps; large (military) force consisting of divisions or armies: 生產建設～ production and construction corps ❷ a general term for any military formation larger than the regiment

【兵器】 bīngqì（名）weapon; weaponry

【兵營】 bīngyíng（名）barracks; military camp

【兵臨城下】 bīng lín chéng xià〈成〉the enemy is at the city gate; the city is in imminent danger

【兵艦】 bīngjiàn（軍艦 jūnjiàn）（名）warship; war vessel

【兵權】 bīngquán（名）control of armed forces

【兵變】 bīngbiàn（名）mutiny

其 qí（代）❶［used within a sentence to refer to sb. or sth. just mentioned］he; she; it; they: 出～不意 catch sb. unawares ❷ his; her; its; their: ～目的在於征求讀者的意見。Its purpose is to solicit the opinions of the readership. ❸ that; such: 查無～事 find that nothing of the kind has ever occurred

【其中】 qízhōng（形）among a certain number of people or things: 我們收到幾百封信，～有許多來自國外。We received several hundred letters, many of which were from abroad.

【其他】 qítā（代）other; else

【其次】 qícì（副）next; secondly: 他是班上最好的學生，～是她。He is the best student in the class, and she comes next.

【其實】 qíshí（副）as a matter of fact; in reality

【其貌不揚】 qí mào bù yáng〈成〉(of a person) look ugly

【其餘】 qíyú（代）the rest

具 jù I（名）tool; appliance; instrument: 廚房用～ kitchen utensils II

（量）（of coffins, corpses and certain other things）：一～擺鐘 a pendulum clock Ⅲ（動）❶ possess (certain qualities or characteristics)：略～輪廓 take tangible shape ❷ prepare; write out：～報 submit a report

【具文】jùwén（名）(of regulations) mere formality

【具名】jùmíng（動）sign; append one's signature (to a document)

【具有】jùyǒu（動）possess：～愛國熱情 be imbued with patriotic enthusiasm

【具結】jùjié（動）〈舊〉submit a paper to the government accepting responsibility for the action taken：～完案 sign a paper stating that a case is closed

【具備】jùbèi（動）[often followed by an abstract object] have：～同等資格 have equal (or equivalent) qualifications

【具體】jùtǐ（形）concrete; specific

典 diǎn Ⅰ（名）❶ standard ② standard work：經～ classics ❸ allusion：用～ use allusions ❹ ceremony ❺（Diǎn）a surname Ⅱ（動）mortgage

【典故】diǎngù（名）allusion

【典型】diǎnxíng Ⅰ（名）model; typical example Ⅱ（形）typical

【典雅】diǎnyǎ（形）elegant; graceful

【典當】diǎndàng（動）mortgage; pawn

【典範】diǎnfàn（名）example; model; paradigm

【典禮】diǎnlǐ（名）ceremony：畢業～ graduation ceremony; commencement

【典籍】diǎnjí（名）ancient works

兼 jiān Ⅰ（形）double; twofold：～程前進 march at double speed Ⅱ（副）simultaneously; concurrently：軟硬～施 use both hard and soft tactics

【兼任】jiānrèn Ⅰ（動）hold an additional post; act concurrently as：教授～系主任。The professor is concurrently the head of the department. Ⅱ（形）part-time：～設計師 a part-time designer

【兼收並蓄】jiān shōu bìng xù〈成〉introduce divergent views on a subject; invite scholars of different schools of thought to join an academic institution

【兼併】jiānbìng（動）annex (territory or property, etc.)

【兼備】jiānbèi（動）be qualified in both or many ways：才貌～ possessed of both beauty and talent

【兼管】jiānguǎn（動）be concurrently in charge of

【兼課】jiānkè（動）take on an additional or spare-time teaching job

【兼職】jiānzhí（名）concurrent job

【兼顧】jiāngù（動）take two or more things into consideration：～集體利益和個人利益 take into account the interest of both the collective and the individual

【兼聽則明，偏信則暗】jiān tīng zé míng, piān xìn zé àn〈成〉listen to all sides, and you will see the whole picture; heed one side alone, and you will get only a one-sided view

冀 jì（名）another name for Hebei (Province)

冂 部

冉 rǎn Ⅰ (副) 〈書〉 slowly; gradually: ～～上升 rise slowly Ⅱ (Rǎn) (名) a surname

冊 cè Ⅰ (名) book; volume: 紀念～ album Ⅱ (量) volume: 藏書百萬～ have a million books in the stacks

【冊子】cèzi (名) book

再 zài (副) ❶ again; once more: 半小時後～試一次。 Try it again in half an hour. ❷ still; in a greater degree: ～吃點。 Have some more. ／～大一點就好了。 If only it were a bit larger! ❸ [indicating what would happen if something should continue]: 你～這樣下去就毀了自己。 You will ruin yourself if you go on like this. ❹ then; before: 準備好了～出發。 Get everything ready before you start off.

【再入境】zàirùjìng (動) re-entry: ～簽證 re-entry visa

【再三】zàisān (副) over and over again; again and again

【再不】zàibu (連) 〈口〉 or else; or: 給我一支鋼筆，～一支鉛筆也行。 Give me a pen, or else a pencil.

【再生產】zàishēngchǎn (名) 〈經〉 reproduction

【再次】zàicì (副) once more; once again

【再見】zàijiàn (套) goodbye; see you again

【再版】zàibǎn Ⅰ (動) reprint Ⅱ (名) second edition

【再度】zàidù (副) again; once more: ～動手術 have another operation

【再婚】zàihūn (動) remarry; marry again

【再現】zàixiàn (動) reappear; recur; be reproduced

【再接再厲】zài jiē zài lì 〈成〉 make continued efforts; make a fresh attempt with redoubled efforts

【再會】zàihuì (套) goodbye; see you again

【再說】zàishuō Ⅰ (動) put off till some later time: 等他回來～。 Let's wait until he comes back. Ⅱ (連) what's more; moreover; besides: 我不太想去，一天也晚了。I don't feel like going; besides, it's getting late.

冒 mào Ⅰ (動) ❶ emit; issue forth; send out: 爐子～着火花。 Flames are leaping up from the stove. ❷ brave; risk: 頂風～雨 brave wind and rain ／～不必要的風險 take unnecessary risks Ⅱ ❶ boldly; recklessly: ～喊一聲 call out thoughtlessly ❷ falsely: ～取錢款 draw money under false pretences Ⅲ (Mào) (名) a surname

【冒火】màohuǒ (動) burn with anger

【冒天下之大不韙】mào tiān xià zhī dà bù wěi 〈成〉 risk universal disapproval or opposition

【冒犯】màofàn (動) offend (one's superior)

【冒失】màoshi (形) rash; thoughtless

【冒失鬼】màoshiguǐ (名) reckless fellow; harum-scarum; madcap

【冒充】màochōng (動) pretend to be; pass oneself off as: ～記者 pass oneself off as a reporter / ～專家 pose as an expert

【冒尖】 màojiān（動）❶ be a little more than: 八歲剛～ be a little over eight years old ❷ stand out: ～的學生 top students

【冒名】 màomíng（動）assume another person's name

【冒名頂替】 mào míng dǐng tì（成）pass oneself as sb. else and act under this assumed name

【冒昧】 màomèi（動）make bold (to); venture: 我～提幾點建議。I venture to make a few suggestions.

【冒風險】 màofēngxiǎn（動）run risks

【冒頂】 màodǐng（名）〈礦〉roof fall

【冒進】 màojìn（動）advance incautiously

【冒牌】 màopái（名）counterfeit of a popular trade mark; imitation: ～醫生 quack; charlatan

【冒牌貨】 màopáihuò（名）fake goods

【冒號】 màohào（名）〈語〉colon

【冒領】 màolǐng（動）falsely claim (money, etc.) as one's own

【冒頭】 màotóu（動）appear; became noticeable; begin to crop up

【冒險】 màoxiǎn（動）run a risk; take risks: ～家 adventurer

【冒險主義】 màoxiǎn zhǔyì（名）adventurism

冕 miǎn（名）crown

冖 部

冗 rǒng（形）superfluous; redun-

dant; supernumerary

【冗長】 rǒngcháng（形）(of writing or speech) lengthy and wordy

【冗員】 rǒngyuán（名）redundant personnel; supernumerary

【冗雜】 rǒngzá（形）(of affairs) miscellaneous; jumbled

冠 guān（名）❶ hat: 衣～楚楚 be immaculately dressed ❷〈生理〉corona
see also guàn

【冠心病】 guānxīnbìng（名）〈醫〉coronary heart disease

【冠冕堂皇】 guān miǎn táng huáng（成）fine-sounding; sanctimonious

冠 guàn Ⅰ（動）put on a hat Ⅱ（名）first place
see also guān

【冠軍】 guànjūn（名）champion

冢 zhǒng（名）tomb; grave

冥 míng Ⅰ（形）❶ dark; sombre ❷ deep; profound: ～思出神 deep in contemplation ❸ stupid; ignorant: ～頑不靈 stupid and stubborn Ⅱ（名）the nether world

【冥王星】 míngwángxīng（名）〈天〉Pluto

【冥想】 míngxiǎng（動）be deep in thought; meditate

【冥器】 míngqì（名）funerary objects

冤 yuān（名）❶ wrong; injustice: 伸～ redress a grievance ❷ hatred; enmity: 結～ sow enmity; incur the enmity of

【冤仇】 yuānchóu（名）enmity; rancour

【冤枉】 yuānwang Ⅰ（動）wrong; falsely charge Ⅱ（形）not

worthwhile: 花～錢 not get one's money's worth

【冤屈】yuānqū Ⅰ(動) wrong; treat unjustly Ⅱ(名) injustice

【冤案】yuān'àn (名) unjust verdict

【冤家】yuānjia (名) enemy; foe

【冤家路窄】yuān jiā lù zhǎi〈成〉enemies often meet face to face on a narrow path; enemies can scarcely avoid each other

【冤假錯案】yuān jiǎ cuò àn (名) unjust, frame-up and wrong cases

冪 mì (名)〈數〉power

【冪級數】mìjíshù (名)〈數〉power series

冫 部

冬 dōng Ⅰ(名) winter Ⅱ(象) dong

【冬天】dōngtiān (冬季 dōngjì) (名) winter

【冬瓜】dōngguā (名) white gourd

【冬眠】dōngmián (動)〈生〉hibernate

冰 bīng Ⅰ(名) ice: 滴水成～〈俗〉(so cold that) dripping water freezes; freezing cold Ⅱ(動) ❶ make one feel cold: 剛到中秋,水就有點～腿了。It is only mid-autumn, and yet my legs feel cold in the water. ❷ ice; cool sth. by putting ice on, in or around it Ⅲ(形) iced: ～西瓜 iced watermelon

【冰刀】bīngdāo (名)〈體〉blade of an ice skate

【冰川】bīngchuān (名) glacier: ～期 (冰河時代) glacial epoch (period); ice age

【冰山】bīngshān (名) iceberg

【冰上運動】bīngshàng yùndòng (名) sports on the ice

【冰天雪地】bīng tiān xuě dì〈成〉a world of frozen ice and drifting snow; vast expanse of ice and snow

【冰冷】bīnglěng (形) ice-cold; icy

【冰島】Bīngdǎo (名) Iceland: ～人 Icelander / ～語 Icelandic (language)

【冰凍】bīngdòng (動) freeze

【冰凍三尺,非一日之寒】bīng dòng sān chǐ, fēi yī rì zhī hán〈成〉it takes more than one cold day for the river to freeze three feet deep; the trouble is deep-rooted

【冰袋】bīngdài (名)〈醫〉ice bag

【冰球】bīngqiú (名)〈體〉❶ ice hockey: ～場 ice hockey rink ❷ puck

【冰場】bīngchǎng (名) skating rink

【冰棍兒】bīnggùnr (冰棒 bīngbàng) (名) ice lolly; popsicle

【冰塊】bīngkuài (名) lump of ice; ice cube

【冰雹】bīngbáo (名) hail; hailstone; hailstorm

【冰箱】bīngxiāng (名) refrigerator; icebox; fridge; freezer

【冰鞋】bīngxié (名) ice skate; skating boot

【冰糖】bīngtáng (名) crystal or rock sugar: ～葫蘆 candied haw stick

【冰磚】bīngzhuān (名) brick ice cream

【冰錐】bīngzhuī (冰柱 bīngzhù) (名) icicle

【冰激凌】bīngjīlíng (冰淇淋 bīngqílín) (名) ice cream

【冰點】bīngdiǎn (名)〈物〉freezing point

【冰镇】bīngzhèn（形）iced: ～酸梅汤 iced plum juice

【冰释】bīngshì（动）（of misgivings, misunderstandings, etc.）melt; vanish; be instantly dispelled

况 kuàng Ⅰ（名）❶ condition: 情～瞬息万变。The situation is fast changing. ❷（Kuàng）a surname Ⅱ（连）❶ in addition; let alone; not to mention: 连专家们都不清楚这件事，更何～我们这班门外汉。Even the experts are not clear about the matter, let alone us laymen.

【况且】kuàngqiě（连）moreover

冷 lěng Ⅰ（形）❶ cold: ～血动物 cold-blooded animal; heartless person ❷ unfriendly; frosty: ～言～语 sarcastic remarks ❸ deserted; silent: 孤村～寂。❹ unfamiliar; little seen: ～僻的词 words not in common use ❺ unwelcome: ～货 goods that don't sell well Ⅱ（Lěng）（名）a surname Ⅲ（动）❶（方）（of food）become cool: 等面一下来再吃 eat the noodles after they get cool ❷ cold shoulder; slight: ～了他几天 give him the cold shoulder for several days

【冷水】lěngshuǐ（名）cold water: 给他的计划泼～ throw cold water on his scheme; discourage him from going on with the scheme

【冷不防】lěngbufáng（副）unexpectedly; suddenly: ～被石头绊了一下 stumble accidentally over a stone

【冷汗】lěnghàn（名）cold sweat: 出～ break into a cold sweat

【冷冰冰】lěngbīngbīng（形）frosty; icy; frigid

【冷冷清清】lěnglěng qīngqīng（冷清lěngqing）（形）❶ desolate; lonely ❷ dreary and dull

【冷门儿】lěngménr（名）profession or branch of learning that attracts few people Ⅱ（形）not much in demand: ～货 goods not in popular demand

【冷板凳】lěngbǎndèng（名）unenviable post; cold reception: 坐了两年～ be neglected for two years

【冷却】lěngquè（动）cool: ～系统 cooling system

【冷若冰霜】lěng ruò bīng shuāng〈成〉distant and cold: 她这个人～。She is an iceberg.

【冷宫】lěnggōng（名）limbo; disfavour: 打入～ consign to limbo; put on the back shelf

【冷冻】lěngdòng（动）freeze: ～室（箱）freezer

【冷气】lěngqì（名）air conditioning: ～机 air conditioner

【冷笑】lěngxiào Ⅰ（名）sneer Ⅱ（动）give a grim laugh

【冷淡】lěngdàn（形）❶ not lively; not brisk ❷ cold; distant; aloof; indifferent: 对人～ be indifferent to everybody; give sb. the cold shoulder Ⅱ（动）cold-shoulder: 对他这样～是不对的。It is not right to cold-shoulder him.

【冷眼】lěngyǎn（名）❶（with a）cool head ❷ sneer; apathy

【冷饮】lěngyǐn（名）cold drink

【冷遇】lěngyù（名）cold reception: 受到～ get the cold shoulder; get a cold reception

【冷场】lěngchǎng（名）uncomfortable silence（when an actor forgets

his words on the stage or when nobody takes the floor at a meeting)

【冷落】lěngluò Ⅰ(形) desolate; deserted Ⅱ(动) give a cold reception to (sb.)

【冷暖】lěngnuǎn (名) ❶ (of weather) change in temperature ❷ well-being: 群众的～ public welfare; well-being of the masses ❸ (of human relationship) fickleness: 人情～。Men's feelings are changeable.

【冷酷】lěngkù(形) cold-blooded; relentless; ruthless

【冷枪】lěngqiāng (名) sniper's shot: 打～ shoot from a hidden place; snipe

【冷箭】lěngjiàn (名) arrow shot from a hidden place; sneak attack

【冷盘】lěngpán (名) cold dish

【冷静】lěngjìng (形) sober; cool-headed; composed

【冷餐】lěngcān (名) buffet

【冷战】lěngzhàn (名) cold war

【冷战】lěngzhan (名)〈口〉shiver; shudder: 浑身直打～ shiver all over

【冷飕飕】lěngsōusōu (形)〈口〉chilly; cold and windy

【冷藏】lěngcáng (动) keep in cold storage

冶 yě (动) smelt

【冶金】yějīn (名) metallurgy

【冶炼】yěliàn (动) smelt

冽 liè (形) cold

冼 Xiǎn (名) a surname

凄 qī (形) ❶ chilly; desolate ❷ sad; wretched

【凄切】qīqiè (形) dreary and sad: 寒蝉～。Cicadas sing dolefully in the cold.

【凄风苦雨】qī fēng kǔ yǔ〈成〉desolate circumstances; wretched weather

【凄凉】qīliáng (形) desolate; bleak

【凄婉】qīwǎn (形)(of sound) plaintive: ～的笛声 the plaintive notes of a flute

【凄惨】qīcǎn (形) wretched; miserable

【凄厉】qīlì (形)(of voice, sound) woeful and shrill

凌 líng Ⅰ(名) ❶ ice ❷ (Líng) a surname Ⅱ(动) ❶ insult; overbear: 他真盛气～人。He's most domineering. ❷ rise high; soar ❸ approach

【凌空】língkōng (动) soar into the skies; hover

【凌辱】língrǔ (动) humiliate; insult; affront

【凌晨】língchén (副) before dawn

【凌云】língyún (形) lofty: ～壮志 lofty aspirations

【凌乱】língluàn (形) messy; disorderly

【凌驾】língjià (动) domineer; override: ～一切的中心任务 the overriding task

【凌厉】línglì (形) speedy and forceful

凍 dòng (动) ❶ freeze ❷ feel freezing cold

【凍结】dòngjié (动) freeze: ～物价 freeze prices

【凍疮】dòngchuāng (名) chilblain

【凍僵】dòngjiāng (动) be numb with cold

淨 jìng Ⅰ(形) ❶ clean; pure: 擦～ wipe sth. clean ❷ net: ～賺 net profit Ⅱ(副) only; nothing but: 這 幾天～下雨。It has been raining nonstop these days. Ⅲ(名) general term for the character type with a fiery or savage temper called "painted faces" in traditional Chinese opera

【淨化】jìnghuà(動) purify; make clean

【淨手】jìngshǒu(動) ❶ wash one's hands ❷〈婉〉relieve oneself

【淨收入】jìngshōurù(名) net income

【淨重】jìngzhòng(名) net weight

【淨盡】jìngjìn(副) completely; with nothing left: 消滅～ completely wipe out

凋 diāo(動) wither

【凋敝】diāobì(形) destitute; depressed: 民生～。The people eked out a miserable existence.

【凋零】diāolíng(形) whithered and desolate

【凋謝】diāoxiè(動) whither away; fall into decay

准 zhǔn(動) allow; permit: 不～ 喧嘩。Be quiet.

【准予】zhǔnyǔ(動) approve; permit: 每人～攜帶 20 公斤行李。 Each passenger is allowed 20 kilos of personal luggage.

【准許】zhǔnxǔ(動) allow; permit

凜 lǐn ❶ cold ❷ stern ❸ afraid; fearful

【凜冽】lǐnliè(形) bitingly

【凜然】lǐnrán(形) solemn; awe-inspiring: ～不可侵犯 have a forbid-

ding and awe-inspiring manner

【凜凜】lǐnlǐn(形) ❶ cold: 寒風～。 The cold wind cut one to the marrow. ❷ stern; forbidding

凝 níng(動) ❶ coagulate; congeal ❷ concentrate one's attention

【凝固】nínggù(動) solidify

【凝固點】nínggùdiǎn(名)〈物〉solidifying point

【凝思】níngsī(名) be deep in thought

【凝神】níngshén(動) concentrate one's attention

【凝視】níngshì(動) fix one's gaze; stare

【凝結】níngjié(動) condense; coagulate

【凝聚】níngjù(動) condense; cohere: ～力 cohesive force

【凝滯】níngzhì(形) stagnant; dull

【凝練】níngliàn(形) concise; condensed

【凝聽】níngtīng(動) listen attentively (to)

几　部

几 jī(名) small, low table: 茶～兒 tea poy; tea table

凡 fán Ⅰ(形) ordinary; commonplace Ⅱ(副) in all: 全書～20 卷。 The book consists of twenty volumes all told. Ⅲ(名) ❶ general drift; essentials: 修辭學發～ Introduction to Rhetoric ❷ the human world

【凡人】fánrén(名) ❶ ordinary person ❷ mortal being

【凡士林】 fánshìlín (名) vaseline

【凡世】 fánshì (名) this mortal world

【凡事】 fánshì (名) everything; anything: ～ 都要慎重考慮. Give careful thought to everything you do.

【凡是】 fánshì (形) every; all: ～ 新生都須體檢. All new students are required to undergo a medical examination.

【凡庸】 fányōng (形) medio

凱 kǎi I (形) victorious; triumphant: 奏～而歸 return in triumph II (Kǎi) (名) a surname

【凱旋】 kǎixuán (名) triumphal return

【凱歌】 kǎigē (名) song of triumph; paean

凳 dèng (名) bench; stool

凵 部

凶 xiōng (名) misfortune: ～ 吉難卜 hard to tell how it will turn out; not know what's in store

【凶兆】 xiōngzhào (名) ill omen

【凶多吉少】 xiōng duō jí shǎo 〈成〉 most likely, the prospects are grim rather than bright; promise more evil than good

凹 āo (形) concave; dented

【凹凸不平】 āo tū bù píng (形) rough; uneven

【凹面鏡】 āomiànjìng (名) concave mirror

【凹透鏡】 āotòujìng (名) concave lens

【凹陷】 āoxiàn (形) hollow; depressed

凸 tū (形) protruding; bulging; raised

【凸面】 tūmiàn (名) convex

【凸透鏡】 tūtòujìng (名) convex lens

出 chū I (動) ❶ go out; come out: ～ 去! Get out of here! ❷ appear; show up: ～ 場 come on the stage; appear on the arena ❸ exceed: ～ 圈兒 go too far; overstep the bounds ❹ issue; give: ～ 了個主意 come up with an idea ❺ yield; produce ❻ take place; happen ❼ put forth; vent: ～ 汗 perspire; sweat II (副) ❶ [used after a verb to indicate outward movement]: 倒 ～ pour out ❷ [used to indicate completion]: 作 ～ 決議 adopt a resolution ❸ [used to indicate identification]: 看不～ cannot make out

【出力】 chūlì (動) exert oneself; make a vigorous effort II (副) energetically

【出入】 chūrù I (動) come in and go out: ～ 國境 cross the border II (名) divergence: 這兩種說法有 ～。 There is discrepancy between these two statements.

【出證】 chūrùzhèng (名) pass

【出人意料】 chū rén yì liào 〈成〉 unexpectedly; contrary to one's expectations

【出人頭地】 chū rén tóu dì 〈成〉 rise head and shoulders above others; tower over others in ability

【出土】 chūtǔ (動) be unearthed: ～

文物 unearthed historical relics

【出口】chūkǒu Ⅰ(动) ❶ speak; say: 難以～ too embarrassing to bring up the matter ❷ export Ⅱ (名) ❶ exit ❷ export

【出毛病】chū máobìng (动) go wrong; break down: 錄音機～了。 The recorder is out of order.

【出去】chūqu (动) go out; get out

【出去】chūqu (副) [used after a verb to indicate outward movement]: 跑～迎接他 run out to meet him

【出示】chūshì (动) show; produce: ～通行證 show one's pass

【出生】chūshēng (动) be born

【出任】chūrèn (动) assume the post of

【出色】chūsè (形) splendid; outstanding

【出名】chūmíng (形) famous; well-known

【出身】chūshēn (名) ❶ family background ❷ one's earlier occupation

【出车】chūchē (动) ❶ dispatch a car, bus, etc. ❷ (of a driver) start; set out; be out driving

【出兵】chūbīng (动) dispatch troops

【出没】chūmò (动) appear and disappear suddenly: ～無常 appear suddenly and unpredictably

【出岔子】chū chàzi (动) go wrong: ～了嗎? Is there something amiss?

【出於】chūyú (介) out of; because of: ～責任心 actuated by a sense of responsibility

【出来】chūlái (动) come out; appear

【出来】chūlái (动) [used after a verb to indicate an outward movement or completion of an action]: 說～! Out with it!

【出征】chūzhēng (动) go on an expedition

【出事】chūshì (动) have an accident: 不會～。 Nothing will go wrong.

【出使】chūshǐ (动) serve as an envoy (to a foreign country); be sent abroad on a diplomatic mission

【出奇】chūqí (副) unusually; exceptionally: 快得～ wonderfully fast

【出奇制勝】chū qí zhì shèng 〈成〉 gain victory by launching a surprise attack on the enemy

【出版】chūbǎn (动) publish: ～自由 freedom of the press

【出界】chūjiè (副)〈體〉 outside; out of bounds

【出轨】chūguǐ (动) ❶ (of a train) be derailed ❷ overstep the limit

【出面】chūmiàn (动) act in one's own name or on sb. else's behalf: 他可以代我們～。 He may act on our behalf.

【出品】chūpǐn (名) product

【出差】chūchāi (动) travel on (official) business; go on a business trip

【出神】chūshén (动) be lost in thought; be in a trance; be preoccupied with sth.

【出洋相】chū yángxiàng (动) make an exhibition of oneself

【出風頭】chū fēngtou (动) be in the limelight; cut a smart figure

【出庭】chūtíng (动) appear in court

【出家】chūjiā (动) become a Buddhist monk or nun

【出马】chūmǎ (动) ❶ go into action; assume a post ❷ take up a matter: 親自～ take up the matter oneself; attend to the matter personally

【出借】chūjiè（動）lend; loan

【出師】chūshī（動）❶ complete one's apprenticeship ❷ dispatch troops on an expedition

【出氣】chūqì（形）vent one's spleen (on sb.)

【出納】chūnà（名）❶ act of receiving and paying out money or bills ❷ cashier

【出席】chūxí（動）attend; be present (at a meeting, party, etc.)

【出息】chūxi（名）(of a person) promise; bright future: 没 ～ be a good-for-nothing

【出租】chūzū（動）hire out; let: ～汽車 taxi

【出院】chūyuàn（動）be discharged from hospital

【出格】chūgé（動）exceed the sense of propriety; act improperly: 這太～了。This is going too far.

【出處】chūchù（名）source (of a quotation or allusion)

【出產】chūchǎn（動）yield; produce

【出國】chūguó（動）go abroad

【出現】chūxiàn（動）appear; become visible

【出售】chūshòu（動）sell

【出動】chūdòng（動）❶ (of a group) set out; start off ❷ go into action; turn out: 防暴警察全體～。The riot police turned out in force. ❸ call out; dispatch: ～二十架直升飛機 dispatch 20 helicopters

【出診】chūzhěn（動）(of a doctor) visit a patient

【出衆】chūzhòng（形）outstanding; out of the common: 人才～ of outstanding ability

【出超】chūchāo（名）trade surplus; favourable balance of trade

【出發】chūfā（動）❶ set out; start off ❷ start from; proceed from: 從全局利益～ proceed from considerations of overall public interest

【出發點】chūfādiǎn（名）starting point

【出勤】chūqín I（動）show up for work II（名）attendance: ～率 attendance rate

【出嫁】chūjià（動）(of a girl) get married

【出路】chūlù（名）way out; outlet: 唯一的～ the only way out

【出境】chūjìng（動）leave a country: ～手續 exit formalities

【出爾反爾】chū ěr fǎn ěr〈成〉one breaks a promise sooner than one makes it; be capricious

【出價】chūjià（動）bid; offer a price

【出賣】chūmài（動）❶ sell ❷〈貶〉betray; sell out: ～國家利益 barter away the interests of the nation

【出錯】chūcuò（動）make a mistake; 容易～ be liable to error

【出頭】chūtóu（動）❶ extricate oneself from difficulty or predicament ❷ step forward: ～干涉 step forward to intervene

【出頭露面】chū tóu lòu miàn〈成〉be in the spotlight; make public appearances

【出謀劃策】chū móu huà cè〈成〉give counsel; mastermind (a project or scheme)

【出擊】chūjī（動）launch an attack; make an assault

【出醜】chūchǒu（動）make a fool of oneself

【出類拔萃】chū lèi bá cuì〈成〉preeminent; be out of the common run: ～的人 the best and the brightest (people)

【出籠】 chūlóng （动）❶ (of steamed bread, etc.) be right off the steamer ❷〈贬〉appear; come out into the open

【出让】 chūràng（动）sell (one's belongings)

函 hán（名）letter; 來～ your letter

【函件】 hánjiàn（名）mail

【函授】 hánshòu（动）give instruction by mail; offer a correspondence course; ～生 correspondence-course student

【函数】 hánshù（名）〈数〉function

【函购】 hángòu（动）order by mail

刀 部

刀 dāo Ⅰ（名）knife; sword Ⅱ（量）(of paper) one hundred sheets: 一～纸 one hundred sheets of paper

【刀叉】 dāochā（名）knife and fork

【刀口】 dāokǒu（名）❶ blade ❷ cut; incision ❸ crucial point

【刀山火海】 dāo shān huǒ hǎi〈成〉a mountain of daggers and a sea of flames; a most dangerous place or a most revere trial

【刀兵】 dāobīng（名）❶ arms ❷ war

【刀枪】 dāoqiāng（名）swords and spears; weapons

刁 diāo Ⅰ（形）cunning; sly; knavish Ⅱ（名）(Diāo) a surname

【刁悍】 diāohàn（形）sly and savage

【刁滑】 diāohuá（形）cunning; crafty

【刁难】 diāonàn（动）deliberately raise difficulty or create trouble for sb.

刃 rèn（名）❶ edge (of a knife, sword, etc.); blade: 雙～剃刀片 a double-edged razor blade ❷ sword; knife

【刃具】 rènjù（名）〈机〉cutting tool

切 qiē（动）cut; carve (cooked meat): 把烤牛肉一～開 carve up the roast beef

see also qiè

【切片】 qiēpiàn Ⅰ（动）cut into slices Ⅱ（名）〈醫〉section

【切削】 qiēxiāo（名）〈机〉cutting: 機械～ machine cutting

【切除】 qiēchú（名）〈醫〉removal; excision

【切丝】 qiēsī（动）shred (meat, vegetables, etc.)

【切磋】 qiēcuō（动）compare notes and learn from each other: ～琢磨 (of fellow students or disciples) discuss academic or professional problems and swap experience

【切槽】 qiēcáo（名）grooving

【切断】 qiēduàn（动）cut off; sever

切 qiè Ⅰ（形）❶ close (to) ❷ eager; anxious: 求勝心～ be eager for success Ⅱ（副）be sure to: ～不可鲁莽行事。 One should never act rashly. Ⅲ（动）❶ correspond to; fit ❷ feel (the pulse)

see also qiē

【切中】 qièzhòng（动）(of opinion or meaning) hit the nail on the head

【切切】 qièqiè（副）be sure to: ～此記 never forget for a moment

【切合】 qièhé（动）fit in with; correspond with

【切忌】qièjì (动) be sure to avoid: ~滋长骄傲情绪. Of all things guard against the growth of conceit.

【切近】qièjìn (动) be close to

【切身】qièshēn (形) ❶ of what is closely connected with one's interests: ~利益 one's immediate or vital interests ❷ personal: 根据~体验 in light of one's personal experience

【切脉】qièmài (动) feel the pulse

【切记】qièjì (动) must keep in mind

【切骨之仇】qiè gǔ zhī chóu (成) inveterate hatred

【切实】qièshí Ⅰ (形) in conformity with objective needs: 这個主意~可行。 The idea is feasible. Ⅱ (副) seriously: ~改進工作条件 take serious steps to improve working conditions

【切齿】qièchǐ (动) grind one's teeth in anger or hatred

【切肤之痛】qiè fū zhī tòng (成) a deep sorrow; an acute pain; bitter experience

【切题】qiètí (动) be appropriate to the subject matter

分 fēn Ⅰ (动) ❶ divide; separate: ~爲五部分 fall into five parts ❷ distribute; assign: 把书~赠大家 give a copy of this book to each of them / ~清敌友 draw a clear distinction between friends and enemies Ⅱ (名) ❶ branch; part: 郵電~局 branch post office / ~校 branch school ❸ point: 得三~ score three points ❹ fraction: 五~之三 three fifths Ⅲ (量) ❶ minute (1/60 of an hour) ❷ fen (1/100 of one yuan RMB)

see also fèn

【分子】fēnzǐ (名) ❶ 〈数〉 numerator ❷ 〈化〉 molecule

【分寸】fēncùn (名) sense of propriety: 做事有~ act with propriety

【分工】fēngōng Ⅰ (动) divide up the work Ⅱ (名) division of labour

【分化】fēnhuà (动) split up; divide

【分手】fēnshǒu (动) bid farewell

【分心】fēnxīn (动) divert one's attention; be side-tracked

【分支】fēnzhī (名) branch; offshoot

【分文不取】fēn wén bù qǔ (动) be free of charge; be given gratis

【分水嶺】fēnshuǐlǐng (名) watershed

【分句】fēnjù (名) 〈语〉 clause

【分母】fēnmǔ (名) 〈数〉 denominator

【分米】fēnmǐ (名) decimetre (dm)

【分而治之】fēn ér zhì zhī (动) divide and rule

【分貝】fēnbèi (名) 〈物〉 decibel (db)

【分佈】fēnbù (动) distribute; scatter: 人口~ population distribution

【分别】fēnbié (动) ❶ part; bid farewell ❷ differentiate ❸ respectively: ~通知他們 notify each of them

【分批】fēnpī (副) in batches; in separate groups

【分身】fēnshēn (动) take time out to attend to sth. else: 難以~ have no time to spare for anything else

【分肥】fēnféi (动) share out profits (usu. ill-gotten); divide up the spoils

【分居】fēnjū Ⅰ (动) live apart Ⅱ (名) separation

【分泌】fēnmì (动) 〈生〉 secrete: ~

物 secretion

【分析】fēnxī Ⅰ (动) analyse Ⅱ (名) analysis

【分明】fēnmíng Ⅰ (形) clearcut; distinct: 黑白~ as distinct as white is from black Ⅱ (副) clearly; evidently

【分歧】fēnqí (名) difference; divergence: 消除~ sink the differences

【分红】fēnhóng (动) give bonus payments (to employees); pay dividends (to shareholders)

【分洪】fēnhóng (名) flood diversion

【分派】fēnpài (动) assign; allot

【分界线】fēnjièxiàn (名) demarcation line

【分庭抗禮】fēn tíng kàng lǐ 〈成〉 stand up to each other with rival claims

【分家】fēnjiā divide up family property among the chief members

【分娩】fēnmiǎn (名) childbirth

【分配】fēnpèi Ⅰ (动) allocate; assign: 給他們~工作 allocate jobs to them Ⅱ (名) allocation; assignment

【分配形式】fēnpèi xíngshì (名) form of distribution

【分清】fēnqīng (动) distinguish

【分野】fēnyě (名) line of demarcation

【分组】fēnzǔ (动) divide into groups

【分崩離析】fēn bēng lí xī (动) crumble; collapse; disintegrate; fall apart

【分發】fēnfā (动) distribute; hand out

【分割】fēngē (动) carve up; separate

【分開】fēnkāi (动) separate

【分散】fēnsàn (动) disperse; diffuse; distract: ~注意力 distract attention

【分期】fēnqī (副) by stages: 工程將~完成。The project will be completed by stages.

【分期付款】fēnqī fùkuǎn (动) pay by instalments

【分裂】fēnliè (动) split; separate; break with

【分裂主義】fēnliè zhǔyì (名) separatism

【分道揚鑣】fēn dào yáng biāo 〈成〉 part company, each pursuing his own course

【分號】fēnhào (名) ❶ semicolon ❷ branch firm or company: 上海~ Shanghai branch

【分隔】fēngé (动) partition; isolate

【分解】fēnjiě (动) resolve; decompose

【分數】fēnshù (名) ❶ 〈数〉 fraction ❷ mark; grade

【分憂】fēnyōu (动) share sb.'s sorrows

【分辨】fēnbiàn (动) distinguish: ~是非 distinguish between right and wrong

【分機】fēnjī (名) extension (telephone): ~號碼 extension number

【分頭】fēntóu (副) separately (by forming people into groups for different purposes)

【分曉】fēnxiǎo Ⅰ (名) outcome: 有待~ remain to be seen Ⅱ (形) clear: 一定問個~。Make sure what it is all about.

【分離】fēnlí (动) separate; part

【分類】fēnlèi Ⅰ (动) classify Ⅱ (名) classification

【分辯】fēnbiàn (动) defend oneself against a charge: 不容~ refuse to accept any explanation

【分赃】fēnzāng（动）divide up the booty

【分摊】fēntān（动）share（the expenses）; pay equally

分 fēn（名）❶ component; content: 盐～ salt content ❷ duty: 尽本～ do one's part ❸ limit: 恰如其～ most appropriate
see also fèn

【分子】fènzǐ（名）element; member

【分内】fènnèi（形）within one's duty

【分外】fènwài Ⅰ（形）outside one's duty Ⅱ（副）extraordinarily

【分量】fènliàng（名）weight

刊 kān Ⅰ（动）❶ publish: 创～号 first issue ❷ correct; emend; delete Ⅱ（名）periodical; supplement of a newspaper

【刊物】kānwù（名）publication

【刊登】kāndēng（动）publish in a newspaper or periodical; carry: ～一篇文章 carry an article

【刊载】kānzài（动）publish in a newspaper or periodical

刑 xíng（名）❶ penalty; punishment: 三年徒～ three years' imprisonment ❷ torture: 受～致死 be tortured to death

【刑法】xíngfǎ（名）〈法〉criminal law; penal code

【刑具】xíngjù（名）〈法〉instruments of torture

【刑事】xíngshì（名）〈法〉criminal: ～犯 criminal offender

【刑场】xíngchǎng（名）execution ground

【刑期】xíngqī（名）〈法〉prison term; term of penalty

【刑罚】xíngfá（名）penalty; punish-

ment

列 liè Ⅰ（动）line up; list: 把下週要做的事～出来。List the things to be done next week. Ⅱ（形）many; each: 到會的～位代表 all delegates to the conference Ⅲ（名）❶ row; rank; file ❷ train: 專～ special train Ⅳ（量）line; procession: 一長～小汽車 a procession of cars

【列支敦士登】Lièzhīdūnshìdēng（名）Liechtenstein: ～人 Liechtensteiner

【列兵】lièbīng（名）〈军〉private

【列車】lièchē（名）（passenger）train: 特快～ special express

【列車员】lièchēyuán（名）（train）attendant

【列車时刻表】lièchē shíkè biǎo（名）train schedule; railway timetable

【列島】lièdǎo（名）archipelago

【列席】lièxí（动）be present（at a meeting）without the right to vote; attend as an observer

【列國】lièguó（名）（various）countries

【列隊】lièduì（动）line up

【列強】lièqiáng（名）big powers

【列舉】lièjǔ（动）list; enumerate

刎 wěn（动）cut the throat: 自～ kill oneself; commit suicide

初 chū Ⅰ（形）❶ early: ～春 early spring ❷ first in order: ～版 first edition / ～九 the ninth day of the lunar month ❸ elementary: ～級英語 elementary English ❹ original: ～願 one's original intention Ⅱ（名）❶ beginning: 月（年）～ at the beginning of the month（year）❷（Chū）a surname

【初中】chūzhōng（名）（short for 初

级中学 chūjí zhōngxué) junior middle school

【初生之犊不畏虎】chū shēng zhī dú bù wèi hǔ〈成〉a new-born calf has no fear for the tiger; young people are daring

【初出茅庐】chū chū máo lú〈成〉at the start of one's career; be still a tiro

【初交】chūjiāo（名）new acquaintance

【初次】chūcì（副）for the first time

【初步】chūbù（形）initial; tentative: ~ 计划 tentative plan

【初等】chūděng（形）elementary: ~ 数学 elementary mathematics

【初期】chūqī（名）early days; early stage (or period)

【初诊】chūzhěn（名）first visit (to a doctor or hospital)

【初试】chūshì（名）❶ preliminary examination ❷ first attempt

【初露锋芒】chū lù fēng máng〈成〉reveal one's talent for the first time

判 pàn Ⅰ（动）sentence; appraise; judge; deliver a verdict: ~ 三年徒刑 be sentenced to three years' imprisonment Ⅱ（形）[used to indicate difference] marked: ~ 若两人 look as if one was a quite different person

【判刑】pànxíng（动）pass sentence

【判决】pànjué Ⅰ（动）bring in a verdict Ⅱ（名）court decision; judgment: 最终 ~ final verdict

【判决书】pànjuéshū（名）court verdict

【判别】pànbié（动）distinguish; tell apart: ~ 是非 distinguish between right and wrong

【判定】pàndìng（动）judge; decide

【判明】pànmíng（动）ascertain; verify

【判处】pànchǔ（动）sentence; condemn

【判罪】pànzuì（动）convict; declare guilty

【判断】pànduàn Ⅰ（动）judge; decide Ⅱ（名）judgment; assertion

别 bié Ⅰ（动）❶ part; separate; leave: 依依惜 ~ be reluctant to part ❷ differentiate; distinguish: 分门 ~ 类 classify; sort; assort ❸ pin; fasten (with a pin or clip): 在胸前 ~ 一枚徽章 pin a badge on one's breast ❹ don't: ~ 见怪。I meant no offence. ❺ [used with 是 to express misgivings, etc.]: ~ 是他出事了吧? Could it be that he had an accident? Ⅱ（名）❶ parting; separation ❷ another; other: ~ 体 a different calligraphic style ❸ difference: 天壤之 ~ as far removed as heaven from earth; a world of difference

see also biè

【别人】biéren（名）others; other people

【别出心裁】bié chū xīn cái〈成〉come up with a totally different idea from that of others

【别名】biémíng（名）alternative name; alias; by-name

【别字】biézì（名）❶ Chinese character incorrectly written or pronounced: 唸 ~ mispronounce a character ❷ alias

【别有天地】bié yǒu tiān dì〈成〉an altogether different world; a place of enchanting beauty

【别有用心】bié yǒu yòng xīn〈成〉

be actuated by ulterior motives

【别有风味】bié yǒu fēng wèi〈成〉have a distinctive flavour

【别具一格】bié jù yī gé〈成〉have a style of one's own

【别针】biézhēn（名）❶ pin; safety pin ❷ brooch

【别处】biéchù Ⅰ（名）another place Ⅱ（副）elsewhere

【别提】biétí（副）so much so that no words can adequately express it: 大廳裏～多擠了。It is hard to describe how crowded the hall was.

【别开生面】bié kāi shēng miàn〈成〉break fresh ground; usher in a new form of art

【别管】biéguǎn Ⅰ（连）〈口〉no matter (who, what, etc.): ～到哪兒，您都需要它。You will need it wherever you go. Ⅱ（动）❶ never mind (about): ～我,我没有什麼問題。Don't bother about me. I am all right. ❷ leave sb. or sth. alone: ～他。Leave him alone.

【别墅】biéshù（名）villa; country house

【别緻】biézhì（形）novel and interesting; unique and attractive; original

【别離】biélí Ⅰ（动）leave; take leave of; part from Ⅱ（名）parting; separation

别 biè

see also bié

【别扭】bièniu（形）❶ difficult to deal with; troublesome; refractory ❷ awkward; vexed: 心裏～feel out of sorts ❸ at odds: 鬧～be at odds ❹ (of speech, writing, etc.) not smooth; awkward

【利】lì Ⅰ（名）❶ benefit; advantage: ～大於弊 have more advantages than disadvantages; do more good than harm ❷ profit; interest: 營～ make profits Ⅱ（动）benefit: ～人 be of benefit to people Ⅲ（形）❶ favourable: 有～的條件 favourable conditions ❷ sharp: ～刃 sharp dagger

【利己】lìjǐ（形）egoistic: ～主義 egoism

【利比亞】Lìbǐyà（名）Libya: ～人 Libyan

【利比里亞】Lìbǐlǐyà（名）Liberia: ～人 Liberian

【利令智昏】lì lìng zhì hūn〈成〉be blinded by greed for gain

【利用】lìyòng（动）❶ utilize; make use of: 我想一這個機會講幾句。I wish to avail myself of this opportunity to say a few words. ❷ take advantage of

【利於】lìyú（动）be of benefit to sb. or sth; be favourable for

【利害】lìhài（名）gain and loss: 這事和我們～攸關。We all have a stake in this matter.

【利害】lìhai（形）terrible; serious; formidable: 這一着棋十分～。This is a formidable move.

【利息】lìxī(利錢 lìqián)（名）interest

【利益】lìyì（名）benefit; interests: ～集團 interest group

【利率】lìlǜ（名）〈經〉interest rate

【利落】lìluo（形）❶ deft; agile: 幹活～ work with dexterity ❷ neat; orderly: 穿着乾淨～ be neatly dressed ❸ finished; settled: 這事基本上辦～了。The matter is as good as settled.

【利诱】lìyòu（动）lure by offer of material advantage; try to buy over

【利润】lìrùn（名）profit: ～留成制 profit retention scheme

【利弊】lìbì（名）advantages and disadvantages; pros and cons: 此事～参半。This matter cuts both ways.

【利欲熏心】lì yù xūn xīn〈成〉be consumed by thirst for gain

【利器】lìqì（名）❶ sharp weapon ❷ sophisticated weapon ❸ good tool

刨 páo（动）❶ dig; excavate: ～花生 dig（up）peanuts ❷ exclude: ～去他还有两人。There are two more, not counting him.

【刨根儿】páogēnr（动）get to the root of a matter

删 shān（动）delete; strike out; cross out: 把无关紧要的细节都～去。Delete the unnecessary details.

【删改】shāngǎi（动）revise

【删除】shānchú（动）delete; strike out

【删节】shānjié（动）abridge

【删节号】shānjiéhào（名）ellipsis（mark）

【删繁就简】shān fán jiù jiǎn〈成〉prune an essay

刻 kè Ⅰ（动）carve; inscribe: 石～ stone inscription Ⅱ（名）moment: 立～ immediately; right away / 此～ now; at this moment Ⅲ（形）❶ incisive; biting ❷ of the highest degree: ～意 painstakingly Ⅳ（量）quarter of an hour: 四点三～ four forty-five

【刻不容缓】kè bù róng huǎn〈成〉brook no delay; most urgent

【刻字】kèzì（动）engrave words or characters on a seal, etc.

【刻板】kèbǎn（形）stiff; rigid

【刻毒】kèdú（形）（of words, etc.）malicious; acrid; spiteful

【刻苦】kèkǔ（副）❶ assiduously; painstakingly ❷ frugally

【刻骨】kègǔ（形）long established; ingrained: ～铭心 be deeply engraved on one's mind / ～仇恨 deep-rooted hatred

【刻画】kèhuà（动）portray; represent in words or other artistic means

【刻薄】kèbó（形）caustic; acrimonious: 尖酸～ tart and mean

券 quàn（名）ticket; coupon: 有奖债～ lottery bond / 餐～ meal ticket

刺 cì Ⅰ（名）thorn; splinter: 肉中～ a thorn in the thigh Ⅱ（动）❶ prick; stab: 从背后一刀～进去 stab sb. in the back ❷ assassinate: 遇～ be assassinated ❸ irritate: ～耳 grate on the ear ❹ satirize: 讥～ ridicule

【刺刺不休】cì cì bù xiū〈成〉talk on and on; babble

【刺客】cìkè（名）assassin

【刺骨】cìgǔ（动）chill one to the bone: 寒风～。The cold wind cuts one to the marrow.

【刺探】cìtàn（动）make secret inquiries（usu. about military matters）; spy

【刺眼】cìyǎn（形）❶ dazzling ❷ unpleasant to the eye

【刺猬】cìwei（名）hedgehog

【刺激】cìjī Ⅰ（动）❶ stimulate; irritate: ～生产 stimulate production / ～皮肤 irritate the skin ❷ upset; shock: 受到精神～ be badly shaken

Ⅱ (名) ❶ stimulation; incentive: 物質～ material incentive ❷ shock

【刺繡】cìxiù (名) embroidery

到 dào Ⅰ (動) ❶ reach; come: 飛機幾點～? When is the plane due? ❷ go: ～辦公室去 go to the office Ⅱ (介) to; until: 從早～晚 from morning till night Ⅲ [used after a verb to indicate success]: 見～ have seen / 做～ have done

【到底】dàodǐ (副) ❶ to the end: 進行～ carry sth. through to the end ❷ finally; at last: 試驗～成功了。 The experiment finally succeeded. ❸ [used in an interrogative sentence] ever; on earth: 她～在哪裏? Where on earth can she be? ❹ after all

【到處】dàochù (副) everywhere; in all places

【到場】dàochǎng (動) be present

【到達】dàodá (動) arrive; reach

【到期】dàoqī (動) fall due; expire

【到職】dàozhí (動) assume office

刷 shuā Ⅰ (名) brush: 鞋～子 shoe brush Ⅱ (動) ❶ brush: ～牙 brush one's teeth ❷ daub; paint or paste with a brush: 粉～房間 whitewash a room ❸ 〈口〉 eliminate in a tournament: 給～下來了 be eliminated Ⅲ (象) swish: 樹葉～～作響。 Leaves were rustling.

see also shuà

【刷洗】shuāxǐ (動) scrub; clean with a brush and water: 把地板～乾淨。 Scrub the floor clean.

【刷新】shuāxīn (動) ❶ renovate ❷ break (a record): ～世界紀錄 break a world record

刷 shuà

see also shuā

【刷白】shuàbái (形) deadly pale

制 zhì Ⅰ (動) ❶ restrain; control; restrict: 軍事管～ military control ❷ draw up; formulate Ⅱ (名) system: 集體所有～ collective ownership

【制止】zhìzhǐ (動) curb; check; stop: ～局勢進一步惡化 prevent the situation from further deteriorating

【制式】zhìshì (名) ❶ rule; formula ❷ model; pattern; system

【制服】zhìfú (名) uniform

【制定】zhìdìng (動) lay down; draw up; draft: ～措施 enact measures

【制訂】zhìdìng (動) work out; formulate: ～政策 make a policy

【制度】zhìdù (名) system; institution

【制約】zhìyuē (動) restrict; restrain

【制高點】zhìgāodiǎn (名) 〈軍〉 commanding elevation

【制動】zhìdòng (動) apply the brakes: ～器 brake

【制裁】zhìcái (動) apply sanctions against: 採取經濟～ take economic sanctions against

【制勝】zhìshèng (動) gain mastery over; subdue

刮 guā (動) ❶ scrape: ～臉 shave (one's face) ❷ plunder; fleece: 搜～ extort ❸ (of wind) blow

【刮目相看】guā mù xiāng kàn 〈成〉 make a fresh appraisal of sb.

剁 duò (動) cut; chop

前 qián Ⅰ (形) ❶ first; front: 名單上的～三名 the first three on the

name list / ～門 front door ❷ preceding; previous; past: ～一封信 the previous letter ❸ former: ～總統 expresident ❹ future: ～程 future Ⅱ (動) go forward: 畏縮不～ hesitate to press forward Ⅲ (副) ago: 六年～ six years ago Ⅳ (介) ❶ in front of: 房～ in front of the house ❷ before: 午～ before noon

【前人】 qiánrén (名) forefathers; predecessors

【前夕】 qiánxī (名) eve

【前方】 qiánfāng Ⅰ (副) (right) in front; ahead Ⅱ (名) front; front line: ～戰士 fighters at the front

【前天】 qiántiān (名) the day before yesterday

【前功盡棄】 qián gōng jìn qì 〈成〉 all previous efforts came o naught

【前年】 qiánnián (名) the year before last

【前任】 qiánrèn (名) predecessor

【前兆】 qiánzhào (名) omen; premonition: 不祥的～ inauspicious omen

【前列】 qiánliè (名) forefront; front rank: 在鬥爭的～ in the forefront of the struggle

【前列腺】 qiánlièxiàn (名) 〈生理〉 prostate (gland): ～炎 prostatitis

【前因後果】 qián yīn hòu guǒ 〈成〉 cause and effect: 事情的～ the whys and wherefores of the event

【前身】 qiánshēn (名) predecessor

【前言】 qiányán (名) preface; foreword

【前車之鑒】 qián chē zhī jiàn 〈成〉 take warning from another's mistake

【前例】 qiánlì (名) precedent: 史無～ without precedent in history

【前沿】 qiányán (名) 〈軍〉 forward position

【前夜】 qiányè (名) eve: 臨行～ on the eve of departure

【前肢】 qiánzhī (名) forelimb; foreleg

【前所未聞】 qián suǒ wèi wén 〈成〉 never heard of before

【前者】 qiánzhě (名) the former

【前奏】 qiánzòu (名) prelude: 官復原職的～ the prelude to his reinstatement

【前面】 qiánmiàn Ⅰ (副) in front: 請～走。Please go ahead. Ⅱ (形) preceding; above: ～一章 the preceding chapter

【前赴後繼】 qián fù hòu jì 〈成〉 advance like rolling waves

【前後】 qiánhòu Ⅰ (副) ❶ in front and behind ❷ from beginning to end: 蓋這座圖書館～用了兩年時間。It took two whole years to build this library. Ⅱ (介) around; about: 新年～ around the New Year

【前哨】 qiánshào (名) outpost

【前途】 qiántú (名) future; prospect

【前進】 qiánjìn (動) march forward; advance

【前景】 qiánjǐng (名) prospect; vista: 光明的～ bright prospects

【前程】 qiánchéng (名) prospect; future

【前提】 qiántí (名) ❶ 〈邏〉 premise ❷ prerequisite

【前置詞】 qiánzhìcí (名) 〈語〉 preposition

【前綫】 qiánxiàn (名) front; front line

【前綴】 qiánzhuì (名) 〈語〉 prefix

【前鋒】 qiánfēng (名) ❶ vanguard ❷ (of football, basketball, etc.)

forward

【前輩】qiánbèi（名）elder; older generation

【前燈】qiándēng（名）headlight

【前臂】qiánbì（名）forearm

【前額】qián'é（名）forehead; brow

【前驅】qiánqū（名）forerunner; pioneer

剃 tì（動）shave

【剃刀】tìdāo（名）razor

【剃頭】tìtóu（動）❶ have one's head shaved ❷ have a haircut

剌 là（形）rude and eccentric

尅 kè（動）❶ set a deadline ❷ digest food

【尅扣】kèkòu（動）keep for oneself part of what should be given to others

削 xiāo（動）pare; peel: ～果皮 peel fruit

see also xuē

削 xuē（動）pare; cut

see also xiāo

【削足適履】xuē zú shì lǚ（成）cut the feet to fit the shoes; apply measures mechanically in complete disregard of reality

【削弱】xuēruò（動）weaken; reduce

【削減】xuējiǎn（動）cut; reduce: ～軍費 cut back on military spending

【削價】xuējià（動）cut prices: ～處理 sell at reduced prices

則 zé Ⅰ（名）❶ standard; norm; example: 以身作～ set an example for others ❷ rule; regulation: 細則 detailed rules and regulations Ⅱ（連）❶［used to indicate causation or

given conditions］: 不平～鳴。 Where there is injustice there will be protest. ❷［used to indicate concession or contrast］: 他頭腦冷靜, 他的弟弟～有點腦急躁。He is cool-headed while his younger brother is a bit impatient. Ⅲ（量）item; piece: 新聞三～ three items of news

剎 chà（名）Buddhist temple: 古～ ancient temple

see also shā

【剎那】chànà（名）Ksana（Sanskrit）; split second; twinkling of an eye: 一～間 in an instant

剎 shā（動）stop; check

see also chà

【剎車（煞車）】shāchē Ⅰ（動）brake; stop immediately Ⅱ（名）brake

剜 wān（動）cut out; scoop out

剖 pōu（動）❶ cut open; slice: 解～ dissect ❷ explain: 我曾向他～白幾句。I have made some explanations to him.

【剖明】pōumíng（動）reveal; explain

【剖析】pōuxī（動）dissect; analyse: ～事理 analyse the whys and wherefores

【剖面】pōumiàn（名）section: ～圖 sectional drawing

【剖視圖】pōushìtú（名）cutaway view

【剖開】pōukāi（動）cut or rip open

【剖腹產】pōufùchǎn（名）〈醫〉Caesarean section

剛 gāng Ⅰ（形）firm; strong; unyielding Ⅱ（副）❶ just; exactly: 時間～合適 just the right time ❷ barely; just: ～成年 be just of age / ～起床 have just got up

【刚巧】gāngqiǎo（副）as it happens

【刚正】gāngzhèng（形）resolute and upright

【刚好】gānghǎo（副）❶ just; exactly ❷ by chance: 他～出去了。He happens to be out.

【刚果】Gāngguǒ（名）the Gongo: ～人 Congolese

【刚直不阿】gāng zhí bù ē〈成〉be upright and never stoop to fawning or favouritism

【刚劲】gāngjìng（形）firm and vigorous

【刚刚】gānggāng（副）just only

【刚健】gāngjiàn（形）(of a person's character or style) vigorous; strong

【刚愎自用】gāng bì zì yòng〈成〉pig-headed; opinionated

【刚强】gāngqiáng（形）(of a person's character or will) firm and unyielding

【刚毅】gāngyì（形）resolute and unswerving

【刚才】gāngcái（副）just now

剔 tī（动）❶ scrape meat off a bone ❷ pick: ～指甲 pick one's fingernails ❸ pick out the bad ones and throw them away: 挑～ find fault with

【剔红】tīhóng（名）carved lacquerware

【剔除】tīchú（动）discard; eliminate

剥 bāo（动）shell; peel; flay
see also bō

剥 bō
see also bāo

【剥削】bōxuē Ⅰ（动）exploit: 被～

者 the exploited Ⅱ（名）exploitation

【剥落】bōluò（动）(of paint, bark, etc.) flake off; come off

【剥蚀】bōshí（动）denude; erode; wear out

【剥夺】bōduó（动）deprive … of; strip … of; deny: ～权利 deprive sb. of his rights

【剥离】bōlí（动）detach (covering, skin, etc.); tear off; peel off

剪 jiǎn Ⅰ（名）❶ scissors; clippers: 指甲～ finger-nail clippers ❷ scissor-shaped tool: 火～ fire tongs Ⅱ（动）❶ scissor; clip; trim; prune ❷ get rid of; remove; annihilate

【剪刀】jiǎndāo（剪子 jiǎnzi）（名）scissors; clippers; shears

【剪刀差】jiǎndāochā（名）scissors differential (difference); price scissors

【剪毛机】jiǎnmáojī（名）shearing machine

【剪除】jiǎnchú（动）get rid of; wipe out

【剪纸】jiǎnzhǐ（名）〈工美〉paper-cut

【剪彩】jiǎncǎi（动）cut the ribbon (at a ceremony)

【剪接】jiǎnjiē（动）edit (a film)

【剪票】jiǎnpiào（动）punch a ticket

【剪报】jiǎnbào（名）newspaper cutting; newspaper clipping

【剪裁】jiǎncái（动）❶ (in dressmaking) cut out ❷ (in writing) prune away superfluities

【剪贴】jiǎntiē（动）(in collecting reference materials) clip and paste

【剪影】jiǎnyǐng（名）❶ (in papercutting) silhouette ❷ character sketch; profile

【剪輯】jiǎnjí（名）montage; film editing; re-editing (of a recording of a film or play for broadcast)：電影錄音～ edited highlights of a film's sound recording

副 fù I（形）deputy; vice-; secondary：～部長 vice-minister ／ ～教授 associate professor II（動）tally with; be true to：名～其實 be true to the name III（量）：一～網球拍 a pair of tennis bats ／ 一～象棋 a set of Chinese chess

【副手】fùshǒu（名）assistant

【副本】fùběn（名）duplicate; copy

【副刊】fùkān（名）supplement

【副作用】fùzuòyòng（名）by-effect

【副官】fùguān（名）adjutant

【副食】fùshí（名）non-staple food

【副食店】fùshídiàn（名）grocery

【副產品】fùchǎnpǐn（名）by-product

【副詞】fùcí（名）〈語〉adverb

【副業】fùyè（名）sideline; side occupation

【副歌】fùgē（名）〈樂〉refrain

【副標題】fùbiāotí（名）subtitle

剐 guǎ（動）❶ cut; slit：袖口～破了。The sleeve got slit open. ❷ cut to pieces (a form of capital punishment in ancient times)

割 gē（動）cut

【割草】gēcǎo（動）mow：～機 mower

【割裂】gēliè（動）split; separate; isolate

【割愛】gē'ài（動）〈婉〉part with what one values

【割據】gējù（動）set up by force a separatist regime within a state

【割禮】gēlǐ（名）〈宗〉circumcision

【割斷】gēduàn（動）sever; cut off

【割讓】gēràng（動）cede：～領土 cession of territory

創 chuāng I（名）wound：精神～傷 trauma II（動）damage：重～敵軍 inflict heavy casualties on the enemy
see also chuàng

創 chuàng（動）initiate; establish; create：～世界記錄 set a world record
see also chuāng

【創立】chuànglì（動）found; originate：～新學説 found a new theory

【創見】chuàngjiàn（名）original idea

【創作】chuàngzuò I（動）produce (literary or artistic works); write II（名）literary and artistic creation

【創始】chuàngshǐ（動）start; initiate：～人 founder; originator

【創建】chuàngjiàn（動）found; set up; establish

【創造】chuàngzào（動）create; initiate：～奇迹 work wonders

【創新】chuàngxīn（動）innovate; blaze a new trail

【創業】chuàngyè（動）pioneer a cause; start an enterprise

【創辦】chuàngbàn（動）set up; inaugurate

【創舉】chuàngjǔ（名）unprecedented act; pioneering work

剩 shèng I（形）surplus; remainder：人口過～ overpopulation II（動）be left over; remain：只～三塊錢。There are only three yuan left.

【剩下】shèngxia（動）be left; remain

【剩飯】shèngfàn（名）leftovers：殘

羹～ leftovers

【剩餘】shèngyú（形）surplus: ～資金 surplus capital

剝 piāo Ⅰ（動）rob; plunder Ⅱ（形）agile; nimble

【剝悍】piāohàn（形）nimble and intrepid

【剝掠】piāolüè（動）loot; pillage

【剝竊】piāoqiè Ⅰ（動）plagiarize Ⅱ（名）plagiarism

剿 chāo（動）plagiarize
see also jiǎo

剿 jiǎo（動）suppress（by force of arms）: ～匪 suppress bandits
see also chāo

【剿滅】jiǎomiè（動）wipe out; annihilate

劃 huá（動）❶ scratch; cut the surface of: ～根火柴 strike a match / ～玻璃 cut glass ❷ paddle; row ❸ pay; be worth-while
see also huà

【劃子】huázi（名）rowing boat; sampan

【劃算】huásuàn（動）❶ calculate; weigh ❷ be worth-while

劃 huà（動）divide; differentiate: ～清界限 make a clear distinction ❷ appropriate; allocate: ～賬 transfer funds to another's account ❸ plan: 策～ plot
see also huá

【劃一】huàyī（形）standardized; uniform

【劃分】huàfēn（動）divide; differentiate

【劃定】huàdìng（動）delimit; designate

【劃時代】huàshídài（形）epoch-making: ～的大事 an epoch-making event

【劃撥】huàbō（動）transfer; appropriate

劈 pī（動）❶ split; slice: ～倒一棵樹 cleave a tree down ❷ strike: 樹枝被雷～斷了。Lightning struck off the tree branches.
see also pǐ

【劈啪】pīpā（象）crackle: 遠處傳來的～槍聲 the distant crackle of rifle fire

【劈頭蓋臉】pī tóu gài liǎn（副）❶ right in the face ❷ ruthlessly: 他把兒子～罵了一通。He gave his son a good dressing down.

劈 pǐ（動）divide; part: ～成兩半 divide into two halves
see also pī

【劈叉】pǐchà（動）do the splits

【劈柴】pǐchái（名）firewood

劇 jù Ⅰ（名）❶ play; drama: 電視連續～ TV play series ❷（Jù）a surname Ⅱ（形）acute; drastic; sharp: ～毒 deadly poisonous

【劇本】jùběn（名）dramatic composition; script（for a play）; scenario（for a film）; libretto（for an opera）

【劇目】jùmù（名）list of theatrical performances; repertoire

【劇作家】jùzuòjiā（名）playwright

【劇烈】jùliè（形）acute; drastic; sharp

【劇情】jùqíng（名）plot（of a play）: ～簡介 synopsis

【劇場】jùchǎng（劇院 jùyuàn）（名）theatre; play-house

【劇團】jùtuán（名）troupe; theatrical

company

【剮變】jùbiàn（名）drastic change

剮 guǎ（動）cut off; chop off

【剮子手】guǎzishǒu（名）❶ exexcutioner ❷ slaughterer

劍 jiàn（名）sword; sabre; foil

【劍拔弩張】jiàn bá nǔ zhāng〈成〉sabre-rattling; all set for a showdown; at daggers drawn

【劍柄】jiànbǐng（名）handle of a sword; hilt

【劍術】jiànshù（名）art of fencing; swordsmanship

【劍鞘】jiànqiào（名）scabbard

劉 Liú（名）a surname

【劉海】liúhǎi（名）fringe（of hair）; bang

劑 jì Ⅰ（名）❶ medicament; pharmaceutical preparation: 打一針强心 ~ give sb. an injection of cardiac stimulant ❷ agent: 乾燥 ~ drying agent Ⅱ（量）dose; decoction: 吃五 ~ 中藥 take five decoctions of herbal medicine

【劑子】jìzi（名）small piece cut out of a large chunk of dough（for making dumplings, etc.）

【劑量】jìliàng（名）dosage; dose

劏 huō（動）❶ slit or cut with a knife ❷ hoe

力 部

力 lì Ⅰ（名）❶ power; strength: ~ 大無窮 have herculean strength ❷ ability: 腦 ~ intellectual power ❸ force Ⅱ（動）try one's best; do one's utmost: 工作不 ~ be inefficient

【力不從心】lì bù cóng xīn〈成〉one's ability falls short of one's ambition; find oneself unequal to the occasion

【力不勝任】lì bù shèng rèn〈成〉be incompetent for the task

【力戒】lìjiè（動）avoid in every possible way; guard against: ~ 驕傲自滿 guard against conceit and arrogance

【力求】lìqiú（動）strive; do one's best: ~ 立能奏效 made every possible effort to achieve instant success

【力爭】lìzhēng（動）strive for; struggle for: ~ 在明春之前完成這項工程 strive for the completion of the project by next spring

【力所不及】lì suǒ bù jí〈成〉beyond one's ability

【力所能及】lì suǒ néng jí〈成〉within one's power

【力氣】lìqi（名）❶ physical strength ❷ effort: 費 ~ have to put in a good deal of effort

【力量】lìliàng（名）strength; power; force

【力圖】lìtú（動）try hard; strive: ~ 推卸責任 make every attempt to shirk responsibility

【力學】lìxué（名）mechanics

功 gōng（名）❶ merit: 立 ~ perform meritorious service ❷ success; result: 教育之 ~ the result of education ❸ skill: 基本 ~ basic skills

【功臣】gōngchén（名）person who has made great contributions

【功利】gōnglì（名）utility; material

【功利主義】gōnglì zhǔyì（名）utilitarianism

【功效】gōngxiào（名）effect; efficacy

【功能】gōngnéng（名）function

【功率】gōnglǜ（名）〈物〉power

【功敗垂成】gōng bài chuí chéng〈成〉sustain a crushing defeat when success is in sight

【功勛】gōngxūn（名）exploit; meritorious deed

【功勞】gōngláo（名）credit; comtribution

【功業】gōngyè（名）achievements

【功德】gōngdé（名）merits and virtues

【功課】gōngkè（名）school-work; homework

【功虧一簣】gōng kuī yī kuì〈成〉lack of a final effort spoils the chance of success; let slip a chance of success for want of a final effort

【功績】gōngjī（名）significant contributions

加 jiā I（動）❶ add: 錯上~錯 one mistake on top of another ❷ increase; augment; enhance ❸ add sth. to; append: 火上~油 add fuel to the flames ❹［used after a monosyllabic adverb and before a verb］: 嚴~批駁 sternly refute II（Jiā）（名）a surname

【加入】jiārù（動）❶ mix; add ❷ join: ~工會 join the trade union

【加工】jiāgōng（動）process: 這篇文章發表前應該進一步~。We should touch up this article before it is published.

【加以】jiāyǐ I（動）［used to introduce a multi-syllabic verb or verbal noun that takes the preceding noun as its object］: 局面必須~控制。The situation must be brought under control. II（連）moreover; furthermore; in addition

【加快】jiākuài（動）quicken; accelerate

【加法】jiāfǎ（名）〈數〉addition

【加侖】jiālún（名）gallon

【加油】jiāyóu（動）❶ apply oil to; lubricate ❷ refuel ❸ make greater efforts ❹［an exclamation used at athletic contests］go it; step on it

【加固】jiāgù（動）strengthen; reinforce; fortify: ~ 防禦工事 reinforce the defences

【加重】jiāzhòng（動）❶ render (become) weightier: ~ 負擔 add to one's load ❷ aggravate; worsen

【加急電報】jiājí diànbào（名）urgent telegram

【加速】jiāsù（動）speed up; accelerate; hasten: ~器 accelerator

【加倍】jiābèi（動）double; be twice as much (many); redouble: ~償還 pay twice the amount for

【加納】Jiānà（名）Ghana: ~ 人 Ghanaian

【加班】jiābān（動）work overtime: ~費 overtime pay

【加班加點】jiābān jiādiǎn（動）work extra hours; work overtime

【加深】jiāshēn（動）deepen; widen (a rift): ~人們對宇宙的認識 deepen our understanding of the universe

【加冕】jiāmiǎn（名）coronation

【加強】jiāqiáng（動）strengthen; intensify: ～管理 improve the management

【加温】jiāwēn（动）warm; warm up

【加紧】jiājǐn（动）intensify; step up

【加蓬】Jiāpéng（名）Gabon: ～人 Gabonese

【加剧】jiājù（动）aggravate; heighten; sharpen: 病势～。The patient's condition is worsening.

【加码】jiāmǎ（动）❶ raise the price ❷ increase the quota

【加热】jiārè（动）heat; heat up: ～器 heater

劣 liè（形）bad; inferior

【劣迹】lièjì（名）misdeeds

【劣马】lièmǎ（名）❶ old or worthless horse ❷ untamed horse

【劣根性】liègēnxìng（名）ingrained bad habit

【劣绅】lièshēn（名）wicked gentry

【劣等】lièděng（形）of low quality; inferior

【劣势】lièshì（名）unfavourable situation: 处于～ be at a disadvantage

【劣质】lièzhì（形）inferior (in quality)

劫 jié Ⅰ（动）❶ rob; plunder: 拦路 抢～ mug ❷ take control by force: ～机 hijack a plane Ⅱ（名）disaster: 浩～ catastrophe

【劫持】jiéchí（动）❶ kidnap ❷ hijack (a vehicle, plane, etc.)

【劫掠】jiélüè（动）loot; plunder; maraud

【劫狱】jiéyù（动）raid a prison to free an inmate

助 zhù（动）help; assist; aid: 资～ give financial aid to / 有～于很好 地掌握汉语 help acquire a good command of Chinese

【助手】zhùshǒu（名）assistant; aide

【助长】zhùzhǎng（动）encourage; foster; whet: ～不正之风 encourage the unhealthy social trends

【助威】zhùwēi（动）cheer: 观众为 自方的队伍热烈～。The home crowd cheered their team enthusiastically.

【助教】zhùjiào（名）teaching assistant

【助理】zhùlǐ（名）assistant: ～研究 员 assistant research fellow/ 部长 ～ assistant minister

【助产士】zhùchǎnshì（名）midwife

【助动词】zhùdòngcí（名）〈语〉auxiliary verb

【助词】zhùcí（名）〈语〉auxiliary word

【助兴】zhùxìng（动）add to the fun

【助学金】zhùxuéjīn（名）stipend; student grant

【助听器】zhùtīngqì（名）hearing aid; audiphone

努 nǔ

【努力】nǔlì（动）strive; make great effort: ～取得更大的进步 strive for greater progress

【努嘴】nǔzuǐ（动）pout one's lips (as a signal)

劾 hé（动）expose sb.'s wrong doings or crimes: 弹～ impeach

勃 bó Ⅰ（副）suddenly Ⅱ（形）thriving; exuberant: 蓬～发展 vigorous development

【勃勃】bóbó（形）flourishing; exuberant: 兴致～ full of zest

【勃然】bórán（副）❶ violently ❷ vigorously

【勃發】bófā (動) ❶ prosper; thrive ❷ break out

【勃興】bóxīng Ⅰ (動) grow vigorously Ⅱ (名) vigorous growth

勁 jìn (名) ❶ bodily strength: 費 ~兒的工作 a tough job ❷ vigour; zeal: 幹~ drive ❸ air; look: 裝模 作樣的~兒 airs and graces ❹ interest; gusto: 這個電影沒～。The film is dull.

see also jìng

【勁頭】jìntóu (名) 〈口〉 ❶ drive; urge ❷ physical strength

勁 jìng (形) strong; tough: ~草 sturdy grass

see also jìn

【勁旅】jìnglǚ (名) crack troops

【勁敵】jìngdí (名) formidable opponent

勇 yǒng (形) brave; courageous; bold: ~冠三軍 distinguished for martial valour

【勇於】yǒngyú (動) dare to; be bold in: ~改革 be bold in carrying out reforms

【勇往直前】yǒng wǎng zhí qián 〈成〉 stride ahead bravely

【勇氣】yǒngqì (名) courage; nerve

【勇敢】yǒnggǎn (形) brave; courageous

【勇猛】yǒngměng (形) strong and fearless; valiant

勉 miǎn (動) ❶ strive: 勤~ work diligently ❷ urge; encourage

【勉強】miǎnqiǎng Ⅰ (動) ❶ manage with an effort of will: ~熬了一夜 managed to stay up all night ❷ force: 不要~他做違心的事。

Don't force him to do what is against his will. Ⅱ (副) ❶ reluctantly; unwillingly: ~接受 accept reluctantly ❷ barely enough: 這車~能坐下五 個人。The car is just big enough for five people. Ⅲ (形) inadequate: ~的理由 a thin excuse

【勉為其難】miǎn wéi qí nán 〈成〉 undertake to do what is apparently beyond one's ability

【勉勵】miǎnlì (動) encourage: ~人 們更加努力地工作 encourage people to work even harder

勘 kān (動) ❶ collate; check against the authentic text ❷ investigate on the spot; survey

【勘探】kāntàn (動) prospect (for); explore 地質~隊 geological prospecting team

【勘測】kāncè (動) survey

【勘誤】kānwù (動) correct printing errors: ~表 errata; corrigenda

【勘察】kānchá (動) (prior to opening up a mine or starting a construction project) examine; prospect

【勘驗】kānyàn (動) investigate (into an accident or crime) on the spot

勒 lè (動) ❶ rein up; stop: ~馬 rein in a horse ❷ coerce; compel: ~派稅款 force (sb.) to pay levies

see also lēi

【勒令】lèlìng (動) force (sb.) by an order; order: ~他交出走私貨物 order that he surrender the smuggled goods

【勒索】lèsuǒ (動) extort; blackmail

勒 lēi (動) tighten (rope, etc.): ~死 strangle

see also lè

務 wù I（名）business; affair: 國～ state affairs II（動）❶ be engaged in ❷ must

【務必】wùbì（動）must; be sure to: ～準時到達。Be sure to turn up on time.

【務虛】wùxū（動）discuss guidelines and principles

【務農】wùnóng（動）be engaged in farming

【務實】wùshí（動）❶ tackle concrete problems ❷ be pragmatic

動 dòng（動）❶ move: ～如脫兔 move like a hare ❷ use: ～腦筋 use one's brains ❸ touch; move: 大～肝火 vent one's spleen ❹ start: ～工 start building

【動人】dòngrén（形）touching; moving

【動力】dònglì（名）❶ power ❷ motivation; impetus

【動土】dòngtǔ（動）break ground

【動心】dòngxīn（動）（of one's desire, interest, etc.）be aroused

【動手】dòngshǒu（動）❶ start work ❷ touch: 請勿～。Please don't touch. ❸ resort to fists

【動手術】dòngshǒushù（動）❶ perform an operation ❷ have an operation

【動不動】dòngbudòng（副）easily; often: ～就生氣 get angry easily

【動用】dòngyòng（動）use; draw on

【動向】dòngxiàng（名）trend: 時局～ the trend of the situation

【動名詞】dòngmíngcí（名）〈語〉 gerund

【動身】dòngshēn（動）start out; leave

【動作】dòngzuò（名）movement;
action

【動武】dòngwǔ（動）begin to fight; resort to arms

【動物】dòngwù（名）animal: ～學 zoology

【動物園】dòngwùyuán（名）zoo

【動脈】dòngmài（名）〈生理〉artery: ～硬化 arteriosclerosis

【動氣】dòngqì（動）become angry; fly into a rage

【動容】dòngróng（動）be visibly moved

【動員】dòngyuán（動）mobilize: ～令 mobilization order

【動產】dòngchǎn（名）movables; movable property

【動情】dòngqíng（動）❶ be moved ❷ fall in love

【動畫片】dònghuàpiàn（名）animated cartoon

【動筆】dòngbǐ（動）start writing

【動詞】dòngcí（名）〈語〉verb

【動搖】dòngyáo（動）shake; waver

【動亂】dòngluàn（名）turbulance; unrest; rior

【動態】dòngtài（名）developments: 國際形勢的最新～ the latest international developments

【動輒】dòngzhé（副）on every possible occasion: ～破口大罵 let loose a stream of abuse at the slightest provocation

【動靜】dòngjing（名）people moving or speaking; activity: 偵察敵人的～ gather intelligence about the enemy's activities

【動彈】dòngtan（動）move

【動盪】dòngdàng（名）turbulence; upheaval; disturbance

【動機】dòngjī（名）motive; intention

【動議】dòngyì (名) motion

【動聽】dòngtīng (形) pleasant to the ear; persuasive

勞 láo I (名) ❶ labour; work: 按 ～分配 to each according to his work ❷ toil; hard labour: 不～而 獲 gain without pain ❸ meritorious service: 立下功～ render meritorious service ❹ (Láo) a surname II (動) present gifts and greetings (to sb. for his outstanding service): 慰 ～邊防軍 bring gifts and greetings to the frontier guards

【勞改】láogǎi (動) (short for 勞動 改造 láodòng gǎizào) reform through labour

【勞保】láobǎo (名) ❶ (short for 勞 動保護 láodòng bǎohù) labour protection ❷ (short for 勞動保險 láodòng bǎoxiǎn) labour insurance

【勞苦】láokǔ I (動) toil; hard labour II (形) toiling; labouring

【勞務】láowù (名) labour; service: ～市場 labour market

【勞教】láojiào (名) (short for 勞動 教養 láodòng jiàoyǎng) re-education (of juvenile delinquents, etc.) through labour

【勞累】láolèi (形) fatigued; tired out: 不要過分～。Don't overwork yourself.

【勞逸】láoyì (名) work and rest: ～ 結合 alternate work with rest

【勞動】láodòng I (動) ❶ work; labour: ～密集型工業 labour-intensive industry / 體力～ manual labour/ 腦力～ mental labour ❷ physical labour: ～鍛鍊 temper oneself through physical labour/ ～ 紀律 labour discipline II (動) do manual labour

【勞動力】láodònglì (名) (for short 勞力 láolì) labour force

【勞資】láozī (名) labour and management; labour and capital: ～糾 紛 disputes between workers and management

【勞碌】láolù (形) busy; working hard

【勞模】láomó (名) (short for 勞動 模範 láodòng mófàn) model worker

【勞駕】láojià (套) [when asking sb. to make way or to do sth.]: ～，～. Excuse me. / ～把窗戶打開。 Would you mind opening the windows?

【勞蘭系統】láolán xìtǒng (名) long range navigation; LORAN

助 xūn (名) merit; contribution

【助章】xūnzhāng (名) medal

【助爵】xūnjué (名) (a title of nobility) Lord

勝 shèng I (名) victory; win: 反敗 爲～ turn defeat into victory; turn the tide II (動) ❶ defeat; beat: 以 少～多 defeat a numerically superior enemy; defeat the enemy despite their numerical superiority ❷ be superior; surpass: 略～一籌 be slightly superior; be a cut above (others) ❸ endure; bear: 不～枚 舉 too numerous to enumerate III (形) wonderful; fascinating; enchanting

【勝仗】shèngzhàng (名) victorious battle; victory: 打～ win a battle; score a success

【勝地】shèngdì (名) scenic spot; recort: 避暑～ summer resort

【勝任】shèngrèn (動) be competent: 不能～這項工作 not be equal to

the task

【胜利】shènglì Ⅰ(名) triumph; success: ~在望。Victory is in sight. Ⅱ(副) victoriously; successfully

【胜券】shèngquàn (名) chance of winning: 穩操 ~ be absolutely sure of success

【胜负】shèngfù (名) victory and (or) defeat: 比賽不分 ~。The game ended in a draw.

【胜败】shèngbài (名) victory and (or) defeat

【胜诉】shèngsù (动) win a lawsuit

势 shì (名) ❶ power; influence: 人多 ~衆 dominate by sheer force of numbers ❷ momentum; trend: ~頭愈來愈大 gain momentum ❸ aspect of a natural phenomenon: 地 ~ low-lying terrain ❹ gesture; sign: 姿 ~ 優美 graceful pose ❺ state of affairs; circumstances

【势力】shìlì (名) power; influence: 習慣 ~ force of habit

【势力範圍】shìlì fànwéi (名) sphere of influence

【势不可当】shì bù kě dāng 〈成〉irresistible: 這種歷史潮流 ~。This historical trend is irresistible.

【势不两立】shì bù liǎng lì 〈成〉cannot coexist by any means; absolutely antagonistic

【势必】shìbì (副) inevitably; unavoidably: 他這樣做 ~要引起别人的誤解。What he does is bound to cause misunderstanding.

【势在必行】shì zài bì xíng 〈成〉be imperative (in view of the situation)

【势利】shìlì (形) snobbish

【势利眼】shìlìyǎn (名) ❶ snobbishness ❷ snob

【势均力敌】shì jūn lì dí 〈成〉 be evenly matched

【势头】shìtóu (名) ❶ momentum; impetus ❷〈口〉tendency; situation

勤 qín Ⅰ(形) diligent Ⅱ(副) frequently; often: ~寫家信 often write home Ⅲ(名) ❶ attendance; duty: 缺 ~ absence from duty ❷ diligence: 業精於 ~ Scholarly achievement results from diligence.

【勤快】qínkuài (形) diligent (in doing physical labour)

【勤勉】qínmiǎn (动) work earnestly

【勤务】qínwù (名) duty; service

【勤务兵】qínwùbīng (名) orderly (in an army unit)

【勤劳】qínláo (形) hard-working

【勤俭】qínjiǎn (动) be diligent and thrifty

【勤奋】qínfèn (动) work tirelessly

【勤恳】qínkěn (动) be diligent and earnest

【勤雜工】qínzágōng (名) odd-job man

募 mù (动) raise; collect; recruit

【募化】mùhuà (动) collect alms

【募兵】mùbīng (动) recruit persons for the army; enlist persons for service in the armed forces

【募兵制】mùbīngzhì (名) mercenary system

【募捐】mùjuān (动) raise a fund; collect contributions

【募集】mùjí (动) raise; collect: ~錢款 raise money

励 Ⅱ Ⅰ(动) encourage Ⅱ(Lì) (名) a surname

【励精圖治】lì jīng tú zhì 〈成〉make determined efforts to make the

country prosperous

話。Keep your voice low, please.

勸 quàn（動）advise; admonish; urge：～他休息休息 advise him to take a rest

【勸告】quàngào（動）exhort; admonish; caution

【勸阻】quànzǔ（動）dissuade sb. from doing sth.：力加～ strongly advise against doing sth.

【勸架】quànjià（動）try to stop a quarrel or fight; mediate（between two quarrelling parties）

【勸勉】quànmiǎn（動）give advice and encouragement to sb.：互相～ encourage each other

【勸酒】quànjiǔ（動）try to make a guest drink more（at a dinner party）

【勸解】quànjiě（動）❶ advise sb. not to worry ❷ mediate

【勸說】quànshuō（動）try to persuade or convince sb.

【勸慰】quànwèi（動）console; comfort

【勸導】quàndǎo（動）advise; exhort

勺 部

勺 sháo（名）spoon; ladle

【勺子】sháozi（名）ladle; scoop

勻 yún Ⅰ（形）even: 均～ well-distributed Ⅱ（動）spare：～出一點時間 spare some time

【勻稱】yúnchèn（形）well-balanced; well-proportioned

【勻整】yúnzhěng（形）even and well spaced

勿 wù（副）no; not：請～高聲談

勾 gōu（動）❶ cross out; cancel: 一筆～銷 write off with one stroke ❷ delineate：～出草圖 draw a sketch ❸ collude with; gang up with

see also gòu

【勾引】gōuyǐn（動）seduce; tempt

【勾心鬥角】gōu xīn dòu jiǎo〈成〉scheme against each other; engage in factional strife

【勾留】gōuliú（動）stop over

【勾通】gōutōng（動）collude with; collaborate with secretly

【勾畫】gōuhuà（動）draw the outline of; delineate; sketch

【勾結】gōujié（動）work in cahoots with

【勾搭】gōuda（動）❶ entice ❷ collude with

勾 gòu

see also gōu

【勾當】gòudàng（名）lousy business; dirty deal

包 bāo Ⅰ（動）❶ wrap; roll up (in)：～餛飩 make won ton（soup dumplings）❷ surround; encircle ❸ include; contain; cover ❹ undertake; contract：這任務我～了。I volunteer to do the job. ❺ ensure; assure; guarantee：～您喜歡。I am sure you will like it. ❻ order; hire; charter Ⅱ（名）❶ bag; sack; satchel; other similar soft container：(手)提～ handbag ❷（量）bundle; package; pack：一～棉花 a bale of cotton

【包工】bāogōng Ⅰ (动) contract for a job Ⅱ (名) job contract: ～头 labour contractor

【包子】bāozi (名) steamed stuffed bun

【包心菜】bāoxīncài (名)〈方〉cabbage

【包抄】bāochāo (动) outflank

【包含】bāohán (动) ❶ include; contain; consist of ❷ imply; embody

【包庇】bāobì (动) harbour; shelter; screen

【包治百病】bāozhì bǎibìng (动) guarantee to cure all diseases: ～的药方 remedy for all ills; panacea; cure-all

【包括】bāokuò (动) include; comprise; consist of

【包容】bāoróng Ⅰ (形) tolerant: 大度～ broad-minded Ⅱ (动) contain; hold

【包紮】bāozā (动) wrap; tie up; bandage: ～伤口 bandage (dress) a wound

【包产】bāochǎn (动) contract for fixed output quotas: ～到户 fixing of farm output quotas for individual households

【包袱】bāofu (名) ❶ bundle ❷ cloth wrapping ❸ burden; load; liability: 思想～ load on one's mind

【包涵】bāohan (动)〈谦〉forgive; excuse; bear with: 请多多～。I earnestly beg your pardon.

【包厢】bāoxiāng (名) box (at a theatre, opera house, etc.)

【包场】bāochǎng (动) book all the seats or a block of seats in a theatre or cinema

【包饭】bāofàn (动) board; get or supply meals regularly at a moderate rate

【包围】bāowéi (动) surround; encircle; besiege: ～圈 ring of encirclement

【包圆兒】bāoyuánr (动)〈口〉buy up; finish off

【包管】bāoguǎn (动) assure; guarantee: ～没问题。I can assure you everything will be all right.

【包装】bāozhuāng Ⅰ (动) pack Ⅱ (名) packing

【包裹】bāoguǒ Ⅰ (名) parcel; bundle Ⅱ (动) wrap up; bind up

【包销】bāoxiāo (动) act as the sole sales agent

【包机】bāojī (名) chartered plane

【包办】bāobàn (动) undertake to do everything by oneself: ～代替 handle matters of collective responsibility arbitrarily and without prior consultation with others concerned

【包办婚姻】bāobàn hūnyīn (名) arranged marriage; arranged match

【包藏祸心】bāo cáng huò xīn〈成〉harbour evil intentions; with malicious intent

【包罗万象】bāo luó wàn xiàng〈成〉all-inclusive and all-embracing

【包揽】bāolǎn (动) monopolize everything

匈 xiōng

【匈牙利】Xiōngyálì (名) Hungary: ～人 Hungarian/ ～语 Hungarian (language)

匍 pú

【匍匐】púfú (动) ❶ crawl; creep: ～前進 move forward on all fours ❷ lie prostrate

匕 部

匕 bǐ

【匕首】bǐshǒu（名）dagger

化 huà（动）❶ change; turn: ～干 戈爲玉帛 bury the hatchet ❷ convert; influence ❸ melt; dissolve: ～凍了。It's thawing. ❹ burn up ❺ [used after certain nouns and adjectives to form verbs]: 正常～ normalize / 惡～ worsen ❻ simplified term for chemistry

【化石】huàshí（名）fossil

【化名】huàmíng（名）alias; assumed name

【化合】huàhé（名）〈化〉chemical combination

【化合物】huàhéwù（名）〈化〉chemical compound

【化身】huàshēn（名）incarnation; embodiment

【化妝】huàzhuāng（动）put on make-up; make up: ～品 cosmetics

【化肥】huàféi（名）chemical fertilizer

【化爲烏有】huà wéi wū yǒu〈成〉disappear into nothing; go out of existence

【化痰】huàtán（动）reduce phlegm

【化裝】huàzhuāng（动）❶ make up ❷ masquerade

【化學】huàxué（名）chemistry

【化學元素】huàxué yuánsù（名）chemical element

【化膿】huànóng（动）fester; suppurate

【化驗】huàyàn（名）chemical examination; laboratory test: ～室 laboratory

【化纖】huàxiān（名）chemical fibre

北 běi Ⅰ（名）north: 天南海～ all over the country; all over the world Ⅱ（动）be beaten: 屢戰屢～ suffer defeats in numerous battles

【北上】běishàng（动）go up north

【北方】běifāng（名）north Ⅱ（形）northern: ～方言 northern dialect

【北斗星】běidǒuxīng（名）（Big）Dipper

【北冰洋】Běibīngyáng（名）Arctic Ocean

【北回歸綫】běihuíguīxiàn（名）the Tropic of Cancer

【北京猿人】Běijīng yuánrén（名）〈考古〉Peking Man（*Sinanthropus pekinensis*）

【北美洲】Běiměizhōu（名）North America

【北部】běibù（名）northern section (part)

【北國】běiguó（名）north-land: ～風光 northern scenery

【北極】běijí（名）North Pole; Arctic: ～光 northern lights; aurora borealis

【北極星】běijíxīng（名）North Star; Polaris

【北極熊】běijíxióng（名）polar bear

【北緯】běiwěi（名）north（northern）latitude

【北邊】běibiān（北面 běimiàn）（名）north side（part）: 在～ in the north

匙 chí（匙子 chízi）（名）spoon

匚 部

【匹】pǐ Ⅰ（量）❶〔of certain draught animals〕：一～驢 a donkey ❷〔of cloth〕bolt：兩～綢子 two bolts of silk Ⅱ（動）be equal to

【匹夫】pǐfū（名）commoner；ordinary person：國家興亡，～有責。Every citizen should hold himself responsible for the weal or woe of his nation.

【匹配】pǐpèi（動）❶ marry ❷ match

【匹敵】pǐdí（動）rival；match：無可～ without a rival；peerless

【匠】jiàng（名）❶ workman skilled in a craft；craftsman：木～ carpenter；joiner ❷ person of outstanding achievement in a certain field；master：巨～ great master

【匠人】jiàngrén（名）craftsman；artisan

【匠心】jiàngxīn（名）ingenuity；originality

【匣】xiá（名）small box

【匪】fěi（名）bandit；robber

【匪首】fěishǒu（名）bandit chief；ringleader

【匪徒】fěitú（名）bandit

【匪患】fěihuàn（名）banditry

【匪幫】fěibāng（名）bandit gang

【匾】biǎn（名）❶（wooden）tablet；horizontal inscribed board（usu. hung over the door or on the wall）：橫～ horizontal inscribed board ❷

silk banner embroidered with words of praise ❸ big round shallow split-bamboo container for silkworm raising, etc.

【匾額】biǎn'é（名）tablet；horizontal inscribed board

【匿】nì（動）hide；conceal

【匿名】nìmíng（形）anonymous：～信 anonymous letter

【匿跡】nìjī（動）go into hiding

【區】Ōu（名）a surname
　　see also qū

【區】qū Ⅰ（名）❶ district；area：市中心～ brsiness centre of a city；downtown～ 邊～ border region ❷ an administrative division：經濟特～ special economic zone Ⅱ（動）distinguish；differentiate
　　see also Ōu

【區分】qūfēn（動）distinguish；differentiate：～兩種類型的產品 distinguish between the two types of products

【區別】qūbié Ⅰ（動）distinguish：兩者～甚大。There is a world of difference between the two. Ⅱ（名）difference；distinction

【區區】qūqū（形）trivial；trifling；petty：～小事 trifling matter／～之數，何必擔憂？Why worry about such a trifling sum of money？

【區域】qūyù（名）area；region

【區域性】qūyùxìng（形）regional

【匯】huì（動）❶ converge：～爲巨川 converge into a mighty river ❷ collect：～集 gather together ❸ remit：～錢 remit money（to sb.）

【匯合】huìhé（動）converge；join

【匯兌】huìduì（名）remittance

【匯率】huìlǜ（名）exchange rate

【匯票】huìpiào（名）draft; bill of exchange; money order

【匯款】huìkuǎn I（動）remit money II（名）remittance

【匯報】huìbào（動）report; give an account of: ～會 report-back meeting

【匯編】huìbiān I（動）compile II（名）compilation; corpus

【匯總】huìzǒng（動）gather; pool

匱 kuì（形）deficient; scanty

【匱乏】kuìfá（形）running short: 物資～ scarcity of material resources

十 部

十 shí I（數）ten: ～進制 the decimal system II（形）upmost: ～惡不赦 guilty of the most heinous crimes

【十一】Shí-Yī（名）October 1, National Day of the PRC

【十一月】shíyīyuè（名）❶ November ❷ eleventh month of the lunar year

【十二分】shíèrfēn（副）extremely; thoroughly: ～抱歉 terribly sorry

【十二月】shíèryuè（名）❶ December ❷ twelfth month of the lunar year

【十之八九】shí zhī bā jiǔ（十有八九 shí yǒu bā jiǔ）（副）in nine cases out of ten; most probably

【十分】shífēn（副）thoroughly; extremely: ～滿意 very pleased; more than satisfied

【十月】shíyuè（名）❶ October ❷ tenth month of the lunar year

【十成】shíchéng（形）hundred per cent

【十全十美】shí quán shí měi〈成〉perfect in all aspects; flawless

【十字架】shízìjià（名）cross; crucifix

【十字路口】shízì lùkǒu（名）crossroads

【十足】shízú（形）absolute; complete; sheer: 有～的理由不參加這次會議 have every reason not to attend this meeting

【十拿九穩】shí ná jiǔ wěn〈成〉be pretty sure (of success); be as good as assured

【十項全能運動】shí xiàng quánnéng yùndòng（名）〈體〉decathlon

【十萬火急】shí wàn huǒ jí（形）most urgent; extremely urgent

千 qiān I（數）❶ thousand ❷ a great number of II（名）（Qiān）a surname

【千瓦】qiānwǎ（名）kilowatt (kw)

【千方百計】qiān fāng bǎi jì〈成〉in every conceivable way; by hook or by crook

【千斤頂】qiānjīndǐng（名）〈機〉(hoisting) jack

【千古】qiāngǔ（形）through the ages; eternal: 一失足成～恨。A slip may cause eternal regret.

【千克】qiānkè（名）kilogram (kg)

【千里迢迢】qiān lǐ tiáo tiáo〈成〉form a thousand li away; all the way from afar

【千辛萬苦】qiān xīn wàn kǔ〈成〉untold hardships

【千言萬語】qiān yán wàn yǔ〈成〉innumerable words: ～也不能表達他的心意。No words can express what is in his heart.

【千金】qiānjīn（名）❶ a large sum of money: ～難買 priceless ❷〈敬〉daughter

【千周】qiānzhōu（名）kilocycle（kc）

【千秋萬代】qiān qiū wàn dài（成）generation after generation; for all generations to come

【千軍萬馬】qiān jūn wàn mǎ（成）a mighty army

【千差萬別】qiān chā wàn bié（成）very in a thousand and one ways

【千鈞一髮】qiān jūn yī fà〈成〉hang by a hair; be faced with impending danger

【千絲萬縷】qiān sī wàn lǚ（成）innumerable ties and links

【千萬】qiānwàn Ⅰ（數）ten million Ⅱ（動）be sure to; must: ～記住我對你講的話。Be sure to remember what I told you.

【千載難逢】qiān zǎi nán féng（成）once in a blue moon

【千篇一律】qiān piān yī lǜ（成）（of writing）be monotonous; lacking originality and inventiveness

【千頭萬緒】qiān tóu wàn xù（成）extremely complicated; a thousand things to attend to

【千錘百煉】qiān chuí bǎi liàn（成）❶ be well-tempered ❷（of literary works）carefully polished

【千變萬化】qiān biàn wàn huà（成）rapid and manifold changes; volatile

廿 niàn（數）twenty

卅 sà（數）thirty

午 wǔ（名）noon; midday

【午休】wǔxiū（名）midday break; lunch hour

【午夜】wǔyè（名）midnight

【午前】wǔqián（名）before noon; forenoon; morning

【午後】wǔhòu（名）afternoon

【午飯】wǔfàn（名）lunch

【午睡】wǔshuì（名）afternoon nap; nap after lunch

【午餐】wǔcān（名）lunch; luncheon: 工作～ working luncheon

【午餐肉】wǔcānròu（名）luncheon meat

升 shēng Ⅰ（動）❶ move upwards: 旭日東～。The sun is rising in the east. ❷ promote to a higher position or rank; upgrade: ～級 escalate Ⅱ（名）litre

【升平】shēngpíng（形）peaceful: ～日子 time of peace

【升官】shēngguān（動）be promoted（in one's official rank, position, etc.）: ～發財 gain power and wealth

【升級】shēngjí（動）❶ go up one grade in school ❷ be promoted in position or rank ❸（of war）escalate

【升值】shēngzhí（動）〈經〉appreciate

【升格】shēnggé（動）（of status, position, etc.）upgrade; go up: 外交關係～ upgrade diplomatic relations

【升旗】shēngqí（動）hoist a flag

【升學】shēngxué（動）enter a higher school

半 bàn Ⅰ（副）❶ half: 對～分 go halves with sb. in sth. ❷ partly: 窗戶～開着。The window is left half open. ❸ halfway; in the middle: ～路 halfway（on one's journey）Ⅱ（形）very little: 一鱗爪的知識 fragmentary knowledge

【半工半读】bàn gōng bàn dú (动) study at school or college on a part-work basis; part work, part study

【半…不…】bàn…bù… (similar in meaning to 半…半…, but with a bad connotation): 半死不活 more dead than alive / 半生不熟 (of food) underdone or half-cooked; (of a lesson) not fully mastered

【半天】bàntiān (副) for quite a while; for some time

【半斤八两】bàn jīn bā liǎng 〈成〉 six of one and half a dozen of the other; equally unsatisfactory

【半月刊】bànyuèkān (名) fortnightly; semimonthly (magazine / periodical); biweekly

【半…半…】bàn…bàn… [used before two opposite words to indicate that the two contradictory states exist side by side]: 半信半疑 half-believing, half-doubting / 半睡半醒 half asleep, half awake / 半吞半吐 be mealy-mouthed; hesitate to speak one's mind / 半文半白 a mixture of the literary and vernacular styles

【半百】bànbǎi (数) fifty: 年过半百 over fifty years old

【半成品】bànchéngpǐn (名) semi-finished product

【半吊子】bàndiàozi (名) ❶ flippant and impulsive person ❷ poorly educated or unskillful person ❸ careless person lacking in perseverance

【半决赛】bànjuésài (名) 〈体〉 semifinal

【半身不遂】bàn shēn bù suí (名) 〈医〉 hemiplegia; paralysis of one side of the body

【半夜】bànyè (副) in the middle of the night: 半夜三更 in the depth of the night; in the small hours (of the morning)

【半空中】bànkōngzhōng (副) 〈口〉 in the sky; in midair: 悬在半空中 suspended in midair

【半音】bànyīn (名) 〈乐〉 semitone: 半音阶 chromatic scale

【半晌】bànshǎng Ⅰ (名) 〈方〉 half of the day: 后半晌 afternoon Ⅱ (副) for some time; for quite a while: 他半晌缍回来. It was quite some time before he came back.

【半饥半饱】bàn jī bàn bǎo 〈成〉 underfed; half-starving

【半径】bànjìng (名) radius

【半岛】bàndǎo (名) peninsula

【半途而废】bàn tú ér fèi 〈成〉 stop (give up) halfway; leave sth. unfinished

【半瓶醋】bànpíngcù (名) 〈口〉 person with merely a superficial knowledge of sth.

【半球】bànqiú (名) hemisphere: 南半球 the Southern Hemisphere

【半票】bànpiào (名) half-price ticket

【半场】bànchǎng (名) half of a game: 上(下)半场 the first (second) half of a game or performance

【半道儿】bàndàor (副) 〈口〉 on the way; halfway; midway

【半圆】bànyuán Ⅰ (名) semicircle Ⅱ (形) semicircular

【半载】bànzǎi (名) half a year; six months

【半截】bànjié Ⅰ (形) half: 半截粉笔 half a piece of chalk Ⅱ (副) halfway: 事情做了一半他就走了.

He left when he was halfway through with his work.

【半旗】bànqí（名）half-mast: 下 ~ 誌哀 fly a flag at half-mast as a sign of mourning

【半價】bànjià（名）fifty per cent discount in price: ~ 出售 sell at half price

【半數】bànshù（名）half: 不到 ~ less than half; the minority

【半輩子】bànbèizi（名）half a lifetime: 大 ~ for the greater part of one's life

【半導體】bàndǎotǐ（名）❶ semiconductor ❷〈口〉transistor radio

【半機械化】bànjīxièhuà（形）semimechanized

【半點】bàndiǎn（名）the least bit

【半邊天】bànbiāntiān（名）❶ half the sky ❷ women, who make up half the population

卉 huì（名）grass: 花 ~ flowers and grasses

卒 zú（名）❶ soldier ❷〈象棋〉pawn

協 xié Ⅰ（形）joint Ⅱ（動）cooperate; assist

【協力】xiélì（動）join in a common effort; cooperate

【協同】xiétóng（動）work in coordination with; cooperate

【協助】xiézhù（動）assist; help

【協作】xiézuò（名）cooperation; coordination

【協定】xiédìng（名）agreement; convention: 雙邊貿易 ~ bilateral trade agreement / 軍事 ~ military convention

【協奏曲】xiézòuqǔ（名）concerto

【協商】xiéshāng（動）consult; be in consultation with; confer

【協會】xiéhuì（名）association; society

【協調】xiétiáo（動）harmonize; coordinate

【協議】xiéyì（名）agreement: 廢止 ~ annul an agreement

卓 zhuó（形）outstanding; extraordinary

【卓有成效】zhuó yǒu chéng xiào（形）highly effective; fruitful: 採取 ~ 的措施以控制通貨膨脹 adopt very effective measures to curb inflation

【卓見】zhuōjiàn（名）brilliant idea; wise counsel

【卓絕】zhuōjué（形）extraordinary; extreme: 英勇 ~ actuated by extraordinary courage

【卓越】zhuōyuè（形）outstanding; brilliant; excellent

【卓著】zhuōzhù（形）distinguished; outstanding; prominent: 功績 ~ make outstanding contributions

【卓識】zhuóshí（名）sagacious insight

卑 bēi（形）❶ low; debased; depraved; vile: 自 ~ 感 inferiority complex ❷ inferior (in quality)

【卑下】bēixià（形）mean and low; humble

【卑劣】bēiliè（形）(of one's quality, speech, conduct, etc.) base; mean; contemptible

【卑怯】bēiqiè（形）cowardly and contemptible; abject

【卑躬屈膝】bēi gōng qū xī〈成〉servile and spineless; bow and scrape

【卑微】bēiwēi (形) petty and low (in position)

【卑鄙】bēibǐ (形) mean; base; dishonourable: ～伎俩 dirty trick

【卑鄙無恥】bēi bǐ wú chǐ 〈成〉mean and shameless

【卑賤】bēijiàn (形) ❶ low and humble (in social station) ❷ mean and low (in manner)

南 nán (名) ❶ south: 這屋子朝～。The house faces south. ❷ (Nán) a surname

【南方】nánfāng (名) south

【南半球】nánbànqiú (名) the Southern Hemisphere

【南北對話】nánběi duìhuà (名) North-South dialogue

【南瓜】nánguā (名) pumpkin

【南風】nánfēng (名) south wind

【南南合作】nánnán hézuò (名) South-South cooperation

【南部】nánbù (名) southern part; south

【南極】nánjí (名) the South Pole; the Antarctic Pole

【南腔北調】nán qiāng běi diào 〈成〉have a mixed accent; talk with a mixture of accent

【南斯拉夫】Nánsīlāfū (名) Yugoslavia: ～人 Yugoslav

【南轅北轍】nán yuán běi zhé 〈成〉go in the diametrically opposite direction to one's purpose; act in contravention of

博 bó I (形) ❶ ample; abounding; vast (in scope) ❷ learned; erudite; well-read; well-informed: 學識淵～ erudite II (動) gain; earn

【博士】bóshì (名) ❶ court academician (in ancient China) ❷ doctor (academic degree): 授予～學位 confer the doctor's degree on sb.

【博古通今】bó gǔ tōng jīn 〈成〉be familiar with things past and present; both learned and well-informed

【博取】bóqǔ (動) court; try to win: ～信任 win sb.'s confidence

【博物館】bówùguǎn (博物院 bówùyuàn) (名) museum

【博茨瓦納】Bócíwǎnà (名) Botswana: ～人 Botswanian

【博得】bódé (動) win; earn; gain: ～青睞 find favour in sb.'s eyes; be in sb.'s good graces

【博愛】bó'ài (名) fraternity; love for mankind; universal love

【博學】bóxué (形) erudite; learned; of wide learning

【博覽】bólǎn (動) read extensively

【博覽會】bólǎnhuì (名) (international) fair; exposition

卜 部

卜 bǔ I (動) ❶ predict; foretell: 勝負未～ cannot predict which side will win ❷ look into a crystal ball; practise divination II (名) ❶ crystal gazing ❷ (Bǔ) a surname

【卜卦】bǔguà I (動) divine (by the Eight Diagrams) II (名) divination (by the Eight Diagrams)

卞 Biàn (名) a surname

卡 kǎ I (動) ❶ check; stop; hold up: 因交通堵塞，車被～住了。The car was held up in a traffic jam. ❷ block: ～住出口處 block the exit

❸ press with the part of the hand between the thumb and the index finger: 緊緊～住他的脖子 seize sb. tightly by the throat Ⅱ（名）❶（short for 卡車 kǎchē）truck; lorry: 十輪～ ten-wheel lorry ❷（short for 卡片 kǎpiàn）card: 信用～ credit card Ⅲ（量）〈物〉（short for 卡路里 kǎlùlǐ）calorie: 千～ kilocalorie

see also qiǎ

【卡片】kǎpiàn（名）card: ～目錄 card catalogue

【卡車】kǎchē（名）truck; lorry

【卡通】kǎtōng（名）cartoon: ～片 animated cartoon

【卡塔爾】Kǎtǎ'ěr（名）Qater: ～人 Qatari

卡 qiǎ Ⅰ（動）❶ wedge; be jammed: ～在兩人中間 be sandwiched in between two persons ❷ clip Ⅱ（名）❶ clip: 髮～ hair pin; hair clasp ❷ checkpost: 設～ set up a checkpost

see also kǎ

【卡刀】qiǎdāo（名）〈機〉swaging clamp

【卡子】qiǎzi（名）❶ clip; fastener ❷ checkpost

【卡具】qiǎjù（名）〈機〉clamping apparatus; fixture

占 zhān（動）practise divination

【占卜】zhānbǔ（動）practise divination; divine

【占卦】zhānguà（名）divination; crystal gazing

【占星】zhānxīng（動）divine by astrology

卦 guà（名）divinatory symbols: 占

～ divination

卩 部

卯 mǎo

【卯眼】mǎoyǎn（名）mortise

【卯榫】mǎosǔn（名）mortise and tenon

印 yìn Ⅰ（名）❶ seal; stamp: 文件上蓋上～ affix a seal to a document ❷ print; mark: 腳～ foot-print Ⅱ（動）print; have sth. printed: 將原稿付～ send a manuscript to the press / 深深～在記憶中 deeply engraved in sb.'s memory

【印花】yìnhuā（名）❶〈紡〉printing ❷ revenue stamp; stamp

【印泥】yìnní（名）red ink paste used for seals

【印刷】yìnshuā（名）printing: 廠 printing house; press

【印度】Yìndù（名）India: ～人 Indian

【印度尼西亞】Yìndùníxīyà（名）Indonesia: ～人 Indonesian / ～語 Indonesian (language)

【印度教】Yìndùjiào（名）〈宗〉Hinduism

【印染】yìnrǎn（動）print and dye (textiles)

【印盒】yìnhé（名）seal box

【印章】yìnzhāng（名）seal; stamp

【印象】yìnxiàng（名）impression

【印發】yìnfā（動）print and distribute; issue: ～傳單 print and distribute handbills

【印數】yìnshù（名）〈印〉printing; impression: 第三次～一萬冊 a

third impression (printing) of 10,000 copies

【印證】 yìnzhèng (動) corroborate; verify

【印鑒】 yìnjiàn (名) specimen seal impression

危 wēi I (名) ❶ danger; jeopardy: 轉～爲安 turn danger into safety; pull through ❷ (Wēi) a surname II (動) endanger; jeopardize III (形) ❶ dying; critical: 病～ be terminally ill ／ ～房 crumbling house ❷ proper; upright: 正襟～坐 sit bolt upright

【危亡】 wēiwáng (形) at stake; in peril

【危在旦夕】 wēi zài dàn xī 〈成〉 be in imminent danger; (of a patient) be dying; (of a place under enemy attack) may fall at any moment

【危地馬拉】 Wēidìmǎlā (名) Guatemala: ～人 Guatemalan

【危局】 wēijú (名) critical situation; crisis

【危急】 wēijí (形) critical; imminently dangerous: 局勢～。The situation is explosive.

【危害】 wēihài (動) harm; impair: ～國民經濟 be harmful to the national economy

【危機】 wēijī (名) crisis

【危險】 wēixiǎn I (名) danger; peril: 有～ be risky; be in danger II (形) dangerous; perilous: ～區 danger zone

【危難】 wēinàn (名) peril; disaster: ～之際 in the hour of desperate danger

即 jí I (動) ❶ approach; be near; contact: 若～若離 seem so near and yet so far away ❷ assume; be enthroned ❸ be; mean: 時間～金錢。Time is money. II (副) ❶ right now: 當～做出決定 make a prompt decision ❷ immediately; at once: 勝利～在眼前。Victory is in sight. ❸ impromptu; extempore ❹ namely; that is: 只有兩個人缺席，～王大夫和張大夫。Only two people are absent, namely Dr. Wang and Dr. Zhang. III (連) even though; even

【即日】 jírì (副) ❶ today; this day ❷ in a few days: ～公演 (of a film, play, etc.) coming soon

【即刻】 jíkè (副) instantly; in no time; right away

【即使】 jíshǐ (連) even thouth: ～你的日程排得很緊，長城還是值得再看的。The Great Wall is worth seeing again even if you've got a tight programme.

【即便】 jíbiàn (連) even if: ～下大雨我們也要出發。We would start off even if it rained hard.

【即時】 jíshí (副) at once; immediately

【即席】 jíxí (副) impromptu; offhand: ～發言 make an impromptu speech; speak off-hand

【即將】 jíjiāng (副) very soon: ～通知他 will soon notify him

【即景】 jíjǐng (動) write or paint on the spur of the moment: ～詩 occasional verse ／ 農村～ village sketch

卵 luǎn (名) egg; ovum

【卵石】 luǎnshí (名) cobble; pebble

【卵巢】 luǎncháo (名)〈生理〉ovary

【卵翼】 luǎnyì (動) take sb. under one's wing; shelter

卷 juǎn I (名) (动) roll; reel: 膠～ roll film II (量) roll; reel: 一～綫 a reel of thread
see also juàn

卷 juàn I (名) ❶ book: 開～有益。 Reading is a profitable occupation. ❷ exam paper: 交～ hand in one's exam paper ❸ files; records; official papers II (量) volume (of a book): 第一～ Volume 1
see also juǎn

【卷子】juànzi (名) exam paper: 改 ～ go over exam papers

【卷宗】juànzōng (名) ❶ folder (for official papers) ❷ file; dossier

【卷軸】juànzhóu (名) scroll

卹 xù (动) ❶ sympathize; have pity on ❷ give relief; compensate

【卹金】xùjīn (名) pension for the disabled or the family of the deceased

卻 què I (动) ❶ move back: ～步 step back; shrink back ❷ reject; decline: 盛情難～ it would be hard to decline such a kind invitation II [used after certain verbs to indicate the completion of an action]: 我早已忘～此事。 I have long since forgotten about it. III (連) but; yet; however: 文章雖短,～很有力。 Short as it is, the essay is forceful.

卸 xiè (动) ❶ unload; remove: ～船 unload a ship / ～下炮衣 dismantle a gun of its covering ❷ relieve; shirk

【卸任】xièrèn (动) be relieved of one's office

【卸車】xièchē (动) unload a vehicle; unload

【卸貨】xièhuò (动) unload cargo; unload

【卸責】xièzé (动) shirk one's responsibility

【卸裝】xièzhuāng (动) remove stage makeup and costume

厂 部

厄 è I (名) ❶ disaster; hardship ❷ strategic point II (动) be in distress

【厄瓜多爾】Èguāduō'ěr (名) Ecuador: ～人 Ecuadorian

【厄運】èyùn (名) misfortune

厚 hòu (形) ❶ thick ❷ deep; profound: 深情～誼 deep friendly sentiment ❸ magnanimous

【厚古薄今】hòu gǔ bó jīn (成) attach weight to the past rather than the present

【厚此薄彼】hòu cǐ bó bǐ (成) treat one with kindness while looking upon the other with disfavour

【厚度】hòudù (名) thickness

【厚望】hòuwàng (名) great expectations: 有負～ disappoint sb.'s expectations

【厚道】hòudao (形) kind and sincere

【厚意】hòuyì (名) profound kindness

【厚顏無恥】hòuyán wúchǐ (形) brazen; shameless

原 yuán I (形) ❶ primary; original; former: ～址 former address; original site ❷ raw; crude: ～糧 unprocessed grain II (名) ❶ area of

【原子】yuánzǐ（名）atom

【原子反應堆】yuánzǐ fǎnyìngduī（名）atomic reactor

【原子核】yuánzǐhé（名）atomic nucleus

【原子能】yuánzǐnéng（名）atomic energy

【原子彈】yuánzǐdàn（名）atom bomb

【原木】yuánmù（名）log

【原文】yuánwén（名）original text; the original

【原主】yuánzhǔ（名）original owner

【原色】yuánsè（名）〈物〉primary colours

【原先】yuánxiān（副）originally; initially

【原因】yuányīn（名）cause; reason

【原有】yuányǒu（形）original

【原判】yuánpàn（名）〈法〉original sentence

【原告】yuángào（名）〈法〉（of a civil case）plaintiff;（of a criminal case）prosecutor

【原材料】yuáncáiliào（名）raw and unprocessed materials

【原形畢露】yuán xíng bì lù〈成〉reveal one's true features

【原來】yuánlái Ⅰ（形）original; former Ⅱ（副）[used to indicate the discovery of the truth]: ～是你幹的! So it was you who did it!

【原始】yuánshǐ（形）❶ original; primary: ～生產方式 primary mode of production ❷ primitive; primeval: ～森林 virgin forest/ ～文化 primitive culture

【原委】yuánwěi（名）whole course of an event; whole story from beginning to end

【原油】yuányóu（名）crude oil

【原狀】yuánzhuàng（名）status quo ante; original state

【原版】yuánbǎn（名）original edition（of a book, etc.）

【原封】yuánfēng（形）untouched; intact: ～不動 be kept intact

【原型】yuánxíng（名）〈機〉prototype

【原則】yuánzé（名）principle

【原原本本】yuán yuán běn běn〈成〉from first to last; in great detail: 我把這事～地告訴你。Let me tell you the whole story from beginning to end.

【原理】yuánlǐ（名）principle; tenet

【原野】yuányě（名）open country

【原動力】yuándònglì（名）motive power; motivation

【原棉】yuánmián（名）〈紡〉raw cotton

【原著】yuánzhù（名）original work; original

【原煤】yuánméi（名）raw coal

【原意】yuányì（名）original meaning（intention）

【原稿】yuángǎo（名）original manuscript; master copy

【原價】yuánjià（名）cost price

【原諒】yuánliàng（動）forgive; pardon

【原職】yuánzhí（名）former post

【原籍】yuánjí（名）native place

厥 jué（動）pass out; lose consciousness: 昏～過去 fall unconscious

厭 yàn（動）❶ detest; loathe ❷ be tired of; be fed up with: 聽～了 be tired of listening to all this ❸ satisfy; satiate: 學而不～ learn with untiring zeal

【厭世】yànshì (動) be weary with life and the world

【厭倦】yànjuàn (動) be tired of; be weary of

【厭惡】yànwù (動) detest; dislike

【厭煩】yànfán (動) be sick of; feel annoyed: 令人～ be boring

【厭戰】yànzhàn (動) be war-weary

厲

厲 I I (形) ❶ strict; harsh ❷ fierce; severe: 正顏～色 put on a stern expression II (Lì) (名) a surname

【厲行】lìxíng (動) make every effort to carry out; practise

【厲兵秣馬】lì bīng mò mǎ〈成〉be battle-ready; buckle on one's armour

【厲害】lìhai (形) serious; fierce; formidable; terrible: 對他～點 get tough with him

【厲聲】lìshēng (副) in a stern voice

厶 部

去 qù I (動)❶ leave; go: ～圖書館 go to the library ❷ lose; remove: 大勢已～。The situation is beyond salvation. / ～掉衣服上的油污 remove grease from one's clothes ❸ be apart from: 相～不遠 be not far from II (形) of the preceding year: ～冬今春 last winter and this spring III (副) ❶ [used after a verb to indicate the direction of the action] away (from the speaker): 出～ get out ❷ [used after a verb to indicate the continua-

tion of an action]: 說下～ go on; carry on (talking)

【去皮】qùpí (動) skin; remove the peel of

【去世】qùshì (動) (of adults) die; pass away

【去年】qùnián (名) last year

【去向】qùxiàng (名) direction in which sb. has gone; whereabouts: 他的～不明。His whereabouts is unknown.

【去污粉】qùwūfěn (名) household cleanser; cleanser

【去垢劑】qùgòujì (名)〈化〉detergent

【去骨】qùgú (動) bone: ～鷄 boned chicken

【去處】qùchù (名) place to go; whereabouts

【去雄】qùxióng (動) emasculate; castrate

【去聲】qùshēng (名)〈語〉falling tone; the fourth tone (in Chinese pronunciation)

叁 sān (數) [the elaborate form of the numeral 三, used on cheques, banknotes, etc.] three

參 cān (動)❶ join; be involved in ❷ refer ❸ pay one's respects to see also cēn; shēn

【參加】cānjiā (動) ❶ join; take part in: ～座談 attend a seminar / ～演出 take part in a performance ❷ give (advice, etc.)

【參考】cānkǎo I (動) consult; make reference to II (名) reference: ～書目 bibliography

【參見】cānjiàn (動) see (also); vide

【參拜】cānbài (動) pay one's respects to

【参军】cānjūn（动）enlist; join the army; join the services

【参看】cānkàn（参阅 cānyuè）（动）refer to; see

【参照】cānzhào I（动）refer to II（介）in the light of; with reference to

【参谋】cānmóu I（名）staff officer: 总～部 general staff II（动）advise; give advice

【参赞】cānzàn（名）counsellor

【参议员】cānyìyuán（名）senator

【参议院】cānyìyuàn（名）（for short 参院 cānyuàn）senate

【参观】cānguān（动）visit; look round

参 cēn
see also cān; shēn

【参差不齐】cēn cī bù qí〈成〉uneven: 他们的水平～。Their levels very.

参 shēn（名）ginseng
see also cān; cēn

又 部

又 yòu（副）❶ [used to indicate repetition or continuation]: 他～来了。He has come again. ❷ [used to indicate the simultaneous existence of several conditions or qualities]: 他们在一起总是～说～笑。You often find them chatting and laughing when they are together. ❸ [used in a negative sentence for emphasis]: 你～不是不会。You certainly know how to do it. ❹ [used to indicate sth. additional]: 四～二

分之一 four and a half

【又及】yòují（名）postscript（PS）

叉 chā I（名）❶ fork: 刀～ knife and fork ❷ cross: 交～路口 cross-roads II（动）fork: ～起一块肉 pick up a piece of meat with a fork
see also chá; chǎ

【叉车】chāchē（名）forklift

【叉腰】chāyāo（动）stand（with arms）akimbo

叉 chá（动）block up: 拖拉机把路～住了。The road was blocked by a tractor.
see also chā; chǎ

叉 chǎ（动）（of legs, etc.）fork: ～着腿 with one's legs apart
see also chā; chá

友 yǒu I（名）friend II（形）friendly: ～邦 friendly country

【友人】yǒurén（名）friend

【友好】yǒuhǎo I（名）good friend II（形）friendly

【友情】yǒuqíng（名）friendship; cordial feelings

【友爱】yǒu'ài（名）friendliness

【友谊】yǒuyì（名）friendship

反 fǎn（动）❶ oppose; resist ❷ turn ❸ return; counter

【反之】fǎnzhī（连）otherwise; on the contrary

【反戈一击】fǎn gē yī jī〈成〉turn round to hit back at one's former comrades

【反比例】fǎnbǐlì（名）〈数〉in verse proportion

【反正】fǎnzhèng I（动）set things to rights II（副）in any case; anyway

【反目】fǎnmù（动）fall out（esp. between husband and wife)

【反而】fǎn'ér（连）but; instead

【反光】fǎnguāng Ⅰ（动）reflect Ⅱ（名）reflected light

【反抗】fǎnkàng（动）resist; revolt

【反攻】fǎngōng（名）counterattack; counteroffensive

【反作用】fǎnzuòyòng（名）reaction

【反帝】fǎndì Ⅰ（名）anti-imperialism Ⅱ（形）anti-imperialist

【反面】fǎnmiàn Ⅰ（名）reverse side Ⅱ（形）❶ negative ❷ opposite: ~意见 dissenting views

【反叛】fǎnpàn（动）revolt (often by going over to the enemy side)

【反映】fǎnyìng（动）❶ reflect; mirror ❷ report: ~群众意见 transmit the views of the public

【反省】fǎnxǐng（动）make a self-criticism after reviewing one's own conduct

【反咬一口】fǎn yǎo yī kǒu〈成〉make false countercharges

【反革命】fǎngémìng（名）counter-revolution

【反封建】fǎnfēngjiàn Ⅰ（名）anti-feudalism Ⅱ（形）anti-feudalist

【反刍】fǎnchú（动）chew the cud; ruminate

【反悔】fǎnhuǐ（动）withdraw one's promise or pledge; go back on one's word

【反射】fǎnshè Ⅰ（动）reflect Ⅱ（名）〈生〉reflex: 条件~ conditioned reflex

【反特】fǎntè（名）counter espionage

【反躬自问】fǎn gōng zì wèn〈成〉examine one's own conscience

【反唇相讥】fǎn chún xiāng jī〈成〉speak with biting sarcasm in retaliation

【反动】fǎndòng（形）reactionary

【反常】fǎncháng（形）abnormal

【反问】fǎnwèn Ⅰ（动）ask a question in retort Ⅱ（名）rhetorical question

【反间】fǎnjiàn（动）sow distrust or discord among the enemy

【反复】fǎnfù Ⅰ（形）❶ changeable: ~无常 fickle ❷ repeated Ⅱ（名）relapse; reversal: 事情可能又有~。There might be an unexpected twist in the event.

【反感】fǎngǎn（名）aversion; resentment

【反话】fǎnhuà（名）ironical remark

【反义词】fǎnyìcí（名）〈语〉antonym

【反驳】fǎnbó（动）refute; retort

【反对】fǎnduì（动）oppose; combat: ~官僚主义 combat bureaucracy

【反对票】fǎnduìpiào（名）negative vote

【反对党】fǎnduìdǎng（名）opposition party

【反扑】fǎnpū（动）launch a counter-attack after suffering a reverse

【反击】fǎnjī（动）counterattack

【反应】fǎnyìng Ⅰ（动）react; respond Ⅱ（名）reaction; response

【反应堆】fǎnyìngduī（名）〈物〉reactor: 核~ nuclear reactor

【反馈】fǎnkuì（名）feedback

【反响】fǎnxiǎng（名）repercussions

及

及 jí Ⅰ（副）in the nick of time; while it is not too late Ⅱ（动）❶ reach; attain; come to: 遍~全国 extend all over the country ❷ [used in negative statements only] be as good as: 我数学不~小李。I am not as good as Xiao Li in maths. Ⅲ（连）and: 孔子~其门徒 Confucius and his disciples / 以~and; along with; as well as

【及早】jízǎo (副) as soon as possible; at an early date

【及至】jízhì (连) not until; when: ～去冬問題纔得到解決。The problem was not solved until last winter.

【及格】jígé (动) pass (a test, exam, etc.); qualify: 考試不～ fail the exam

【及時】jíshí Ⅰ (副) in time; on time: ～趕到現場 arrive at the scene in good time Ⅱ (形) timely: ～雨 timely rain; timely help

取 qǔ (动) ❶ get; fetch: ～信件 collect one's mail ❷ invite; court: 自～滅亡 court destruction; dig one's own grave ❸ adopt; assume: 採～適當措施 adopt appropriate measures

【取巧】qǔqiǎo (动) gain advantage or evade difficulty by trickery: 投機～ take advantage of opportunities to advance one's interests

【取代】qǔdài (动) replace: 沒有人可以～他的位置。Nobody is able to replace him.

【取而代之】qǔ ér dài zhī 〈成〉 take sb.'s place

【取決】qǔjué (动) depend on; be decided by: 會議是否在露天舉行～於天氣。Whether the meeting will be held outdoors depends on the weather.

【取材】qǔcái (动) derive materials (from)

【取長補短】qǔ cháng bǔ duǎn 〈成〉learn from others' strong points to make up for one's deficiencies

【取消】qǔxiāo (动) cancel; abolish: ～一切不合理的規章制度 abolish all unreasonable rules and regulations

【取笑】qǔxiào (动) ridicule; make fun of; laugh at

【取悅】qǔyuè (动) try to win favour from sb.; try to please

【取得】qǔdé (动) acquire; obtain: 工作～進展 make progress in one's work / ～聯繫 make contact

【取捨】qǔshě (动) accept or discard; choose: 有所～ have the option to accept or refuse

【取景】qǔjǐng (动) choose a view as the background for a photograph or painting

【取道】qǔdào (动) take the route through; via: ～武漢, 前往廣州 go to Guangzhou by way of Wuhan

【取勝】qǔshèng (动) gain victory; achieve success; win: 不能以暴力～ cannot achieve success by brute force

【取經】qǔjīng (动) ❶ go on a long journey (to India) for the Buddhist canon of scriptures ❷ learn from sb.'s experience

【取暖】qǔnuǎn (动) warm oneself (by a fire, etc.)

【取締】qǔdì (动) ban; outlaw; prohibit

【取樂】qǔlè (动) have fun; revel; make merry; seek sensual pleasure

【取樣】qǔyàng Ⅰ (动) take a sample Ⅱ (名) sampling

叔 shū (名) ❶ uncle; father's younger brother ❷ address for a man about one's own father's age ❸ husband's younger brother: 小～子 brother-in-law (husband's younger brother)

【叔父】shūfù（名）uncle; father's younger brother

【叔母】shūmǔ（名）uncle's wife; aunt

【叔伯】shūbai（形）of the same grandfather or great grandfather on the father's side: ～弟兄（姐妹）cousins on the paternal side

【叔叔】shūshu（名）〈口〉❶ uncle; father's younger brother ❷ uncle（child's address for any man about his father's age）

受 shòu（动）❶ accept; receive: ～礼 accept a gift ❷ suffer; sustain: ～歧视 be discriminated against ❸ endure; bear: 不能再忍～了 can no longer tolerate it

【受用】shòuyòng（动）benefit from; enjoy: ～不盡 draw endless benefit

【受刑】shòuxíng（动）be tortured; undergo torture

【受旱】shòuhàn（动）suffer from drought

【受灾】shòuzāi（动）be afflicted by a natural disaster

【受命】shòumìng（动）receive a mandate; receive instructions

【受苦】shòukǔ（动）suffer（hardships）

【受挫】shòucuò（动）suffer a setback: ～而不氣餒 never feel deflated despite setbacks

【受託】shòutuō（动）be commissioned; be asked（to do sth.）

【受害】shòuhài（动）be injured; be killed; be victimized: ～者 victim; the injured party

【受氣】shòuqì（动）be bullied; be browbeaten

【受辱】shòurǔ（动）be insulted; be humiliated; be abused

【受訓】shòuxùn（动）undergo training

【受益】shòuyì（动）gain from; get benefit: ～非淺 be greatly benefited

【受累】shòulèi（动）be given much trouble: 叫您～了。Sorry to have put you to so much trouble.

【受理】shòulǐ（动）〈法〉accept a case for prosecution

【受寒】shòuhán（受涼 shòuliáng）（动）catch cold

【受援】shòuyuán（动）receive aid: ～國 recipient country

【受賄】shòuhuì（动）take bribes

【受傷】shòushāng（动）be wounded; be injured: 作戰～ be wounded in action

【受罪】shòuzuì（动）have a terrible time: 聽他胡扯那麽長的時間真是活～。It was sheer torture to hear him talk rubbish for such a long time.

【受罰】shòufá（动）be punished; be penalized; be fined

【受精】shòujīng（动）be fertilized: ～卵 fertilized egg; zygote

【受潮】shòucháo（动）become damp

【受獎】shòujiǎng（动）be rewarded; be given an award

【受審】shòushěn（动）stand trial

【受難】shòunàn（动）suffer a disaster; be afflicted

【受騙】shòupiàn（动）be swindled; be fooled

【受權】shòuquán（动）be authorized

【受驚】shòujīng（动）be frightened; be startled; be taken aback

叛 pàn（动）betray; rebel against

【叛逆】pànnì Ⅰ（动）rebel; revolt Ⅱ

（名）rebel

【叛逃】pàntáo（动）defect

【叛徒】pàntú（名）traitor; renegade

【叛国】pànguó（动）betray one's country

【叛国罪】pànguózuì（名）treason

【叛乱】pànluàn（名）rebellion; revolt; mutiny: 武装～ armed rebellion

【叛离】pànlí（动）defect; desert

【叛变】pànbiàn（动）betray; defect

叙 xù（动）❶ talk; chat: ～～旧 chat about the old days ❷ narrate; describe: 简～ make a brief statement

【叙别】xùbié（动）pay a farewell call

【叙利亚】Xùlìyà（名）Syria: ～人 Syrian

【叙事】xùshì（动）narrate; recount: ～诗 narrative poetry

【叙述】xùshù（动）describe; narrate: 这篇文章仔细地～了事情发生的经过。This article describes in detail how the incident happened.

【叙说】xùshuō（动）tell; narrate; relate

【叙谈】xùtán（动）talk; chat: ～学习 come together and exchange views about studies

叢 cóng Ⅰ（动）crowd together: 杂草～生 be overgrown with weeds Ⅱ（名）❶ clump: 灌木～ a clump of bushes ❷ group of people or things: 人～ a crowd of people ❸（Cóng）a surname

【叢林】cónglín（名）forest; jungle

【叢书】cóngshū（名）(of books) series

【叢集】cóngjí（动）gather together

口 部

口 kǒu Ⅰ（名）❶ mouth ❷ opening: 售票窗～ wicket; box office window ❸ cut: 包扎伤～ bandage up a wound ❹ knife edge: 刀～锋利。The knife has a sharp edge. ❺ pass (of the Great Wall) ❻ gateway: 出入～岸 port of call Ⅱ（量）❶ [of family members, wells, pigs, etc.]: 三～之家 a family of three ❷ mouthful: 喝～茶 take a sip of tea

【口才】kǒucái（名）ability to speak with fluency, power and aptness; eloquence

【口子】kǒuzi（名）❶ opening ❷ cut ❸〈口〉one's own spouse: 我们那～进城了。My mate has gone downtown. ❹ people: 他们家有三～。There are three people in their family.

【口口声声】kǒukou shēngshēng（副）(say) repeatedly or constantly

【口水】kǒushuǐ（名）saliva

【口令】kǒulìng（名）❶ word of command ❷ password

【口吃】kǒuchī（动）stammer; stutter

【口舌】kǒushé（名）❶ quarrel: 一场～ a quarrel ❷ persuading: 他费了很多～，缴使他们平息下来。It took a lot of persuading for him to pacify them.

【口技】kǒujì（名）vocal mimicry

【口角】kǒujué（名）quarrel; squabble

【口吻】kǒuwěn（名）way of speaking: 以玩笑的～ speak jokingly

【口服】kǒufú（动）❶ be apparently convinced: 心服～ be truly persuaded ❷ to be taken orally

【口供】kǒugòng（名）〈法〉verbal deposition; testimony

【口味】kǒuwèi（名）❶ taste of food ❷ personal taste (for food, etc.)

【口红】kǒuhóng（名）lipstick

【口音】kǒuyīn（名）❶ voice ❷ accent: 她～重。She has a strong accent.

【口信】kǒuxìn（名）(oral) message: 捎个～ pass on a message

【口是心非】kǒu shì xīn fēi〈成〉say one thing but mean another

【口香糖】kǒuxiāngtáng（名）chewing gum

【口若悬河】kǒu ruò xuán hé〈成〉talk incessantly and eloquently

【口哨儿】kǒushàor（名）whistling; whistle: 吹～ whistle

【口径】kǒujìng（名）❶ bore; calibre ❷ requirements; specification ❸ line of action; statement: 对～〈口〉(of suspects) agree not to show discrepancy in their statements

【口气】kǒuqì（名）❶ (of speech) tone: 他～是不赞成的。His tone is one of disapproval. ❷ the way one speaks; manner of speech: 他的～狂妄自大。He sounds self-important and arrogant. ❸ what is implied in one's speech: 听你的～好像有希望。You sound hopeful.

【口袋】kǒudài（名）pocket

【口袋】kǒudai（名）beg; sack

【口授】kǒushòu（动）❶ dictate ❷ teach orally

【口腔】kǒuqiāng（名）〈生理〉oral cavity: ～外科医师 oral surgeon

【口琴】kǒuqín（名）mouth organ; harmonica: 吹～ play the mouth organ

【口渴】kǒukě（形）thirsty; parched

【口罩】kǒuzhào（名）mouth mask; gauze mask

【口号】kǒuhào（名）slogan

【口试】kǒushì（名）oral examination

【口福】kǒufú（名）luck to be treated to good food: 一～不浅 be lucky enough to enjoy delicacies

【口语】kǒuyǔ（名）spoken language

【口紧】kǒujǐn（形）tight-lipped; able to keep one's mouth shut

【口齿】kǒuchǐ（名）enunciation; articulation: ～伶俐 speak fluently

【口头】kǒutóu（形）oral; verbal; in words (as against in deeds): ～禅 pet phrase

【口粮】kǒuliáng（名）grain ration

【口译】kǒuyì（名）oral interpretation

古 gǔ Ⅰ（形）ancient; old Ⅱ（Gǔ）（名）a surname

【古人】gǔrén（名）the ancients

【古巴】Gǔbā（名）Cuba: ～人 Cuban

【古文】gǔwén（名）classical Chinese

【古代】gǔdài（名）ancient times; antiquity

【古老】gǔlǎo（形）ancient; age-old

【古色古香】gǔ sè gǔ xiāng（形）antique; quaint

【古板】gǔbǎn（形）old-fashioned and stubborn

【古物】gǔwù（名）historical relics

【古玩】gǔwán（名）antique; curio

【古怪】gǔguài（形）eccentric; abnormal

【古典】gǔdiǎn（形）classical: ～文学 classical literature

【古典主义】gǔdiǎn zhǔyì（名）classicism

【古往今來】gǔ wǎng jīn lái〈成〉past and present; from time immemorial

【古迹】gǔjì（名）historic site; place of historic interest

【古都】gǔdū（名）ancient capital

【古稀】gǔxī（名）seventy years of age

【古雅】gǔyǎ（形）of classical elegance

【古話】gǔhuà（名）old saying

【古董】gǔdǒng（名）❶ antique ❷ old die-hard; museum piece

【古樸】gǔpǔ（形）of classical simplicity

【古籍】gǔjí（名）ancient books

【古蘭經】Gǔlánjīng（名）〈宗〉the Koran

可 kě Ⅰ（動）❶ permit; approve: 未經許 ~ without permission ❷ may; can: 兩者不 ~ 偏廢。Neither should be neglected. ❸ be worth (doing); -able: 一本 ~ 讀的書 a good book to read Ⅱ（副）❶ but; yet: 別看他年紀小，~ 彈得一手好鋼琴。Young as he is, the boy plays the piano wonderfully well. ❷ [used for emphasis]: 花 ~ 美了。These flowers are really beautiful. ❸ [used in interrogative sentences for emphasis]: 你 ~ 知道他是誰? Who do you think he is?

see also kè

【可口】kěkǒu（形）tasty; delicious

【可以】kěyǐ Ⅰ（動）can; may: ~ 這樣說。You can put it that way. Ⅱ〈口〉❶ passable; tolerable: 他舞跳得還 ~。She's not a bad dancer. ❷ awful; terrible: 他吵得真 ~。

He made such a terrible scene.

【可可】kěkě（名）cocoa

【可巧】kěqiǎo（副）by coincidence; luckily

【可行】kěxíng（形）feasible; practicable: 我看這方案 ~。I think the plan is feasible.

【可行性研究】kěxíngxìng yánjiū（名）feasibility study

【可見】kějiàn（口）thus; therefore: 由此 ~ thus it can be seen

【可怕】kěpà（形）fearful; dreadful

【可取】kěqǔ（形）desirable; advisable: 一無 ~ worthless

【可是】kěshì（連）[often preceded by another conjunction, e.g., 雖然, etc.] but; yet: 雖然陰霾滿空，~ 大家熱情很高。Everyone was in high spirits although the weather was very gloomy.

【可恨】kěhèn（形）hateful; abhorrent

【可恥】kěchǐ（形）shameful; disgraceful

【可能】kěnéng Ⅰ（形）possible; likely; probable: 盡一切 ~ do what is humanly possible Ⅱ（名）possibility; likelihood Ⅲ（副）maybe; possibly

【可氣】kěqì（形）annoying; vexing

【可笑】kěxiào（形）funny; ridiculous; ludicrous

【可乘之機】kě chéng zhī jī〈成〉opportunity that can be utilized

【可耕地】kěgēngdì（名）arable land

【可惜】kěxī（副）unfortunately: ~ 他不在家。Unfortunately he wasn't in.

【可望而不可即】kě wàng ér bù kě jí〈成〉be beyond reach; unattainable

【可悲】kěbēi（形）sad; tragic

【可貴】kěguì（形）valuable; commendable

【可欺】kěqī（形）❶ easily fooled ❷ easily bullied

【可喜】kěxǐ（形）gratifying; welcome: 這真是～的事。This is really gratifying.

【可惡】kěwù（形）detestable; despicable

【可敬】kějìng（形）worthy of respect; honourable

【可愛】kě'ài（形）lovely; charming: 小姑娘多～! What a lovely little girl!

【可疑】kěyí（形）suspicious; fishy: 這家伙是個～人物。This chap is a suspicious character.

【可歌可泣】kě gē kě qì〈成〉can move people to song and tears

【可靠】kěkào（形）reliable; trustworthy

【可憐】kělián Ⅰ（形）pitiful; piteous Ⅱ（副）pitifully; miserably: 馬瘦得～。The horse is wretchedly bony. Ⅲ（動）feel pity for; have compassion on

【可蘭經】Kělánjīng（名）〈宗〉Koran

可 kè
see also kě

【可汗】kèhán（名）khan

叵 pǒ

【叵測】pǒcè（形）〈貶〉unfathomable; unpredictable: 心懷～ cherish ulterior motives

右 yòu Ⅰ（名）right; righ side Ⅱ（形）right

【右派】yòupài（名）rightist

【右首】yòushǒu（名）the right-hand side; the right

【右傾】yòuqīng（名）right deviation

【右翼】yòuyì（名）❶〈軍〉right wing; right flank ❷ the Right

【右邊】yòubiān（名）the right side; the right

司 sī Ⅰ（動）take charge of: ～綫員 linesman Ⅱ（名）❶ department (in a ministry) ❷（Sī）a surname

【司令】sīlìng（名）commander

【司法】sīfǎ（名）justice; judicature: ～部長 Minister of Justice

【司空見慣】sī kōng jiàn guàn〈成〉no rare occurrence; familiar sight: 這些事現在已是～了。Such things are no rare occurrences nowadays.

【司馬】Sīmǎ（名）a surname

【司徒】Sītú（名）a surname

【司務長】sīwùzhǎng（名）❶ mess officer ❷ company quartermaster

【司儀】sīyí（名）master of ceremonies

【司機】sījī（名）driver; chauffeur

【司爐】sīlú（名）stoker

召 zhào（動）assemble; convene; summon

【召之即來】zhào zhī jí lái〈成〉assemble at the first call; be at sb.'s beck and call

【召回】zhàohuí（動）recall; call back

【召見】zhàojiàn（動）❶ call in (a subordinate) ❷〈外〉summon (an envoy) to an interview

【召喚】zhàohuàn（動）call; summon

【召集】zhàojí（動）call together; assemble; convene: 把村民們一～在 一起 call all the villagers together

【召開】zhàokāi（動）convene; hold (a meeting)

叮 dīng（動）❶（of mosquitos, etc.）bite ❷ press sb. for an answer

【叮嚀】dīngníng (動) give repeated exhortations

【叮囑】dīngzhǔ (動) urge time and again

叩 kòu (動)❶ knock (at the door, etc.) ❷ kowtow

【叩頭】kòutóu (動) kowtow

另 lìng (形) other; another: ～有高就 have another and better appointment

【另外】lìngwài Ⅰ (副) moreover; besides: 我借了兩本小說，～還有一本雜誌。I borrowed two novels and a magazine as well. Ⅱ (形) other; another: ～找個時間再商量 find time to talk the matter over again

【另起爐灶】lìng qǐ lú zào 〈成〉❶ start anew ❷ go one's own way

【另眼相看】lìng yǎn xiāng kàn 〈成〉 see sb. in a new light; treat sb. with special favour

【另請高明】lìng qǐng gāo míng 〈成〉 seek the counsel of a better qualified person

叨 dāo
see also tāo

【叨叨】dāodao (動) talk endlessly

叨 tāo (動) get (benefit): ～光 much obliged to you for your kindness
see also dāo

叼 diāo (動) hold in the mouth

叫 jiào Ⅰ (動)❶ shout; cry: 大聲～ shout loudly ❷ call; greet: 把他們都～到這裏來。Ask them in. ❸

name; give a name to ❹ summon; send for; hire (a taxi, etc.); order (dishes, etc.): 快去～大夫! Send for the doctor at once! ❺ ask (sb. to do sth.); tell (sb. to do sth.): ～他走開。Tell him to get away. ❻ allow; let: 別～他來。Don't let him come here. ❼ be: 那真～好! That is really wonderful! Ⅱ (介) [used in a passive construction to introduce the agent] by: ～風颳跑了 be blown away by the wind

【叫好】jiàohǎo (動) shout brave; give cheers

【叫屈】jiàoqū (動) cry out against an injustice

【叫花子】jiàohuāzi (名) 〈口〉 beggar

【叫苦】jiàokǔ (動) complain; grumble; air one's grievances

【叫座兒】jiàozuòr (動) be a box-office success

【叫喊】jiàohǎn (動) cry; yell; shout

【叫喚】jiàohuàn (動) yell; cry out

【叫賣】jiàomài (動) hawk one's wares

【叫醒】jiàoxǐng (動) wake sb. up

【叫嚷】jiàorǎng (動) shout; yell

【叫囂】jiàoxiāo (動) 〈貶〉 clamour; raise a hullabaloo

叱 chì (動) bawl; rebuke

【叱吒風雲】chì zhà fēng yún 〈成〉 all-conquering; all-powerful

【叱責】chìzé (動) upbraid; scold

叭 bā (象) sharp cracking sound: ～的一聲折斷了。It broke with a snap.

【叭兒狗(巴兒狗)】bārgǒu (名)❶ pekingese; lapdog ❷ flatterer

史 shǐ (名) ❶ history ❷ (Shǐ) a surname

【史册】shǐcè (名) history book; annals: 载入～ be recorded in the annals of history; go down in history

【史前】shǐqián (形) before recorded history; prehistoric

【史书】shǐshū (史籍 shǐjí) (名) history; annals

【史料】shǐliào (名) historical data

【史无前例】shǐ wú qián lì 〈成〉 unprecedented (in history)

【史诗】shǐshī (名) epic (poem)

【史实】shǐshí (名) historical facts

【史学】shǐxué (名) history; historical studies

句 jù I (名) 〈语〉 sentence: 词～ wording II (量): 一～话也听不进 refuse to listen to a single word of advice

【句子】jùzi (名) 〈语〉 sentence

【句型】jùxíng (名) 〈语〉 sentence pattern

【句号】jùhào (名) 〈语〉 full stop; period

吉 jí I (形) lucky; auspicious; fortunate: 在～庆的日子里 in the auspicious days II (名) ❶ good luck: 逢凶化～ turn misfortune into a blessing ❷ (Jí) short for Jilin (Province)

【吉卜赛人】Jíbǔsàirén (名) Gypsy

【吉凶未卜】jí xiōng wèi bǔ 〈成〉 the fate hangs in the balance

【吉他】jítā (名) guitar

【吉布提】Jíbùtí (名) Djibouti: ～人 Djiboutian

【吉兆】jízhào (名) good omen; lucky sign

【吉利】jílì (形) lucky; propitious

【吉祥】jíxiáng (形) lucky; auspicious: ～物 mascot

【吉普车】jípǔchē (名) jeep

吏 lì (名) official

吁 xū (动) sigh: 气喘～～ be out of breath

吐 tǔ (动) ❶ spit: ～沫 spit ❷ put out: ～舌头 stick out one's tongue ❸ tell; speak see also tù

【吐诉】tǔsù (动) tell; pour out; pour forth

【吐穗儿】tǔsuìr (动) 〈农〉 ear up

【吐露】tǔlù (动) reveal: ～实情 tell the truth

吐 tù (动) ❶ vomit: ～血 spit blood ❷ disgorge; surrender see also tǔ

【吐沫】tùmo (名) saliva; spittle

同 tóng I (形) same: ～岁 of the same age / ～辈 of the same generation / ～姓 have the same surname; be one's namesake II (副) together: 有福～享, 有难～当 share joys and sorrows; stick together through thick and thin III (介) ❶ together with: 我～你一起唱。 Let me join you in singing. ❷ [used to introduce a comparison]: 他的脾气～我们有些不一样。 He is somewhat different from us in temperament.

【同一】tóngyī (形) one and the same; identical

【同上】tóngshàng (名) ditto; ibid.; *idem*

【同工同酬】tóng gōng tóng chóu 〈成〉

equal pay for equal work

【同仁】tóngrén（名）colleague; fellow member (of an organization)

【同心】tóngxīn（动）be at one: ～协力 work in unison; act in concert

【同化】tónghuà（动）assimilate

【同甘共苦】tóng gān gòng kǔ〈成〉share joys and sorrows; share weal and woe

【同名】tóngmíng（动）share the same name or title; be one's namesake

【同行】tóngxíng（动）travel together

【同行】tóngháng Ⅰ（形）in the same line; of the same occupation Ⅱ（名）person of the same trade

【同伴】tóngbàn（名）mate; companion

【同志】tóngzhì（名）comrade

【同位素】tóngwèisù（名）〈化〉isotope

【同位语】tóngwèiyǔ（名）〈语〉appositive

【同床异梦】tóng chuáng yì mèng〈成〉sleep in one bed but dream different dreams; be strange bedfellows

【同房】tóngfáng（动）〈婉〉（man and wife) make love; have sex

【同居】tóngjū（动）cohabit; live together

【同事】tóngshì（名）colleague

【同性】tóngxìng（形）❶ of the same sex: ～恋 homosexuality ❷ of the same nature

【同宗】tóngzōng（名）have a common ancestor; be of the same clan

【同胞】tóngbāo Ⅰ（形）born of the same parents Ⅱ（名）compatriot; fellow countryman

【同时】tóngshí（副）❶ at the same time; meanwhile ❷ moreover; besides

【同案犯】tóng'ànfàn（名）partner in a crime; accomplice

【同情】tóngqíng（动）sympathize (with sb.): 對他的不幸遭遇表示～ express sympathy for his misfortune

【同鄉】tóngxiāng（名）person from the same village, town, county or province; fellow townsman; fellow provincial

【同等】tóngděng（形）of the same rank or status; equal: ～學力 with identical educational level

【同期】tóngqī（名）corresponding period: 達到去年～的水平 reach the same level as in the same period of last year

【同感】tónggǎn（名）same feeling; similar impression

【同盟】tóngméng（名）alliance; coalition; league: 結成軍事～ from a military aliance / 攻守～ agreement between culprits to shield each other

【同意】tóngyì（动）agree; approve; assent (to)

【同義詞】tóngyìcí（名）〈语〉synonym

【同路】tónglù（动）take the same road: ～人 fellow traveller

【同夥】tónghuǒ（名）partner; associate; confederate

【同樣】tóngyàng Ⅰ（形）same; similar; identical Ⅱ（副）alike; likewise

【同謀】tóngmóu Ⅰ（动）conspire with sb. Ⅱ（名）conspirator; accomplice

【同學】tóngxué Ⅰ（动）study in the same school Ⅱ（名）schoolmate: 同班～ classmate

【同聲傳譯】tóngshēng chuányì（名）

simultaneous interpretation

【同歸於盡】tóng guī yú jìn〈成〉perish together

吊 diào（動）❶ hang; suspend ❷ lift or lower with a rope ❸ revoke

【吊死】diàosǐ（動）hang by the neck; hang: 他～了。He hanged himself.

【吊車】diàochē（名）〈機〉crane

【吊銷】diàoxiāo（動）revoke: ～他的駕駛執照 revoke his driving licence

【吊燈】diàodēng（名）pendant lamp

【吊橋】diàoqiáo（名）drawbridge; suspension bridge

【吊環】diàohuán（名）〈體〉swinging rings

吃 chī（動）❶ eat: ～了嗎?（a daily greeting）Have you eaten?（How are you?）❷ eat at: ～食堂 have one's meals in the canteen ❸ live on: ～民脂民膏 live on the flesh and blood of the people ❹ wipe out: ～掉一個車（in chess）take off a castle ❺ exhaust; be a strain: ～不住勁 cannot stand the strain ❻ absorb ❼ suffer; sustain: ～一拳 get a blow

【吃一塹，長一智】chī yī qiàn, zhǎng yī zhì〈成〉a fall into the pit, a gain in your wit

【吃力】chīlì（形）laboured; strenuous: 他呼吸很～。He is breathing with difficulty. / 工作很～。The work is strenuous.

【吃大鍋飯】chī dàguōfàn（動）everyone eats from the same big pot (as opposed to better pay for better work)

【吃不消】chī bu xiāo（動）cannot

endure: 長途跋涉她～。She cannot endure the hardship of a long journey.

【吃不開】chī bu kāi（動）be unpopular; get nowhere: 這種自吹自擂的話是～的。People won't swallow such boastful remarks.

【吃白食】chī báishí（動）eat at others' expense

【吃老本】chī lǎoběn（動）live on one's past gains; rest on one's laurels

【吃香】chīxiāng（動）〈口〉be popular; be in great demand

【吃重】chīzhòng（形）strenuous; arduous

【吃苦】chīkǔ（動）endure hardships

【吃苦頭】chīkǔtóu（動）suffer: 不吸取教訓就要～。You are bound to suffer for it if you don't take warning from your experience.

【吃透】chītòu（動）have a thorough grasp (understanding) of

【吃現成飯】chī xiànchéngfàn（動）enjoy the fruits of other people's labour

【吃得消】chī de xiāo（動）can stand (exertion, hardship, etc.)

【吃得開】chī de kāi（動）be popular

【吃軟不吃硬】chī ruǎn bù chī yìng〈口〉yield to soft tactics but can withstand high-handed pressure

【吃飯】chīfàn（動）❶ have a meal ❷ make a living: 靠打獵～ make a living by hunting

【吃喝玩樂】chī hē wán lè（動）eat, drink and be merry; seek pleasure

【吃裏爬外】chī lǐ pá wài〈成〉benefit a rival group at the expense of one's own

【吃緊】chījǐn（形）pressing; tense;

critical: 形势～。The situation is tense.

【吃醋】chīcù (动) be jealous

【吃亏】chīkuī (动) ❶ suffer a loss ❷ be at a disadvantage: ～在技术落后 be at a disadvantage because of out-dated technology

【吃惊】chījīng (动) be surprised; be startled: 大吃一惊 be greatly surprised

吆 yāo

【吆喝】yāohe (动) cry; shout; yell

合 hé

合 hé I (动) ❶ close; shut: ～拢 converge ❷ join; combine: ～力 join forces ❸ suit; agree: 正～我意。Your wishes are mine. ❹ be equal to; add up to: 费用一～一百圆。The expenses total 100 *yuan*. II (形) whole: ～村居民 the inhabitants of the entire village

【合口】hékǒu (动) ❶ (of a wound) heal up ❷ (of food) be to one's taste

【合乎】héhū (动) correspond to; accord with; tally with: ～价值规律 conform to the law of values

【合伙】héhuǒ (动) enter into partnership

【合同】hétong (名) contract: ～工 contract worker

【合同制】hétongzhì (名) contract system

【合成】héchéng (动) compose; compound: ～橡胶 synthetic rubber

【合成词】héchéngcí (名)〈语〉compound word

【合作】hézuò (动) cooperate; collaborate

【合身】héshēn (动) (of clothes) fit

【合并】hébìng (动) merge; amalgamate

【合金】héjīn (名) alloy: ～钢 alloy steel

【合法】héfǎ (形) legal; lawful; legitimate: ～权益 legitimate rights and interests

【合拍】hépāi (动) [oft. used metaphorically] beat in time: 与时代～ be in keeping with the times

【合计】héjì (动) amount to; add up to; total

【合计】héji (动) ❶ think over; figure out ❷ consult

【合格】hégé (形) qualified; up to standard: ～产品 standard product

【合唱】héchàng (名) chorus: ～团 chorus

【合理】hélǐ (形) rational; reasonable

【合情合理】hé qíng hé lǐ (形) fair and reasonable

【合群】héqún (动) be gregarious; be sociable

【合意】héyì (动) suit; be to one's liking

【合资企业】hézī qǐyè (名) joint venture

【合适】héshì (形) suitable; appropriate

【合算】hésuàn (形) worthwhile: 这不～。This doesn't pay.

【合影】héyǐng I (名) group photo II (动) have a group picture taken

【合剂】héjì (名)〈药〉mixture

【合谋】hémóu I (动) conspire; plot together II (名) conspiracy

名 míng

名 míng I (名) ❶ first name ❷ name; title ❸ fame; reputation II (形) famous; well-known: ～作家 famous writer III (量) [of persons]: 十～运动员 ten athletes

【名人】míngrén（名）celebrity; well-known figure: ～錄 who's who

【名下】míngxià（副）under sb.'s name; belonging to: 把成績全記在一個人～ claim all credit for one single individual

【名手】míngshǒu（名）celebrated artist; masterhand; ace player

【名不副實】míng bù fù shí〈成〉not be worthy of one's title; not deserve the high reputation one enjoys

【名不虛傳】míng bù xū chuán〈成〉fully deserve the high reputation one enjoys

【名片】míngpiàn（名）visiting card; calling card

【名册】míngcè（名）roll; register

【名目】míngmù（名）items; names of things

【名正言順】míng zhèng yán shùn〈成〉be appropriate and justified

【名字】míngzì（名）❶ name ❷ given name; first name

【名次】míngcì（名）position in a name list; place in a competition

【名列前茅】míng liè qián máo〈成〉be at the top of the list of successful examinees; come out at the top

【名存實亡】míng cún shí wáng〈成〉be practically nonexistent except in name; exist only in name

【名利】mínglì（名）fame and wealth: 不計～ have no thought either for fame or personal gain

【名言】míngyán（名）famous saying

【名家】míngjiā（名）celebrated master: ～之作 the work of a master

【名流】míngliú（名）distinguished figures; luminaries

【名氣】míngqì（名）fame; reputation: 極有～的人 a man of the highest credit / 這家報紙～不大 This newspaper is not so well-known.

【名產】míngchǎn（名）famous product

【名堂】míngtang（名）❶ variety; item: 他們的晚會準有不少～。They will offer a variety of items at the evening party. ❷ achievement; result: 他們調查了三天，一點～也沒有。They had no findings after three days of investigation. ❸ reason: 他一言不發，這裏面一定有～。There must be some reason for his silence.

【名望】míngwàng（名）good reputation; prestige

【名副其實】míng fù qí shí〈成〉one's reputation is justified by one's ability; be worthy of the name

【名詞】míngcí（名）❶〈語〉noun ❷ term

【名勝】míngshèng（名）scenic spot

【名單】míngdān（名）name list; roster

【名貴】míngguì（形）famous; rare: 一幅～的畫 a scroll of famous painting

【名揚四海】míng yáng sì hǎi〈成〉gain worldwide fame; be world-famous

【名著】míngzhù（名）masterpiece: 古典～ celebrated classics

【名牌】míngpái（名）❶ well-known brand: ～大學 prestigious university ❷ name-plate

【名落孫山】míng luò sūn shān〈成〉fail in a competitive examination

【名義】míngyì Ⅰ（名）name: 以國家的～ in the name of the state Ⅱ（形）nominal: ～上的國家元首

nominal head of state

【名稱】míngchēng（名）name; designation

【名數】míngshù（名）〈數〉concrete number

【名聲】míngshēng（名）reputation: 好～ a good reputation

【名額】míng'é（名）quota of people: 錄取～有限。The quota of people to be enrolled is limited.

【名譽】míngyù Ⅰ（名）honour; reputation Ⅱ（形）honorary: ～學位 honorary degree

各 gè（形）each; every; all: ～盡所能 from each according to his ability

【各人】gèrén（名）each one

【各不相謀】gè bù xiāng móu〈成〉they hold no consultation among themselves, each acting in his own way

【各自】gèzì（代）each; everyone: ～爲政。Each acts in his own way.

【各有千秋】gè yǒu qiān qiū〈成〉each has his strong points

【各式各樣】gè shì gè yàng（形）of various kinds

【各行各業】gè háng gè yè（名）all walks of life

【各行其是】gè xíng qí shì〈成〉each does what he considers proper (whether it is right or wrong)

【各別】gèbié（形）❶ different: ～處理 handle individual cases according to their peculiarities ❷ peculiar; unusual: 這人真～。This chap is really peculiar.

【各抒己見】gè shū jǐ jiàn〈成〉each voices his own views

【各奔前程】gè bèn qián chéng〈成〉

each follows the course of his own; each goes his own way

【各界】gèjiè（名）various circles: ～人士 public figures from various circles

【各個】gègè Ⅰ（形）each; every Ⅱ（副）one by one; separately; individually

【各級】gèjí（名）different levels: ～組織 organizations at different levels

【各執一詞】gè zhí yī cí〈成〉each sticks to his own version

【各得其所】gè dé qí suǒ〈成〉each is in his proper place; each has a role to play

向 xiàng Ⅰ（名）❶ direction: 雙～選擇 mutual selection; two-way selection ❷（Xiàng）a surname Ⅱ（動）❶ favour; side with: 她總是～着最小的孩子。She is always partial to her youngest child. ❷ face; turn towards: 葵花～陽。Sunflowers turn towards the sun. Ⅲ（介）towards: ～南走去 walk in the south direction / ～日本出口 export to Japan

【向上】xiàngshàng Ⅰ（動）make progress Ⅱ（副）upward; up

【向下】xiàngxià（副）downwards; down

【向心力】xiàngxīnlì（名）〈物〉centripetal force

【向日葵】xiàngrìkuí（名）sunflower

【向來】xiànglái（副）always; all along

【向往】xiàngwǎng（動）long for; look forward to: ～自由 long for freedom

【向前】xiàngqián（副）forward; ahead: ~ 看 look ahead; look to the future

【向陽】xiàngyáng (動) ❶ face the sun ❷ (of a house) face south; have a southern exposure

【向導】xiàngdǎo (名) guide

后 hòu (名) queen; empress

吝 lìn (形) stingy

【吝惜】lìnxī (動) stint; begrudge: 不一力量地幫助別人 spare no efforts to help others

【吝嗇】lìnsè (形) stingy; close-fisted

【吝嗇鬼】lìnsèguǐ (名) miser; niggard

吞 tūn (動) ❶ swallow; gulp: 狼～虎咽 wolf down; gobble up ❷ annex; take possession of: 侵～公款 embezzle public funds

【吞吐】tūntǔ (動) swallow and spit; take in and send away; handle: 港口的～量是多少? What's the handling capacity of the port?

【吞沒】tūnmò (動) ❶ embezzle ❷ engulf

【吞吞吐吐】tūn tūn tǔ tǔ〈成〉speak hesitantly; hem and haw

【吞併】tūnbìng (動) annex; incorporate (a country, business, etc.)

【吞食】tūnshí (動) eat; devour

【吞噬】tūnshì (動) swallow; engulf

否 fǒu I (動) deny; say no II (連) whether; if: 我不知他是～能來。I don't know whether he will be able to come.

【否決】fǒujué (動) reject; veto

【否決權】fǒujuéquán (名) veto power

【否定】fǒudìng (動) negate

【否則】fǒuzé (連) otherwise

【否認】fǒurèn (名) deny

君 jūn (名) ❶ monarch; sovereign ❷ (polite form of address for a man) gentleman; you: 祝～早日康復。Wish you a speedy recovery.

【君子】jūnzǐ (名) noble man; gentleman

【君子協定】jūn zǐ xié dìng〈成〉gentlemen's agreement

【君王】jūnwáng (名) king; monarch

【君主】jūnzhǔ (名) monarch

【君權】jūnquán (名) sovereignty; monarchical power

吭 háng (名) throat: 引～高歌 sing lustily
see also kēng

吭 kēng (動) speak; utter: 他連～都不一一聲。He didn't even utter a word.
see also háng

【吭聲】kēngshēng (吭 氣 kēngqì) (動) [often used in the negative] say a word: 他受了很多累,可是從來不～。He never complained even though he had gone through so much.

呆 ái (形) [used only in the expression 呆板] rigid; stiff
see also dāi

【呆板】áibǎn (形) stiff; rigid; inflexible: ～的規定 rigid regulation

呆 dāi (形) ❶ foolish; slow-witted ❷ dumb-struck: 兩眼發～ have a vacant look
see also ái

【呆若木鷄】dāi ruò mù jī〈成〉be

struck dumb; be utterly petrified

【呆滞】dāizhì Ⅰ (形) dull; lifeless Ⅱ (动) stagnate: 资金~。Capital lies idle.

呀 yā Ⅰ (叹) ah; oh: ~, 天快亮了。Oh, day is breaking. Ⅱ (象) creak

吠 fèi (动) bark; yap

呃 è

【呃逆】ènì (名) 〈医〉hiccup

吧 bā (象) ❶ sound of snapping: ~的一声, 树枝折断了。The branch snapped. ❷ puff (sound of puffing at a pipe, etc.)

see also ba

【吧嗒】bādā (动) smack: ~着嘴 smack one's lips

【吧嗒】bādā (象) sound of smacking

吧 ba (助) ❶ [used at the end of a sentence to indicate agreement or approval]: 好, 我們等着瞧~。All right, we'll wait and see. ❷ [used at the end of a sentence to indicate doubt, hesitation or conjecture]: 這樣不行~? It won't do, will it? ❸ [used at the end of a sentence to indicate suggestion, request or command]: 坐下~。Do sit down! ❹ [used to indicate a pause implying an alternative supposition, often in a dilemma]: 把消息告訴他~, 不好; 不告訴他~, 他又會不高興的。It's no good breaking the news to him now; but if we don't, he will be displeased.

see also bā

吼 hǒu (动) roar; howl; bellow: 寒風怒~。The cold wind is roaring.

呐 nà

【呐喊】nàhǎn (动) shout; cry out

吵 chǎo

see also chǎo

【吵吵】chāochao (动) make a lot of noise; make a row

吵 chǎo (动) ❶ make a noise: 大~大閙 make a scene ❷ quarrel: 同他~翻天 have a terrible row with him

see also chāo

【吵架】chǎojià (动) quarrel; row: 跟人~ quarrel with sb.

【吵閙】chǎonào Ⅰ (动) ❶ pick up a row ❷ disturb others with noise Ⅱ (形) noisy

【吵嘴】chǎozuǐ (动) quarrel; squabble

【吵嚷】chǎorǎng (动) clamour; make a racket

吴 Wú (名) a surname

吟 yín (动) sing; recite

【吟咏】yínyǒng (动) recite rhythmically

【吟詩】yínshī (动) recite a poem

【吟誦】yínsòng (动) chant; recite

吩 fēn

【吩咐】fēnfu (动) instruct; order

呈 chéng Ⅰ (动) ❶ appear; assume: ~綠色 be green in colour ❷ submit (to a superior) Ⅱ (名) document submitted to a superior; petition; memorial: 辭~ letter of resignation

【呈現】chéngxiàn (动) show; appear: 雨後天空又~出一片蔚藍

色。The rain over, the sky turned a bright blue again.

【呈報】 chéngbào（動）submit a report (to a superior)

【呈遞】 chéngdì（動）present; submit

吸

xī（動）❶ breathe in; inhale: ～口氣 take a breath ❷ absorb; assimilate ❸ attract; draw

【吸力】 xīlì（名）suction; attraction

【吸引】 xīyǐn（動）attract; draw: ～大量觀眾 attract a large audience

【吸引力】 xīyǐnlì（名）force of attraction; attraction: 動畫片對孩子們富有～。Cartoons have a strong appeal for children.

【吸奶器】 xīnǎiqì（名）breast pump

【吸收】 xīshōu（動）❶ absorb; suck up: ～外資 absorb foreign capital ❷ recruit; enrol: ～新會員 admit new members

【吸血鬼】 xīxuèguǐ（名）blood-sucker; vampire

【吸附】 xīfù（名）absorption

【吸取】 xīqǔ（動）absorb; learn: ～某人的經驗 learn from sb.'s experience / ～精神力量 draw moral strength

【吸毒】 xīdú（動）take drugs: ～者 drug addict

【吸煙】 xīyān（動）smoke

【吸塵器】 xīchénqì（名）dust catcher; vacuum cleaner

【吸熱】 xīrè（名）heat absorption

【吸墨紙】 xīmòzhǐ（名）blotting paper

【吸聲】 xīshēng（名）sound absorption

【吸蟲】 xīchóng（名）fluke

【吸鐵石】 xītiěshí（名）magnet

吹

chuī（動）❶ blow: 把火柴～滅 blow out a match ❷ play (a wind instrument) ❸ (of wind, etc.) lash; pound: 風～雨打 be buffeted by wind and rain; be weather-beaten ❹ boast: ～得天花亂墜 give a fantastic account of sth. ❺〈口〉break off; come to nothing: 計劃告～。The plan fell flop.

【吹牛】 chuīniú（動）boast; brag: ～拍馬 boast and flatter

【吹毛求疵】 chuī máo qiú cī〈成〉be fault-finding; be nit-picking; pick holes

【吹灰之力】 chuī huī zhī lì〈成〉very small effort: 不費～ as easy as blowing off dust; require very little effort

【吹吹打打】 chuī chuī dǎ dǎ（動）perform with wind and percussion instruments

【吹吹拍拍】 chuī chuī pāi pāi〈成〉boasting and toadying

【吹拂】 chuīfú（動）(of a breeze) brush; flick off

【吹風】 chuīfēng（動）❶ be exposed to the wind ❷ dry (hair, etc.) with a blower ❸〈口〉brief on inside information

【吹奏】 chuīzòu（動）play (a wind instrument): ～樂 wind music; band music

【吹捧】 chuīpěng（動）flatter; extol profusely

【吹鼓手】 chuīgǔshǒu（名）❶ trumpeter ❷ eulogist

【吹噓】 chuīxū（動）boast of; brag about

吻

wěn（動）kiss

【吻合】 wěnhé（動）coincide; tally

with

呂 Lǚ (名) a surname

吮 shǔn (动) suck

【吮吸】shǔnxī (动) suck

含 hán (动) ❶ keep (sth.) in the mouth for a while ❷ contain: ~泪 with eyes misting over with tears ❸ nurse; harbour: ~怨 nurse a grievance

【含血喷人】hán xuè pēn rén〈成〉attack sb. viciously; spit poison

【含辛茹苦】hán xīn rú kǔ〈成〉undergo great hardships

【含沙射影】hán shā shè yǐng〈成〉insinuate

【含苞】hánbāo (动)〈书〉be in bud

【含垢忍辱】hán gòu rěn rǔ〈成〉suffer deep humiliation

【含笑】hánxiào (副) with a smile

【含冤】hányuān (动) suffer a gross injustice

【含量】hánliàng (名) content

【含义】hányì (名) meaning; implication

【含蓄】hánxù (形) ❶ implicit; veiled ❷ reserved

【含糊】(含胡 hánhu) (形) ❶ ambiguous; vague: ~其辞 speak in vague terms ❷ careless: 一点也不能~ call for the closest attention

告 gào (动) ❶ tell; inform: 奔走相~ run around passing on news to one another ❷ accuse; sue ❸ ask for; request: ~贷 ask for a loan ❹ declare; announce

【告示】gàoshi (名) public notice; bulletin

【告别】gàobié (动) take leave; say goodbye: ~茶会 farewell tea-party

【告知】gàozhī (动) inform; notify

【告状】gàozhuàng (动) ❶ sue ❷ lodge a complaint against

【告急】gàojí (动) report an emergency and ask for help

【告假】gàojià (动) ask for leave

【告捷】gàojié (动) ❶ win victory ❷ report a victory

【告密】gàomì (动) inform against sb.: ~者 informer

【告终】gàozhōng (动) end up: 以失败~ end up in defeat

【告发】gàofā (动) inform against or report (an offender to the police, law court or government)

【告诉】gàosù (动) tell; let know; inform

【告诫】gàojiè (动) exhort; warn

【告辞】gàocí (动) take leave (of the host) (by the guest)

【告警】gàojǐng (动) report an emergency and ask for help or increased vigilance

【告饶】gàoráo (动) beg for mercy; ask to be forgiven (for one's offence)

咏 yǒng (动) ❶ sing; chant; recite: 歌~ singing ❷ narrate in verse

【咏叹】yǒngtàn (动) chant; sing: 反复~ chant the same lines again and again

【咏赞】yǒngzàn (动) praise; eulogize

味 wèi I (名) ❶ taste; flavour: 有酸~ have a sour taste ❷ smell; scent; odour: 有鱼腥~ smell of fish; fishy ❸ interest: 听得津津有~ listen with great interest II (量)

〈中藥〉ingredient（of a prescription）：三～藥 three ingredients of herbal medicine

【味同嚼蠟】wèi tóng jiáo là〈成〉be dry and tasteless; be insipid

【味道】wèidao（名）taste：這種咖啡～很好。This coffee tastes good.

【味精】wèijīng（名）MSG; gourmet powder; monosodium glutamate

【味覺】wèijué（名）sense of taste

呵 hē（動）❶ scold; rebuke ❷ exhale

【呵欠】hēqiàn（名）yawn

【呵斥】hēchì（動）rebuke; scold

【呵呵】hēhē（象）：～大笑 laugh heartily

咕 gū（象）（of hens, etc.）cluck;（of turtle-doves, etc.）coo

嗬 zā（動）❶ click one's tongue ❷ sip; suck：～一口白蘭地酒 take a sip of brandy ❸ enjoy slowly; savour

【嗬嘴】zāzuǐ（動）click one's tongue to express admiration or surprise

呸 pēi（嘆）bah; pooh：～! 諒你也不敢。Bah! I dare you to.

呢 ne（助）❶ [used at the end of an interrogative sentence]：他爲什麼不來～? Why didn't he come? ❷ [used at the end of a statement to give emphasis]：八點鐘纔開始～。It will not begin till eight o'clock. ❸ [used to indicate that the action is in progress]：他在工作～。He is working. ❹ [used to make a pause within a sentence]：現在～, 跟過去大不一樣了。Nowadays, things are quite different.

see also ní

呢 ní（名）woollen cloth

see also ne

【呢子】nízi（名）woollen cloth

【呢喃】nínán（名）（of swallows）twittering

【呢絨】níróng（名）woollen fabric

咖 gā

see also kā

【咖喱】gālí（名）curry

咖 kā

see also gā

【咖啡】kāfēi（名）coffee：牛奶～ white coffee / 煮～ make coffee

【咖啡因】kāfēiyīn（咖啡鹼 kāfēijiǎn）（名）caffeine

【咖啡館】kāfēiguǎn（名）café

【咖啡過濾壺】kāfēi guòlǜhú（名）percolator

咔 kā

【咔嘰】kǎjī（名）〈紡〉khaki

咀 jǔ（動）❶ chew ❷ ruminate

【咀嚼】jǔjué（動）❶ chew ❷ ponder; ruminate（over）

呷 xiā（動）sip：～一口酒 take a sip of wine

呻 shēn

【呻吟】shēnyín（動）groan; moan

咒 zhòu Ⅰ（名）incantation Ⅱ（動）curse; abuse

【咒罵】zhòumà（動）curse; abuse; damn

咄 duō

【咄咄怪事】duō duō guài shì〈成〉gross absurdity

【咄咄逼人】duō duō bī rén (形) domineering; aggressive

呼 hū I (动) ❶ shout; cry out ❷ call: 一～百诺 have hundreds at one's beck and call ❸ breathe; exhale II (象) howl: 北风～～地吹。The north wind is howling.

【呼叫】hūjiào (动) call out; shout

【呼吸】hūxī I (动) breathe II (名) breath; respiration

【呼哨】hūshào (动) whistle

【呼救】hūjiù (动) call for help; signal SOS

【呼喊】hūhǎn (动) call out; shout

【呼唤】hūhuàn (动) call

【呼号】hūháo (动) cry; wail

【呼号】hūhào (名) call signal

【呼啸】hūxiào (动) howl; whistle

【呼应】hūyìng (动) echo each other's sentiment

【呼声】hūshēng (名) voice; call

【呼噜】hūlū (名)〈口〉snore

【呼吁】hūyù (动) appeal to; call on: ～书 appeal; petition

咋 zǎ (代)〈方〉how; why: ～办? What can we do?

咆 páo

【咆哮】páoxiào (动) roar: ～如雷 roar with anger

呱 gū (名)〈书〉cry of a baby
see also guā

【呱呱坠地】gū gū zhuì dì (动)(of a baby) be born into the world

呱 guā
see also gū

【呱呱】guāguā (象) sound made by ducks, frogs or crows; caw; croak

【呱嗒】guādā (象) clack; clatter

呦 yōu (叹) [used to indicate surprise]: ～! 出了什麼事? Why! What's happened?

命 mìng I (名) ❶ life: 丧～ lose one's life; die ❷ fate; fortune: 算～ tell sb.'s fortune / 宿～论 fatalism ❸ order; instruction: 奉～ follow instructions II (动) instruct; order: ～其早日返回 instruct sb. to return at an early date

【命中】mìngzhòng (动) hit the target

【命令】mìnglìng I (名) order; command II (动) order: ～部队撤退 order the troops to withdraw

【命名】mìngmíng (动) give a name to; name

【命在旦夕】mìng zài dàn xī〈成〉be on one's last legs; one's life hangs in the balance

【命脉】mìngmài (名) lifeline; lifeblood

【命案】mìng'àn (名) homicide; murder

【命根子】mìnggēnzi (名) lifeblood; one's most precious thing

【命途多舛】mìng tú duō chuǎn〈成〉one's life is full of setbacks and frustrations

【命笔】mìngbǐ (动) commit to paper; begin to write

【命运】mìngyùn (名) fate; destiny

【命题】mìngtí I (动) set the examination paper II (名) proposition

和 hé I (形) ❶ gentle; mild: ～风 gentle breeze ❷ harmonious; in amity: 兄弟～睦。The brothers live in peace. II (名) ❶ peace: 媾～

sign a peace treaty ❷ sum: 總~
sum total ❸ (Hé) a surname Ⅲ
(連) and Ⅳ(介) with; to: 你最好
~他通通气。You had better keep
him informed about it.

see also hè; huó; huò

【和平】hépíng（名）peace

【和平共处】hépíng gòngchǔ（名）
peaceful coexistence

【和好】héhǎo（動）restore friendly
relations

【和局】héjú（名）drawn game; tie;
draw

【和服】héfú（名）kimono

【和尚】héshang（名）Buddhist monk

【和事佬】héshìlǎo（名）peace-maker
(who usu. does not bother about the
question of right and wrong)

【和約】héyuē（名）peace treaty

【和衷共济】hé zhōng gòng jì〈成〉
work in unison to tide over difficulties

【和善】héshàn（形）kindly; genial

【和会】héhuì（名）peace conference

【和解】héjiě（動）be reconciled (after a quarrel)

【和睦】hémù（形）harmonious; ami-
cable: ~相處 live in harmony

【和暖】hénuǎn（形）warm

【和煦】héxù（形）nice and warm

【和畅】héchàng（形）(of wind) gentle and pleasant

【和谈】hétán（名）peace talks

【和盘托出】hé pán tuō chū〈成〉tell
the whole truth about sth.; make a
clean breast of sth.

【和谐】héxié（形）harmonious

【和颜悦色】hé yán yuè sè〈成〉look
kindly and amiable

【和蔼】hé'ǎi（形）kindly; affable

和 hè（動）❶ join in the singing:
一唱百~。A proposal attracts numerous supporters. ❷ compose a
poem in reply, using the same
rhyme sequence

see also hé; huó; huò

和 huó（動）mix (an ingredient)
with water, etc.: ~泥 mix clay
with water

see also hé; hè; huò

【和稀泥】huóxīní（動）try to plaster
over the differences at the expense
of principle

和 huò Ⅰ（動）mix; blend Ⅱ（量）
[used to indicate the frequency of
action]: 洗了兩~ have rinsed
(sth.) twice

see also hé; hè; huó

咎 jiù Ⅰ（名）blame: 他的失败不能
归~於他缺乏决心。His failure was
not to be attributed to his lack of determination. Ⅱ（動）censure; hold
(sb.) responsible: 既往不~ let's
forget about the past; forget and
forgive; let bygones be bygones

【咎由自取】jiù yóu zì qǔ〈成〉have
nobody but oneself to blame

周 zhōu Ⅰ（名）❶ circumference;
periphery: 學校四~都種着樹。
The school is surrounded by trees on
all sides. ❷ circle; circuit: 繞地球
一~ make a circuit of the earth ❸
week ❹〈電〉cycle ❺ (Zhōu) a
surname Ⅱ（形）❶ whole; all over:
~身濕透 be drenched to the skin
❷ thoughtful; considerate: 照顧不
~ not be properly attended to

【周末】zhōumò（名）weekend

【周年】zhōunián (名) anniversary

【周全】zhōuquán (形) comprehensive; thorough; complete

【周折】zhōuzhé (名) twists and turns; reverses: 經過最初階段的一番～,他的路子總走對。After the initial setbacks, he was on the right track.

【周波】zhōubō (名)〈電〉cycle

【周長】zhōucháng (名) perimeter; circumference

【周到】zhōudào (形) thoughtful; considerate

【周密】zhōumì (形) careful; circumspect: ～考慮 give careful thought to

【周旋】zhōuxuán (動) ❶ deal with (people): 與政敵～ have to contend with one's political opponents ❷ mix with other people; rub shoulders with: 作為一名記者,他得和各種人～。As a reporter, he rubs shoulders with all sorts of people.

【周報】zhōubào (周刊 zhōukān) (名) weekly

【周期】zhōuqī (名) period; cycle

【周遊】zhōuyóu (動) travel round; tour: ～世界 travel round the world

【周圍】zhōuwéi (副) around; round: 樓房～的草坪 the lawns around the buildings

【周詳】zhōuxiáng (形) circumspect and elaborate: 計劃～ carefully mapped out

【周歲】zhōusuì (名) one full year (of age): 這個女孩兩～了。The little girl is two years old.

【周濟】zhōujì (動) help out (the needy); give relief to

【周轉】zhōuzhuǎn (名)〈經〉turn-over: 資本～ turnover of capital

哀 āi I (名) ❶ sorrow ❷ mourning: 致～ pay one's respects to the deceased II (動) lament; feel sad for

【哀求】āiqiú (動) implore; beg piteously

【哀思】āisī (名) sad feelings; grief: 表達我們的～ express our grief

【哀怨】āiyuàn (形) plaintive

【哀悼】āidào I (動) mourn (the death of sb.) II (名) condolences: 表示～ express condolences

【哀痛】āitòng (形) profound grief; deep sorrow

【哀傷】āishāng (形) sad; grieved

【哀愁】āichóu (名) sorrow; sadness

【哀鳴】āimíng I (動) cry woefully II (名) sad cry

【哀歌】āigē (名) mournful song; dirge; elegy

【哀嘆】āitàn (動) lament; bewail

【哀憐】āilián (動) have compassion for (the misfortune of others)

【哀樂】āiyuè (名) funeral music

咨 zī (動) consult; take counsel

【咨文】zīwén (名) report by the head of government on state affairs

【咨詢】zīxún (動) seek advice from; consult: ～機構 advisory body

咬 yǎo (動) ❶ bite: ～一口蛋糕 take a bite of the cake ❷ accuse: 亂～好人 make random charges against innocent people ❸ pronounce: 他連個簡單的字都～不準。He cannot even pronounce a simple word correctly.

【咬文嚼字】yǎo wén jiáo zì〈成〉pay excessive attention to language details; be nitpicking about the choice of words

【咬牙切齒】yǎo yá qiè chǐ〈成〉grind one's teeth: 恨得～ gnash one's teeth in hatred

【咬耳朵】yǎo ěrduo（動）〈口〉whisper

【咬住】yǎozhù（動）❶ bite into ❷ refuse to let go: ～人家的錯誤不放 deliberately keep referring to sb.'s fault

【咬定】yǎodìng（動）insist; say sth. with certainty

【咬緊牙關】yǎojǐn yáguān（動）grit one's teeth

咳 hāi（嘆）[used to indicate warning, greeting, regret, surprise, etc]: ～,是你啊! Hey, it's you!
see also ké

咳 ké（動）cough
see also hāi

【咳嗽】késou（動）cough

咩 miē（象）baa; bleat

咪 mī

【咪咪】mīmī Ⅰ（象）mew; miaow Ⅱ（形）smiling: 笑～ smile genially; all smiles

咦 yí（嘆）well; why: ～,你怎麼了? Why, what's wrong with you?

哇 wā（象）sound of vomiting, crying, etc.

【哇啦】wālā（象）sound of confused voices made by a crowd

哎 āi（嘆）[used before a sentence to indicate commitment, surprise, discontent or regret] oh; hey; why

【哎呀】āiyā（嘆）❶ [used independently or before a sentence to express surprise] oh; dear me; my: ～,我忘了! Oh, dear, I forgot. ❷ [used before a sentence to indicate impatience or a mild criticism]: ～,真討厭! Oh, damn it!

【哎喲】āiyō（嘆）❶ [used in expressions of surprise] gosh ❷ [a cry of pain, distress] ow: ～,真冷! Gosh! It is freezing.

哄 hōng（名）hubbub; din: ～～ in a hubbub; noisily

【哄動】hōngdòng（動）cause a great sensation

【哄堂大笑】hōng táng dà xiào〈成〉all the people in the hall burst out laughing heartily

【哄傳】hōngchuán（動）(of rumours) spread far and wide

哄 hǒng（動）❶ fool; deceive; kid ❷ coax
see also hōng; hòng

【哄騙】hǒngpiàn（動）cheat; swindle; hoodwink

哄 hòng（名）uproar; disturbance: 起～ kick up a row
see also hōng; hǒng

哐 kuāng（象）loud clattering noise; crash: ～啷一聲,盤碗從桌上摔下去了。The dishes fell from the table with a clatter.

咧 liě（動）grin: ～嘴大笑 grin from ear to ear

品 pǐn Ⅰ（名）❶ article; goods: 紀念～ souvenir ❷ grade; class: 下～ low grade ❸ quality; character: ～學兼優 good both in character and at studies II (动) evaluate; sample

【品行】pǐnxíng (名) conduct; behaviour

【品性】pǐnxìng (名) moral character

【品级】pǐnjí (名) (of goods) grade; class

【品格】pǐngé (名) ❶ (of person) behaviour; character ❷ characteristic feature as regards artistic quality and style

【品脱】pǐntuō (名) pint

【品评】pǐnpíng (动) judge; appraise

【品尝】pǐncháng (动) taste; savour

【品种】pǐnzhǒng (名) ❶ breed; strain ❷ variety; assortment

【品貌】pǐnmào (名) ❶ appearance ❷ moral conduct and appearance

【品德】pǐndé (名) moral character; morality

【品质】pǐnzhì (名) ❶ (of a person) character; quality ❷ (of goods, etc.) quality

【品类】pǐnlèi (名) category; class

呲 cī (动) 〈口〉scold; give a dressing-down: 挨～(儿) get a scolding

咽 yān (名) pharynx; throat

【咽喉】yānhóu (名) ❶ throat: ～发炎 inflammation of the throat ❷ vital passage; key link: 两洋之间的～ the vital link between the two oceans

哈 hā I (动) exhale II (象) ha; ha-ha: ～～大笑 burst into loud laughter III (叹) [used to indicate satisfaction] ha; aha
see also hǎ

【哈欠】hāqian (名) yawn

【哈尼族】Hānízú (名) the Hani nationality

【哈哈镜】hāhājìng (名) distorting mirror

【哈腰】hāyāo (动) bend or bow

【哈尔滨】Hā'ěrbīn (名) Harbin (capital of Heilongjiang Province)

【哈萨克族】Hāsàkèzú (名) the Kazak nationality

哈 hǎ
see also hā

【哈巴狗】hǎbagǒu (名) pekinese (a small breed of pet dog)

哆 duō

【哆嗦】duōsuo (动) shiver; tremble

咯 gē
see also kǎ

【咯吱】gēzhī (象) creak

【咯咯】gēgē (象) cluck; chuckle; titter

【咯噔】gēdēng (象) click

咯 kǎ (动) cough up; spit: ～痰 cough up phlegm
see also gē

【咯血】kǎxiě I (动) spit blood II (名) 〈医〉haemoptysis

咱 zán (代) [including both the speaker and the person (persons) spoken to] we

【咱们】zánmen (代) [including the speaker and the person (persons) spoken to] we: ～走吧。Let's go.

咿 yī (象) squeak; creak

【咿呀】yīyā I (动) creak: 门一一声开了。The door opened with a creak. II (名) prattle; babble

哌 pài

【哌嗪】pàiqín (名) 〈化〉piperazine

哞 mōu (象) (cow's cry) moo; low

唐 Táng (名) a surname

【唐人街】Tángrénjiē (名) China Town

【唐三彩】tángsāncǎi (名) 〈工美〉 (replica of) tricolour glazed pottery of the Tang Dynasty

【唐突】tángtū (形) rude; brusque; abrupt

【唐詩】tángshī (名) Tang poetry; poetry of the Tang Dynasty

哥 gē (名) elder brother

【哥哥】gēge (名) elder brother

【哥特式】gētèshì (形) 〈建〉Gothic: ～建築 Gothic architecture

【哥倫比亞】Gēlúnbǐyà (名) Colombia: ～人 Colombian

【哥斯達黎加】Gēsīdálíjiā (名) Costa Rica: ～人 Costa Rican

哲 zhé (名) wise man; sage: 先～ the sages of old

【哲人】zhérén (名) sage; philosopher

【哲理】zhélǐ (名) philosophical theory

【哲學】zhéxué (名) philosophy

唇 chún (名) lip

【唇舌】chúnshé (名) talking: 大費 ～ take a great deal of persuading

【唇膏】chúngāo (名) lipstick

【唇齒相依】chún chǐ xiāng yī 〈成〉 be as close to each other as the lips and the teeth; be closely related and interdependent

唁 yàn (動) extend condolences

【唁函】yànhán (名) letter of condolence

【唁電】yàndiàn (名) telegram of condolence; message of condolence

哼 hēng (動) ❶ groan from pain; snort ❷ croon; hum: ～曲子 hum a tune

see also hng

哼 hng (嘆) [used to show displeasure or doubt] humph: ～, 你又遲到了。Humph, you're late again.

see also hēng

哮 xiào (動) ❶ wheeze ❷ roar

【哮喘】xiàochuǎn (名) asthma

哺 bǔ (動) nurse; feed (a baby)

【哺育】bǔyù (動) ❶ feed (an infant) ❷ nurture; foster

【哺乳】bǔrǔ (動) nurse; breast-feed; suckle

【哺乳動物】bǔrǔ dòngwù (名) mammal

【哺養】bǔyǎng (動) feed; rear

哽 gěng (動) choke

【哽咽】gěngyè (名) sob; choke with sobs

哪 nǎ (代) ❶ which: 兩部電影～部更好? Of the two films, which is better? ❷ any: 這些工具中一件都行。Any of these tools will do. ❸ [used in a rhetorical question]: 不努力～能成功? How can you win success without hard work?

【哪怕】nǎpà (連) even if; even though: ～你本領再大, 沒有羣眾的支持也不會成功。However capable you may be, you'll never succeed without popular support.

【哪些】nǎxiē (代) which; who; what: ～書? What books? / 他們中

~人參加了會議? Who among them attended the meeting?

【哪個】nǎgè (代) ❶ which: ~學校 which school ❷ who: ~是負責的? Who is in charge here?

【哪能】nǎnéng (副) how can: 他~那樣看待人呢? How can he treat people like that?

【哪裏】nǎli (副) ❶ where: 你去~? Where are you going? /他不管走到~,都帶着本雜誌。Wherever he goes, he has a magazine with him. ❷ [used in a rhetorical question to indicate negation]: 我~知道會趕上下雨。Little did I expect to run into a shower.

【哪樣】nǎyàng (代) what kind of; what: 你要~的鉛筆? What kind of pencil do you want?

唧 jī I (動) squirt; spout: ~了我一身水。I was squirted all over with water. II (象) chirp, whisper, etc.

【唧唧】jījī (象) ❶ chirp ❷ whisper: ~咕咕半天 talk in whispers for a long while

【唧筒】jītǒng (名) pump

哨 shào (名) ❶ sentry post; post: 觀察~ observation post ❷ whistle

【哨子】shàozi (名) whistle

【哨兵】shàobīng (名) sentry; sentinel

【哨所】shàosuǒ (名) sentry post; post

員 yuán I (名) ❶ person engaged in some field of activity: 司令~ commander / 服務~ attendant ❷ member: 會~ member of an association II (量) 運動場上的一一猛將 an ace atlhlete

【員工】yuángōng (名) staff members and workers

唄 bei (助) ❶ [used to indicate plain common sense]: 不懂,就好好學~。Well, if you don't know how to do it, start learning now. ❷ [used to indicate agreement with reluctance]: 想去就去~。Well, go if you like.

哩 li

【哩哩啦啦】līlīlālā 〈口〉 scattered; on and off: 會~地開了一個月。The meeting went on and off for a whole month.

哭 kū (動) weep; cry: ~鼻子 start snivelling

【哭泣】kūqì (動) shed silent tears; sob

【哭笑不得】kūxiào bude (動) find oneself caught in a ludicrously embarrassing situation; caught between laughter and tears

【哭哭啼啼】kūkutítí (動) wail endlessly; keep crying

【哭喪着臉】kūsāng zhe liǎn (動) pull a long face; look dismal

哦 ó (嘆) [used to indicate doubt]: ~,他來過? Oh, has he been here?
see also ò

哦 ò (嘆) [used to indicate understanding or realization]: ~,是你。Oh, it's you.
see also ó

唆 suō (動) instigate; incite: 教~犯 abettor

【唆使】suōshǐ (動) instigate; abet; incite

唉 ǎi（嘆）❶（a response to sb.'s call or request）yes; O.K. ❷ cry of distress
see also ài

【唉聲嘆氣】ài shēng tàn qì〈成〉heave sighs（of pain, regret, sorrow, etc.）

唉 ài Ⅰ（嘆）oh; alas（sigh of sadness, regret, distress or pity）: ～, 沒有希望了。Oh, it's hopeless! Ⅱ（象）sound of sighing; alas
see also āi

商 shāng Ⅰ（動）discuss; consult: 他們磋～了很久，但未能達成協議。They spent much time discussing the problem without reaching agreement. Ⅱ（名）❶ commerce; business: 與鄰國通～ do business with neighbouring countries ❷ merchant; businessman: 批發～ wholesale dealer ❸（數）quotient ❹（Shāng）a surname

【商人】shāngrén（名）businessman; merchant

【商行】shānghǎng（名）trading company; commercial firm

【商定】shāngdìng（動）agree on; settle through consultation or discussion

【商店】shāngdiàn（名）shop; store

【商界】shāngjiè（名）commercial circles

【商洽】shāngqià（動）take up（a matter）with sb.; consult with

【商亭】shāngtíng（名）stall; stand; kiosk

【商約】shāngyuē（名）commercial treaty

【商品】shāngpǐn（名）commodity; goods

【商品交易會】shāngpǐn jiāoyìhuì（名）trade fair

【商品經濟】shāngpǐn jīngjì（名）commodity economy: 計劃～ planned commodity economy

【商務】shāngwù（名）commercial affairs: ～簽證 business visa

【商船】shāngchuán（名）merchant ship; merchantman

【商販】shāngfàn（名）pedlar; small retailer

【商情】shāngqíng（名）market conditions

【商港】shānggǎng（名）commercial port

【商場】shāngchǎng（名）shopping mall; market; bazaar

【商隊】shāngduì（名）trade caravan

【商量】shāngliang（動）consult; discuss: 把這事和朋友們～一下 consult with one's friends about this matter

【商會】shānghuì（名）chamber of commerce

【商業】shāngyè（名）commerce; trade: ～區 business district; shopping centre

【商榷】shāngquè（商討 shāngtǎo）（動）discuss: 有事與你～ have something to discuss with you

【商標】shāngbiāo（名）trade mark

【商調】shāngdiào（動）arrange for a transfer

【商談】shāngtán（動）discuss; exchange views

【商議】shāngyì（動）confer; disucss

啟 qǐ（動）❶ open ❷ enlighten ❸ start; initiate

【啟示】qǐshì Ⅰ（動）enlighten Ⅱ（名）

revelation; enlightenment

【啓事】 qǐshì (名) notice; announcement

【啓封】 qǐfēng (動) ❶ unseal; break the seal ❷ open an envelop or wrapper

【啓航港】 qǐhánggǎng (名) port of embarkation

【啓發】 qǐfā (動) enlighten; inspire: 我從此書中得到許多~。 I am very much enlightened by this book.

【啓蒙】 qǐméng (動) ❶ teach beginners ❷ enlighten

【啓齒】 qǐchǐ (動) bring up a matter (usu. to ask a favour): 不便~ find it hard to bring up the matter

問 wèn (動) ❶ ask; inquire: ~東~西 ask all sorts of irrelevant questions; be inquisitive ❷ interrogate; examine: 審～囚犯 interrogate a prisoner ❸ pay attention to; show interest in: 從不過～ never bother about sth.

【問心有愧】 wèn xīn yǒu kuì 〈成〉 be conscience-stricken; feel guilty; have a guilty conscience

【問心無愧】 wèn xīn wú kuì 〈成〉 have a clear conscience

【問世】 wènshì (動) be published; come out

【問安】 wèn'ān (動) pay one's respects to (one's senior): 請代向他~。 Please send him my respects.

【問好】 wènhǎo (動) give one's regards to; give one's best wishes to

【問長問短】 wèn cháng wèn duǎn 〈成〉 inquire after sb. or sth. with real concern

【問津】 wènjīn (動) 〈書〉 inquire about: 無人~。 Nobody cares to ask about it.

【問候】 wènhòu (動) send one's regards (respects) to; greet

【問訊】 wènxùn (動) inquire; ask

【問訊處】 wènxùnchù (名) information desk; information office; inquiry office

【問答】 wèndá (名) questions and answers

【問道於盲】 wèn dào yú máng 〈成〉 take the blind as one's guide; ask the wrong person for help

【問寒問暖】 wèn hán wèn nuǎn 〈成〉 inquire after sb. affectionately

【問號】 wènhào (名) question mark

【問罪】 wènzuì (動) condemn; denounce; censure

【問題】 wèntí (名) ❶ question; problem: 緊急~ an urgent problem ❷ trouble: 他的肺出~了。 There's something wrong with his lungs. ❸ the point; the thing: ~不在這裏。 This is not the point.

【問題單】 wèntídān (名) questionnaire

啐 cuì (動) spit

啞 yǎ (形) ❶ dumb; mute: 聾~人 deafmute ❷ hoarse; husky: 哭~了嗓子 cry oneself hoarse

【啞口無言】 yǎ kǒu wú yán 〈成〉 be speechless; get tongue-tied

【啞吧】 yǎba (名) dumb person

【啞鈴】 yǎlíng (名) 〈體〉 dumb-bell

【啞嗓子】 yǎsǎngzi (名) husky voice; hoarse voice

【啞劇】 yǎjù (名) dumb show; mime

【啞謎】 yǎmí (名) puzzle; riddle

啦 la (助) [used at the end of a sentence to indicate exclamation, interrogation, etc]: 您回來~! So you have come back!

啪 pā (象) bang

【啪嗒】pādā (象) clatter; patter

啄 zhuó (動) peck

【啄木鳥】zhuómùniǎo (名) woodpecker

啜 chuò (動) sob

【啜泣】chuòqì (動) sob

啊 ā (嘆)(a cry of surprise or amazement) oh; ah: ~,多可愛的孩子! Oh, what a lovely child!
see also á; ǎ; à; a

啊 á (嘆) ❶ Pardon? ❷ [used at the beginning of a sentence to press for an answer]: ~,你到底喜歡不喜歡? Well, do you like it or not?
see also ā; ǎ; à; a

啊 ǎ (嘆)〈口〉[used at the beginning of a sentence to express doubt]: ~,你這話可當真? Do you really mean it?
see also ā; á; à; a

啊 à (嘆) ❶ [used to indicate commitment] yes: ~,我就來。Yes, I am coming. ❷ [used to denote sudden realization] oh: ~,原來如此! Oh, I see. ❸ [used to indicate admiration] oh: ~,真是美極了! Oh, how beautiful it is!
see also ā; á; ǎ; a

啊 a (助) ❶ [used at the end of a sentence to indicate surprise, admiration, warning, etc.]: 別上當~! Don't be taken in! ❷ 〈口〉[used before a pause to attract attention]:

他~,纏滿不在乎呢! Well, he couldn't care less!
see also ā; á; ǎ; à

唬 hǔ (動) bluff; intimidate

啃 kěn (動) ❶ gnaw; bite (at) constantly ❷ take pains to study: 這本書太難,~不動。The book is too difficult for me to understand even if I am prepared to put in a good deal of effort.

唱 chàng Ⅰ (動) ❶ sing ❷ call: ~名 call the roll Ⅱ (名) song; singing (in Chinese opera): 小~ ditty

【唱反調】chàng fǎndiào (動) sing a different tune

【唱片】chàngpiān (名) record; disc: 放~ play a record / 激光~ compact disc

【唱高調】chàng gāodiào (動) use high-sounding words

【唱對臺戲】chàng duìtáixì (動) put on a rival performance or show

【唱機】chàngjī (名) gramophone; phonograph; record player

【唱獨角戲】chàng dújiǎoxì (動) put on a one-man show; go it alone

【唱戲】chàngxì (動) become an actor or actress (in Beijing opera)

唸 niàn (動) ❶ read (aloud): ~報 read a newspaper ❷ study; attend school: ~大學 go to college; be in college

【唸叨】niàndao (動) talk about frequently: 他老~已去世的妻子。He is always talking about his deceased wife.

【唸珠】niànzhū (名)〈宗〉beads; rosary

【唸經】niànjīng (動) chant Buddhist

scriptures

哈 shǎ (代)〈方〉what: 你叫～? What's your name? / 你要～? What can I do for you?

唾 tuò Ⅰ (名) saliva Ⅱ (动) spit

【唾手可得】tuò shǒu kě dé〈成〉within easy reach

【唾沫】tuòmo (名) saliva; spittle

【唾液】tuòyè (名) saliva

【唾弃】tuòqì (动) forsake; reject; repudiate

【唾骂】tuòmà (动) curse vehemently; shout abuse at

唯 wéi (副) alone; only
see also wěi

【唯心主义】wéixīn zhǔyì (唯心論 wéixīnlùn) (名)〈哲〉idealism

【唯物主义】wéiwù zhǔyì (唯物論 wéiwùlùn) (名)〈哲〉materialism

【唯物辩证法】wéiwù biànzhèngfǎ (名)〈哲〉materialist dialectics

唯 wěi
see also wéi

【唯唯诺诺】wěi wěi nuò nuò〈成〉be a yes man; be subservient

啤 pí

【啤酒】píjiǔ (名) beer

售 shòu (动) sell: 零～ retail

【售货亭】shòuhuòtíng (名) kiosk

【售货员】shòuhuòyuán (名) shop assistant; salesman (saleswoman)

【售票员】shòupiàoyuán (名) ticket seller; booking-office clerk; box-office clerk; (bus) conductor

【售票处】shòupiàochù (名) ticket office; ticket window; booking office (at the railway station or a theatre)

善 shàn Ⅰ (形) ❶ good; kind: ～行 good conduct ❷ friendly: 親～ on friendly terms ❸ familiar: 面～ look familiar ❹ wise; fine: ～策 wise strategy Ⅱ (动) ❶ be good at: ～處難局 be a good trouble-shooter ❷ be apt to; be prone to: 多愁～感 sentimental / ～疑 suspicious ❸ do well: ～始～終 pursue a matter properly from start to finish Ⅲ (副) properly: ～自爲謀 be able to shift for oneself

【善心】shànxīn (名) kindness; mercy

【善本書】shànběnshū (名) valuable book; rare book

【善良】shànliáng (形) good and honest; kind-hearted

【善於】shànyú (动) be good at; be skilled in: ～處理這種事務 be adept at handling such matters

【善後】shànhòu (动) settle problems consequent upon an unfortunate event; smooth out the aftermath

【善終】shànzhōng (动) ❶ die a natural death ❷ end well

【善意】shànyì (名) good will

【善罷甘休】shàn bà gān xiū〈成〉[often used in negative sentences] be willing to let go or give up

喜 xǐ Ⅰ (动) ❶ be happy; be overjoyed: 聞過則～ be glad to have one's error pointed out ❷ be fond of; like: ～游泳 be keen on swimming Ⅱ (名) ❶ happy event: 雙～臨門 be blessed with double happiness ❷ pregnancy: 她有～了。She's expecting.

【喜不自勝】xǐ bù zì shèng〈成〉be beside oneself with joy

【喜出望外】xǐ chū wàng wài〈成〉be overjoyed; be pleasantly surprised

【喜好】xǐhào〈動〉like; love

【喜色】xǐsè〈名〉joyous expression: 滿臉 ~ appear happy and contented

【喜形於色】xǐ xíng yú sè〈成〉with joy written on one's face; be visibly pleased

【喜事】xǐshì〈名〉❶ happy event ❷ wedding

【喜怒無常】xǐ nù wú cháng〈成〉have alternate fits of joy and anger; be subject to changing moods; be moody and unpredictable

【喜訊】xǐxùn〈名〉happy news

【喜悅】xǐyuè〈形〉happy; delighted

【喜氣洋洋】xǐ qì yáng yáng〈成〉beaming with joy

【喜笑顏開】xǐ xiào yán kāi〈成〉be all smiles; beam with joy

【喜報】xǐbào〈名〉report of good news

【喜滋滋】xǐzīzī〈動〉be pleased; be self-contented

【喜新厭舊】xǐ xīn yàn jiù〈成〉be fond of sth. new and tired of sth. old; be fickle in love

【喜愛】xǐ'ài〈動〉like: ~ 運動 be keen on sports

【喜聞樂見】xǐ wén lè jiàn〈成〉be delighted to see and hear; enjoy: 這類電視節目是大家～的。Everybody enjoys such TV programmes.

【喜劇】xǐjù〈名〉comedy

【喜慶】xǐqìng I〈形〉happy; joyous II〈動〉celebrate III〈名〉happy event

【喜鵲】xǐquè〈名〉magpie

【喜歡】xǐhuan I〈動〉like; love; take to: ～聽音樂 love music II〈形〉happy; glad: 非常～ be greatly pleased

喪 sāng〈名〉funeral; mourning: 治～ make funeral arrangements
see also sàng

【喪服】sāngfú〈名〉mourning dress; funeral costume

【喪事】sāngshì〈名〉funeral arrangements

【喪禮】sānglǐ〈名〉funeral (service)

【喪鐘】sāngzhōng〈名〉funeral bell; (death) knell

喪 sàng〈動〉lose
see also sāng

【喪心病狂】sàng xīn bìng kuáng〈成〉wicked and unscrupulous; perverse

【喪失】sàngshī〈動〉lose; forfeit: ～良機 lose a very good chance

【喪命】sàngmìng〈動〉lose one's life; get killed

【喪氣】sàngqì〈動〉be downcast; feel frustrated; lost heart

【喪家之犬】sàng jiā zhī quǎn〈成〉stray cur

【喪偶】sàng'ǒu〈動〉〈書〉bereaved of one's spouse, esp. one's wife

【喪魂落魄】sàng hún luò pò〈成〉frightened out of one's senses

【喪膽】sàngdǎn〈動〉be panic-stricken; lose one's nerve

【喪權辱國】sàng quán rǔ guó〈成〉lose sovereignty and bring humiliation upon the nation

喧 xuān〈形〉noisy

【喧賓奪主】xuān bīn duó zhǔ〈成〉the voice of the host is drowned by the hilarity of the guests; the secondary usurps the position of the primary

【喧鬧】xuānnào（名）noise; uproar

【喧嘩】xuānhuá（動）make a deafening noise: 一片～聲 a confused hubbub

【喧嚷】xuānrǎng（名）outcry; clamour

【喧囂】xuānxiāo Ⅰ（形）noisy: ～的人羣 a noisy crowd Ⅱ（名）noise; clamour

喀 kā（象）noise of coughing or vomiting

【喀麥隆】Kāmàilóng（名）Cameroon: ～人 Cameroonian

【喀嚓】kāchā（象）noise of cracking or snapping: 椅子的一條腿～一聲斷了。One leg of the chair broke with a crack.

啼 tí（動）❶ cry; wail ❷ crow; twitter: 處處聞～鳥 hear birds singing all around

【啼笑皆非】tí xiào jiē fēi〈成〉not know whether to laugh or cry; be caught between laughter and tears

喏 nuò（嘆）[used to attract attention]: ～, 你的鑰匙在這兒。Look, here is your key!

喵 miāo（象）miaow; mew

喃 nán

【喃喃】nánnán（象）mutter; mumber

喇 lǎ

【喇叭】lǎba（名）❶ trumpet; horn; klaxon: 吹～ blow the trumpet ❷ loudspeaker or any other hornlike device for producing sound: 汽車～ car horn

【喇嘛】lǎma（名）〈宗〉lama

【喇嘛教】lǎmajiào（名）〈宗〉Lamaism

喋 dié（動）talk endlessly

【喋血】diéxuè（動）shed a good deal of blood: ～沙場。A good deal of blood was shed on the battlefield.

【喋喋不休】dié dié bù xiū（動）babble; rattle away

喳 chā（象）whispering or twittering sound

see also zhā

【喳喳】chāchā（象）sound of jabbering: 嘁嘁～～ chatter away

【喳喳】chācha（動）whisper

喳 zhā（象）chatter; chirp: 麻雀在樹上～～地叫。Sparrows are chirping on the trees.

see also chā

喔 wō（象）cock's crow

喂 wèi Ⅰ（嘆）hello; hey: ～, 你找誰？Hey, who are you looking for? Ⅱ（動）feed; spoon-feed: ～孩子 feed a baby

【喂奶】wèinǎi（動）breast-feed; suckle

【喂養】wèiyǎng（動）feed; raise

喝 hē（動）drink

see also hè

喝 hè（動）yell

see also hē

【喝倒彩】hè dàocǎi（動）make cat-calls

【喝彩】hècǎi（動）acclaim; cheer

單 dān Ⅰ（形）❶ single: ～幹 do

sth. by oneself; go it alone ❷ odd:
~數 odd numbers ❸ thin; unlined:
~衣 unlined garment Ⅱ (副) only;
merely Ⅲ (名) bill; list: 菜~
menu / 賬~ bill / 傳~ handbill
see also Shàn

【單刀直入】dān dāo zhí rù〈成〉
come right to the point

【單方面】dānfāngmiàn (副) unilat-
erally

【單行本】dānxíngběn (名) offprint;
separate edition

【單身】dānshēn (形) single; unmar-
ried: ~漢 bachelor

【單位】dānwèi (名) ❶ unit of measurement: 貨幣~ monetary unit ❷
institution; organization: 工作~
work unit

【單純】dānchún Ⅰ (形) pure; simple: 思想~ unsophisticated Ⅱ (副)
only; merely: ~追求數量 pay exclusive attention to quantity; place
exclusive emphasis on quantity

【單程】dānchéng (名) one way: ~
票 single or one-way ticket

【單詞】dāncí (名) word

【單槓】dāngàng (名)〈體〉 horizontal bar

【單槍匹馬】dān qiāng pǐ mǎ〈成〉
single-handed

【單價】dānjià (名)〈經〉 unit price

【單調】dāndiào (形) monotonous;
unvaried

【單據】dānjù (名) receipt; voucher

【單獨】dāndú (副) alone; separately

【單薄】dānbó (形) ❶ thin; little:
穿得~ be thinly clad (esp. on cold
days) ❷ weak

單 Shàn (名) a surname
see also dān

喘 chuǎn (名) ❶ pant; gasp ❷
asthma

【喘吁吁】chuǎnxūxū (形) panting
and puffing

【喘氣】chuǎnqì (動) ❶ pant; gasp;
be out of breath ❷ take a breather

【喘息】chuǎnxī Ⅰ (動) gasp for air Ⅱ
(名) breathing space; respite

喻 yù Ⅰ (動) ❶ understand; know:
不言而~ it goes without saying ❷
explain; expound: 曉~ give explicit instructions Ⅱ (名) ❶ analogy:
比~ analogy; metaphor ❷ (Yù) a
surname

喊 hǎn (動) ❶ shout ❷ call: ~醫
生 call for a doctor

【喊叫】hǎnjiào (動) shout at the top
of one's voice; yell

啾 jiū

【啾啾】jiūjiū (象) (of birds) chirp

喚 huàn (動) call

【喚起】huànqǐ (動) ❶ arouse: ~民
眾 arouse the masses ❷ call up: ~
童年的回憶 call up the memories of
one's childhood

【喚醒】huànxǐng (動) wake up;
awaken

喉 hóu (名) larynx; throat

【喉舌】hóushé (名) mouthpiece

【喉嚨】hóulóng (名) throat

嗖 sōu (象) whiz: ~的一聲飛過
去了 whiz by / 冷~~的風 chilly
wind

喙 huì (名) ❶ beak; snout ❷
mouth: 無庸置~ no need to comment

哟 yō (嘆) [used to express surprise]: ~，是你呀! Oh! It's you!
see also yo

哟 yo (助) [used at the end of a sentence]: 大家齊用力 ~! Come on, put some beef into the job, everybody!
see also yō

喬 qiáo
【喬木】qiáomù (名) 〈植〉arbor; tree
【喬其紗】qiáoqíshā (名) 〈紡〉georgette
【喬裝打扮】qiáo zhuāng dǎ bàn 〈成〉disguise oneself
【喬遷】qiáoqiān (動) ❶ move into a new house in a better neighbourhood; move (house) ❷ have a promotion

嗇 sè (形) stingy; close-fisted

嗙 pǎng (動) 〈方〉brag: 胡吹亂 ~ brag fantastically about oneself

嗎 mǎ
see also ma
【嗎啡】mǎfēi (名) morphine

嗎 ma (助) [used at the end of a declarative sentence to turn it into a question]: 你要去動物園 ~? Are you going to the zoo? / 問我 ~? Me?
see also mǎ

嗜 shì (動) have a special liking for; crave for
【嗜好】shìhào (名) ❶ hobby ❷ addiction

嗑 kè (動) crack between the front teeth: ~ 葵花子 crack sunflower seeds

嗝 gé (名) ❶ belch ❷ hiccup

嗒 dā (象) clatter (of horse's hoofs); rattle (of a machine gun)

嗔 chēn (動) be annoyed
【嗔怪】chēnguài (動) blame

嗓 sǎng (名) ❶ throat; larynx ❷ voice
【嗓子】sǎngzi (名) ❶ throat; larynx ❷ voice: ~ 不好 have not a good voice; lose one's voice
【嗓門兒】sǎngménr (名) voice: 尖 ~ high-pitched voice
【嗓音】sǎngyīn (名) voice: ~ 不好聽 have an unpleasant voice

嗯 ńg (嘆) [used to indicate doubt]: ~! 發生了什麼事? Hem? What's happened?
see also ňg; ng

嗯 ňg (嘆) [used to indicate surprise or disapproval]: ~，他不去? Hey! He is not going, is he?
see also ńg; ng

嗯 ng (嘆) [used to indicate response]: ~，好吧。Yes, all right.
see also ńg; ňg

嗤 chī (動) sneer (at)
【嗤之以鼻】chī zhī yǐ bí 〈成〉snort with contempt; laugh sb. to scorn
【嗤笑】chīxiào (動) sneer at; laugh at

嗆 qiāng (動) choke: 喝飲料 ~ 着了 choke on one's drink
see also qiàng

嗆 qiàng（動）choke: 這股惡味～得他幾乎透不過氣來。This nasty smell nearly choked him.
see also qiāng

嗡 wēng（象）buzz; drone

嗅 xiù（動）smell
【嗅覺】xiùjué（名）sense of smell

嗥 háo（動）growl; howl

嗚 wū（象）toot; hoot: ～的一聲, 他的汽車飛馳過去了。He honked his horn and sped past.
【嗚呼】wūhū I（嘆）alas; alack II（動）die: 一命～ kick the bucket
【嗚咽】wūyè（動）sob

嘉 jiā I（形）good; wonderful; fine: ～賓 welcome (honoured) guest II（動）commend; applaud: 可～ be praiseworthy
【嘉許】jiāxǔ（動）of one's superior) praise; appreciate; commend
【嘉獎】jiājiǎng（動）commend and give a reward to; cite

嘗 cháng I（動）taste; experience: 艱苦備～ suffer all kinds of hardship II（副）[used in negative statements] ever: 未～去過 have never been there
【嘗試】chángshì（動）try

嘧 mì
【嘧啶】mìdìng（名）〈化〉pyrimidine

嘀 dí
【嘀咕】dígu（動）❶ speak in a low voice; mutter ❷ have doubts: 心裏有些～ have some misgivings

嘛 ma（助）[used at the end of a

sentence to emphasize the obviousness of the statement]: 事實勝於雄辯～。Facts speak louder than words. / 他講的是真話～! He was telling the truth!

嗾 sǒu
【嗾使】sǒushǐ（動）instigate; incite

嗷 áo（象）scream (with pain)
【嗷嗷待哺】áo áo dài bǔ（成）(of starving refugees or children) suffer piteously from lack of food

嘈 cáo（形）noisy
【嘈雜】cáozá（形）noisy; clamorous: 人聲～ a confusion of many voices

嘔 ǒu（動）vomit; throw up
【嘔心瀝血】ǒu xīn lì xuè（成）take great pains; make the greatest effort
【嘔吐】ǒutù（動）vomit; throw up

嗽 sòu（動）cough

嗃 hē（嘆）[used to express astonishment]ah; oh: ～, 這景色真美。Oh, what a beautiful view!

嘟 dū I（象）honk; beep II（動）〈方〉pout
【嘟嚕】dūlū I（量）cluster: 一～葡萄 a bunch of grapes II（動）trill
【嘟囔】dūnang（動）mutter; mumble

嘆 tàn（動）❶ sigh: ～了口氣 heave a sigh ❷ acclaim: 讚～不止 praise profusely ❸ chant; intone; sing
【嘆氣】tànqì（動）sigh
【嘆息】tànxī（動）sigh
【嘆賞】tànshǎng（動）have great ad-

miration for

嘞 lei I （助）〈口〉[used in a similar way as 了，but with a note of light-heartedness]: 好～，我就來。OK, I'm coming.

嘎 gā
【嘎巴】gābā （象）crack; snap
【嘎吱】gāzhī （象）creak

噓 shī （嘆）[used to demand silence] hush
see also xū

嘘 xū I （動）❶ breathe out slowly ❷ sigh ❸ scald; burn: ～了手 scald one's hand (by hot steam) II （嘆）sh; hush: ～，別說話。Hush! Don't speak.
see also shī

嗶 bì
【嗶嘰】bìjī （名）serge; beige

嘍 lóu
【嘍羅】lóuluo （名）lackey; stooge

嘣 bēng （象）sound of sth. throbbing, bursting, banging, etc.: 嘎～ sound of cracking nuts with one's teeth

嘁 qī
【嘁嘁喳喳】qī qī chā chā （象）prattle on; chatter away; gibber

嘮 láo
【嘮叨】láodao （動）nag: ～個没完 nag endlessly

噎 yē （動）choke: 讓飯～住了 be choked by food / 把眼淚～回去 choke back one's tears

嘻 xī I （動）smile; giggle: 笑～～ smiling face II （嘆）cry of surprise
【嘻嘻哈哈】xīxī hāhā （形）happy and gay

嘩 huā （象）gurgle
see also huá

嘩 huá （名）noise; clamour: 喧～ hubbub; uproar
see also huā
【嘩然】huárán （形）in an uproar; with a burst of public clamour
【嘩眾取寵】huá zhòng qǔ chǒng 〈成〉try to win popularity by catering to the transient sentiment of the public
【嘩變】huábiàn （名）mutiny

噴 pēn （動）❶ spurt; jet; gush: 鮮血從傷口裏～出來。Blood gushed out from the wound. ❷ spray; sprinkle: 給家具～漆 spray the furniture with paint
see also pèn
【噴火器】pēnhuǒqì （名）〈軍〉flame projector
【噴泉】pēnquán （名）fountain
【噴射】pēnshè （動）spurt; jet: ～泵 jet pump
【噴氣式】pēnqìshì （形）jet-propelled: ～飛機 jet aircraft
【噴氣發動機】pēnqì fādòngjī （名）jet engine
【噴粉器】pēnfěnqì （名）〈農〉duster
【噴壺】pēnhú （名）watering can; sprinkling can
【噴槍】pēnqiāng （名）spray gun
【噴嚏】pēntì （名）sneeze
【噴薄】pēnbó （動）(of sun) burst forth; emerge
【噴霧器】pēnwùqì （名）sprayer; at-

omizer

【噴灑】pēnsǎ（動）spray; sprinkle

噴 pèn

see also pēn

【噴香】pènxiāng（形）fragrant; savoury

噁 è

【噁心】ěxin Ⅰ（動）feel sick Ⅱ（形）disgusting

嘶 sī Ⅰ（動）neigh Ⅱ（形）hoarse; raucous

【嘶啞】sīyǎ（形）hoarse; husky

嘲 cháo（動）ridicule; deride; satirize

【嘲弄】cháonòng（動）mock

【嘲笑】cháoxiào（動）deride; ridicule

【嘲諷】cháofěng（動）jeer (at)

嘹 liáo

【嘹亮】liáoliàng（形）clarion; sonorous

嘿 hēi（嘆）hey: ～，雨 停 了。Hey, the rain has stopped.

噗 pū（象）puff: 火車～～地噴着氣開進車站。The train puffed into the station.

嘰 jī（象）sound of chirping

【嘰咕】jīgu（嘰嘰咕咕 jījī gūgū）（象）mutter; whisper: 你們嘰嘰咕咕地說什麼? What are you muttering about?

【嘰嘰喳喳】jījī zhāzhā（動）chirp; twitter or giggle: 鳥兒在樹上～地叫個不停。Birds keep chirping in the trees.

【嘰嘰嘎嘎】jījī gāgā（象）creak;

laughing: 他們上樓時樓梯～響。The stairs creaked as they walked up.

噎 è（形）appalling; sad

【噎耗】èhào（名）sad tidings; news announcing the death of one's close relative or friend

噻 sāi

【噻吩】sāifēn（名）〈化〉thiophene

【噻唑】sāizuò（名）〈化〉thiazole

噤 jìn Ⅰ（動）be silent Ⅱ（名）shiver: 打寒～ shiver with cold

【噤若寒蟬】jìn ruò hán chán（成）be like a cicada in cold weather; be scared to death

噸 dūn（名）ton

【噸位】dūnwèi（名）tonnage

噱 xué

【噱頭】xuétóu（名）amusing tricks

嘴 zuǐ（名）❶ mouth: 張～open one's mouth ❷ anything shaped or functioning like a mouth: 煙～兒 cigarette holder

【嘴巴】zuǐbā（名）mouth

【嘴快】zuǐkuài（動）have a big mouth

【嘴唇】zuǐchún（名）lip

【嘴甜】zuǐtián（動）be ready with honeyed words; be honey-mouthed

【嘴笨】zuǐbèn（形）be clumsy of speech

【嘴緊】zuǐjǐn（動）know how to keep one's mouth shut

【嘴臉】zuǐliǎn（名）〈貶〉ugly countenance

器 qì（名）❶ utensil; ware; implement: 陶～ pottery ❷ organ: 泌尿

~ urinary organs ❸ talent; endowment: 成~ become a useful person

【器皿】qìmǐn（名）kitchen utensils

【器件】qìjiàn（名）parts of an apparatus

【器材】qìcái（名）material; equipment: 照相~ photographic equipment

【器官】qìguān（名）organ: 生殖~ reproductive organs; genitals

【器具】qìjù（名）utensil; appliance

【器重】qìzhòng（动）regard highly; have a high opinion of

【器械】qìxiè（名）❶ apparatus; instrument ❷ weapon

【器乐】qìyuè（名）instrumental music

噪 zào（名）❶（of birds, insects, etc.）chirp; cheep: 鹊~ the cheeping of a magpie ❷ clamour; hubbub: 聒~ noisy; clamorous

【噪音】zàoyīn（名）noise

嗳 ǎi（叹）[used before a sentence to express disagreement] oh, no; why: ~，你搞錯啦! Oh, no, you are mistaken.
see also ài

嗳 ài（叹）[ejaculation showing regret or annoyance]: ~，來不及了! Oh, it's late.
see also ǎi

噙 qín（动）hold（in the mouth or the eyes）: ~着眼淚 with one's eyes filled with tears

噬 shì（动）bite

嚓 cā（象）noise produced by friction

嚎 háo（动）howl; wail

嚏 tì（动）sneeze

【嚏噴】tìpen（名）sneeze: 打~ sneeze

嚔 huò（叹）[used to express surprise]: ~! 下雨了。Oh! It's raining.

嚇 hè（动）threaten; intimidate
see also xià

嚇 xià（动）frighten; scare
see also hè

【嚇唬】xiàhu（动）frighten; intimidate

嘯 xiào（动）❶ whistle ❷ roar; howl

嚙 niè

【嚙齒動物】nièchǐ dòngwù（名）rodent

嚨 lóng（名）throat

嚥 yàn（动）swallow

【嚥氣】yànqì（动）breathe one's last; die

嚴 yán Ⅰ（形）❶ tight: 把窗子關~ shut the window tight ❷ strict; severe: 紀律很~ keep strict discipline Ⅱ（Yán）（名）a surname

【嚴正】yánzhèng（形）solemn; serious; strict: ~聲明 make a solemn statement

【嚴冬】yándōng（名）severe winter

【嚴守】yánshǒu（动）❶ strictly observe（discipline）❷ rigidly guard（a secret）

【嚴防】yánfáng（动）be on sharp guard against; keep a strict vigilance over

【嚴明】yánmíng（形）strict and impartial

【嚴重】yánzhòng（形）grave; serious:～的住房問題 serious problem of housing shortage; serious housing problem

【嚴峻】yánjùn（形）stern; grave; harsh: 形勢依然～。The situation is still grave.

【嚴陣以待】yán zhèn yǐ dài〈成〉be combat-ready; be fully prepared for battle

【嚴格】yángé（形）strict:～要求學生 be strict with one's students

【嚴密】yánmì（形）tight; close: 瓶口封得很～。The bottle is tightly sealed. / 部署～ make careful arrangements

【嚴詞】yáncí（名）harsh words:～駁斥 refute sternly

【嚴寒】yánhán（形）bitter cold; freezing cold

【嚴肅】yánsù（形）serious; earnest: 神情～ look stern / 治學態度～ be a serious scholar; be a man of sound scholarship

【嚴禁】yánjìn（動）strictly forbid

【嚴實】yánshi Ⅰ（形）tight; close Ⅱ（副）safely: 把錢藏～ put the money in a safe place

【嚴酷】yánkù（形）bitter; merciless:～的剝削 ruthless exploitation

【嚴厲】yánlì（形）stern; austere: 對下屬太～ be too severe with one's subordinates

【嚴辦】yánbàn（動）deal with severely

【嚴謹】yánjǐn（形）strict and cautious: 辦事～ be cautious in one's work / 結構～的論文 a well-orga-

nized research paper

【嚴懲】yánchéng（動）punish severely

嚷 rāng
see also rǎng

【嚷嚷】rāngrang（動）〈口〉❶ yell; shout ❷ make widely known: 別把這件事～出去。Don't say a word about it to anybody.

嚷 rǎng（動）shout; yell: 別～了。Don't make such a noise.
see also rāng

嚣 xiāo（形）clamorous; noisy: 喧～ clamour; din

【囂張】xiāozhāng（形）arrogant; rampant; blatant: 他氣焰～。He's overbearing.

嚼 jiáo（動）chew; munch
see also jué

【嚼舌頭】jiáoshétou（嚼舌 jiáoshé; 嚼舌根 jiáoshégen）（動）❶ stir up trouble; gossip: 他喜歡～。He is fond of gossip. ❷ argue

嚼 jué（動）chew
see also jiáo

囊 náng（名）bag; sack; pocket: 飽私～ line one's pockets

【囊空如洗】náng kōng rú xǐ〈成〉without a penny to one's name; penniless

【囊括】nángkuò（動）include; encompass

【囊腫】nángzhǒng（名）〈醫〉cyst

【囊蟲】nángchóng（名）cysticercus

囈 yì（名）talk in one's sleep

【囈語】yìyǔ（名）❶ talk in one's sleep ❷ delirium; ravings; rigmarole

嘱 zhǔ Ⅰ（动）enjoin; advise; admonish: 她～代爲問好。She asks me to send you her best regards. Ⅱ（名）instructions; advice: 遵～ in compliance with your instructions

【嘱咐】zhǔfù（动）exhort; enjoin: ～孩子過馬路時要小心 tell the child to watch out when crossing the street

【嘱託】zhǔtuō（动）ask; entrust: 他～我爲他買票。He asked me to get a ticket for him.

口 部

四 sì（数）four

【四人帮】Sìrénbāng（名）the Gang of Four (a counter-revolutionary clique, formed in the Cultural Revolution, overthrown in 1976)

【四川】Sìchuān（名）Sichuan (Province)

【四下裏】sìxiàli（副）〈口〉(all) around; everywhere

【四月】sìyuè（名）❶ April ❷ fourth month of the lunar year

【四方】sìfāng Ⅰ（形）square; cubic Ⅱ（副）from all sides: ～支援 support from all quarters

【四化】sìhuà（名）Four Modernizations; modernization of industry, of agriculture, of national defence, and of science and technology

【四分五裂】sì fēn wǔ liè〈成〉break up; fall apart; disintegrate

【四不象】sìbùxiàng（名）❶（动）David's deer; mi-lu ❷ nondescript;

neither fish, flesh, nor good red herring

【四平八穩】sì píng bā wěn〈成〉❶ very steady; well balanced ❷ over-cautious

【四合院】sìhéyuàn（名）siheyuan, quadrangle courtyard house

【四季】sìjì（名）four seasons

【四肢】sìzhī（名）arms and legs; the four limbs

【四周】sìzhōu（副）all around

【四面】sìmiàn（副）on all sides: ～八方（from）all directions

【四重奏】sìchóngzòu（名）〈乐〉(instrumental) quartet

【四重唱】sìchóngchàng（名）〈乐〉(vocal) quartet

【四海】sìhǎi（名）the four seas; the whole country; the entire world

【四处】sìchù（副）everywhere; all around

【四捨五入】sì shě wǔ rù〈成〉〈数〉rounding (up); raise or take off decimal points to make a round number

【四散】sìsàn（动）disperse in all directions

【四聲】sìshēng（名）four tones of standard Chinese pronunciation

【四邊】sìbiān（四周 sìzhōu）（副）on four sides; all around

囚 qiú Ⅰ（动）imprison; jail Ⅱ（名）prisoner; convict

【囚犯】qiúfàn（名）prisoner; convict; jailbird

【囚車】qiúchē（名）prisoners' van

【囚牢】qiúláo（名）prison; jail

【囚室】qiúshì（名）prison cell

【囚禁】qiújìn（动）imprison; put in jail

因 yīn Ⅰ(名) reason; cause Ⅱ(介) because of; due to: ～天氣不好 because of bad weather

【因小失大】 yīn xiǎo shī dà 〈成〉 suffer a big loss for a little gain

【因公】 yīngōng (副) on business; while on duty: ～出國 go abroad on official business

【因而】 yīn'ér (連) thus; as a result

【因此】 yīncǐ (副) therefore; hence; so

【因地制宜】 yīn dì zhì yí 〈成〉 take measures in light of local conditions

【因材施教】 yīn cái shī jiào 〈成〉 teach according to the students' abilities

【因果】 yīnguǒ (名) cause and effect

【因陋就簡】 yīn lòu jiù jiǎn 〈成〉 make do with the available facilities; practise thrift

【因病】 yīnbìng (副) because of illness

【因素】 yīnsù (名) factor; element

【因為】 yīnwèi (連) because; since; for

【因循守舊】 yīn xún shǒu jiù 〈成〉 cling to old practices and refuse to accept new things: 他是個貨真價實的～分子。He is a real stick-in-the-mud.

【因勢利導】 yīn shì lì dǎo 〈成〉 guide sth. along its natural course of development; guide tactfully

【因噎廢食】 yīn yē fèi shí 〈成〉 stop eating altogether just because of a hiccup; give up a major undertaking on account of a slight risk

【因緣】 yīnyuán (名) ❶ cause ❷ predestined bond

【因襲】 yīnxí (動) follow; copy

回 huí Ⅰ(動) ❶ return; go back: ～國 return to one's country ❷ turn round ❸ wind; circle: 峰～路轉。The path zigzags up the mountain. ❹ answer: ～話 reply Ⅱ(量) [used to indicate frequency of action]: 去過好幾～ have been there several times Ⅲ (名) ❶ chapter (in a classical Chinese novel) ❷ the Hui nationality

【回升】 huíshēng (動) rise again (after a fall)

【回心轉意】 huí xīn zhuàn yì 〈成〉 come round; repent: 使人～ bring sb. round

【回民】 huímín (名) people of the Hui nationality

【回去】 huíqu (動) return; go back

【回合】 huíhé (名) round; bout

【回扣】 huíkòu (名) commission

【回收】 huíshōu (動) collect; reclaim

【回光返照】 huí guāng fǎn zhào 〈成〉 the transient show of returning strength before death; a sudden spurt of activity before collapse

【回見】 huíjiàn (動) 〈套〉 see you later

【回來】 huílái (動) return; come back

【回味】 huíwèi Ⅰ(名) after-taste Ⅱ (動) ponder over some past experience; chew the cud

【回拜】 huíbài Ⅰ(動) return a visit Ⅱ (名) return visit

【回春】 huíchūn Ⅰ(名) return of spring Ⅱ(動) restore one to health: 妙手～ be able to bring the dying back to life; effect a miraculous cure

【回首】 huíshǒu (動) ❶ return round ❷ 〈書〉 book back; recollect

【回音】huíyīn（名）❶ echo ❷ reply

【回族】Huízú（名）the Hui nationality

【回访】huífǎng I（动）return a visit II（名）return call

【回教】Huíjiào（名）〈旧〉Islam

【回旋】huíxuán（动）❶ circle round ❷ manoeuvre: ～餘地 room for manoeuvre

【回报】huíbào（动）❶ report back ❷ repay; requite ❸ retaliate

【回答】huídá（动）answer; reply

【回复】huífù（动）reply（a letter, telegram, etc.）

【回绝】huíjué（动）decline; refuse

【回敬】huíjìng（动）requite a person for his kindness or gift; do（give）sth. in return

【回溯】huísù（动）recall; look back upon

【回想】huíxiǎng（动）recall; recollect

【回避】huíbì（动）evade; dodge

【回荡】huídàng（动）resound; reverberate

【回忆】huíyì（动）recollect; recall: ～錄 reminiscences; memoirs

【回头】huítóu I（动）❶ turn one's head ❷ mend one's ways II（副）〈口〉later: ～見。See you later.

【回头是岸】huí tóu shì àn〈成〉repent and you are saved; turn from one's evil ways

【回擊】huíjī（动）fight back; counterattack

【回聲】huíshēng（名）echo

【回歸綫】huíguīxiàn（名）〈地〉tropic: 南～ the Tropic of Capricorn / 北～ the Tropic of Cancer

【回顧】huígù（动）look back; review

【回響】huíxiǎng（名）reverberation; echo

囡 nān（名）〈方〉child

困 kùn I（动）❶ land oneself in inextricable difficulty: 久～於病 have been afflicted by a lingering disease ❷ besiege; pin down: 被～在孤島上 get stranded on a remote island II（形）tired; fatigued; weary

【困乏】kùnfá（形）tired; fatigued; fagged

【困守】kùnshǒu（动）be entrenched against a siege

【困苦】kùnkǔ（形）（of life）full of hardships; in dire poverty

【困惑】kùnhuò（形）puzzled; bewildered

【困窘】kùnjiǒng（形）distressed and embarrassed; in straitened circumstances

【困境】kùnjìng（名）embarrassing situation; fix: 處於～ get into a fix

【困擾】kùnrǎo（动）trouble; distress

【困難】kùnnán I（名）hardship; difficulty II（形）poverty-stricken

囤 dùn（名）grain bin see also tún

囤 tún（动）hoard; store see also dùn

【囤積】túnjī（动）hoard for speculation: ～居奇 hoard for profiteering

囫 hú

【囫圇吞棗】hú lún tūn zǎo〈成〉swallow the dates whole; read sth. hastily without understanding

固 gù I（形）solid; firm II（副）❶ firmly; resolutely: ～請 at one's insistent request ❷ originally; in the first place

【固守】gùshǒu (动) defend tenaciously

【固有】gùyǒu (形) intrinsic; inherent; innate: ～文化 native culture

【固定】gùdìng Ⅰ(形) fixed; regular: ～汇率 fixed exchange rate Ⅱ(动) fix; regularize

【固若金汤】gù ruò jīn tāng〈成〉impregnable

【固习】gùxí (名) deep-rooted habit

【固执】gùzhí Ⅰ(形) obstinate Ⅱ(动) stick to; cling to: ～己见 be opinionated

【固然】gùrán (副) no doubt; of course

【固体】gùtǐ (名)〈物〉solid: ～燃料 solid fuel

囹 líng

【囹圄】língyǔ (名) prison: 身陷～ be in prison

圃 pǔ (名) garden: 花～ flower nursery

圈 juān (动)❶ pen in; confine to a pen ❷〈口〉put into prison
see also juàn; quān

圈 juàn (名) pen (for livestock); sty
see also juān; quān

【圈肥】juànféi (名) barnyard manure

圈 quān Ⅰ(名) circle; ring: 把椅子圈成～ arrange the chairs in a circle / 轮～ wheel ring Ⅱ(动)❶ mark with a circle: 把～ make a small circle over one's name to show that one has read the document ❷ encircle: 把苗牀～起来 fence up

the seedbeds
see also juān; juàn

【圈子】quānzi (名) circle; ring: 飞机打了几个～然后着着陆。The airplane circled several times before it landed. / 小～ (of core members) inner ring

【圈占】quānzhàn (名) enclosure (of land)

【圈套】quāntào (名) snare; trap: 设～ set a trap

【圈点】quāndiǎn (动)❶ punctuate with a small circle or a dot at the end of each clause or sentence in a Chinese essay ❷ make small circles or dots in a piece of writing to show that the words or sentences deserve special attention

國 guó Ⅰ(名)❶ country; state; nation ❷ (Guó) a surname Ⅱ(形) of the state; national: ～寶 national treasure

【國土】guótǔ (名) territory

【國內】guónèi (形) internal; domestic

【國手】guóshǒu (名) national champion; grand master

【國王】guówáng (名) king

【國立】guólì (形) national

【國民】guómín (形) national: ～經濟 national economy / ～生產總值 gross national product (GNP) / ～收入 national income

【國外】guówài (形) external; overseas; abroad

【國有化】guóyǒuhuà (名) nationalization

【國防】guófáng (名) national defence: ～力量 defence capability

【國君】guójūn (名) monarch

【國事】guóshì（名）state affairs: ～訪問 state visit

【國法】guófǎ（名）law

【國度】guódù（名）country; state; nation

【國界】guójiè（名）national boundaries

【國計民生】guó jì mín shēng〈成〉the national economy and the people's livelihood

【國恥】guóchǐ（名）national humiliation

【國家】guójiā（名）country; state; nation: ～所有制 state ownership

【國書】guóshū（名）letter of credence; credentials

【國宴】guóyàn（名）state banquet

【國庫】guókù（名）state treasury

【國庫券】guókùquàn（名）treasury bond

【國務】guówù（名）state affairs: ～委員 state councillor

【國務院】guówùyuàn（名）the State Council; the State Department (of the United States)

【國產】guóchǎn（形）made in one's own country; of native make

【國貨】guóhuò（名）native product

【國教】guójiào（名）state religion

【國情】guóqíng（名）state of a country

【國都】guódū（名）national capital

【國畫】guóhuà（名）traditional Chinese painting

【國策】guócè（名）fundamental policy of a state

【國會】guóhuì（名）Congress; Diet; Parliament

【國葬】guózàng（名）state funeral

【國債】guózhài（名）national debt

【國事】guóbīn（名）state guest: ～館 state guest-house

【國粹】guócuì（名）a nation's cultural heritage

【國歌】guógē（名）national anthem

【國旗】guóqí（名）national flag

【國境】guójìng（名）❶ territory ❷ border

【國際】guójì（形）international: ～關係 international relations

【國際主義】guójì zhǔyì（名）internationalism

【國際慣例】guójì guànlì（名）international practice

【國慶節】Guóqìngjié（名）National Day

【國徽】guóhuī（名）national emblem

【國營】guóyíng（形）state-operated; state-run

【國難】guónàn（名）national calamity

【國籍】guójí（名）nationality

【國體】guótǐ（名）state system

圍 wéi I（動）surround; encircle; besiege: ～着 gather around II（副）around; round: 周～長滿了向日葵。There are sunflowers growing all around. III（量）arm span

【圍巾】wéijīn（圍脖兒 wéibór）（名）muffler; scarf; shawl

【圍攻】wéigōng（動）❶ lay siege to ❷ make converging attacks on

【圍困】wéikùn（動）besiege; pin down

【圍棋】wéiqí（名）weiqi; go: 八段～手 level 8 weiqi master

【圍裙】wéiqún（名）apron

【圍剿】wéijiǎo（動）(of government troops) surround and destroy (bandits, etc.)

【圍墾】wéikěn（動）build dykes around marshes or tideland for land reclamation

【圍嘴兒】wéizuǐr（名）bib

【圍牆】wéiqiáng（名）enclosing wall (of a garden, courtyard, etc.)

【圍繞】wéirǎo I（動）centre on; revolve around: ～着質量控制的問題進行討論。The discussion centred on quality control. II（介）(move) around

【圍攏】wéilǒng（動）throng around

【圍殲】wéijiān（動）surround and wipe out

圍 yuán（名）garden; park; place for public recreation: 遊樂～ amusement park

【園丁】yuándīng（名）gardener

【園田】yuántián（名）vegetable garden

【園地】yuándì（名）❶ garden plot ❷ field; scope (for certain activity)

【園林】yuánlín（名）garden; park: ～師 landscape gardener

【園藝】yuányì（名）horticulture

圓 yuán I（名）circle II（形）❶ round: ～桌會議 round-table conference ❷ tactful; satisfactory III（動）cause to look satisfactory: 自～其說 justify oneself one way or another

【圓心】yuánxīn（名）centre of a circle

【圓形】yuánxíng（形）round; circular: ～劇場 amphitheatre

【圓周】yuánzhōu（名）circumference

【圓柱】yuánzhù（名）cylinder; column

【圓括號】yuánkuòhào（名）round parentheses

【圓通】yuántōng（形）flexible; accommodating

【圓珠筆】yuánzhūbǐ（名）ball-pen

【圓規】yuánguī（名）compasses

【圓寂】yuánjì（名）〈宗〉nirvana

【圓圈】yuánquān（名）circle; ring

【圓場】yuánchǎng（名）help to smooth things over between disputing parties: 打～ mediate

【圓椎】yuánzhuī（名）cone

【圓筒】yuántǒng（名）cylinder

【圓號】yuánhào（名）〈樂〉French horn; horn

【圓滑】yuánhuá（形）slippery; slick; smooth

【圓滿】yuánmǎn（形）satisfactory; complete: ～結束 come to a satisfactory conclusion

【圓夢】yuánmèng（動）interpret a dream

【圓舞曲】yuánwǔqǔ（名）〈樂〉waltz

【圓領汗衫】yuánlǐng hànshān（名）T-shirt

團 tuán I（形）round: ～～轉 run round in circles II（名）❶ ball: 擠作一～ huddle together ❷ organization; group; league: 參觀～ visiting group ❸ (short for 中國共產主義青年團 Zhōngguó Gòngchǎn Zhǔyì Qīngniántuán) the Communist Youth League of China ❹〈軍〉regiment III（動）unite IV（量）ball: 兩～麵 two lumps of dough / 把毛綫繞成三～ roll the wool into three balls

【團伙】tuánhuǒ（名）criminal band; gang

【團粉】tuánfěn（名）cooking starch

【團員】tuányuán（名）❶ member (of a delegation) ❷ member of the

Communist Youth League

【團結】tuánjié Ⅰ（動）unite; rally Ⅱ（名）unity; solidarity: ～就是力量。Unity is strength.

【團圓】tuányuán（名）reunion

【團聚】tuánjù（動）reunite: 親人～family reunion

【團體】tuántǐ（名）group; organization: ～操 group callisthenics / ～旅行 group tour

圖 tú Ⅰ（名）picture; chart: 畫一幅～ make a sketch Ⅱ（動）❶ scheme; plot ❷ seek; attempt: 不能只～快而不顧質量。It won't do to put speed before quality.

【圖片】túpiàn（名）picture; photograph

【圖形】túxíng（名）graph; figure: ～交通標誌 pictogram

【圖表】túbiǎo（名）chart; diagram; table

【圖案】tú'àn（名）pattern; design: ～美麗的綢緞 silk with a beautiful pattern

【圖釘】túdīng（名）drawing pin

【圖紙】túzhǐ（名）blueprint; drawing

【圖書】túshū（名）books

【圖書館】túshūguǎn（名）library: 公共～ lending library

【圖章】túzhāng（名）seal; stamp; chop

【圖像】túxiàng（名）picture; image; pattern

【圖畫】túhuà（名）drawing; picture

【圖景】tújǐng（名）prospect; outlook

【圖解】tújiě Ⅰ（名）❶ diagram; graph ❷ illustration Ⅱ（動）explain through diagrams; illustrate

【圖樣】túyàng（名）pattern; design; drawing

【圖謀】túmóu（動）plot; design: ～不軌 engage in conspiratorial and unlawful activities

土　部

土 tǔ Ⅰ（名）❶ earth; soil: 一堆～ a heap of earth ❷ land: 領～完整 territorial integrity Ⅱ（形）❶ local: ～著 native; aborigines / ～話 local dialect ❷ indigenous: ～法 indigenous method ❸ rustic; unrefined: ～包子 clodhopper

【土方】tǔfāng（名）❶ cubic metre of earth ❷ earthwork ❸〈中醫〉folk recipe

【土木】tǔmù（名）building; construction: 大興～ go in for large-scale construction

【土地】tǔdì（名）❶ land; ground; soil: ～改革 land reform ❷ territory

【土耳其】Tǔ'ěrqí（名）Turkey: ～人 a Turk / ～語 Turkish (language)

【土耳其浴室】Tǔ'ěrqí yùshì（名）Turkish bath; sweat-bath house

【土豆】tǔdòu〈口〉potato: ～泥 mashed potato

【土建】tǔjiàn（名）(short for 土木工程建築 tǔmù gōngchéng jiànzhù) building; construction

【土政策】tǔzhèngcè（名）unauthorized departmental policy (as contrasted with the policy of the central government)

【土氣】tǔqì（形）rustic: 土裏～ rustic; boorish

【土匪】tǔfěi（名）bandit

【土產】tǔchǎn（名）local product

【土壤】tǔrǎng（名）soil

圭 guī

【圭亞那】Guīyànà（名）Guyana: ～人 Guyanese

地 de（助）[used after an adverb or an adverbial phrase]: 聚精會神～聽報告 listen to a talk with rapt attention

see also dì

地 dì（名）❶ earth: 天～ heaven and earth ❷ land; field: 好～ fertile soil ❸ ground; floor ❹ place; locality: 本一人 local people ❺ situation; position: 設身處～ place oneself in sb. else's position ❻ background: 白～紅花 red flowers on a white background ❼ distance: 二里～ a distance of two *li*（one kilometre）

see also de

【地力】dìlì（名）land fertility

【地上】dìshàng（副）on the ground

【地下】dìxià（形）underground: ～宮殿 underground palace

【地下室】dìxiàshì（名）basement

【地大物博】dì dà wù bó（成）vast in territory and abundant in resources

【地方】dìfāng（名）locality: 中央和～ central administration and local governments

【地方】dìfang（名）❶ place ❷ space; room: 騰個～ make room for ❸ part: 小說中最有趣的一～ the most interesting part of the novel

【地皮】dìpí（名）land; ground

【地主】dìzhǔ（名）❶ landlord ❷ host

【地平綫】dìpíngxiàn（名）horizon

【地位】dìwèi（名）position; status: 經濟～ economic status

【地址】dìzhǐ（名）address

【地形】dìxíng（名）topography

【地利】dìlì（名）favourable terrain; favourable geographical conditions

【地步】dìbù（名）❶ situation; predicament ❷ extent

【地板】dìbǎn（名）floor

【地段】dìduàn（名）area; block

【地界】dìjiè（名）boundary

【地面】dìmiàn（名）land surface; ground

【地契】dìqì（名）title deed（for land）

【地峽】dìxiá（名）isthmus

【地租】dìzū（名）land rent

【地帶】dìdài（名）zone; belt

【地基】dìjī（名）foundation

【地理】dìlǐ（名）geography

【地球】dìqiú（名）the earth; the globe

【地區】dìqū（名）area; district; region

【地域】dìyù（名）region; district

【地動儀】dìdòngyí（名）seismograph

【地痞】dìpǐ（名）riffraff; local ruffian

【地殼】dìqiào（名）〈地〉earth crust

【地堡】dìbǎo（名）bunker; underground shelter

【地窖】dìjiào（名）cellar

【地毯】dìtǎn（名）carpet; rug

【地道】dìdào（名）tunnel

【地道】dìdao（形）❶ genuine;（of food）typical ～的北京風味 typical Beijing flavour ❷ perfect; idiomatic: 講～的英語 speak flawless English

【地雷】dìléi（名）land mine

【地勤】dìqín（名）〈航空〉ground service

【地势】dìshì（名）terrain

【地图】dìtú（名）map: ～集 atlas

【地狱】dìyù（名）hell

【地盘】dìpán（名）domain; sphere of influence

【地热】dìrè（名）〈地〉terrestrial heat

【地震】dìzhèn（名）earthquake: ～学 seismology

【地质】dìzhì（名）geology: ～学家 geologist

【地点】dìdiǎn（名）place; spot

【地铁】dìtiě（名）underground railway; subway; tube; metro

在 zài Ⅰ（动）❶ exist; be alive: 家母已經不～了。My mother is dead. ❷ rest with; depend on: 事～人爲。Everything depends on the human factor. Ⅱ（介）[used to indicate time, place, condition, etc.]: ～晚上讀報 read mewspapers in the evening / ～目前情況下 under present condition Ⅲ（副）[used to indicate an action in progress]: 他～聽音樂。He is listening to music.

【在乎】zàihu（动）care（about）; mind: 他毫不～别人怎麼想。He doesn't care in the least what others think.

【在世】zàishì（动）be living

【在行】zàiháng（动）be good at（a skill, etc.）

【在劫难逃】zài jié nán táo〈成〉what is destined cannot be avoided

【在押】zàiyā（动）be under detention; be in custody

【在於】zàiyú（动）❶ lie in; rest

with: 主要困難～缺少經費。The chief difficulty lies in the shortage of funds. ❷ be determined by; depend on: 成功往往～堅持。Success very often depends on perseverance.

【在所不辞】zài suǒ bù cí〈成〉will never balk: 赴湯蹈火，～。I will not hesitate to lay down my life for the cause.

【在所难免】zài suǒ nán miǎn〈成〉be hardly avoidable

【在家】zàijiā（动）be at home

【在座】zàizuò（动）be present（at a banquet, meeting, etc.）: ～的有許多知名學者和外國專家。Present at the banquet were many distinguished scholars and foreign experts.

【在望】zàiwàng（动）❶ be visible; be in sight: 勝利～。Victory is in sight. ❷ be round the corner

【在理】zàilǐ（形）reasonable; right

【在野】zàiyě（动）be out of office

【在场】zàichǎng（动）be on the spot; be on the scene

【在握】zàiwò（动）be within one's grasp; have sth. in one's pocket

【在意】zàiyì（动）[usu. used in the negative] mind; care about: 他批評過於嚴厲，但我並不～。His criticism is a bit too harsh, but I don't mind.

【在职】zàizhí（动）be at one's post; be on the job: ～培訓 on-the-job training

坊 fáng（名）workshop; mill

坑 kēng Ⅰ（名）hole; hollow: 刨～兒 dig a pit Ⅱ（动）do harm to sb.; get sb. into trouble: 這簡直是～人。This is deliberately getting peo-

ple into trouble.

【坑坑窪窪】kēngkengwāwā （形）
(of a road or surface of an object)
rugged

【坑害】kēnghài（動）harm people by
vicious means; entrap

【坑道】kēngdào（名） ❶ underground tunnel ❷〈礦〉gallery

址 zhǐ（名）location; site: 通訊地
~ mailing address

均 jūn Ⅰ（形）equal; even; fair: 貧
富不~ contrast between wealth and
poverty Ⅱ（副）❶ equally; evenly;
fairly: 雙方勢~力敵。The two
sides are evenly matched. ❷ all;
without exception; invariably: 各項
指標~已達到。All the targets have
been met.

【均分】jūnfēn（動）divide into equal
parts: 大家~食品。The food is
shared out equally among us.

【均匀】jūnyún（副）evenly; regularly:
呼吸~ breathe evenly

【均等】jūnděng（形）equal; fair: 機
會~ equal opportunity

【均勢】jūnshì（名）balance of power;
parity: 保持~ maintain the equilibrium

【均衡】jūnhéng（形）balanced; harmonious; even: ~ 裁軍 balanced
reduction of armaments

坍 tān（動）collapse; fall; cave in

【坍塌】tāntā（動）collapse; cave in;
fall

坎 kǎn（名）❶ ridge; natural or
man-made long and narrow elevation
of land, stones, etc.: 石~ flood-
control stone ridge ❷ hollow; pit:
我從心一裏感謝您。I thank you

from the bottom of my heart.

【坎肩兒】kǎnjiānr（名）〈口〉sleeveless jacket (usu. padded or lined and
worn over a sweater)

【坎坷】kǎnkě（形）❶ rough; rugged: 這條路~不平。This road is
bumpy. ❷ uncertain and full of
misfortunes: 他一生~。Life for
him was a series of frustrations.

坂 bǎn（名）slope of a hill

坐 zuò（動）❶ sit; take a seat: ~
下歇歇 sit down and have a break
❷ travel by; ride in (car, boat,
plane, etc.): ~公共汽車去上班
go to work by bus ❸ (of a building)
have its back towards: 我的房間~
北朝南。My room faces south. ❹
put (a pan, pot, kettle, etc.) on a
fire: 把鍋~在爐子上 put the pot
on the stove ❺ (of a gun, rifle,
etc.) recoil; kick back: 無~力炮
recoilless gun

【坐月子】zuò yuèzi（動）be confined
(in childbirth)

【坐井觀天】zuò jǐng guān tiān〈成〉
look at heaven from the bottom of a
well; have a limited outlook

【坐立不安】zuò lì bù ān〈成〉be on
pins and needles; be worried and
restless

【坐失良機】zuò shī liáng jī〈成〉
watch a golden opportunity slip
through one's fingers

【坐吃山空】zuò chī shān kōng〈成〉
squander away one's fortune in idleness

【坐位】zuòwèi（名）seat

【坐牢】zuòláo（動）be put in prison;
be in jail

【坐冷板凳】zuò lěng bǎn dèng〈成〉

❶ be left out in the cold ❷ cool one's heels ❸ hold an office with nominal duties

【坐享其成】zuò xiǎng qí chéng〈成〉enjoy the fruits of others' work without having to lift a finger

【坐班】zuòbān〈动〉❶ do work in an office; do office work ❷ be on duty

【坐视】zuòshì〈动〉sit by and watch: ～不救 watch on the sidelines and refuse to help

【坐等】zuòděng〈动〉sit back and wait

【坐落】zuòluò〈动〉(of a building, house, etc.) be located; be situated

【坐墊】zuòdiàn〈名〉cushion

垃 lā

【垃圾】lājī〈名〉garbage

【垃圾桶】lājītǒng〈名〉garbage bin

坪 píng〈名〉level ground: 草～ lawn

坷 kē

【坷拉】kēlā〈名〉〈方〉clod

坩 gān

【坩堝】gānguō〈名〉〈化〉crucible

坯 pī〈名〉❶ blank ❷ adobe

坡 pō〈名〉slope

【坡度】pōdù〈名〉slope; gradient

坦 tǎn〈形〉❶ level; even: 平～ smooth ❷ calm; unruffled ❸ straightforward; frank: 爲人～直 be straightforward to others

【坦白】tǎnbái Ⅰ〈形〉frank; candid: ～地講 frankly speaking Ⅱ〈动〉confess; own up

【坦克】tǎnkè〈名〉〈軍〉tank

【坦桑尼亞】Tǎnsāngníyà〈名〉Tanzania: ～人 Tanzanian

【坦率】tǎnshuài〈形〉candid; frank; outspoken

【坦然】tǎnrán〈形〉unperturbed; free of misgivings

坤 kūn〈形〉female: ～鞋 woman's shoe

坳 ào〈名〉depression in a mountain range

垂 chuí〈动〉❶ hang; droop: 下～ droop ❷ go down; be handed down: 名～青史 go down in history ❸ approach: ～暮 approaching dusk; towards evening

【垂死】chuísǐ〈形〉dying; on one's last legs: 做～掙扎 put up a last-ditch struggle

【垂危】chuíwēi〈形〉terminally ill; dying from a serious injury or wound

【垂直】chuízhí〈形〉vertical; perpendicular

【垂涎】chuíxián〈动〉covet; gloat on

【垂釣】chuídiào〈动〉angle

【垂頭喪氣】chuí tóu sàng qì〈成〉crest-fallen; dejected; downcast

型 xíng〈名〉❶ mould; pattern ❷ model; type: 重～卡車 heavy-duty truck

【型號】xínghào〈名〉model; type

垣 yuán〈名〉wall: 城～ city wall

垮 kuǎ〈动〉collapse; break down

【垮臺】kuǎtái〈动〉collapse; fall

城 chéng〈名〉❶ city ❷ city wall; wall: 萬里長～ the Great Wall ❸

town; urban areas: ～鄉差別 difference between town and country

【城市】 chéngshì (名) city; town

【城門】 chéngmén (名) city gate

【城郊】 chéngjiāo (名) outskirts; suburbs

【城區】 chéngqū (名) city proper

【城堡】 chéngbǎo (名) castle

【城裏人】 chénglǐrén (名) townspeople; city dweller

【城樓】 chénglóu (名) gatetower: 在天安門～上 on the rostrum of Tian An Men

【城壕】 chénghǎo (名) moat

【城牆】 chéngqiáng (名) city wall

【城關】 chéngguān (名) area just outside a city gate

垛 duǒ (名) buttress; battlements
see also duò

垛 duò I (動) stack; pile up II (名) pile; stack: 乾草～ haystack
see also duǒ

垢 gòu I (名) ❶ dirt; filth ❷ humiliation: 含～忍辱 suffer insult and injury II (形) dirty; filthy

埂 gěng (名) ❶ ridge between fields ❷ earth dyke

埋 mái (動) bury: 石碑有一半～在土裏。The tombstone is half-buried in the earth. ❷ hide; conceal: 他隱姓～名周遊世界。She travelled around the world incognito.
see also mán

【埋伏】 máifu (動) ambush; lie in wait for

【埋没】 máimò (動) ❶ bury ❷ stifle; neglect: ～功績 neglect

sb.'s contributions

【埋汰】 máitai (形)〈方〉dowdy; indecent

【埋葬】 máizàng (動) bury

【埋頭】 máitóu (動) bury oneself in; be immersed in: ～工作 concentrate on one's work

【埋藏】 máicáng (動) lie hidden: ～在地下的煤和鐵 the coal and iron deposits lying underground

埋 mán
see also mái

【埋怨】 mányuàn (動) blame; complain

埃 āi I (名) dust II (量) angstrom (Å)

【埃及】 Āijí (名) Egypt: ～人 Egyptian

【埃塞俄比亞】 Āisài'ébǐyà (名) Ethiopia: ～人 Ethiopian

培 péi

【培土】 péitǔ (動) heap up earth around the roots of a plant

【培育】 péiyù (動) breed; rear: ～新一代 bring up a new generation

【培訓】 péixùn I (動) train; cultivate: ～班 training course II (名) training: 職業～ vocational training

【培植】 péizhí (動) cultivate; foster

【培養】 péiyǎng (動) ❶ nurture; train: ～初級外交官 train junior diplomats ❷ culture: ～疫苗 culture vaccine

執 zhí (動) ❶ hold; grasp: ～手同行 walk hand in hand ❷ persist in; adhere to: 固～己見 adhere stubbornly to one's own opinions ❸ carry out; execute

【執行】zhíxíng（動）carry out; execute: ～計劃 carry out a plan

【執法】zhífǎ（動）enforce the law

【執拗】zhíniù（形）stubborn; headstrong

【執政】zhízhèng（動）be in power; be in office

【執迷不悟】zhí mí bù wù〈成〉persist in one's wrong course without awaking

【執筆】zhíbǐ（動）do the actual writing: 我們一起討論一下原則，由他～。Let's get together and discuss the principle involved, and he'll do the writing.

【執意】zhíyì（動）insist on（doing sth.）: ～要親自去一趟 insist on going oneself

【執照】zhízhào（名）licence

堵 dǔ I（動）block; stop: ～漏洞 plug the leak II（量）一～高牆 a big wall

域 yù（名）region; territory

埝 niàn（名）low earth bank between fields

堆 duī I（動）pile up; stack II（名）pile; heap

【堆積】duījī（動）pile up

埠 bù（名）❶ pier; wharf ❷ port; port city

堅 jiān（形）❶ solid; hard: ～甲利兵 strong armour and sharp weapons ❷ firm; persevering: 其志甚～ very firm in one's determination II（副）resolutely; firmly; unyieldingly III（名）❶ fortified defences; fortification: 無～不摧 break through any strongly fortified position; overrun all fortifications ❷（Jiān）a surname

【堅不可摧】jiān bù kě cuī〈成〉impregnable; strong enough to resist or withstand any attack

【堅守】jiānshǒu（動）adhere to; stick to: ～自己的信念 adhere to one's belief

【堅如磐石】jiān rú pán shí〈成〉firm as a rock

【堅決】jiānjué I（形）resolute; determined; resolved II（副）resolutely; firmly; steadfastly

【堅固】jiāngù（形）strong; impregnable; solid

【堅定】jiāndìng I（形）firm; unswerving; staunch II（動）fortify; consolidate; strengthen: ～克服困難的決心 fortify one's determination to overcome difficulties

【堅定不移】jiān dìng bù yí〈成〉unswerving; unshakable; steadfast

【堅果】jiānguǒ（名）nut

【堅信】jiānxìn（動）have profound faith in; firmly believe; be strongly convinced

【堅持】jiānchí（動）persevere in; persist in; adhere to: ～錯誤觀點 cling to mistaken views

【堅持不懈】jiān chí bù xiè〈成〉persevering; persistent: ～的努力 persevering effort

【堅貞不屈】jiān zhēn bù qū〈成〉remain loyal and unyielding; stand firm and dauntless

【堅苦卓絕】jiān kǔ zhuó jué〈成〉display a spirit of extraordinary courage and fortitude in adverse circumstances: ～的長期鬥爭 a prolonged course of extremely arduous struggle

【堅強】jiānqiáng Ⅰ（形） staunch; powerful; strong Ⅱ（動） make strong and powerful; strengthen

【堅硬】jiānyìng（形） hard; solid; tough; strong

【堅韌】jiānrèn（形） tenacious; tough

【堅韌不拔】jiān rèn bù bá（堅忍不拔 jiān rěn bù bá）〈成〉 indomitable; unyielding; tenacious of purpose

【堅實】jiānshí（形） strong; solid; sturdy

【堅毅】jiānyì（形） characterized by steadfastness and fortitude; resolute: 他是個有～意志的人。He is a man of iron will.

【堅壁】jiānbì（動） put provisions in a cache against enemy seizure

【堅壁清野】jiān bì qīng yě〈成〉 strengthen fortifications, evacuate civilians and hide all provisions

基 jī Ⅰ（名）❶ foundation; groundwork: 壩～ the base of a dam ❷ 〈化〉base; radical: 甲～ methyl Ⅱ（形）basic; primary: ～幹 hardcore; backbone

【基石】jīshí（名） foundation stone; corner-stone

【基本】jīběn（形）❶ fundamental; basic; rudimentary: ～功 basic training ❷ main; chief; principal: ～上 in the main; more or less / ～工資 base salary

【基本建設】jīběn jiànshè（名）（for short 基建 jījiàn）capital construction

【基地】jīdì（名）base: 海軍～ naval base

【基因】jīyīn（名）gene: 遺傳～ gene

【基於】jīyú（副）in view of; on account of: ～種種原因，我們做出了這一決定。We made the decision for a variety of reasons.

【基金】jījīn（名）fund

【基金會】jījīnhuì（名）foundation: 中國兒童福利～ Foundation for Children's Welfare of China

【基督】Jīdū（名） Christ: ～教 Christianity / ～徒 Christian

【基準】jīzhǔn（名）❶〈測〉datum ❷ criterion standard; yardstick

【基層】jīcéng（名）grassroots: ～單位 grassroots unit

【基調】jīdiào（名）❶〈樂〉fundamental key; keynote ❷ the central theme; tone: 確定了會議的～ set the tone for the meeting

【基數】jīshù（名）❶〈數〉cardinal number ❷〈統計〉base

【基點】jīdiǎn（名）❶ centre; starting point; base ❷〈測〉datum mark

【基礎】jīchǔ（名）foundation; basis; ground-work: 打下堅實的～ lay a solid foundation Ⅱ（形）basic: ～設施 infrastructure

堂 táng Ⅰ（名）❶ principal room of a traditional Chinese house: ～屋 central room of such a house / 四世同～ four generations live under the same roof ❷ hall; large room: 禮～ auditorium Ⅱ（形）(of a relation) on the paternal side: ～姐妹 female cousins on the paternal side Ⅲ（量）(in a school) class; period: 兩～中國古典文學課 two classes in classical Chinese literature

【堂皇】tánghuáng（形） grandiose; majestic: 富麗～ gorgeous and magnificent

【堂堂】 tángtáng〈形〉❶ (of a man) handsome and impressive ❷ having noble aspirations: ～中華兒女 worthy sons and daughters of the Chinese nation

【堂堂正正】 tángtáng zhèngzhèng〈成〉❶ open and aboveboard ❷ (of a person) having a noble and dignified carriage

報 bào I〈動〉❶ announce; report: 通風～信 disclose secret information to sb.; tip sb. off ❷ respond; reply: ～以微笑 respond with a smile ❸ repay; recompensate; revenge: 投桃～李 give a plum in return for a peach; requite sb. for a benefit II〈名〉❶ newspaper; journal; periodical: 見～ be reported in the newspapers ❷ report; bulletin: 新聞簡～ news bulletin ❸ telegram: 打電～ send a telegram ❹ retribution; heaven's reward or punishment

【報分】 bàofēn〈動〉〈體〉call the score (in contests)

【報仇】 bàochóu〈動〉avenge; revenge; get even with: 爲他～ avenge him

【報仇雪恨】 bào chóu xuě hèn〈成〉revenge a gross injustice

【報戶口】 bào hùkǒu〈動〉register the birth of a baby with the police; apply for personal residence: 報臨時戶口 register for temporary residence

【報刊】 bàokān〈名〉newspapers and periodicals

【報考】 bàokǎo〈動〉apply or register for an (entrance) examination

【報名】 bàomíng〈動〉enter one's name for; sign up for: ～單 application form

【報社】 bàoshè〈名〉general office of a newspaper

【報告】 bàogào I〈動〉report II〈名〉report; speech; talk; lecture: 做～ make a report; make a speech

【報告人】 bàogàorén〈名〉speaker; lecturer

【報表】 bàobiǎo〈名〉forms and questionnaires: (for reporting to the higher-up) 財務～ accounting report

【報到】 bàodào〈動〉report for duty; register: 新生～時間 time for the new students to register

【報界】 bàojiè〈名〉the press; journalistic circles

【報信】 bàoxìn〈動〉inform; pass on a message to: 通風～ tip off; leak information to

【報案】 bào'àn〈動〉report a case to the plice

【報效】 bàoxiào〈動〉offer service to repay sb.'s kindness

【報恩】 bào'ēn〈動〉repay sb. for his kindness

【報務員】 bàowùyuán〈名〉telegraph operator; radio operator; radioman

【報時】 bàoshí〈動〉tell time (usu. over the radio or phone)

【報紙】 bàozhǐ〈名〉newspaper

【報國】 bàoguó〈動〉serve one's country wholeheartedly

【報捷】 bàojié〈動〉announce) report a military victory or the success of a project

【報章雜誌】 bàozhāng zázhì〈名〉newspapers and magazines

【報答】 bàodá〈動〉repay; requite; reciprocate: ～他的好意 repay (reciprocate) his kindness

【報單】bàodān（名）taxation form; declaration form

【報道】bàodào（報導 bàodǎo）Ⅰ（動）report; cover Ⅱ（名）news report; coverage

【報喜】bàoxǐ（動）announce good news; proclaim glad tidings

【報復】bàofù Ⅰ（動）retaliate; vindicate; revenge: 打擊～ retaliate Ⅱ（名）retaliation; reprisal; vengeance

【報話機】bàohuàjī（名）walkie-talkie

【報酬】bàochou（名）pay; reward; honorarium

【報幕】bàomù（動）announce the items on a (theatrical) programme

【報價】bàojià（名）〈經〉quotation; quoted price

【報數】bàoshù（動）count off

【報銷】bàoxiāo（動）❶ claim reimbursement ❷ register expended articles ❸〈口〉wipe out (enemy); write off

【報賬】bàozhàng（動）❶ present a bill of expenses ❷ turn in an account for reimbursement

【報廢】bàofèi（動）scrap; discard: 這部車～了。The car is no longer serviceable; The car ought to be put out to pasture.

【報憂】bàoyōu（動）disclose bad news: 報喜不～ show the bright side of things only

【報應】bàoyìng（名）〈宗〉retribution; judgment; nemesis

【報償】bàocháng（名）repayment; compensation; reward

【報關】bàoguān（動）declare at the customs: 進口～ customs entry

【報警】bàojǐng（動）❶ give an alarm ❷ report an incident to the police

【報攤】bàotān（名）news stall; newsstand

堰 yàn（名）weir

堪 kān（動）❶ can; may: 後果～憂。The consequences would be dreadful. ❷ be able to endure or stand: 不～設想 be unthinkable

堞 dié（名）battlements

堤 dī（名）dyke

【堤岸】dī'àn（名）embankment

【堤壩】dībà（名）dykes and dams

場 cháng Ⅰ（名）❶ level, open ground: 在～上幹活 work on the threshing ground ❷ fair; market place: 趕～ go to the fair Ⅱ（量）[used to denote the process of sth. happening]: 一～風暴 a storm / 吵了一～～ kick up a row
see also chǎng

【場院】chángyuàn（名）threshing ground

場 chǎng Ⅰ（名）❶ site; ground: 網球～ tennis court ❷ farm: 奶牛～ dairy farm ❸ stage: 下～ off stage ❹ (of drama) scene: 三幕四～話劇 a play of three acts and four scenes Ⅱ（量）(of sports or recreation): 一～雜技表演 an acrobatic show
see also cháng

【場地】chǎngdì（名）(broad) place: 施工～ construction site

【場合】chǎnghé（名）occasion: 説話看～ suit one's words to the occasion

【場所】chǎngsuǒ（名）arena; place; ground: 娛樂～ places of amusement

【場面】chǎngmiàn（名）❶（in a film or drama）scene ❷ spectacle; scene: 動人的～ moving scene ❸ facade; appearance: 撐～ preserve appearances

堡 bǎo（名）fort; fortress: 橋頭～ bridgehead
see also bǔ

【堡壘】bǎolěi（名）fortress; bastion; bulwark; stronghold

堡 bǔ（名）[used mostly in place names] walled village
see also bǎo

塗 tú（動）❶ spread on; paint: ～層 coating ❷ scribble; scrawl ❸ blot out

【塗改】túgǎi（動）alter: ～編號 alter the serial number

【塗抹】túmǒ（動）❶ smear; daub ❷ scrawl

【塗料】túliào（名）coating（material）; paint

【塗脂抹粉】tú zhī mǒ fěn〈成〉prettify; whitewash

塞 sāi I（動）stuff; cram: 把文件～進抽屜 cram papers into a drawer II（名）stopper; cork
see also sài; sè

【塞子】sāizi（名）stopper; cork; plug

塞 sài（名）strategic stronghold: 要～ fortress
see also sāi; sè

【塞內加爾】Sàinèijiā'ěr（名）Senegal: ～人 Senegalese

【塞外】sàiwài（名）land beyond (north of) the Great Wall

【塞舌爾】Sàishé'ěr（名）Seychelles: ～人 Seychellois

【塞拉利昂】Sàilālì'áng（名）Sierra Leone: ～人 Sierra Leonian

【塞浦路斯】Sàipǔlùsī（名）Cyprus: ～人 Cypriot

【塞翁失馬】sài wēng shī mǎ〈成〉(misfortune may be) a blessing in disguise

塞 sè
see also sāi; sài

【塞音】sèyīn（名）〈語〉plosive

【塞擦音】sècāyīn（名）〈語〉affricate

塑 sù（動）mould: ～～尊佛像 mould a statue of Buddha

【塑料】sùliào（名）plastics: ～袋 plastic bag

【塑造】sùzào（動）❶ mould ❷（in literature）portray

【塑像】sùxiàng（名）statue; sculpture: 半身～ bust

塘 táng（名）❶ embankment: 河～ river embankment ❷ pool of water: 池～ pond ❸ bathing pool: 澡～ public bathroom

塔 tǎ（名）❶ tower ❷（Buddhist）pagoda ❸ dagoba

【塔吊】tǎdiào（名）tower crane; derrick

【塔臺】tǎtái（名）〈航空〉control tower

【塔樓】tǎlóu（名）tower-shaped building

填 tián（動）❶ fill; cram; stuff: 把坑～平 fill up the hollow ❷ fill in; write: ～月報表 fill in a monthly progress form

【填空】tiánkòng（動）❶ fill a vacancy ❷ fill in blanks（in a quiz, etc.）

【填補】tiánbǔ（動）fill（a gap, etc.）：～一項空白 fill in a gap

【填寫】tiánxiě（動）fill in（a form, etc.）：～登記表 fill in a registration form

塌 tā（動）❶ collapse; cave in ❷ sink; be depressed: 他的肩膀往下～了。His shoulders drooped. ❸ calm down; settle down: 下心來工作 get down to work

【塌方】tāfāng Ⅰ（動）cave in Ⅱ（名）landslide; landslip

【塌陷】tāxiàn（動）sink; cave in

塢 wù（名）area which is lower than the rest of the surface; depression: 船～ dock

塊 kuài Ⅰ（名）piece; cube; lump: 一堆磚～ a heap of bricks Ⅱ（量）❶ piece; plot（of land）: 一～巧克力 a bar of chocolate / 一～肥皂 a cake of soap ❷〈口〉yuan: 一～錢 一公斤 one yuan per kilogram

【塊煤】kuàiméi（名）lump coal

塾 shú（名）old-style private school

塵 chén（名）❶ dust; dirt: 粉～ powder-like waste ❷ this world: 看破紅～ see through the vanities of this mortal world

【塵土】chéntǔ（名）dust; dirt: ～飛揚 raise a cloud of dust

【塵世】chénshì（名）this mortal human world; this mortal life

【塵埃】chén'āi（名）dust

【塵暴】chénbào（名）〈氣〉 dust storm

境 jìng（名）❶ border;（national）boundary: 驅逐出～ deport; expel from a country ❷ area; land ❸ circumstances; condition: 處於順（逆）～ be in favourable（adverse）circumstances

【境內】jìngnèi（副）within the borders; in the country

【境地】jìngdì（名）circumstances; state: 處於進退兩難的～ be in a dilemma

【境況】jìngkuàng（名）（financial）circumstances: ～不佳 in straitened circumstances

【境界】jìngjiè（名）❶（of land）boundary; border ❷ state; realm: 達到高度的藝術～ attain a high level of art

【境遇】jìngyù（名）fortune; lot

墊 diàn Ⅰ（動）❶ put a pad under sth. to raise it or make it level; pad ❷ pay for sb.（on a loan basis）: 你身邊如果沒有錢, 我可以～上。I can pay for you if you have no money with you. Ⅱ（名）cushion; pad

【墊子】diànzi（名）mat; cushion

【墊肩】diànjiān（名）shoulder pad

【墊圈】diànquān（名）〈機〉washer

塹 qiàn（名）moat; chasm

【塹壕】qiànháo（名）〈軍〉trench; entrenchment

墟 xū（名）❶ ruins ❷ fair; market: 趕～ go to market

墓 mù（名）tomb; grave: 陵～ mausoleum

【墓地】mùdì（名）graveyard; cemetery

【墓室】mùshì (名) coffin chamber

【墓碑】mùbēi (名) tombstone; gravestone

【墓誌銘】mùzhìmíng (名) inscription on a tombstone; epitaph

墅 shù (名) villa: 別～ villa; country house

墩 dūn I (名) ❶ mound ❷ block of stone or wood II (量) cluster: 一～草 a cluster of grass

【墩布】dūnbù (名) mop

增 zēng (動) increase: 該市人口大～。The population of the city has greatly increased. / ～產 increase production

【增白劑】zēngbáijì (名) 〈化〉brightening agent; brightener

【增加】zēngjiā (動) increase; raise: 出口逐年～。The exports have been increasing from year to year. / ～定額 raise the quota

【增刊】zēngkān (名) supplement (to a newspaper or periodical); supplementary issue

【增生】zēngshēng (名) 〈醫〉hyperplasia; proliferation; multiplication

【增光】zēngguāng (動) add to the glory: 爲國～ win honours for the country

【增收】zēngshōu (動) increase income; earn more

【增色】zēngsè (動) add to the beauty (brilliance, prestige, etc.) of; rise: 貿易在逐年～。Trade is gradually increasing. / ～見識 enrich one's experience

【增訂】zēngdìng (動) revise and enlarge (a book)

【增值】zēngzhí (名) 〈經〉appreciation; increment

【增進】zēngjìn (動) enhance; promote: ～了解 promote understanding

【增添】zēngtiān (動) add; replenish: ～新品種 increase new varieties / ～他的憂慮 add to his anxieties

【增強】zēngqiáng (動) strengthen; enhance: ～責任心 heighten the sense of responsibility / ～體質 build up one's physique

【增援】zēngyuán (動) 〈軍〉reinforce

【增補】zēngbǔ (動) supplement; add

墳 fén (名) grave; tomb

【墳地】féndì (名) graveyard; cemetery

【墳墓】fénmù (名) tomb; grave

墜 zhuì I (動) ❶ fall; drop: 搖搖欲～ tottering ❷ weigh down: 豐滿的穀穗～下頭去。The plump ears of the rice make the stalks droop. II (名) weight; hanging object: 耳～ ear pendant

【墜毀】zhuìhuǐ (動) (of a plane, etc.) crash

【墜落】zhuìluò (動) fall; drop: ～海中 crash into the sea

墮 duò (動) fall; sink

【墮胎】duòtāi (名) (induced) abortion

【墮落】duòluò (動) degenerate

墨 mò I (名) ❶ ink; ink stick ❷ learning: 胸無點～ practically illiterate II (形) black; dark

【墨水】mòshuǐ (名) ❶ ink ❷ book learning: 他肚子裏還有點~。He is not entirely without learning.

【墨水瓶】mòshuǐpíng (名) ink bottle

【墨斗魚】mòdǒuyú (名) cuttlefish; inkfish

【墨汁】mòzhī (名) liquid Chinese ink

【墨西哥】Mòxīgē (名) Mexico: ~人 Mexican

【墨守成規】mò shǒu chéng guī 〈成〉cling to old conventions; follow the routine

【墨迹】mòjì (名) ❶ ink mark ❷ (sb.'s) treasured handwriting or painting

【墨家】Mòjiā (名) ❶ Mohist School ❷ Mohist

【墨盒】mòhé (名) Chinese ink box

【墨綠】mòlǜ (名) dark green

【墨鏡】mòjìng (名) sun-glasses

【墨寶】mòbǎo (名) ❶ priceless scrolls of calligraphy or painting ❷ 〈敬〉your treasured handwriting or painting

壅 yōng (動) ❶ block; obstruct: ~塞 blocked up; jammed ❷ heap soil or fertilizer around the roots of plants: ~土 hilling

壇 tán (名) ❶ altar ❷ area of soil slightly raised for growing flowers: 花~ flower bed ❸ plaform; forum; tribune: 文學論~ forum on literature ❹ circles; world: 文~ literary circles

壁 bì (名) ❶ wall: 四~ the four walls (of a room) ❷ anything resembling a wall; wall-like structure: 細胞~ cell wall ❸ cliff: 懸崖峭~ overhanging cliff and sheer precipice ❹ breastwork; rampart: 作~上觀 watch the fighting from the rampart; sit by and watch; be an onlooker or bystander

【壁虎】bìhǔ (名) gecko; house lizard

【壁畫】bìhuà (名) fresco; mural painting: 敦煌~ Dunhuang frescoes (Gansu Province, Northwest China, dating from 36 A.D.)

【壁報】bìbào (牆報 qiángbào) (名) wall newspaper; handwritten wall bulletin

【壁毯】bìtǎn (名) tapestry; wall tapestry

【壁燈】bìdēng (名) wall lamp; bracket light

【壁壘】bìlěi (名) rampart; breastwork

【壁壘分明】bì lěi fēn míng 〈成〉diametrically opposed; sharply divided

【壁壘森嚴】bì lěi sēn yán 〈成〉❶ strongly fortified and closely guarded ❷ sharply divided

【壁櫥】bìchú (名) built-in wardrobe (cabinet)

【壁爐】bìlú (名) fireplace

墾 kěn (動) turn over the soil; cultivate land; reclaim (wasteland)

【墾荒】kěnhuāng (動) reclaim wasteland

【墾區】kěnqū (名) reclamation area

壕 háo (名) ditch: 戰~ trench

壓 yā (動) ❶ press; weigh down: 用書把紙~住 put a book on a piece of paper to hold it down ❷ control; hold down; quell: ~住怒火 control one's anger ❸ suppress; crack down: ~敵人投降 force the enemy to surrender / 倚勢~人 abuse one's power and boss people about ❹ shelve; pigeonhole: 信～在他那裏都三天了。He has held up the letter for three days. ❺ keep long in stock: ～貨 cargoes kept long in stock (at a port or station)

【壓力】yālì（名）pressure: 屈服於～ yield to pressure / 在公衆～下 under popular pressure

【壓力鍋】yālìguō（名）pressure cooker

【壓平】yāpíng（動）flatten

【壓低】yādī（動）lower; cut; reduce: ～嗓子 lower one's voice

【壓抑】yāyì（動）constrain; hold back; depress: ～感情 control one's feelings

【壓制】yāzhì（動）suppress; smother: ～批評 gag criticism

【壓迫】yāpò Ⅰ（動）oppress Ⅱ（名）oppression

【壓服】yāfú（動）overwhelm; coerce: 企圖～ try to browbeat sb. into submission

【壓垮】yākuǎ（動）crush; fall apart under pressure: 人民的意志是無法～的。The will of the people cannot be crushed.

【壓倒】yādǎo（動）overwhelm; suddue: ～多數 overwhelming majority

【壓軸戲】yāzhóuxì（名）last and best item on a theatrical programme

【壓歲錢】yāsuìqián（名）money given to children as a Spring Festival gift

【壓路機】yālùjī（名）road roller; roller

【壓榨】yāzhà（動）❶ squeeze; press: ～大豆造油 press soya-beans to yield oil ❷ exploit: ～奴隸 exploit the slaves

【壓價】yājià（動）force the price down; reduce the price

【壓縮】yāsuō（動）compress; cut; reduce: ～篇幅 shorten an article / ～餅乾 ship biscuit / ～開支 cut down expenditure

【壓榨】yāzhà（動）crush; squash

【壓彎】yāwān（動）bend

【壓驚】yājīng（動）help sb. get over a shock (usu. with drinks)

壑 hè（名）gully; big pool; ravine

壘 lěi Ⅰ（動）build（with bricks, stones or earth）; pile up: ～河壩 build a river embankment Ⅱ（名）❶ rampart ❷（of baseball and softball）base: 全～打 home run

【壘球】lěiqiú（名）softball

壟 lǒng（名）❶ ridge in a field ❷ raised path between fields

【壟斷】lǒngduàn Ⅰ（動）monopolize Ⅱ（名）monopoly

【壟斷資本】lǒngduàn zīběn（名）monopoly capital

【壟斷價格】lǒngduàn jiàgé（名）monopoly price

壞 huài Ⅰ（形）bad; evil: ～名聲 bad reputation Ⅱ（動）go bad; be out of order: 鷄蛋～了。It's a rotten egg. Ⅲ（副）badly; extremely; very: 急～了 be awfully anxious

【壞人】huàirén（名）wicked person; villain; evil-doer

【壞分子】huàifènzǐ（名）offender; evildoer

【壞死】huàisǐ（名）necrosis

【壞血病】huàixuèbìng（名）scurvy

【壞事】huàishì Ⅰ（名）bad thing; evil deed Ⅱ（動）make matters worse

【壞處】huàichu（名）harm; disadvantage

【壞蛋】huàidàn（名）〈罵〉bad egg; scoundrel; rascal

【壞話】huàihuà（名）unkind comments about sb.; unpleasant words

壜 tán（名）earthen jar or jug: ～子 earthen jar

【壜壜罐罐】tántán guànguàn（名）pots and pans; kitchen utensils; household articles

壤 rǎng（名）❶ soil: 土～ soil ❷ earth ❸ area: 僻～ remote place

【壤土】rǎngtǔ（名）〈農〉loam

壩 bà（名）❶ dam ❷ dyke; embankment ❸ [used in place names] flatland; plain

士 部

士 shì（名）❶ scholar ❷（commendable form of address）: 王女～ Madam Wang／愛國志～ noble-minded patriot ❸ person (of a certain profession）: 鬥牛～ matador ❹ noncommissioned officer; private: 戰～ soldier; private ❺ bodyguard, a piece in Chinese chess

【士大夫】shìdàfū（名）〈舊〉feudal scholar-officials; literati

【士兵】shìbīng（名）private; soldier; serviceman

【士卒】shìzú（名）rank-and-file; soldiers; men

【士氣】shìqì（名）morale

【士紳】shìshēn（名）(landed) gentry

壯 zhuàng Ⅰ（形）❶ strong; robust; stout: 年輕力～ young and strong ❷ grand; majestic Ⅱ（動）strengthen: ～膽 embolden; boost sb.'s courage Ⅲ（Zhuàng）（名）the Zhuang nationality

【壯大】zhuàngdà（動）strengthen; grow in strength

【壯工】zhuànggōng（名）unskilled labourer

【壯士】zhuàngshì（名）heroic man; warrior

【壯年】zhuàngnián（名）prime of life

【壯志】zhuàngzhì（名）great aspiration; lofty ambition

【壯烈】zhuàngliè（形）brave and noble; heroic: ～犧牲 meet one's death like a hero

【壯實】zhuàngshi（形）strong; sturdy

【壯舉】zhuàngjǔ（名）heroic undertaking; remarkable feat

【壯闊】zhuàngkuò（形）grand; magnificent; grandiose

【壯麗】zhuànglì（形）magnificent; majestic; splendid

【壯觀】zhuàngguān（形）magnificent; imposing

壹 yī（數）[the elaborate form of the numeral used on cheques, banknotes, etc.] one

壺 hú（名）kettle; pot: 茶～ teapot

壽 shòu Ⅰ（名）❶ longevity ❷ life; age: 人～保險 life insurance ❸ birthday: ～禮 birthday present (usu. for an elderly person) Ⅱ（形）〈婉〉for burial: ～衣 gravecloth; shroud

【壽辰】shòuchén（名）birthday（of an old person）

【壽命】shòumìng（名）life span: 平均～ life expectancy

【壽星】shòuxīng（名）❶ God of Longevity ❷ elderly person for whom a birthday celebration is being held

【壽終正寢】shòu zhōng zhèng qǐn〈成〉❶ die of a ripe old age; die ❷ come to an end（often with a touch of sarcasm）

夂 部

夏 xià（名）❶ summer ❷（Xià）a surname

【夏天】xiàtiān（名）summer

【夏令】xiàlìng（名）summer-time; summer

【夏令營】xiàlìngyíng（名）summer camp

【夏季】xiàjì（名）summer; summer-time; summer season

【夏曆】xiàlì（名）traditional Chinese calendar; lunar calendar

夕 部

夕 xī（名）❶ sunset; dusk ❷ evening; night

【夕陽】xīyáng（名）setting sun

【夕煙】xīyān（名）evening mist

【夕照】xīzhào（名）evening sunglow

外 wài Ⅰ（形）❶ external; foreign: ～商 foreign trader ❷ outside; outer: ～牆 outer walls ❸ other: ～埠 other towns and cities ❹（relatives）of one's mother, sister or daughter: ～孫（～孫女）grandson（granddaughter）/ ～祖父（～祖母）grandpa（grandma）/ ～甥（～甥女）nephew（niece）❺ in addition; extra: 一客份飯 ～加一瓶啤酒 a table d'hôte and a bottle of beer Ⅱ（名）foreign country: 對～開放 open to the outside world / 對～關係 foreign relations

【外人】wàirén（名）❶ stranger ❷ outsider

【外文】wàiwén（外語 wàiyǔ）（名）foreign language

【外引】wàiyǐn（動）introduce from other localities or foreign countries

【外交】wàijiāo（名）diplomacy; foreign affairs: ～官 diplomat / ～部 Foreign Ministry / ～部長 foreign minister / 建立（斷絕）～關係 establish（sever）diplomatic relations

【外地】wàidì（名）parts of the country other than where one is; other palace

【外行】wàiháng（名）layman; amateur

【外向】wàixiàng（形）extroverted

【外向型】wàixiàngxíng（形）❶ export-oriented: ～經濟 export-oriented economy ❷ extrovert

【外快】wàikuài（名）additional income（for an extra job, etc.）

【外形】wàixíng（名）shape

【外來】wàilái（形）foreign; outside: ～電話 incoming call

【外事】wàishì（名）foreign affairs

【外長】wàizhǎng（名）（short for 外交部長 wàijiāo bùzhǎng）foreign

minister

【外表】wàibiǎo（名）appearance; surface; veneer

【外界】wàijiè（名）outside world: 與~隔絕 be cut off from the outside world / ~有種種謠言. There are all sorts of rumours in various circles.

【外科】wàikē（名）〈醫〉surgical department: ~醫生 surgeon

【外面】wàimian（副）outside: 去~散步 go out for a walk

【外屋】wàiwū（名）outer room; anteroom

【外星人】wàixīngrén（名）extraterrestrial; ET

【外流】wàiliú（名）drain; outflow: 資金~ outflow of funds / 制止人才~ halt the brain drain

【外套】wàitào（外衣 wàiyī）（名）overcoat

【外帶】wàidài I（名）tyre;（rubber）cover II（副）in addition

【外國】wàiguó（名）foreign country: ~人 foreigner; alien / ~語 foreign language

【外殼】wàiké（名）（empty）shell; outer casing

【外貿】wàimào（名）（short for 對外貿易 duìwài màoyì）foreign trade

【外鄉】wàixiāng（名）another part of the country: ~人 person from another locality

【外援】wàiyuán（名）foreign aid

【外電】wàidiàn（名）reports from foreign news agencies

【外匯】wàihuì（名）foreign exchange: ~券 foreign exchange certificate（FEC）/ ~匯率 foreign exchange rate

【外傳】wàizhuàn（名）anecdotes;

unofficial biography

【外傷】wàishāng（名）wound; external injury: 腿部一處受~ receive an injury to the leg

【外債】wàizhài（名）foreign debt

【外資】wàizī（名）foreign capital

【外賓】wàibīn（名）foreign guest（visitor）

【外僑】wàiqiáo（名）foreign national

【外貌】wàimào（名）（of a person）features; appearance

【外幣】wàibì（外鈔 wàichāo）（名）foreign currency: ~兌換處 money exchange

【外調】wàidiào（動）❶ transfer a person from one work unit to another ❷ transfer goods from one locality to another

【外銷】wàixiāo（形）earmarked for sale abroad or in other localities

【外層空間】wàicéng kōngjiān（名）outer space

【外邊】wàibian（外頭 wàitou）（副）❶ outside ❷ away from home: 我在~待了好幾年了. I've been away from home for several years.

【外籍】wàijí（形）of foreign nationality: ~專家 foreign expert

【外觀】wàiguān（名）appearance; veneer

多 duō I（形）❶ many; much ❷ more than: 十~年 more than ten years ❸ much more: 清楚了~ much clearer II（副）❶ how: 你要待~久? How long are you going to stay? ❷ [used in exclamatory sentences]how; what: 她唱得~好啊! How well she sings! / ~好的天氣! What a nice day!

【多久】duōjiǔ（副）how long

【多才多艺】duō cái duō yì〈形〉versatile: ~的人 a versatile man

【多方】duōfāng〈副〉in many ways: ~求援 seek assistance from many quarters

【多少】duōshǎo Ⅰ〈名〉amount; number: ~不等 very in number Ⅱ〈副〉somewhat; more or less Ⅲ〈代〉how many; how much: ❶ [used in interrogative sentences] 礼堂里有~人? How many people are there in the auditorium? ❷ [used to indicate an uncertain quantity] 要~，拿~。Take as much as you want.

【多心】duōxīn〈形〉oversensitive

【多半】duōbàn Ⅰ〈形〉most; mostly Ⅱ〈副〉most likely

【多此一举】duō cǐ yī jǔ〈成〉make an unnecessary move

【多米尼加】Duōmǐníjiā〈名〉Dominica: ~人 Dominican

【多多益善】duō duō yì shàn〈成〉the more the better

【多灾多难】duō zāi duō nàn〈形〉disaster-ridden; long-suffering

【多事】duōshì〈形〉❶ meddle-some ❷ eventful: ~之秋 troubled times

【多面手】duōmiànshǒu〈名〉person of many parts; versatile person

【多哥】Duōgē〈名〉Togo: ~人 Togolese

【多情】duōqíng〈形〉endowed with a romantic temperament

【多国公司】duōguógōngsī〈名〉multinational corporation

【多云】duōyún〈形〉cloudy

【多愁善感】duō chóu shàn gǎn〈形〉excessively sentimental

【多么】duōme〈副〉how; what: ~巨大的变化! How great the changes are! / ~可爱的孩子! What a lovely child!

【多疑】duōyí〈形〉suspicious

【多数】duōshù〈名〉majority: ~票 majority vote

【多余】duōyú〈形〉superfluous; unnecessary

【多嘴】duōzuǐ〈动〉make unwarranted remarks

【多谋善断】duō móu shàn duàn〈成〉resourceful and decisive

【多亏】duōkuī〈副〉owing to; fortunately: ~他的指导，我们缆取得一些成绩。We owe it all to his guidance that we have scored some achievements.

【多谢】duōxiè〈套〉thanks a lot

【多边】duōbiān〈形〉multilateral

凤 sù〈形〉long-standing; long-cherished

【凤愿】sùyuàn〈名〉long-cherished wish

夜 yè〈名〉night; evening: ~生活 night life

【夜大学】yèdàxué〈名〉evening university; sparetime school

【夜以继日】yè yǐ jì rì〈成〉day and night

【夜半】yèbàn〈名〉midnight

【夜市】yèshì〈名〉night market

【夜光】yèguāng〈形〉luminous: ~镖 luminous watch

【夜车】yèchē〈名〉night train: 开~ work deep into the night; burn the midnight oil

【夜盲】yèmáng〈名〉night blindness; nyctalopia

【夜长梦多】yè cháng mèng duō〈成〉unexpected problems often crop up

in the course of a long delay; There is many a slip between the cup and the lip.

【夜郎自大】 yè láng zì dà 〈成〉 be ludicrously conceited (like the King of Yelang)

【夜班】 yèbān（名）night shift

【夜航】 yèháng（名）night flight

【夜宵】 yèxiāo（名）night snack

【夜校】 yèxiào（名）evening school; night school

【夜晚】 yèwǎn（名）night

【夜場】 yèchǎng（名）evening show

【夜間】 yèjiān（副）at night

【夜壺】 yèhú（名）chamber pot

【夜幕】 yèmù（名）darkness of night; night: ～來臨。Night began to fall.

【夜餐】 yècān（名）night snack

【夜闌人靜】 yè lán rén jìng〈成〉in the dead of night; in the silent hours of the night

【夜總會】 yèzǒnghuì（名）nightclub

【夜鶯】 yèyīng（名）night-ingale

夠 gòu I（形）enough; sufficient II（動）reach: ～不着 be out of reach

【夠嗆】 gòuqiàng（形）〈方〉terrible: 累得～ be dog-tired

夢 mèng（名）dream

【夢幻】 mènghuàn（名）illusion

【夢見】 mèngjiàn（動）see in a dream; dream of: 她常常～童年的朋友。She often dreamt about her childhood friends.

【夢鄉】 mèngxiāng（名）dreamland; dream

【夢遊症】 mèngyóuzhèng（名）somnambulism; sleepwalking

【夢寐以求】 mèng mèi yǐ qiú〈成〉crave for sth. day and night; long for

【夢寐難忘】 mèng mèi nán wàng〈成〉cannot forget; always keep in mind

【夢話】 mènghuà（名）❶ talk in one's sleep ❷ nonsense: 你又在説～了。You are daydreaming.

【夢想】 mèngxiǎng I（動）dream of: ～成爲名演員 dream of becoming a famous actor II（名）dream; wishful thinking: ～變成了現實。The dream has come true. / 這純屬～。It is nothing but an idle dream.

【夢境】 mèngjìng（名）dreamland; dream: 多年後他再見到她, 宛如～。After so many years, he saw her again, as if in a dream.

【夢囈】 mèngyì（名）❶ talk in one's sleep ❷ ravings

【夢魘】 mèngyǎn（名）〈醫〉nightmare

夥 huǒ I（名）partner; companion: 散～ part company II（量）group; band: 一～人 a group of people

【夥同】 huǒtóng（動）be in league with; act in collusion with

【夥伴】 huǒbàn（名）partner; companion

【夥計】 huǒji（名）❶ partner ❷ shop assistant; salesclerk

大 部

大 dà I（形）❶ big; large: ～樓 a large building ❷ eldest: ～哥 elder (eldest) brother ❸ earlier or later than: ～前年 two years before last / ～後天 three days from now ❹ old: 小孩兒多～了? How old is the child? Ⅱ (副) greatly; on a big scale: 禁止～吃～喝 ban feasting at public expense Ⅲ 〈敬〉your: ～作 your celebrated work Ⅳ (Dà) (名) a surname

see also dài

【大力】dàlì Ⅰ (名) great effort Ⅱ (副) with great efforts; vigorously: ～支持 extend vigorous support to

【大人】dàrén (名) adult

【大人物】dàrénwù (名) VIP; bigwig

【大刀闊斧】dà dāo kuò fǔ 〈成〉 boldly and resolutely

【大大】dàdà (副) greatly; considerably

【大凡】dàfán (副) in most cases

【大小】dàxiǎo (名) ❶ size: ～相同 be of the same size ❷ seniority: 不分～ regardless of seniority in age ❸ adults and children

【大千世界】dàqiān shìjiè (名) boundless universe

【大方】dàfāng (名) expert: 貽笑～ incur the disdian of experts

【大方】dàfang (形) ❶ generous: 用錢～ be liberal with money ❷ natural; easy-mannered ❸ tasteful: 她衣着～。She's dressed in good taste.

【大戶】dàhù (名) ❶ rich and powerful family ❷ large family

【大白】dàbái (動) come to light: 真相～。The truth has come out.

【大半】dàbàn Ⅰ (名) more than half Ⅱ (副) very likely

【大失所望】dà shī suǒ wàng (形) bitterly disappointed

【大本營】dàběnyíng (名) ❶ headquarters ❷ base camp

【大甩賣】dàshuǎimài (名) big sale

【大地】dàdì (名) the earth

【大好】dàhǎo (形) excellent: ～風光 beautiful scenery

【大江】dàjiāng (名) ❶ long river ❷ Changjiang (Yangtze) River

【大衣】dàyī (名) overcoat

【大多】dàduō (副) mostly; chiefly

【大多數】dàduōshù (名) great majority: 絶～ the overwhelming majority

【大同小異】dà tóng xiǎo yì 〈成〉 very similar but with minor differences

【大有文章】dà yǒu wén zhāng 〈成〉 there is sth. more to it than you can think of; the matter is more complicated than it appears

【大有作爲】dà yǒu zuò wéi 〈成〉 be able to fully develop one's talents; be able to accomplish much

【大西洋】Dàxīyáng (名) Atlantic Ocean

【大臣】dàchén (名) minister (of a monarch)

【大合唱】dàhéchàng (名) cantata; group singing; chorus

【大名鼎鼎】dàmíng dǐngdǐng (形) famous; well-known

【大伯】dàbó (名) father's elder brother; uncle

【大批】dàpī (形) large quantities of

【大豆】dàdòu (名) soya bean

【大志】dàzhì (名) lofty ambition

【大亨】dàhēng (名) magnate

【大局】dàjú (名) overall situation: 顧全～ bear the overall public interest in mind

【大快人心】dà kuài rén xīn 〈成〉(of punishment of evildoers) to the immense gratification of the public

【大材小用】dà cái xiǎo yòng 〈成〉

assign talented people to petty jobs; a waste of talent

【大言不惭】dà yán bù cán〈成〉boast brazenly

【大吹大擂】dà chuī dà lèi〈成〉give sth. unusually wide publicity; raise a great fanfare

【大吹法螺】dà chuī fǎ luó〈成〉blow one's own trumpet

【大抵】dàdǐ（副）approximately

【大典】dàdiǎn（名）solemn ceremony（held by the state）

【大事】dàshì Ⅰ（名）major event Ⅱ（副）in a big way: ~宣扬 give wide publicity

【大河】dàhé（名）❶ long river ❷ Huanghe（Yellow）River

【大使】dàshǐ（名）ambassador

【大使馆】dàshǐguǎn（名）embassy

【大放厥词】dà fàng jué cí〈成〉talk a lot of rubbish

【大便】dàbiàn Ⅰ（名）stool Ⅱ（动）go to stool; move the bowels

【大度】dàdù（形）generous; tolerant; broad-minded

【大计】dàjì（名）plan of far-reaching importance: 百年~ a programme of long-term importance

【大约】dàyuē（副）approximately; about

【大是大非】dà shì dà fēi（名）cardinal principle of right and wrong

【大逆不道】dà nì bù dào〈成〉heinous crime; gross treachery

【大相径庭】dà xiāng jìng tíng〈成〉act in direct contradiction; hold divergent views

【大气】dàqì（名）〈气〉atmosphere: ~污染 air pollution

【大家】dàjiā（名）everyone; all

【大员】dàyuán（名）〈旧〉high-ranking official

【大致】dàzhì（副）roughly; more or less

【大师】dàshī（名）❶ grand master: 艺术~ grand master of art ❷ title used to address a Buddhist monk

【大师傅】dàshīfu（名）cook; chef

【大庭广众】dà tíng guǎng zhòng〈成〉before a large audience: ~之下 on public occasions

【大海捞针】dà hǎi lāo zhēn〈成〉look for a needle in a haystack

【大略】dàlüè Ⅰ（副）roughly; approximately Ⅱ（名）general idea; gist: 计划的~ a gist of the plan

【大赦】dàshè Ⅰ（名）amnesty Ⅱ（动）grant amnesty to

【大陆】dàlù（名）continent; mainland

【大陆架】dàlùjià（名）continental shelf

【大进大出】dàjìn dàchū（动）import and export on a big scale

【大部分】dà bùfen（名）majority; greater part; most

【大理石】dàlǐshí（名）marble

【大动脉】dàdòngmài（名）❶ main artery ❷ trunk railway

【大扫除】dàsǎochú（名）thorough cleanup; spring-cleaning

【大张旗鼓】dà zhāng qí gǔ〈成〉in a big way; with a flourish

【大规模】dàguīmó Ⅰ（副）on a large scale Ⅱ（形）massive; extensive: ~毁灭性武器 weapon of mass destruction

【大量】dàliàng（形）❶ plenty of; a large number of ❷ magnanimous; large-minded

【大街】dàjiē（名）main street; avenue; thoroughfare

【大众】dàzhòng Ⅰ（名）the masses; the public Ⅱ（形）popular

【大运河】Dàyùnhé（名）Grand Canal

【大智若愚】dà zhì ruò yú〈成〉a man of great wisdom often appears slow-witted

【大提琴】dàtíqín（名）violoncello

【大发雷霆】dà fā léi tíng〈成〉fly into a fury

【大厦】dàshà（名）large building; mansion; edifice

【大脑】dànǎo（名）〈生理〉cerebrum

【大势】dàshì（名）general trend

【大肆】dàsì（副）unrestrainedly

【大话】dàhuà（名）boast

【大意】dàyì（名）general idea; gist

【大意】dàyi（形）careless

【大腹便便】dà fù pián pián〈成〉big-bellied

【大义凛然】dà yì lǐn rán〈成〉unyielding and awe-inspiring in defence of justice

【大概】dàgài Ⅰ（名）overall picture Ⅱ（形）approximate Ⅲ（副）probably

【大纲】dàgāng（名）outline: 教学 ～ syllabus

【大写】dàxiě（名）❶ elaborate form of a numeral in Chinese ❷ capitalization

【大选】dàxuǎn（名）general election

【大模大样】dà mó dà yàng〈成〉assume an air of self-importance

【大静脉】dàjìngmài（名）〈生理〉vena cava

【大学】dàxué（名）university; college: ～生 college student; undergraduate

【大锅饭】dàguōfàn（名）big rice pot: 吃～（with everybody）eating from the same big pot; get regular pay without reference to work

【大胆】dàdǎn（形）❶ bold; courageous ❷ audacious

【大粪】dàfèn（名）human excrement; night soil

【大声疾呼】dàshēng jíhū（动）cry out to draw attention to matters of immediate urgency; cry out to warn people of the grave situation

【大权】dàquán（名）power; authority

【大体】dàtǐ Ⅰ（副）generally; on the whole; basically Ⅱ（名）leading principle

【大惊小怪】dà jīng xiǎo guài〈成〉kick up a big fuss over a trivial matter

【大显身手】dà xiǎn shēn shǒu〈成〉brilliantly exercise one's talent

【大观】dàguān（名）grand view

大 dài
see also dà

【大夫】dàifu（名）doctor; physician

天 tiān Ⅰ（名）❶ sky; heaven ❷ day: 白～ daytime ❸ time: ～晚了。It's getting late. ❹ season: 冬～ winter ❺ weather: ～不好 nasty weather ❻ nature: ～敌 natural enemy ❼ God: ～哪! My goodness! Ⅱ（形）overhead: ～车 overhead travelling crane

【天才】tiāncái（名）❶ genius; gift: ～的创作 work of genius ❷ gifted person; genius

【天大】tiāndà（形）extremely big; enormous; huge: ～的笑话! What a big joke!

【天下】tiānxià（名）❶ world; the whole of China: 愿～太平。May

peace reign on earth! ❷ rule; domination: 那裏全是他一個人的～。 He has all the say there.

【天子】 tiānzǐ (名) Son of Heaven; emperor

【天分】 tiānfèn (名) talent; (natural) endowment

【天井】 tiānjǐng (名) ❶ courtyard; patio ❷ skylight

【天天】 tiāntiān (副) every day

【天文】 tiānwén (名) astronomy: ～館 planetarium / ～臺 astronomical observatory

【天平】 tiānpíng (名) scales; balance

【天生】 tiānshēng (形) born; innate; congenital: 他～是個歌手。 He is a born singer.

【天仙】 tiānxiān (名) ❶ goddess from the celestial sphere ❷ beautiful girl: 她真是個～。 She is really a beauty.

【天主教】 Tiānzhǔjiào (名) Catholicism; Roman Catholic Church

【天地】 tiāndì (名) ❶ heaven and earth; universe: 這種事爲～所不容! Heaven forbid! ❷ range of activities; world: 孩子的小～ children's small world

【天色】 tiānsè (名) colour of sky; time of the day: ～還早。 It is still early.

【天安門】 Tiān'ānmén (名) Tian An Men (Gate of Heavenly Peace)

【天良】 tiānliáng (名) conscience

【天災】 tiānzāi (名) natural calamity: ～人禍 natural and man-made calamities

【天空】 tiānkōng (名) sky

【天使】 tiānshǐ (名) angel

【天性】 tiānxìng (名) one's nature; natural disposition

【天花】 tiānhuā (名) 〈醫〉 smallpox

【天花板】 tiānhuābǎn (名) ceiling

【天底下】 tiān dǐxia (副) 〈口〉 on earth; in the world: ～沒有人會相信的。 Nobody on earth would believe it.

【天府之國】 tiān fǔ zhī guó 〈成〉 (usu. referring to Sichuan Province) Nature's storehouse; land of plenty

【天津】 Tiānjīn (名) Tianjin

【天亮】 tiānliàng (名) dawn; daybreak

【天南地北】 tiān nán dì běi 〈成〉 ❶ far apart ❷ from various places: 來自～的青年人 young people from all over the land

【天南海北】 tiān nán hǎi běi 〈成〉 ❶ all over the country ❷ rambling; armless: 兩人～地一直談到早晨兩三點鐘。 They kept talking at random till the small hours of the morning.

【天氣】 tiānqì (名) weather: ～預報 weather forecast

【天真】 tiānzhēn (形) naive; unsophisticated; innocent

【天倫之樂】 tiān lún zhī lè 〈成〉 family bliss: 享受～ enjoy a happy family life

【天堂】 tiāntáng (名) heaven; paradise

【天涯海角】 tiān yá hǎi jiǎo 〈成〉 (remotest) corners of the earth; faraway places

【天窗】 tiānchuāng (名) 〈建〉 skylight: 打開～說亮話 frankly speaking

【天然】 tiānrán (形) natural: ～氣 natural gas

【天資】 tiānzī (名) talent; gift

【天意】 tiānyì（名）Heaven's design; God's will

【天經地義】 tiān jīng dì yì〈成〉 irrefutable cardinal principle; perfectly correct proposition

【天綫】 tiānxiàn（名）aerial; antenna

【天賦】 tiānfù Ⅰ（形）inborn; endowed by nature Ⅱ（名）talent; genius;（natural）endowment

【天機】 tiānjī（名）❶ mysterious Heaven's design or secret: ～不可洩漏。This secret is to be jealously guarded.

【天橋】 tiānqiáo（名）overline bridge; overhead bridge

【天險】 tiānxiǎn（名）natural barrier

【天壇】 Tiāntán（名）Temple of Heaven（in Beijing）

【天曉得】 tiān xiǎode〈口〉Heaven knows; who knows

【天邊】 tiānbiān（名）horizon; remotest place

【天藍】 tiānlán（形）azure; sky blue

【天職】 tiānzhí（名）bounden duty

【天鵝】 tiān'é（名）swan

【天鵝絨】 tiān'éróng（名）velvet

【天翻地覆】 tiān fān dì fù〈成〉❶ earth-shaking changes: 發生～的變化 experience tremendous changes ❷ tremendous commotion: 鬧得～ create enough commotion to upset everybody and everything; create a pandemonium

【天體】 tiāntǐ（名）heavenly body

夫 fū（名）❶ man; labourer: 漁～ fisherman ❷ husband

【夫人】 fūrén（名）❶ Madame; Mrs. ❷ wife

【夫子】 fūzǐ（名）❶ master ❷ learned scholar ❸ pedant

【夫婦】 fūfù（夫妻 fūqī）（名）husband and wife

太 tài Ⅰ（形）❶ highest; remotest: ～古 remote antiquity ❷ most senior: ～公〈方〉great-grandfather Ⅱ（副）❶ excessively; too much: 做得～過了。That's going too far. ❷ [used in praises]extremely: 那～好了。That's great indeed. ❸ [used in negative sentences]very: 不～高 not very tall

【太子】 tàizǐ（名）crown prince

【太太】 tàitai（名）❶ Mrs.; Madame ❷ madam; lady ❸ one's wife: 我～ my wife

【太平】 tàipíng（名）（social）peace: ～門 exit / ～ 梯 fire escape

【太平洋】 Tàipíngyáng（名）the Pacific（Ocean）

【太平間】 tàipíngjiān（名）mortuary

【太后】 tàihòu（名）mother of an emperor; queen mother: 西～ Empress Dowager

【太空】 tàikōng（名）outer space; space: ～時代 space age

【太陽】 tàiyáng（名）❶ sun: ～帽 sun helmet; topee / ～鏡 sunglasses / ～穴 temple（of the head）❷ sunshine

【太陽系】 tàiyángxì（名）solar system

【太陽能】 tàiyángnéng（名）solar energy

【太極拳】 tàijíquán（名）*taijiquan*, a type of traditional Chinese shadow boxing

夭 yāo（動）die young

【夭亡】 yāowáng（動）die young

【夭折】 yāozhé（動）❶ die young ❷ come to a premature end

夯

夯 hāng Ⅰ(名) rammer; ram Ⅱ (動) pound; ram

【夯土機】 hāngtǔjī (名) rammer

【夯歌】 hānggē (名) rammer's work chant

央

央 yāng Ⅰ(名) centre Ⅱ(動) ❶ entreat; beg ❷ end: 樂未～。 The joy is inexhaustible.

【央告】 yānggào (動) beg; implore

【央求】 yāngqiú (動) entreat; plead

失

失 shī Ⅰ(動) ❶ lose; miss: 喪～信心 lose heart; lose confidence ❷ slip; fail to grasp: ～口 a slip of the tongue ❸ get lost: 在林中走～ get lost in the woods ❹ fail to achieve one's objective ❺ turn abnormal Ⅱ (名) mishap; fault: 這是我的過～。 It's my fault.

【失火】 shīhuǒ (動) catch fire; be on fire

【失手】 shīshǒu (動) lose hold of and drop

【失去】 shīqù (動) lose: ～機會 miss an opportunity

【失主】 shīzhǔ (名) owner of lost property

【失地】 shīdì (名) lost territory

【失色】 shīsè (動) ❶ (of one's face) turn pale with fright ❷ be outshone; be overshadowed

【失守】 shīshǒu (失陷 shīxiàn) (動) (of a defended place) fall into enemy hands; be occupied by the enemy

【失血】 shīxuè (動) lose blood

【失利】 shīlì (動) lose (a battle, game, etc.)

【失足】 shīzú (動) ❶ miss one's footing ❷ 〈婉〉 take a false step in life; go to pieces morally: 一～成千古恨。 A false step in life may cause eternal regret. / ～青少年 juvenile delinquent; ex-juvenile delinquent

【失明】 shīmíng (動) go blind: 雙目～ go blind in both eyes

【失事】 shīshì (動) have an accident: 飛機～，無一生還。 The plane crashed and there were no survivors.

【失物】 shīwù (名) lost article; lost property: ～招領處 Lost and Found (Office)

【失信】 shīxìn (動) fail to keep one's promise; not keep one's word

【失修】 shīxiū (動) be in disrepair

【失約】 shīyuē (動) break an appointment

【失重】 shīzhòng (名) 〈物〉 weightlessness; zero gravity

【失效】 shīxiào (動) be no longer effective or valid; expire

【失眠】 shīmián (名) sleeplessness; insomnia

【失真】 shīzhēn (動) (of a voice, image, etc.) lack fidelity; not be faithful to the original

【失敗】 shībài Ⅰ(動) ❶ lose (a war, game, etc.) ❷ fail Ⅱ(名) failure; defeat

【失常】 shīcháng (形) abnormal; not one's usual self

【失掉】 shīdiào (動) ❶ lose: ～理智 lose one's reason ❷ miss; let slip: ～時機 miss an opportunity

【失控】 shīkòng (動) be out of control

【失陪】 shīpéi 〈口〉〈套〉 excuse me for having to leave now

【失望】 shīwàng (動) ❶ lose hope; lose heart ❷ be disappointed

【失策】shīcè(失計 shījì)(名) miscalculation; unwise move; wrong move

【失散】shīsàn (動)❶ (of family members, etc.) be out of touch with each other ❷ be scattered; be lost: ～的文稿 missing manuscripts

【失傳】shīchuán (動) not be handed down from past generations; get lost in the course of time

【失當】shīdàng (形) improper; injudicious: 處置～ mishandle; not handle with propriety

【失落】shīluò (動) lose; be misisng: 有～感 feel lost

【失勢】shīshì (動) lose one's power and influence; be out of favour; fall into disgrace

【失業】shīyè (動) lose one's job; be out of employment: ～救濟 unemployment benefit / ～者 the unemployed

【失意】shīyì (動) be frustrated: ～政客 disgraced politician

【失算】shīsuàn (動) miscalculate

【失態】shītài (動) behave inappropriately

【失誤】shīwù (名) fault; mistake: 工作中的～ mistakes that occur in one's work

【失實】shīshí (形) untrue; unfounded

【失調】shītiáo (動)❶ be out of balance: 比例～ be out of proportion ❷ have not recuperated after an illness, childbirth, etc.

【失踪】shīzōng (動) [mostly used to refer to persons] be missing

【失學】shīxué (動) drop out of school

【失聲】shīshēng (動)❶ let out a cry ❷ be choked (with tears) or unable to cry out in extreme grief

【失禮】shīlǐ (動)❶ show discourtesy ❷ apologize for his impolite behaviour

【失職】shīzhí (名) dereliction of duty; negligence in work

【失寵】shīchǒng (動) fall from grace; be in disgrace

【失竊】shīqiè (動) have sth. stolen; have one's house burgled

【失戀】shīliàn (動) be disappointed in love; be jilted

【失靈】shīlíng (動) (of a machine, apparatus, etc.) not work; not work properly

夷 yí Ⅰ (形) safe Ⅱ (動)❶ raze; level ❷ exterminate Ⅲ (名)〈貶〉 foreigner

【夷爲平地】yí wéi píngdì (動) raze to the ground; completely destroy

夾 gā
see also jiā; jiá

【夾肢窩】gāzhiwō (名) armpit

夾 jiā Ⅰ (動)❶ fix or hold sth. by applying force on both sides; place in between; clip; pinch: 手上～着一支雪茄 with a cigar between one's fingers ❷ intersperse; intermingle; mix Ⅱ (名)❶ clip; clamp; pincer: 領帶～ tiepin ❷ folder
see also gā; jiá

【夾子】jiāzi (名)❶ clip; peg; tongs ❷ folder; billfold; wallet

【夾心】jiāxīn (形) sandwiched; with filling

【夾生】jiāshēng (形) half-cooked; underdone: ～飯 half-cooked rice; job done crudely; half-digested knowledge

【夾攻】jiāgōng（动）attack in a pincer movement: 左右 ~ be under crossfire from left and right

【夾板】jiābǎn（名）❶ splints: 石膏 ~ plastic splints ❷ boards for holding sth. in between

【夾帶】jiādài（动）carry sth. secretly by hiding it under one's garment or elsewhere; smuggle

【夾道】jiādào Ⅰ（名） passage-way; narrow lane Ⅱ（动）(of people) line the road: ~ 欢迎 line the streets to greet guests of honour

【夾縫】jiāfèng（名）crack; narrow space between two objects

【夾雜】jiāzá（动）be mxied with; be blended with

夾 jiá（形）(of clothes) lined; having a lining
see also gā; jiā

【夾被】jiábèi（名） double-layered quilt

【夾襖】jiá'ǎo（名） lined jacket (coat)

奉 fèng Ⅰ（动）❶ present or receive with respect: ~ 命行事 act on instructions ❷ respect; believe in: 信 ~ 基督教 believe in Christianity Ⅱ（Fèng）（名）a surname

【奉公守法】fèng gōng shǒu fǎ〈成〉observe laws and government orders; be dutiful and law-abiding

【奉行】fèngxíng（动）pursue; follow

【奉告】fènggào（动）inform; acquaint with details

【奉承】fèngcheng（动）flatter

【奉命】fèngmìng（动）receive or obey orders

a gift to sb.

【奉陪】fèngpéi（动）keep sb. company

【奉養】fèngyǎng（动）support; provide for

【奉還】fènghuán（动）〈敬〉return

【奉勸】fèngquàn（动）advise; warn

【奉獻】fèngxiàn（动）offer respectfully

奈 nài

【奈何】nàihé（副）[often used in a rhetorical question or a statement to indicate a state of helplessness]why, how, what: 无可 ~ have to bow to the impossible; nothing can be done about it / ~ 問道於盲 Why take a blind man as your guide?

奇 jī（形）(of a number) odd
see also qí

【奇數】jīshù（名）odd number

奇 qí（形）❶ strange; unusual ❷ unexpected ❸ surprising; astonishing
see also jī

【奇幻】qíhuàn（形）magical; bizarre and changeful

【奇兵】qíbīng（名）surprise raiders

【奇妙】qímiào（形）wonderful; marvellous

【奇形怪狀】qí xíng guài zhuàng〈成〉(of shape) grotesque; queer in appearance

【奇怪】qíguài（形）strange; odd

【奇迹】qíjì（名）miracle; wonder

【奇特】qítè（形）peculiar; unusual

【奇恥大辱】qí chǐ dà rǔ〈成〉dreadful shame and disgrace

【奇缺】qíquē（形） in exceedingly short supply

【奇货可居】qí huò kě jū〈成〉hoard sth. as a rare commodity in expectation of a better price

【奇异】qíyì（形）❶ queer; bizarre: ~的特性 peculiar characteristic ❷ curious: 用~的目光盯着某人 look curiously at sb.

【奇景】qíjǐng（名）magnificent view

【奇遇】qíyù（名）❶ fortuitous meeting ❷ adventure

【奇装异服】qí zhuāng yì fú〈成〉outlandish clothes

【奇闻】qíwén（名）strange story

【奇谈】qítán（名）tall story: ~怪论 absurd argument

【奇丽】qílì（形）magnificent; of exceptional charm

【奇袭】qíxí（名）surprise attack; raid

【奇观】qíguān（名）wonder; miraculous sight

奄 yǎn

【奄奄一息】yǎn yǎn yī xī〈成〉dying; on the brink of death

奏 zòu（动）❶ play (music): ~迎宾曲 play the tune of welcome / 齐~ play in unison ❷ achieve; produce

【奏效】zòuxiào（动）achieve the desired effect; yield results; prove effective

【奏鸣曲】zòumíngqǔ（名）〈乐〉sonata

【奏乐】zòuyuè（动）play music; strike up a tune

奎 kuí

【奎宁】kuíníng（名）〈药〉quinine

奔 bēn（动）❶ run; move quickly:

飞~ run at top speed; run like mad ❷ hurry; rush ❸ flee; run away see also bèn

【奔忙】bēnmáng（动）bustle about: 终日~ be busy running about all day

【奔走】bēnzǒu（动）❶ be on the run ❷ rush about (on business)

【奔走相告】bēn zǒu xiāng gào〈成〉go about telling one another of the news

【奔命】bēnmìng（动）rush around on errands: 疲於~ be kept constantly on the run; be rushed off one's feet

【奔波】bēnbō（动）dash around; be constantly on the move; hustle and bustle

【奔放】bēnfàng（形）free and vigorous; unbounded; bold and uninhibited: 热情~ full of enthusiasm

【奔逃】bēntáo（动）flee; take to one's heels

【奔流】bēnliú Ⅰ（动）flow on rapidly; rush on in a torrent; pour Ⅱ（名）rushing torrent

【奔跑】bēnpǎo（动）run; dash

【奔驰】bēnchí（动）run quickly; speed; race: 汽车在高速公路上。The car is racing on the superhighway.

【奔泻】bēnxiè（动）(of torrents) pour down; flow swiftly

【奔腾】bēnténg（动）❶ gallop: 萬马~ like a thousand horses galloping ❷ surge forward; roll on in waves: 洪水~而下。The flood poured down the valley.

【奔袭】bēnxí（名）〈军〉long-range raid

奔 bèn Ⅰ（动）❶ head for; be

bound for: 各~前程。Each pursues his own course. ❷〈口〉approach (in age): ~七十的人 a man approaching seventy ❸ try to get sth. done: 你如果需要這種技術信息，我可以替你去~。If you need this kind of technical information, I can try and get it for you. Ⅱ（介）towards; to: ~草原去 head for the grassland
see also bēn

【奔命】bènmìng（動）〈口〉❶ strain one's utmost efforts to do sth. ❷ travel nonstop

【奔頭】bèntour（名）〈口〉good prospect; sth. to look forward to

契 qì Ⅰ（名）contract; deed Ⅱ（動）agree; be congenial

【契友】qìyǒu（名）bosom friend; close associate

【契合】qìhé（動）agree with; accord with

【契約】qìyuē（名）contract; deed

【契機】qìjī（名）turning point; juncture

套 tào Ⅰ（名）❶ cover; sheath: 相機~ camera case ❷ thing that covers: ~鞋 overshoes ❸ knot; noose: 落入圈~ fall into a trap; walk into a trap ❹ harness ❺ padding; batting: 棉花被~ cotton padding of a quilt ❻ formula; conventionality: 不落俗~ free from conventions; unconventional Ⅱ（動）❶ cover with: ~上工作服 slip on one's work clothes ❷ overlap: ~種 intercrop; interplant ❸ harness (a horse, etc.): ~車 hitch up (a horse, etc.) to a cart ❹ model on; imitate: ~用某人愛說的一句話 to

borrow sb.'s favourite phrase ❺ draw out (the truth): ~供 trick the accused into confession ❻ draw sb. over to one's side: ~交情 try to forge a relationship with sb. Ⅲ（量）set; suit; suite: 一~ 紀念郵票 a series of commemorative stamps / 一~ 茶具 a tea set

【套房】tàofáng（名）suite（of rooms）; connecting rooms

【套間】tàojiān（名）inner room (of a flat)

【套匯】tàohuì（動）buy in hard currency illegally

【套語】tàoyǔ（名）polite formula

【套褲】tàokù（名）leg sheaths; leggings

【套購】tàogòu（動）purchase (state-controlled commodities) by illegal means

奚 xī（名）a surname

【奚落】xīluò（動）deride; scoff

奢 shē（形）luxurious; extravagant; excessive: 窮~極慾 live in luxury and extravagance / ~望 extravagant hope

【奢侈】shēchǐ（形）luxurious; extravagant

【奢華】shēhuá（形）extravagant; luxurious; sumptuous

奠 diàn（動）❶ establish; found: ~都 establish a capital ❷ make offerings to the dead: 祭~ a memorial ceremony

【奠定】diàndìng（動）firmly establish: ~基礎 lay the groundwork for

【奠基】diànjī（動）lay the foundation

【奠基人】diànjīrén（名）founder

【奠基石】diànjīshí（名）cornerstone

奥 ào (形) profound; abstruse; mysterious: 含義深~ with abstruse implications

【奥地利】 Àodìlì (名) Austria: ~人 Austrian

【奥妙】 àomiào I (形) secret; profound; wonderful; subtle II (名) secret; subtlety: 没有看出其中的~ fail to see what is behind it

【奥林匹克運動會】 Àolínpǐkè Yùndònghuì (名) (for short 奥運會 Àoyùnhuì) Olympic Games

【奥秘】 àomì (名) mystery; secret: 大自然的~ secrets of nature

奪 duó (動) ❶ seize; snatch ❷ strive for: ~標 win a championship ❸ decide: 定~ make the final decision

【奪目】 duómù (動) dazzle: 鮮艷~ brilliantly colourful

【奪取】 duóqǔ (動) seize; capture

【奪權】 duóquán (動) seize power

獎 jiǎng I (動) award; reward: 得~ win a prize II (名) award; reward; prize

【獎杯】 jiǎngbēi (名) (prize) cup; trophy

【獎金】 jiǎngjīn (名) bonus; cash award; premium: 諾貝爾~ the Nobel Prize

【獎券】 jiǎngquàn (名) raffle ticket

【獎狀】 jiǎngzhuàng (名) certificate of merit; honorary credential; citation

【獎品】 jiǎngpǐn (名) prize; award

【獎章】 jiǎngzhāng (名) medal; decoration

【獎賞】 jiǎngshǎng (名) award; reward

【獎學金】 jiǎngxuéjīn (名) scholarship; grant; fellowship

【獎勵】 jiǎnglì I (動) commend and reward; award; reward II (名) award; reward; encouragement

【獎懲】 jiǎngchéng (名) rewards and penalties (sanctions): ~條例 regulations for rewards and penalties

奮 fèn (動) ❶ pluck up ❷ raise

【奮不顧身】 fèn bù gù shēn 〈成〉 dash straight ahead with no thought for one's own safety

【奮勇】 fènyǒng (動) muster up one's courage: 自告~ volunteer one's service

【奮起】 fènqǐ (動) rise; strive: ~抵抗侵略 rise to resist aggression

【奮鬥】 fèndòu (動) struggle; strive

【奮發】 fènfā (動) make a great effort: ~圖强 strive hard to build up one's homeland

【奮戰】 fènzhàn (動) fight bravely

【奮臂高呼】 fèn bì gāo hū (動) raise one's arms and shout at the top of one's voice

女 部

女 nǚ (名) ❶ woman; female: 男~平等 equality between men and women / ~乘務員 stewardess; air hostess ❷ daughter; girl: 養~ adopted daughter

【女人】 nǚrén (名) woman

【女工】 nǚgōng (名) woman worker

【女子】 nǚzǐ (名) woman; girl: ~單(雙)打 women's singles (doubles)

【女士】 nǚshì (名) [a polite form of

address for a woman]: lady; madam

【女王】 nǚwáng（名）queen

【女生】 nǚshēng（名）woman student; schoolgirl

【女巫】 nǚwū（名）witch; sorceress

【女性】 nǚxìng（名）❶ female sex ❷ woman

【女兒】 nǚ'ér（名）daughter

【女朋友】 nǚpéngyou（名）girl-friend

【女服務員】 nǚfúwùyuán（名）waitress; stewardess; woman attendant

【女紅】 nǚgōng（名）needle-work

【女孩】 nǚhái（名）girl

【女皇】 nǚhuáng（名）empress

【女郎】 nǚláng（名）maiden; girl

【女神】 nǚshén（名）goddess

【女高音】 nǚgāoyīn（名）〈樂〉soprano

【女廁所】 nǚcèsuǒ（名）ladies' room; women's room

【女婿】 nǚxù（名）❶ son-in-law ❷〈口〉husband

【女裏女氣】 nǚlǐnǚqì（形）〈貶〉（of a man）effeminate; womanish; feminine

奶 nǎi Ⅰ（名）❶ breasts ❷ milk Ⅱ（動）breast-feed: ～孩子 breast-feed a baby

【奶牛】 nǎiniú（名）milk cow; milch cow

【奶奶】 nǎinai（名）❶（paternal）grandmother; grandma ❷ [a respectful form of address for an old woman] granny

【奶油】 nǎiyóu（名）cream

【奶品】 nǎipǐn（名）milk products; dairy products

【奶粉】 nǎifěn（名）milk powder; powdered milk

【奶瓶】 nǎipíng（名）feeding bottle;

milk bottle

【奶罩】 nǎizhào（名）brassiere; bra

【奶酪】 nǎilào（名）cheese

【奶媽】 nǎimā（名）wet nurse

【奶瘡】 nǎichuāng（名）mastitis

【奶頭】 nǎitóu（名）❶ nipple; teat; tit ❷ nipple（of a feeding bottle）

【奶嘴】 nǎizuǐ（名）nipple（of a feeding bottle）

奴 nú（名）slave

【奴才】 núcai（名）flunkey; stooge

【奴化】 núhuà（動）enslave

【奴役】 núyì（動）enslave; hold in subjection

【奴僕】 núpú（名）servant; valet

【奴隸】 núlì（名）slave: ～制度 slavery

【奴顔婢膝】 nú yán bì xī〈成〉servile; obsequious

妄 wàng（形）❶ absurd; preposterous ❷ rash; impertinent: 膽大～爲 bold and reckless

【妄自菲薄】 wàng zì fěi bó〈成〉be unduly humble; think too lowly of oneself: 不要～。Don't belittle yourself.

【妄自尊大】 wàng zì zūn dà〈成〉be ridiculously conceited and self-important

【妄動】 wàngdòng（動）act recklessly

【妄想】 wàngxiǎng（動）vainly hope

【妄圖】 wàngtú（動）make a futile attempt to

奸 jiān Ⅰ（形）❶ evil; sinister; villainous ❷〈口〉selfish; self-seeking: 這個人可真～。This chap is so selfish and calculating. ❸ treacherous; disloyal Ⅱ（名）❶

traitor; informer ❷ illicit sexual relations: 强～ rape / 輪～ gang rape

【奸污】 jiānwū（動）rape; seduce

【奸臣】 jiānchén（名）treacherous courtier

【奸邪】 jiānxié（形）wily and wicked

【奸計】 jiānjì（名）evil plot; wicked scheme

【奸笑】 jiānxiào（名）wicked grin

【奸商】 jiānshāng（名）unscrupulous and deceitful merchant; profiteer

【奸細】 jiānxi（名）enemy agent

【奸淫】 jiānyín Ⅰ（名）illicit sexual relations Ⅱ（動）rape; seduce

【奸雄】 jiānxióng（名）arch careerist

【奸詐】 jiānzhà（形）perfidious; deceitful; treacherous

【奸猾】 jiānhuá（形）sly; cunning; crafty

【奸險】 jiānxiǎn（形）deceitful and sinister; treacherous

妃 fēi（名）❶ imperial concubine ❷ wife of a prince

好 hǎo Ⅰ（形）❶ good; fine; nice: ～日子 good life ❷ friendly; kind: 他倆關係很～。 They are on very good terms. ❸ be in good health: 病全～了 be fully recovered ❹ [used as a polite formula]: 你～! Hello!（or How do you do）❺ [used to indicate approval or displeasure]: ～，該你發言了! Well, it's your turn to speak. / ～，你又遲到了。 Well, you are late again. ❻ [used to indicate a request]: 我看看～嗎? Could I have a look? Ⅱ（副）❶ easily: 他能否來不一說。 It's difficult to say if he'll be able to come. / 這～辦。 No problem. ❷ exceedingly: ～燙! Ouch, it's so

hot! ❸ [used to indicate completion of an action]: 飯做～了。 Dinner is ready. Ⅲ（動）[used to indicate a greeting]: 向你的夫人問～。 Give your wife my best regards.

see also hào

【好比】 hǎobǐ（動）can be compared to; be like

【好不】 hǎobù（副）how; what: ～淒涼! How sad it is!

【好歹】 hǎodǎi Ⅰ（名）❶ advantage and disadvantage: 不識～ not know what is good for one ❷ misfortune; mishap Ⅱ（副）❶ anyhow: ～吃點什麼。 Let's have a bite, anyhow. ❷ in any case; at any rate: 我們～也要把這事幹完。 We'll finish the work one way or the other.

【好手】 hǎoshǒu（名）dab hand; expert

【好心】 hǎoxīn（名）good intention; good will

【好在】 hǎozài（副）luckily; fortunately

【好似】 hǎosì（好像 hǎoxiàng）（動）seem; be like

【好事多磨】 hǎo shì duō mó〈成〉the road to happiness is paved with setbacks

【好笑】 hǎoxiào（形）funny; ridiculous

【好家伙】 hǎojiāhuo（嘆）my goodness; good heavens

【好處】 hǎochù（名）benefit; profit; gain

【好感】 hǎogǎn（名）good impression; soft spot: 對她有～ have a soft spot for her

【好話】 hǎohuà（名）❶ good advice ❷ compliments

【好意】 hǎoyì（名）good intention;

kindness

【好意思】 hǎoyìsi（動）be thick-skinned; have the cheek to: 他竟然～當面扯謊。He had the cheek to tell such a barefaced lie.

【好漢】 hǎohàn（名）true man; hero

【好端端】 hǎoduānduān（形）for no reason at all: ～的, 怎麼發起火來了? Why are you flaring up when nothing goes wrong?

【好辦】 hǎobàn（形）easy to do

【好轉】 hǎozhuǎn（動）be better; improve

好 hào（動）❶ like; love; be fond of: ～出風頭 like to be in the limelight ❷ be liable to; be apt to: ～忘事 be apt to forget things; be forgetful

see also hǎo

【好大喜功】 hào dà xǐ gōng〈成〉crave for power and glory

【好吃懶做】 hào chī lǎn zuò〈成〉have a fondness for food but an aversion to work; be lazy and gluttonous

【好奇】 hàoqí（形）curious: 出於～心 out of curiosity

【好事】 hàoshì（動）be meddlesome; poke one's nose into other people's affairs

【好客】 hàokè（形）hospitable

【好高騖遠】 hào gāo wù yuǎn〈成〉set one's sights too high

【好逸惡勞】 hào yì wù láo〈成〉be fond of ease and comfort while showing an aversion to work

【好強】 hàoqiáng（形）eager to excel

【好勝】 hàoshèng（形）have a strong desire to outshine others

【好惡】 hàowù（名）prejudice: 這是個人～問題。This is a matter of personal prejudice.

【好戰】 hàozhàn（形）bellicose; war-like

她 tā（代）she; her

【她們】 tāmen（代）(of females) they; them: ～的 their

如 rú Ⅰ（動）❶ be like or similar to: ～魚得水 feel just like fish in water / ～畫 be picturesque ❷ [used in negative sentences] be as...as: 他的身體不～以前。He is not as fit as before. / 以別人都不一也 consider oneself second to none Ⅱ（介）❶ according to: ～期到達 show up right on schedule ❷ such as Ⅲ（連）if: ～合力去做, 我們定會成功。We'll succeed if we join our efforts.

【如下】 rúxià（動）as follows: 説明～。Explanations are given below.

【如今】 rújīn（副）these days; nowadays

【如火如荼】 rú huǒ rú tú〈成〉vigorously; fervently

【如出一轍】 rú chū yī zhé〈成〉(of two things) be identical

【如此】 rúcǐ（副）so: 他～狂妄, 真叫人受不了。He was so arrogant that nobody could stand him.

【如同】 rútóng（介）like; as: 他看上去～往年一樣年輕。He looks as young as ever.

【如何】 rúhé（代）how; what: 你對此人印象～? What is your impression of him?

【如坐針氈】 rú zuò zhēn zhān〈成〉be plunged into a state of tension and suspense; be on pins and needles

【如果】 rúguǒ（連）if

【如法炮製】rú fǎ páo zhì〈成〉act exactly in the same way as others have done; follow sb.'s example

【如虎添翼】rú hǔ tiān yì〈成〉like adding wings to a tiger; further consolidate one's strength

【如故】rúgù（副）❶ remain unchanged ❷ like old friends: 一見～ be friends with sb. at the first meeting

【如飢似渴】rú jī sì kě〈成〉act with great eagerness; thirst after

【如常】rúcháng（副）as usual: 平靜～ peaceful as usual

【如喪考妣】rú sàng kǎo bǐ〈成〉be lugubrious; look as if newly bereft of both parents

【如意】rúyì（動）have one's wishes fulfilled: 祝萬事～。Wish you success in everything.

【如意算盤】rú yì suàn pan〈成〉what is unlikely to come true; wishful thinking

【如雷貫耳】rú léi guàn ěr〈成〉(of one's name) resound like thunder; well-known: 久聞大名，～。I've long heard of your great fame.

【如夢初醒】rú mèng chū xǐng〈成〉as if suddenly waking up from a dream

【如實】rúshí（副）strictly according to facts: ～向上級反映情況 report the facts as they are to the higher authorities

【如數】rúshù（副）according to a specified number or amount: 債務～還清 pay off all one's debts

【如數家珍】rú shù jiā zhēn〈成〉as if counting one's family treasures; recount a story or enumerate facts at one's fingertips

【如膠似漆】rú jiāo sì qī〈成〉be passionately attached to each other

【如獲至寶】rú huò zhì bǎo〈成〉as if one had acquired a rare treasure

【如臨大敵】rú lín dà dí〈成〉as if faced with a formidable foe

【如願以償】rú yuàn yǐ cháng〈成〉achieve what one has wished for; realize one's dream

【如釋重負】rú shì zhòng fù〈成〉feel greatly relieved

妆 zhuāng Ⅰ（動）make up: 梳～ dress and make up Ⅱ（名）❶ stage costume ❷ trousseau

【妆飾】zhuāngshì（動）adorn; dress up

【妆奩】zhuānglián（名）trousseau

妥 tuǒ（形）❶ proper; appropriate; meet ❷［used after a verb to indicate proper completion of the action］settled; finished: 已經商～了。The matter has been settled through consultation.

【妥協】tuǒxié（動）come to terms; compromise

【妥善】tuǒshàn Ⅰ（副）appropriately; satisfactorily Ⅱ（形）proper: ～措施 proper measure

【妥貼】tuǒtiē（動）fitting and proper

【妥當】tuǒdang（形）appropriate; reliable

妨 fāng（動）harm: 不～試試 no harm trying
see also fáng

妨 fáng（動）hamper; obstruct
see also fāng

【妨害】fánghài（動）harm; impair

【妨礙】fáng'ài（動）hinder; impede

妒 dù (动) envy; be jealous of

【妒忌】dùjì (动) be jealous of: ～心 jealousy

姸 yán (名) beauty

妓 jì (名) prostitute; whore

【妓女】jìnǚ (名) prostitute; whore

【妓院】jìyuàn (名) brothel; whorehouse

姊 bǐ (名) one's deceased mother: 如丧考～ (look) as if one had lost one's parents; be in deep sorrow

妞 niū (名)〈口〉girl

妙 miào (形) ❶ wonderful; fine: 這個想法一極了。It's a splendid idea! ❷ clever; miraculous: 這一着真～。This is a clever move.

【妙不可言】miào bù kě yán〈成〉too wonderful for words

【妙手回春】miào shǒu huí chūn〈成〉raise sb. from the dead; bring a patient back to life

【妙計】miàojì (名) wise move; subtle scheme

【妙品】miàopǐn (名) ❶ fine quality goods ❷ masterpiece

【妙訣】miàojué (名) knack; key: 學會其中～ learn the knack

【妙語】miàoyǔ (名) witty remark; clever saying

【妙趣橫生】miào qù héng shēng〈成〉very witty and humorous

【妙藥】miàoyào (名) sure remedy; panacea

【妙齡】miàolíng (形) (of woman) young: ～女郎 young woman

妊 rèn (动) be pregnant

【妊娠】rènshēn (名) pregnancy; gestation

【妊婦】rènfù (名) pregnant woman; expectant mother

妖 yāo Ⅰ (名) devil; demon Ⅱ (形) ❶ evil; wicked ❷ coquettish; seductive

【妖言】yāoyán (名) fallacies calculated to misguide people: ～惑衆 mislead people by spreading fallacies

【妖怪】yāoguài (名) monster; demon

【妖風】yāofēng (名) evil wind; evil trend

【妖術】yāoshù (名) black art; witchcraft; sorcery

【妖裏妖氣】yāolǐ yāoqì (形) seductive and alluring

【妖精】yāojing (名) ❶ evil spirit ❷ seductive woman

【妖艷】yāoyàn (妖冶 yāoyě) (形) (usu. of a woman) pretty and coquettish; seductive

【妖魔】yāomó (名) evil spirit; goblin

【妖魔鬼怪】yāomó guǐguài (名) demons and devils

妾 qiè (名) concubine

妻 qī (名) wife

【妻子】qīzi (名) wife

【妻離子散】qī lí zǐ sàn〈成〉with one's family broken up in a disaster

委 wěi Ⅰ (动) ❶ entrust; commit; appoint: ～任書 certificate of appointment ❷ throw away: ～棄 discard; abandon ❸ shift (blame, etc.) onto others: ～罪他人 the blame on sb. else Ⅱ (形) ❶ indirect; roundabout ❷ languid; spiritless: ～頓 weary; exhausted Ⅲ (名) ❶ end: 事情的原～ the beginning and end of the story; the whole story ❷ (簡) committee: 經～ the Economic Commission ❸ (簡) committee member: 常～ member of a standing committee

【委内瑞拉】Wěinèiruìlā(名) Venezuela: ～人 Venezuelan

【委托】wěituō(動) entrust; commission: 把這件事～他辦 entrust him with the task

【委任】wěirèn(動) appoint; designate

【委曲求全】wěi qū qiú quán〈成〉compromise in order to preserve one's own interests; tolerate sth. unpleasant for the sake of overall interests

【委屈】wěiqu Ⅰ(動) ❶ feel wrongly blamed ❷ put (sb.) to inconvenience; wrongly blame Ⅱ (名) grievance: 訴說～ air one's grievances

【委派】wěipài(動) appoint; designate

【委員】wěiyuán(名) member of a committee

【委婉】wěiwǎn(名) mild; indirect; tactful: ～語 euphemism

【委實】wěishí(副) really; indeed; truly: 我～不知道。Honestly, I have no idea.

【委靡】wěimǐ(形) spiritless; listless

妹 mèi(名)younger sister

【妹夫】mèifu(名) husband of one's younger sister; brother-in-law

【妹妹】mèimei(名) (younger) sister

姑 gū Ⅰ(名) ❶ aunt (father's sister) ❷ sister-in-law (husband's sister) ❸ nun Ⅱ (副) provisionally; for the time being

【姑父】gūfu(名) uncle (husband of the father's sister)

【姑且】gūqiě(副) for the time being: ～不談 leave the matter aside for the time being

【姑妄言之】gū wàng yán zhī〈成〉see no harm in venturing an opinion

【姑妄聽之】gū wàng tīng zhī〈成〉see no harm in listening to what sb. has to say

【姑娘】gūniang(名)girl; maiden

【姑息】gūxī(動) tolerate; appease; indulge

【姑息養奸】gū xī yǎng jiān〈成〉unprincipled tolerance breeds evil

【姑嫂】gūsǎo(名)sisters-in-law

姐 jiě(名) ❶ elder sister ❷ [general address for young woman]: 李小～ Miss Li / 大～ elder sister (a term of endearment for a woman of one's age group)

【姐夫】jiěfu(姐丈 jiězhàng)(名) elder sister's husband; brother-in-law: 大～ eldest sister's husband

【姐姐】jiějie(名)elder sister

【姐妹】jiěmèi(姊妹 zǐmèi)(名) sisters

妯 zhóu

【妯娌】zhóuli(名) wives of brothers; sisters-in-law

姓 xìng(名)surname; family name

【姓氏】xìngshì(名)surname

【姓名】xìngmíng(名) full name; name

姍 shān

【姍姍來遲】shān shān lái chí〈成〉arrive late

姊 zǐ（名）elder sister

【姊妹】zǐmèi（名）sisters

始 shǐ Ⅰ（名）beginning; start Ⅱ（動）start: 學期開～以來 since the beginning of the term

【始末】shǐmò（名）the whole story

【始祖】shǐzǔ（名）earliest ancestor（traced genealogically）

【始料不及】shǐ liào bù jí〈成〉quite unexpected

【始終】shǐzhōng（副）all along; all the time: 他的態度一不變。His attitude has never changed.

【始終如一】shǐ zhōng rú yī〈成〉remain unchanged; remain loyal to the very end

姿 zǐ（名）❶ posture; gesture: 舞～ dancing posture ❷ looks; appearance

【姿色】zǐsè（名）(of a woman) fine features; good looks

【姿勢】zǐshì（名）posture; carriage: ～優美 have an elegant carriage

【姿態】zǐtài（名）❶ posture; carriage ❷ attitude; pose: 擺出一副大師的～ assume the pose of a grand master

姜 Jiāng（名）a surname

威 wēi Ⅰ（名）impressive strength or awe-inspiring dignity Ⅱ（副）by force

【威力】wēilì（名）might; prowess

【威士忌】wēishìjì（名）whisky: ～蘇打 whisky and soda

【威名】wēimíng（名）great renown won by virtue of one's tremendous prowess

【威武】wēiwǔ Ⅰ（名）force; power: ～不能屈 not to be cowed by force Ⅱ（形）of overwhelming might

【威風】wēifēng（名）awe-inspiring pose; arrogance backed up by power

【威信】wēixìn（名）prestige and credit: ～掃地 be completely discredited

【威脅】wēixié Ⅰ（動）threaten; intimidate Ⅱ（名）threat: ～利誘 threat and inducement

【威望】wēiwàng（名）reputation and prestige

【威逼】wēibī（動）coerce; threaten by force

【威嚇】wēihè（動）intimidate; cow; menace

【威懾】wēishè（動）deter; discourage (from acting) by instilling fear: ～力量 deterrent

姹 chà（形）charming

【姹紫嫣紅】chà zǐ yān hóng〈成〉brilliant purples and reds; beautiful flowers

姘 pīn（動）have an affair with

【姘居】pīnjū（動）cohabit (illegally)

【姘頭】pīntou（名）lover; mistress

姨 yí（名）❶（one's maternal) aunt ❷ one's wife's sister: 小～子 one's wife's younger sister

【姨父】yífu（名）one's maternal aunt's husband; uncle

【姨太太】yítàitai（名）concubine

【姨母】yímǔ（名）maternal aunt; aunt

【姨表】yíbiǎo（名）maternal cousin

娃 wá (名) baby; child
【娃娃】wáwa (名) ❶ baby ❷ doll: 泥～ clay doll

姥 lǎo
【姥姥】lǎolao (名)〈方〉(maternal) grandma

姻 yīn (名) ❶ marriage ❷ affinity; relation by marriage
【姻兄弟】yīnxiōngdi (名) brother-in-law
【姻緣】yīnyuán (名) predestined (matrimonial) bond; marriage
【姻親】yīnqīn (名) relation by marriage

姚 Yáo (名) a surname

娘 niáng (名) ❶ mother; mum ❷ a form of address for an elderly married woman ❸ young woman
【娘胎】niángtāi (名) mother's womb: 從～裏帶來的 inborn; innate
【娘家】niángjia (名) a married woman's parents' home

姬 Jī (名) a surname

娓 wěi
【娓娓】wěiwěi (副) ❶ (talk) tirelessly ❷ (talk) fascinatingly: ～動聽 speak with eloquence

娟 juān (形) beautiful; elegant; lovely
【娟秀】juānxiù (形) elegant; graceful

娛 yú (動) amuse: 自～ amuse oneself
【娛樂】yúlè Ⅰ (動) amuse Ⅱ (名) a-

musement; entertainment; recreation: ～活動 recreation activities

娥 é Ⅰ (形) beautiful Ⅱ (名) pretty young woman: 宮～ maid of honour

娩 miǎn (名) childbirth; delivery: 分～ childbirth; parturition

婆 pó (名) ❶ old woman: 老太～ old woman ❷ mother-in-law; husband's mother ❸ grandmother
【婆家】pójia (名) husband's family
【婆娑】pósuō (形) whirling; dancing gracefully: 樹影～。The shadows cast by the trees flicked on the ground.
【婆婆】pópo (名) ❶ mother-in-law; husband's mother ❷〈方〉grandmother
【婆婆媽媽】pópomāmā (形) dawdling; fussy
【婆羅門】Póluómén (名) Brahman
【婆羅門教】Póluóménjiào (名) Brahmanism

娶 qǔ (動) marry (a woman)

婁 Lóu (名) a surname
【婁子】lóuzi (名) trouble; error: 出～ get into trouble / 捅大～ make a grievous mistake

婉 wǎn (形) ❶ gracious; gentle: 委～詞 euphemism / ～拒 decline politely ❷ graceful; agreeable
【婉言】wǎnyán (名) polite (tactful) words: ～相勸 tactfully offer one's advice
【婉轉】wǎnzhuǎn (形) ❶ indirect; tactful: 措詞～ couched in polite terms ❷ (of singing, chirping, etc.) agreeable; sweet; charming

娸 biāo

【娸】biāozi （名）〈貶〉prostitute; whore; harlot: ～養的〈罵〉son of a bitch; bastard

婦 fù

（名）❶ married woman ❷ woman ❸ wife: 夫～ husband and wife

【婦女】fùnǚ （名）woman

【婦女節】Fùnǚjié （名）Women's Day

【婦產科】fùchǎnkē （名）(department of) gynaecology and obstetrics

【婦產醫院】fùchǎn yīyuàn （名）maternity hospital

【婦聯】fùlián （名）women's association

【婦孺】fùrú （婦幼 fùyòu）（名）women and children

婀 ē

【婀娜】ēnuó （形）graceful

娼 chāng

（名）prostitute

【娼妓】chāngjì （名）prostitute

【娼婦】chāngfù （名）〈罵〉whore

婢 bì

（名）slave girl; servant-girl

【婢女】bìnǚ （名）slave girl; servant-girl

婚 hūn

Ⅰ（動）wed; marry Ⅱ（名）marriage; wedding

【婚姻】hūnyīn （名）marriage

【婚約】hūnyuē （名）engagement; marriage contract

【婚配】hūnpèi （動）marry

【婚期】hūnqī （名）wedding day

【婚禮】hūnlǐ （名）wedding; marriage ceremony

媒 méi

（名）❶ intermediary ❷ matchmaker; go-between

【媒人】méirén （名）matchmaker; go-between

【媒介】méijiè （名）intermediary; medium: 大眾傳播～ mass media

【媒婆】méipó （名）professional woman matchmaker

【媒質】méizhì （名）〈物〉medium

婿 xù

（名）❶ son-in-law ❷ husband

媚 mèi

Ⅰ（形）charming; lovely Ⅱ（動）flatter; curry favour with

【媚外】mèiwài （動）be servile to foreign powers

【媚骨】mèigǔ （名）servility

嫂 sǎo

（名）elder brother's wife; sister-in-law

【嫂子】sǎozi （名）〈口〉elder brother's wife; sister-in-law

嫁 jià

（動）❶ (of a woman) take a husband; marry ❷ transfer; shift

【嫁妝】jiàzhuang （名）dowry

【嫁接】jiàjiē （動）(of a plant) graft

【嫁禍於人】jià huò yú rén （成）lay one's own fault at sb. else's door; shift one's blame onto another

嫉 jí

（動）❶ be jealous of; envy ❷ hate; detest; loathe: 憤世～俗 detest the evil practices of society

【嫉妒】jídù （動）be jealous of; feel envy at

【嫉恨】jíhèn （動）hate (sb.) out of jealousy

嫌 xián

Ⅰ（動）dislike; grudge; complain of: ～他沒有禮貌 complain of his bad manners Ⅱ（名）suspicion: 招～ incur suspicion

【嫌惡】xiánwù （動）detest; abhor

【嫌棄】xiánqì（動）dislike and reject

【嫌疑】xiányí（名）suspicion：～犯 suspect

媾 gòu（動）❶ wed：婚～ be joined in wedlock ❷ reconcile ❸ mate：交～ have sex

【媾和】gòuhé（動）make peace

媽 mā（名）❶〈口〉mum; mother ❷ informal address for any woman about one's parent's age：大～ aunt

【媽媽】māma（名）mama; mother

媼 ǎo（名）old woman

媳 xí（名）son's wife

【媳婦】xífu（名）❶ son's wife; daughter-in-law ❷ wife; married woman

媲 pì

【媲美】pìměi（動）match in excellence or beauty

嫡 dí（形）❶ of the main branch in family genealogy：～子 son by one's own wife (as distinct from a son by one's concubine in older days) ❷ most closely related：～派 one's own clique (in military or political circles)

【嫡系】díxì（名）❶ those closest to the leader of a clique in political infighting ❷ those troops under the direct command of a warlord

【嫡親】díqīn（名）blood relations

嫣 yān

【嫣紅】yānhóng（形）bright red

【嫣然一笑】yānrán yī xiào（動）give a winsome smile

嫩 nèn（形）❶ tender; delicate; (of cooked meat) rare：嬰孩的嫩皮膚 the delicate skin of a baby /～豆腐 tender bean curd /～煎的菜 sauté (food) ❷ (of colour) light：～色 pale-coloured ❸ inexperienced; immature

嫖 piáo（動）visit brothels; go whoring

嫗 yù（名）〈書〉old woman

嫦 cháng

【嫦娥】Cháng'é（名）name of the legendary goddess of the moon

嬉 xī（動）play

【嬉皮士】xīpíshì（名）hippy; hippie

【嬉皮笑臉】xī pí xiào liǎn〈成〉be frivolous; wear a roguish smile one one's face

【嬉鬧】xīnào（動）have fun; play

嫻 xián（形）❶ skilled：～於繪畫 be good at painting ❷ refined; polite; expert

【嫻雅】xiányǎ（形）refined and elegant

【嫻熟】xiánshú（形）skilled; expert

【嫻靜】xiánjìng（形）gentle and refined

嬋 chán

【嬋娟】chánjuān Ⅰ（形）(of a woman) lovely; graceful Ⅱ（名）moon

嫵 wǔ

【嫵媚】wǔmèi（形）charming; lovely

嬌 jiāo Ⅰ（形）(of a child, flower) lovely; charming Ⅱ（動）spoil; pamper：這小孩～壞了。The child is spoiled.

【嬌小玲瓏】jiāo xiǎo líng lóng〈成〉

petite and dainty

【嬌客】jiāokè（名）son-in-law

【嬌氣】jiāoqi（形）〈贬〉❶（of a person）weak-willed and afraid of hardship ❷ be easily upset by criticism

【嬌嫩】jiāonen（形）delicate; fragile: 她看起來有點～。She looks a little fragile.

【嬌滴滴】jiāodīdī（形）affectedly sweet: ～的聲音 a sweet girlish voice

【嬌慣】jiāoguàn（動）pamper; indulge: 從小～壞了 be pampered from childhood / be spoiled by doting parents when a child

嬴 Yíng（名）a surname

媛 ài（名）〈敬〉[used only in the set phrase 令媛] your beloved daughter

婴 yīng（名）baby; infant

【嬰兒】yīng'ér（名）baby; infant

嬸 shěn（名）❶ aunt; wife of father's younger brother ❷ a form of address for a married woman about one's mother's age; aunt; auntie: 大～ Auntie

【嬸母】shěnmǔ（名）aunt; wife of father's younger brother

孀 shuāng（名）widow: 遺～ sb.'s widow

子 部

子 zǐ（名）❶ son: 幼～ youngest

son ❷ person: 女～ woman ❸ seed: 菜～ vegetable seed / 蓮～ lotus seed ❹ egg: 魚～ roe / 蠶～ silkworm egg ❺ sth. small and hard: 珠～ bead ❻ [used as a suffix to form a noun]: 桌～ table / 瞎～ blind person / 墊～ mat

【子女】zǐnǚ（名）sons and daughters; children

【子公司】zǐgōngsī（名）subsidiary

【子午綫】zǐwǔxiàn（名）〈地〉meridian (line)

【子弟】zǐdì（名）sons and younger brothers; younger generation: 職工～ children of the workers and staff

【子夜】zǐyè（名）midnight

【子音】zǐyīn（名）〈語〉consonant

【子宫】zǐgōng（名）uterus; womb

【子孫】zǐsūn（名）children and grandchildren; descendants

【子彈】zǐdàn（名）bullet

【子爵】zǐjué（名）viscount

孓 jié

【孓孒】jiéjué（名）wriggler; larvae of the mosquito

【孑然一身】jié rán yī shēn〈成〉be all alone without any relatives; be alone and friendless

孔 kǒng Ⅰ（名）❶ hole: 打～ punch a hole; perforate ❷（Kǒng）a surname Ⅱ（量）(of cave dwellings, etc.): 兩～窰洞 two cave dwellings

【孔孟之道】Kǒng Mèng zhī dào（名）Confucian and Mencian doctrines

【孔雀】kǒngquè（名）peacock: ～開屏 a peacock spreading its tail

【孔道】kǒngdào（名）passage; pass; access to a place

【孔廟】Kǒngmiào（名）Confucian

temple

孕 yùn (形) pregnant: 有 ~ be
(big) with child; be pregnant

【孕育】yùnyù (动) be pregnant
with: ~ 着几种可能的结局 be
pregnant with several possibilities

【孕妇】yùnfù (名) pregnant woman

【孕期】yùnqī (名) pregnancy

字 zì (名) ❶ character; word: 常
用 ~ common words ❷ pronunciation (of a character or word): 咬~
articulation ❸ style of a written or
printed character: 草 ~ a Chinese
character written in the cursive hand
/ 斜体 ~ italic type ❹ calligraphy;
script: 以 ~ 画闻名 noted for one's
calligraphy and painting

【字句】zìjù (名) words and expressions; wording

【字母】zìmǔ (名) letter; alphabet:
小写 ~ small letter

【字典】zìdiǎn (名) dictionary

【字帖】zìtiè (名) copybook (for calligraphy)

【字面】zìmiàn (名) literal (sense of
the word): ~上 literally

【字迹】zìjì (名) handwriting

【字条】zìtiáo (名) brief note

【字纸篓】zìzhǐlǒu (名) wastepaper
basket; wastebasket

【字眼】zìyǎn (名) wording; diction:
抠 ~ find fault with words and
phrases

【字斟句酌】zì zhēn jù zhuó 〈成〉
choose every word and every sentence carefully; speak or write with
great care

【字里行间】zì lǐ háng jiān 〈成〉 between the lines: ~ 的意思不难看
清楚。The implication is easy to

read between the lines.

【字幕】zìmù (名) captions; subtitles

【字样】zìyàng (名) ❶ model of
written characters ❷ (written or
printed) words

【字据】zìjù (名) signed paper (e. g.
receipt, IOU, contract, etc.)

【字体】zìtǐ (名) style of calligraphy;
typeface

存 cún (动) ❶ exist; live: 残 ~
survive ❷ store; deposit ❸
reserve; retain: ~ 疑 leave the
question open ❹ leave (a car, a bicycle, etc.) in a bicycle park: ~自
行车 park one's bicycle ❺ harbour;
cherish: 不 ~ 偏见 have no prejudice

【存亡】cúnwáng (动) live or die;
survive or perish: 生死 ~ 的斗争 a
life-and-death struggle

【存心】cúnxīn Ⅰ (副) deliberately;
on purpose: ~ 叫人为难 deliberately try to embarrass sb. Ⅱ (动) intend: ~ 不良 harbour evil intentions

【存在】cúnzài Ⅰ (动) exist; be; survive Ⅱ (名) existence; being: 军事
~ military presence

【存在主义】cúnzài zhǔyì (名) exis-
tentialism

【存车处】cúnchēchù (名) bicycle or
car park; parking lot

【存放】cúnfàng (动) place for safe-
keeping: 把行李 ~ 在这里。Deposit
your luggage here.

【存根】cúngēn (名) stub; counter-
foil

【存货】cúnhuò (名) goods in stock:
清点 ~ stocktaking

【存款】cúnkuǎn (名) deposit; bank

savings

【存项】cúnxiàng (名) credit balance; surplus

【存折】cúnzhé (名) deposit book; bankbook

【存档】cúndàng (动) put on file

孝 xiào (名) ❶ filial piety ❷ mourning

【孝子】xiàozǐ (名) ❶ filial son ❷ son in mourning

【孝顺】xiàoshùn (名) show filial obedience

【孝敬】xiàojìng (动) ❶ give presents (to one's elder or superior) ❷ show filial respect (to one's parents)

孜 zī

【孜孜不倦】zī zī bù juàn 〈成〉assiduously; untiringly

孟 Mèng (名) a surname

【孟加拉】Mèngjiālā (形) Bengal: ~人 Bengalese / ~语 Bengali (language)

【孟加拉国】Mèngjiālāguó (名) Bangladesh

【孟浪】mènglàng (形) rash; reckless

孢 bāo

【孢子】bāozǐ (名) 〈植〉spore

孤 gū I (名) orphan: ~寡 orphans and widows II (形) alone; single III (代) [used by feudal princes]: I

【孤本】gūběn (名) the only existing copy of a book; only manuscript of an unpublished book

【孤立】gūlì (形) isolated: ~地看问题 look at a problem in isolation

【孤立主义】gūlìzhǔyì (名) isolationism

【孤儿】gū'ér (名) orphan: ~院 orphanage

【孤注一掷】gū zhù yī zhì 〈成〉 risk everything on a single throw

【孤芳自赏】gū fāng zì shǎng 〈成〉 pride oneself on being aloof from the world; be narcissistic

【孤军作战】gū jūn zuò zhàn 〈成〉 fight without support; fight single-handed

【孤苦伶仃】gū kǔ líng dīng 〈成〉 live alone in wretched circumstances; lonely and helpless

【孤陋寡闻】gū lòu guǎ wén 〈成〉 ignorant and ill-informed

【孤家寡人】gū jiā guǎ rén 〈成〉 a man alienated from the public; a leader who has lost popular support

【孤寂】gūjì (形) lonely

【孤单】gūdān (形) alone and friendless; solitary

【孤傲】gū'ào (形) proud and standoffish

【孤零零】gūlínglíng (形) all alone; with nobody to rely upon

【孤掌难鸣】gū zhǎng nán míng 〈成〉 cannot clap with a single hand; cannot achieve anything without mass support

【孤僻】gūpì (形) eccentric and unsociable

【孤独】gūdú (形) lonely

【孤孀】gūshuāng (名) widow

季 jì (名) ❶ season: 四~如春 It is like spring all the year round. / 西红柿旺~ tomato season ❷ last month of a season: ~春 (夏、秋、冬) the last month of spring (summer, autumn, winter) ❸ crop: 一年收两~稻 reap two crops of rice a

year ❹ (Jì) a surname

【季刊】jìkān（名）quarterly（publication)

【季度】jìdù（名）quarter of a year

【季風】jìfēng（名）monsoon

【季節】jìjié（名）season: 游泳 ～ swimming season ／ ～差價 seasonal variations in price

孩 hái（名）childhood; infancy

【孩子氣】háiziqì（名）childishness

【孩提】háití（名）early childhood; infancy

孫 sūn（名）❶ grandchild ❷ relative of the grandchild's generation: 外 ～ grandson on the daughter's side ❸ generations below that of the grandchild: 曾 ～ great grandson ❹ (Sūn) a surname

【孫女】sūnnǚ（名）granddaughter

【孫子】sūnzi（名）grandson

孰 shú（代）〈書〉❶ who; which one: ～優～劣 (of the two) which is superior and which inferior ❷ what: 是可忍，～不可忍? If this is to be tolerated, what is not?

孱 chán（形）frail; weak; feeble

【孱弱】chánruò（形）feeble; delicate (in health)

孵 fū（名）hatch; incubate

【孵化】fūhuà（名）incubation

【孵化器】fūhuàqì（名）incubator

學 xué Ⅰ（動）❶ learn; study: ～英文 learn (study) English ／ ～音樂 take music lessons ❷ imitate: ～他爸爸講話時的怪樣子 imitate his dad's mannerisms in speech Ⅱ（名）❶ learning; knowledge: 飽～之士

a learned man ❷ school: 輟 ～ leave school

【學士】xuéshì（名）bachelor: 文(理)～ Bachelor of Arts (Science)

【學分】xuéfēn（名）credit

【學生】xuésheng（名）student; pupil

【學年】xuénián（名）school year; academic year

【學舌】xuéshé（動）mechanically repeat; parrot

【學究】xuéjiū（名）pedant

【學位】xuéwèi（名）academic degree; degree

【學府】xuéfǔ（名）institution of higher learning; college; university

【學者】xuézhě（名）scholar

【學制】xuézhì（名）❶ educational system ❷ length of schooling

【學風】xuéfēng（名）attitude towards study: 沒有良好的 ～ have no serious attitude towards study

【學科】xuékē（名）branch of learning; discipline

【學派】xuépài（名）school of thought

【學時】xuéshí（名）class hour

【學徒】xuétú（名）trainee; apprentice

【學校】xuéxiào（名）school

【學員】xuéyuán（名）trainee; student

【學院】xuéyuàn（名）college; institute

【學術】xuéshù（名）learning; academic research: 進行～ 研究 do research

【學問】xuéwèn（名）knowledge; learning; academic attainments

【學習】xuéxí（動）study; learn

【學報】xuébào（名）school journal

【學費】xuéfèi（名）school fee; tuition

【學期】xuéqī（名）term; semester

【學會】xuéhuì Ⅰ（動）learn; master: ～一門外語 master a foreign language Ⅱ（名）institute; learned society

【學業】xuéyè（名）one's studies: 完成～ complete one's education

【學說】xuéshuō（名）theory; doctrine

【學潮】xuécháo（名）student unrest

【學歷】xuélì（名）record of schooling; formal education; academic record

【學識】xuéshí（名）learning; knowledge

【學籍】xuéjí（名）student status: 開除～ expel sb. from school; send sb. down (from a university)

【學齡】xuélíng（名）school age

孺 rú（名）child: ～子 child; lad

孽 niè（名）sin; evil

孿 luán（名）twin: ～生兄弟 twin brothers

宀 部

它 tā（代）it

【它們】tāmen（代）they; them

宇 yǔ（名）❶ house: 屋～ house ❷ space; universe

【宇宙】yǔzhòu（名）universe; cosmos

【宇宙航行】yǔzhòu hángxíng（ for short 宇航 yǔháng）（名）astronavigation; space travels

【宇宙飛船】yǔzhòu fēichuán（名）spacecraft

【宇航員】yǔhángyuán（名）astronaut; spaceman

守 shǒu（動）❶ guard; safeguard: ～備部隊 garrison force ❷ keep watch: ～夜 keep night watch ❸ observe; adhere to: ～約 keep a promise ❹ be close to; be near: ～着水的地方,可以多種稻子。More rice may be grown in the fields nearby the water.

【守口如瓶】shǒu kǒu rú píng〈成〉be tight-lipped

【守法】shǒufǎ（動）observe the laws and decrees; abide by the law: ～公民 law-abiding citizen

【守門員】shǒuményuán（名）〈體〉goalkeeper

【守軍】shǒujūn（名）defenders; defending troops

【守則】shǒuzé（名）rules; regulations

【守候】shǒuhòu（動）❶ wait for: ～家鄉的消息 wait anxiously for news from one's hometown ❷ watch over: 護士日夜～着傷員。The nurses looked after the wounded soldiers day and night.

【守時】shǒushí（動）be punctual

【守財奴】shǒucáinú（名）niggard; miser

【守勢】shǒushì（名）the defensive: 處於～ be on the defensive

【守歲】shǒusuì（動）see the old year out and usher the new year in

【守寡】shǒuguǎ（動）remain a widow

【守衛】shǒuwèi（動）guard; defend

【守舊】shǒujiù（動）stick to outmoded values, practices, etc.; be conservative

【守護】shǒuhù（動）defend; safeguard: ～祖國的邊疆 safeguard the frontiers of one's country

【守靈】shǒulíng（動）stand as guards at the bier; keep vigil by the coffin

宅 zhái（名）residence; house: 住～ residential quarters

安 ān Ⅰ（形）peaceful; quiet; calm: 心神不～ feel anxious Ⅱ（動）❶ be content: ～於現狀 be contented with one's lot; be contented with the existing state of affairs ❷ soothe; steady; tranquillize: ～神 steady one's nerves ❸ install: ～空調 have an air-conditioner installed ❹ set up: ～關卡 set up a checkpost ❺ bring (a charge against sb.) ❻ harbour (intentions, usu. evil ones): 他～的是什麼心? What tricks has he up his sleeve? Ⅲ（名）❶ safety; security: 公～局 public security bureau ❷ (Ān) a surname Ⅳ（副）[an interrogative word used in rhetorical questions]: ～能不聞不問? How can we keep aloof?

【安之若素】ān zhī ruò sù〈成〉go on as usual despite discomfort or difficulty

【安分】ānfèn（形）law-abiding: ～守己 law-abiding and honest

【安心】ānxīn（動）feel calm and relaxed: ～工作 be pleased with one's job

【安生】ānshēng（動）❶ live in peace ❷ (of a child) be quiet and still

【安民告示】ān mín gào shì（名）notice to reassure the public

【安好】ānhǎo（形）well; in good health

【安危】ānwēi（名）safety or danger: 不顧個人～ with no thought for one's own safety

【安全】ānquán Ⅰ（形）safe; secure Ⅱ（名）safety; security: ～感 sense of security

【安全係數】ānquán xìshù（名）safety coefficient

【安全帶】ānquándài（名）safety belt

【安如泰山】ān rú Tàishān〈成〉solid and firm like Mount Tai

【安身】ānshēn（動）have somewhere to live: 無處～ have nowhere to live; become homeless

【安定】āndìng Ⅰ（形）stable Ⅱ（動）stabilize Ⅲ（名）stability: ～團結 stability and unity

【安放】ānfàng（動）put sth. in place

【安居樂業】ān jū lè yè〈成〉live in peace and work in contentment

【安息】ānxī（動）❶ rest in peace ❷ be sound asleep

【安家】ānjiā（動）settle in: ～落戶 settle down

【安家費】ānjiāfèi（名）settlement allowance

【安哥拉】Āngēlā（名）Angola: ～人 Angolan

【安眠藥】ānmiányào（名）sleeping tablet

【安排】ānpái（動）arrange; make arrangements for: ～你明天去參觀這家工廠 arrange for you to visit the factory tomorrow

【安培】ānpéi（量）〈電〉ampere

【安逸】ānyì（形）carefree and comfortable: 過著～的生活 lead a life of ease and comfort; be comfortably off

【安理會】Ānlǐhuì（名）(short for 安全理事會 Ānquán Lǐshìhuì) the (UN) Security Council

【安插】ānchā（动）assign (sb. to a job); plant

【安道爾】Āndào'ěr（名）Andorra: ~人 Andorran

【安頓】āndùn（动）(help) settle in; put in a proper place; make proper arrangements for

【安詳】ānxiáng（形）serene; composed: 舉止~ calm and unhurried in manner

【安歇】ānxiē（动）❶ go to bed; retire (for the night) ❷ take a rest

【安葬】ānzàng（动）bury (the dead)

【安置】ānzhì（动）❶ put in a proper place: ~行李 find a proper place for luggage ❷ find accommodation for ❸ find a job for

【安裝】ānzhuāng（动）mount; install: 在辦公室裏~一臺電話 have a telephone installed in the office

【安寧】ānníng（形）❶ tranquil; peaceful ❷ composed; free from worry

【安撫】ānfǔ（动）console; reassure; pacify

【安慰】ānwèi（动）comfort; console

【安樂】ānlè Ⅰ（名）peace and comfort Ⅱ（形）peaceful and comfortable: ~死 euthanasia; mercy killing

【安靜】ānjìng Ⅰ（形）peaceful; quiet: 請~。Be quiet, please. Ⅱ（副）quietly

【安營】ānyíng（动）pitch a camp

【安徽】Ānhuī（名）Anhui (Province)

【安穩】ānwěn（形）steady; stable

完 wán Ⅰ（形）intact; perfect: ~人 perfect man Ⅱ（动）❶ run out; exhaust: 賣~了 all sold out; out of stock ❷ finish; be concluded: 說個沒~沒了 be long-winded; keep nagging ❸ pay (taxes)

【完了】wánle（动）be over; end: 作業做~ finish one's homework

【完工】wángōng（动）(of a project, etc.) be completed

【完好】wánhǎo（形）intact; undamaged

【完成】wánchéng（动）complete; fulfil; attain: 工程不久就可以~。The project will be completed before long.

【完全】wánquán Ⅰ（副）completely; totally Ⅱ（形）complete; intact

【完事】wánshì（动）〈口〉finish (a job, etc.); be through with: 他一~就回家了。He went home as soon as he got the work done.

【完美】wánměi（形）perfect; flawless

【完畢】wánbì（动）be completed; be concluded; be over: 操練~。The drill is over.

【完蛋】wándàn（动）〈口〉be ruined; collapse; be finished: 事情既是這樣, 他~了。As it is, he is finished.

【完結】wánjié（动）come to an end; be over

【完備】wánbèi（形）complete; adequate: 有不~的地方, 請多提意見。Please feel free to give your comments if there is any shortcoming.

【完善】wánshàn（形）perfect; impeccable; consummate

【完滿】wánmǎn（形）full; perfect; satisfactory

【完整】wánzhěng（形） complete; intact:保存～ kept intact／領土～ territorial integrity

【完璧歸趙】wán bì guī Zhào〈成〉return a thing intact to its owner; return a thing to its owner in good condition

宋 Sòng（名）a surname

宏 hóng（形）great; grand; magnificent

【宏大】hóngdà（形）great; grand

【宏旨】hóngzhǐ（名）theme; main idea

【宏偉】hóngwěi（形）grand; magnificent

【宏圖】hóngtú（名） lofty ideal; grand plan

【宏論】hónglùn（名） far-sighted views

【宏願】hóngyuàn（名）noble ambitions

【宏觀】hóngguān（形）macroscopic:～世界 macrocosm／～控制 macro-control

宗 zōng Ⅰ（名）❶ ancestor ❷ sect; school: 正～ orthodox; genuine; authentic ❸ aim; purpose: 萬變不離其～。The central purpose remains unaltered despite milliard outward changes. Ⅱ（量）：一～買賣 a deal／一～喜事 a happy event

【宗旨】zōngzhǐ（名）aim; purpose

【宗派】zōngpài（名） faction; sect: ～鬥爭 factional infighting

【宗教】zōngjiào（名）religion:～儀式 ritual

【宗族】zōngzú（名）clan

定 dìng Ⅰ（動）❶ decide; settle ❷

order; book: ～貨 order goods ❸ fix; fasten Ⅱ（形）❶ calm; tranquil: 生活安～ lead a peaceful life ❷ fixed; unchangeable: ～量 fixed quantity Ⅲ（副）surely; certainly Ⅳ（Dìng）（名）a surname

【定名】dìngmíng（動）name; designate

【定見】dìngjiàn（名）definite opinion; fixed idea

【定局】dìngjú Ⅰ（動）finalize Ⅱ（名）foregone conclusion

【定居】dìngjū（動）settle down

【定弦】dìngxián（動）tune up

【定性】dìngxìng（動）❶ determine the kinds of constituents of a substance ❷ determine the nature of a legal case

【定律】dìnglǜ（名）law: 物質不滅～ law of indestructibility of matter

【定型】dìngxíng（動）get into shape: 產品～ fix the type of the product

【定神】dìngshén（動）❶ compose oneself ❷ concentrate one's attention: ～細看 gaze at sth. with fixed attention

【定案】dìng'àn（動）decide (on a plan); give the final verdict (on a case) Ⅱ（名）verdict

【定員】dìngyuán（名） stipulated number of staff members or passengers

【定時】dìngshí（形）regular; at regular times

【定時炸彈】dìngshí zhàdàn（名）time bomb

【定時器】dìngshíqì（名）timer

【定產】dìngchǎn（名）fixed output quota

【定理】dìnglǐ（名）theorem

【定做】dìngzuò（動）have (clothing,

etc.) made to order

【定期】dìngqī Ⅰ(副) regularly; periodically Ⅱ(动) set a date

【定量供應】dìngliàng gōngyìng(名) rationing

【定睛】dìngjīng(动) fix one's eyes on

【定義】dìngyì(名) definition

【定罪】dìngzuì(动) convict

【定語】dìngyǔ(名)〈语〉attribute: ～从句 attributive clause

【定奪】dìngduó(动) decide; make a final decision

【定稿】dìnggǎo Ⅰ(动) finalize a draft Ⅱ(名) final version

【定價】dìngjià Ⅰ(动) fix a price Ⅱ(名) price

【定論】dìnglùn(名) final conclusion

【定調子】dìngdiàozi(动) set the tone

【定額】dìng'é(名) quota

【定額工資】dìng'é gōngzī(名) wages based on work quotas

宜 yí(形) suitable; appropriate: 不合時～ out of keeping with the times Ⅱ(动) should; ought to: 事不～遲。The matter admits of no delay.

官 guān(名) ❶ government official; officer ❷ organ: 感～ sense organ ❸ (Guān) a surname

【官方】guānfāng(形) official: ～聲明 official statement

【官司】guānsi(名)〈口〉lawsuit

【官吏】guānlì(名)〈舊〉government officials

【官邸】guāndǐ(名) official residence

【官官相護】guān guān xiāng hù〈成〉all bureaucrats shield each other

【官能】guānnéng(名)(organic) function; sense

【官員】guānyuán(名) official

【官倒】guāndǎo(名) racketeering by government officials or departments

【官倒爺】guāndǎoyé(名) bureaucrat-profiteer

【官場】guānchǎng(名) officialdom; official circles

【官腔】guānqiāng(名) official jargon

【官話】guānhuà(名) ❶ mandarin ❷ bureaucratic jargon

【官銜】guānxián(名) official title

【官僚】guānliáo(名) bureaucrat

【官僚主義】guānliáo zhǔyì(名) bureaucracy

【官價】guānjià(名) official price

【官樣文章】guānyàng wénzhāng(名) ❶ bureaucratic jargon; officialese ❷ mere formality

【官職】guānzhí(名) government post

宛 wǎn Ⅰ(形) winding; zigzag Ⅱ(名)(Wǎn) a surname Ⅲ(动) look as if; seem

【宛如】wǎnrú(宛若 wǎnruò)(介)(just) like: 回首前塵，～一夢。When I look back upon the past, it seems like a dream.

宣 xuān(动) declare; announce

【宣布】xuānbù(动) declare; announce: ～戒嚴 declare martial law

【宣告】xuāngào(动) proclaim; declare: ～結束 have come to an end

【宣言】xuānyán(名) declaration; manifesto

【宣判】xuānpàn(动) pronounce

judgment: 法官～他終身監禁。
The judge pronounced a life sentence on him.

【宣揚】xuānyáng（動）advocate;
propagate: 大肆～ give wide publicity to

【宣傳】xuānchuán Ⅰ（動）propagate;
publicize: ～新的經濟政策 publi-
cize the new economic policies Ⅱ
（名）propaganda: ～機器 propa-
ganda machine

【宣稱】xuānchēng（動）assert; declare: 他～已重新控制了局面。He
asserted that he had regained control
of the situation.

【宣誓】xuānshì（動）take an oath:
總統昨晨～就職。The president
was sworn in yesterday morning.

【宣戰】xuānzhàn（動）declare war

【宣講】xuānjiǎng（動）give publicity
to: ～計劃生育的重要意義 give
publicity to the significance of birth
control

【宣讀】xuāndú（動）read out（in
public）; present: ～論文 present
one's paper

宦 huàn（名）❶ official ❷ eunuch

【宦官】huànguān（名）eunuch

【宦海】huànhǎi（名）officialdom: ～
升沉 political ups and downs

室 shì（名）❶ room ❷ office: 調
度～ dispatcher's office

【室內】shìnèi（形）indoor: ～裝飾
用品 articles for interior decoration

【室內樂】shìnèiyuè（名）〈樂〉cham-
ber music

【室外】shìwài（形）outdoor: ～運動
outdoor exercise

客 kè Ⅰ（名）❶ visitor; guest: 會

～室 reception room ❷ passenger;
traveller: ～車 passenger train; bus
❸ customer: 招徠顧～ solicit customers ❹ roving person engaged in
a particular pursuit: 政治掮～ political broker Ⅱ（動）settle or stay
away from one's home: ～座教授
visiting（guest）professor Ⅲ（形）
objective（as against subjective）Ⅳ
（量）［of food sold by the portion］
serving: 兩～冰激凌 two ice
creams

【客人】kèrén（名）guest; visitor

【客戶】kèhù（名）client

【客串】kèchuàn（動）（of an amateur
actor）play a part in a professional
performance

【客店】kèdiàn（名）inn

【客房】kèfáng（名）hotel room;
guest room

【客家】Kèjiā（名）the Hakkas: ～話
Hakka

【客氣】kèqi（形）❶ polite: 請不要
～。Make yourself at home. ❷
modest; humble

【客套】kètào Ⅰ（名）conventional
polite expressions Ⅱ（動）make polite remarks

【客商】kèshāng（名）visiting businessman

【客隊】kèduì（名）〈體〉visiting
team

【客飯】kèfàn（名）❶ canteen meal
specially prepared for visitors ❷ set
meal; table d'hôte.

【客滿】kèmǎn（形）（of hotels,
restaurants, theatres, etc.）full

【客機】kèjī（名）passenger plane

【客觀】kèguān（形）objective（as a-
gainst subjective）

【客廳】kètīng（名）drawing room;

sitting room

宰 zǎi (动) ❶ slaughter; butcher: ~ 羊 butcher sheep ❷ govern; reign: ~ 制 rule; dominate

【宰相】 zǎixiàng (名) chief minister (in feudal China)

【宰杀】 zǎishā (动) slaughter; kill

【宰割】 zǎigē (动) trample underfoot; oppress and exploit

害 hài I (名) evil; harm II (形) harmful; destructive III (动) ❶ harm; kill: ~人不浅 do people no small harm ❷ contract: ~病 be taken ill ❸ feel

【害怕】 hàipà (动) fear; be afraid of

【害处】 hàichu (名) harm

【害群之马】 hài qún zhī mǎ 〈成〉 a black sheep; a rotten apple in the barrel

【害臊】 hàisào (害羞 hàixiū) (动) feel ashamed; be bashful

家 jiā I (名) ❶ family: 养 ~ support one's family ❷ home; residence ❸ school of thought ❹ specialist; expert: 史学 ~ historian II (形) ❶ 〈谦〉 [used to refer to one's senior or elder relatives] my: ~ 母 my mother ❷ domesticated; domestic: ~ 畜 domestic animal III (量) [of households, firms, etc.]: 这 ~ 饭馆 this restaurant / 三 ~ 副食店 three groceries

【家小】 jiāxiǎo (名) 〈口〉 wife and children; wife

【家用】 jiāyòng (名) running expenses of a family

【家伙】 jiāhuo (名) 〈口〉 ❶ implement; weapon ❷ chap; guy

【家长】 jiāzhǎng (名) ❶ head of a family ❷ parent or guardian of a child

【家长制】 jiāzhǎngzhì (名) patriarchal system

【家底儿】 jiādǐr (家底 jiādǐ) (名) family property (usu. accumulated over a long period of time); possessions of an organization: ~ 厚 have substantial financial resources

【家政学】 jiāzhèngxué (名) home economics; domestic science

【家书】 jiāshū (家信 jiāxìn) (名) letter to or from home

【家庭】 jiātíng (名) family: ~ (联产) 承包责任制 system of contracted household responsibility (with remuneration related to output)

【家庭妇女】 jiātíng fùnǚ (名) housewife

【家破人亡】 jiā pò rén wáng 〈成〉 with one's family broken up and its members dead

【家家户户】 jiā jiā hù hù 〈成〉 each and every household

【家务】 jiāwù (名) household duties; domestic affairs; housework: 料理 ~ attend to domestic duties; keep house

【家教】 jiājiào (名) upbringing; domestic discipline: 没有 ~ lack breeding

【家眷】 jiājuàn (名) ❶ wife and children ❷ wife

【家族】 jiāzú (名) clan; family

【家产】 jiāchǎn (名) family property

【家常】 jiācháng (名) domestic routine: 拉 ~ chitchat

【家常便饭】 jiācháng biànfàn (名) ❶ homely meal ❷ daily routine

【家禽】 jiāqín (名) poultry

【家鄉】jiāxiāng（名）native place; hometown

【家喻戶曉】jiā yù hù xiǎo〈成〉be a household word; be known to every household: 這個新的規定應該做到～。This new stipulation should be made known to all.

【家當】jiādàng（名）〈口〉family property

【家園】jiāyuán（名）native place; home

【家電】jiādiàn（名）(short for 家用電器 jiāyòng diànqì) electrical home appliance

【家境】jiājìng（名）financial condition of a family

【家醜】jiāchǒu（名）family disgrace; skeleton in the cupboard: ～不可外揚 Don't wash your dirty linen in public.

【家譜】jiāpǔ（名）family tree; genealogy

【家屬】jiāshǔ（名）family dependents

【家蠶】jiācán（名）silkworm

宵 xiāo（名）night: 熬了個通～ stay up all night

【宵禁】xiāojìn（名）curfew

宴 yàn I（名）banquet; feast II（動）entertain at a banquet

【宴席】yànxí（名）banquet

【宴會】yànhuì（名）banquet; dinner party

【宴會廳】yànhuìtīng（名）banquet hall

【宴請】yànqǐng（動）give a banquet in sb.'s honour; invite sb. to dinner

宮 gōng（名）❶ palace: 故～博物院 Palace Museum ❷ temple ❸

（Gǒng）a surname

【宮廷】gōngtíng（名）❶ palace ❷ royal or imperial court

【宮殿】gōngdiàn（名）palace

【宮燈】gōngdēng（名）palace lantern

容 róng I（動）❶ hold; contain: 這間會議室能～五十人。The meeting room can hold fifty people. ❷ tolerate: 大量～人 be tolerant and broadminded ❸ allow; permit: 不～分說 allow for no explanations II（名）❶ appearance; looks: 愁～滿面 look worried / 整頓市～ tidy up the appearance of the city ❷（Róng）a surname

【容光煥發】róng guāng huàn fā〈成〉look radiant with health

【容身】róngshēn（動）take refuge: ～之地 a place where one can live and work peacefully

【容忍】róngrěn（動）tolerate; put up with: 不能～這種侮辱 cannot put up with such an insult

【容易】róngyì（形）❶ easy ❷ likely; liable: ～出錯 be liable to error

【容納】róngnà（動）hold; accommodate; contain

【容許】róngxǔ（動）allow; permit: 決不～這樣的事情再次發生 should not allow this sort of thing to happen again

【容量】róngliàng（名）capacity

【容貌】róngmào（容顏 róngyán）（名）(of a person) appearance; looks; features

【容積】róngjī（名）volume; holding space

【容器】róngqì（名）container

密 mì Ⅰ (形) ❶ dense; thick: 秧苗 插得太～了。The seedlings are transplanted too closely. ❷ intimate; close: ～友 close associate; bosom friend ❸ secret; classified Ⅱ (名) ❶ secret: 保～ keep a secret ❷ (Mì) a surname

【密切】mìqiè Ⅰ (形) intimate; close: 他俩關係～。They are on intimate terms with each other. Ⅱ (副) closely; carefully: ～注視事態發展 follow closely the development of the situation

【密件】mìjiàn (名) confidential paper (letter); classified material

【密佈】mìbù (形) densely covered: 濃雲～ covered with dark clouds

【密使】mìshǐ (名) secret envoy

【密室】mìshì (名) secret chamber

【密約】mìyuē (名) ❶ secret agreement; secret treaty ❷ secret rendezvous

【密度】mìdù (名) density

【密封】mìfēng Ⅰ (動) seal up: 把氣 體～在瓶子裏 seal up the gas in a battle Ⅱ (形) sealed; airtight: ～的 信件 letter sealed with wax / 錶殼 是～的。The watchcase is airtight.

【密封艙】mìfēngcāng (名) airtight cabin

【密紋唱片】mìwén chàngpiàn (名) long-playing record; microgroove record

【密閉】mìbì (形) airtight

【密商】mìshāng (動) hold secret counsel with

【密探】mìtàn (名) secret agent; spy

【密密麻麻】mìmi mámá (形) close and countless; thickly dotted

【密密層層】mìmi céngcéng (形)

close; dense; layer upon layer: ～ 的灌木叢 impenetrable thicket

【密集】mìjí (形) dense; crowded: 技術～型 technology-intensive / 人 口～地區 densely-populated area

【密植】mìzhí (名) 〈農〉 close planting

【密電】mìdiàn (名) cipher telegram; code telegram

【密碼】mìmǎ (名) cipher; cipher code

【密談】mìtán (名) talk behind closed doors; secret negotiation

【密謀】mìmóu (動) conspire; plot

寇 kòu (名) ❶ bandit; brigand; invader ❷ (Kòu) a surname

寄 jì (動) ❶ commit in trust: 我們 ～希望於年輕一代。We lay our hopes on the younger generation. ❷ send by post; mail: 用郵包～ send sth. by parcel post ❸ depend on for support ❹ lodge: ～居友人家裏 lodge at a friend's house

【寄人籬下】jì rén lí xià〈成〉 place oneself under sb.'s patronage

【寄予】jìyǔ (動) ❶ put (hope, etc.) on: ～厚望 place high hopes on sb. ❷ give; bestow; confer: ～ 無微不至的關懷 show solicitous concern for sb.'s well-being

【寄生】jìshēng Ⅰ (名) parasitism Ⅱ (形) parasitic

【寄生蟲】jìshēngchóng (名) parasite

【寄存】jìcún (寄放 jìfàng) (動) deposit; hand over for safekeeping: 把 行李～友人處 leave one's luggage at a friend's house

【寄託】jìtuō (動) ❶ deposit; entrust: 把孩子～給他 entrust the children to his care ❷ express one's (hope, emotion, etc); give expression to: ～我們的深情厚誼 give expression to our profound feelings

【寄宿】jìsù (動) ❶ 學校 boarding school ❷ put up; lodge

【寄養】jìyǎng (動) ❶ entrust a child to sb. ❷ (of a child) be brought up in another's home: ～在祖母家 be brought up by one's grandmother

【寄賣】jìmài(寄售 jìshòu)(動) consign for sale; put up for sale at a second-hand shop

寂 jì (形) ❶ quiet; silent; noiseless ❷ lonely: 孤～ alone and friendless

【寂寞】jìmò (形) lonely; solitary; forlorn: ～萬分 extremely lonely

【寂靜】jìjìng (形) quiet; noiseless: ～無聲。No sound is audible.

宿 sù Ⅰ (動) stay overnight: 寄～ 在朋友家 put up at a friend's house Ⅱ (形) long-standing: ～疾 chronic trouble Ⅲ (名) (Sù) a surname see also xiǔ

【宿舍】sùshè (名) hostel; dormitory: 單身～ living quarters for single men or women; bachelor quarters

【宿命論】sùmìnglùn (名) fatalism

【宿怨】sùyuàn (名) old grudge

【宿營】sùyíng (動) camp: ～地 campsite

【宿願】sùyuàn (名) long-cherished wish: 以償～ so as to fulfil a long-cherished wish

宿 xiǔ (量) : 他們談了一～。They kept talking the whole night. see also sù

寒 hán (形) ❶ cold ❷ poor; impoverished: 出身清～ born into an impoverished intellectual family

【寒心】hánxīn (動) ❶ be sadly disillusioned ❷ shudder

【寒衣】hányī (名) winter clothes

【寒冷】hánlěng (形) cold

【寒流】hánliú (名) 〈氣〉 cold current

【寒帶】hándài (名) 〈地〉 frigid zone

【寒假】hánjià (名) winter vacation

【寒暑表】hánshǔbiǎo (名) thermometer

【寒暄】hánxuān (名) polite conversation following the exchange of greetings

【寒意】hányì (名) a nip in the air: 一絲～ a chill in the air; a hint of winter in the air

【寒微】hánwēi (形) of humble background; of low station in life

【寒酸】hánsuān (形) ungracious in behaviour; shabby

【寒潮】háncháo (名) 〈氣〉 cold wave

【寒磣】hánchen Ⅰ (形) ❶ ugly; unpresentable: 長相～ look ugly ❷ shameful Ⅱ(動) hold sb. to ridicule: 覺得～ feel small; feel ashamed

【寒噤】hánjìn (名) shiver; chill: 她打了個～。She felt a chill running down her spine.

富 fù Ⅰ (形) ❶ rich; wealthy ❷ plentiful; full of Ⅱ (名) wealth

【富有】fùyǒu (形) full of; rich in

【富足】fùzú (形) plentiful; rich

【富翁】fùwēng (名) man of wealth

【富庶】fùshù (形) populous and rich in resources

【富貴】fùguì (名) wealth and rank

【富裕】fùyù (形) well-to-do: 過著～ 的生活 live comfortably off

【富強】fùqiáng (形) rich and strong:

~ 的國家 prosperous and powerful nation

【富源】fùyuán（名）natural resources

【富豪】fùháo（名）magnate

【富餘】fùyu（形）surplus; spare: ~ 的時間 spare time

【富麗堂皇】fùlì tánghuáng（形）magnificent

【富饒】fùráo（形）rich in resources

寓 yù Ⅰ（動）❶ reside; live ❷ imply; contain: ~ 意深遠 endowed with a profound meaning Ⅱ（名）residence: 客~ lodgings

【寓言】yùyán（名）fable; allegory; parable

【寓所】yùsuǒ（名）residence; abode

寐 mèi（動）sleep: 夜不能 ~ cannot fall asleep at night

寧 níng Ⅰ（形）peaceful; quiet Ⅱ（名）short for the Ningxia Hui Autonomous Region
see also nìng

【寧夏】Níngxià（名）Ningxia

【寧夏回族自治區】Níngxià Huízú Zìzhìqū（名）the Ningxia Hui Autonomous Region

【寧靜】níngjìng（形）peaceful; quiet; tranquil

寧 nìng（副）(would) rather
see also níng

【寧可】nìngkě（副）(would) rather: 我 ~ 現在不談這件事 I'd rather not talk about it now.

【寧死不屈】nìng sǐ bù qū〈成〉prefer death to dishonour

【寧缺毋濫】nìng quē wú làn〈成〉would rather go without than have

sth. trashy

寨 zhài（名）❶ camp; stockade; stronghold ❷ stockaded village

寞 mò（形）lonely; deserted: 心情寂 ~ feel lonely and bored

寡 guǎ（形）❶ few; scant: ~ 聞 ill-informed ❷ being a widow

【寡人】guǎrén（名）(royal)"We"; I, the sovereign

【寡不敵眾】guǎ bù dí zhòng〈成〉cannot hold out against overwhelming odds

【寡婦】guǎfu（名）widow

【寡廉鮮恥】guǎ lián xiǎn chǐ〈成〉corrupt and shameless

【寡頭】guǎtóu（名）oligarch: ~ 政治 oligarchy

寥 liáo（形）❶ few; sparse ❷ deserted; empty

【寥若晨星】liáo ruò chén xīng〈成〉as few as the stars at dawn

【寥落】liáoluò（形）scanty; sparse

【寥廓】liáokuò（形）vast; immense

【寥寥】liáoliáo（形）very few: ~ ~ 無幾 can be counted on the fingers

寢 qǐn（名）❶ sleep: 尚未就 ~ have not retired yet for the night ❷ bedroom

【寢具】qǐnjù（名）bedding

【寢食】qǐnshí（名）sleeping and eating: ~ 不安 unable to sleep or eat quietly

【寢室】qǐnshì（名）bedroom

實 shí Ⅰ（形）❶ solid: 把窟窿填了。Fill up the hole. ❷ true; sincere: ~ 話 ~ 說 tell the truth ❸ actual; real: ~ 情 the true story; the actual state of affairs Ⅱ（名）❶ reality: 名存～亡 cease to exist except in name ❷ fruit; seed

【實力】shílì（名）strength

【實心】shíxīn（形）❶（of a ball, etc.）solid ❷ sincere; unfeigned: ～話 honest and sincere remark

【實心實意】shí xīn shí yì〈成〉in earnest; in all sincerity

【實用】shíyòng（形）practical; suitable for actual use

【實用主義】shíyòng zhǔyì（名）pragmatism: ～者 pragmatist

【實地】shídì（副）on the spot: ～考察 on-the-spot inspection

【實行】shíxíng（動）carry out; implement

【實在】shízài Ⅰ（形）true; real; tangible; honest: 他這個人很～。He is very down-to-earth. Ⅱ（副）indeed: ～記不起來了 really can't remember

【實況】shíkuàng（形）live: ～轉播 live broadcast

【實足】shízú（形）full; solid; good: ～年齡 exact age / 一噸煤 a full ton of coal

【實例】shílì（名）example; instance

【實物】shíwù Ⅰ（名）material object: ～交換 barter trade Ⅱ（形）in kind: 以～提供援助 provide aid in kind

【實施】shíshī（動）implement; enforce

【實效】shíxiào（名）practical result; real effect: 講求～ pay special attention to practical results

【實習】shíxí（名）practice; field study

【實現】shíxiàn（動）realize; materialize

【實報實銷】shí bào shí xiāo（動）reimburse what one has spent on official business

【實測】shícè（動）survey; measure: ～數據 date collected in a survey

【實惠】shíhuì Ⅰ（名）real benefit; tangible benefit; substantial profit Ⅱ（形）substantial

【實業】shíyè（名）business; industry and commerce; industry

【實際】shíjì Ⅰ（名）reality: 不符合～ incompatible with reality Ⅱ（形）❶ actual; specific: ～行動 concrete action ❷ practical: 不切～ unrealistic; unpractical

【實踐】shíjiàn Ⅰ（動）practise; fulfil (one's promise) Ⅱ（名）practice: ～出真知。Genuine knowledge comes from practice.

【實彈】shídàn（名）〈軍〉live ammunition

【實質】shízhì（名）substance; essence: ～上不同 be different in essence

【實績】shíjì（名）actual contribution (in work); tangible achievement

【實權】shíquán（名）real authority or power

【實體】shítǐ（名）❶〈哲〉substance ❷〈法〉entity

【實驗】shíyàn（名）experiment; test: ～室 laboratory

察

chá（動）scrutinize; examine; investigate

【察言觀色】chá yán guān sè〈成〉weigh a person's words and watch his mood

【察看】chákàn（動）observe; examine: ～風向 check the direction in which the wind blows

【察覺】chájué（動）sense; become

aware of

寬 kuān Ⅰ (形) ❶ wide; broad ❷ lenient: 從 ~ 處理 be dealt with lightly ❸ well-to-do: 手頭比以往 ~ 了些 be somewhat better off than before Ⅱ (名) ❶ width: 這條路 ~ 四米。 The road is four metres wide. ❷ (Kuān) a surname Ⅲ (動) extend (a limit); relax: 放 ~ 期限 extend the time limit

【寬大】 kuāndà (形) ❶ spacious; large ❷ lenient

【寬心】 kuānxīn (動) feel relieved; set one's mind at ease

【寬宏大量】 kuān hóng dà liàng 〈成〉 generous; broadminded; magnanimous

【寬待】 kuāndài (動) treat leniently

【寬厚】 kuānhòu (形) kind and generous; benign

【寬度】 kuāndù (名) width

【寬限】 kuānxiàn (動) extend a time limit: ~ 期 grace period

【寬窄】 kuānzhǎi (名) width

【寬容】 kuānróng (形) tolerant; lenient; forbearing

【寬恕】 kuānshù (動) pardon; forgive; condone

【寬敞】 kuānchang (形) spacious; commodious

【寬裕】 kuānyù (形) well-off; ample

【寬廣】 kuānguǎng (形) vast; broad: ~ 的原野 vast open country

【寬銀幕】 kuānyínmù (形) 〈電〉 widescreen

【寬慰】 kuānwèi (動) ❶ comfort: 在這種情況下, 我沒有辦法 ~ 她。 Under these circumstances I can do nothing to comfort her. ❷ feel reassured: 聽到這個消息我心裏緣 ~

些。 I felt a little reassured at the news.

【寬闊】 kuānkuò (形) wide; broad

【寬鬆】 kuānsōng (形) (of clothes) loose-fitting: ~ 的 褲子 baggy trousers

寮 liáo (名) small house: 茶 ~ (small) teahouse

審 shěn Ⅰ (動) ❶ examine; check over ❷ interrogate; try: ~ 問罪犯 interrogate a criminal Ⅱ (形) careful

【審判】 shěnpàn (動) bring to trial; try

【審批】 shěnpī (名) examine and approve

【審定】 shěndìng (動) check, revise and approve

【審查】 shěnchá (動) examine; investigate; check

【審訂】 shěndìng (動) examine and revise

【審計】 shěnjì (動) audit: ~ 員 auditor

【審看】 shěnkàn (動) ❶ censor (a film or play) ❷ examine; scrutinize

【審美】 shěnměi (形) aesthetic: ~ 觀 aesthetic perception

【審核】 shěnhé (動) examine and verify; verify

【審校】 shěnjiào (動) examine and revise

【審時度勢】 shěn shí duó shì 〈成〉 give careful consideration to the current situation

【審訊】 shěnxùn (動) 〈法〉 interrogate; try

【審理】 shěnlǐ (動) 〈法〉 try (a case); hear

【審問】 shěnwèn (動) interrogate; cross-examine

【審結】shěnjié（動）try and wind up a case

【審慎】shěnshèn（形）careful; cautious; circumspect

【審閱】shěnyuè（動）make comments and give the final approval

【審議】shěnyì（動）consider; examine and deliberate

【審驗】shěnyàn（動）check; examine

寫 xiě（動）❶ write: 這個故事～得很好。The story is well written. ❷ portray; describe

【寫生】xiěshēng（動）paint from life; sketch from nature

【寫字檯】xiězìtái（名）writing desk; desk

【寫作】xiězuò（名）writing: 練～ practise writing / 以～爲生 make a living by writing

【寫真】xiězhēn Ⅰ（動）❶ draw a portrait ❷ describe sth. realistically Ⅱ（名）portrait

【寫照】xiězhào（名）portrayal; portraiture

【寫稿】xiěgǎo（動）write for (a magazine, newspaper, etc.)

寰 huán（名）extensive region

【寰球】huánqiú（寰宇 huányǔ）（名）the globe; the earth; the whole world

寵 chǒng（動）dote on; love dearly: ～壞 spoil sb.

【寵兒】chǒng'ér（名）favourite; pet

【寵愛】chǒng'ài（動）dote on

寶 bǎo Ⅰ（名）treasure: 如獲至～ as if one had found a treasure Ⅱ（形）precious; treasured: ～劍 (trea-

sured) double-edged sword Ⅲ（代）〈敬〉〈舊〉[said of a friend's family or shop]your: ～號 your shop

【寶石】bǎoshí（名）precious stone

【寶貝】bǎobèi（名）❶ treasure ❷ darling; baby ❸ an incompetent or eccentric: 他真是個～。He is quite a character.

【寶庫】bǎokù（名）treasure house (trove): 知識～ a storehouse of knowledge

【寶座】bǎozuò（名）throne

【寶貴】bǎoguì（形）valuable; rewarding: ～的經驗 rewarding experience

【寶塔】bǎotǎ（名）pagoda; dagoba

【寶藏】bǎozàng（名）mineral deposits

【寶寶】bǎobao（名）little darling

寸 部

寸 cùn Ⅰ（名）unit of length, = 1/30 metre Ⅱ（形）small; short

【寸心】cùnxīn（名）❶ innermost thought ❷ modest acknowledgement: 略表～ be a modest acknowledgement of one's appreciation

【寸步難行】cùn bù nán xíng〈成〉cannot move an inch

寺 sì（名）temple

【寺院】sìyuàn（名）monastery; temple

【寺廟】sìmiào（名）temple

封 fēng Ⅰ（動）❶ seal: ～別人的嘴 seal sb.'s lips ❷ confer (title or land) upon Ⅱ（量）幾～信 several letters Ⅲ（名）(Fēng) a surname

【封存】fēngcún（动）seal up for sefekeeping

【封地】fēngdì（名）fief

【封官許願】fēng guān xǔ yuàn〈成〉promise appointments and other favours

【封建】fēngjiàn（形）feudal

【封建主義】fēngjiàn zhǔyì（名）feudalism

【封面】fēngmiàn（名）front cover

【封條】fēngtiáo（名）sealing strip

【封閉】fēngbì（动）❶ seal ❷ close down

【封閉療法】fēngbì liáofǎ（名）〈醫〉block therapy

【封鎖】fēngsuǒ（动）blockade；close off

【封蠟】fēnglà（名）sealing wax

射 shè（动）❶ shoot；fire：～出一發子彈 fire a shot ❷ discharge；emit：輻～ radiate ❸ allude to sb. or sth：影～ throw out innuendoes against；make veiled attacks on

【射手】shèshǒu（名）marksman；shooter

【射門】shèmén（动）〈體〉shoot (at the goal)

【射流】shèliú（名）〈物〉efflux

【射程】shèchéng（名）range (of fire)

【射綫】shèxiàn（名）〈物〉ray

【射箭】shèjiàn Ⅰ（动）shoot an arrow Ⅱ（名）〈體〉archery

【射擊】shèjī Ⅰ（动）shoot；fire Ⅱ（名）shooting

專 zhuān Ⅰ（动）❶ concentrate：～心 concentrate one's attention on ❷ monopolize：～賣 monopoly Ⅱ（形）

special；for a particular person or purpose：～號 special issue (of a periodical)

【專一】zhuānyī（形）single-minded；devoted

【專用】zhuānyòng（动）serve a particular purpose；be for use by a particular unit

【專刊】zhuānkān（名）special issue

【專列】zhuānliè（名）speical train

【專車】zhuānchē（名）special train

【專利】zhuānlì（名）patent

【專長】zhuāncháng（名）speciality；special field of study；special skill

【專門】zhuānmén（形）special；specialized：～知識 specialized knowledge

【專制】zhuānzhì Ⅰ（名）autocracy Ⅱ（形）autocratic：君主～ autocratic monarchy

【專注】zhuānzhù（动）concentrate one's attention on；devote oneself to

【專政】zhuānzhèng（名）dictatorship

【專科學校】zhuānkē xuéxiào（名）technical college；vocational training school

【專修】zhuānxiū（动）specialize in；major in

【專案】zhuān'àn（名）special case

【專家】zhuānjiā（名）expert；specialist

【專員】zhuānyuán（名）(administrative) commissioner：新聞～ press attaché

【專區】zhuānqū（名）prefecture

【專程】zhuānchéng（名）special trip：～來京拜訪 make a special trip to Beijing to see sb.

【專款】zhuānkuǎn（名）fund earmarked for special use；special fund

【專誠】zhuānchéng（副）specially；

這個蛋糕是～爲你做的。The cake is specially made for you.

【專業】zhuānyè（名）special field of study: ～戶 rural household engaged exclusively or principally in a certain line of agricultural sideline

【專橫】zhuānhèng（形）unjust and cruel; despotic

【專機】zhuānjī（名）special plane

【專斷】zhuānduàn（動）act arbitrarily

【專題】zhuāntí（名）special topic: 作～報告 give a lecture on a special topic

【專職】zhuānzhí（名）full-time job

【專欄】zhuānlán（名）special column: ～作家 columnist

將 jiāng Ⅰ（介）❶ with; by means of; by: ～鷄蛋碰石頭 use eggs to smash a rock; a futile attempt ❷ [used before the direct object of a transitive verb in an inverted phrase or sentence]: ～失物還給主人 restore lost property to its owner Ⅱ（動）❶ be going to; be about to; will; shall: 天～破曉。Dawn is breaking. ❷〈象棋〉check ❸ challenge; goad: 我們～他一下，使他明確表態。We goaded him into clarifying his stand. Ⅲ（副）[used between a verb and a complement of direction]: 叫～起來 start to scream / 走～進去 walk right in Ⅳ（名）(Jiāng) a surname
see also jiàng

【將死】jiāngsǐ（動）checkmate

【將近】jiāngjìn（動）be close to; approach: ～一千噸 nearly a thousand tons

【將來】jiānglái Ⅰ（名）future: 人類的～ the future of mankind Ⅱ（副）in (the) future

【將軍】jiāngjūn Ⅰ（名）ranking officer; general Ⅱ（動）❶〈象棋〉check ❷ put sb. in a fix: 用難題將他一軍 taunt him with an embarrassing question

【將要】jiāngyào（動）will; shall; be going to; be about to

【將計就計】jiāng jì jiù jì〈成〉beat sb. at his own game; make sb. stew in his own juice

【將息】jiāngxī（動）rest; recuperate

【將就】jiāngjiù（動）make do with; put up with: 我們只好～現在的安排。We have to put up with the present arrangement.

【將養】jiāngyǎng（動）rest; convalesce: 他還得～個把月纔能康復。He will have to rest for a month or so before he is well again.

【將錯就錯】jiāng cuò jiù cuò〈成〉make the best of an error without rectifying it

將 jiàng（名）general; military commander: 少～ major general
see also jiāng

【將士】jiàngshì（名）officers and men; commanders and fighters

【將官】jiàngguān（名）〈口〉high-ranking officer; general

【將領】jiànglǐng（名）high-ranking officer

尉 wèi（名）❶ junior officer: 準～ warrant officer ❷（Wèi) a surname
see also yù

【尉官】wèiguān（名）junior officer

尉 yù
see also wèi

【尉遲】Yùchí（名）a surname

尊 zūn Ⅰ（動）respect; esteem: 中國有～師的傳統。China has the tradition of respecting teachers. / 自～ self-respect Ⅱ（敬）your: ～姓 your name Ⅲ（量）一～大炮 a cannon

【尊重】zūnzhòng（動）respect; esteem; value: 我們～你的意見。We all value your advice.

【尊崇】zūnchóng（動）worship; venerate

【尊貴】zūnguì（形）honourable; respectable; noble

【尊敬】zūnjìng（動）respect; esteem; revere

【尊稱】zūnchēng（名）respectful form of address

【尊嚴】zūnyán Ⅰ（名）dignity; honour Ⅱ（形）dignified

尋 xín
see also xún

【尋死】xínsǐ（動）❶ attempt suicide ❷ commit suicide

【尋思】xínsi（動）consider; think over: 獨自～ be alone and deep in thought

【尋開心】xínkāixīn（動）❶ pull sb.'s leg ❷ seek pleasure

【尋短見】xínduǎnjiàn（動）attempt suicide; commit suicide

尋 xún（動）look for; seek
see also xín

【尋找】xúnzhǎo（動）look for: ～借口 look for an excuse

【尋求】xúnqiú（動）seek: ～保護 seek protection / ～政治避難 seek political asylum

【尋味】xúnwèi（動）chew sth. over; consider carefully: 這件事耐人～。This matter gives us plenty of food for thought.

【尋根究底】xún gēn jiū dǐ（成）get to the roots of things; make a thorough investigation

【尋常】xúncháng（形）ordinary; common: ～百姓 ordinary people

【尋訪】xúnfǎng（動）look for; make inquiries about

【尋覓】xúnmì（動）seek; look for

【尋機】xúnjī（動）seek opportunities; look for a chance

【尋釁】xúnxìn（動）provoke; pick a quarrel

對 duì Ⅰ（動）❶ answer; reply: 無言以～ have nothing to say in reply; feel tongue tied ❷ face ❸ check: 校～ read the proofs ❹ add; mix: ～水 add some water Ⅱ（形）correct; right; suitable Ⅲ（名）pair; couple: 一～鴛鴦 a pair of love-birds Ⅳ（介）towards; to: ～工作的態度 attitude towards work

【對口】duìkǒu（動）be in line with: ～的工作 a job suited to one's professional training

【對內】duìnèi（形）internal; domestic

【對手】duìshǒu（名）opponent; rival

【對比】duìbǐ（名）contrast

【對不起】duì bu qǐ（動）❶（套）be sorry; excuse me; pardon me ❷ let down

【對牛彈琴】duì niú tán qín〈成〉speak to the wrong audience; cast pearls before swine

【對白】duìbái（名）dialogue（in a drama or film）

【對半】duìbàn（副）fifty-fifty: ～分

divide in half

【對付】duìfu（動）❶ cope with; tackle ❷ make do: 能～着看英文報了 can manage to read English-language newspapers

【對立】duìlì（名）antagonism; opposition

【對外】duìwài（形）external; foreign: ～政策 foreign policy

【對抗】duìkàng Ⅰ（動）oppose; resist Ⅱ（名）confrontation; antagonism

【對於】duìyú（介）to; on; for.: ～這個問題我有保留。I have reservations on this question.

【對岸】duì'àn（名）the other side of the river

【對門】duìmén（名）house(s) on the opposite side

【對待】duìdài（動）treat; deal with

【對勁】duìjìn❶ suit; be satisfactory ❷ get along well

【對峙】duìzhì Ⅰ（動）confront each other; stand eyeball to eyeball Ⅱ（名）confrontation

【對面】duìmiàn（形）❶ opposite: 街～ across the street ❷ right in front

【對症下藥】duì zhèng xià yào〈成〉prescribe medicine according to each particular case; find a solution for each specific situation

【對得起】duì de qǐ（動）not disappoint sb.'s hopes; be worthy of sb.'s confidence

【對策】duìcè（名）countermeasure

【對開】duìkāi Ⅰ（動）❶（of trains, buses or ships）run from opposite directions ❷ divide into two halves Ⅱ（名）〈印〉folio

【對象】duìxiàng（名）❶ target; object ❷ boyfriend（girlfriend）

【對照】duìzhào（動）compare; collate: ～原文修改譯文 check the translation against the original and make corrections

【對話】duìhuà（名）dialogue

【對稱】duìchèn（名）symmetry

【對臺戲】duìtáixì（名）rival show

【對蝦】duìxiā（名）prawn

【對質】duìzhì（名）confrontation between the accuser and the defendant

【對頭】duìtóu（形）❶ correct; right ❷ normal: 神色不～ not look quite oneself

【對聯】duìlián（名）couplet

【對應】duìyìng（動）correspond

導 dǎo（動）❶ lead; guide ❷ conduct; transmit

【導火綫】dǎohuǒxiàn（名）❶ fuse ❷ incident that triggers hostilities

【導言】dǎoyán（名）introductory remarks; foreword

【導航】dǎoháng Ⅰ（動）navigate Ⅱ（名）navigation

【導師】dǎoshī（名）teacher; tutor

【導致】dǎozhì（動）lead to; cause; result in

【導遊】dǎoyóu Ⅰ（名）❶ tourist guide ❷ guidebook Ⅱ（動）guide a tour

【導遊圖】dǎoyóutú（名）tourist map

【導源】dǎoyuán（動）originate; derive

【導演】dǎoyǎn Ⅰ（動）direct (a film or stage performance) Ⅱ（名）director (of a film, play, etc.)

【導綫】dǎoxiàn（名）lead; wire

【導彈】dǎodàn（名）(guided) missile

【導體】dǎotǐ（名）conductor: 半～ semiconductor

小 部

【小】xiǎo Ⅰ(形) ❶ little; small: ～规模 small scale ❷ young: ～女儿 the youngest daughter ❸ [used as a prefix before a surname, given name or ordinal number among brothers and sisters, usu. of a young or younger person]: ～张 Little Zhang; Xiao Zhang Ⅱ(副) for a short time: ～住数日 just stay for a few days

【小刀】xiǎodāo (名) pocket knife

【小人】xiǎorén (名) base person; villain

【小人书】xiǎorénshū (名)〈口〉picture-story book

【小人物】xiǎorénwù (名) unimportant person; nobody; nonentity; small potato

【小工】xiǎogōng (名) unskilled labourer

【小子】xiǎozi (名) ❶ boy; son ❷ fellow; chap

【小丑】xiǎochǒu (名) clown; buffoon

【小心】xiǎoxīn (动) take care; be careful: ～轻放 handle with care

【小心翼翼】xiǎo xīn yì yì〈成〉cautious; cagey

【小五金】xiǎowǔjīn (名) hardware; metal goods for domestic use

【小市民】xiǎoshìmín (名) urban petty bourgeois

【小册子】xiǎocèzi (名) pamphlet; booklet; brochure

【小生产】xiǎoshēngchǎn (名) small-scale production: ～者 small producer

【小巧玲珑】xiǎo qiǎo líng lóng〈成〉small and exquisite

【小本经营】xiǎoběn jīngyíng (名) business with a small capital; small business

【小吃】xiǎochī (名) snack; refreshments; cold dishes; collation: ～店 snack bar

【小米】xiǎomǐ (名) millet

【小名】xiǎomíng (名) pet name for a child; nickname

【小伙子】xiǎohuǒzi (名) youngster; lad; young chap

【小百货】xiǎobǎihuò (名) small articles of daily use

【小车】xiǎochē (名) ❶ handcart; wheelbarrow ❷ (sedan) car

【小姑】xiǎogū (名) sister-in-law; husband's younger sister

【小姐】xiǎojiě (名) ❶ Miss ❷ young lady

【小事】xiǎoshì (名) trifle; trifling matter

【小两口】xiǎoliǎngkǒu (名)〈口〉young couple

【小叔子】xiǎoshūzi (名) husband's younger brother; brother-in-law

【小朋友】xiǎopéngyǒu (名) children

【小夜曲】xiǎoyèqǔ (名) serenade

【小拇指】xiǎomuzhǐ (名) little finger

【小儿科】xiǎo'érkē (名)〈医〉(department of) paediatrics

【小金库】xiǎojīnkù (名) private treasure of an orgnization (outside the control of the financial authorities concerned)

【小便】xiǎobiàn Ⅰ(动) urinate; pass water Ⅱ(名) urine

【小看】xiǎokàn (动) look down upon; despise

【小品】xiǎopǐn (名) short essay; short artistic creation

【小型】xiǎoxíng (形) small-sized; miniature: ～客车 minibus; coaster

【小孩儿】xiǎoháir (名) child

【小气】xiǎoqi (形) ❶ stingy; mean ❷ narrow-minded

【小时】xiǎoshí (名) hour

【小恩小惠】xiǎo ēn xiǎo huì〈成〉petty favours

【小产】xiǎochǎn (名) miscarriage; abortion

【小贩】xiǎofàn (名) pedlar; vendor; hawker

【小康】xiǎokāng (形) fairly well-off: ～之家 a fairly well-off family

【小麦】xiǎomài (名) wheat

【小偷】xiǎotōu (名) petty thief; pick pocket

【小组】xiǎozǔ (名) group

【小圈子】xiǎoquānzi (名) clique; coterie

【小商品】xiǎoshāngpǐn (名) small commodities: ～经济 small commodity economy

【小菜】xiǎocài (名) pickled vegetables; pickles

【小费】xiǎofèi (名) tip; gratuity

【小结】xiǎojié (名) brief summary

【小报告】xiǎobàogào (名) secret information, usu. false, given by sb. to his superior about sb. else

【小道消息】xiǎodào xiāoxi (名) grapevine (news); hearsay

【小提琴】xiǎotíqín (名) violin: ～手 voilinist

【小集团】xiǎojítuán (名) clique; faction

【小肠】xiǎocháng (名) small intestine: ～疝气 hernia

【小号】xiǎohào (名)〈乐〉trumpet

【小节】xiǎojié (名) ❶ trifle; small matter ❷〈乐〉bar; measure

【小脑】xiǎonǎo (名) cerebellum

【小农】xiǎonóng (名) small farmer; peasant: ～经济 small-scale peasant economy

【小葱】xiǎocōng (名) shallot; chive

【小脚】xiǎojiǎo (名) bound foot

【小腿】xiǎotuǐ (名) shank

【小说】xiǎoshuō (名) novel; fiction: 短篇～ short story

【小算盘】xiǎosuànpan (名) selfish calculations

【小调】xiǎodiào (名) ❶ ditty ❷〈乐〉minor

【小数】xiǎoshù (名)〈数〉decimal

【小写】xiǎoxiě (名) small letter

【小卖部】xiǎomàibù (名) ❶ canteen; small shop ❷ buffet; snack counter

【小标题】xiǎobiāotí (名) subheading; subtitle

【小学】xiǎoxué (名) elementary school; primary school: ～生 pupil

【小声】xiǎoshēng (名) low voice; whisper

【小聪明】xiǎocōngming (名) cleverness in trivial matters

【小题大作】xiǎo tí dà zuò〈成〉a storm in a teacup; make much ado about nothing

【小轿车】xiǎojiàochē (名) sedan (car); limousine

【小苏打】xiǎosūdá (名) sodium bicarbonate

【小辫儿】xiǎobiànr (名) braid; pigtail

少 shǎo I (形) few; little: 活下来

的人很～。There were few survivors. / 他最近很～露面。He hardly ever appears in public lately. Ⅱ(動) ❶ be short of; lack: 我們還～兩張票。We are still short of two tickets. ❷ lose; be missing: 這本書～了幾頁。A few pages are missing from this book. Ⅲ(副) a little while; a moment: 請～等一等。Please wait a moment.
see also shào

【少不得】shǎo bu dé (少不了 shǎo bu liǎo) cannot do without; be indispensable: 我們～還要請教您 We may have to seek your counsel again.

【少見多怪】shǎo jiàn duō guài 〈成〉 consider many things strange for want of knowledge and experience; a man who has seen little gets excited easily

【少許】shǎoxǔ (形)〈書〉a little; a few; a wee bit

【少量】shǎoliàng (形) a small amount (of); a small number (of); a little

【少數】shǎoshù (名) ❶ minority ❷ a small number

【少數民族】shǎoshù mínzú (名) minority nationality

少 shào (形) young: 全家老～ all members of the family; old and young
see also shǎo

【少女】shàonǚ (名) girl

【少不更事】shào bù gēng shì 〈成〉 young and inexperienced

【少年】shàonián (名) ❶ boyhood or girlhood ❷ boy or girl; youngster

【少年先鋒隊】shàonián xiānfēngduì (名) Young Pioneers

【少年宮】shàoniángōng (名) Children's Palace

【少壯】shàozhuàng (形) young and full of vigour

【少婦】shàofù (名) young married woman

尖 jiān Ⅰ(名) ❶ pointed end of anything; tip: 鋼筆～ pen nib ❷ best of the kind; topnotch: 冒～兒 stand out; be in the limelight Ⅱ(形) ❶ having a point; pointed ❷ (of sound, voice, etc.) high-pitched and piercing ❸ (of senses) sharp; sensitive: 他眼睛很～。He has sharp eyes.

【尖刀】jiāndāo (名) sharp knife; dagger

【尖子】jiānzi (名) ace; best of the kind: 這學生是個～。He is a topnotch student.

【尖兵】jiānbīng (名) ❶ (of troops) vanguard ❷ pioneer; trailblazer

【尖利】jiānlì (形) ❶ sharp; cutting: ～的刺刀 sharp bayonet / ～的筆調 poignant style ❷ (of sound, voice, etc.) shrill: 聲音～ shrill voice

【尖刻】jiānkè (形) (of words, remarks, etc.) caustic; poignant; sharp

【尖脆】jiāncuì (形) (of a voice) high-pitched and crisp

【尖端】jiānduān Ⅰ(名) pointed end; acme Ⅱ(形) most advanced; highly sophisticated: ～技術 sophisticated technology

【尖酸刻薄】jiānsuān kèbó (形) acerbic; harsh or bitter in manner, speech, etc.

【尖銳】jiānruì (形) ❶ having a

pointed blade; sharp ❷ incisive; penetrating: ~深刻的分析 penetrating in-depth analysis ❸ (of sound) high-pitched and piercing ❹ of great intensity; acute: 冲突～化了。 The conflict has intensified.

【尖嘴薄舌】jiān zuǐ bó shé〈成〉have a sharp tongue

尚 shàng I (副)〈書〉still; yet: 年紀～幼 be still too young /～不可知 be yet unknown II (動) esteem; value: ～武精神 emphasis on military affairs; pursuit of military ideals III (名)(Shàng) a surname

【尚且】shàngqiě (連) [used as an intensifier to indicate an extreme or hypothetical case] even: 騎車～來不及, 何況步行。 One can't even get there in time by bike, let alone on foot.

【尚未】shàngwèi (副)〈書〉not yet: ～到達 has not yet arrived

尤 部

尤 yóu I (形) extraordinary; outstanding: 無恥之～ the worst of the shameless II (副) particularly; especially: ～妙 especially wonderful III (動) blame: 怨天～人 complain about one's lot and lay the blame on everybody IV (名) ❶ fault: 以儆效～ serve as a warning to those who might follow suit ❷ (Yóu) a surname

【尤其】yóuqí (副) particularly; especially: 他愛看電影, ～是記錄片。 He likes to see films, especially

documentaries.

就 jiù I (動) ❶ move close to; come near to: ～着燈看書 read in the lamp light ❷ undertake; take; have: ～座 take one's seat ❸ accomplish; effect; make: 決議草案已擬～。 A draft resolution is ready. ❹ take advantage of: ～勢應下來 make use of the opportunity to comply with sb.'s request ❺ suit; accommodate: ～他的方便 at his convenience ❻ (of eating or drinking) go with: 泡菜～稀飯 pickled vegetables to go with rice gruel II (副) ❶ right away; in no time: 他～來。 He is coming. ❷ as early as; already: 他們從小～認識了。 They have known each other since childhood. ❸ no sooner...than: 他一進來～認出了我。 He recognized me the minute he stepped in. ❹ [used to indicate the natural outcome of a certain premise introduced by 只要 (as long as), 要是 (if), 既然 (now that), etc.]: 他既然來了, 我～跟他說說吧。 Now that he is here, I may as well talk to him. ❺ as many (much) as: 一天～收到了一百份申請。 As many as 100 applications arrived in one single day. ❻ [placed between two identical words or phrases to indicate tolerance or accommodation]: 他不去～不去吧。 Let him stay behind if he doesn't want to go. ❼ [used to indicate that it has been the case all along]: 我早～知道要出事。 I knew from the start that we would get into trouble. ❽ only; just: 我們～這麼一間房。 This is the only room we have. ❾ [used to indicate firmness or resolution]: 他～是不作承諾。He flatly refused to commit himself. ❿ [used for emphasis] exactly; right: 郵局～在拐角。The post office is right at the corner. Ⅲ〈介〉with regard to; in the light of; on; about: ～事情的本身來説 as far as it goes Ⅳ〈連〉even if: 你～再加錢我也不幹。I would back out even if you should increase my pay.

【就手】jiùshǒu〈副〉〈口〉without going out of one's way: 你今天如果去買東西，～替我捎些信封來好嗎？Could you get me some envelopes if you go shopping today?

【就任】jiùrèn〈動〉assume office; take up one's post

【就此】jiùcǐ〈副〉now; here; thus; at this point: 會議～結束。The conference was thus concluded.

【就地】jiùdì〈副〉right on the spot: ～伏法 be executed on the spot

【就地取材】jiù dì qǔ cái〈成〉make use of indigenous materials

【就近】jiùjìn〈副〉nearby; at the nearest place: ～入學 go to a school in the neighbourhood

【就位】jiùwèi〈動〉take one's place: 請大家～。Will everybody please take his or her place?

【就伴兒】jiùbànr〈動〉go together on a trip

【就事論事】jiù shì lùn shì〈成〉deal with matters on their own merits; take sth. as it is

【就便】jiùbiàn〈副〉while it is convenient: 他到上海出差時要～去看幾個老朋友。He wants to take the opportunity of his business trip to Shanghai to visit some old friends.

【就要】jiùyào〈動〉be about to; be going to: 天～黑了。It's getting dark. / 他們～離開北京了。They are leaving Beijing soon.

【就是】jiùshì Ⅰ〈副〉❶ [used at the end of a sentence, often followed by 了 for emphasis]: 讓他去～了。Well, let him go by all means. ❷ [used in response to a statement] exactly; absolutely: 我們不能坐失良機。—～，沒錯兒。We cannot sit back and let slip the golden opportunity. —Absolutely. Ⅱ〈連〉[often followed by 也] even if: ～再大的困難，也阻攔不了我們前進。No difficulty, however great, could deter us from forging ahead. Ⅲ〈動〉be; mean: 我想到的問題～這個。This is exactly the problem I have in mind.

【就是説】jiùshìshuō〈口〉that is to say; in other words

【就業】jiùyè Ⅰ〈動〉be employed; get a job Ⅱ〈名〉employment: ～機會 job opportunities

【就義】jiùyì〈動〉be killed for a just cause; be martyred

【就算】jiùsuàn〈連〉〈口〉granting that; even though; supposing: ～問題已基本解決了，過去的失誤也應該引以爲戒。We should take warning from our mistake even though the matter is as good as settled.

【就緒】jiùxù〈動〉be properly arranged; be ready: 晚會已準備～。Preparations for the evening party have been completed.

【就範】jiùfàn〈動〉come to terms; yield; be subdued

【就餐】jiùcān〈動〉have a meal: ～時間 meal time

【就職】jiùzhí（動）take up one's post; take office: 宣誓 ~ be sworn in

【就醫】jiùyī（動）receive medical care; see a doctor

【就讓】jiùràng（連）〈口〉even if: ~ 他來當經理也無濟於事。It wouldn't help matters even if he should be appointed the manager.

尷

gān

【尷尬】gāngà（形）❶ in a dilemma ❷ awkward; embarrassed: 神態 ~ look embarrassed

尸 部

尹

yǐn（名）❶ official title in ancient China ❷（Yǐn）a surname

尺

chǐ（名）❶ chi, a Chinese unit of length (1/3 of a metre): 英 ~ foot ❷ ruler: 卷 ~ tape measure ❸ anything in the shape of a ruler: 計算 ~ slide rule

【尺寸】chǐcun（名）measurement; size: 鞋的 ~ size of the shoes

【尺度】chǐdù（名）criterion; yardstick

尼

ní（名）Buddhist nun

【尼日利亞】Nírìlìyà（名）Nigeria: ~ 人 Nigerian

【尼日爾】Nírì'ěr（名）the Niger: ~ 人 Nigerois

【尼古丁】nígǔdīng（名）nicotine

【尼加拉瓜】Níjiālāguā（名）Nicaragua: ~ 人 Nicaraguan

【尼姑】nígū（名）(Buddhist) nun

【尼泊爾】Níbo'ěr（名）Nepal: ~ 人 Nepalese / ~ 語 Nepali

【尼庵】ní'ān（名）Buddhist nunnery

【尼龍】nílóng（名）nylon

局

jú Ⅰ（名）❶ chessboard ❷ circumstances; situation: 事關大 ~。 This concerns the overall situation. ❸ bureau; shop: 電信 ~ telecommunications bureau ❹ trap: 騙 ~ swindle Ⅱ（量）(of chess or other games) game; set; innings: 打了個平 ~ end in a draw Ⅲ（動）constrain; restrain

【局外人】júwàirén（名）outsider

【局長】júzhǎng（名）director of a bureau

【局促】júcù（形）❶ (of a place) cramped: ~ 的住房 cramped quarters ❷ (of time) short ❸ (of manner) reserved: ~ 不安 ill at ease

【局面】júmiàn（名）state of affairs at certain period of time

【局限】júxiàn（動）limit; restrain; confine: 不 ~ 於文學題目 not limited to literary topics

【局限性】júxiànxìng（名）limitations

【局部】júbù Ⅰ（名）part (of a whole) Ⅱ（形）local; partial: 天氣預報明日 ~ 地區有小陣雨。The weather forecast says that there will be occasional showers in some areas tomorrow.

【局勢】júshì（名）(politifcal or military) situation: ~ 緊張。The situation is tense.

屁

pì（名）wind (from bowels); fart: 放 ~ break wind; talk nonsense; shit

【屁股】pìgu（名）❶ buttocks; bottom ❷ (of an animal or bird) rump

❸ end; butt: 香煙～ cigarette end

【屁話】pìhuà（名）nonsense; shit

尿 niào Ⅰ（名）urine Ⅱ（動）urinate; make water
see also suī

【尿布】niàobù（名）diaper

【尿盆】niàopén（名）urinal

【尿素】niàosù（名）〈化〉urea; carbamide

【尿道】niàodào（名）〈生理〉urethra

尿 suī（名）urine
see also niào

尾 wěi Ⅰ（名）❶ tail: 夾着～巴 with one's tail between one's legs ❷ end: 有頭無～ start sth. without carrying it through to the end ❸ remaining part; last stage: 做掃～工作 wind up the work; give finishing touches Ⅱ（量）(of fish)：四～鯉魚 four carps

【尾巴】wěiba（名）❶ tail ❷ taillike part: 電影的～部分 the tail end of a film ❸ servile follower

【尾數】wěishù（名）❶〈數〉number after the decimal point ❷ small amount after a round figure

【尾隨】wěisuí（動）❶ follow; tail after ❷ shadow; tail

【尾翼】wěiyì（名）〈航空〉empennage; tail surface

【尾聲】wěishēng（名）❶〈樂〉coda ❷ epilogue ❸ end: 接近～ drawing to an end

屆 jiè Ⅰ（動）fall due: ～期奉還 return (sth.) at the appointed time Ⅱ（量）[of certain periodic terms or events]: 歷～政府 all previous governments /第六～全國運動會 the Sixth National Games

【屆時】jièshí（副）when it falls due; at the appointed time

【屆滿】jièmǎn（副）when one's term of office expires

居 jū Ⅰ（動）❶ reside; live: 定～北京 settle down in Beijing ❷ be in a certain position; rank: 產量～全國第一位 rank first in the country in terms of output ❸ claim; assert; allege: 以功臣自～ consider oneself a hero who has rendered meritorious services to the state ❹ keep in store; hoard: 視爲奇貨可～ regard it as a rare commodity worth hoarding ❺ stand still; stay put: 歲月不～。Time flies. Ⅱ（名）❶ residence: 遷入新～ move into a new place of residence ❷（Jū）a surname

【居心】jūxīn Ⅰ（動）〈貶〉have (ulterior) motives: ～不善 harbour evil intentions Ⅱ（名）〈貶〉(dishonourable) motives: 你這樣做是何～? What are you up to in doing that?

【居民】jūmín（名）inhabitant; resident

【居功自傲】jū gōng zì ào〈成〉become arrogant on account of one's past achievements

【居多】jūduō（動）make up the majority of: 這個省的人口以少數民族～。The population of the province is mainly composed of ethnic minorities.

【居安思危】jū ān sī wēi〈成〉don't lose vigilance in days of peace

【居住】jūzhù（動）inhabit; reside; live

【居委會】jūwěihuì（名）（short for

居民委員會 jūmín wěiyuánhuì)
neighbourhood committee

【居室】jūshì（名）room（for living in）: 一套三～的房子 a three-room flat

【居留】jūliú Ⅰ（動）reside Ⅱ（名）residence: ～證 residence permit / ～權 right of permanent residence （for an alien）

【居高臨下】jū gāo lín xià〈成〉look down from a vantage point; be in a superior position

【居間】jūjiān（副）（act as a mediator）between two parties: ～說合 act as a go-between

【居然】jūrán（副）❶ contrary to one's expectation: 這麼大的事你～給忘了! You shouldn't have forgotten such an important matter, should you? ❷ go so far as to

屈 qū Ⅰ（動）❶ bend; stoop ❷ be in the wrong 深知理～ deeply conscious that one is in the wrong ❸ yield to; submit: 威武不能～ will never yield to force Ⅱ（名）❶ wrong; injustice: 含冤負～ suffer a gross injustice ❷（Qū）a surname

【屈才】qūcái（動）assign a man of great talent to a petty job

【屈服】qūfú（動）submit; yield: 不～於外來壓力 refuse to bow to outside pressure

【屈指可數】qū zhǐ kě shǔ〈成〉can be counted on one's fingers

【屈辱】qūrǔ（名）humiliation; disgrace

【屈從】qūcóng（動）obey against one's own will; submit to

【屈尊】qūzūn（動）condescend: 盼閣下～一位臨賜教 hope you will condescend to come and give your guidance

【屈膝】qūxī（動）go down on one's knees; knuckle under（to sb.）: 不肯～投降 refuse to surrender

屏 bǐng（動）❶ reject; get rid of; remove ❷ hold（one's breath）
see also píng

【屏除】bǐngchú（動）remove; banish; do away with: ～雜念 dismiss all distracting considerations

【屏氣】bǐngqì（屏息 bǐngxī）（動）hold one's breath; bate one's breath

【屏棄】bǐngqì（動）discard; abandon

屏 píng Ⅰ（動）screen; shield Ⅱ（名）screen
see also bǐng

【屏風】píngfēng（名）screen

【屏幕】píngmù（名）（of television）screen

【屏障】píngzhàng（名）protective screen; shield

【屏蔽】píngbì Ⅰ（動）screen; shield Ⅱ（名）shield; barrier

屎 shǐ（名）❶ shit; excrement; dung ❷ secretion（of the eye, ear, etc.）: 眼～ gum（at the corners of the eyes）/ 耳～ earwax

屍 shī（名）corpse; dead body

【屍骨】shīgǔ（尸骸 shīhái）（名）skeleton（of a corpse）: ～未寒 so soon after sb.'s death

【屍體】shītǐ（尸首 shīshǒu）（名）dead body; corpse

屋 wū（名）❶ house ❷ room

【屋子】wūzi（名）room

【屋脊】wūjǐ（名）ridge（of a roof）

【屋頂】wūdǐng（名）roof

【屋檐】wūyán（名）eaves

展 zhǎn I (動) ❶ spread out; unfold: 舒～雙臂 stretch one's arms / ～翅 spread the wings ❷ extend; prolong: ～期 extend a time limit ❸ give free play to: 一籌莫～ at one's wits end II (名) ❶ exhibition: 美～ art exhibition / 書～ book fair ❷ (Zhǎn) a surname

【展出】 zhǎnchū (動) put on display; exhibit

【展示】 zhǎnshì (動) display; reveal: ～光明的前景 open up a bright prospect

【展品】 zhǎnpǐn (名) exhibit; item on display

【展望】 zhǎnwàng (動) look ahead: ～未來 look to the future

【展現】 zhǎnxiàn (動) unfold before one's eyes

【展開】 zhǎnkāi (動) ❶ spread out; unfold: 把畫卷～ unfold a picture scroll ❷ launch; carry out: ～競賽 launch a competition

【展銷會】 zhǎnxiāohuì (名) commodity fair

【展覽】 zhǎnlǎn I (動) put on display; exhibit II (名) exhibition

屑 xiè (名) bits; scraps; fragments: 把紙～扔進紙簍。Throw these scraps of paper into the waste basket.

屐 jī (名) ❶ clog; wooden shoe ❷ shoe

屠 tú I (動) ❶ kill (animals); slaughter: ～刀 butcher's knife ❷ massacre II (名) (Tú) a surname

【屠夫】 túfū (名) ❶ butcher ❷ cold-blooded ruler

【屠宰】 túzǎi (動) slaughter (animals): ～場 slaughter-house

【屠殺】 túshā (動) slaughter; massacre: ～無辜 massacre innocent people

屙 ē (動) 〈方〉 discharge (excrement)

屜 tì (名) ❶ tray (for steaming food): 籠～ steamer ❷ drawer

屢 lǚ (副) repeatedly

【屢次】 lǚcì (副) many times; again and again

【屢見不鮮】 lǚ jiàn bù xiān 〈成〉 be no rare occurrence

【屢教不改】 lǚ jiào bù gǎi 〈成〉 refuse to change one's behaviour or mend one's ways despite repeated admonition

屣 xǐ (名) shoe

層 céng I (名) ❶ layer; stratum; tier: 多～次 multilayered ❷ storey; floor: 底～ ground floor; rock-bottom II (量) layer: 一～灰 a layer of dust

【層出不窮】 céng chū bù qióng 〈成〉 appear one after another

【層次】 céngcì (名) order; arrangement

【層層】 céngcéng (副) tier upon tier: ～下達 (instructions) from one administrative level to another

履 lǚ I (名) shoe II (動) ❶ walk on; tread on: 如～薄冰 as if walking gingerly on thin ice; be extra-careful ❷ carry out

【履行】 lǚxíng (動) fulfil; honour: ～合同 carry out a contract / ～諾

言 keep one's promise

【履約】lǚyuē（動）honour an agreement

【履帶】lǚdài（名）caterpillar tread

【履歷】lǚlì（名）biographical sketch; résumé

屬 shǔ Ⅰ（名）❶ category; class; division: 稀有金～ rare metals ❷〈生〉genus ❸ family member: 家～ family dependents Ⅱ（動）❶ be subordinate; be under; be affiliated: 國務院直屬機關 government organs directly under the State Council ❷ belong to: 勝利終～我們。Victory will be ours. ❸ be: 純～捏造 be a sheer fabrication ❹ be born in the year named after (one of the 12 animals representing the Earthly Branches of the Cycle): 他～龍。He was born in the year of the dragon.

【屬地】shǔdì（名）dependency; possession

【屬性】shǔxìng（名）〈邏〉property; attribute; basic character

【屬於】shǔyú（動）belong to; be part of

【屬實】shǔshí（動）be true: 這一切都～。All this is true.

屮 部

屯 tún Ⅰ（動）❶ gather; store up: 聚草～糧 store up fodder and grain ❷ station (troops) Ⅱ（名）village: ～子 village

【屯墾】túnkěn（動）station troops for opening up wasteland

山 部

山 shān（名）❶ hill; mountain ❷ (Shān) a surname

【山川】shānchuān（名）mountains and rivers; landscape

【山口】shānkǒu（名）(mountain) pass

【山水】shānshuǐ（名）❶ water running down from a mountain ❷ natural scenery with hills and waters ❸〈美術〉traditional Chinese painting of mountains and waters; landscape

【山毛櫸】shānmáojǔ（名）〈植〉beech

【山地】shāndì（名）❶ mountainous area ❷ fields on a hill

【山西】Shānxī（名）Shanxi (Province)

【山羊】shānyáng（名）goat

【山村】shāncūn（名）mountain village

【山谷】shāngǔ（名）mountain valley; glen

【山芋】shānyù（名）〈方〉sweet potato

【山坳】shān'ào（名）col

【山東】Shāndōng（名）Shandong (Province)

【山河】shānhé（名）mountains and rivers; the land of a country

【山林】shānlín（名）mountain forest

【山坡】shānpō（名）hillside; mountain slope

【山城】shānchéng（名）mountain city

【山洞】shāndòng（名）cave; cavern;

grotto

【山洪】shānhóng（名）mountain torrents

【山炮】shānpào（名）mountain gun; mountain artillery

【山泉】shānquán（名）mountain spring

【山珍海味】shān zhēn hǎi wèi〈成〉exotic foods; rare dishes; delicacies

【山峰】shānfēng（名）mountain peak; mountain top

【山脊】shānjǐ（山梁 shānliáng）（名）ridge (of a mountain or hill)

【山脉】shānmài（名）mountain range

【山茶花】shāncháhuā（名）camellia

【山崩】shānbēng（名）landslide; landslip

【山顶】shāndǐng（名）summit (top) of a mountain; hilltop

【山庄】shānzhuāng（名）mountain villa; country house

【山岗】shāngāng（名）hillock

【山货】shānhuò（名）❶ mountain products ❷ rustic goods made of earthenware, wood, bamboo, etc.

【山区】shānqū（名）mountainous region

【山雀】shānquè（名）〈动〉tit

【山崖】shānyá（名）cliff

【山沟】shāngōu（名）gully; ravine

【山路】shānlù（名）mountain path

【山脚】shānjiǎo（名）foot of a mountain

【山腰】shānyāo（名）mountainside; half way up the mountain

【山楂】shānzhā（名）❶（Chinese）hawthorn ❷ haw

【山楂糕】shānzhāgāo（名）haw jelly

【山盟海誓】shān méng hǎi shì〈成〉(of lovers) pledge eternal fidelity

【山歌】shāngē（名）folk song of mountain areas

【山寨】shānzhài（名）fortified mountain village; mountain fortress

【山穷水尽】shān qióng shuǐ jìn〈成〉at the end of one's tether; in a desperate situation

【山涧】shānjiàn（名）mountain stream; mountain creek

【山猫】shānmāo（名）leopard cat; lynx

【山头】shāntóu（名）❶ hilltop; top of a mountain ❷ faction; clique

【山墙】shānqiáng（名）〈建〉gable

【山岳】shānyuè（名）lofty mountains

【山岭】shānlǐng（名）mountain ridge

【山药】shānyào（名）〈植〉Chinese yam

【山麓】shānlù〈名〉mountain foot

【山峦】shānluán（名）chain of mountains

【山鹬】shānyù（名）woodcock

岌 jí

【岌岌】jíjí（形）precarious; on the verge of collapse: ～可危 faced with impending disaster; perilous

屹 yì

【屹立】yìlì（动）stand erect; stand firm

岑 Cén（名）a surname

岔 chà（动）❶ branch off: 分～ (of a road) diverge into a byroad ❷ turn off: ～上了小路 turn off to a path

【岔口】chàkǒu（名）fork (in a road)

【岔子】chàzi（名）❶ side road ❷ trouble; untoward turn of events

出 ～ have trouble; go wrong ❸ flaw; fault: 找 ～ pick a quarrel

【岔開】chàkāi（動）❶ diverge ❷ change the topic: 把話題 ～ change the subject of conversation ❸ stagger: 把會議時間 ～ stagger the dates for the meetings

【岔道兒】chàdàor（名） sideroad; byroad

岡 gāng（名）mountain ridge

【岡比亞】Gāngbǐyà（名） the Gambia: ～人 Gambian

岸 àn（名）shore; bank: 沿 ～ along the coast (river bank)

【岸然】ànrán（形）dignified: 道貌 ～ look enormously dignified

【岸標】ànbiāo（名） shore mark; coast beacon

岬 jiǎ（名）❶ narrow piece of land jutting into a large body of water; cape ❷ narrow space between two mountains

岳 yuè（名）❶ high mountain ❷ wife's parents or uncles ❸（Yuè）a surname

【岳父】yuèfù（名）wife's father; father-in-law

【岳母】yuèmǔ（名）wife's mother; mother-in-law

岱 dài（名）another name for Tai-shan Mountain (Mt. Tai)

峡 xiá（名）gorge

【峡谷】xiágǔ（名）gorge; canyon

峭 qiào（形）❶ high and steep ❷ stern: ～直 strict and severe

【峭立】qiàolì（動）stand steep and erect; tower

【峭拔】qiàobá（形）❶ steep ❷ (of style in writing) powerful; vigorous: 筆鋒 ～ precise and vigorous style of writing

【峭壁】qiàobì（名）cliff; precipice

峪 yù（名）valley; ravine

峻 jùn（形）❶ high; towering ❷ stern; grave; rigorous: 形勢嚴 ～。 The situation is grave.

【峻峭】jùnqiào（形）high and precipitous

【峻嶺】jùnlǐng（名）high mountain

峨 é（形）high

峰 fēng（名）❶ peak: 名聲的最高 ～ the pinnacle of fame ❷ hump

岛 dǎo（名）island: 半 ～ peninsula

【岛國】dǎoguó（名）island country; insular country

【岛嶼】dǎoyǔ（名）islands and islets

崇 chóng Ⅰ（形）high: ～ 山峻嶺 lofty and steep mountains Ⅱ（動）worship; admire: 尊 ～ worship; revere Ⅲ（名）（Chóng）a surname

【崇拜】chóngbài（動）worship: 個人 ～ personality cult

【崇高】chónggāo（形）lofty; sublime; noble

【崇敬】chóngjìng（動）esteem; respect; admire

崖 yá（名）cliff

【崖壁】yábì（名）precipice; cliff

崎 qí（形）
【崎嶇】qíqū（形）(of mountain paths) rugged; rough

崛 jué（動）rise steeply

【崛起】juéqǐ（動）❶ (of mountains, etc.) rise steeply ❷ appear (as a political force)

崗 gǎng（名）❶ hillock; mound ❷ sentry; post: 下～ be off duty
【崗位】gǎngwèi（名）post
【崗哨】gǎngshào（名）❶ sentry; sentinel ❷ sentry post
【崗樓】gǎnglóu（名）watchtower

崢 zhēng
【崢嶸】zhēngróng（形）❶ (of mountains) lofty and steep; towering ❷ outstanding; extraordinary: ～歲月 eventful years; years of youthful ebullience

崩 bēng（動）❶ burst; break apart; collapse: 山～ landslide ❷ burst; crack: 談～了。Negotiations broke down. ❸ hit by a bursting piece: 玻璃片～了眼睛 have one's eye hit by a flying piece of glass ❹〈口〉shoot dead; execute by shooting ❺ (of a sovereign) pass away: 駕～ (of a monarch) pass away
【崩裂】bēngliè（動）crack; burst apart; split
【崩塌】bēngtā（動）collapse; cave in; crumble: 坑道～。The tunnel caved in.
【崩潰】bēngkuì Ⅰ（動）fall apart; collapse; crumble Ⅱ（名）collapse; breakdown: 經濟～ economic debacle

崔 Cuī（名）a surname

嵯 cuó
【嵯峨】cuó'é（形）(of a mountain) high and steep

嵌 qiàn（動）inlay; embed: ～有珠

寶的花瓶 vase embedded with jewels

崴 wǎi（動）sprain

崽 zǎi（名）❶〈方〉son; brat ❷ young animal; whelp

嵐 lán（名）misty haze or vapour (in the hills)

嶄 zhǎn
【嶄新】zhǎnxīn（形）brand-new

嶙 lín
【嶙峋】línxún（形）❶ craggy ❷ thin; skinny: 瘦骨～ a beg of bones

嶺 lǐng（名）mountain; ridge; mountain range

嶼 yǔ（名）small island; islet

巍 wēi（形）towering; very high
【巍峨】wēi'é（形）(of a mountain or building) towering
【巍然】wēirán（形）(of a mountain, building, etc.) towering; massive and majestic
【巍巍】wēiwēi（形）very high; towering

巋 kuī
【巋然】kuīrán（形）towering: ～屹立 stand erect and steadfast

巔 diān（名）summit; peak

巒 luán（名）hill; mountain

巖 yán（名）rock; cliff
【巖石】yánshí（名）rock; crag
【巖洞】yándòng（名）grotto
【巖漿】yánjiāng（名）magma
【巖層】yáncéng（名）rock stratum

《 部

川 chuān（名）❶ river ❷（Chuān）short for Sichuan (Province)

【川流不息】chuān liú bù xī〈成〉(of vehicles, people, etc.) go by in a continuous stream: ～的汽车 a stream of cars

州 zhōu（名）(autonomous) prefecture

巡 xún（动）patrol; make one's rounds

【巡查】xúnchá（动）make a tour of inspection; inspect

【巡洋艦】xúnyángjiàn（名）cruiser

【巡迴】xúnhuí（动）go on circuit; tour: ～講演 make a lecture tour

【巡航】xúnháng（动）cruise

【巡航導彈】xúnháng dǎodàn（名）cruise missile

【巡視】xúnshì（动）make an inspection tour

【巡邏】xúnluó（动）patrol; be on one's beat

巢 cháo（名）❶ nest: 鷹～ eagle's nest ❷ den; lair: 傾～出動 turn out in full force

【巢穴】cháoxué（名）lair; hide-out

工 部

工 gōng Ⅰ（名）❶ worker; workman; working class ❷ work; labour

❸（construction）project: 動～ start a project ❹ industry ❺ manday Ⅱ（動）be good at; be expert in: ～書善畫 be good at calligraphy and painting

【工人】gōngrén（名）worker; workman

【工力】gōnglì（名）skill; craftsmanship

【工夫】gōngfu（名）❶ time: 没～ have no time ❷ effort; energy; work: 下～ make an effort ❸ skill

【工件】gōngjiàn（名）workpiece

【工地】gōngdì（名）construction site

【工序】gōngxù（名）process; working procedure

【工作】gōngzuò Ⅰ（名）work; job Ⅱ（動）work: ～日 working day

【工作服】gōngzuòfú（名）work uniform

【工事】gōngshì（名）defence works

【工具】gōngjù（名）tool; instrument; means

【工具書】gōngjùshū（名）reference book

【工段】gōngduàn（名）❶ section of a construction project ❷ workshop section

【工科】gōngkē（名）engineering course

【工效】gōngxiào（名）work efficiency

【工時】gōngshí（名）man-hour

【工商界】gōngshāngjiè（名）industrial and commercial circles; business circles

【工商業】gōngshāngyè（名）industry and commerce

【工場】gōngchǎng（名）workshop

【工運】gōngyùn（名）labour movement

【工程】gōngchéng（名）engineering; project

【工程師】gōngchéngshī（名）engineer

【工筆畫】gōngbǐhuà（名）〈美術〉traditional Chinese painting characterized by fine and delicate brush-work

【工資】gōngzī（名）wages; pay; salary

【工業】gōngyè（名）industry: ～家 industrialist ／ ～國 industrialized nation

【工會】gōnghuì（名）trade union

【工廠】gōngchǎng（名）mill; factory; plant

【工潮】gōngcháo（名）labour unrest; workers' strike

【工整】gōngzhěng（形）（of handwriting）neat

【工頭】gōngtóu（名）foreman

【工藝】gōngyì（名）craft; technology: ～美術 industrial art; arts and crafts

【工齡】gōnglíng（名）length of service

巧 qiǎo（形）❶ clever; deft: 這姑娘的手真～。The girl is quite clever with her fingers. ❷ fortuitous; opportune: 湊～ by accident; by chance ❸ artful; cunning: 有張～嘴 have a glib tongue

【巧立名目】qiǎo lì míng mù〈成〉invent all sorts of excuses (to extort money or achieve other wicked purposes)

【巧合】qiǎohé（名）coincidence

【巧妙】qiǎomiào（形）subtle; wise

【巧克力】qiǎokèlì（名）chocolate

【巧取豪奪】qiǎo qǔ háo duó〈成〉rob by trick or by force

【巧遇】qiǎoyù（名）chance meeting

【巧奪天工】qiǎo duó tiān gōng〈成〉exquisite skill surpassing the work of nature

巨 jù I（形）huge; vast; tremendous II（名）(Jù) a surname

【巨人】jùrén（名）giant

【巨大】jùdà（形）enormous; colossal

【巨型】jùxíng（形）giant; large-size: ～噴氣客機 jumbo jet ／ ～運輸機 jumbo freighter

【巨細】jùxì（形）(of matters) big and small: 事無～都親自處理 attend in person to all matters, big or small

【巨著】jùzhù（名）magnum opus; monumental work; voluminous work

【巨輪】jùlún（名）❶ mighty wheel ❷ large ship; ocean-going liner

【巨頭】jùtóu（名）tycoon; baron; great leader; 紡織業～ textile magnate

【巨額】jù'é（名）huge sum: ～資金 a huge amount of capital

【巨變】jùbiàn（名）great change

左 zuǒ I（名）❶ left; the left side ❷ (Zuǒ) a surname II（形）left; radical: 極"～" ultra-"Left"

【左右】zuǒyòu I（名）left and right sides: ～夾攻 attack from both sides II（副）about; around; or so: 一個星期～ a week or so III（動）control; manipulate: 少數人怎能～輿論? How can a handful of people sway public opinion?

【左右手】zuǒyòushǒu（名）right-hand man

【左右逢源】zuǒ yòu féng yuán〈成〉go on smoothly one way or the

other; butter one's bread on both sides

【左右爲難】zuǒ yòu wéi nán〈成〉be caught between the devil and the deep sea; be in an awkward position

【左派】zuǒpài（名）❶ the Left; the leftwing ❷ Leftist

【左首】zuǒshǒu（名）left-hand side

【左傾】zuǒqīng（名）"Left" deviation: ～機會主義 "Left" opportunism

【左撇子】zuǒpiězi（名）left-handed person; lefty

【左翼】zuǒyì（名）❶〈軍〉left wing ❷ the left wing

【左邊】zuǒbiān（名）left side; left

【左證】zuǒzhèng（名）evidence; proof

巫 wū（名）❶ witch; wizard ❷（Wū）a surname

【巫師】wūshī（名）wizard

【巫術】wūshù（名）witchcraft

【巫婆】wūpó（名）witch

【巫醫】wūyī（名）witch doctor

差 chā（名）❶ difference: 溫～ range of temperature; temperature difference ❷ error; deviation: 誤～ 檢測 error detection
see also chà; chāi

【差別】chābié（名）discrepancy; difference

【差異】chāyì（名）difference; discrepancy

【差距】chājù（名）gap; disparity: 找～ find out how far one lags behind

【差價】chājià（名）difference in price: 地區～補貼 regional weighting (allowance)

【差錯】chācuò（名）❶ mistake; slip

❷ mishap: 機器出了～。Something went wrong with the machine.

【差額】chà'é（名）balance; difference: 國際收支～ balance of international payments

差 chà I（動）❶ differ: 相～無幾 differ very little ❷ fall short of: ～ 十分十二點 ten to twelve II（形）❶ not good; inferior: 條件並不太 ～。Conditions are not so bad. ❷ wrong: 理解～了 misunderstand or misinterpret the meaning
see also chā; chāi

【差不多】chà bu duō I（副）almost; nearly: ～好了(完了) about to finish II（形）❶ similar: 顏色～ about the same colour ❷ passable: 這還 ～。That's more like it.

【差不多的】chàbuduōde（名）average person: ～都能幹這活 This is what any ordinary person can do.

【差不離兒】chà bu lír I（副）almost; nearly II（形）❶ passable ❷ almost used up

【差勁】chàjìn（形）no good; disappointing: 他的表現太～了。His performance is too disappointing.

【差點兒】chàdiǎnr I（副）almost: ～忘了。I nearly forgot. II（形）not up to the mark: 他的手藝～。His workmanship is not good enough.

差 chāi I（動）send (sb. on an errand): ～人去找大夫 send (sb.) for a doctor II（名）errand; mission
see also chā; chà

【差遣】chāiqiǎn（動）❶ send (sb. on an errand) ❷ appoint

【差使】chāishi（名）official post

【差事】chāishi（名）❶ official post ❷ errand

【差遣】chāiqiǎn（动）send（sb. on an errand）; assign: 听人～ run errands for sb.; be at sb.'s beck and call

己 部

己 jǐ I（名）❶ oneself: ～所不欲，勿施於人。Do not do unto others as you would not have them do unto you. ❷ the sixth of the ten Celestial Stems II（形）one's own: 坚持～见 stick to one's own views
【己方】jǐfāng（名）one's own side

已 yǐ I（动）stop; cease: 赞嘆不～ shower praise on II（副）already: 我～看过道部电影。I've already seen the film
【已往】yǐwǎng（形）past; before
【已知】yǐzhī（形）known: ～数〈数〉known number
【已故】yǐgù（形）deceased; late: ～總统 the late president
【已婚】yǐhūn（形）married
【已经】yǐjīng（副）already

巴 bā I（动）❶ look forward to: 朝～夜望 long to see sb. day and night ❷ cling to; stick to: ～在牆上 creep on the wall II（名）(Bā) a surname III [suffix, unstressed in speech]: 泥～ mud
【巴不得】bābude（动）wish anxiously; have a strong desire to; long to
【巴巴多斯】Bābāduōsī（名）Barbados: ～人 Barbadian
【巴布亞新幾内亚】Bābùyà Xīnjǐnèiyà（名）Papua New Guinea: ～人 Papua New Guinean
【巴西】Bāxī（名）Brazil: ～人 Brazilian
【巴林】Bālín（名）Bahrain: ～人 Bahraini
【巴拉圭】Bālāguī（名）Paraguay: ～人 Paraguayan
【巴哈馬】Bāhāmǎ（名）Bahamas: ～人 Bahamian
【巴拿馬】Bānámǎ（名）Panama: ～人 Panamanian
【巴望】bāwàng（动）〈方〉look forward to; expect eagerly
【巴基斯坦】Bājīsītǎn（名）Pakistan: ～人 Pakistani
【巴勒斯坦】Bālèsītǎn（名）Palestine: ～人 Palestinian
【巴结】bājie（动）curry favour with; fawn on
【巴掌】bāzhang（名）palm; hand: 打一～ slap sb. on the face

巷 hàng（名）tunnel
see also xiàng

巷 xiàng（名）lane; alley
see also hàng

巾 部

巾 jīn（名）towel; scarf; kerchief
【巾帼】jīnguó（名）woman: ～英雄 heroine

市 shì I（名）❶ market; bazaar: 夜～ night fair ❷ city; municipality; town: 直辖～ municipality directly under the central government Ⅱ（形）of traditional Chinese system of weights and measures (as distinguished from the metric system): ~ 斤 jin, equivalent to 0.5 kilogram

【市民】shìmín（名）city resident; urban dweller; townspeople

【市長】shìzhǎng（名）mayor

【市郊】shìjiāo（名）suburb; outskirts

【市面】shìmiàn（名）business situation; market; trade: ~ 不景氣 sluggish market

【市政】shìzhèng（名）municipal administration

【市容】shìróng（名）appearance of a city: 參觀 ~ go sightseeing in the city

【市區】shìqū（名）urban area; city proper

【市場】shìchǎng（名）market; marketplace: ~ 機制 market mechanism

【市集】shìjí（名）fair

【市價】shìjià（名）market price

【市儈】shìkuài（名）（貶）unscrupulous businessman; philistine: ~ 作風 philistinism

【市鎮】shìzhèn（名）(small) town

布 bù（名）cloth: 尼龍 ~ nylon fabric

【布丁】bùdīng（名）pudding

【布匹】bùpǐ（名）(cotton) piece goods

【布帛】bùbó（名）cottons and silks

【布隆迪】Bùlóngdí（名）Burundi: ~ 人 Burundian

【布鞋】bùxié（名）cloth shoe

【布穀鳥】bùgǔniǎo（名）cuckoo

帆 fān（名）sail

【帆布】fānbù（名）canvas

【帆船】fānchuán（名）sailing boat

希 xī（動）hope: ~ 認真對待。We hope you'll give it serious attention.

【希罕】xīhan Ⅰ（形）rare; exceptional: ~ 事兒 rare thing; rarity Ⅱ（動）value as a rarity; cherish: 我的家鄉就在海邊，没人一見貝殼。My hometown is close to the sea and nobody there is much interested in sea shells.

【希奇】xīqí（形）rare; curious; uncommon: 這種作法並不~。This is no uncommon practice.

【希望】xīwàng Ⅰ（動）hope; wish: ~你工作更努力。We hope you'll work even harder. Ⅱ（名）hope; expectation: 成功的 ~ 很小了。There is little hope of success.

【希圖】xītú（動）attempt; try: ~ 蒙蔽羣眾 in an attempt to hoodwink the public

【希臘】Xīlà（名）Greece: ~ 人 Greek ／ ~ 語 Greek (language)

帚 zhǒu（名）broom

帖 tiē（形）❶ submissive; subservient: 服服 ~ ~ obedient; docile ❷ proper; appropriate
see also tiě; tiè

帖 tiě Ⅰ（名）❶ written invitation: 招待會請 ~ invitation card for a reception ❷ note; card Ⅱ（量）〈中醫〉dose; draught
see also tiē; tiè

帖 tiè（名）book of models of calligraphy or painting
see also tiē; tiě

帕 pà（名）handkerchief

帛 bó (名) silk

【帛畫】 bóhuà (名) (in ancient China) painting on silk

帝 dì (名) ❶ the Supreme Being: 上～ God ❷ emperor; monarch ❸ imperialism

【帝子】 dìzǐ (名) children of an emperor

【帝王】 dìwáng (名) emperor

【帝制】 dìzhì (名) monarchy

【帝國】 dìguó (名) empire

【帝國主義】 dìguó zhǔyì (名) imperialism: ～者 imperialist

帥 shuài Ⅰ (名) commander in chief: 最高統～ the supreme commander ❷ (Shuài) a surname Ⅱ (形) beautiful; smart

【帥氣】 shuàiqi (形) 〈口〉 smart-looking; dashing

席 xí (名) ❶ seat: 貴賓～ seats for distinguished guests ❷ banquet; dinner: 酒～ feast ❸ (Xí) a surname

【席次】 xící (名) ❶ order of seats; seating arrangement: 打亂～ upset the seating arrangement

【席位】 xíwèi (名) seat: 合法～ rightful seat

【席卷】 xíjuǎn (動) sweep over; take away everything: 風暴～全國。The storm swept through the whole country.

師 shī (名) ❶ teacher; master worker: ～生 teacher and student / ～徒 master and disciple (or apprentice) ❷ model; fine example: 爲人～表 be a paragon of virtue and learning ❸ person skilled in a certain trade: 設計～ designer ❹ 〈軍〉 divison: ～團 division ❺ troops; armed units ❻ (Shī) a surname

【師父】 shīfu (名) master worker

【師長】 shīzhǎng (名) ❶ 〈敬〉 teacher ❷ 〈軍〉 division commander

【師資】 shīzī (名) qualified teachers

【師範】 shīfàn (形) teacher training: ～大學 normal university

【師德】 shīdé (名) ethics of the teaching profession

帶 dài Ⅰ (名) ❶ belt; band; tie; strap; lace; ribbon: 鞋～ shoelace ❷ zone; area; region: 沿海一～ coastal region Ⅱ (動) ❶ bring; take; carry: ～個口信 take a verbal message ❷ lead: ～路 act as guide ❸ have sth. attached: ～帽子的大衣 a parka ❹ bear; have: 面～病容 look ill

【帶孝】 dàixiào (動) wear mourning (for one's deceased parent)

【帶勁】 dàijìn (形) ❶ vigorous; energetic: 走路～ walk briskly ❷ interesting; wonderful: 這本小說真～。This novel is really fascinating.

【帶動】 dàidòng (動) ❶ push forward; spur on

【帶魚】 dàiyú (名) hairtail; tape fish

【帶領】 dàilǐng (動) lead

【帶頭】 dàitóu (動) take the lead

常 cháng Ⅰ (形) ❶ ordinary; common: 不同尋～ unusual; extraordinary ❷ constant: ～青樹 evergreen tree Ⅱ (副) frequently; regularly Ⅲ (Cháng) a surname

【常年】 chángnián (副) ❶ year in, year out; all the year round ❷ in the average year: ～產量 annual output

【常任】chángrèn（形）permanent: ～理事 member of the permanent council

【常言】chángyán（名）saying: ～道 as the saying goes

【常客】chángkè（名）frequent visitor

【常務】chángwù（形）day-to-day business: ～理事 executive director

【常常】chángcháng（副）often; usually

【常規】chángguī Ⅰ（名）❶ convention ❷〈醫〉routine: 尿～ routine urine test Ⅱ（形）conventional

【常情】chángqíng（名）normal practice; natural inclination: 人之～ the way of the world; human nature

【常設】chángshè（形）standing: ～代理機構 permanent agency

【常備不懈】cháng bèi bù xiè（成）be perpetually prepared against any eventuality

【常備軍】chángbèijūn（名）standing army

【常態】chángtài（名）normal practice: 一反～ act contrary to one's normal practice

【常駐】chángzhù（形）permanent; resident: ～代表 permanent representative

【常識】chángshí（名）❶ general knowledge ❷ common sense

帳 zhàng（名）camp; tent 蚊～ mosquito net

【帳子】zhàngzi（名）mosquito net

【帳篷】zhàngpeng（名）tent

帷 wéi（名）curtain

【帷子】wéizi（名）curtain

【帷幕】wéimù（名）large curtain; stage curtain; cloth partition（in a big room）

幅 fú Ⅰ（名）❶ width of cloth: 雙～ double width ❷ width: 振～ amplitude Ⅱ（量）：一～地圖 a map

【幅度】fúdù（名）range: 選擇的～很大。There is a wide range of possible choices.

【幅員】fúyuán（名）territory: ～遼闊 vast in territory

帽 mào（名）cap; hat: 貝雷～ beret / 鋼筆～ cap of a pen

【帽子】màozi（名）❶ cap; hat ❷ label; tag: 扣～ slap a label（on sb.）/ 摘～ restore sb.'s good reputation; rehabilitate sb.

【帽舌】màoshé（名）peak; visor

【帽店】màodiàn（名）hat shop

【帽帶】màodài（名）hat-band

【帽徽】màohuī（名）insignia on a cap

幌 huǎng（名）curtain; screen

【幌子】huǎngzi（名）❶ shop sign; signboard ❷ pretence; cover; pretext

幕 mù（名）❶ curtain; screen ❷〈戲劇〉act: 獨一劇 one-act play

【幕布】mùbù（名）curtain;（cinema）screen

【幕後】mùhòu（形）backstage; behind-the-scenes: ～人物 men behind the scenes / ～活動 behind-the-scenes activities

【幕間休息】mùjiān xiūxi（名）interval; intermission

【幕僚】mùliáo（名）assistant; aide

幔 màn（名）curtain: 窗～ window curtain

幣 bì (名)　money; currency; (legal) tender: 人民～ Renminbi (currency of the PRC)

【幣制】bìzhì (名) currency system; monetary system

【幣值】bìzhí (名) value of the currency

幢 chuáng (名) ❶ (in ancient China) pennant; streamer ❷ stone pillar inscribed with Buddha's name or Buddhist scripture
see also zhuàng

【幢幢】chuángchuáng (動)(of shadows) flicker; dance

幢 zhuàng (量) [of buildings]: 一～新樓 a new building
see also chuáng

幫 bāng Ⅰ (動) help; assist; aid Ⅱ (名) gang; clique; band: 結成～會 form a secret society Ⅲ (量) group (of people): 一～小朋友 a troop of children

【幫工】bānggōng Ⅰ (動) help in farm work Ⅱ (名) assistant; helper; hired farmhand

【幫子】bāngzi (名) ❶ outer leaf (of cabbage) ❷ upper (of a shoe)

【幫手】bāngshou (名) helper; assistant

【幫兇】bāngxiōng (名) accomplice; henchman; jackal

【幫忙】bāngmáng (動) help; assist: 來，幫～吧! Come on, lend us a hand!

【幫助】bāngzhù Ⅰ (動) help, assist Ⅱ (名) assistance; aid: 在他的～下 with his assistance

【幫派】bāngpài Ⅰ (名) faction Ⅱ (形) factional

【幫倒忙】bāng dàománg (動) mean to bring help but end up causing trouble; do more harm than good

【幫腔】bāngqiāng (動) ❶ chime in; echo sb. ❷ sing in accompaniment (behind the scenes in a traditional Chinese opera) ❸ speak in support of sb.'s argument

【幫閑】bāngxián Ⅰ (動) serve as a hack writer for the rich and powerful Ⅱ (名)〈貶〉parasite; hack: ～文人 hack writer

【幫辦】bāngbàn Ⅰ (動) assist in the management of Ⅱ (名) deputy: 助理國務卿～ Deputy Assistant Secretary (of the US Department of State)

【幫襯】bāngchèn (動) assist

干 部

干 gān (名) involvement: 與他不相～ have nothing to do with him

【干戈】gāngē (名) ❶ weapons ❷ war: 免動～ refrain from appealing to arms; prevent the outbreak of war

【干支】gānzhī (名) the Heavenly Stems and Earthly Branches

【干係】gānxi (名) involvement; implication

【干涉】gānshè Ⅰ (動) interfere; intervene: ～別國內政 interfere in the internal affairs of another nation Ⅱ (名) intervention; involvement: 武裝～ armed intervention

【干連】gānlián (名) involvement: 這事我們多少都有些～。We are all involved one way or another.

【干預】gānyù（動）intervene; meddle

【干擾】gānrǎo Ⅰ（動）disturb; interfere Ⅱ（名）interference: 不受～ free from interference

平 píng Ⅰ（形）❶ flat; smooth: 臥 lie flat; ❷ be on a par; equal in position: 論考試成績他們是～列 的。They are on a par in examination results. ❸ calm; quiet: 你先 把氣～下去再說。You must first of all cool down. ❹ average; ordinary: 年成～～。The harvest is about average. Ⅱ（動）❶ level; even: ～整土地 level the land ❷ pacify; appease ❸ put down; suppress: ～叛 quell a rebellion Ⅲ （名）(Píng) a surname

【平凡】píngfán（形）ordinary; common

【平日】píngrì（副）usually; ordinarily

【平反】píngfǎn（動）rehabilitate; redress (a wrong)

【平方】píngfāng（名）〈數〉square: ～公里 square kilometre

【平方根】píngfānggēn（名）〈數〉 square root

【平分】píngfēn（動）divide equally

【平分秋色】píng fēn qiū sè〈成〉(of two contending parties) have an equal share of honour or power

【平心而論】píng xīn ér lùn〈成〉to do justice to sb. (or sth.); in fairness to sb.

【平心靜氣】píng xīn jìng qì〈成〉 cool and patient

【平民】píngmín（名）commoner; common people

【平生】píngshēng Ⅰ（名）one's life-

time; one's whole life: ～的志願 one's lifelong aspiration Ⅱ（副）in all one's life: 他～工作嚴謹。He has always had a rigorous style of work.

【平白無故】píng bái wú gù〈成〉 without rhyme or reason

【平安】píng'ān（形）safe and sound; well

【平行】píngxíng（形）❶ of equal rank: ～單位 units of equal rank ❷ parallel; simultaneous: ～作業 simultaneous operations ❸ parallel: ～綫 parallel lines

【平地一聲雷】píng dì yī shēng léi 〈成〉❶ a meteoric rise of fame in the academic or political world ❷ an unexpected happy event

【平局】píngjú（名）draw; tie

【平足】píngzú（名）〈醫〉flatfoot

【平均】píngjūn（形）❶ average ❷ equally shared

【平均主義】píngjūn zhǔyì（名）egalitarianism

【平步青雲】píng bù qīng yún〈成〉 suddenly rise to a position of importance

【平定】píngdìng（動）❶ calm down: 她情緒已一下來。She has calmed down. ❷ suppress; quell

【平房】píngfáng（名）one-storey house; bungalow

【平和】pínghé（形）❶（of one's temperament, speech or conduct) moderate; gentle ❷（of medicine) mild

【平坦】píngtǎn（形）(of land, etc.) flat; smooth

【平昔】píngxī（副）in former times

【平易近人】píng yì jìn rén〈成〉 modest and unassuming; easy of access

【平信】píngxìn (名) ordinary mail

【平面】píngmiàn (名) plane; flat surface

【平面几何】píngmiàn jǐhé (名) plane geometry

【平时】píngshí (副) ❶ in normal times; usually ❷ in peacetime

【平素】píngsù (副) usually; as a rule

【平息】píngxī (动) ❶ subside: 風暴 已逐漸～。The storm has gradually subsided. ❷ suppress: ～騷亂 put down a riot

【平原】píngyuán (名) plain; flatlands

【平起平坐】píng qǐ píng zuò〈成〉(of two persons) occupy positions of equal importance; be on an equal footing

【平常】píngcháng Ⅰ(形) ordinary; common: 節目很～。The programme was not really above average.Ⅱ(副) generally; as a rule: 他～睡得很晚。He usually stays up rather late.

【平淡】píngdàn (形) dull; insipid

【平庸】píngyōng (形) mediocre; dull: ～之輩 mediocrities

【平等】píngděng (名) equality

【平絨】píngróng (名)〈紡〉velveteen

【平滑】pínghuá (形) smooth

【平裝】píngzhuāng (名) paperback

【平台】píngtái (名) platform; terrace

【平輩】píngbèi (形) of the same generation

【平鋪直敘】píng pū zhí xù〈成〉❶ narrate in a plain, simple way ❷ narrate in a flat, dull style

【平靜】píngjìng (形) quiet; tranquil

【平衡】pínghéng (名) balance; equilibrium: 恢復～ restore the equilibrium

【平衡木】pínghéngmù (名)〈體〉balance beam

【平穩】píngwěn (形) steady; stable

【平爐】pínglú (名)〈冶〉open hearth furnace

年 nián (名) ❶ year ❷ age: 他～長五歲。He is five years older. / 晚～ old age ❸ harvest: 豐～ rich harvest ❹ New Year: ～夜 the eve of the lunar New Year ❺ (Nián) a surname

【年月】niányuè (名)〈口〉❶ days; years ❷ age; time

【年代】niándài (名) ❶ years; time; period: 在和平～ in peacetime ❷ decade: 二十世紀三十～ in the 1930's

【年份】niánfèn (名) ❶ a certain year (particularly concerned with book-keeping and finances) ❷ age (of a thing)

【年成】niánchéng (名) harvest: 看來今年～不壞。It seems we are going to have a good harvest this year.

【年表】niánbiǎo (名) chronological table

【年初】niánchū (名) the first few days of a year

【年底】niándǐ (名) end of a year

【年度】niándù (名) year: 財政～ fiscal year

【年紀】niánjì (名) a person's age

【年限】niánxiàn (名) fixed number of years

【年級】niánjí (名) grade in a school

【年息】niánxī (名) annual interest

【年終】niánzhōng (名) the end of a

year: ～報告 year-end report

【年貨】niánhuò（名）food and other items purchased for the Spring Festival

【年假】niánjià（名）❶ New Year holidays ❷ winter vacation ❸ annual leave

【年畫】niánhuà（名）New Year picture (painting)

【年景】niánjǐng（名）a year's harvest

【年富力强】nián fù lì qiáng〈成〉in the prime of life

【年號】niánhào（名）title of an emperor's reign

【年會】niánhuì（名）annual session

【年歲】niánsuì（名）❶（of a person）age ❷ years; time: 因爲～久遠，大家都把這件事忘了。Since it happened such a long time ago, we have all forgotten about it.

【年輕】niánqīng（名）young

【年輪】niánlún（名）〈植〉annual ring

【年糕】niángāo（名）New Year cake (made of glutinous rice flour)

【年曆】niánlì（名）year calendar: ～卡 calendar card

【年邁】niánmài（形）aged; advanced in years

【年頭】niántóu（名）❶ year ❷ years; long time: 他在這兒有～了。He has been here for years. ❸ a year's harvest

【年齡】niánlíng（名）age: ～組 age group／～結構 age structure

【年譜】niánpǔ（名）（of a scholar, statesman, etc.）chronicle of sb.'s life

【年鑒】niánjiàn（名）yearbook; almanac

幸 xìng Ⅰ（名）❶ happiness;

rejoice: 爲她的成功而深感慶～ rejoice at her success ❷ good luck: 萬～ by sheer luck Ⅱ（副）fortunately; luckily: ～未招來麻煩。Fortunately, I didn't get into trouble.

【幸存】xìngcún（動）survive: ～者 survivor

【幸而】xìng'ér（副）fortunately; luckily

【幸好】xìnghǎo（幸虧 xìngkuī）（副）fortunately; luckily: ～我們趕上了進城的末班車。Luckily we were in time for the last bus to the city.

【幸免】xìngmiǎn（動）escape by sheer luck: 無一～。No one survived.

【幸事】xìngshì（名）good luck; happy event; blessing

【幸運】xìngyùn（形）lucky; blessed

【幸運兒】xìngyùn'ér（名）child of fortune; lucky person

【幸福】xìngfú（名）happiness

幹 gàn Ⅰ（名）trunk; main part: ～渠 trunk canal Ⅱ（動）do; make Ⅲ（形）able; capable

【幹才】gàncái（名）capable person

【幹事】gànshi（名）office employee

【幹活】gànhuó（動）work; be on the job

【幹勁】gànjìn（名）vigour; enthusiasm

【幹部】gànbù（名）cadre; functionary

【幹掉】gàndiào（動）〈口〉do in; kill

【幹嗎】gànmá（副）〈口〉why; what for: 他來～? What did he come for? ／～來這一套? Why all this nonsense?

【幹綫】gànxiàn（名）trunk line

【幹練】gànliàn（形）capable and experienced

幺 部

【幻】huàn Ⅰ（形）unreal; imaginary; illusory Ⅱ（名）extraordinary change

【幻術】huànshù（名）magic; conjury

【幻象】huànxiàng（名）phantom; mirage

【幻滅】huànmiè（動）vanish like soap bubbles

【幻想】huànxiǎng（名）illusion; fantasy

【幻境】huànjìng（名）dreamland; fairyland

【幻燈】huàndēng（名）slide show: ~片（lantern）slide

【幻覺】huànjué（名）hallucination

【幼】yòu Ⅰ（形）young: ~芽 young shoot Ⅱ（名）children; the young: 敬老愛~ respect the old and love the young

【幼小】yòuxiǎo（形）young and small

【幼年】yòunián（名）childhood

【幼兒】yòu'ér（名）infant; baby; child

【幼兒園】yòu'éryuán（名）kindergarten; nursery school

【幼苗】yòumiáo（名）seedling

【幼教】yòujiào（名）(short for 幼兒教育 yòu'ér jiàoyù) preschool education

【幼稚】yòuzhì（形）❶ young ❷ childish; naïve; infantile: ~病 infantile disorder

【幼蟲】yòuchóng（名）larva

【幽】yōu（形）❶ quiet; tranquil; darkish: ~谷 tranquil valley ❷ secret; hidden: ~居 live a secluded life ❸ of the nether world: ~靈 phantom

【幽門】yōumén（名）〈生理〉pylorus

【幽深】yōushēn（形）deep and quiet

【幽雅】yōuyǎ（形）quiet and in good taste

【幽暗】yōu'àn（形）dim; gloomy

【幽會】yōuhuì（名）lovers' rendezvous

【幽禁】yōujìn（動）put under house arrest; throw into prison

【幽魂】yōuhún（名）ghost; apparition

【幽靜】yōujìng（形）quiet and peaceful

【幽默】yōumò Ⅰ（形）humorous Ⅱ（名）humour: ~感 sense of humour

【幾】jǐ（副）nearly; approximately; all but: ~瀕滅絕 be almost on the verge of extinction
see also jī

【幾乎】jīhū（副）almost; practically: ~動武 barely short of coming to blows

【幾】jǐ（形）❶ how many: 你有一個孩子? How many children have you? ❷ several; some; odd: 八十~歲 over eighty years old; in one's eighties
see also jī

【幾分】jǐfēn（副）a little; somewhat; rather: 有~好奇 be a bit curious

【幾內亞】Jǐnèiyà（名）Guinea: ~人 Guinean

【幾何】jǐhé Ⅰ(形) how much: 價值
~? What is the price? How much is
it (are they)? Ⅱ(名) geometry: ~
學 geometry

【幾兒】jǐr (副)〈口〉on what day;
when: 他~去東北? When is he
leaving for the Northeast?

【幾時】jǐshí (副) what time; when:
我~有空就來. I'll drop by when
I'm free.

【幾許】jǐxǔ (副) how much; how
many: 尚有~? How much is left?

广 部

序 xù Ⅰ(名) ❶ order; sequence:
秩~混亂 in disorder ❷ preface:
作~ write a preface Ⅱ(動) arrange
in order

【序文】xùwén (序言 xùyán) (名)
preface; foreword

【序曲】xùqǔ (名) overture

【序幕】xùmù (名) prologue; prelude: 爲一場大戰拉開了~ serve
as a prelude to a major battle

【序數】xùshù (名) ordinal number;
ordinal

庇 bì (動) shelter; protect: 包~逃
犯 shield an escaped convict

【庇護】bìhù Ⅰ(動) shield; harbour;
give refuge to Ⅱ(名) protection;
aegis

【庇護所】bìhùsuǒ (名) sanctuary; a-
sylum; refuge

店 diàn (名) ❶ shop; store: 百貨
~ department store ❷ inn

【店主】diànzhǔ (名) shopkeeper

【店員】diànyuán (名) shop assistant;
salesman

府 fǔ (名)（official）residence;
mansion: 總督~ governor's residence

【府上】fǔshang (名)〈敬〉your
home

【府邸】fǔdǐ (名) residence (esp. of
a senior officer)

【府綢】fǔchóu (名) poplin

底 dǐ (名) ❶ lowest or last part:
湖~ the bottom of a lake／月~ the
end of a month ❷ origin; base;
sth. stored in a file: 留~ keep a
duplication on file

【底下】dǐxià (副) ❶ under; below;
beneath ❷ later; afterwards

【底子】dǐzi (名) ❶ bottom ❷ foundation: 數學~好 have a good
grounding in mathematics

【底片】dǐpiàn (名)〈攝〉negative;
plate

【底細】dǐxi (名) inside story

【底層】dǐcéng (名) ❶ bottom: 社
會~ rock bottom of society ❷
ground floor

【底稿】dǐgǎo (名) first draft;
manuscript

度 dù Ⅰ(名) ❶ linear measure ❷
degree: 攝氏 10~ 10℃／45~角
45° angle ❸〈電〉kilowatt-hour: 1
~ 電 one kilowatt-hour ❹ limit;
extent: 勞累過~ be overworked ❺
(Dù) a surname Ⅱ(動) pass;
spend: ~假 spend one's vacation Ⅲ
(量) time: 再~聲明 reiterate
see also duó

【度日如年】dù rì rú nián〈成〉 eke

out one's miserable existence, each day dragging on like a year

【度外】dùwài（動）not take into consideration: 個人安危, 置之～ have no thought for one's personal safety

【度量】dùliàng（名）tolerance

【度量衡】dùliànghéng（名）weights and measures

度 duó（動）estimate
see also dù

庫 kù（名）storehouse: 冷～ cold storage; freezer

【庫存】kùcún（名）stock: 清點～ take stock; stock-taking

【庫房】kùfáng（名）warehouse

座 zuò I（名）❶ seat; place: 讓～ offer one's seat to sb. ❷ stand; pedestal: 青銅雕像的～兒 pedestal of the bronze statue II（量）江上一～大橋 a bridge across a river

【座子】zuòzi（名）❶ stand; pedestal ❷ saddle (of a bicycle, motorcycle)

【座上客】zuòshàngkè（名）guest (of honour)

【座右銘】zuòyòumíng（名）motto; maxim

【座次】zuòcì（名）order of seats

【座位】zuòwèi（名）seat; place: 安排～ seating arrangement

【座無虛席】zuò wú xū xí〈成〉the hall is packed to capacity; have a full house

【座談】zuòtán（動）have a discussion: ～會 forum; discussion

【座鐘】zuòzhōng（名）desk clock

庭 tíng（名）❶ front courtyard ❷ law court: ～長 presiding judge /

休～。Court is adjourned.

【庭院】tíngyuàn（名）courtyard

【庭園】tíngyuán（名）garden

庶 shù I（形）multitudinous; miscellaneous: ～務處 general affairs office II（名）collateral branch of a family: ～出 born of a concubine

【庶民】shùmín（名）common people; commoner

庵 ān（名）❶ hut ❷ Buddhist nunnery

康 kāng（名）❶ good health ❷ well-being; welfare ❸（Kāng）a surname

【康莊大道】kāng zhuāng dà dào〈成〉broad road or avenue

【康復】kāngfù I（動）be restored to health; recuperate II（名）rest and recuperation

【康樂】kānglè（形）healthy and blissful

庸 yōng I（形）commonplace; mediocre: ～人 mediocre perosn II（動）[used in the negative] need: 無～諱言 no need to beat around the bush; needless to say

【庸人自擾】yōng rén zì rǎo〈成〉fuss about nothing only to trouble oneself

【庸才】yōngcái（名）mediocrity

【庸俗】yōngsú（形）vulgar: ～刊物 vulgar publications

【庸碌】yōnglù（形）mediocre

【庸醫】yōngyī（名）quack; charlatan

廊 láng（名）porch; passage: 走～ corridor; passage-way

廐 jiù（名）stable; shed for domestic animals

厢 xiāng（名）❶ wingroom; wing ❷ (railway) carriage

【厢房】xiāngfáng（名）wingroom

厕 cè（名）toilet; W.C.

【厕所】cèsuǒ（名）toilet; lavatory

廉 lián Ⅰ（形）❶ incorruptibly honest: 為政清～ be incorruptibly honest as a government official ❷ inexpensive; cheap Ⅱ（名）(Lián) a surname

【廉正】liánzhèng（形）upright

【廉政】liánzhèng（名）clean government

【廉恥】liánchǐ（名）sense of shame

【廉價】liánjià（形）cheap: ～出售 sell at low prices; sell cheap

【廉潔】liánjié（形）honest

【廉潔奉公】lián jié fèng gōng〈成〉be incorruptibly honest in the discharge of duties

厦 shà（名）edifice; mansion

廓 kuò Ⅰ（形）extensive; vast Ⅱ（名）outline; contour

廖 Liào（名）a surname

厨 chú（名）kitchen

【厨房】chúfáng（名）kitchen

【厨師】chúshī（名）cook; chef

厮 sī（副）[early vernacular usage] with each other: ～打 come to blows

廣 guǎng Ⅰ（形）❶ broad; spacious ❷ numerous: 大庭～眾之下 in public; before a large audience Ⅱ（動）expand; spread: 推～ popular-

ize

【廣大】guǎngdà（形）❶ broad; extensive; vast ❷ (of people) numerous

【廣西】Guǎngxī（名）　Guangxi (Zhuang Autonomous Regon)

【廣泛】guǎngfàn（形）extensive; widespread

【廣告】guǎnggào（名）advertisement

【廣告牌】guǎnggàopái（名）billboard

【廣東】Guǎngdōng（名）Guangdong (Province)

【廣度】guǎngdù（名）scope; range

【廣柑】guǎnggān（名）orange

【廣袤】guǎngmào（名）length and breadth of land

【廣博】guǎngbó（形）(of a person's knowledge) extensive; wide

【廣場】guǎngchǎng（名）(public) square

【廣開言路】guǎng kāi yán lù〈成〉open up every avenue for people to air their views

【廣義】guǎngyì（名）broad sense

【廣漠】guǎngmò（形）a vast expanse of

【廣播】guǎngbō（名）broadcast

【廣播電臺】guǎngbō diàntái（名）radio station

【廣闊】guǎngkuò（形）vast; spacious

廟 miào（名）temple

【廟宇】miàoyǔ（名）temple; monastery

【廟會】miàohuì（名）fair

廢 fèi Ⅰ（動）abolish; give up Ⅱ（形）waste; useless

【廢止】fèizhǐ（動）abrogate; repeal

【廢物】 fèiwù (名) ❶ waste; refuse ❷ good-for-nothing

【廢品】 fèipǐn (名) ❶ scrap; waste ❷ reject

【廢除】 fèichú (動) abolish; annul

【廢料】 fèiliào (名) waste: 工業～ industrial waste

【廢紙】 fèizhǐ (名) waste paper: ～ 簍 waste paper basket

【廢棄】 fèiqì (動) discard; abandon: 把～的土地變成良田 turn the wasteland into fertile fields

【廢話】 fèihuà (名) nonsense: 少～ stop your nonsense; shut up

【廢置】 fèizhì (動) get rid of as useless; discard

【廢寢忘食】 fèi qǐn wàng shí 〈成〉 (so absorbed in an undertaking as to) forget one's meals and rest

【廢墟】 fèixū (名) ruins

【廢黜】 fèichù (動) depose; dethrone

【廢鐵】 fèitiě (名) scrap iron

廠 chǎng (名) factory; mill: 電影 製片～ film studio

【廠址】 chǎngzhǐ (名) address (location) of a factory

【廠房】 chǎngfáng (名) workshop; factory building

【廠長】 chǎngzhǎng (名) director of a factory: ～負責制 director responsibility system; manager responsibility system

【廠商】 chǎngshāng (名) manufacturer; firm

廬 lú (名) hut

【廬山真面目】 Lú Shān zhēn miàn mù 〈成〉 one's true features (colours); the truth of the matter

廳 tīng (名) ❶ hall; lounge: 客～

sitting room / 舞～ ballroom; dance hall ❷ vestibule: 兩室一～的套房 a flat of two rooms and a vestibule ❸ office ❹ department of a provincial government

廴 部

廷 tíng (名) imperial court; monarchical government: 宮～政變 palace coup

延 yán (動) ❶ prolong; lengthen: 鐵路～到河港。The railway was extended to the river port. ❷ delay; postpone: 會議向後～了。 The meeting has been postponed.

【延伸】 yánshēn (動) stretch; extend: 小路～到遠方。The path stretches far into the distance.

【延長】 yáncháng (動) lengthen; extend: ～逗留時間 prolong one's stay

【延期】 yánqī (動) postpone; put off: 會議～到後天舉行。The meeting will be put off till the day after tomorrow.

【延誤】 yánwù (動) delay: 此事應迅速處理,不得～。The matter should be dealt with without delay.

【延遲】 yánchí (動) put off; delay

【延緩】 yánhuǎn (動) postpone; defer: ～還債 defer the payment of debt

【延請】 yánqǐng (動) employ; hire: ～外國專家 hire foreign experts

【延擱】 yángē (動) delay

【延續】 yánxù (動) last; go on: 森林 大火～了一月。The forest fire

lasted a month.

建 jiàn (動) ❶ build; construct ❷ establish; set up ❸ propose; suggest: ～個議 have a suggestion to make

【建立】jiànlì (動) ❶ found; establish ❷ build; forge; form: ～聯繫 come into contact with; establish relations

【建交】jiànjiāo (動) establish diplomatic relations

【建材】jiàncái (名) (short for 建築材料 jiànzhù cáiliào) building materials

【建制】jiànzhì (名) organizational system; structure of establishment

【建造】jiànzào (動) construct; build

【建國】jiànguó (動) ❶ found a state ❷ engage in national reconstruction

【建設】jiànshè I (動) build; construct II (名) construction

【建設性】jiànshèxìng (形) constructive

【建樹】jiànshù I (動) make a contribution; score an achievement II (名) achievement; attainment

【建築】jiànzhù I (動) construct; build II (名) ❶ architecture ❷ building; relatively permanent construction

【建議】jiànyì I (動) make a suggestion; put forward a proposal II (名) proposal; suggestion

廾 部

弁 biàn (名) ❶ 〈舊〉 man's conical cap worn on ceremonious occasions

❷ low-ranking military officer: 馬 ～ (officer's) bodyguard

弄 lòng (名) lane; alley
see also nòng

【弄堂】lòngtáng (名) lane; alleyway

弄 nòng (動) ❶ play with; fool with: 別玩～槍。Don't meddle with the gun. ❷ do; make: ～幾個菜 cook a few dishes / 把腳～傷了 hurt one's foot ❸ get; fetch: ～幾本小説來讀 get some novels to read
see also lòng

【弄巧成拙】nòng qiǎo chéng zhuō 〈成〉 try to be smart but fail miserably

【弄好】nònghǎo (動) ❶ do sth. well ❷ get (sth.) done: 你的論文～了沒有? Is your dissertation in order?

【弄清】nòngqīng (動) make clear; understand fully: ～問題 clear up the matter

【弄虛作假】nòng xū zuò jiǎ 〈成〉 practise deception; fraudulent practice

【弄錯】nòngcuò (動) make a mistake; mistake: ～人 mistake one person for another

【弄糟】nòngzāo (動) make a mess of; spoil: 她把事情全～了。He messed up everything.

【弄壞】nònghuài (動) ruin; spoil: 把玩具～ damage the toy

弈 yì I (名) go II (動) play chess

弊 bì (動) ❶ harm; disadvantage; demerit: ～多利少 have more disadvantages than advantages; do more harm than good ❷ fraud; malpractice: 營私舞～ abuse of office and corruption

【弊病】bìbìng（名）fault; defect; drawback; disadvantage

【弊端】bìduān（名）abuse; malady; evil

弋 部

式 shì（名）❶ type; style; fashion: 手提～打字機 portable typewriter ❷ form; pattern; model: 被動～ passive form ❸ ceremony; rite: 閱兵～ military review（parade）❹ formula: 方程～ equation ❺〈語〉mode of speech: 命令～ imperative mood

【式子】shìzi（名）❶ posture; pose ❷〈數〉formula

【式樣】shìyàng（名）mode; fashion; style

弓 部

弓 gōng Ⅰ（名）bow Ⅱ（動）bend; bow

【弓子】gōngzi（名）❶ bow（of a stringed instrument）❷ bow-shaped thing

引 yǐn（動）❶ lead; guide; conduct: ～入歧途 lead sb. astray ❷ lure; attract: ～入毀滅的道路 lure sb. to destruction ❸ leave: ～退 retire（from office）❹ cause; e-voke: ～起極大的憤慨 arouse great indignation ❺ quote; cite: ～

自書中的一段文章 a passage quoted from a book

【引力】yǐnlì（名）〈物〉gravitation: 萬有～ universal gravitation

【引人入勝】yǐn rén rù shèng〈成〉（of a literary passage or scenery）be a scene of enchanting beauty; be very fascinating

【引人注目】yǐn rén zhù mù〈成〉conspicuous; eye-catching

【引子】yǐnzi（名）prelude; prologue; introductory remarks

【引水】yǐnshuǐ（動）❶ draw or di-vert water: ～入田 divert water in-to the fields ❷ pilot a ship into harbour

【引文】yǐnwén（名）quotation

【引以爲戒】yǐn yǐ wéi jiè〈成〉take warning or draw lessons from a mis-take

【引用】yǐnyòng（動）quote; cite

【引伸】yǐnshēn（動）extend（the original meaning of a word）: "鏡子"這個詞可以～爲"鑒"的意思。The word "mirror" can be extended to mean "warning" in Chinese.

【引見】yǐnjiàn（動）introduce; pre-sent

【引言】yǐnyán（名）foreword; intro-duction

【引咎】yǐnjiù（動）〈書〉take the blame on oneself: ～自責 take the blame and reproach oneself

【引信】yǐnxìn（名）detonator; fuse

【引起】yǐnqǐ（動）arouse; cause; e-voke: ～爭論 stir up controversy / ～深思 be thought-provoking

【引航】yǐnháng Ⅰ（動）pilot Ⅱ（名）pilotage

【引狼入室】yǐn láng rù shì〈成〉in-vite a wolf into the fold; open the door to the enemy

【引進】yǐnjìn（動）❶ recommend ❷ introduce; import

【引渡】yǐndù（動）extradite

【引經據典】yǐn jīng jù diǎn〈成〉quote from classics; quote chapter and verse

【引誘】yǐnyòu（動）lure; seduce; tempt

【引號】yǐnhào（名）quotation mark; quote

【引導】yǐndǎo（動）guide; conduct

【引薦】yǐnjiàn（動）recommend

【引擎】yǐnqíng（名）engine

【引證】yǐnzhèng（動）cite as evidence

【引爆】yǐnbào（動）ignite; detonate

弔 diào

【弔唁】diàoyàn（動）condole

弘 hóng（形）great; grand; magnificent

【弘大】hóngdà（形）grand

弛 chí（動）relax; slacken：紀律鬆～。The discipline is lax.

【弛緩】chíhuǎn（形）calm down; relax

弟 dì（名）younger brother

【弟子】dìzǐ（名）disciple; pupil

【弟兄】dìxiong（名）brothers

弦 xián（名）❶ bowstring; string ❷ spring (of a watch or clock)

【弦外之音】xián wài zhī yīn〈成〉implication; allusion

【弦樂】xiányuè（名）string music

【弦樂隊】xiányuèduì（名）string orchestra

【弦樂器】xiányuèqì（名）stringed instrument

弧 hú（名）arc

【弧光】húguāng（名）arc light; arc

【弧形】húxíng（名）arc; curve

【弧度】húdù（名）〈數〉radian

弩 nǔ（名）crossbow

【弩弓】nǔgōng（名）crossbow

弭 mǐ（動）suppress; remove

【弭亂】mǐluàn（動）quash (quell) a rebellion

弱 ruò（形）❶ weak; feeble：體質虛～ be of a weak constitution ❷ young ❸ [used after a fraction or decimal] a little less than：四分之一～ a little less than one-fourth

【弱小】ruòxiǎo（形）small and weak

【弱不禁風】ruò bù jīn fēng〈成〉be of a delicate constitution

【弱肉強食】ruò ròu qiáng shí〈成〉law of the jungle

【弱者】ruòzhě（名）the weak

【弱點】ruòdiǎn（名）weak point; weakness

張 zhāng Ⅰ（動）❶ open; spread：醫生讓病人～開嘴。The doctor told the patient to open his mouth. / ～開手臂 stretch out one's arms; open one's arms; expand：虛～聲勢 make a false show of strength / 擴～ enlarge; expand ❸ look：東～西望 look around ❹ open a new shop：開～ open a business Ⅱ（量）：一～明信片 a postcard / 兩～桌子 two tables Ⅲ（名）(Zhāng) a surname

【張力】zhānglì（名）〈物〉tension：表面～ surface tension

【張口結舌】zhāng kǒu jié shé〈成〉
gape in astonishment

【張牙舞爪】zhāng yá wǔ zhǎo〈成〉
show one's fangs and claws; make
ferocious threatening gestures

【張狂】zhāngkuáng（形）　insolent;
impertinent

【張皇失措】zhāng huáng shī cuò〈成〉
be scared out of one's wits

【張冠李戴】zhāng guān Lǐ dài〈成〉
put Zhang's hat on Li's head; fasten
one person's story on another
person; mistake one thing for another

【張掛】zhāngguà（動）hang up（a
picture, curtain, etc.)

【張望】zhāngwàng（動）look around

【張貼】zhāngtiē（動）put up（a notice, poster, etc.)

【張揚】zhāngyáng（動）make widely
known; make public: 他四處～這
件醜聞。He spread the scandal all
around.

【張燈結彩】zhāng dēng jié cǎi〈成〉
decked with lanterns and silk festoons

【張嘴】zhāngzuǐ（動）❶ open one's
mouth: 他一就是罵人。He never
opens his mouth without starting to
curse. ❷ ask for a loan or a favour:
不好意思～借錢 find it embarras-
ing to ask for a loan

【張羅】zhāngluo（動）❶ take care
of; look after: ～女兒的婚事 busy
preparing for one's daughter's wedding ❷ raise（funds）: 爲展覽會～
一筆款子 raise a sum of money for
the exhibition ❸ entertain; attend
to: ～顧客 attend to customers

弼 bì（動）assist: 輔～ assist a

monarch in governing a country

強 jiàng（形）stubborn; obstinate:
脾氣倔～ as stubborn as a mule;
mulish
see also qiáng; qiǎng

【強嘴】jiàngzuǐ（動）talk back in defiance

強 qiáng（形）❶ strong; powerful:
體格～ physically strong ❷ better:
今年莊稼比去年～。This year's
crops are better than last year's. ❸
of high degree: 信心～ have strong
confidence ❹ slightly more than:
四分之一～ a little over one quarter
see also jiàng; qiǎng

【強人】qiángrén（名）❶　strong
man; powerful or capable person ❷
gangster

【強力霉素】qiánglìméisù（名）〈藥〉
doxycycline

【強大】qiángdà（形）mighty; powerful

【強心劑】qiángxīnjì（名）〈藥〉car-
diae stimulant; cardiotonic

【強加】qiángjiā（動）impose; ob-
trude: 把自己的意志～給別人 im-
pose one's will on others

【強似】qiángsì（動）exceed; surpass: 一九八八年的國民收入～前
一年。The national income of 1988
exceeded that of the previous year.

【強行】qiángxíng（副）by force: 在
委員會～通過一項計劃 railroad a
plan through a committee

【強行軍】qiángxíngjūn（名）　forced
march

【強有力】qiángyǒulì（形）strong;
forceful: 發動一次～的反擊 launch
a vigorous counterattack

【强佔】qiángzhàn（動）occupy by force

【强壮】qiángzhuàng（形）strong; sturdy: 體格～ of sturdy build

【强固】qiánggù（形）strong; solid

【强弩之末】qiáng nǔ zhī mò〈成〉a powerful arrow reaching the end of its long flight; a spent force

【强制】qiángzhì（動）compel; force: ～勞動 forced labour; penal servitude

【强的松】qiángdísōng（名）〈藥〉prednisone

【强度】qiángdù（名）strength; intensity: 電流～ current intensity

【强姦】qiángjiān（動）rape; assault: ～民意 outrage public opinion

【强勁】qiángjìn（形）strong; powerful: 北風～，橫掃整個平原。The north wind is strong, sweeping across the entire plain.

【强烈】qiángliè（形）strong; intense: 深造的～願望 intense desire to pursue advanced study

【强盜】qiángdào（名）robber; bandit

【强國】qiángguó（名）powerful nation; power

【强健】qiángjiàn（形）physically strong; hale and hearty

【强盛】qiángshèng（形）(of a country) strong and prosperous

【强硬】qiángyìng（形）strong; vigorous: 提出～的抗議 lodge a strong protest

【强韌】qiángrèn（形）tough; tenacious: 有～的意志力 tenacious of purpose

【强溶劑】qiángróngjì（名）〈化〉strong solvent

【强酸】qiángsuān（名）strong acid

【强暴】qiángbào Ⅰ（形）voilent; ferocious: ～行爲 brutality Ⅱ（名）violence; brute force

【强調】qiángdiào（動）emphasize; stress

【强權】qiángquán（名）might; power

【强權政治】qiángquán zhèngzhì（名）power politics

強

qiǎng（形）forced; unnatural: ～笑 forced smile
see also jiàng; qiáng

【强人所難】qiǎng rén suǒ nán〈成〉force sb. to do what is beyond his ability or against his will

【强求】qiǎngqiú（動）insist on; impose: ～別人 impose sth. upon others

【强使】qiǎngshǐ（動）force; compel

【强逼】qiǎngbī（强迫 qiǎngpò）（動）force; compel

【强詞奪理】qiǎng cí duó lǐ〈成〉chop logic to defend one's position

【强辯】qiǎngbiàn（動）resort to sophistry

彈

dàn（名）bullet; bomb
see also tán

【彈弓】dàngōng（名）catapult

【彈丸】dànwán（名）❶ pellet; shot ❷ head of a bullet ❸ small piece of land

【彈子】dànzǐ（名）❶ marble ❷ billiard: ～房 billiard room

【彈道】dàndào（名）trajectory: ～導彈 ballistic missile

【彈無虛發】dàn wú xū fā〈成〉every shot hit the mark

【彈藥】dànyào（名）ammunition: ～庫 ammunition depot

彈 tán I（動）❶ shoot（with the function of a spring）：～球 play marbles ❷ spring; bounce ❸ flick; flip ❹ fluff：～花機 cotton fluffer ❺ play（a stringed instrument）：～吉他 play the guitar ❻ impeach; attack：～劾 impeach II（形）elastic see also dàn

【彈力】tánlì（名）elasticity; stretch：～襪 stretch socks

【彈性】tánxìng（名）elasticity; resilience：～好 springy

【彈奏】tánzòu（動）play（a stringed musical instrument）

【彈詞】táncí（名）〈曲藝〉storytelling to the accompaniment of stringed instruments, popular in Southeast China

【彈跳】tántiào（動）spring; bounce

【彈壓】tányā（動）suppress or crack down on（a riot）

【彈簧】tánhuáng（名）spring：～摺刀 spring blade knife

彌 mí I（動）fill：煙霧～漫 be filled with smoke II（副）even more：欲蓋～彰。The cover-up effort only serves to make the story more notorious.

【彌天大謊】mí tiān dà huǎng〈成〉a flat lie; a big lie

【彌合】míhé（動）close; bridge：～分歧 bridge the gap; sink the differences

【彌留】míliú（動）be dying; be on one's deathbed

【彌勒】Mílè（名）〈宗〉Maitreya

【彌補】míbǔ（動）make up; remedy

【彌漫】mímàn（動）permeate; fill：園裏～着花香。The garden is permeated with the fragrance of flowers.

【彌撒】mísa（名）〈宗〉Mass

【彌縫】míféng（動）gloss over a fault

彎 wān I（形）curved; twisted：～～的小溪 a meandering brook II（動）bend：～腰 bend the back III（名）turn; curve：你直説了吧，别繞～子。You'd better come straight to the point and not beat about the bush.

【彎子】wānzi（名）bend; turn

【彎曲】wānqū（形）winding; zigzag

【彎路】wānlù（名）roundabout way; tortuous course：走～ take a roundabout way

彐 部

彗 huì
【彗星】huìxīng（名）〈天〉comet

彝 yí
【彝族】Yízú（名）Yi nationality

彡 部

形 xíng（名）❶ shape; form：呈球～ in the shape of a ball ❷ body; entity

【形式】xíngshì（名）form：新的藝術～ a new art form

【形成】xíngchéng（動）form; take shape：～風氣 become a common practice／～良好的衞生習慣 form a good habit of personal hygiene

【形而上學】xíng'érshàngxué（名）

metaphysics

【形形色色】xíng xíng sè sè〈成〉all sorts of; of every description: ~的政客 politicians of every hue

【形狀】xíngzhuàng（名）form; shape

【形迹】xíngjì（名）behaviour; conduct; expression: ~可疑 look fishy

【形容】xíngróng（動）describe; portray: 無法 ~ defy description; beyond description; indescribable

【形容詞】xíngróngcí（名）〈語〉adjective

【形象】xíngxiàng（名）image; figure; profile: 改進自己的 ~ improve one's own image

【形勢】xíngshì（名）situation; circumstances: ~惡化。The situation is deteriorating.

【形態】xíngtài（名）form; shape

【形影不離】xíng yǐng bù lí〈成〉be inseparable; be on intimate terms

【形影相吊】xíng yǐng xiāng diào〈成〉alone and friendless

【形體】xíngtǐ（名）❶ shape; body: ~和精神 body and spirit ❷〈語〉form and structure

彤 tóng（形）red

彬 bīn

【彬彬】bīnbīn（形）refined; gentle; polite: ~有禮 gentle and polite

彪 biāo Ⅰ（名）tiger cub Ⅱ（形）tigerlike

【彪大漢】biāo xíng dà hàn〈成〉burly chap; husky fellow

彩 cǎi Ⅰ（名）❶ colour: 絢麗多 ~ bright and colourful ❷ coloured silk (ribbon): 剪 ~ cut the ribbon ❸ applause; cheers: 連聲喝 ~ cheer

again and again ❹ variety; splendour: 增添光 ~ add lustre to ❺ prize ❻〈婉〉wound: 掛 ~ wounded in action Ⅱ（形）❶ coloured ❷ multicoloured

【彩色】cǎisè（形）colour: ~照片 colour photo / ~電視 colour TV

【彩車】cǎichē（名）float (in a parade)

【彩虹】cǎihóng（名）rainbow

【彩排】cǎipái（名）dress rehearsal

【彩票】cǎipiào（名）lottery ticket

【彩陶】cǎitáo（名）painted pottery

【彩墨畫】cǎimòhuà（名）ink painting with colour

彭 Péng（名）a surname

彰 zhāng（形）evident; conspicuous: 欲蓋彌 ~。Attempts to cover things up can only result in making them conspicuous.

影 yǐng（名）❶ shadow; reflection ❷ trace; dim impression ❸ photograph; picture: 近 ~ a recent photo ❹ motion picture; film

【影子】yǐngzi（名）❶ shadow; reflection: ~內閣 shadow cabinet ❷ trace; dim impression: 這事我連點 ~都不知道。I haven't the faintest idea of the matter.

【影片】yǐngpiàn（名）film; movie

【影印】yǐngyìn（動）photocopy; xerox

【影迷】yǐngmí（名）film fan

【影射】yǐngshè Ⅰ（動）allude to; insinuate: 這部小說的主角~作者的一個朋友。The hero of the novel alludes to one of the author's friends. Ⅱ（名）indirect reference; innuendo

【影院】yǐngyuàn（名）cinema; movies

【影集】yǐngjí（名）photograph album

【影評】yǐngpíng（名）film review

【影響】yǐngxiǎng I（名）influence; impact: 對他～很大 exert a great influence on him II（動）influence; affect: 嚴重～產品的質量 seriously affect the quality of the products

彳 部

彷 páng

【彷徨】pánghuáng（動）walk back and forth; feel uncertain about the best course to take; hesitate

役 yì I（名）❶ labour ❷ servant ❸ military service: 現～ on active service ❹ battle; campaign II（動）enslave

【役使】yìshǐ（動）work (an animal); enslave

往 wǎng I（動）go: 來～的行人 passing pedestrians II（副）to; towards: 飛～上海 fly to Shanghai III（形）past; former
see also wàng

【往日】wǎngrì（副）in former days; in the past

【往年】wǎngnián（副）in the past years; formerly

【往返】wǎngfǎn（動）make a round trip: ～於京滬之間 travel between Beijing and Shanghai

【往來】wǎnglái（動）❶ go and come; come and go: ～車輛 traffic; outbound and inbound vehicles ❷

contact; communication: 我們沒什麼～。We don't see much of each other.

【往往】wǎngwǎng（副）very often: 上課～遲到 be often late for class

【往昔】wǎngxī（副）before; in the past

【往事】wǎngshì（名）past events; the past: ～歷歷在目。The past is still fresh in one's memory.

【往常】wǎngcháng（副）(as) used to be the case: 比～起早 get up earlier than usual

往 wàng（介）to; towards: 江水～東流。The river flows east.
see also wǎng

【往後】wànghòu（副）from now on; later: ～怎麼辦? What shall we do in the days to come?

征 zhēng（動）❶ start a military campaign: 出～ go on an expedition ❷ go on a journey: ～途 journey to a distant place

【征服】zhēngfú（動）conquer; overcome

【征討】zhēngtǎo（動）go on a punitive expedition

彼 bǐ（代）❶ that; the other; those: ～時 at that time; then ❷ the other party

【彼一時, 此一時】bǐ yī shí, cǐ yī shí〈成〉It was like that then, but it is different now.

【彼此】bǐcǐ（代）each other; one another: 不分～。What one has, the other is welcome to.（share the last penny with sb.）

【彼此彼此】bǐcǐ bǐcǐ〈套〉[routine expression indicating reciprocity]:

你幹得不錯。一~。You have done a good job. — Well, so have you.

【彼岸】bǐ'àn（名）the other shore

徂 cú（介）to: 自東~西 from east to west

待 dāi（動）stay: ~在屋裏不出門 shut oneself up in the room
see also dài

待 dài（動）❶ wait for: ~機 wait for a chance ❷ treat; entertain: ~客 entertain guests ❸ be about to: 正~出發 be starting off
see also dāi

【待人接物】dài rén jiē wù〈成〉the way one gets along with people

【待命】dàimìng（動）wait for orders

【待遇】dàiyù（名）❶ treatment ❷ pay; salary; wages

【待續】dàixù（動）to be continued

律 lǜ Ⅰ（名）❶ law; rule ❷（Lǜ）a surname Ⅱ（動）bridle; discipline: ~己甚嚴 be very strict in selfdiscipline

【律師】lǜshī（名）lawyer; attorney

【律詩】lǜshī（名）Chinese classical poem of eight lines with a strict tone pattern and rhyme scheme

很 hěn（副）very; quite: ~難得 very difficult indeed

徇 xùn

【徇私】xùnsī（徇情 xùnqíng）（動）act unfairly from selfish motives; practise favouritism

後 hòu Ⅰ（名）❶ back; rear ❷ offspring Ⅱ（副）later; after: 飯~ after dinner

【後人】hòurén（名）❶ later genera-

tions ❷ posterity

【後方】hòufāng（名）rear; base

【後天】hòutiān Ⅰ（名）day after tomorrow Ⅱ（形）postnatal; acquired

【後代】hòudài（名）❶ later periods (in history) ❷ later generations; offspring

【後世】hòushì（名）successive generations

【後生可畏】hòu shēng kě wèi〈成〉the younger generation is to be treated with due respect; the young will surpass the old

【後果】hòuguǒ（名）consequence; aftermath

【後門】hòumén（名）❶ back door ❷ backdoor dealings

【後者】hòuzhě（名）the latter

【後事】hòushì（名）❶ subsequent developments (as in a novel) ❷ funeral arrangements

【後肢】hòuzhī〈動〉hind legs

【後來】hòulái（副）afterwards; later

【後來居上】hòu lái jū shàng〈成〉the younger generation will surpass the older generation

【後盾】hòudùn（名）strong backing; support

【後勁】hòujìn（名）❶（of alcoholic drinks）aftereffect ❷ reserve strength; stamina

【後面】hòumiàn（副）❶ at the back; behind: 留在~ stay behind ❷ later; afterwards

【後退】hòutuì（動）draw back; retreat

【後記】hòujì（名）postscript

【後悔】hòuhuǐ（動）regret; repent

【後院】hòuyuàn（名）backyard

【後起之秀】hòu qǐ zhī xiù（名）young people of promise; new star

【後患】hòuhuàn（名）future trouble: ～無窮 be a source of endless trouble

【後進】hòujìn（形）less advanced; backward

【後備】hòubèi（名）reserve: ～部隊 reserve units

【後援】hòuyuán（名）reinforcements

【後勤】hòuqín（名）rear service; logistics

【後跟】hòugēn（名）heel

【後路】hòulù（名）❶（of an army）supply line in the rear; route of retreat ❷ room for manoeuvre

【後裔】hòuyì（名）descendant; offspring

【後臺】hòutái（名）❶ backstage ❷ backer

【後綴】hòuzhuì（名）〈語〉suffix

【後輩】hòubèi（名）❶ younger generation; junior member ❷ descendants

【後遺症】hòuyízhèng（名）❶ sequelae ❷ adverse effect of some mishandled matter

【後衛】hòuwèi（名）❶ rear ❷（of sports）full back; guard

【後繼】hòujì（動）carry on: ～有人 no lack of worthy successors

【後顧】hòugù（動）❶ take care of things left behind: 無～之憂 have nothing to worry about back at home ❷ look backward

徒 tú Ⅰ（副）❶ on foot: ～涉 wade through ❷ merely: ～託空言 be couched in merely empty words ❸ in vain; for nothing: ～然消耗人力物力 waste manpower and material resources Ⅱ（形）empty: ～手 barehanded; unarmed Ⅲ（名）❶ ap-

prentice; student: 學～工 apprentice ❷（religious）follower; disciple: 基督～ Christian ❸〈貶〉person: 不法之～ lawless person ❹ imprisonment

【徒工】túgōng（名）（worker）apprentice

【徒子徒孫】tú zǐ tú sūn（成）〈貶〉adherents; henchmen

【徒刑】túxíng（名）imprisonment: 判處無期～ be sentenced to life imprisonment; get a life sentence

【徒步】túbù（副）on foot: ～旅行 trekking

【徒弟】túdì（名）apprentice; disciple

【徒勞】túláo（動）make futile efforts: ～無功 do fruitless work

徑 jìng Ⅰ（名）❶ path; trail ❷ way; means ❸ diameter Ⅱ（副）directly; straight

【徑自】jìngzì（副）without telling anybody; directly: 他一言不發，～出去了。He left directly without a word.

【徑直】jìngzhí（副）directly: ～飛赴倫敦 take the nonstop flight to London; fly nonstop to London

【徑賽】jìngsài（名）〈體〉track events: 田～ track and field meet

徐 Xú（名）a surname

【徐徐】xúxú（副）slowly; gently: 春風～吹過。A spring breeze blew gently past.

徘 pái

【徘徊】páihuái（動）❶ wander about; walk to and for ❷ hesitate

徙 xǐ（動）move: ～居 move house

得 dé（動）❶ get; gain: ～益

proft (from) ❷ suit: ～法 do sth. properly ❸ be ready; complete: 信寫～了。The letter is finished. ❹ be satisfied: 揚揚自～ feel complacent ❺ may; can
see also de; děi

【得力】délì Ⅰ(形) capable: ～助手 able assistant Ⅱ(動) benefit (from)

【得寸進尺】dé cùn jìn chǐ〈成〉give him an inch and he'll take an ell; have an insatiable desire

【得心應手】dé xīn yìng shǒu〈成〉work with ease and proficiency

【得天獨厚】dé tiān dú hòu〈成〉enjoy rich gifts from nature

【得不償失】dé bù cháng shī〈成〉the gain is outweighed by the loss

【得失】déshī(名) gain and loss; advantages and disadvantages

【得志】dézhì(動) be successful in one's career

【得到】dédào(動) get; obtain

【得病】débìng(動) fall ill

【得逞】déchěng(動) prevail; succeed

【得勝】déshèng(動) win a victory

【得過且過】dé guò qiě guò〈成〉live without aim; muddle along

【得當】dédàng(副) properly; with propriety

【得勢】déshì(動) be in power

【得意】déyì(形) exultant; complacent: ～忘形 be dizzy with success

【得罪】dézuì(動) offend

【得獎】déjiǎng(動) win a prize

【得寵】déchǒng(動) be in sb.'s good graces

【得體】détǐ(副) properly

得 de(助)❶[used after a verb to indicate possibility]: 買～到 be available in the market ❷[used after a verb or an adjective to indicate result or degree]: 熱～很 extremely hot
see also dé; děi

得 děi(動)❶ need; require: 真～注意 demand serious attention ❷ must; have to: 我們～快做決定。We must make a prompt decision.
see also de; dé

從 cōng
see also cóng

【從容】cōngróng(形)❶ unhurried; unruffled ❷ (of time or money) ample: 手頭～ have enough money and to spare

從 cóng Ⅰ(動)❶ follow: ～征 go on an expedition ❷ obey: 力不～心。One's ability falls short of one's wishes. ❸ be engaged in; join: ～商 go into business Ⅱ(介) from; since: ～頭到尾 from start to finish ～那以後 since then Ⅲ(副)[used before a negative]ever: ～未見過 have never seen Ⅳ(形) of secondary importance: 有主有～ be arranged in proper order Ⅴ(名) (Cóng) a surname
see also cōng

【從中作梗】cóng zhōng zuò gěng〈成〉put a spoke in sb.'s wheel

【從犯】cóngfàn(名) accessary

【從此】cóngcǐ(副) from now (then) on

【從而】cóng'ér(連) thus; thereby; as a result

【從長計議】cóng cháng jì yì〈成〉refuse to consider a matter till a later time; shelve a matter

【從來】cónglái（副）always; ever: ~没去過上海 have never been to Shanghai

【從事】cóngshì（動）❶ be engaged in: ~考古工作 be engaged in archaeology ❷ deal with; act: 軍法~ be dealt with according to military law

【從前】cóngqián（副）in the past; before; once upon a time

【從速】cóngsù（副）as soon as possible

【從師】cóngshī（動）be apprenticed to

【從略】cónglüè（動）be omitted

【從善如流】cóng shàn rú liú〈成〉follow good advice willingly

【從屬】cóngshǔ（形）subordinate

御 yù I（動）❶ drive（a carriage）❷ manage; control: 駕~ control II（形）imperial: ~用 for imperial use

【御旨】yùzhǐ（名）imperial edict

【御花園】yùhuāyuán（名）imperial garden

復 fù I（動）❶ recover; resume: ~課 resume classes ❷ return; repeat: 周而~始 come full circle ❸ reply; answer II（副）again: 年一~年 year after year

【復工】fùgōng（動）return to work（after stoppage）

【復仇】fùchóu（動）revenge

【復古】fùgǔ（動）go back to the ancients

【復刊】fùkān（動）resume publication

【復查】fùchá（動）recheck; reexamine

【復信】fùxìn I（動）answer a letter II（名）reply

【復活】fùhuó I（動）revive II（名）revival; resurrection

【復活節】Fùhuójié（名）Easter

【復核】fùhé（動）reexamine

【復員】fùyuán I（動）demobilize: ~軍人 demobilized armyman II（名）demobilization

【復原】fùyuán（動）recover; recuperate from an illness

【復辟】fùbì（動）stage a comeback

【復會】fùhuì（動）resume a session

【復興】fùxīng（名）rebirth: 文藝~ the Renaissance

【復舊】fùjiù（動）restore the old ways

【復蘇】fùsū I（動）regain consciousness; recover II（名）recovery; resurgence: 經濟~ economic recovery

循 xún（動）abide by; follow

【循序漸進】xún xù jiàn jìn〈成〉advance step by step; make steady progress

【循規蹈矩】xún guī dǎo jǔ〈成〉never stray from the rules and regulations; stick to convention; toe the line: ~的孩子 an obedient and docile child

【循循善誘】xún xún shàn yòu〈成〉guide with skill and patience

【循環】xúnhuán I（動）circulate II（名）cycle; circulation: 惡性~ vicious circle

微 wēi I（形）❶ tiny; small: ~乎其~ infinitesimal; negligible ❷ micro: 縮~膠片 microfiche; microfilm ❸ profound; abstruse: ~言大義 profound remarks pregnant with meaning II（動）decline; dwindle

【微小】wēixiǎo（形）tiny; slight: 成功的可能性是極其～的。The chances of success are very slim.

【微分】wēifēn（名）〈數〉differential

【微不足道】wēi bù zú dào〈成〉insignificant; negligible

【微生物】wēishēngwù（名）microorganism; microbe

【微妙】wēimiào（形）subtle; delicate: ～的局面 delicate situation

【微波】wēibō（名）〈電子〉microwave: ～爐 microwave oven

【微風】wēifēng（名）breeze

【微型】xēixíng（形）mini-; miniature: ～軸承 miniature bearing

【微弱】wēiruò（形）faint; feeble; slight: ～的多數 narrow majority

【微笑】wēixiào（名）smile

【微細】wēixì（形）tiny; small: ～的差別 slight difference

【微粒】wēilì（名）particle; fine grain

【微機】wēijī（微電腦 wēidiànnǎo）（名）microcomputer

【微積分】wēijīfēn（名）〈數〉calculus

【微薄】wēibó（形）meagre; scant: ～的貢獻 meagre contribution

【微觀】wēiguān（形）microscopic; microcosmic; micro-: ～經濟學 microeconomics

徭 yáo

【徭役】yáoyì（名）corvée; forced labour

徹 chè（形）thorough; penetrating

【徹底】chèdǐ I（形）thorough: ～勝利 complete victory II（副）completely

【徹夜】chèyè（副）throughout the night; all night

【徹骨】chègǔ（副）to the bone: 寒風。～The cold wind cuts one to the marrow.

【徹頭徹尾】chè tóu chè wěi〈成〉out and out; downright: ～的捏造 downright fabrication

德 dé（名）❶ virtue; morality; integrity ❷ favour; kindness

【德行】déxíng（名）moral conduct

【德育】déyù（名）moral education

【德高望重】dé gāo wàng zhòng（形）(of a person) be of eminent virtue and high prestige

【德國】Déguó（名）Germany: ～人 German

【德語】Déyǔ（名）German (language)

徵 zhēng I（動）❶ conscript; recruit ❷ levy; collect (taxes, etc.) ❸ solicit; ask for: ～文 solicit articles II（名）sign; portent: 特～ characteristic

【徵用】zhēngyòng（動）requisition; expropriate

【徵兆】zhēngzhào（名）sign; portent

【徵收】zhēngshōu（動）levy; impose: ～煙酒稅 impose duties on tobacco and wine

【徵兵】zhēngbīng（動）conscript; draft

【徵求】zhēngqiú（動）solicit; ask for: ～意見 solicit comments

【徵候】zhēnghòu（名）sign: 打噴嚏常常是感冒的～。Sneezing is often a sign of having caught cold.

【徵集】zhēngjí（動）❶ collect; gather ❷ recruit; enlist

【徵税】zhēngshuì（動）levy taxes

【徵詢】zhēngxún（動）solicit sb.'s counsel

【徵募】zhēngmù（動）recruit; enlist

【徵聘】zhēngpìn（動）invite applications for a job; advertise a vacancy

【徵調】zhēngdiào（名）requisition; draft

【徵購】zhēnggòu（動）purchase by the state

【徵糧】zhēngliáng（動）impose grain levies

徵 huī（名）emblem; badge; insignia: 軍～ army emblem

【徵章】huīzhāng（名）badge; insignia

心 部

心 xīn（名）❶ heart; mind; feeling; motive: 全～全意 heart and soul／開～ feel happy／良～ conscience ❷ centre; core: 核～ core; nucleus／重～ the centre of gravity／江～ the middle of the river

【心力】xīnlì（名）mental and physical efforts: ～交瘁 tire oneself out both mentally and physically

【心口】xīnkǒu（名）pit of the stomach

【心不在焉】xīn bù zài yān〈成〉absent-minded

【心中有數】xīn zhōng yǒu shù〈成〉feel sure of sth.; be fully confident

【心目】xīnmù（名）one's mind; one's view: 在别人的～中 in the eyes of other people

【心平氣和】xīn píng qì hé〈成〉in a calm state of mind; composed and even-tempered; in a placid mood

【心甘情願】xīn gān qíng yuàn〈成〉be willing and ready; of one's free will

【心安理得】xīn ān lǐ dé〈成〉have an easy conscience; feel no qualms (about)

【心地】xīndì（名）heart; moral character: ～善良 kind-hearted

【心血】xīnxuè（名）painstaking effort

【心血來潮】xīn xuè lái cháo〈成〉be seized with a sudden impulse; have a brain wave

【心如刀割】xīn rú dāo gē〈成〉have one's heart wrung with sorrow; be torn with grief

【心有餘悸】xīn yǒu yú jì〈成〉have a lingering fear; shudder at the mere thought of

【心灰意懶】xīn huī yì lǎn〈成〉be dispirited; be discouraged; lose heart

【心坎】xīnkǎn（名）bottom of one's heart

【心肝】xīngān（名）❶ conscience: 没～ conscienceless ❷ darling; dear

【心花怒放】xīn huā nù fàng〈成〉be highly exhilarated; be wild with joy

【心事】xīnshì（名）sth. that weighs on one's mind

【心直口快】xīn zhí kǒu kuài〈成〉be frank and outspoken; speak one's mind freely

【心服口服】xīn fú kǒu fú〈成〉be genuinely convinced; admit sb.'s superiority sincerely

【心明眼亮】xīn míng yǎn liàng〈成〉be keen in judgment

【心狠】xīnhěn (形) cruel; brutal

【心思】xīnsi (名) ❶ thought; idea: 看出别人的~ read sb.'s mind ❷ thinking: 白费~ waste one's efforts ❸ state of mind; mood: 没~去 not feel like going; not in the mood to go

【心急】xīnjí (形) impatient; short-tempered

【心计】xīnjì (名) calculation; fore-thought

【心神不定】xīn shén bù dìng 〈成〉 be restless; feel perturbed

【心律】xīnlǜ (名) 〈医〉 rhythm of the heart; palpitations; heartbeats: ~不齐 irregular heartbeats; heartbeat irregularities

【心胸】xīnxiōng (名) breadth of mind: ~开阔 broad-minded / ~狭窄 narrow-minded

【心病】xīnbìng (名) ❶ worry; anxiety ❷ secret concern; sensitive point; trauma

【心疼】xīnténg (动) ❶ love dearly ❷ make one's heart ache

【心悦诚服】xīn yuè chéng fú 〈成〉 admire sb. in all sincerity; be thoroughly convinced

【心得】xīndé (名) what one learns from one's study or work; appreciation

【心悸】xīnjì (名) 〈医〉 palpitation

【心理】xīnlǐ (名) psychology; mentality: ~学家 psychologist

【心情】xīnqíng (名) state of mind; mood: ~愉快 in a happy frame of mind

【心软】xīnruǎn (形) tender-hearted; soft-hearted

【心术】xīnshù (名) intention; motive: 他~不正. His heart is not in its right place.

【心细】xīnxì (形) careful; cautious

【心虚】xīnxū (形) ❶ with a guilty conscience ❷ lacking in confidence

【心眼儿】xīnyǎnr (名) ❶ bottom of one's heart: 一个~工作 work whole-heartedly ❷ intention: ~好 kind-hearted; good-natured ❸ intelligence; cleverness: 有~ be smart ❹ breadth of mind: ~小 narrow-minded

【心硬】xīnyìng (形) hard-hearted; callous

【心寒】xīnhán (形) bitterly disappointed

【心焦】xīnjiāo (形) anxious; troubled

【心绞痛】xīnjiǎotòng (名) 〈医〉 angina pectoris

【心爱】xīn'ài (形) beloved; treasured

【心肠】xīncháng (名) heart: 好~ have a kind heart

【心烦】xīnfán (形) annoyed; upset

【心意】xīnyì (名) ❶ kindly feelings: 作为我们的一点~ as a token of our regard ❷ intention; purpose

【心腹】xīnfù Ⅰ(名) trusted subordinate; trusted follower Ⅱ(形) confidential: ~话 confidential talk

【心腹之患】xīn fù zhī huàn 〈成〉 hidden grave danger (within an organization, country, etc.)

【心里】xīnli (副) in the heart; in the mind: 记在~ keep in mind

【心里话】xīnlihuà (名) one's innermost thoughts and feelings

【心慈手软】xīn cí shǒu ruǎn 〈成〉 soft and kind-hearted

【心慌】xīnhuāng (形) confounded; flustered

【心慌意亂】xīn huāng yì luàn〈成〉all in a flutter; nervous and flustered

【心照不宣】xīn zhào bù xuān〈成〉have a tacit understanding

【心亂如麻】xīn luàn rú má〈成〉be much confused and perplexed; have one's mind all in a tangle

【心猿意馬】xīn yuán yì mǎ〈成〉feel restless and waver in purpose

【心電圖】xīndiàntú(名)〈醫〉electrocardiogram

【心酸】xīnsuān(形)grieved; sad

【心態】xīntài(名)mentality; psychology; state of mind

【心境】xīnjìng(名)state of mind; mood

【心領神會】xīn lǐng shén huì〈成〉take the hint; understand tacitly

【心滿意足】xīn mǎn yì zú〈成〉be fully satisfied; rest content

【心潮澎湃】xīn cháo péng pài〈成〉filled with excitement; feel an upsurge of emotion

【心機】xīnjī(名)scheming: 枉費~。One's schemes will come to naught.

【心頭】xīntóu(名)heart; mind: 銘刻~ engraved in one's mind

【心曠神怡】xīn kuàng shén yí〈成〉feel relaxed and happy; be in a cheerful frame of mind

【心願】xīnyuàn(名)desire; wish; aspiration

【心懷鬼胎】xīn huái guǐ tāi〈成〉harbour evil designs; have ulterior motives

【心臟】xīnzàng(名)heart: ~病 heart disease; heart trouble

【心驚膽戰】xīn jīng dǎn zhàn〈成〉shudder with fright; tremble with terror

【心靈】xīnlíng Ⅰ(形)clever; alert Ⅱ(名)heart; spirit

必 bì Ⅰ(副)certainly; definitely; necessarily: 未～可靠 not necessarily authentic (reliable) Ⅱ(動)must; be bound to: ～讀書籍 required reading

【必不可少】bì bù kě shǎo(形)indispensable; absolutely necessary

【必由之路】bì yóu zhī lù〈成〉the only path: 成功的~ the way to success

【必定】bìdìng(副)certainly; bound to; without fail: ~成功 be sure to succeed

【必要】bìyào Ⅰ(形)necessary; indispensable; essential Ⅱ(名)need

【必要性】bìyàoxìng(名)necessity

【必要前提】bìyào qiántí(名)prerequisite; precondition

【必修課】bìxiūkè(名)requirement; required (compulsory) course

【必恭必敬】bì gōng bì jìng〈成〉be all reverence

【必然】bìrán Ⅰ(形)inevitable; necessary: ~規律 inexorable law Ⅱ(副)surely; certainly; be bound to Ⅲ(名)necessity

【必須】bìxū(動)must; have (got) to; should

【必需】bìxū(形)essential; necessary; vital

【必需品】bìxūpǐn(名)necessity: 生活~ necessaries of life

忘 wàng(動)❶ forget ❷ overlook: ~了另一方面 lose sight of the other side

【忘乎所以】wàng hū suǒ yǐ〈成〉forget oneself

【忘年交】wàngniánjiāo〈名〉 very good friends regardless of disparity in age

【忘我】wàngwǒ〈动〉be selfless

【忘记】wàngjì〈动〉forget; neglect

【忘恩负义】wàng ēn fù yì〈成〉 be ungrateful

【忘掉】wàngdiào〈动〉forget

忙 máng Ⅰ〈形〉busy: 整天～家务 be fully occupied with household chores / ～得不可开交 be as busy as a bee Ⅱ〈动〉hurry: 别～! No hurry!

【忙人】mángrén〈名〉busy person

【忙中有错】máng zhōng yǒu cuò〈成〉 haste makes waste

【忙于】mángyú〈动〉be busy with

【忙活】mánghuo〈动〉〈口〉be busy: 这几個小淘氣真夠媽媽～的。These naughty children keep their mother busy all day.

【忙裏偷閑】máng lǐ tōu xián〈成〉 snatch a moment's leisure from a busy schedule

【忙碌】mánglù〈动〉go about one's business all day; be busily engaged

【忙亂】mángluàn〈动〉hustle and bustle

忖 cǔn〈动〉guess; think over

【忖度】cǔnduó〈动〉speculate

志 zhì Ⅰ〈名〉❶ will; aspiration: 壮～ lofty ideal ❷ records; annals: 日～ daily record ❸ mark; sign: 友誼日益增長的標～ sign of growing friendship Ⅱ〈动〉record; keep in mind

【志士】zhìshì〈名〉people of high resolve and moral integrity: 愛國～ patriot

【志大才疏】zhì dà cái shū〈成〉 have great ambitions but no real talent

【志向】zhìxiàng〈名〉ideal; aspiration

【志同道合】zhì tóng dào hé〈成〉 cherish common ideals and hold identical views

【志哀】zhì'āi〈动〉do sth. as a sign of mourning

【志氣】zhìqì〈名〉aspiration; ambition; resolve: ～昂揚 have a lofty aspiration

【志趣】zhìqù〈名〉inclination; natural bent

【志願】zhìyuàn Ⅰ〈名〉wish; will; aspiration: 違反個人的～作出這樣的決定 make such a decision against one's own will Ⅱ〈动〉volunteer: 暑期内～参加勞動 volunteer manual labour during the summer vacation

忌 jì〈动〉❶ be jealous of; be envious of: ～恨 be eaten up with jealousy and hatred ❷ avoid: ～過度勞累和過度激動 avoid overexertion and overexcitement ❸ give up: ～煙 give up smoking

【忌辰】jìchén〈名〉anniversary of the death of one's parent, ancestor, or any celebrated public figure

【忌妒】jìdu〈动〉be jealous of; envy

【忌憚】jìdàn〈名〉fear; apprehension: 肆無～ act shamelessly and unscrupulously

【忌諱】jìhuì Ⅰ〈名〉taboo: 小心别犯了他的～。Take care not to violate his taboo. Ⅱ〈动〉❶ avoid as a taboo: 這裏～用這個字 This word is taboo here. ❷ refrain from doing sth. to avoid possible consequences: 寫文章最～空洞無物。In writing, the most dangerous thing is lack of substance.

忍 rěn（动）endure; tolerate: 一再~ bear and forbear / ~住這口氣 restrain one's anger

【忍心】rěnxīn（动）have the heart to: 我不~把這一不幸消息告訴她。I didn't have the heart to break the sad news to her.

【忍不住】rěnbuzhù（动）cannot help (doing sth.): 他疼得一叫起來了。He couldn't help screaming with pain.

【忍冬】rěndōng（名）〈植〉honeysuckle

【忍受】rěnshòu（动）endure; stand: 無法~ unbearable

【忍耐】rěnnài（动）restrain one's feeling; be patient

【忍俊不禁】rěn jùn bù jīn〈成〉cannot suppress a smile

【忍氣吞聲】rěn qì tūn shēng〈成〉suffer in silence; swallow an insult

【忍辱負重】rěn rǔ fù zhòng〈成〉suffer humiliation willingly in an attempt to fulfil an important mission

【忍無可忍】rěn wú kě rěn〈成〉be driven beyond endurance; reach the limit of one's endurance

【忍讓】rěnràng（动）exercise forbearance; be yielding

忐 tǎn

【忐忑】tǎntè（形）perturbed; uneasy

忭 biàn（形）happy; glad: 不勝欣~ be overjoyed

忱 chén（名）true sentiment; sincerity: 愛國熱~ patriotic enthusiasm

快 kuài Ⅰ（形）❶ fast; speedy: ~遞 express delivery ❷ (of a knife, axe or scissors) sharp ❸ (of mind) quick ❹ straight-forward: ~嘴 outspoken person ❺ happy; glad: 不~ displeased Ⅱ（副）❶ soon: 天~晴了。It will soon clear up. ❷ fast; quickly: 跑得~ run fast Ⅲ（动）hurry: ~點! Hurry up!

【快刀斬亂麻】kuài dāo zhǎn luàn má〈成〉cut the Gordian knot; act decisively to resolve all complicated issues

【快車】kuàichē（名）express train or bus

【快門】kuàimén（名）〈攝〉shutter

【快板兒】kuàibǎnr（名）*kuaibanr*, rhythmic monologue to the accompaniment of bamboo clappers (a form of Chinese folk entertainment)

【快活】kuàihuo（形）happy; joyful; merry

【快要】kuàiyào（动）be about to; be going to: 勝利~到來。Success is in sight.

【快馬加鞭】kuài mǎ jiā biān〈成〉at top speed

【快報】kuàibào（名）(wall) bulletin; poster

【快艇】kuàitǐng（名）speed-boat; motorboat

【快樂】kuàilè（形）happy; gratified

【快餐】kuàicān（名）fast food; snack

忸 niǔ

【忸怩】niǔní（形）bashful; shy

忡 chōng

【忡忡】chōngchōng（形）careworn: 憂心~ weighed down with anxieties

忠 zhōng （形）loyal; faithful; devoted

【忠心耿耿】zhōng xīn gěng gěng 〈成〉be devoted heart and soul (to a friend or cause)

【忠告】zhōnggào （名）advice; exhortation

【忠言逆耳】zhōng yán nì ěr 〈成〉good advice often sounds unpleasant to the ear

【忠贞】zhōngzhēn （形）loyal and steadfast: ～不渝 unswervingly loyal

【忠厚】zhōnghòu （形）honest and kind

【忠诚】zhōngchéng （形）faithful; loyal: ～老實 faithful and trustworthy

【忠實】zhōngshí （形）faithful; devoted: ～可靠 faithful and reliable

念 niàn I （动）think of; miss: 留～ keep sth. as a souvenir II （名）thought; idea: 信～ belief; faith

【念物】niànwù （名）souvenir; keepsake; memento

【念念不忘】niàn niàn bù wàng 〈成〉always keep in mind; never forget to mention; always talk about

【念頭】niàntou （名）thought; idea

忽 hū I （动）neglect; overlook; ignore II （副）suddenly

【忽而】hū'ér （副）alternately; by turns: 雪～下，～停. It snowed intermittently.

【忽略】hūlüè （动）neglect; overlook

【忽視】hūshì （动）ignore; overlook; neglect

【忽然】hūrán （副）suddenly; all of a sudden

怦 pēng （象）rhythm of the pounding of one's heart: 他激動得心～～跳。His heart throbbed with excitement.

怯 qiè （形）timid; chicken-hearted

【怯弱】qièruò （形）timorous and soft

【怯陣】qièzhèn （动）feel frightened before going into battle; get nervous before a big audience

【怯場】qièchǎng （动）have stage fright; feel nervous before a large audience

【怯懦】qiènuò （形）cowardly

怵 chù （动）fear; be apprehensive: 令人～心 make one tremble with fear

怙 hù （动）❶ rely on ❷ persist

【怙惡不悛】hù è bù quān 〈成〉persist in evil and refuse to mend

怖 bù （动）fear: 令人感到恐～ be terrifying

怪 guài I （形）strange; unusual II （动）blame: 我不好。I am to blame. III （副）quite; very: ～不好意思的 feel somewhat embarrassed IV （名）monster; demon: 鬼～ demon

【怪不得】guài bu de （副）no wonder: ～他没起牀，他昨夜十一點才睡。No wonder he is still in bed; he stayed up until eleven last night.

【怪異】guàiyì （形）strange; weird; eerie

【怪罪】guàizuì （动）blame

【怪誕】guàidàn （形）strange; fantastic: ～不經的故事 a tall tale

【怪僻】guàipì （形）odd: 脾氣～ eccentric

【怪模怪様】guài mú guài yàng（形）outlandish in manners; bizarre

【怪癖】guàipǐ（名）odd habit

怛 dá（形）sad; miserable

怏 yàng

【怏怏不樂】yàng yàng bù lè（動）feel sad; be unhappy

性 xìng Ⅰ（名）❶ nature; character: 生～懶惰 be lazy by nature / 没有人～ be inhuman ❷ sex: 兩～ both sexes ❸〈語〉gender Ⅱ [used as a suffix to indicate a property or characteristic]: 複雜～ complication / 嚴重～ gravity

【性生活】xìngshēnghuó（名）sexual life

【性交】xìngjiāo（名）sexual intercourse

【性別】xìngbié（名）sex

【性命】xìngmìng（名）life: ～攸關 a matter of life and death

【性急】xìngjí（形）impatient; impetuous

【性病】xìngbìng（名）venereal disease (V. D.)

【性格】xìnggé（名）nature; disposition: ～内(外)向 be introverted (extroverted)

【性能】xìngnéng（名）performance; function; property

【性情】xìngqíng（名）temperament; temper: ～古怪 be eccentric

【性感】xìnggǎn（形）sexy

【性慾】xìngyù（名）sexual desire

【性質】xìngzhì（名）nature; character: 具有政治～ of a political nature

【性器官】xìngqìguān（名）sexual organs; genitals

【性關係】xìngguānxi（名）sexual relations

怕 pà（動）❶ be afraid of; fear ❷ I'm afraid; perhaps: 天～要下雨。It's going to rain, I'm afraid.

【怕生】pàshēng（動）(of a child) be shy with strangers

【怕死】pàsǐ（動）fear death

【怕事】pàshì（動）be afraid of getting into trouble; be afraid to commit oneself

【怕羞】pàxiū（形）shy; bashful

怡 yí（形）〈書〉joyful

【怡然自得】yí rán zì dé（形）happy and gratified; selfsatisfied

思 sī Ⅰ（動）❶ think; reflect; ponder ❷ miss; long for Ⅱ（名）thought; thinking: 鄉～ homesickness

【思考】sīkǎo（思量 sīliang）（動）turn sth. over in one's mind; consider: 認真～問題 give serious consideration to the problem

【思念】sīniàn（動）miss; think of fondly

【思索】sīsuǒ（動）consider carefully in order to find a solution: ～問題 examine the question carefully

【思想】sīxiǎng（名）thought; thinking; ideology: 偉大的～家 a great thinker

【思路】sīlù（名）line of thinking: 沿着這個～ follow this line of thinking / 他的～被打斷了。His train of thought was interrupted.

【思維】sīwéi Ⅰ（名）thought; thinking Ⅱ（動）think; ponder

【思潮】sīcháo（名）❶ current of

the time; trend: 文學 ～ literary current / 社會 ～ social trend ❷ one's thoughts: ～起伏, 憂慮萬端 feel a surge of disquieting thoughts

【思慮】sīlǜ〈動〉ponder over; consider: ～周到 consider carefully

怎 zěn〈代〉how; why: ～辦? What is to be done?

【怎麼】zěnme〈代〉❶ [used as an interrogative]: 他～不來? Why didn't he come? / 你～哭了? What are you crying for? / 這字～讀? How do you pronounce this word? ❷ [used to indicate the nature, condition, manner in general]: 你該～辦就～辦。Do what you ought to do. ❸ [used in the negative to indicate inadequacy]: 水不～多了。There isn't much water left. / 我不～認識他。I am not well acquainted with him.

【怎麼樣】zěnmeyàng〈代〉❶ how: 這部電影～? How do you like the film? ❷ [an euphemism used in the negative]: 他的法語不～。His French is not so good.

【怎樣】zěnyàng〈代〉❶ how: 你近來～? How have you been keeping recently? ❷ [used to indicate the nature, condition, manner in general]: 這裏沒有多大變化, 人們過去～生活, 現在還是～生活。There has been little change here. The people live the way they used to.

怱 cōng〈副〉hurriedly

【怱忙】cōngmáng〈副〉in a hurry: ～離開 hurry off

【怱怱】cōngcōng〈副〉in a hurry

【怱促】cōngcù〈副〉in haste: 走得太～了 leave in a terrible hurry

急 jí I〈形〉❶ rash; worried: ～不可待 seem to be in a tearing hurry ❷ urgent; pressing; imperative: ～事 urgent business; matter of great urgency / 緊～ state of emergency ❸ annoyed; angry: 他有點～了。He went into a huff. II〈副〉fast; swiftly: ～轉彎 take a sudden turn III〈名〉emergency; urgency: 告～ appeal for emergency help IV〈動〉be ready to help: ～人之急 always ready to help people in need

【急中生智】jí zhōng shēng zhì〈成〉hit upon a wise move to get out of trouble

【急切】jíqiè I〈副〉❶ impatiently; urgently: ～需要幫助 be in dire need of aid ❷ in a hurry II〈形〉impatient; anxious

【急件】jíjiàn〈名〉urgent paper; urgent mail for immediate delivery

【急忙】jímáng〈副〉hurriedly: ～離去 leave in a hurry

【急如星火】jí rú xīng huǒ〈成〉so urgent as to require immediate attention

【急迫】jípò〈形〉pressing; imperative

【急性子】jíxìngzi〈形〉impatient: 他是個～的人。He's an impetuous man.

【急於】jíyú〈動〉be anxious to; be impatient to: 不要～下結論。Don't draw hasty conclusions.

【急促】jícù〈形〉❶ hurried; hasty: ～的敲門聲 rapid knocks on the door ❷ (of time) pressing: 我們的時間很～。We have very little time to spare.

【急剎車】jí shāchē〈動〉❶ put on the brake suddenly ❷ bring to an emergency halt

【急風暴雨】jí fēng bào yǔ〈成〉tempest; storm

【急流】jíliú（名）rapids; rushing current

【急流勇退】jí liú yǒng tuì〈成〉retire from politics when one reaches the zenith of one's power

【急起直追】jí qǐ zhí zhuī〈成〉lose no time in trying to catch up

【急速】jísù（副）rapidly

【急救】jíjiù（名）first aid

【急診】jízhěn（名）emergency treatment; emergency care

【急腹症】jífùzhèng（名）〈醫〉acute abdominal disease; acute abdomen

【急需】jíxū Ⅰ（動）need badly：~ 處理 cry out for immediate attention Ⅱ（名）crying need

【急劇】jíjù（形）rapid; sudden; drastic：局勢~惡化. The situation took an abrupt turn for the worse.

【急轉直下】jí zhuǎn zhí xià〈成〉（of a situation）take a sudden turn

【急躁】jízào（形）❶ fidgety ❷ impatient; imprudent

怨 yuàn Ⅰ（名）hatred; enmity：宿~ inveterate hatred Ⅱ（動）blame; complain：埋~ complain; grumble

【怨天尤人】yuàn tiān yóu rén〈成〉blame heaven and all people on earth except oneself

【怨言】yuànyán（名）grumble; complaint：毫無~ without complaint

【怨恨】yuànhèn（名）resentment; ill will; hatred

【怨氣】yuànqì（名）grudge; complaint; resentment：並無~ bear no grudge

【怨聲載道】yuàn shēng zài dào〈成〉hear voices of discontent everywhere

怠 dài（形）lazy; slack

【怠工】dàigōng Ⅰ（動）go slow; stage a slowdown Ⅱ（名）slowdown

【怠惰】dàiduò（形）lazy

【怠慢】dàimàn（動）cold-shoulder：~客人 slight a visitor

怒 nù Ⅰ（名）wrath; fury：~火滿腔 boil with fury Ⅱ（副）furiously; vigorously：心花~放 be wild with joy

【怒火】nùhuǒ（名）rage：~ 中燒 burn with anger

【怒不可遏】nù bù kě è〈成〉be unable to restrain one's fury

【怒吼】nùhǒu（動）roar; howl; bellow

【怒氣】nùqì（名）anger; fury; wrath

【怒族】Nùzú（名）the Nu nationality

【怒號】nùháo（動）roar angrily

【怒潮】nùcháo（名）raging tide

【怒衝衝】nùchōngchōng（副）in a fury; angrily

【怒髮衝冠】nù fà chōng guān〈成〉bristle with anger; fly into a towering rage

【怒濤】nùtāo（名）raging waves

恃 shì（動）rely（on）; depend（on）

【恃強凌弱】shì qiáng líng ruò〈成〉presume on one's strength to bully the weak

恒 héng（形）❶ permanent; lasting ❷ usual; constant

【恒心】héngxīn（名）perseverance; constancy

【恒星】héngxīng（名）〈天〉（fixed）star

【恒溫】héngwēn（名）constant temperature

【恒齒】héngchǐ(名)〈生理〉permanent tooth

恢 huī(形)extensive; vast

【恢復】huīfù(動)restore; recover; resume:～外交關係 resume diplomatic relations

恨 hèn Ⅰ(動)hate Ⅱ(名)regret:遺～ eternal regret

【恨事】hènshì(名)regrettable occurrence

【恨鐵不成鋼】hèn tiě bù chéng gāng〈成〉be exasperated with sb. for his failing to make desired progress

恍 huǎng(副)seemingly:～如昨日 feel as if it were yesterday

【恍惚】huǎnghū Ⅰ(形)in a trance; absent-minded Ⅱ(副)dimly; faintly:～聽見 seem to have heard

【恍然大悟】huǎng rán dà wù〈成〉be suddenly enlightened

恫 dòng

【恫嚇】dònghè(動)threaten; intimidate

恰 qià Ⅰ(形)proper; suitable Ⅱ(副)just; exactly:～在那個關鍵的時刻他不見了。It was just at this juncture that he was absent.

【恰巧】qiàqiǎo(副)by chance; as it happens:他～在場。He happened to be on the spot.

【恰好】qiàhǎo(副)just right; just in time

【恰如其分】qià rú qí fèn〈成〉appropriate; no more and no less

【恰當】qiàdàng(形)appropriate; suitable

恬 tián(形)❶ tranquil; serene:～靜 tranquil; quiet ❷ unruffled; unperturbed

【恬不知恥】tián bù zhī chǐ〈成〉be impudent; have no sense of shame

恪 kè(副)prudently and respectfully

【恪守】kèshǒu(動)faithfully adhere to

恙 yàng(名)illness

恣 zì(形)unbridled; unrestrained

【恣意】zìyì(形)wilful; wanton; unscrupulous

恥 chǐ(名)shame; humiliation

【恥辱】chǐrǔ(名)shame; disgrace; ignominy

【恥笑】chǐxiào(動)ridicule; scoff at; jeer

恐 kǒng Ⅰ(名)terror; apprehension Ⅱ(動)threaten; cow Ⅲ(副)perhaps:～不可靠。It's perhaps unreliable.

【恐怖】kǒngbù(名)terror:～主義 terrorism

【恐怕】kǒngpà(副)❶ I'm afraid:～他不會同意。I'm afraid he won't agree. ❷ perhaps; probably

【恐慌】kǒnghuāng Ⅰ(動)be seized with panic Ⅱ(名)panic; alarm

【恐龍】kǒnglóng(名)dinosaur

【恐嚇】kǒnghè(動)threaten; intimidate

恭 gōng(形)respectful; reverent:～聽 listen respectfully / 玩世不～ be cynical

【恭賀】gōnghè(動)congratulate:

~新禧 Happy New Year

【恭順】gōngshùn（形）respectful and obedient

【恭喜】gōngxǐ（动）congratulate

【恭敬】gōngjìng（形）courteous（to elders and guests）; respectful

【恭維】gōngwéi（动）flatter

【恭謹】gōngjǐn（形）respectful and cautious

恩 ēn（名）favour; kindness

【恩人】ēnrén（名）benefactor

【恩怨】ēnyuàn（名）gratitude and grievance（usu. referring to the latter）: 不計個人～ put personal grievances aside; not be swayed by personal feelings

【恩情】ēnqíng（名）true kindness

【恩將仇報】ēn jiāng chóu bào〈成〉return evil for good; repay kindness with malevolence

【恩愛】ēn'ài（名）conjugal affection; matrimonial bliss

【恩賜】ēncì I（动）favour; charity II（名）bestow gifts

【恩德】ēndé（恩典 ēndiǎn; 恩惠 ēnhuì）（名）kindness; favour

息 xī I（名）❶ breath: 奄奄一～ at one's last gasp ❷ news; message: 消～ news ❸ interest: 月～ monthly interest ❹ rest II（动）❶ stop; cease: ～兵 stop fighting ❷ grow; multiply: 休養生～ recuperate and multiply

【息事寧人】xī shì níng rén〈成〉❶ bring about a reconciliation between two disputing parties; mediate a settlement ❷ make concessions to avoid getting into further trouble

【息怒】xīnù（动）appease sb.'s anger; calm sb. down

【息息相關】xī xī xiāng guān〈成〉be closely related; be intimately bound up with

恕 shù I（动）forgive; excuse; condone: 不能饒～的錯誤 unpardonable mistake II（套）please pardon me(us) for: ～我直言。Forgive me for speaking bluntly.

【恕不奉陪】shù bù fèng péi〈套〉excuse me（for not keeping you company）

悦 yuè I（形）happy; merry; pleased: 喜～ joyous II（动）please; delight

【悦目】yuèmù（形）pleasant to the eye; pleasant

【悦耳】yuè'ěr（形）pleasant to the ear; melodious

【悦服】yuèfú（动）obey cheerfully

悖 bèi（形）❶ contrary to ❷ erroneous; absurd; perverse

【悖入悖出】bèi rù bèi chū〈成〉ill-gotten, ill-spent

【悖謬】bèimiù（形）absurd; perverse; preposterous

悚 sǒng（形）horrified

悟 wù（动）realize; understand

【悟性】wùxìng（名）comprehension; ability to understand

悄 qiāo

【悄悄】qiāoqiāo（副）stealthily; quietly: ～地走掉 sneak away; steal away

悍 hàn（形）❶ intrepid ❷ fierce; brutal

【悍然】hànrán（副）outrageously: ～不顧 in utter disregard of

悔 huǐ

【悔改】huǐgǎi（动）repent and mend one's ways

【悔恨】huǐhèn（动）regret deeply

【悔悟】huǐwù（动）realize one's error and feel repentant

【悔过】huǐguò（动）be repentant

【悔罪】huǐzuì（动）show penitence

悛 quān（动）repent; mend one's ways：怙恶不～ persist in doing evil and refuse to mend one's ways

患 huàn Ⅰ（名）❶ trouble; disaster ❷ worry：忧～ anxiety Ⅱ（动）contract; suffer from：～癌症 suffer from cancer

【患者】huànzhě（名）patient; victim of a disease

【患病】huànbìng（动）suffer from an illness

【患得患失】huàn dé huàn shī〈成〉worry about personal gains and losses

【患难】huànnàn（名）hardship; adversity：同甘苦，共～ share joys and sorrows

悉 xī（动）know; learn：欣～ glad to know; pleased to learn

【悉心】xīxīn（动）concentrate one's attention on; be entirely devoted to：～工作 throw oneself into the work heart and soul

悠 yōu Ⅰ（形）❶ distant; remote ❷ leisurely Ⅱ（动）swing; sway

【悠久】yōujiǔ（形）long; age-old

【悠然】yōurán（形）carefree and leisurely：～自得 be carefree and self-satisfied

【悠闲】yōuxián（形）leisurely

【悠扬】yōuyáng（形）（of music）melodious

【悠荡】yōudàng（动）swing; sway

您 nín（代）〈敬〉you

惋 wǎn

【惋惜】wǎnxī（动）feel sorry; sympathetic; regret：他如此浪费时间，我深為～。I am sorry that he is wasting his time like that.

悴 cuì（形）❶ worried ❷ gaunt

惦 diàn（动）have at heart

【惦记】diànjì（惦念 diànniàn）（动）be concerned about; worry about

情 qíng（名）❶ feeling; emotion：母～ affection between mother and son ❷ favour; mercy：不留～ show no mercy ❸ love; passion：妇 mistress ❹ situation; condition：军～ military situation

【情人】qíngrén（名）sweetheart; lover

【情分】qíngfèn（名）friendship; affection

【情夫】qíngfū（名）lover

【情不自禁】qíng bù zì jìn（动）cannot control oneself：他～地搂抱她。He was seized with a sudden impulse and took her in his arms.

【情由】qíngyóu（名）hows and whys

【情有可原】qíng yǒu kě yuán〈成〉pardonable; forgivable

【情形】qíngxíng（名）situation; condition

【情况】qíngkuàng（名）situation; circumstances

【情投意合】qíng tóu yì hé〈成〉be congenial to each other; be completely in agreement

【情侣】qínglǚ（名）lovers; sweethearts

【情面】qíngmiàn（名）sensibilities; feelings: 顾全～ take care not to offend sb.'s feelings

【情急智生】qíng jí zhì shēng〈成〉hit upon a bright idea when the situation is getting desperate

【情书】qíngshū（名）love letter

【情理】qínglǐ（名）reason; sense: ～难容 contrary to reason and the code of social behaviour

【情报】qíngbào（名）information; intelligence

【情景】qíngjǐng（名）scene; sight: 难忘的～ unforgettable scene

【情感】qínggǎn（名）feeling; emotion

【情节】qíngjié（名）❶（of a novel, etc.）plot ❷ circumstances（of an event）

【情义】qíngyì（名）natural affection as between relatives, friends, etc.

【情意】qíngyì（名）good will; affection

【情歌】qínggē（名）love song

【情敌】qíngdí（名）rival in love

【情调】qíngdiào（名）mood: 悲观主义的～ pessimistic mood

【情趣】qíngqù（名）❶ temperament; natural bent ❷ taste; appeal; interest

【情绪】qíngxù（名）❶ state of mind; mood: 急躁～ impetuosity ❷ moodiness; depression: 她在闹～。She has fallen into a bad mood.

【情谊】qíngyì（名）friendship; affection

【情欲】qíngyù（名）lust; sexual desire

【情操】qíngcāo（名）noble sentiment: 革命志士的～ the noble sentiment of a devoted revolutionary

【情愿】qíngyuàn（动）❶ be willing to ❷ prefer; would rather: 他～走着去。He would rather go on foot.

怅 chàng（形）disappointed

【怅惘】chàngwǎng（形）depressed

惜 xī（动）❶ cherish; care for: 不～任何代价 at any price ❷ feel sorry: 痛～ deeply regret

【惜力】xīlì（动）spare oneself; not try one's best: 不～ spare no effort

【惜别】xībié（动）part reluctantly

悼 dào（动）mourn

【悼念】dàoniàn（动）mourn; lament

【悼词】dàocí（名）funeral oration

惘 wǎng（动）be disappointed

【惘然】wǎngrán（形）depressed; dejected

惕 tì（形）cautious; wary: 日夜～属 be on the alert day and night

悸 jì（动）（of the heart）palpitate: 心有余～ feel the lingering tremors of the heart

惆 chóu（形）rueful; dejected

【惆怅】chóuchàng（名）melancholy; dejection

惟 wéi（副）only; alone

【惟一】wéiyī（形）sole; only: ～的抉择 the only possible choice; Hobson's choice

【惟有】wéiyǒu（副）only; alone: 大家都愿意去，～他不愿意去。Everybody is ready to go except him.

【惟利是图】wéi lì shì tú〈成〉〈贬〉seek nothing but profit; be only interested in profit; profit before everything

【惟命是聽】wéi mìng shì tīng (唯命是從 wéi mìng cóng) 〈成〉be at sb.'s beck and call

【惟恐】wéikǒng (連) for fear of: ~ 走錯了一步棋 for fear of making a false move

【惟獨】wéidú (副) only: ~ 他没有出席。He alone was absent.

悲 bēi I (形) ❶ sad; melancholy ❷ merciful: 發慈 ~ have pity; be merciful II (名) sorrow: 樂極生 ~。When joy reaches the extreme, sorrow is in the wake. III (動) lament; deplore; pity: ~天憫人 lament the corruption of social morals and pity the suffering multitude

【悲壯】bēizhuàng (形) sad but stirring

【悲哀】bēi'āi I (名) grief; sorrow; sadness II (形) sorrowful; woeful

【悲痛】bēitòng (形) painfully unhappy; grieved

【悲喜交集】bēi xǐ jiāo jí 〈成〉with a mixture of joy and sorrow

【悲傷】bēishāng (形) sad; grievous; sorrowful

【悲鳴】bēimíng (動) wail; whine; make a plaintive cry

【悲嘆】bēitàn (動) bemoan; bewail; sigh with sadness

【悲慘】bēicǎn (形) tragic; pitiful; pathetic

【悲歌】bēigē I (名) song of lamentation; elegy II (動) sing fervently solemn songs

【悲劇】bēijù (名) tragedy

【悲憤】bēifèn I (名) bitter resentment II (形) sad and indignant

【悲歡離合】bēi huān lí hé 〈成〉meetings and partings, joys and sorrows

【悲觀】bēiguān (形) pessimistic: ~ 失望 be plunged into despair

【悲觀主義】bēiguān zhǔyì (名) pessimism

惠 huì (名) ❶ favour; benefit ❷ (Huì) a surname

【惠存】huìcún (動) 〈敬〉please keep this as a memento

【惠臨】huìlín (名) 〈敬〉your gracious presence

惡 è I (名) evil; crime II (形) ❶ evil; vile ❷ brutal; fierce
see also wù

【惡人】èrén (名) villain

【惡化】èhuà (動) deteriorate; worsen

【惡劣】èliè (形) bad; evil: ~環境 dreadful circumstances

【惡有惡報】è yǒu è bào 〈成〉evil is rewarded with evil; sow the wind and reap the whirlwind

【惡作劇】èzuòjù (名) practical joke; mischief

【惡性】èxìng (形) malignant; vicious: ~腫瘤 malignant tumour; cancer

【惡果】èguǒ (名) adverse effect; disastrous consequence

【惡毒】èdú (形) vicious; malicious: ~誹謗 venomous slander

【惡臭】èchòu (名) stink

【惡習】èxí (名) bad habit

【惡貫滿盈】è guàn mǎn yíng 〈成〉be guilty of countless crimes and fully deserve damnation

【惡棍】ègùn (名) ruffian

【惡感】 ègǎn (名) resentment; ill will

【惡意】 èyì (名) malice; malevolence

【惡夢】 èmèng (名) nightmare

【惡霸】 èbà (名) despot

【惡魔】 èmó (名) demon

惡 wù (動) hate; dislike: 厭 ～ detest
see also è

惑 huò (動) ❶ be puzzled; be perplexed: 大 ～ 不解 be greatly perplexed ❷ mislead; dupe: 造謠 ～ 衆 invent stories to misguide the public

悶 mēn I (形) stuffy; close: 屋子裏太 ～ 。 The room is a bit too close. II (動) cover closely: 把茶 ～ 一 ～ 。 Let the tea brew for a while.
see also mèn

【悶氣】 mēnqì (形) stuffy

【悶熱】 mēnrè (形) sultry; oppressively hot

【悶頭】 mēntóu (副) in sulky silence: ～ 抽煙 keep smoking in silence

【悶聲不響】 mēn shēng bù xiǎng (動) remain silent and sulky

悶 mèn (形) ❶ bored; vexed: ～ 坐着 sit bored ❷ tightly closed; airtight
see also mēn

【悶子車】 mènzichē (名) box wagon; boxcar

【悶氣】 mènqì (名) sulkiness; pent-up resentment: 生 ～ be in the sulks; nurse bottled-up resentment

【悶悶不樂】 mèn mèn bù lè 〈成〉 be in low spirits; feel bored

【悶雷】 mènléi (名) ❶ muffled thunder ❷ heavy blow

【悶葫蘆】 mènhúlu (名) puzzle: 他的話真是個 ～ 。 What he said is really a puzzle.

意 yì (名) ❶ meaning; idea: 大 ～ main idea ❷ wish; intention: 真 ～ one's real intention ❸ expectation: 不 ～ 在那裏碰到他 meet him there quite unexpectedly ❹ trace; suggestion: 寒 ～ a chill in the air

【意大利】 Yìdàlì (名) Italy: ～ 人 Italian / ～ 語 Italian (language)

【意中人】 yìzhōngrén (名) sweetheart

【意外】 yìwài I (名) accident II (形) unexpected: ～ 收穫 unexpected gains

【意向】 yìxiàng (名) intention: ～ 書 letter of intent

【意志】 yìzhì (名) will; determination

【意見】 yìjiàn (名) ❶ idea; view; opinion: 發表 ～ air one's opinion ❷ objection; complaint: 對旅行計劃有 ～ object to the itinerary

【意見簿】 yìjiànbù (名) customers' book; vistors' book; comment book

【意念】 yìniàn (名) idea; thought

【意味】 yìwèi I (動) imply; mean: 他的話 ～ 着什麼? What's implied in his remarks? II (名) ❶ implication; meaning ❷ overtone; touch: 諷刺 ～ a touch of irony

【意思】 yìsi (名) ❶ meaning; sense: 詞的 ～ the meaning of a word ❷ opinion; view: 我的 ～ 是這個問題明天再議。 To my mind, we can sleep on the question. ❸ token of gratitude or appreciation: 一點小 ～ a little gift as a token of one's appreciation ❹ interest; fun: 這本小

説一點～也没有。The novel is not interesting at all. ❺ touch; hint; sign: 有春天的～了。There is a hint of spring in the air.

【意料】yìliào（動）expect; anticipate: ～之外 contrary to one's expectation

【意氣】yìqì（名）❶ spirit; enthusiasm: ～風發 fired with boundless enthusiasm ❷ disposition; temperament: ～相投 have similar tastes; be temperamentally compatible ❸ personal feeling: ～用事 be swayed by personal feelings

【意想】yìxiǎng（動）imagine; expect

【意會】yìhuì（動）sense; comprehend

【意義】yìyì（名）❶ meaning; sense ❷ significance; importance: 具有重大～ be of great significance

【意境】yìjìng（名）artistic conception

【意圖】yìtú（名）intention

【意願】yìyuàn（名）wish; aspiration

【意識】yìshí Ⅰ（名）consciousness Ⅱ（動）be conscious of; realize

【意識形態】yìshí xíngtài（名）ideology

【意譯】yìyì（名）free translation

恽 Yùn（名）a surname

悒 qiè（動）be satisfied: 意願不～ feel somewhat displeased

【悒意】qièyì（動）feel pleased or gratified

惰 duò（形）lazy

【惰性】duòxìng（名）inertia

慨 kǎi（形）❶ indignant ❷ deeply moved ❸ generous; bountiful: ～允惠臨 kindly promise to come

【慨然】kǎirán（副）❶ with emotion: ～長嘆 heave a deep sigh ❷ generously: ～相贈，作爲紀念 be generous enough to give one sth. as a memento

【慨嘆】kǎitàn（動）sigh with deep feeling

側 cè（形）sad

【側隱】cèyǐn（名）pity; compassion: ～之心 compassion

惺 xīng

【惺忪】xīngsōng（形）with one's eyes still heavy with sleep

【惺惺】xīngxīng（形）clever

【惺惺作態】xīng xīng zuò tài〈成〉affected and insincere

愕 è（形）stunned; astonished

【愕然】èrán（形）astonished

愣 lèng Ⅰ（形）❶ dumb struck; astounded: 嚇得他發～。He was struck dumb with horror. ❷〈口〉reckless: 這小子真～。This chap is a real hothead. Ⅱ（副）recklessly

【愣頭愣腦】lèng tóu lèng nǎo〈口〉stupid; fool-hardy

愉 yú（形）pleased; happy; cheerful

【愉快】yúkuài（形）happy; cheerful: 心情～ be in a cheerful mood / ～的日子 pleasant days

愎 bì（形）wilful; perverse; stubborn: 剛～自用 self-opinionated; head-strong; turn a deaf ear to advice

惶 huáng（名）fear; anxiety: 驚～ alarmed; scared

【惶恐】huángkǒng（形）frightened; terrified

【惶惶】 huánghuáng（形）alarmed; wildly scared: ~不可终日 be in a state of perpetual anxiety; be on tenterhooks

【惶惑】 huánghuò（形）perplexed and alarmed

恼 nǎo（动）❶ be angry; be annoyed: 气~ be irritated ❷ be worried: 苦~ be vexed

【恼火】 nǎohuǒ（形）annoyed; irritated

【恼恨】 nǎohèn I（动）resent; hate II（名）hatred

【恼怒】 nǎonù（形）angry; enraged; exasperated

【恼羞成怒】 nǎo xiū chéng nù〈成〉feel ashamed of oneself and, as a result, fly into a rage

慈 cí（形）kind; compassionate: 心~ kindhearted

【慈母】 címǔ（名）(loving) mother

【慈祥】 cíxiáng（形）(usu. said of an elderly person) benign; kindly

【慈善】 císhàn（形）charitable; philanthropic: ~家 philanthropist

【慈悲】 cíbēi（名）mercy; pity

【慈爱】 cí'ài（名）affection（of the old for the young）

惹 rě（动）❶ cause; court; incur: ~许多麻烦 cause a good deal of trouble ❷ offend; provoke: 这人脾气大，~不得。This chap is quick-tempered. We can't afford to offend him.

【惹事】 rěshì（动）make trouble

【惹是生非】 rě shì shēng fēi〈成〉stir up controversy and create trouble

【惹祸】 rěhuò（动）get into trouble;

stir up trouble

想 xiǎng（动）❶ think: 敢~敢干。Dare to think and dare to act. / 我也这样~。That's what I think too. ❷ miss: 母亲~着远行的儿子。The mother missed her son who had gone on a long journey. ❸ want to; would like to: 他~去散步。He feels like going for a walk. ❹ suppose; reckon: 我~他会喜欢的。I reckon he would like it.

【想入非非】 xiǎng rù fēi fēi〈成〉indulge in fantastic ideas; daydream

【想不到】 xiǎng bu dào（形）unexpected: ~发生了这种事。We didn't expect that such a thing could happen.

【想不开】 xiǎng bu kāi（动）take things to heart

【想方设法】 xiǎng fāng shè fǎ〈成〉try every means; leave no stone unturned

【想必】 xiǎngbì（副）presumably; most probably: ~他不会来了。Most probably he won't come.

【想见】 xiǎngjiàn（动）infer; gather: 由此可以~，经济形势多么严峻。One can infer from this how grave the economic situation is.

【想来】 xiǎnglái（副）presumably

【想念】 xiǎngniàn（动）long to see again; miss

【想到】 xiǎngdào（动）think of; have at heart

【想法】 xiǎngfa（名）idea; opinion: 我同意你的~。I entirely agree with you.

【想家】 xiǎngjiā（动）be homesick

【想起】 xiǎngqǐ（动）remember; recall: ~过去的岁月 recall the past

days

【想通】xiǎngtōng（动）come round; straighten out one's thinking: 他 还在 还 没 ～。He is still not convinced.

【想望】xiǎngwàng（动）yearn for; desire

【想得开】xiǎng de kāi（动）look at the bright side of things; not take things to heart

【想象】xiǎngxiàng（动）imagine; fancy

【想象力】xiǎngxiànglì（名）imagination

【想当然】xiǎngdāngrán（动）take（sth.）for granted; assume（sth.）as a matter of course

感 gǎn Ⅰ（动）❶ feel; sense ❷ move; touch: 人至深 move one deeply ❸ be affected Ⅱ（名）sense; feeling: 自豪～ sense of pride

【感人肺腑】gǎn rén fèi fǔ（成）touch one's heart

【感化】gǎnhuà（动）（of a person's moral character or outlook on life）influence subtly

【感召】gǎnzhào（名）influence; call

【感光】gǎnguāng（名）〈摄〉sensitization

【感受】gǎnshòu Ⅰ（动）catch; be infected with Ⅱ（名）experience; impression

【感性】gǎnxìng（形）perceptual: ～认识 perceptual knowledge

【感官】gǎnguān（名）sense organ

【感冒】gǎnmào（动）cold Ⅱ（名）❶ catch a cold ❷ have a touch of flu

【感染】gǎnrǎn（动）❶ be infected with ❷ influence; infect

【感恩】gǎn'ēn（动）feel indebted

【感恩节】Gǎn'ēnjié（名）Thanksgiving Day

【感动】gǎndòng（动）move; touch: 故事深深地～了他。He was deeply moved by the story.

【感情】gǎnqíng（名）❶ feeling; emotion: 悲伤的～ a feeling of sadness ❷ affection

【感慨】gǎnkǎi（动）sigh deeply; sigh wistfully

【感想】gǎnxiǎng（名）impressions; reflections

【感叹】gǎntàn（动）sigh sadly; lament

【感叹号】gǎntànhào（名）〈语〉exclamation mark

【感激】gǎnjī（动）feel grateful

【感谢】gǎnxiè（动）thank; be grateful: ～不尽 cannot thank sb. enough

【感触】gǎnchù（名）thoughts and feelings

【感觉】gǎnjué Ⅰ（名）sense; feeling; perception Ⅱ（动）feel; sense

愚 yú Ⅰ（形）foolish; stupid: ～人节 All Fools' Day Ⅱ（动）fool; dupe

【愚弄】yúnòng（动）fool; dupe

【愚昧】yúmèi（形）ignorant

【愚笨】yúbèn（形）stupid; dull-witted; clumsy

【愚蠢】yúchǔn（形）foolish; stupid; silly

爱 ài Ⅰ（动）❶ love ❷ like; be fond of: 喜 ～ 唱 歌 be fond of singing ❸ cherish; treasure Ⅱ（名）love; affection Ⅲ（副）easily; readily; frequently: ～感冒 be liable to colds

【爱人】àirén（名）husband or wife;

sweetheart

【爱…不…】ài…bù… 〈口〉[used before reduplicated verbs, meaning 'do as you like']: 爱理不理 (of attitude) indifferent

【爱不释手】ài bù shì shǒu 〈成〉examine sth. with admiring fondness; be so delighted with an object that one is reluctant to part with it

【爱好】àihào I 〈名〉interest; hobby II 〈动〉be keen on; be fond of: ～者 fan; enthusiast; amateur

【爱克斯光】àikèsīguāng 〈名〉 X-ray: ～透视 X-ray examination

【爱面子】ài miànzi 〈动〉be intent on saving face; be afraid of losing face

【爱屋及乌】ài wū jí wū 〈成〉 love me, love my dog

【爱财如命】ài cái rú mìng 〈成〉 love money as if it were one's own life

【爱国】àiguó I 〈动〉love one's country II 〈形〉patriotic: ～心 patriotic sentiment; patriotism

【爱情】àiqíng 〈名〉love (between man and woman)

【爱惜】àixī 〈动〉make the best use of; use sparingly

【爱莫能助】ài mò néng zhù 〈成〉unable to extend help, though not without regret; wish one could be of help to sb.

【爱称】àichēng 〈名〉pet or affectionate name

【爱尔兰】Ài'ěrlán 〈名〉Ireland: ～人 the Irish; Irishman

【爱慕】àimù 〈动〉admire; adore

【爱怜】àilián 〈动〉be deeply attached to; cherish

【爱戴】àidài 〈名〉popular support

【爱护】àihù 〈动〉take good care of;

cherish

【爱恋】àiliàn 〈动〉fall in love with; fall for

愈 yù I 〈副〉[used in duplicate] the more… the more: ～快～好 the sooner the better II 〈动〉recover; get well: 病～ recover from an illness

【愈加】yùjiā 〈副〉all the more; even more: ～糊塗起來 become even more confused

【愈合】yùhé 〈动〉〈医〉heal up

【愈來愈】yù lái yù 〈副〉more and more; increasingly: ～好 become better and better

愁 chóu 〈动〉worry; be distressed

【愁苦】chóukǔ 〈名〉distress; vexation

【愁眉】chóuméi 〈名〉knitted brows: ～苦臉 look dejected

【愁容】chóuróng 〈名〉woeful expression

【愁悶】chóumèn 〈动〉be overcome with pent-up feelings of sadness; feel downcast

【愁腸】chóucháng 〈名〉feelings of sadness and anxiety: ～百結 overcome with deep sorrow

慌 huāng I 〈形〉flustered; nervous; scared: 别～。Don't panic. II 〈副〉[used after 得 as a complement] awfully; unbearably: 悶得～ be bored beyond endurance

【慌忙】huāngmáng 〈形〉hurried; in great haste

【慌張】huāngzhāng 〈形〉flurried; flustered

慄 lì 〈动〉tremble; shiver

慎 shèn (形) careful; discreet: 此事必須~之又~。You can't be too careful about the matter.

【慎重】shènzhòng (形) cautious; prudent: ~行事 act cautiously

愠 yùn (形) angry; annoyed: 面有~色 look rather annoyed; look angry

愴 chuàng (形) sad; sorrowful: ~然淚下 shed tears sadly

愧 kuì (動) feel ashamed: 自~不如 feel that one is not as good as another either in talent or in skill

【愧色】kuìsè (名) look as ashame

【愧疚】kuìjiù (動) feel ashamed and regretful

【愧恨】kuìhèn (動) be over taken by remorse and a sense of shame

態 tài (名) ❶ form; condition: 醜~百出 cut a contemptible figure ❷ 〈物〉state: 固~ solid state ❸ 〈語〉voice: 被動語~ passive voice

【態度】tàidu (名) ❶ manner; demeanor: ~和藹 affable manner ❷ attitude; stand: 明確的~ clear stand; unequivocal attitude

【態勢】tàishì (名) posture; situation: 保持進攻的~ maintain an offensive posture

慷 kāng

【慷慨】kāngkǎi (形) ❶ heroic; vehement: ~就義 go to one's death like a hero / ~陳詞 speak vehemently ❷ generous; charitable: ~的援助 generous assistance

【慷慨激昂】kāng kǎi jī áng (成) impassioned; passionate: ~的演說 impassioned speech

慚 cán (動) feel ashamed: 自~形穢 feel small

【慚愧】cánkuì (形) feel ashamed

慳 qiān

【慳吝】qiānlìn (形) stingy; mean

慪 òu (動)〈方〉❶ irritate; annoy ❷ be irritated: 他正爲這事~氣。He is feeling very bad about this.

慢 màn Ⅰ (形) ❶ slow: 幹活~ slow at one's work ❷ arrogant; rude: 怠~客人 neglect a guest Ⅱ (動) postpone

【慢車】mànchē (名) local (train); slow train

【慢坡】mànpō (名) gentle slope

【慢性】mànxìng (形) ❶ slow in taking effect: ~中毒 cumulative poisoning ❷ chronic: ~胃炎 chronic gastritis

【慢性子】mànxìngzi (名) ❶ unexcitable character ❷ slow coach

【慢性病】mànxìngbìng (名) chronic disease

【慢待】màndài (動) treat impolitely

【慢條斯理】màntiáo sīlǐ (副) unhurriedly; slowly

【慢動作】màndòngzuò (名) slow motion

【慢悠悠】mànyōuyōu (副) leisurely

【慢說】mànshuō (動) let alone; to say nothing of: ~摩托車，他連自行車都不會騎。He can't even ride a bicycle, let along a motorbike.

【慢慢騰騰】mànmàn tēngtēng (形) slowly; unhurriedly

【慢鏡頭】mànjìngtóu (名)〈電影〉

slow motion

慣 guàn Ⅰ (形) accustomed to; habituated to Ⅱ (動) indulge; spoil (a child)

【慣技】guànjì (名) old tricks

【慣性】guànxìng (名)〈物〉inertia

【慣例】guànlì (名) usual practice; convention

【慣竊】guànqiè (名) confirmed thief

惨 cǎn Ⅰ (形) ❶ miserable; tragic ❷ cruel; brutal Ⅱ (副) terribly; badly: 股票價格～跌 drastic fall of stock prices

【惨不忍睹】cǎn bù rěn dǔ〈成〉(of a tragic scene) too horrible to look at

【惨白】cǎnbái (形) pale; pallid

【惨叫】cǎnjiào (動) give a blood-curdling scream

【惨死】cǎnsǐ (動) die a tragic death

【惨狀】cǎnzhuàng (名) tragic condition (or sight)

【惨重】cǎnzhòng (形) heavy; grievous; disastrous

【惨案】cǎn'àn (名) ❶ massacre ❷ murder case

【惨敗】cǎnbài (名) fiasco; crushing defeat; ignominious defeat

【惨淡】cǎndàn (形) gloomy; bleak

【惨淡經營】cǎn dàn jīng yíng〈成〉take great pains to carry on under difficult circumstances (esp. in building a business from scratch)

【惨痛】cǎntòng (形) bitter; traumatic

【惨無人道】cǎn wú rén dào〈成〉inhuman; cruel and savage

【惨劇】cǎnjù (名) tragedy; calamity

慶 qìng Ⅰ (動) celebrate Ⅱ (名) ❶

anniversary worthy of celebration: 國～ National Day ❷ (Qìng) a surname

【慶大霉素】qìngdàméisù (名)〈藥〉gentamicin

【慶典】qìngdiǎn (名) celebration; event for jubilation

【慶幸】qìngxìng (動) rejoice (at an unexpected outcome) 家人幸免於難,深爲～。I rejoice over the narrow escape of my close relatives.

【慶祝】qìngzhù (動) celebrate: ～他的六十壽辰 celebrate the 60th anniversary of his birthday

【慶賀】qìnghè (動) congratulate; celebrate

慧 huì (形) clever; bright

【慧心】huìxīn (名) wisdom

【慧眼】huìyǎn (名) keen insight

【慧黠】huìxiá (形) clever and cunning

慕 mù (動) admire; look up to: 令人敬～ command admiration and respect

【慕名】mùmíng (動) hear with admiration and respect about sb.'s name: ～而來 pay sb. a visit out of admiration and respect for his name

憂 yōu Ⅰ (動) worry Ⅱ (名) sorrow; anxiety: 解～ relieve sorrow

【憂心忡忡】yōu xīn chōng chōng〈成〉be extremely worried

【憂患】yōuhuàn (名) misery; distress

【憂愁】yōuchóu (形) distressed; sorrowful; worried

【憂傷】yōushāng (形) sad; mournful; distressed

【憂慮】yōulù (形) worried; anxious

【憂鬱】yōuyù（形）melancholy; depressed

憨 hān（形）❶ foolish; silly ❷ naive; simple; ingenuous

【憨直】hānzhí（形）simple and straightforward

【憨厚】hānhòu（形）simple and honest

慰 wèi（動）console; comfort; relieve: 聊以自～ may well be something to console oneself with

【慰安婦】wèiānfù（名）comfort woman

【慰問】wèiwèn（動）convey greetings to sb. as an appreciation of his services; extend sympathy to: ～死者家屬 offer condolences to the bereaved

【慰問信】wèiwènxìn（名）sympathy note; note of appreciation

【慰勞】wèiláo（動）bring gifts to sb. for his splendid performance

慮 lù（動）❶ think; consider; contemplate: 考～ think over ❷ worry; feel anxious: 無憂無～ be carefree

慾 yù（名）desire; wish: 利～熏心 overcome with avarice

【慾望】yùwàng（名）desire; longing; lust

【慾壑難填】yù hè nán tián〈成〉greed is hard to satisfy; avarice is insatiable

慫 sǒng

【慫恿】sǒngyǒng（動）instigate; goad

憲 xiàn（名）❶ decree; statute ❷ constitution

【憲兵】xiànbīng（名）military police; gendarme

【憲法】xiànfǎ（名）constitution

【憲政】xiànzhèng（名）constitutional government; constitutionalism

【憲章】xiànzhāng（名）charter

憧 chōng

【憧憧】chōngchōng（形）flickering; moving: 鬼影～ shadows flickering about like dancing ghosts

【憧憬】chōngjǐng（動）long for: ～着幸福的明天 look forward to a happy future

憐 lián（動）❶ pity; commiserate ❷ love

【憐惜】liánxī（動）feel pity for

【憐憫】liánmǐn（動）commiserate with

憎 zēng（動）hate; detest; abominate: 可～ detestable

【憎恨】zēnghèn（動）hate; detest

【憎惡】zēngwù（動）abhor; loathe; dislike

憤 fèn Ⅰ（動）flare up Ⅱ（名）anger; indignation: 洩私～ give vent to personal spite

【憤世嫉俗】fèn shì jí sú〈成〉detest the human world for its social injustice

【憤恨】fènhèn（動）be filled with indignation and hatred

【憤怒】fènnù（名）wrath; fury; indignation

【憤然】fènrán（副）angrily: ～離去 leave in a fit of anger

【憤慨】fènkǎi（形）indignant

【憤激】fènjī（動）feel indignant

【憤憤】fènfèn（形）indignant

【憤懣】fènmèn（形）resentful; in a fit of pique

愍 mǐn（名）pity; 憐～ take pity on

憬 jǐng

【憬悟】jǐngwù（動）awake（to）; realize（one's mistake, etc.）

慣 kuì（形）muddleheaded; befuddled

憔 qiáo

【憔悴】qiáocuì（形）❶（of a person）in bad shape; haggard; gaunt ❷（of a plant）withered

憑 píng I（動）❶ lean on; lean against ❷ rely on: 她被提升現職全～才幹。She got her present promotion by sheer ability. II（名）evidence; proof: 不足爲～ cannot be taken as evidence III（連）no matter: ～他說什麼,你都不要信他。Don't believe him no matter what he says.

【憑空】píngkōng（副）without foundation: ～ 指控別人 accuse sb. without a shred of evidence

【憑眺】píngtiào（動）enjoy a panoramic view from a high place

【憑單】píngdān（名）certificate; voucher

【憑據】píngjù（名）evidence; proof

【憑藉】píngjiè（動）rely on: ～武力 resort to force / ～語言表達思想 rely on language to express our thoughts

【憑證】píngzhèng（名）proof; certificate

憋 biē（動）❶ hold back; keep down; restrain: ～住不說 hold back

one's tongue ❷ suffocate; be stuffy

【憋氣】biēqì（動）❶ be stuffy; be stifling ❷ suffocate with resentment; feel injured and resentful

【憋悶】biēmèn（動）feel oppressed; be depressed

憩 qì（名）rest

【憩息】qìxī（動）take a rest

憊 bèi（形）tired out; exhausted: 疲～ fatigued; exhausted

憶 yì（動）recall

【憶舊】yìjiù（動）recollect the past

懂 dǒng（動）understand; know

【懂行】dǒngháng（動）know the ropes

【懂事】dǒngshì（形）sensible; well-behaved

憾 hàn（名）regret: 引以爲～ cannot mention it without regret

【憾事】hànshì（名）matter for regret

懈 xiè（動）slacken; relax: 努力不～ strive persistently

【懈怠】xièdài（形）slack; sluggish; indolent

懊 ào（形）❶ regretful; remorseful ❷ annoyed; vexed

【懊悔】àohuǐ（動）regret; repent: ～莫及 be overtaken by deep remorse

【懊惱】àonǎo（動）be annoyed; be vexed; be upset

【懊喪】àosàng（形）dismayed; dejected; depressed

應 yīng I（動）❶ answer; respond: 他冷冷地～了一聲。He replied

coldly. ❷ promise (to do sth.): 這事她已～下來了。 She has promised to attend to it. II (動) should; ought to: 你～更細心些。 You should be more careful.

see also yīng

【應允】 yīngyǔn (動) assent; consent

【應有盡有】 yīng yǒu jìn yǒu 〈成〉 everything that one needs is available: 旅館裏各種設備～。 The hotel is furnished with all modern facilities.

【應當】 yīngdāng (動) should; ought to

【應該】 yīnggāi (動) should; ought to; must

應 yìng (動) ❶ answer; echo: 答～ answer; reply ❷ comply with; suit; 他已適～這裏的環境。 He has got used to the environment here. ❸ deal with; handle ❹ accept; 倉卒～戰 go into battle in haste

see also yīng

【應付】 yìngfu (動) ❶ deal with; handle: ～裕如 handle the situation with ease ❷ do sth. perfunctorily ❸ make do: 這件襯衫還可以～一陣兒。 This shirt can last for some time yet.

【應用】 yìngyòng (動) apply

【應用文】 yìngyòngwén (名) practical writing (as business letters, official correspondence, etc.)

【應考】 yìngkǎo (動) sit for an examination: ～的人數近千。 There were nearly 1,000 candidates taking the examination.

【應承】 yìngchéng (動) promise; consent

【應急】 yìngjí (動) meet an emergency; cope with an urgent situation

【應時】 yìngshí I (形) seasonable; in season II (副) at once; immediately

【應接不暇】 yìng jiē bù xiá 〈成〉 have too many visitors or matters to attend to

【應景】 yìngjǐng (動) do sth. for a certain occasion: ～之作 occasional poem; occasional essay

【應運而生】 yìng yùn ér shēng 〈成〉 arise at the right historic moment

【應答】 yìngdá (動) answer; reply

【應酬】 yìngchóu (名) social life; social intercourse

【應徵】 yìngzhēng (動) ❶ be recruited or conscripted; enlist: ～入伍 be conscripted ❷ respond to a call for contributions to a publication

【應諾】 yìngnuò (動) promise; consent

【應邀】 yìngyāo (動) accept sb.'s invitation: ～出席大會 attend the conference on invitation

【應聲蟲】 yìngshēng chóng (名) yes-man

【應驗】 yìngyàn (動) come true; be realized: 他的預言已經～了。 His prediction has come true.

【應變】 yìngbiàn (動) prepare for all eventualities; meet a contingency

懇 kěn I (副) earnestly; in sincerity II (動) beseech; beg; implore

【懇切】 kěnqiè (形) earnest and ardent

【懇求】 kěnqiú (動) beseech; beg

【懇談】 kěntán (動) talk (with sb.) in all sincerity

懦 nuò (形) cowardly; weak-kneed

【懦夫】 nuòfū (名) coward

【懦弱】 nuòruò (形) weak; cowardly:

~無能 weak and inept

懲 chéng（動）punish; penalize: 嚴 ~ severely punish

【懲戒】chéngjiè（動）mete out a punishment to sb. so that he may take warning from it; chasten

【懲前毖後】chéng qián bì hòu〈成〉learn from past errors to avoid future mistakes

【懲罰】chéngfá I（動）punish; penalize II（名）punishment; penalty

【懲辦】chéngbàn（動）mete out punishment to; penalize; punish

懷 huái I（名）❶ bosom: 孩子睡在媽媽~裏。The baby is sleeping in his mother's arms. ❷ mind: 正中下~。This fits in exactly with my wishes. II（動）❶ cherish; harbour: 滿 ~希望 cherish high hopes ❷ think of; yearn for: ~鄉 be homesick

【懷孕】huáiyùn（動）be pregnant

【懷抱】huáibào I（名）bosom; embrace: 撲向她母親的~ throw herself into her mother's arms II（動）cherish: ~遠大理想 cherish great aspirations

【懷念】huáiniàn（動）think about; remember with fondness

【懷恨】huáihèn（動）nurse grievances; bear a grudge

【懷疑】huáiyí（動）doubt; suspect

【懷錶】huáibiǎo（名）pocket watch

【懷舊】huáijiù（動）miss old days or old friends; be filled with nostalgia

懶 lǎn（形）❶ lazy (as opposed to industrious) ❷ weary; sluggish: 身子發 ~ feel weary

【懶洋洋】lǎnyāngyāng（形）lacking in energy or enthusiasm; listless; lackadaisical

【懶得】lǎnde（動）be reluctant to; be disinclined to: 我今天~上街。I don't feel like going to town today.

【懶惰】lǎnduò（形）lazy; idle

【懶散】lǎnsǎn（形）slothful; sluggish

【懶漢】lǎnhàn（名）idler; sluggard

懵 měng（形）muddled; ignorant

【懵懂】měngdǒng（形）benighted; muddleheaded

懸 xuán I（動）hang; suspend: ~空 suspended in midair II（形）❶ unsettled; pending: 事情還~着呢。The matter remains pending. ❷ dangerous: 好~，過馬路時差點讓車壓了。What a near thing! I narrowly missed being run over by a passing car while I was crossing the road. ❸ far apart

【懸吊】xuándiào（動）suspend in midair

【懸而未決】xuán ér wèijué（形）unsettled; pending: ~的問題 outstanding issue

【懸念】xuánniàn I（動）continue to think about sb. who is elsewhere; miss: 不勝~ miss sb. very much II（名）suspense: 引起讀者的~ keep the reader in suspense

【懸案】xuánàn（名）❶ unsettled law case ❷ unresolved question

【懸殊】xuánshū（名）wide gap; big difference: 社會地位的~ disparity in social standing

【懸掛】xuánguà（動）hang up; fly: ~國旗 hang up the national flag

【懸梯】xuántī（名）hanging ladder

【懸崖】xuányá（名）steep cliff;

precipice

【懸崖勒馬】xuán yá lè mǎ 〈成〉rein in at the edge of a cliff; stop doing evil before it is too late

【懸賞】xuánshǎng （動）solicit help by offering a reward: ～尋人 reward for information about the whereabouts of a missing person / ～緝拿逃犯 reward for the capture of an escaped convict

【懸燈結彩】xuán dēng jié cǎi 〈成〉hang up lanterns and festoons

懺 chàn （動）repent

【懺悔】chànhuǐ （動）❶ repent ❷ 〈宗〉confess (one's sins to God or a priest)

懾 shè （動）〈書〉fear; terrify: ～於淫威 be cowed by sb.'s despotic power

【懾服】shèfú （動）❶ yield to sb. out of fear ❷ cow sb. into submission

懼 jù （動）fear; dread: 毫無所～ have absolutely nothing to fear

【懼怕】jùpà （動）be afraid of; fear

戀 liàn （動）love; be attached to

【戀家】liànjiā （動）be homesick; be unwilling to leave home

【戀愛】liàn'ài （名）love: 談～ be in love; fall in love

【戀歌】liàngē （名）love song

【戀戀不捨】liàn liàn bù shě 〈成〉hate to part

戈 部

戈 gē （名）❶ spear; lance ❷ weapon; war: 兵～ weapons of war / 動兵～ start war ❸ (Gē) a surname

【戈壁】gēbì （名）the Gobi Desert

戍 shù （動）defend; guard: 衛～部隊 garrison forces

【戍邊】shùbiān （動）guard the frontier

戎 róng （名）〈書〉❶ army; war: ～裝 military uniform ❷ (Róng) a surname

成 chéng Ⅰ（動）❶ accomplish; succeed: 辦～ get sth. done ❷ become; turn into: ～爲專家 become an expert ❸ be all right: 那不～! That won't do! Ⅱ（名）❶ achievement: 收～ harvest ❷ (Chéng) a surname Ⅲ（形）❶ mature; fully developed: ～熟 mature ❷ established: ～規 convention; established practice ❸ capable: 他可真～! He is really resourceful! ❹ (in considerable amount): ～年累月 year in, year out Ⅳ（量）one tenth: 增加一～ increase by 10 per cent

【成人】chéngrén Ⅰ（動）grow up; become an adult Ⅱ（名）adult

【成分】chéngfen （名）composition; component; ingredient

【成天】chéngtiān （副）〈口〉all day long

【成文】chéngwén Ⅰ（名）existing writing Ⅱ（形）written: ～法 written law

【成心】chéngxīn（副）deliberately: ～跟人作對 go out of one's way to oppose sb.

【成本】chéngběn（名）cost

【成功】chénggōng Ⅰ（動）succeed Ⅱ（名）success

【成立】chénglì Ⅰ（動）❶ establish; set up ❷（of ideas, opinion, etc.）be tenable: 這個論點從事實出發能～。This argument is tenable for it is based on facts. Ⅱ（名）establishment

【成交】chéngjiāo（動）strike a bargain; clinch a deal

【成名】chéngmíng（動）rise to fame: ～成家 establish oneself as a well-known authority

【成年】chéngnián Ⅰ（動）come of age Ⅱ（副）all the year round

【成全】chéngquán（動）help sb. to realize his wish or long-cherished dream

【成材】chéngcái（動）❶（of trees）become timber ❷（of a person）become useful member of society

【成見】chéngjiàn（名）bias; preconceived idea: 對他抱～ be prejudiced against him

【成批】chéngpī（副）in batches: ～生產 mass production

【成災】chéngzāi（動）cause disaster

【成果】chéngguǒ（名）achievement; fruit: 取得～ yield positive results

【成長】chéngzhǎng（動）grow up; become mature

【成性】chéngxìng（副）〈貶〉by nature; being sb.'s second nature: 貪婪～ greedy by nature

【成事不足，敗事有餘】chéng shì bù zú, bài shì yǒu yú〈成〉incapable of

doing any good but quite capable of spoiling the show

【成風】chéngfēng（動）become a prevailing practice in society

【成品】chéngpǐn（名）finished product; end product

【成家】chéngjiā（動）❶（of a man）get married: ～立業 get married and embark on a career ❷ establish oneself as an authority

【成效】chéngxiào（名）effect; result

【成套】chéngtào（名）complete set

【成員】chéngyuán（名）member

【成敗】chéngbài（名）success or failure: ～在所不計 not care whether one will end up in success or failure; not consider the chances of success and failure

【成堆】chéngduī（動）pile up; be in heaps

【成就】chéngjiù Ⅰ（名）achievement; success Ⅱ（動）achieve; accomplish

【成為】chéngwéi（動）become; turn into: ～事實 materialize

【成群】chéngqún（副）in groups: ～結隊 move in crowds

【成語】chéngyǔ（名）idiom; set phrase

【成熟】chéngshú（形）ripe; mature

【成親】chéngqīn（成婚 chénghūn）（動）get married

【成績】chéngjī（名）achievement: ～單 school report; academic report

戒 jiè Ⅰ（動）❶ avoid; guard against: ～驕～躁 guard against conceit and impetuosity ❷ give up: ～煙 give up smoking Ⅱ（名）❶ ring: 鑽～ diamond ring ❷〈宗〉monastic discipline

【戒心】jièxīn（名）vigilance; guard;

有～ be on one's guard

【戒指】jièzhǐ（名）ring（worn on a finger）

【戒律】jièlǜ（名）religious discipline; taboo: 數不盡的清規～ countless taboos

【戒備】jièbèi（動）keep a sharp lookout; guard

【戒嚴】jièyán（動）impose a curfew; proclaim martial law

我 wǒ（代）❶ I; me ❷ my: ～哥哥 my elder brother ❸ we; us ❹ our: ～校 our school ❺ self: 大～ the greater self; the collective

【我行我素】wǒ xíng wǒ sù（成）go one's own way（regardless of what others may say）; do as I please

【我們】wǒmén（代）we; us

或 huò Ⅰ（副）perhaps; maybe Ⅱ（連）or; either...or... Ⅲ（副）～早～晚 sooner or later / ～是你去, ～是我去。Either you or I am to go.

【或者】huòzhě Ⅰ（連）perhaps; maybe Ⅱ（連）or; either...or...

【或許】huòxǔ（副）perhaps; maybe

【或然】huòrán（形）probable

戚 qī（名）❶ relative: 親～ relative ❷ sorrow; distress ❸（Qī）a surname

戟 jǐ（名）halberd: 三叉～ trident

戡 kān（動）quell; put down by force

戥 děng（動）weigh（precious metal, medicine, etc.）

【戥子】děngzi（名）small steelyard（for weighing gold, medicine, etc.）

截 jié Ⅰ（動）❶ cut or sever（sth. long and slender in shape）: ～去左臂 amputate the left arm ❷ stop; obstruct; block: ～擊機 interceptor Ⅱ（量）section; division: 他活兒做了半～就走了。He left when he was halfway through with his work.

【截止】jiézhǐ（動）close; terminate: ～日期 deadline

【截至】jiézhì（介）by（a certain time）; till; up to: ～消息時 up to the time the news is released

【截然】jiérán（副）distinctly; categorically: 這類型是跟那種類型～不同的。This type is a far cry from that one.

【截獲】jiéhuò（動）intercept and seize: ～走私物品 intercept smuggled goods

【截斷】jiéduàn（動）❶ cut off; sever ❷ interrupt; intercept

戮 lù（動）kill; slaughter

戰 zhàn Ⅰ（名）war; battle; fight: 反～ 運動 antiwar movement Ⅱ（動）❶ fight: 爲獨立而～ fight for independence ❷ shiver; tremble: 嚇得打～ shiver with fright

【戰士】zhànshì（名）soldier; fighter

【戰友】zhànyǒu（名）comrade-in-arms

【戰火】zhànhuǒ（名）flames of war: 在那～紛飛的歲月裏 in those war-ridden years

【戰犯】zhànfàn（名）war criminal

【戰功】zhàngōng（名）outstanding military exploits: 立～ distinguish oneself in action / 赫赫～ brilliant achievements in war

【戰役】zhànyì（名）campaign; battle

【戰局】zhànjú（名）war situation

【戰利品】zhànlìpǐn（名）spoils of war; war trophies

【戰果】zhànguǒ（名）fruits of victory; success; victory

【戰例】zhànlì（名）a specific example of a battle (in military science)：有名的～ a famous battle

【戰爭】zhànzhēng（名）war; warfare：～狂人 war maniac

【戰俘】zhànfú（名）prisoner of war (P.O.W.)

【戰後】zhànhòu（形）postwar

【戰前】zhànqián（形）prewar

【戰鬥】zhàndòu Ⅰ（動）fight; combat Ⅱ（名）battle; fighting

【戰鬥力】zhàndòulì（名）combat effectiveness; fighting capacity

【戰時】zhànshí（名）wartime

【戰敗】zhànbài（動）❶ be defeated; lose the war ❷ defeat; triumph over

【戰略】zhànlüè（名）strategy：～物資 strategic materials

【戰術】zhànshù（名）(military) tactics

【戰勝】zhànshèng（動）defeat; triumph over; overcome：～疾病 triumph over disease

【戰備】zhànbèi（名）preparation against war

【戰場】zhànchǎng（名）battlefield

【戰無不勝】zhàn wú bù shèng（成）triumph in every battle; invincible; ever-victorious

【戰鼓】zhàngǔ（名）battle drum

【戰慄】zhànlì（動）shiver; tremble

【戰綫】zhànxiàn（名）battle line; front

【戰端】zhànduān（名）the beginning of a war：重啟～。War broke out again.

【戰戰兢兢】zhànzhàn jīngjīng（形）❶ trembling with fright ❷ cautious; very careful

【戰壕】zhànháo（名）trench

【戰艦】zhànjiàn（名）warship

戲 xì Ⅰ（名）play; drama; opera; show Ⅱ（動）play with; sport

【戲目】xìmù（名）(theatrical) programme

【戲曲】xìqǔ（名）traditional opera

【戲弄】xìnòng（動）play with; make fun of; tease

【戲法】xìfǎ（名）trick; jugglery：～人人會變，各有巧妙不同。Many are the magicians, but each has his own tricks.

【戲迷】xìmí（名）theatre fan

【戲班】xìbān（名）theatrical troupe

【戲院】xìyuàn（名）theatre

【戲臺】xìtái（名）stage

【戲劇】xìjù（名）drama; play

戴 dài Ⅰ（動）❶ wear; put on：～着帽子 wear a hat ❷ esteem; support：愛～ love and respect Ⅱ（名）(Dài) a surname

戳 chuō（動）jab; poke; prod：用手指頭～他 poke him with a finger

【戳兒】chuōr（戳子 chuōzi）（名）（口）stamp; seal：郵～ post mark

【戳穿】chuōchuān（動）❶ puncture; pierce through ❷ expose：～鬼把戲 lay bare sb.'s dirty tricks

【戳破】chuōpò（動）puncture：～輪胎 puncture the tyre

户 部

户 hù（名）❶ household; family ❷ status: 門當～對 well matched in social status ❸（bank）account: 開個～ open an account

【户口】hùkǒu（名）residence registration; census registration: 報～ register for residence

【户主】hùzhǔ（名）head of a household

【户樞不蠹】hù shū bù dù〈成〉sth. in constant motion is not likely to corrode

【户頭】hùtóu（名）bank account

【户籍】hùjí（名）local census register; registered permanent residence

房 fáng（名）❶ house ❷ room ❸（Fáng）a surname

【房子】fángzi（名）❶ house ❷ room

【房地産】fángdìchǎn（名）real estate

【房東】fángdōng（名）landlord; landlady

【房事】fángshì（名）sexual intercourse（between husband and wife）

【房客】fángkè（名）tenant

【房租】fángzū（名）(house) rent

【房産】fángchǎn（名）house property

【房頂】fángdǐng（名）roof

【房間】fángjiān（名）room: 雙人～ double room

【房檐】fángyán（名）eaves

戾 lì Ⅰ（名）crime Ⅱ（形）cruel; unreasonable

所 suǒ Ⅰ（名）❶ place: 公共場～ public place ❷ institution; office: 邊防哨～ frontier guard post Ⅱ（量）(of buildings or institutions): 一～公寓 an apartment house / 一～中學 a middle school Ⅲ（助）❶ [used together with 爲 or 被 to form a passive construction]: 爲人民～唾棄 spurned by the people ❷ [used before a transitive verb to form a past participle modifying the noun that follows]: 這是衆～周知的事實。This is a fact known to all. ❸ [often used in a noun clause 是…的 between the subject and the verb]: 那是大家～希望看到的。That is what everybody would very much like to see. ❹ [used before two verbs to form a nominal phrase]: ～見～聞 what one sees and hears / ～作～爲 what one does and how one behaves

【所以】suǒyǐ（連）therefore; so; that's why: 他遲到了，～挨了批評。He was criticized for being late.

【所以然】suǒyǐrán（名）whys and wherefores: 他想了半天，也没想出～來。He thought hard but failed to get to the root of the matter.

【所有】suǒyǒu Ⅰ（動）own; possess; hold: 這家企業爲國家～。This enterprise is owned by the state. Ⅱ（名）all one possess: 一身之外别無～。I have not a single penny to bless myself with. Ⅲ（形）all; every: 使出～力量 make every effort

【所有制】suǒyǒuzhì（名）ownership（system）: 集體～ collective ownership

【所有權】suǒyǒuquán（名）owner-ship

【所在】suǒzài（名）place where sth. exists: 這正是困難～. This is exactly where the difficulty lies (where the shoe pinches).

【所在地】suǒzàidì（名）site; location

【所長】suǒcháng（名）what one is good at; one's speciality: 一無～ have no special skill to his credit

【所得】suǒdé（名）earnings; income: 一無～ gain nothing; make a fruitless attempt

【所得稅】suǒdéshuì（名）income tax

【所謂】suǒwèi（形）❶ so-called ❷ what is meant by: 互相讓步就是一種對雙方都有利的妥協。What is meant by mutual concession is a compromise to the advantage of both sides.

【所屬】suǒshǔ（形）❶ under one's command; under one's jurisdiction; under: 市政府～各部門 departments under the municipal government ❷ in charge; competent (authority): 向～領導機關報告 report to the competent authorities

扁 biǎn（形）❶ flat: 壓～ be crushed flat ❷ undervalued: 把人看～了 underestimate sb.

【扁平】biǎnpíng（形）flat

【扁豆】biǎndòu（名）lentil; string bean

【扁桃腺】biǎntáoxiàn（名）tonsil: ～炎 tonsillitis

【扁圓】biǎnyuán（形）oblate

【扁擔】biǎndan（名）carrying pole; shoulder pole

扇 shàn I（名）fan II（量）[of door, windows, etc.]: 一～屏風 a screen

【扇子】shànzi（名）fan

【扇貝】shànbèi（名）scallop; fan shell

【扇車】shànchē（名）winnowing machine; winnower

【扇形】shànxíng I（形）fan-shaped II（名）〈數〉sector

扈 hù（名）❶ retinue ❷（Hù）a surname

扉 fēi（名）door leaf

【扉頁】fēiyè（名）〈印〉title page

手　部

手 shǒu I（名）❶ hand ❷ person possessing a special skill 棋～ skilful chess player II（動）hold in the hand: 做到人～一冊 make sure that everyone has a copy III（形）handy; small and easy to carry: 焊工～冊 the welder's handbook (manual) IV（量）(of skill or proficiency): 寫得一～好字 write in a neat hand

【手工】shǒugōng I（名）❶ handwork; craftsmanship: ～業 handicraft industry / ～藝 handicraft ❷〈口〉charge for a piece of handwork II（形）handmade

【手巾】shǒujīn（名）face towel

【手下】shǒuxià I（副）❶ under sb.'s leadership or supervision: 他～有十個人。He has a team of ten persons working under him. ❷（of things） be with one ❸ at sb.'s hands: 敗在某人的 ～ suffer a defeat in a contest with sb.; be defeated by sb. in a contest Ⅱ (名) financial condition: 到每月底 ～就緊 be always hard up by the end of a month

【手下留情】shǒu xià liú qíng〈成〉 show mercy in meting punishment to an offender; be lenient

【手心】shǒuxīn（名）❶ palm of the hand ❷ sphere of control

【手不釋卷】shǒu bù shì juàn〈成〉 (of a scholar) be extremely studious

【手巧】shǒuqiǎo（形）deft; dexterous

【手印】shǒuyìn（名）❶ impression of a hand finger-print: 按 ～ affix one's thumbprint (fingerprint)

【手忙腳亂】shǒu máng jiǎo luàn〈成〉 dash about, hardly knowing what to do; be in a flurry

【手快】shǒu kuài（形）deft (of the hand); quick-moving

【手杖】shǒuzhàng（名）(walking) stick

【手抄本】shǒuchāoběn（名）hand-written text (of an ancient novel, play, etc.); hand-written script

【手扶拖拉機】shǒufú tuōlājī（名） walking tractor

【手法】shǒufǎ（名）❶ (of artistic and literary works) technique: 中國傳統建築的獨特 ～ the unique techniques of traditional Chinese architecture ❷ trick; tactics: 兩面 ～ double-dealing tactics

【手背】shǒubèi（名）back of the hand

【手段】shǒuduàn（名）❶ means; method: 用各種可能的 ～ by all possible means ❷ trick; dirty

means: 耍 ～ play dirty tricks

【手指甲】shǒuzhǐjia（名）finger nail

【手指頭】shǒuzhítou（手指 shǒuzhǐ） （名）finger

【手勁兒】shǒujìnr（名）strength of the wrist; muscular strength of the hand

【手風琴】shǒufēngqín（名）accordion

【手氣】shǒuqi（名）luck (such as in gambling)

【手套】shǒutào（名）glove; mitten

【手紙】shǒuzhǐ（名）toilet paper

【手球】shǒuqiú（名）handball

【手軟】shǒuruǎn（動）be soft-hearted

【手術】shǒushù（名）surgical operation: ～室 operating room; operating theatre / ～臺 operating table

【手推車】shǒutuīchē（名）handcart; pushcart; wheelbarrow

【手掌】shǒuzhǎng（名）palm

【手腕】shǒuwàn（名）❶ wrist: ～子 wrist ❷ trick; artifice: 使 ～ play tricks

【手提】shǒutí（形）portable: ～式錄音機 portable tape recorder / ～箱 suitcase / ～包 handbag

【手提行李】shǒutí xíngli（名）hand luggage; carry-on (baggage)

【手無寸鐵】shǒu wú cùn tiě〈成〉 (of ordinary civilians) unarmed

【手絹】shǒujuàn（手帕 shǒupà）（名） handkerchief

【手腳】shǒujiǎo（名）❶ action: ～不靈 be clumsy; be all thumbs; have difficulty moving about ❷ 〈方〉trick: 背地做 ～ play dirty tricks behind sb.'s back

【手勢】shǒushì（名）gesture; gesticulation

【手電筒】shǒudiàntǒng（名）electric torch; flash-light

【手銬】shǒukào（名）handcuffs

【手槍】shǒuqiāng（名）pistol: 左輪 ~ revolver

【手榴彈】shǒuliúdàn（名）（hand）grenade

【手緊】shǒujǐn（形）❶ tightfisted; stingy ❷ short of money

【手舞足蹈】shǒu wǔ zú dǎo〈成〉dance for joy; jump for joy; run about with joyful gesticulation

【手稿】shǒugǎo（名）manuscript (usu. of a well-known figure)

【手頭】shǒutóu Ⅰ（副）on hand: 我 ~只有一本英語詞典。I have only one English dictionary on hand. Ⅱ（名）financial circumstance: ~不寬裕 be somewhat short of money; be hard up

【手錶】shǒubiǎo（名）wrist-watch

【手臂】shǒubì（名）arm

【手鬆】shǒusōng（形）open-handed; generous with one's money

【手邊】shǒubiān（副）on hand; ready for use: 我~沒零錢。I have no change on me.

【手藝】shǒuyì（名）craftsmanship: ~人 artisan

【手續】shǒuxù（名）procedure; formalities: ~費 commission; handling fee / 合乎~ comply with the required formalities

【手鐲】shǒuzhuó（名）bracelet

才 cái（名）❶ talent; ability: 口 ~ eloquence ❷ person of a certain type（in terms of talent and ability）: 奇~ person of rare talent

【才子】cáizǐ（名）man of outstanding literary talent

【才能】cáinéng（名）knowledge and ability

【才氣】cáiqì（名）literary talent: ~過人 have outstanding talent

【才智】cáizhì（名）ability and wisdom

【才華】cáihuá（名）（literary or artistic）talent

【才幹】cáigàn（名）ability; capability

【才學】cáixué（名）intelligence and scholarship

扎 zhā（動）❶ prick: 她給樹枝~了一下。She pricked herself on a thorn. ❷ plunge into; get into: 一頭~進圖書館 shut oneself up in the library

【扎手】zhāshǒu Ⅰ（動）prick the hand Ⅱ（形）difficult to deal with; thorny: ~的問題 a thorny problem

【扎伊爾】Zhāyī'ěr（名）Zaire: ~人 Zairian

【扎針】zhāzhēn（動）〈中醫〉give or have an acupuncture treatment

【扎根】zhāgēn（動）take root: 在人們的心中深深~ strike root deep down in the hearts of the people

【扎堆】zhāduī（動）gather together; flock together

【扎眼】zhāyǎn（形）dazzling; garish; showy

【扎實】zhāshí（形）❶ strong; sturdy ❷ solid; down-to-earth: 基礎~ have a solid foundation

打 dá（量）dozen: 一~鉛筆 a dozen pencils
see also dǎ

打 dǎ Ⅰ（動）❶ beat; strike: ~鼓 beat a drum ❷ catch: ~魚 go fish-

ing ❸ buy: ～酒 buy wine ❹ fight: ～起来了 come to blows ❺ gather in: ～柴 gather firewood ❻ knit: ～毛襪子 knit woollen socks ❼ play: ～籃球 play basketball ❽ pack: ～行李 pack up ❾ send; dispatch: ～電報 send a telegram ❿ fetch: ～開水 fetch boiled water ⓫ do: ～零工 do odd jobs ⓬ break: 玻璃杯～了。The glass is broken. II〔介〕from：～哪兒來? Where did you come from?
see also dá

【打手】dǎshou（名）hatchet man; thug

【打火機】dǎhuǒjī（名）lighter

【打牙祭】dǎ yájì（動）〈方〉treat oneself occasionally to a nice meal

【打仗】dǎzhàng（動）fight a battle; go to war

【打字】dǎzì（動）type：～機 typewriter / ～員 typist

【打成一片】dǎ chéng yī piàn（動）integrate：同羣衆～ integrate with the masses

【打交道】dǎ jiāodao（動）deal with

【打劫】dǎjié（動）rob; plunder：趁火～ plunder a burning house; take advantage of a confused situation to harm sb.

【打扮】dǎban（動）dress up; decorate

【打抱不平】dǎ bàobùpíng（動）defend a wronged person; cry out against an injustice

【打官司】dǎ guānsi（動）go to court; start a lawsuit

【打官腔】dǎ guānqiāng（動）speak like a bureaucrat; resort to officialese

【打油詩】dǎyóushī（名）doggerel

【打招呼】dǎ zhāohu（動）❶ greet; say hello to ❷ give advance information

【打架】dǎjià（動）come to blows; fight

【打胎】dǎtāi（名）induced abortion

【打盹兒】dǎdǔnr（動）doze off; take a nap

【打倒】dǎdǎo（動）overthrow

【打消】dǎxiāo（動）dispel：～疑慮 dispel one's misgivings

【打破】dǎpò（動）break：～世界記錄 break a world record

【打針】dǎzhēn（動）give or receive an injection

【打氣】dǎqì（動）❶ pump up; inflate ❷ encourage; boost the morale of

【打氣筒】dǎqìtǒng（名）tyre pump

【打埋伏】dǎ máifu（動）❶ lie in ambush ❷ hold sth. back ❸ withhold information about sth.

【打草驚蛇】dǎ cǎo jīng shé〈成〉put the adversary on guard by thoughtless action

【打敗】dǎbài（動）defeat; be defeated

【打掃】dǎsǎo（動）clean; tidy up

【打動】dǎdòng（動）touch a responsive chord：～人心 touch one's heart

【打場】dǎcháng（動）thresh

【打量】dǎliang（動）❶ observe: 把他～了一番 look him up and down ❷ suppose; judge

【打亂】dǎluàn（動）upset：～座次 upset the seating arrangement

【打碎】dǎsuì（動）smash; break to pieces

【打落水狗】dǎ luòshuǐgǒu（動）beat a drowning cur; deal a discredited person a smashing blow

【打電話】dǎdiànhuà (動) make a phone call; ring up; call

【打算】dǎsuàn I (動) plan; intend II (名) intention; plan; calculation

【打趣】dǎqù (動) banter; hold sb. to ridicule

【打撈】dǎlāo (動) salvage

【打賭】dǎdǔ (動) bet; wager

【打磨】dǎmó (動) polish

【打點】dǎdiǎn (動) get ready: ～行裝 pack up

【打鼾】dǎhān (動) snore

【打擊】dǎjī (動) ❶ deal sb. a blow: 給予侵者以殲滅性的～ deal the invaders a smashing blow ❷ strike: ～樂器 percussion instrument

【打獵】dǎliè I (動) hunt II (名) hunting

【打斷】dǎduàn (動) ❶ break ❷ interrupt

【打翻】dǎfān (動) overturn

【打聽】dǎtīng (動) ask about; pry into: ～朋友的下落 inquire about a friend's whereabouts

【打顫】dǎzhàn (動) shiver; tremble: 氣得～ tremble with anger

【打攪】dǎjiǎo (動) disturb; trouble

扔 rēng (動) ❶ throw; fling: 不要亂～紙屑雜物。No littering. ❷ throw away; discard: 把它～掉吧。Throw it away.

扒 bā (動) ❶ hold on to: ～着欄杆 hold on to the balustrade ❷ pull down; demolish: ～房 pull down a house ❸ strip; take off: ～皮 peel; skin

see also pá

扒 pá (動) ❶ rake (together): ～草 rake the weeds together ❷ 〈方〉scratch: ～癢 scratch an itch ❸ stew; braise; broil; grill: ～鴨 braised duck / ～對蝦 broiled prawns / ～雜拌 mixed grill

see also bā

【扒手】páshǒu (名) pick-pocket

【扒竊】páqiè (動) steal; pick sb.'s pocket

扛 káng (動) carry on the shoulder

【扛長活】káng chánghuó (扛活 kánghuó; 扛長工 káng chánggōng) 〈口〉 work on a farm as a hired labourer; toil as a regular farm-hand

扣 kòu I (動) ❶ button up; buckle up ❷ place a cup, bowl, etc. upside down over sth. ❸ detain; apprehend ❹ deduct ❺ discount ❻〈體〉smash a ball II (名) button; buckle; knot: 繫個繩～ tie a knot on the rope

【扣子】kòuzi (名) ❶ button ❷ knot

【扣押】kòuyā (動) ❶ hold in custody ❷ detain

【扣除】kòuchú (動) deduct: ～所得稅 deduct the income tax

【扣留】kòuliú (動) detain; hold in custody: ～人質 hold sb. hostage

【扣殺】kòushā (動) 〈體〉 smash (the ball)

【扣帽子】kòu màozi (動) pin a label on (sb.); label (sb.)

【扣壓】kòuyā (動) withhold

扦 qiān (名) needle-shaped piece of metal, bamboo, etc; spike

托 tuō I (動) ❶ support with one's hand or palm; support; hold: 茶盤～着一個茶壺和幾個茶杯。The tray holds a teapot and several cups.

❷ set off; serve as a contrast: 綠葉
～紅花 green leaves set off red
flowers ❸ entrust: ～他辦這件事
entrust him with this task ❹ give as
an excuse: ～病不去 refuse to go
on the pretext of ill health ❺ owe
to: ～您的福, 一切都很順利。We
owe it to you that all goes well. Ⅱ
(名) support; base: 茶～ tea tray

【托人情】tuō rénqíng (動) seek sb.'s
good offices

【托子】tuōzi (名) base; support;
pad

【托付】tuōfù (動) entrust; commit
to sb.'s care: 把孩子～給鄰居
leave the child in the care of a
neighbour

【托幼】tuōyòu (名) nurseries and
kindergartens: 興辦～事業 set up
nurseries and kindergartens

【托兒所】tuō'érsuǒ (名) day-care
centre; nursery

【托拉斯】tuōlāsī (名)〈經〉trust

【托詞】tuōcí Ⅰ (動) find an excuse:
～不到 fail to turn up on some pretext Ⅱ (名) excuse; pretext

【托運】tuōyùn (動) ship (unaccompanied baggage) on a passenger ticket; check: ～貨物 unaccompanied
goods / ～行李 unaccompanied baggage

【托管】tuōguǎn (名) trusteeship

【托盤】tuōpán (名) tray

抖

抖 dǒu (動) ❶ shake; shiver: 嚇
得發～ shudder with fear / ～掉毯
子上的土 shake the dust off the
blanket ❷ pluck up; rouse

【抖動】dǒudòng (動) shake; vibrate

【抖擻】dǒusǒu (動) enliven; muster
up

抗

抗 kàng (動) ❶ resist; withstand;
ward off ❷ refuse; oppose; reject:
違～命令 defy or disobey orders ❸
match sth. or sb. against: 與之～
衡 contend with sb. or sth.

【抗旱】kànghàn Ⅰ (動) fight a
drought Ⅱ (形) (of vegetation)
drought resistant

【抗災】kàngzǎi (動) combat a natural disaster

【抗拒】kàngjù (動) resist; disobey

【抗洪】kànghóng (動) resist a flood
disaster

【抗稅】kàngshuì (動) refuse to pay
taxes

【抗菌素】kàngjūnsù (抗生素
kàngshēngsù) (名)〈藥〉antibiotic

【抗震】kàngzhèn (形) antiseismic

【抗戰】kàngzhàn (名) (short for 抗
日戰爭 Kàng Rì Zhànzhēng)
(China's) War of Resistance against
Japan (1937-1945)

【抗擊】kàngjī (動) resist; repulse

【抗藥性】kàngyàoxìng (名)〈醫〉re-
sistance to the action of a drug: 有
～ be drug-resistant

【抗議】kàngyì (動) protest (against)

【抗體】kàngtǐ (名)〈醫〉antibody

扶

扶 fú (動) ❶ support (with the
hand): ～老人回家 support the old
man home ❷ hold: ～杖而行 walk
with a stick ❸ help

【扶手】fúshou (名) ❶ armrest ❷
handrail; banisters

【扶手椅】fúshǒuyǐ (名) armchair

【扶助】fúzhù (動) help; assist

【扶持】fúchí (動) help; take care of

【扶病】fúbìng (副) despite ill health:
～出席 attend a meeting despite ill

health

【扶梯】fútī（名）staircase

【扶植】fúzhí（动）shore up; back up

【扶搖直上】fú yáo zhí shàng（成）rise steeply

【扶養】fúyǎng（动）provide for; bring up

技 jì（名）skill; technique; craft: 雕蟲小～ petty skill

【技工】jìgōng（名）skilled worker

【技巧】jìqiǎo（名）technique

【技能】jìnéng（名）skill; ability; technique

【技師】jìshī（名）technician; technical expert

【技校】jìxiào（名）(short for 技術學校 jìshù xuéxiào) technical school

【技術】jìshù（名）skill; technology: ～員 technician /～轉讓 technology transfer

【技藝】jìyì（名）craft; performing skill: ～高超 superb skill

找 zhǎo（动）❶ look for; seek: 替我～個座位。Please find a seat for me. /～～事故的原因 find out the cause of the accident ❷ want to see; call on; approach: 會計～你。The accountant wants to see you. ❸ give change: 我得～你五分錢。I should give you five fen change.

【找死】zhǎosǐ（动）court death

【找事】zhǎoshì（动）❶ hunt for a job ❷ pick a quarrel

【找麻煩】zhǎo máfan（动）❶ look for trouble ❷ cause sb. trouble: 他給我們找了好多麻煩。He caused us a lot of trouble.

【找尋】zhǎoxún（动）look for; seek

【找補】zhǎobu（动）make up a deficiency

【找碴兒】zhǎochár（动）find fault; pick a quarrel

扼 è（动）❶ grip; grasp ❷ guard; control

【扼守】èshǒu（动）guard

【扼制】èzhì（动）control; check

【扼要】èyào（形）to the point: 作～的説明 make a brief statement

【扼殺】èshā（动）strangle; throttle

抒 shū（动）express; vent

【抒情】shūqíng Ⅰ（动）express one's emotion Ⅱ（形）lyric: ～詩 lyric poetry

【抒發】shūfā（动）express; give expression to: ～感情 give expression to one's emotion

【抒寫】shūxiě（动）describe; express; relate

抉 jué（动）pick out; select

【抉擇】juézé（动）make one's option: 只得等待，別無～ have no choice but to wait

扭 niǔ（动）❶ turn round: ～頭 turn one's head ❷ twist; wrench ❸ sprain: ～了手腕 sprain one's wrist ❹ tussle with: 兩個摔跤手～在一起。The wrestlers grappled with each other. ❺ swing: ～秧歌 snake a yangko dance

【扭打】niǔdǎ（动）wrestle; grapple

【扭送】niǔsòng（动）seize and turn over (to security authorities); drag sb. off to: 把扒手～派出所 turn the pick-pocket over to the police station

【扭捏】niǔnie（形）affectedly shy

【扭轉】niǔzhuǎn（动）❶ turn round ❷ reverse; turn back: ～時局 turn

the tide

【扭擺】niǔbǎi (動) rock; reel or sway

把 bǎ I (動) ❶ grasp; grip: ～住鐵鏈 take a firm hold of the chain ❷ control; keep hold of; monopolize ❸ guard; watch: ～球門 (in football, etc.) be the goalkeeper ❹ be close to: ～在拐角 be at the street corner II (名) ❶ handle (of a pushcart, etc.): 自行車～ the handle bar of a bike ❷ bundle; bunch: 草～ straw bundle III (量) ❶ [of sth. with a handle]: 一～傘 an umbrella ❷ a handful of: 一～花生 a handful of peanuts ❸ [used with some abstract nouns]: 加一勁 put in more effort; redouble one's effort ❹ about: 個一星期 a week or so IV (介) ❶ [this usage of 把 often causes inverted order]: ～窗打開 open the window ❷ [this usage of 把 is often called for when such verbs as 忙, 累, 氣, 急, 高興, etc. come at the end]: 這消息～他樂壞了. He was overjoyed at the news.

see also bà

【把手】bǎshou (名) handle; knob; handle bar (of a bike, etc.): 門～ door handle

【把兄弟】bǎxiōngdì (名) sworn brothers

【把守】bǎshǒu (動) guard

【把門】bǎmén (動) stand watch at the door (gate)

【把柄】bǎbǐng (名) handle: 給人以～ give sb. a handle

【把持】bǎchí (動) 〈貶〉control; monopolize; dominate: ～一個部門 control a department

【把風】bǎfēng (動) keep watch; be on the lookout

【把酒】bǎjiǔ (動) raise one's wine cup

【把舵】bǎduò (動) steer; hold the rudder; be at the helm

【把握】bǎwò I (動) hold; grasp; take hold of: ～原則 never deviate from what is a matter of principle II (名) assurance; certainty: 有～ be confident

【把勢】bǎshì (名) ❶ 〈口〉wushu (martial arts); Chinese boxing gestures: 練～ practise martial arts ❷ person skilled in a trade: 瓜～ professional melon grower

【把頭】bǎtou (名) ❶ labour contractor ❷ gangmaster

【把戲】bǎxì (名) ❶ acrobatics; jugglery ❷ trick; game: 耍鬼～ play dirty tricks

【把關】bǎguān (動) ❶ guard (hold) a pass ❷ check quality, safety measures, etc.: 層層～ check quality at all levels

把 bà (名) ❶ grip; handle; stock; haft; helve: 刀～兒 knife handle ❷ stem (of leaf, flower or fruit): 梨～兒 pear stem

see also bǎ

【把子】bàzi (名) handle

抄 chāo (動) ❶ copy; make a fair copy of ❷ plagiarize ❸ search and confiscate ❹ take a short cut: ～敵人後路 attack the enemy's rear ❺ go off with: ～走兩本書 make off with two books ❻ fold one's hands in one's sleeves on front

【抄本】chāoběn (名) hand-copied book: 手～ hand-written copy

【抄件】chāojiàn（名）copy; duplicate

【抄送】chāosòng（动）copy to

【抄家】chāojiā（动）ransack sb.'s home

【抄写】chāoxiě（动）copy by hand; transcribe

【抄录】chāolù（动）make a copy of

【抄袭】chāoxí（动）❶ plagiarize ❷ copy mechanically other people's experience ❸ attack the rear or flank of

扯 chě（动）❶ tear: 把信～得粉碎 tear the letter to pieces ❷ pull: ～住 grasp tightly ❸ chat

【扯皮】chěpí（动）resort to endless dispute; squabble over petty issues

【扯后腿】chě hòutuǐ（动）hold sb. back from an undertaking

【扯淡】chědàn I（动）〈方〉talk nonsense II（名）nonsense

【扯谎】chěhuǎng（动）lie; tell a lie

批 pī I（动）❶ write comments or instructions on（a report, etc.）❷ criticize II（量）lot; load; group: 一～书 a batch of books 一～人 a group of people

【批示】pīshì（名）instructions or comments（written on a report, etc.）

【批改】pīgǎi（动）correct: ～学生作文 correct students' compositions

【批判】pīpàn（动）criticize; repudiate

【批判现实主义】pīpàn xiànshí zhǔyì（名）critical realism

【批註】pīzhù（动）annotate with comments

【批发】pīfā（动）wholesale

【批评】pīpíng I（动）criticize II（名）criticism

【批准】pīzhǔn（动）approve; ratify

【批驳】pībó（动）refute; confute

【批语】pīyǔ（名）❶ commentary on an essay ❷ comments on a report, memo, etc.

【批阅】pīyuè（动）read and write comments on

扮 bàn（动）play the part of; dress up as; disguise oneself as: 女～男装 a woman disguised as a man / 梳妆打～ deck oneself out; dress up

【扮相】bànxiàng（名）make-up of an actor or actress

【扮装】bànzhuāng I（动）play the role of II（名）make-up

【扮演】bànyǎn（动）play the role of; act

抛 pāo（动）❶ throw; cast ❷ leave behind; abandon ❸ disclose

【抛物线】pāowùxiàn（名）〈数〉parabola

【抛售】pāoshòu（动）sell sth. in large quantities（either to force down the price or to forestall a price drop）

【抛弃】pāoqì（动）abandon; discard: ～旧观念 discard old ideas

【抛砖引玉】pāo zhuān yǐn yù〈成〉venture one's commonplace opinions to elicit valuable views from other people; set the ball rolling

【抛头露面】pāo tóu lù miàn〈成〉〈贬〉（be compelled by circumstances to）make public appearances

【抛锚】pāomáo（动）❶ cast anchor ❷（of a vehicle）break down

投 tóu（动）❶ throw; toss; cast: ～球手（baseball）pitcher ❷ put

in: 向市场～放新产品 put new products on the market ❸ throw oneself into: ～河自尽 drown oneself in the river ❹ cast (light, glance, etc.) ❺ mail; send: ～书晚报 write a letter to the *Evening News* ❻ join; take part in ❼ cater to; agree; suit: 情～意合 find themselves temperamentally compatible

【投入】tóurù (动) put into: ～生产 put into production

【投合】tóuhé (动) ❶ be congenial; get along well ❷ cater to: ～消费者的需要 cater to the needs of consumers

【投考】tóukǎo (动) sign up for an entrance examination

【投向】tóuxiàng (名) trend of purchasing; orientation of investment

【投身】tóushēn (动) join in; throw oneself into

【投奔】tóubèn (动) hung to (a friend) for support or protection; seek the protection (of a man of influence)

【投降】tóuxiáng I (动) surrender; capitulate II (名) capitulation; surrender

【投射】tóushè (动) cast (light, a glance, shadow, etc.)

【投案自首】tóu'àn zìshǒu (动) give oneself up to the police

【投产】tóuchǎn (动) go into operation

【投票】tóupiào (动) cast a ballot; vote: 去～ go to the polls

【投宿】tóusù (动) put up for the night; stay overnight (at an inn, hotel, etc.)

【投诉】tóusù (动) lodge a complaint with the authorities

【投资】tóuzī I (动) invest II (名) investment: ～環境 investment environment (climate) / ～所得利润 return on investment

【投递】tóudì (动) deliver; send: ～员 postman

【投標】tóubiāo (动) bid (for); submit a tender; make a bid

【投敌】tóudí (动) defect to the enemy

【投稿】tóugǎo (动) contribute an article to a newspaper or journal

【投靠】tóukào (动) seek patronage with

【投彈】tóudàn (动) ❶ release a bomb ❷ throw a hand-grenade

【投親靠友】tóu qīn kào yǒu (动) go and live with one's relatives or friends

【投機】tóujī I (形) congenial; harmonious: 我们一路上談得很～。We had a very agreeable chat on the way. II (动) speculate: 政治～ political opportunism / ～倒把 speculate and profiteer

【投擲】tóuzhì (动) throw; fling

【投篮】tóulán (动) 〈篮球〉shoot

抑

抑 yì (动) restrain; curb

【抑制】yìzhì (动) restrain; check: ～不住自己的激动 cannot restrain one's excitement

【抑鬱】yìyù (形) depressed; disheartened

折

折 shé (动) ❶ break; snap: 我的錶带～了。The band of my wristwatch is broken. ❷ suffer a loss in money matters
see also zhē; zhé

【折本】shéběn (动) lose money in

business

【折耗】shéhào（動）damage; loss

折 zhē（動）turn over: ~跟頭 turn a somersault
see also shé; zhé

【折騰】zhēteng（動）❶ toss about: 他~了一夜没睡。He tossed about in bed, unable to fall asleep the whole night. ❷ do sth. over and over again: 他把家具擺過來擺過去，~了一天。He busied himself the whole day arranging and rearranging his furniture. ❸ cause physical or mental suffering: 牙痛真~人。A toothache is a torture.

折 zhé I（動）❶ break; snap: 樹枝被大風吹~了。A branch snapped in the strong wind. / 骨~ fracture ❷ lose: 損兵~將（of an army）suffer heavy casualties ❸ bend; change direction: ~回原路 turn back on the road one came / 百~不撓 unbending; undaunted ❹ admire; be convinced: ~服 be convinced; be persuaded ❺ convert into: 按照牌價把美元~成人民幣 change U. S. dollars into Rinminbi according to the list price II（名）discount: 打九~ give a 10% discount
see also shé; zhē

【折子戲】zhézixì（名）high-lights from operas

【折合】zhéhé（動）convert one currency into another; amount to

【折扣】zhékòu（名）discount; rebate

【折射】zhéshè（名）〈物〉refraction

【折衷】zhézhōng（動）compromise: 擬出一個~方案 work out a compromise

【折衷主義】zhézhōng zhǔyì（名）eclecticism

【折價】zhéjià（動）convert property into cash; evaluate in terms of money

【折磨】zhémó（動）afflict; torment: 飽受癌症的~ be tortured by cancer

【折舊】zhéjiù（名）〈經〉depreciation

扳 bān（動）pull; switch: ~倒 pull down

【扳子】bānzi（名）spanner; wrench

【扳手】bānshou（名）❶ level（on a machine）❷ spanner; wrench

【扳道工】bāndàogōng（名）〈交〉switchman; pointsman

【扳機】bānjī（名）trigger: 扣~ press the trigger

抓 zhuā（動）❶ clutch; grab; seize: ~住當前時機調整物價 seize the present opportunity to readjust the commodity prices / 她跌倒時一把~住我的衣袖。She clutched at my sleeve as she fell. ❷ arrest; catch: 當場~住小偷 catch a thief red-handed ❸ scratch: 他~~腦袋答不出來。He scratched his head without a reply. ❹ pay special attention to; stress: ~質量 stress the quality / ~勞動紀律 pay proper attention to labour discipline ❺ take charge of: ~日常工作 look after day-to-day business

【抓差】zhuāchāi（動）draft sb. for a particular job; press sb. into service

【抓緊】zhuājǐn（動）take a firm hold on: ~時機 let slip no opportunity

【抓藥】zhuāyào（動）have a prescription of Chinese herbal medicine filled

【抓辫子】zhuā biànzi （動） seize hold of sb.'s minor fault to criticize or denounce him

【抓阄兒】zhuājiūr （動）draw lots

承 chéng （動） ❶ undertake（to do a job）; accept orders for: ～製各式服裝 accept orders for making all kinds of garments ❷ carry on: 繼～ inherit ❸〈套〉be thankful for: ～您慷慨資助. We are grateful to you for your generous financial assistance.

【承包】chéngbāo （動） contract: 經營責任制 the contracted managerial responsibility system

【承先啓後】chéng xiān qǐ hòu〈成〉（of learning, enterprise, etc.）serve as a link between two generations

【承受】chéngshòu （動） bear; endure: ～巨大壓力 be under great pressure; withstand immense pressure

【承蒙】chéngméng （動）〈套〉be grateful: ～光臨,無任感荷. I am indebted to you for your gracious presence.

【承認】chéngrèn （動）❶ admit; acknowledge: 不～有罪 plead not guilty ❷ recognize; give diplomatic recognition to

【承諾】chéngnuò Ⅰ（動）promise Ⅱ（名）commitment

【承擔】chéngdān （動）assume; take on: ～責任 accept responsibility for

【承辦】chéngbàn （動）undertake: ～住房建築工程 undertake housing projects

拌 bàn （動）mix; mingle; stir and mix: 用鹽～一～ mix a little salt into sth.

【拌匀】bànyún （動）mix thoroughly; mix even

【拌和】bànhuo （動）mix: 把水泥和沙子～起來 mix cement with sand

【拌種】bànzhǒng （名）〈農〉 seed dressing

【拌嘴】bànzuǐ （動） exchange rude remarks; quarrel

拉 lā （動）❶ pull; haul: ～上窗簾 draw the window curtain ❷ transport（by a vehicle）: 用卡車～煤 transport coal by truck ❸ move （troops）❹ play（a musical instrument）: ～大提琴 play the cello ❺ give help: ～他一把 lend him a hand ❻ implicate; involve: 把他～下水 drag sb. into the mire of corruption ❼ try to establish certain ties: ～交情 try to forge some sort of social relationships ❽ loosen the bowels: ～屎 empty the bowels ❾〈方〉talk: ～家常 make small talk; chitchat

see also lá

【拉丁文】Lādīngwén （名） Latin （language）

【拉丁美洲】Lādīng Měizhōu （名） Latin America

【拉下臉】lāxiàliǎn （動）❶ not spare sb.'s feelings ❷ look displeased; pull a long face

【拉手】lāshou （名）handle （of a door, drawer, etc.）

【拉平】lāpíng （動）even up; make equal

【拉扯】lāche （動）〈口〉❶ pull; drag ❷ bring up（a child）❸ implicate; involve ❹ try to win sb. over to one's own side; rope in ❺ chitchat

【拉肚子】lā dùzi（动）have diarrhoea; have loose bowels

【拉扯】lāchě chě（动）〈口〉❶ drag sb. about ❷ engage in idle talk ❸ puff up one another

【拉拉队】lālāduì（名）rooters; cheering squad: ～长 cheer leader

【拉后腿】lā hòutuǐ（动）〈口〉be a hindrance to sb.; hold sb. back

【拉倒】lādǎo（动）〈口〉forget it; leave it at that: 不干～。You might as well quit if you don't feel like it.

【拉开】lākāi（动）❶ draw open: ～门 pull the door open ❷ space out; widen the gap

【拉杂】lāzá（拉拉杂杂 lālā zázá）（形）（of writing, narration）not well-organized; rambling

【拉锁儿】lāsuǒr（拉链 lāliàn）（名）zipper

【拉关系】lā guānxi（动）〈贬〉try to form a relationship with sb.

【拉拢】lālǒng（动）draw sb. over to one's own side by dubious means

拉 lá（动）cut; slit: ～块牛肉 cut off a chunk of beef
see also lā

挂 zhǔ（动）lean on（a stick, etc.）

抨 pēng

【抨击】pēngjī（动）assail; denounce

抹 mā（动）wipe; clean: ～玻璃 wipe the panes clean
see also mǒ; mò

【抹布】mābù（名）rag; wiper

【抹脸】māliǎn（动）suddenly change one's countenance; put on a stern expression

抹 mò（动）❶ put on; apply: 往地

板上～蜡 wax the wooden floor ❷ wipe: ～嘴 wipe one's mouth ❸ delete; erase: 把这个字～了。Cross out these words.
see also mā; mǒ

【抹杀】mǒshā（动）write off; obliterate; deny: ～他的功劳是不公平的。It is unfair to deny his contributions.

【抹黑】mǒhēi（动）blacken sb.'s reputation; smear; discredit: 这家伙就是要给我们脸上～。This chap is deliberately trying to bring discredit on us.

抹 mò（动）daub; plaster: 往墙上～灰 plaster a wall
see also mā; mǒ

拒 jù（动）❶ resist; spurn: ～人于千里之外 give a wide berth to sb. ❷ refuse; turn down; decline: ～不执行自己的诺言 refuse to make good one's own promise

【拒付】jùfù（动）refuse payment

【拒捕】jùbǔ（动）resist arrest

【拒绝】jùjué（动）❶ refuse: ～签字 refuse to sign（a document, petition, etc.）❷ turn down; reject: ～邀请 decline an invitation

拔 bá（动）❶ pull up; pull out: 连根～起 uproot ❷ suck（draw）out sth. poisonous: ～毒 draw out pus from an affected part ❸ choose（select）the best people: 选～人才 select talented persons ❹ stand out; surpass: 出类～萃的演员 an outstanding actor ❺ capture; seize（a city, forts, etc.）❻ lift; raise: ～腿就跑 run off at once; dash off; take to one's heels ❼〈口〉put sth. in cold water

【拔火罐】bá huǒguàn〈动〉cup: ~
疗法 cupping treatment

【拔火罐】báhuǒguàn〈名〉detachable
stovepipe (used to make the fire
draw)

【拔牙】báyá〈动〉pull out (extract)
a tooth; have a tooth out

【拔尖】bájiān〈形〉top-flight; outstanding

【拔河】báhé〈名〉tug of war

【拔苗助长】bá miáo zhù zhǎng〈成〉
pull the seedlings upward to help
them grow faster; spoil things by a
ridiculous desire for quick success

【拔除】báchú〈动〉eradicate; wipe
out: ~ 祸根 remove the root of
trouble

【拔高】bágāo〈动〉lift; raise: ~ 嗓
子 raise one's voice to a high pitch

【拔丝】básī Ⅰ〈动〉〈机〉draw wire
Ⅱ〈形〉sugar-coated: ~ 山药 candied yam (served hot when sugar
can be drawn out in threads)

【拔节】bájié〈名〉〈农〉jointing; e-
longation

【拔脚】bájiǎo〈动〉take to one's
feet: ~ 就走 take to one's heels

拓 tà〈动〉make rubbings
　　see also tuò

【拓片】tàpiàn〈名〉rubbing

【拓本】tàběn〈名〉book of rubbings

拓 tuò〈动〉open up (a road, path,
etc.): ~ 宽街道 widen a road
　　see also tà

【拓荒】tuòhuāng〈动〉　open up
wasteland: ~ 者 pioneer

抿 mǐn〈动〉❶ slightly close: ~ 起
嘴 press one's lips together ❷ sip:
~ 酒 sip wine ❸ brush; smooth: ~

了~头发 pat one's hair into shape

拂 fú〈动〉❶ flick: ~ 去灰尘
whisk the dust off ❷ touch: 春风 ~
面。The spring breeze caresses
one's cheeks.

【拂拭】fúshì〈动〉wipe; clean

【拂袖而去】fú xiù ér qù〈成〉leave
in a huff

【拂晓】fúxiǎo〈副〉before dawn

披 pī〈动〉❶ throw on (clothes):
~ 上一条围巾 throw a scarf over
one's shoulders ❷ open; unfurl ❸
(of bamboo, wood, etc.) cleave;
split

【披肝沥胆】pī gān lì dǎn〈成〉lay
bare one's heart; be boundlessly loyal

【披肩】pījiān〈名〉cape; shawl

【披风】pīfēng〈名〉cloak

【披星戴月】pī xīng dài yuè〈成〉
work from dawn to dusk; travel day
and night

【披荆斩棘】pī jīng zhǎn jí〈成〉
cleave a path through the jungle;
blaze new roads despite tremendous
difficulties

【披头散发】pī tóu sàn fà〈成〉with
hair hanging loose and dishevelled;
dishevelled

【披露】pīlù〈动〉❶ publish; an-
nounce ❷ disclose; impart

招 zhāo Ⅰ〈动〉❶ beckon: 他 ~ 手
要我走近些。He beckoned to me to
come closer. ❷ recruit; enrol: ~
护士 recruit nurses ❸ provoke: ~
事 invite trouble ❹
confess; admit: 不打自 ~ confess
of one's own accord; give oneself
away Ⅱ〈名〉trick; device; move:

這真是個高～. It's really an ingenious move.

【招生】zhāoshēng（動）enrol new students

【招考】zhāokǎo（動）admit (students, trainees, etc.) by examination

【招收】zhāoshōu（動）recruit; enrol

【招兵】zhāobīng（動）recruit soldiers

【招兵買馬】zhāo bīng mǎi mǎ〈成〉raise an army; enlist followers

【招供】zhāogòng（名）confess; own up

【招呼】zhāohu（動）❶ call: 母親在～孩子。Mother is calling her child. ❷ greet; say hello to: 親切地～客人 greet the guests cordially ❸ tell; inform: ～他該走了 warn him it's time to leave ❹ look after: ～病人 look after the patient

【招架】zhāojià（動）resist; withstand: 覺得外來壓力難以～ find it hard to withstand outside pressure

【招待】zhāodài Ⅰ（動）entertain; receive: ～朋友 entertain one's friends Ⅱ（名）waiter or waitress

【招待所】zhāodàisuǒ（名）hostel; guesthouse

【招待會】zhāodàihuì（名）reception

【招展】zhāozhǎn（動）flutter; wave

【招致】zhāozhì（動）❶ recruit; take in ❷ cause; bring about: ～財產損失 cause damage to property

【招貼】zhāotiē（名）poster; placard

【招牌】zhāopái（名）shop sign; signboard

【招搖撞騙】zhāo yáo zhuàng piàn〈成〉swindle by false pretences

【招募】zhāomù（動）recruit; enlist

【招聘】zhāopìn（動）invite applications for a job

【招惹】zhāorě（動）provoke; incur; incite

【招認】zhāorèn（動）confess one's crime

【招領】zhāolǐng（動）put up a "claim lost property" notice

【招標】zhāobiāo（動）invite tenders; invite bids

【招攬】zhāolǎn（動）solicit (customers or business)

押 yā（動）❶ mortgage; pawn: 以汽車作一借款 borrow money on the security of one's car ❷ detain; keep in custody: 那個殺人犯已被～起來了。The murderer has been taken into custody. ❸ escort

【押金】yājīn（名）(cash) deposit; security: 支付電視機的～ pay a deposit on a TV set

【押送】yāsòng（動）send under escort

【押解】yājiè（動）escort (a prisoner)

【押韻】yāyùn（名）rhyme: ～詩 rhymed poetry

抻 chēn（動）〈口〉draw out; stretch

【抻麵】chēnmiàn Ⅰ（動）draw out dough into noodles by hand Ⅱ（名）hand-pulled noodles

抽 chōu（動）❶ take out: 從錢包裏～出五元 take out a 5-yuan note from the wallet ❷ take (a part from the whole): ～時間 find time (to do sth.) ❸ (of a plant) sprout: ～芽 bud ❹ draw; inhale: ～水 pump water ❺ shrink: 這窗簾～水了。The curtain shrank after washing.

❻ lash; whip

【抽打】chōudǎ (动) whip; lash; flog

【抽身】chōushēn (动) get away (from one's work)

【抽空】chōukòng (抽功夫 chōu gōngfu) (动) find time (to do sth.)

【抽泣】chōuqì (动) sob

【抽查】chōuchá (动) sample; spot-check

【抽风】chōufēng (名)〈医〉convulsions

【抽纱】chōushā (名) drawn-work

【抽屉】chōuti (名) drawer

【抽税】chōushuì (动) levy a tax

【抽象】chōuxiàng (形) abstract

【抽烟】chōuyān (动) smoke

【抽搐】chōuchù Ⅰ(动) twitch Ⅱ(名)〈医〉spasm

【抽调】chōudiào (动) transfer

【抽签】chōuqiān (动) draw lots

拐 guǎi Ⅰ(动) ❶ turn: 往東 ~ turn east ❷ abduct; swindle ❸ limp Ⅱ(名) crutch

【拐杖】guǎizhàng (名) cane; walking stick

【拐角】guǎijiǎo (名) corner: 街 的 ~ at the corner of the street / 房子 的 ~ in the corner of the room

【拐棍】guǎigùn (名) walking stick; cane

【拐骗】guǎipiàn (动) abduct; swindle

【拐彎】guǎiwān (动) turn a corner

【拐彎抹角】guǎi wān mò jiǎo (成) beat about the bush

拈 niān (动) pick up (with the thumb and one or two fingers): ~ 筆 pick up a writing brush

【拈輕怕重】niān qīng pà zhòng (成)

choose easy jobs and steer away from hard ones

【拈閹】niānjiū (动) draw lots

拙 zhuō (形) ❶ clumsy; awkward ❷〈谦〉my: ~見 my humble opinion

【拙劣】zhuōliè (形) clumsy and inferior: ~伎俩 clumsy tactics

【拙笨】zhuōbèn (形) clumsy; awkward

拇 mǔ

【拇指】mǔzhǐ (名) ❶ thumb ❷ big toe

拎 līng (动)〈方〉carry in one's hand: ~了一籃子菜 carry a basket of vegetables

拖 tuō (动) ❶ pull; drag ❷ delay; retard: 問題一一再一没有解决. The problem remained unsolved after repeated delays.

【拖欠】tuōqiàn (动) be behind in payment: ~房租 be in arrears with rent

【拖曳車】tuōyèchē (名) breakdown van; tow truck

【拖把】tuōbǎ (名) mop

【拖車】tuōchē (名) trailer; trailer coach

【拖延】tuōyán (动) delay; put off; be dilatory: 採取~戰術 adopt delaying tactics; playing for time

【拖拉】tuōlā (形) slow in action; dilatory

【拖拉機】tuōlājī (名) tractor

【拖泥带水】tuō ní dài shuǐ (成) (of writing or work) messy; sloppy

【拖後腿】tuō hòutuǐ (动) be a drag on sb.; hold sb. back

【拖累】tuōlèi （动）❶ weigh down: 受家务的 ～ be weighed down with household chores ❷ implicate; involve

【拖堂】tuōtáng （动）prolong a class

【拖轮】tuōlún （拖船 tuōchuán）（名）tugboat; towboat

【拖鞋】tuōxié （名）slipper

拃 zhǎ Ⅰ（动）measure by handspans Ⅱ（量）span: 两～长 two spans long

抱 bào Ⅰ（动）❶ hold in the arms; hug; embrace: ～着小孩 carry a baby in one's arms ❷ bear (a grudge against sb.); cherish (an illusion about sth. or sb.); entertain (high hopes of sb.): ～成见 be prejudiced (against sb.) ❸ have one's first child or grandchild ❹ adopt (a baby) ❺ hang together ❻ hatch eggs Ⅱ（量）armful: 一～柴草 an armful of firewood

【抱不平】bào bùpíng （动）feel indignant at an injustice done to sb.: 打～ seek to redress a wrong

【抱成一团】bào chéng yī tuán （动）❶ gang up ❷ get into a clinch

【抱佛脚】bào fó jiǎo （动）（literally）hug Buddha's legs and beseech: 临时～ seek help at the eleventh hour; cram for exams at the last minute

【抱定】bàodìng （动）hold firmly: 主意 hold on to a decision

【抱屈】bàoqū （动）nurse a grievance

【抱负】bàofù （名）aspiration; ambition

【抱恨】bàohèn （动）be filled with remorse for: ～终天 regret sth. for the rest of one's life

【抱怨】bàoyuàn （动）grumble; complain

【抱病】bàobìng （动）be ill; be in poor health: ～工作 work regularly despite ill health

【抱残守缺】bào cán shǒu quē 〈成〉be content with deficient knowledge and refuse to improve oneself

【抱愧】bàokuì （动）feel ashamed

【抱歉】bàoqiàn （动）be sorry for; be apologetic for; regret

【抱养】bàoyǎng （动）adpot (a child)

拘 jū Ⅰ（动）❶ arrest; apprehend: ～押 take into custody ❷ restrain; limit: 文章长短不～。No limit is set on the length of an essay. Ⅱ（形）rigid; stiff: ～泥细节 be overparticular about details

【拘束】jūshù （动）❶ restrain; restrict: 不要过分～孩子们的活动。Don't place undue restrictions on the activities of the children. ❷ feel uncomfortable; be embarrassed: 在這麼多的知名學者面前，他有些～。He feels shy and ill at ease in the presence of so many distinguished scholars.

【拘泥】jūnì （动）rigidly conform to; be inflexible about: 过分～小节 be overparticular about small matters; be punctilious

【拘捕】jūbǔ （动）arrest; apprehend: 首犯已被～。The principal culprit has been placed under arrest.

【拘留】jūliú Ⅰ（动）detain; take into custody Ⅱ（名）detention: ～所 house of detention

【拘禁】jūjìn （动）take into custody; detain

【拘谨】jūjǐn （形）overcautious; prim

拍 pāi Ⅰ (動) ❶ clap; slap; pat: ～那孩子的頭 pat the child on the head / ～桌子 pound the table ❷ take (a picture); shoot (a film) ❸ send (a telegram, etc.) ❹ flatter; toady: ～馬屁 lick sb.'s spittle; fawn on Ⅱ (名) ❶ bat; racket: 羽毛球～ badminton racket ❷ 〈樂〉 beat; time: 合～ be on the beat; be in step with; be in harmony with

【拍子】 pāizi (名) ❶ bat; racket ❷ 〈樂〉 beat; time

【拍手】 pāishǒu (動) clap one's hands: ～稱快 clap one's hands in approval; clap and cheer

【拍打】 pāida (動) pat; beat

【拍板】 pāibǎn Ⅰ (名) clappers Ⅱ (動) ❶ rap the gavel ❷ have the final say: 這事我無法～定案。I have no final say in the matter.

【拍紙簿】 pāizhǐbù (名) (writing) pad

【拍照】 pāizhào (動) take a photograph; have a photograph taken

【拍賣】 pāimài (名) auction: ～市場 auction market

【拍攝】 pāishè (動) take pictures; shoot films

抵 dǐ (動) ❶ support; prop: ～住門 prop the door ❷ resist ❸ be equal to; offset: 收支相～ maintain a balance of revenue and expenditure ❹ arrive: ～滬 arrive in Shanghai

【抵抗】 dǐkàng (動) resist

【抵押】 dǐyā (動) mortgage

【抵制】 dǐzhì (動) resist; boycott

【抵消】 dǐxiāo (動) offset; counteract

【抵達】 dǐdá (動) arrive

【抵罪】 dǐzuì (動) pay for one's crime

【抵賴】 dǐlài (動) deny by lies or sophistry

【抵擋】 dǐdǎng (動) withstand; resist: ～不住外來壓力 be unable to withstand outside pressure

【抵禦】 dǐyù (動) resist; hold out against

【抵償】 dǐcháng (動) compensate

【抵觸】 dǐchù (動) conflict; contradict

拆 chāi (動) ❶ take apart: ～玩具 disassemble a toy ❷ tear open: ～信 open a letter ❸ demolish: ～牆 pull down a wall

【拆東牆，補西牆】 chāi dōng qiáng, bǔ xī qiáng (成) tear down the east wall to repair the west wall; rob Peter to pay Paul

【拆穿】 chāichuān (動) expose: ～西洋鏡 strip off the camouflage

【拆卸】 chāixiè (動) dismantle; dismount

【拆除】 chāichú(拆掉 chāidiào) (動) demolish; dismantle: ～腳手架 remove the scaffolding

【拆開】 chāikāi (動) ❶ disassemble; dismantle ❷ (of letters, etc.) tear open

【拆散】 chāisǎn (動) break (a set)

【拆散】 chāisàn (動) break up (a family, etc.)

【拆毀】 chāihuǐ (動) demolish: ～柏林牆 demolish the Berlin wall

【拆線】 chāixiàn (動) 〈醫〉 remove the stitches

【拆臺】 chāitái (動) cut the ground from under sb.'s feet: 這是拆我的臺。This is letting me down.

【拆牆腳】 chāi qiángjiǎo (動) pull

away a prop; undermine: 你的所作所爲就是拆他的牆腳。What you do is undermining public confidence in him.

拗 ào

see also niù

【拗口】àokǒu（形）difficult to articulate clearly

拗 niù（形）stubborn; obstinate: 她脾氣很～。She is very stubborn.

see also ào

拜 bài Ⅰ（動）❶ make obeisance to sb. ❷ enter into a certain relationship with sb.: 結～兄弟 become sworn brothers Ⅱ（名）courtesy call: 回～ return call Ⅲ〈敬〉[used before a verb]: ～望 pay one's respects to sb.

【拜年】bàinián（動）pay a New Year call; extend New Year greetings

【拜見】bàijiàn（動）〈敬〉make a formal call on

【拜金主義】bàijīn zhǔyì（名）mammonism

【拜師】bàishī（動）acknowledge sb. as one's master

【拜託】bàituō（動）〈敬〉ask; ask a favour of sb.: 這件事就～你好嗎？Could I leave the matter with you?

【拜訪】bàifǎng（動）pay a visit; call on

【拜會】bàihuì（動）pay a formal or courtesy call (on)

【拜謁】bàiyè（動）〈敬〉❶ pay one's respects to sb. ❷ pay homage to (a monument, etc.)

【拜謝】bàixiè（動）〈敬〉thank sincerely

拳 quán（名）❶ fist ❷ boxing;

pugilism: 太極～ taijiquan, a kind of shadow-boxing

【拳打腳踢】quándǎ jiǎotī（動）hit and kick; beat up

【拳拳】quánquán（形）sincere: ～之意 my sincere intention

【拳頭】quántou（名）fist

【拳擊】quánjī（名）boxing; pugilism

挈 qiè（動）❶ lift; raise: 提綱～領 grasp the main points; state in brief ❷ take along: ～眷南歸 return to the south accompanied by one's family

按 àn Ⅰ（動）❶ press; push down: ～電鈴 press the bell ❷ hold sth. back; shelve: 此事只好～下不提。We'll have to put the matter aside. ❸ restrain; control; hold back ❹ keep a tight grip on; keep one's hand on Ⅱ（介）❶ in accordance with; in the light of: ～制度辦事 handle matters according to the regulations ❷ per; by: ～月交房租 pay rent monthly Ⅲ（名）note; remarks; comment

【按兵不動】àn bīng bù dòng〈成〉hold troops back from battle; take no action; bide one's time

【按脈】ànmài（動）feel (take) the pulse

【按時】ànshí（副）on time; on schedule

【按理】ànlǐ（副）normally; it stands to reason...

【按捺不住】ànnà bù zhù（動）cannot restrain or control: ～心頭怒火 cannot control one's temper

【按部就班】àn bù jiù bān〈成〉❶ work by the rules of procedure ❷ follow conventional ways in doing things

【按钮】ànniǔ（名）push button: ~控制 push-button control

【按期】ànqī（副）on schedule; according to schedule: ~付款 pay regularly

【按劳分配】àn láo fēn pèi〈成〉to each according to his work

【按照】ànzhào（介）according to; in accordance with; in terms of: ~我們的經驗 in the light of our experience

【按語】ànyǔ（名）note; comment

【按需分配】àn xū fēn pèi〈成〉to each according to his needs

【按摩】ànmó（动）massage: ~療法 massotherapy

挖 wā（动）dig; unearth: ~河泥 dredge

【挖苦】wāku（动）deride; taunt

【挖掘】wājué（动）dig out; uproot

【挖掘】wājué（动）excavate; tap: ~潜力 tap potentialities

【挖牆脚】wā qiángjiǎo（动）〈口〉undermine; cut the ground from under sb.'s feet

拼 pīn（动）❶ piece together: 把各方面的信息~起来。Piece together information from various sources. ❷ be ready to risk all

【拼法】pīnfǎ（名）spelling

【拼命】pīnmìng Ⅰ（动）risk one's life Ⅱ（副）with all one's might; in desperation: ~奔跑 run like crazy

【拼音】pīnyīn Ⅰ（动）combine sounds into syllables Ⅱ（名）pinyin (Chinese phonetic transcription)

【拼音文字】pīnyīn wénzì（名）alphabetic writing

【拼音字母】pīnyīn zìmǔ（名）phonetic alphabet

【拼凑】pīncòu（动）put (odds and ends) together; knock together

【拼搏】pīnbó（动）strive strenuously

【拼盘】pīnpán（名）assorted cold dishes; hors d'oeuvres

【拼寫】pīnxiě（动）spell

持 chí（动）❶ hold by the hand: ~刀行兇 assail sb. with a knife or dagger ❷ maintain: 各~己见 each sticking to his own view ❸ manage: 主~會議 chair a meeting ❹ confront: 僵~局面 stalemate

【持久】chíjiǔ（形）lasting; enduring: ~力 stamina; sustaining power

【持平】chípíng（形）just; impartial; evenhanded

【持有】chíyǒu（动）hold: ~健康證明 hold a health certificate

【持重】chízhòng（形）prudent; discreet

【持家】chíjiā（动）keep house

【持續】chíxù Ⅰ（动）sustain; last Ⅱ（形）sustained: ~努力 make a sustained effort

拮 jié

【拮据】jiéjū（形）hard up: 手頭~run short of money

拷 kǎo（动）torture; beat hard with a stick, whip, etc.

【拷打】kǎodǎ（动）flog; beat up

【拷贝】kǎobèi（名）〈電影〉copy

【拷問】kǎowèn（动）extort confession by torture

拱 gǒng Ⅰ（动）❶ fold: ~手 fold hands before the chest (to show respect) ❷ surround; encircle: 四山環~ surrounded on all sides by mountains ❸ arch; hunch ❹ push; prop up Ⅱ（名）arch

【拱門】gǒngmén（名）〈建〉arched door

【拱頂】gǒngdǐng（名）〈建〉vault

【拱衛】gǒngwèi（動）guard on all sides

【拱橋】gǒngqiáo（名）〈建〉arch bridge

拭 shì（動）wipe

【拭目以待】shì mù yǐ dài〈成〉wait and see

拷 kuà（動）❶ carry on the arm: 兩個小女孩一起胳膊向學校走去。Two little girls, arm in arm, are walking towards the school. ❷ carry over the shoulder, across the neck or at the waist: ～着槍 with a rifle slung over the shoulder

【拷包】kuàbāo（名）satchel

拯 zhěng

【拯救】zhěngjiù（動）save; rescue

搜 zhuāi（動）pull; drag: 這抽屜～不開。This drawer won't open.

指 zhī
see also zhí; zhǐ

【指甲】zhījia（名）fingernail

指 zhí
see also zhī; zhǐ

【指頭】zhítou（名）❶ finger ❷ toe

指 zhǐ Ⅰ（名）finger: 食～ index finger Ⅱ（動）❶ point at; point to: 羅盤的針～向北方。The needle of a compass points to the north. ❷ point out; refer to: ～出錯誤 point out the errors ❸ count on; rely on
see also zhī; zhí

【指引】zhǐyǐn（動）guide; lead

【指日可待】zhǐ rì kě dài〈成〉in the offing: 和平解決，～。A peaceful settlement is in sight.

【指手劃腳】zhǐ shǒu huà jiǎo〈成〉❶ gesticulate ❷ give uncalled-for advice or ineffective orders

【指示】zhǐshì Ⅰ（動）instruct; order Ⅱ（名）instruction

【指正】zhǐzhèng（動）correct; make a comment or criticism: 我要是説得不對，請～。Please correct me if I'm wrong.

【指令】zhǐlìng（名）order; instruction: ～性計劃 mandatory planning

【指名】zhǐmíng（動）mention by name: 我不願～道姓。I don't want to name names.

【指明】zhǐmíng（動）point out; demonstrate

【指定】zhǐdìng（動）appoint; assign: 在～的時間見面 meet at the appointed time

【指使】zhǐshǐ（動）instigate; incite

【指派】zhǐpài（動）appoint; assign; name: 他被～爲經理。He was appointed manager.

【指南】zhǐnán（名）guide; guidebook

【指南針】zhǐnánzhēn（名）compass

【指紋】zhǐwén（名）fingerprint

【指針】zhǐzhēn（名）❶ indicator; pointer ❷ guiding principle

【指桑罵槐】zhǐ sāng mà huái〈成〉abuse by innuendoes; attack by inference or implication

【指教】zhǐjiào〈套〉give advice or guidance: 希望多多～。I hope you will not hesitate to give us advice.

【指控】zhǐkòng（動）charge; accuse: 他被～受賄。He was accused of taking bribes.

【指望】zhǐwàng Ⅰ(动) look forward to; look to: ~他们早日归来 look forward to their early return Ⅱ(名) prospect; hope: 几乎没有成功的~。 There is little chance of success.

【指责】zhǐzé (动) censure; denounce

【指挥】zhǐhuī Ⅰ(动) command; direct; conduct: ~交通 direct traffic / ~部队 command troops Ⅱ(名) ❶ commander; director ❷ 〈乐〉 conductor

【指挥部】zhǐhuībù (名) command post; headquarters

【指路牌】zhǐlùpái (名) signpost; guidepost

【指标】zhǐbiāo (名) target; quota; norm

【指导】zhǐdǎo (动) instruct; direct

【指靠】zhǐkào (动) depend on; count on: 你可以~他的帮助。You can count on him for support.

【指数】zhǐshù (名) index number; index

【指点】zhǐdiǎn (动) instruct; show how: ~他开机器 show him how to operate the machine

挑 tiāo Ⅰ(动) ❶ choose; pick; single out: ~花了眼 be at a loss what to select (from a dazzling variety of things); be too choosy ❷ carry (on a shoulder pole): ~子 carrying pole with its load Ⅱ(量) (of sth. carried on a shoulder pole) load: 一~土 two basketfuls of earth see also tiǎo

【挑剔儿】tiāocìr (动) 〈口〉 find fault; nitpick; be fastidious: 爱~ be fault-finding

【挑肥拣瘦】tiāo féi jiǎn shòu (成) 〈贬〉 choose whatever is to one's advantage; be choosy

【挑剔】tiāoti (动) be fastidious; be fault-finding

【挑拣】tiāojiǎn (动) pick and choose: 挑三拣四 be choosy

【挑选】tiāoxuǎn (动) choose; pick out

挑 tiǎo (动) ❶ raise (with a pole) ❷ poke: 把刺儿~出来 pick out a thorn (splinter) / ~明 lay all the cards on the table ❸ incite; abet see also tiāo

【挑大梁】tiǎo dàliáng (动) play the part of a mainstay; play a key role

【挑逗】tiǎodòu (动) tease; tantalize

【挑起】tiǎoqǐ (动) excite; provoke

【挑唆】tiǎosuo (动) incite; abet; goad

【挑动】tiǎodòng (动) provoke; excite; rouse

【挑拨】tiǎobō (动) sow discord: ~离间 foment dissension

【挑战】tiǎozhàn (动) challenge

【挑衅】tiǎoxìn (名) provocation: ~行动 a provocative act

拴 shuān (动) tie; tether

【拴绑】shuānbǎng (动) tie up; fasten; truss up

拾 shí Ⅰ(动) pick up (from the ground): 把玩具从地上~起来。 Pick up the toys from the floor. Ⅱ(数) [the elaborate form of the numeral 十, used on cheques, banknotes, etc.] ten

【拾取】shíqǔ (动) ❶ pick up (from the ground) ❷ collect; gather

【拾金不昧】shí jīn bù mèi (成) not

pocket the money one has picked up somewhere

【拾音器】shíyīnqì（名）pickup (of a phonograph)

【拾掇】shíduo（动）❶ tidy up; put in good order: 把你書桌上的東西～～。Tidy up your desk. ❷ gather ❸ repair: 手錶走時不準，得一～一下。The watch does not keep good time and needs to be fixed. ❹〈口〉punish; discipline

【拾零】shílíng（名）[often used in newspaper headings] titbits; sidelights

括 kuò（动）❶ contract (muscles) ❷ comprise; include: 包～一切費用 all charges included

【括弧】kuòhú（名）parenthesis: 有～ be in parentheses

【括號】kuòhào（名）bracket

拿 ná I（动）❶ take; hold: ～着書 have a book in one's hand / 把信～走 take the letter away ❷ capture; seize: ～住三個罪犯 capture three criminals / ～下一座城 take a city ❸ decide; be sure of: 我已～定了主意。I have made up my mind. II（介）with: ～鎬挖坑 dig a pit with a pick

【拿大頂】nádàdǐng（名）〈體〉handstand

【拿手】náshǒu（形）good at; skilled in: 做蛋糕她很～。She is good at making cakes.

【拿手好戲】ná shǒu hǎo xì〈成〉one's best skill; one's speciality

【拿主意】ná zhǔyi（动）make up one's mind; decide

【拿住】názhù（动）❶ apprehend; arrest ❷ hold firmly

【拿架子】nájiàzi（动）put on airs; get on one's high horse

【拿開】nákāi（动）take away

【拿辦】nábàn（动）arrest and deal with according to law

【拿獲】náhuò（动）apprehend; arrest

捕 bǔ（动）capture; seize; arrest: 追～逃犯 chase (hunt) down an escaped criminal (convict)

【捕食】bǔshí（动）prey on

【捕風捉影】bǔ fēng zhuō yǐng〈成〉indulge in groundless suspicion

【捕捉】bǔzhuō（动）catch; seize: ～昆蟲 catch insects / ～戰機 seize the most opportune moment to give battle

【捕獲】bǔhuò（动）capture; catch; arrest: 當場～殺人兇手 catch the murderer red-handed

【捕獲量】bǔhuòliàng（名）(of fish, etc.) catch

【捕鯨船】bǔjīngchuán（名）whaling vessel; whaler

挟 xié（动）❶ hold sth. under the arm: ～着書包 carry one's school bag under the arm ❷ coerce; force

【挟制】xiézhì（动）force sb. into doing one's bidding

【挟持】xiéchí（动）hold sb. under duress; coerce sb. into submission

振 zhèn（动）❶ shake; wield: ～臂 raise one's arm ❷ rouse (oneself); be roused to action: 一蹶不～ unable to pick oneself up again after a setback

【振作】zhènzuò（动）pull oneself together

【振振有辭】zhèn zhèn yǒu cí〈成〉

hold forth at great length

【振动】zhèndòng (名)〈物〉vibration: ~計 vibro-meter

【振奮】zhènfèn (動) ❶ rouse oneself; bestir oneself ❷ inspire; stimulate: ~人心的講話 an inspiring speech

【振興】zhènxīng (動) develop vigorously; prosper: ~中華 rejuvenate the Chinese nation

【振蕩】zhèndàng (名) ❶〈物〉vibration ❷〈電〉oscillation

捂 wǔ (動) cover; mask: ~着耳朵 cover one's ears

【捂蓋子】wǔgàizi (動) conceal the truth

挪 nuó (動) move; shift: 把書架~到另一間屋裏 move the book-shelf to another room

【挪用】nuóyòng (動) ❶ divert (funds) ❷ embezzle: ~公款 embezzle public funds

【挪威】Nuówēi (名) Norway: ~人 Norwegian / ~語 Norwegian (language)

【挪動】nuódòng (動) move; shift

捎 shāo (動) take sth. to sb.: 我想請李先生~一封信給他。I am thinking of asking Mr. Li to kindy hand-deliver a letter to him.

【捎腳兒】shāojiǎor (動) pick up passengers or goods on the way; give sb. a lift

捍 hàn (動) defend; guard

【捍衛】hànwèi (動) defend; safeguard; protect

捏 niē (動) ❶ hold between the fingers; pinch: ~住 keep hold of

❷ knead with the fingers; mould: ~生麵團 knead dough ❸ fabricate; make up

【捏一把汗】niē yī bǎ hàn (動) sweat with fear or anxiety

【捏合】niēhé (動) bring together

【捏造】niēzào (動) fabricate; make up: ~證據 fabricate evidence

捌 bā (數) [the elaborate form of the numeral 八, used on cheques, banknotes, etc.] eight

捐 juān Ⅰ (動) ❶ relinquish; give up ❷ donate; contribute Ⅱ (名) tax

【捐助】juānzhù (動) donate; contribute

【捐稅】juānshuì (名) levies and taxes: 繳納~ pay taxes and levies to the state

【捐棄】juānqì (動) abandon; discard: ~前嫌 bury the hatchet

【捐款】juānkuǎn Ⅰ (動) contribute a sum of money Ⅱ (名) donation; contribution

【捐軀】juānqū (動) lay down one's life; die a martyr

【捐贈】juānzèng (動) present; donate: 向孤兒院~一萬元 donate 10,000 yuan to an orphanage

【捐獻】juānxiàn (動) donate; offer: 把收藏的古幣~給博物館 offer one's collection of ancient coins to the museum

捉 zhuō (動) catch; capture; seize: ~小偷 catch a thief

【捉弄】zhuōnòng (動) make fun of; tantalize

【捉迷藏】zhuōmícáng (動) play hide-and-seek

【捉拿】zhuōná (動) arrest; capture:

~逃犯 arrest an escaped convict

【捉摸】zhuōmō〔动〕predict; ascertain: 不可~ unpredictable; inconceivable

【捉襟见肘】zhuō jīn jiàn zhǒu〈成〉have too many difficulties to cope with

捆 kǔn Ⅰ〔动〕tie up Ⅱ〔量〕bundle: 两~稻子 two bundles of rice

【捆紮】kǔnzā〔动〕bind; bundle up

【捆绑】kǔnbǎng〔动〕truss up; bind up

捋 lǚ〔动〕stroke; smooth: ~绳子 straighten out the ropes

挫 cuò〔名〕setback: 受~ meet with setbacks

【挫折】cuòzhé Ⅰ〔名〕setback; failure Ⅱ〔动〕hamper; weaken

【挫败】cuòbài Ⅰ〔名〕frustration; defeat Ⅱ〔动〕beat

【挫伤】cuòshāng Ⅰ〔名〕bruise Ⅱ〔动〕hurt; discourage; frustrate: ~他的情绪 hurt his feelings

挺 tǐng Ⅰ〔形〕errect; straight: 穿着笔~的西装 wear a well-pressed suit Ⅱ〔动〕❶ straighten up: ~起腰板 straighten one's back ❷ endure; hold out; pull through: ~得住 can manage to hold out Ⅲ〔副〕very; pretty: 跑得~快 run pretty fast Ⅳ〔量〕两~机枪 two machine guns

【挺立】tǐnglì〔动〕stand errect

【挺身】tǐngshēn〔动〕❶ square one's shoulders ❷ come out boldly (against sth.): ~而出 step forward bravely

【挺拔】tǐngbá〔形〕❶ errect and tall ❷ forceful; vigorous

【挺直】tǐngzhí Ⅰ〔动〕straighten up Ⅱ〔形〕❶ straight and strong: ~的胸脯 square and strong shoulders ❷ (of clothes) well-pressed

【挺进】tǐngjìn〔动〕(of troops) press forward

【挺举】tǐngjǔ〔名〕〈体〉(of weightlifting) clean and jerk

挽 wǎn Ⅰ〔动〕❶ pull; draw; tug: ~着他的肩膀，放声大哭 cry bitterly over his arm ❷ roll up (sleeves, etc.) Ⅱ〔形〕elegiac: ~诗 elegy

【挽回】wǎnhuí〔动〕redeem; retrieve: 无可~的损失 irretrievable loss

【挽留】wǎnliú〔动〕urge sb. to stay on at his post

【挽救】wǎnjiù〔动〕save; rescue; redeem

【挽歌】wǎngē〔名〕dirge; elegy

【挽联】wǎnlián〔名〕elegiac couplet

挨 āi Ⅰ〔动〕❶ be (get) close to; be next to: ~着墙走 skirt along the wall Ⅱ〔副〕in sequence; one by one; by turns: ~户通知 notify each and every household

see also ái

【挨次】āicì〔副〕one by one

【挨近】āijìn〔动〕approach; be close to

【挨门逐户】āi mén zhú hù〈成〉from door to door; from house to house

【挨个儿】āigèr〔副〕one after another: ~来 take turns

挨 ái〔动〕❶ suffer; endure: ~批评 be reprimanded ❷ tide over: ~过那困难的岁月 tide over those

difficult years
see also āi

【挨擼】áilū (動)〈口〉be given a dressing-down

控 kòng (動) ❶ accuse; charge: 被～ be accused of; be charged with ❷ control; command: 失～get out of control

【控告】kònggào (動) lodge a charge (against sb.) with the (judicial) authorities; lodge a complaint (against sb.) with an organ of state

【控制】kòngzhì (動) control: ～着局勢 be in control of the situation

【控制論】kòngzhìlùn (名)〈數〉cybernetics

【控訴】kòngsù (動) impeach; indict

接 jiē (動) ❶ touch; be close to: ～吻 kiss ❷ connect; link up: 上氣不～下氣 be out of breath ❸ catch hold of: ～球 catch a ball ❹ meet with; welcome: 迎～客人 meet a guest ❺ receive: ～到電報 receive a telegram / ～電話 answer the telephone ❻ take over; replace: ～他的工作 take over his job

【接力】jiēlì (名) relay: 八百米～800-metre relay

【接二連三】jiē èr lián sān〈成〉one after another; repeatedly

【接生】jiēshēng Ⅰ(動) aid in the delivery of a baby Ⅱ(名) midwifery

【接合】jiēhé (動) join together

【接收】jiēshōu (動) ❶ receive: ～來電 receive a telegram ❷ take over (property, organization, etc.) in accordance with law or decree ❸ (of an organization) admit; accept: ～新會員 admit new members

【接見】jiējiàn (動) meet with (guests, visitors, etc.); give an interview to (journalists, etc.)

【接近】jiējìn (動) be close to; approach: 現已～假期。The vacation is drawing near. / ～官方的人士 sources close to the government

【接受】jiēshòu (動) accept; take: ～教職 accept a teaching position

【接待】jiēdài (動) receive (guests, visitors, etc.): ～室 reception room

【接洽】jiēqià (動) consult with sb. about; make arrangements for: ～日程安排 make arrangements concerning the itinerary

【接風】jiēfēng (動) give a dinner in honour of a newly arrived guest

【接連】jiēlián (形) continual; successive: ～警告 give repeated warnings

【接納】jiēnà (動) admit (into an organization); accept

【接氣】jiēqì (形) coherent: 不～incoherent; disorganized

【接通】jiētōng (動) (in telephoning) put through; get through; 請給我～上海。Will you please put me through to Shanghai?

【接班】jiēbān (動) take over the duties from the previous shift

【接班人】jiēbānrén (名) successor

【接着】jiēzhe (動) ❶ catch (with one's hands): 我往下扔, 你在下面～。Catch it as I throw it down. ❷ go on (to do sth.); carry on: ～談吧。Go on, please.

【接替】jiētì (動) take the place of; succeed: 我們也許要派人去～他。Perhaps we will have to send somebody to replace him.

【接種】jiēzhòng (動)〈醫〉inoculate: ～牛痘 be vaccinated

【接踵】jiēzhǒng （副）（of people） one after another; in succession: ～而來 come in succession

【接頭】jiētóu （動）❶ connect（two threads）❷〈口〉contact: 他要我一到這裏就跟你～。He wanted me to contact you as soon as I got here. ❸ know well about（a matter, business, etc.）: 不～ have no idea

【接頭兒】jiētóur （名）joint（between two threads）

【接應】jiēyìng （動）❶ reinforce: ～前綫部隊 reinforce the troops at the front ❷ supply（of goods, etc.）: 電力～不上。Electricity is in short supply.

【接濟】jiējì （動）give financial or material aid to; send relief to

【接觸】jiēchù Ⅰ（動）❶ contact; touch: ～到放射性物質 be exposed to radioactive material ❷ have contact with: 與讀者保持～ keep in touch with the reading public ❸ engage: 與敵前哨～ skirmish with the enemy's advance guards Ⅱ（名）contact: ～傳染病 contagious disease

【接壤】jiērǎng （動）be contiguous to; have a common border with

探 tàn Ⅰ（動）❶ explore; sound; probe: ～口氣 sound sb. out ❷ visit; call on: ～監 visit a prisoner ❸ stretch forward; lean out: ～身 bend forward（for a better look）Ⅱ（名）spy; detective: 暗～ secret agent

【探戈】tàngē （名）tango

【探明】tànmíng （動）ascertain; verify

【探風】tànfēng （動）probe; find out

about the situation

【探索】tànsuǒ （動）explore（a secret or mystery）; seek（truth）

【探討】tàntǎo （動）inquire into; investigate; look into: ～這個計劃的可行性 study the feasibility of this plan

【探訪】tànfǎng （動）visit; go in search of: ～親友 visit one's relatives and friends

【探問】tànwèn （動）❶ try to fish for（information）: 我～他的意圖。I tried to sound him out. ❷ inquire after（sb.）

【探望】tànwàng （動）❶ look out and about ❷ visit; call on（living far away）: ～遠客他鄉的友人 visit one's friends who live far away from home

【探視】tànshì （動）visit a patient in a hospital ward; visit a prisoner: ～時間 visiting hours（in a hospital）

【探測】tàncè （動）measure; probe; fathom

【探照燈】tànzhàodēng （名）searchlight

【探親】tànqīn （動）go on home leave

【探險】tànxiǎn （動）explore: ～旅行 make an expedition / 到南極～ go on an expedition to the Antarctic

【探礦】tànkuàng （動）go prospecting

【探聽】tàntīng （動）make inquiries: ～失踪人員的下落 make inquiries about the missing persons

掠 lüè （動）❶ take by force; plunder ❷ flit; skim: 流星～空而過。A meteor darted across the sky.

【掠取】lüèqǔ （動）take by force; plunder

【掠美】lüèměi （動）claim credit for

sb. else's achievement

【掠過】lüèguò（動）sweep past; skim over; fly past

【掠奪】lüèduó（動）plunder; pillage

掂 diān（動）weigh in the hand

【掂斤播兩】diān jīn bō liǎng〈成〉be prone to petty calculations

【掂量】diānliáng（動）❶ weigh in the hand ❷ weigh up; consider

掖 yē（動）tuck in

捐 qián（動）〈方〉carry on the shoulder

【捐客】qiánkè（名）broker

捲 juǎn（動）❶ roll up: 薄餅～烤鴨片 pieces of roast duck rolled up in thin pancakes ❷ sweep away; carry along: 汽車一起塵土，飛馳而過。The car sped past, raising a cloud of dust.

【捲入】juǎnrù（動）be involved in; be implicated in

【捲土重來】juǎn tǔ chóng lái〈成〉stage a comeback

【捲尺】juǎnchǐ（名）tape measure

【捲心菜】juǎnxīncài（名）〈方〉cabbage

【捲煙】juǎnyān（名）cigarette

【捲髮】juǎnfà Ⅰ（名）curly hair; permed hair Ⅱ（動）have one's hair permed

【捲鋪蓋】juǎn pūgai〈口〉pack up and leave; be sacked; quit the job

捧 pěng Ⅰ（動）❶ hold in both hands: ～着個壜子 hold a jar in one's hands ❷ extol; toady Ⅱ（量）double handful: 一～米 a double handful of rice

【捧場】pěngchǎng（動）❶ applaud and cheer（a performer, etc.）; serve as a claque ❷ extol; flatter

【捧腹】pěngfù（動）split one's sides

掛 guà（動）❶ hang; put up: 把大衣～在衣鈎上。Hang the overcoat on the hook. ❷ hitch; get caught: 釘子～住衣服。I caught my dress on a nail. ❸ be concerned about: 牽～ worry about ❹ register: ～耳鼻喉科 register for ENT

【掛一漏萬】guà yī lòu wàn〈成〉the list cannot be exhaustive

【掛失】guàshī（動）report the loss of sth.

【掛名】guàmíng（形）nominal; titular

【掛羊頭賣狗肉】guà yáng tóu mài gǒu ròu〈成〉tout for business under a false signboard; engage in dirty dealings behind a facade of honesty

【掛車】guàchē（名）trailer

【掛念】guàniàn（動）continue to worry about（sb. or sb.'s state of health）; continue to think about sb.; miss

【掛帥】guàshuài（動）be in command; take command

【掛彩】guàcǎi（動）❶ hang up silk festoons on festive occasions ❷ be wounded in action

【掛毯】guàtǎn（名）tapestry

【掛號】guàhào（動）❶ register（at a hospital, etc.）: ～處 registration office ❷ send by registered mail: ～信 registered letter

【掛齒】guàchǐ（動）mention

【掛鎖】guàsuǒ（名）padlock

【掛麵】guàmiàn（名）noodles; vermicelli

捷 jié Ⅰ（形）quick; swift: 敏～

agile II (名) triumph; victory; success: 連戰皆 ~ win all battles in succession

【捷足先登】jié zú xiān dēng 〈成〉 he who is swift of foot is among the first to arrive

【捷克斯洛伐克】jiékèsīluòfákè (名) Czechoslovakia: ~人 Czechoslovak; Czechoslovakian

【捷徑】jiéjìng (名) short-cut; royal road

【捷報】jiébào (名) tidings of victory; report of success: ~傳來，舉國歡欣 The whole nation is jubilant over the glad tidings of victory.

措 cuò (動) arrange; place: 手足無 ~ be at a loss

【措手不及】cuò shǒu bù jí 〈成〉 be caught unawares: 叫人 ~ take sb. unawares

【措施】cuòshī (名) measure; step: ~不力 take inadequate measures

【措置】cuòzhì (動) handle; manage: ~裕如 handle matters efficiently

【措辭】cuòcí (名) wording: ~含糊 couched in equivocal terms

捺 nà I (動) restrain; repress: 按 ~不住心頭怒火 cannot hold back one's anger II (名) (of a Chinese character) right-falling stroke

掩 yǎn (動) ❶ cover; conceal: ~面哭泣 hide one's face and weep ❷ shut; close: 門半~着 The door is left ajar.

【掩耳盜鈴】yǎn ěr dào líng 〈成〉 stuff one's ears while stealing a bell; act like an ostrich

【掩埋】yǎnmái (動) bury

【掩飾】yǎnshì (動) gloss over; cover up: ~過失 gloss over one's error / ~焦急的心情 try to hide one's anxiety

【掩蓋】yǎngài (動) cover; conceal: ~罪行 cover up one's crime

【掩蔽】yǎnbì (動) cover up; shelter

【掩藏】yǎncáng (動) hide; conceal

【掩護】yǎnhù (動) screen; cover: 在夜幕~下 under cover of night

掘 jué (動) dig; excavate

【掘土機】juétǔjī (名) 〈機〉 excavator

掇 duō (動) pick: 拾~ tidy up

掃 sǎo (動) ❶ sweep (with a broom): ~煙囪 sweep a chimney ❷ remove; eliminate: ~盲 eliminate illiteracy ❸ move swiftly from one side to the other: 他~了她一眼。He flashed her a glance.
see also sào

【掃地】sǎodì (動) ❶ sweep the floor ❷ (of reputation, honour, etc.) be dragged in the dust: 威信~ with one's prestige ruined; be thoroughly discredited

【掃尾】sǎowěi (動) round off one's work: 進行工程的~工作 wind up the final phase of the project

【掃除】sǎochú (動) clear away; eliminate; wipe out: ~垃圾 clear away the rubbish / ~惡習 eradicate bad habits

【掃射】sǎoshè (動) strafe

【掃雪車】sǎoxuěchē (名) snow plough

【掃描】sǎomiáo (動) 〈電〉 scan: ~器 scanner

【掃雷】sǎoléi (動) clear (away) mines: ~器 mine-sweeper

【掃墓】sǎomù（動）pay respects to a dead person at his grave

【掃蕩】sǎodàng（動）mop up

【掃興】sǎoxìng I（動）feel disappointed II（形）disappointing

掃 sào

see also sǎo

【掃帚】sàozhou（名）broom

【掃帚星】sàozhouxīng（名）❶〈天〉comet ❷ person that brings bad luck

捫 mén（動）feel (by hand)

【捫心自問】mén xīn zì wèn〈成〉search one's heart; search one's conscience

排 pái I（動）❶ line up; arrange: 把架上的書～好 arrange the books on the shelf／～在別人後面 line up behind the others ❷ discharge; remove:～澇 drain flooded farmland ❸ rehearse:～戲 rehearse a play II（名）❶ row; line: 站成一～ stand in a row ❷〈軍〉platoon ❸ raft ❹ pie: 蘋果～ apple pie ❺ steak; chop: 牛～ beef steak III（量）row; line:一～柏樹 a row of cypresses

see also pǎi

【排山倒海】pái shān dǎo hǎi〈成〉move with irresistible force

【排比】páibǐ（名）〈語〉parallelism

【排水】páishuǐ（動）drain off water:～噸位 displacement tonnage／～量 displacement

【排斥】páichì（動）exclude; reject

【排外】páiwài I（形）exclusive; antiforeign II（名）exclusivism; xenophobia; antiforeignism

【排印】páiyìn（動）typeset and print

【排行】páiháng（名）seniority among brothers and sisters: 他～老大。He is the eldest of the children.

【排列】páiliè（動）arrange in order; rank

【排污】páiwū（動）drain waste; dispose of hazardous substances

【排字】páizì（動）typeset; compose

【排卵】páiluǎn（動）〈生〉ovulate

【排尾】páiwěi（名）last person in a row

【排長】páizhǎng（名）platoon leader

【排版】páibǎn（動）typeset

【排洩】páixiè（動）❶ drain ❷ excrete

【排除】páichú（動）dispel; remove:～障礙 remove obstacles／～其它可能性 rule out all other possibilities

【排骨】páigǔ（名）spareribs

【排球】páiqiú（名）volleyball

【排場】páichang（名）ostentatious show

【排隊】páiduì（動）line up; queue up

【排解】páijiě（動）mediate; intercede

【排練】páiliàn（排演 páiyǎn）I（動）rehearse II（名）rehearsal

【排憂解難】pái yōu jiě nàn（動）help relieve people of worries and difficulties

【排頭】páitóu（名）first person in a row

【排擠】páijǐ（動）squeeze sb. out

【排灌】páiguàn（名）irrigation and drainage

排 pǎi

see also pái

【排子車】pǎizichē（名）〈方〉handcart

掉 diào I（動）❶ fall; drop ❷

fade: 不~色 be colourfast ❸ lose ❹ turn; move: ~過身 turn round ❺ lay behind Ⅱ(助)[used after some verbs to indicate the completion of an action]: 燒~ burn out

【掉以輕心】diào yǐ qīng xīn〈成〉relax one's vigilance; take a casual attitude

【掉包】diàobāo(動)stealthily replace sth. valuable by sth. worthless

【掉隊】diàoduì(動)drop out; fall behind

【掉頭】diàotóu(動)turn back; look over one's shoulder

【掉轉】diàozhuǎn(動)turn round

授 shòu(動)❶ award; accord; confer: ~以碩士學位 confer on sb. a master's degree ❷ teach; instruct; lecture: 講~新課 offer a new course

【授予】shòuyǔ(動)confer; award: ~她榮譽證書 award her a certificate of honour

【授意】shòuyì(動)give(drop)a hint for sb. to do sth.

【授獎】shòujiǎng(動)award a prize

【授精】shòujīng(動)inseminate: 人工~ artificial insemination

【授課】shòukè(動)give lessons

【授權】shòuquán(動)authorize; delegate power

採 cǎi(動)❶ pick; pluck: ~蓮花 pick lotus flowers ❷ gather; collect: ~風 collect folk songs ❸ select: ~辦(select and)purchase ❹ mine; exploit: ~油 extract oil/開~天然氣 extract natural gas

【採用】cǎiyòng(動)adopt; employ

【採伐】cǎifá(動)fell(trees)

【採光】cǎiguāng(名)〈建〉lighting

【採取】cǎiqǔ(動)take; adopt: ~預防措施 take preventive measures

【採納】cǎinà(動)adopt; accept: ~他的意見 take his advice

【採訪】cǎifǎng(動)(of a journalist)cover; interview: ~一個會議 cover a conference

【採掘】cǎijué(動)〈礦〉dig; excavate

【採集】cǎijí(動)gather; collect: ~礦物標本 take ore samples

【採煤】cǎiméi(名)coal mining: ~工人 coal miner

【採摘】cǎizhāi(動)pick; pluck: ~葡萄 gather grapes

【採購】cǎigòu(動)purchase; procure

【採礦】cǎikuàng(名)mining: ~工業 mining industry

掙 zhēng

see also zhèng

【掙扎】zhēngzhá(動)struggle: 在困境中~ struggle to get out of a difficult situation; fight against odds

掙 zhèng(動)❶ struggle to get free: ~脫封建枷鎖 shake off feudal fetters ❷ earn: ~工資 earn a salary / 你一月~多少錢? How much do you earn a month?

see also zhēng

捻 niǎn Ⅰ(動)twist with one's fingers: ~一個紙捻兒 twist up a paper spill Ⅱ(名)spill

捨 shě(動)❶ abandon; give up: ~命 give up one's life ❷ give alms

【捨己爲人】shě jǐ wèi rén〈成〉risk one's life for another

【捨本逐末】shě běn zhú mò〈成〉

overlook the fundamentals while paying attention to the details

【捨死忘生】 shě sǐ wàng shēng〈成〉go to sb.'s rescue with no thought for one's own safety

【捨身】 shěshēn（動）lay down one's life

【捨近求遠】 shě jìn qiú yuǎn〈成〉seek after what is distant but neglect what is near; seek from a far what lies close at hand

【捨得】 shěde（動）be willing to spend (time, money, effort, etc.); be ready to dispense with sth.

【捨棄】 shěqì（動）abandon; discard

掄 lūn（動）brandish; wield

捶 chuí（動）beat (with a stick of fist); pound

掬 jū（動）hold in both hands: 笑容可～ smile broadly; be all smiles

掏 tāo（動）❶ draw out; take out: 從兜裏～出圓珠筆 take a ball pen out of one's pocket ❷ dig (a hole); scoop ❸ steal from sb.'s pocket

【掏腰包】 tāo yāobāo（動）〈口〉❶ foot a bill: 是他掏的腰包。He paid the bill. ❷ steal from sb.'s pocket: 給人掏了腰包 have sth. stolen by a pickpocket

掐 qiā I（動）❶ pinch; nip: ～豆角 pick fresh kidney beans ❷ cut off; sever: ～電綫 disconnect the wire II（量）一～鹽 a pinch of salt

推 tuī（動）❶ push: ～了他一把 give him a push ❷ plane; cut: ～草機 lawn mower ❸ promote; pursue ❹ deduce; infer ❺ decline (an of-

fer, etc.) ❻ shirk (responsibility) ❼ postpone: 會議往後～了一天。The meeting was put off until the next day. ❽ hold in high esteem ❾ elect; select

【推力】 tuīlì（名）thrust

【推子】 tuīzi（名）clippers

【推土機】 tuītǔjī（名）bull-dozer

【推心置腹】 tuī xīn zhì fù〈成〉confide in sb.: 與他～地交談 have a heart-to-heart talk with him

【推出】 tuīchū（動）bring to the fore; present: ～三臺新戲 present three new operas

【推行】 tuīxíng（動）carry out; practise: ～獨立自主的外交政策 pursue an independent foreign policy

【推托】 tuītuō（動）goive an excuse (for not doing sth.)

【推定】 tuīdìng（動）❶ elect; select ❷ conclude by inference

【推波助瀾】 tuī bō zhù lán〈成〉pour oil on the flame

【推卸】 tuīxiè（動）shirk; shift: ～事故責任 shirk all responsibility for an accident

【推拿】 tuīná（名）〈中醫〉massage

【推倒】 tuīdǎo（動）❶ overturn; overthrow ❷ repudiate; reject

【推動】 tuīdòng（動）promote; spur: ～經濟改革 spur on economic reforms

【推理】 tuīlǐ I（名）〈邏〉inference; deduction II（動）deduce

【推移】 tuīyí（動）❶ (of time) elapse; pass ❷ (of a situation, social tendency, etc.) develop; evolve; progress

【推進】 tuījìn（動）❶ promote; forward; further ❷〈軍〉drive

【推脱】 tuītuō（動）evade (responsibility, work, etc.）

【推崇】tuīchóng（動）hold in esteem

【推陳出新】tuī chén chū xīn〈成〉weed out the old to bring forth the new

【推測】tuīcè（動）infer; gather; guess

【推想】tuīxiǎng（動）gather; reckon

【推廣】tuīguǎng（動）spread; popularize：～良種小麥 extend the use of a fine variety of wheat

【推敲】tuīqiāo（動）deliberate; cogitate：仔細～文字 weigh one's words carefully; choose the correct word

【推算】tuīsuàn（動）calculate; compute; reckon

【推遲】tuīchí（動）put off; defer; delay

【推論】tuīlùn（名）inference; corollary

【推銷】tuīxiāo（動）promote sales; promote the marketing of：～員 salesman

【推選】tuīxuǎn（動）elect; select

【推舉】tuījǔ I（動）elect; select II（名）〈舉重〉(clean and) press

【推薦】tuījiàn（動）recommend

【推斷】tuīduàn（動）infer; deduce

【推翻】tuīfān（動）❶ overthrow; topple; subvert ❷ repudiate; reject; cast off：～原有的協定 scrap the original agreement

【推辭】tuīcí（動）decline

【推讓】tuīràng（動）decline（ an offer, position, etc. out of politeness or modesty）

捭

捭 bǎi（動）separate; part

【捭闔】bǎihé（動）open and close（as in 縱橫捭闔 zònghéng bǎihé）

掀

掀 xiān（動）lift

【掀起】xiānqǐ（動）❶ lift ❷ surge：大海～巨浪。The sea was surging high. ❸ start; bring about：～高潮 bring about an upsurge

【掀動】xiāndòng（動）lift; set in motion

【掀開】xiānkāi（動）raise; open

掌

掌 zhǎng I（名）❶ palm：鼓～ clap hands; applaud ❷（of certain animals）paw：鴨～ duck's foot; duck's web（as a dish）❸ shoe sole or heel：前～ shoe sole ❹ horseshoe II（動）❶ be in charge of; control：～權 wield power ❷ strike with the palm of one's hand

【掌勺】zhǎngsháo（動）be the chef

【掌印】zhǎngyìn（動）keep the seal; be in power

【掌故】zhǎnggù（名）anecdotes

【掌舵】zhǎngduò（動）be at the helm

【掌握】zhǎngwò（動）❶ grasp; master：～第一手資料 have first-hand information／～游泳的要領 learn the ABC of swimming ❷ take into one's hands; control：～時機 seize the opportunity／～保險櫃的鑰匙 keep the key to the safe

【掌管】zhǎngguǎn（動）be in charge of; control：～財權 in charge of financial matters

【掌聲】zhǎngshēng（名）clapping; applause

【掌櫃】zhǎngguì（名）shopkeeper; manager

掣

掣 chè（動）❶ pull ❷ draw：～回手 draw back one's hand

【掣肘】chèzhǒu（動）hold sb. back

by the elbow; keep in check

掰 bāi（動）break sth. off with fingers and thumb: ～玉米 break off corncobs

【掰開】bāikāi（動）break into two with one's hands

【掰腕子】bāi wànzi（動）do arm wrestling

揮 huī（動）❶ wave; wield: ～手告別 wave sb. goodbye ❷ wipe away: ～汗 wipe the sweat from one's face ❸ scatter; disperse

【揮金如土】huī jīn rú tǔ〈成〉spend money lavishly

【揮動】huīdòng（動）brandish; wave

【揮發】huīfā（動）volatilize: ～油 volatile oil

【揮舞】huīwǔ（動）wave; brandish

【揮霍】huīhuò（動）spend freely; squander（wealth）

搓 cuō（動）rub between one's plams

【搓板】cuōbǎn（名）wash-board

揍 zòu（動）beat; hit; strike: 把孩子～了一頓 give the child a beating

揀 jiǎn（動）choose; select; pick: ～你所喜歡的。Pick what you like.

【揀選】jiǎnxuǎn（動）choose; select; pick

揶 yé

【揶揄】yéyú（動）ridicule; mock

描 miáo（動）❶ copy; trace ❷ retouch

【描述】miáoshù（動）describe

【描紅】miáohóng（動）（in Chinese calligraphy）learn to write by trac-

ing over characters printed in red

【描圖】miáotú（動）trace designs: ～員 tracer

【描寫】miáoxiě（動）describe; portray

【描繪】miáohuì（動）depict; describe: 這幾部小說～了東北的農村生活。All these novels depict rural life in the Northeast.

揠 yà（動）pull up

【揠苗助長】yà miáo zhù zhǎng〈成〉pull the seedlings upward to help them grow; haste makes waste

揉 róu（動）knead; rub: ～麵 knead dough

握 wò（動）❶ hold; grasp ❷ control

【握手】wòshǒu（動）shake hands

【握手言和】wò shǒu yán hé〈成〉❶ shake hands and make up ❷ draw（in a match）

【握手言歡】wò shǒu yán huān〈成〉shake hands and become friends again; be reconciled

【握別】wòbié（動）shake hands at the time of parting; bid farewell

【握拳】wòquán（動）clench one's fist

提 dī

see also tí

【提防】dīfáng（動）guard against

提 tí（動）❶ carry in the hand（sth. having a handle, straps, etc.）: ～一桶水 carry a pail of water ❷ lift; raise: ～幹 promote a worker to be a staff member ❸ move up: 雨季～早來臨。The rainy season came earlier than

usual. ❹ point out; put forth: ～建議 put forward one's suggestion / ～要求 make a request ❺ extract; take out: ～款 draw money from a bank / ～純 purify; refine ❻ mention; bring up: ——到這件事他就好笑. He would laugh heartily whenever I brought up the matter. ❼ bring a prisoner or detainee to court: ～審 bring to trial
see also dī

【提升】tíshēng (動) promote; elevate: ～爲正教授 be promoted to full professorship

【提心吊膽】tí xīn diào dǎn〈成〉be on tenterhooks; have one's heart in one's mouth

【提包】tíbāo (名) handbag; bag

【提示】tíshì (動) prompt; hint

【提出】tíchū (動) put forward; raise: ～不同意見 put forth different views

【提成】tíchéng (動) deduct a percentage (from a sum of money)

【提名】tímíng (動) nominate

【提交】tíjiāo (動) submit to; refer to: 這項議案將～大會審議. This proposal will be submitted to the general assembly for deliberation.

【提拔】tíbá (動) promote (sb. to a higher rank)

【提法】tífǎ (名) wording; formulation

【提取】tíqǔ (動) ❶ extract; recover; reclaim: 從廢液中～銀 extract silver from waste liquid ❷ draw out from safe-keeping: ～行李 claim one's luggage

【提供】tígōng (動) provide; give: ～服務 cater; offer services

【提前】tíqián (動) move forward; advance: ～三天完成計劃 fulfil the plan three days ahead of schedule

【提神】tíshén (動) refresh oneself

【提倡】tíchàng (動) advocate; encourage; uphold: ～自力更生 advocate self-reliance

【提案】tí'àn (名) motion; bill

【提高】tígāo (動) raise; increase: ～效率 increase efficiency

【提級】tíjí (動) promote to a higher rank

【提留】tíliú (動) retain a percentage of the total profits for the enterprise's own use

【提起】tíqǐ (動) ❶ mention: 没人～他. Nobody ever spoke of him. ❷ arouse; call: ～精神, 奮勇前進. Square your shoulders and forge ahead.

【提貨】tíhuò (動) pick up goods

【提單】tídān (名) bill of lading (B/L)

【提琴】tíqín (名) the violin family: 小～ violin / 中～ viola / 大～ violoncello

【提煉】tíliàn (動) refine; extract: 從原油中～汽油 extract petrol from crude oil

【提綱】tígāng (名) outline

【提醒】tíxǐng (動) remind; warn

【提議】tíyì (動) suggest; propose

揚 yáng (動) ❶ raise; lift: ～帆 raise the sail; set sail ❷ winnow: ～穀子 winnow the millet ❸ spread: 消息很快傳～開來. The news spread quickly.

【揚水站】yángshuǐzhàn (名) pumping station

【揚名】yángmíng (動) become famous

【揚言】 yángyán （動） openly threaten

【揚長而去】 yáng cháng ér qù 〈成〉 go away haughtily; stalk off

【揚長避短】 yáng cháng bì duǎn 〈成〉 utilize the advantages and avoid the disadvantages; make amends for one's weaknesses by exploiting one's strengths

【揚眉吐氣】 yáng méi tǔ qì 〈成〉 feel happy and proud

【揚場】 yángcháng （名） winnowing

【揚揚得意】 yángyáng déyì （形） proud and self-satisfied; complacent

【揚棄】 yángqì （動） ❶ discard ❷ 〈哲〉 sublate

【揚聲器】 yángshēngqì （名） loudspeaker

揭 jiē I （動）❶ tear off: 把手指上 的橡皮膏一下來 take the adhesive tape off one's finger ❷ remove (the cover); lift (the lid) ❸ expose; reveal: ～他的老底 show sb.'s true features; rake up sb.'s past II （名） (Jiē) a surname

【揭示】 jiēshì （動）❶ reveal; disclose: ～社會發展的普遍規律 bring to light a universal law governing social development ❷ announce to the public: ～牌 notice board

【揭穿】 jiēchuān （動） bring to light; lay bare: ～他的陰謀詭計 lay bare all his tricks and schemes

【揭發】 jiēfā （動） reveal; uncover: ～政治上的腐敗現象 uncover political corruption

【揭開】 jiēkāi （動） disclose; open up: ～未來的新篇章 open up a new page for the future

【揭短兒】 jiēduǎnr （揭 短 jiēduǎn） （動） expose sb.'s faults or weaknesses

【揭幕】 jiēmù （動） unveil (a monument, etc.) II （名） inauguration: 這是歷史上新時代的～。 This inaugurated a new era in history.

【揭曉】 jiēxiǎo （動） be announced; be made public: 考試成績已經～。 The exam results have come out.

【揭露】 jiēlù （動） lay bare; reveal: ～他不可告人的動機 lay bare his ulterior motives

揣 chuāi （動） keep inside one's clothes: ～着手 tuck one's hands in the opposite sleeves
see also chuǎi

揣 chuǎi （動） estimate; guess; reckon
see also chuāi

【揣測】 chuǎicè （動） surmise; conjecture

【揣摩】 chuǎimó （動） try to figure out

揢 kāi （動） wipe

【揢油】 kāiyóu （動） 〈口〉 sponge off; obtain petty advantages at the expense of others or the state

援 yuán （動）❶ pull by hand; hold: 攀～ climb up by holding on to sth. ❷ help; assist; support ❸ quote; cite

【援引】 yuányǐn （動） quote; cite

【援助】 yuánzhù （動） help; support; aid: 伸出～之手 stretch a helping hand

【援例】 yuánlì （動） cite a precedent

【援軍】 yuánjūn （名） reinforcements

【揆救】yuánjiù（动）rescue; extricate from danger

揪 jiū（动）clutch; grab; seize: ～住那根绳子别放。Hold on to the rope and don't let go.

【揪出】jiūchū（动）uncover; ferret out: ～不法之徒 ferret out unlawful scoundrels

【揪辫子】jiū biànzi〈口〉seize on sb.'s casual remark or a slip of the tongue to launch an attack

插 chā（动）❶ insert; stick in: 把窗户～上 bolt the window ❷ interpolate: ～话 chip in

【插入】chārù（动）❶ insert ❷〈电〉plug in

【插手】chāshǒu（动）meddle in: ～别国内政 interfere in the internal affairs of another country / 不用你～。Mind your own business.

【插曲】chāqǔ（名）❶〈乐〉interlude ❷ song in a film or play ❸ episode: 历史的～ an episode in history

【插班】chābān（动）put a transfer student in an appropriate class

【插秧】chāyāng（动）transplant rice seedlings

【插座】chāzuò（名）socket

【插图】chātú（名）illustration; plate

【插销】chāxiāo（名）❶ latch; bolt (for a door, window, etc.) ❷〈电〉plug

【插嘴】chāzuǐ（插口 chākǒu）（动）cut in; chip in

【插头】chātóu（名）〈电〉plug

换 huàn（动）❶ exchange: 交～留学生 exchange international students ❷ change

【换车】huànchē（动）change trains or buses

【换防】huànfáng（动）〈军〉relieve a garrison

【换季】huànjì（动）change dress between seasons

【换取】huànqǔ（动）exchange sth. for; get in return

【换班】huànbān（动）change shifts; relieve a person

【换汤不换药】huàn tāng bù huàn yào〈成〉change only the form but not the content

【换算】huànsuàn（名）conversion

搜 sōu（动）❶ search; rummage ❷ collect; gather

【搜身】sōushēn（动）search a person; frisk

【搜刮】sōuguā（动）obtain money from the people by all unscrupulous means; extort

【搜查】sōuchá（动）search; ransack

【搜捕】sōubǔ（动）track down; hunt; pursue and arrest

【搜索】sōusuǒ（动）search for; tract down; reconnoitre: ～在战争中失踪的人员 search for the missing persons in war

【搜集】sōují（动）collect; amass: ～罪证 collect criminal evidence

【搜寻】sōuxún（动）search high and low; rummage

【搜腰包】sōu yāobāo（动）search sb. for money

【搜罗】sōuluó（动）collect; recruit: ～人才 search for talent

搞 gǎo（动）❶ do; be engaged in; make: ～计划生育 carry out family planning / ～研究 be engaged in research work ❷ establish; set up ❸ get hold of: ～點東西吃 get sth. to eat ❹ play (tricks): ～鬼 play tricks

【搞活】gǎohuó (動) ❶ invigorate; enliven: ～經濟 enliven the economy

搪 táng (動) ❶ keep out; stave off: ～飢 stave off hunger ❷ stall off; stall; evade; go through the motions: ～差事 loaf on the job

【搪瓷】tángcí (名) enamel

【搪塞】tángsè (動) give a vague answer; stall sb. off; do sth. half-heartedly

搧 shān (動) ❶ fan: ～扇子 fan oneself

【搧風機】shānfēngjī (名) ventilating fan

【搧動】shāndòng (動) flap: 那隻鳥～翅膀走了。The bird flew away flapping its wings.

搏 bó Ⅰ (動) ❶ fight; wrestle ❷ pounce on: ～兔 pounce on a rabbit ❸ throb; beat Ⅱ (名) ❶ fight: 肉～戰 hand-to-hand combat ❷ beat: 脈～不規律 irregular pulse

【搏鬥】bódòu Ⅰ (動) wrestle; struggle; combat: 與暴徒～ grapple with the rioters Ⅱ (名) fight; struggle

【搏動】bódòng (動) throb; pulsate; beat rhythmically

搭 dā (動) ❶ put up: ～棚子 put up a shed ❷ carry; lift: 把桌子～進屋裏 move the table into the room ❸ hang: 把洗的衣服～在繩子上 hang the laundry on a line ❹ take; ride: ～公共汽車進城 take a bus to town

【搭伙】dāhuǒ (動) ❶ go into partnership with ❷ have regular meals at the canteen: 在學校～ eat in the school canteen

【搭配】dāpèi Ⅰ (動) make a proportionate arrangement Ⅱ (名) collocation

【搭訕】dāshàn (動) find sth. to say so as to smooth over an awkward situation

【搭救】dājiù (動) rescue

【搭檔】dādàng Ⅰ (動) collaborate; cooperate Ⅱ (名) partner

搽 chá (動) put in; apply (to the skin, etc.): 在患處～藥水 apply the lotion to the affected part (of the body)

【搽粉】cháfěn (動) powder; dab (one's face) with powder

搔 sāo (動) scratch: ～頭不知所措 scratch one's head, not knowing what to do

【搔癢】sāoyǎng (動) scratch an itch

捅 tǒng (動) ❶ poke; jab: 被人從背後～了一刀 be stabbed in the back ❷ disclose; reveal: 這事別～了出去。Never breathe a word about it to anybody.

【捅馬蜂窩】tǒng mǎfēngwō 〈口〉stir up a hornets' nest; bring a hornets' nest about one's ears

【捅婁子】tǒng lóuzi 〈口〉get (oneself or others) into trouble through a blunder

損 sǔn Ⅰ (動) ❶ lose; diminish: 企業虧～ loss incurred by an enterprise ❷ harm; damage; impair Ⅱ (形) 〈方〉❶ sarcastic; ironical: 別～他了。Don't speak so sarcastically about him. ❷ mean; wicked: ～到家 dreadfully mean

【损人利己】 sǔn rén lì jǐ〈成〉 seek personal advantage at the expense of others

【损公肥私】 sǔn gōng féi sī〈口〉 seek private gain at public expense

【损失】 sǔnshī Ⅰ (动) lose; suffer a loss Ⅱ (名) loss; amount lost: ～惨重 suffer heavy losses

【损害】 sǔnhài (动) harm; impair; mar

【损耗】 sǔnhào (名) ❶ loss; depletion; wear and tear: 转运～ loss incurred in transit ❷〈商〉 wastage; spoilage

【损益】 sǔnyì (名) ❶ decrease and increase ❷ loss and gain

【损伤】 sǔnshāng Ⅰ (动) harm; injure: 跌打～ injury sustained from a fall Ⅱ (名) loss

【损坏】 sǔnhuài (动) damage; ruin; spoil: ～别人名誉 damage sb.'s reputation

揾 èn (动) press

抢 qiǎng (动) ❶ snatch; take forcibly: 她把我正在读的书～走了。She snatched away the book I was reading. ❷ rush: 他们～进去, 看看究竟出了什么事。They rushed in to see what was happening. ❸ compete with each other for a lead: ～着参加篮球队 compete to be the first to join the basketball team

【抢手货】 qiǎngshǒuhuò (名) goods in great demand; goods that sell like hot cakes

【抢白】 qiǎngbái (动) rebuke sb. to his face; chide; satirize sb. to his face

【抢收】 qiǎngshōu (动) rush-harvest

【抢先】 qiǎngxiān (动) strive or manage to be the first: ～说话 snatch the first chance to speak

【抢劫】 qiǎngjié (动) rob; mug

【抢拍】 qiǎngpāi (动) ❶ lose no time in shooting (a film) ❷ seize the opportune moment to snap a shot

【抢修】 qiǎngxiū (动) rush-repair

【抢时间】 qiǎngshíjiān (动) race against time

【抢救】 qiǎngjiù (动) rescue; save: ～危重病人 rescue a patient who is critically ill

【抢夺】 qiǎngduó (动) seize; wrest

【抢种】 qiǎngzhòng (动) rush-plant

【抢险】 qiǎngxiǎn (动) (in case of emergency) rush to the rescue to avoid or reduce loss; rush to save a dangerous situation

【抢购】 qiǎnggòu (名) stampede to buy things; panic buying

摇 yáo (动) shake; wave: 在风中～来～去 sway in the wind

【摇曳】 yáoyè (动) flicker; sway: 烛影～。The candle flickered.

【摇身一变】 yáo shēn yī biàn〈成〉 make a sudden change in one's identity

【摇尾乞怜】 yáo wěi qǐ lián〈成〉 beg piteously for mercy

【摇晃】 yáohuàng (动) sway; rock: 船～得厉害。The ship is rocking to and fro.

【摇动】 yáodòng (动) shake; swing: ～手臂 wave one's hand

【摇椅】 yáoyǐ (名) rocking chair

【摇摇欲坠】 yáo yáo yù zhuì〈成〉 liable to collapse any moment; on its last legs; tottering: 企图保住～的统治 attempt to shore up a tottering regime

【摇旗呐喊】yáo qí nà hǎn〈成〉beat the drum for; shout support for

【摇滚乐】yáogǔnyuè（名）rock and roll; big beat

【摇头】yáotóu（动）shake one's head

【摇头晃脑】yáo tóu huàng nǎo〈成〉look ostensibly self-satisfied; look smug or conceited

【摇头摆尾】yáo tóu bǎi wěi〈成〉show smug satisfaction

【摇钱树】yáoqiánshù（名）person or thing that is the source of profit; goose that lays golden eggs; money-spinner

【摇摆】yáobǎi（动）sway; rock: ~乐 swing music

【摇篮】yáolán（名）cradle: ~曲 lullaby

携 xié（动）❶ carry; take along: ~枪 carry a gun / ~眷 bring along one's family ❷ take hold of（sb.'s hand）

【携手】xiéshǒu（副）hand in hand: ~并肩 file abreast hand in hand

【携带】xiédài（动）carry; take along: 他总是随身~一本词典和一个笔记本。He always carries with him a dictionary and a notebook.

捣 dǎo（动）❶ pestle; beat; smash ❷ disturb; upset

【捣鬼】dǎoguǐ（动）play tricks; make trouble

【捣蛋】dǎodàn（动）do mischief: ~鬼 troublemaker

【捣毁】dǎohuǐ（动）destroy; smash

【捣乱】dǎoluàn（动）make trouble; create disturbances

搬 bān（动）❶ move; remove; take away（sth. cumbersome or heavy）: 把行李~进来 move the luggage in here ❷ move（house）: ~进新居 move into a new house ❸ copy（mechanically）; apply（indiscriminately）: 照~ copy slavishly

【搬弄】bānnòng（动）❶ meddle with; play with ❷ show off; trot out; display: ~小聪明 show off one's cleverness

【搬弄是非】bān nòng shì fēi〈成〉tell tales; sow discord; incite dissension

【搬家】bānjiā（动）move house; move

【搬运】bānyùn（动）carry; transport: ~费 transportation charges

【搬运工人】bānyùn gōngrén（名）porter; docker; longshoreman

【搬迁】bānqiān（动）（of a factory, plant, etc.）move to another place

摩 mā
see also mó

【摩挲】māsa（动）stroke gently: 把衣服~平 smooth one's clothes with one's hands

摩 mó（动）❶ touch: 抚~ caress ❷ study; ponder（over）: 揣~ try to figure out
see also mā

【摩天】mótiān（形）skyscraping: ~大厦 skyscraper

【摩托车】mótuōchē（名）motorcycle

【摩托艇】mótuōtǐng（名）motorboat

【摩洛哥】Móluògē（名）Morocco: ~人 Moroccan

【摩纳哥】Mónàgē（名）Monaco: ~人 Monacan

【摩拳擦掌】mó quán cā zhǎng〈成〉itch for a fight; be eager for a try

【摩登】módēng（形）modern; fashionable

【摩擦】mócā I（動）rub against sth. II（名）friction; conflict:～生熱。Friction generates heat. / 兩個政治派別之間的～ friction between two political factions

【摩擦音】mócāyīn（名）〈語〉fricative

摯 zhì（形）sincere; earnest

【摯友】zhìyǒu（名）bosom friend

摘 zhāi（動）❶ pick; pluck:～一串葡萄 pluck a cluster of grapes ❷ select; make extracts from

【摘引】zhāiyǐn（動）quote

【摘抄】zhāichāo I（動）make extracts II（名）extract; excerpt

【摘要】zhāiyào I（動）summarize; make a summary II（名）summary; précis

【摘除】zhāichú（動）〈醫〉excise; remove

【摘記】zhāijì I（動）take notes II（名）extract; excerpt

【摘帽子】zhāimàozi（動）❶ take off one's cap ❷ take a political label off sb.; rehabilitate

【摘錄】zhāilù I（動）make extracts II（名）extract; excerpt

摔 shuāi（動）❶ fall; tumble:～了一大跤 have a bad fall ❷ plunge: 航天飛機突然～進海裏。The space shuttle shuddenly plunged into the sea. ❸（cause to）fall and break: 別把眼鏡～了。Don't break your glasses. ❹ throw; fling

【摔打】shuāida（動）❶ beat;

knock:～鞋上的土 knock the dirt off one's shoes ❷ be tempered: 在艱苦的生活中～ be tempered in hardships

【摔跤】shuāijiāo（動）❶ tumble; trip up ❷〈體〉wrestling

【摔跟頭】shuāi gēntou（動）〈口〉❶ trip up; fall over ❷ make a big mistake: 你這樣下去會～的。You are bound to make an awful blunder if you go on like this.

摸 mō（動）❶ touch; feel: 別～電綫。Don't touch the electric wire. / 這種紙一～上去很光滑。This paper feels smooth. ❷ feel for; fumble:～着黑找手電筒 fumble in the dark for the torch ❸ feel out; try to find out

【摸底】mōdǐ（動）❶ try to feel out: 想知道考試結果,還要到老師那兒～。We'll have to feel the teacher out on the results of the examination. ❷ know well: 對情況～ be clear about the situation

【摸索】mōsuo（動）❶ fumble; grope: 在黑暗中～ grope in the dark ❷ try to find out; seek:～出了一些經驗 have gained some experience

【摸黑】mōhēi（動）feel about in the dark

摳 kōu（動）❶ dig out with a finger or sth. small and pinted:～耳朵 pick one's ear ❷ delve into: 死～書本 read books mechanically and without real understanding

【摳字眼兒】kōu zìyǎnr〈口〉be too fastidious in the choice of words

摺 zhé I（動）fold:～尺 folding

ruler II (名) booklet for keeping accounts; folder: 存～ bankbook; savings book

【摺門】zhémén (名) folding door

【摺扇】zhéshàn (名) folding fan

【摺叠】zhédié (動) fold: 把毯子～得整整齊齊 fold up the blanket neatly

搂 lōu (動) ❶ gather: ～乾草 rake up hay ❷ tuck up ❸ obtain by unfair means; extort
see also lǒu

【摟錢】lōuqián (動) extort money

摟 lǒu (動) hug; embrace
see also lōu

【摟抱】lǒubào (動) hug; cuddle

摑 guāi (動) slap; box (sb.'s ear)

撂 liào (動) ❶ put down ❷ leave off

【撂挑子】liào tiāozi (動) throw up one's work; give up one's job

【撂倒】liàodǎo (動) knock down; shoot down

摞 luò I (動) pile up; stack up II (量) pile; stack: 一～書 a pile of books

摧 cuī (動) smash; break; destroy

【摧枯拉朽】cuī kū lā xiǔ (成) as easy as crushing deadwood

【摧殘】cuīcán (動) ruin; devastate: 受到精神～ suffer an emotional trauma

【摧毀】cuīhuǐ (動) smash; destroy

摜 guàn (動) ❶ hurl; fling ❷ fall

【摜紗帽】guàn shāmào (動) 〈方〉hand in one's resignation

摹 mó (動) copy; imitate: ～帖 copy a model of calligraphy

【摹本】móběn (名) copy; facsimile

撞 zhuàng (動) ❶ dump against; run into; collide: 兩輛車一在一起了。Two vehicles collided. / 我在街上～上了他。I ran into him in the street. ❷ strike; knock: 被過路的車～了 be knocked down by a passing car ❸ test: ～運氣 try one's luck ❹ act rashly; run about wildly: 橫衝直～ dash about everywhere like crazy; dash around madly

【撞見】zhuàngjiàn (動) meet by chance; run into

【撞擊】zhuàngjī (動) strike; ram

【撞鎖】zhuàngsuǒ (名) spring lock

【撞騙】zhuàngpiàn (動) swindle; defraud: 招搖～ bluff and swindle

撤 chè (動) ❶ remove: 把桌布～下來 take away the tablecloth ❷ withdraw: 後～ retreat

【撤回】chèhuí (動) recall: ～談判人員 recall the negotiating team ❷ withdraw: ～要求 withdraw a demand

【撤兵】chèbīng (動) pull back troops; withdraw troops

【撤退】chètuì (動) retreat

【撤除】chèchú (動) dismantle; remove

【撤換】chèhuàn (動) replace: 把他～下來 send sb. to replace him

【撤銷】chèxiāo (動) dismiss; cancel: ～過時的規定 abolish outmoded regulations

【撤離】chèlí (動) evacuate; leave

【撤職】chèzhí (動) dismiss sb. from office

捞 lāo (动) ❶ fish up; scoop up from the water or any other liquid ❷ obtain through irregular channels: ～外快 have an extra income; go moonlighting / ～一把 seek illegal gains

【捞稻草】lāo dàocǎo (动) seize what one regards as an opportunity for unleashing an attack on sb.

撻 tà (动) ❶ flog; whip; lash

【撻伐】tàfá (动) ❶ send a punitive expedition ❷ lash out (at); censure

撓 náo (动) ❶ hinder: 對人横加阻～ create obstacles for sb. ❷ bend; yield: 百折不～ unyielding despite reverses ❸ scratch

【撓頭】náotóu (动) ❶ scratch one's head ❷ be hard to tackle: ～的事 a hard nut to crack; a thorny problem

撕 sī (动) tear; rip; split

【撕碎】sīsuì (动) tear to shreds

【撕毁】sīhuǐ (动) tear up; abandon: ～合同 tear up a contract

撒 sā (动) ❶ let go; cast: ～腿跑 take to one's heels / ～手不管 wash one's hands of the business ❷ throw off all restraint; let oneself go: ～嬌 behave like a spoiled child
see also sǎ

【撒手】sāshǒu (动) let go (of)

【撒旦】sādàn (名) 〈宗〉 Satan

【撒尿】sāniào (动) 〈口〉 piss; pee; make water

【撒拉族】Sālāzú (名) the Salar (Sala) nationality

【撒氣】sāqì (动) ❶ (of a ball, tyre, etc.) leak; get a flat; deflate ❷ give vent to one's anger: 他常拿

妻子～。He often vented his ill temper upon his wife.

【撒野】sāyě (动) act wildly

【撒潑】sāpō (动) behave like a shrew

【撒賴】sālài (动) act shamelessly

【撒謊】sāhuǎng (动) 〈口〉 tell a lie

撒 sǎ (动) ❶ scatter; spread: 在田裏～糞 spread manure over a field ❷ spill; drop: ～了一地的牛奶 spill the milk all over the floor
see also sā

【撒種】sǎzhǒng (动) sow seeds

撅 juē (动) ❶ stick up; turn upwards: ～着尾巴 stick up the tail ❷ 〈口〉 break: ～一根樹枝當作拐棍兒 break a branch for use as a walking stick

【撅嘴】juēzuǐ (动) pout (one's lips)

撩 liāo (动) ❶ lift: ～裙子 hold up one's skirt ❷ sprinkle
see also liáo

撩 liáo (动) tease; flirt
see also liāo

【撩逗】liáodòu (动) tantalize; tease

【撩撥】liáobō (动) ❶ banter ❷ provoke

撰 zhuàn (动) write; compose: ～文 write an essay

【撰寫】zhuànxiě (动) write; compose

撥 bō Ⅰ (动) ❶ move with finger or stick; poke: ～算盤 work on an abacus ❷ turn; dial: ～(電話)號 dial (a phone number) ❸ ～弦 pluck the strings (of a guitar, etc.) ❹ appropriate; allot; set a-

side: 调～物资 allocate supplies Ⅱ
(量) (of people) batch; group: 轮
～儿 by turns

【撤正】bōzhèng (动) set right

【撤弄】bōnong (动) ❶ fiddle with:
～键盘 fiddle with the keyboard ❷
stir up; incite; rouse: ～是非 stir
up trouble; sow discord ❸ manipulate

【撤刺】bōlà (象) splash: ～一声,
他跳到河里 He jumped into the
river with a splash.

【撤款】bōkuǎn Ⅰ (动) issue or allocate funds Ⅱ (名) appropriation

【撤乱反正】bō luàn fǎn zhèng 〈成〉
reduce chaos to order; set things to
rights

撤 piē (动) ❶ discard; do away
with ❷ skim: ～去鸡汤上油 skim
the fat from the chicken soup
see also piě

【撤开】piēkāi (动) put aside; by-
pass: 目前先把这个问题～。Let's
put the matter aside for the time being.

【撤弃】piēqì (动) abandon; forsake

撤 piě Ⅰ (动) throw; cast Ⅱ (名)
left-falling stroke (in a Chinese
character)
see also piē

撑 chēng (动) ❶ support: 两手～
着下巴 rest one's chin in both hands
❷ punt with a pole: ～船 punt (a
boat) with a pole ❸ keep up (in
spite of difficulty): ～日子 eke out
a minimal living ❹ open: ～开口袋
open one's pocket ❺ burst: 别吃～
着。Don't overeat yourself.

【撑杆跳高】chēnggān tiàogāo (名)

pole vault

【撑腰】chēngyāo (动) support; back
up: 有人～ have sb's backing

撮 cuō Ⅰ (动) ❶ gather; bring together ❷ brush dust or dirt into a
dustpan ❸ pick up between the
thumbs and a finger ❹ extract Ⅱ
(量) pinch: 一小～ a handful of
see also zuǒ

【撮合】cuōhe (动) act as a go-between

【撮弄】cuōnòng (动) ❶ play tricks
on; make fun of ❷ instigate; stir up

【撮要】cuōyào Ⅰ (名) abstract Ⅱ
(动) make a précis

撮 zuǒ (量) tuft: 一～头发 a tuft
of hair
see also cuō

挥 dǒn (动) brush off the dust: ～
子 duster

撲 pū (动) ❶ rush at: 向他猛～过
去 pounce on him ❷ flap; pat: ～
打身上的雪花 brush the snowflakes
off oneself ❸ dedicate oneself to an
undertaking: 一心～在工作上 be
wholeheartedly devoted to one's
work

【撲克】pūkè (名) ❶ playing cards
❷ poker

【撲空】pūkōng (动) find that the
person one wants to see is gone: 你
最好先和他约好时间, 免得～。
You'd better make an appointment
with him to make sure he is there.

【撲面】pūmiàn (动) blow against
one's face: 和风～ The gentle
wind stroked our cheeks.

【撲哧】pūchī (象) ❶ titter; snigger
❷ fizz

【撲粉】pūfěn（動）dab powder

【撲通】pūtōng（象）thump; plop: ～一聲坐在靠椅上 flop into an arm-chair／～一聲掉進水裏 drop into the water with a plop

【撲滅】pūmiè（動）put out; extinguish; exterminate

【撲簌】pūsù（動）(of tears) trickle down

【撲騰】pūtēng（象）thump; thud

播 bō（動）❶ spread: 新聞聯～ broadcast news over a radio（TV）network ❷ sow; seed: ～種青草 sow a plot of land with grass

【播弄】bōnòng（動）❶ order sb. about ❷ stir up（trouble or purpose）: ～是非 sow discord

【播送】bōsòng（動）broadcast; transmit: ～音樂節目 broadcast a music programme

【播音】bōyīn（動）broadcast; be on the air: 開始～ go on the air

【播種】bōzhòng Ⅰ（動）sow seeds Ⅱ（名）sowing: ～期 sowing season

【播種】bōzhǒng（動）sow; seed: 玉米的～面積 acreage sown to maize

撬 qiào（動）pry off: 溜門～鎖 secretly break the lock and force open the door; break into a house

撫 fǔ（動）❶ caress; stroke ❷ comfort; console ❸ protect; nurture

【撫育】fǔyù（動）nurture; take care of: ～孤兒 take care of orphans

【撫卹】fǔxù（動）comfort and assist a person who has sustained injuries in performing his duty; comfort and give assistance to a bereaved family

【撫卹金】fǔxùjīn（名）compensation; pension

【撫愛】fǔ'ài（動）caress; stroke fondly

【撫養】fǔyǎng（動）foster; bring up: ～孩子 bring up children

【撫摩】fǔmó（動）stroke

【撫慰】fǔwèi（動）console; solace

擅 shàn Ⅰ（副）arbitrarily: ～斷 make an arbitrary decision Ⅱ（動）be good at; be adept in: 她～於國畫。She is adept in Chinese painting.

【擅自】shànzì（副）without authorization; arbitrarily; without leave: ～作主 act alone without asking for instructions

【擅長】shàncháng（動）be good at; be adept in: ～書法 be good at calligraphy

【擅離職守】shàn lí zhí shǒu（動）leave one's post without asking for permission（usu. at a critical moment）

擁 yōng（動）❶ embrace; hug ❷ surround; gather round: 熱情的聽眾～着他。He was surrounded by an enthusiastic crowd of listeners. ❸ crowd; swarm: 人們～進體育場。People crowded into the stadium. ❹ support

【擁有】yōngyǒu（動）possess; have; own: ～一家企業 own a business

【擁抱】yōngbào（動）embrace; hug

【擁戴】yōngdài（動）choose sb. as leader and give him full support

【擁擠】yōngjǐ Ⅰ（動）crowd Ⅱ（形）crowded; thronged

【擁護】yōnghù（動）uphold; support; endorse

擀 gǎn (动) roll: ~餃子皮 roll out dumpling wrappers

擂 lèi (动) hit; strike
see also léi; lèi

擂 léi (动) grind; pulverize
see also lěi; lèi

擂 léi (动) drum; beat (the drum)
see also lěi; léi

【擂臺】 lèitái (名) ring; arena (for contests in martial arts): 打 ~ pick up the gauntlet

撼 hàn (动) shake

【撼動】 hàndòng (动) shake; topple

掰 pī (动) strip off: ~ 玉米 pick corn

擋 dǎng I (动) ❶ block; be in the way ❷ cover; shelter II (名) ❶ cover ❷ gear: 换 ~ shift gears

【擋駕】 dǎngjià (动) decline to see a visitor

【擋箭牌】 dǎngjiànpái (名) ❶ shield ❷ excuse

據 jù I (动) ❶ occupy; appropriate: 把他人的財物 ~ 爲己有 appropriate sb.'s private property ❷ rely on; draw on: ~ 險頑抗 depend on a strategic pass to offer fierce resistance II (介) in accordance with; on the basis of: ~ 實報道 give a truthful account III (名) evidence; basis: 有根有 ~ be well-founded; be well supported by evidence

【據理力爭】 jù lǐ lì zhēng 〈成〉 make vigorous representations on just grounds

【據傳】 jùchuán (副) allegedly; it is

rumoured that; rumour has it that

【據説】 jùshuō (副) allegedly; it is said that

擄 lǔ (动) take prisoner; capture

【擄掠】 lǔlüè (动) pillage; loot

操 cāo I (动) ❶ hold; have in hand: 穩~勝券 be certain of success ❷ do; be engaged in ❸ speak (a language): ~英語 speak English II (名) ❶ exercise; drill: 做早 ~ do morning exercises ❷ conduct: 節 ~ moral integrity

【操之過急】 cāo zhī guò jí 〈成〉 act with undue haste

【操心】 cāoxīn (动) worry about; bother about

【操行】 cāoxíng (名) (of a student) behaviour; conduct

【操作】 cāozuò (动) operate; work: ~規程 operating instructions

【操持】 cāochí (动) manage: ~家務 keep house

【操場】 cāochǎng (名) playground

【操勞】 cāoláo (动) ❶ work hard: ~ 過度 be overworked ❷ take pains

【操練】 cāoliàn (名) (in military and physical training, etc.) drill

【操縱】 cāozòng (动) ❶ operate; control ❷ manipulate (underhandedly): ~選舉 manipulate the elections

擇 zé (动) choose; select: 選 ~ select
see also zhái

【擇善而從】 zé shàn ér cóng 〈成〉 make sure of what is exemplary behaviour and follow it

擇 zhái (动) choose; select; pick:

~白菜 trim cabbage

see also zé

擒 qín (動) capture; catch

【擒拿】qínná (動) bring to book; place under arrest

揀 jiǎn (動) pick up; collect: 把玩具～起來。Pick up the toys.

【揀了芝蔴, 丢了西瓜】jiǎn le zhīmɑ, diū le xīguā〈口〉pick up sesame seeds while leaving behind watermelons; concentrate on trivial details to the neglect of what is essential; penny wise and pound foolish

【揀漏】jiǎnlòu (動) stop leakage in the roof; plug leaks

擔 dān (動) ❶ carry on the shoulder ❷ undertake; bear

see also dàn

【擔心】dānxīn (動) worry

【擔任】dānrèn (動) hold the post of

【擔保】dānbǎo (動) assure; guarantee

【擔待】dāndài (動) ❶ forgive ❷ shoulder (responsibility)

【擔負】dānfù (動) shoulder; bear

【擔架】dānjià (名) stretcher

【擔風險】dān fēngxiǎn (動) take risks

【擔當】dāndāng (動) take on; bear: ～艱巨的工作 take on arduous jobs

【擔驚受怕】dān jīng shòu pà (動) be filled with worry and anxiety

擔 dàn Ⅰ (名) load; task Ⅱ (量): 一～水 two buckets of water (carried on a shoulder pole)

see also dān

擊 jī (動) ❶ strike: 迎～敵軍 give battle to the enemy ❷ assault; at-

tack: 不堪一～ cannot stand a single blow ❸ collide; lash: 浪～礁嚴。The waves are lashing the reef. ❹ witness: 目～記 eyewitness account

【擊中】jīzhòng (動) hit: ～敵機 hit the enemy plane /一語～要害 hit the nail on the head

【擊沉】jīchén (動) sink (a ship)

【擊退】jītuì (動) beat back; drive back: ～進犯的敵軍 beat back the invading enemy

【擊破】jīpò (動) smash; defeat

【擊敗】jībài (動) defeat; beat

【擊毀】jīhuǐ (動) hit and destroy

【擊落】jīluò (動) shoot down; down

【擊劍】jījiàn (名) fencing

【擊潰】jīkuì (動) inflict a crushing defeat on; rout

【擊斃】jībì (動) shoot dead; kill

擎 qíng (動) prop up; lift up

擘 bò (名) thumb: 醫學界巨～ authority in the medical profession

擰 níng (動) ❶ twist; wring: 把濕衣服～乾 wring out the wet clothes ❷ pinch; tweak: 他～了一下那孩子的耳朵。He gave the child's ear a little tweak.

see also nǐng

擰 nǐng (動) ❶ wrench; screw: ～開 unscrew / ～緊 screw sth. on tight ❷ wrong; mistake: 他把問題弄～了。He has a mistaken idea of the matter.

see also níng

擯 bìn (動) abandon; discard; oust

【擯除】bìnchú (動) get rid of; dispense with: ～萬難 overcome all

difficulties

【擯棄】bìnqì（動） discard; cast away; abandon: ～舊惡 bury the hatchet

擦 cā（動）❶ rub; scrape ❷ clean by wiping: ～玻璃 clean window panes ❸ apply: ～藥膏 apply medical ointment to ❹ brush; touch lightly against: ～邊球〈兵乓球〉edge ball ❺ grate; scrape（into shreds）

【擦亮】cāliàng（動） polish; shine; furbish: ～眼睛 keep one's eyes open; keep a sharp lookout for

【擦拭】cāshì（動） clean; cleanse: ～機床 clean a machine tool

【擦掉】cādiào（動） rub out（off, away）; wipe away（off）

擠 jǐ（動）❶ crowd; swarm; pack: ～得喘不過氣來 so crowded that one could hardly breathe ❷ squeeze in; squash in: ～進會場 push one's way into an assembly hall ❸ squeeze; press: ～牛奶 milk a cow

【擠兌】jǐduì（名）a run on the bank to draw out money

【擠眉弄眼】jǐ méi nòng yǎn〈成〉make eyes; wink

撞 tái（動）❶ lift; raise: ～價 force up prices ❷（of two or more people）carry: ～傷員 carry a wounded soldier（on a stretcher）

【撞槓】táigàng（動）〈口〉argue unreasonably; bicker; squabble: ～抬嘴 argue fiercely and fall to quarrelling

【撞頭】táitóu（動）❶ raise one's head ❷ gain ground: 不良傾向正在～。Unhealthy social trends are

on the rise. ❸ start a new line of writing in private or official correspondence as a sign of respect for the addressee

【撞舉】táiju（動）give sb. favours; praise or promote sb.: 他這樣不識～,不會對他有什麼好處的。His failure to accept favours with good grace will do him no good.

【撞轎子】táijiàozi（動）praise sb. lavishly and often unctuously to build up his prestige

擱 gē（動）❶ put; place ❷ put aside: 把計劃～起來 shelve the plan
see also gé

【擱淺】gēqiǎn（動）❶（of ships）be stranded ❷ come to a standstill; reach a stalemate

【擱置】gēzhì（動）lay aside（matter; business）; shelve

擱 gé（動）gear; stand; endure: 滌綸～洗。Polyester washes well.
see also gē

擬 nǐ（動）❶ draw up; draft: ～發言稿 draft one's speech ❷ intend; plan: ～採納他的建議 intend to adopt his suggestions ❸ imitate: 模～ imitate; copy; simulate

【擬人】nǐrén Ⅰ（名）〈語〉personification Ⅱ（動）personify

【擬訂】nǐdìng（動）draw up; work out

【擬議】nǐyì Ⅰ（名）proposal; recommendation Ⅱ（動）draw up; draft; propose: ～的解決方案 the proposed solution

擤 xǐng

【擤鼻涕】xǐngbítì（動） blow one's nose

擴 kuò (動) expand; extend; amplify; enlarge

【擴大】 kuòdà (動) extend; enlarge: ~會議 enlarged session / ~化 magnify; exceed the bounds

【擴印】 kuòyìn (動)〈攝〉enlarge and print

【擴充】 kuòchōng (動) augment; expand; increase

【擴建】 kuòjiàn (動) (of a plant, mine, business building, etc.) extend: 飯店的~工程 the extension project of the hotel

【擴音器】 kuòyīnqì (名) ❶ microphone ❷ loudspeaker ❸ audio amplifier

【擴軍備戰】 kuòjūn bèizhàn (名) arms expansion and preparation for war

【擴展】 kuòzhǎn (動) expand; enlarge

【擴張】 kuòzhāng (動) (of influence, ambition, etc.) expand; broaden

【擴張主義】 kuòzhāng zhǔyì (名) expansionism

【擴散】 kuòsàn (動) spread; proliferate

擻 zhì (動) throw; hurl; fling: 一~千金 ready to squander a thousand pieces of gold at one go / ~鐵餅 discus throw

撣 niǎn (動) ❶ drive out; expel: 把某人從公司~走 oust sb. from the company ❷ 〈方〉catch up: 努力~上 do one's best to catch up (with sb.)

擾 rǎo (動) ❶ harass; disturb: 內心紛~ feel seriously perturbed ❷ bother: 我吃了他一頓好飯, 但太

打~他了。I enjoyed his meal, but it was such a bother to him.

【擾亂】 rǎoluàn (動) disturb; upset: ~市場 disrupt the market

擺 bǎi (動) ❶ put; set; arrange: ~刀叉 lay the knives and forks ❷ sway; wave: ~手 wave one's hand ❸ show off: ~老資格 show off one's seniority; put on the airs of a veteran

【擺平】 bǎipíng (動) treat (both sides) fairly; be even-handed

【擺佈】 bǎibu (動) manipulate: 任人~ allow oneself to be dictated to

【擺弄】 bǎinòng (動) ❶ fiddle with; play with (sth.) ❷ order about; manipulate (sb.); twist sb. round one's (little) finger

【擺事實, 講道理】 bǎi shì shí, jiǎng dào li (成) present the facts and reason things out; produce facts to back up one's argument

【擺架子】 bǎijiàzi (動) put on airs; be pretentious

【擺動】 bǎidòng (動) swing; sway; oscillate

【擺脫】 bǎituō (動) free oneself from; shake off; get rid of: ~貧困 shake off poverty

【擺設】 bǎishè (動) decorate; furnish: 房間裏~得很講究。The room is elegantly furnished.

【擺設兒】 bǎisher (名) furnishings; ornaments: 小~ knickknack

【擺渡】 bǎidù I (動) ferry across II (名) ferry

【擺龍門陣】 bǎi lóngménzhèn 〈口〉 have a chat; engage in chitchat

【擺闊氣】 bǎikuòqi (動) parade a penchant for luxury; vie for extravagance; flaunt one's wealth

【攏攤子】bǎi tānzi（動）keep a stall

攀 pān（動）❶ climb; scale: ~牆 climb over a wall ❷ forge ties of social relationship with people in high position: 高 ~ seek connections with people of superior social status

【攀折】pānzhé（動）pick; pluck

【攀登】pāndēng（動）climb; scale

【攀談】pāntán（動）chat

【攀緣】pānyuán（動）climb; clamber

【攀龍附鳳】pān lóng fù fèng〈成〉curry favour with people of power and influence

【攀親】pānqīn（動）❶ claim kinship ❷ arrange a match

攏 lǒng（動）❶ add up; total ❷ hold together; hold in place: 把孩子~在懷裏 hold the child in one's arms ❸ approach; reach: 快~工地了。The worksite is right ahead. ❹ comb

【攏子】lǒngzi（名）comb with close fine teeth

【攏共】lǒnggòng（副）in all; in total: 醫院裏~有 300 張病牀。The hospital has a total of 300 beds.

【攏岸】lǒng'àn（動）come alongside the shore

攔 lán（動）bar; hold back; dam up: 誰也 ~ 不住他。Nobody can stop him.

【攔阻】lánzǔ（動）obstruct; hinder; block; bar

【攔河壩】lánhébà（名）dam

【攔路】lánlù（動）❶ block the way: ~虎 formidable obstacle; stumbling block ❷ hold up: ~搶劫 waylay; mug

【攔腰】lányāo（副）by the waist; in the middle: ~切斷敵給綫 cut the enemy supply line in the middle

【攔截】lánjié（動）intercept; waylay: ~敵機 intercept enemy planes / 被一羣歹徒~了 be waylaid by gangsters

攙 chān（動）❶ support by the arm: ~着病人站起來 assist the patient to his feet ❷ mix: 往牛奶裏~水 add water to the milk

【攙扶】chānfú（動）support sb. with one's hand

【攙和】chānhuo（動）mix

【攙雜】chānzá（動）mix up; mingle: 一些流氓阿飛~到人羣裏。A handful of hooligans mingled with the crowd.

攝 shè（動）❶ absorb; take in ❷ take a photograph or picture of; shoot ❸ act as agent

【攝氏溫度計】shèshì wēndùjì（名）centigrade thermometer; Celsius thermometer

【攝取】shèqǔ（動）❶ absorb; assimilate: ~養分 assimilate nutrient materials ❷ take（a photograph）; shoot（a film）

【攝政】shèzhèng（動）act as regent

【攝像機】shèxiàngjī（名）pickup camera

【攝製】shèzhì（動）produce（a film）

【攝影】shèyǐng（動）❶ take a photograph or picture ❷ shoot a film

【攝影機】shèyǐngjī（名）camera

攤 tān I（動）❶ unfold; spread out: ~開雙手 spread out one's hands ❷ fry a thin layer of batter: ~鷄蛋餅 make a pancake with a mixture of flour and egg ❸ share out: 費用均～ share the expenses equally Ⅱ（名）vendor's stall or stand: 擺菜～of a vegetable vendor Ⅲ（量）(of blood, mud, etc.) pool; puddle: 一～稀泥 a muddy puddle

【攤子】tānzi（名）❶（vendor's）stall; booth; stand ❷ setup; organizational arrangement: 收拾爛～ clear up an awful mess

【攤派】tānpài（動）divide and share out; assign; allot: 每人的工作都～好了。Work has been assigned to everybody.

【攤販】tānfàn（名）street pedlar

【攤牌】tānpái（動）show-down: 該是時候和你老板～的時候了。It's time for a show-down with your boss.

攢 zǎn（動）accumulate; save: ～錢買汽車 save money for a car / ～郵票 collect stamps

攣 luán（名）contraction: 痙～spasm

攫 jué（動）seize; snatch; catch

【攫取】juéqǔ（動）seize by force; plunder

攥 zuàn（動）grip; grasp; clutch: 她很害怕，～住了我的手。She gripped my hand in fear.

攪 jiǎo（動）❶ disturb; harass: 胡～pester ❷ stir; mix: 用匙子把咖啡～一～。Stir the coffee with a spoon.

【攪拌】jiǎobàn（動）mix; blend: ～混凝土 mix cement

【攪和】jiǎohuo（動）❶ stir; blend ❷ make a mess of: 瞎～ mess things up

【攪動】jiǎodòng（動）stir; blend

【攪渾】jiǎohún（動）〈口〉blend; mix: 把水～ muddy the water; deliberately cause confusion

【攪亂】jiǎoluàn（動）mess up; disrupt: ～我們的旅行安排 mess up our travel arrangements

【攪擾】jiǎorǎo（動）disturb; pester; trouble: 不要～他。Don't disturb him.

攬 lǎn（動）❶ put the arms round; embrace; hug: 媽媽把小孩～在懷裏。The mother took the child into her arms ❷ tie up ❸ take sth. upon oneself; canvass: ～生意 tout for business ❹ keep a tight grip on: ～權 keep a firm grip on power

攮 nǎng（動）stab

【攮子】nǎngzi（名）dagger

支 部

支 zhī Ⅰ（動）❶ prop up; put up; erect: ～上簾子 prop up the curtain / ～～涼棚 erect a mat shelter ❷ sustain; bear: 累得～不住 too tired to hold out any longer ❸ pay or draw (money): 從銀行～一千塊錢 draw 1,000 yuan from the bank ❹ send away; order about: 毫不客氣地把他～走了 send him away rudely Ⅱ（名）❶ branch: ～行 branch office ❷ watt: 15～光的燈泡 a 15-watt bulb ❸〈紡〉count: 85一紗 85-count yarn Ⅲ（量）❶［of stick-like things］: 一～粉筆 a stick of chalk / 一～香煙 a cigarette ❷ [for songs or melodies]: 一～民歌 a folk song ❸ [of army units]: 一～部隊 a contingent of troops

【支出】zhīchū Ⅰ (動) pay (money); disburse Ⅱ (名) expenses; expenditure

【支付】zhīfù (動) pay; defray

【支吾】zhīwu (動) equivocate; prevaricate: ～ 其詞 mince one's words; hum and haw

【支取】zhīqǔ (動) draw (money)

【支使】zhīshǐ (動) ❶ order about ❷ send away

【支持】zhīchí Ⅰ (動) ❶ sustain; hold out: 他一不住了，只好認輸。As he could no longer hold out, he had to concede defeat. ❷ support; second: 我一你的意見。I second your suggestion. Ⅱ (名) support

【支架】zhījià (名) support; stand

【支柱】zhīzhù (名) pillar; mainstay; brace

【支流】zhīliú (名) ❶ tributary; affluent ❷ minor aspects

【支配】zhīpèi (動) ❶ arrange; allocate: 很好地一課外活動時間 properly allocate the time for extracurricular activities ❷ control; dominate; manipulate: 受人 ～ be manipulated by sb.

【支氣管】zhī qìguǎn (名) bronchus: ～ 炎 brochitis

【支部】zhībù (名) branch (of an organization)

【支票】zhīpiào (名) cheque; check

【支隊】zhīduì (名) detachment

【支援】zhīyuán Ⅰ (動) support; aid; help Ⅱ (名) support; help

【支解】zhījiě (動) dismember

【支撐】zhīcheng (動) prop up; support; sustain: 用拱門～的屋頂 a

roof supported by arches

【支點】zhīdiǎn (名)〈物〉fulcrum

【支離破碎】zhī lí pò suì〈成〉shattered to pieces; fallen apart

<h1 style="text-align:center">支 部</h1>

【收】shōu (動) ❶ bring in; bring together: 招～新生 recruit new students ❷ receive; accept: ～受禮物 accept gifts ❸ take what one has the right to get back or what originally belongs to one: ～房租 collect rent / 沒 ～ confiscate/ ～ 歸國有 nationalize ❹ gather in: ～麥子 get in the wheat ❺ gain (economic profit): 國內稅 ～ inland revenue ❻ restrain (one's emotion or action); check: ～淚 refrain from tears ❼ arrest: ～監 imprison ❽ conclude; stop (work): 現在可以～了。It's time to knock off.

【收入】shōurù Ⅰ (名) income: 非法 ～ illegal earning Ⅱ (動) include: 這個選集～了許多當代散文作家的作品。Many modern prose writers are included in the anthology.

【收工】shōugōng (動) (of people working in the fields or on a construction site) knock off; call it a day

【收支】shōuzhī (名) income and expenses

【收成】shōucheng (名) crop; harvest

【收件人】shōujiànrén (名) addressee; consignee

【收回】shōuhuí (動) ❶ take back; recall: 所有借給學生的書，都～

了。We've collected all the books lent to the students. ❷ withdraw or retract (a command, request, proposal, etc.)

【收兵】shōubīng（动）call back troops from battle

【收尾】shōuwěi（名）❶ final phase (of a project, etc.) ❷ ending; concluding remarks (of a book, an essay, etc.)

【收到】shōudào（动）achieve; receive: ～良好的效果 achieve good results

【收看】shōukàn（动）tune in (to) (a television programme)

【收拾】shōushi（动）❶ tidy up; clear up: 厨房太乱了，要～～。The kitchen is in a mess and should be tidied up. ❷ pack up: ～行装 pack things up for a journey ❸ repair: 把皮箱～一下 have the suitcase repaired ❹〈口〉punish; settle 5 〈口〉kill; finish off

【收信人】shōuxìnrén（名）addressee (of a letter)

【收音机】shōuyīnjī（名）radio set: 听～ listen to the radio

【收效】shōuxiào（动）gain results; produce effect: ～甚大 reap great benefits

【收留】shōuliú（动）take in and provide for

【收起】shōuqǐ（动）put an end to; put away: ～你们那一套拙劣手法吧! Stop playing those clumsy tricks of yours!

【收容】shōuróng（动）take in; provide living quarters, etc. for: 难民～所 refugee camp

【收益】shōuyì（名）profit; proceeds

【收货人】shōuhuòrén（名）consignee

【收票员】shōupiàoyuán（名）ticket collector

【收费】shōufèi（动）charge; require payment: ～公路 toll road (highway)

【收复】shōufù（动）recover; take back

【收场】shōuchǎng Ⅰ（动）bring to a conclusion: 忽忽～ wind up a matter in haste Ⅱ（名）end; outcome

【收割】shōugē（动）harvest; reap: ～機 harvester

【收集】shōují（动）collect: ～废品 collect waste

【收买】shōumǎi（动）❶ purchase ❷ buy over: ～民心 buy popular support

【收税】shōushuì（动）collect taxes

【收款人】shōukuǎnrén（名）payee

【收发室】shōufāshì（名）office for incoming and outgoing mail

【收养】shōuyǎng（动）adopt (a child)

【收盘】shōupán（名）〈经〉closing quotation: ～价 closing price (on the exchange)

【收审】shōushěn（动）take into custody for interrogation

【收据】shōujù（收条 shōutiáo）（名）receipt: 开张～ write a receipt

【收录机】shōulùjī（名）radio cassette recorder

【收购】shōugòu（动）buy from various localities: ～羊毛 purchase wool

【收缩】shōusuō（动）❶ shrink: 这种毛衣不～。This kind of woollen sweater won't shrink. ❷ concentrate: 敌军把主力～在交通綫上。The enemy concentrated their main force along the communication lines.

【收藏】shōucáng（动）collect: ～古

董 collect curios and antiques

【收穫】 shōuhuò Ⅰ (动) harvest Ⅱ (名) gains; positive results: 很有～的經歷 rewarding experience

【收聽】 shōutīng (动) tune in (to a radio programme); listen in to (the radio): ～天氣預報 listen to the weather forecast over the radio

【收攤兒】 shōutānr (动) let's stop work for the day; let's call it a day

攻 gōng (动) ❶ attack; assault ❷ accuse; charge: 羣起而～之。 Many rose to point a finger at him. ❸ study; major in

【攻打】 gōngdǎ (动) attack

【攻克】 gōngkè (动) capture (city, enemy fort, etc.); overcome (technical difficulty, problem, etc.)

【攻陷】 gōngxiàn (动) capture (city, enemy fort, etc.)

【攻堅】 gōngjiān (动) attack fortified positions

【攻勢】 gōngshì (名) offensive

【攻擊】 gōngjī (动) ❶ attack; assault ❷ slander; calumniate

【攻讀】 gōngdú (动) study assiduously; specialize in

改 gǎi (动) ❶ change; transform ❷ touch up; polish: ～文章 polish an article ❸ correct; rectify: ～卷子 correct papers

【改口】 gǎikǒu (动) take back what one has said; change one's tune

【改日】 gǎirì (副) another day: ～再來 come again some other day

【改正】 gǎizhèng (动) correct; rectify

【改行】 gǎiháng (动) change one's profession

【改良】 gǎiliáng (动) improve; reform

【改良主義】 gǎiliáng zhǔyì (名) reformism

【改邪歸正】 gǎi xié guī zhèng 〈成〉 turn over a new leaf

【改弦更張】 gǎi xián gēng zhāng 〈成〉 change the way of doing things and start afresh

【改弦易轍】 gǎi xián yì zhé 〈成〉 change course; change one's attitude

【改建】 gǎijiàn (动) rebuild; renovate

【改革】 gǎigé (名) reform; restructuring: 物價～ price reform

【改悔】 gǎihuǐ (动) repent

【改造】 gǎizào (动) transform; remould

【改掉】 gǎidiào (动) abolish; get rid of

【改動】 gǎidòng Ⅰ (动) change; alter; modify Ⅱ (名) change

【改組】 gǎizǔ (动) reorganize; reshuffle

【改進】 gǎijìn (动) improve

【改道】 gǎidào (动) change the route of one's journey; change its course (of a river)

【改期】 gǎiqī (动) change a fixed date

【改善】 gǎishàn (动) improve; better: ～經濟環境 improve the economic environment

【改過自新】 gǎi guò zì xīn 〈成〉 turn over a new leaf; amend one's ways

【改朝換代】 gǎi cháo huàn dài 〈成〉 overthrow the old regime and inaugurate a new one; undergo a dynastic change

【改嫁】 gǎijià (动) (of a woman) remarry

【改編】 gǎibiān (动) ❶ adapt; rewrite ❷ (of troops) reorganize; re-designate

【改寫】gǎixiě (動) rewrite; adapt

【改選】gǎixuǎn Ⅰ (動) reelect; elect Ⅱ (名) reelection; election

【改錐】gǎizhuī (名) screwdriver

【改頭換面】gǎi tóu huàn miàn〈成〉change the appearance; put on a new facade

【改變】gǎibiàn (動) change; alter

【改觀】gǎiguān (動) take on a fresh look

放 fàng (動) ❶ release; free: ～包袱 disburden oneself ❷ give free reign to: ～聲高唱 sing lustily ❸ put; lay: 把書～在書架上 lay down the book on the bookshelf ❹ show; play: ～錄像 show a video

【放工】fànggōng (動) knock off work

【放大】fàngdà (動) enlarge; magnify

【放大鏡】fàngdàjìng (名) magnifying glass

【放下屠刀，立地成佛】fàng xià tú dāo, lì dì chéng fó〈成〉lay down your butcher's knife and you will become a Buddha; repent and you will turn over a new leaf

【放心】fàngxīn (動) be at ease; be free from anxiety

【放火】fànghuǒ (動) set fire to: ～罪 arson / ～犯 arsonist

【放手】fàngshǒu (動) ❶ let go (of) ❷ abandon all restrictions

【放出】fàngchū (動) give out; emit

【放行】fàngxíng (動) let pass: 免稅～ allow sth. to be brought in duty-free

【放任】fàngrèn Ⅰ (動) leave alone Ⅱ (名) laissez faire

【放任自流】fàng rèn zì liú (動) let persons or things drift along

【放屁】fàngpì (動) ❶ fart; break wind ❷ talk nonsense; shit

【放牧】fàngmù (動) graze

【放空氣】fàng kōngqì (動) spread rumours; deliberately create an impression

【放毒】fàngdú (動) spew venom

【放風】fàngfēng (動) ❶ let prisoners out for stretching their limbs in the yard ❷ leak information

【放映】fàngyìng (動) show; project (a film)

【放映機】fàngyìngjī (名) projector

【放哨】fàngshào (動) stand sentry

【放射】fàngshè Ⅰ (動) radiate Ⅱ (名) radiation

【放逐】fàngzhú (動) ostracize; banish; exile

【放假】fàngjià (動) have a holiday or vacation

【放款】fàngkuǎn (動) grant a loan to

【放過】fàngguò (動) let slip: ～機會 let slip an opportunity

【放晴】fàngqíng (動) (of weather) clear up

【放棄】fàngqì (動) relinquish; give up

【放電】fàngdiàn (動) discharge electricity

【放置】fàngzhì (動) lay; put

【放學】fàngxué (動) (of pupils) go home after school

【放蕩】fàngdàng (形) spend one's life in dissipation; dissolute

【放蕩不羈】fàng dàng bù jī〈成〉loose and unconventional

【放縱】fàngzòng Ⅰ (動) fail to impose necessary discipline; indulge Ⅱ

（形）unruly; without manners

【放鬆】fàngsōng（動）relax; slacken

政 zhèng（名）❶ politics; political affairs: ~綱 political programme / 從 ~ enter politics ❷ government: 當 ~ be in power; be in office / 簡 ~ streamlined administration ❸ certain administrative aspects of government: 財~ (public) finance

【政見】zhèngjiàn（名）political view

【政局】zhèngjú（名）political situation

【政法】zhèngfǎ（名）politics and law

【政府】zhèngfǔ（名）government

【政委】zhèngwěi（名）political commissar

【政協】zhèngxié（名）(short for) the Chinese People's Political Consultative Conference

【政治】zhèngzhì（名）politics

【政界】zhèngjiè（名）political circles; government circles

【政客】zhèngkè（名）politician

【政策】zhèngcè（名）policy

【政敵】zhèngdí（名）political opponent

【政論】zhènglùn（名）political article or essay: ~家 political commentator

【政黨】zhèngdǎng（名）political party

【政權】zhèngquán（名）regime; political power

【政變】zhèngbiàn（名）coup d'état

【政體】zhèngtǐ（名）system of government

故 gù Ⅰ（名）❶ incident; happenings: 變 ~ unexpected misfortune ❷ reason; cause: 無緣無 ~

without reason or cause ❸ friend; acquaintance: 親 ~ relatives and friends Ⅱ（形）old; former Ⅲ（副）on purpose: ~作鎮定 pretend to be calm and unruffled Ⅳ（動）die; pass away Ⅴ（連）therefore

【故人】gùrén（名）old friend

【故土】gùtǔ（名）native land

【故技】gùjì（名）old trick

【故弄玄虛】gù nòng xuán xū〈成〉juggle with mystifying ideas

【故步自封】gù bù zì fēng〈成〉stick to old things and refuse to change

【故居】gùjū（名）former residence

【故事】gùshi（名）❶ story; tale ❷ plot

【故宮】gùgōng（名）the Imperial Palace

【故都】gùdū（名）old capital

【故鄉】gùxiāng（名）native place; hometown

【故意】gùyì（副）deliberately; intentionally

【故障】gùzhàng（名）(of machinery or equipment) trouble; fault

【故態復萌】gù tài fù méng〈成〉relapse into one's old bad habit

效 xiào Ⅰ（名）effect: 生 ~ take effect / 療~ curative effect Ⅱ（動）❶ imitate: 仿 ~ follow the example of ❷ devote to; render service

【效力】xiàolì Ⅰ（動）render a service to; serve: 我可以爲你~。You can count on me for help. Ⅱ（名）effect

【效法】xiàofǎ（動）follow sb.'s example

【效果】xiàoguǒ（名）effect; result

【效忠】xiàozhōng（動）be loyal to: 宣誓 ~ swear allegiance to

【效能】xiàonéng（名）function; efficacy

【效益】xiàoyì（名）beneficial result: 經濟～ economic results

【效率】xiàolǜ（名）efficiency

【效勞】xiàoláo（動）be at sb.'s service; render a service to: 我願～。I'm at your disposal.

敖 Áo（名）a surname

教 jiāo（動）teach

see also jiào

【教書】jiāoshū（動）teach

教 jiào Ⅰ（動）teach; instruct; educate: 嚴加管～ take in hand Ⅱ（名）❶ education: 文～部門 cultural and educational departments ❷ religion: 信～ believe in a religion ❸（Jiào）a surname

see also jiāo

【教工】jiàogōng（名）faculty and administrative personnel

【教士】jiàoshì（名）priest; pastor; clergyman: 傳～ missionary

【教材】jiàocái（名）teaching material; textbook

【教廷】jiàotíng（名）the Holy See

【教育】jiàoyù Ⅰ（名）education Ⅱ（動）educate

【教皇】jiàohuáng（名）Pope

【教室】jiàoshì（名）classroom; lecture hall

【教研室】jiàoyánshì（名）teaching and research division

【教科書】jiàokēshū（教本 jiàoběn）（名）textbook

【教案】jiào'àn（名）teaching notes

【教師】jiàoshī（名）teacher: 小學～ primary school teacher / 大學～ university teacher

【教唆】jiàosuō（動）abet; encourage a crime: ～犯 abettor

【教員】jiàoyuán（名）teacher; instructor

【教徒】jiàotú（名）religious follower or believer

【教訓】jiàoxun Ⅰ（名）lesson (drawn from a failure or an error) Ⅱ（動）scold; reprimand: ～～他 give him a dressing-down; teach him a lesson

【教條】jiàotiáo（名）dogma; doctrine

【教條主義】jiàotiáo zhǔyì（名）dogmatism

【教務長】jiàowùzhǎng（名）Dean of Studies; Dean of the Academic Department

【教務處】jiàowùchù（名）Dean's Office; Academic Department

【教授】jiàoshòu Ⅰ（名）professor: 副～ reader; associate professor Ⅱ（動）give lessons in; lecture in; teach

【教堂】jiàotáng（名）church; cathedral; chapel: 聖保羅～ St. Paul's Cathedral

【教規】jiàoguī（名）〈宗〉canon

【教程】jiàochéng（名）course（of study）

【教會】jiàohuì（名）church（including the Roman Catholic Church, the Orthodox Church, the Protestant Church, etc.）

【教誨】jiàohuì（名）teaching; education

【教養】jiàoyǎng（名）❶ training and education of the younger generation ❷ breeding; culture ❸（short for 勞動教養 láodòng jiàoyǎng）reform through labour

【教練】jiàoliàn Ⅰ（動）train; instruct Ⅱ（名）coach; instructor; trainer

【教導】jiàodǎo Ⅰ（動）teach; instruct Ⅱ（名）guidance; instructions: 您的～將永銘於心。Your words will be engraved on my mind.

【教導員】jiàodǎoyuán（名）instructor

【教學】jiàoxué（名）❶ teaching; instruction ❷ instruction and learning: ～相長。Teaching benefits teachers as well as students.（To teach is to learn.）

【教齡】jiàolíng（名）(of a teacher) length of service

救 jiù（動）❶ rescue; save: 搶～ rescue; salvage; give emergency treatment (to a patient) / ～死扶傷 rescue the dying and heal the wounded ❷ help; relieve

【救火】jiùhuǒ（動）put out a fire: ～車 fire engine / ～隊 fire brigade

【救生衣】jiùshēngyī（名）life vest; life jacket

【救生員】jiùshēngyuán（名）lifeguard

【救生圈】jiùshēngquān（名）life buoy

【救生艇】jiùshēngtǐng（名）lifeboat

【救災】jiùzāi（動）provide relief for victims of natural disaster

【救助】jiùzhù（動）rescue and render help to sb.

【救命】jiùmìng（動）save sb.'s life

【救活】jiùhuó（動）bring back to life

【救急】jiùjí（動）help tide over a difficulty; rush emergency aid

【救星】jiùxīng（名）saviour; liberator

【救援】jiùyuán（動）rescue; render help; aid: ～工作 rescue operation

【救濟】jiùjì Ⅰ（動）relieve; provide relief to Ⅱ（名）relief

【救護】jiùhù（動）give first aid; rescue

【救護車】jiùhùchē（名）ambulance

敕 chì（名）imperial decree: ～封 designated by imperial decree

敢 gǎn Ⅰ（形）bold; courageous Ⅱ（動）❶ dare: ～作～爲的人 a person of great daring ❷ be sure: 我～說他會改變主意。I am certain that he will change his mind. Ⅲ〈謙〉make bold; venture: ～問 venture to ask

【敢於】gǎnyú（動）dare: ～正視現實 have the courage to face reality squarely

敗 bài Ⅰ（動）❶ defeat; beat: 擊～對手 defeat one's rival ❷ be defeated or beaten: 驕必～。Pride goes before a fall. ❸ fail ❹ spoil; make a mess of: ～事 spoil the show ❺ counteract; remove; dispel: ～毒 counter inflammation (toxin) ❻ fade; wither; decay; rot: 花開～了。The flowers have withered. Ⅱ（形）❶ defeated ❷ spoiled; bad; degenerated

【敗子】bàizǐ（名）(short for 敗家子 bàijiāzǐ) prodigal; spendthrift

【敗火】bàihuǒ（動）〈中醫〉relieve inflammation or internal heat

【敗北】bàiběi（動）be defeated; be put on rout

【敗仗】bàizhàng（名）defeat; lost battle: 打～ lose a battle

【敗血症】bàixuèzhèng（名）〈醫〉septicaemia

【敗退】bàituì（動）retreat in defeat

【敗胃】bàiwèi（動）upset one's

stomach

【敗陣】bàizhèn（動）be defeated on the battlefield

【敗筆】bàibǐ（名）❶ faulty stroke (in calligraphy or painting) ❷ unhappy expression in a piece of writing

【敗訴】bàisù（動）lose a lawsuit

【敗落】bàiluò（動）decline in fortune

【敗興】bàixìng（動）be dejected; be disappointed：～而歸 return disappointed

【敗類】bàilèi（名）scum; black sheep

【敗壞】bàihuài Ⅰ（動）ruin; corrupt; destroy; spoil：～名聲 tarnish one's reputation Ⅱ（形）bad; rotten：道德～ morally degenerate

【敗露】bàilù（動）〈貶〉be exposed; be uncovered

敏 mǐn（形）agile; quick

【敏捷】mǐnjié（形）quick; nimble：才思～ be quick-witted

【敏感】mǐngǎn（形）sensitive：～問題 a sensitive issue / 對灰塵～ be allergic to dust

【敏銳】mǐnruì（形）sharp; keen

敦 dūn（形）honest; sincere

【敦促】dūncù（動）urge

【敦厚】dūnhòu（形）honest and sincere

【敦睦】dūnmù（動）promote relations of peace and friendship

【敦實】dūnshí（形）sturdy

散 sàn Ⅰ（動）come loose; fall apart：木箱～了。The wooden box fell apart. Ⅱ（形）loose; scattered：～居 live scattered

see also sàn

【散文】sǎnwén（名）prose：～詩 prose poem; free verse

【散光】sǎnguāng（名）〈醫〉astigmatism

【散兵】sǎnbīng（名）❶ skirmisher ❷ stray soldiers; stragglers

【散沙】sǎnshā（名）loose sand：一盤～ a sheet of loose sand; without any cohesion

【散記】sǎnjì（名）random notes; sidelights

【散貨】sǎnhuò（名）bulk cargo

【散裝】sǎnzhuāng（形）not packaged：我買些～糖果。I bought some sweets loose.

【散漫】sǎnmàn（形）undisciplined; desultory

散 sàn（動）❶ disband; disperse：電影～場了。The film show is over. / 人羣～了。The crowd dispersed. ❷ distribute; scatter ❸ dispel; let out：開開電風扇，～～熱氣。Turn on the electric fan to cool the air.

see also sǎn

【散心】sànxīn（動）divert oneself (from anxiety)

【散失】sànshī（動）❶ scatter and disappear; be lost：文件已經找回了。The missing papers have been recovered. ❷（of moisture, etc.）be lost; evaporate

【散伙】sànhuǒ（動）❶ dissolve partnership ❷ part company

【散佈】sànbù（動）spread; scatter：～細菌 disseminate germs / ～着許多小島嶼 strewn with many islets

【散步】sànbù（動）take a walk; go for a stroll

【散發】sànfā（動）❶ give off;

emit: 那條魚～着腥味兒。That fish gives off a strong smell. ❷ distribute; hand out: ～學習材料 hand out materials for study

【散開】sànkāi (動) disperse; scatter

【散會】sànhuì (動) (of a meeting) break up; adjourn

【散播】sànbō (動) spread; disseminate

【散熱器】sànrèqì (名) radiator

【散攤子】sàntānzi (動) 〈口〉break up

敝 bì I (形) shabby; ragged; tattered II (代) 〈謙〉my; our: ～姓 my name (surname)

【敝帚自珍】bì zhǒu zì zhēn 〈成〉cherish one's old broom; things which are worthless to others may be of value to the owner

敞 chǎng (形) ❶ spacious ❷ open: ～着蓋 with the lid off

【敞亮】chǎngliàng (形) ❶ (of room, etc.) spacious and light ❷ clear (in one's mind): 心裏～了 feel enlightened

【敞開】chǎngkāi (動) open: ～思想 speak one's mind without reservation

【敞開兒】chǎngkāir (副) 〈口〉unrestrictedly: ～喝 drink one's fill

敬 jìng I (動) ❶ respect; regard; esteem: 佇立肖像之前, 肅然起～ stand before the portrait in respectful silence ❷ present with respect: ～茶 offer sb. a cup of tea II (副) respectfully: ～謝不敏。I apologize for my inability to comply with your wishes. III (名) (Jìng) a surname

【敬而遠之】jìng ér yuǎn zhī 〈成〉

keep a respectful distance from sb.

【敬仰】jìngyǎng (動) revere; admire: 受人～的領導人 a revered leader

【敬老院】jìnglǎoyuàn (名) home for the aged

【敬佩】jìngpèi (動) admire; hold in high esteem

【敬畏】jìngwèi (動) revere; be in awe of

【敬重】jìngzhòng (動) venerate; respect highly

【敬愛】jìngài I (動) respect and love II (形) beloved; respected

【敬意】jìngyì (名) esteem; regard; tribute: 聊表～ serve as a token of respect for you

【敬禮】jìnglǐ I (動) salute II (名) 〈敬〉[used as the formal ending of a letter]: 此致～ respectfully(cordially) yours

敲 qiāo (動) knock; beat: ～鐘 toll the bell

【敲打】qiāodǎ (動) beat; strike: ～鑼鼓 beat gones and drums

【敲竹槓】qiāozhúgàng (動) swindle; fleece

【敲定】qiāodìng (動) finalize; decide: ～這樁交易 clinch the deal

【敲門磚】qiāomén zhuān (名) stepping stone

【敲骨吸髓】qiāo gǔ xī suǐ 〈成〉exploit cruelly

【敲詐】qiāozhà (動) blackmail; extort

敵 dí I (名) enemy; foe II (動) ❶ resist; withstand: 所向無～ be invincible ❷ match; rival: 勢均力～ be evenly matched

【敵人】dírén (名) enemy

【敌手】díshǒu（名）rival; opponent; adversary

【敌情】díqíng（名）enemy's manoeuvre

【敌国】díguó（名）enemy state

【敌意】díyì（名）hostility; enmity

【敌忾】díkài（名）hatred for the foe

【敌对】díduì（形）hostile; antagonistic

敷 fū（动）❶ apply: 在伤口上～药 apply ointment to a wound ❷ extend; spread ❸ be sufficient

【敷衍】fūyǎn（动）do or say sth. hastily without care or interest; be perfunctory

【敷衍了事】fū yǎn liǎo shì〈成〉go through the motions of the business

【敷衍塞责】fū yǎn sè zé〈成〉get one's work done in a perfunctory manner

【敷设】fūshè（动）lay; build: ～铁路 build a railway

数 shǔ（动）❶ count: ～一～有多少人 count and see how many people there are ❷ be counted as: 在北京～这个幼儿园最好。This kindergarten is counted as the best in Beijing.

see also shù; shuò

【数一数二】shǔ yī shǔ èr〈成〉as one of the very best; rank high

【数得着】shǔ de zháo（动）〈口〉be counted among the best: 班里～的优秀生 be reckoned as one of the best students in the class; be among the top students in the class

【数落】shǔluo（数说 shǔshuō）（动）〈口〉❶ reproach; censure; criticize sb. by enumerating his mistakes ❷ enumerate verbally; give a verbal list of

【数数儿】shǔ shùr（动）〈口〉count; reckon

数 shù Ⅰ（名）❶ number; amount: 总～ total amount ❷（数）number: 实（虚）～ real (imaginary) number ❸〈语〉number; figure ❹ knowledge about how things stand: 对计划是否可行心中无～ not know for certain if the plan is feasible ❺ destiny; fate: 他大～已尽。His days are numbered. Ⅱ（形）several: ～十人 dozens of people

see also shǔ; shuò

【数目】shùmù（名）amount; number

【数字】shùzì（数目字 shùmùzì）（名）figure; numeral: ～手表 digital watch

【数珠】shùzhū（名）〈宗〉beads

【数控】shùkòng（名）〈机〉numerical control (NC)

【数词】shùcí（名）〈语〉numeral

【数量】shùliàng（名）amount; quantity; number: 既要保证～,也要保证质量。It is necessary to guarantee not only sufficient quantity but also good quality.

【数码】shùmǎ（名）❶ numeral ❷ number; amount

【数据】shùjù（名）data: ～处理 data processing

【数学】shùxué（名）mathematics

【数额】shù'é（名）amount; number

数 shuò（副）frequently; time and again

see also shǔ; shù

整 zhěng Ⅰ（形）❶ whole; complete; entire: 忙了一～天 be busy for the whole day ❷ neat; tidy; orderly Ⅱ（动）❶ put in order; rectify: ～隊 get the ranks in good order ❷ repair; mend: 桌子壞了～一～。Repair the rickety table. ❸ make sb. suffer: 隨便～人 punish sb. without good reason

【整天】zhěngtiān（副）whole day; all day long

【整改】zhěnggǎi（动）improve and rectify

【整形】zhěngxíng（名）〈醫〉plastic: ～手術 plastic operation

【整枝】zhěngzhī（动）〈農〉prune; train

【整治】zhěngzhì（动）❶ renovate; repair ❷ punish; give sb. a lesson

【整風】zhěngfēng（动）rectify the incorrect style of work

【整修】zhěngxiū（动）renovate

【整個】zhěnggè（形）whole; entire: ～學期 the whole term

【整流】zhěngliú（名）〈電〉rectification

【整容】zhěngróng Ⅰ（动）tidy up one's appearance Ⅱ（名）face-lifting; cosmetic surgery

【整理】zhěnglǐ（动）put in order; arrange: ～筆記 sort out one's notes / ～牀舖 fix one's bed

【整頓】zhěngdùn（动）rectify; reorganize; put in order

【整裝待發】zhěng zhuāng dài fā（成）be all packed up and ready to set out

【整齊】zhěngqí（形）orderly; tidy; well-arranged

【整編】zhěngbiān（动）reorganize (troops)

【整潔】zhěngjié（形）neat and tidy

【整數】zhěngshù（名）❶〈數〉integer; whole number ❷ round number

【整整】zhěngzhěng（形）whole;

full: ～三天 three whole days

【整黨】zhěngdǎng（动）consolidate the party organization

【整體】zhěngtǐ（名）whole; entirely

敛

敛 liǎn（动）❶ hold back; curb ❷ collect; levy

【敛迹】liǎnjī（动）go into hiding and make no public appearances; lie low

【敛容】liǎnróng（动）（of one's face）suddenly turn serious; put on a grave countenance

【敛財】liǎncái（动）acquire wealth by dishonest means; seek wealth greedily

【敛錢】liǎnqián（动）collect fees or donations

斃

斃 bì（动）❶ die; get killed: 倒～ drop dead ❷ kill; shoot dead; finish off

【斃命】bìmìng（动）〈貶〉die; die a violent death; get killed

文 部

文 wén Ⅰ（名）❶ character; script ❷ language: 法～ the French language ❸ writing; article; essay: 散～ prose Ⅱ（形）❶（of language）literary: 這種題材不應寫得太～了。A literary style would be out of place for such a topic. ❷ civilian, civil

【文人】wénrén（名）scholar; man of letters; writer

【文才】wéncái（名）literary talent

【文工團】wéngōngtuán（名）song and dance ensemble

【文化】wénhuà（名）❶ culture: 中國～ Chinese culture ❷ literacy; education: 他～水平高。He is well-educated.

【文火】wénhuǒ（名）slow fire: 用～炖鷄 stew the chicken over a slow fire

【文不對題】wén bù duì tí〈成〉be irrelevant; be beside the point

【文本】wénběn（名）text; version

【文字】wénzì（名）❶ character; writing: ～學 philology / ～史料 written historical record ❷ language; diction: ～通順 smooth and fluent in language

【文件】wénjiàn（名）document

【文件夾】wénjiànjiā（名）file

【文告】wéngào（名）proclamation; official document

【文身】wénshēn（名）tattoo

【文言】wényán（名）classical Chinese: ～文和白話文 classical and vernacular Chinese

【文官】wénguān（名）civil official

【文具】wénjù（名）stationery; writing equipment: ～店 stationer's

【文盲】wénmáng（名）❶ illiterate ❷ illiteracy

【文明】wénmíng Ⅰ（名）civilization: 西方～ Western civilization Ⅱ（形）civilized: ～禮貌 civilized behaviour / 他很講～。He has very good manners.

【文武】wénwǔ（形）civil and military: ～全才 be a politician and soldier; be an all-round man

【文物】wénwù（名）cultural relics: ～保護 protection of cultural relics

【文采】wéncǎi（名）literary gift

【文科】wénkē（名）liberal arts

【文思】wénsī（名）creative flow

【文風】wénfēng（名）style of writing

【文風不動】wén fēng bù dòng〈成〉make no move; not turn a hair

【文庫】wénkù（名）library; series (of books issued in a single format by a publisher)

【文書】wénshū（名）❶ document; papers ❷ copy clerk; office worker

【文娛】wényú（名）recreation; entertainment

【文弱】wénruò（形）frail; feeble

【文教】wénjiào（名）culture and education

【文彩】wéncǎi（名）rich colours

【文理】wénlǐ（名）(of writing) logic: coherence: ～不通 full of grammar mistakes and badly organized; unreadable

【文章】wénzhāng（名）❶ article; essay; writing ❷ hidden meaning; implication: 他的話裏大有～。Much is implied in his remark.

【文筆】wénbǐ（名）style of writing

【文過飾非】wén guò shì fēi〈成〉whitewash one's faults

【文集】wénjí（名）anthology; collected works

【文萊】Wénlái（名）Brunei

【文雅】wényǎ（形）elegant; cultivated; refined

【文電】wéndiàn（名）documents; telephone and telegraphic messages

【文豪】wénháo（名）great writer; literary titan

【文摘】wénzhāi（名）abstract; digest

【文稿】wéngǎo（名）manuscript; draft

【文廟】wénmiào（名）Confucian temple

【文選】wénxuǎn（名）selected readings; selected works

【文質彬彬】wén zhì bīn bīn〈成〉refined; well-mannered

【文憑】wénpíng（名）diploma; certificate

【文靜】wénjìng（形）gentle and quiet; demure

【文學】wénxué（名）literature: ～家 writer / ～批評 literary criticism

【文壇】wéntán（名）literary circles; world of letters

【文職】wénzhí（名）civil service: ～人員 civilian staff

【文辭】wéncí（名）❶ diction; language ❷ a piece of writing

【文藝】wényì（名）literature and art: ～理論 theory of literature and art

【文牘主義】wéndú zhǔyì（名）red tape

【文獻】wénxiàn（名）document; literature: 關於第二次世界大戰的～ literature on World War Two

【文體】wéntǐ（名）❶ style; literary form: ～學 stylistics ❷（short for 文娛體育 wényú tǐyù）recreation and sports

斑 bān I（名）spot; stain; speck: 雀～ freckles II（形）mottled; striped: ～竹 mottled bamboo

【斑白】bānbái（形）grey; hoary

【斑馬】bānmǎ（名）zebra: ～綫 zebra crossing

【斑紋】bānwén（名）stripe; streak; mottle

【斑疹傷寒】bānzhěn shānghán（名）〈醫〉typhus

【斑斑】bānbān（形）full of stains or spots: 血迹～ bloodstained

【斑鳩】bānjiū（名）mourning dove; turtle-dove

【斑駁】bānbó（形）mottled; motley

【斑點】bāndiǎn（名）spot; speckle

斐 fěi

【斐然】fěirán（形）❶ characteristic of literary talent: ～成章 written in a fine literary style ❷ marked: 成績～ achieve remarkable success

【斐濟】Fěijì（名）Fiji: ～人 Fijian

斗 部

斗 dǒu（名）❶ dou unit of dry measure for grain: 三～米 three dou of rice ❷ a dou measure ❸ funnel-shaped thing: 煙～ tobacco pipe

【斗室】dǒushì（名）very small room

【斗笠】dǒulì（名）bamboo hat

【斗篷】dǒupeng（名）cape; cloak

【斗膽】dǒudǎn（動）〈謙〉venture: ～問一句 make bold to ask a question

料 liào I（動）expect; predict: 没～到天會下雹子。We didn't expect it would hail. II（名）❶ material: 木～ lumber ❷ fodder

【料子】liàozi（名）dress material

【料事如神】liào shì rú shén〈成〉foresee with amazing accuracy

【料酒】liàojiǔ（名）cooking wine

【料峭】liàoqiào（形）chilly: 春寒～。There is a chill in the spring air.

【料理】liàolǐ（動）handle; manage

【料想】liàoxiǎng（动）guess; anticipate

【料器】liàoqì（名）glassware

斜 xié（形）slanting; inclined; oblique: ～屋頂 a slanting roof

【斜角】xiéjiǎo（名）〈数〉oblique angle

【斜坡】xiépō（名）slope

【斜面】xiémiàn（名）〈数〉inclined plane

【斜紋】xiéwén（名）〈纺〉twill (wave)

【斜視】xiéshì Ⅰ（名）〈医〉strabismus Ⅱ（动）look sideways; look askance

【斜路】xiélù（名）wrong path: 青年人不警惕就會走上～。Young people will go astray if they are not on the alert.

【斜綫】xiéxiàn（名）oblique line

【斜邊】xiébiān（名）〈数〉hypotenuse

【斜體字】xiétǐzì（名）italics

斟 zhēn（动）pour (wine or tea) into a cup: ～茶 pour sb. a cup of tea

【斟酌】zhēnzhuó（动）ponder over; deliberate: 措詞必須仔細～。We must consider the wording very carefully.

斡 wò

【斡旋】wòxuán Ⅰ（动）mediate: 從中～ mediate between the disputing parties Ⅱ（名）〈法〉good offices

斤 部

斤 jīn（名）jin（= 1/2 kilogram）

【斤斤計較】jīn jīn jì jiào〈成〉haggle over every penny; be particular even about trifling matters

【斤兩】jīnliǎng（名）weight: 缺斤短兩 give short weight

斥 chì（动）❶ denounce; scold: 怒～ angrily rebuke ❷ exclude: 互相排～的 mutually exclusive

【斥力】chìlì（名）〈物〉repulsion

【斥責】chìzé（动）rebuke; upbraid

斧 fǔ（名）axe

【斧正】fǔzhèng（动）〈敬〉make corrections

【斧頭】fǔtóu（斧子 fǔzi）（名）axe

斬 zhǎn（动）cut; chop: ～首 behead / 披荆～棘 hack a way forward through the brambles; hack one's way through tremendous difficulties

【斬草除根】zhǎn cǎo chú gēn〈成〉exterminate sth. root and branch; eradicate

【斬釘截鐵】zhǎn dīng jié tiě〈成〉categorically; resolutely

【斬假石】zhǎnjiǎshí（名）〈建〉artificial stone; imitation stone

斯 sī Ⅰ（代）this Ⅱ（名）（Sī）a surname

【斯文】sīwen（形）polite; gentle; urbane

【斯里蘭卡】Sīlǐlánkǎ（名）Sri Lanka: ～人 Sri Lankan

【斯威士蘭】Sīwēishìlán（名）Swaziland: ～人 Swazi

新 xīn Ⅰ（形）new; fresh: ～發現 new dicoveries Ⅱ（名）（Xīn）short for the Xinjiang Uygur Autonomous Region

【新人】xīnrén（名）❶ people of a new type ❷ new talent: 體壇～a new figure in sports circles ❸ newly-married couple; bride

【新手】xīnshǒu（名）new hand; tyro

【新生】xīnshēng Ⅰ（形）newly born; newborn Ⅱ（名）❶ new life; re-birth ❷ new student

【新加坡】Xīnjiāpō（名）Singapore: ～人 Singaporean

【新交】xīnjiāo（名）new friend

【新年】xīnnián（名）New Year

【新式】xīnshì（形）new-style; new; modern: ～裝備 up-to-date equipment

【新名詞】xīnmíngcí（名）new term

【新西蘭】Xīnxīlán（名）New Zea-land: ～人 New Zealander

【新秀】xīnxiù（名）new talent; ris-ing star

【新兵】xīnbīng（名）new recruit

【新近】xīnjìn（副）recently

【新房】xīnfáng（名）bridal chamber

【新居】xīnjū（名）new home

【新奇】xīnqí（形）new; strange: ～的事物 novelties

【新版】xīnbǎn（名）new edition

【新星】xīnxīng（名）❶〈天〉nova ❷ rising star; new talent: 劇壇～a new star in the theatrical firma-ment

【新風】xīnfēng（名）new custom; new practice

【新型】xīnxíng（名）new type; new model

【新郎】xīnláng（名）bridegroom

【新紀元】xīnjìyuán（名）new era

【新娘】xīnniáng（名）bride

【新婚】xīnhūn（形）newly-married: ～夫婦 newlyweds

【新陳代謝】xīn chén dài xiè（名）metabolism

【新聞】xīnwén（名）news: ～界 the press

【新興】xīnxīng（形）rising; new: ～港市 new port city

【新穎】xīnyǐng（形）new; novel: 款式～的服裝 dresses in novel styles

【新鮮】xīnxiān（形）❶ fresh: ～水果 fresh fruit/ ～事物 new things

【新疆】Xīnjiāng（名）Xinjiang; the Xinjiang Uygur Autonomous Region

断 duàn Ⅰ（動）❶ cut; break ❷ cease; discontinue: 笑聲～了。The laugh stopped short. ❸ judge; de-cide Ⅱ（副）[used only in negative sentences] absolutely; undoubtedly: ～無此事。There is nothing of the kind.

【断句】duànjù（動）punctuate

【断奶】duànnǎi（動）wean

【断言】duànyán（動）assert; allege

【断炊】duànchuī（動）run out of food

【断定】duàndìng（動）conclude

【断後】duànhòu（動）❶ cover a re-treat; fight a rearguard action ❷ have no offspring

【断送】duànsòng（動）forfeit; ruin: ～前途 ruin one's future

【断根】duàngēn（動）(of illness) be completely cured

【断氣】duànqì（動）breathe one's last; die

【断案】duàn'àn（動）pass judgment on a lawsuit

【断章取義】duàn zhāng qǔ yì〈成〉distort the meaning by quoting iso-lated sentences; quote out of context

【断然】duànrán Ⅰ（形）resolute Ⅱ

（副）absolutely; categorically: ～拒絕 categorically reject

【斷絕】duànjué（動）cut off; sever

【斷腸】duàncháng（形）heart-broken

【斷頭臺】duàntóutái（名）guillotine

【斷斷續續】duànduàn xùxù（副）off and on: 我在那裏～住了二十年。I lived there off and on for twenty years.

方 部

方 fāng I（名）❶ direction: 南～ the south ❷ side; party: 有關各～ all parties concerned ❸ method; way: 多～設法 try in various ways ❹ prescription ❺（Fāng）a surname II（形）❶ square ❷ upright III（副）just: ～纔 just now; a moment ago

【方丈】fāngzhàng（名）Buddhist abbot

【方子】fāngzi（名）prescription

【方式】fāngshì（名）way; fashion; mode: 生活～ way of life; life style

【方向】fāngxiàng（名）direction: ～問題 a matter of orientation

【方向舵】fāngxiàngduò（名）〈航空〉rudder

【方向盤】fāngxiàngpán（名）〈汽車〉steering wheel

【方位】fāngwèi（名）bearings; position; orientation

【方言】fāngyán（名）dialect

【方法】fāngfǎ（名）method; way: ～論 methodology

【方面】fāngmiàn（名）respect; aspect; side

【方便】fāngbiàn I（形）❶ convenient; proper: 爲～起見 for the sake of convenience II（動）❶ facilitate ❷〈婉〉with money to spare: 手頭不～ have no money to spare

【方案】fāng'àn（名）plan

【方針】fāngzhēn（名）policy; principle

【方格】fānggé（名）check

【方程】fāngchéng（名）〈數〉equation

【方圓】fāngyuán（名）❶ neighbourhood; vicinity ❷ circumference

【方興未艾】fāng xīng wèi ài〈成〉be gaining momentum

於 yú（介）❶［used similarly as 在］in; at; on: 建～1959 年 be built in 1959 ❷［used similarly as 向］to; for: 有求～我 need my assistance ❸［used similarly as 對, 對於］to; for: 有益～健康 beneficial to one's health ❹［used similarly as 到, 給］to: 獻身～科學事業 dedicate oneself to science ❺［used similarly as 自, 從］from: 出～惡意 out of spite ❻［used to indicate comparison］than: 大～ bigger than

【於今】yújīn（副）❶ up to now; since now ❷ now; at present

【於是】yúshì（連）thereupon; as a result; hence

施 shī I（動）❶ carry out; put into operation: ～暴 resort to violence ❷ give; bestow: ～恩 bestow favours ❸ apply; spread on: ～用除草劑 use herbicide II（名）（Shī）a surname

【施工】shīgōng（名）construction: ～質量 quality of construction

【施主】shīzhǔ（名）donor; benefac-

【施加】shījiā（动）exert（pressure; influence; etc.）on

【施行】shīxíng（动）❶ bring into effect; come into force: 自公佈之日起～ come into effect from the day of promulgation ❷ perform; carry out

【施放】shīfàng（动）discharge: ～催泪弹 use tear gas

【施肥】shīféi（动）apply fertilizer(to crops)

【施政】shīzhèng（动）administer state affairs: ～方针 guiding principles for administration

【施展】shīzhǎn（动）display; give full play to: ～種花招 play various tricks

【施捨】shīshě Ⅰ（动）give alms Ⅱ（名）alms

旁 páng Ⅰ（名）❶ side: 在小河～ at the riverside ❷ lateral radical of a Chinese character Ⅱ（代）other; else: 我要和～的大夫商量一下。 I'll have to consult other doctors.

【旁人】pángrén（名）other people

【旁白】pángbái（名）aside（in a play）

【旁門】pángmén（名）side door

【旁若無人】páng ruò wú rén〈成〉behave as if there were no one else on the scene; cocksure and arrogant

【旁敲側擊】páng qiāo cè jī〈成〉make indirect accusations; make veiled attacks; make oblique references

【旁徵博引】páng zhēng bó yǐn〈成〉cite a wealth of supporting evidence; be well-documented

【旁邊】pángbiān（名）side: 馬路～ by the side of the street

【旁證】pángzhèng（名）circumstantial evidence

【旁聽】pángtīng（动）audit（a class）: ～生 auditor

【旁觀】pángguān（动）stand by; look on

【旁觀者】pángguānzhě（名）spectator; onlooker

旅 lǚ Ⅰ（动）travel Ⅱ（名）〈军〉❶ brigade ❷ troops; army: 强兵勁～ seasoned soldiers and crack troops

【旅行】lǚxíng（动）travel; go on a trip

【旅行支票】lǚxíng zhīpiào（名）traveller's cheque

【旅行社】lǚxíngshè（名）travel agency

【旅行指南】lǚxíng zhǐnán（名）guidebook

【旅行袋】lǚxíngdài（名）travelling bag; carry-all

【旅行證件】lǚxíng zhèngjiàn（名）travel document

【旅社】lǚshè（名）hotel

【旅伴】lǚbàn（名）travelling companion

【旅店】lǚdiàn（名）inn; tavern

【旅居】lǚjū（动）live in a place other than one's hometown; reside abroad

【旅長】lǚzhǎng（名）brigade commander

【旅客】lǚkè（名）hotel guest; passenger

【旅途】lǚtú（名）journey: 踏上～ set off on a journey

【旅程】lǚchéng（名）journey

【旅費】lǚfèi（名）travel expenses; travel money

【旅遊】lǚyóu（名）tourism: ～設施

tourist facilities

【旅遊車】lǚyóuchē (名) tourist bus (coach); tourist train

【旅遊業】lǚyóuyè (名) tourist industry; tourism

【旅遊鞋】lǚyóuxié (名) sneakers

【旅館】lǚguǎn (名) hotel: 汽車 ~ motel/ ~服務員 hotel attendant

旋 xuán (動) ❶ revolve; spin; move around: 輪子飛 ~。The wheels are spinning at a dizzy speed. ❷ return; come back: 凱 ~ return in triumph
see also xuàn

【旋律】xuánlǜ (名)〈樂〉melody

【旋鈕】xuánniǔ (名)〈機〉knob

【旋渦】xuánwō (名) whirlpool; eddy

【旋繞】xuánrào (動) wind; curl up

【旋轉】xuánzhuàn (動) go round and round; revolve; rotate

旋 xuàn Ⅰ (形) whirling Ⅱ (副) (act) off-handedly: ~ 用 ~ 買 refuse to buy sth. until it is badly needed
see also xuán

旌 jīng (名) ancient type of banner

【旌旗】jīngqí (名) flags; banners

族 zú (名) ❶ race; nationality: 各 ~ 人民 the people of all nationalities / 異 ~ alien race ❷ clan: ~ 長 clan elder ❸ family: 水 ~ 館 aquarium

旗 qí (名) flag; banner

【旗手】qíshǒu (名) standard-bearer

【旗杆】qígān (名) flagpole

【旗袍】qípáo (名) tight-fitting Chinese frock

【旗開得勝】qí kāi dé shèng〈成〉

win success from the start; score an initial victory

【旗號】qíhào (名)〈貶〉banner; flag: 打着利他主義的 ~ under the cover of altruism

【旗鼓相當】qí gǔ xiāng dāng〈成〉be evenly matched

【旗語】qíyǔ (名) semaphore; flag signal

【旗幟】qízhì (名) banner; flag

【旗幟鮮明】qí zhì xiān míng〈成〉take a clear-cut stand

【旗艦】qíjiàn (名) flagship

旛 fān (名) streamer

无 部

既 jì Ⅰ (副) previously; already: 達 到 ~ 定目標 achieve the set goal Ⅱ (連) ❶ [often followed by 且、又、也, etc.] both... and; as well as; in addition to: ~ 聰明又用功 both intelligent and hard-working ❷ now that; since: 話 ~ 出口, 就不能收回 了。You can't take back the word you have said.

【既成事實】jìchéng shìshí (名) fait accompli

【既定】jìdìng (形) fixed; set: ~ 方 針 set policy

【既往不咎】jì wǎng bù jiù〈成〉not censure sb. for his past misdeeds; forgive all past faults

【既得利益】jìdé lìyì (名) vested interest

【既然】jìrán (連) now that; as; inasmuch as: ~ 天氣不太冷, 咱們 就去吧。Let's go then since it isn't very cold.

日 部

【日】 rì (名) ❶ sun: 旭～ the rising sun ❷ daytime: 夜以繼～ day and night ❸ 節～ holiday/ 周～ week days ❹ day by day: ～有起色 change for the better with each passing day ❺ time: 平～ usually; ordinarily

【日子】 rìzi (名) ❶ day; date: ～已經安排定了。The date has been fixed. ❷ time: 我好些～沒見到他了。I haven't seen him for quite some time. ❸ life; livelihood: 過好～ lead a happy life

【日久天長】 rì jiǔ tiān cháng 〈成〉 with the passage of time

【日本】 Rìběn (名) Japan: ～人 Japanese

【日用】 rìyòng (形) of everyday use

【日用品】 rìyòngpǐn (名) daily necessities; articles of everyday use

【日托】 rìtuō (名) day-care; day-care centre

【日光】 rìguāng (名) sunlight; sunbeam

【日光浴】 rìguāngyù (名) sunbath

【日光燈】 rìguāngdēng (名) fluorescent lamp

【日來】 rìlái (副) recently

【日夜】 rìyè (名) day and night

【日食】 rìshí (名)〈天〉solar eclipse

【日界綫】 rìjièxiàn (名) date line; International Date Line

【日班】 rìbān (名) day shift

【日記】 rìjì (名) diary

【日益】 rìyì (副) day by day; more and more: ～繁榮 become more and more prosperous

【日值】 rìzhí (名) payment for a workday; earning in a day

【日常】 rìcháng (形) daily; everyday: ～工作 daily routine; day-to-day work

【日理萬機】 rì lǐ wàn jī 〈成〉 have numerous affairs of state to deal with every day

【日報】 rìbào (名) daily (paper)

【日場】 rìchǎng (名) day show; matinée

【日程】 rìchéng (名) schedule; programme; itinerary: 列入議事～ place on the agenda

【日晷】 rìguǐ (名) sundial

【日期】 rìqī (名) date

【日照】 rìzhào (名) sunshine

【日新月異】 rì xīn yuè yì 〈成〉 make rapid progress; change fast

【日漸】 rìjiàn (副) day by day; gradually

【日語】 Rìyǔ (名) Japanese (language)

【日誌】 rìzhì (名) daily record; journal

【日暮途窮】 rì mù tú qióng 〈成〉 have reached the dead end

【日曆】 rìlì (名) calendar

【日積月累】 rì jī yuè lěi 〈成〉 accumulate day by day

【日薄西山】 rì bó xī shān 〈成〉 the sun is setting; approach one's end

【旦】 dàn (名) ❶ dawn: 通宵達～ throughout the night ❷ day: 元～ New Year's Day ❸ female character in Beijing opera

【早】 zǎo Ⅰ (名) ❶ morning: 他一大

~就開會去了。He went to the meeting early in the morning. ❷〈套〉good morning Ⅱ（副）❶ long ago: 那是很～的事了。It happened long ago. ❷ early; soon: ～點回來。Come back as soon as possible. Ⅲ（形）early: ～年 one's early years

【早上】zǎoshang（名）（early）morning

【早已】zǎoyǐ（副）long ago; for a long time: 火車～開走了。The train left long ago.

【早日】zǎorì（副）soon; at an early date: ～作出決定 make a decision at an early date

【早先】zǎoxiān（副）previously; in the past

【早安】zǎo'ān〈套〉good morning

【早車】zǎochē（名）morning train or coach

【早退】zǎotuì（動）leave earlier than is scheduled; leave early without permission

【早班】zǎobān（名）morning shift

【早晚】zǎowǎn Ⅰ（名）morning and evening Ⅱ（副）sooner or later: ～他會想通的。He'll come round sooner or later.

【早晨】zǎochén（名）（early）morning

【早婚】zǎohūn（名）early marriage

【早產】zǎochǎn（名）〈醫〉premature birth

【早期】zǎoqī（名）early stage; early period

【早場】zǎochǎng（名）performance of a play or film given in the morning; morning show

【早稻】zǎodào（名）early（season）rice

【早熟】zǎoshú（形）❶ precocious: ～的孩子 precocious child ❷ early-maturing: ～品種 early-ripe variety

【早餐】zǎocān（早飯 zǎofàn）（名）breakfast

【早操】zǎocāo（名）morning exercises

【早點】zǎodiǎn（名）（light）breakfast

旨 zhǐ（名）❶ purport; purpose: 開一個～在增進國際間相互了解的大會 convene a conference for the promotion of international understanding ❷ decree: 聖～ imperial decree

旬 xún（名）❶ period of ten days: 上（中、下）～ the first（second, third）ten days of a month ❷ every ten years（of age）年近七～ be getting on for seventy

旮 gā

【旮旯兒】gālár（名）〈方〉nook; corner

旭 xù

【旭日】xùrì（名）rising sun

旱 hàn（名）drought

【旱田】hàntián（名）dry farmland; dry land

【旱災】hànzāi（名）drought

【旱季】hànjì（名）dry season

【旱路】hànlù（名）overland route: 走～ travel by land

【旱稻】hàndào（名）upland rice; dry rice

【旱獺】hàntǎ（名）〈動〉marmot

昔 xī（名）past: 今～ today and yesterday; the present and the past

【昔日】xīrì（副）in the past; in the old days

旺 wàng（形）prosperous; thriving: 火燒得很～。The fire is burning briskly.

【旺季】wàngjì（名）peak; busy season: 旅遊～ tourist season／～價格 peak rate; peak fare

【旺盛】wàngshèng（形）vigorous; luxuriant: 精力～ be full of vigour

【旺銷】wàngxiāo（動）sell like hot cakes; sell very well

昌 chāng（形）prosperous

【昌盛】chāngshèng（形）flourishing; prosperous

昆 kūn（名）❶ elder brother: ～仲（elder and younger）brothers ❷ descendant: 後～ descendants

【昆曲】kūnqǔ（名）Kunqu opera

【昆蟲】kūnchóng（名）insect

明 míng I（形）❶ bright; luminous: 陽光～媚 bright sunshine ❷ clear; manifest: 表～自己的立場 state one's own position ❸ open; unequivocal: 有話～說 Speak out if you have anything on your mind. II（名）sight: 失～ lose one's sight; go blind III（動）know; understand: 不～真相 fail to see what the situation is really like

【明天】míngtiān（明日 míngrì）（名）tomorrow

【明火執仗】míng huǒ zhí zhàng〈成〉commit robbery in broad daylight

【明令】mínglìng（名）explicit order or instruction

【明白】míngbai I（形）clear; apparent; explicit: 做了～的回答 answer in explicit terms II（動）know; understand: 我不～他到底想說什麼。I don't know what on earth he is driving at.

【明白人】míngbairén（名）sensible person

【明目張膽】míng mù zhāng dǎn〈成〉flagrantly; brazenly

【明年】míngnián（名）next year

【明快】míngkuài（形）❶（of writing）lucid and fluent ❷（of personality）frank; straightforward

【明明】míngmíng（副）obviously; certainly: 他～是在撒謊。Obviously he is lying.

【明知】míngzhī（動）know well; be fully aware of

【明知故犯】míng zhī gù fàn（動）commit a crime knowingly; violate a rule not by mistake but by choice

【明知故問】míng zhī gù wèn（動）ask deliberately

【明爭暗鬥】míng zhēng àn dòu〈成〉fight both in the open and behind the scenes

【明亮】míngliàng I（形）bright: 燈光～的教室 a brightly lit classroom／～的星星 bright stars II（動）become clear: 這篇文章使他心裏一亮了。The article made him see the light.

【明星】míngxīng（名）star: 電影～ film（movie）star

【明信片】míngxìnpiàn（名）postcard

【明淨】míngjìng（形）bright and clean

【明朗】mínglǎng（形）❶ bright and clear: ～的星空 a bright starry sky ❷ obvious; clear: 態度～ take a clear-cut stand ❸ frank and cheerful; forthright: ～的風格 a forthright style

【明哲保身】 míng zhé bǎo shēn〈成〉 act wisely and keep out of harm's way; be worldly-wise and play safe

【明晃晃】 mínghuǎnghuàng (形) luminous; shining

【明眼人】 míngyǎnrén (名) person who is quick to judge and understand; person of good judgment

【明智】 míngzhì (形) wise; sensible

【明媚】 míngmèi (形) (of scenery) bright and lovely; radiant and charming: 河山~ a land of enchanting beauty

【明晰】 míngxī (形) clear; distinct

【明喻】 míngyù (名) simile

【明溝】 mínggōu (名) open drain; open sewerage

【明察秋毫】 míng chá qiū háo〈成〉 be observant enough not to let even a small detail escape one's notice; have penetrating insight

【明槍暗箭】 míng qiāng àn jiàn〈成〉 overt and covert attacks

【明暢】 míngchàng (形) (of writing) effortlessly clear and fluent; of an easy style

【明澈】 míngchè (形) clear; limpid: ~的溪流 clear stream

【明碼】 míngmǎ (名) ❶ plain code ❷ clearly marked price

【明確】 míngquè I (形) clear; definite: ~的態度 a clear-cut attitude II (動) make clear; define: ~我們面臨的任務 clearly define the tasks confronting us

【明燈】 míngdēng (名) bright lamp; beacon

【明辨是非】 míng biàn shì fēi〈成〉 clearly distinguish between right and wrong

【明瞭】 míngliǎo I (動) understand: ~這個詞的意思 be clear about the meaning of the word II (形) clear: 他的講話簡單~。 His speech is concise and easy to understand.

【明擺着】 míngbǎizhe (形) obvious: 你的計劃一行不通。 It is obvious that your plan won't work.

【明證】 míngzhèng (名) clear evidence

【明礬】 míngfán (名)〈化〉alum

【明顯】 míngxiǎn (形) clear; apparent; evident: ~的用心 obvious intention

易 yì I (形) easy; simple: 輕而~舉 easy to do II (動) ❶ change: 會議將~地進行。 The meeting will be resumed at a different venue. ❷ exchange: 以物~物 barter

【易如反掌】 yì rú fǎn zhǎng〈成〉 extremely easy; hands down: 我贏他~。 I can beat him hands down.

【易拉罐】 yìlāguàn (名) pop-top can: ~飲料 pop-top beverage

【易貨】 yìhuò (動) barter

【易碎】 yìsuì (形) breakable; fragile

【易腐】 yìfǔ (形) perishable: ~物 perishables

【易燃】 yìrán (形) combustible; inflammable: ~品 inflammables; combustibles

昂 áng I (動) hold (one's head) high II (形) high; soaring: 情緒激~ be very excited; boil with indignation

【昂首】 ángshǒu (動) straighten one's back or square one's shoulders

【昂首闊步】 áng shǒu kuò bù〈成〉 march ahead in big strides

【昂貴】ángguì（形）costly; expensive

【昂然】ángrán（副）proudly: ～挺立 stand erect and proud

【昂揚】ángyáng（形）high in morale; in high spirits: 鬥志～ show one's mettle

昏 hūn Ⅰ（名）dusk: 黄～ dusk Ⅱ（形）❶ dark; gloomy ❷ confused; muddled

【昏天黑地】hūn tiān hēi dì〈成〉❶ pitch-dark ❷ a world of darkness and chaos

【昏沉】hūnchén（形）❶ dim ❷ dazed

【昏花】hūnhuā（形）dim-sighted; blurred

【昏迷】hūnmí（名）stupor; coma; unconsciousness

【昏眩】hūnxuàn（形）dizzy; giddy

【昏庸】hūnyōng（形）fatuous

【昏黄】hūnhuáng（形）dusky; dim; faint

【昏厥】hūnjué（名）faint; swoon

【昏暗】hūn'àn（形）dark; dim

【昏聵】hūnkuì（形）decrepit and muddleheaded

春 chūn（名）❶ spring ❷ vitality: 青～ youth; youthfulness ❸ love; lust: ～心 longing for love ❹（Chūn）a surname

【春天】chūntiān（名）spring; springtime

【春光】chūnguāng（名）splendid scene of spring: ～明媚 bright and enchanting scene of springtime

【春色】chūnsè（名）spring scenery

【春季】chūnjì（名）spring; spring season

【春卷】chūnjuǎn（名）spring roll

【春風】chūnfēng（名）spring breeze: 滿面～（of facial expression）beam with joy

【春耕】chūngēng（名）spring ploughing

【春節】Chūnjié（名）Spring Festival（the first day or the first few days of the first month of the Lunar New Year）

【春意】chūnyì（名）breath of spring; savour of springtime

【春聯】chūnlián（名）Spring Festival couplet（posted on the door）

昧 mèi（動）❶ be ignorant of; be unclear about: ～於事理 fail to see the truth of the matter ❷ hide; conceal

【昧心】mèixīn（動）do sth. against one's conscience

【昧心話】mèixīnhuà（名）deliberate lie

是 shì Ⅰ（形）correct; right: 各行其～ each does what he thinks is right; each goes his own way Ⅱ（副）yes: ～, 馬上就辦。Yes, I'll see to it at once. Ⅲ（動）❶［used as a linking verb between the subject of a sentence and its noun complement］be: 她、護士。She is a nurse. ❷［used to indicate existence］窗外～小溪。Outside the window is a brook. ❸［said with stress to emphasize affirmation］那個劇就～好。That play is very good indeed. ❹［used at the beginning of a sentence for emphasis］～他救了這個孩子。It was he who rescued the child. ❺［followed by 的 to introduce an explanation or categorization] be: 我的自行車～綠色的。 My bike is a green one. ❻ [used in an alternative or disjunctive question] be...or: 這本書～圖書館借的，還～私人的? Is the book borrowed from the library, or is it a private copy? ❼ [used before a noun to emphasize each and every one of the kind]: ～好電影他都去看。He never misses a single good film. ❽ [used to indicate concession]:這個工作難～難，卻很有意思。Though demanding, the job is very interesting. ❾ [used before a noun to indicate suitability]: 放的不～地方 be put in a wrong place

【是否】shìfǒu (連) whether or not: 他～能勝任，很成問題。It is questionable if he is equal to his task.

【是的】shìde (副) yes; that's right: ～，我們大家都很想念他。Yes, we all miss him very much.

【是非】shìfēi (名) ❶ right and wrong: ～觀念 sense of right and wrong ❷ dispute; gossip: ～之地 a place where one often gets into trouble for one reason or another

【是非曲直】shì fēi qū zhí (成) rights and wrongs

【是味兒】shìwèir (動) 〈口〉 ❶ be palatable ❷ be at ease: 覺得不～ sense that there's something wrong

昭 zhāo (形) clear; evident

【昭雪】zhāoxuě (動) rehabilitate

【昭然若揭】zhāo rán ruò jiē (成) obvious to all

【昭著】zhāozhù (形) clear; evident: 臭名～ have fallen into disrepute; be notorious

【昭彰】zhāozhāng (形) conspicuous; evident

映 yìng (動) ❶ reflect; mirror: 湖裏～出柳樹的倒影。The willows are reflected in the lake. ❷ project a film: 放～電影 show a film

【映山紅】yìngshānhóng (名) 〈植〉 azalea

【映射】yìngshè (動) shine upon

【映象】yìngxiàng (名) image

【映襯】yìngchèn (動) set off: 白雪～紅梅，分外綺麗。The white snow sets off the red plum blossoms beautifully.

星 xīng (名) ❶ star: 滿天～斗。The sky is dotted with stars. ❷ bit; particle: 一～半點 a wee bit

【星斗】xīngdǒu (名) stars

【星火】xīnghuǒ (名) spark

【星辰】xīngchén (名) stars

【星星】xīngxing (名) ❶ 〈口〉 star ❷ tiny speck

【星座】xīngzuò (名) constellation

【星球】xīngqiú (名) heavenly body; star: ～大戰計劃 star wars; SDI

【星雲】xīngyún (名) 〈天〉 nebula

【星期】xīngqī (名) week

【星期一】xīngqīyī (名) Monday

【星期二】xīngqī'èr (名) Tuesday

【星期三】xīngqīsān (名) Wednesday

【星期四】xīngqīsì (名) Thursday

【星期五】xīngqīwǔ (名) Friday

【星期六】xīngqīliù (名) Saturday

【星期日】xīngqīrì (名) Sunday

【星號】xīnghào (名) asterisk

【星際】xīngjì (形) interplanetary; interstellar

【星羅棋佈】xīng luó qí bù (成) scattered here and there either like stars in the sky or like men on a chessboard

昨 zuó (名) yesterday

【昨天】 zuótiān (名) yesterday

【昨晚】 zuówǎn (名) yesterday evening; last night

晉 jìn Ⅰ (動) ❶ enter; move forward ❷ advance in rank; promote Ⅱ (名) ❶ (Jìn) another name for Shanxi (Province) ❷ (Jìn) a surname

【晉升】 jìnshēng (動) be promoted to a higher position

【晉見】 jìnjiàn (動) pay a call on one's superior

【晉級】 jìnjí (動) be promoted

時 shí Ⅰ (名) ❶ time; times: 一~間 for a time ❷ set time: 定~炸彈 time bomb ❸ season: 應~瓜果 melons and fruits of the season ❹ hour: 晚十一~ at 10 p.m. ❺ (語) tense ❻ (Shí) a surname Ⅱ (形) present: ~價 current price Ⅲ (副) from time to time; at times: ~有發生 happen every now and then / 質量~好~壞。The quality fluctuates.

【時代】 shídài (名) ❶ times; era ❷ period in one's life: 幼年~ childhood

【時而】 shí'ér (副) ❶ sometimes; now and then ❷ [when repeated in the same sentence] sometimes ... sometimes...: ~互相吹捧、~反唇相譏 lavish mutual praise at times but hold up each other to ridicule on other occasions

【時光】 shíguāng (名) time: ~過得真快。Time flies.

【時至今日】 shí zhì jīnrì (副) at this eleventh hour; even to this day

【時局】 shíjú (名) present political situation

【時刻】 shíkè Ⅰ (名) time; moment; juncture: ~表 timetable; schedule Ⅱ (副) constantly; at all times

【時事】 shíshì (名) current affairs

【時宜】 shíyí (名) need of the times: 不合~ unsuitable for the present occasion; not in agreement with the times

【時差】 shíchā (名) ❶ time difference; jet lag ❷ 〈天〉equation of time

【時限】 shíxiàn (名) time limit; deadline

【時效】 shíxiào (名) ❶ effectiveness for a given period of time ❷ 〈法〉 prescription

【時速】 shísù (名) speed per hour: ~/英里 miles per hour; MPH

【時務】 shíwù (名) present circumstances; trends of the times

【時候】 shíhòu (名) ❶ time: 你等了多少~啦? How long have you been waiting? ❷ (point of) time: 你出去的~有人給你打電話。Someone phoned you up when you were out.

【時時】 shíshí (副) often

【時針】 shízhēn (名) ❶ hands of a clock or watch ❷ hour hand

【時常】 shícháng (副) often

【時區】 shíqū (名) time zone

【時期】 shíqī (名) age; era

【時運】 shíyùn (名) fortune; chance

【時間】 shíjiān (名) ❶ time (as opposed to space): ~與空間的關係 the relation between time and space ❷ point of time: 出發~ time of departure ❸ period of time: 我去的~不會很長。I shan't be long.

【時間性】shíjiānxìng（名）time factor：～在信息時代尤其重要。The time factor is especially important in the era of information.

【時節】shíjié（名）❶ season ❷ time

【時勢】shíshì（名）time and circumstances

【時新】shíxīn（形）usu. of dress styles）modern; fashionable; in vogue

【時裝】shízhuāng（名）fashionable clothes：～表演 fashion show

【時髦】shímáo（形）fashionable; à la mode

【時態】shítài（名）〈語〉tense

【時弊】shíbì（名）ills of the time; current social maladies

【時機】shíjī（名）opportunity; opportune time：～成熟了。The time is ripe.

【時興】shíxīng（時行 shíxíng）（形）in fashion; faddish

【時鮮】shíxiān（名）fruits, vegetables, fish, fowl, etc. which are in season

【時鐘】shízhōng（名）clock

晃 huǎng（動）❶ shine brightly：太陽一得我睜不開眼。The glare of the sun dazzled me. ❷ flash past
see also huàng

晃 huàng（動）swing; shake
see also huǎng

【晃悠】huàngyou（動）sway back and forth; hobble along

【晃蕩】huàngdàng（動）rock; sway; swing

晁 Cháo（名）a surname

晌 shǎng（名）part of the day：後

半 ～ afternoon; the latter part of the day／～午 at noon

晝 zhòu（名）daytime; day：～夜 day and night

晨 chén（名）morning：凌～ before dawn

【晨星】chéngxīng（名）❶ stars at dawn：寥若～ as few as the stars at dawn ❷ morning star

【晨曦】chénxī（名）aurora; light at dawn

晤 wù（動）meet; interview

【晤面】wùmiàn（動）meet

【晤談】wùtán（動）hold a talk; talk

晦 huì Ⅰ（名）❶ last day of a lunar month ❷ night Ⅱ（形）dark; obscure; dim

【晦氣】huìqì（形）unlucky

【晦澀】huìsè（形）obscure

晚 wǎn Ⅰ（名）evening; night：昨～ yesterday evening／今～ this evening Ⅱ（形）❶ late; later：～稻 late rice ❷ junior; younger

【晚上】wǎnshang Ⅰ（名）evening; night：～好! Good evening! Ⅱ（副）in the evening; at night

【晚安】wǎn'ān〈套〉good night

【晚年】wǎnnián（名）old age; one's later years

【晚班】wǎnbān（名）night shift

【晚婚】wǎnhūn Ⅰ（動）marry late Ⅱ（名）late marriage

【晚報】wǎnbào（名）evening paper

【晚間】wǎnjiān（名）night; evening：～新聞 evening news

【晚期】wǎnqī（名）final phase

【晚會】wǎnhuì（名）evening party：音樂～ musical evening

【晚節】wǎnjié（名）integrity in later life: 保持～ maintain one's integrity in old age

【晚輩】wǎnbèi（名）younger generation; one's juniors

【晚餐】wǎncān（晚飯 wǎnfàn）（名）supper; dinner

【晚點】wǎndiǎn（動）(of a train, liner, etc.) be behind the schedule; be late

【晚霞】wǎnxiá（名）evening glow; sunset glow

普 pǔ（形）general; universal: ～天同慶 universal jubilation

【普及】pǔjí（動）popularize; universalize

【普及本】pǔjíběn（名）popular edition

【普查】pǔchá（名）general survey: 人口～ census

【普通】pǔtōng（形）ordinary; common: ～人 ordinary people

【普通話】pǔtōnghuà（名）putonghua; common speech of the Chinese language; standard Chinese (pronunciation); mandarin

【普遍】pǔbiàn（形）universal; common: ～感興趣的事 matter of common interest

【普選】pǔxuǎn（名）general election: ～權 universal suffrage

【普魯卡因】pǔlǔkǎyīn（名）（藥）procaine

景 jǐng Ⅰ（名）❶ scenery; sight: 遠～ distant view; perspective ❷ state of affairs; circumstances; vista: 遠～規劃 long-range planning ❸ setting (of a play or film) ❹ scene (of a play) ❺（Jǐng）a surname Ⅱ（動）respect; esteem

【景色】jǐngsè（名）scenery; sight: 西湖～ the sights of West Lake

【景仰】jǐngyǎng（景慕 jǐngmù）（動）esteem; admire

【景況】jǐngkuàng（名）circumstance; condition

【景物】jǐngwù（名）scenery; landscape

【景氣】jǐngqi（名）boom; prosperity: 不～ depression

【景泰藍】jǐngtàilán（名）cloisonné

【景深】jǐngshēn（名）（攝）depth of field

【景象】jǐngxiàng（名）scene; spectacle: 一片欣欣向榮的～ a picture of peace and prosperity; a thriving scene

【景頗族】Jǐngpōzú（名）the Jingpo (Chingpo) nationality

【景緻】jǐngzhi（名）(beautiful) scenery; (fine) view

晾 liàng（動）❶ air-dry; air ❷ dry in the sun; sun

晴 qíng（形）(of weather) clear; fine

【晴天霹靂】qíng tiān pī lì〈成〉a bolt from the blue

【晴雨表】qíngyǔbiǎo（名）barometer

【晴空萬里】qíng kōng wàn lǐ〈成〉vast clear sky

【晴朗】qínglǎng（形）bright and clear; sunny

暑 shǔ（名）heat; summer: ～天 on hot summer days / 避～勝地 summer resort

【暑假】shǔjià（名）summer vacation

【暑期】shǔqī（名）summer vacation period: ～學生夏令營 student summer camp

晰 xī（形）clear; lucid: 明～ distinct

晶 jīng Ⅰ（形）sparkling; glittering Ⅱ（名）crystal

【晶莹】jīngyíng（形）transparent and sparkling

【晶体】jīngtǐ（名）crystal

【晶体管】jīngtǐguǎn（名）transistor

智 zhì（名）wisdom; intelligence; wit: 急中生～ become resourceful in a desperate situation

【智力】zhìlì（名）intelligence; intellect: 高超的～ superior intelligence

【智利】Zhìlì（名）Chile: ～人 Chilean

【智取】zhìqǔ（动）take by strategy

【智育】zhìyù（名）intellectual education

【智能】zhìnéng（名）intellect; intelligence: 人工～ artificial intelligence

【智商】zhìshāng（名）intelligence quotient (IQ)

【智慧】zhìhuì（名）wisdom

【智谋】zhìmóu（名）resourcefulness; wit: 钦佩他的～勇略 admire sb. for his courage and resourcefulness

【智囊团】zhìnángtuán（名）brain trust

暄 xuān（形）soft; fluffy: 很～的蛋糕 a fluffy cake

暗 àn（形）❶ dark; dull: 阴～ dark; gloomy ❷ hidden; secret: 明来～往 have overt and covert contacts with sb. ❸ unclear; hazy: 若明若～ (of situation) murky

【暗中】ànzhōng（副）❶ in the dark ❷ in private

【暗示】ànshì Ⅰ（动）hint (at); drop a hint Ⅱ（名）hint

【暗地】àndì（副）secretly, in secrecy

【暗含】ànhán（动）imply

【暗室】ànshì（名）〈摄〉darkroom

【暗送秋波】àn sòng qiū bō〈成〉cast sidelong glances; make indirect overtures

【暗害】ànhài（动）assassinate; stab sb. in the back

【暗记】ànjì（名）secret mark

【暗笑】ànxiào（动）laugh in one's sleeve

【暗杀】ànshā Ⅰ（动）murder; assassinate Ⅱ（名）assassination; attempt on sb.'s life

【暗娼】ànchāng（名）unlicensed prostitute

【暗淡】àndàn（形）gloomy; dismal

【暗盒】ànhé（名）〈摄〉magazine; cassette

【暗探】àntàn（名）special agent; private detective

【暗堡】ànbǎo（名）bunker

【暗道】àndào（名）secret tunnel (path)

【暗无天日】àn wú tiān rì〈成〉dark and cruel rule; hell on earth

【暗暗】àn'àn（副）secretly; inwardly; to oneself

【暗沟】àngōu（暗渠 ànqú）（名）underdrain

【暗伤】ànshāng（名）❶ internal injury ❷ internal damage (to an object)

【暗号】ànhào（名）secret signal (sign); countersign; cipher

【暗算】ànsuàn Ⅰ（动）scheme against Ⅱ（名）machination

【暗语】ànyǔ（名）secret words: 用

~講話 talk in code

【暗潮】àncháo（名）undercurrent

【暗箭】ànjiàn（名）arrow shot from a hidden position: ~難防。It is hard to guard against a sniper's attack.

【暗箱】ànxiāng（名）〈攝〉dark chamber of a camera

【暗礁】ànjiāo（名）submerged reef (rock)

【暗鎖】ànsuǒ（名）mortise lock

【暗藏】àncáng（動）conceal; hide

暈 yūn Ⅰ（形）dizzy; giddy Ⅱ（動）faint; swoon: ~倒 be in a fainting fit; fall into a faint
see also yùn

【暈厥】yūnjué（名）〈醫〉syncope; faint

【暈頭轉向】yūn tóu zhuàn xiàng〈成〉disoriented; become confused and lose one's bearings

暈 yùn Ⅰ（動）feel giddy; be dizzy Ⅱ（名）〈氣〉halo: 日~ solar halo
see also yūn

【暈車】yùnchē（形）carsick; trainsick; bussick

【暈船】yùnchuán（形）seasick

【暈機】yùnjī（形）airsick

暉 huī（名）sunshine; sunlight

暇 xiá（名）free time: 有(無)~ be free (busy)

暖 nuǎn Ⅰ（形）warm: ~風 warm breeze Ⅱ（動）warm up: 烤火取~ warm oneself by the fire

【暖色】nuǎnsè（名）warm colour

【暖房】nuǎnfáng（名）〈方〉greenhouse

【暖和】nuǎnhuo（形）warm

【暖流】nuǎnliú（名）〈氣〉warm current

【暖氣】nuǎnqì（名）central heating: ~片（heating）radiator

【暖烘烘】nuǎnhōnghōng（形）nice and warm

【暖壺】nuǎnhú（暖瓶 nuǎnpíng）（名）thermos flask; thermos bottle; thermos

【暖簾】nuǎnlián（名）quilted door curtain

暨 jì（連）and: 總統先生~夫人 His Excellency Mr. President and his wife

暢 chàng（形）❶ unimpeded; fluent ❷ uninhibited; gratified: 心情舒~ be relaxed and happy

【暢快】chàngkuài（形）carefree and cheerful

【暢所欲言】chàng suǒ yù yán〈成〉speak out freely

【暢通】chàngtōng（形）unimpeded; unobstructed: ~無阻 be open to traffic; run smoothly

【暢游】chàngyóu（動）enjoy a good swim

【暢遊】chàngyóu（動）go on a sightseeing trip

【暢飲】chàngyǐn（動）drink one's fill

【暢談】chàngtán（動）talk animatedly; talk breezily

【暢銷】chàngxiāo Ⅰ（動）sell well: ~海内外 have a ready market at home and abroad Ⅱ（形）best selling: ~書 best seller / ~貨 fast-selling commodity

暫 zàn Ⅰ（形）of short duration: 短~的停留 short stay; stopover Ⅱ（副）temporarily; for the time being

【暫且】zànqiě（副）for the time being; for the present: ～把問題擱置起來 shelve the matter for the present

【暫行】zànxíng（形）provisional; temporary: ～辦法 provisional measure

【暫定】zàndìng Ⅰ（動）be tentatively fixed: 你的工資～每月一百元。Your monthly salary is tentatively fixed at a hundred *yuan* Ⅱ（形）tentative; provisional: ～計劃 tentative plan

【暫時】zànshí（形）transient; temporary: ～的安排 temporary arrangement

【暫停】zàntíng Ⅰ（動）suspend: ～宣判 suspend judgment Ⅱ（名）〈體〉time-out

【暫緩】zànhuǎn（動）postpone; defer: 比賽～舉行。The game is postponed.

暮 mù（名）❶ dusk; sunset ❷ late: ～秋 late autumn

【暮色】mùsè（名）dusk; twilight

【暮年】mùnián（名）old age; evening of one's life

【暮氣】mùqì（名）sluggishness; languor

【暮靄】mù'ǎi（名）evening haze

暴 bào（形）❶ sudden and violent: ～風雨 tempest ❷ brutal; fierce; cruel: 態度粗～ be rude ❸ violent; impetuous: 脾氣～ have a violent temper

【暴力】bàolì（名）violence: 使用～ resort to violence

【暴光】bàoguāng Ⅰ（動）expose (camera film, etc.) to light Ⅱ（名）exposure: ～表 exposure meter

【暴行】bàoxíng（名）atrocity; brutality; outrage

【暴君】bàojūn（名）tyrant; despot

【暴利】bàolì（名）excessive profit

【暴雨】bàoyǔ（名）torrential rain; rainstorm

【暴政】bàozhèng（名）tyranny; tyrannical rule

【暴虐】bàonüè（形）tyrannical; despotic; cruel

【暴風】bàofēng（名）squall; hurricane

【暴風雨】bàofēngyǔ（名）tempest; rainstorm: ～般的掌聲 stormy applause; tempestuous applause

【暴風雪】bàofēngxuě（名）blizzard; snowstorm

【暴病】bàobìng（名）sudden severe illness

【暴徒】bàotú（名）hooligan; thug; riffraff

【暴烈】bàoliè（形）violent; vehement: 性情～ fiery temper

【暴動】bàodòng（名）insurrection; insurgence; riot

【暴跌】bàodiē（動）slump; fall drastically (in market price)

【暴飲暴食】bào yǐn bào shí〈口〉eat and drink immoderately

【暴發】bàofā（動）❶ break out; erupt; flare up ❷ gain access to wealth and power all of a sudden

【暴發戶】bàofāhù（名）parvenu; upstart

【暴亂】bàoluàn（名）riot

【暴跳如雷】bào tiào rú léi〈成〉stamp about in a towering rage

【暴漲】bàozhǎng（動）(of prices, rivers, etc.) rise sharply; soar; skyrocket

【暴躁】bàozào (形) irascible; hot-tempered; irritable

【暴露】bàolù (動) expose; lay bare; betray: ~文學 literature of exposure

【暴露無遺】bào lù wú yí 〈成〉 be completely exposed

暱 nì (形) close; intimate: 親~ affectionate; intimate

曆 lì (名) calendar: 陰~ lunar calendar

【曆法】lìfǎ (名) calendar

【曆書】lìshū (名) almanac

曇 tán

【曇花】tánhuā (名) broad-leaved epiphyllum: ~一現 a transient success

曉 xiǎo I (名) dawn; daybreak: 破~ dawn II (動) ❶ know; understand: 通~德語 be well versed in German ❷ tell; let sb. know: ~以利害 warn sb. of the consequences

【曉得】xiǎode (動) know: 我~了。I see.

曙 shǔ (名) daybreak; dawn

【曙光】shǔguāng (名) (light at) dawn

曖 ài (形) (of daylight) dim

【曖昧】àimèi (形) ❶ [of attitude or intention] ambiguous; equivocal ❷ 〈貶〉[of behaviour or relationship] dubious; murky

曠 kuàng I (形) ❶ open and spacious ❷ relaxed; free from worries: ~達 open-minded II (名) (Kuàng) a surname

【曠工】kuànggōng (動) stay away from work without permission

【曠日持久】kuàng rì chí jiǔ 〈成〉 prolonged; long-drawn-out

【曠野】kuàngyě (名) open country

【曠課】kuàngkè (動) stay away from school without permission; play truant

曝 pù (動) expose to the sun

【曝光】pùguāng (攝) exposure

【曝光表】pùguāngbiǎo (名) exposure meter

【曝曬】pùshài (動) be tanned by the sun

曦 xī (名) 〈書〉 sunlight

曬 shài (動) ❶ (of the sun) shine upon ❷ dry in the sun; sun: 皮膚~得很黑 get tanned

【曬煙】shàiyān (名) sun-cured tabacco

【曬臺】shàitái (名) flat roof (for drying clothes, etc.)

【曬圖】shàitú (名) make a blueprint

日 部

曰 yuē (動) 〈書〉 ❶ say ❷ call; name

曲 qū I (形) ❶ bent; winding: 面 curved surface ❷ wrong: 歪~ twist; distort II (名) ❶ bend (of a river, etc.) ❷ (Qū) a surname see also qǔ

【曲尺】qūchǐ (名) carpenter's square

【曲折】qūzhé I (形) tortuous; winding II (名) complications: 個中~殊難細述. It is hard to describe in detail all the complications of the story.

【曲別針】qūbiézhēn（名）paper clip

【曲直】qūzhí（名）right and wrong: 是非～ the rights and wrongs of a matter

【曲柄】qūbǐng（名）（機）crank

【曲突徙薪】qū tū xǐ xīn〈成〉provide against all eventualities

【曲軸】qūzhóu（名）（機）crankshaft; bent axle

【曲棍球】qūgùnqiú（名）❶ field hockey ❷ hockey ball

【曲解】qūjiě（動）distort, misinterpret

【曲意逢迎】qū yì féng yíng〈成〉curry favour with sb. by all means

曲 qū（名）❶ music (of a song): 爲歌詞譜～ set a song to music ❷ song; tune: 流行歌～ popular songs
see also qǔ

【曲子】qǔzi（名）song; tune

【曲高和寡】qǔ gāo hè guǎ〈成〉too highbrow to be appreciated by the multitude

【曲調】qǔdiào（名）tune; melody

【曲藝】qǔyì（名）quyi, ballad singing and other folk art forms

曳 yè（動）drag; haul

【曳光彈】yèguāngdàn（名）tracer bullet

更 gēng I（動）change; replace; alter II（名）night watch
see also gèng

【更正】gēngzhèng（動）have some corrections to make; correct

【更衣】gēngyī（動）change one's clothes: ～室 locker room

【更迭】gēngdié（動）alternate

【更始】gēngshǐ（動）make a new start; start afresh

【更動】gēngdòng（動）change

【更番】gēngfān（副）by turns; repeatedly: ～轟炸 bomb repeatedly

【更替】gēngtì（動）replace; substitute

【更新】gēngxīn（動）renew; renovate; update: ～知識 update one's knowledge

更 gèng（副）❶ more; still more ❷ further: ～有甚者 what is even worse
see also gēng

【更加】gèngjiā（副）more; even more: 幹得～起勁 work even harder

書 shū I（名）❶ book: ～本知識 book knowledge ❷ letter; correspondence: 來～ your letter ❸ document; papers: 畢業證～ diploma; graduation certificate ❹ style of calligraphy: 草～ running (cursive) hand II（動）write down; record: 值得大～特～ deserve to be recorded in letters of gold; be worthy of special mention

【書包】shūbāo（名）satchel; schoolbag

【書刊】shūkān（名）books and magazines

【書目】shūmù（名）booklist; catalogue

【書皮】shūpí（名）book cover; book jacket

【書生】shūshēng（名）scholar; student; intellectual: 他～氣太重。He is hopelessly bookish.

【书市】shūshì（名）book fair

【书名】shūmíng（名）(book) title

【书夹】shūjiā（名）book end

【书局】shūjú（名）publishing house

【书店】shūdiàn（名）bookshop; bookstore

【书法】shūfǎ（名）calligraphy: ～家 calligrapher

【书房】（书斋 shūzhāi）（名）study

【书架】shūjià（名）bookshelf; book rack

【书面】shūmiàn（形）in writing: ～声明 written statement

【书亭】shūtíng（名）bookkiosk

【书信】shūxìn（名）letter; correspondence

【书展】shūzhǎn（名）book exhibition

【书桌】shūzhuō（名）(writing) desk

【书记】shūjì（名）❶ (party) secretary: ～处 secretariat ❷ clerk

【书库】shūkù（名）stacks

【书评】shūpíng（名）book review

【书画】shūhuà（名）Chinese painting and calligraphy

【书呆子】shūdāizi（名）bookworm; pedant

【书写】shūxiě（动）write: ～工具 writing instrument

【书橱】shūchú（书柜 shūguì）（名）bookcase

【书签】shūqiān（名）bookmark

【书籍】shūjí（名）books

【书摊】shūtān（名）bookstall; bookstand

【曹】cáo（名）❶ people of the same kind or group: 吾～ we ❷ (Cáo) a surname

【曼】màn（形）❶ graceful ❷ prolonged

【曼延】mànyán（动）stretch; extend: 小路～曲折。A footpath zigzags into the distance.

【曼声】mànshēng（名）measured tones: ～低语 speak in a low, deliberate voice

【曾】céng（副）once; ever: 未～当过教员 have never been a teacher before

see also Zēng

【曾经】céngjīng（副）over; once: 我们～见过面。We have met each other before.

【曾】Zēng（名）a surname

see also céng

【曾祖父】zēngzǔfù（名）(paternal) great-grandfather

【曾祖母】zēngzǔmǔ（名）(paternal) great-grandmother

【曾孙】zēngsūn（名）great-grandson

【曾孙女】zēngsūnnǚ（名）great-granddaughter

【替】tì I（动）replace; substitute; supercede: 冒名顶～ take sb.'s place under an assumed name II（介）for; on behalf of: ～他难过 be sorry for him

【替代】tìdài（动）replace; substitute

【替死鬼】tìsǐguǐ（名）〈口〉scapegoat

【替身】tìshēn（名）(of a person) ❶ substitute; replacement: 即使你想不干，也得找个～。Even if you want to throw up your job, you'll have to find somebody to replace you. ❷ scapegoat

【替换】tìhuan（动）replace; substitute; relieve: 你去～他一下。

You'll go and relieve him, won't you?

【替罪羊】tìzuìyáng（名）scapegoat

最

zuì（副）most: ～要緊 the most important

【最大】zuìdà（形）maximum: ～功率 maximum power

【最少】zuìshǎo（副）at least

【最多】zuìduō（副）at most

【最好】zuìhǎo I（形）best; first-rate: 他～的朋友 his best friend II（副）preferably; had better: 你～先幹完你的工作。You'd better finish your work first.

【最近】zuìjìn I（形）nearest II（副）❶ lately; recently: 我～沒見到他。I haven't seen him lately. ❷ soon; in the near future: 他～就走。He is leaving soon.

【最低】zuìdī（形）lowest; minimum: ～年齡 minimum age

【最初】zuìchū I（形）first; initial; original: ～幾天 the first few days II（副）at first; initially

【最佳】zuìjiā（形）best: ～選擇 best option

【最後】zuìhòu I（形）final; last; ultimate: ～通牒 ultimatum II（副）at last; finally; eventually

【最高】zuìgāo（形）highest; supreme: ～級會議 summit

【最終】zuìzhōng（形）final; ultimate: ～目的地 final destination

【最惠國】zuìhuìguó（名）most-favoured-nation: ～待遇 most-favoured-nation treatment

會

huì I（名）❶ meeting; conference ❷ chief city; capital: 省～ provincial capital ❸ association; society; union: 學生～ students' union／教～ church ❹ chance: 機～ opportunity ❺〈口〉a short period of time: 等一～ wait a moment II（動）❶ assemble: 在大廳～齊 assemble in the hall ❷ be able to; be sure to: 她～講德語。She speaks German.／他～來。He is sure to come. ❸ understand: 心領神～ readily take a hint; show tacit understanding ❹ meet; see: ～見某人 meet sb.

see also kuài

【會心】huìxīn（會意 huìyì）（形）understanding; knowing: ～的微笑 a knowing smile

【會合】huìhé（動）meet; join

【會同】huìtóng（動）act in cooperation with

【會客】huìkè（動）receive a visitor: ～室 reception room

【會面】huìmiàn（動）meet; see

【會師】huìshī（動）join forces

【會員】huìyuán（名）member: ～國 member state

【會商】huìshāng（動）hold a consultation

【會堂】huìtáng（名）assembly hall; hall

【會晤】huìwù（動）meet

【會診】huìzhěn（名）consultation (of doctors)

【會場】huìchǎng（名）meeting place; assembly hall

【會費】huìfèi（名）membership dues

【會話】huìhuà（名）dialogue; conversation

【會演】huìyǎn（名）joint performance

【會談】huìtán（名）talks: 首腦～ summit meeting

【會餐】huìcān I（動）dine together II

（名）dinner party

【會議】huìyì（名）meeting; conference

會 kuài
see also huì

【會計】kuàijì（名）❶ accounting: 成本 ~ cost accounting ❷ bookkeeper; accountant: ~師 accountant

月 部

月 yuè（名）❶ moon ❷ month: 五 ~ May

【月子】yuèzi（名）❶ month of confinement after childbirth ❷ time of expected childbirth

【月中】yuèzhōng（名）middle of a month

【月刊】yuèkān（名）monthly magazine; monthly

【月光】yuèguāng（名）moonlight

【月色】yuèsè（名）moonlight

【月份】yuèfèn（名）month

【月份牌】yuèfènpái（名）calendar

【月初】yuèchū（名）beginning of a month

【月底】yuèdǐ（名）end of a month

【月季】yuèjì（名）〈植〉Chinese rose

【月亮】yuèliang（名）moon

【月息】yuèxī（名）monthly interest

【月桂樹】yuèguìshù（名）laurel; bay tree

【月票】yuèpiào（名）monthly ticket; commutation ticket

【月球】yuèqiú（名）moon

【月報】yuèbào（名）❶ monthly magazine; monthly ❷ monthly report

【月經】yuèjīng（名）menses; menstruation; period

【月暈】yuèyùn（名）lunar halo

【月餅】yuèbǐng（名）moon cake

【月蝕】yuèshí（名）〈天〉lunar eclipse

【月臺】yuètái（名）railway platform: ~票 platform ticket

【月曆】yuèlì（名）monthly calendar

【月薪】yuèxīn（名）monthly salary

有 yǒu（動）❶ have; possess: 他 ~一幅新畫。He has a new car. ❷ there is: 房前~一口井。There is a well in front of the house. ❸ happen; occur: 經濟~了新的發展。The economy has developed in new dimensions. ❹ [used to indicate an estimate or comparison]: 這片果樹 ~上千棵吧。There must be over one thousand fruit trees here. ❺ [used before people, place, or time to mean "certain"]: ~一次 once/ ~人贊成，~人反對。Some people are for it, and some against it.

【有力】yǒulì（形）forceful; powerful; weighty

【有口皆碑】yǒu kǒu jiē bēi〈成〉be praised by all; enjoy great popularity; win universal acclaim

【有口難分】yǒu kǒu nán fēn〈成〉find it difficult to vindicate oneself

【有方】yǒufāng（動）have the right method or way: 教導~ provide a correct course of instruction

【有心】yǒuxīn Ⅰ（動）have a mind to; intend to Ⅱ（副）deliberately; intentionally

【有用】yǒuyòng（形）useful

【有生力量】yǒushēng lìliàng（名）effective forces

【有生以来】yǒushēng yǐlái（副）since one was born

【有史以来】yǒushǐ yǐlái（副）since the beginning of recorded history; since the dawn of human civilization

【有目共睹】yǒu mù gòng dǔ（成）known to everyone; be obvious to all

【有色】yǒusè（形）coloured: 對～人種的歧視 colour bar / ～金屬 non-ferrous metal

【有名】yǒumíng（形）well-known; famous; renowned

【有名無實】yǒu míng wú shí（成）exist only in name; impressive but worthless

【有利】yǒulì（形）beneficial; favourable

【有形】yǒuxíng（形）tangible; visible

【有言在先】yǒu yán zài xiān（成）make explicit remarks on a matter before-hand; forewarn

【有助於】yǒuzhùyú（動）contribute to; help: ～問題的解決 be conducive to the solution of the problem

【有的放矢】yǒu dì fàng shǐ（成）do sth. with a definite objective in view; aim one's arrow at the target

【有的是】yǒudeshì（動）have plenty of: ～機會 have a lot of opportunities

【有始有終】yǒu shǐ yǒu zhōng（成）pursue an undertaking properly from start to finish

【有始無終】yǒu shǐ wú zhōng（成）begin a task but fail to pursue it to the end

【有神論】yǒushénlùn（名）theism

【有待】yǒudài（動）remain（to be done）: ～進一步考慮 await further consideration; require further deliberation

【有限】yǒuxiàn（形）limited; finite: ～公司 limited company

【有軌電車】yǒuguǐ diànchē（名）tramcar; streetcar

【有恃無恐】yǒu shì wú kǒng（成）do evil without fear on account of one's powerful backing

【有勇無謀】yǒu yǒng wú móu（成）have physical courage but lack resourcefulness

【有害】yǒuhài（形）harmful; detrimental

【有效】yǒuxiào（形）effective; valid: ～期 period of validity

【有時】yǒushí（副）sometimes; at times

【有益】yǒuyì（形）beneficial; useful

【有條不紊】yǒu tiáo bù wěn（成）kept in good order; methodically: 文章雖長,但～。It's a lengthy but well-organized essay.

【有救】yǒujiù（動）can be cured or remedied; be remediable

【有理】yǒulǐ（形）reasonable; justified

【有爲】yǒuwéi（形）promising; capable: 年青～ young and promising

【有朝一日】yǒu zhāo yī rì（成）there will be a day; some day

【有過之無不及】yǒu guò zhī wú bù jí（貶）go even farther than people of that ilk

【有備無患】yǒu bèi wú huàn（成）preparedness prevents disaster

【有意】yǒuyì Ⅰ（動）be inclined to; intend to Ⅱ（副）deliberately; on purpose

【有意思】yǒu yìsi（形）interesting;

amusing

【有意識】yǒu yìshi（副）consciously

【有綫】yǒuxiàn（形）wired: ～電視 cable TV

【有數】yǒushù Ⅰ（動）know how things stand: 他講話心裏～。He knows what he is talking about. Ⅱ（形）a limited number; only a few: 捲進去的只是～的幾個人。Only a few people have got involved.

【有餘】yǒuyú（動）have more than enough

【有趣】yǒuqù（形）interesting; a-musing

【有錢】yǒuqián（形）rich; wealthy

【有賴】yǒulài（動）depend on; rely on: 一切～於她自己的努力。Everything depends on her own effort.

【有機】yǒujī（形）organic: ～體 organism

【有機可乘】yǒu jī kě chéng〈成〉have loopholes that can be exploited; find an opportunity which can be taken advantage of

【有點】yǒudiǎn Ⅰ（形）some; a little: 還～事要幹 still have something else to attend to Ⅱ（副）somewhat; a bit: ～餓了 feel a bit hungry

【有聲有色】yǒu shēng yǒu sè〈成〉vivid and graphic; lifelike and dramatic

【有關】yǒuguān Ⅰ（動）have sth. to do with; relate to: 與許多人～ concern many people Ⅱ（形）relevant; concerned: 準備好～的文件 get all the relevant papers ready

【有識之士】yǒu shí zhī shì（名）person of insight

服 fú Ⅰ（名）clothes: 便～ plain clothes Ⅱ（動）❶ serve: ～兵役 conscripted for military service ❷ obey; believe ❸ be accustomed to: 不～水土 not be used to the climate; not be acclimatized
see also fù

【服役】fúyì（動）be conscripted for military service

【服侍】fúshì（動）serve; attend to

【服毒】fúdú（動）take poison

【服氣】fúqì（動）be convinced; regard sb.'s statement or criticism as fair; be persuaded that one is in the wrong

【服務】fúwù Ⅰ（動）serve Ⅱ（名）service: ～行業 service industry

【服務員】fúwùyuán（名）❶ waiter; waitress ❷ attendant

【服務臺】fúwùtái（名）information desk; reception desk

【服從】fúcóng（動）obey; submit to

【服喪】fúsāng（動）be in mourning

【服飾】fúshì（名）dress

【服罪】fúzuì（動）plead guilty

【服裝】fúzhuāng（名）clothing; costume

【服裝店】fúzhuāngdiàn（名）❶ tailor's ❷ garment shop

【服輸】fúshū（動）concede defeat

服 fú（量）：一～湯藥 a dose of herbal medicine
see also fú

朋 péng（名）friend: 良～ good friend

【朋友】péngyou（名）friend

【朋比爲奸】péng bǐ wéi jiān〈成〉act in collusion with

【朋黨】péngdǎng（名）cabal; junto

朗 lǎng（形）❶ bright; clear: 明～

的天 clear skies ❷ (of a voice) clear and loud

【朗朗】 lǎnglǎng（象）sound of pupils reading aloud

【朗誦】 lǎngsòng Ⅰ（動）recite Ⅱ（名）recitation

【朗讀】 lǎngdú（動）read aloud

朔 shuò（名）❶ new moon ❷ first day of a lunar month ❸ north

【朔月】 shuòyuè（名）new moon

望 wàng Ⅰ（動）❶ look into the distance: 麥田一～無際。The wheat field stretches as far as the eye can see. ❷ pay a visit to: 看～傷病員 visit the sick and wounded ❸ hope; look forward to: ～早日答復。I look forward to an early reply. Ⅱ（名）❶ prestige; repute ❷ (Wàng) a surname

【望文生義】 wàng wén shēng yì〈成〉take the words too literally and make a wrong interpretation

【望而生畏】 wàng ér shēng wèi〈成〉the sight inspires awe in everybody; stand in awe of; forbidding

【望洋興嘆】 wàng yáng xīng tàn〈成〉be overawed by the sheer magnitude of a task

【望風】 wàngfēng（動）keep watch; be on the lookout

【望梅止渴】 wàng méi zhǐ kě〈成〉console oneself with imagined happiness

【望眼欲穿】 wàng yǎn yù chuān〈成〉look eagerly forward to; expect eagerly

【望遠鏡】 wàngyuǎnjìng（名）telescope: 雙筒～ binoculars

【望塵莫及】 wàng chén mò jí〈成〉lag far behind; cannot hope to catch up

期 qī Ⅰ（名）❶ a period of time; stage ❷ scheduled time: 如～完成 fulfil on schedule / 任～ term of office Ⅱ（動）❶ make an appointment: 不～而遇 come across ❷ hope; expect Ⅲ（量）issue: 過～的刊物 back numbers of periodicals

【期刊】 qīkān（名）periodical

【期限】 qīxiàn（名）time limit; deadline

【期待】 qīdài（動）hope; expect

【期望】 qīwàng（名）hope; expectation: 不辜負人民的～ not disappoint the hopes of the people

【期間】 qījiān（名）time; period; course

朝 cháo Ⅰ（名）❶ court; government ❷ dynasty Ⅱ（動）pay respects to (a sovereign) Ⅲ（介）towards: ～着河邊走去 walk towards the riverside
see also zhāo

【朝代】 cháodài（名）dynasty

【朝見】 cháojiàn（動）have an audience with (the sovereign)

【朝廷】 cháotíng（名）imperial government; imperial court

【朝拜】 cháobài（動）pay homage to (a sovereign); go on a pilgrimage to

【朝聖】 cháoshèng（名）pilgrimage

【朝鮮】 Cháoxiān（名）Korea: ～人 Korean / ～語 Korean (language)

朝 zhāo（名）❶ morning: ～霞 rosy clouds in the morning ❷ day: 今～ today; the present
see also cháo

【朝夕】 zhāoxī（副）❶ morning and evening; all the time: ～相處 be

together all the time ❷ a short
time: ～之間 within a day

【朝三暮四】zhāo sān mù sì 〈成〉
shift and veer; capricious; inconsistent

【朝不保夕】zhāo bù bǎo xī 〈成〉 in
a precarious situation; in a critical
state

【朝令夕改】zhāo lìng xī gǎi 〈成〉
constantly change policies; be inconsistent in policy

【朝思暮想】zhāo sī mù xiǎng 〈成〉
long for sb. or sth. day and night;
yearn day and night

【朝氣】zhāoqì（名）vigour; ardour;
vitality: ～蓬勃 full of youthful vitality

【朝陽】zhāoyáng（名）morning sun

【朝暉】zhāohuī（名）morning sunlight

朦 méng

【朦朧】ménglóng（形）dim; hazy;
darkish: 月色～ dim moonlight

木 部

木 mù Ⅰ（名）❶ tree: 花～ flowers
and trees (in a park or garden) ❷
wood; timber: 朽～ rotten wood ❸
(Mù) a surname Ⅱ（形）❶ wooden:
～桌椅 wooden desks and chairs ❷
numb; insensible: 他的手指頭全凍
～了。All his fingers are numb with
cold. / 這孩子很～。The child is
quite dull.

【木乃伊】mùnǎiyī（名）mummy

【木工】mùgōng（名）❶ woodwork
❷ joiner; carpenter

【木已成舟】mù yǐ chéng zhōu 〈成〉
what's done is done; the die is cast

【木瓜】mùguā（名）❶ Chinese flowering quince ❷〈方〉papaya

【木耳】mù'ěr（名）arboreal fungus;
(edible) fungus

【木匠】mùjiàng（名）❶ joiner; carpenter

【木材】mùcái（名）timber; lumber

【木刻】mùkè（名）woodcut; wood
engraving

【木板】mùbǎn（名）plank; board

【木版畫】mùbǎnhuà（名）woodcut

【木炭】mùtàn（名）charcoal

【木星】mùxīng（名）〈天〉Jupiter

【木柴】mùchái（名）firewood

【木屐】mùjī（名）wooden sandal;
clog

【木馬】mùmǎ（名）❶ hobbyhorse;
rocking horse ❷〈體〉vaulting
horse; pommel horse

【木料】mùliào（名）timber; lumber;
wood

【木船】mùchuán（名）wooden boat

【木偶】mù'ǒu（名）wooden figure;
puppet: ～戲 puppet show

【木魚】mùyú（名）wooden clapper

【木筏】mùfá（木排 mùpái）（名）raft

【木棉】mùmián（名）silk cotton;
kapok

【木琴】mùqín（名）xylophone

【木然】mùrán（形）stupefied

【木雕】mùdiāo（名）wood engraving

【木器】mùqì（名）wooden furniture

【木頭】mùtou（名）wood: ～人
blockhead

【木蘭花】mùlánhuā（名）magnolia

未 wèi（副）not yet; not: 尚～決
定 not decided yet / 他～出席會
議。He didn't attend the meeting.

【未了】 wèiliǎo（形）unfinished: ～的工作 unfinished work

【未卜先知】 wèi bǔ xiān zhī〈成〉able to foresee accurately

【未必】 wèibì（副）not necessarily: 天～下雨。Maybe it's not going to rain.

【未可厚非】 wèi kě hòu fēi〈成〉should not lay too much blame on sb. for his fault

【未老先衰】 wèi lǎo xiān shuāi〈成〉age prematurely

【未成年】 wèichéngnián（形）not yet of age; under age

【未決】 wèijué（形）unsettled; undecided; open

【未免】 wèimiǎn（副）rather; a bit too: ～有點傲氣 a bit arrogant

【未定】 wèidìng（形）undecided; not fixed; not final: 他的度假地點～。He has not yet decided where he will be going for his holidays.

【未來】 wèilái（名）future: ～學 futurology

【未雨綢繆】 wèi yǔ chóu móu〈成〉provide for a rainy day; take due precautions

【未知數】 wèizhīshù（名）❶（數）the unknown ❷ unknown quantity; sth. unknown: 他去不去還是個～。It is still uncertain whether he will go or not.

【未便】 wèibiàn（動）find it hard to: 目前～表態 find it inappropriate to take a stand at present

【未能】 wèinéng（動）fail to; be unable to: ～及時趕到 fail to arrive in time

【未婚】 wèihūn（形）unmarried; single

【未婚夫】 wèihūnfū（名）fiancé

【未婚妻】 wèihūnqī（名）fiancée

【未遂】 wèisuì（形）abortive; unsuccessful: ～政變 abortive coup d'état

【未曾】 wèicéng（副）never; not yet: ～想到 … It has never occurred to one that…

【未詳】 wèixiáng（形）unknown; unclear: 地址～。The address is not clear.

【未嘗】 wèicháng（副）〈書〉❶ not yet: 他一天～進食。He did not eat anything for the whole day. ❷［used before a negative word to form a double negative］: ～沒有困難 not without difficulty

末 mò（名）❶ tip; end: 春～ at the end of spring ❷ nonessentials: 叙述故事的本～ tell the story from beginning to end ❸ powder; dust

【末了】 mòliǎo（副）at last; finally: 他～還是同意了。He agreed in the end.

【末日】 mòrì（名）end; doom

【末代】 mòdài（名）last reign of a dynasty: ～皇帝 the last emperor

【末年】 mònián（名）last years of a dynasty or reign

【末尾】 mòwěi（名）end: 文章的～ the end of an essay; the concluding paragraph of an essay

【末班車】 mòbānchē（名）last bus; last train: 乘～進城 take the last bus to the city

【末梢】 mòshāo（名）tip; end

【末期】 mòqī（名）last stage; end: 三十年代～ in the late thirties

【末路】 mòlù（名）dead end; impasse

【末葉】 mòyè（名）last years (of a century or dynasty)

本 běn Ⅰ（名）❶ stem or root (of a

plant): 木～ 植物 woody plant ❷ foundation; fundamentals; origin: 國以民爲～。 The people are the foundation of a country. ❸ capital; principal: 生產成～ cost of pruduction ❹ book: 記事～ notebook ❺ edition: 袖珍～ pocket edition Ⅱ (量) book; copy: 三～小册子 three brochures Ⅲ (形) ❶ this; current; present: ～世紀 this century ❷ one's own; native: ～市 this city ❸ essential; fundamental: ～部 headquarters ❹ original Ⅳ (副) ❶ [used in the statement of a past fact that has ceased to be true] originally; formally: 事情～不如此。(Originally) it was not like this. ❷ [used before such an auxiliary verb as 當 or 可 in a subjunctive statement to indicate what should be or should have been]: ～當 should (be); should have (been) Ⅴ(介) in accordance with; based on

【本人】 běnrén (名) ❶ I; me ❷ oneself: 今天他～來。He will come in person today.

【本子】 běnzi (名) writing pad; notebook; exercise book

【本土】 běntǔ (名) ❶ native place ❷ metropolitan territory

【本分】 běnfèn Ⅰ(名) one's duty Ⅱ (形) contented with one's lot: 守～ law-abiding; know one's place

【本文】 běnwén (名) ❶ this article; this text ❷ the text (as distinguished from notes, headings, illustrations, etc.); the main body of a book; the original words (used by the author as distinguished from notes, commentary, translation, paraphrase, etc.)

【本末】 běnmò (名) the complete story; the beginning and end of; the ins and outs

【本末倒置】 běn mò dào zhì 〈成〉 put the side issues ahead of the central theme

【本地】 běndì Ⅰ(名) this place; here Ⅱ(形) local; native: ～特產 local speciality

【本行】 běnháng (名) ❶ one's line; one's profession ❷ this bank; this firm

【本色】 běnsè (名) ❶ natural colour: ～布 grey (cloth) ❷ true qualities: 英雄的～ inherent traits of a hero

【本利】 běnlì (名) ❶ investment and profit ❷ principal and interest

【本身】 běnshēn (代) itself: 這～並不重要。This in itself is a matter of little consequence.

【本位】 běnwèi (名) ❶ standard: 金～ gold standard (of a currency) ❷ one's own department

【本位主義】 běnwèi zhǔyì (名) departmentalism; departmental egoism

【本屆】 běnjiè (形) current: ～會議 current session

【本金】 běnjīn (名) ❶ (of deposits and loans) principal ❷ capital

【本事】 běnshì (名) original story; source material

【本事】 běnshi (名) ability; skill

【本性】 běnxìng (名) nature; innate quality

【本來】 běnlái Ⅰ(形) original Ⅱ(副) ❶ originally; formerly: ～挺受歡迎 used to be very popular ❷ of course; certainly; it goes without saying: 公共財物～應當愛護。Public property should of course be protected.

【本來面目】běn lái miàn mù〈成〉true colours (features)

【本科】běnkē(名)undergraduate course; regular course (of a college or university)

【本草】běncǎo(名)general term for Chinese herbal medicine:《～綱目》Compendium of Materia Medica

【本家】běnjiā(名)member of the same clan; distant relative bearing the same family name

【本能】běnnéng(名)instinct

【本息】běnxī(名)principal and interest

【本國】běnguó Ⅰ(名)one's own country Ⅱ(形)of one's own country: ～語 mother tongue

【本着】běnzhe(介)in accordance with; in line with

【本鄉本土】běn xiāng běn tǔ〈成〉homeland; one's native place

【本義】běnyì(名)primary or original meaning

【本意】běnyì(名)original idea; true intention: 歪曲作者的～ misrepresent the author's intention

【本領】běnlǐng(名)ability; skill

【本質】běnzhì(名)essence; (fundamental) nature; substance

【本錢】běnqián(名)capital investment; asset: 身體是～。Good health is an asset.

【本壘】běnlěi(名)〈棒、壘球〉home base

【本職】běnzhí(名)one's own job (work, post): 做好～工作 perform one's duties conscientiously

札 zhá(名)❶ thin pieces of wood used for writing on in ancient China ❷〈書〉letter

【札記】zhájì(名)reading notes

朽 xiǔ(形)rotten; decayed

【朽木】xiǔmù(名)❶ rotten wood ❷ worthless person

朴 Piáo(名)a surname

朱 zhū Ⅰ(形)vermillion; bright red Ⅱ(名)(Zhū)a surname

【朱紅】zhūhóng(形)bright red; vermillion

【朱漆】zhūqī(名)red paint; red lacquer

朵 duǒ(量):一～花 a flower / 一～雲 a cloud

束 shù Ⅰ(動)❶ tie; bundle up; fasten: ～緊腰帶 tighten one's belt ❷ restrain; keep within bounds Ⅱ(名)(Shù)a surname Ⅲ(量)bundle; bunch; beam: 小女孩把一～鮮花獻給貴賓。The little girl presented a bouquet to the guest of honour. / 一～光 a light beam; a ray of light

【束之高閣】shù zhī gāo gé〈成〉tie sth. up and place it on a high shelf; lay sth. aside and forget about it; shelve

【束手】shùshǒu(動)have one's hands tied up; be in a helpless situation

【束手待斃】shù shǒu dài bì〈成〉await certain death in face of imminent danger; be a sitting duck

【束手無策】shù shǒu wú cè〈成〉feel helpless; be unable to find a way out; at the end of one's rope

【束縛】shùfù Ⅰ(動)tie up; fetter Ⅱ(名)restriction; bondage; fetters

杆 gān (名) pole

杜 dù I (动) stop; prevent II (名) (Dù) a surname
【杜絕】dùjué (动) eradicate
【杜撰】dùzhuàn (动) make up; fabricate

村 cūn (名) village
【村莊】cūnzhuāng (名) village
【村鎮】cūnzhèn (名) villages and townships

材 cái (名) ❶ timber: 木已成～. The tree has grown into useful timber. ❷ material: 照相器～ photographic supplies ❸ talent; aptitude: 因～施教 teach a person according to his aptitude ❹ capable person: 棟樑之～ person of great calibre
【材料】cáiliào (名) ❶ material: 金屬～ metal ❷ material; data: 第一手～ first-hand information ❸ stuff: 他是辦企業的～. He is cut out for an entrepreneur. ❹ ingredients (of food, medicine, etc.)

杖 zhàng (名) cane; stick: 手～ walking stick

杞 Qǐ (名) a surname
【杞人憂天】Qǐ rén yōu tiān〈成〉like the man of Qi who feared that the sky might fall; be burdened with unnecessary worries

李 lǐ (名) ❶ plum tree ❷ plum ❸ (Lǐ) a surname
【李子】lǐzi (名) ❶ plum ❷ plum tree

杈 chā (杈子 chāzi) (名) wooden fork; hayfork

杈 chà (名) (of a tree, etc.) branch: 樹～兒 branch of a tree
see also chā

杏 xìng (名) apricot
【杏仁】xìngrén (名) almond
【杏脯】xìngfǔ (名) preserved apricot

杉 shā (名)〈植〉China fir
see also shān
【杉木】shāmù (名) China fir
【杉篙】shāgāo (名)〈建〉fir pole

杉 shān (名)〈植〉Chinese fir
see also shā

東 dōng (名) ❶ east ❷ host; owner: 作～ stand sb. a treat; play the host / 房～ landlord
【東山再起】Dōng Shān zài qǐ〈成〉return to power; regain office
【東半球】dōngbànqiú (名) the eastern hemisphere
【東西】dōngxī (名) east and west: ～關係 the East-West relations
【東西】dōngxi (名) ❶ thing: 有～吃 have sth. to eat ❷ [used to express affection or disgust for a person or animal] creature: 可愛的小～ a lovely little thing / 不要臉的～. What a skunk.
【東拉西扯】dōng lā xī chě (动) ramble haphazardly
【東拼西湊】dōng pīn xī còu (动) scrape together; do patch work (in writing)
【東帝汶】Dōngdìwén (名) East Timor
【東家】dōngjia (名) master; boss
【東張西望】dōng zhāng xī wàng (动) look about curiously; look here and

there

【東道】dōngdào〈名〉host: ～國 host country

【東鄉族】dōngxiāngzú〈名〉the Dongxiang nationality

【東經】dōngjīng〈地〉east longitude

杭 Háng〈名〉a surname

枕 zhěn〈名〉pillow

【枕巾】zhěnjīn〈名〉towel used to cover a pillow

【枕木】zhěnmù〈鐵道〉sleeper; tie

【枕套】zhěntào〈名〉pillow-case

【枕頭】zhěntou〈名〉pillow

枉 wǎng I〈形〉crooked; erroneous: 矯～過正 overcorrect a wrong II〈動〉❶ twist; distort: 貪贓～法 take bribes and break the law ❷ wrong; do sb. an injustice: 冤～好人 do wrong to a good, honest person; unjustly blame an innocent person III〈副〉in vain

【枉費】wǎngfèi〈動〉waste: ～功夫 a waste of time and energy

【枉然】wǎngrán〈形〉fruitless; futile; in vain: 一切努力都是～。All effort is in vain.

枝 zhī I〈名〉branch; twig: 橄欖～ olive branch II〈量〉: 一～蠟燭 a candle / 一～圓珠筆 a ball pen

【枝節】zhījié〈名〉❶ minor matter; side issue ❷ unexpected difficulty: 橫生～ deliberately cause complications

林 lín〈名〉❶ forest; woods ❷ forestry ❸〈Lín〉a surname

【林子】línzi〈名〉woods; forest

【林立】línlì〈動〉stand tall and erect in large numbers: 這一帶工廠～。There are numerous factory buildings in this area.

【林海】línhǎi〈名〉vast stretch of wooded country

【林帶】líndài〈名〉forest belt

【林場】línchǎng〈名〉tree farm

【林業】línyè〈名〉forestry

【林蔭道】línyīndào〈名〉boulevard

杯 bēi I〈名〉❶ cup: 酒～ wine glass; wine cup ❷ glass; mug: 量～ measuring glass ❸ cup; trophy: 捧回獎～ win the (prize) cup II〈量〉cup; glass; mug: 一～啤酒 a mug of beer

【杯子】bēizi〈名〉cup; glass; tumbler

【杯水車薪】bēi shuǐ chē xīn〈成〉trying to put out a cartload of burning firewood with a cup of water; ridiculously futile measure

【杯中物】bēizhōngwù〈名〉wine; liquor

【杯盤狼藉】bēi pán láng jí〈成〉(after a feast) with wine cups and plates still scattered on the table

杏 yǎo

【杳無音信】yǎo wú yīn xìn〈成〉have never been heard of ever since

枘 ruì〈名〉tenon

枇 pí

【枇杷】pípa〈名〉loquat

松 sōng〈名〉❶ pine: ～樹 pine (tree) / ～子 pine nut ❷〈Sōng〉a surname

【松花蛋】sōnghuādàn（松花 sōnghuā）〈名〉preserved egg

【松香】sōngxiāng（名）rosin; colophony

【松鼠】sōngshǔ（名）squirrel

枚 méi Ⅰ（量）［used for small objects］: 一～校徽 a school badge / 三一奖章 three medals Ⅱ（名）（Méi）a surname

【枚举】méijǔ（动）enumerate: 不胜～ far too many to enumerate

析 xī（动）❶ separate; divide ❷ analyse: 辨～ distinguish and analyse

【析义】xīyì（动）analyse the meaning

【析疑】xīyí（动）resolve a doubt

板 bǎn Ⅰ（名）❶ board; plank; plate: 黑～ blackboard ❷ shutters (of a shop) ❸ clappers (a percussion instrument) ❹ musical beat; metre: 一～一眼 following a set pattern; scrupulous and methodical Ⅱ（形）stiff; dull; stony: 辨事死～ mechanical in handling matters Ⅲ（动）look serious: ～着面孔 pull a long face; put on a stern expression

【板子】bǎnzi（名）❶ board; plank ❷ flogging board (used as an instrument of torture or corporal punishment, made of bamboo or wood)

【板牙】bǎnyá（名）❶ front tooth; incisor ❷ molar ❸〈机〉screw die; threading die

【板胡】bǎnhú（名）banhu, a two-stringed Chinese musical instrument

【板栗】bǎnlì（名）chestnut

【板眼】bǎnyǎn（名）❶ metre or measure in traditional Chinese music ❷ orderliness: 他说话做事很有～。He is methodical in whatever he says or does.

【板结】bǎnjié（动）(of soil) harden; become hard and impervious

【板报】bǎnbào（名）〈口〉blackboard newspaper

【板凳】bǎndèng（名）bench or stool (usu. made of wood)

【板壁】bǎnbì（名）wooden partition

【板鸭】bǎnyā（名）dried salted duck

【板擦儿】bǎncār（名）blackboard eraser

果 guǒ Ⅰ（名）❶ fruit: 结～ bear fruit ❷ result; consequence: 前因后～ cause and effect Ⅱ（形）resolute; determined Ⅲ（副）really: 事情～然如此。This is exactly the case.

【果汁】guǒzhī（名）fruit juice

【果品】guǒpǐn（名）fruit

【果真】guǒzhēn（副）really; truly

【果脯】guǒfǔ（名）preserved fruit; sweetmeat

【果敢】guǒgǎn（形）determined and daring

【果然】guǒrán（副）really; as expected; indeed

【果园】guǒyuán（名）orchard

【果实】guǒshí（名）fruit

【果树】guǒshù（名）fruit tree

【果断】guǒduàn（形）resolute; decisive

【果酱】guǒjiàng（名）jam

柒 qī（数）［the elaborate form of the numeral 七, used on cheques, banknotes, etc.］seven

染 rǎn（动）❶ dye: 把头发～黑 have one's hair dyed black ❷ catch (a disease); acquire (a bad habit, etc.): ～疾 contract a disease / 沾

~官僚主義作風 be contaminated with the bureaucratic style of work

【染色】 rǎnsè (名) dyeing; colouring: ~工 dyer

【染色體】 rǎnsètǐ (名)〈生〉chromosome

【染坊】 rǎnfáng (名) dyehouse; dyeworks

【染缸】 rǎngāng (名) dye vat; dye jigger

【染指】 rǎnzhǐ (動) infringe upon; have a finger in the pie

【染料】 rǎnliào (名) dyestuff; dye

【染髮藥水】 rǎnfà yàoshuǐ (名) hairdye

柬 jiǎn (名) general term for letters, cards and notes: 書~ letter

【柬帖】 jiǎntiě (名) note

【柬埔寨】 jiǎnpǔzhài (名) Cambodia; Kampuchea: ~人 Cambodian; Kampuchean

【柬邀】 jiǎnyāo (動) send sb. an invitation

某 mǒu (代) certain; some: 張~ a certain Zhang/ 一種條件 some condition(s)

【某人】 mǒurén (代) somebody

【某事】 mǒushì (代) something

【某某】 mǒumǒu (代) so-and-so: ~將軍 General so-and-so; a certain general / ~工廠 a certain factory

柱 zhù (名) post; pillar; column

【柱子】 zhùzi (名) post; pillar

【柱石】 zhùshí (名) pillar; mainstay

柿 shì (名) persimmon

【柿子】 shìzi (名) persimmon

【柿餅】 shìbǐng (名) dried persimmon

柜 jǔ (名)〈植〉tree of the elm family; *Zelkawa accuminata*

柯 kē (名) a surname

柄 bǐng (名) ❶ handle; shaft: 錘~ handle of a hammer (of a flower, leaf or fruit) stem: 葉~ stem of a leaf ❸ laughing stock; handle: 給人抓住把~ give sb. a handle (against oneself) / 成爲笑~ becoem a laughing-stock ❹ power; authority: 權~ one's power (authority)

柑 gān (名) mandarin orange

【柑橘】 gānjú (名) tangerine

枯 kū (形) ❶ (of a plant, etc.) withered; shrivelled ❷ (of a well, river, etc.) dry; dried up: 海~石爛 (even if) the sea may run dry and the rocks crumble ❸ dull; joyless; ~寂的生活 cheerless and solitary life

【枯木逢春】 kū mù féng chūn〈成〉be revitalized; be rejuvenated

【枯水期】 kūshuǐqī (名) dry season

【枯黃】 kūhuáng (形) withered and yellow

【枯萎】 kūwěi (形) withered and wilted; faded

【枯竭】 kūjié (形) dry up; be exhausted: 他的精力似乎永遠不會~。His energy seems almost inexhaustible.

【枯燥】 kūzào (形) dull and dry

枢 jiù (名) coffin with a corpse inside

【柩車】 jiùchē (名) hearse

枷 jiā (名) cangue

【枷鎖】jiāsuǒ（名）fetters; yoke; shackles

查 chá（動）❶ check; examine: ～身份證 check identity cards ❷ investigate: ～無實據。Investigations provide no reliable evidence. ❸ consult: ～有關參考書籍 consult all relevant books
see also Zhā

【查收】cháshōu（動）❶ check and accept ❷（in a letter）find sth. enclosed: 隨信寄去簡歷, 請～。Please find enclosed my resumé.

【查抄】cháchāo（動）make a list of a criminal's property and confiscate it

【查明】chámíng（動）ascertain; find out: ～原委 find out all the details of the story from beginning to end

【查封】cháfēng（動）seal up; close down: ～走私貨物 seal up contraband

【查看】chákàn（動）examine; inspect

【查問】cháwèn（動）question; interrogate

【查禁】chájìn（動）prohibit: ～賭博 ban gambling

【查詢】cháxún（動）inquire: ～他的下落 inquire about his whereabouts

【查對】cháduì（動）check up; verify

【查閱】cháyuè（動）consult; look up: ～檔案 look up the archives

【查辦】chábàn（動）investigate an error or crime and deal with the offender accordingly

【查點】chádiǎn（動）tally; check the number or amount of

【查獲】cháhuò（動）ferret out; hunt down and seize: ～毒品 track down drugs

【查驗】cháyàn（動）check; examine: ～行李 inspect the luggage

查 Zhā（名）a surname
see also chá

柚 yóu
see also yòu

【柚木】yóumù（名）〈植〉teak

柚 yòu（名）shaddock; pomelo; grapefruit
see also yóu

枳 zhǐ（名）〈植〉trifoliate orange

柞 zuò（名）oak（quercus）

【柞絲綢】zuòsīchóu（名）pongee; tussah silk

【柞蠶】zuòcán（名）tussah

柵 zhà（名）pailing; railing

【柵欄】zhàlán（名）rails; bars; fence

柏 bǎi（名）cypress

【柏油】bǎiyóu（名）tar; pitch: ～路 asphalt road

【柏樹】bǎishù〈植〉cypress

柳 liǔ（名）❶ willow ❷（Liǔ）a surname

【柳條】liǔtiáo（名）willow twig; wicker: ～帽 wicker helmet

【柳絮】liǔxù（名）willow catkins

栀 zhī

【栀子】zhīzi（名）〈植〉Cape jasmine

柔 róu（形）❶ soft; supple; pliable: 柳樹的一條～ the pliable twigs of willows ❷ gentle; mild: 性顏溫～ be gentle in disposition

【柔和】róuhé（形）soft; gentle

【柔情】róuqíng（名）tender affection

【柔软】róuruǎn（形）soft; lithe

【柔道】róudào（名）judo

【柔韌】róurèn（形）pliable

【柔嫩】róunèn（形）tender

【柔麗】róulì（形）gentle and lovely

架 jià I（名）❶ structure for supporting sth.; frame: 衣帽～ clothes tree ❷ quarrel; exchange of blows; fight: 無法勸～ unable to stop the quarrel II（動）❶ erect; prop up: 江上一起一座橋梁 build a bridge across the river ❷ fend off; sustain: 壓力太大, 招～不住。The pressure is too great to withstand. ❸ take sb. away by force: 綁～ kidnap III（量）[of things with props or mechanism]: 一一鋼琴 a piano / 三～收音機 three radios

【架子】jiàzi（名）❶ frame; structure for supporting sth. ❷ outline; framework ❸ airs; arrogance: 沒～ modest and unassuming; be easy to approach ❹ posture; pose: 拉開～ strike a pose

【架不住】jiàbuzhù（動）❶ cannot sustain; cannot withstand: 好漢一人多。Even a brave man would be overwhelmed by so many opponents. ❷ be no match for: ～這些人能言善辯 be no match for these people in argument

【架次】jiàcì（名）sortie; one operational flight made by one aircraft

【架空】jiàkōng（動）❶ be constructed on stilts ❷ be without basis ❸ strip sb. of real power while paying him lip service: 實際上他被～了。As a matter of fact he was rendered unable to exercise his authority.

【架設】jiàshè（動）set up; erect: ～電話綫 set up telephone lines

【架勢】jiàshi（名）〈口〉posture; pose: 擺出咄咄逼人的～ assume a threatening posture

案 àn（名）❶ table; desk: 條～ long narrow table（traditional Chinese furniture）❷（law）case: 破～ crack a（criminal）case ❸ record; file of documents: 備～ put on record ❹ proposal or plan submitted for approval: 初步方～ preliminary plan

【案子】ànzi（名）❶ long table; trestle table: 乒乓球～ ping-pong table ❷〈口〉（law）case

【案由】ànyóu（名）gist of a case; brief

【案件】ànjiàn（名）（law）case: 刑事～ criminal case

【案板】ànbǎn（名）chopping or kneading board

【案卷】ànjuàn（名）files; records

【案情】ànqíng（名）（details of a）case

【案頭】àntóu（副）on the desk: ～詞典 desk dictionary / 一～日曆 desk calendar

栽 zāi（動）❶ plant; grow: 我們新～了許多果樹。We have newly planted many fruit trees. ❷ trip; tumble: 一了一跤 have a fall ❸ frame up: ～贓 frame up a case against sb.

【栽培】zāipéi（動）❶ cultivate; grow ❷ train; foster

【栽跟頭】zāi gēntou（動）❶ fall; tumble ❷ suffer a setback

【栽種】zāizhòng（動）plant; grow

栗 lì (名) ❶ chestnut ❷ (Lì) a surname

【栗子】lìzi (名) chestnut

【栗色】lìsè (名) dark brownish colour; maroon

校 jiào (动) proofread; check: 初~ first reading of galley proofs
see also xiào

【校正】jiàozhèng (动) examine and correct; proofread and make corrections

【校订】jiàodìng (动) collate; revise: ~本 revised version

【校准】jiàozhǔn (动) calibrate; regulate: ~機器 calibrate a machine

【校对】jiàoduì Ⅰ (动) check; proofread: 把譯文跟原文~一下 check the translation against the original Ⅱ (名) proofreader

【校樣】jiàoyàng (名) proof (sheet)

【校閱】jiàoyuè (动) read through and revise

校 xiào (名) ❶ school ❷ field officer
see also jiào

【校友】xiàoyǒu (名) alumnus; alumna

【校刊】xiàokān (名) school magazine; college journal

【校址】xiàozhǐ (名) location of a school, college or university; address of a school, college or university

【校官】xiàoguān (名) field officer

【校長】xiàozhǎng (名) headmaster; principal; president

【校舍】xiàoshè (名) school building

【校園】xiàoyuán (名) school yard; campus

【校曆】xiàolì (名) school calendar; university calendar

【校徽】xiàohuī (名) school badge

核 hé Ⅰ (名) ❶ stone; pit; core: 杏~ apricot-pit / 無~葡萄 seedless grapes ❷ nucleus: 細胞~ cell nucleus Ⅱ (动) examine; check
see also hú

【核子】hézǐ (名)〈核〉nucleon

【核心】héxīn (名) nucleus; core; kernel: ~成員 core member

【核反應】héfǎnyìng (名) nuclear reaction: ~堆 nuclear reactor

【核定】hédìng (动) approve and ratify

【核武器】héwǔqì (名) nuclear weapon

【核計】héjì (动) assess; calculate

【核桃】hétao (名) walnut

【核試驗】héshìyàn (名) nuclear test

【核對】héduì (动) check; verify

【核算】hésuàn (名) business accounting: ~單位 accounting unit

【核聚變】héjùbiàn (名) nuclear fusion

【核實】héshí (动) verify; check

【核導彈】hédǎodàn (名) nuclear missile

【核彈頭】hédàntóu (名) nuclear warhead

【核輻射】héfúshè (名) nuclear radiation

【核戰爭】hézhànzhēng (名) nuclear war

【核爆炸】hébàozhà (名) nuclear explosion

核 hú (名)〈口〉stone; core
see also hé

桂 guì (名) ❶ cassia-bark tree ❷

laurel ❸ sweet-scented osmanthus ❹（Guì）another name for the Guangxi Zhuang Autonomous Region ❺（Guì）a surname

【桂冠】guìguān（名）laurel：～詩人 poet laureate

【桂圓】guìyuán（龍眼 lóngyǎn）（名）longan

桓 Huán（名）a surname

框 kuàng Ⅰ（名）frame Ⅱ（動）❶ draw a line around ❷ restrict; restrain：～死 impose rigid restrictions on
see also kuàng

【框子】kuàngzi（名）frame（of a relatively small size）：眼鏡～ rims（of eyeglasses）

【框框】kuàngkuang（名）❶ frame ❷ convention; accepted rule：打破舊的條條～ aboish all old regulations nd restrictions

框 kuàng（名）frame：安門～ install a door frame
see also kuàng

桎 zhì

【桎梏】zhìgù（名）shackles; yoke

根 gēn Ⅰ（名）❶ root：樹～ the root of a tree ❷ base; bottom：牆～ the base of a wall ❸ cause; origin ❹ counterfoil：存～ stub Ⅱ（副）thoroughly Ⅲ（量）（of long and thin objects）：一～竹竿 a bamboo pole

【根本】gēnběn Ⅰ（形）basic; essential; fundamental Ⅱ（副）❶ at all; simply：～不同意 not agree at all ❷ thoroughly; completely; for good and all

【根由】gēnyóu（名）cause; origin

【根究】gēnjiū（動）investigate thoroughly; trace

【根底】gēndǐ（名）❶ cause; root：追問～ ask for detailed information ❷ foundation：英語～好 have a solid foundation in English

【根治】gēnzhì（動）bring about a permanent cure for; bring under permanent control

【根除】gēnchú（動）root out; eliminate

【根基】gēnjī（名）basis; foundation

【根深蒂固】gēn shēn dì gù〈成〉deep-rooted; ingrained

【根絕】gēnjué（動）eradicate; exterminate：～艾滋病 eradicate AIDS

【根源】gēnyuán（名）source; origin; root

【根據】gēnjù Ⅰ（介）on the basis of; according to：～公報精神 in accordance with the spirit of the communiqué Ⅱ（名）basis; grounds：科學～ scientific basis

栩 xǔ

【栩栩】xǔxǔ（形）vivid; lively

【栩栩如生】xǔ xǔ rú shēng〈成〉lifelike; true to life; animated

桐 tóng（名）paulownia; phoenix tree; tung tree：～油 tung oil

栓 shuān（名）❶ bolt; plug：消火～ fire hydrant; fireplug ❷ stopper; cork

株 zhū Ⅰ（名）trunk; stem Ⅱ（量）[of trees and other plants]：一～柳樹 a willow tree

【株連】zhūlián（動）involve（in a

criminal case); implicate

【株距】zhūjù (名)〈農〉spacing in the rows

桅 wéi (名) mast

【桅杆】wéigān (名) mast

格 gé (名)❶ square; check: 方～ square; check ❷ standard; norm ❸ quality; manner: 風～ style ❹〈語〉case: 所有～ the possessive case

【格子】gézi (名) check; lattice

【格外】géwài (副) exceptionally; especially

【格式】géshì (名) form; pattern

【格言】géyán (名) maxim; motto

【格局】géjú (名) pattern; layout

【格林納達】Gélínnàdá (名) Grenada;～人 Grenadian

【格律】gélǜ (名) tonal and rhyme patterns in classical Chinese poetry

【格格不入】gé gé bù rù〈成〉not congenial to one's nature

【格鬥】gédòu (動) grapple; be locked in a fist-fight

【格調】gédiào (名) style; taste

柏 jiǔ (烏柏 wūjiù) (名)〈植〉Chinese tallow tree

桃 táo (名)❶ peach: ～核雕 peach-stone carving ❷ sth. shaped like a peach: 棉～ cotton boll / 紅～ (of playing cards) heart

【桃色】táosè (形)❶ pink ❷ of illicit relationship between a man and a woman: ～事件 a sex scandal

【桃李】táolǐ (名) peaches and plums; one's students or disciples:～滿天下 (of someone having a long teaching career) have pupils everywhere

【桃花】táohuā (名) peach blossom

【桃脯】táofǔ (名) preserved peach

桑 sāng (名)❶ white mulberry; mulberry ❷ (Sāng) a surname

【桑梓】sāngzǐ (名)〈書〉one's native place

【桑甚】sāngshèn (名) mulberry

【桑樹】sāngshù (名) mulberry tree

【桑蠶】sāngcán (名) silkworm

柴 chái (名)❶ firewood: 砍～ cut wood (for use as fuel) ❷ (Chái) a surname

【柴火】cháihuo (名)〈口〉firewood; faggot

【柴米油鹽】chái mǐ yóu yán〈成〉fuel, rice, oil and salt; essentials for subsistence

【柴油】cháiyóu (名) diesel oil

【柴草】cháicǎo (名) sticks, twigs, branches or straw for use as fuel; faggot

桌 zhuō Ⅰ (名) table; desk Ⅱ (量):一～菜 a table of dishes

【桌子】zhuōzi (名) table; desk

【桌布】zhuōbù (名) tablecloth

【桌面兒上】zhuōmiànrshang (副) on the table; above-board: 將 觀點擺 到～上 lay the cards on the table

梁 liáng (名)❶ beam ❷ bridge: 橋～ bridge ❸ ridge ❹ (Liáng) a surname

【梁上君子】liáng shàng jūnzǐ〈婉〉thief

梓 zǐ (名)〈植〉Chinese catalpa

梳 shū Ⅰ (名) comb Ⅱ (動) comb (hair, etc.): ～頭 comb one's hair;

dress one's hair

【梳子】shūzi（名）comb

【梳妆】shūzhuāng（动）(of a woman) dress her hair and make herself up: ~臺 dressing table / ~用品 toiletry

【梳洗】shūxǐ（动）dress one's hair and wash one's face

梯 tī I（名）ladder; stairs: ~子 ladder; stepladder II（形）terraced: 階~教室 lecture theatre

【梯田】tītián（名）〈農〉terraced fields

【梯隊】tīduì（名）〈軍〉echelon (formation)

械 xiè（名）❶ tool: 器~ apparatus; instrument ❷ weapon: 缴~ lay down one's arms; disarm

【械鬥】xièdòu（动）fight with weapons (between groups of people)

梗 gěng I（名）stalk; stem: 菠菜~ spinach stalk II（动）❶ straighten; stiffen: ~着脖子 crane one's neck ❷ block; obstruct: 從中作~ put a spoke in sb.'s wheel

【梗直】gěngzhí（形）honest and frank; outspoken

【梗阻】gěngzǔ（动）block; hamper: 山川~ separated by mountains and rivers

【梗概】gěnggài（名）outline; gist

【梗塞】gěngsè I（动）❶ block; obstruct: 道路~ The road is blocked. II（名）infarction: 心肌~ myocardial infarction

梧 wú

【梧桐】wútóng（名）Chinese parasol (tree)

梵 fàn（名）Buddhist: ~文 Sanskrit

【梵蒂岡】Fàndìgāng（名）Vatican

桶 tǒng（名）pail; bucket; drum: 石油每~價格 oil price per barrel

梢 shāo（名）tip; thin end of a twig, etc.: 樹~ the top of a tree

桿 gǎn I（名）shaft or arm of sth: 鋼筆~ pen-holder II（量）[of sth. with a shaft]: 一~旗 a flag

【桿菌】gǎnjūn（名）〈微〉becillus

梆 bāng I（名）watchman's clapper (hollow, usu. made of wood or bamboo)II（象）rat-tat; rat-a-tat

【梆子】bāngzi（名）❶ watchman's clapper ❷ wooden clappers (musical instrument for beating time) ❸〈梆子腔 bāngziqiāng）local operas in north China performed to the accompaniment of wooden clappers: 陝西~ Shaanxi opera

梏 gù（名）wooden handcuffs

梅 méi（名）plum: 烏~ smoked plum; park plum

【梅子】méizi（名）plum

【梅花】méihuā（名）plum blossom

【梅花鹿】méihuālù（名）sika; spotted deer

【梅毒】méidú（名）〈醫〉syphilis

梭 suō（名）〈紡〉shuttle: 穿~外交 shuttle diplomacy

【梭子】suōzi I（名）❶〈紡〉shuttle ❷ cartridge clip II（量）(cartridge) clip

【梭鏢】suōbiāo（名）spear

梨 lí（名）❶ pear ❷ pear tree

條 tiáo Ⅰ(名) ❶ twig; spray ❷ strip; long and narrow piece: ~幅 vertical scroll / 打白~ pay with IOU'S ❸ item; point: ~目 clause (in a treaty, etc.); entry (in a dictionary) ❹ orderliness: 井井有~ in perfect order Ⅱ(量) ❶ (of long and slender things): 兩~腿 two legs / 一~牛仔褲 a pair of jeans / 三~黃瓜 three cucumbers ❷ item; point: 提兩~意見 make two suggestions

【條子】 tiáozi (名) ❶ strip ❷ short informal note: 開~ write a brief note

【條件】 tiáojiàn (名) ❶ condition; term: 創造有利~ create favourable conditions ❷ circumstance; state: 身體~ (state of) health ❸ requirement; qualification: 無~投降 unconditional surrender

【條例】 tiáolì (名) regulations; rules

【條約】 tiáoyuē (名) treaty; pact

【條紋】 tiáowén (名) stripe; streak

【條條框框】 tiáotiáo kuàngkuàng (名) 〈貶〉 conventions; trammels

【條理】 tiáolǐ (名) orderliness; good organization: 工作有~ work methodically

【條款】 tiáokuǎn (名) article; provision; terms and conditions

棄 qì (動) abandon; forsake

【棄置】 qìzhì (動) discard; jettison; throw overboard

【棄嬰】 qìyīng (名) foundling

【棄舊圖新】 qì jiù tú xīn 〈成〉 turn over a new leaf; reject the old for the new

【棄權】 qìquán (動) ❶ abstain from voting: 三票~ three abstentions ❷

forfeit the right to play; forfeit

棗 zǎo (名) jujube; (Chinese) date

【棗泥】 zǎoní (名) jujube paste

【棗紅】 zǎohóng (形) brownish red; claret

【棗樹】 zǎoshù (名) jujube tree; date tree

棘 jí (名) ❶ sour jujube ❷ prickly shrub: 荊~叢生 overgrown with thistles and prickly shrubs

【棘手】 jíshǒu (形) hard to resolve; thorny; knotty: ~的事情 a thorny matter

棕 zōng (名) ❶ palm (tree) ❷ palm fibre; coir: ~繩 coir rope

【棕色】 zōngsè (形) brown

【棕櫚】 zōnglǘ (名) palm; hemp palm

棺 guān (名) coffin

【棺材】 guāncai (名) coffin

椁 guǒ (名) outer coffin

棒 bàng Ⅰ(名) stick; club; truncheon: 接力~ relay baton Ⅱ(形) 〈口〉 good; strong; robust: 身體 很~ in very good health ❷ great; capital: 太~了! That's capital!

【棒子】 bàngzi (名) ❶ stick; club ❷ 〈方〉 maize; corn

【棒球】 bàngqiú (名) baseball: ~場 baseball diamond (field) / ~投球手 pitcher / ~擊球手 batter

棲 qī (動) ❶ (of birds) perch on a tree ❷ live or stay

【棲身】 qīshēn (動) stay or live: 無 處~ have nowhere to stay

【棲息】 qīxī (動) (of birds) dwell

棱 léng（名）❶ edge; line at which a surface ends: 三～鏡 triangular prism ❷ ridge; raised narrow strip on anything: 瓦～（楞）紙 corrugated paper

【棱角】léngjiǎo（名）❶ edges and corners ❷ pointedness; sharpness: 不露～ refrain from displaying one's true worth

棟 dòng Ⅰ（名）ridge-pole Ⅱ（量）(of buildings): 一～房子 a house

【棟梁】dòngliáng（名）ridge-pole and beam: 社會～ the pillars of society

棋 qí（名）chess game: 國際象～ (international) chess

【棋子】qízǐ（名）chessman

【棋迷】qímí（名）chess fan

【棋逢對手】qí féng duì shǒu（成）find one's match in a chess game; encounter a rival of equal ability or skill

【棋盤】qípán（名）chess-board

【棋譜】qípǔ（名）chess manual

植 zhí（動）plant; grow: 荒山～上了樹。The barren hills have been planted with trees.

【植物】zhíwù（名）plant; flora: ～園 botanical garden

【植保】zhíbǎo（名）(short for 植物保護 zhíwù bǎohù) plant protection

【植被】zhíbèi（名）vegetation

森 sēn

【森林】sēnlín（名）forest: ～保護區 forest preserve

【森嚴】sēnyán（形）strict; august: 人口戒備～。The entrance is heavily guarded.

棧 zhàn（名）❶ warehouse: 貨～ warehouse ❷ inn: 客～ inn ❸ shed; pen: 馬～ stable

【棧房】zhànfáng（名）warehouse; storehouse

【棧道】zhàndào（名）a plank road: 修～ build a plank road along the cliff face

椅 yǐ（名）chair: 扶手～ armchair

【椅子】yǐzi（名）chair

極 jí Ⅰ（名）❶ extreme; acme: 藝術上登峰造～ reach the acme of perfection in art ❷ ultra: ～左分子 ultraleftist ❸〈地〉pole: 南(北)～ South (North) Pole ❹ the throne: 登～ ascend the throne; come to the throne ❺〈電〉電～ electrode ❻〈物〉: 磁～ magnetic pole Ⅱ（動）reach the extreme: ～必反。Things turn into their opposites when they reach the extreme. Ⅲ（形）❶ utmost; ultimate: ～量 maximum doze ❷ polar: ～光 aurora Ⅳ（副）extremely; to the utmost: 快～了 exceedingly fast

【極力】jílì（動）do one's utmost; make every effort: ～主張 vehemently advocate

【極刑】jíxíng（名）death penalty; capital punishment: 處以～ be executed

【極其】jíqí（副）extremely; most: 後果～嚴重 fraught with very grave consequences

【極限】jíxiàn（名）❶ limit; maximum: 速度達到～ reach the maximum speed ❷〈數〉limit

【極度】jídù（副）exceedingly; extremely: ～疲勞 dog-tired; tired

out

【極盛】jíshèng（名）zenith; prime; heyday: 當時正是波斯的～時期。Persia was then at the height of its splendour.

【極端】jíduān Ⅰ（名）extreme; farthest end: 從一個～走向另一個～ go from one extreme to the other Ⅱ（副）extremely; exceedingly

【極樂世界】jílè shìjiè（名）〈宗〉 Sukhavati; world of utmost bliss

【極點】jídiǎn（名）extreme; utmost: 聰明到了～ extremely clever

【極權主義】jíquán zhǔyì（名）totalitarianism

椒 jiāo（名）hot spice plant

【椒鹽】jiāoyán（名）mixture of salt and roast prickly ash (a condiment)

棵 kē（量）(usu. of plants): 兩～蘋果樹 two apple trees

【棵兒】kēr（名）size of a plant: 揀～大的白菜砍 chop off only those big cabbages

棍 gùn（名）❶ rod; stick ❷ scoundrel; rascal: 惡～ ruffian

棚 péng（名）shed: 天～ canopy / 自行車～ bicycle shed

【棚戶】pénghù（名）〈方〉slum-dweller

椎 zhuī（名）vertebra: 胸～ thoracic vertebra

【椎骨】zhuīgǔ（名）〈生理〉vertebra

棉 mián Ⅰ（名）cotton: 藥～ cotton wool Ⅱ（形）cotton-padded

【棉大衣】miándàyī（名）cotton-padded overcoat

【棉毛衫】miánmáoshān（名）cotton (interlock) jersey

【棉毛褲】miánmáokù（名）cotton (interlock) drawers

【棉布】miánbù（名）cotton cloth

【棉田】miántián（名）cotton field

【棉衣】miányī（名）cotton-padded clothes

【棉花】miánhuā（名）cotton

【棉籽】miánzǐ（名）cotton seed

【棉紗】miánshā（名）cotton yarn

【棉桃】miántáo（名）cotton boll

【棉紡】miánfǎng（名）cotton spinning

【棉紡廠】miánfǎngchǎng（名）cotton mill

【棉紡織品】miánfǎngzhīpǐn（名）cotton textiles; cotton goods

【棉被】miánbèi（名）cotton-padded quilt

【棉毯】miántǎn（名）cotton blanket

【棉帽】miánmào（名）cotton-padded cap

【棉絮】miánxù（名）❶ cotton fibre ❷ cotton wadding (for bedding)

【棉鈴】miánlíng（名）cotton boll

【棉線】miánxiàn（名）cotton thread

【棉鞋】miánxié（名）cotton-padded shoes

【棉褲】miánkù（名）cotton-padded trousers

【棉織品】miánzhīpǐn（名）cotton textiles; cotton goods; cotton fabrics

【棉襖】mián'ǎo（名）cotton-padded jacket

榔 láng

【榔頭】lángtou（名）hammer

楔 xiē（名）❶ wedge ❷ peg

【楔子】xiēzi（名）❶ wedge ❷ peg

❹ prologue in some modern novels

椿 chūn (名)〈植〉Chinese toon

楝 liàn (名) chinaberry

椰 yē (名) coconut
【椰子】yēzi (名) coconut palm; coconut: ～樹 coconut tree

楠 nán
【楠木】nánmù (名)〈植〉nanmu (*Phoebe nanmu*)

楚 chǔ Ⅰ (名) ❶ pang; pain: 凄～ wretched; miserable ❷ (Chǔ) a surname Ⅱ (形) neat; clear: 衣冠～～ be immaculately dressed

楂 chá (名) short bristly hair or beard
see also zhā

楂 zhā (名) ❶ (Chinese) hawthorn ❷ haw
see also chá

概 gài (形) ❶ general; approximate ❷ without exception: ～不負責 take no responsibility for whatever may happen
【概況】gàikuàng (名) general situation; survey
【概念】gàiniàn (名) concept; conception
【概括】gàikuò (動) sum up; generalize
【概要】gàiyào (名) essentials; outline
【概率】gàilǜ (名)〈數〉probability
【概略】gàilüè (名) summary; synopsis
【概莫能外】gài mò néng wài〈成〉there can be no exception whatever

【概算】gàisuàn (名)〈經〉budgetary estimate
【概論】gàilùn (名) outline; introduction

楫 jí (名) oar; paddle: 舟～ vessel; boat

楊 yáng (名) ❶ poplar ❷ (Yáng) a surname
【楊柳】yángliǔ (名) ❶ poplar and willow ❷ willow
【楊梅】yángméi (名) red bayberry

楷 kǎi (名) ❶ model; fine example ❷ (in Chinese calligraphy) regular script: 正～ regular script
【楷書】kǎishū (名) (in Chinese calligraphy) regular script
【楷模】kǎimó (名) fine example
【楷體】kǎitǐ (名) ❶ regular script ❷ block letter

榆 yú
【榆樹】yúshù (名) elm

楸 qiū (名)〈植〉Chinese catalpa

楓 fēng (名)〈植〉maple

槌 chuí (名) mallet: 木～ mallet

椽 chuán (名) rafter
【椽子】chuánzi (名) rafter

業 yè (名) ❶ line of business; trade: 第三產～ tertiary industry ❷ profession; job: 以教書爲～ be a teacher by profession ❸ course of study: 畢～ finish school; graduate ❹ cause; enterprise: 祖國統一大～ the cause of the reunification of our motherland ❺ estate; property
【業主】yèzhǔ (名) proprietor

【業務】yèwù（名）business; professional work: ～很强的工程師 a fully qualified engineer

【業餘】yèyú（形）❶ sparetime: ～學校 sparetime school ❷ amateur: ～攝影師 an amateur photographer

【業績】yèjì（名）achievement

榮 róng Ⅰ（形）luxuriant; flourishing: 繁～ prosperous; thriving Ⅱ（名）❶ honour; glory: 引爲殊～ regard it as a privilege ❷（Róng）a surname

【榮幸】róngxìng（形）privileged; honoured: 不勝～ feel greatly honoured

【榮辱】róngrǔ（名）honour or dishonour: ～與共 throw in one's lot with sb.

【榮華富貴】rónghuá fùguì（名）honour and wealth

【榮耀】róngyào（名）glory; honour; splendour

【榮譽】róngyù（名）honour; credit: ～稱號 glorious title

榕 róng（名）〈植〉banyan

【榕樹】róngshù（名）banyan (tree)

榨 zhà（動）squeeze out; extract; press: ～油 extract oil

【榨取】zhàqǔ（動）❶ squeeze; extract ❷ exploit; extort

【榨菜】zhàcài（名）hot pickled mustard tuber

榜 bǎng（名）❶ list of successful candidates (as in civil service examinations or school entrance examinations): 選民～ list of eligible voters ❷ notice; announcement

【榜樣】bǎngyàng（名）model; good example: 樹立～ set a good example

構 gòu Ⅰ（動）construct; form Ⅱ（名）literary work: 佳～ an excellent work

【構成】gòuchéng（動）form; constitute

【構件】gòujiàn（名）〈機〉component; part

【構思】gòusī Ⅰ（動）conceive (the plot of a story, etc.) Ⅱ（名）plot

【構造】gòuzào（名）structure; construction

【構陷】gòuxiàn（動）incriminate sb. by foul means

【構圖】gòutú（名）〈美術〉design of a picture; composition

【構築】gòuzhù（動）build; construct

榛 zhēn（名）〈植〉hazel

槓 gàng（名）❶ thick stick ❷ bar: 高低～ uneven bars ❸ thick line: 劃～ underline

【槓桿】gànggǎn（名）lever: ～作用 leverage

【槓鈴】gànglíng（名）〈體〉barbell

榻 tà（名）couch; bed

橙 qī

【橙木】qīmù（名）〈植〉alder

槍 qiāng（名）❶ spear ❷ gun; rifle: 雙筒～ double-barrelled gun ❸ anything in the shape of a gun: 焊～ welding gun

【槍手】qiāngshǒu（名）marksman; gunner

【槍支】qiāngzhī（名）firearms

【槍刺】qiāngcì（名）bayonet

【槍法】qiāngfǎ（名）marksmanship

【槍林彈雨】qiāng lín dàn yǔ〈成〉a shower of bullets; in the midst of a fierce battle

【槍栓】qiāngshuān（名）rifle bolt

【槍殺】qiāngshā（動）shoot dead

【槍桿】qiānggǎn（名）barrel of a gun; gun; arms

【槍靶】qiāngbǎ（名）target; mark

【槍管】qiāngguǎn（名）barrel of a gun

【槍榴彈】qiāngliúdàn（名）rifle grenade

【槍膛】qiāngtáng（名）bore（of a gun）

【槍彈】qiāngdàn（名）bullet; cartridge

【槍聲】qiāngshēng（名）shot; report of a gun: 稀疏的～ sound of sporadic gunfire

【槍斃】qiāngbì（動）execute（by shooting）; shoot dead

槐 huái（名）locust tree

榴 liú（名）pomegranate

【榴彈炮】liúdànpào（名）howitzer

樟 zhāng（名）camphor tree

【樟腦】zhāngnǎo（名）camphor

【樟腦丸】zhāngnǎowán（名）camphor ball; mothball

【樟樹】zhāngshù（名）camphor tree

樣 yàng（名）❶ shape; form: 那人長得什麼～? What does the man look like? ❷ model; sample: 血～ blood sample ❸ sort; kind: 各種各～的人 people of all sorts

【樣子】yàngzi（名）❶ shape; appearance: 這個人～很難看。This man is ugly. ❷ facial expression; manner; air: 露出焦急的～ wear a

worried look ❸ example; model: 給別人做個～ set an example to the others ❹ likelihood: 看～車能及時趕到。Most likely the car will be here in time.

【樣本】yàngběn（名）❶ sample book ❷〈印〉specimen

【樣式】yàngshì（名）style; pattern: 最新～的時裝 the latest fashion

【樣板】yàngbǎn（名）model; example

【樣品】yàngpǐn（名）sample; specimen

椿 zhuāng Ⅰ（名）stake; pile Ⅱ（量）[of events, matters, etc.]: ～～往事湧上心頭。The past events flashed back across one's mind.

槽 cáo（名）❶ trough; manger ❷ groove; slot; channel: 開～ slotting

標 biāo Ⅰ（名）❶ superficiality; symptom: 治～不治本 relieve the symptoms rather than cure the disease; offer temporary relief but no permanent relief ❷ mark; sign; indication: 路～ route mark; road sign ❸ prize; award: 奪～ win the championship ❹ tender; bidding: 中～者 successful bidder Ⅱ（動）mark; label; indicate

【標尺】biāochǐ（名）❶〈測〉surveyor's rod ❷〈水〉staff gauge ❸〈軍〉rear sight

【標本】biāoběn（名）sample; specimen

【標兵】biāobīng（名）❶ pacesetter: 被樹爲～ be cited as a pacesetter ❷ marker; parade guard

【標明】biāomíng（動）mark; indicate: 這些文件必須～編號。These documents must be marked with serial numbers.

【標記】biāojì (名) mark; sign

【標準】biāozhǔn I (名) standard; criterion; norm: 採用國際～ adopt international standards II (形) standard; typical

【標準化】biāozhǔnhuà (名) standardization

【標新立異】biāo xīn lì yì (成) come up with an apparently novel idea as a show of one's originality

【標語】biāoyǔ (名) slogan; poster: ～牌 placard

【標誌】biāozhì I (名) mark; symbol: 交通～ traffic sign II (動) indicate; symbolize; mark

【標榜】biāobǎng (動) ❶ give favourable publicity to; flaunt ❷ brag; praise excessively: 自我～ blow one's own trumpet; self advertisement ❸ profess; claim: 中立 profess to be neutral; claim neutrality

【標槍】biāoqiāng (名) javelin: 擲～ javelin throw

【標價】biāojià I (動) price; mark the price II (名) marked price; tag price

【標燈】biāodēng (名) beacon light

【標緻】biāozhì (形) (of a woman) pretty; lovely

【標點】biāodiǎn (名) punctuation: 加～符號 punctuate (a piece of writing)

【標題】biāotí (名) heading; title: 小～ subheading

【標籤】biāoqiān (名) label; tag: 貨運～ cargo label; shipping tag

模 mó I (名) example; model;

standard: 爲人楷～ be an example for others to follow II (動) imitate
see also mú

【模本】móběn (名) model copy

【模仿】mófǎng (動) imitate; copy

【模型】móxíng (名) model; pattern: 汽車～ the model of a car

【模特兒】mótèr (名) model: 時裝～ fashion model/ 人體～ artist's model

【模棱兩可】mó léng liǎng kě (形) equivocal; ambiguous

【模糊】móhu I (形) vague; dim: 我對這件事只有一些～的概念。I have only a hazy notion of the matter. II (動) confuse; blur: ～是非界限 blur the distinction between righ and wrong

【模範】mófàn (名) model; good example: 勞動～ a model worker

【模擬】mónǐ (動) imitate; simulate

模 mú (名) model; mould; pattern; form: 木～ wooden form
see also mó

【模子】múzi (名) mould

【模具】mújù (名) mould; matrix; die

【模樣】múyàng I (名) look; appearance: 姊妹倆～差不離。The two sisters look very much alike. II (形) approximate; about: 這個孩子有十幾歲～。The boy is in his teens.

【模壓】múyà (名) mould pressing

樞 shū (名) ❶ door hinge ❷ pivot; hub: 電訊中～ telecommunication centre

【樞紐】shūniǔ (名) pivot; hub: 起着～的作用 play a pivotal role

械 qī

【橄樹】qīshù（名）maple

橄 gǎn

【橄欖】gǎnlǎn（名）〈植〉olive: ～油 olive oil

【橄欖球】gǎnlǎnqiú（名）American football; Rugby

樓 lóu（名）❶ storeyed building; tower ❷ storey; floor: 三 ～ the second floor; the third floor (American)

【樓上】lóushàng（名）upstairs

【樓下】lóuxià（名）downstairs

【樓房】lóufáng（名）storeyed building

【樓梯】lóutī（名）stairs;

樊 fán（名）❶ fence ❷（Fán）a surname

【樊籠】fánlóng（名）cage

【樊籬】fánlí（名）❶ fence ❷ restriction

橡 xiàng（名）❶ oak ❷ rubber tree

【橡皮】xiàngpí（名）❶ rubber: ～圖章 rubber stamp ❷ eraser; rubber

【橡膠】xiàngjiāo（名）rubber

樅 cōng（名）〈植〉fir

槳 jiǎng（名）oar

樂 lè I（形）happy; joyous: ～園 paradise II（動）❶ take delight in; enjoy (doing sth.): ～於爲您效勞 would be glad to be of service to you ❷〈口〉〈方〉laugh III（名）❶ happiness: 享天倫之～ enjoy the bliss of a happy family life (with one's father or brothers) ❷（Lè）a surname

see also yuè

【樂天】lètiān（名）carefree: 他是個 ～派。He takes everything easy.

【樂呵呵】lèhēhē（形）cheerful; jovial

【樂得】lèdé（動）be only too glad to (do sth.)

【樂極生悲】lè jí shēng bēi〈成〉when joy reaches its extremity, it turns into sorrow; after joy comes sorrow

【樂滋滋】lèzīzī（形）〈口〉pleased; gratified; satisfied: 他聽了表揚心裏一。He was pleased to hear the compliments.

【樂意】lèyì I（副）willingly; readily: 她一留下來看孩子。She readily agreed to stay behind to take care of the children. II（形）happy: 心裏老大不一 feel rather displeased

【樂趣】lèqù（名）pleasure; joy; delight: 讀書的 ～ the pleasure of reading

【樂觀】lèguān I（形）optimistic II（名）optimism

樂 yuè（名）❶ music: 交響～ symphonic music ❷（Yuè）a surname

see also lè

【樂池】yuèchí（名）orchestra pit; orchestra

【樂曲】yuèqǔ（名）musical composition; music: 譜成～ set to music

【樂理】yuèlǐ（名）〈樂〉music theory

【樂章】yuèzhāng（名）〈樂〉movement

【樂隊】yuèduì（名）orchestra; band: 銅管～ brass band

【樂團】yuètuán（名）philharmonic society; philharmonic orchestra

【樂器】yuèqì（名）musical instrument

【樂譜】yuèpǔ（名）music score

桡 ráo（名）oar

【桡骨】ráogǔ（名）〈生理〉radius

【桡動脈】ráodòngmài（名）〈生理〉radial artery

樹 shù Ⅰ（名）tree: 植～造林 afforestation Ⅱ（動）❶ grow; cultivate ❷ set up; uphold; erect: ～新風 encourage new social practices ／～碑立傳（literally）erect a monument to sb. and recount his deeds

【樹木】shùmù Ⅰ（名）trees Ⅱ（動）plant trees

【樹皮】shùpí（名）bark（of a tree）

【樹立】shùlì（動）set up; establish; build: ～信心 build up one's confidence

【樹杈】shùchà（名）crotch（of a tree）

【樹枝】shùzhī（名）（tree）branch; twig; bough

【樹林】shùlín（名）forest; woods

【樹苗】shùmiáo（名）sapling

【樹脂】shùzhī（名）resin

【樹幹】shùgàn（名）（tree）trunk

【樹葉】shùyè（名）tree leaf

【樹蔭】shùyīn（名）（tree）shade

【樹敵】shùdí（動）antagonize; make enemies: 他這個人～太多。He has made too many enemies.

【樹墩】shùdūn（名）（tree）stump

【樹叢】shùcóng（名）grove; small wood

横 héng Ⅰ（形）horizontal Ⅱ（副）❶ across; crosswise: ～渡大西洋 sail across the Atlantic ❷ turbulent-ly; profusely: 老淚～流。Tears criss-crossed the old cheeks. Ⅲ（名）（of Chinese characters）horizontal stroke

see also hèng

【横生】héngshēng（動）❶ grow all around: 蔓草～ be rank with weeds ❷ be full of: 妙趣～ with frequent sparkles of humour

【横生枝節】héng shēng zhī jié（成）problems crop up unexpectedly; create side issues

【横行】héngxíng（動）run wild: ～霸道 behave or rule like a despot

【横格紙】hénggézhǐ（名）lined paper

【横梁】héngliáng（名）crossbeam

【横掃】héngsǎo（動）sweep away; wipe out

【横豎】héngshù（副）〈口〉in any case; anyway: 别急，他～要來的。Don't worry. He'll show up anyway.

【横衝直撞】héng chōng zhí zhuàng（成）push one's way like crazy; run amok

【横徵暴斂】héng zhēng bào liǎn〈成〉levy exorbitant taxes

横 hèng（形）❶ unreasonable; perverse; savage: 蠻～ savage and unreasonable ❷ unexpected

see also héng

【横死】hèngsǐ（動）die a violent death

【横事】hèngshì（名）unexpected occurence

【横財】hèngcái（名）ill-gotten riches

【横禍】hènghuò（名）unexpected misfortune

【横暴】hèngbào（形）ruthless

橛 jué (名) short wooden stake

【橛子】juézi (名) short wooden stake; wooden pin

橘 jú (名) tangerine: 蜜~ tanger- ine

【橘子】júzi (名) tangerine

【橘子水】júzishuǐ (名) orangeade

【橘汁】júzhī (名) orange juice

橢 tuǒ

【橢圓】tuǒyuán (名) 〈數〉ellipse; oval

橙 chén (橙子 chénzi) (名) orange see also chéng

橙 chéng (名) ❶ orange ❷ orange colour: ~黃 orange (colour) see also chén

【橙子】chéngzi (名) orange

樺 huà (名) birch

樸 pǔ (形) simple; plain

【樸直】pǔzhí (形) simple and straightforward

【樸素】pǔsù (形) (of colour, style) light-coloured; simpled and plain

【樸實】pǔshí (形) ❶ simple; mod- est and unassuming ❷ sincere and honest

橇 qiāo (名) sledge; sled

橋 qiáo (名) bridge: 立交~ traffic flyover

【橋孔】qiáokǒng (名) bridge open- ing

【橋拱】qiáogǒng (名) bridge arch

【橋面】qiáomiàn (名) bridge floor; roadway

【橋梁】qiáoliáng (名) bridge

【橋牌】qiáopái (名) (game or) bridge

【橋塔】qiáotǎ (名) 〈建〉bridge tower

【橋墩】qiáodūn (名) (bridge) pier

【橋頭】qiáotóu (名) either end of a bridge

【橋頭堡】qiáotóubǎo (名) ❶ 〈軍〉 bridgehead ❷ 〈建〉bridgetower

【橋欄】qiáolán (名) bridge railing

樵 qiáo (名) firewood; faggot

【樵夫】qiáofū (名) woodman; wood- cutter

機 jī (名) ❶ machine; machinery: 洗衣~ washing machine ❷ aircraft: 轟炸~ bomber ❸ crucial link (of a matter): 契~ juncture ❹ opportunity; chance: 一綫生~ a slim chance of survival; a gleam of hope II (形) ❶ flexible; crafty: ~ 敏 alert and dexterous ❷ organic: 有~化學 organic chemistry

【機井】jījǐng (名) motor-pumped well

【機車】jīchē (名) locomotive

【機牀】jīchuáng (名) machine tool: 精密~ precision machine tool

【機宜】jīyí (名) guidelines (tactics) for action under specific circum- stances

【機制】jīzhì I (形) machine-made II (名) machanism: 競爭~ mecha- nism of competition

【機要】jīyào (形) classified; confi- dential

【機能】jīnéng (名) 〈生〉function; faculty

【機動】jīdòng (動) ❶ flexible; mo- bile ❷ keep in reserve for emergen- cy use: ~資金 reserve fund ❸ motor-driven: ～車輛 motor-driven (motor) vehicle

【機密】jīmì Ⅰ (形) classified; confidential Ⅱ (名) secret; classified information: 洩露～ disclose secret information; divulge a secret plan

【機組】jīzǔ (名) ❶ unit; set: 發電～ generating unit ❷ aircrew; flying crew

【機械】jīxiè Ⅰ (名) machinery: ～工業 engineering industry / ～工程師 mechanical engineer Ⅱ (形) mechanical; rigid: ～的規定 rigid rules

【機械化】jīxièhuà Ⅰ (動) mechanize: 實現農業～ mechanize farming Ⅱ (名) mechanization

【機場】jīchǎng (名) airport; airdrome; airstrip

【機遇】jīyù (名) good luck; opportunity; chance

【機智】jīzhì (形) resourceful; witty

【機羣】jīqún (名) air fleet; aircraft flying in formation

【機會】jīhuì (名) chance; opportunity: ～均等 equal opportunities

【機會主義】jīhuì zhǔyì (名) opportunism

【機構】jīgòu (名) ❶ part of a device or machine that transmits or transforms motion; mechanism: 齒輪～ gear mechanism ❷ organ; setup; institution; government agency: 行政～ administrative setup

【機槍】jīqiāng (名) (short for 機關槍 jīguānqiāng) machine gun

【機緣】jīyuán (名) good luck; lucky coincidence

【機器】jīqi (名) machine; machinery: ～製造業 machine-building industry / 戰爭～ war machine

【機器人】jīqirén (名) robot

【機關】jīguān (名) ❶ office; institution; organ: ～工作人員 office clerk; government employee / ～刊物 organ ❷ intrigue; scheme; machination: 暗設～ lay a trap for sb. in secrecy ❸ mechanical contrivance; mechanism: 傳動～ transmission mechanism

【機警】jījǐng (形) alert; astute

【機靈】jīling (形) clever; intelligent; smart: 小～鬼兒 clever youngster

檀 tán (名) ❶ wingceltis ❷ (Tán) a surname

【檀香】tánxiāng (名) 〈植〉 white sandalwood: ～扇 sandalwood fan

檁 lǐn (名) 〈建〉 purlin

檔 dàng (名) ❶ pigeonholes ❷ files: 存～ put on file ❸ grade: 高 (低) ～商品 high (low-) grade goods

【檔案】dàng'àn (名) files; archives; records

檢 jiǎn (動) ❶ check up; examine: 體～ medical check-up ❷ restrain; control: 言語失～ make indiscreet remarks

【檢字表】jiǎnzìbiǎo (名) index of Chinese characters

【檢字法】jiǎnzìfǎ (名) indexing system of Chinese characters

【檢查】jiǎnchá Ⅰ (動) check; inspect; censor; review Ⅱ (名) self-criticism: 做～ make a self-criticism

【檢修】jiǎnxiū (動) overhaul; check and repair

【檢疫】jiǎnyì (名) quarantine

【檢索】jiǎnsuǒ（動）look up（data, etc.）

【檢討】jiǎntǎo Ⅰ（名）　self-criticism Ⅱ（動）review：～自己的錯誤 criticize oneself for the mistake one has made

【檢測】jiǎncè（動）examine（machines and equipment）

【檢察】jiǎnchá（動）prosecute：最高人民～院 Supreme People's Procuratorate

【檢察官】jiǎncháguān（名）prosecutor；prosecuting attorney

【檢察長】jiǎncházhǎng（名）chief prosecutor

【檢閱】jiǎnyuè（動）review（troops, etc.）；inspect

【檢閱臺】jiǎnyuètái（名）reviewing stand

【檢舉】jiǎnjǔ（動）inform against；impeach；accuse

【檢點】jiǎndiǎn（動）❶ make a careful check of ❷ restrain from improper behaviour；be discreet：有失～ lack discretion

【檢驗】jiǎnyàn（動）inspect；test；verify：實踐是～真理的唯一標準。Truth can only be verified through practice.

檜 yán（名）eaves

檄 xí

【檄文】xíwén（名）official statement（in ancient China）denouncing an enemy or a traitor

檸 níng

【檸檬】níngméng（名）lemon
【檸檬水】níngméngshuǐ（名）lemonade

檳 bīng

【檳榔】bīnglang（名）❶ betel nut；areca nut ❷ betel palm；areca

檯 tái（名）table；desk：～布 tablecloth

【檯球】táiqiú（名）❶ billiards；pool ❷ snooker ❸ billiard ball
【檯燈】táidēng（名）desk lamp
【檯曆】táilì（名）desk calendar

櫃 guì（名）❶ cupboard；cabinet：衣～ wardrobe ❷ counter
【櫃臺】guìtái（名）counter；bar

檻 kǎn（名）threshold：門～ threshold

櫥 chú（名）cabinet；closet；cupboard：壁～ built-in wardrobe or cupboard；closet

【櫥窗】chúchuāng（名）❶ show window ❷ glass-fronted billboard
【櫥櫃】chúguì（名）cupboard

櫓 lǔ（名）scull

櫟 lì（名）oak

櫪 lì（名）manger

欄 lán（名）❶ railing；fence；banisters ❷ fold；pen；sty：羊～ sheepfold ❸（of newspapers, periodicals, etc.）column：專～作家 columnist

【欄杆】lángān（名）banisters；railing

櫻 yīng（名）❶ cherry ❷ oriental cherry
【櫻花】yīnghuā（名）oriental cherry
【櫻桃】yīngtáo（名）cherry

權

quán I (名) ❶ power: 掌握大~ wield power ❷ right: 人~ human rights / 特~ privilege ❸ advantageous position: 主動~ initiative ❹ (Quán) a surname II (動) weigh; consider; assess: ~其輕重 assess the relative importance of the matter

【權力】quánlì (名) power; authority: 國家~ state power / ~之爭 power struggle

【權且】quánqiě (副) for the time being: ~把這事擱一擱。Let's put the matter aside for the moment.

【權利】quánlì (名) right: 保障公民的~ safeguard the rights of the citizens

【權宜】quányí (形) expedient: ~之計 expediency

【權柄】quánbǐng (名) power; authority

【權威】quánwēi (名) ❶ authority: ~著作 authoritative work ❷ expert: 他是近代史的~。He is an authority on modern history.

【權限】quánxiàn (名) limits of authority; jurisdiction: 這是他~之內的事。This is within his jurisdiction.

【權益】quányì (名) rights and interests

【權術】quánshù (名) political intrigue

【權貴】quánguì (名) influential officials; bigwigs

【權勢】quánshì (名) power and influence

【權衡】quánhéng (動) weigh; balance: ~輕重 weigh the relative importance

欠 部

欠

qiàn (動) ❶ be short of; lack: 做事~考慮 act thoughtlessly ❷ owe: ~人十元錢 owe sb. 10 *yuan* ❸ raise slightly (a part of the body): 從座位上~起身子 half rise from one's seat ❹ yawn

【欠伸】qiànshēn (動) yawn and stretch one's limbs

【欠缺】qiànquē (形) lacking: 他的經驗還很~。He is not experienced enough.

【欠債】qiànzhài (動) be in debt

次

cì I (形) ❶ second; next: ~日 the next day / 分清主~ distinguish between what is primary and what is secondary ❷ inferior; second-rate II (名) order; sequence: 名~ order of prize winners or that of successful candidates in an examination III (量) time: 三番五~ again and again

【次序】cìxù (名) order: ~顛倒 not in the right order

【次要】cìyào (形) secondary; minor

【次品】cìpǐn (名) substandard product; defective goods

【次等】cìděng (形) second-class; second-rate

【次數】cìshù (名) number of times

欣

xīn (形) happy; joyous; glad

【欣欣向榮】xīn xīn xiàng róng (成) be prosperous; be thriving: 文學藝術~。Art and literature are flourishing.

【欣悉】xīnxī (動) be glad to hear; be

delighted to learn

【欣然】xīnrán（副）〈書〉joyfully; gladly; graciously: ～接受邀請 accept the invitation with pleasure; graciously accept the invitation

【欣喜】xīnxǐ（形）glad; happy: ～若狂 wild with joy

【欣賞】xīnshǎng（動）enjoy; admire; appreciate: 他獨自站在那裏～大自然的美。He stood there alone, admiring the beauty of nature.

【欣慰】xīnwèi（形）pleased; gratified: 對他迅速康復感到～ be pleased at his speedy recovery

欲

欲 yù（動）❶ wish; long for: 隨心所～ have one's own way; do whatever one wishes ❷ be about to; be on the verge of: 搖搖～墜 teeter on the brink of collapse; tottering

【欲速則不達】yù sù zé bù dá〈成〉more haste, less speed

【欲蓋彌彰】yù gài mí zhāng〈成〉attempt to cover up the truth only to make it more conspicuous

【欲罷不能】yù bà bù néng〈成〉cannot stop even one wishes to

【欲擒故縱】yù qín gù zòng〈成〉give the enemy some leeway in order to catch him later

款

款 kuǎn（名）❶ sum of money: 銀行貸～ bank loan ❷ section of an article in a decree, charter, treaty, etc. ❸ name of the artist or recipient inscribed on a piece of calligraphy or painting: 上～ name of the recipient ／ 下～ signature of the artist

【款子】kuǎnzi（名）sum of money

【款式】kuǎnshì（名）style; pattern:

～新穎的服裝 dresses of novel designs

【款待】kuǎndài（動）treat; entertain 承你們盛情～ grateful to you for your kind hospitality

【款項】kuǎnxiàng（名）fund; sum of money

欺

欺 qī（動）❶ deceive; cheat ❷ bully

【欺人之談】qī rén zhī tán〈成〉a wilful lie

【欺上瞞下】qī shàng mán xià〈成〉deceive those above and hoodwink those below

【欺生】qīshēng（動）behave rudely to strangers; cheat or deal unfairly with strangers

【欺世盜名】qī shì dào míng〈成〉gain fame under false pretences

【欺負】qīfu（動）bully; browbeat

【欺凌】qīlíng（動）bully and humiliate

【欺軟怕硬】qī ruǎn pà yìng〈成〉browbeat the weak but fear the strong

【欺詐】qīzhà（動）cheat; defraud

【欺壓】qīyā（動）ride roughshod over

【欺騙】qīpiàn（動）deceive; hoodwink; cheat

欽

欽 qīn

【欽佩】qīnpèi（動）admire; respect

【欽差大臣】qīnchāi dàchén（名）imperial envoy

歇

歇 xiē（動）❶ have a rest; rest: 我們～一會吧。Let's have a break. ❷ stop

【歇工】xiēgōng（動）stop work; knock off

【歇班】xiēbān（動）be off duty

【歇晌】xiēshǎng（動）take a midday rest; take an afternoon nap

【歇息】xiēxi（動）❶ take a rest ❷ go to bed; put up for the night

【歇宿】xiēsù（動）put up for the night

【歇斯底里】xiēsīdǐlǐ（名）hysteria

【歇業】xiēyè（動）go out of business

【歇腳】xiējiǎo（動）stop（on the way）to have a rest

歉 qiàn（名）❶ apology: 爲遲到道 ～ apologize for being late ❷ crop failure

【歉年】qiànnián（名）lean year

【歉收】qiànshōu（動）have a poor harvest

【歉意】qiànyì（名）apology: 請接受我的～。Please accept my apologies.

歌 gē I（名）song II（動）sing: 載 ～載舞 sing and dance．

【歌手】gēshǒu（名）singer; vocalist

【歌功頌德】gē gōng sòng dé（動）extol sb.'s virtues and achievements

【歌曲】gēqǔ（名）song

【歌咏】gēyǒng（名）singing

【歌唱】gēchàng（動）sing

【歌唱家】gēchàngjiā（名）singer

【歌詞】gēcí（名）words of a song

【歌喉】gēhóu（名）singing voice

【歌頌】gēsòng（動）extol; sing the praises of; eulogize

【歌舞】gēwǔ（名）song and dance

【歌舞升平】gē wǔ shēng píng（成）put on a facade of peace and prosperity

【歌舞團】gēwǔtuán（名）song and dance troupe

【歌劇】gējù（名）opera

【歌劇院】gējùyuàn（名）opera house

【歌謠】gēyáo（名）ballad; folk song

【歌譜】gēpǔ（名）music of a song

歐 Ōu（名）a surname

【歐化】ōuhuà（動）Europeanize; Westernize

【歐姆】ōumǔ（名）〈物〉ohm

【歐洲】Ōuzhōu（名）Europe: ～ 共同體 the European Community

【歐陽】Ōuyáng（名）a surname

歡 huān（副）❶ joyfully; happily: ～慶五一 celebrate May Day ❷〈方〉vigorously; in full swing: 幹得～ work vigorously

【歡心】huānxīn（名）favour; liking: 博取～ curry sb.'s favour

【歡天喜地】huān tiān xǐ dì〈成〉be filled with boundless joy: ～迎新年 usher in the New Year with great joy

【歡迎】huānyíng I（動）welcome; greet: ～詞 welcoming speech II（形）welcome

【歡呼】huānhū（動）hail; cheer

【歡欣鼓舞】huān xīn gǔ wǔ〈成〉be filled with great joy

【歡度】huāndù（動）spend joyfully; celebrate（a festival）: ～聖誕節 celebrate Christmas; spend the Christmas holidays / ～晚年 enjoy the evening of one's life

【歡送】huānsòng（動）send off: ～會 farewell party

【歡喜】huānxǐ I（形）happy; delighted II（動）like; have a liking for

【歡暢】huānchàng（形）elated

【歡聚】huānjù（動）gather happily together

【歡樂】huānlè (形)(usu. said of a crowd of people) happy; joyous

【歡聲雷動】huān shēng léi dòng〈成〉resound with thunderous cheers

【歡騰】huānténg (動) jump with joy

止 部

止 zhǐ I (動) stop; cease: 他血流不~。He bled profusely. II (介) to; till: 至十月五日~ by October 5 III (副) only: 不~一公里 more than a kilometre

【止血】zhǐxuè (動) stop bleeding

【止步】zhǐbù (動) halt; stop

【止咳】zhǐké (動) relieve a cough

【止痛】zhǐtòng (動) stop pain: ~藥 painkiller

【止境】zhǐjìng (名) end; limit: 貪婪是無~的。Avarice knows no limits.

正 zhēng
see also zhèng

【正月】zhēngyuè (名) first month of the lunar year

正 zhèng I (形) ❶ straight; upright: 坐~ sit straight / ~東 due east ❷ upright; decent; proper: 品行端~ honest and correct in behaviour ❸ right; pure: ~色 pure colour ❹ principal; chief: ~文 main text; body of a book ❺ positive: ~負數 positive and negative numbers II (動) correct; set right: 修~ revise / 以~視聽 so as to clarify the issues to the public III (副) ❶ just; exactly: 這~合我意。It suits me perfectly. / 這~是我想要看到的。This is just what I wanted to see. ❷ [used to indicate an action in progress]: 會上~在討論這個問題。The problem is under discussion at the meeting.
see also zhēng

【正大光明】zhèng dà guāng míng〈成〉upright and honourable; fair and square

【正比】zhèngbǐ (名)〈數〉direct ratio

【正午】zhèngwǔ (名) high noon

【正中下懷】zhèng zhòng xià huái〈成〉fit in with exactly what one wishes for

【正方形】zhèngfāngxíng (名) square

【正巧】zhèngqiǎo (副) ❶ by coincidence; happen to: 我~認識他。I happen to know him. ❷ just in time; just at the right moment: 他回來得~, 有人找他。He came back at the right moment as someone was looking for him.

【正好】zhènghǎo (副) ❶ just right; just in time: 他~趕上末班車。He was just in time for the last bus. / 這條裙子我穿~。The skirt fits me nicely. ❷ as it happens: 他~不在家。He happened to be out.

【正式】zhèngshì (形) formal; official: 在~場合 on a formal occasion

【正門】zhèngmén (名) front door; main entrance

【正直】zhèngzhí (形) honest and upright

【正法】zhèngfǎ (動) execute (a criminal): 就地~ execute on the spot

【正宗】zhèngzōng I (名) orthodox school II (形) standard

【正面】zhèngmiàn Ⅰ（名）❶ front; facade: 紀念碑的～ the facade of a monument ❷ the right side; the obverse side: 紙的～ the right side of the paper Ⅱ（形）positive: ～人物 positive character Ⅲ（副）directly; openly: 請一說出你的看法。Please tell me exactly what you have in mind.

【正派】zhèngpài（形）upright; decent

【正品】zhèngpǐn（名）quality goods

【正音】zhèngyīn Ⅰ（動）correct one's pronunciation Ⅱ（名）standard pronunciation: ～詞典 pronouncing dictionary

【正軌】zhèngguǐ（名）right track: 納入～ bring sth. onto the correct path

【正氣】zhèngqì（名）healthy social trend

【正常】zhèngcháng（形）regular; normal: 心率不～ irregular heartbeats

【正規】zhèngguī（形）regular; standard: ～軍 regular army

【正視】zhèngshì（動）face squarely; look sb. in the face: ～出現的新情況 face up to the new circumstances

【正統】zhèngtǒng（形）orthodox

【正當】zhèngdāng（形）just when; at a time when: ～他要出門時，下起雨來了。He was going out when it began to rain.

【正當】zhèngdàng（形）legitimate; proper; rightful: ～權益 legitimate rights and interests

【正電】zhèngdiàn（名）positive electricity

【正殿】zhèngdiàn（名）main hall (in a palace or temple)

【正經】zhèngjing（形）❶ decent; respectable ❷ serious: 我說的是～事。I meant business.

【正楷】zhèngkǎi（名）(in Chinese calligraphy) regular script

【正義】zhèngyì Ⅰ（名）justice Ⅱ（形）just; righteous: ～的事業 just cause

【正誤】zhèngwù（動）correct misprints: ～表 errata; corrigenda

【正確】zhèngquè（形）correct; right

【正點】zhèngdiǎn（副）(of a train, ship, etc.) on schedule; on time

【正題】zhèngtí（名）subject of a talk or essay: 偏離～ stray from the subject

【正廳】zhèngtīng（名）❶ main hall ❷ stalls (in a theatre)

此 cǐ Ⅰ（代）this: ～行 this trip Ⅱ（副）❶ this moment: 從～以後 from now on ❷ this place: 由～往左 turn left from here ❸ this; like this: 長～以往 if things go on like this; if things continue this way

【此外】cǐwài（副）besides; moreover; furthermore

【此地】cǐdì（名）here; this place

【此刻】cǐkè（副）right now; at this moment

【此後】cǐhòu（副）after this; thereafter; henceforth

【此時】cǐshí（副）now; at present; at the moment

【此致】cǐzhì（套）[used at the end of a letter] with: ～敬禮 with best regards

【此起彼伏】cǐ qǐ bǐ fú〈成〉as one wave subsides, another rises, rise one after another

【此處】cǐchù（副）here

【此路不通】cǐ lù bù tōng 〈成〉❶ not a through road; no thoroughfare (road sign) ❷ blind alley

步 bù Ⅰ (名) ❶ step; pace: 前進一大～ take a big stride forward ❷ stage; phase: 逐～發展 develop by stages ❸ state; situation: 落到這一～ get into such a fix ❹ move: 一～好棋 a marvelous move (in chess) Ⅱ (動) ❶ walk: 漫～街頭 go for stroll in the street ❷ tread: ～其後塵 follow in sb.'s footsteps; trail sb. in his wake

【步子】bùzi (名) pace; step

【步伐】bùfá (名) step; pace

【步行】bùxíng (動) walk; go on foot

【步兵】bùbīng (名) ❶ foot soldier; infantryman ❷ infantry

【步槍】bùqiāng (名) rifle

【步調】bùdiào (名) pace: ～協調 act in concert

【步驟】bùzhòu (名) step; measure: 採取～ take steps (measures)

武 wǔ Ⅰ (形) ❶ military; martial: 文～雙全 competent in both civilian and military affairs ❷ brave; valiant: 英～ heroic Ⅱ (名) ❶ force: 用～ use force ❷ (Wǔ) a surname

【武力】wǔlì (名) ❶ force; violence ❷ military force; armed force

【武士】wǔshì (名) warrior; fighter

【武打】wǔdǎ (名) acrobatic fighting

【武功】wǔgōng (名) ❶ acrobatic skill ❷ skill in martial arts

【武官】wǔguān (名) ❶ military officer ❷ military attaché

【武庫】wǔkù (名) arsenal

【武鬥】wǔdòu (動) fight; resort to violence

【武術】wǔshù (名) wushu; martial arts

【武裝】wǔzhuāng Ⅰ (名) arms; military equipment Ⅱ (形) armed: ～力量 armed froces /～中立 armed neutrality Ⅲ (動) furnish with weapons; equip with something that adds strength to oneself: 用知識～自己 arm oneself with knowledge

【武器】wǔqì (名) weapon; arms; weaponry

【武斷】wǔduàn (形) arbitrary

【武藝】wǔyì (名) skill in martial arts

【武警】wǔjǐng (名) armed police

歧 qí Ⅰ (名) fork; branch Ⅱ (形) different; variant

【歧途】qítú (名) wrong road: 走入～ go astray

【歧視】qíshì (動) discriminate against

【歧義】qíyì (名) various interpretations

【歧路】qílù (名) branch road; forked road

歪 wāi (形) ❶ not in the correct position; awry ❷ foul; evil

【歪曲】wāiqū (動) distort; misrepresent: ～別人原來的意圖 misrepresent sb.'s original intentions

【歪歪扭扭】wāiwāi niǔniǔ (形) askew; crooked: ～的字 sloppy handwriting

【歪風邪氣】wāi fēng xié qì 〈成〉 unhealthy social trends

【歪斜】wāixié (形) askew; slanting; crooked

歲 suì Ⅰ (名) year: 去～ last year Ⅱ (量) years of age: 百～老人 centenarian

【歲月】suìyuè（名）years; time: 隨著～的流逝 with the passage of time

【歲末】suìmò（名）end of the year

【歲數】suìshu（名）〈口〉age; years (of age): 上了～的人 person who is getting on in years; person of advanced age

歷 I（動）go through; experience: ～險 undergo a dangerous experience II（副）all over; one by one: ～覽名山大川 visit all celebrated mountains and mighty rivers

【歷代】lìdài（名）past dynasties (ages)

【歷史】lìshǐ（名）history: ～學家 historian

【歷史唯物主義】lìshǐ wéiwù zhǔyì（名）historical materialism

【歷次】lìcì（形）all previous (occasions)

【歷任】lìrèn I（動）serve successively as II（形）successive: ～外長 all the previous foreign ministers

【歷年】lìnián（副）over the years

【歷屆】lìjiè（形）all previous; successive: ～內閣 all the previous cabinets

【歷來】lìlái（副）always; all along

【歷時】lìshí（動）last (a period of time): ～三天的騷亂 the riot that lasted three days

【歷程】lìchéng（名）course: 人生的～ life's journey

【歷歷】lìlì（副）clearly; vividly

【歷歷可數】lìlì kě shǔ〈成〉can be clearly noticed

【歷歷在目】lìlì zài mù〈成〉be still fresh in one's mind; it seems as if everything were happening right before one's eyes

歸 guī I（動）❶ return; go back to ❷ converge; come together ❸ be placed (in sb.'s charge): 這個系～他管 He is in charge of the department. II（名）(Guī) a surname

【歸心似箭】guī xīn sì jiàn〈成〉be seized with a desire to return home promptly; be anxious to return

【歸功】guīgōng（動）be attributed to

【歸於】guīyú（動）❶［used with abstract nouns］belong to ❷ result in; end in

【歸併】guībìng（動）merge into; be incorporated into

【歸咎】guījiù（動）put the blame on; lay the blame on sb.'s door

【歸案】guī'àn（動）bring to book; bring to justice

【歸納】guīnà（動）induce; conclude; summarize: ～法 induction

【歸途】guītú（名）way home; return journey

【歸根結底】guī gēn jié dǐ〈成〉in the final analysis

【歸宿】guīsù（名）ending; destination: 人生的～ the destination of one's life's journey

【歸結】guījié I（動）sum up II（名）end

【歸順】guīshùn（動）give allegiance to

【歸罪】guīzuì（動）put the blame on sb.

【歸僑】guīqiáo（名）returned overseas Chinese

【歸還】guīhuán（動）return; give back

【歸檔】guīdàng（動）place on file

【歸屬】guīshǔ（動）belong to: 無所

~ belong nowhere

【歸攏】guīlǒng（動）put together

歹 部

歹 dǎi（形）bad; evil; vicious: 爲非作~ do evil of all kinds

【歹人】dǎirén（名）evildoer

死 sǐ Ⅰ（動）die: ~於肺炎 die of pneumonia Ⅱ（形）❶ dead: ~屍 dead body; corpse ❷ desperate: ~守 put up a stubborn resistance ❸ deadly; irreconcilable: ~對頭 implacable adversary ❹ stiff; rigid ❺ impassable Ⅲ（副）❶ utterly; extremely: 高興~了 extremely delighted / 他氣得半~。He was overcome with rage. ❷ to the last: ~抱着舊觀點不放 cling tenaciously to outmoded views Ⅳ（名）death

【死力】sǐlì（名）all one's strength: 出~ with all one's strength; for all one's worth

【死氣氛】sǐqìqi（名）sheer strength; brute force: 靠~打不開,得用巧勁。You can't open it by sheer strength, you have to have the knack.

【死亡】sǐwáng（名）death; doom: ~人數 fatalities

【死水】sǐshuǐ（名）stagnant water: 一潭~ a pool of stagnant water; (of atmosphere or condition) lifelessness; dullness

【死心】sǐxīn（名）abandon one's hope or idea: 不到黃河不~ refuse to give up until all hope is gone

【死心眼兒】sǐxīnyǎnr Ⅰ（形）obsti-

nate Ⅱ（名）person having a one-track mind

【死心塌地】sǐ xīn tā dì〈成〉be dead set on

【死不瞑目】sǐ bù míng mù〈成〉will not close one's eyes if one dies; will turn in one's grave

【死去活來】sǐ qù huó lái〈成〉half dead; be mad with grief: 被打得~ be brutally beaten

【死皮賴臉】sǐ pí lài liǎn〈成〉brazen-faced and unreasonable

【死刑】sǐxíng（名）〈法〉death sentence; capital punishment

【死扣兒】sǐkòur（死結 sǐjié）（名）fast knot

【死板】sǐbǎn（形）rigid; inflexible; mechanical

【死命】sǐmìng（副）desperately

【死者】sǐzhě（名）the deceased

【死活】sǐhuó Ⅰ（名）[used in negative sentences] life or death: 不管別人~ do not care what would befall others Ⅱ（副）〈口〉(not) for all the world: ~不答應 would not consent to anything

【死勁兒】sǐjìnr（副）〈口〉with all one's strength: ~追 be in hot pursuit of

【死鬼】sǐguǐ（名）[often used in cursing or joking] devil; you devil

【死氣沉沉】sǐ qì chén chén〈成〉spiritless; dull

【死記硬背】sǐ jì yìng bèi〈成〉mechanical memorizing; learn by rote

【死硬】sǐyìng（形）❶ inflexible; rigid ❷ obstinate: ~分子 diehard

【死傷】sǐshāng（名）casualities

【死罪】sǐzuì（名）capital offence

【死路】sǐlù（名）❶ dead end ❷ fatal road: 一條~ a road to ruin

【死脑筋】sǐnǎojīn（名）one-track mind

【死衚衕】sǐhútòng（名）blind alley; cul-de-sac

【死敌】sǐdí（名）sworn enemy

【死缓】sǐhuǎn（名）〈法〉（short for 死刑缓刑 sǐxíng huǎnxíng）death sentence with a two-year reprieve and forced labour

【死难】sǐnàn（动）❶ die in an accident: ～者 victim (of an accident or disaster) ❷ die for a revolutionary cause

【死党】sǐdǎng（名）diehard followers

【死读书】sǐ dúshū（动）read without understanding

殁 mò（动）die

殂 cú（动）die

殃 yāng Ⅰ（名）disaster; catastrophe: 使人们遭 ～ bring disaster to the people Ⅱ（动）bring calamity to

殆 dài Ⅰ（名）danger Ⅱ（副）almost; nearly: ～ 不可得 seldom available

殊 shū Ⅰ（形）❶ different; divergent: 複印件與原本無～。The photocopy looks exactly the same as the original text. ❷ special; outstanding; peculiar: 特 ～ 情况 an exceptional case Ⅱ（副）very; extremely: ～ 难从命 find it very difficult to comply with the request

【殊不知】shūbùzhī（动）little imagine: 你以爲是事實，～ 其中大有文章。You think it is a fact, but there is a lot more to it than you can think of.

【殊死】shūsǐ（形）desperate; last-ditch: 进行 ～ 的 斗争 carry on a life-and-death struggle

【殊途同归】shū tú tóng guī（成）reach the same destination via different routes; achieve the same goal, though in different ways; all roads lead to Rome

殉 xùn（动）sacrifice one's life for

【殉国】xùnguó（动）die for one's country

【殉葬】xùnzàng（动）be buried alive with a dead person: ～品 burial object

【殉职】xùnzhí（动）die at one's post

【殉难】xùnnàn（动）die a martyr

殖 zhí（动）breed; multiply

【殖民主义】zhímín zhǔyì（名）colonialism

【殖民地】zhímíndì（名）colony

残 cán Ⅰ（形）❶ incomplete; deficient: ～本 incomplete text ❷ remnant: ～月 waning moon ❸ savage; ferocious: 凶～暴虐 brutal and savage Ⅱ（动）destroy; injure: 摧 ～身 体 ruin one's health; undermine one's constitution

【残存】cáncún（形）remnant

【残局】cánjú（名）❶ closing phase of a game or chess ❷ messy situation that emerges after defeat, military or otherwise: 收拾 ～ pick up the pieces

【残忍】cánrěn（形）cruel; brutal

【残兵败将】cán bīng bài jiàng（成）remnants of a defeated army

【残迹】cánjī（名）relics; remains; vestiges

【殘品】cánpǐn（名）defective goods

【殘害】cánhài（動）persecute; kill

【殘疾】cánjí（名）deformity: ～人 the handicapped; the disabled

【殘缺】cánquē（形）fragmentary; incomplete

【殘殺】cánshā（動）slaughter; kill in cold blood

【殘酷】cánkù（形）cruel; ruthless

【殘廢】cánfèi Ⅰ（形）disabled: ～軍人 disabled soldier Ⅱ（名）disabled person; handicapped person

【殘餘】cányú（名）remnants; survivals

【殘暴】cánbào（形）ruthless; ferocious

【殘骸】cánhái（名）wreckage

【殘羹剩飯】cán gēng shèng fàn〈成〉leftovers; crumbs from the table

殛 jí（動）kill: 遭雷～ be struck dead by lightning

殞 yǔn（動）die; perish

【殞命】yǔnmìng（動）〈書〉lose one's life; be killed

殫 dān（動）use up; exhaust: ～精竭慮 rack one's brains

殓 liàn（動）place a body in a coffin

殯 bìn（動）❶ lay a coffin in a memorial hall ❷ carry it to the grave or crematory

【殯車】bìnchē（名）hearse

【殯葬】bìnzàng（動）funeral and burial; interment

【殯儀館】bìnyíguǎn（名）the undertaker's; funeral parlour

殲 jiān（動）(in military operations) annihilate; wipe out: ～敵無數

wipe out countless enemy troops

【殲滅】jiānmiè（動）annihilate; destroy

【殲滅戰】jiānmièzhàn（名）battle of annihilation; war of annihilation

【殲擊機】jiānjījī（名）fighter plane

殳 部

段 duàn Ⅰ（名）❶ section; part ❷（Duàn）a surname Ⅱ（量）：一～時間 a period of time/ 一～文章 a paragraph of an essay

【段落】duànluò（名）❶ paragraph ❷ period; phase

殷 yīn Ⅰ（形）❶ ardent ❷ hospitable Ⅱ（名）（Yīn）a surname

【殷切】yīnqiè（形）earnest; eager: ～希望 eager hopes

【殷富人家】yīnfù rénjiā（名）well-off family

【殷勤】yīnqín（形）eagerly attentive; solicitous: 獻～ dance attendance on

【殷墟】Yīnxū（名）〈考古〉Yin Dynasty ruins

【殷實】yīnshí（形）well-off; rich

殺 shā Ⅰ（動）❶ kill; slay ❷ fight: ～出重圍 break through a tight encirclement ❸ weaken; reduce: ～～他的威風 deflate his arrogance ❹〈方〉cause a sharp stinging pain: 肥皂水～眼睛。Soapy water makes the eyes smart. ❺ express (resentment): 拿人～氣 vent one's spleen on others Ⅱ（副）extremely: 悶～ be bored stiff

【殺一儆百】shā yī jǐng bǎi〈成〉execute one man to give a warning to a hundred

【殺人】 shārén（動）kill a person; murder: ～不眨眼 murder in cold blood / ～越貨 murder sb. after robbing him

【殺身成仁】 shā shēn chéng rén〈成〉lay down one's life in a righteous cause

【殺風景】 shā fēngjǐng（動）spoil the fun; dampen one's enthusiasm

【殺害】 shāhài（動）kill; murder

【殺氣】 shāqì（名）air of fiendish ferocity

【殺菌】 shājūn（動）disinfect; sterilize

【殺傷】 shāshāng（動）inflict casualties on

【殺戮】 shālù（動）slaughter; massacre

【殺頭】 shātóu（動）behead; execute

【殺蟲劑】 shāchóngjì（名）insecticide; pesticide

【殺雞取卵】 shā jī qǔ luǎn〈成〉kill the goose that lays golden eggs; sacrifice long-range interests for transient needs

殼 ké（名）shell: 花生～兒 peanut shell
see also qiào

殼 qiào（名）shell; crust: 地～ the earth's crust
see also ké

殿 diàn I（名）hall; palace; temple II（副）at the rear

【殿下】 diànxià（名）Your Highness; His (Her) Highness

【殿後】 diànhòu（動）bring up the rear

毀 huǐ（動）❶ destroy; damage; ruin ❷ slander; calumniate

【毀滅】 huǐmiè（動）destory; exterminate

【毀損】 huǐsǔn（動）impair; damage; injure

【毀謗】 huǐbàng（動）slander; libel; vilify

【毀壞】 huǐhuài（動）damage; ruin

【毀譽】 huǐyù（名）praise or censure: ～參半 praise mixed with censure

毅 yì（形）resolute; steadfast

【毅力】 yìlì（名）willpower; will

【毅然】 yìrán（副）firmly; resolutely

毆 ōu（動）beat; hit

【毆打】 ōudǎ（動）beat up; hit

毋　部

毋 wú（副）〈書〉[used to introduce a prohibition or admonition]no; not: ～因小失大. Don't risk things of importance for the sake of trifles.

【毋庸】 wúyōng（動）need not: ～置疑 no doubt; undoubtedly

【毋寧】 wúníng（副）（not so much...）as; rather ...(than): 與其說他是學者，～說他是政客. He is more a politician than a scholar.

母 mǔ I（名）mother II（形）female: ～兔 doe

【母牛】 mǔniú（名）cow

【母老虎】 mǔlǎohǔ（名）❶ tigress ❷ vixen; virago

【母系】 mǔxì（形）maternal; matriarchal

【母性】mǔxìng （名） motherhood; maternity

【母校】mǔxiào （名） Alma Mater; one's old school

【母愛】mǔ'ài （名）maternal love

【母語】mǔyǔ （名）❶ mother tongue ❷ parent language

【母親】mǔqīn （名）mother

【母鷄】mǔjī （名）hen

每 měi I （形） every; each: 一兩星期一次 once every other week/ 一公斤十元 ten yuan a kilo II （副）❶ every time: 他一回進城都要逛逛商店。 She goes window-shopping every time she is in town. ❷ every

【每每】měiměi （副） often: 他一獨坐無言, 若有所思。 He often sits alone silent as if deep in thought.

【每况愈下】měi kuàng yù xià 〈成〉 get worse and worse; steadily worsen; deteriorate

【每逢】měiféng （副）on every occasion

【每當】měidāng （連）whenever

毒 dú I （名）❶ poison ❷ narcotics: 吸一者 drug addict ❸ pernicious influence II （動） poison III （形） heartless; cruel

【毒手】dúshǒu （名） deadly means; murder: 下一 resort to deadly means

【毒化】dúhuà （動） exert a harmful influence upon people; poison （one's body or mind）

【毒計】dújì （名） venomous scheme or design

【毒草】dúcǎo （名）poisonous weeds

【毒害】dúhài I （動）poison; corrupt II （名）venom

【毒氣】dúqì （名）poison gas

【毒蛇】dúshé （名）poisonous snake

【毒辣】dúlà （形）ruthless

【毒藥】dúyào （名）poison

比 部

比 bǐ I （動）❶ compare; draw a parallel between: 甲與乙相一 compare A with B ❷ emulate; compete with: 一一一 make a comparison; compete （with） ❸ liken to: 把松柏一作高風亮節 liken the pine and cypress to moral integrity to do sth. the same way as: 將心一心 think as others would think in similar circumstances ❺ make gestures; gesticulate ❻ copy; model after II （介）❶ ［used to indicate difference in degree, manner, etc.］than: 長江一黃河長。 The Yangtze River is longer than the Yellow River. ❷ as...as; （just） like: 壽一南山。 May you live as long as Mt. Nanshan. （birthday greeting） ❸ to （in a score）: 二一一我們贏了。 （The score is） 2 to 1 in our favour. III （名） ratio; proportion: 反（正）一 inverse （direct） ratio

【比上不足,比下有餘】bǐ shàng bù zú, bǐ xià yǒu yú 〈成〉 inferior to the advanced but superior to the laggards; middling; tolerable

【比方】bǐfāng I （名）analogy: 打個一 draw an analogy II （副）for instance: 一說 suppose; let's say

【比分】bǐfēn （名）〈體〉 score: 一接近 a close game

【比不上】bǐ bu shàng （動） cannot compare with; be inferior to

【比如】bǐrú（副）for instance; such as: ～說 say; let's say

【比利時】Bǐlìshí（名）Belgium: ～人 Belgian

【比例】bǐlì（名）❶ proportion; ratio: ～失調 imbalance ❷ scale: 百萬分之一一的地圖 map on a scale of 1:1,000,000

【比重】bǐzhòng（名）❶〈物〉specific gravity ❷ proportion: 旅遊業在國民經濟中的～ the percentage of the tourist industry in the national economy

【比率】bǐlǜ（名）ratio; rate

【比着】bǐzhe（動）copy; model after: ～葫蘆畫瓢 copy mechanically

【比得上】bǐ de shàng（動）compare favourably with

【比畫】bǐhua（動）gesticulate; make gestures; use sign language: 用手～大小 show the size by gestures

【比喻】bǐyù I（名）parable; metaphor; allegory: 用～的方法 by（means of）analogy II（動）liken to: 以河流～生命。Life is compared to a river.

【比照】bǐzhào I（動）❶ copy; model on ❷ contrast II（介）in the light of; with reference to

【比較】bǐjiào I（動）compare; contrast: 兩相～ compare the two II（名）comparison III（副）relatively; quite; fairly: 漢語講得～好 speak Chinese fairly well IV（形）comparative: ～文學 comparative literature V（介）[used to indicate difference in manner, degree, etc.]: ～過去有所改進 show some improvement as compared with the past

【比價】bǐjià（名）parity（rate）; rate

of exchange: 美元與日元的～ the exchange rate of the American dollar for the Japanese yen

【比鄰】bǐlín I（形）（close）neighbour: 天涯若～。（for bosom friends living far apart）The end of the earth seems as close as one's neighbourhood. II（動）adjoin; be close（next）to III（形）near; next to

【比擬】bǐnǐ I（名）analogy; comparison; parallel II（動）liken; compare; parallel: 無可～ cannot be compared

【比賽】bǐsài I（名）match; tournament; competition: ～場地 competition arena; ground; court II（動）compete（in a contest）; have a match（game, contest, etc.）: 同中國隊～ play against the Chinese team

毗 pí（動）adjoin; border on

【毗連】pílián（毗鄰 pílín）（動）border on; be adjacent to

毖 bì（動）caution: 懲前～後 avoid future errors by learning from past ones

毛 部

毛 máo I（名）❶ hair; feather ❷ wool: 純羊～ pure wool / 合成～ synthetic wool ❸ mildew: mould ❹ mao（one-tenth of a yuan RMB）❺（Máo）a surname II（形）❶ little; very young: ～丫頭 a chit of a girl ❷ semifinished ❸ careless; imprudent: ～手～腳 careless; haphazardly ❹ panicky; frightened:

那部電影使他心裏發~。That film strikes terror into his heart. ❺ gross Ⅲ (動) (of currency) depreciate; become less in value: 英鎊 ~了。The pound is depreciating in value.

【毛巾】máojīn (名) towel

【毛巾被】máojīnbèi (名) towelling coverlet

【毛孔】máokǒng (名) 〈生理〉pore (of the skin)

【毛毛雨】máomáoyǔ (名) drizzle

【毛布】máobù (名) coarse cotton cloth

【毛皮】máopí (名) fur; pelt

【毛竹】máozhú (名) mao bamboo

【毛衣】máoyī (名) woollen sweater; sweater

【毛衣針】máoyīzhēn (名) knitting needle

【毛收入】máoshōurù (名) gross income

【毛豆】máodòu (名) green soya bean

【毛里求斯】Máolǐqiúsī (名) Mauritius: ~人 Mauritian

【毛里塔尼亞】Máolǐtǎníyà (名) Mauritania: ~人 Mauritanian

【毛利】máolì (名) gross profit

【毛坯】máopī (名) semifinished product

【毛重】máozhòng (名) gross weight

【毛孩子】máoháizi (名) little child; mere child

【毛玻璃】máobōlí (名) frosted glass

【毛病】máobìng (名) ❶ trouble; complaint: 洗衣機出~了。The washing machine doesn't work. ❷ illness ❸ shortcoming; flaw: 他最大的~是高傲自大。His failing is arrogance.

【毛紡】máofǎng (名) wool spinning: ~廠 woollen mill

【毛料】máoliào (名) woollen cloth; woollen material

【毛茸茸】máoróngróng (形) hairy; downy: ~的小兔子 downy little rabbit

【毛骨悚然】máo gǔ sǒng rán 〈成〉 shudder with fear; make one's flesh creep

【毛票】máopiào (名) 〈口〉 banknotes of one, two or five jiao denominations; one-jiao, two-jiao, or five-jiao note

【毛細血管】máoxì xuèguǎn (名) 〈生理〉blood capillary

【毛筆】máobǐ (名) writing brush

【毛毯】máotǎn (名) woollen blanket

【毛遂自薦】máo suì zì jiàn 〈成〉recommend oneself for a position; offer one's services

【毛線】máoxiàn (名) knitting wool; woollen yarn

【毛髮】máofà (名) hair

【毛蝦】máoxiā (名) shrimp

【毛糙】máocào (形) careless; crude

【毛澤東思想】Máo Zédōng sīxiǎng (名) Mao Zedong Thought

【毛氈】máozhān (名) felt

【毛蟲】máochóng (毛毛蟲 máomáochóng) (名) caterpillar

【毛織品】máozhīpǐn (名) ❶ woollen fabric; woollen goods ❷ woollen knitwear

【毛藍】máolán (名) darkish blue

【毛難族】Máonánzú (名) the Maonan nationality

【毛躁】máozao (形) ❶ hot-headed; fiery-tempered ❷ careless

【毛驢】máolǘ (名) donkey

毫 háo I (名) ❶ fine long hair ❷ writing bruth II (形) milli-: ～米 millimetre (mm) III (副) [used in the negative] in the least; at all: ～ 不奇怪 not at all surprising / ～無 道理 absolutely groundless

【毫毛】háomáo (名) hair on the human or animal body: 不能损伤一根 ～ cannot do him the least harm

【毫釐】háolí (名) slightest degree: 失之～, 謬以千里。The slightest error can lead one miles away in the wrong direction.

毯 tǎn (名) rug; blanket: 壁 ～ tapestry

【毯子】tǎnzi (名) blanket

毽 jiàn (名) shuttlecock

【毽子】jiànzi (名) shuttlecock: 踢 ～ play the shuttlecock

氂 máo (名)

【氂牛】máoniú (名) yak

氅 chǎng (名) overcoat: 大 ～ overcoat

氈 zhān (名) felt: ～鞋 felt shoe

【氈子】zhānzi (名) felt rug; felt blanket

氏 部

氏 shì (名) ❶ family name: 姓 ～ surname /無名 ～ anonym ❷ née: 張王 ～ Mrs. Zhang née Wang ❸ (form of address for a famous person, es. a specialist) 華 ～溫度 計 Fahrenheit thermometer

【氏族】shìzú (名) clan: ～社會 clan society

民 mín I (名) the people; civilian: 平 ～ common people; commoner II [used as a suffix] persons pursuing a certain occupation: 農 ～ farmer; peasant III (形) folk: ～ 歌 folk song

【民工】míngōng (名) labourer (engaged in public works)

【民心】mínxīn (名) feeling of the people; popular support; public sentiment: 得 (失) ～ gain (lose) the support of the people

【民不聊生】mín bù liáo shēng 〈成〉 the people find it difficult to survive; life for the people is intolerable

【民生】mínshēng (名) people's livelihood

【民用】mínyòng (形) for civil use; civil

【民主】mínzhǔ I (名) democracy II (形) democratic

【民主黨派】mínzhǔ dǎngpài (名) (of Chinese politics) democratic parties

【民兵】mínbīng (名) militia; militiaman

【民法】mínfǎ (名) civil law

【民房】mínfáng (名) private house; house owned by a citizen

【民事】mínshì (形) civil: ～訴訟法 civil procedure law

【民俗】mínsú (名) folk custom: ～ 學 folklore

【民政】mínzhèng (名) civil administration

【民航】mínháng (名) civil aviation: 中國～ CAAC (General Administra-

【民航機】mínhángjī (名) airliner

【民脂民膏】mín zhī mín gāo (名) people's wealth obtained by sweat and blood

【民情】mínqíng (名) ❶ general condition of the people ❷ public sentiment; popular mood

【民族】mínzú (名) nation; nationality; ethnic group

【民族風味菜】mínzú fēngwèicài (名) ethnic cuisine

【民族學】mínzúxué (名) ethnology

【民衆】mínzhòng (名) the people; the masses; the populace; the public

【民間】mínjiān (形) ❶ folk; among the people: 他的書在～很流行。His books are highly popular. ❷ non-governmental: ～貿易 people-to-people trade

【民間工藝品】mínjiān gōngyìpǐn (名) folk arts and crafts

【民間文學】mínjiān wénxué (名) folk literature

【民間故事】mínjiān gùshì (名) folk tale; folk story

【民間傳說】mínjiān chuánshuō (名) folklore

【民間藝術】mínjiān yìshù (名) folk art

【民賊】mínzéi (名) traitor to the people

【民意】mínyì (名) will of the people; public opinion

【民意測驗】mínyì cèyàn (名) public opinion poll

【民樂】mínyuè (名) traditional instrumental music

【民辦】mínbàn (形) run by the community; non-governmental: ～企業 enterprise run by the community

【民憤】mínfèn (名) public indignation; enmity of the people

【民謠】mínyáo (名) folk rhyme; ballad

【民警】mínjǐng (名) people's police; police; policeman

【民權】mínquán (名) civil rights; civil liberties

气 部

氖 nǎi (名) 〈化〉 neon (Ne)

氙 xiān (名) 〈化〉 xenon (Xe)

氛 fēn (名) atmosphere

氨 ān (名) ammonia

【氨水】ānshuǐ (名) ammonia water; aqua ammoniae

【氨氣】ānqì (名) ammonia

【氨基酸】ānjīsuān (名) amino acid

氧 yǎng (名) 〈化〉 oxygen (O)

【氧化】yǎnghuà (動) oxidize

【氧氣】yǎngqì (名) oxygen

氣 qì I (名) ❶ gas: 廢～ waste gas ❷ air; atmosphere: ～溫 air temperature ❸ breath: 倒抽一口～ catch one's breath ❹ weather: 多麼好的天～! What a nice day! ❺ airs; manner: 他書生～十足。He is a typical naive intellectual. ❻ spirit; morale: 勇～ courage ❼ smell; odour: 魚腥～ a fishy smell II (動) ❶ get angry; enrage: ～得說不出話來 be choked with anger ❷ bully: 受～ be bullied

【氣力】qìlì (名) ❶ strength ❷ effort: 不費什麼～ require little effort; effortlessly

【氣孔】qìkǒng (名) air vent

【氣功】qìgōng (名) qigong (a traditional Chinese system of deep breathing exercises)

【氣色】qìsè (名) complexion

【氣氛】qìfēn (名) atmosphere: 節日～ holiday atmosphere

【氣泡】qìpào (名) air buddle; bubble

【氣味】qìwèi (名) smell; flavour

【氣味相投】qì wèi xiāng tóu 〈成〉 be of similar taste; be birds of a feather

【氣昂昂】qì'áng'áng (形) in high spirits

【氣呼呼】qìhūhū (形) in a huff

【氣度】qìdù (名) tolerance; generosity of spirit

【氣派】qìpài (名) manner; bearing

【氣泵】qìbèng (名)〈機〉air pump

【氣急敗壞】qì jí bài huài 〈成〉flurried and exasperated

【氣候】qìhòu (名) climate: ～學 climatology

【氣流】qìliú (名) air current; jet stream

【氣息】qìxī (名) ❶ breath ❷ flavour: 時代～ the spirit of the times

【氣息奄奄】qì xī yǎn yǎn 〈成〉gasp one's last; on one's last legs

【氣焊】qìhàn (名)〈機〉gas welding

【氣球】qìqiú (名) balloon

【氣象】qìxiàng (名) ❶ atmospheric phenomena ❷ meteorology ❸ look; scene: 一一新 take on a new look

【氣象雷達】qìxiàng léidá (名) weather radar

【氣象預報】qìxiàng yùbào (名) weather forecast

【氣象萬千】qì xiàng wàn qiān 〈成〉(of scenes or things) present a spectrum of magnificent sights

【氣象臺】qìxiàngtái (名) meteorological observatory

【氣喘】qìchuǎn Ⅰ(名)〈醫〉asthma Ⅱ(動) pant: ～吁吁地吐出幾個字 pant out a few words

【氣窗】qìchuāng (名) transom window; fanlight

【氣惱】qìnǎo (形) annoyed; angry

【氣焰】qìyàn (名) arrogance; swagger: ～囂張 overweening arrogance

【氣短】qìduǎn (動) ❶ be out of breath ❷ lose heart

【氣量】qìliàng (名) tolerance; forbearance

【氣筒】qìtǒng (名) inflator; bicycle pump

【氣概】qìgài (名) mettle; spirit

【氣節】qìjié (名) moral integrity

【氣勢】qìshì (名) grandeur; momentum

【氣勢洶洶】qì shì xiōng xiōng 〈成〉in a threatening manner

【氣勢磅礴】qì shì páng bó 〈成〉in a grand and powerful manner; magnificent

【氣槍】qìqiāng (名) air gun

【氣墊】qìdiàn (名) air cushion

【氣墊船】qìdiànchuán (名) hovercraft

【氣管】qìguǎn (名) windpipe; trachea

【氣管炎】qìguǎnyán (名) tracheitis

【氣餒】qìněi (動) feel disheartened; lose heart

【氣魄】qìpò (名) ❶ daring; courage and breadth of vision ❷ grandeur; magnificence

【氫質】qìzhì (名) ❶ temperament; disposition ❷ inborn qualities

【氫衝衝】qìchōngchōng (形) furious; exasperated

【氫錘】qìchuí (名)〈機〉pneumatic hammer

【氫頭上】qìtóushang (副) in a fit of anger

【氫憤】qìfèn (形) angry; indignant

【氫壓】qìyā (名)〈氣〉atmospheric pressure

【氫體】qìtǐ (名) gas

氫 qīng (名)〈化〉hydrogen (H)

【氫氣】qīngqì (名) hydrogen

【氫彈】qīngdàn (名) hydrogen bomb

氮 dàn (名)〈化〉nitrogen (N)

【氮肥】dànféi (名) nitrogenous fertilizer

氰 qíng (名)〈化〉cyanogen; dicyanogen

【氰化物】qínghuàwù (名) cyanide

【氰酸】qíngsuān (名) cyanic acid

氬 yà (名)〈化〉argon (Ar)

氯 lǜ (名)〈化〉chlorine (Cl)

【氯綸】lǜlún (名)〈紡〉polyvinyl chloride fibre

水 部

水 shuǐ (名) ❶ water ❷ river: 漢 ~ the Han River ❸ general term for all waters: ~陸兩棲 amphibious ❹ liquid; juice: 染髮~ hair dye ❺ (Shuǐ) a surname

【水力】shuǐlì (名) hydraulic power

【水土】shuǐtǔ (名) ❶ water and soil: ~保持 water and soil conservation ❷ climate and natural environment: 不服~ not be acclimatized

【水上旅館】shuǐshàng lǚguǎn (名) floating hotel; boatel

【水上運動】shuǐshàng yùndòng (名) aquatic sports

【水分】shuǐfèn (名) ❶ moisture ❷ exaggeration: 上報費用中~很大。 The reported cost is much inflated.

【水手】shuǐshǒu (名) seaman; sailor

【水文】shuǐwén (名) hydrology

【水井】shuǐjǐng (名) (water) well

【水牛】shuǐniú (名) (water) buffalo

【水仙】shuǐxiān (名)〈植〉narcissus; daffodil

【水田】shuǐtián (名) paddy field

【水平】shuǐpíng Ⅰ (名) level (in a graded scale of values); standard: 業務~ vocational level Ⅱ (形) horizontal

【水印】shuǐyìn (名) ❶〈美術〉watercolour block printing ❷ watermark

【水池】shuǐchí (水池子 shuǐchízi) (名) pond; cistern

【水利】shuǐlì (名) ❶ water conservancy ❷ irrigation works; water conservancy facilities

【水坑】shuǐkēng (名) puddle; pool

【水兵】shuǐbīng (名) (naval) sailor; blue jacket

【水車】shuǐchē (名) water-wheel

【水位】shuǐwèi (名) water level: 警戒~ warning water level; warning stage

【水災】shuǐzāi (名) flood

【水表】shuǐbiǎo (名) water meter

【水泡】shuǐpào (名) ❶ bubble ❷

（水疱 shuǐpào）blister

【水性】shuǐxìng（名） ability in swimming; swimming skill: 他～好。He is a good swimmer.

【水果】shuǐguǒ（名）fruit: ～冰淇淋 sundae

【水泥】shuǐní（名）cement

【水洩不通】shuǐ xiè bú tōng〈成〉be so crowded that no one can get through

【水垢】shuǐgòu（水碱 shuǐjiǎn）（名）incrustation; scale

【水泵】shuǐbèng（名）water pump

【水星】shuǐxīng（名）〈天〉Mercury

【水流】shuǐliú（名）❶ general term for rivers, streams, etc. ❷（water）flow

【水库】shuǐkù（名）reservoir

【水彩】shuǐcǎi（名）water-colour

【水产】shuǐchǎn（名）aquatic product

【水球】shuǐqiú（名）water polo

【水桶】shuǐtǒng（名）bucket; pail

【水族】shuǐzú（名）aquatic animals: ～馆 aquarium

【水深火热】shuǐ shēn huǒ rè〈成〉abyss of misery; in deep water

【水壶】shuǐhú（名）kettle

【水痘】shuǐdòu（名）chicken pox

【水道】shuǐdào（名）❶ water course ❷ waterway; water route

【水晶】shuǐjīng（名）crystal

【水渠】shuǐqú（名）canal; ditch

【水乡】shuǐxiāng（名）land of rivers and lakes

【水运】shuǐyùn（名）water transport

【水禽】shuǐqín（名）aquatic birds; waterfowl

【水塔】shuǐtǎ（名）water tower

【水塘】shuǐtáng（名）（natural）pond

【水溝】shuǐgōn（名）ditch; gutter

【水路】shuǐlù（名）water route: 走～（travel）by water

【水源】shuǐyuán（名）❶ water-head ❷ source of water

【水閘】shuǐzhá（名） water gate; sluice

【水準】shuǐzhǔn（名）level; standard

【水暖工】shuǐnuǎngōng（名）plumber

【水落石出】shuǐ luò shí chū〈成〉the rocks emerge when the water subsides; doubts will disappear when facts are known; the truth will come out

【水電站】shuǐdiànzhàn（名）（short for 水力發電站 shuǐlì fādiànzhàn）hydraulic power station

【水蒸汽】shuǐzhēngqì（名） steam; water vapour

【水管】shuǐguǎn（名） water-pipe: 污～ sewage pipe

【水餃】shuǐjiǎo（名）jiaozi; dumpling

【水榭】shuǐxiè（名）waterside pavilion

【水銀】shuǐyín（名）〈化〉mercury; quicksilver

【水蜜桃】shuǐmìtáo（名） honey peach

【水稻】shuǐdào（名）paddy; rice: ～田 paddy field

【水箱】shuǐxiāng（名）water tank

【水質】shuǐzhì（名）quality of water

【水澆地】shuǐjiāodì（名） irrigated land

【水墨畫】shuǐmòhuà（名）〈美術〉ink and wash（painting）

【水龍頭】shuǐlóngtóu（名）（water）tap; faucet: 擰開（關上）～ turn on (off) the tap

【水壓】 shuǐyā (名) hydraulic pressure; water pressure

【水翼船】 shuǐyìchuán (名) hydrofoil

【水獺】 shuǐtǎ (名) otter

【水壩】 shuǐbà (名) dam

永 yǒng (副) forever; always; eternally: ～誌不忘 will always bear in mind

【永久】 yǒngjiǔ (形) permanent; everlasting

【永生】 yǒngshēng Ⅰ (名)〈宗〉 eternal life Ⅱ (形) immortal

【永別】 yǒngbié (名) part forever

【永恒】 yǒnghéng (形) eternal; everlasting

【永垂不朽】 yǒng chuí bù xiǔ〈成〉 live forever in the hearts of the people: 人民英雄～。Eternal glory to the people's heroes.

【永訣】 yǒngjué (動) be separated forever

【永遠】 yǒngyuǎn (副) always; forever

汁 zhī (名) juice: 蘋果～ apple juice

求 qiú Ⅰ (動) ❶ ask; request; implore: ～某人寬恕 ask sb.'s pardon ❷ strive for; try to obtain: 實事求是 seek truth from facts Ⅱ (名) demand: 供過於～。Supply exceeds demand.

【求之不得】 qiú zhī bù dé〈成〉 be a godsend: ～的機會 a rare golden opportunity

【求全】 qiúquán (動) ❶ demand perfection ❷ hope that sth. will turn out to be a complete success

【求全責備】 qiú quán zé bèi〈成〉 blame others for failing to be perfect; nitpick

【求同存異】 qiú tóng cún yì〈成〉 seek common ground and put aside differences

【求見】 qiújiàn (動) seek an audience with sb.; ask for an interview

【求助】 qiúzhù (動) appeal to sb. for assistance

【求和】 qiúhé (動) ❶ sue for peace ❷ (of the losing side) strive for a draw

【求知】 qiúzhī (動) be in quest of knowledge: ～慾 desire for knowledge

【求得】 qiúdé (動) obtain; secure

【求婚】 qiúhūn (動) propose marriage (to sb.); propose

【求教】 qiújiào (動) seek advice; consult

【求救】 qiújiù (動) cry for help; call out for rescue

【求情】 qiúqíng (動) ask a favour; ask sb. to put in a good word

【求援】 qiúyuán (動) ask for help

【求愛】 qiú'ài (動) woo; court

【求學】 qiúxué (動) ❶ attend school ❷ pursue one's studies

【求職】 qiúzhí (動) hunt for a job; seek employment

【求饒】 qiúráo (動) beg for mercy

尔 cuān (動) quick-boil: ～丸子 quick-boiled meatballs with soup

汗 hàn (名) sweat; perspiration: 出冷～ break into a cold sweat

【汗毛】 hànmáo (名) fine hair on the human body

【汗衫】 hànshān (名) undershirt; T-shirt

【汗馬功勞】 hàn mǎ gōng láo〈成〉

meritorious services in war

【汗流浹背】hàn liú jiā bèi〈成〉
sweat all over

【汗腺】hànxiàn (名)〈生理〉sweat
gland

污 wū (形) ❶ dirty; foul ❷ corrupt: 貪官～吏 corrupt officials/ 貪
～犯 grafter; embezzler

【污水】wūshuǐ (名) foul water;
waste water; sewage

【污言穢語】wū yán huì yǔ (名) foul
language

【污泥】wūní (名) mud; sludge

【污垢】wūgòu (名) dirt; filth

【污染】wūrǎn Ⅰ (動) pollute; con-
taminate Ⅱ (名) pollution: 空氣
(水)～ air (water) pollution /精神
～ moral pollution

【污染物】wūrǎnwù (名) pollutant

【污辱】wūrǔ (動) ❶ insult; humiliate ❷ molest; assault

【污濁】wūzhuó (形) dirty; filthy:
～的水 muddy water

【污點】wūdiǎn (名) stain

【污穢】wūhuì (形) foul; filthy

江 jiāng (名) ❶ river ❷ the
Changjiang (Yangtze) River ❸
(Jiāng) a surname

【江山】jiāngshān (名) ❶ rivers and
mountains; land ❷ state; country;
state power: 半壁～ half the
country's territory

【江山易改, 本性難移】jiāng shān yì
gǎi, běn xìng nán yí〈成〉rivers and
mountains can be changed, but it is
hard to alter a person's character

【江西】Jiāngxī (名) Jiangxi (Province)

【江米】jiāngmǐ (名) glutinous rice

【江米酒】jiāngmǐjiǔ (名) fermented
glutinous rice

【江南】jiāngnán (名) ❶ area to the
south of the lower reaches of the
Yangtze, i. e., the southern parts of
Jiangsu and Anhui and the north of
Zhejiang ❷ regions south of the
Yangtze

【江湖】jiānghú (名) ❶ towns and
villages all over the country: 走～
travel from place to place performing acrobatics or selling fake tonics
and herbs / ～醫生 quack doctor ❷
strolling entertainer; quack doctor,
etc.

【江湖騙子】jiānghú piànzi (名)
mountebank; charlatan

【江輪】jiānglún (名) steamer for inland navigation

【江蘇】Jiāngsū (名) Jiangsu (Province)

汲 jí (動) draw (water): ～水於井
draw water from a well

【汲汲】jíjí (形) anxious: ～於富貴
crave wealth and power; go after
wealth and rank

【汲取】jíqǔ (動) draw: ～別國的經
驗 draw on the experience of other
countries

汛 xùn (名) flood: 春～ spring
flood

【汛期】xùnqī (名) flood season

汐 xī (名) nighttide

池 chí (名) ❶ pond; pool: ～鹽
lake salt ❷ pit; anything in the
shape of a pool: 硯～ inkstone ❸
(Chí) a surname

【池塘】chítáng (名) pond

汝 rǔ (代)〈書〉you

汞 gǒng (名)〈化〉mercury (Hg)

汯 hóng (名) deluge; big flood

【汯瀣一氣】hóng xiè yī qì〈成〉act in cahoots; birds of a feather flock together

沈 Shěn (名) a surname

沉 chén I (動) ❶ sink: 石～大海 like a stone dropped into the sea ❷ [used in an abstract sense] sink; keep down: ～下臉來 pull a long face ❸ be calm: ～不住氣 cannot keep calm II (形) ❶ deep: 陰～ cloudy; gloomy ❷ heavy: 心情～重 be in the doldrums; be laden with sorrow

【沉沉】chénchén (形) ❶ heavy: ～的穀穗 heavy ears of grain ❷ deep; dull: 死氣～ lifeless; stagnant

【沉沒】chénmò (動) sink

【沉住氣】chénzhùqì (動) be calm

【沉迷】chénmí (動) indulge in: ～於聲色之好 indulge in sensual pleasure

【沉思】chénsī (名) ponder; be deep in thought

【沉重】chénzhòng (形) ❶ heavy: ～的擔子 heavy burden ❷ serious: 病情～ be critically ill

【沉浮】chénfú (動) rise and fall

【沉浸】chénjìn (動) be immersed in

【沉冤】chényuān (名) long-standing gross injustice

【沉寂】chénjì I (形) quiet; still II (名) silence; stillness

【沉淪】chénlún (動) sink into depravity; degenerated; be degraded

【沉着】chénzhuó I (形) composed; calm II (副) calmly

【沉悶】chénmèn (形) ❶ (of weather, etc.) depressing; dull ❷ (of one's mood) depressed ❸ (of one's character) dull

【沉湎】chénmiǎn (動) indulge in: ～於酒色 be excessively fond of wine and women

【沉痛】chéntòng (形) ❶ very sad ❷ bitter: ～的教訓 painful lesson

【沉溺】chénnì (動) wallow in; indulge in

【沉睡】chénshuì (動) be sound asleep

【沉醉】chénzuì I (形) dead drunk II (動) be intoxicated: ～在節日的歡樂裏 be intoxicated by the joys of the festive occasion

【沉澱】chéndiàn I (動) precipitate II (名) sediment

【沉靜】chénjìng (形) ❶ quiet; calm ❷ (of one's character, mood or facial expression) calm; placid

【沉默】chénmò (形) ❶ quiet ❷ reticent: ～寡言的人 a man of few words

沁 qìn (動) seep; ooze

【沁人心脾】qìn rén xīn pí〈成〉refreshing to the mind

汪 wāng I (動) gather; accumulate: 眼裏～着淚水。One's eyes filled with tears. II (量) (of liquid) puddle: 路上一～～的水。There are puddles of water on the road. III (名) (Wāng) a surname IV (象) bark

【汪汪】wāngwāng I (形) tearful: 他們淚～地分別了。They parted in tears. II (象) bark; yelp: 聽見狗～地叫 hear dogs barking

【汪洋】wāngyáng (形) (of waters)

vast: ～大海 a boundless expanse of sea

沛 pèi (形) abundant; exuberant: 雨水充～ have plentiful rainfall

沏 qī (动) infuse: ～茶 make tea

沐 mù (动) wash one's hair

【沐浴】 mùyù (动) bathe; take a bath

【沐猴而冠】 mù hóu ér guàn 〈成〉 a worthless person in stately dress

汰 tài (动) eliminate; dismiss: 淘～赛 tournament

决 jué I (动) ❶ decide; resolve: 悬而未～的问题 an outstanding issue ❷ put to death; execute: 依法处～ be executed in accordance with the law ❸ (of dams, dykes, etc.) burst; break suddenly and violently II (副) [used before negative terms] definitely; absolutely: ～非小事 by no means a trifling matter

【决一雌雄】 jué yī cí xióng 〈成〉 fight to determine which side is the victor

【决口】 juékǒu I (动) (of dams, dykes, etc.) burst II (名) breach

【决不】 juébù (副) never; by no means: ～同意 can never agree to

【决心】 juéxīn I (动) be determined (to do sth.): 他～把试验进行下去。He is determined to carry on the experiment. II (名) determination; resolve: 下～ make up one's mind; be determined

【决定】 juédìng I (动) decide; resolve II (名) decision: 做～ make a decision

【决计】 juéjì I (动) decide; make up one's mind II (副) definitely; absolutely

lutely

【决斗】 juédòu I (名) ❶ duel ❷ decisive fight II (动) have a duel

【决裂】 juéliè (动) break with; break off relations with: 与传统观念～ break with conventional ideas

【决胜】 juéshèng (动) determine the victory of a battle

【决策】 juécè I (动) decide on a policy II (名) policy decision 做出重大～ make a major policy decision

【决意】 juéyì (动) make up one's mind

【决算】 juésuàn (名) final accounts (of revenue and expenditure)

【决战】 juézhàn (名) decisive battle (campaign): 决一死战 fight to the bitter end

【决赛】 juésài (名) 〈体〉 final: 半～ semi-final

【决议】 juéyì (名) decision; resolution: 通过～ pass (adopt) a resolution

沙 shā I (名) ❶ sand ❷ paste; mush: 澄～ sweetened bean paste ❸ (Shā) a surname II (形) (of voice) hoarse; husky

【沙丁鱼】 shādīngyú (名) sardine

【沙子】 shāzi (名) ❶ sand ❷ small grains; pellets

【沙文主义】 shāwén zhǔyì (名) chauvinism

【沙丘】 shāqiū (名) (sand) dune

【沙坑】 shākēng (名) 〈体〉 jumping pit

【沙洲】 shāzhōu (名) shoal; sandbar

【沙皇】 shāhuáng (名) tsar

【沙浴】 shāyù (名) sand-bath

【沙特阿拉伯】 Shātè Ālābó (名) Saudi Arabia: ～人 Saudi Arabian

【沙眼】shāyǎn（名）trachoma

【沙啞】shāyǎ（形）hoarse; husky: ~的嗓子 a husky voice

【沙袋】shādài（名）sandbag

【沙場】shāchǎng（名）battlefield: 戰死~ killed in action

【沙發】shāfā（名）sofa

【沙漠】shāmò（名）desert

【沙漏】shālòu（名）hourglass; sand filter

【沙龍】shālóng（名）salon

【沙鍋】shāguō（名）earthenware pot; casserole

【沙礫】shālì（名）grit

【沙瓤】shāráng（名）mushy watermelon pulp

【沙灘】shātān（名）sandy beach; beach

汩 gǔ

【汩汩】gǔgǔ（象）gurgle

沖 chōng（動）pour water on; rinse; develop; flush

【沖印】chōngyìn（動）〈攝〉develop and print

【沖刷】chōngshuā（動）wash away; sweep away

【沖垮】chōngkuǎ（動）wash away; smash: ~河堤 burst the embankment

【沖洗】chōngxǐ（動）❶ wash; rinse ❷〈攝〉develop (film)

【沖淡】chōngdàn（動）❶ dilute ❷ play down: ~事件的意義 play down the significance of the event

【沖劑】chōngjì（名）〈中藥〉instant herbal mixture

泛 fàn I（動）❶ float on the water ❷ be tinged with: 東方~白。The east is tinged with grey. ❸ flood;

overflow II（形）extensive: ~讀 extensive reading

【泛泛】fànfàn（形）general; superficial: 把文章一地讀了一遍 have roughly gone over the article

【泛指】fànzhǐ（動）not refer to anything specifically; speak in general terms

【泛濫】fànlàn（動）❶ overflow ❷ spread unchecked

汽 qì（名）steam; vapour

【汽化】qìhuà（名）〈物〉vaporization

【汽水】qìshuǐ（名）soft drink; soda water

【汽車】qìchē（名）motorcar; automobile: 小型公共~ minibus

【汽車司機】qìchē sījī（名）chauffeur; driver

【汽車保險】qìchē bǎoxiǎn（名）automobile insurance

【汽車站】qìchēzhàn（名）bus stop

【汽車票】qìchēpiào（名）bus ticket

【汽車售票員】qìchē shòupiàoyuán（名）conductor

【汽車停車場】qìchē tíngchēchǎng（名）car park

【汽車觀光旅遊】qìchē guānguāng lǚyóu（名）coach tour

【汽油】qìyóu（名）petrol; gasoline; gas

【汽缸】qìgāng（名）〈機〉cylinder

【汽船】qìchuán（名）steamship; steamer

【汽笛】qìdí（名）steam whistle; siren

【汽艇】qìtǐng（名）motorboat

【汽輪機】qìlúnjī（名）steam turbine

【汽錘】qìchuí（名）〈機〉steam hammer

沃 wò（形）rich; fertile

【沃土】wòtǔ（名）rich soil

没 méi

see also mò

【没日没夜】méirì méiyè（副）day and night: ～地工作 work day and night

【没心没肺】méixīn méifèi（形）ungrateful; cruel; heartless

【没心眼】méixīnyǎn（形）naive; candid

【没什麼】méishénme I（名）nothing important: 你説什麼? ——What did you just say? — Nothing important. II（動）that's all right; it doesn't matter

【没皮没臉】méipí méiliǎn（動）be shameless

【没出息】méichūxi（形）good for nothing; spineless

【没有】méiyǒu I（動）not have; there is not: 他～真心的朋友。He has no real friends. / 我們～共同語言。We have no common language. II（副）❶ not: 圖書館還～關門。The library hasn't closed yet. ❷ [used as a negative answer to a question] no: 你去過故宫嗎? ——～。Have you been to the Palace Museum? — No. III（形）less than; not so (as)...as: 這所房子～那一所大。This house is not so big as that one.

【没有説的】méiyǒu shuōde（形）❶ perfect; impeccable: 論人品, 他可是～。In character he is impeccable. ❷ without question; needless to say: ～, 他會支持我們。Undoubtedly he'll give us support.

【没良心】méiliángxīn（動）have no conscience; be ungrateful

【没完没了】méiwán méiliǎo（形）interminable; endless

【没治】méizhì（副）〈口〉❶ (of person or thing) beyond cure: 他這個人可真是～了。He's hopeless. ❷ extremely good: 電影好得～了。The film is really wonderful.

【没事】méishì（動）be free; be at leisure; it doesn't matter; never mind: 對不起, 打擾了。——～。Sorry to have troubled you. — That's all right.

【没事找事】méishì zhǎoshì（動）❶ invite trouble ❷ find fault (with); be fastidious (about)

【没法子】méifǎzi can't help it; there's no way out

【没門兒】méiménr（動）〈口〉❶ not a chance ❷ [used to express disagreement]: nothing doing 你想蒙我? ～! Are you kidding me? No go!

【没羞】méixiū（動）be shameless; have no sense of shame

【没深没淺】méishēn méiqiǎn（形）flippant

【没詞兒】méicír（動）〈口〉be unable to make a retort; become tongue-tied in an argument

【没輕没重】méiqīng méizhòng（形）❶ tactless ❷ frivolous

【没精打采】méijīng dǎcǎi（形）listless; dispirited; lackadaisical

【没趣】méiqù（動）feel slighted; feel rejected

【没影兒】méiyǐngr（形）〈口〉❶ without a trace ❷ groundless

【没頭没腦】méitóu méinǎo（形）❶ stupid; heedless: 這傢伙真是～。This chap has no brains. ❷ without any clue: 這個問題～。The question completely baffled us.

【没错儿】méicuòr（动）〈口〉can't be wrong

【没关系】méi guānxi（动）it's nothing; that's all right; never mind

【没辙】méizhé（动）〈口〉can do nothing; be at a loss what to do 我可真是～了。I'm really at a loss.

没 mò（动）❶ sink; submerge: 被洪水淹～ be submerged by flood ❷ overflow; be up to: 河水～腰。The river is waistdeep. ❸ confiscate; take away ❹ end: ～齿不忘 never forget in one's lifetime
see also méi

【没收】mòshōu（动）confiscate

【没奈何】mònàihé（动）be helpless: 他非要去，我也～。He insisted on going and there was nothing I could do.

【没顶】mòdǐng（动）be drowned: ～之灾 got drowned

【没落】mòluò（动）decline; be on the decline: ～的贵族之家 a declining aristocratic family

沓 dá（量）pile; pad: 一～钞票 a wad of banknotes
see also tà

沓 tà（副）quickly and in large numbers
see also dá

泣 qì Ⅰ（动）weep; sob Ⅱ（名）tears

注 zhù（动）❶ pour: 伤口流血如～。Blood gushed out from the wound. ❷ concentrate: 引人～目 become the focus of attention

【注入】zhùrù（动）pour into; instil

【注目】zhùmù（动）fix one's eyes

upon

【注定】zhùdìng（动）be destined: 他的企图～失败。His attempt is doomed to failure.

【注重】zhùzhòng（动）lay stress on; place emphasis on

【注射】zhùshè（动）〈医〉inject

【注视】zhùshì（动）gaze at; watch closely: ～局势的发展 follow closely the development of the events

【注意】zhùyì Ⅰ（动）pay attention to; take care: ～不要得罪他。Take care not to offend him. Ⅱ（名）attention

泳 yǒng（名）swimming: 蛙～ breaststroke

泌 mì（动）secrete

【泌尿科】mìniàokē（名）〈医〉urological department

【泌尿器官】mìniào qìguān（名）〈医〉urinary organs

沫 mò（名）foam

法 fǎ Ⅰ（名）❶ law ❷ method; way ❸ model; example Ⅱ（动）follow; take as a model

【法人】fǎrén（名）legal person: ～团体 body corporate

【法子】fǎzi（名）way; method; measure

【法令】fǎlìng（名）laws and decrees

【法西斯】fǎxīsī（名）fascist

【法西斯主义】fǎxīsī zhǔyì（名）fascism

【法典】fǎdiǎn（名）code: 刑～ criminal code／民～ civil code

【法官】fǎguān（名）judge; justice

【法定】fǎdìng（形）legal; lawful: ～

年龄 legal age ／ ～人数 quorum

【法制】fǎzhì（名）legal system

【法治】fǎzhì（名）rule by law

【法度】fǎdù（名）❶ law ❷ norm

【法律】fǎlǜ（名）law

【法郎】fǎláng（名）franc

【法纪】fǎjì（名）law and discipline

【法则】fǎzé（名）law; rule

【法案】fǎ'àn（名）bill

【法庭】fǎtíng（名）(law) court

【法院】fǎyuàn（名）(law) court

【法规】fǎguī（名）laws and regulations

【法国】Fǎguó（名）France: ～人 Frenchman; Frenchwoman

【法术】fǎshù（名）magic

【法场】fǎchǎng（名）place of execution; execution ground

【法语】Fǎyǔ（名）French (language)

【法网】fǎwǎng（名）net of justice

【法办】fǎbàn（动）punish by law

【法学】fǎxué（名）science of law; jurisprudence: ～家 jurist

【法医】fǎyī（名）forensic expert; coroner

【法宝】fǎbǎo（名）magic weapon

【法警】fǎjǐng（名）bailiff

河 hé（名）river

【河山】héshān（名）rivers and mountains; land; territory

【河北】Héběi（名）Hebei (Province)

【河床】héchuáng（名）riverbed

【河岸】hé'àn（名）river bank

【河南】Hénán（名）Henan (Province)

【河马】hémǎ（名）hippopotamus; river horse

【河流】héliú（名）rivers

【河堤】hédī（名）river dike

【河渠】héqú（名）rivers and canals; waterways

汁 gān

【汁水】gānshuǐ（名）swill; slops

沽 gū（动）❶ buy ❷ sell: 待價而 ～ ready to offer one's service at a price

【沽名钓誉】gū míng diào yù〈成〉angle for fame and compliments; crave popular acclaim; court popularity

沸 fèi（动）boil: 人声鼎～ seething with hubbub

【沸点】fèidiǎn（名）〈物〉boiling point

【沸腾】fèiténg（动）❶ boil ❷ seethe: ～的工地生活 bustling activity at the worksite

泓 hóng Ⅰ（形）(of water) deep Ⅱ（量）一～清水 an expanse of fresh water

泯 mǐn（动）get rid of; lose: ～除成见 do away with prejudices

【泯灭】mǐnmiè（动）erase; obliterate: 给大家留下了不可～的印象 leave an indelible impression on all people

泥 ní（名）❶ mud; mire ❷ mashed vegetable or fruit: 土豆～ mashed potato

see also nì

【泥人】nírén（名）〈工美〉clay figurine

【泥土】nítǔ（名）❶ earth; soil ❷ clay

【泥巴】níbā（名）〈方〉mud; mire

【泥瓦匠】níwǎjiàng（名）bricklayer;

plasterer; tiler; mason

【泥石流】níshíliú（名）〈地〉mud-rock flow

【泥坑】níkēng（名）quagmire; mire; morass

【泥沙】níshā（名）silt

【泥沙俱下】ní shā jù xià〈成〉a case of bad people mingling with good ones

【泥塑】nísù（名）clay sculpture

【泥塘】nítáng（名）mire; bog

【泥浆】níjiāng（名）slurry; mud

【泥泞】níníng（形）muddy; miry

【泥鳅】níqiū（名）loach

泥 nì（动）cover or daub with plaster, putty, etc.: ～墙 plaster a wall
see also ní

波 bō（名）❶ wave; ripple: 碧～荡漾 the blue ripples (of a lake, etc.) ❷〈物〉wave: 电(光、声)～ electric (light, sound) wave ❸ upheaval; unexpected turn of events: 风～ disturbance; storm

【波及】bōjí（动）affect; involve

【波折】bōzhé（名）twists and turns; ups and downs; setback

【波长】bōcháng（名）wavelength

【波段】bōduàn（名）〈无〉wave band: ～开关 waver; band switch

【波浪】bōlàng（名）wave; roller

【波纹】bōwén（名）❶ ripple; ruffle ❷ corrugation: ～纸板 corrugated cardboard

【波动】bōdòng Ⅰ（动）fluctuate; waver Ⅱ（名）undulation; fluctuation: 市场的～ market fluctuation

【波涛】bōtāo（名）surge; billow;

white horses: ～汹涌 waves roaring and surging ahead

【波澜】bōlán（名）billow; great wave; surge

【波澜壮阔】bō lán zhuàng kuò〈成〉surge ahead with tremendous force

【波兰】Bōlán（名）Poland: ～人 Pole / ～语 Polish (language)

沼 zhǎo（名）pool; pond

【沼气】zhǎoqì（名）biogas; methane

【沼泽】zhǎozé（名）marsh; swamp

沾 zhān（动）❶ be stained with: ～满了鲜血的手 blood-stained hands ❷ touch: 说话不～边儿 not speak to the point ❸ gain (some advantage by being related to sb.): ～便宜 gain some advantage ❹ wet; soak: 热泪～衣 tears falling on one's clothes

【沾手】zhānshǒu（动）❶ touch with one's hand ❷ have a hand in: 这事你不必～。You don't have to get involved in the matter.

【沾光】zhānguāng（动）benefit by sb's influence

【沾沾自喜】zhān zhān zì xǐ〈成〉be self-complacent; be pleased with oneself

【沾染】zhānrǎn（动）be infected with; be tainted with: ～坏习气 be contaminated by evil social practices

【沾亲带故】zhān qīn dài gù〈成〉have ties of kinship or friendship (with people)

沮 jǔ Ⅰ（动）stop; obstruct; hold back Ⅱ（形）(of facial expression) gloomy; downcast
see also jù

【沮丧】jǔsàng（形）downcast; dejected; disheartened

沮 jù (形) marshy; swampy

see also jǔ

油 yóu I (名) oil; fat: 花生 ~ peanut oil II (动) ❶ paint; varnish: 这桌子刚 ~ 过。The table is freshly painted. ❷ be stained with grease: 真可惜，我的新裙子 ~ 了。It's too bad my new skirt has got some grease stains on it. III (形) oily; slick

【油水】yóushuǐ (名) ❶ grease ❷ profit on the side; perks; gain

【油井】yóujǐng (名) oil well

【油田】yóutián (名) oilfield

【油布】yóubù (名) oilcloth; tarpaulin

【油灰】yóuhuī (名)〈建〉putty

【油印】yóuyìn (名) mimeograph

【油门】yóumén (名)〈机〉❶ throttle ❷〈口〉accelerator

【油泥】yóuní (名) greasy filth; grease

【油砂】yóushā (名)〈石油〉oil sand

【油泵】yóubèng (名)〈机〉oil pump

【油条】yóutiáo (名) deep-fried dough sticks

【油脂】yóuzhī (名) oil; fat

【油库】yóukù (名) oil depot

【油料作物】yóuliào zuòwù (名) oil-bearing crops

【油船】yóuchuán (名) (oil) tanker

【油菜】yóucài (名) rape: ~ 籽 rapeseed

【油画】yóuhuà (名) oil painting

【油腔滑调】yóu qiāng huá diào〈成〉unctuous; glibtongued

【油滑】yóuhuá (形) oily; slick; slippery

【油饼】yóubǐng (名) deep-fried dough cake

【油管】yóuguǎn (名)〈石油〉oil pipe

【油漆】yóuqī (名) paint: 当心 ~ mind the fresh paint

【油膏】yóugāo (名)〈药〉ointment

【油层】yóucéng (名)〈石油〉oil reservoir

【油墨】yóumò (名) printing ink

【油箱】yóuxiāng (名) fuel tank

【油灯】yóudēng (名) oil lamp; paraffin lamp

【油头粉面】yóu tóu fěn miàn〈成〉foppish in appearance

【油头滑脑】yóu tóu huá nǎo〈成〉slick; sly

【油腻】yóunì (形) greasy; oily

【油毡】yóuzhān (名)〈建〉asphalt felt

【油矿】yóukuàng (名) ❶ oil deposit ❷ oil field

【油罐】yóuguàn (名) oil tank

泱 yāng

【泱泱】yāngyāng (形) vast; great; magnificent: ~ 大國 a great country

泅 qiú (动) swim

【泅水】qiúshuǐ (动) swim

泡 pāo (名) sth. puffy and soft: 豆腐 ~ beancurd puff

see also pào

【泡桐】pāotóng (名) paulownia

泡 pào I (名) ❶ bubble ❷ bubble-shaped thing: 燈 ~ (light) bulb II (动) steep; soak: ~ 茶 make tea

see also pāo

【泡沫】pàomò (名) foam; suds

【泡沫塑料】pàomò sùliào (名)

foamed plastics

【泡沫劑】pàomòjì (名) foaming agent

【泡泡紗】pàopàoshā (名)〈紡〉seersucker

【泡菜】pàocài (名) pickled vegetables

【泡湯】pàotāng (動)〈俗〉❶ (of money) be wasted ❷ (of hope, plan, etc.) be dashed to pieces

【泡影】pàoyǐng (名) forlorn hope; bubble: 化爲～ vanish; melt into thin air

沿 yán I (名) edge; border: 邊～ edge; fringe II (動) follow: 相～成習 be handed down as a custom from generation to generation III (介) along: ～大街走 go (walk) along the boulevard
see also yàn

【沿用】yányòng (動) continue to use

【沿岸】yán'àn (副) along the river bank; along the coast

【沿河】yánhé (名) along the river

【沿革】yángé (名) development; evolution

【沿途】yántú (副) on the way; during one's journey: ～一派豐收景象 a scene of bumper harvest all the way during my journey

【沿海】yánhǎi (形) coastal; littoral: ～省份 coastal provinces

【沿着】yánzhe (介) along: ～河邊種了柳樹。The bank of the river is lined with the willows.

【沿街】yánjiē (副) along the street

【沿綫】yánxiàn (副) along the (railway) line

【沿邊】yánbiān (名) trim; braid

【沿襲】yánxí (動) follow: ～舊傳統 follow the old tradition

沿 yàn (名) bank; water's edge: 溝～ edge of a ditch
see also yán

泊 bó (動) ❶ anchor; be at anchor: 停～ lie at anchor ❷ live temporarily: 飄～在他鄉 (of a person) drift around away from home
see also pō

【泊位】bówèi (名)〈交〉berth

泊 pō (名) pool; lake: 湖～ lakes
see also bó

治 zhì (動) ❶ rule; govern; run ❷ treat (a disease); cure: 一種新藥～好了他的病。A new remedy cured him of his illness. ❸ study; research: ～學 pursue one's studies ❹ punish: ～罪 punish sb. (for an offence) ❺ control; harness; exterminate: ～河 harness a river

【治本】zhìběn (動) get a permanent cure

【治安】zhì'ān (名) public order; public security

【治國】zhìguó (動) run a country

【治理】zhìlǐ (動) ❶ govern; administer ❷ harness; tame; bring under control: ～沙漠 control the desert

【治喪】zhìsāng (動) make funeral arrangements: ～委員會 funeral committee

【治標】zhìbiāo (動) give temporary relief

【治療】zhìliáo (動) treat; cure

泰 tài I (形) ❶ peaceful; calm ❷ blessed; prosperous: 國～民安 prosperity for the country and peace for the people Ⅱ (名)（Tài）a surname

【泰山】Tàishān（名）❶ Mount Taishan（in Shandong Province）❷（tàishān）father-in-law

【泰國】Tàiguó（名）Thailand: ～人 Thai; Thailander

【泰然】tàirán（形）calm; selfpossessed

泵 bèng（名）pump: 液壓～ hydraulic pump

泉 quán（名）spring; fountain

【泉水】quánshuǐ（名）spring water; spring: 礦～ mineral water

【泉源】quányuán（名）❶ fountainhead; springhead ❷ source: 靈感的～ source of inspiration

洋 yáng Ⅰ（名）ocean: 遠隔重～ separated by oceans Ⅱ（形）foreign: 留～ study abroad

【洋人】yángrén（名）foreigner

【洋奴】yángnú（名）flunkey of a foreign boss; worshipper of anything foreign

【洋白菜】yángbáicài（名）cabbage

【洋行】yángháng（名）〈舊〉foreign firm

【洋灰】yánghuī（名）cement

【洋服】yángfú（名）Western-style clothes

【洋相】yángxiàng（名）silly sight: 出～ make an exhibition of oneself; make a fool of oneself in public

【洋洋】yángyáng（形）magnificent; numerous: ～灑灑 at great length

【洋洋自得】yáng yáng zì dé〈成〉complacent; smug

【洋娃娃】yángwáwa（名）doll

【洋財】yángcái（名）big fortune: 發

～ make a big fortune

【洋氣】yángqi（形）outlandish: 穿得很～ stylishly dressed

【洋鬼子】yángguǐzi（名）foreign devil

【洋琴】yángqín（名）dulcimer

【洋葱】yángcōng（名）onion

【洋溢】yángyì（動）be filled with; be permeated with: 熱情～ be full of enthusiasm

【洋槐】yánghuái（名）〈植〉locust

【洋鎬】yánggǎo（名）pickaxe

洲 zhōu（名）continent: 亞～ Asia

【洲際導彈】zhōujì dǎodàn（名）intercontinental missile

洪 hóng Ⅰ（形）big; great; vast Ⅱ（名）❶ flood: 山～ mountain flood ❷（Hóng）a surname

【洪水】hóngshuǐ（名）flood

【洪水猛獸】hóng shuǐ měng shòu〈成〉scourges as fearful as floods and fierce animals

【洪亮】hóngliàng（形）sonorous

【洪流】hóngliú（名）mighty tide; mighty social trends

【洪峰】hóngfēng（名）flood peak

【洪都拉斯】Hóngdūlāsī（名）Honduras: ～人 Honduran

【洪爐】hónglú（名）furnace

洌 liè（形）(of liquid) clear

津 jīn（名）❶ saliva ❷ sweat; perspiration ❸（Jīn）short for Tianjin

【津巴布韋】Jīnbābùwéi（名）Zimbabwe: ～人 Zimbabwean

【津津有味】jīn jīn yǒu wèi〈成〉with great interest: 說得～ talk about sth. with great gusto

【津津樂道】jīn jīn lè dào〈成〉dwell

upon with gusto; talk about with relish

【津液】jīnyè（名）❶〈中醫〉body fluid ❷ saliva

【津貼】jīntiē（名）allowance; subsidy

洞 dòng I（名）hole; care II（副）thoroughly: ～悉其奸 see through sb.'s trick

【洞穴】dòngxué（名）cave; den

【洞房】dòngfáng（名）bridal chamber

【洞若觀火】dòng ruò guān huǒ〈成〉see things as clearly as a blazing fire

【洞悉】dòngxī（動）know clearly

【洞察】dòngchá（動）see through

洩 xiè（動）❶ let out; leak; discharge ❷ give vent to: 一～積怨 give vent to his pent-up grievancy

【洩洪】xièhóng（動）release floodwater

【洩氣】xièqì I（動）lose heart; be disheartened II（形）disappointing; frustrating

【洩密】xièmì（動）give away a secret

【洩漏】xièlòu（動）leak; let out; disclose

洽 qià（動）❶ contact; consult: 請與辦公室接～。Please contact the general office. ❷ be in harmony: 感情融～ be on very good terms

【洽談】qiàtán（洽商 qiàshāng）（動）negotiate; talk over with

【洽購】qiàgòu（動）❶ contact for purchase ❷ negotiate the purchase of

洗 xǐ（動）❶ wash up; wash: ～盤

子 wash dishes / 乾～ dryclean ❷ kill; butcher: 血～ massacre; bloodbath

【洗心革面】xǐ xīn gé miàn〈成〉reform oneself completely; make a new start in life

【洗手不幹】xǐ shǒu bù gàn〈成〉❶（of an offender）turn over a new leaf ❷ wash one's hands of the business

【洗衣板】xǐyībǎn（名）washboard

【洗衣店】xǐyīdiàn（名）laundry

【洗衣粉】xǐyīfěn（名）washing powder; detergent

【洗衣機】xǐyījī（名）washing machine; washer

【洗耳恭聽】xǐ ěr gōng tīng〈成〉listen respectfully; be all ears

【洗劫】xǐjié（名）loot; pillage

【洗刷】xǐshuā（動）❶ scrub; clean: ～澡盆 scrub the bathtub ❷ wash off: ～ 罪名 clear oneself of a charge

【洗染店】xǐrǎndiàn（名）laundering and dyeing shop; cleaners and dyers

【洗牌】xǐpái（動）shuffle the cards

【洗滌】xǐdí（動）wash: ～池 sink

【洗滌劑】xǐdíjì（名）detergent

【洗塵】xǐchén（動）give a dinner in honour of a visitor from after

【洗澡】xǐzǎo（動）take a bath

【洗頭】xǐtóu（動）wash one's hair; shampoo

【洗禮】xǐlǐ I（動）baptize II（名）❶ baptism ❷ test: 經受艱苦鬥爭的 ～ go through the test of arduous struggle

【洗臉】xǐliǎn（動）wash one's face: ～毛巾 face towel

【洗臉盆】xǐliǎnpén（名）wash-basin

洗 Xiǎn（名）a surname

活 huó Ⅰ（动）live; be alive: 他～了很大年纪。He lived to a ripe old age. Ⅱ（形）❶ lively ❷ movable ❸ vivid; lifelike Ⅲ（名）job; work

【活力】huólì（名）vigour; vitality; dynamism

【活字典】huózìdiǎn（名）walking dictionary

【活佛】huófó（名）〈宗〉Living Buddha

【活命】huómìng（动）eke out a miserable existence

【活受罪】huóshòuzuì（动）〈口〉be in a living hell; suffer terribly

【活计】huójì（名）❶ job; work ❷ needle work ❸ handicraft; handiwork

【活页】huóyè（形）(of book, notebook, etc.) loose-leaf

【活动】huódòng Ⅰ（动）❶ move about; exercise: 早晨～～有好处。It's good to do some exercises every morning. ❷ use one's influence on sb.'s behalf Ⅱ（形）❶ unstable; loose: 这张桌子直～。This table is rickety. ❷ mobile Ⅲ（名）activity; manoeuvre: 社会～ social activities

【活象】huóxiàng（动）be the spitting image of

【活期】huóqī（形）(of money deposits in a bank) current

【活期储蓄】huóqī chǔxù（名）current deposit

【活塞】huósāi（名）〈机〉piston

【活该】huógāi（动）〈口〉serves sb. right

【活路】huólù（名）means of subsistence; way out

【活泼】huópo（形）lively; active;

vivacious

【活宝】huóbǎo（名）a funny fellow; somewhat clownish person

【活跃】huóyuè（形）active; brisk; lively Ⅱ（动）enliven; animate: ～农村经济生活 enliven rural economic life

【活灵活现】huólíng huóxiàn（形）vivid; lifelike

汹 xiōng

【汹汹】xiōngxiōng（形）❶ (of waves) roaring ❷ violent; vehement: 气势～ be fierce and obstreperous

【汹涌澎湃】xiōngyǒng péngpài（形）surging; billowing: ～的大海波涛 the surging tide of the sea

派 pài Ⅰ（名）❶ school; faction; sect: 小说的新流～ a new school of fiction／保守～ the conservatives ❷ manner; bearing Ⅱ（动）dispatch; assign: ～人去办 send sb. to do the work Ⅲ（量）❶ [of schools of thought] 两～观点 views of two different schools ❷ (of scene, weather, sound, language, etc.)一～新气象 a new thriving atmosphere

【派生】pàishēng（动）derive

【派生词】pàishēngcí（名）〈语〉derivative

【派出所】pàichūsuǒ（名）(local) police station

【派别】pàibié（名）school; faction; sect

【派系】pàixì（名）clique; faction

【派性】pàixìng（名）factionalism

【派遣】pàiqiǎn（动）send; dispatch

【派头】pàitóu（名）〈贬〉air; bearing; manner: 傲慢的～ an air of

arrogance

流 liú Ⅰ (动) ❶ flow: 溪水～得很
快。The stream flows along rapidly.
❷ shed: ～泪 shed tears ❸ move;
spread: ～入大城市 drift into big
cities Ⅱ (名) ❶ current; stream:
顺～而行 sail down the stream ❷
rate; class: 一～演员 topnotch act-
or

【流亡】 liúwáng (动) go into exile

【流亡政府】 liúwáng zhèngfǔ (名)
government-in-exile

【流水】 liúshuǐ (名) flowing water

【流水作业】 liúshuǐ zuòyè (名) assembly line method

【流水线】 liúshuǐxiàn (名) assembly
line

【流水账】 liúshuǐzhàng (名) day-to-
day account; dull journal of the daily
routine

【流民】 liúmín (名) vagrant; tramp

【流失】 liúshī (动) (of soil) erosion

【流血】 liúxuè (动) bleed

【流行】 liúxíng (形) prevalent; in
fashion; popular: ～歌曲 popular
song/ ～音乐 pop music

【流行性感冒】 liúxíngxìng gǎnmào
(名) influenza; flu

【流行病】 liúxíngbìng (名) epidemic
disease

【流沙】 liúshā (名) quicksand

【流利】 liúlì (形) fluent; flowing: 讲
一口～的法语 speak fluent French

【流言蜚语】 liú yán fēi yǔ 〈成〉 rumours and slanders; malicious gossip

【流氓】 liúmáng (名) hooligan; rascal

【流放】 liúfàng (动) exile; banish

【流芳百世】 liú fāng bǎi shì 〈成〉
leave a good name in history

【流派】 liúpài (名) school; sect;

trend

【流毒】 liúdú (名) very harmful influence

【流星】 liúxīng (名) meteor

【流速】 liúsù (名) current velocity

【流浪】 liúlàng (动) wander; rove:
～者 vagrant

【流连】 liúlián (动) be reluctant to
leave; linger on: ～忘返 be reluctant to leave a place

【流逝】 liúshì (动) (of time) pass;
fly; elapse

【流通】 liútōng (动) circulate

【流寇】 liúkòu (名) roving bandits

【流产】 liúchǎn Ⅰ (动) abortion; miscarriage Ⅱ (动) fail to materialize

【流域】 liúyù (名) valley; basin

【流动】 liúdòng Ⅰ (动) flow Ⅱ (形)
mobile: ～人口 floating population

【流动资本】 liúdòng zīběn (名) cir-
culating capital

【流量】 liúliàng (名) volume of flow

【流传】 liúchuán (动) spread; hand
down: 消息很快～开来。The news
soon spread far and wide. /从老一
辈～下来的传说 the legend handed
down from the forefathers

【流感】 liúgǎn (名) (short for 流行
性感冒 liúxíngxìng gǎnmào) influenza; flu

【流落】 liúluò (动) wander about
homeless and penniless: ～他乡 be
penniless and stranded in a strange
land

【流脑】 liúnǎo (名) (short for 流行
性脑脊髓膜炎 liúxíngxìng nǎo-
jǐsuǐmóyán) epidemic cerebrospinal
meningitis

【流畅】 liúchàng (形) (of writing)
smooth; fluent

【流线型】 liúxiànxíng (形) stream-

lined】liúbì（名）evil social practices;
prevailing abuses

【流食】liúzhì（名）liquid food

【流彈】liúdàn（名）stray bullet

【流蕩】liúdòng（動）wander; rove

【流竄】liúcuàn（動）（of bandits or
enemy forces）rove; run about

【流離失所】liú lí shī suǒ（成）drift
along homeless; live a vagrant life

【流露】liúlù（動）show; betray: ～
不滿的感情 betray a feeling of discontent

【流體】liútǐ（名）〈物〉fluid

浪 làng Ⅰ（名）wave; billow: 風平
～靜。The wind and the waves have
subsided.（All is quiet.）Ⅱ（形）un-
restrained; selfindulgent: ～迹天涯
roam about all over the world/ 流～
漢 tramp; vagrant

【浪子】làngzǐ（名）profligate young
man; idler: ～回頭 return of the
prodigal son

【浪花】lànghuā（名）❶ spray ❷ a
particular episode in one's life

【浪費】làngfèi（動）run to waste;
waste; use（manpower, money,
time, etc.）unsparingly

【浪漫】làngmàn（形）romantic

【浪潮】làngcháo（名）tide; tidal
wave（forceful and widespread
movement in public opinion, action,
etc.）: 抗議的～ wave of protests

【浪蕩】làngdàng Ⅰ（動）loiter about;
lounge about Ⅱ（形）lewd: ～子弟
profligate sons

【浪頭】làngtou（名）〈口〉❶ billow;
breaker ❷ trend

涕 tì（名）❶ tears ❷ mucus of the
nose: 流鼻～ have a running nose

浦 pǔ（名）❶ [usu. used in place
names] bank or mouth of a river ❷
（Pǔ）a surname

浙 Zhè（名）short for Zhejiang
Province

【浙江】Zhèjiāng（名）Zhejiang
（Province）

浹 jiā（動）soak through; saturate;
drench

浸 jìn（動）immerse; soak

【浸沒】jìnmò（動）be immersed

【浸泡】jìnpào（動）soak; souse

【浸透】jìntòu（動）soak; saturate

【浸膏】jìngāo（名）〈藥〉extract

【浸潤】jìnrùn Ⅰ（動）soak; infiltrate;
permeate Ⅱ（名）〈醫〉infiltration

【浸禮】jìnlǐ（名）〈宗〉baptism

消 xiāo（動）❶ disappear; fade: 煙
～火滅。The smoke dissolved and
the fire went out. ❷ remove; dispel ❸ divert oneself; while away
（the time）❹ need; take: 把這篇
文章讀完只～一會兒功夫。It only
takes a while to read the article
through.

【消亡】xiāowáng（動）perish; die
out; wither away

【消化】xiāohuà（動）digest: ～系統
digestive system

【消火栓】xiāohuǒshuān（名）fire
hydrant

【消失】xiāoshī（動）disappear; vanish; fade away: 從人們的記憶中～
fade from people's memory

【消沉】xiāochén（形）low-spirited;
downcast

【消防】xiāofáng（動）fight fire: ～
隊 fire brigade / ～車 fire engine

【消炎】xiāoyán (動)〈醫〉reduce inflammation

【消毒】xiāodú (動) sterilize; disinfect

【消音器】xiāoyīnqì (名) muffler

【消耗】xiāohào (動) consume; expend: ～能源 consume the sources of energy

【消除】xiāochú (動) eliminate; remove; do away with: ～偏見 get rid of one's prejudice

【消氣】xiāoqì (動) be appeased; be mollified

【消息】xiāoxi (名) news; information

【消逝】xiāoshì (動)(of time) pass; elapse

【消散】xiāosàn (動) disperse; dissipate

【消費】xiāofèi (動) consume: ～者 consumer

【消極】xiāojí (形) ❶ negative: ～影響 negative influence ❷ passive; inactive: ～態度 passive attitude

【消滅】xiāomiè (動) exterminate; annihilate; wipe out: ～蚊子 exterminate mosquitoes / ～赤字 wipe out the deficit

【消遣】xiāoqiǎn Ⅰ (動) divert oneself Ⅱ (名) diversion; pastime

【消瘦】xiāoshòu (動) become thin

【消融】xiāoróng (動) melt

【消磨】xiāomó (動) wear off; fritter away: ～時間 kill time

涓 juān (名) tiny stream

【涓涓】juānjuān (形) slowly trickling: ～細流 tiny trickling stream

涉 shè (動) ❶ wade; ford: 跋山～水 cross mountains and rivers ❷

experience; undergo: ～世不深 be ignorant of the ways of the world ❸ involve: 牽～ involve

【涉及】shèjí (動) involve; concern: ～到許多方面的問題 touch on many aspects of the problems

【涉禽】shèqín (名) wading bird; wader

【涉嫌】shèxián (動) be under suspicion

【涉獵】shèliè (動) browse: ～羣書 browse among many books

浮 fú Ⅰ (動) float Ⅱ (形) ❶ superficial ❷ frivolous ❸ excessive: 人～於事 more staff members than jobs require; be overstaffed

【浮力】fúlì (名)〈物〉buoyancy

【浮沉】fúchén (動) ❶ drift along: 隨俗～ play to the gallery ❷ have ups and downs: 宦海～ political ups and downs

【浮財】fúcái (名) movable property

【浮現】fúxiàn (動) appear; emerge

【浮動】fúdòng (動) ❶ float ❷ fluctuate: 人心～ a feeling of insecurity among the populace

【浮動工資】fúdòng gōngzī (名) fluctuating salary

【浮動匯率】fúdòng huìlǜ (名) floating exchange rate

【浮萍】fúpíng (名)〈植〉duckweed

【浮華】fúhuá (形) florid; ostentatious: ～生活 a lavish life style

【浮腫】fúzhǒng (名)〈醫〉dropsy

【浮誇】fúkuā (形) fantastically boastful or exaggerative

【浮誇風】fúkuāfēng (名) work style characterized by boasting and exaggeration

【浮塵】fúchén (名) floating dust

【浮標】fúbiāo（名）buoy

【浮雕】fúdiāo（名）relief

【浮橋】fúqiáo（名）floating bridge

【浮躁】fúzào（形）rash; impulsive

涂 Tú（名）a surname

浴 yù（名）bath: 淋～ shower bath/ 冷水～ cold bath

【浴巾】yùjīn（名）bath towel; wash towel

【浴血】yùxuè（動）be bathed in blood: ～奮戰 fight a bloody battle

【浴衣】yùyī（名）bathrobe

【浴池】yùchí（名）public bathhouse; public bath

【浴盆】yùpén（名）bathtub; tub

【浴室】yùshì（名）bathroom; bath

【浴場】yùchǎng（名）outdoor bathing place

浩 hào（形）❶ great; vast; grand ❷ numerous

【浩大】hàodà（形）vast; huge; enormous

【浩如煙海】hào rú yān hǎi〈成〉(of data, documents, etc.) voluminous; a tremendous amount of

【浩劫】hàojié（名）great calamity; catastrophe

【浩氣】hàoqì（名）nobility of character

【浩渺】hàomiǎo（形）(of water) vast; boundless: 煙波～。Mists and waves stretch far beyond the horizon.

【浩蕩】hàodàng（形）vast and mighty: ～的江河 torrential rivers

【浩翰】hàohàn（形）boundless; vast

【浩繁】hàofán（形）huge and multifarious

海 hǎi Ⅰ（名）❶ sea; big lake ❷ a great number of: 火～ a sea of flames ❸（Hǎi）a surname Ⅱ（形）very big; enormous

【海口】hǎikǒu（名）❶ seaport ❷ boast: 誇～ brag unashamedly

【海外】hǎiwài（形）abroad; overseas: ～同胞 countryman residing abroad

【海市蜃樓】hǎi shì shèn lóu（名）mirage

【海米】hǎimǐ（名）dried shrimps

【海地】Hǎidì（名）Haiti: ～人 Haitian

【海防】hǎifáng（名）coast defence

【海岸】hǎi'àn（名）coast; seashore: ～綫 coastline

【海拔】hǎibá（名）height above sea level; elevation

【海味】hǎiwèi（名）choice seafood

【海底】hǎidǐ（名）sea floor

【海底撈針】hǎi dǐ lāo zhēn〈成〉an impossible task; search for a needle in a haystack

【海洛因】hǎiluòyīn（名）heroin

【海南】Hǎinán（名）Hainan (Province)

【海軍】hǎijūn（名）navy: ～陸戰隊 marine corps; marines

【海洋】hǎiyáng（名）seas and oceans: ～法 law of the sea / ～學 oceanography

【海枯石爛】hǎi kū shí làn〈成〉even if the seas run dry and the rocks crumble: ～，此心不變。My loyalty will remain unchanged for ever.

【海峽】hǎixiá（名）strait; channel: 英吉利～ the English Channel / 臺灣～ the Taiwan Straits

【海豹】hǎibào（名）seal

【海员】hǎiyuán（名）seaman; sailor; marine

【海产】hǎichǎn（名）marine product

【海域】hǎiyù（名）sea area; marine space

【海豚】hǎitún（名）dolphin

【海参】hǎishēn（名）sea cucumber

【海带】hǎidài（名）kelp

【海盗】hǎidào（名）pirate: ～版 pirate edition

【海港】hǎigǎng（名）seaport; harbour

【海报】hǎibào（名）poster; playbill

【海量】hǎiliàng ❶（名）magnanimity: 請～包涵 crave your pardon ❷ enormous capacity for drinking

【海运】hǎiyùn（名）sea transportation; shipping

【海蜇】hǎizhé（名）jellyfish

【海绵】hǎimián（名）❶ sponge ❷ foam rubber

【海誓山盟】hǎi shì shān méng〈成〉solemnly pledge eternal love

【海轮】hǎilún（名）seagoing vessel

【海啸】hǎixiào（名）tsunami; seismic sea wave

【海阔天空】hǎi kuò tiān kōng〈成〉(of a chat) unrestrained and far-ranging; rambling

【海滨】hǎibīn（名）seashore; seaside

【海关】hǎiguān（名）customhouse; customs

【海疆】hǎijiāng（名）coastal areas and territorial seas

【海鸥】hǎi'ōu（名）sea gull

【海滩】hǎitān（名）beach

【海湾】hǎiwān（名）bay; gulf

涎 xián（名）saliva: 垂～欲滴 start drooling; with one's mouth watering (with envy or greed)

浚 jùn（动）dredge; scoop earth from the bottom of a river, canal, etc.: 疏～河道 dredge a river

淙 cóng

【淙淙】cóngcóng（象）sound of flowing water

淀 diàn（名）shallow lake

淳 chún（形）simple and honest

【淳厚】chúnhòu（形）honest and kind

【淳樸】chúnpǔ（形）honest; simple

凉 liáng（形）❶ cold; cool; chilly: 天～了。It's getting cold. ❷ disheartened; disappointed: 他讀完考卷,心就～了。His heart sank when he read through the examination paper.

see also liàng

【凉水】liángshuǐ（名）❶ cold drinking water ❷ unboiled water

【凉快】liángkuai Ⅰ（形）refreshing and cool; cool: 下雨後天～多了。It got much cooler after the rain. Ⅱ（动）refresh and cool oneself

【凉亭】liángtíng（名）pavilion

【凉粉】liángfěn（名）bean jelly

【凉爽】liángshuǎng（形）refreshingly cool

【凉菜】liángcài（名）cold dish

【凉帽】liángmào（名）summer hat

【凉棚】liángpéng（名）mat shed

【凉蓆】liángxí（名）summer bed-mat

【凉臺】liángtái（名）balcony; verandah

【凉鞋】liángxié（名）sandals

【凉飕飕】liángsōusōu（形）chilly

凉 liàng（动）make sth. cool

see also liáng

淬 cuì

【淬礪】cuìlì (動) temper oneself through hardship

液 yè (名) fluid; liquid

【液化】yèhuà (名) liquefaction

【液化氣】yèhuàqì (名) liquid gas

【液態】yètài (名) liquid state

【液壓】yèyā (名) hydraulic pressure

【液體】yètǐ (名) liquid

淤 yū Ⅰ (名) silt; sludge Ⅱ (動) silt up; clog up

【淤血】yūxuè (名) extravasated blood

【淤泥】yūní (名) silt; sludge

【淤塞】yūsè (動) silt up; clog up: 水道～了。The water course is silted up.

【淤積】yūjī (動) silt up; form sediment

【淤灌】yūguàn (動) 〈農〉warp

淚 lèi (名) tear: 傷心落～ shed sad tears; weep sadly

【淚水】lèishuǐ (名) tears; teardrops

【淚汪汪】lèiwāngwāng (形) (of eyes) tearful

【淚花】lèihuā (名) tears in the eyes

【淚珠】lèizhū (名) teardrop

【淚痕】lèihén (名) tear stains

深 shēn Ⅰ (形) ❶ deep: 這兒水～。The water is deep here. / 在～海中 in the deep sea ❷ profound: 學問～ have profound learning ❸ (of feelings) deep; strong: 她對母親感情很～。She is greatly attached to her mother. ❹ (of time) late; long ❺ penetrating; in-depth; profound: 影響很～ have a great impact (on) ❻ (of colour) deep;

dark: ～綠 dark green Ⅱ (副) deeply; greatly: ～受浪漫派詩人影響 be greatly influenced by Romantic poets

【深入】shēnrù Ⅰ (動) go deep into: ～淺出 explain profound ideas in plain language Ⅱ (形) thorough; deepgoing; in-depth: ～的調查 thorough investigation

【深入人心】shēn rù rén xīn 〈成〉win the wholehearted support of the public; be very popular

【深化】shēnhuà (形) deepen; intensify

【深水】shēnshuǐ (形) deepwater: ～碼頭 deepwater wharf

【深仇大恨】shēn chóu dà hèn 〈成〉intense hatred: 懷著～ harbour inveterate hatred for

【深切】shēnqiè (形) heartfelt; deep and sincere: 表示～的慰問 express deep and sincere solicitude

【深沉】shēnchén (形) ❶ (denoting intensity) deep: ～的哀悼 profound condolences ❷ (of sound or voice) deep; dull ❸ (of a person's character) deep

【深更半夜】shēn gēng bàn yè 〈成〉in the dead of night

【深究】shēnjiū (動) go deep into (a problem)

【深刻】shēnkè (形) deep; profound: ～的理解 profound understanding

【深夜】shēnyè (副) at midnight: 捱到～ sit up very late at night

【深呼吸】shēnhūxī (名) deep breathing

【深居簡出】shēn jū jiǎn chū 〈成〉live in seclusion; go out only on rare occasions

【深度】shēndù（名）❶ depth: 河道的～ the depth of the river ❷ profundity; depth: 有～的分析 penetrating analysis

【深厚】shēnhòu（形）❶ deep; profound ❷ firm; solid

【深重】shēnzhòng（形） extremely grave

【深思】shēnsī（动） ponder over

【深思熟虑】shēn sī shú lǜ〈成〉think deeply and carefully

【深耕】shēngēng（名）deep ploughing

【深造】shēnzào（动）pursue further studies

【深海】shēnhǎi（名）deep sea

【深处】shēnchù（名）depths; recesses: 大洋～ the depths of the ocean

【深浅】shēnqiǎn（名）❶ depth: 水的～ the depth of the water ❷ sense of propriety: 办事不知～ act indiscreetly

【深情】shēnqíng（名）deep feeling

【深深】shēnshēn（副）deeply; profoundly

【深渊】shēnyuān（名）abyss: 如临～ feel as if sitting on the brink of an abyss

【深恶痛绝】shēn wù tòng jué〈成〉have intense hatred for

【深奥】shēn'ào（形）abstruse; profound

【深远】shēnyuǎn（形）far-reaching

【深谋远虑】shēn móu yuǎn lǜ〈成〉think deeply and plan far ahead

【深邃】shēnsuì（形）❶ deep ❷ abstruse; profound

淡 dàn（形）❶ light; thin; mild: ～色 light colour ❷ slack: ～季 slack season ❸ indifferent: 冷～客人 slight a guest ❹ insipid: 菜～了。The dish needs a little more salt.

【淡水】dànshuǐ（名）fresh water

【淡忘】dànwàng（动） fade from one's memory

【淡泊】dànbó（动） seek neither fame nor wealth

【淡雅】dànyǎ（形）elegant and in good taste

【淡漠】dànmò（形）❶ indifferent; apathetic ❷ faint; hazy

【淡薄】dànbó（形）❶ not dense; thin ❷ not intimate: 對她感情～ grow distant towards her ❸ faint: 印象～ have only a hazy idea of sth.

清 qīng Ⅰ（形）❶ clear; pure: 泉水又～又凉。The fountain is cold and clear. ❷ clear; distinct: 把自己的意思说～ make oneself clear ❸ quiet: 冷～ desolate; lonely ❹ free from corruption Ⅱ（动）❶ take inventory; check up: ～仓 make an inventory of all the stock; stocktaking ❷ settle accounts Ⅲ（副）completely; thoroughly: ～债 pay off a debt

【清一色】qīngyīsè（形）homogeneous; identical

【清白】qīngbái（形）clean; unblemished: ～的名聲 unblemished reputation

【清冷】qīnglěng（形）chilly

【清秀】qīngxiù（形）delicate: 眉目～的女孩 a girl of delicate features

【清官】qīngguān（名）honest and upright official

【清明】qīngmíng Ⅰ（名）(Qingming) Pure Brightness (a Chinese festival on April 5th or 6th for visiting family graveyards) Ⅱ（形）clear and bright

【清查】qīngchá（動）check

【清風】qīngfēng（名）cool breeze

【清俊】qīngjùn（形）cute; delicately attractive

【清洗】qīngxǐ（動）❶ rinse; clean: ～消毒炊具 cleanse and sterilize cooking utensils ❷ purge: ～不良分子 expel undesirable elements (from a political party)

【清香】qīngxiāng（名）delicate scent

【清音】qīngyīn（名）〈語〉voiceless sound

【清除】qīngchú（動）clear away; eradicate

【清脆】qīngcuì（形）（of voice）clear; ringing

【清淨】qīngjìng（名）peace and quiet

【清高】qīnggāo（形）indifferent to fame and material pursuits

【清朗】qīnglǎng（形）clear and bright

【清真】qīngzhēn（形）Islamic; Muslim

【清真寺】qīngzhēnsì（名）mosque

【清真教】Qīngzhēnjiào（名）Islam; Islamism

【清涼】qīngliáng（形）cool and refreshing: ～飲料 cold drink

【清涼油】qīngliángyóu（名）essential balm

【清教徒】Qīngjiàotú（名）Puritan

【清貧】qīngpín（形）impoverished: 家道～。His family lived in reduced circumstances.

【清理】qīnglǐ（動）clear up; sort out

【清淡】qīngdàn（形）❶ light; delicate (in colour, taste or smell): 一杯的綠茶 a cup of weak green tea ❷ light; not greasy: 醫生建議吃～的食物。The doctor suggested a light diet. ❸（of business）dull, slack

【清甜】qīngtián（名）❶（of voice）sweet, mellifluous; dulcet ❷（of feeling）refreshing and heart-warming

【清晨】qīngchén（清早 qīngzǎo）（名）early morning

【清爽】qīngshuǎng（形）❶（of weather or air）cool and fresh; pleasantly cold and brisk: 秋氣～。The autumn air is brisk. ❷ free from care: 任務完成了,心裏也～了。I am free from worry now that my work is done.

【清規戒律】qīng guī jiè lǜ（成）restrictions and taboos

【清單】qīngdān（名）complete list; detailed account

【清寒】qīnghán（形）❶ poor; impoverished ❷ clear and cold

【清閑】qīngxián（形）idle; undisturbed: ～的生活 quiet and undisturbed life

【清晰】qīngxī（形）distinct; clear

【清湯】qīngtāng（名）consommé; light soup

【清雅】qīngyǎ（形）elegant; graceful

【清楚】qīngchu Ⅰ（形）clear; distinct Ⅱ（動）be clear about: 我不～你在說什麼。I don't understand what you are talking about.

【清廉】qīnglián（形）honest and upright: 為政～ clean government

【清新】qīngxīn（形）fresh; refreshing

【清嗓子】qīngsǎngzi（動）clear one's throat

【清蒸】qīngzhēng（動）steam in clear soup: ～鱖魚 steamed mandarin fish

【清瘦】qīngshòu（形）thin; lean

【清算】qīngsuàn（動）❶ clear (accounts) ❷ settle with sb. by listing his crimes; settle account with; liquidate

【清漆】qīngqī（名）varnish

【清澈】qīngchè（形）clear; limpid

【清稿】qīnggǎo（名）fair copy; clean copy

【清樣】qīngyàng（名）final proof

【清賬】qīngzhàng（動）clear an account

【清談】qīngtán（名）idle talk

【清潔】qīngjié（形）clean

【清潔工】qīngjiégōng（名）sanitation worker; street cleaner

【清熱藥】qīngrèyào（名）antipyretic

【清燉】qīngdùn（動）stew in clear soup

【清靜】qīngjìng（形）quiet

【清醒】qīngxǐng Ⅰ（形）(of one's mind) clear Ⅱ（動）come to

【清償】qīngcháng（動）pay off; liquidate

【清點】qīngdiǎn（動）check; make an inventory (of)

淋 lín（動）drench: 讓雨～了 be caught in the rain; get soaked in the downpour

【淋巴】línbā（名）〈生理〉lymph: ～結炎 lymphnoditis

【淋浴】línyù（名）shower (bath)

【淋漓】línlí（形）❶ dripping: 汗水 ～ sweat profusely ❷ free; unconstrained

【淋漓盡致】lín lí jìn zhì〈成〉give a vivid and minute description

涯 yá（名）margin; limit

淺 qiǎn（形）❶ shallow ❷ short (in time):他在公司的日子還～。He has not been long with the company. ❸ simple; easy to understand: 這些教材很～。These textbooks are simple and easy. ❹ (of colour) light: ～綠 pale green

【淺見】qiǎnjiàn（名）humble opinion; superficial view: 就～所及 in my humble opinion; as far as I can see

【淺近】qiǎnjìn（形）simple and plain: ～易懂 very simple and easy to understand

【淺易】qiǎnyì（形）simple and easy

【淺陋】qiǎnlòu（形）(of knowledge and experience) meagre; shallow: 我對日語知識還很～。I have only a smattering of Japanese.

【淺嘗】qiǎncháng（動）dabble: ～輒止 dabble in the subject and feel satisfied with what little knowledge one has

【淺薄】qiǎnbó（形）superficial: 她對情況的了解很～。She has a very superficial understanding of the situation.

【淺灘】qiǎntān（名）shallows; shoal

【淺顯】qiǎnxiǎn（形）plain; simple

淹 yān（動）flood; inundate: 水把村子全～了。The whole village was flooded.

【淹死】yānsǐ（動）drown; be drowned

【淹沒】yānmò（動）submerge; flood

涮 shuàn（動）❶ rinse: 把瓶子～乾淨 rinse the bottle clean ❷ instant-boil (thin slices of meat, etc.): ～羊肉 instant-boiled (or rinsed) mutton

【涮锅子】shuànguōzi (动) instant-boil mutton in a (Mongolian) pot; hot pot

涵 hán I (动) contain II (名) culvert

【涵洞】hándòng (名) culvert

【涵义】hányì (名) meaning

【涵养】hányǎng (名) large-mindedness; ability to exercise self-restraint

淌 tǎng (动) flow; drip: ~汗 drip with sweat

淑 shū (形) (of a woman) gentle and kind; graceful; refined

混 hún (形) muddleheaded; stupid: ~蛋 bastard; idiot
see also hùn

混 hùn (动) ❶ mix; blend ❷ drift along: ~日子 muddle along
see also hún

【混合】hùnhé (名) mix; blend

【混血儿】hùnxuè'ér (名) half-breed; half-caste

【混同】hùntóng (动) confuse; confound

【混纺】hùnfǎng (动) 〈纺〉 blend: ~织物 blend fabric

【混淆】hùnxiáo (动) confuse; mix up: ~视听 confuse public opinion

【混帐】hùnzhàng (名) 〈骂〉 scoundrel; bastard

【混乱】hùnluàn (名) chaos; disorder

【混战】hùnzhàn (名) aimless fight with warring parties constantly changing sides; tangled warfare

【混凝土】hùnníngtǔ (名) concrete

【混杂】hùnzá (动) blend; mix

涸 hé (动) (of water) run dry

淪 lún (动) ❶ sink ❷ decline; fall

【淪亡】lúnwáng (动) (of a country) fall into the hands of the enemy; be subjugated

【淪陷】lúnxiàn (动) (of territory) be occupied by foreign aggressors; fall

【淪陷区】lúnxiànqū (名) enemy-occupied area

【淪落】lúnluò (动) sink low in society: ~天涯 drop out of ordinary society and become a tramp

淆 xiáo (动) mix up; confuse: 混~是非 confuse right and wrong

添 tiān (动) add; append: ~油加醋 add inflammatory details (to a narration)

【添置】tiānzhì (动) acquire; purchase

【添砖加瓦】tiān zhuān jiā wǎ 〈成〉 contribute one's little bit to; do what little one can to help

淘 táo (动) ❶ wash in a container: ~米做饭 wash and cook rice ❷ dredge: ~下水道 dredge the sewer ❸ consume; spend: ~神之处，容当面謝。I'll personally extend my thanks to you for the trouble you have taken on my behalf.

【淘汰】táotài (动) eliminate: ~赛 elimination contest

【淘金】táojīn (名) pan; wash gold: ~热 gold rush

【淘气】táoqì (形) naughty; mischievous

淼 miǎo (形) vast: 浩~的大海 the vast sea

洎 xuàn

【洎染】xuànrǎn（动）　exaggerate; play up：這樣一件小事，用不着如此～。We shouldn't play up such a trifling incident.

渡 dù（动）❶ cross over：～河 cross a river ❷ tide over：～過危機 tide over a crisis

【渡口】dùkǒu（名）place from which a ferryboat leaves; ferry

【渡船】dùchuán（名）ferryboat

【渡槽】dùcáo（名）aqueduct

游 yóu Ⅰ（动）swim Ⅱ（名）❶ part of a river; reach：下～ lower reaches (of a river) ❷（Yóu）a surname

【游泳】yóuyǒng（动）swim：～褲 swimming trunks

【游移】yóuyí（动）(of attitude; policy, etc.) waver; vacillate

【游禽】yóuqín（名）natatorial bird

【游蕩】yóudàng（动）wander; rove

【游擊隊】yóujīduì（名）guerrillas

【游擊戰】yóujīzhàn（名）guerrilla war

【游藝】yóuyì（名）entertainment; recreation：～室 recreation room

渾 hún（形）❶ muddy; turbid ❷ muddleheaded; stupid ❸ whole; all over：～身是汗 sweat all over ❹ simple and natural; unsophisticated：～厚 (of writing, painting, etc.) characterized by simplicity and vigour

【渾水摸魚】hún shuǐ mō yú〈成〉fish in troubled waters

【渾渾噩噩】hún hún è è〈成〉ignorant and muddleheaded

【渾然一體】hún rán yī tǐ〈成〉an integrated whole

【渾濁】húnzhuó（形）muddy; turbid

滋 zī（动）grow; cause：～事 create trouble

【滋生】zīshēng（动）❶ grow; multiply; breed：～疾病的地方 breeding ground of disease ❷ cause; incite：～事端 create disturbances

【滋長】zīzhǎng（动）grow; develop; engender; generate：～官僚主義 foster the growth of bureaucracy

【滋味】zīwèi（名）taste; flavour

【滋補】zībǔ（形）nourishing; nutritious

【滋養】zīyǎng Ⅰ（动）nourish Ⅱ（名）nourishment

【滋潤】zīrùn Ⅰ（形）moist Ⅱ（动）moisten

【滋擾】zīrǎo（动）create disturbances; harass

湊 còu（动）❶ put together; pool：～足人數 rope in enough people to make up the required number ❷ happen to do sth.：正～上好天。It happened to be a fine day. ❸ move closer：往前～ move closer to the front

【湊巧】còuqiǎo（副）as it happens; by chance

【湊合】còuhe（动）❶ gather together：～在一起跳舞 get together for dancing ❷ made do：～用這個筆尖 make do with this nib

渤 bó

【渤海】Bóhǎi（名）the Bohai Sea (to the east of North China)

渠 qú（名）canal; channel

【渠道】qúdào（名）❶ irrigation

canal ❷ medium; channel: 通過官方 ~ through official channels

湮 yān

【湮沒】yānmò (動) be forgotten; pass into oblivion: 他們的名字早已 ~ 無聞。Their names have long passed into oblivion.

湛 zhàn (形) ❶ profound; deep: 深 ~ profound and thorough ❷ crystal clear

港 gǎng (名) ❶ port; harbour: 海 ~ port; harbour ❷ (Gǎng) short for Xianggang (Hong Kong)

【港口】gǎngkǒu (名) port; harbour

【港務局】gǎngwùjú (名) port office

【港灣】gǎngwān (名) harbour; bay

湖 hú (名) lake

【湖北】Húběi (名) Hubei (Province)

【湖泊】húpō (名) lakes

【湖南】Húnán (名) Hunan (Province)

【湖濱】húbīn (名) lakeside

湘 Xiāng (名) another name for Hunan Province: ~ 繡 Hunan embroidery

渣 zhā (名) ❶ dregs; dross ❷ crumbs

【渣滓】zhāzǐ (名) dregs; scum; residue: 人類的 ~ scum of the earth

減 jiǎn (動) ❶ subtract; deduct; minus ❷ reduce; decrease; decline; drop

【減少】jiǎnshǎo (動) reduce; retrench; cut down: ~ 支出 cut down expenditure

【減色】jiǎnsè (動) reduce the lively atmosphere of; diminish the lustre of: 這些高層建築使風景大爲 ~。These towering buildings detract greatly from the beauty of the natural scenery.

【減刑】jiǎnxíng (動) reduce penalty; commute a sentence

【減低】jiǎndī (動) reduce; cut down

【減免】jiǎnmiǎn (動) ❶ mitigate or annul (a punishment) ❷ reduce or remit (taxation, debt, etc.): ~ 稅 tax reductions and exemptions

【減法】jiǎnfǎ (數) subtraction

【減肥】jiǎnféi (動) reduce one's weight

【減退】jiǎntuì (動) subside; abate; come down: 他的體溫 ~ 了。His temperature has dropped.

【減速】jiǎnsù (動) gear down; slow down

【減弱】jiǎnruò (動) weaken; abate; subside: 風勢 ~。The wind has abated.

【減員】jiǎnyuán (名) (of troops) depletion

【減產】jiǎnchǎn (名) decline in production; drop in crop yields

【減號】jiǎnhào (名) minus sign; sign of subtraction (-)

【減輕】jiǎnqīng (動) lighten; ease; alleviate; ~ 工作量 lighten one's workload

【減價】jiǎnjià (動) reduce the price; (of price) come down

【減壓】jiǎnyā (動) reduce pressure

湧 yǒng (動) ❶ gush; pour; surge: 幾千人 ~ 上街頭。Thousands of people spilled onto the street. ❷ emerge from the water or

mist: 雨過天晴，～出一輪明月。
The sky cleared up after the rain
and there emerged a bright moon.

【湧現】yǒngxiàn（動）emerge in
large quantities

溉 gài（動）irrigate

渺 miǎo（形）❶ remote and indistinct; uncertain: ～無音信 hear
nothing about sb.; never hear from
sb. ❷ insignificant; negligible

【渺小】miǎoxiǎo（形）insignificant;
tiny

【渺茫】miǎománg（形）❶ remote
and vague: 煙霧～。The mist
stretched far into the distance. ❷
uncertain; questionable: 前途～。
The future is full of uncertainties.

測 cè（動）❶ survey; measure: ～
海深 fathom the sea ❷ predict; estimate: 莫～高深 cannot tell what
is in sb.'s mind

【測定】cèdìng（動）survey and determine

【測量】cèliáng（動）survey; gauge

【測試】cèshì（動）test (a machine,
etc.)

【測繪】cèhuì（動）survey and map:
～學 cartography

【測驗】cèyàn Ⅰ（動）test Ⅱ（名）
test; quiz

湯 tāng（名）❶ hot water; boiling
water: 溫～ lukewarm water ❷
soup; broth: 鷄～ chicken soup ❸
(Tāng) a surname

【湯勺】tāngsháo（名）(soup) ladle

【湯加】Tāngjiā（名）Tonga: ～人
Tongan

【湯匙】tāngchí（名）tablespoon

【湯圓】tāngyuán（名）(stuffed)
dumplings (made from glutinous rice
flour, served in soup)

【湯藥】tāngyào（名）〈中醫〉decoc-
tion of Chinese medicine

【湯麵】tāngmiàn（名）noodles in
soup

渴 kě Ⅰ（形）thirsty: 不解～ cannot quench one's thirst Ⅱ（副）
earnestly; zealously: ～求 passionately desire

【渴望】kěwàng（動）long for; hanker for: 我～去巴黎旅遊。I long
for a trip to Paris.

渦 wō（名）whirlpool

【渦流】wōliú（名）whirlpool; eddy

【渦輪】wōlún（名）turbine: ～噴氣
機 turbojet (plane)

湍 tuān（形）(of a current) rapid

【湍急】tuānjí（形）(of a current)
rapid

渝 yú（動）(of one's feeling or attitude) change: 始終不～ remain unchanged; be constant to the end

渙 huàn（動）dissolve; vanish

【渙散】huànsàn（形）slack: 士氣
～。The morale is low.

淵 yuān Ⅰ（名）deep water; abyss:
苦難的深～ abyss of misery Ⅱ（形）
deep: ～深 (of learning) deep; profound

【淵博】yuānbó（形）(of learning)
broad and profound: 學識～ erudite

【淵源】yuānyuán（名）source; origin

溶 róng（動）dissolve: 易～於水
easily dissolve in water

【溶化】rónghuà（动）dissolve

【溶洞】róngdòng（名）cave with stalactites and stalagmites

【溶液】róngyè（名）〈化〉solution

【溶解】róngjiě（动）dissolve

【溶解度】róngjiědù（名）solubility

【溶质】róngzhì（名）〈化〉solute

【溶剂】róngjì（名）〈化〉solvent

滂 pāng

【滂沱】pāngtuó（形）torrential; pouring: 大雨～。It is pouring.

溯 sù（动）❶ go upstream ❷ recall; trace back; recollect

【溯源】sùyuán（动）trace back to the source; trace the origin

溢 yì（动）overflow

【溢出】yìchū（动）overflow; spill over

溝 gōu（名）❶ ditch: 陰～ sewer ❷ furrow; groove

【溝通】gōutōng（动）link up; connect

【溝渠】gōuqú（名）irrigation canals

【溝壑】gōuhè（名）gully; ravine

涟 lián（名）ripples

【涟漪】liányī（名）ripples

滇 Diān（名）another name for Yunnan Province

滅 miè（动）❶（of a light, fire, etc.）go out: 火～了。The fire went out. ❷ put off; extinguish: 請把燈～了。Turn off the light, please. ❸ destroy; wipe out: ～族 exterminate the whole clan

【滅口】mièkǒu（动）get rid of a witness or an accomplice

【滅亡】mièwáng（动）be subjugated; perish; die out

【滅火】mièhuǒ（动）put out a fire

【滅火器】mièhuǒqì（名）extinguisher

【滅迹】mièjī（动）destroy the evidence of a crime

【滅頂】mièdǐng（动）be drowned

【滅頂之災】miè dǐng zhī zāi（名）the disaster of getting drowned; overwhelming disaster

【滅絕】mièjué（动）❶ become extinct ❷ destroy completely: ～種族 genocide

【滅絕人性】miè jué rén xìng〈成〉inhuman; brutal

源 yuán（名）source; origin: 詞～ origin of a word; etymological dictionary

【源泉】yuánquán（名）source; fountainhead

【源流】yuánliú（名）source and course; origin and development

【源遠流長】yuán yuǎn liú cháng〈成〉long established; of long standing

【源源】yuányuán（副）in a steady stream; incessantly

溺 nì（动）❶ drown ❷ indulge in: 沉～於酒色 indulge in sensual pleasure

【溺愛】nì'ài（动）indulge; spoil; dote on: ～子女 indulge one's children

滑 huá Ⅰ（形）❶ slippery; smooth ❷ cunning; crafty; sly Ⅱ（动）slip; slide: 道路泥濘～倒了 slip and fall on the muddy road

【滑冰】huábīng（动）skate: ～場 skating rink / 花樣～ figure skating

【滑行】huáxíng（動）slide; coast

【滑坡】huápō（名）〈地〉landslide; landslip

【滑梯】huátī（名）slide（for children）

【滑雪】huáxuě（動）ski

【滑翔】huáxiáng（動）glide: ～機 glider

【滑溜】huáliu（形）〈口〉smooth

【滑稽】huáji（形）funny; comical

【滑輪】huálún（名）pulley; block

【滑膩】huáni（形）satiny; soft; creamy

【滑頭】huátóu I（名）sly old fox II（形）sly; slick

溫 wēn I（形）warm; lukewarm II（動）❶ warm up: 把粥～一～ warm up the porridge ❷ review III（名）❶ temperature ❷（Wēn）a surname

【溫文爾雅】wēn wén ěr yǎ（形）civil and polite

【溫存】wēncún（形）tender; kind; gentle

【溫牀】wēnchuáng（名）breeding ground; hotbed: 產生腐敗的～ a hotbed of corruption

【溫和】wēnhé（形）mild; temperate; gentle: ～派 the moderates／氣候～ mild climate

【溫和】wēnhuo（形）lukewarm

【溫差】wēnchā（名）difference in temperature

【溫柔】wēnróu（形）gentle; mild

【溫泉】wēnquán（名）hot spring

【溫厚】wēnhòu（形）gentle and kind-hearted

【溫度】wēndù（名）temperature

【溫度計】wēndùjì（溫度表 wēndùbiǎo）（名）thermometer

【溫室】wēnshì（名）greenhouse; hothouse

【溫室效應】wēnshì xiàoyìng（名）greenhouse effect

【溫故知新】wēn gù zhī xīn〈成〉review what has been learnt to gain fresh insight; recall the past so as to understand the present better

【溫習】wēnxí（動）review: ～功課 go over old lessons

【溫帶】wēndài（名）temperate zone

【溫情】wēnqíng（名）feeling of tenderness; tender-heartedness

【溫順】wēnshùn（形）docile; tame

【溫暖】wēnnuǎn（形）warm

【溫馴】wēnxùn（動）（of animals）tame; meek

【溫飽】wēnbǎo（名）sufficient food and clothing: 靠教書勉強維持～ manage to make a living by teaching

【溫靜】wēnjìng（形）gentle and quiet; demure

【溫濕】wēnshī（形）warm and humid

滔 tāo（動）inundate; flood

【滔天】tāotiān（形）❶（of billows）huge ❷ monstrous; atrocious: 罪惡～ outrageous crime

【滔滔不絕】tāo tāo bù jué〈成〉pour out a torrent of words; burst out in a torrent of speech

溪 xī（名）stream; brook

滄 cāng（形）❶（of waters）dark blue ❷ cold

【滄海】cānghǎi（名）vast blue sea

【滄桑】cāngsāng（名）（short for 滄海桑田 cānghǎi sāngtián）the vicissitudes; change of world events: 世事～ the vicissitudes of life

凖 zhǔn I（名）standard; criterion

水 ~ level; standard Ⅱ (形) ❶ accurate; exact: 瞄 ~ take good aim ❷ quasi-; para-: ~光波 quasi-optical wave / ~軍事機構 para-military organization Ⅲ (副) definitely; surely: 我~來。Surely I'll come.

【準則】zhǔnzé (名) norm; standard

【準星】zhǔnxīng (名) front sight (of a gun)

【準時】zhǔnshí (形) punctual; on time: 他 ~ 到達。He arrived on time.

【準備】zhǔnbèi (動) ❶ prepare: ~考試 prepare for the exam / ~晚飯 prepare dinner ❷ intend; plan: 我們 ~ 明天討論這個問題。We're going to discuss the question tomorrow.

【準確】zhǔnquè (形) accurate; exact; precise

【準繩】zhǔnshéng (名) criterion; yardstick: 以法律爲~ with the law as yardstick

溜 liū Ⅰ (動) ❶ slide: 書從膝蓋上 ~ 下來。The book slid off his knee. ❷ sneak away: ~出會場 sneak out of the meeting hall Ⅱ (形) smooth; slippery

see also liù

【溜之大吉】liū zhī dà jí (成) take to one's heels

【溜冰】liūbīng (動) skate: ~ 場 skating rink

【溜達】liūda (動) go for a walk; stroll

【溜鬚拍馬】liū xū pāi mǎ (成) be a toad-eater; toady

溜 liù (名) ❶ torrent: 隨大 ~ follow the crowd ❷ row: 一~白楊樹 a row of poplars

see also liū

溴 xiù (名) 〈化〉 bromine (Br)

滕 Téng (名) a surname

演 yǎn (動) ❶ perform; act: ~主角 play the leading role ❷ develop; evolve

【演化】yǎnhuà (名) evolution

【演出】yǎnchū Ⅰ (動) show; give a performance Ⅱ (名) performance: ~隊 troupe

【演示】yǎnshì (動) demonstrate; show

【演技】yǎnjì (名) acting skill; acting

【演奏】yǎnzòu (動) play (a musical instrument)

【演員】yǎnyuán (名) actor; actress: ~表 cast

【演唱】yǎnchàng (動) sing an aria

【演習】yǎnxí (名) manoeuvre; exercise

【演義】yǎnyì (名) historical romance

【演算】yǎnsuàn (動) make mathematical calculations; calculate

【演說】yǎnshuō (名) speech; address: 就職~ inaugural speech

【演播】yǎnbō (動) perform in a radio or TV programme; broadcast live

【演講】yǎnjiǎng (動) give a lecture; make a speech

【演戲】yǎnxì (動) ❶ put on a play ❷ act in a play

【演繹】yǎnyì (名) deduction: 歸納和~ induction and deduction

【演變】yǎnbiàn Ⅰ (動) develop; e-volve Ⅱ (名) evolution

滴 dī Ⅰ (動) drip Ⅱ (量) (of liquid) drop: 一~水 a drop of water

【滴水成冰】dī shuǐ chéng bīng (成)

even dripping water freezes; freezing cold

【滴水穿石】dī shuǐ chuān shí〈成〉constant dripping wears away stone

【滴答】dīdā〈象〉ticktack; patter

湝 hǔ〈名〉waterside

漉 lù〈动〉filter

滚 gǔn〈动〉❶ roll; trundle: ~下山坡 roll down the slope ❷ boil: ~开的水 boiling water ❸〈骂〉get away: ~出去! Get out!

【滚瓜烂熟】gǔn guā làn shú〈成〉have sth. at one's fingertips; learn by heart

【滚珠】gǔnzhū〈名〉〈机〉ball: ~轴承 ball bearing

【滚动】gǔndòng〈动〉roll; trundle

【滚滚】gǔngǔn〈动〉roll; billow; surge: ~向前 roll ahead; surge forward

【滚烫】gǔntàng〈形〉boiling hot; scorching hot

滬 Hù〈名〉another name for Shanghai

漾 yàng〈动〉❶ ripple ❷ overflow: 奶~出来了。The milk is spilling over.

渍 zì〈名〉stain; sludge: 墨~ ink stain; ink spot / 油~ grease spot; oil sludge

渐 jiàn〈副〉gradually; progressively; little by little

【渐次】jiàncì〈副〉gradually

【渐进】jiànjìn〈动〉advance or develop gradually

【渐渐】jiànjiàn〈副〉by degrees; gradually

潄 shù〈动〉rinse (the mouth): 洗~ 用具 toilet articles

【潄口】shùkǒu〈动〉rinse the mouth; gargle: ~杯 tooth glass; mug (for gargling or teeth-cleaning)

漂 piāo〈动〉float; drift
see also piǎo; piào

【漂泊】piāobó〈动〉wander from place to place; drift along

【漂浮】piāofú Ⅰ〈动〉float: ~在水面的海草 the seaweed floating on the surface of the water Ⅱ〈形〉(of work style) incapable of getting down to brass tacks; superficial

【漂流】piāoliú〈动〉❶ drift about ❷ rove

漂 piǎo〈动〉❶ bleach ❷ rinse away (soap, dirt, etc.)
see also piāo; piào

【漂白】piǎobái〈动〉bleach

【漂白粉】piǎobáifěn〈名〉bleaching powder

漂 piào
see also piāo; piǎo

【漂亮】piàoliang〈形〉❶ beautiful; handsome; pretty ❷ excellent; splendid: 干得~ make a splendid job of it

【漂亮話】piàolianghuà〈名〉fine words; high-sounding words: 说～ pay lip service

漢 hàn〈名〉❶ the Han Dynasty (206 BC-220 AD) ❷ the Han nationality: ~人 the Hans ❸ Chinese language ❹ man: 老~ old man

【漢白玉】hànbáiyù〈名〉white marble

【漢奸】hànjiān〈名〉traitor (to the

Chinese people)

【漢字】hànzì（名）Chinese character

【漢族】Hànzú（名）the Han nationality

【漢語】hànyǔ（名）Chinese (language)：～拼音 pīnyīn (the Chinese phonetic alphabet)

【漢學】hànxué（名）❶ the Han school of classical philology ❷ Sinology：～家 Sinologist

滿 mǎn I（形）❶ full; filled: 大廳裏人都～了。The hall is filled to capacity. ／～街是人。The street was crowded with people. ❷ conceited; proud：～招損。Pride goes before a fall. ❸ satisfied: 心懷不～ feel discontented; be filled with resentment II（副）completely; entirely; fully: 有了這筆錢, 我們～可以買臺冰箱了。With the money, we can well afford a refrigerator. III（動）expire; be over: 合同期已～。The contract has expired. IV（名）(Mǎn) a surname

【滿口】mǎnkǒu（副）(speak) profusely：～答應 promise readily ／～胡說 talk sheer nonsense

【滿天】mǎntiān（副）all over the sky：～星斗。The sky is dotted with stars.

【滿心】mǎnxīn（動）(one's heart) be filled with：～憂慮 filled with anxiety

【滿分】mǎnfēn（名）full mark

【滿月】mǎnyuè I（名）full moon II（動）(of a baby) be a month old

【滿不在乎】mǎn bùzàihu（動）not care at all: 他對這事一～。He couldn't care less about it.

【滿打滿算】mǎndǎ mǎnsuàn（副）taking everything into account; at

most; all included: 這項工程～三萬元就夠了。This project requires at most a sum of thirty thousand yuan.

【滿目瘡痍】mǎn mù chuāng yí〈成〉misery and devastation greets the eye everywhere

【滿足】mǎnzú（動）❶ feel satisfied: ～現狀 be content with the things as they are ❷ satisfy: ～人們對消費品的需求 meet people's need for consumer goods

【滿身】mǎnshēn（副）all over one's body：～是泥 be splashed all over with mud

【滿門】mǎnmén（名）the whole family

【滿面】mǎnmiàn（滿臉 mǎnliǎn）（副）all over the face: 氣得～通紅 flush with anger

【滿面春風】mǎn miàn chūn fēng〈成〉one's face glows with joy; beam with happiness

【滿城風雨】mǎn chéng fēng yǔ〈成〉create a stir; become the talk of the town

【滿座】mǎnzuò（名）full house; house full: 場場～ have a capacity audience for every show

【滿員】mǎnyuán（形）❶ (of an army) at full strength ❷ all seats taken: 這輛旅遊車已經～。This tourist coach is full. ／This coach is fully booked up.

【滿師】mǎnshī（動）serve out an apprenticeship

【滿族】Mǎnzú（名）the Man (Manchu) nationality

【滿眼】mǎnyǎn（動）❶ (one's yes) brim with: 他～淚水。His eyes filled with tears. ❷ come into full view: ～花紅柳綠。Red flowers and green willows met my eye all around.

【滿堂紅】mǎntánghóng（名）all-round success

【滿堂灌】mǎntángguàn（動）cram students in classroom instruction); spoon-feed

【滿腔】mǎnqiāng（動）be filled with: ～怒火 boil with anger

【滿期】mǎnqī（動）expire: 我的護照再過三天就～了。My passport expires in three days.

【滿登登】mǎndēngdēng（形）full: 糧倉裝得～。The granary is full.

【滿意】mǎnyì（形）satisfactory; gratifying: 結果還～。The result is satisfactory

【滿腹】mǎnfù（動）be filled with: 牢騷 ～ be full of complaints; nurse lots of grievances

【滿腹狐疑】mǎn fù hú yí〈成〉full of suspicion; very suspicious

【滿載】mǎnzài（形）fully loaded: ～西瓜的卡車 a lorry fully loaded with watermelons

【滿載而歸】mǎn zài ér guī〈成〉return with a wealth of fruitful gains

【滿腦子】mǎnnǎozi（動）(mind) be crammed with; have one's head filled with: ～餿主意 be full of lousy ideas

【滿額】mǎn'é（動）fulfil the (enrolment, employment, etc.) quota

【滿懷】mǎnhuái I（動）be filled with; cherish: ～愛國精神 be imbued with patriotism II（名）bosom: 撞了個～ bump right into sb.

漚 òu（動）soak; macerate; ret: ～肥 make compost

滯 zhì（形）stagnant; sluggish

【滯留】zhìliú（動）be delayed: 因要事在滬～數日 be detained for a few days in Shanghai by urgent business

【滯銷】zhìxiāo（動）(of a commodity) not be in demand

漆 qī I（名）❶ lacquer; paint ❷ (Qī) a surname II（動）paint; varnish

【漆工】qīgōng（名）❶ lacquering; painting ❷ lacquerer; lacquer man; painter

【漆布】qībù（名）varnished cloth

【漆包線】qībāoxiàn（名）enamel-insulated wire

【漆革】qīgé（名）patent leather

【漆畫】qīhuà（名）lacquer painting

【漆黑】qīhēi（形）pitch-dark

【漆黑一團】qīhēi yìtuán（形）❶ completely dark: 他把形勢說成～。He painted a gloomy picture of the situation ❷ be in the dark: 他的意圖如何我仍然～。I am still in the dark about his intentions.

【漆器】qīqì（名）lacquerware; lacquerwork

【漆樹】qīshù（名）lacquer tree

漲 zhǎng（動）(of water, prices, etc.) rise: 河水繼續往上～。The river continues to rise.
see also zhàng

【漲潮】zhǎngcháo（名）rising tide; flood tide

【漲價】zhǎngjià（動）rise in price; mark up

漲 zhàng（動）❶ swell after absorbing water: 木板泡～了。The plank swelled in water. ❷ (of the head) be filled to excess with a rush of blood: ～紅了臉（one's face) flush

see also zhǎng

漏 lòu（動）❶ leak: 屋頂～了。The roof leaks. / 走～了消息。leak information ❷ miss; leave out: ～了一個問號。A question mark is missing.

【漏勺】lòusháo（名）strainer; colander

【漏斗】lòudǒu（名）funnel

【漏洞】lòudòng（名）❶ leak; hole ❷ loophole; flaw: 填塞～ close a hole; plug a loophole

【漏稅】lòushuì（名）tax evasion

【漏網】lòuwǎng（動）escape punishment; be at large: 如～之魚 like a fish which has slipped out of the fisherman's net

【漏瘡】lòuchuāng（名）anal fistula

漠 mò Ⅰ（名）desert Ⅱ（形）indifferent

【漠不關心】mò bù guān xīn〈成〉be indifferent (to); be apathetic

【漠視】mòshì（動）pay no attention to; ignore: ～僱員的抗議 turn a deaf ear to the employees' protest

【漠然】mòrán（副）indifferently: 對名利～置之 be indifferent to fame and wealth

【漠漠】mòmò（形）❶ misty; foggy ❷ vast and silent: ～的荒原 vast wasteland

漫 màn Ⅰ（動）overflow; flood: 河水～上兩岸。The river overflowed its banks. Ⅱ（副）all over; everywhere Ⅲ（形）❶ casual; random: 這些學生很散～。These students

are far from well-disciplined. ❷ long: 路～～。The road stretched endlessly.

【漫山遍野】màn shān biàn yě〈成〉over the mountains and on the plains: ～而來 rush in from after all over the place

【漫天】màntiān（副）❶ all over the sky: ～塵土。The dust covered the sky. ❷ limitless: ～要價。They ask exhorbitant prices.

【漫不經心】màn bù jīng xīn（副）carelessly; absent-mindedly

【漫步】mànbù（動）stroll; roam

【漫長】màncháng（形）long; endless: ～的時間 over a prolonged period of time

【漫捲】mànjuǎn（動）(of a flag) flutter

【漫畫】mànhuà（名）caricature; cartoon: ～家 cartoonist

【漫遊】mànyóu（動）travel; roam

【漫筆】mànbǐ（名）random notes

【漫無邊際】màn wú biān jì〈成〉❶ extend endlessly ❷ stray far from the subject

【漫溢】mànyì（動）overflow; brim over

【漫漫】mànmàn（形）endless; long

【漫談】màntán（名）casual talk; informal discussion: 美學～ random talk on aesthetics

【漫罵】mànmà（動）abuse: 恣意～ indulge in a stream of abuse

漁 yú Ⅰ（名）fishing: ～港 fishing port Ⅱ（動）fish for (profit)

【漁民】yúmín（名）fisherman

【漁利】yúlì Ⅰ（動）fish for profits at others' expense Ⅱ（名）ill-gotten gains; spoils

【渔具】yújù （名） fishing tackle (gear)

【渔产】yúchǎn （名） aquatic products

【渔船】yúchuán （名） fishing boat

【渔场】yúchǎng （名） fishing ground; fishery

【渔业】yúyè （名） fishery

【渔轮】yúlún （名） fishing vessel

涤 dí （动） wash; rinse

【涤卡】díkǎ （名）〈纺〉 dacron knaki

【涤纶】dílún （名）〈纺〉 polyester

【涤荡】dídàng （动） wash away; sweep away (off)

渗 shèn （动） ooze; seep: 水似乎从水管裂口～出。Water seems to have seeped through a crack in the pipe. / 地面～水 water oozed from the ground

【渗入】shènrù （动） ❶ seep into; filter into ❷ (of influence, ideas, etc., often derogatory) infiltrate

【渗透】shèntòu Ⅰ （动） seep through; filter through Ⅱ （名） infiltration; penetration: 文化～ cultural infiltration

【渗漏】shènlòu （名） seepage and leakage

浆 jiāng Ⅰ （名） thick liquid: 豆～ soya-bean milk Ⅱ （动） starch
see also jiàng

【浆果】jiāngguǒ （名） small soft fruit such as grape and tomato

【浆洗】jiāngxǐ （动） wash and starch: 把我的衬衫拿去～。Have my shirts washed and starched.

浆 jiàng （形） thick
see also jiāng

【浆糊】jiànghu （名） paste

澈 chè （形）(of water) clear: 明～ bright and clear; transparent

涝 lào （动） waterlogging; flooding: 旱～保收田 farmland which ensures stable yields despite drought or excessive rain

【涝灾】làozāi （名） crop failure resulting from waterlogging

洁 jié （形） clean; spotless

【洁白】jiébái （形） white and clean

【洁身自好】jié shēn zì hào 〈成〉 ❶ resist moral contamination and preserve one's integrity ❷ stand aloof in all matters for fear of getting into trouble

【洁净】jiéjìng （形） clean; unsoiled

浇 jiāo （动） ❶ pour or spray (liquid) on: 面条裏～点辣椒油 sprinkle some chilli oil over the noodles / 借酒～愁 drown one's sorrow in drink ❷ irrigate; water: ～菜地 water the vegetable plot

【浇灌】jiāoguàn （动） ❶ irrigate: ～稻田 irrigate the paddy fields ❷ pour into a mould

澎 pēng （动） splash; spatter: ～了一身水 be splashed all over with water

【澎湃】pēngpài （动） surge: 浪涛～。The waves surge high.

潭 tán （名） ❶ pond: 一～清水 a pond of crystal-clear water ❷ pit; depression: 泥～ morass; quagmire

潮 cháo Ⅰ （名） ❶ tide: 低～ low tide ❷ upsurge; upheaval: 文艺思～ literary current Ⅱ （形） damp

【潮水】cháoshuǐ （名） tide; tidal water

【潮汐】cháoxī（名）tide; morning and evening tides

【潮流】cháoliú（名）❶ tide ❷ current; trend: 時代～ current of the times

【潮氣】cháoqì（名）moisture

【潮濕】cháoshī（形）damp; moist; humid

潸 shān（副）〈書〉in tears

【潸然淚下】shān rán lèi xià〈成〉shed tears

潛 qián Ⅰ（動）hide; go under Ⅱ（形）latent; hidden Ⅲ（副）secretly; stealthily

【潛入】qiánrù（動）❶ sneak into; steal in ❷ dive; submerge

【潛力】qiánlì（名）potential

【潛水】qiánshuǐ（動）dive; go under water

【潛水艇】qiánshuǐtǐng（名）submarine; U-boat

【潛在】qiánzài（形）latent; potential: ～需求 latent demand

【潛伏】qiánfú（動）hide; lie in ambush: ～的危機 hidden crisis

【潛伏期】qiánfúqī（名）〈醫〉incubation period

【潛泳】qiányǒng（名）underwater swimming

【潛逃】qiántáo（動）abscond

【潛流】qiánliú（名）undercurrent; underflow

【潛移默化】qián yí mò huà〈成〉exert an imperceptible influence on sb.'s character, thinking, etc.

【潛意識】qiányìshí（名）subconsciousness

【潛藏】qiáncáng（動）hide

潤 rùn Ⅰ（形）moist; sleek: 光～的皮膚 smooth skin Ⅱ（動）❶ moisten; lubricate: 她的眼睛濕～了。Her eyes moistened. ❷ embellish Ⅲ（名）profit; benefit: 純利～ net profits

【潤色】rùnsè（潤飾 rùnshì）（動）（of writing）polish

【潤滑】rùnhuá（動）lubricate

【潤滑油】rùnhuáyóu（名）lubricating oil; lubricant

澗 jiàn（名）brook; gully; ravine

潺 chán（象）sound of flowing water

【潺潺】chánchán（象）murmuring; babbling: 溪水～ murmuring stream

澄 chéng（形）（of water）clear see also dèng

【澄清】chéngqīng Ⅰ（形）transparent; crystal clear Ⅱ（動）clear up; clarify

【澄澈】chéngchè（形）limpid; transparent

澄 dèng（動）（of liquid）settle see also chéng

潑 pō Ⅰ（動）spill; splash: ～了一地水 splash water all over the floor Ⅱ（形）❶ shrewish; vixenish ❷ aggressive

【潑皮】pōpí（名）rascal; scoundrel

【潑冷水】pō lěngshuǐ（動）throw cold water on; discourage

【潑婦】pōfù（名）shrew; vixen

【潑辣】pōlà（形）❶ shrewish; vixenish ❷ bold and energetic ❸ pungent（in style）

【潑灑】pōsǎ（動）splash

潰 kuì（動）❶（of a dam or dyke）break; burst ❷ break through（an encirclement）❸ be routed: 擊～敵軍 put the enemy troops to rout

【潰決】kuìjué（動）（of a dam or dyke）burst; give way

【潰逃】kuìtáo（動）flee pell-mell

【潰退】kuìtuì（動）retreat in disorder

【潰敗】kuìbài Ⅰ（動）be routed; be defeated Ⅱ（名）debacle

【潰瘍】kuìyáng（名）〈醫〉ulcer: 十二指腸～ duodenal ulcer

【潰爛】kuìlàn（動）〈醫〉fester; ulcerate

潘 Pān（名）a surname

潷 bì（動）〈口〉strain; decant: ～藥 strain a decoction from boiled medicinal herbs

澱 diàn（名）sediment

【澱粉】diànfěn（名）starch

澡 zǎo（名）bath: 洗冷水～ take a cold bath

【澡盆】zǎopén（名）bathtub

【澡堂】zǎotáng（名）public baths; bathhouse

澤 zé Ⅰ（名）❶ pool; pond: 沼～ marsh; swamp ❷ lustre（of metals, pearls, etc.）Ⅱ（形）damp; moist

濃 nóng（形）❶ thick; dense: 霧 thick（heavy）fog ❷（of degree or extent）high; strong: 臭氣很～ very offensive smell; strong smell

【濃度】nóngdù（名）concentration; density

【濃厚】nónghòu（形）❶ -thick; dense ❷（of atmosphere, colour,

interest, etc.）strong: ～的東方色彩 a strong oriental flavour

【濃烈】nóngliè（形）❶（of fragrance）strong; rich ❷（of emotion, etc.）intense; passionate

【濃密】nóngmì（形）dense; thick

【濃重】nóngzhuó（形）❶（of fog, smoke, etc.）dense; thick; turbid ❷（of voice）gruff; husky; deep

【濃縮】nóngsuō（動）〈化〉concentrate: ～鈾 enriched uranium

【濃鬱】nóngyù（形）rich; strong

濁 zhuó（形）❶ dirty; turbid; muddy: ～水 muddy water ❷（of voice）loud and raucous: ～聲～氣 shout loud

【濁音】zhuóyīn（名）〈語〉voiced sound

激 jī Ⅰ（動）❶（of water）swash; send up 一石～起千層浪。A tossed stone raises numerous ripples ring upon ring. ❷ catch a chill; fall ill from getting wet in a cold rain: 他被雨～着了。He caught a bad cold after he got soaked in a downpour. ❸ excite; stir; arouse: 感～不盡 be most grateful ❹ chill（by putting in cold water）: 把瓜用涼水～一～。Chill the melon in cold water. Ⅱ（形）acute radical; fierce: 過～ extremist; radical

【激化】jīhuà（動）intensify; exacerbate

【激切】jīqiè（形）（of words）vehement; fervent

【激光】jīguāng（名）laser

【激昂】jī'áng（形）impassioned; fervent; vehement: 慷慨～的講話 impassioned speech

【激怒】jīnù（動）enrage; infuriate

【激烈】jīliè（形）acute; vigorous; violent: ~的戰鬥 fierce fighting

【激流】jīliú（名）torrent; rapids

【激起】jīqǐ（動）arouse; evoke; draw forth: ~抗議浪潮 give rise to a wave of protests

【激素】jīsù（名）hormone

【激動】jīdòng（動）excite; stir; inflame: 他~得熱淚盈眶。He was so touched that his eyes brimmed with tears.

【激將】jījiàng（動）goad sb. into action: ~法 the trick of working people up by sarcasm or irony

【激情】jīqíng（名）fervour; passion

【激進】jījìn（形）radical: ~分子 radical (element)

【激發】jīfā（動）arouse; stir up: ~他的學習熱情 kindle his enthusiasm for study

【激增】jīzēng（動）soar; go up by a large margin: 存款~。Bank deposits have shot up.

【激蕩】jīdàng（動）❶ surge; be turbulent ❷ excite: 愛國熱情~着他。He was fired with a strong sense of patriotism.

【激憤】jīfèn Ⅰ（動）be roused to indignation Ⅱ（形）indignant: 羣情~。Popular indignation runs high.

【激戰】jīzhàn（名）fierce fighting

【激勵】jīlì（動）encourage; inspire: ~士氣 boost the morale

澳 ào（名）❶ inlet of the sea ❷（Ào）short for 澳門 Àomén

【澳大利亞】Àodàlìyà（名）Australia: ~人 Australian

【澳門】Àomén（名）Aomen; Macao

濱 bīn Ⅰ（名）shore; bank: 海~公園 seaside park Ⅱ（介）by; on; bor-

dering on: ~海 bordering on the sea

濠 háo（名）moat

濟 jǐ

see also jì

【濟濟】jǐjǐ（形）(of people) a large number of: 各界人士~一堂。The hall is crowded with many people from different circles.

濟 jì（動）❶ ferry; cross a river: 和衷共~ make a concerted effort to overcome difficulties ❷ rescue; assist: 救~災民 give relief to disaster victims ❸ be of benefit; succeed: 事終不~。The matter ended in failure.

see also jǐ

【濟事】jìshì（動）[used mostly in negative statements] be of use; help matters: 勸説不~。It's no use trying to bring him around by persuasion.

濤 tāo（名）billow; breaker: 波~洶湧 roaring waves

濫 làn Ⅰ（動）flood Ⅱ（形）excessive; immoderate; exorbitant: ~要價 ask an exorbitant price

【濫用】lànyòng（動）abuse

【濫伐】lànfá（動）fell trees indiscriminately: 濫砍~ indiscriminate tree-felling

【濫竽充數】làn yú chōng shù〈成〉(of incompetent people or inferior goods) be there just to swell the total

【濫調】làndiào（名）trite remarks; platitude

澀 sè（形）❶ unsmooth; rough: 齒

輪發～，該上油了。The gear does not work smoothly. It needs oiling. ❷ puckery; astringent ❸ obscure; hard to understand: 晦～obscure

【澀味】sèwèi（名）astringent taste

濕 shī（形）wet; humid; dank: 淋淋 sopping wet; soaked through

【濕度】shīdù（名）humidity; moisture: ～表 hygrometer

【濕氣】shīqì（名）❶ moisture; wetness ❷〈中醫〉eczema; fungus infection of hand or foot

【濕疹】shīzhěn（名）〈醫〉eczema

【濕透】shītòu（動）be wet through: 全身～ be drenched to the skin

【濕漉漉】shīlùlù（形）dripping wet; damp

【濕熱】shīrè（形）humid and hot

【濕潤】shīrùn（形）moist

濛 méng（形）drizzly; misty

【濛濛】méngméng（形）drizzly; misty: 細雨～。It is drizzling. / 遠處煙霧～。There are misty clouds in the far distance.

瀉 xiè（動）❶（of river, etc.）rush down; roll on (down) ❷ have diarrhoea

【瀉肚】xièdù（動）have diarrhoea; have loose bowels

【瀉藥】xièyào（名）laxative

【瀉鹽】xièyán（名）Epsom salts

瀆 dú（動）slight: ～犯 show no respect for

【瀆職】dúzhí（名）dereliction of duty

瀘 lù（動）filter

【瀘色鏡】lùsèjìng（名）（colour）filter

【瀘紙】lùzhǐ（名）filter paper

【瀘器】lùqì（名）filter

濺 jiàn（動）splash; spatter: 火花飛～。Sparks flew about.

【濺落】jiànluò（動）〈宇航〉splash down

瀑 pù（名）waterfall

【瀑布】pùbù（名）waterfall; cataract

瀏 liú

【瀏覽】liúlǎn（動）glance through; browse: ～各種教材 browse through various textbooks

瀚 hàn（形）vast

瀝 lì（動）❶ drip ❷ filter

【瀝青】lìqīng（名）pitch; asphalt

瀕 bīn（動）❶ border on; be close to (a river, sea, etc.) ❷ be on the verge of: ～死 be dying; be at the last gasp

【瀕危】bīnwēi（動）❶ be on the edge of great danger ❷ be on one's last legs; be critically ill

【瀕於】bīnyú（動）be close to: ～瓦解 be on the edge of collapse

【瀕臨】bīnlín（動）❶ border on; be close by: ～大西洋 be by the Atlantic ❷ be on the brink of: ～破產 be on the verge of bankruptcy

瀟 xiāo

【瀟瀟】xiāoxiāo（名）❶ whistling and pattering: 風雨～ the whistling of wind and pattering of rain ❷ drizzy

【瀟灑】xiāosǎ（形）elegant with natural grace

瀾 lán（名）billows; breakers: 狂～raging tide; desperate situation

灌 guàn (動) ❶ irrigate ❷ fill; pour

【灌木】guànmù (名) bush; shrub

【灌注】guànzhù (動) pour sth. into

【灌溉】guàngài Ⅰ (動) irrigate Ⅱ (名) irrigation

【灌腸】guàncháng (名)〈醫〉enema

【灌輸】guànshū (動) imbue; instil

灑 sǎ (動) sprinkle; spill; shed: 給花~水 sprinkle water on the flowers

【灑水車】sǎshuǐchē (名) watering car; sprinkler

【灑淚】sǎlèi (動) shed tears

【灑脫】sǎtuō (形) free and easy; relaxed

灘 tān (名) ❶ beach ❷ shoal

灣 wān (名) ❶ bend (of a river) ❷ gulf; bay

火 部

火 huǒ Ⅰ (名) ❶ fire: 滅~ put out a fire ❷ firearms; ammunition: 開~ open fire ❸ anger; temper: 發~ lose one's temper Ⅱ (形) ❶ fiery; flaming: ~紅的太陽 a flaming sun ❷ urgent; pressing: ~急 most urgent

【火力】huǒlì (名) fire power; fire: ~點 firing point / ~發電廠 thermal power plant

【火山】huǒshān (名) volcano: ~口 crater

【火上加油】huǒ shàng jiā yóu〈成〉 add fuel to the fire

【火化】huǒhuà (動) cremate

【火中取栗】huǒ zhōng qǔ lì〈成〉 pull sb.'s chestnuts out of the fire

【火石】huǒshí (名) flint

【火把】huǒbǎ (名) torch

【火車】huǒchē (名) train: ~頭 locomotive

【火災】huǒzāi (名) fire; conflagration

【火坑】huǒkēng (名) fiery pit; hell upon earth

【火花】huǒhuā (名) spark

【火併】huǒbìng (名) open strife between members of the same faction

【火炬】huǒjù (名) torch

【火苗】huǒmiáo (名) flame

【火炮】huǒpào (名) cannon; gun

【火星】huǒxīng (名) ❶ spark ❷ Mars

【火柴】huǒchái (名) match

【火速】huǒsù (副) at top speed; posthaste

【火焰】huǒyàn (名) flame

【火腿】huǒtuǐ (名) ham

【火葬】huǒzàng (動) cremate: ~場 crematorium; crematory

【火綫】huǒxiàn (名) front line

【火辣辣】huǒlàlà (形) scorching; burning

【火種】huǒzhǒng (名) kindling; tinder

【火箭】huǒjiàn (名) rocket

【火險】huǒxiǎn (名) fire insurance

【火燒眉毛】huǒ shāo méi máo〈成〉 imminent; very urgent; of great urgency

【火藥】huǒyào (名) gun-powder; powder

【火警】huǒjǐng (名) fire alarm

【火爐】huǒlú (名) stove

【火鸡】huǒjī (名) turkey

灰 huī Ⅰ (名) ❶ ash ❷ dust ❸ lime; (lime) mortar Ⅱ (形) ❶ grey ❷ disheartened; discouraged

【灰心】huīxīn (形) discouraged; disappointed

【灰白】huībái (形) greyish white; ashen; pale

【灰色】huīsè Ⅰ (名) grey Ⅱ (形) ❶ pessimistic; gloomy ❷ obscure; ambiguous

【灰暗】huī'àn (形) dingy

【灰尘】huīchén (名) dust; dirt

【灰锰氧】huīměngyǎng (名) potassium permanganate

【灰烬】huījìn (名) ashes

灼 zhuó Ⅰ (动) burn; scorch Ⅱ (形) thorough; penetrating

【灼见】zhuójiàn (名) penetrating and insightful views

【灼热】zhuórè (形) scorching hot

灸 jiǔ (名) 〈中醫〉 moxibustion

災 zāi (名) disaster; calamity: 火 ~ fire

【災民】zāimín (名) people of a stricken area; victims of a natural disaster

【災害】zāihài (名) disaster; calamity

【災荒】zāihuāng (名) famine

【災情】zāiqíng (名) condition of a disaster

【災區】zāiqū (名) afflicted (or stricken) area

【災禍】zāihuò (名) disaster; catastrophe

【災難】zāinàn (名) catastrophe; suffering; disaster

炕 kàng (名) kang; brick bed that can be heated from below

【炕桌兒】kàngzhuōr (名) small, low table used on the kang

【炕蓆】kàngxí (名) kang mat

炎 yán Ⅰ (形) hot; burning: 赤日 ~~。 It's blazingly hot. Ⅱ (名) inflammation: 腦 ~ encephalitis

【炎症】yánzhèng (名) inflammation

【炎涼】yánliáng (形) warm or cold towards people of higher or lower social positions; snobbish: 世態 ~ snobbishness of human society

【炎熱】yánrè (形) sweltering; exceedingly hot

炔 quē (名) 〈化〉 alkyne

炒 chǎo (动) stir-fry: 爆 ~ quick-fry

【炒米花】chǎo mǐhuā (名) puffed rice

【炒菜】chǎocài Ⅰ (动) stir-fry meat or vegetables Ⅱ (名) stir-fried dish

【炒麵】chǎomiàn (名) ❶ chow mein; fried noodles ❷ parched flour

炊 chuī (动) cook a meal

【炊具】chuījù (名) cooking utensils; kitchenware

【炊事】chuīshì (名) cooking; kitchen work: ~ 員 cook; messcook

【炊煙】chuīyān (名) smoke from cooking fire

炙 zhì (动) roast: ~肉 roast meat

【炙手可熱】zhì shǒu kě rè 〈成〉 (of senior officials) imperious and haughty

炫 xuàn (动) ❶ dazzle ❷ show off

【炫示】xuànshì（動）show off; display: ～自己的學識 show off one's learning

【炫耀】xuànyào（動）show off; make a display of: 公開～實力 make an open display of strength

炬 jù（名）torch: 目光如～ dart a piercing glance

炳 bǐng（形）bright; splendid

炯 jiǒng（形）shining; glistening

【炯炯】jiǒngjiǒng（形）（of eyes）bright; shining: 目光～有神 with a pair of sharp, penetrating eyes

炸 zhá（動）deep-fry: ～魚 fried fish / ～土豆片（fried）potato chips; chips
see also zhà

炸 zhà（動）❶ explode; burst: 我倒進開水，玻璃杯就～了。The glass burst after I poured boiling water into it. ❷ blow up; blast: 炸敵人軍火庫 blow up an enemy arsenal / ～得粉碎 be smashed to pieces; be blown to bits ❸ flare up: 他一聽見這消息就～了。He flew into a violent rage at the news.
see also zhá

【炸彈】zhàdàn（名）bomb

【炸藥】zhàyào（名）（charges）explosive; dynamite: 烈性～ high explosive

炮 bāo（動）quick fry
see also páo; pào

炮 páo prepare Chinese medicine by roasting
see also bāo; pào

【炮製】páozhì（動）❶ prepare

（Chinese medicine）❷〈貶〉cococt; cook up

炮 pào（名）cannon; artillery
see also bāo; páo

【炮火】pàohuǒ（名）gunfire; artillery fire

【炮手】pàoshǒu（名）gunner; bombardier

【炮灰】pàohuī（名）cannon fodder

【炮兵】pàobīng（名）artillery; artilleryman

【炮位】pàowèi（名）emplacement

【炮筒子】pàotǒngzi（名）〈口〉loudmouth

【炮艇】pàotǐng（名）gunboat

【炮臺】pàotái（名）fort; battery

【炮樓】pàolóu（名）blockhouse

【炮彈】pàodàn（名）（artillery）shell

【炮擊】pàojī（動）bombard; shell

【炮轟】pàohōng（動）bombard; shell

【炮艦】pàojiàn（名）gunboat

炭 tàn（名）❶ charcoal ❷ coal: 煤～工業 coal industry

烤 kǎo Ⅰ（動）roast; bake; broil: 北京～鴨 roast Beijing duck / ～白薯 baked sweet potatoes / 一片～麵包 a piece of toast Ⅱ（形）scorching

【烤火】kǎohuǒ（動）warm oneself by a fire

【烤肉】kǎoròu（名）grilled meat; roast meat

【烤羊肉串】kǎo yángròuchuàn（名）shish kebab; shashlik

【烤爐】kǎolú（烤箱 kǎoxiāng）（名）oven

烘 hōng（動）❶ dry sth. or warm oneself by the fire ❷ set off（by contrast)

【烘托】hōngtuō(動)❶ (of Chinese painting) give a pale background to an object so as to make it stand out clearly ❷ set off by contrast

【烘烤】hōngkǎo(動)toast; bake

【烘箱】hōngxiāng(名)oven

烙 lào(動)❶ press with a hot iron; brand: ～印 brand ❷ bake (in a pan or griddle): ～餡兒餅 bake meat pie (on a pan)

【烙餅】làobǐng(名)pancake

【烙鐵】làotie(名)❶ flat-iron ❷ soldering iron

烈 liè Ⅰ(形)strong; violent; vehement: 他性子～。He has a fiery temper. Ⅱ(名)❶ martyr: 先～ fallen heroes; martyrs ❷ heroic deeds

【烈士】lièshì(名)a person of high endeavour; revolutionary martyr

【烈火】lièhuǒ(名)blazing fire

【烈日】lièrì(名)scorching sun

【烈性】lièxìng(形)❶ fierce; fiery; unyielding ❷ strong: ～炸藥 high explosive

【烈酒】lièjiǔ(名)strong liquor; spirits

【烈屬】lièshǔ(名)family member of a martyr

烏 wū Ⅰ(名)crow Ⅱ(形)black; dark

【烏七八糟】wū qī bā zāo(形)❶ at sixes and sevens; terribly messy ❷ filthy; obscene

【烏干達】Wūgāndá(名)Uganda: ～人 Ugandan

【烏木】wūmù(名)〈植〉ebony

【烏有】wūyǒu(名)naught; nothing:

化爲～ vanish like soap bubbles; disappear from the earth

【烏合之衆】wū hé zhī zhòng〈成〉a horde of ruffians; rabble; mob

【烏托邦】Wūtuōbāng(名)Utopia

【烏拉圭】Wūlāguī(名)Uruguay: ～人 Uruguayan

【烏亮】wūliàng(形)shining black

【烏紗帽】wūshāmào(名)official post

【烏梅】wūméi(名)dark plum

【烏魚】wūyú(名)snake-headed fish

【烏黑】wūhēi(形)pitch-dark; jet-black

【烏雲】wūyún(名)dark cloud

【烏賊】wūzéi(名)cuttlefish; ink-fish

【烏煙瘴氣】wū yān zhàng qì〈成〉filthy surroundings; foul atmosphere

【烏鴉】wūyā(名)crow

【烏龍茶】wūlóngchá(名)oolong tea

【烏龜】wūguī(名)tortoise

烹 pēng(動)boil; cook

【烹飪】pēngrèn(名)cooking; cuisine

【烹調】pēngtiáo(動)cock

焐 wù(動)warm up: ～腳 warm one's feet

焊 hàn(動)weld; solder: 電～ electric welding

【焊工】hàngōng(名)❶ welding; soldering ❷ welder; solder

【焊條】hàntiáo(名)welding rod

【焊接】hànjiē Ⅰ(動)weld; solder Ⅱ(名)welding; soldering

【焊槍】hànqiāng(名)welding torch; (welding) blowpipe

烽 fēng(名)beacon; signal

【烽火】 fēnghuǒ (名) ❶ beacon-fire ❷ war

【烽火臺】 fēnghuǒtái (名) beacon tower

【烽煙四起】 fēng yān sì qǐ 〈成〉 the flames of war rise all around

焙 bèi (動) bake (dry over a slow fire)：烘 ～ cure (tea, tobacco leaves or medicinal herbs)

【焙乾】 bèigān (動) dry over a fire

【焙燒】 bèishāo (動) roast; bake

焰 yàn (名) flame

【焰火】 yànhuǒ (名) fireworks

煮 zhǔ (動) boil; cook：～麵條 boil noodles ／ ～飯 cook rice

焚 fén (動) burn

【焚化】 fénhuà (動) burn; cremate

【焚毀】 fénhuǐ (動) burn; burn down

無 wú Ⅰ (名) nothing：一 ～ 所有 have nothing that one may call one's own Ⅱ (動) not have：～直接聯繫 have no direct connection Ⅲ (副) regardless of：事 ～ 大小都要親自 過 問 personally attend to all matters, be they big or small

【無力】 wúlì (形) ❶ weak; feeble：四肢 ～ feel weak in the limbs ❷ unable; incapable：我 ～ 解決你的 問題。I am in no position to solve your problem.

【無干】 wúgān (動) have no connection with; be completely irrelevant：顯然 ～ be obviously irrelevant

【無上】 wúshàng (形) supreme; highest：至 高 ～ 的 職 責 the supreme duty

【無比】 wúbǐ (形) matchless; incomparable; peerless

【無不】 wúbù (副) universally; without exception：～ 歡欣鼓舞 All jumped with joy.

【無方】 wúfāng (副) not properly：治廠 ～ not run a factory properly; mismanage a factory

【無心】 wúxīn Ⅰ (動) not feel like; have no inclination; be in no mood to：～ 參加晚會 be in no mood to go to the evening party Ⅱ (形) unintentional：他是 ～ 幹的。He did not do it on purpose.

【無孔不入】 wú kǒng bù rù 〈成〉 lose no chance (in doing evil)

【無中生有】 wú zhōng shēng yǒu 〈成〉 sheer fabrication

【無以復加】 wú yǐ fù jiā 〈成〉 extremely：兇狠得 ～ extremely savage

【無用】 wúyòng (形) useless; worthless

【無可比擬】 wú kě bǐ nǐ 〈成〉 without equal; without parallel：這種奉獻精神是 ～。This spirit of dedication is without parallel.

【無可奉告】 wú kě fèng gào 〈成〉 have nothing to say; have no comment to make：對你提出的問題，我 ～。I have no comment to make on your question.

【無可奈何】 wú kě nài hé 〈成〉 have no way out; have no option：他 ～，只好取消了這個約會。He has no alternative but to cancel the appointment.

【無可爭辯】 wú kě zhēng biàn (形) indisputable

【無功受祿】 wú gōng shòu lù 〈成〉 receive emolument without rendering any service; get an undeserved reward

【無色】wúsè（形）colourless

【無名】wúmíng（形）❶ nameless; anonymous; unknown: ～作家 anonymous writer; obscure writer / ～小卒 a nobody / ～英雄 unsung hero ❷ indescribable; indefinable

【無名指】wúmíngzhǐ（名）third finger; ring finger

【無米之炊】wú mǐ zhī chuī〈成〉cook without rice; make bricks without straw

【無休止】wúxiūzhǐ（形）incessant; endless; ceaseless

【無地自容】wú dì zì róng〈成〉wish one could vanish from under one's feet; be extremely ashamed

【無私】wúsī（形）selfless; disinterested: ～援助 disinterested assistance

【無形】wúxíng（形）invisible: ～貿易 invisible trade / ～商品 intangible goods

【無形中】wúxíngzhōng（副）virtually; imperceptibly; unknowingly: 他～成了我們的對手。He has virtually become our rival. / 他～染上了酒癮。He got addicted to drinking before he was aware of it.

【無足輕重】wú zú qīng zhòng〈成〉of little significance; unimportant

【無妨】wúfáng（副）might as well: 你～坦率地亮出自己的觀點。You might as well frankly state your own views.

【無怪】wúguài（副）no wonder; little wonder: 他們走了三個小時的路，～他們這麼累。No wonder they are so tired, they have walked for three hours nonstop.

【無奈】wúnài Ⅰ（動）have no choice; cannot but: ～出此下策 have no

choice but to make this unwise move Ⅱ（連）but: 她本想出國，～小孩没有人照料，只好不去。She planned to go abroad, but she had to give up the trip because there was nobody to look after her child.

【無味】wúwèi（形）tasteless; dull; insipid

【無非】wúfēi（副）nothing but; only: 我～是開個玩笑。I was only joking.

【無知】wúzhī Ⅰ（形）ignorant Ⅱ（名）ignorance: ～比貧困更可怕。Ignorance is worse than poverty.

【無狀】wúzhuàng（形）ill-mannered

【無法】wúfǎ（動）be unable to; cannot: ～得出結論 be unable to draw a conclusion

【無法無天】wú fǎ wú tiān〈成〉no law under heaven; defy all law and discipline

【無所不在】wú suǒ bù zài〈成〉exist everywhere; ubiquitous

【無所不知】wú suǒ bù zhī〈成〉know everything

【無所不爲】wú suǒ bù wéi〈成〉resort to any means to achieve wicked purposes

【無所事事】wú suǒ shì shì〈成〉loaf around doing nothing

【無所適從】wú suǒ shì cóng〈成〉not know the direction in which to follow

【無所謂】wúsuǒwèi（動）❶ cannot be taken as; cannot be regarded as: 我只是籠統地講，～針對什麼人。I was talking in general; it was not directed against anybody in particular. ❷ be indifferent to: 我真是～。It really doesn't matter with me.

【無事生非】wú shì shēng fēi〈成〉deliberately create trouble

【無事忙】wú shì máng〈成〉make much ado about nothing; be a busybody

【無花果】wúhuāguǒ (名)〈植〉fig

【無的放矢】wú dì fàng shǐ〈成〉shoot without a target; be aimless

【無底洞】wúdǐdòng (名) bottomless pit

【無拘無束】wú jū wú shù〈成〉uninhibited; free from convention: ～討論 discuss freely; have a free exchange of views

【無依無靠】wú yī wú kào〈成〉with no one to turn to or rely on; alone and friendless

【無度】wúdù (形) excessive; without restraint

【無故】wúgù (副) without reason; with no excuse: ～曠課 absent from class with no excuse

【無畏】wúwèi (形) dauntless; fearless; brave; heroic

【無垠】wúyín (形) boundless; vast

【無限】wúxiàn (形) infinite; boundless

【無限期】wúxiànqī (副) of indefinite duration; indefinitely: 會議～推遲。The meeting has been put off indefinitely.

【無風不起浪】wú fēng bù qǐ làng〈成〉there is no smoke without fire; everything has a cause

【無計可施】wú jì kě shī〈成〉reach the end of one's tether; at one's wits' end

【無神論】wúshénlùn (名) atheism: ～者 atheist

【無政府主義】wúzhèngfǔ zhǔyì (名) anarchism: ～者 anarchist

【無軌電車】wúguǐ diànchē (名) trolley; trolleybus

【無效】wúxiào (形) invalid; ineffective; null and void

【無恥】wúchǐ (形) shameless; audacious

【無害】wúhài (形) harmless

【無核】wúhé (形) non-nuclear; nuclear-free: ～區 nuclear-free zone / ～國家 non-nuclear country

【無益】wúyì (形) useless; unprofitable; without benefit

【無恙】wúyàng (形) in good health

【無能】wúnéng (形) incapable; incompetent: ～之輩 nonentities; incompetents

【無能為力】wú néng wéi lì〈成〉be in no position to help; be powerless: ～,只好袖手旁觀。Unable to help, one can only stand by and watch.

【無病呻吟】wú bìng shēn yín〈成〉sigh sadly for imaginary worries; (of literary works) be affected in style and devoid of true feeling

【無記名投票】wújìmíng tóupiào (名) secret ballot

【無家可歸】wú jiā kě guī〈成〉homeless

【無條件】wútiáojiàn (形) unconditional

【無息貸款】wúxī dàikuǎn (名) interest-free loan

【無時無刻】wú shí wú kè (副) all the time; always

【無聊】wúliáo (形) ❶ senseless; boring: ～的問題 a silly question ❷ bored; weary: ～得要命 be bored to death

【無情】wúqíng (形) merciless; pitiless; heartless: ～無義 heartless and faithless

【無常】wúcháng （形）changeable; capricious: 天氣變化～。The weather is capricious.

【無異】wúyì （副）not different from; as good as: 這～於自殺。This is tantamount to suicide.

【無堅不摧】wú jiān bù cuī （成）be able to smash the stiffest resistance

【無從】wúcóng （動）not know how (to do sth.）; be unable to (decide what to do): ～下筆 (of writing) not know where to start

【無理】wúlǐ （形）without rhyme or reason: ～要求 unreasonable demand

【無理取鬧】wú lǐ qǔ nào （成）deliberately provoke a row; be unreasonable and make a scene

【無產者】wúchǎnzhě （名）proletarian

【無產階級】wúchǎn jiējí （名）proletariat

【無視】wúshì （動）disregard; ignore: 他～我的忠告, 結果出了事。He disregarded my advice and got into trouble.

【無動於衷】wú dòng yú zhōng （成）remain indifferent; be apathetic

【無國籍】wúguójí （形）stateless: ～者 stateless alien

【無陪同包價旅行】wúpéitóng bāojià lǚxíng （名）inclusive independent tour; IIT

【無牽無掛】wú qiān wú guà （形）be carefree; have nothing to worry about

【無辜】wúgū Ⅰ（形）innocent Ⅱ（名）innocent person

【無須】wúxū （副）need not; not have to; be unnecessary: ～解釋 need no explanation

【無幾】wújǐ （形）few; little: 相差～。The difference is negligible.

【無量】wúliàng （形）boundless; incalculable; limitless: 功德～ be immensely beneficial

【無期徒刑】wúqī túxíng （名）life imprisonment

【無惡不作】wú è bù zuò 〈成〉be capable of any evil; stop at nothing in doing evil

【無痛分娩】wútòng fēnmiǎn （名）(of childbirth) painless delivery

【無補】wúbǔ （形）useless; of no help: 無原則的批評於事～。Unprincipled criticism won't help matters.

【無愧】wúkuì （動）have nothing to be ashamed of; be worthy of: ～於人民的信賴 be worthy of the people's trust

【無罪】wúzuì （形）innocent; not guilty

【無暇】wúxiá （動）have no time; be fully occupied: ～會客 be too busy to receive guests

【無意】wúyì Ⅰ（動）have no intention: ～出席會議 have no desire to attend the meeting Ⅱ（副）unintentionally; by chance: ～中發現 discover by chance

【無意識】wúyìshì （形）unconscious

【無傷大雅】wú shāng dà yǎ 〈成〉do no harm; not matter much; be harmless

【無微不至】wú wēi bù zhì 〈成〉meticulously; pay attention to every detail: ～地關懷 take care of sb. in every possible way

【無與倫比】wú yǔ lún bǐ 〈成〉peerless; unrivalled; beyond comparison

【無疑】wúyí （副）no doubt; undoubtedly

【無端】wúduān（副）for no reason whatever：～發怒 get angry for no conceivable reason

【無綫】wúxiàn（名）wireless; cordless：～電報 wireless telegram; radiotelegram／～電話 radiotelephone

【無綫電】wúxiàndiàn（名）radio：～傳真 radiofacsimile／～導航 radio range

【無隙可乘】wú xì kě chéng〈成〉invulnerable; leave no loophole

【無精打采】wú jīng dǎ cǎi〈成〉disappointed and low-spirited

【無窮】wúqióng（形）endless; infinite：後患～ engender endless trouble

【無敵】wúdí（形）invincible; unrivalled; unmatched：所向～ be all-conquering

【無數】wúshù（形）❶ innumerable; countless ❷ uncertain; unsure：我心中～。I'm not sure about it.

【無論】wúlùn（連）no matter…：～你是誰，都無權這樣做。You have no right to do so, no matter who you are.

【無論如何】wúlùn rúhé（副）in any case; at all costs：這種條件～也不能答應。Such terms are unacceptable in any case.

【無稽之談】wú jī zhī tán〈成〉nonsense; groundless rumour

【無價之寶】wú jià zhī bǎo〈成〉invaluable asset; priceless treasure

【無影無踪】wú yǐng wú zōng〈成〉vanish without a trace; nowhere to be found

【無影燈】wúyǐngdēng（名）〈醫〉shadowless lamp

【無緣無故】wú yuán wú gù〈成〉for no reason at all; without rhyme or reason

【無懈可擊】wú xiè kě jī〈成〉beyond reproach; invulnerable

【無賴】wúlài Ⅰ（形）shameless Ⅱ（名）rascal; scoundrel

【無機】wújī（形）inorganic：～化學 inorganic chemistry

【無謂】wúwèi（形）meaningless; senseless; nonsensical：～的爭論 meaningless argument

【無獨有偶】wú dú yǒu ǒu〈成〉be no isolated case

【無頭案】wútóu'àn（名）criminal case without any clues; unsolved mystery

【無縫鋼管】wúfèng gāngguǎn（名）seamless steel tube

【無聲】wúshēng（形）soundless; silent; noiseless：寂然～ silent and still

【無償】wúcháng（形）gratis; free; without pay：～服務 gratuitous service

【無償債能力】wú chángzhài nénglì（名）insolvency

【無濟於事】wú jì yú shì〈成〉to no purpose; fruitless; in vain

【無雙】wúshuāng（形）peerless; unique

【無題】wútí（形）untitled; titleless

【無邊無際】wúbiān wújì（形）vast; boundless; infinite：～的海洋 boundless sea

【無關】wúguān（動）not affect or concern; be irrelevant to：這與我們的討論～。This is irrelevant to our discussion.／～大局 not affect the overall situation／～緊要 be of no importance; not matter

【無關痛癢】wú guān tòng yǎng〈成〉

pointless; superficial: ~的話 inane remarks

【無繩電話】 wúshéng diànhuà (名) cordless telephone

【無黨派人士】 wúdǎngpài rénshì (名) people without party affiliation; nonparty personage

【無權】 wúquán (動) have no right to; not be entitled to

然 rán I (形) ❶ right; correct: 不以爲 ~ disapprove of ❷ so; like that: 快走吧,不 ~ 就遲到了。Hurry up or else you'll be late. II [suffix of certain adverbs and adjectives indicating the state of affairs]: 突 ~ suddenly / 愕 ~ astounded

【然而】 rán'ér (連) yet; but; however: 這事很怪,~ 卻是真的。It is strange, yet it is a fact.

【然後】 ránhòu (副) then; afterwards: 學 ~ 知不足。Learn and you will find yourself deficient in knowledge.

焦 jiāo I (形) ❶ burnt; scorched: 飯燒 ~ 了。The rice is burnt. ❷ anxious; worried: 令人心 ~ make one worried; cause anxiety II (名) ❶ coke: 煉 ~ 爐 coke oven ❷ (Jiāo) a surname

【焦土】 jiāotǔ (名) scorched earth; a heap of rubble; a lot of debris

【焦油】 jiāoyóu (名) tar

【焦急】 jiāojí (形) anxious; worried: ~ 萬狀 anxious beyond description

【焦炭】 jiāotàn (名) coke

【焦黃】 jiāohuáng (形) ❶ brown ❷ (of face) sallow

【焦慮】 jiāolǜ (動) be deeply worried; be eaten up with anxiety

【焦頭爛額】 jiāo tóu làn é〈成〉 (of enemy troops) be battered right and left; be thrown into utter confusion; be in a tight corner

【焦點】 jiāodiǎn (名) focal point; focus: 爭論的 ~ bone of contention; focal point of disagreement

【焦躁】 jiāozào (形) impatient; full of anxiety

煎 jiān (動) ❶ light-fry in a little oil ❷ simmer: ~ 中藥 decoct Chinese medicinal herbs

【煎熬】 jiān'áo (動) be in torment; 受盡 ~ suffer all kinds of torments

【煎餅】 jiānbing (名) thin pancake

煸 biān (動) stir-fry before stewing

煉 liàn (動) temper; smelt; refine

【煉丹】 liàndān (名) alchemy

【煉油】 liànyóu (名) oil refining: ~ 廠 refinery

【煉乳】 liànrǔ (名) condensed milk

【煉焦】 liànjiāo (名) coking

【煉鋼】 liàngāng (名) steel-making: ~ 廠 steelworks

【煉鐵】 liàntiě (名) iron-smelting

煙 yān (名) ❶ smoke: 滿屋是 ~。The room is filled with smoke. ❷ tobacco; cigarette: 一條 ~ a carton of cigarettes ❸ opium

【煙土】 yāntǔ (名) crude opium

【煙火】 yānhuǒ (名) ❶ smoke and fire ❷ fireworks

【煙斗】 yāndǒu (名) tabacco pipe

【煙斗絲】 yāndǒusī (名) pipe tabacco

【煙民】 yānmín (名) opium addicts

【煙灰】 yānhuī (名) tabacco ash; cigarette ash

【煙灰缸】 yānhuīgāng (名) ashtray

【煙囪】 yāncōng (名) chimney

【煙具】yānjù（名）smoking set

【煙油】yānyóu（名）tabacco tar

【煙草】yāncǎo（名）tabacco

【煙鬼】yānguǐ（名）❶ heavy smoker ❷ opium addict; drug user

【煙消雲散】yān xiāo yún sàn〈成〉vanish like smoke; completely disappear

【煙袋】yāndài（名）❶ tabacco pouch ❷ small-bowled long-stemmed pipe

【煙盒】yānhé（名）cigarette case

【煙道】yāndào（名）〈建〉flue（pipe）

【煙絲】yānsī（名）pipe tabacco; cut tabacco

【煙筒】yāntong（名）stovepipe; chimney

【煙葉】yānyè（名）tabacco leaf; leaf tabacco

【煙幕】yānmù（名）smoke screen: 放～ put up a smoke screen / ～彈 smoke bomb

【煙頭】yāntóu（名）cigarette end; cigarette stub

【煙嘴】yānzuǐ（名）cigarette holder

【煙霧】yānwù（名）smoke; mist; haze

【煙癮】yānyǐn（名）❶ craving to smoke ❷ opium addiction

煤 méi（名）coal: 蜂窩～ honeycomb briquet

【煤田】méitián（名）coalfield

【煤油】méiyóu（名）kerosene

【煤油燈】méiyóudēng（名）kerosene lamp

【煤油爐】méiyóulú（名）kerosene stove

【煤矸石】méigānshí（名）gangue

【煤炭】méitàn（名）coal

【煤倉】méicāng（名）coal bunker

【煤耗】méihào（名）coal consumption

【煤氣】méiqì（名）gas; coal gas

【煤氣中毒】méiqì zhòngdú（名）gas poisoning; carbon monoxide poisoning

【煤氣管】méiqìguǎn（名）gas pipe

【煤氣罐】méiqìguàn（名）gas tank

【煤氣竈】méiqìzào（名）gas range; gas cooker

【煤球】méiqiú（名）（egg-shaped）briquet

【煤渣】méizhā（名）（coal）cinder

【煤場】méichǎng（名）coal yard

【煤焦油】méijiāoyóu（名）coal tar

【煤煙】méiyān（名）❶ smoke from coal combustion ❷ soot

【煤塵】méichén（名）coal dust

【煤玉】méiyù（名）coal玉 méiyù）jet; black amber

【煤層】méicéng（名）coal seam; coal bed

【煤窯】méiyáo（名）coalpit

【煤礦】méikuàng（名）coal mine: ～工人 coal miner

煳 hú（形）(of food) burnt

煩 fán Ⅰ（形）❶ vexed; annoyed ❷ lengthy; involved Ⅱ（動）be annoyed; be fed up

【煩冗】fánrǒng（形）❶ complicated ❷ tedious

【煩勞】fánláo（動）bother; trouble

【煩悶】fánmèn（形）unhappy; in a bad mood; moody

【煩惱】fánnǎo（形）vexed; worried

【煩瑣】fánsuǒ（形）tedious; trivial

【煩瑣哲學】fánsuǒ zhéxué（名）❶ scholasticism ❷ hairsplitting

【煩擾】fánrǎo（動）❶ bother ❷ feel upset

【烦躁】fánzào（形）irritable; irascible

煨 wēi（动）❶ stew; simmer ❷ roast in fresh cinders

煌 huáng（形）bright; brilliant: 灯火辉～ brilliantly illuminated

焕 huàn（形）shining; glowing

【焕发】huànfā（动）glow: 容光～ glow with health

【焕然一新】huàn rán yī xīn〈成〉take on a fresh look

照 zhào Ⅰ（动）❶ shine; illuminate: 电光把屋子都～亮了。The lightning lit up the room. ❷ reflect; mirror: ～镜子 look at oneself in the mirror ❸ take a picture（photograph）; shoot: 我给他～了一张相。I took a photograph of him. / 去医院～X 光 go to hosptial for an X ray ❹ look after; attend to ❺ check against: 对～ compare ❻ understand: 心～不宣 have a tacit understanding Ⅱ（名）❶ sunlight: 夕～ glow of sunset ❷ photograph; picture ❸ licence; certificate: 驾驶执～ driving licence Ⅲ（介）❶ in the direction of; towards: ～敌人开枪 shoot at the enemy; open fire on the enemy ❷ according to; in accordance with: ～理说 theoretically speaking

【照片】zhàopiàn（名）photograph; picture

【照本宣科】zhào běn xuān kē〈成〉read straight from the text; read item by item mechanically

【照抄】zhàochāo（动）❶ copy word for word ❷ plagiarize

【照例】zhàolì（副）as a rule;

usually: 他～每天晚饭后散步。As a rule, he takes a walk after dinner.

【照明】zhàomíng（动）illuminate: ～弹 flare

【照看】zhàokàn（动）take care of; keep an eye on: ～孩子 take care of the children

【照相】zhàoxiàng（动）take a photograph; have one's photograph taken: ～馆 photo studio

【照相机】zhàoxiàngjī（名）camera

【照料】zhàoliào（动）take care of; attend to; mind

【照射】zhàoshè（动）shine; illuminate

【照常】zhàocháng（形）as usual: ～办公 office opens as usual

【照发】zhàofā（动）❶ issue as before ❷（of a document or telegram）approved for distribution

【照搬】zhàobān（动）copy blindly

【照会】zhàohuì Ⅰ（动）present a note to（a government）Ⅱ（名）（diplomatic）note

【照管】zhàoguǎn（动）look after; be in charge of

【照样】zhàoyàng（副）❶ after（a pattern）❷ still; as before

【照办】zhàobàn（动）do accordingly

【照应】zhàoying（动）look after; take care of

【照旧】zhàojiù（形）as before; unchanged: 一切～。Everything remains unchanged.

【照耀】zhàoyào（动）shine; illuminate

【照顾】zhàogu（动）❶ show consideration for; take account of: ～到各个方面 take account of the different aspects or the different parties concerned ❷ look after; attend to: ～

老人 care for the old people

煦 xù（形）〈書〉warm

煞 shā（動）❶ put a stop to; halt;
check ❷ tighten
see also shà

【煞尾】shāwěi Ⅰ（動）bring to an
end; wind up Ⅱ（名）final stage;
ending

煞 shà Ⅰ（副）very; exceedingly Ⅱ
（名）demon; fiend
see also shā

【煞白】shàbái（形）ashen

【煞有介事】shà yǒu jiè shì〈成〉do
things as if in all seriousness; act as
if in real earnest

【煞費苦心】shà fèi kǔ xīn〈成〉
spare no effort; make a painful effort: ～，事終無望。He made a futile effort to accomplish his aim.

熔 róng（動）melt; smelt

【熔化】rónghuà（動）melt

【熔解】róngjiě（名）〈物〉fusion

【熔煉】róngliàn（動）smelt

【熔劑】róngjì（名）〈冶〉flux

【熔點】róngdiǎn（名）〈物〉melting
point

【熔爐】rónglú（名）❶ smelting furnace ❷ crucible; furnace

【熔巖】róngyán（名）〈地〉lava

煽 shān（動）instigate; incite

【煽風點火】shān fēng diǎn huǒ〈成〉
instigate trouble

【煽動】shāndòng（動）instigate; incite

熒 yíng

【熒光屏】yíngguāngpíng（名）fluo-
rescent screen

【熒光燈】yíngguāngdēng（名）fluo-
rescent lamp

熘 liū（動）quick-fry: ～肉片 pork
slices sauté

熄 xī（動）put out; extinguish

【熄滅】xīmiè（動）go out: 火～了。
The fire has gone out.

【熄燈】xīdēng Ⅰ（動）turn off the
light Ⅱ（名）lights-out

熙 xī

【熙熙攘攘】xī xī rǎng rǎng〈成〉
busy and noisy with people coming
and going

熏 xūn（動）smoke: 牆被煙～黑
了。The walls were blackened by
smoke.

【熏肉】xūnròu（名）smoked meat

【熏染】xūnrǎn（動）contaminate;
gradually corrupt: 受社會不良傾向
的～ be influenced by unhealthy social trends

【熏魚】xūnyú（名）smoked fish

【熏陶】xūntáo（動）nurture; exercise an imperceptible and salutary
influence on

熊 xióng（名）❶ bear ❷（Xióng）a
surname

【熊掌】xióngzhǎng（名）bear's paw
(a rare delicacy)

【熊熊】xióngxióng（形）flaming: ～
烈火 roaring fire

【熊貓】xióngmāo（名）panda

熟 shóu（形）〈口〉cooked: ～肉
cooked meat
see also shú

熟 shú Ⅰ（形）❶ ripe: 條件成～

conditions are ripe ❷ cooked ❸ processed: ～鐵 wrought iron ❹ familiar: 這人看着眼～。This man looks familiar. ❺ skilled: 技術純～ highly skilled Ⅱ(副) deeply; profoundly: 深思～慮 careful consideration

see also shóu

【熟人】shúrén (名)(old) acquaintance; friend

【熟手】shúshǒu (名) skilled worker; experienced person

【熟字】shúzì (名) word already learnt

【熟客】shúkè (名) frequenter; frequent visitor

【熟食】shúshí (名) ready food; cooked food

【熟記】shújì (動) learn by heart; commit to memory

【熟能生巧】shú néng shēng qiǎo〈成〉practice makes perfect

【熟悉】shúxī (動) know well; be well acquainted with; be conversant with

【熟習】shúxí (動) be well versed in or proficient in (a skill or subject): ～會計業務 be practised in accounting

【熟視無睹】shú shì wú dǔ〈成〉take no notice of or turn a blind eye to (familiar malpractices)

【熟睡】shúshuì (動) be sound asleep

【熟語】shúyǔ (名) idiom; idiomatic expression

【熟練】shúliàn (形) skilful; proficient: ～操作 skilful operation

【熟識】shúshí (動) be familiar with; know well

熵 shāng (名)〈物〉entropy

熬 āo (動)〈方〉cook in water; boil; simmer; stew

see also áo

熬 áo (動) ❶ boil; simmer; stew: ～藥 decoct (Chinese) medicinal herbs ❷ endure; bear; stand: ～出頭 live through hard times

see also āo

【熬夜】áoyè (動) stay up late at night; burn the midnight oil

【熬煎】áojiān (名) torture; suffering

熱 rè Ⅰ(名) ❶ heat: 輻射～ radiant heat ❷ fever: 退～ bring down one's fever ❸ craze; fad: 足球～ football craze Ⅱ(形) ❶ hot: 天越來越～。It's getting hotter every day. ❷ ardent; passionate: 親～ affectionate Ⅲ(動) heat up: 把水一～ heat up the water

【熱天】rètiān (名) hot weather; hot season

【熱切】rèqiè (形) earnest

【熱心】rèxīn (形) warm-hearted; enthusiastic

【熱水浴】rèshuǐyù (名) hot bath

【熱水瓶】rèshuǐpíng (名)〈口〉thermos bottle (flask)

【熱水袋】rèshuǐdài (名) hot-water bottle (bag)

【熱火朝天】rè huǒ cháo tiān〈成〉reach a high tide of mass movement and enthusiasm; seethe with activity

【熱乎】rèhu (nice and) warm: 水還～。The water is still warm.

【熱血】rèxuè (名) righteous ardour: ～沸騰 fervent; impassioned

【熱忱】rèchén (名) zeal; warmheartedness

【熱身賽】rèshēnsài (名)〈體〉 warm-up match

【熱狗】règǒu (名) hot dog

【熱門】rèmén (形) popular; in great demand

【熱度】rèdù (名) ❶ (degree of) heat ❷ fever; temperature

【熱能】rènéng (名)〈物〉 heat (thermal) energy

【熱浪】rèlàng (名)〈氣〉 heat wave; hot wave

【熱烈】rèliè (形) ardent; heated

【熱氣】rèqì (名) steam; heat: ~騰騰 bubbling with life

【熱衷】rèzhōng (動) ❶ hanker after; pine for: ~賺錢 all out to make money ❷ be keen on: ~數學 be passionately fond of mathematics

【熱核】rèhé (形) thermonuclear

【熱核反應】rèhé fǎnyìng (名)〈物〉 thermonuclear reaction

【熱貨】rèhuò (名) goods in great demand

【熱情】rèqíng Ⅰ (名) enthusiasm; zeal Ⅱ (形) enthusiastic; warm-hearted

【熱望】rèwàng (動) ardently hope

【熱帶】rèdài (名) tropics: ~雨林 tropical rain forest

【熱處理】rèchǔlǐ (名)〈機〉 heat treatment

【熱淚盈眶】rè lèi yíng kuàng (成) eyes filled with tears

【熱量】rèliàng (名)〈物〉 quantity of heat

【熱飲】rèyǐn (名) hot drinks

【熱源】rèyuán (名) heat source

【熱愛】rè'ài (動) love ardently

【熱誠】rèchéng (形) warm and sincere; cordial

【熱電】rèdiàn (名)〈物〉 pyroelectricity; thermoelectricity

【熱電廠】rèdiànchǎng (名) heat and power plant

【熱綫】rèxiàn (名) ❶〈物〉 heat ray ❷ hot line

【熱敷】rèfū (名)〈醫〉 hot compress

【熱潮】rècháo (名) upsurge

【熱鬧】rènào Ⅰ (形) (of a scene) lively; busy: 市內的~街道 busy streets of the town Ⅱ (名) fun: 看~ watch the fun

【熱輻射】rèfúshè (名)〈物〉 heat (thermal) radiation

【熱點】rèdiǎn (名) ❶ hot spot ❷ tourist attraction

【熱壓】yèyā (名)〈化〉 hot pressing

【熱戀】rèliàn (動) be passionately in love

熨 yùn (動) iron; press: ~平褲子上的皺紋 iron out the creases in a pair of trousers

【熨斗】yùndǒu (名) iron: 電~ electric iron

燙 tàng Ⅰ (動) ❶ burn; scald: ~嘴 scald one's lips ❷ heat up (with sth. hot); iron: ~褲子 iron a pair of trousers ❸ perm: 冷~ cold wave Ⅱ (形) very hot

【燙金】tàngjīn (名)〈印〉 gilding: ~封面 gilded cover

【燙傷】tàngshāng (名) scald

【燙髮】tàngfà (動) have a perm; have one's hair permed

熾 chì (形) ablaze

【熾烈】chìliè (形) ❶ burning fiercely ❷ fervent

【熾熱】chìrè (形) ❶ redhot: ~的太陽 scorching sun ❷ passionate

燉 dùn (動) ❶ stew: ~肉 stewed

meat ❷ warm sth. by putting the container in hot or boiling water

燧 suì (名) flint

【燧石】 suìshí (名) flint

燒 shāo Ⅰ (動)❶ burn: ～焦的木頭 burnt wood / ～煤 burn coal ❷ cook; heat; bake: ～菜 cook a dish / ～石灰 heat limestone ❸ fry and then stew: 紅～牛肉 braised beef ❹ run a fever: 不～了。The fever is down. Ⅱ (名) fever: 他發高～。He is running a high fever.

【燒火】 shāohuǒ (動) make a fire; light a fire

【燒杯】 shāobēi (名)〈化〉beaker

【燒香】 shāoxiāng (名) burn joss sticks (before an idol)

【燒酒】 shāojiǔ (名) white spirit; liquor

【燒瓶】 shāopíng (名)〈化〉flask

【燒傷】 shāoshāng (名)〈醫〉burn

【燒餅】 shāobǐng (名) sesame seed cake

【燒鹼】 shāojiǎn (名)〈化〉caustic soda

【燒藍】 shāolán (形)〈工美〉enameling

燎 liáo (動) burn; be ablaze

【燎泡】 liáopào (名) blister (caused by burns or scalds)

【燎原】 liáoyuán (動)(of fire) spread far and wide; set the prairie aflame

燜 mèn (動) braise; stew: 紅～豬肉 pork braised in brown sauce

燈 dēng (名) lamp; light: 紅綠～ traffic light

【燈火】 dēnghuǒ (名) light: ～管制 blackout

【燈光】 dēngguāng (名)❶ lamp-light ❷ (stage) lighting

【燈泡】 dēngpào (名) electric bulb

【燈塔】 dēngtǎ (名) light-house; beacon

【燈罩】 dēngzhào (名) lamp-shade

【燈節】 Dēngjié (名) the Lantern Festival (the 15th day of the 1st lunar month)

【燈謎】 dēngmí (名) lantern riddles

【燈籠】 dēnglong (名) lantern

燃 rán (動) burn; kindle; light: 紙張易～。Paper burns easily.

【燃放】 ránfàng (動) set off (fireworks, etc.)

【燃眉之急】 rán méi zhī jí (成) a matter of great urgency

【燃料】 ránliào (名) fuel

【燃燒】 ránshāo Ⅰ (動) burn Ⅱ (名) combustion; inflammation

【燃燒彈】 ránshāodàn (名) incendiary bomb

燕 yàn (名) swallow

【燕子】 yànzi (名) swallow

【燕尾服】 yànwěifú (名) swallow-tailed coat; tailcoat

【燕麥】 yànmài (名) oats

【燕窩】 yànwō (名) (edible) bird's nest

營 yíng Ⅰ (名)❶ battalion ❷ camp; barracks: 兵～ army barracks Ⅱ (動)❶ run; operate; manage: 私～ privately-operated ❷ seek: 結黨～私 gang up for private gains

【營火】 yínghuǒ (名) camp-fire

【營生】 yíngshēng (動) earn a living

【營地】 yíngdì (名) camping ground

【營利】yínglì（動）seek profits

【營房】yíngfáng（名）barracks

【營長】yíngzhǎng （名） battalion commander

【營救】yíngjiù（動）save; rescue

【營業】yíngyè（動）do business: ～時間 business hours / ～執照 business licence

【營業員】yíngyèyuán（名）shop assistant

【營養】yíngyǎng（名）nourishment; nutrition

【營養學】yíngyǎngxué（名）dietetics: ～家 dietitian

【營壘】yínglěi（名）❶ barracks and the surrounding walls ❷ camp

燦 càn（形）bright: 金～～ golden; bright and dazzling

【燦爛】cànlàn（形）bright; splendid: 光輝～ magnificent

燥 zào（形）dry: 口乾舌～ one's lips are parched

燭 zhú（名）candle

【燭臺】zhútái（名）candle-stick

燴 huì（動）❶ braise: ～豆腐 braised bean-curd ❷ cook (rice or shredded pancakes) with meat and vegetables

燼 jìn（名）cinder; embers; ashes

爆 bào（動）❶ burst; explode; pop: 氣球～了。The balloon has burst. ❷ quick-fry: 葱～牛肉 quick-fried beef slices with scallion

【爆玉米花】bào yùmǐhuā（名）popcorn

【爆竹】bàozhú（炮仗 pàozhàng）（名）firecracker: 燃放～ set off firecrackers

【爆肚兒】bàodǔr（名） quick-boiled tripe (a North China delicacy)

【爆炸】bàozhà Ⅰ（動）explode; blast Ⅱ（名）explosion: ～物 explosive

【爆裂】bàoliè（動）crack; burst

【爆發】bàofā（動）break out; erupt: 內戰～了。Civil war broke out.

爍 shuò（形）bright: 星星在閃～。The stars are twinkling.

爐 lú（名）stove; oven; furnace

【爐火純青】lú huǒ chún qīng〈成〉(of learning, skill, etc.) reach perfection

【爐灰】lúhuī（名）ashes (in or from a stove)

【爐箅子】lúbìzi（名）grate

【爐竈】lúzào（名） stove; cooking range

爛 làn Ⅰ（形）❶ sodden; soft: 牛肉不～。The beef is a bit tough. ❷ rotten; decaying ❸ ragged; tattered: 破～衣裳 ragged clothes ❹ messy; confused; in disorder: ～攤子 a messy organization, unit, etc. Ⅱ（動）rot; corrupt

【爛漫】lànmàn（形）❶ fresh and beautiful in colour ❷ ingenuous; unaffected: 天真～ lovely and innocent

【爛糊】lànhu（形）(of food) soft and mushy

【爛熟】lànshú（形）❶ (of food) thoroughly cooked ❷ be well acquainted with; be very skilled in: 數據記得～ have the data at one's fingertips

【爛醉】lànzuì（形）dead drunk

【爛攤子】làntānzi（名）a shambles;

an awful mess

爪 部

爪 zhǎo（名）claw; talon: 鷹～
eagle's talons
see also zhuǎ

【爪牙】zhǎoyá（名）lackey; flunkey

爪 zhuǎ（名）claw; paw; talon
see also zhǎo

爭 zhēng（動）❶ argue; dispute:
在這個問題上我不和你～。I won't
argue with you on this problem. /
～個水落石出 argue the matter out
❷ contend; strive; vie: ～錦標
vie with one another for the championship / ～霸 contend for hegemony

【爭光】zhēngguāng（動）bring credit
to

【爭先恐後】zhēng xiān kǒng hòu〈成〉
dash ahead for fear of falling behind;
demonstrate an earnest desire to
participate in some activity or work

【爭吵】zhēngchǎo（動）squabble;
quarrel; bicker

【爭取】zhēngqǔ（動）strive for; win
over: ～持久和平 strive for a lasting peace / ～人民的大多數 win
over the majority of the people

【爭氣】zhēngqì（動）work hard to
win honour for oneself or one's
country

【爭執】zhēngzhí（動）dispute with;
be at odds with

【爭奪】zhēngduó（動）fight for;
contend for: ～市場 strive to capture the market

【爭端】zhēngduān（名）dispute;
conflict: 解決～ settle a dispute

【爭論】zhēnglùn（名）argument; debate; controversy

【爭議】zhēngyì（名）controversy:
有～的問題 controversial problem

【爭辯】zhēngbiàn（動）argue; debate

【爭權奪利】zhēng quán duó lì〈成〉
jockey for power and scramble for
profit

爬 pá（動）❶ crawl; creep ❷
climb; scramble: ～上梯子 climb
up the ladder

【爬行】páxíng（動）crawl; creep

【爬行動物】páxíng dòngwù（名）
reptile

【爬泳】páyǒng（名）〈體〉crawl

【爬蟲】páchóng（名）reptile

為 wéi Ⅰ（動）❶ act; do: 所作所
～ what one does ❷ become; turn:
成～旅遊勝地 become a tourist attraction ❸ be: 一百公分～一米。A
hundred centimetres makes a metre.
Ⅱ（介）❶ as: 指定他～隊長。He
was appointed leader of the team. /
作～軍人要服從命令。As a soldier
you must obey orders. ❷ [used to
introduce the agent in a passive
structure, followed by 所]by: ～人
所不齒 be held in contempt by people
see also wèi

【為人】wéirén（動）the way one behaves in society: ～爽直 be frank
and straightforward

【為止】wéizhǐ（副）up to; till: 到目
前～ up to now; upto the very present

【爲主】 wéizhǔ（動）[preceded by 以] be the most important; give priority to: 本地產品以棉花～。The main produce of this region is cotton.

【爲生】 wéishēng（動）make a living; eke out one's livelihood

【爲非作歹】 wéi fēi zuò dǎi（成）perpetrate crimes of all sorts

【爲所欲爲】 wéi suǒ yù wéi（成）〈貶〉do whatever appeals to one; do everything at will

【爲首】 wéishǒu（形）[preceded by 以] headed by; led by: 以他～的代表團 a delegation headed by him

【爲限】 wéixiàn（動）not exceed (a period of time): 以三日～ within the limit of three days; in three days

【爲重】 wéizhòng（動）[preceded by 以] put (sth.) ahead of everything else: 以長期友誼～ value above anything else long-standing friendship

【爲時過早】 wéi shí guò zǎo（副）much too early (to do sth.): 現在作出判斷～。It is premature to pass any judgment yet.

【爲期】 wéiqī（動）not exceed a time-limit; last: 會議～十天。The conference will last ten days.

【爲數】 wéishù（動）amount; number: ～甚少 be very small in number; amount to very little

【爲難】 wéinái Ⅰ（形）awkward; embarrassing: 叫人～的問題 embarrassing question Ⅱ（動）create trouble for

爲 wèi（介）❶ [used to indicate the object of an action]: ～人民服務 serve the people ❷ [used to indicate the aim or goal]: ～世界和平而努力 work for world peace ❸ [used to indicate the cause]: ～勝利而歡欣鼓舞 jump for joy at one's victory

see also wéi

【爲了】 wèile（介）for; in order to

【爲什麼】 wèi shénme（副）what for; why: 你～遲到？ Why are you late?

【爲此】 wèicǐ（副）to this end; for this reason

爵 jué（名）❶ peerage; rank of a peer: 加官晉～ promote to a higher rank ❷ ancient 3-legged wine cup

【爵士】 juéshì（名）❶ knight ❷ Sir

【爵士樂】 juéshìyuè（名）jazz

父 部

父 fù（名）❶ father ❷ male relative of the elder generation: 叔(伯)～ uncle

【父母】 fùmǔ（名）parents

【父兄】 fùxiōng（名）father and elder brothers

【父老】 fùlǎo（名）elders (male)

【父系】 fùxì（名）paternity

【父親】 fùqīn（名）father

【父權制】 fùquánzhì（名）patriarchy

爸 bà（名）pa; dad; father

【爸爸】 bàba（名）papa; dad; father

爹 diē（名）father; dad: ～～ daddy; pa

爺 yé（名）❶ grandfather ❷ uncle: 王大～ Uncle Wang

【爺們】 yémen（名）man; menfolk

【爺爺】yéye（名）grandpa; grandfather

爻 部

爽 shuǎng（形）❶ clear; bright: 神清目 ~ relaxed and refreshed ❷ (of human character) frank; candid: ~ 直 candid; straightforward ❸ well; fine; in good health

【爽口】shuǎngkǒu（形）refreshingly pleasant to one's palate

【爽快】shuǎngkuai（形）❶ refreshed: 精神 ~ feel refreshed ❷ frank; straightforward

【爽身粉】shuǎngshēnfěn（名）talcum powder

【爽朗】shuǎnglǎng（形）❶ (of weather) bright and refreshing ❷ open-hearted; hearty: 這個人很 ~,有说有笑。He is frank-hearted, cheerful sort of person.

爾 ěr Ⅰ（代）❶ you ❷ that: ~ 時 at that time Ⅱ（副）like this; so: 果 ~ if so

【爾後】ěrhòu（副）thereafter

【爾虞我詐】ěr yú wǒ zhà〈成〉cheat each other; practise cheating on each other

爿 部

牀 chuáng（名）bed: 舖 ~ make the bed

【牀單】chuángdān（名）sheet

【牀舖】chuángpù（名）bed

【牀頭櫃】chuángtóuguì（名）bedside table

牆 qiáng（名）wall

【牆角】qiángjiǎo（名）corner (of a room or a building)

【牆根】qiánggēn（名）foot of a wall

【牆紙】qiángzhǐ（名）wall paper

【牆報】qiángbào（名）wall newspaper

【牆腳】qiángjiǎo（名）❶ foot of a wall ❷ foundation: 挖 ~ undermine sb.'s position, reputation or prestige

【牆壁】qiángbì（名）wall

片 部

片 piān
see also piàn

【片子】piānzi（名）❶ (roll of) film ❷ film; movie: 拍 ~ shoot a film ❸ gramophone record; disc

片 piàn Ⅰ（名）❶ flat and thin piece; slice: 土豆 ~ (potato) chips /明 信 ~ postcard ❷ subdivision: 分 ~ 傳達 relay official instructions or reports in subdivisions Ⅱ（形）fragmentary; incomplete Ⅲ（量）❶ tablet; slice: 兩 ~ 阿司匹林 two tablets of aspirin ❷ stretch; expanse (of land or water): 一 ~ 草原 a stretch of grasslands / 天空一 ~ 蔚藍色。The sky is a bright blue.
see also piān

【片甲不存】piàn jiǎ bù cún（片甲不留 piàn jiǎ bù liú）〈成〉be completely wiped out

【片言】piànyán（名）a few words

【片刻】piànkè（名）a moment; a little while

【片面】piànmiàn（形）❶ unilateral: ~之詞 unilateral statement ❷ one-sided: ~的觀點 a lopsided view

【片面性】piànmiànxìng（名）one-sidedness

【片紙隻字】piàn zhǐ zhī zì（名）just a few lines; brief note: 她没有给我 ~。She hasn't dropped me a line.

【片劑】piànjì（名）tablet

【片斷】piànduàn（名）（of writing, novel, life, etc.）part; passage; episode

版 bǎn（名）❶ printing plate or block: 照相~ process plate ❷ edition（of a book）: 修訂~ revised edition ❸ page（of a newspaper）: 頭~ front page

【版本】bǎnběn（名）edition

【版次】bǎncì（名）number of the edition（such as the first or second edition）

【版面】bǎnmiàn（名）❶ printing space of a page in a book, magazine or newspaper ❷ layout of a printed page: ~設計 layout

【版税】bǎnshuì（名）royalty（on a book published）

【版畫】bǎnhuà（名）picture printed from an engraved or etched plate

【版圖】bǎntú（名）territory（of a country）

【版權】bǎnquán（名）copyright

牌 pái（名）❶ plate; board: 佈告 ~ bulletin board ❷ brand: 你用什麼~的香皂? What brand of soap do you use? /那輛汽車是什麼~的? What make is that car? ❸ cards;

dominoes: 打撲克~ play cards

【牌子】páizi（名）❶ tablet; sign ❷ trademark

【牌坊】páifāng（名）memorial archway

【牌照】páizhào（名）licence（tag）; number plate: 自行車~ bicycle number plate

【牌號】páihào（名）❶ shop sign ❷ trade mark; brand

【牌價】páijià（名）❶ list price ❷ market quotation

【牌樓】páilóu（名）decorated arch

牒 dié（名）document; certificate: 最後通~ ultimatum

牙 部

牙 yá（名）❶ tooth ❷ ivory

【牙牀】yáchuáng（名）〈生理〉gum

【牙刷】yáshuā（名）toothbrush

【牙科】yákē（名）dentistry: ~醫生 dentist; dental surgeon

【牙痛】yátòng（名）toothache

【牙買加】Yámǎijiā（名）Jamaica: ~人 Jamaican

【牙膏】yágāo（名）toothpaste

【牙齒】yáchǐ（名）tooth

【牙雕】yádiāo（名）ivory carving

【牙簽】yáqiān（名）toothpick

牛 部

牛 niú（名）❶ ox; cow ❷（Niú）a surname

【牛奶】niúnǎi（名）milk

【牛皮】niúpí（名）❶ oxhide ❷ boasting; bragging: 吹～ talk big; brag

【牛皮纸】niúpízhǐ（名）brown paper; kraft (paper)

【牛皮癣】niúpíxuǎn（名）〈醫〉psoriasis

【牛仔裤】niúzǎikù（名）jeans

【牛肉】niúròu（名）beef

【牛角】niújiǎo（名）ox horn

【牛角尖】niújiǎojiān（名）detail of no great significance: 鑽～ wasting time on insignificant details; split hairs

【牛勁】niújìn（名）❶ tremendous effort; great strength: 費了～ make a Herculean effort ❷ stubbornness; obstinacy

【牛虻】niúméng（名）gadfly

【牛馬】niúmǎ（名）beasts of burden

【牛排】niúpái（名）beefsteak; steak

【牛痘】niúdòu（名）smallpox pustule; vaccine pustule

【牛黃】niúhuáng（名）〈中藥〉bezoar

【牛棚】niúpéng（名）cowshed

【牛脾氣】niúpíqì（名）pigheadedness; obstinacy

【牛鼻子】niúbízi（名）❶ nose or muzzle of an ox ❷ key; crux: 牽～ lead an ox by the halter; grasp the key link

【牛糞】niúfèn（名）cow dung

【牛犢】niúdú（名）calf

【牛欄】niúlán（名）cattle pen

牝 pìn（形）(of certain birds and animals) female: ～馬 mare

牟 móu I（動）angle for; seek II （名）(Móu) a surname

【牟利】móulì（動）seek profit

【牟取】móuqǔ（動）seek: ～暴利 seek staggering profits

牢 láo I（名）prison; jail II（形）firm; fast: ～不可破 indestructible; unbreakable

【牢牢】láoláo（副）firmly: 他～地控制着局勢。He is firmly in control of the situation.

【牢固】láogù（形）firm; solid

【牢記】láojì（動）bear firmly in mind

【牢靠】láokào（動）❶ (of furniture, etc.) firm; solid ❷ reliable; trustworthy: 他這個人很～。He is very reliable.

【牢騷】láosāo（名）complaint: 發～ grumble; complain

牡 mǔ（形）male: ～鹿 stag

【牡丹】mǔdān（名）peony

【牡蠣】mǔlì（名）oyster

牧 mù（動）herd; graze: ～羊 pasture sheep

【牧民】mùmín（名）herdsman

【牧羊人】mùyángrén（名）shepherd

【牧草】mùcǎo（名）herbage; forage grass

【牧師】mùshī（名）clergyman; priest

【牧區】mùqū（名）pastoral area

【牧場】mùchǎng（名）ranch; pasture; ground for grazing; stock farm

【牧童】mùtóng（名）shepherd boy; cowboy

【牧業】mùyè（名）animal husbandry

【牧歌】mùgē（名）❶ pastoral song ❷〈樂〉madrigal

物 wù（名）❶ thing; matter: 萬～ everything under the sun ❷ content; substance: 言之有～

speech or essay which is informative or persuasive

【物力】wùlì（名）material resources

【物以類聚】wù yǐ lèi jù〈成〉 birds of a feather flock together; like attracts like

【物色】wùsè（動）look for; scout for: ～運動員 scout for potential athletes

【物品】wùpǐn（名）thing; article: 零星～ odds and ends

【物產】wùchǎn（名）produce; products

【物理】wùlǐ（名）physics

【物理療法】wùlǐ liáofǎ（名）physical therapy; physiotherapy

【物極必反】wù jí bì fǎn〈成〉a thing will switch in the opposite direction when pushed to the extreme; extremes meet

【物資】wùzī（名）goods; materials; commodities

【物價】wùjià（名）commodity price: ～指數 commodity price index

【物質】wùzhì Ⅰ（名）matter; substance Ⅱ（形）material: ～刺激 material incentive

【物證】wùzhèng（名）material evidence

【物議】wùyì（名）public criticism: 免招～ avoid incurring criticism from the public

【物體】wùtǐ（名）matter; body; substance

牲 shēng（名）❶ domestic animal; livestock ❷ animal sacrifice

【牲口】shēngkou（名）draught animal; beast of burden

【牲畜】shēngchù（名）livestock

特 tè Ⅰ（形）special; uncommon:

～價 special（discount）rate; bargain price Ⅱ（副）❶ specially; specifically: 他～地來表示歡迎。He has come specially to apologize. ❷ very: ～好 superb Ⅲ（名）spy; secret agent: ～工人員 special agent

【特立尼達和多巴哥】Tèlìnídá hé Duōbāgē（名）Trinidad and Tobago

【特色】tèsè（名）characteristic; unique feature: ～風味菜 speciality dish

【特別】tèbié Ⅰ（形）special; uncommon: ～會議 special session Ⅱ（副）❶ especially; exceptionally: 他的議論～動聽。His argument sounded particularly eloquent. ❷ for a special purpose: ～派人到那裏進行現場調查 send sb. there specially to make an on-the-spot investigation

【特技】tèjì（名）stunt; trick: ～飛行 stunt flying; aerobatics

【特快】tèkuài（名）〈交〉（short for 特別快車 tèbié kuàichē）express（train）: ～專遞 special delivery; express delivery

【特長】tècháng（名）one's special field; one's speciality

【特使】tèshǐ（名）special envoy

【特派】tèpài（形）specially appointed; accredited: ～員 commissioner

【特級】tèjí（形）superfine; special grade: ～廚師 expert chef

【特殊】tèshū（形）special; uncommon: 搞～化 (of a senior official) seek personal privileges

【特務】tèwu（名）spy; secret agent: 從事～活動 be engaged in espionage

【特許】tèxǔ（名）special permission: 進口～證 speical import licence

【特异】tèyì(形)peculiar; unusual: ~功能 extrasensory perception

【特产】tèchǎn(名)special product (of a locality): ~商店 speciality store

【特区】tèqū(名)(short for 经济特区 jīngjì tèqū)special (economic) zone

【特赦】tèshè(动)grant special pardon; grant special amnesty

【特等】tèděng(形)special class; top class: ~舱(of a passenger ship)stateroom; state cabin; luxury cabin

【特征】tèzhēng(名)feature; characteristics

【特邀】tèyāo(动)specially invite

【特点】tèdiǎn(名)characteristic; feature

【特护】tèhù(动)provide special care: 他已改成~了。He has been transferred to speical care.

【特权】tèquán(名)privilege; prerogative

牵

牵 qiān(动)❶ lead; pull: ~着孩子的手 lead the child by the hand ❷ involve: 他也~进这椿醜闻裏头去了。He was also involved in the scandal.

【牵牛花】qiānniúhuā(名)morning-glory

【牵引】qiānyǐn(动)pull; draw; haul: ~车 tractor; towing car

【牵扯】qiānchě(动)involve; implicate

【牵制】qiānzhì(动)pin down; contain

【牵连】qiānlián(动)involve; implicate

【牵涉】qiānshè(动)involve; concern

【牵动】qiāndòng(动)directly affect: ~一髮而动全局。A small change in anything would affect the situation as a whole.

【牵挂】qiānguà(名)worry; care: 了無~ be free from care

【牵累】qiānlèi(动)❶ tie down: 受两个幼小孩子的~ be tied down by two small children ❷ involve: 这场官司~了他。He was involved in the lawsuit.

【牵强附会】qiān qiǎng fù huì〈成〉draw far-fetched analogies

【牵肠挂肚】qiān cháng guà dù〈成〉be overcome with deep anxiety

【牵线】qiānxiàn(动)❶ pull strings ❷ act as intermediary; act as go-between

【牵头】qiāntóu(动)❶ take the lead; pioneer: ~项目 key project ❷ act as intermediary; act as go-between

犁

犁 lí Ⅰ(名)plough: 雙鏵~ double-shared plough Ⅱ(动)plough

犀

犀 xī

【犀牛】xīniú(名)rhinoceros

【犀利】xīlì(形)sharp; penetrating; incisive: ~的刀鋒 sharp(keen)knife / ~的目光 sharp eyes; keen insight

【犀角】xījiǎo(名)rhinoceros horn

犄

犄 jī

【犄角】jījiǎo(名)corner: 屋子~ corner of a room

【犄角】jījiao(名)horn; antler

犍

犍 jiān(名)bullock; castrated bull

犖

犖 luò(形)〈書〉outstanding

【犖犖】luòluò（形）obvious; salient

犒 kào（動）offer food and drink to troops as a general reward

【犒勞】kàoláo（動）offer food and drink to troops for splendid service

犟 jiàng（形）stubborn; obstinate

犢 dú（名）calf

犧 xī

【犧牲】xīshēng I（名）sacrifice: 作出巨大～ make a great sacrifice II（動）sacrifice; give up: ～生命 lay down one's life

【犧牲品】xīshēngpǐn（名）victim

犬 部

犬 quǎn（名）dog; cur

【犬牙】quǎnyá（名）❶ canine tooth ❷ fang (of a dog)

【犬牙交錯】quǎnyá jiāocuò（形）interlocking jigsaw

【犬馬之勞】quǎn mǎ zhī láo〈成〉faithful service (as of a dog or a horse to its master): 效～ render you a faithful service; be at your disposal

【犬齒】quǎnchǐ（名）canine tooth

犯 fàn I（動）❶ violate; offend ❷ invade: 來～之敵 invading enemy ❸ recur: 他的心臟病又～了。He had another heart attack. II（名）criminal: 嫌疑～ suspect

【犯人】fànrén（名）prisoner

【犯不着】fàn bu zháo（形）〈口〉not be worth the trouble

【犯法】fànfǎ（動）break (violate) the law

【犯病】fànbìng（動）fall ill; have a relapse

【犯規】fànguī（動）break (violate) the rules

【犯愁】fànchóu（動）worry; suffer from the blues

【犯罪】fànzuì（動）commit a crime

犰 qiú

【犰狳】qiúyú（名）armadillo

狀 zhuàng（名）❶ form; shape; appearance: 他～甚醜陋。He has ugly features. ❷ condition; state: 慘～ miserable condition ❸ written complaint; plaint: 供～ written confession ❹ certificate: 獎～ certificate of merit

【狀元】zhuàngyuan（名）❶（of the imperial examination system）the one who heads the list of successful candidates; zhuangyuan ❷ the very best (in a field)

【狀況】zhuàngkuàng（名）condition; state: 實際～ the reality

【狀態】zhuàngtài（名）state; state of affairs: 處於危險～ be in a dangerous state; be in danger

【狀語】zhuàngyǔ（名）〈語〉adverbial

狄 Dí（名）a surname

狂 kuáng（形）❶ mad; insane ❷ vehement; intense: ～風 strong wind ❸ wild; uninhibited: ～瀾 raging tide／欣喜若～ wild with joy ❹ presumptuous; arrogant: ～夫 arrogant fellow

【狂人】kuángrén（名）madman; maniac

【狂妄】kuángwàng（形）extremely arrogant

【狂风暴雨】kuángfēng bàoyǔ（名）violent storm; hurricane

【狂欢】kuánghuān（名）public merrymaking and feasting: ～節 carnival

狒 fèi

【狒狒】fèifèi（名）〈动〉baboon

狙 jū

【狙击】jūjī（动）〈军〉snipe

【狙击手】jūjīshǒu（名）〈军〉sniper

狎 xiá

【狎昵】xiánì（动）be unduly intimate with

狗 gǒu（名）dog

【狗仗人势】gǒu zhàng rén shì〈成〉act as a bully on the strength of powerful backing

【狗血喷頭】gǒu xuè pēn tóu〈成〉curse savagely

【狗尾续貂】gǒu wěi xù diāo〈成〉add an unworthy sequel to a masterpiece

【狗急跳墙】gǒu jí tiào qiáng〈成〉a cornered beast will fight desperately; a desperate person is capable of anything

【狗腿子】gǒutuǐzi（名）cat's paw; henchman

【狗窝】gǒuwō（名）kennel

【狗熊】gǒuxióng（名）black bear

狍 páo（名）roe deer

狐 hú（名）fox

【狐臭】húchòu（名）body odour; bromhidrosis

【狐狸】húli（名）fox

【狐狸尾巴】húli wěiba（名）fox's tail: 露出 ～ expose one's cloven hoof

【狐假虎威】hú jiǎ hǔ wēi〈成〉play the bully by dint of one's influential connections

【狐媚】húmèi（动）bewitch; enchant

【狐群狗党】hú qún gǒu dǎng〈成〉a gang of scheming scoundrels

【狐疑】húyí（名）suspicion; misgivings

狩 shòu（名）hunting（esp. in winter）

【狩猎】shòuliè（动）hunt

狡 jiǎo（形）sly; wily; cunning: ～計 nasty trick

【狡兔三窟】jiǎo tù sān kū〈成〉a wily hare always has several possible hideouts

【狡诈】jiǎozhà（形）cunning and deceitful

【狡猾】jiǎohuá（形）cunning; foxy

【狡赖】jiǎolài（动）quibble; prevaricate

【狡黠】jiǎoxiá（形）crafty; treacherous

【狡辩】jiǎobiàn Ⅰ（动）use false deceptive arguments; equivocate Ⅱ（名）sophistry

狠 hěn Ⅰ（形）cruel; ruthless; merciless Ⅱ（副）❶ firmly; resolutely ❷ with all one's might: ～命地幹 work for all one is worth

【狠心】hěnxīn（形）hard-hearted; heartless

【狠毒】hěndú（形）vicious; venomous

狼 láng（名）wolf

【狼子野心】láng zǐ yě xīn〈成〉　a wicked person with wild ambitions

【狼心狗肺】láng xīn gǒu fèi〈成〉❶ unscrupulous and heartless ❷ absolutely ungrateful

【狼狗】lánggǒu（名）wolf-hound; police dog

【狼狈】lángbèi（形）embarrassed; indigent: 十分～ embarrassed beyond description

【狼狈为奸】láng bèi wéi jiān〈成〉collude with each other (in doing evil)

【狼藉】lángjí（形）❶ messy; in total disorder: 杯盘～ a terrible mess of plates and dishes on the dining table ❷ discredited; notorious: 声名～ be thoroughly discredited

狭 xiá（形）narrow

【狭小】xiáxiǎo（形）　narrow and small

【狭窄】xiázhǎi（形）cramped; narrow: 思路～ narrow in one's views / ～的住房 cramped living quarters

【狭隘】xiá'ài（形）narrow: 道路～ a narrow path / 心胸～ narrow-minded

【狭路相逢】xiá lù xiāng féng〈成〉(of enemies) meet each other on a narrow path; the confrontation is inevitable

【狭义】xiáyì（名）narrow sense: ～地说 in a narrow sense

狸 lí（名）racoon dog

【狸猫】límāo（名）leopard cat

猝 cù（形）sudden: ～不及防 be caught unawares

【猝然】cùrán（副）suddenly and unexpectedly

猜 cāi（动）❶ guess: ～一～ make a guess ❷ suspect: 两小无～ (of a little girl and a little boy) be innocent childhood playmates

【猜中】cāizhòng（动）guess right; make out: ～一個謎語 solve a riddle

【猜拳】cāiquán（动）play the finger-guessing game (usu. while drinking)

【猜测】cāicè（名）guess; conjecture; surmise: 純屬～ mere conjecture

【猜想】cāixiǎng（动）guess; suppose; suspect

【猜疑】cāiyí Ⅰ（动）suspect; be suspicious Ⅱ（名）suspicion: 引起～ arouse suspicion

【猜谜】cāimí（动）❶ guess riddles ❷ guess; conjecture

猛 měng Ⅰ（形）violent; fierce: 炮火很～。There was heavy gunfire. Ⅱ（副）suddenly: ～一轉身 turn around suddenly

【猛力】měnglì（副）vigorously: ～關上門 slam the door shut

【猛士】měngshì（名）brave fighter

【猛不防】měngbùfáng（副）suddenly; unexpectedly: ～他們撞了個滿懷。Unexpectedly, they bumped into each other.

【猛劲儿】měngjìnr（名）❶ spurt: 比賽快結束了，他一跑到底。He put on a spurt towards the end of the race. ❷ vigour: 他幹什麼事都有股～。Whatever he undertakes, he never fails to display vigour and energy.

【猛烈】měngliè（形）violent; vigorous; ferocious: 向敌人～开火 open fire fiercely at the enemy

【猛进】měngjìn（动）press forward

【猛禽】měngqín（名）bird of prey

【猛然】měngrán（副）abruptly; suddenly: ～出现 appear suddenly

【猛犸】měngmǎ（名）mammoth

【猛醒】měngxǐng（动）suddenly see the light; suddenly awake to

【猛兽】měngshòu（名）beast of prey

猖 chāng

【猖狂】chāngkuáng（形）ferocious; outrageous

【猖獗】chāngjué Ⅰ（动）run rampant Ⅱ（形）unbridled; raging

猙 zhēng

【猙狞】zhēngníng（形）ferocious; fierce; malignant

猞 shē

【猞猁】shēlì（名）lynx

猶 yóu（副）❶ as if; like: 此类人～毒蛇猛兽。This kind of people are like poisonous snakes and ferocious animals. ❷ still: 言～在耳。The words still ring in my ears.

【犹太人】Yóutàirén（名）Jew; Jewess

【犹太教】Yóutàijiào（名）Judaism

【犹如】yóurú（副）as if; like: ～大梦初醒 as if waking up from a dream

【犹豫】yóuyù（形）hesitant; undecided

猢 hú

【猢狲】húsūn（名）macaque; monkey

猩 xīng（名）orang-utan

【猩红热】xīnghóngrè（名）〈医〉scarlet fever

【猩猩】xīngxing（名）orang-utan: 大～ gorilla

猥 wěi（形）❶ multifarious; multitudinous: ～杂 miscellaneous ❷ obscene; base

【猥亵】wěixiè Ⅰ（形）obscene; indecent Ⅱ（动）behave indecently (to a woman): ～幼女 molest a small girl

猴 hóu（名）monkey

猿 yuán（名）ape

【猿人】yuánrén（名）apeman: 北京～ Peking Man

【猿猴】yuánhóu（名）apes and monkeys

猾 huá（形）cunning; foxy; sly

狮 shī（名）lion

【狮子】shīzi（名）lion: ～舞 lion dance

【狮身人面像】shīshēn rénmiàn xiàng（名）Sphinx

獐 zhāng（名）river deer

【獐子】zhāngzi（名）river deer

狱 yù（名）❶ prison; jail: 出～ come out of prison ❷ lawsuit; case

【狱吏】yùlì（名）prison guard; warder

獠 liáo

【獠牙】liáoyá（名）bucktooth: 青面～ have ugly ferocious features

独 dú Ⅰ（形）only Ⅱ（副）alone; singly

【獨一無二】dú yī wú èr〈成〉with-out equal; peerless

【獨夫民賊】dúfū mínzéi（名）ruth-less ruler spurned by the people; tyrant

【獨木橋】dúmùqiáo（名）❶ single-plank bridge ❷ hazardous path

【獨白】dúbái（名）monologue

【獨立】dúlì Ⅰ（動）stand along Ⅱ（名）independence Ⅲ（副）inde-pendently

【獨出心裁】dú chū xīn cái〈成〉put forward an original plan; adopt a to-tally different approach

【獨自】dúzì（副）alone; on one's own

【獨佔】dúzhàn（動）obtain exclusive control of: ~ 鰲頭 head the list of successful candidates; win first prize

【獨身】dúshēn Ⅰ（副）all along: ~ 在外 live alone in a strange land Ⅱ（形）unmarried; single: ~ 主義 celibacy

【獨角戲】dújiǎoxì（名）monodrama: 唱 ~ act a one-man show; do sth. singlehanded

【獨到】dúdào（形）out of the ordi-nary run; unique

【獨奏】dúzòu（名）（instrumental）solo

【獨特】dútè（形）unique; peculiar

【獨唱】dúchàng（名）（vocal）solo

【獨創】dúchuàng（名）original con-tribution

【獨裁】dúcái（名）dictatorship: ~ 者 dictator

【獨當一面】dúdāng yīmiàn（動）be in sole charge of a department; work on one's own

【獨幕劇】dúmùjù（名）one-act play

【獨樹一幟】dú shù yī zhì〈成〉set up a new banner; establish one's own school（of art, philosophy, etc.）

【獨龍族】Dúlóngzú（名）the Drung nationality

【獨斷專行】dú duàn zhuān xíng〈成〉act peremptorily; be despotic

【獨霸】dúbà（動）reign supreme

【獨攬】dúlǎn（動）monopolize

獰 níng（形）ferocious; hideous

【獰笑】níngxiào（動）give a grim smile

獲 huò（動）❶ capture; obtain ❷ reap; harvest: 收 ~ bring in the crops

【獲得】huòdé（動）acquire; get; ob-tain: ~ 好評 be favourably received

【獲悉】huòxī（動）learn（of news, etc.）

【獲勝】huòshèng（動）win

【獲釋】huòshì（動）be released; be set free

獸 shòu Ⅰ（名）beast; animal: 禽不如 worse than a beast Ⅱ（形）beastly; brutal; bestial

【獸行】shòuxíng（名）bestial（bru-tal）behaviour

【獸性】shòuxìng（名）beastliness; bestiality; animal passions

【獸慾】shòuyù（名）bestial lust; car-nal desire

【獸醫】shòuyī（名）veterinary sur-geon; veterinarian

【獸類】shòulèi（名）beasts; animals

猭 guǎng（形）rough; boorish; un-couth

【猭悍】guǎnghàn（形）intrepid

獵 liè（動）hunt: 出 去 打 ~ go

hunting

【獵戶】lièhù（獵人 lièrén）（名）hunter

【獵手】lièshǒu （名）huntsman; hunter

【獵狗】liègǒu（名）hound

【獵奇】lièqí（動）hunt for novelties

【獵取】lièqǔ（動）hunt; seek

【獵物】lièwù（名）prey; quarry; game

【獵捕】lièbǔ（動）catch or trap（wild animals, fowls, etc.）

【獵場】lièchǎng（名）preserve; hunting ground

【獵槍】lièqiāng（名）hunting rifle; shotgun; sporting gun

獻 xiàn（動）offer; dedicate; donate

【獻身】xiànshēn（動）dedicate oneself to; lay down one's life for: ～於公共衛生事業 dedicate one's life to public health

【獻花】xiànhuā Ⅰ（動）present a bouquet of flowers Ⅱ（名）floral tribute

【獻花圈】xiànhuāquān（動）lay a wreath

【獻策】xiàncè（動）give advice

【獻詞】xiàncí（名）（congratulatory）message

【獻媚】xiànmèi（動）curry favour with

【獻演】xiànyǎn（動）present; perform

【獻醜】xiànchǒu（動）〈謙〉excuse me for my poor skill

【獻禮】xiànlǐ（動）present a gift; celebrate a festive occasion by contributing sth.：以辛勤勞動向五一節～。Greet May Day by working extra hard.

獺 tǎ（名）otto

獼 mí

【獼猴】míhóu（名）macaque; rhesus monkey; monkey

【獼猴桃】míhóutáo（名）*yangtao（Actinidia chinensis）*

獾 huān（名）badger

【獾油】huānyóu（名）ointment made from badger grease for treating burns

玄 部

玄 xuán（形）❶ black; dark ❷ fantastic; unreliable: 這真是說～了。This is a cock-and-bull story!

【玄妙】xuánmiào（形）subtle; mysterious; complicated: 事情～，難以捉摸。The whole thing is too complicated and difficult to understand.

【玄青】xuánqīng（名）deep black

【玄虛】xuánxū（名）trick; mystery: 這是故弄～。This is pulling the wool over sb.'s eyes.

率 lǜ（名）rate; ratio: 兌換 ～ rate of exchange
see also shuài

率 shuài Ⅰ（動）lead: ～兵 lead an army Ⅱ（形）❶ straight-forward; unreserved: 坦～地交換意見 have a frank exchange of views ❷ rash; reckless: 草～決定 make a hasty decision
see also lǜ

【率先】shuàixiān（副）first: ～發言

be the first to speak

【率直】shuàizhí (形) frank; forthright

【率領】shuàilǐng (動) lead; command

玉 部

玉 yù (名) jade

【玉石】yùshí (名) jade

【玉石俱焚】yù shí jù fén 〈成〉 everything is committed to the flames, be it jade or stone; indiscriminate and total destruction

【玉米】yùmǐ (名) maize; corn: ~花 popcorn / ~片 cornflakes / ~粥 corn porridge; maize gruel

【玉潔冰清】yù jié bīng qīng 〈成〉 pure and noble

【玉雕】yùdiāo (名) jade carving

【玉器】yùqì (名) jade object; jadeware

【玉簪】yùzān (名) jade hairpin

【玉璽】yùxǐ (名) imperial jade seal

【玉蘭片】yùlánpiàn (名) slices of tender bamboo shoots

王 wáng I (名) ❶ king; monarch ❷ prince ❸ (Wáng) a surname II (形) royal

【王八】wángba (名) ❶ tortoise ❷ 〈罵〉 cuckold: ~蛋 bastard; son of a bitch

【王子】wángzǐ (名) son of a king; prince

【王后】wánghòu (名) queen

【王位】wángwèi (名) throne

【王法】wángfǎ (名) law of the country: 目無~ lawless

【王室】wángshì (名) ❶ royal family ❷ imperial court; royal court

【王冠】wángguān (名) crown

【王宮】wánggōng (名) (royal) palace

【王國】wángguó (名) ❶ kingdom ❷ domain; realm

【王朝】wángcháo (名) ❶ dynasty ❷ imperial court; royal court

【王牌】wángpái (名) trump card

【王漿】wángjiāng (蜂王漿 fēngwángjiāng) (名) royal jelly

【王儲】wángchǔ (名) crown prince

玖 jiǔ (數) [the elaborate form of the numeral 九, used on cheques, banknotes, etc.] nine

玩 wán I (動) ❶ play ❷ resort to (improper means): ~花招 play a trick ❸ trifle with; neglect: ~世不恭 be cynical II (名) object of appreciation: 古~商 antique dealer

【玩弄】wánnòng (動) ❶ play fast and loose (with women) ❷ juggle with: ~數字遊戲 juggle with figures ❸ employ (improper means, etc.): ~障眼法 pull the wool over people's eyes

【玩忽】wánhū (動) neglect; trifle with: ~職守 neglect one's duty

【玩具】wánjù (名) toy

【玩物】wánwù (名) plaything; toy

【玩兒命】wánrmìng (動) 〈口〉 risk one's own life: ~地幹 work like mad / ~地跑 race ahead for what one is worth

【玩笑】wánxiào (名) joke; fun; jest: 她跟我開了一個~。She played a joke on me.

【玩意兒】wányìr (名) 〈口〉 ❶ toy ❷ thing; gadget

玫 méi

【玫瑰】méiguì（名）rose

珂 kē

（名）❶ jadelike, semi-precious stone ❷ ornament on a bridle

珐 fà

【珐琅】fàláng（名）enamel

玻 bō

【玻利維亞】Bōlìwéiyà（名）Bolivia：~人 Bolivian

【玻璃】bōli（名）glass：彩色~ stained glass

【玻璃板】bōlibǎn（名）plate glass；glass top (of a desk)

【玻璃杯】bōlibēi（名）(drinking) glass；tumbler

【玻璃棉】bōlimián（名）glass wool

【玻璃鋼】bōligāng（名）glass fibre reinforced plastics

玷 diàn

（名）flaw in jade

【玷污】diànwū（動）smear；blemish：~名聲 sully sb.'s reputation

【玷辱】diànrǔ（動）humiliate；disgrace

玲 líng

【玲瓏】línglóng（形）❶ exquisite；refined；delicate：~的牙雕 exquisite ivory carving ❷ nimble；agile：~活潑的姑娘 lively, petite girl

【玲瓏剔透】líng lóng tī tòu（形）(usu. of handicraft, esp. those hollowed-out) exquisitely wrought (with clear outlines of an ingenious design)

珍 zhēn

Ⅰ（形）precious；valuable Ⅱ（名）treasure：稀世奇~ an extremely rare treasure；rarity of rari-

ties Ⅲ（動）value highly；treasure

【珍品】zhēnpǐn（名）treasure

【珍重】zhēnzhòng（動）❶ treasure；value ❷ take good care of oneself

【珍珠】zhēnzhū（名）pearl

【珍惜】zhēnxī（動）treasure；value

【珍視】zhēnshì（動）prize；cherish；value：我們都~這個良機。We all cherish this good opportunity.

【珍異】zhēnyì（形）rare

【珍貴】zhēnguì（形）valuable；precious；priceless

【珍愛】zhēn'ài（動）love dearly；cherish

【珍藏】zhēncáng（動）keep (rare editions, art treasures, etc.) as of great value

【珍寶】zhēnbǎo（名）treasure；jewellery

珊 shān

【珊瑚】shānhú（名）coral

【珊瑚島】shānhúdǎo（名）coral island

【珊瑚礁】shānhújiāo（名）coral reef

班 bān

Ⅰ（名）❶ class：畢業~ graduating class ❷ team：道~ railway or highway maintenance squad ❸ shift；duty：上白~ be on the day shift ❹ squad Ⅱ（量）❶ group of people；bunch：一~小伙子 a group of youngsters ❷ run (in regular transportation service)：航~ flight

【班子】bānzi（名）❶ team；group；body：另behnu外組織~進行調查 orga-nize another team to investigate the case ❷ theatrical troupe

【班主任】bānzhǔrèn（名）school-teacher in charge of a class；class adviser

【班次】bāncì（名）❶ order of classes of grades at school ❷ number of runs or flights ❸ flight number (of an airliner)

【班车】bānchē（名） regular bus; scheduled transport (usu. for employees going to and from work)

【班底】bāndǐ（名）❶ ordinary members of an old-time theatrical troupe (not including the leading players) ❷ core members of an organization

【班房】bānfáng（名）〈口〉jail: 進了～ be in jail

【班长】bānzhǎng（名）❶ squad leader ❷ class monitor ❸ team leader

【班门弄斧】Bān mén nòng fǔ（成）show off one's skill with the axe before Lu Ban, the legendary master carpenter; show off before an expert

【班级】bānjí（名） classes (and grades)

【班组】bānzǔ（名）team; group

【班机】bānjī（名）airliner; scheduled flight

珠 zhū（名）❶ pearl ❷ beadlike thing: 滿額汗～ with one's brow beaded with sweat 水～ drops of water

【珠算】zhūsuàn（名）calculation with an abacus

【珠宝】zhūbǎo（名）pearls and jewels; jewelry

珞 luò

【珞巴族】Luòbāzú（名）the Lhoba nationality

琉 liú

【琉璃】liúlí（名）coloured glaze

【琉璃瓦】liúliwǎ（名）glazed tile

琅 láng

【琅琅】lángláng（象）sound of tinkling; sound of reading aloud

球 qiú（名）❶ ball: 足～ football; soccer ❷ anything in the shape of a ball: 衛生～ mothballs ❸ the globe; the earth ❹〈數〉sphere

【球形】qiúxíng（形）spherical; globular: ～閥 spherical valve

【球果】qiúguǒ（名）〈植〉cone

【球拍】qiúpāi（名） (tennis, badminton, etc.) racket; (pingpong) bat

【球门】qiúmén（名）〈體〉goal

【球门柱】qiúménzhù（名）〈體〉goalpost

【球迷】qiúmí（名）(ball game) fan

【球风】qiúfēng（名） sportsmanship (of a player)

【球面】qiúmiàn（名）spherical surface

【球茎】qiújīng（名）〈植〉corm

【球队】qiúduì（名）〈體〉team: 籃～ basketball team

【球场】qiúchǎng（名）〈體〉playground; tennis court; football field, etc.

【球菌】qiújūn（名）〈微〉coccus

【球网】qiúwǎng（名）net (for ball games)

【球鞋】qiúxié（名） gym shoes; sneakers

【球磨機】qiúmójī（名）〈機〉ball mill

【球坛】qiútán（名）ball-playing circles; ball-playing world

【球胆】qiúdǎn（名）bladder (of a ball)

【球赛】qiúsài（名）ball game; match

【球類運動】qiúlèi yùndòng（名）ball games

【球藝】qiúyì（名）ball game skills

【球體】qiútǐ（名）spheroid

現 xiàn Ⅰ（形）present; current: ～政府 the present government / ～將這本書寄給你。I am now sending you the book by mail. Ⅱ（副）acting in such a way as to meet an immediate need or challenge; extempore: ～學　～教 teach while learning Ⅲ（動）show: ～原形 show one's colours; reveal one's true features

【現世】xiànshì（名）this life

【現代】xiàndài Ⅰ（形）modern; contemporary Ⅱ（名）modern times

【現代化】xiàndàihuà（名）modernization

【現成】xiànchéng（形）ready-made: 吃～飯 enjoy the fruits of another's labours

【現存】xiàncún（形）in stock; in existence: ～版本 extant edition

【現任】xiànrèn Ⅰ（形）incumbent; present: ～外長 the present foreign minister Ⅱ（動）currently hold the office of: 他～這所大學的校長。He is now the president of this university.

【現行】xiànxíng（形）in force; in effect; current: ～體制 the present system / ～法規 laws and decrees in effect

【現有】xiànyǒu（形）available; existing

【現在】xiànzài（副）now; at present

【現役】xiànyì（形）on service; on active service

【現身說法】xiàn shēn shuō fǎ（動）advise or warn by recounting one's own experience

【現狀】xiànzhuàng（名）current situation; status quo

【現金】xiànjīn（名）cash; ready money

【現象】xiànxiàng（名）phenomenon

【現場】xiànchǎng（名）scene (of an event); spot: ～調查 on-the-spot investigation

【現款】xiànkuǎn（現錢 xiànqián）（名）cash; money on hand; ready money

【現實】xiànshí Ⅰ（名）reality Ⅱ（形）❶ actual; real ❷ practical; realistic: ～的辦法 a practical measure; a realistic approach

【現實主義】xiànshí zhǔyì（名）realism: ～者 realist

理 lǐ Ⅰ（名）❶ texture; vein ❷ reason; commonsense; truth: 不講～ refuse to see reason ❸ natural sciences ❹ short for science or physics Ⅱ（動）❶ manage ❷ tidy up: 整～房間 tidy up the room ❸ pay attention to (often used in the negative): 我根本沒～他。I took no notice of him whatsoever.

【理工科】lǐgōngkē（名）science and engineering

【理由】lǐyóu（名）reason; cause; grounds: 毫無～ completely groundless

【理性】lǐxìng（名）reason; senses

【理事】lǐshì（名）council member; director

【理事會】lǐshìhuì（名）council

【理直氣壯】lǐ zhí qì zhuàng〈成〉speak confidently with one's head held up

【理屈词穷】lǐ qū cí qióng〈成〉be unable to advance any further argument

【理所当然】lǐ suǒ dāng rán〈成〉as a matter of course

【理科】lǐkē（名）natural sciences

【理财】lǐcái（动）manage money affairs

【理智】lǐzhì（名）senses; mind

【理顺】lǐshùn（动）put in good order; straighten out: ～工業發展與環境保護的關係 straighten out the relationships between industrial development and environmental protection

【理睬】lǐcǎi（动）take notice of; pay attention to

【理會】lǐhuì（动）❶ understand ❷ heed

【理解】lǐjiě（动）understand; comprehend

【理想】lǐxiǎng Ⅰ（名）ideal; goal Ⅱ（形）ideal; satisfactory: ～的休假地 ideal holiday resort

【理想國】lǐxiǎngguó（名）ideal society; Utopia

【理論】lǐlùn（名）theory

【理髮】lǐfà（名）haircut; hairdo: ～員 barber; hairdresser

【理髮館】lǐfàguǎn（名）barber's shop

【理虧】lǐkuī（理屈 lǐqū）on precarious grounds: 他明明是～嘛。He's obviously in the wrong.

【理療】lǐliáo（名）physiotherapy

【理應】lǐyīng（动）should; be obliged to

琵 pí

【琵琶】pípa（名）pipa（a 4-stringed Chinese musical instrument）

琴 qín（名）general name for certain musical instruments: 七弦～ heptachord

【琴弦】qínxián（名）string（of a musical instrument）

【琴馬】qínmǎ（名）〈樂〉bridge（of a stringed instrument）

【琴書】qínshū（名）story-telling in the form of ballads sung with musical accompaniment

【琴鳥】qínniǎo（名）lyre-bird

【琴凳】qíndèng（名）music stool

【琴撥】qínbō（名）plectrum

【琴鍵】qínjiàn（名）key（on a musical instrument）

琪 qí（名）fine jade

琢 zhuó（动）chisel; carve: 精雕細～ exquisitely carved
see also zuó

【琢磨】zhuómó（动）❶（of jade）carve and polish ❷（of literary works）polish; refine

琢 zuó
see also zhuó

【琢磨】zuómó（动）turn sth. over in one's mind; ponder: ～問題 ponder upon a problem

琥 hǔ

【琥珀】hǔpò（名）amber

瑟 sè

【瑟瑟】sèsè（象）（of wind）rustle

【瑟縮】sèsuō（动）huddle oneself up

瑕 xiá（名）flaw; shortcoming

【瑕疵】xiácī（名）flaw; minor defect

【瑕瑜互見】xiá yú hù jiàn〈成〉have both merits and demerits

瑞 ruì（形）auspicious; lucky

【瑞士】Ruìshì（名）Switzerland: ～人 Swiss

【瑞典】Ruìdiǎn（名）Sweden: ～人 Swede; the Swedish/ ～語 Swedish (language)

【瑞雪】ruìxuě（名）timely snow

瑜 yú（名）❶ fine jade ❷ virtue; merit: 瑕不掩～。Minor defects do not outweigh the merits.

瑪 mǎ

【瑪瑙】mǎnǎo（名）agate

瑣 suǒ（形）trivial; petty; trifling

【瑣事】suǒshì（名）trivial matters; trivia; trivialities

【瑣細】suǒxì（形）trifling; trivial; petty

【瑣碎】suǒsuì（形）trivial; petty and numerous

瑤 yáo（名）precious jade

【瑤族】Yáozú（名）Yao nationality

瑰 guī（形）rare; extraordinary; marvellous

【瑰瑋】guīwěi（形）❶ extraordinary ❷ (of style) florid; ornate

【瑰寶】guībǎo（名）treasure; rarity; gem

【瑰麗】guīlì（形）splendid; magnificent

璞 pú（名）uncut jade

璣 jī（名）pearl not exactly round in shape: 字字珠～ every word a gem; graceful writing

環 huán Ⅰ（名）❶ ring; hoop: 花～ garland ❷ link: 重要的一～ a key link Ⅱ（動）surround; encircle: ～城賽跑 round-the-city race

【環行】huánxíng（動）go around: ～鐵路 circuit railway

【環抱】huánbào（動）surround; encircle: 羣山～ nestling among the hills

【環球】huánqiú（形）❶ round the world ❷ global: ～旅行 round-the-world tour; transglobe expedition

【環視】huánshì（動）look around

【環節】huánjié（名）❶ link ❷ segment

【環境】huánjìng（名）environment; surroundings: ～保護 environmental protection

【環繞】huánrǎo（動）surround; centre around

【環顧】huángù（動）look round

璧 bì（名）flat, round piece of carved jade with a hole in its centre

【璧還】bìhuán（動）〈敬〉❶ return sth. (with thanks) ❷ decline a gift (with thanks)

璽 xǐ（名）imperial (royal) seal

瓊 qióng（名）fine jade

【瓊脂】qióngzhī（名）agaragar; agar

瓜　部

瓜 guā（名）melon; gourd; squash: 黃～ cucumber

【瓜子】guāzǐ（名）melon seeds

【瓜分】guāfēn（動）carve up; divide up; partition

【瓜田李下】guā tián lǐ xià〈成〉in suspicious circumstances

【瓜葛】guāgé（名）connection: 他

跟這一醜聞並無～。He has no connection with the scandal.

【瓜熟蒂落】guā shú dì luò〈成〉when a melon is ripe, it falls off its stem; things can be easily done when conditions are ripe

瓢 piáo（名）gourd ladle

【瓢潑大雨】piáopō dàyǔ（名）pouring rain; downpour

【瓢蟲】piáochóng（名）ladybird

瓣 bàn Ⅰ（名）❶ petal: 玫瑰花～ rose petals ❷ section; segment (of fruit or bean) ❸ valve; lamella: 安全～ safety valve ❹ piece; fragment: 破成幾～ be broken into pieces Ⅱ（量）section: 一～大蒜 a clove of garlic

【瓣膜】bànmó（名）〈生理〉valve

瓤 ráng（名）pulp; pith: 沙～西瓜 water-melon with mushy pulp

瓦 部

瓦 wǎ Ⅰ（名）❶（roof）tile ❷〈電〉watt Ⅱ（形）of baked clay: ～罐 earthern jar
see also wà

【瓦匠】wǎjiang（瓦工 wǎgōng）（名）bricklayer; plasterer

【瓦房】wǎfáng（名）tile-roofed house

【瓦特】wǎtè（名）〈電〉watt

【瓦斯】wǎsī（名）gas: 催淚～ tear gas

【瓦解】wǎjiě（動）fall apart; collapse

【瓦藍】wǎlán（形）（often of the sky) light blue

【瓦礫】wǎlì（名）debris; rubble

瓦 wà（動）tile (a roof)
see also wǎ

瓷

瓷 cí（名）porcelain; china

【瓷實】císhi（形）〈方〉solid; firm

【瓷磚】cízhuān（名）ceramic tile

【瓷雕】cídiāo（名）〈工美〉porcelain carving

【瓷器】cíqì（名）china; porcelain

瓶

瓶 píng（名）bottle; flask

【瓶子】píngzi（名）bottle

【瓶塞】píngsāi（名）bottle stopper; cork

【瓶膽】píngdǎn（名）glass liner (of a thermos bottle)

甄

甄 zhēn Ⅰ（動）discriminate; distinguish Ⅱ（名）(Zhēn) a surname

【甄別】zhēnbié（動）examine and distinguish; screen

【甄拔】zhēnbá（動）select

甕

甕 wèng（名）urn; jar

【甕中之鱉】wèng zhōng zhī biē〈成〉be like a turtle in an urn; be trapped

【甕聲甕氣】wèng shēng wèng qì（形）in a low, muffled voice

甘 部

甘 gān Ⅰ（形）❶ sweet ❷ willing: 不～失敗 not be resigned to defeat; not take defeat lying down; unwilling to accept defeat Ⅱ（名）❶ (Gān) short for Gansu Province ❷ (Gān) a surname

【甘心】gānxīn Ⅰ(形) willing Ⅱ(動) resign oneself to

【甘休】gānxiū (動) be willing to give up; be ready to let it go

【甘油】gānyóu (名)〈化〉glycerine

【甘苦】gānkǔ (名) joys and sorrows; (of work or experience) difficulty: 不知其中~ be ignorant of the difficulty involved

【甘拜下風】gān bài xià fēng〈成〉sincerely admire sb. for his superiority (in knowledge or skill); sincerely concede defeat

【甘草】gāncǎo (名)〈中藥〉licorice root

【甘肅】Gānsù (名) Gansu (Province)

【甘蔗】gānzhe (名) sugarcane

【甘霖】gānlín (名) timely rain

【甘薯】gānshǔ (名) sweet potato

【甘願】gānyuàn (副) willingly

【甘露】gānlù (名) sweet dew

甚 shèn (副) ❶ very; rather: ~爲不滿 be very much displeased ❷ more than: 關心別人~於關心自己 care for others more than one does for oneself

【甚至】shènzhì (連) even: 這一點~小學生也知道。This is understood even by school-children.

甜 tián (形) ❶ sweet: 愛吃~食 have a sweet tooth ❷ (of sleep) sound: 睡得很~ be sound asleep ❸ agreeable; pleasant: 他話說得很~。His mouth overflows with honey.

【甜言蜜語】tián yán mì yǔ〈成〉honeyed words; flattery

【甜菜】tiáncài (名) beet; beetroot

【甜蜜】tiánmì (形) sweet; joyous

【甜頭】tiántou (名) ❶ sweetish flavour; pleasant taste ❷ benefit; gain; profit: 嘗到~ begin to enjoy the benefit; have a foretaste of sth.

【甜點心】tiándiǎnxin (名) dessert

【甜麵醬】tiánmiànjiàng (名) sweet sauce made from fermented flour

生 部

生 shēng Ⅰ(動) ❶ give birth to: 在北京出~ be born in Beijing ❷ grow: 荊棘叢~ be overgrown with brambles ❸ generate; create; have: ~事 make trouble ❹ make (a fire): ~爐子做飯 light a stove to cook a meal Ⅱ(名) ❶ life (as opposed to death): 死裏逃~ escape by the skin of one's teeth ❷ livelihood; living: ~計 means of livelihood ❸ all one's life: 畢~的事業 work of a lifetime ❹ pupil; learner: 畢業~ graduate ❺ male role (in traditional Chinese opera) Ⅲ(形) ❶ living; lively: ~龍活虎 full of vim and vigour ❷ unripe: 這西瓜是~的。This water-melon is not ripe. ❸ (of food) raw; uncooked: ~麵團 dough ❹ crude; unprocessed: ~橡膠 raw rubber ❺ unfamiliar: 陌~的面孔 unfamiliar faces ❻ stiff; mechanical: 態度~硬 be stiff in manner Ⅳ(副) [used before some words that express emotion or sensation] very: 口~疼。The cut hurts very much.

【生人】shēngrén (名) stranger

【生力軍】shēnglìjūn (名) fresh reinforcement; vital new force

【生日】shēngrì（名）birthday

【生手】shēngshǒu（名）green-horn

【生火】shēnghuǒ（動）make a fire; build a fire; light a stove

【生水】shēngshuǐ（名）unboiled water

【生平】shēngpíng（名）lifetime; life story：～簡介 biographical sketch

【生存】shēngcún（動）survive; subsist：～鬥爭 struggle for existence

【生死】shēngsǐ（名）life and death：～攸關的問題 a question of vital importance

【生米煮成熟飯】shēng mǐ zhǔ chéng shú fàn〈成〉What's done cannot be undone; it's a fait accompli

【生吞活剝】shēng tūn huó bō〈成〉accept an idea uncritically

【生冷】shēnglěng（形）（of food）cold or raw

【生肖】shēngxiào（屬相 shǔxiang）（名）any of the twelve animals representing the year in which a person was born

【生育】shēngyù（動）bear（children）：節制～ birth control ／ ～年齡 childbearing age

【生來】shēnglái（副）❶ from one's birth ❷ by nature：他～就喜歡音樂。He loves music by nature.

【生命】shēngmìng（名）life：～力 vitality ／ ～綫 lifeline

【生怕】shēngpà（生恐 shēngkǒng）（動）be afraid that; take care not to：處處小心，～得罪人 act very cautiously so as to offend nobody

【生物】shēngwù（名）❶ living things：～實驗衛星 biosatellite ❷ biology：～學 biology

【生性】shēngxìng Ⅰ（副）by nature：

～固執 be obstinate by nature; have a stubborn disposition Ⅱ（名）natural disposition; nature

【生長】shēngzhǎng（動）grow up; grow

【生活】shēnghuó Ⅰ（名）❶ life：過着幸福的～ live a happy life ／ ～方式 mode of life; way of life ❷ livelihood：～條件 living conditions／ ～水平 standard of living Ⅱ（動）live

【生計】shēngjì（名）livelihood

【生前】shēngqián（副）during the lifetime of the deceased

【生病】shēngbìng（動）fall ill

【生財】shēngcái（動）get rich：～有道 know how to make money

【生根】shēnggēn（動）take root：～結果 strike root and bear fruit

【生氣】shēngqì Ⅰ（動）get angry Ⅱ（名）vitality; vigour; liveliness

【生效】shēngxiào（動）take effect; go into force：從即日起～ come into effect as from this very day

【生造】shēngzào（動）coin（a word or expression）

【生涯】shēngyá（名）career：開始政治～ embark on a political career

【生理】shēnglǐ（名）physiology：～鹽水 physiological saline

【生動】shēngdòng（形）vivid; lively; graphic：～描寫 graphic description

【生動活潑】shēngdòng huópo（形）vivid and vigorous; sprightly

【生產】shēngchǎn Ⅰ（動）❶ produce; turn out ❷ give birth to a baby Ⅱ（名）production; manufacture：～率 productivity ／ ～綫 production line ／ ～責任制 production responsibility system

【生產方式】shēngchǎn fāngshì（名）mode of production

【生產手段】shēngchǎn shǒuduàn（名）means of production

【生產過剩】shēngchǎn guòshèng（名）overproduction

【生產勞動】shēngchǎn láodòng（名）productive labour

【生產關係】shēngchǎn guānxì（名）relations of production

【生啤酒】shēngpíjiǔ（名）draught beer; bitter

【生詞】shēngcí（生字 shēngzì）（名）new word（for a learner）

【生就】shēngjiù（動）be endowed with: ～一副好嗓子 be gifted with a good voice

【生疏】shēngshū（形）❶ unfamiliar; inexperienced: 業務～unfamiliar with one's work ❷ rusty（through lack of practice）: 她的英語～了。Her English is rusty. ❸ not intimate

【生殖】shēngzhí（名）reproduction: ～器 reproductive organs; genitals

【生硬】shēngyìng（形）stiff; rigid; inflexible; awkward

【生絲】shēngsī（名）raw silk

【生路】shēnglù（名）means of livelihood: 別無～cannot find any other means of livelihood; there is no other way out

【生意】shēngyì（名）a natural scene full of life and vitality

【生意】shēngyi（名）business: 做皮貨～的人 a fur dealer

【生搬硬套】shēng bān yìng tào〈成〉copy sth. mechanically in total disregard of specific conditions

【生態】shēngtài（名）ecology: ～平衡 ecological balance

【生疑】shēngyí（動）become suspicious

【生漆】shēngqī（名）crude lacquer

【生銹】shēngxiù（動）（of iron, etc.）become rusty

【生僻】shēngpì（形）rarely seen; uncommon

【生髮精】shēngfàjīng（名）hair growth tonic

【生豬】shēngzhū（名）live pig

【生機】shēngjī（名）❶ vitality ❷ chance of survival

【生薑】shēngjiāng（名）〈口〉green ginger; ginger

【生離死別】shēng lí sǐ bié〈成〉part never to meet again; part for ever

【生鐵】shēngtiě（名）pig iron

產

產 chǎn Ⅰ（動）❶ give birth to; reproduce ❷ produce; yield: 多～（的）prolific Ⅱ（名）❶ product; produce: 水～aquatic product ❷ estate; property; assets: 私～private property

【產生】chǎnshēng（動）yield; give rise to: ～副作用 produce side effects

【產地】chǎndì（名）producing area; producing centre: 水果～fruit-growing area

【產卵】chǎnluǎn（動）（of fish, etc.）spawn;（of insects）oviposit;（of birds, etc.）lay eggs

【產物】chǎnwù（名）outcome; product

【產科】chǎnkē（名）❶ obstetrical department ❷ obstetrics

【產品】chǎnpǐn（名）product; produce: 名優～brand product

【產院】chǎnyuàn（名）maternity hospital

【产值】chǎnzhí（名）output value

【产假】chǎnjià（名）maternity leave

【产量】chǎnliàng（名）output; yield

【产业】chǎnyè（名）❶ estate; property; assets ❷ industry: ～革命 the Industrial Revolution

【产业工人】chǎnyè gōngrén（名）industrial worker

【产权】chǎnquán（名）property right

甥 shēng（外甥 wàisheng）（名）nephew; sister's son

【甥女】shēngnǚ（外甥女 wàishengnǚ）（名）niece; sister's daughter

用 部

用 yòng Ⅰ（动）❶ use; employ; apply ❷ [used mostly in the negative] need: 不～细讲。There is no need to go into detail. Ⅱ（名）❶ expenses: 军事费～ military expenditure ❷ usefulness; use: 公～ for public use

【用人】yòngrén（动）❶ choose a person for a job: 他不会～。He does not know how to select the right persons for the right jobs. ❷ need employees

【用力】yònglì（动）exert oneself; use strength to accomplish sth.: ～把门推开 push hard to open the door

【用户】yònghù（名）consumer; user

【用心】yòngxīn Ⅰ（副）attentively; intently: ～学习 concentrate on one's studies Ⅱ（名）intention; motive: 他～是好的。He meant well.

【用功】yònggōng（形）diligent; hard-working

【用兵】yòngbīng（动）❶ deploy troops in war ❷ use military forces

【用法】yòngfǎ（名）use; usage

【用具】yòngjù（名）utensils; instrument; tool: 炊事～ kitchen utensils

【用事】yòngshì（动）act: 意气～ act on impulse

【用武】yòngwǔ（动）resort to force; exercise one's talents: 无～之地 cannot display one's military genius; have nowhere to display one's abilities

【用品】yòngpǐn（名）articles for use

【用途】yòngtú（名）use

【用处】yòngchu（名）use; function: 电脑的～很大。The computer is extremely useful.

【用费】yòngfèi（名）expense; cost

【用场】yòngchǎng（名）use: 这些人派不上～。We have no use for such people.

【用意】yòngyì（名）intention; purpose

【用语】yòngyǔ（名）❶ wording ❷ phraseology; term

甩 shuǎi（动）❶ swing; wave: 袖子一～就走了 go away with a sweep of the arm ❷ throw; cast: 向他～鸡蛋和西红柿 throw eggs and tomatoes at him ❸ throw off; jettison; abandon ❹ leave sb. behind

【甩手】shuǎishǒu（动）❶ swing one's arm ❷ refuse to have anything more to do with: ～不干 wash one's hands of the business

【甩卖】shuǎimài（动）dump; put up for sale

甫 fǔ (副) just: 行裝~卸 have just unpacked

甬 yǒng

【甬道】yǒngdào (名) ❶ passageway in a courtyard or graveyard ❷ corridor

甭 béng (动)〈方〉needn't: ~客氣. Please don't stand on ceremony.

田 部

田 tián (名) ❶ farmland; field: ~間管理 field management ❷ (Tián) a surname

【田地】tiándì (名) ❶ farmland ❷ plight; fix: 我不知道他已病到這步~. I didn't know he was so very ill.

【田徑】tiánjìng (名)〈體〉track and field

【田野】tiányě (名) field; open country; expanse of farmland

【田園】tiányuán (名) countryside; country: ~詩 idyl(l); pastoral poetry

由 yóu Ⅰ (名) cause; reason: 根~ root cause Ⅱ (动) ❶ be attributable to: 咎~自取 have only oneself to blame for the mistake ❷ obey: ~着性子 act on impulse Ⅲ (介) ❶ by; through: ~此門進 enter by this door / 這事~他負責. He is responsible for it. ❷ on the basis of: 人體是~各種細胞組成的. The human body is composed of various kinds of cells. ❸ from: ~天津出發 set out from Tianjin

【由不得】yóubude (动) ❶ have no say (in a matter): 這事~你. It is not up to you to decide. ❷ cannot help: 聽眾~大笑起來. The audience couldn't help bursting into laughter.

【由於】yóuyú (介) owing to; due to

【由來】yóulái (名) origin; cause

【由來已久】yóu lái yǐ jiǔ (成) longstanding

【由衷】yóuzhōng (形) sincere; heartfelt

甲 jiǎ (名) ❶ the first of the Ten Celestial Stems, often used as an ordinal referring to the first item in a series: ~天下 number one in the world; second to none ❷ [used as a substitute for sth. indefinite] A: ~組同乙組比賽. Group A plays against Group B. ❸ shell; carapace ❹ nail: 剪指~ trim one's nails ❺ armour: 盔~ suit of armour ❻ 〈舊〉grassroots unit of civil administration ❼ (Jiǎ) a surname

【甲板】jiǎbǎn (名) deck (of a ship)

【甲狀腺】jiǎzhuàngxiàn (名) thyroid gland

【甲骨文】jiǎgǔwén (名) script on tortoise shells or animal bones of the Shang Dynasty (c. 16th-11th century B.C.) in ancient China

【甲魚】jiǎyú (名) turtle with a soft shell

【甲殼】jiǎqiào (名) crust: ~動物 crustacean

【甲蟲】jiǎchóng (名) beetle

申 shēn Ⅰ (动) state; express; declare: 重~己見 reiterate one's

views Ⅱ (名) (Shěn) a surname

【申斥】 shēnchì (动) scold (one's subordinate); reprimand

【申明】 shēnmíng (动) declare; state

【申述】 shēnshù (动) state; explain in detail

【申冤】 shēnyuān (动) ❶ redress an injustice ❷ apeal for redress of a wrong

【申诉】 shēnsù (动) appeal

【申报】 shēnbào (动) ❶ report to a higher body ❷ declare sth. (to the customs): 你有需要～的物品吗? Have you anything to declare?

【申请】 shēnqǐng (动) apply for; request: ～人 applicant / ～表 application form

【申辩】 shēnbiàn (动) plead one's case; defend oneself

男 nán (名) man; male: 一～一女 a man and a woman / ～演员 actor

【男人】 nánrén (名) ❶ man ❷ menfolk

【男人】 nánren (名)〈口〉husband

【男子】 nánzǐ (名) man; male

【男子汉】 nánzǐhàn (名) man

【男生】 nánshēng (名) man student; boy student; schoolboy

【男低音】 nándīyīn (名)〈乐〉bass

【男性】 nánxìng (名) male sex

【男儿】 nán'ér (名) man

【男朋友】 nánpéngyou (名) boyfriend

【男孩】 nánhái (名) boy

【男高音】 nángāoyīn (名)〈乐〉tenor

【男厕所】 náncèsuǒ (名) gents'; men's (lavatory)

【男爵】 nánjué (名) baron

甾 zāi (名)〈化〉steroid

畏 wèi (动) ❶ fear; dread: 无～

be fearless ❷ respect; esteem: 令人敬～ command respect; inspire awe

【畏怯】 wèiqiè (形) cowardly; faint-hearted

【畏首畏尾】 wèi shǒu wèi wěi〈成〉be filled with misgivings; be timid and overcautious

【畏途】 wèitú (名) dangerous path; risky job

【畏罪】 wèizuì (动) fear punishment for one's offence: ～潜逃 run away to escape punishment

【畏避】 wèibì (动) flinch from; shy away from

【畏缩】 wèisuō (名) shrink; wince

【畏难】 wèinán (动) shrink from difficulty

【畏惧】 wèijù (动) dread; fear

界 jiè (名) ❶ bounds; boundary ❷ scope; range: 開闊眼～ broaden one's vision ❸ circle; world: 教育～ educational circles ❹ world; kingdom: 動物～ the animal world ❺〈地〉group: 新生～ the Cenozoic Group

【界內球】 jiènèiqiú (名)〈體〉in bounds; ball

【界外球】 jièwàiqiú (名)〈體〉out-of-bounds; out

【界限】 jièxiàn (名) ❶ dividing line; bounds ❷ limit; extreme: 超過～ beyond the limit

【界碑】 jièbēi (名) boundary tablet; boundary marker

【界綫】 jièxiàn (名) boundary; demarcation line: 軍事分～ military demarcation line

畝 mǔ (名) mu, a unit of area (= 0.0667 hectares)

畜 chù（名）livestock：家～ domestic animal

see also xù

【畜生】chùsheng（名）❶ animal ❷〈詈〉beast; brute

畜 xù（動）raise domestic animals

see also chù

【畜牧】xùmù（動）raise livestock or poultry：～場 animal farm

【畜牧業】xùmùyè（名）animal husbandry

【畜產】xùchǎn（名）livestock products; animal products

【畜養】xùyǎng（動）raise（domestic animals）

畔 pàn（名）❶ border（of a field）❷ side; bank（of a lake, river, etc.）

留 liú（動）❶ stay; remain：～在朋友家過夜 stay overnight at a friend's ❷ detain; ask（sb.）to stay：～客 ask a visitor to stay ❸ keep; retain：手頭總～一本好字典 always keep a good dictionary at hand ❹ wear; grow：～辮子 wear plaits（pigtails）❺ leave：把奶～到明天喝 leave the milk over for tomorrow

【留一手】liú yīshǒu（動）hold back one or two knacks（when passing on one's skills）; have a card up one's sleeve

【留心】liúxīn（動）be careful; pay attention to

【留成】liúchéng（名）profit retention

【留存】liúcún（動）keep; preserve

【留任】liúrèn（動）retain the office

【留守】liúshǒu（動）stay behind for rounding-off work or liaison duty

【留守處】liúshǒuchù（名）rear office

【留步】liúbù〈套〉don't bother to see me out; let's say good-bye here

【留言】liúyán（動）leave a message; offer one's comments on departure

【留言簿】liúyánbù（名）visitors' book

【留念】liúniàn（動）keep sth. as a memento

【留後路】liú hòulù（動）leave a way for retreat

【留神】liúshén（動）look out; mind; be on guard（against）

【留級】liújí（動）（of a student）repeat the year's studies

【留情】liúqíng（動）show mercy

【留宿】liúsù（動）❶ put sb. up for the night ❷ stay overnight

【留傳】liúchuán（動）hand down to posterity

【留意】liúyì（動）be careful; beware

【留影】liúyǐng（動）have a picture taken as a memento

【留駐】liúzhù（動）be stationed

【留餘地】liú yúdì（動）leave room for; allow a margin for

【留學】liúxué（動）study abroad

【留學生】liúxuéshēng（名）❶ person studying abroad：外國～ foreign student ❷ returned student or scholar

【留聲機】liúshēngjī（名）gramophone; phonograph

【留職停薪】liúzhí tíngxīn（動）be on long leave without pay

【留難】liúnàn（動）deliberately make things difficult

【留戀】liúliàn（動）linger on; be reluctant to leave; have nostalgia for

畚 běn (動)〈方〉scoop up (with a dustpan)
【畚箕】běnjī (名)〈方〉❶ dustpan ❷ bamboo or wicker scoop

畦 qí (名) small plot of land surrounded by ridges: 菜～ vegetable bed

畢 bì Ⅰ (動) finish; complete; accomplish: 工作完～後 after finishing the job Ⅱ (形) whole; entire; complete Ⅲ (副) entirely; completely; altogether: 鋒芒～露 make a showy display of one's ability
【畢生】bìshēng (副) for life; all one's life: ～向往 a lifelong yearning
【畢其功於一役】bì qí gōng yú yī yì 〈成〉accomplish the entire task at one stroke
【畢竟】bìjìng (副) after all; in the last analysis; when all is said and done
【畢業】bìyè Ⅰ (動) finish school; graduate Ⅱ (名) graduation
【畢業生】bìyèshēng (名) graduate
【畢業典禮】bìyè diǎnlǐ (名) commencement; graduation ceremony
【畢業設計】bìyè shèjì (名) graduation project
【畢業論文】bìyè lùnwén (名) thesis; dissertation
【畢業證書】bìyè zhèngshū (名) diploma; graduation certificate

異 yì (形) ❶ different ❷ unusual; extraordinary; strange: 優～的成績 outstanding achievements ❸ surprising: 感到詫～ be surprised
【異己】yìjǐ (名) dissident: 排除～ get rid of those who hold different views
【異口同聲】yì kǒu tóng shēng 〈成〉in one voice; in chorus; unanimously
【異化】yìhuà (名) alienation
【異乎尋常】yì hū xún cháng (形) unusual; extraordinary: 他具有～的勇氣。He is a man of extraordinary courage.
【異同】yìtóng (名) similarities and differences
【異曲同工】yì qū tóng gōng 〈成〉these writings, though by different people, have the identical hallmark of excellence; reach the same end by different means
【異性】yìxìng (名) opposite sex
【異軍突起】yì jūn tū qǐ 〈成〉a new force suddenly coming to the fore
【異國】yìguó (名) foreign country
【異教】yìjiào (名) paganism; heathenism
【異族】yìzú (名) foreign nation; alien race
【異常】yìcháng Ⅰ (形) strange; unusual: 他今天態度有點～。He is a bit odd today. Ⅱ (副) extremely: ～激動 very excited
【異彩】yìcǎi (名) magnificent splendour
【異鄉】yìxiāng (名) foreign land; strange place
【異想天開】yì xiǎng tiān kāi 〈成〉have fantastic ideas; indulge in wishful thinking
【異端】yìduān (名) heresy
【異樣】yìyàng (形) ❶ unusual; extraordinary ❷ different
【異議】yìyì (名) objection: 對方案沒有～ have no objection to the plan

略 lüè I (名) plan: 策～ stratagem II (動) leave out: ～去最後一段 delete the last paragraph III (形) sketchy; brief: ～作停留 make a brief stay; stop over IV (副) slightly; a little: 天氣～有好轉。The weather seems to be clearing up a little bit.

【略見一斑】lüè jiàn yī bān〈成〉get a bird's-eye view of sth.

【略知一二】lüè zhī yī èr〈成〉know a thing or two about sth.; have a rough idea of sth.

【略略】lüèlüè (副) slightly: ～有些得意 feel a bit smug

【略勝一籌】lüè shèng yī chóu〈成〉somewhat superior by comparison; a cut above

【略微】lüèwēi (副) a little; a bit: ～有點累 feel a little tired

【略語】lüèyǔ (名) abbreviation

【略圖】lüètú (名) sketch; brief diagram

畫 huà I (名) ❶ drawing; painting; picture: 油～ oil painting ❷ stroke (of a Chinese character) II (動) draw; paint: ～圖解 draw a diagram / ～一張畫 draw a picture

【畫布】huàbù (名) canvas (for painting)

【畫冊】huàcè (名) picture album

【畫卷】huàjuàn (名) picture scroll

【畫虎類狗】huà hǔ lèi gǒu〈成〉any poor imitation is bound to be ludicrous; attempt something too ambitious and end up in failure

【畫室】huàshì (名) studio

【畫展】huàzhǎn (名) art exhibition

【畫家】huàjiā (名) painter

【畫蛇添足】huà shé tiān zú〈成〉spoil sth. by making a superfluous effort

【畫報】huàbào (名) pictorial

【畫廊】huàláng (名) ❶ painted corridor ❷ (picture) gallery

【畫筆】huàbǐ (名) painting brush

【畫像】huàxiàng I (動) make a portrait; portray II (名) portrait

【畫餅充飢】huà bǐng chōng jī〈成〉draw a cake to relieve hunger; seek imaginary satisfaction

【畫龍點睛】huà lóng diǎn jīng〈成〉put the finishing touches to sth.

畬 shē

【畬族】Shēzú (名) the She nationality

番 fān (名) time; occasion: 使產量翻了一～ double the output

【番茄】fānqié (名) tomato: ～醬 ketchup; tomato paste

【番號】fānhào (名) designation

【番薯】fānshǔ (名) sweet potato

當 dāng I (動) ❶ be; act as: ～組長 act as group leader ❷ bear; answer for: 敢作敢～ act boldly whatever the consequences ❸ take charge of; manage: ～權 be in power ❹ resist: 銳不可～ be irresistible ❺ should; ought to II (形) equal: 旗鼓相～ be well-matched III (副) in sb.'s presence; to sb.'s face IV (連) while; at the moment: 我們出發時，天下起雪來。We were setting off when it began to snow. V (象) ding-dong

see also dàng

【當之無愧】dāngzhī wúkuì (動) certainly deserve; be worthy of

【當心】dāngxīn (動) be careful; look

out: ～臺階。Mind the steps.

【當今】dāngjīn（副）at present; now

【當仁不讓】dāng rén bù ràng〈成〉never decline to shoulder a responsibility

【當代】dāngdài（名）our time: ～詩歌 contemporary poetry

【當年】dāngnián（副）❶ in those years: ～這裏是一所學校。There used to be a school here in those days. ❷ in the prime of life: 小伙子正～ a young man in his prime

【當地】dāngdì（形）local: ～新聞 local news

【當兵】dāngbīng（動）join the army; enlist

【當即】dāngjí（副）right now; immediately

【當局】dāngjú（名）the authorities

【當局者迷】dāng jú zhě mí〈成〉those who are in the game do not see as clearly as they should

【當初】dāngchū（副）originally; at the beginning; initially

【當空】dāngkōng（副）in the sky

【當事人】dāngshìrén（名）person or party concerned

【當前】dāngqián Ⅰ（形）present; current: ～的政局 the current political situation Ⅱ（動）face; confront: 大敵～ be confronted with the formidable adversary

【當面】dāngmiàn（副）face to face; in sb.'s presence

【當時】dāngshí（副）then; at that time

【當家】dāngjiā（動）❶ manage household affairs ❷ have the final say

【當務之急】dāng wù zhī jí（名）matter of great urgency

【當道】dāngdào（動）❶ stand in the way ❷ wield power

【當場】dāngchǎng（副）on the spot

【當然】dāngrán（副）❶ of course; certainly ❷ rightfully

【當眾】dāngzhòng（副）in public

【當機立斷】dāng jī lì duàn〈成〉make a prompt decision

當 dàng Ⅰ（形）suitable; right: 處得～ handle with propriety Ⅱ（動）❶ be equal to: 以一～十 pit one against ten ❷ think; guess: 我～你走了。I thought you were gone. ❸ regard as: ～貴賓看待 treat sb. as a distinguished guest ❹ pawn
see also dāng

【當年】dàngnián（副）in the same year

【當時】dàngshí（副）at that very moment

【當真】dàngzhēn Ⅰ（動）believe; take seriously: 把玩笑～ take the joke seriously Ⅱ（副）really: 你～不幹了？Do you really want to throw up your job?

【當票】dàngpiào（名）pawn ticket

【當做】dàngzuò（動）❶ treat as ❷ take for: 上次我把你姐姐～你了。I took your sister for you last time.

【當鋪】dàngpù（名）pawnshop

畸 jī（形）❶ irregular; abnormal; deformed: ～變 distortion ❷ lopsided; unbalanced

【畸形】jīxíng Ⅰ（名）deformity; malformation: 先天～ congenital malformation Ⅱ（形）abnormal; misshapen

疆 jiāng（名）❶ border; frontier

❷ limit; end; bound

【疆土】jiāngtǔ（疆域 jiāngyù）（名）territory; domain

【疆界】jiāngjiè（名）boundary

【疆場】jiāngchǎng（名）battlefield; battle ground

疇 chóu（名）❶ farmland ❷ kind; category

疊 dié（動）❶ pile up ❷ overlap ❸ fold

【疊牀架屋】dié chuáng jià wū〈成〉build one house on top of another

疋 部

疏 shū Ⅰ（動）❶ dredge (a river, canal etc.) ❷ disperse; spread widely：～開隊形 open formation ❸ neglect; overlook Ⅱ（形）❶ thinly scattered; sparse ❷ (of family or social relations) distant; not intimate with ❸ unfamiliar：生～ be unfamiliar with ❹ scanty; hollow：才～學淺 have small talent and scanty knowledge; be an indifferent scholar Ⅲ（名）（Shū）a surname

【疏放】shūfàng（形）〈書〉unrestrained ❷ (of writing) unconventional

【疏忽】shūhu Ⅰ（名）negligence; carelessness; oversight Ⅱ（動）neglect

【疏浚】shūjùn（動）dredge (a river, canal, etc.)

【疏通】shūtōng（動）❶ dredge (a river, canal, etc.) ❷ mediate; remove misunderstanding between two or more parties

【疏散】shūsàn Ⅰ（動）evacuate; disperse Ⅱ（形）scattered; straggling

【疏遠】shūyuǎn Ⅰ（動）estrange; alienate Ⅱ（形）(of relations) not close; cold; estranged

【疏落】shūluò（形）sparse; scattered; few and far between

【疏漏】shūlòu（名）slip; oversight; omission due to carelessness

【疏導】shūdǎo（動）❶ dredge (a river, canal, etc.) ❷ disperse (a crowd) through persuasion ❸ enlighten; remove discontent or resentment by reasoning and persuasion

【疏鬆】shūsōng Ⅰ（形）loose; puffy; (of soil) porous Ⅱ（動）loosen

疑 yí Ⅰ（名）doubt; suspect Ⅱ（形）uncertain; doubtful：存～ leave the question open

【疑心】yíxīn（動）doubt; suspect：我~他在玩弄把戲。I suspect that he is playing tricks.

【疑神疑鬼】yí shén yí guǐ〈成〉be perpetually obsessed by suspicion; foster groundless suspicion; be suspicious

【疑案】yí'àn（名）❶ disputed case ❷ mystery

【疑問】yíwèn（名）question; doubt

【疑雲】yíyún（名）misgivings; doubt

【疑惑】yíhuò（動）feel uncertain; have doubts

【疑義】yíyì（名）doubt

【疑團】yítuán（名）doubts; suspicions

【疑慮】yílǜ（名）doubt; apprehensions：滿懷~ a mind full of misgivings

【疑點】yídiǎn（名） questionable point; suspicious point

【疑難】yínán（形）difficult; puzzling；～問題 knotty problem

【疑懼】yíjù（名）misgivings

疒 部

疔 dīng（名）malignant boil

疝 shàn（名）hernia

【疝氣】shànqì（名）〈醫〉hernia

疙 gē

【疙瘩】gēda（名） pimple; lump; knot: 滿是～的臉 a pimpled face / 我心上的～已去掉了。The load is off my mind.

疚 jiù（動）feel remorseful: 深感內～ feel deep remorse

疣 yóu（名）〈醫〉wart

疤 bā（名）❶ scar: 瘡～ scar ❷ flaw on a utensil

【疤痕】bāhén（名）scar

疥 jiè（名）scabies

【疥瘡】jièchuāng（名）scabies

疫 yì（名）epidemic disease: 瘟～ pestilence; plague

【疫苗】yìmiáo（名）vaccine

【疫情】yìqíng（名） epidemic situation

症 zhèng（名）disease; illness: 絕～ fatal illness; mortal disease / 後遺～ sequelae; aftermath

【症狀】zhèngzhuàng（名）symptom

疴 kē（名）disease; illness: 沈～ incurable disease

病 bìng Ⅰ（名）❶ illness; disease; sickness; ailment: 裝～ pretend illness ❷ fault; trouble: 一種通～ a common weakness（failing）Ⅱ（動）be ill; fall sick; feel unwell: 一得很厲害 be very ill Ⅲ（形）sick; sickly: ～容滿面 look ill

【病人】bìngrén（病 員 bìngyuán）（名）patient; invalid; sick person: 住院～ inpatient / 門診～ outpatient

【病入膏肓】bìng rù gāo huāng〈成〉the disease is beyond cure

【病包兒】bìngbāor（名）〈口〉sickly person

【病危】bìngwēi（形）critically ill

【病因】bìngyīn（名）cause of disease

【病牀】bìngchuáng（名）❶ hospital bed ❷ sickbed

【病房】bìngfáng（病室 bìngshì）（名）ward; sickroom

【病例】bìnglì（名）(medical) case

【病毒】bìngdú（名）〈醫〉virus: 計算機～ computer virus

【病故】bìnggù（動）die of illness

【病根】bìnggēn（名） ❶ lingering chronic disease ❷ root cause（of trouble）

【病逝】bìngshì（動）die of illness

【病情】bìngqíng（病 況 bìngkuàng）（名）condition of patient: ～公報 medical bulletin

【病假】bìngjià（名）sick leave: 請～ ask for sick leave

【病從口入】bìng cóng kǒu rù〈成〉disease goes in by the mouth

【病菌】bìngjūn（名）germs;（pathogenic）bacteria

【病愈】bìngyù（动）recover（from illness）; be cured of a disease; get well

【病态】bìngtài（名）morbidity: ～心理 morbid (abnormal) psychology

【病历】bìnglì（病案 bìng'àn）（名）medical record; case history (of a patient)

【病虫害】bìngchónghài（名）plant insect pest(s)

【病灶】bìngzào（名）focus; foci (of infection)

【病魔】bìngmó（名）curse of disease; serious chronic illness: ～缠身 afflicted with a chronic disease

疲 pí（形）tired; fatigued

【疲乏】pífá（形）tired; fatigued

【疲於奔命】pí yú bèn mìng〈成〉be dog-tired from running about on business

【疲倦】píjuàn（形）weary; fatigued

【疲劳】píláo（形）weary; tired

【疲塌】pítā（形）sluggish; indolent

【疲惫】píbèi（形）exhausted; worn out

痂 jiā（名）scab

疽 jū（名）〈中醫〉subcutaneous ulcer

疹 zhěn（名）rash: 麻～ measles

疾 jí Ⅰ（名）❶ disease; illness ❷ suffering; pain; hardship Ⅱ（动）detest: ～惡如仇 detest evils and evil-doers like sworn enemies Ⅲ（副）fast; swiftly: ～進 march with speed

【疾言厲色】jí yán lì sè〈成〉make angry remarks with a stern face

【疾苦】jíkǔ（名）hardships; sufferings

【疾風知勁草】jí fēng zhī jìng cǎo〈成〉strong winds test the strength of grass; adversity is the acid test of a man's character

【疾病】jíbìng（名）illness; ailment; disorder

痄 zhà

【痄腮】zhàsai（名）〈醫〉mumps

疱 pào（名）blister; bleb

【疱疹】pàozhěn（名）❶ bleb ❷ herpes

疼 téng（动）❶ ache; hurt: 頭～得厲害 have a bad headache / 你這兒～嗎? Does it hurt? ❷ love; adore; dote on

【疼痛】téngtòng（动）ache; hurt

【疼愛】téng'ài（动）love; adore

痍 yí（名）〈書〉wound

痔 zhì（名）haemorrhoids

【痔瘡】zhìchuāng（名）piles; haemorrhoids

痕 hén（名）mark; trace: 傷～ a scar from a wound

【痕迹】hénjī（名）trace; vestige

疵 cī（名）flaw; blemish; defect

痊 quán

【痊愈】quányù（动）fully recover from an illness; get well

痧 shā（名）〈中醫〉acute disease such as cholera and sunstroke

【痧子】shāzi（名）〈方〉measles

痣 zhì（名）nevus; mole

痘 dòu（名）❶ smallpox ❷ vaccine: 種～ vaccinate; be vaccinated / ～苗 vaccine

痞 pǐ (名) ❶ lump in the abdomen ❷ ruffian; rascal

痦 wù

【痦子】wùzi (名) nevus; mole

痙 jìng

【痙攣】jìngluán (名) spasm; convultions: 面部～ facial spasm

痛 tòng I (动) ache; hurt: ～得厉害. It hurts terribly. II (名) ❶ pain; ache: 牙～ toothache ❷ sorrow; grief III (副) to one's heart's content; thoroughly: ～改前非 thoroughly mend one's ways/ ～擊 deal a deadly blow at

【痛心】tòngxīn (形) grieved; bitterly regretful

【痛心疾首】tòng xīn jí shǒu〈成〉filled with indignation and hatred

【痛切】tòngqiè (副) with intense sorrow

【痛斥】tòngchì (动) bitterly denounce

【痛快】tòngkuai I (形) happy; contented II (副) ❶ to one's satisfaction: 吃個～ eat one's fill ❷ without hesitation; frankly: 痛痛快快地交代 own up without the least hesitation

【痛恨】tònghèn (动) hate bitterly

【痛苦】tòngkǔ (名) pain; misery; agony

【痛哭】tòngkū (动) wail: ～流涕 cry bitterly; cry one's eyes out

【痛處】tòngchù (名) tender spot: 碰到他的～ touch his sore spot

【痛惜】tòngxī (动) deplore; deeply regret

【痛惡】tòngwù (动) abhor; hate bitterly

【痛感】tònggǎn (动) feel most keenly

【痛癢】tòngyǎng (名) ❶ suffering; hardship ❷ importance; significance: 無關～ of no consequence

痢 lì

【痢疾】lìji (名) dysentery

【痢特靈】lìtèlíng (名)〈藥〉furazolidone

瘁 cuì (形) exhausted; tired out

痰 tán (名) sputum; phlegm

【痰盂】tányú (痰桶 tántǒng) (名) spittoon

痼 gù

【痼疾】gùjí (名) refractory disease; deep-seated illness

【痼癖】gùpǐ (名) ingrained eccentricity

痱 fèi

【痱子】fèizi (名) prickly heat

【痱子粉】fèizifěn (名) prickly-heat powder

痴 chī (形) ❶ foolish; idiotic: 白～ idiot ❷ crazy about ❸ deranged; insane

【痴人說夢】chī rén shuō mèng〈成〉tale told by an idiot; fantastic nonsense

【痴心】chīxīn (名) infatuation: ～妄想 wishful thinking; idle dream

【痴情】chīqíng (名) passionate love, often unrequited

【痴獃】chīdāi I (形) dull-witted II (名) dementia: 老年性～症 senile

dementia

瘓 wěi (名) paralysis; impotence

瘧 nüè (名) malaria
【瘧疾】nüèjí (名) malaria; ague

瘍 yáng (名) sore; ulcer

瘋 fēng (形) mad; insane; frenzied
【瘋人院】fēngrényuàn (名) lunatic asylum
【瘋子】fēngzi (名) mad person; lunatic
【瘋狂】fēngkuáng (形) frantic; crazy
【瘋狗】fēnggǒu (名) mad dog
【瘋癲】fēngdiān (形) insane

瘦 shòu (形) ❶ thin; skinny ❷ lean ❸ (of clothes, shoes, etc.) tight ❹ barren; infertile
【瘦小】shòuxiǎo (形) thin and small
【瘦子】shòuzi (名) thin person
【瘦肉】shòuròu (名) lean meat
【瘦長】shòucháng (形) tall and thin; lanky
【瘦弱】shòuruò (形) thin and weak; frail

瘊 hóu (名) wart

瘟 wēn (名) 〈中醫〉 acute infectious disease: 鷄～ chicken pest
【瘟疫】wēnyì (名) pestilence; plague
【瘟神】wēnshén (名) god of plague

瘡 chuāng (名) ❶ sore; boil ❷ would: 刀～ sword wound
【瘡疤】chuāngbā (名) scar

瘠 jí (形) ❶ thin and weak: ～瘦 thin ❷ (of land) barren; poor: 土地貧～ poor and unproductive land

【瘠薄】jíbó (形) (of land) barren; unproductive: 土質～ poor soil

瘤 liú (名) tumour

瘢 bān (名) scar on skin
【瘢痕】bānhén (名) scar
【瘢點】bāndiǎn (名) freckles

瘴 zhàng (名) miasma
【瘴氣】zhàngqì (名) miasma

瘸 qué (動) limp; be lame: 一～一拐地走路 limp along
【瘸子】quézi (名) 〈口〉 lame person; cripple

癆 láo (名) tuberculosis; TB

癍 bān (名) pigmentary deposits on the skin; flecks; blotch

療 liáo (動) give medical treatment; cure
【療法】liáofǎ (名) therapy: 針灸～ acupuncture and moxibustion (therapy)
【療效】liáoxiào (名) curative effect
【療程】liáochéng (名) course of medical treatment
【療養】liáoyǎng Ⅰ (動) recuperate Ⅱ (名) recuperation
【療養院】liáoyǎngyuàn (名) sanatorium

癌 ái (名) cancer: 肺～ lung cancer
【癌症】áizhèng (名) cancer
【癌擴散】áikuòsàn (名) carcinomatous proliferation; carcinomatosis
【癌轉移】áizhuǎnyí (名) metastasis of cancer

癔 yì
【癔病】yìbìng (名) 〈醫〉 hysteria

癖 pǐ (名) addiction

【癖好】pǐhào (名) hobby; leaning

【癖性】pǐxìng (名) natural inclination

癤 jiē (名) furuncle; boil

【癤子】jiēzi (名) ❶ furuncle; boil ❷ node; knot (in wood)

癟 biē
see also biě

【癟三】biēsān (名)〈方〉city bum; tramp

癟 biě (形) shrunken; deflated: ~榖 shrivelled grain
see also biē

癢 yǎng (動) itch: 背上~~ have an itch on one's back

癥 zhēng

【癥結】zhēngjié (名) crux: 問題的~ the crux of a matter

癩 lài (名) ❶ leprosy ❷〈方〉scabies on the head

【癩子】làizi (名) person affected with scabies on the head

【癩皮狗】làipígǒu (名) ❶ mangy dog ❷〈罵〉scoundrel; disgusting creature

【癩蛤蟆】làiháma (名) toad

癮 yǐn (名) addiction; craving: 煙~不易去. It is difficult to give up smoking altogether.

癬 xuǎn (名) tinea; ringworm

癰 yōng (名)〈醫〉carbuncle

【癰疽】yōngjū (名) ulcer

癱 tān (動) paralyze

【癱子】tānzi (名) person suffering from paralysis; paralytic

【癱瘓】tānhuàn Ⅰ (名) paralysis Ⅱ (動) be paralysed: 鐵路工人罷工使鐵路陷於~. The railwaymen's strike paralysed the train service.

癲 diān (名) mental disorder: 瘋~ insane

【癲癇】diānxián (名)〈醫〉epilepsy

癶 部

登 dēng (動) ❶ ascend; mount: ~山運動 mountaineering ❷ publish; record

【登記】dēngjì (動) register: ~住宿 check in (at a hotel)

【登時】dēngshí (副) [usu. used in recounting past events] immediately

【登峰造極】dēng fēng zào jí〈成〉achieve perfection; reach the apex

【登基】dēngjī (動) ascend the throne

【登陸】dēnglù (動) land: ~艦 landing craft

【登場】dēngchǎng (動) appear on the stage

【登報】dēngbào (動) (of news; articles, etc.) be carried in a newspaper

【登載】dēngzǎi (動) publish (in a newspaper or magazine)

【登臺】dēngtái (動) appear on the stage: 初次~ make one's first appearance on the stage; make one's debut

發 fā Ⅰ (動) ❶ send; deliver: ~信

send off a letter ❷ utter; express ❸ germinate; grow ❹ break out with: ～疹子 break out with a rash ❺ expose; open ❻ turn; become: ～怒 fly into a rage ❼ start Ⅱ(量) (of ammunition): 一一子彈 a bullet

【發人深省】fā rén shěn xǐng〈成〉set one thinking; be thought-provoking

【發火】fāhuǒ (動) get angry; flare up

【發生】fāshēng (動) happen; occur

【發出】fāchū (動) send off; give off: ～呼救信號 dispatch an SOS

【發行】fāxíng (動) publish; issue: ～債券 issue bonds

【發光】fāguāng (動) shine; radiate

【發汗】fāhàn (動) induce perspiration

【發作】fāzuò (動) break out: 脾氣～ fly into a rage/ 心臟病～ have a heart attack

【發佈】fābù (動) issue; release: ～命令 issue orders

【發抖】fādǒu (動) shiver; tremble

【發狂】fākuáng (動) go crazy

【發言】fāyán (動) make a speech

【發言人】fāyánrén (名) spokesman

【發牢騷】fā láosāo (動) grumble; complain

【發放】fāfàng (動) (of government or institution) grant: ～貸款 grant loans

【發昏】fāhūn (動) ❶ feel dizzy ❷ be out of one's mind

【發明】fāmíng Ⅰ(動) invent Ⅱ(名) invention

【發芽】fāyá (動) sprout

【發炎】fāyán〈醫〉Ⅰ(動) inflame Ⅱ (名) inflammation

【發育】fāyù (名) growth; develop-

ment

【發表】fābiǎo (動) publish; issue: ～著作 publish a book

【發亮】fāliàng (動) shine: 天剛～ at the crack of dawn

【發洩】fāxiè (動) give vent to; vent

【發音】fāyīn (名) pronunciation

【發迹】fājì (動) gain access to power and wealth

【發財】fācái (動) make a fortune; get rich

【發家】fājiā (動) make a fortune for the family

【發起】fāqǐ (動) ❶ sponsor; initiate: ～人 sponsor ❷ start; launch

【發射】fāshè (動) fire; launch; emit

【發條】fātiáo (名) spiral power spring; clock-work spring

【發展】fāzhǎn (動) ❶ develop; promote; expand: ～生產力 develop the productive forces ❷ recruit; admit (members into an organization)

【發展中國家】fāzhǎnzhōng guójiā (名) developing country

【發售】fāshòu (動) sell

【發問】fāwèn (動) raise a question

【發現】fāxiàn (動) find; discover

【發球】fāqiú (動) serve a ball

【發票】fāpiào (名) bill; receipt

【發掘】fājué (動) explore; excavate: ～歷史文物 unearth historical relics

【發動】fādòng (動) ❶ start: ～攻勢 start an offensive ❷ mobilize

【發動機】fādòngjī (名) engine

【發揮】fāhuī (動) ❶ expound; elaborate ❷ give play to

【發愣】fālèng (動) be dazed; be stupefied

【發報】fābào (動) transmit (messages): ~機 transmitter

【發揚】fāyáng (動) develop; promote; carry forward

【發窘】fājiǒng (動) feel embarrassed

【發脾氣】fā píqi (動) lose one's temper

【發達】fādá (形) developed; prosperous

【發達國家】fādá guójiā (名) developed country

【發愁】fāchóu (動) worry; be worried about

【發落】fāluò (動) treat; deal with: 從輕～ let sb. off lightly

【發源】fāyuán (動) originate

【發慌】fāhuāng (動) get nervous

【發福】fāfú (動) gain weight

【發電】fādiàn (動) generate electricity

【發電廠】fādiànchǎng (名) power plant

【發電機】fādiànjī (名) generator

【發號施令】fā hào shī lìng〈成〉issue orders; give instructions

【發誓】fāshì (動) pledge; swear; vow

【發獃】fādāi (動) be stupefied; be struck dumb

【發酵】fājiào (動) ferment

【發瘋】fāfēng (動) go mad

【發獎】fājiǎng (動) award prizes

【發霉】fāméi (動) become mouldy

【發奮】fāfèn (發憤 fāfèn) (動) strive firmly: ～讀書 be determined to study hard

【發燒】fāshāo (動) run a fever

【發難】fānàn (動) ❶ raise difficult questions ❷ start a revolt

【發覺】fājué (動) find; discover

白 部

【白】bái I (形) ❶ white: 銀～ silvery white ❷ clear: 案情大～ The case has come to light. ❸ pure, plain, blank: ～飯 plain cooked rice II (副) ❶ in vain; to no avail; to no purpose: ～費心機 rack one's brains in vain ❷ free of charge: ～給 given free of charge III (名) ❶ spoken part in an opera: 旁～ aside ❷ (Bái) a surname IV (動) look scornfully: ～他一眼 look at him scornfully

【白人】báirén (名) white man

【白刃戰】báirènzhàn (名) hand-to-hand combat; bayonet charge

【白天】báitiān (名) daytime; day: 大～ in broad daylight

【白木耳】báimù'ěr (名) white fungus; jelly fungus

【白內障】báinèizhàng (名)〈醫〉cataract: ～摘除術 cataract extraction

【白日做夢】bái rì zuò mèng〈成〉day-dreaming; indulge in wishful thinking

【白手起家】bái shǒu qǐ jiā〈成〉start from scratch

【白白】báibái (副) in vain; for nothing; to no purpose: ～浪費時間 sheer waste of time

【白皮書】báipíshū (名) (of government reports) white paper

【白字】báizì (名) wrongly written or mispronounced Chinese character

【白血病】báixuèbìng (名)〈醫〉leukaemia

【白血球】báixuèqiú（名）white blood cell; leucocyte

【白果】báiguǒ（名）〈植〉gingko; ginkgo

【白金】báijīn（名）platinum

【白宫】Bái Gōng（名）the White House

【白班儿】báibānr（名）day shift

【白晃晃】báihuǎnghuǎng（形）dazzlingly white

【白纸黑字】bái zhǐ hēi zì〈成〉in black and white (written)

【白眼】báiyǎn（名）contemptuous or disdainful look: ～看人 treat sb. scornfully

【白乾儿】báigānr（名）liquor; spirits

【白垩】bái'è（名）chalk: ～粉 whiting

【白垩纪】Bái'èjì（名）〈地〉Cretaceous period

【白昼】báizhòu（名）daytime

【白描】báimiáo（名）❶ traditional Chinese-style line drawing in brush and ink ❷ simple, straightforward style of writing in literary creation

【白菜】báicài（名）Chinese cabbage

【白喉】báihóu（名）〈医〉diphtheria

【白费】báifèi（动）waste: ～力气 waste of energy

【白开水】báikāishuǐ（名）plain boiled water

【白报纸】báibàozhǐ（名）newsprint

【白痴】báichī（名）❶ idiocy ❷ idiot

【白搭】báidā（形）useless; in vain; getting nowhere: 同他再提这件事也是～。It's no good bringing up the matter with him again.

【白话】báihuà（名）vernacular: ～文 vernacular Chinese

【白杨】báiyáng（名）〈植〉poplar; aspen

【白银】báiyín（名）silver

【白熊】báixióng（名）polar bear; white bear

【白皑皑】bái'ái'ái（形）(of snow, frost) white and clean

【白热】báirè（名）white heat; incandescence

【白热化】báirèhuà（动）turn white hot

【白发苍苍】báifà cāngcāng（形）hoary-headed; silver-haired

【白头偕老】bái tóu xié lǎo〈成〉live to a ripe old age and remain a devoted couple

【白炽】báichì（名）white heat

【白糖】báitáng（名）(refined) white sugar

【白薯】báishǔ（名）sweet potato

【白璧无瑕】bái bì wú xiá〈成〉as pure as flawless white jade

【白药】báiyào（名）white styptic powder in Chinese medicine

【白蚁】báiyǐ（名）termite; white ant

【白铁】báitiě（名）galvanized iron

【白厅】Bái Tīng（名）Whitehall

百 bǎi I（数）hundred: 年逾半～ get on for fifty II（形）numerous; all kinds of: ～事通 know-all III（副）very; always: ～听不厌 worth hearing a hundred times

【百分之百】bǎi fēn zhī bǎi I（数）hundred per cent II（副）absolutely; out and out: ～地正确 a hundred percent correct

【百分比】bǎifēnbǐ（名）percentage

【百分制】bǎifēnzhì（名）hundred-mark system

【百分数】bǎifēnshù（名）percentage

【百孔千疮】bǎi kǒng qiān chuāng

〈成〉honeycombed with holes and sores; afflicted with all sorts of evils

【百尺竿头，更进一步】bǎi chǐ gān tóu, gèng jìn yī bù〈成〉go all out for still greater success

【百日咳】bǎirìké （名） whooping cough; pertussis

【百合】bǎihé（名）lily

【百年】bǎinián（名）❶ hundred years; very long time: ～不遇 not to be seen in a hundred years; once in a blue moon ❷ lifetime: ～之後 when sb. is no more

【百年大计】bǎi nián dà jì〈成〉project of long-term importance

【百折不挠】bǎi zhé bù náo〈成〉undaunted despite repeated setbacks; indomitable

【百姓】bǎixìng（名）common people

【百儿八十】bǎi'erbāshí〈口〉a hundred or so

【百依百顺】bǎi yī bǎi shùn〈成〉obedient and subservient; servile

【百花齐放，百家争鸣】bǎi huā qí fàng, bǎi jiā zhēng míng〈成〉let a hundred flowers blossom and a hundred schools of thought contend (a policy for promoting the progress of arts and sciences)

【百思莫解】bǎi sī mò jiě〈成〉feel as perplexed as ever even though one has racked one's brains

【百科全书】bǎikē quánshū（名）encyclopaedia

【百般】bǎibān（副）in a thousand and one ways: ～刁难 resort to every possible measure to make things difficult for sb.

【百倍】bǎibèi（数）hundred-fold; hundred times

【百货】bǎihuò（名） general mer-

chandise: ～商店 department store; general store

【百发百中】bǎi fā bǎi zhòng〈成〉(in archery or shooting) never miss the target; never fail in one's endeavour

【百无聊赖】bǎi wú liáo lài〈成〉be bored beyond endurance

【百万】bǎiwàn（数）million

【百万吨】bǎiwàndūn（名）megaton

【百感交集】bǎi gǎn jiāo jí〈成〉be overcome with all sorts of feelings

【百里挑一】bǎi lǐ tiāo yī〈成〉one in a hundred

【百炼成钢】bǎi liàn chéng gāng〈成〉be tempered into steel; be a long-tested hero of iron nerves

【百叶窗】bǎiyèchuāng（名）(Venetian) blind; shutters

【百闻不如一见】bǎi wén bù rú yī jiàn〈成〉seeing once is better than hearing a hundred times; seeing is believing

【百废俱兴】bǎi fèi jù xīng〈成〉undertake all neglected work

【百战百胜】bǎi zhàn bǎi shèng〈成〉emerge victorious from every battle; ever victorious

【百褶裙】bǎizhěqún（百褶裙 bǎijiǎnqún）（名）skirt with accordion pleats

【百灵鸟】bǎilíngniǎo（名）lark

皂 zào（名）soap: 香～ toilet soap / 浴～ bath soap

的 de（助）❶ [used after an attribute]: 伟大～祖国 the great mother land / 要做～事 Many things remain to be done. ❷ [used after a noun or pronoun to indicate possession]: 我～书 my books ❸ [used after a noun, a pronoun, an adjective, a verbal phrase, etc, as a nominalizer]: 男~ men / 賣水果~ fruit seller

see also dí; dì

的 dí

see also de; dì

【的當】dídàng (形) fitting and proper

【的確】díquè (副) indeed; really

【的確良】díquèliáng (名) 〈紡〉dacron

的 dì (名) bull's eye; target

see also de; dì

皆 jiē (代) all; every: 比比~是 can be found everywhere / 放之四海而~準 be universally applicable

【皆大歡喜】jiē dà huān xǐ 〈成〉to the gratification of all; everybody is delighted

皇 huáng (名) emperor; sovereign

【皇太子】huángtàizǐ (名) crown prince

【皇后】huánghòu (名) empress

【皇帝】huángdì (名) emperor

【皇室】huángshì (名) imperial family; royal family

【皇宮】huánggōng (名) imperial palace

皈 guī

【皈依】guīyī 〈宗〉Ⅰ(動) believe in Buddhism or any other religion Ⅱ (名) religious ceremony at which a person is officially given the name of a Buddhist

皎 jiǎo Ⅰ(形) clear and bright Ⅱ (名) (Jiǎo) a surname

【皎皎】jiǎojiǎo (形) extremely clear and bright: ~的月光 bright moonlight

【皎潔】jiǎojié (形) (of the moon) bright: ~的月亮高懸天上。A bright moon hangs in the sky.

皖 Wǎn (名) another name for Anhui Province

皓 hào (形) ❶ white: 明眸~齒 (of a woman) with bright eyes and white teeth ❷ bright: ~月 the bright moon

皑 ái (形) pure white: 白雪~~。The snow is an endless expanse of whiteness.

皮 部

皮 pí Ⅰ(名) ❶ skin; leather; fruit or vegetable peel ❷ wrapper; cover: 餃子~ dumpling wrapper ❸ sheet: 鐵~ iron sheet ❹ (Pí) a surname Ⅱ(形) ❶ no longer crisp; soggy: 土豆片~了。The potato chips aren't crisp any more. ❷ naughty; mischievous: ~孩子 naughty boys

【皮子】pízi (名) ❶ leather; hide ❷ fur

【皮下注射】píxià zhùshè (名) 〈醫〉hypodermic injection

【皮下組織】píxià zǔzhī (名) 〈生理〉subcutaneous tissue

【皮毛】pímáo (名) ❶ fur ❷ smattering: 對詩歌只懂點~ have only a smattering knowledge of poetry

【皮尺】píchǐ (名) tape measure

【皮包】píbāo（名）handbag; brief-case

【皮包骨頭】pí bāo gǔ tóu（形）all skin and bones; skinny

【皮匠】píjiàng（名）❶ cobbler ❷ tanner

【皮夾子】píjiāzi（名）wallet

【皮炎】píyán（名）〈醫〉dermatitis

【皮革】pígé（名）leather; hide

【皮疹】pízhěn（名）〈醫〉rash

【皮貨】píhuò（名）fur; pelt: ～商 furrier; fur trader

【皮球】píqiú（名）rubber ball; ball

【皮蛋】pídàn（名）preserved egg

【皮帶】pídài（名）leather belt

【皮棉】pímián（名）ginned cotton

【皮筏】pífá（名）skin raft

【皮開肉綻】pí kāi ròu zhàn〈成〉badly bruised from flogging

【皮靴】píxuē（名）leather boots

【皮鞋】píxié（名）leather shoes

【皮箱】píxiāng（名）(leather) suit-case; trunk

【皮影戲】píyǐngxì（名）leather-sil-houette show

【皮膚】pífū（名）skin

【皮膚病】pífūbìng（名）skin disease; dermatosis

【皮膚醫生】pífū yīshēng（名）der-matologist

皱 zhòu Ⅰ（名）wrinkles; lines Ⅱ（動）wrinkle; crease: 我的上衣～了。My coat needs ironing. / ～眉頭 knit one's brows; frown

【皱紋】zhòuwén（名）lines; wrin-kles

【皱褶】zhòuzhě（名）fold

皿 部

皿 mǐn（名）container

盂 yú（名）a broad-mouthed recep-tacle for holding liquid: 痰～ spit-toon

盅 zhōng（名）handleless cup: 酒～ winecup

盆 pén（名）basin; pot: 浴～ bath-tub

【盆地】péndì（名）basin

【盆景】pénjǐng（名）potted landscape

【盆腔】pénqiāng（名）〈生理〉pelvic cavity: ～炎 pelvic infection

【盆湯】péntāng（盆塘 péntáng）（名）bathtub cubicle (in a public bath)

盈 yíng（動）❶ be full of: 豐～ in abundance ❷ have a surplus

【盈利】yínglì（贏利 yínglì）（名）profit; gain

【盈餘】yíngyú（贏餘 yíngyú）（名）surplus

【盈虧】yíngkuī（名）❶（of the moon）wax and wane ❷ profit and loss

益 yì Ⅰ（名）benefit; profit: 有～於 be of benefit to Ⅱ（形）beneficial

【益友】yìyǒu（名）helpful friend; friend and mentor

【益處】yìchu（名）benefit; advan-tage

【益鳥】yìniǎo（名）beneficial bird

【益壽】yìshòu（動）lengthen one's life; contribute to longevity

【益蟲】yìchóng（名）beneficial insect

盎 àng（名）an ancient vessel with a big belly and a small spout
【盎司】àngsī（名）ounce
【盎然】àngrán（形）abundant; full of; overflowing: 生機～ full of vim and vigour

盔 kuī（名）helmet: 頭～ helmet
【盔甲】kuījiǎ（名）suit of armour

盛 chéng（動）❶ ladle: 一～碗湯 fill a bowl with soup ❷ hold: 這個杯子～得半升啤酒。This mug can hold half a litre of beer.
see also shèng
【盛器】chéngqì（名）vessel; receptacle

盛 shèng Ⅰ（形）❶ prosperous; thriving: 太平～世 times of peace and prosperity ❷ vigorous; exuberant: 精力旺～ energetic ❸ magnificent; great: ～典 grand ceremony ❹ great; profound: ～意難卻。It would not be right to decline your kind offer（or invitation）. ❺ popular; prevailing: ～極一時 be in vogue for a time Ⅱ（副）deeply; widely: ～傳 it is widely rumoured that Ⅲ（名）(Shèng) a surname
see also chéng
【盛大】shèngdà（形）grand; great
【盛行】shèngxíng（動）be all the fashion; prevail
【盛況】shèngkuàng（名）grand occasion
【盛衰】shèngshuāi（名）rise and fall; prosperity and decline
【盛夏】shèngxià（名）midsummer
【盛宴】shèngyàn（盛筵 shèngyán）

（名）grand feast; sumptuous dinner: ～招待貴賓 give a banquet in honour of the distinguished guests
【盛氣凌人】shèng qì líng rén（成）domineering; haughty
【盛產】shèngchǎn（動）abound in; be rich in
【盛情】shèngqíng（名）great kindness: 感謝您的～款待 thank you for your gracious hospitality
【盛開】shèngkāi（動）blossom magnificently; be in full bloom
【盛暑】shèngshǔ（名）peak of summer
【盛裝】shèngzhuāng（名）festive dress; gala costume
【盛會】shènghuì（名）grand gathering
【盛贊】shèngzàn（動）praise profusely
【盛譽】shèngyù（名）high repute: 享有～ enjoy a high reputation

盒 hé（名）box; case; casket

盗 dào Ⅰ（動）steal; rob Ⅱ（名）thief; robber
【盜用】dàoyòng（動）use illegally; usurp
【盜汗】dàohàn（動）have a night sweat
【盜賊】dàozéi（名）robber
【盜墓】dàomù（動）rob a tomb: ～者 tomb robber
【盜賣】dàomài（動）steal and sell
【盜竊】dàoqiè（動）steal

盏 zhǎn Ⅰ（名）small cup: 茶～ small tea cup Ⅱ（量）[of lamps]: 一～燈 a lamp

盟 méng（名）alliance

see also míng

【盟友】méngyǒu（名）ally

【盟主】méngzhǔ（名）leader of an alliance

【盟兄弟】méngxiōngdì（名）sworn brothers

【盟約】méngyuē（名）treaty of alliance

【盟軍】méngjūn（名）allied forces

【盟國】méngguó（名）allied country; ally

盟 míng

see also méng

【盟誓】míngshì（動）take an oath

監 jiān I（動）keep a watch over; supervise II（名）jail: 收～ put sb. into prison

【監工】jiāngōng I（動）oversee work II（名）supervisor; overseer

【監考】jiānkǎo I（動）invigilate II（名）proctor; invigilator

【監票】jiānpiào（名）election supervisor; scrutineer

【監視】jiānshì（動）keep watch on; place under surveillance

【監測】jiāncè（動）monitor

【監禁】jiānjìn（動）take into custody; imprison

【監督】jiāndū I（動）supervise; superintend; oversee II（名）❶ supervision ❷ supervisor; superintendent

【監獄】jiānyù（監牢 jiānláo）（名）jail; prison; gaol: 進～ be imprisoned

【監製】jiānzhì（動）supervise the manufacture of

【監察】jiānchá（動）supervise (and inspect)

【監護】jiānhù（名）guardianship

【監護人】jiānhùrén（名）guardian

【監聽】jiāntīng（動）monitor (through listening in)

盡 jǐn I（副）as...as possible: ～早回信 reply as soon as possible II（介）❶ within the limits of; not exceeding: ～着這點錢花。Don't spend more than is in your purse. ❷ [used before expressions of locality] at the farthest end of: ～裏頭 in the innermost part III（動）give priority to: 先～兒童上車。Let the children get on the bus first.

see also jìn

【盡可能】jǐnkěnéng（盡量 jǐnliàng）（副）as far as possible

【盡先】jǐnxiān（副）give top priority to

【盡快】jǐnkuài（副）as soon as possible

【盡管】jǐnguǎn I（連）although; in spite of the fact that II（動）feel free to; do not hesitate to: 如果你要我替你辦點事～告訴我。Do let me know if I can do anything for you.

盡 jìn I（名）❶ end: 無～無休 endless ❷ death: 自～ commit suicide II（動）❶ to the utmost; to the full: ～善～美 height of perfection; perfect III（動）❶ exhaust: 一飲而～ finish one's drink in one gulp ❷ do one's best; make the most of: ～心竭力工作 work wholeheartedly; throw oneself heart and soul into one's work IV（代）all: ～人皆知 be known to all; be public knowledge

see also jǐn

【盡是】jìnshì（動）be full of

【盡情】jìnqíng（副）to one's heart's content

【盡量】jìnliàng（副）to the full: ～吃 eat one's fill; do full justice to the food

【盡義務】jìnyìwù（動）❶ fulfil an obligation ❷ work not for pay but to fulfil an obligation

【盡頭】jìntóu（名）end

【盡興】jìnxìng I（動）enjoy oneself to the full II（副）to one's heart's content

【盡職】jìnzhí（動）be conscientious in fulfilling one's duties

盤 pán I（名）❶ plate; tray: 托～（serving）tray ／ 冷～ hors d'oeuvres; cold dishes ❷ sth. shaped or used as a tray, plate, etc: 棋～ chessboard ❸（Pán）a surname II（動）❶ coil; twine: cross: ～腿 sit with one's legs crossed ❷ build (a brick cooking range, etc.) ❸ check; investigate III（量）❶ (of food) dish: 一～牛肉 a dish of beef ❷ coil: 一～錄像帶 a videotape ❸ game: 一～象棋 a game of Chinese chess

【盤子】pánzi（名）plate; dish

【盤查】pánchá（動）question; check on (a person)

【盤桓】pánhuán（動）linger; loiter

【盤根錯節】pán gēn cuò jié〈成〉entangled and thorny; deep-seated

【盤剝】pánbō（動）practise usury; exploit

【盤問】pánwèn（盤詰 pánjié）（動）interrogate closely

【盤旋】pánxuán（動）❶ spiral; hover about ❷ linger; loiter

【盤算】pánsuàn（動）calculate; con-

template

【盤踞】pánjù（動）occupy illegally; be entrenched in

【盤賬】pánzhàng（動）audit accounts

【盤點】pándiǎn（盤貨 pánhuò）（動）take an inventory of goods; take stock

【盤纏】pánchan（盤川 pánchuān）（名）travelling expenses; travel money

盧 Lú（名）a surname

【盧比】lúbǐ（名）rupee

【盧布】lúbù（名）rouble

【盧旺達】Lúwàngdá（名）Rwanda: ～人 Rwandan

【盧森堡】Lúsēnbǎo（名）Luxembourg: ～人 Luxembourger

盥 guàn（動）wash (one's hands or face)

【盥洗室】guànxǐshì（名）washroom

目 部

目 mù（名）❶ eye: 悦～ pleasant to the eye ❷ item; detail: 賬～ items of an account

【目不暇接】mù bù xiá jiē〈成〉too many things for the eye to take in at once

【目不轉睛】mù bù zhuǎn jīng〈成〉look attentively; fix one's eyes (on)

【目不識丁】mù bù shí dīng〈成〉unable to read; be utterly illiterate

【目中無人】mù zhōng wú rén〈成〉look down on everyone; be very haughty

【目光】mùguāng（名）❶ brightness

of the eye ❷ sight; vision: ～短淺的人 a man without vision; short-sighted person

【目的】mùdì（名）aim; goal; purpose: 預期～ the desired purpose

【目的地】mùdìdì（名）destination

【目空一切】mù kōng yī qiè〈成〉be supercilious; look down on everyone and everything

【目送】mùsòng（動）watch sb. go: ～戰士出征 gaze after the soldiers leaving for the front

【目前】mùqián（副）at present; now: ～還無法下結論 cannot draw a conclusion as yet

【目眩】mùxuàn（形）dizzy; giddy; dazzled

【目視飛行】mùshì fēixíng（名）〈航空〉contact flight; visual flight

【目測】mùcè（動）〈軍〉range estimation

【目無法紀】mù wú fǎ jì（動）have no respect for law and discipline

【目睹】mùdǔ（動）see; witness: 我～其事。I was an eyewitness.

【目標】mùbiāo（名）target; aim; objective: 經濟～ economic objective

【目錄】mùlù（名）❶ catalogue; list: 新產品～ list of the new products ❷ table of contents

【目錄學】mùlùxué（名）bibliography

【目瞪口呆】mù dèng kǒu dāi（形）stunned; dumbfounded

【目擊】mùjī（動）see; witness: ～者 eyewitness; witness

【目鏡】mùjìng（名）eyepiece; ocular

【盯】dīng（動）fix one's eyes on: ～着某人的臉 stare at sb.; give sb. a stare

【盯梢】dīngshāo（動）shadow sb.; tail sb.

【盲】máng（形）blind

【盲人】mángrén（名）blind person

【盲人院】mángrényuàn（名）blind asylum

【盲人摸象】máng rén mō xiàng〈成〉take a part for the whole; draw a conclusion from incomplete data

【盲人瞎馬】máng rén xiā mǎ〈成〉be like a blind man riding a blind horse; head for trouble

【盲文】mángwén（名）braille

【盲目】mángmù（副）blindly; without clear understanding: ～行動 act blindly

【盲流】mángliú（動）(of rural inhabitants) drift into a city

【盲從】mángcóng（動）follow blindly; obey mechanically

【盲動】mángdòng（動）act blindly

【盲腸】mángcháng（名）〈生理〉caecum

【盲腸炎】mángchángyán（名）〈醫〉appendicitis; typhlitis

【直】zhí Ⅰ（形）❶ straight: ～立 stand straight ❷ just; up-right: 理～氣壯 be full of confidence as justice is on one's side ❸ frank; straightforward: 耿～ honest and frank ❹ vertical Ⅱ（動）straighten: ～起身來 straighten up Ⅲ（副）❶ straight; directly: ～奔作案現場 rush straight to the scene of crime ❷ continuously: 那孩子～哭。The child cried all the time.

【直升飛機】zhíshēng fēijī（名）helicopter

【直角】zhíjiǎo（名）〈數〉right angle

【直抒己見】zhí shū jǐ jiàn〈成〉be

plainspoken; speak one's mind

【直言不諱】zhí yán bù huì〈成〉not mince words; speak without reserve

【直系親屬】zhíxì qīnshǔ（名）lineal relative; immediate dependent

【直到】zhídào（介）until; till; up to: 我～昨晚纔知道那件事。I didn't know about it until last night. / ～現在 up to now

【直性子】zhíxìngzi（名）honest and straightforward person

【直徑】zhíjìng（名）〈數〉diameter

【直流電】zhíliúdiàn（名）direct current (D. C.)

【直接】zhíjiē（形）direct; immediate: ～後果 immediate consequence

【直爽】zhíshuǎng（形）frank; forthright

【直率】zhíshuài（形）frank; candid; straightforward

【直達】zhídá（形）through; nonstop: ～火車 through train / ～飛行 nonstop flight

【直腸】zhícháng（名）〈生理〉rectum

【直綫】zhíxiàn（名）straight line

【直截了當】zhí jié liǎo dàng〈成〉in plain terms; categorically: ～地說 to put it bluntly

【直轄】zhíxiá（動）exercise direct jurisdiction over: ～市 municipality directly under the Central Government

【直譯】zhíyì（名）literal translation; word-for-word translation

【直覺】zhíjué（名）〈心〉intuition

【直屬】zhíshǔ（動）directly subordinate to: ～文化部 be directly under the Ministry of Culture

【直觀】zhíguān（動）be directly perceived through the senses; audio-visual: ～教學 object teaching

相 xiāng Ⅰ（副）mutually; each other: 遙遙～望 face each other at a distance Ⅱ（動）see for oneself: 這件衣服她～不中。She doesn't particularly like this coat.

see also xiàng

【相干】xiānggān（動）have sth. to do with; be related to

【相比】xiāngbǐ（動）compare: ～之下 by comparison

【相反】xiāngfǎn（形）opposite; contrary: 態度～ adopt a contrary attitude

【相互】xiānghù（形）mutual; each other: ～學習 learn from each other

【相仿】xiāngfǎng（形）alike; similar: 他們脾氣～。They are alike in temperament.

【相同】xiāngtóng（形）same; identical

【相好】xiānghǎo Ⅰ（動）❶ be temperamentally compatible and on the best of terms ❷ have an affair with Ⅱ（名）lover; mistress

【相安無事】xiāng ān wú shì〈成〉live in harmony

【相似】xiāngsì（動）be similar; resemble

【相投】xiāngtóu（動）get on well with each other: 氣味～ share identical tastes

【相形見絀】xiāng xíng jiàn chù〈成〉be overshadowed; compare unfavourably with

【相依】xiāngyī（動）depend on each other: ～爲命 be mutually dependent and inseparable

【相宜】xiāngyí（形）suitable; opportune

【相抵】xiāngdǐ（動）offset; balance

【相差】xiāngchà（動）differ: 兩者～甚遠。There is a great difference between the two.

【相持】xiāngchí（動）end in a stalemate; come to a deadlock

【相思】xiāngsī（名）secret longings; love-sickness: 單～的痛苦 pangs of unrequited love

【相信】xiāngxìn（動）believe

【相逢】xiāngféng（動）meet; come across

【相連】xiānglián（動）be linked; be adjacent to

【相處】xiāngchǔ（動）get along with: 此人不易～。This chap is difficult to get along with.

【相符】xiāngfú（動）agree with; tally with; match

【相像】xiāngxiàng（動）be alike; resemble each other

【相異】xiāngyì（形）different; diverse; dissimilar

【相等】xiāngděng（動）be equal; be quivalent (to)

【相距】xiāngjù（動）be at a distance: ～很遠 be far apart

【相提並論】xiāng tí bìng lùn〈成〉be on a par with each other; be mentioned in the same breath

【相傳】xiāngchuán Ⅰ（副）according to legend Ⅱ（動）pass on; hand down

【相當】xiāngdāng Ⅰ（動）match; be equal to: 地位～ be well-matched in social status/ ～於一個月的工資 be equivalent to a month's salary Ⅱ（形）suitable; proper: 他做這件工作很～。He is the right person for the job. Ⅲ（副）considerably; quite:

～困難 quite difficult

【相對】xiāngduì（副）❶ opposite; face to face: 隔江～ face each other across the river ❷ relatively; comparatively: ～安全 relatively safe

【相稱】xiāngchèn（動）match; fit: 這件襯衣和她的裙子不～。This blouse does not match her skirt.

【相輔相成】xiāng fǔ xiāng chéng〈成〉complement each other

【相親相愛】xiāng qīn xiāng ài（動）love each other dearly; have a deep affection for each other

【相應】xiāngyìng（形）corresponding; relevant: 做出～的調整 make corresponding adjustments

【相識】xiāngshí Ⅰ（動）know; be acquainted with: 與他～ be acquainted with him Ⅱ（名）acquaintance: 老～ old acquaintance

【相關】xiāngguān（動）be related to

【相勸】xiāngquàn（動）advise; exhort

【相繼】xiāngjì（副）one after another; in succession

相 xiàng（名）❶ looks; appearance: 一副邋遢～ a slovenly appearance / 手～術 palmistry ❷ photograph: ～冊 photo album
see also xiāng

【相片】xiàngpiān（名）photograph; photo

【相角】xiàngjiǎo（名）photo corner

【相面】xiàngmiàn（動）practise physiognomy

【相紙】xiàngzhǐ（名）photographic paper

【相貌】xiàngmào（名）looks; appearance

【相機】xiàngjī（名）camera

【相聲】xiàngsheng（名）cross talk

眉

眉 méi（名）eyebrow; brow

【眉毛】méimao（名）eyebrow: ～胡子一把抓 attend to matters big and small regardless of priority

【眉心】méixīn（名）space between the eyebrows

【眉目】méimù（名）❶ features; appearance ❷ order and sequence: 這篇評論～不清。This commentary is neither concise nor well-organized.

【眉目】méimu（名）chance; possibility: 他找工作的事有～了嗎？Is there any chance of his finding a job?

【眉宇】méiyǔ（名）forehead

【眉批】méipī（名）notes and commentary written in the top margin of a page

【眉來眼去】méi lái yǎn qù〈成〉exchange amorous glances; ogle

【眉飛色舞】méi fēi sè wǔ〈成〉be wild with joy; beam with joy

【眉梢】méishāo（名）tip of the brow: 喜上～ beam with joy

【眉清目秀】méi qīng mù xiù〈成〉have fine features

【眉眼高低】méiyǎn gāodī（名）facial expression

【眉筆】méibǐ（名）eyebrow pencil

【眉開眼笑】méi kāi yǎn xiào〈成〉smile broadly; smile from ear to ear

【眉睫】méijié Ⅰ（名）eyebrows and eyelashes Ⅱ（形）imminent; urgent: 迫在～ impending; extremely urgent

【眉頭】méitóu（名）brows: 皺～knit one's brows; frown; scowl

省

省 shěng Ⅰ（動）❶ economize; be frugal: ～時～力 save time and energy ❷ leave out; cut: ～了一個字 omit one word Ⅱ（名）province see also xǐng

【省份】shěngfèn（名）province

【省吃儉用】shěng chī jiǎn yòng〈成〉live a frugal life

【省事】shěngshì（動）save trouble: 這可以使你～得多。This can save you a lot of trouble.

【省得】shěngde（動）so as to avoid; lest: 把實際情況都告訴他，～他又發牢騷。Tell him the whole truth lest he should complain again.

【省略】shěnglüè（動）cut; omit; delete: ～號 ellipsis; ellipsis dots

【省會】shěnghuì（名）provincial capital

省 xǐng（動）❶ examine oneself: 反躬自～ make a critical examination of one's own conduct; examine one's own conscience ❷ become conscious: 猛～ come to a sudden realization ❸ visit (one's elders) see also shěng

【省悟】xǐngwù（動）awake to the truth

【省親】xǐngqīn（動）visit one's parents or elders

眈

眈 dān

【眈眈】dāndān（動）stare fiercely

盹

盹 dǔn（動）doze: 打～兒 doze off

眨

眨 zhǎ（動）blink; wink: 吃驚地～眼睛 blink with astonishment

【眨眼】zhǎyǎn（名）very short time: 一～就不見了 disappear in

the twinkling of an eye

盼 pàn (動) ❶ expect; look forward to: ～家裏的消息 long for news from home ❷ look: 左顧右～ look around

【盼望】pànwàng (動) look froward to; yearn for: 我們～你早日歸來。We are hoping for your early return.

【盼頭】pàntou (名) hope; promising prospect: 沒～ hopeless

看 kān (動) ❶ look after; tend: ～行李 take care of the luggage ❷ keep under watch
see also kàn

【看守】kānshǒu Ⅰ (動) keep guard over; look after: ～內閣 caretaker cabinet Ⅱ (名) warder

【看押】kānyā (動) detain; take (sb.) into custody

【看門】kānmén (動) guard the gate: ～人 gatekeeper; doorkeeper

【看家】kānjiā Ⅰ (動) stay behind to take charge of temporary duties Ⅱ (形) 〈口〉 special: ～本領 one's special ability or skill

【看家狗】kānjiāgǒu (名) watchdog

【看管】kānguǎn (動) ❶ look after; take charge of ❷ keep watch over; guard

【看護】kānhù Ⅰ (動) nurse: ～病人 使之恢復健康 nurse a patient back to health Ⅱ (名) (hospital) nurse

看 kàn (動) ❶ see; watch: ～圖識字 learn characters (words) from pictures ❷ read: ～小說 read a novel ❸ think; reckon; judge: 你 ～怎麼樣? What do you think of it? ❹ look upon: 小～ look down upon; underestimate ❺ pay a visit

to sb. ❻ take care of: 照～病人 attend to a patient ❼ give medical treatment to: 誰～好了你的病? Who cured you? ❽ be contingent on: ～風使舵 watch the wind and turn the rudder; trim the sails ❾ [used after a verb, often in reduplicated form] and see (whether the idea is correct or whether the method works out successfully): 用用～。Let's have a try and see if it works.
see also kān

【看上】kànshang (看中 kànzhòng) (動) like: 我～這條紅裙子。I like this red skirt.

【看不起】kàn bu qǐ (動) 〈口〉 look down upon; scorn

【看不慣】kàn bu guàn (動) 〈口〉 detest; frown at; find (sth.) repulsive

【看出】kànchū (動) detect; discern: ～某人人品上的缺陷 detect flaws in sb.'s character

【看死】kànsǐ (動) have fixed ideas about sb. or sth.: 不要把他～。Don't think that he will never change for the better.

【看成】kànchéng (動) regard as: 把他～英雄 regard him as a hero

【看見】kànjian (動) meet; notice: 我昨天偶然～他。I ran across him yesterday.

【看到】kàndào (動) come to realize; note: 我們要～問題的嚴重性。We should be aware of the seriousness of the case.

【看法】kànfǎ (名) opinion; view; perception: 你的～如何? What is your opinion?

【看來】kànlai (看樣子 kàn yàngzi) (動) seem; appear; look like: ～我

冤枉你了。Perhaps, I've wrongly blamed you.

【看穿】kànchuān (看透 kàntòu) (动) see through

【看待】kàndài (动) treat; look upon: 作爲貴賓～ be treated as a V.I.P.

【看重】kànzhòng (动) regard as important; set store by: 我們十分～一個人的品德。We set great store by a person's character.

【看病】kànbìng (动) ❶ (of a doctor) see a patient; give medical treatment to a patient ❷ (of a patient) consult a doctor

【看破】kànpò (动) ❶ see through ❷ be disillusioned

【看望】kànwàng (动) call on; pay a visit to (sb.)

【看做】kànzuò (动) consider as: 我們把他～老師。We regard him as our teacher.

【看得起】kàn de qǐ (动)〈口〉have a good opinion of: 我不敢説人們都～她。I am not sure if all people think highly of her.

【看得遠】kàn de yuǎn (动) ❶ look far ❷ have foresight; be farseeing

【看輕】kànqīng (动) make light of: 不要～這椿事。Don't belittle the significance of the matter.

【看齊】kànqí (动) ❶ dress: 向右～! Eyes right! ❷ emulate; catch up with

【看臺】kàntái (名) bleachers; spectators' stand

【看懂】kàndǒng (动) read; comprehend: 他能～古文。He can read classical Chinese.

盾 dùn (名) shield

【盾牌】dùnpái (名) shield

真 zhēn Ⅰ(形) true; real; genuine: ～善美 the true, the good and the beautiful Ⅱ(副) ❶ really; truly: ～好。It's really good. ❷ clearly: 聽得～ hear clearly

【真才實學】zhēn cái shí xué (名) solid learning; real knowledge

【真心】zhēnxīn (形) sincere; whole-hearted: ～實意 with all one's heart; in all sincerity

【真切】zhēnqiè (形) clear; distinct

【真正】zhēnzhèng Ⅰ(形) genuine; real: ～的友誼 true friendship Ⅱ(副) truly; really: 這個人～不簡單。This man is truly remarkable.

【真主】Zhēnzhǔ (名)〈宗〉Allah

【真空】zhēnkōng (名)〈物〉vacuum: 我們不是生活在～裏。We do not live in a vacuum.

【真知】zhēnzhī (名) genuine knowledge

【真知灼見】zhēn zhī zhuó jiàn〈成〉rare wisdom and keen insight

【真相】zhēnxiàng (名) actual state of affairs; truth; facts: ～ 大白。The truth has come out.

【真迹】zhēnjì (名) genuine work (of painting or calligraphy)

【真理】zhēnlǐ (名) truth

【真情】zhēnqíng (名) ❶ actual state of affairs; facts ❷ genuine feelings; real sentiments

【真菌】zhēnjūn (名) fungus

【真誠】zhēnchéng (形) sincere; genuine; earnest: ～的祝願 one's sincere good wishes

【真實】zhēnshí (形) true; real; actual: 這故事不～。The story is not true to life.

【真挚】zhēnzhì（形）sincere; cordial; genuine

【真谛】zhēndì（名）true meaning

【真凭实据】zhēn píng shí jù〈成〉genuine and reliable evidence

眩 xuàn（形）dizzy; giddy

【眩晕】xuànyūn（名）dizziness

眠 mián（名）❶ sleep: 失～ sleeplessness; insomnia ❷ (of a beast) a state like a long sleep: 冬～ hibernation

眷 juàn Ⅰ（名）relatives: 家～ family members; family dependents Ⅱ（动）be concerned about

【眷念】juànniàn（动）miss; think about

【眷属】juànshǔ（名）family (dependents); wife and children

【眷恋】juànliàn（动）have a soft spot for; be warmly attached to a (person or place)

眯 mī（动）half close the eyes
see also mí

【眯盹儿】mīdǔnr（动）take a nap; snooze; doze

【眽缝】mīfeng（动）narrow (one's eyes)

眯 mí（动）get into one's eye: 让沙子～了我的眼。Stone dust got into my eyes.
see also mī

眶 kuàng（名）socket of the eye: 热泪盈～。Tears filled one's eyes.

眼 yǎn（名）❶ eye ❷ small hole: 钻个～ drill a small hole

【眼力】yǎnlì（名）❶ eyesight ❷ ability to judge: 很有～的人 man of

vision; man of insight

【眼下】yǎnxià（副）at the moment; at present; now

【眼巴巴】yǎnbābā（副）❶ eagerly; anxiously: ～地盼他来信 look eagerly forward to hearing from him ❷ helplessly: ～看着他在黑暗中消失了 look helplessly at him disappearing into the darkness

【眼中钉】yǎnzhōngdīng（名）thorn in one's flesh

【眼生】yǎnshēng（动）look unfamiliar: 听众里有几个～的面孔。I saw a few unfamiliar faces among the audience.

【眼皮】yǎnpí（名）eyelid

【眼光】yǎnguāng（名）❶ eye: 大家的～都注视着他。All eyes were fixed on him. ❷ insight; judgement: 我很佩服他的～。I admire him for his insight.

【眼色】yǎnsè（名）glance; wink: 使～ give sb. a wink

【眼尖】yǎnjiān（形）sharp-eyed: 他～，一下子就能把他们看穿。He has sharp eyes and can easily see them through.

【眼见为实】yǎn jiàn wéi shí〈成〉seeing is believing

【眼底】yǎndǐ Ⅰ（名）back part of an eyeball Ⅱ（副）before one's eyes: 全城景物尽收～。The whole city came into view.

【眼花】yǎnhuā（形）dim-sighted

【眼花缭乱】yǎn huā liáo luàn〈成〉be dazzled by a wonderful sight; display or performance

【眼明手快】yǎn míng shǒu kuài〈成〉have sharp eyes and deft hands; be agile and alert

【眼红】yǎnhóng（形）❶ furious;

angry: 氣得～ get into a towering rage ❷ envious; jealous: 不要見別人賺上錢就～。Don't envy other people their high earnings.

【眼界】 yǎnjiè (名) field of vision; view: 開～ open one's eyes; increase one's knowledge

【眼科】 yǎnkē (名)〈醫〉ophthalmology: ～醫生 oculist; eye doctor; eye specialist

【眼前】 yǎnqián (副)❶ before one's eyes: ～是一片稻田。Right in front of us is a stretch of rice fields. ❷ at present; now: ～還不能下結論。No conclusion can be made at present.

【眼看】 yǎnkàn Ⅰ (副) soon; presently: 工程～就要完成了。The project is approaching completion. Ⅱ (動) watch helplessly: 不能～着他受欺負 cannot stand by with folded arms and watch him being bullied

【眼神】 yǎnshén (名) look in one's eyes: 他～中顯出疲乏。He has a tired look in his eyes.

【眼珠】 yǎnzhū (名) eyeball; apple of the eye

【眼高手低】 yǎn gāo shǒu dī〈成〉set a very exacting standard for others but cannot live up to it oneself

【眼球】 yǎnqiú (名) eyeball

【眼眶】 yǎnkuàng (名) orbit; eye socket

【眼圈】 yǎnquān (名) rim of the eye; orbit

【眼淚】 yǎnlèi (名) tears

【眼睛】 yǎnjing (名) eye

【眼罩】 yǎnzhào (名) eyeshade

【眼裏】 yǎnli (副) in one's eyes: 在他～,一切都不成問題。In his eyes, nothing is too difficult.

【眼睫毛】 yǎnjiémáo (名) eyelash

【眼福】 yǎnfú (名) feast for the eyes

【眼熟】 yǎnshú (動) look familiar

【眼皮】 yǎnpí (名) eyelid

【眼藥】 yǎnyào (名) eye ointment; eyedrops

【眼簾】 yǎnlián (名) eye: 映入～ come into view

【眼鏡】 yǎnjìng (名) glasses; spectacles

【眼鏡蛇】 yǎnjìngshé (名) cobra

【眼饞】 yǎnchán (動) be full of envy

眺 tiào (動) look afar from a height

【眺望】 tiàowàng (動) look afar from a height

睒 shǎn (動) blink; twinkle: 一～眼 in the twinkling of an eye; in an instant

睏 kùn Ⅰ (形) sleepy Ⅱ (動)〈方〉sleep: ～覺 go to bed

【睏倦】 kùnjuàn (形) weary; tired and sleepy

督 dū (動) supervise; command

【督促】 dūcù (動) urge; check the implementation of

【督察】 dūchá (動) superintend; supervise

睛 jīng (名) eyeball: 定～一看 take a good look (at)

睫 jié (名) eyelash

【睫毛】 jiémáo (名) eyelash

睦 mù (形) harmonious; peaceful; congruous

【睦鄰】 mùlín (名) good-neighbourliness: ～政策 good-neighbour policy

睹 dū (動) see: 耳聞目～ what one

sees and hears

睐 lài（动）look at: 受到青～ find favour in sb.'s eyes; be in sb.'s good graces

睁 zhēng（动）open (the eyes): 他睏得眼都～不開了。He was so sleepy that he could barely keep his eyes open.

睬 cǎi（动）[used mostly in negative sentences] take notice of: 不理～ ignore; take no notice of

睡 shuì（动）sleep: 熟～ be sound asleep

【睡衣】shuìyī（名）pyjamas

【睡眠】shuìmián（名）sleep

【睡袋】shuìdài（名）sleeping bag (sack)

【睡蓮】shuìlián（名）water lily

【睡醒】shuìxǐng（动）wake up

【睡覺】shuìjiào（名）睡一小覺 have a nap

瞄 miáo（动）aim (at)

【瞄準】miáozhǔn（动）take aim

睽 kuí

【睽睽】kuíkuí（动）gaze: 眾目～之下 in the public gaze; be the focus of public attention; in broad daylight

睾 gāo

【睾丸】gāowán（名）〈生理〉testis; testicle

瞎 xiā Ⅰ（形）blind: 雙眼～了 go blind in both eyes Ⅱ（副）blindly; groundlessly; aimlessly: ～出主意 give wrong advice

【瞎子】xiāzi（名）blind person

【瞎扯】xiāchě（动）❶ talk nonsense

❷ have an idle chat

【瞎信】xiāxìn（名）dead letter

【瞎指揮】xiāzhǐhuī（动）give wrong instructions; not observing objective laws when giving instructions

【瞎話】xiāhuà（名）lie: 說～ tell a lie

【瞎幹】xiāgàn（动）act blindly

【瞎鬧】xiānào（动）act senselessly; act mischievously

瞑 míng（动）close one's eyes; die in peace

【瞑目】míngmù（动）die in peace: 死不～ turn over in one's grave

瞌 kē

【瞌睡】kēshuì（名）doze: 他乘火車好打～。He is apt to doze off on the train.

瞟 piǎo（动）look askance at sb.

瞘 kōu（动）(of eyes) sink in: 她很瘦，眼睛都～進去了。She is very thin and her eyes are sunken.

瞞 mán（动）withhold the truth from; conceal; hide: 這事為什麼～著大家？Why did you keep it secret from others?

【瞞上欺下】mán shàng qī xià〈成〉hoodwink one's superior and bully one's subordinates and the common people

【瞞天過海】mán tiān guò hǎi〈成〉resort to colossal deception and act in complete secrecy

【瞞哄】mánhōng（动）cheat; deceive

瞰 kàn（动）see from above: 俯～全城 have a bird's-eye view of the city

瞠 chēng (动) stare
【瞠目結舌】chēng mù jié shé 〈成〉 stare (watch) dumbfounded

瞥 piē (动) flash a look at
【瞥見】piējiàn (动) catch sight of

瞳 tóng (名) pupil of the eye
【瞳孔】tóngkǒng (名)〈生理〉pupil

瞭 liǎo (动) understand; see clearly
see also liào
【瞭如指掌】liǎo rú zhǐ zhǎng 〈成〉 know sth. like the palm of one's hand; know sth. inside out
【瞭然】liǎorán (动) understand thoroughly; be crystal clear
【瞭解】liǎojiě (动) ❶ understand; know: 完全～這件事 know the matter inside out ❷ look into; try to figure out: ～事情真相 find out the truth

瞭 liào
see also liǎo
【瞭望】liàowàng (动) look out; look afar from a height

瞪 dèng (动) stare; glare

瞬 shùn (名) wink; split second: 轉～ in the twinkling of an eye
【瞬息】shùnxī (瞬間 shùnjiān) (名) twinkling; split second
【瞬息萬變】shùn xī wàn biàn 〈成〉 numerous changes take place in the twinkling of an eye: 局勢～。The situation is fast changing.

瞧 qiáo (动)〈口〉look at; see: ～一～ take a look
【瞧不上眼】qiáobùshàng yǎn (动) regard as unworthy of notice

【瞧不起】qiáobùqǐ (动) look down upon
【瞧見】qiáojiàn (动) see
【瞧着辦】qiáozhebàn (动) do as one sees fit; act at one's discretion
【瞧得起】qiáodeqǐ (动) hold sb. in high regard

瞿 Qú (名) a surname
【瞿麥】qúmài (名) 〈植〉 fringed pink

瞼 jiǎn (名) eyelid

瞻 zhān (动) look upward or forward
【瞻仰】zhānyǎng (动) look at with reverence; pay one's respect to; pay homage to
【瞻念】zhānniàn (动) look to; think of
【瞻前顧後】zhān qián gù hòu 〈成〉 look forward and backward; weigh one's decisions and watch one's steps
【瞻望】zhānwàng (动) look ahead

矗 chù (动) stand upright; tower
【矗立】chùlì (动) tower (above sth.); stand tall and erect

矚 zhǔ (动) gaze; look fixedly at: 舉世～目的成就 an achievement which has attracted world attention

矛 部

矛 máo (名) lance; spear
【矛盾】máodùn Ⅰ (名) contradiction: ～律 the law of contradiction Ⅱ (动) ❶ contradict; conflict (with):

有關事態的相互～的消息 conflicting news about the event / 兩人鬧～了。The two of them fell out. ❷ hesitate: 他對是否去南方旅遊，心裏很～。He is still hesitating about his trip to the South.

【矛盾百出】máo dùn bǎi chū〈成〉teem with contradictions

【矛頭】máotóu（名）spearhead; attack: 文章的～所向是浮誇作風。The article is spearheaded at boasting and exaggeration.

矜 jīn I（動）take pity on; have compassion for II（形）❶ conceited; haughty: 驕～ self-important ❷ restrained; prudent

【矜持】jīnchí（形）reserved; over-cautious

矢 部

矢 shǐ（名）arrow: 無的放～ shoot an arrow without a target; make unfounded statements

【矢口】shǐkǒu（副）completely; firmly: ～抵賴 flatly deny; give a flat denial

知 zhī I（動）know: 只～其名 know sb. by name / 就我所～ as far as I know II（名）knowledge: 愚昧無～ stupidity and ignorance

【知了】zhīliǎo（名）cicada

【知己】zhījǐ（名）bosom friend

【知心】zhīxīn（形）intimate; bosom: 講～話 have a heart-to-heart talk; exchange private views

【知名】zhīmíng（形）well-known;

celebrated; famous: ～人士 public figure; celebrity

【知足】zhīzú（動）be content with one's lot: ～常樂。He who is content will be happy.（Content is happiness.）

【知更鳥】zhīgēngniǎo（名）robin; redbreast

【知底】zhīdǐ（動）know the thing inside out

【知情】zhīqíng（動）be in the know; be well-informed about certain facts

【知道】zhīdào（動）be aware of: ～自己的弱點 be well aware of one's own weakness

【知趣】zhīqù（動）behave sensibly

【知曉】zhīxiǎo（動）know; be aware of

【知識】zhīshi（名）knowledge: 專業～ professional knowledge

【知識分子】zhīshi fènzǐ（名）intellectual

【知識產權】zhīshi chǎnquán（名）intellectual property

【知覺】zhījué（名）consciousness

矩 jǔ（名）❶（carpenter's）square ❷ rule; principle: 蹈～ act on set principles; follow a prescribed procedure ❸〈物〉moment

【矩形】jǔxíng（名）rectangle

【矩陣】jǔzhèn（名）〈數〉matrix

短 duǎn I（形）short II（動）❶ lack ❷ owe: ～人家的錢 owe sb. money III（名）shortcoming

【短小精悍】duǎnxiǎo jīnghàn（形）❶ small in stature but of sturdy build ❷ concise and vigorous in style

【短見】duǎnjiàn（名）❶ shortsighted view ❷ suicide

【短兵相接】duǎn bīng xiāng jiē〈成〉fight at close quarters; fight hand to hand; repartee

【短命】duǎnmìng（动）be short-lived

【短波】duǎnbō（名）shortwave

【短促】duǎncù（形）short: 我們時間～。We are hard pressed for time.

【短缺】duǎnquē（名）shortage

【短淺】duǎnqiǎn（形）shallow; superficial: 目光～ short-sighted; myopic

【短處】duǎnchu（名）shortcoming; weakness

【短跑】duǎnpǎo（名）dash; sprint

【短期】duǎnqī（名）short period: ～目標 short-term objective

【短路】duǎnlù（名）〈電〉short circuit

【短語】duǎnyǔ（名）〈語〉phrase

【短篇小說】duǎnpiān xiǎoshuō（名）short story

【短暫】duǎnzàn（形）short; brief; transient

【短褲】duǎnkù（名）shorts

矮 ǎi（形）❶（of stature）short; low: ～一級 a grade lower ❷

【矮小】ǎixiǎo（形）short and small: 身材～ of short stature

【矮子】ǎizi（名）dwarf

【矮子裏拔將軍】ǎizili bá jiāngjūn〈口〉pick a general from among dwarfs; choose the best from among the mediocrities

【矮稈】ǎigǎn（形）〈農〉of short stem: ～作物 short-stemmed crop

【矮墩墩】ǎidūndūn（形）short and plump; dumpy

矯 jiǎo I（动）❶ rectify; correct

❷ pretend; feign II（形）valiant; robust; vigorous

【矯正】jiǎozhèng（动）correct; set right

【矯形】jiǎoxíng（形）orthopaedic

【矯枉過正】jiǎo wǎng guò zhèng〈成〉overshoot the mark; be overcorrect in righting a wrong

【矯健】jiǎojiàn（形）robust; vigorous; energetic: ～的步伐 vigorous springy step

【矯揉造作】jiǎo róu zào zuò〈成〉affected in manner: 並不～ be without affectation

石 部

石 shí（名）❶ rock; stone: ～板 flagstone; slabstone ❷ stone inscription ❸（Shí）a surname

【石匠】shíjiang（名）stonemason

【石灰】shíhuī（名）lime

【石沉大海】shí chén dà hǎi〈成〉disappear like a stone dropped into the sea; never be seen or heard of again

【石刻】shíkè（名）stone inscription

【石油】shíyóu（名）〈礦〉petroleum; oil: ～輸出國組織 the Organization of Petroleum Exporting Countries (OPEC)

【石英】shíyīng（名）quartz: ～表 quartz watch

【石級】shíjí（名）stone step

【石棉】shímián（名）asbestos

【石窟】shíkū（名）grotto; rock (stone) cave: 敦煌～ the Dunhuang Caves (in Gansu Province, dating from 366 A.D.）

【石碑】shíbēi（名）stele; stone tablet; monolith

【石榴】shíliú（名）pomegranate

【石膏】shígāo（名）gypsum; plaster

【石墨】shímò（名）graphite

【石器】shíqì（名）stone instrument

【石器時代】shíqì shídài（名）Stone Age

【石頭】shítou（石塊兒 shíkuàir）（名）stone; rock

【石雕】shídiāo（名）stone carving

矸 gān

【矸石】gānshí（名）〈礦〉waste（rock）

矽 xī（名）〈化〉silicon（Si）

【矽肺】xīfèi（名）〈醫〉silicosis

研 yán（動）❶ grind: ～藥 pestle medicinal herbs ❷ study: 科～ scientific research

【研究】yánjiū（動）❶ study; research: 學術～ academic research ❷ discuss: 這個問題還要～。The problem needs more deliberation.

【研究生】yánjiūshēng（名）postgraduate; graduate student

【研究員】yánjiūyuán（名）research fellow

【研討】yántǎo（動）discuss; study

【研討會】yántǎohuì（名）symposium; seminar

【研製】yánzhì（動）research and produce; develop

砌 qì（動）build by laying bricks or stones: ～煙囪 construct a chimney

【砌築】qìzhù（動）build by laying bricks or stones

砂 shā（名）sand; grit

【砂土】shātǔ（名）sandy soil

【砂布】shābù（名）abrasive cloth; emery cloth

【砂眼】shāyǎn（名）〈冶〉blowholes; sand holes

【砂箱】shāxiāng（名）〈冶〉sandbox; moulding box

【砂漿】shājiāng（名）〈建〉mortar

【砂輪】shālún（名）〈機〉emery wheel; grinding wheel

【砂糖】shātáng（名）granulated sugar

【砂鍋】shāguō（名）earthern pot; casserole: 打破～問到底 insist on getting to the bottom of the matter

【砂礦】shākuàng（名）placer; placer deposit

【砂礫】shālì（名）gravel; grit

【砂岩】shāyán（名）〈礦〉sandstone

砒 pī（名）arsenic

【砒霜】pīshuāng（名）（white）arsenic

砍 kǎn（動）❶ hew; cut; chop ❷〈方〉hurl（sth.）at

【砍刀】kǎndāo（名）chopper

【砍伐】kǎnfá（動）hew down（trees）

砰 pēng（象）bang: 氣球～地一聲爆炸了。The balloon burst with a bang.

砝 fǎ

【砝碼】fǎmǎ（名）weight（used on a balance）

砸 zá（動）❶ pound; thump: 他使勁～門。He thumped on the door. ❷ break; smash: 花瓶～了。The vase is broken. ❸ fail: 他計劃～了。His plan fell through.

破 pò I (形) ❶ broken; damaged: ~布 rags / 玻璃~了。The glass is broken. ❷ poor in quality: 誰看那個~戲? Who cares for such a lousy performance? II (動) ❶ break; split; cut: ~記錄 break a record ❷ break with; abolish (custom, regulations, ideas) ❸ defeat; rout ❹ spend (money): 我並不要她這樣~鈔。I didn't really want her to go to such a lot of expense. ❺ reveal; lay bare: 識~ see through

【破土】pòtǔ (動) break ground (in construction)

【破天荒】pòtiānhuāng (動) happen for the first time: 這種情況是~的。This is the first time that such a thing has happened.

【破冰船】pòbīngchuán (名) ice-breaker

【破折號】pòzhéhào (名)〈語〉dash

【破例】pòlì (動) make an exception; break a rule

【破案】pò'àn (動) crack a criminal case

【破除】pòchú (動) get rid of; abolish: ~ 情面 not spare anybody's sensibilities

【破格】pògé (動) break a rule: ~提升有才能的年輕人 break a rule to promote talented young people

【破涕】pòtì (動) refrain from tears: ~爲笑 smile away one's tears

【破釜沉舟】pò fǔ chén zhōu〈成〉sink one's boats; be determined to fight to the bitter end

【破產】pòchǎn I (動) go bankrupt II (名) bankruptcy

【破敗】pòbài (形) ruined; dilapidated

【破費】pòfèi (動) spend money; go to some expense: 這頓飯由我付錢,你不必~了。Don't bother to pay. The dinner is on me.

【破裂】pòliè (動) split; break

【破損】pòsǔn (形) damaged; torn: 轉運中並無~ sustain no damage during transit

【破碎】pòsuì (形) broken; shattered

【破落】pòluò (of one's family, fortune) decline: 家道~ sink low in fortune and social status

【破滅】pòmiè (動) be disillusioned; be shattered

【破傷風】pòshāngfēng (名)〈醫〉tetanus

【破綻】pòzhàn (名) flaw; loophole: ~百出。There exists a considerable number of obvious loopholes.

【破曉】pòxiǎo (名) dawn; daybreak

【破獲】pòhuò (動) uncover; ferret out

【破壞】pòhuài (動) wreck; sabotage

【破鏡重圓】pò jìng chóng yuán〈成〉reconciliation or reunion of husband and wife

【破爛】pòlàn I (形) ragged; tattered II (名) junk; odds and ends

【破罐破摔】pò guàn pò shuāi〈成〉throw away a broken pot because it's already broken; give oneself up for lost and act recklessly

砧 zhēn (名) anvil; hammering block

【砧板】zhēnbǎn (名) chopping block

砷 shēn (名)〈化〉arsenic (As)

砥 dǐ (名) whetstone

【砥礪】dǐlì (動) ❶ temper ❷ encourage

硅 guī (名)〈化〉silicon (Si)

硒 xī (名)〈化〉selenium (Se)

硃 zhū (名) cinnabar

【硃砂】zhūshā (名) cinnabar

硫 liú (名)〈化〉sulphur (S)

【硫化】liúhuà (名)〈化〉vulcanization

【硫酸】liúsuān (名)〈化〉sulphuric acid

硬 yìng Ⅰ (形) ❶ hard: ～如磐石 as hard as a rock ❷ tough: ～漢 a tough man ❸ stubborn; obstinate: 死～派 diehards ❹ solid; sound: ～功夫 masterly skill Ⅱ (副) forcibly; doggedly: 他～拉我去。He literally dragged me into going. / ～要自己去 insist upon going there oneself

【硬木】yìngmù (名) hardwood

【硬化】yìnghuà Ⅰ (動) harden; stiffen Ⅱ (名)〈醫〉sclerosis: 動脈～ arteriosclerosis

【硬件】yìngjiàn (名)〈計算機〉hardware

【硬度】yìngdù (名)〈物〉hardness

【硬席】yìngxí (名) hard seat (on a train); hard berth

【硬骨頭】yìnggútou (名) unyielding person

【硬通貨】yìngtōnghuò (名) hard currency

【硬煤】yìngméi (名) hard coal; anthracite

【硬腭】yìng'è (名)〈生理〉hard palate

【硬幣】yìngbì (名) coin

硝 xiāo (名)〈化〉nitre; saltpetre

【硝煙】xiāoyān (名) smoke of gunpowder

【硝酸】xiāosuān (名)〈化〉nitric acid

硯 yàn

【硯臺】yàntái (名) inkstone; inkslab

碇 dìng (名) heavy stone used as an anchor

碗 wǎn (名) bowl

碎 suì Ⅰ (動) break to pieces: 茶杯打得粉～。The teacup is smashed to pieces. Ⅱ (形) ❶ broken; fragmented; fractured: ～屑 bits; scraps ❷ garrulous: 閑言～語 gossip

碰 pèng (動) ❶ touch; collide with: ～了某人的手臂 touch sb. on the arm ❷ meet; encounter: ～到問題 encounter problems ❸ try one's luck: ～～看 take one's chance

【碰巧】pèngqiǎo (副) by chance: 我們～在那裏相遇。We met there by chance.

【碰見】pèngjiàn (動) run into; come across

【碰杯】pèngbēi (動) clink glasses

【碰釘子】pèng dīngzi (動) be rebuffed; be snubbed

【碰運氣】pèng yùnqì (動) try one's luck

【碰撞】pèngzhuàng (動) bump into; collide

【碰壁】pèngbì (動) be balked; be rejected; fail

【碰頭】pèngtóu (動) meet briefly to discuss sth.; put (our, their, etc.) heads together

【碰鎖】pèngsuǒ（名）spring lock

碘 diǎn（名）〈化〉iodine（I）

【碘酒】diǎnjiǔ（名）〈藥〉tincture of iodine

硼 péng（名）〈化〉boron（B）

【硼砂】péngshā（名）borax; sodium borate

【硼酸】péngsuān（名）boric acid

碉 diāo

【碉堡】diāobǎo（名）pillbox

碑 bēi（名）stele; upright stone tablet

【碑文】bēiwén（名）inscribed text on a stone tablet

【碑帖】bēitiè（名）rubbing from a stone inscription（used as a calligraphy model）

碌 liù
see also lù

【碌碡】liùzhóu（名）stone roller

碌 lù（形）❶ mediocre ❷ busy
see also liù

【碌碌】lùlù（形）❶ commonplace: ~無能 mediocre ❷ busy: 終生~ work like a beaver all one's life

碧 bì Ⅰ（名）emerald; green jade Ⅱ（形）green; bluish; greenish blue

【碧玉】bìyù（名）jasper: 小家~ pretty girl of modest family background

【碧血】bìxuè（名）blood shed for a worthy cause: ~丹心 lay down one's life in a noble cause

【碧綠】bìlù（形）emerald green; verdant

磋 cuō

【磋商】cuōshāng Ⅰ（動）consult Ⅱ（名）consultation

磁 cí（名）❶ magnetism ❷ porcelain; china

【磁帶】cídài（名）(magnetic) tape: ~錄音機 tape recorder

【磁鐵】cítiě（名）magnet: ~礦 magnetite

碟 dié（名）small plate; saucer: ~子 small dish

碴 chá（動）〈方〉be cut (by broken glass, etc.)

【碴兒】chár（名）❶ fragment: 碎玻璃~ pieces of broken glass ❷ sharp edge of broken glass, china, etc.: 碗~ the cutting edge of a cracked bowl ❸ sth. that may trigger off a dispute

碩 shuò（形）large; big

【碩士】shuòshì（名）master; graduate holding a master's degree: 文科~ Master of Arts; M.A.

【碩大無朋】shuò dà wú péng〈成〉huge; of immeasurable size

【碩果】shuòguǒ（名）outstanding achievement: 結~ score monumental achievements

碳 tàn（名）〈化〉carbon（C）: ~水化合物 carbohydrate / 二氧化~ carbon dioxide

磅 bàng（名）❶（measure for weight）pound ❷ scales: 過~ weigh (on the scales)
see also páng

【磅秤】bàngchèng（名）scales; platform scale; weighing machine

磅 páng

see also bàng

【磅礴】pángbó Ⅰ（形）overwhelming; majestic Ⅱ（動）pervade

確 què Ⅰ（形）true; authentic: 千真萬～ absolutely true Ⅱ（副）firmly; resolutely

【確切】quèqiè（形）exact; precise

【確立】quèlì（動）establish

【確定】quèdìng Ⅰ（形）definite; certain Ⅱ（動）fix; ascertain; determine

【確保】quèbǎo（動）ensure; guarantee

【確信】quèxìn（動）firmly believe; be convinced

【確診】quèzhěn（動）make a final diagnosis

【確認】quèrèn（動）affirm; confirm

【確實】quèshí Ⅰ（形）true; reliable Ⅱ（副）really; certainly

【確鑿】quèzuò（形）conclusive; reliable

碼 mǎ Ⅰ（名）❶ sign indicating number: 電話～ telephone number／房間號～ room number ❷ things of the same kind: 咱倆說的不是一～事。We are not talking about the same thing. ❸ yard（yd.）Ⅱ（動）pile: 把磚～在院子裏 stack the bricks in the courtyard

【碼頭】mǎtou（名）❶ dock; quay; wharf ❷ port city

【碼頭工人】mǎtou gōngrén（名）docker; longshoreman

【碼頭費】mǎtoufèi（名）wharfage

磕 kē（動）❶ knock（against a hard object）: ～破了膝蓋 graze one's knee ❷ tap（sth. out of a container）: 把花盆裏的土～出來

knock the earth out of the flower pot

【磕巴】kēba〈口〉stutter; stammer: 打～ stutter

【磕碰】kēpèng（動）❶ knock against; bump against: 小心點，別～壞了玻璃酒杯。Take care not to break the wine glasses. ❷ clash; squabble ❸ meet with setbacks; experience frustrations

【磕頭】kētóu（動）kowtow

磊 lěi

【磊落】lěiluò（形）open and aboveboard

碾 niǎn Ⅰ（名）roller Ⅱ（動）grind; husk; crush: 把小麥～成麵粉 grind the wheat into flour

【碾子】niǎnzi（名）roller

【碾米機】niǎnmǐjī（名）rice mill

【碾坊】niǎnfáng（名）grain mill

【碾壓】niǎnyā（動）roll: ～成的金箔 rolled gold

磐 pán

【磐石】pánshí（名）huge solid rock: 堅如～ as solid as a rock

磨 mó（動）❶ rub; wear: 這種布耐～。This cloth wears well. ❷ grind; polish: ～成細粉 grind sth. into powder ❸ sharpen; whet: ～剃刀 sharpen a razor ❹ wear out; wear down: 這場病可把我～壞了。The illness has completely worn me out. ❺ dawdle; waste（time）: 故意～時間 play for time ❻ delete; obliterate: 百世不～ last for ever see also mò

【磨刀石】módāoshí（名）whetstone

【磨刀霍霍】mó dāo huò huò〈成〉whet one's sword for a fight

【磨光】móguāng（動）polish: ～表面 polish the surface

【磨牀】móchuáng（名）grinding machine; grinder

【磨洋工】móyánggōng（動）dawdle along; loaf on one's job

【磨滅】mómiè（動）wear away; obliterate: 不可～ be indelible

【磨練】móliàn（動）temper; harden: ～意志 steel one's will

【磨嘴皮子】mó zuǐpízi（動）talk a lot; talk glibly

【磨難】mónàn（名）hardship; tribulation; adversity

【磨蹭】móceng（動）❶ rub gently: 手在桌上～ rub one's hand lightly along the table ❷ move slowly: 你這樣～會誤飛機的。If you go on dawdling like this, you'll miss your plane.

磨 mò Ⅰ（名）mill; millstones Ⅱ（動）❶ grind; mill: ～玉米 grind maize ❷ turn round (sth. heavy or cumbersome)
see also mó

【磨坊】mòfáng（名）mill

【磨麵機】mòmiànjī（名）flour-milling machine

磬 qìng（名）❶ chime stone ❷ inverted bell (a Buddhist percussion instrument made of copper)

磙 gǔn（名）roller: 石～ stone roller

磚 zhuān（名）brick

【磚坯】zhuānpī（名）unfired brick

【磚茶】zhuānchá（名）brick tea

【磚窰】zhuānyáo（名）brick-kiln

【磚頭】zhuāntou（名）brick

磷 lín（名）〈化〉phosphorus (P)

【磷火】línhuǒ（名）phosphorescent light

【磷光】línguāng（名）〈物〉phosphorescence

【磷肥】línféi（名）〈農〉phosphate fertilizer

磺 huáng（名）sulphur

【磺胺】huáng'àn（名）〈藥〉sulphanilamide

磴 dèng Ⅰ（名）stone step Ⅱ（量）：八～臺階 eight steps (stairs)

礁 jiāo（名）reef; submerged rock, coral, etc.

【礁石】jiāoshí（名）reef; submerged rock

礎 chǔ（名）plinth: 打好基～ lay a solid foundation for

礙 ài（動）obstruct; hinder: 妨～交通 obstruct the traffic

【礙口】àikǒu（動）be too embarrassing to mention

【礙手礙脚】ài shǒu ài jiǎo〈成〉get in the way

【礙事】àishì（動）❶ be in the way [used mainly in negative sentences] matter; be of serious consequence: 他的病不～。His illness is not at all serious.

【礙面子】ài miànzi（動）be unwilling offend sb.'s sensibilities

【礙眼】àiyǎn（動）offend the eye; be an eyesore

礬 fán（名）alum

【礬土】fántǔ（名）alumina

礦 kuàng（名）❶ mineral deposit

❷ ore ❸ mine

【礦工】kuànggōng（名）miner

【礦山】kuàngshān（名）mine：～機械 mining machinery

【礦井】kuàngjǐng（名）〈礦〉shaft; pit

【礦石】kuàngshí（名）ore：鐵～ iron ore

【礦物】kuàngwù（名）mineral

【礦泉水】kuàngquánshuǐ（名）mineral water

【礦區】kuàngqū（名）mining area

【礦產】kuàngchǎn（名）mineral product

【礦業】kuàngyè（採礦業 cǎikuàngyè）（名）mining industry; mining

【礦藏】kuàngcáng（名）mineral resources

礪 I I（名）whetstone II（動）whet; sharpen

礫 II（名）gravel

【礫石路】lìshílù（名）gravel road

示 部

示 shì（動）show; manifest：寫請～報告 draft a memo asking for instructions

【示例】shìlì（動）cite typical examples; demonstrate

【示威】shìwēi I（名）demonstration：遊行～ stage a demonstration II（動）show one's strength

【示弱】shìruò（動）show signs of weakness; take sth. lying down; yield

【示眾】shìzhòng（動）show sb. up (esp. a criminal) before the public

【示意】shìyì（動）communicate by signal; hint：用手勢～ gesture with one's hands／～圖 sketch map

【示範】shìfàn（動）set an example for others to follow; demonstrate：～作用 exemplary role

【示警】shìjǐng（動）give a warning：鳴槍～ fire a warning shot

社 shè（名）❶ agency; association; society：旅行～ travel agency ❷ people's commune：～員 commune member

【社交】shèjiāo（名）social intercourse

【社會】shèhuì（名）society：原始～ primitive society／～風氣 social trends

【社會主義】shèhuì zhǔyì（名）socialism

【社會學】shèhuìxué（名）sociology

【社會關係】shèhuì guānxi（名）❶ social relationship ❷ social connections

【社團】shètuán（名）mass organizations; corporation

【社論】shèlùn（名）editorial

【社稷】shèjì（名）the state; the country

祁 Qí（名）a surname

【祁紅】qíhóng（名）keemun（black tea）

祈 qí（動）❶ pray ❷ crave; entreat

【祈求】qíqiú（動）entreat; pray for

【祈使句】qíshǐjù（名）〈語〉imperative sentence

【祈禱】qídǎo I（動）pray II（名）prayer

祛 qū（動）dispel; remove

【祛除】qūchú（动）dispel; get rid of

祠 cí（名）ancestral temple; memorial temple

【祠堂】cítáng（名）ancestral hall; memorial temple

祖 zǔ（名）❶ grandfather: 曾 ～ great-grandfather ❷ ancestor

【祖父】zǔfù（名）(paternal) grandfather: 外 ～ maternal grandfather

【祖母】zǔmǔ（名）(paternal) grandmother

【祖先】zǔxiān（名）ancestry; forefathers; forebears

【祖宗】zǔzōng（名）ancestry; ancestors

【祖祖辈辈】zǔ zǔ bèi bèi〈成〉from generation to generation

【祖国】zǔguó（名）motherland

【祖传】zǔchuán（动）be handed down from one's ancestors

【祖坟】zǔfén（名）ancestral grave

【祖辈】zǔbèi（名）ancestors; forefathers

【祖籍】zǔjí（名）ancestral home

神 shén Ⅰ（名）❶ god; deity ❷ spirit; mind: 聚精会 ～ with undivided attention ❸ look; expression Ⅱ（形）supernatural; magical: ～力 superhuman strength

【神父】shénfù（神甫 shénfu）（名）priest; Catholic father

【神化】shénhuà Ⅰ（动）deify Ⅱ（名）deification

【神仙】shénxian（名）fairy; immortal

【神出鬼没】shén chū guǐ mò〈成〉appear mysteriously and vanish without a trace

【神乎其神】shén hū qí shén（形）fantastic; miraculous

【神似】shénsì（形）similar in spirit

【神志】shénzhì（名）consciousness; senses: ～清醒过来 recover one's consciousness; come to

【神采】shéncǎi（名）look; expression: ～奕奕 beam with health

【神奇】shénqí（形）magical; power; rare knack; miraculous

【神往】shénwǎng（动）be held spellbound

【神速】shénsù（形）speedy; amazingly quick

【神通】shéntōng（名）magical

【神秘】shénmì（形）mysterious

【神气】shénqì Ⅰ（名）expression; look; air: 摆出一副大气高人一等的～ assume an air of intellectual superiority Ⅱ（形）❶ spirited; vigorous: 她穿上那件衣服，显得很～。She looks very smart in that dress. ❷ arrogant; cocky

【神情】shénqíng（神色 shénsè）（名）expression; look

【神聊】shénliáo（动）chat away on any conceivable topic

【神童】shéntóng（名）child prodigy

【神驰】shénchí（动）wander in one's thoughts

【神殿】shéndiàn（名）shrine

【神话】shénhuà（名）myth; mythology

【神圣】shénshèng（形）sacred; holy

【神经】shénjīng（名）nerve

【神经科】shénjīngkē（名）department of neurology

【神经病】shénjīngbìng（名）❶ neuropathy ❷ mental disorder

【神经衰弱】shénjīng shuāiruò（名）neurasthenia

【神经过敏】shénjīng guòmǐn（形）oversensitive

【神經質】shénjīngzhì（形）neurotic; nervous

【神像】shénxiàng（名）picture or statue of a god or Buddha

【神態】shéntài（名）manner; expression; mien

【神槍手】shénqiāngshǒu（名）expert marksman

【神學】shénxué（名）theology

【神機妙算】shén jī miào suàn〈成〉astonishing foresight and resourcefulness

【神權】shénquán（名）❶ theocracy ❷ rule by divine right

【神靈】shénlíng（名）gods; deities

祝 zhù Ⅰ（動）express good wishes; wish：～你萬事如意。Wish you every success. Ⅱ（名）(Zhù) a surname

【祝酒】zhùjiǔ（動）drink a toast; propose a toast

【祝捷】zhùjié（動）celebrate a victory

【祝詞】zhùcí（名）congratulatory speech; congratulatory message

【祝賀】zhùhè Ⅰ（動）congratulate：～你取得出色的成就。We congratulate you on your outstanding achievement. Ⅱ（名）congratulation

【祝壽】zhùshòu（動）offer birthday congratulations（to an elderly person）

【祝願】zhùyuàn（動）wish

祟 suì（名）evil spirit; ghost; evil doing：作～make trouble

票 piào（名）❶ bank note; bill ❷ ticket：單程～one-way ticket ❸ ballot：選～vote ❹ hostage：綁～

kidnap（for ransom）

【票子】piàozi（名）bank note; paper money

【票友】piàoyǒu（名）amateur actor or actress of Beijing opera

【票房】piàofáng（名）booking office; ticket office

【票面價值】piàomiàn jiàzhí（名）face value; par value; nominal value（of a note, bond, etc.）

【票根】piàogēn（名）counterfoil; stub

【票價】piàojià（名）admission fee（to the theatre, cinema, etc.）

【票箱】piàoxiāng（名）ballot box

【票據】piàojù（名）bill; note; negotiable instrument

【票額】piào'é（名）face value

祭 jì（動）❶ commemorate the death of a relative or friend ❷ offer sacrifices to; worship：～祖 offer sacrifices to one's ancestors

【祭文】jìwén（名）funeral speech; elegiac essay（read aloud at a funeral service）

【祭祀】jìsì（動）offer sacrifices to（gods or one's ancestors）

【祭奠】jìdiàn（動）hold memorial service for the deceased

稟 bǐng（動）〈敬〉❶ beg to report（to one's superior）：回～beg to report or reply（to one's superior）❷ receive; be endowed with

【稟承】bǐngchéng（動）act on（the instructions or advice of sb.）

【稟性】bǐngxìng（名）natural disposition or temperament; natural quality：～溫和 be of a gentle disposition

【稟報】bǐngbào（動）beg to report

(to a superior)

禄 lù (名) official's salary

禁 jīn (動) ❶ withstand; endure: ～得起狂風暴雨 can withstand the bury of the elements ❷ [used in negative construction] refrain: 不～笑了起來 cannot help laughing
see also jìn

【禁不住】jīnbuzhù (動) ❶ cannot withstand: 莊稼～乾旱的天氣。The crops cannot endure dry weather. ❷ cannot refrain from: ～喊起來 cannot help crying out

【禁得住】jīndezhù (動) can withstand: ～巨大外來壓力 be able to withstand tremendous outside pressure

禁 jìn Ⅰ (動) ❶ forbid; interdict: ～果 the forbidden fruit ❷ imprison; jail: 幽～ put under house arrest; imprison Ⅱ (名) ❶ thing forbidden by law or custom; taboo: 犯～ violate a ban ❷ forbidden (restricted) area: ～衛軍 imperial guards
see also jīn

【禁止】jìnzhǐ (動) forbid; prohibit: ～車輛通行 closed to traffic / ～照相 no photographing

【禁忌】jìnjì Ⅰ (名) ❶ taboo: 犯～ violate a taboo ❷〈醫〉contraindication Ⅱ (動) avoid; forgo; abstain from

【禁閉】jìnbì (名) confinement (a disciplinary punishment): 坐～ be placed in confinement

【禁區】jìnqū (名) ❶ forbidden zone; off bounds ❷ preserve (for protection of wildlife and plant)

【禁運】jìnyùn (名) embargo

【禁煙車廂】jìnyān chēxiāng (名) non-smoking compartment

【禁錮】jìngù (動) be taken into custody; confine

【禁獵區】jìnlièqū (名) preserve

福 fú (名) happiness: blessing

【福地】fúdì (名) Promised Land

【福利】fúlì (名) welfare

【福音】fúyīn (名) ❶ Gospel ❷ good news

【福星】fúxīng (名) lucky star: ～高照。One's star is in the ascendant.

【福建】Fújiàn (名) Fujian (Province)

【福氣】fúqi (名) good fortune

禍 huò Ⅰ (名) misfortune; disaster; calamity: 闖～ get into trouble; be in for trouble Ⅱ (動) damage; ruin: ～害 damage

【禍心】huòxīn (名) evil intentions

【禍不單行】huò bù dān xíng〈成〉misfortunes never come singly

【禍首】huòshǒu (名) arch-criminal

【禍胎】huòtāi (名) root cause of the trouble

【禍根】huògēn (名) root cause of the trouble

【禍害】huòhài (名) disaster; scourge

【禍患】huòhuàn (名) disaster; calamity

【禍國殃民】huò guó yāng mín〈成〉bring disaster on one's homeland and fellow citizens

【禍端】huòduān (名) source of the trouble

禪 chán Ⅰ (名)〈宗〉meditation: 參～ practise meditation Ⅱ (形) Buddhist

【禪林】chánlín (名) Buddhist temple

【禪宗】chánzōng（名）Zen; Zen Buddhism

禦 yù（動）resist; keep out

【禦侮】yùwǔ（動）resist invasion

【禦寒】yùhán（動）keep out the cold

禮 lǐ（名）❶ ceremony: 奠基典～ foundation stone laying ceremony ❷ courtesy; etiquette: 敬～ salute ❸ gift: 獻～ present a gift to / 聖誕節～ Christmas gift

【禮花】lǐhuā（名）display of fireworks: 放～ have a display of fireworks

【禮服】lǐfú（名）full dress; dress suit: 夜～ evening dress; evening suit

【禮尚往來】lǐ shàng wǎng lái〈成〉courtesy should be reciprocated

【禮炮】lǐpào（名）salvo; gun salute: 鳴～ fire a gun salute

【禮品】lǐpǐn（禮物 lǐwù）（名）gift; present: ～商店 gift shop

【禮拜】lǐbài（名）❶〈宗〉religious service; church service; worship: ～寺 mosque /～堂 church / 做～ go to church ❷〈口〉week: 上上～ the week before last ❸〈口〉[used before 一，二，...六] day of the week: ～六 Saturday ❹〈口〉Sunday

【禮拜天】lǐbàitiān（禮拜日 lǐbàirì）（名）Sunday

【禮教】lǐjiào（名）Confucian (feudal) code of ethics

【禮堂】lǐtáng（名）auditorium; assembly hall

【禮帽】lǐmào（名）felt hat; bowler (hat); derby: 大～ top hat

【禮遇】lǐyù（名）honours; courteous reception: 給予最高～ accord sb.

the redcarpet treatment or reception

【禮節】lǐjié（名）etiquette; protocol: ～性拜會 courtesy call

【禮輕情意重】lǐ qīng qíng yì zhòng〈成〉the gift may be of small value, but it conveys the sender's deep feeling; a gift of high sentimental value

【禮賓司】lǐbīnsī（名）Department of Protocol

【禮貌】lǐmào（名）politeness; manners; civility

【禮儀】lǐyí（名）etiquette; rite; ritual

【禮讓】lǐràng（動）give precedence to others out of courtesy

禱 dǎo（動）pray

【禱告】dǎogào（動）say one's prayers

内 部

禽 qín（名）birds: 飛～ the fowls of the air

【禽獸】qínshòu（名）❶ birds and beast ❷ beast; human beast; person who behaves like a beast

禾 部

禾 hé（名）standing grain（esp. rice）

【禾苗】hémiáo（名）seedlings（of cereal crops）

【禾場】héchǎng（名）threshing

ground

秃 tū (形) bald; hairless: 光~~的山 barren hill

【秃子】tūzi (名) baldhead

【秃顶】tūdǐng (形) bald; baldish: 他有點~了。He is going bald.

秀 xiù (形) ❶ excellent ❷ beautiful; handsome: ~外慧中 have both outward and inward grace

【秀才】xiùcái (名) ❶ scholar; intellectual ❷ first degree (at county level) of the imperial examination ❸ holder of that degree

【秀美】xiùměi (形) beautiful; elegant

【秀氣】xiùqi (形) delicate; fine: 長得~ have delicate features

【秀麗】xiùlì (形) beautiful; graceful

私 sī Ⅰ (形) ❶ private; personal: ~章 private seal; signet ❷ selfish: ~心 selfishness ❸ illegal; unlicensed: ~貨 contraband; smuggled goods Ⅱ (副) secretly; privately: 竊竊~語 talk in whispers

【私人】sīrén (名) ❶ private: ~產 private property ❷ personal: ~關係 personal relationship

【私下】sīxià (副) in privacy; secretly

【私心】sīxīn (名) selfish motive; selfish ends; selfishness

【私仇】sīchóu (名) personal grudge; private enmity

【私立】sīlì (形) (of a school, hospital, etc.) private; privately-owned

【私生子】sīshēngzǐ (名) illegitimate child; bastard

【私生活】sīshēnghuó (名) private life

【私交】sījiāo (名) ❶ personal friendship ❷ personal friend

【私有】sīyǒu (形) private: ~經濟部門 private (economiic) sector

【私有制】sīyǒuzhì (名) private ownership

【私自】sīzì (副) secretly; without leave; without permission

【私利】sīlì (名) selfish interests; personal gain

【私事】sīshì (名) private or personal affairs

【私奔】sībēn (動) elope

【私念】sīniàn (名) selfish consideration

【私通】sītōng (動) ❶ have undercover communication with: ~敵特 be in secret communication with enemy agents ❷ have illicit relations with; commit adultery

【私情】sīqíng (名) personal friendship or relationship: 徇~ give special treatment to one's friend or relative; practise favouritism

【私產】sīchǎn (名) private property

【私塾】sīshú (名) old-style private school where the tutor taught Confucian classics

【私憤】sīfèn (名) personal grievance

【私營】sīyíng (形) privately-owned; privately-operated

【私囊】sīnáng (名) private purse; one's own pocket: 中飽~ line one's pockets

秉 bǐng (動) ❶ hold; grasp ❷ control; be in charge of: ~政 be in power

【秉公】bǐnggōng (副) impartially; with justice: ~執法 enforce the law strictly

【秉承】bǐngchéng（動）act on（the instructions or advice of sb.）

【秉性】bǐngxìng（名）natural temperament

科 kē I（名）❶ branch of academic or vocational training: 醫～大學 medical university ❷ subdivision of an administrative unit; section: ～長 section chief ❸〈生〉family: 蟒～爬行動物 Boidae reptiles II（動）be sentenced to: 以萬元罰款 impose（on the defendant）a fine of 10,000 *yuan* RMB

【科幻小說】kēhuàn xiǎoshuō（名）（short for 科學幻想小說 kēxué huànxiǎng xiǎoshuō）science fiction

【科技】kējì（名）（short for 科學技術 kēxué jìshù）science and technology

【科盲】kēmáng（名）❶ innumeracy ❷ innumerate

【科研】kēyán（名）（short for 科學研究 kēxué yánjiū）scientific research: ～成果 achievements in scientific research

【科室人員】kēshì rényuán（名）office staff

【科威特】Kēwēitè（名）Kuwait: ～人 Kuwaiti

【科班】kēbān（名）❶ old-type Chinese opera school ❷ regular or professional training: ～出身 university-educated or professionally trained professionally

【科教片】kējiàopiàn（名）（short for 科學教育影片 kēxué jiàoyù yǐngpiàn）popular science film

【科舉】kējǔ（名）imperial examinations for selecting officials

【科學】kēxué（名）science: ～院 academy of sciences / ～專題討論會 scientific symposium

秋 qiū（名）❶ autumn: 初～ early autumn ❷ harvest time: 大～ harvest season in autumn ❸ year: 千～ 萬代 throughout the ages ❹（Qiū）a surname

【秋天】qiūtiān（名）autumn

【秋令】qiūlìng（名）❶ autumn ❷ autumn weather

【秋色】qiūsè（名）autumn scenery

【秋收】qiūshōu（名）autumn harvest

【秋季】qiūjì（名）autumn; the autumn months

【秋後】qiūhòu（副）after autumn; after the autumn harvest

【秋耕】qiūgēng（名）autumn ploughing

【秋海棠】qiūhǎitáng（名）begonia

【秋莊稼】qiūzhuāngjia（名）autumn crops

【秋播】qiūbō（名）autumn sowing

种 Chóng（名）a surname

秒 miǎo（名）second: 兩分三～ two minutes and three seconds

【秒針】miǎozhēn（名）second hand（of a clock or watch）

【秒錶】miǎobiǎo（名）stopwatch

秕 bǐ（名）shrivelled grain; chaff

【秕糠】bǐkāng（名）❶ shrivelled grain and husks; chaff ❷ trash

秦 Qín（名）❶ another name for Shaanxi Province ❷ a surname

秘 bì

see also mì

【秘魯】Bìlǔ（名）Peru: ～人 Peruvian

秘 mì（形）secret
see also bì

【秘方】mìfāng（名）secret recipe

【秘史】mìshǐ（名）secret history; inside story

【秘书】mìshū（名）secretary：～長 secretary-general

【秘书处】mìshūchù（名）secretariat

【秘诀】mìjué（名）secret：養生～ the secret of keeping fit

【秘密】mìmì I（形）secret; confidential：～情報 confidential information II（名）secret：公開的～ open secret／軍事～ military secrets

秤 chèng（名）balance; steelyard：過～ weigh

【秤杆】chènggǎn（名）arm of a steelyard

秣 mò I（名）fodder II（動）feed（animals）

【秣馬厲兵】mò mǎ lì bīng〈成〉be combat-ready; prepare for war

秫 shú（名）gaoliang; sorghum

【秫秸】shújiē（名）sorghum stalk

租 zū I（動）❶ rent; hire ❷ let（out）; rent out：房子～給學生 rent（out）rooms to students II（名）rent

【租户】zūhù（名）tenant; leaseholder

【租用】zūyòng（動）rent; hire：～小汽車 hire a car

【租佃】zūdiàn（動）（of a landlord）rent out land to tenants

【租金】zūjīn（名）rent; rental

【租界】zūjiè（名）concession

【租約】zūyuē（名）lease：繳訂～ renew the lease

【租借】zūjiè（動）rent; hire; lease

【租賃】zūlìn（動）rent; lease; lease out; charter（a bus, ship, etc.）

秧 yāng（名）❶ seedling：稻～ rice seedling ❷ vine; stem：南瓜～ squash vine ❸ young; fry：魚～子（fish）fry

【秧田】yāngtián（名）rice seedling bed

【秧苗】yāngmiáo（名）rice shoot; rice seedling

【秧歌】yāngge（名）yangko（a folk dance）：扭～ snake a yangko; do a drum dance

秩 zhì

【秩序】zhìxù（名）order; sequence：維持～ maintain order

秸 jiē（名）grain stalk（after threshing）

【秸秆】jiēgǎn（名）grain stalk; straw

移 yí（動）❶ move：把桌子～開 move the table away ❷ change：堅定不～ stand firm

【移民】yímín I（名）migrant：入境～ immigrant／出境～ emigrant II（動）migrate

【移交】yíjiāo（動）turn over; transfer：～工作 hand over one's job to a successor

【移居】yíjū（名）migrate

【移風易俗】yí fēng yì sú〈成〉change established customs and habits; transform traditional practices

【移動】yídòng（動）move：向東～ move eastward

【移植】yízhí（動）transplant

税 shuì（名）tax, levy: 個人所得～ personal income tax

【税收】shuìshōu（名）tax revenue

【税務員】shuìwùyuán（名）tax collector

【税率】shuìlǜ（名）tax rate; tariff rate

【税單】shuìdān（名）tax receipt

【税額】shuì'é（名）amount of tax

稍 shāo（副）a little; a bit; slightly: ～有區別 be slightly different

【稍微】shāowēi（稍許 shāoxǔ）（副）a little; a bit; slightly: ～有點窘 be slightly embarrassed

稈 gǎn（名）stalk; stem

程 chéng I（名）❶ regulation: 操作規～ rules of operation ❷ procedure: 會議議～ agenda of a conference ❸ journey; leg of a journey: 歸～ return journey ❹ distance 行～萬里 travel 10,000 li ❺（Chéng）a surname II（動）estimate: 計日～功 be able to count the days needed to complete a project; have the completion of a project in sight

【程式】chéngshì（名）form; formula; pattern

【程序】chéngxù（名）❶ procedure: 遵循一定～ follow a definite procedure ❷（in automation）programme: ～設計 programming

【程度】chéngdù（名）❶ level: 大專～ junior college level ❷ degree; extent: 在某種～上 to some extent

稃 fū（名）husk

稀 xī（形）❶ scarce; rare: 物以～爲貴. A thing is valued when it is rare. ❷ few; sparse: ～～拉拉的白髮 stray white hair ❸ thin; watery: 墨汁太～了. The ink is too thin.

【稀少】xīshǎo（形）few; rare: 人煙～ sparsely populated

【稀有】xīyǒu（形）rare; uncommon: ～動物 rare animal

【稀客】xīkè（名）rare visitor

【稀飯】xīfàn（名）gruel; porridge; congee

【稀疏】xīshū（動）thin; sparse; few: ～零落 sparse and scattered

【稀裏糊塗】xīlǐhútu（形）incapable of thinking clearly; muddleheaded

【稀薄】xībó（形）thin; sparse

【稀鬆】xīsōng（動）❶ make a poor show: 他們幹起活來，哪個也不～。No one is a sluggard when they start to work. ❷ unimportant: ～小事 trifles

【稀釋】xīshì（動）dilute

【稀爛】xīlàn（形）❶ mashed: 嬰兒吃的蔬菜要煮得～。Vegetables for babies should be cooked to a pulp. ❷ completely smashed: 玻璃打得～。The glass is broken to pieces.

稠 chóu（形）❶ dense ❷ thick: 粥很～。The porridge is thick.

【稠密】chóumì（形）dense: 人口～ densely populated

稚 zhì（形）young; childish

【稚子】zhìzǐ（名）child

【稚氣】zhìqì（名）childishness

稗 bài I（名）barnyard grass; tare II（形）insignificant; unofficial

【稗子】bàizi（名）barnyard millet; barnyard grass; tare

【稗官野史】bàiguān yěshǐ（名）unofficial history; anecdotes

稱 chèn（動）match; suit:（衣服）～身（of clothes）fit one well
see also chēng

【稱心】chènxīn（動）be pleased with sth.: ～如意 very satisfactory; gratifying

【稱職】chènzhí（動）be fully qualified for the job; be competent

稱 chēng I（動）❶ weigh: 給我～半公斤花生。I'd like half a kg. of peanuts, please. ❷ call: ～他為活字典 call him a walking dictionary ❸ praise: 著～於世 world-famous II（名）name: 簡～ for short
see also chèn

【稱王稱霸】chēng wáng chēng bà〈成〉act like an overlord; domineer

【稱兄道弟】chēng xiōng dào dì〈成〉(of men) call each other "brother"; be on the best of terms

【稱呼】chēnghu I（動）call; address: 我們～她小妹。We call her Little Sister. II（名）(form of) address

【稱病】chēngbìng（動）plead illness; pretend illness

【稱得起】chēngdeqǐ（動）be worthy of the title; deserve to be called

【稱道】chēngdào（動）commend; mention: 值得～ deserve a commendation; be praiseworthy

【稱號】chēnghào（名）title; designation: 獲得最佳守門員的～ be given the title of "the best goalkeeper"

【稱頌】chēngsòng（動）eulogize

【稱霸】chēngbà（動）seek hegemony; dominate

【稱讚】chēngzàn（動）praise; extol

種 zhǒng I（名）❶ seed: 穀～ grain seeds ❷ strain; breed: 純～ pure breed ❸ race: 有色人～ coloured races ❹〈生〉species II（量）kind; type; variety: 各～人 all sorts of people
see also zhòng

【種子】zhǒngzǐ（名）seed

【種族】zhǒngzú（名）race: ～歧視 racial discrimination / ～隔離 apartheid

【種種】zhǒngzhǒng（形）all kinds of; a variety of: 製造～借口 cook up various excuses

【種類】zhǒnglèi（名）kind; type; category

種 zhòng（動）plant; grow: ～蔬菜 grow vegetables / ～樹 plant trees
see also zhǒng

【種地】zhòngdì（動）do farm work

【種痘】zhòngdòu I（名）vaccination II（動）vaccinate

【種植】zhòngzhí（動）plant; grow

穀 gǔ（名）❶ cereal; grain ❷ millet

【穀子】gǔzi（名）millet; grain

【穀物】gǔwù（名）cereal; grain

【穀倉】gǔcāng（名）granary; barn

稼 jià I（動）sow: 耕～ sow crops II（名）crops: 莊～ crops

【稼穡】jiàsè（動）sow and get in crops

稿 gǎo（名）❶ draft; sketch: 畫～ rough sketch (for a painting) ❷ original text: 手～ manuscript

【稿子】gǎozi（名）draft

【稿件】gǎojiàn（名）contribution;

manuscript

【稿紙】gǎozhǐ（名）manuscript paper

【稿費】gǎofèi（名）author's remuneration; payment for a piece of writing

稽 jī I（動）examine; check; verify: 無～之談 unfounded rumour; sheer nonsense II（名）（Jī）a surname

【稽查】jīchá I（動）verify; ascertain; check II（名）inspector

【稽核】jīhé（動）check; audit; examine

【稽留】jīliú I（動）stay; stop over: ～數日 stay a few days II（名）stay: 稍作～ make a brief stay

稻 dào（名）rice

【稻田】dàotián（名）paddy field

【稻草】dàocǎo（名）rice straw: ～人 scarecrow

穎 yǐng（形）clever; intelligent

【穎悟】yǐngwù（形）(of a teenager) intelligent; bright

【穎慧】yǐnghuì（形）(of a teenager) intelligent; clever

積 jī I（動）accumulate; amass; hoard II（形）long-standing; age-old; of long accumulation

【積分】jīfēn（名）❶〈體〉score ❷〈數〉integral

【積木】jīmù（名）toy building blocks

【積少成多】jī shǎo chéng duō〈成〉take care of the pence and the pounds will take care of themselves

【積存】jīcún（動）keep in store; save (up)

【積怨】jīyuàn（名）pent-up ill-feeling; long-standing grievances

【積重難返】jī zhòng nán fǎn〈成〉evil practices of long standing are hard to eradicate; deep-entrenched evils die hard

【積累】jīlěi I（動）accumulate: ～資金 accumulate funds II（名）accumulation: ～與消費的比例 the ratio between accumulation and consumption

【積習】jīxí（名）ingrained habit: ～難改 long-standing practices cannot be cast off overnight; old habits die hard

【積極】jījí（形）❶ positive (of attitude, outlook, etc.): ～面 positive aspect ❷ active; enthusiastic; vigorous: ～參加 take an active part in / ～性 enthusiasm

【積極分子】jījí fènzǐ（名）activist

【積勞成疾】jī láo chéng jí〈成〉fall ill from overwork

【積聚】jījù（動）accumulate; amass

【積蓄】jīxù I（動）accumulate; save (money): ～大量資金 accumulate a huge amount of capital II（名）savings; deposit: ～可觀 have sizable savings

【積壓】jīyā（動）keep long in stock: ～物資 stockpiled goods / ～在他心頭的憂慮 the worries that weigh on him

【積攢】jīzǎn（動）〈口〉put away; put by: ～下一筆錢 put by some money

穆 mù I（形）solemn; respectful: 靜～ quiet and solemn II（名）（Mù）a surname

【穆斯林】mùsīlín（名）Moslem; Muslim

穌 sū（動）regain consciousness; revive; come to

穗 suì（名）❶ ear of grain: 稻～ ear of rice ❷ tassel; fringe ❸ (Suì) another name for Guangzhou (Canton) ❹ (Suì) a surname
【穗子】suìzi（名）tassel

穢 huì（形）❶ dirty; filthy ❷ ugly; repulsive
【穢土】huìtǔ（名）garbage; dirt
【穢行】huìxíng（名）notorious misbehaviour
【穢聞】huìwén（名）sex scandal

穩 wěn（形）❶ stable; steady: 汽車停～了。The car pulled up. ❷ sure; certain: ～能按時到達 be certain to arrive on time
【穩步】wěnbù（動）steadily: ～發展旅遊業 steadily develop tourism
【穩妥】wěntuǒ（形）safe; reliable: ～的辦法 a sound approach
【穩定】wěndìng Ⅰ（形）stable Ⅱ（動）stabilize: ～局勢 stabilize the situation / ～劑 stabilizer
【穩固】wěngù（形）firm; solid
【穩重】wěnzhòng（形）(of a person) sedate; steady and reliable
【穩紮穩打】wěn zhā wěn dǎ〈成〉act with caution
【穩健】wěnjiàn（形）❶ steady; firm: 步伐～ firm and steady steps ❷ prudent; cautious; careful: 辦事～ cautious in handling matters / ～派 moderates
【穩當】wěndang（形）reliable; dependable; safe and sure: ～的決定 a safe decision
【穩操勝券】wěn cāo shèng quàn〈成〉success is as good as assured; it's in the bag

穴 部

穴 xué（名）cave; hole
【穴位】xuéwèi（名）acupuncture point

究 jiū Ⅰ（動）examine; probe; investigate: 此事必須追～。We must get to the root of the matter. Ⅱ（副）after all; anyway: 他的耐心終～是有限的。There is, after all, a limit to his patience.
【究竟】jiūjìng Ⅰ（名）outcome; what actually took place: 問個～ get to the bottom of the matter Ⅱ（副）❶ [used in interrogative sentences]exactly; on earth: 這事～怎麼辦? How on earth are we to handle the matter? ❷ after all; anyway: 他～是個孩子。He is a child after all.
【究辦】jiūbàn（動）investigate and deal with: 這些事情應根據情況逐一～。These problems should be dealt with one by one as the case may be.

空 kōng Ⅰ（形）empty; vacant: ～～如也 be absolutely empty; have nothing left Ⅱ（名）sky Ⅲ（副）in vain; to no avail: 他的希望落～了。His hopes were dashed to pieces.
see also kòng
【空手】kōngshǒu（副）empty-handed
【空文】kōngwén（名）stipulations that will never come into force: 不

過是一紙～ be merely a scrap of paper

【空中】kōngzhōng (形) aerial; in the sky: 一樓閣 castles in the air / ～小姐(空姐) (air) hostess

【空幻】kōnghuàn (形) illusory; unreal

【空泛】kōngfàn (形) (of a statement, words, etc.) hollow and vague; generalized

【空投】kōngtóu (名) airdrop

【空洞】kōngdòng Ⅰ(名) hole; cavity Ⅱ(形) devoid of substance

【空軍】kōngjūn (名) air force: ～基地 air base

【空前】kōngqián (形) unprecedented: 這是一絕沒的事。This is something that never happened before, nor will it ever happen again. (This is unprecedented and totally unique.)

【空城計】kōngchéngjì〈成〉"empty-city" ploy; a stratagem to outwit the opponents by presenting a bold front to conceal a weak defence

【空氣】kōngqì (名) air; atmosphere

【空虛】kōngxū (形) devoid of substance; hollow

【空運】kōngyùn (動) airlift

【空間】kōngjiān (名) space

【空想】kōngxiǎng (名) idle dream; Utopian scheme

【空話】kōnghuà (名) empty talk; empty rhetoric; lip service

【空對空導彈】kōng duì kōng dǎodàn (名) air-to-air guided missile

【空談】kōngtán (名) idle talk

【空頭】kōngtóu (形) ❶ (in speculation) selling short ❷ nominal: 開～支票 pass off a bad cheque; make an empty promise

【空蕩蕩】kōngdàngdàng (形) desolate; empty: 街道顯得～的。The streets were deserted.

【空曠】kōngkuàng (空闊 kōngkuò) (形) open and boundless: ～的草原 open grassland stretching far into the distance

【空難】kōngnàn (名) plane crash; air disaster

【空歡喜】kōnghuānxǐ (動) rejoice too soon only to be disappointed

空 kòng Ⅰ(動) leave vacant; leave a space: 中間～兩行 leave a double space in between Ⅱ(形) vacant; unused Ⅲ(名) ❶ blank: 留出個～ leave a space ❷ spare time; leisure: 你有～嗎? Are you free?
see also kōng

【空子】kòngzi (名) ❶ gap in space or time: 抽個～到我們這邊來。Come and see us when you have time to spare. ❷ opportunity (usu. for doing evil); loophole

【空白】kòngbái (名) (of a printed sheet, etc.) empty space; blank: ～點 gap / ～支票 blank cheque

【空閑】kòngxián (空暇 kòngxiá) (名) leisure; spare time

【空隙】kòngxì (名) blank space; gap; interval

【空額】kòng'é (空缺 kòngquē) (名) vacancy

穹 qióng Ⅰ(名) ❶ vault ❷ sky Ⅱ(形) ❶ vaulted ❷ deep: ～谷 deep valley

【穹頂】qióngdǐng (名) dome

【穹蒼】qióngcāng (名) the heavens

穿 chuān (動) ❶ put on (clothes, etc.); wear: ～得很樸素 be sim-

ply dressed ❷ pierce through: 戳~
陰謀 expose a plot ❸ cross; get
through: 橫~馬路 cross the street

【穿小鞋】 chuān xiǎoxié〔動〕〔use.
used in the combination 給人小鞋
穿〕give sb. tight shoes to wear;
make things difficult for sb.

【穿針引綫】 chuān zhēn yǐn xiàn〈成〉
act as a go-between

【穿着】 chuānzhuó (名) dress

【穿梭】 chuānsuō (動) shuttle: ~外
交 shuttle diplomacy

【穿插】 chuānchā Ⅰ(副) alternately:
我們可以安排這兩種工作~進行。
We can make these two types of
work alternate. Ⅱ(動)(in writing,
etc.) interweave; weave in: 導言
中~了有趣的軼事。The introduc-
tion was spiced with interesting
anecdotes.

【穿越】 chuānyuè (動) pass through;
cut across

【穿戴】 chuāndài (名) what one
wears: ~入時 be fashionably
dressed; be dressed à la mode

【穿鑿附會】 chuān zuò fù huì〈成〉
give a far-fetched interpretation

突 tū (動) ❶ dash forward;
charge: ~入敵軍陣地 charge into
enemy positions ❷ suddenly: 局勢
一變。 The situation underwent a
sudden change.

【突出】 tūchū Ⅰ(形) ❶ protruding;
protruded ❷ outstanding: 做出~
的貢獻 make outstanding contributions Ⅱ(動) give emphasis to; give
prominence to: ~個人的作用
stress the role of the individual

【突尼斯】 Tūnísī (名) Tunisia: ~人
Tunisian

【突如其來】 tū rú qí lái〈成〉happen

unexpectedly; appear suddenly

【突突】 tūtū〔象〕(of the heart)
thumping; (of a machine, etc.)
chugging

【突飛猛進】 tū fēi měng jìn〈成〉in
an undertaking, academic achievement, etc.) advance rapidly; develop fast; by leaps and bounds

【突起】 tūqǐ (動) ❶ break out; suddenly appear ❷ rise high; tower

【突破】 tūpò (動) ❶ effect a breakthrough ❷ overcome (difficulties,
etc.); break (restrictions, etc.):
產量~萬噸大關。 The output has
topped the 10,000-ton mark.

【突然】 tūrán (副) suddenly; abruptly; all of a sudden

【突圍】 tūwéi (動) break out of an
encirclement

【突擊】 tūjī (動) ❶ assault; storm:
~隊 shock brigade ❷ do rush
work: ~任務 crash project

【突襲】 tūxí (動) make a surprise attack; make a raid

窄 zhǎi (形) ❶ narrow: 這裏路
~。 The road is narrow here. ❷
narrow-minded

窈 yǎo

【窈窕】 yǎotiǎo (形) (of a woman)
gentle and graceful

窒 zhì (動) obstruct; block

【窒息】 zhìxī (動) stifle; suffocate;
choke: 熱得令人感到~ stifling hot

窘 jiǒng Ⅰ(形) ❶ poor; hard up ❷
embarrassed; ill at ease Ⅱ(動)
abash; embarrass: 不要~他。
Don't taunt him.

【窘迫】 jiǒngpò (形) ❶ impoverished; poverty-stricken ❷ sorely pressed; in a predicament: 處境 ～ be caught in a predicament

【窘境】jiǒngjìng（名）awkward position; predicament: 陷 於 ～ be caught in a dilemma

【窘態】jiǒngtài（窘 相 jiǒngxiàng）（名）embarrassed manner: ～百出 be all embarrassment

窖 jiào Ⅰ（名）cellar Ⅱ（動）store up in a pit: 把白薯一起來 store up the sweet potatoes

窗 chuāng（名）window

【窗户】chuānghu（名）window

【窗花】chuānghuā（名）paper-cut for window decoration

【窗臺】chuāngtái（名）windowsill

【窗簾】chuānglián（名）window curtain

窟 kū（名）❶ hole ❷ lair; den

【窟窿】kūlong（名）❶ hole ❷ deficit

窠 kē（名）nest; den; lair

【窠臼】kējiù（名）（of literary and artistic works）stereotype: 擺脫前人的～ free from conventional techniques

窪 wā Ⅰ（形）sunken; concave Ⅱ（名）depression; cavity

【窪地】wādì（名）low-lying area

【窪陷】wāxiàn（形）（of the ground）hollow; sunken

窩 wō Ⅰ（名）❶ nest; den; lair: 狗～ kennel / 匪～ bandits' lair ❷ hollow; pit: 酒～ dimple Ⅱ（動）❶ shelter; hide ❷ hold in; keep: ～火 smoulder with anger ❸ bend:

鋼筋 bend a steel bar Ⅲ（量）❶（of young animals）brood; litter: 一 ～小狗 a litter of puppies ❷（of outlaws）gang; group: 一～土匪 a gang of bandits

【窩工】wōgōng（動）（of work）be held up owing to poor planning or lack of material

【窩心】wōxīn（動）〈方〉simmer with resentment; feel resentful

【窩棚】wōpeng（名）shed; shanty

【窩窩頭】wōwōtóu（名） steamed maize bread

【窩藏】wōcáng（動）hide; harbour: ～逃犯 harbour an escaped criminal

【窩贓】wōzāng（動）harbour stolen goods

【窩囊】wōnang（動）❶ feel slighted or unwanted; be annoyed: 心裏～ feel slighted ❷ worthless; useless

【窩囊廢】wōnangfèi（名）〈方〉dull-headed and chicken-hearted person; worthless person

窮 qióng Ⅰ（形）poor; impoverished Ⅱ（名）end: 無～無盡 endless; interminable Ⅲ（副）extremely: ～兇極惡 extremely atrocious Ⅳ（動）trace back: ～源溯流 trace the origin and development of an affair

【窮人】qióngrén（名）poor people

【窮山惡水】qióng shān è shuǐ〈成〉bare mountains and turbulent waters; a land of scarcity

【窮年累月】qióng nián lěi yuè〈成〉year in, year out

【窮困】qióngkùn（形）impoverished; destitute

【窮兵黷武】qióng bīng dú wǔ〈成〉mobilize the entire national resources for military ventures

【窮苦】qióngkǔ (形) poor; poverty-stricken

【窮途末路】qióng tú mò lù 〈成〉 blind alley; dead end

【窮奢極欲】qióng shē jí yù 〈成〉 lead a life of extravagance and dissipation

【窮極無聊】qióng jí wú liáo 〈成〉 ❶ bored stiff ❷ senseless; shameless

【窮鄉僻壤】qióng xiāng pì rǎng 〈成〉 remote backward region

【窮盡】qióngjìn (名) limit; end: 人類的智慧是無～的。Human wisdom is infinite.

窨 yáo (名) ❶ kiln ❷ coal pit ❸ cave dwelling

【窨子】yáozi (名)〈方〉brothel

【窨洞】yáodòng (名) cave dwelling

窺 kuī (動) peep: ～視孔 peephole

【窺見】kuījiàn (動) have a glimpse of: 從這首詩裏可以～他的胸懷。From this poem we can get a glimpse of his lofty aspirations.

【窺伺】kuīsì (動) observe secretly and bide one's time

【窺探】kuītàn (動) pry (about)

【窺測】kuīcè (動) spy out

窾 qiào (名) ❶ aperture; opening: 七～ the seven apertures (referring to the eyes, ears, nostrils, and mouth in the human head) ❷ key to sth.: 訣～ trick; knack

【窾門】qiàomén (名) key (to a problem); secret of success

竄 cuàn (動) ❶ flee; run about ❷ change: ～改原文 tamper with the original text

【竄犯】cuànfàn (動) invade; raid:

～領空 invade the air space of a country

【竄逃】cuàntáo (動) flee helter-skelter

竈 zào (名) kitchen range; cooking stove

竊 qiè Ⅰ (動) steal; pilfer Ⅱ (副) secretly; stealthily

【竊取】qièqǔ (動) steal

【竊國】qièguó (動) usurp state power

【竊賊】qièzéi (名) thief; burglar

【竊據】qièjù (動) occupy undeservedly; usurp: ～要津 manoeuvre oneself into high position

【竊聽】qiètīng (動) eavesdrop; tap

【竊聽器】qiètīngqì (名) tapping device; bug

【竊竊私語】qiè qiè sī yǔ (動) talk in whispers

立 部

立 lì Ⅰ (動) ❶ stand ❷ set up: ～銅像 erect a bronze statue ❸ establish: ～新風 introduce a new style of work ❹ exist Ⅱ (形) ❶ vertical; erect: ～式鋼琴 upright piano ❷ immediate; instant: 針療後～見好轉。The acupuncture gave instant relief.

【立戶】lìhù (動) open an account with the bank

【立方】lìfāng Ⅰ (名)〈數〉cube Ⅱ (量) cubic metre

【立方體】lìfāngtǐ (名) cube

【立功】lìgōng (動) make outstanding

contributions; render distinguished service

【立正】lìzhèng (動) stand at attention

【立交橋】lìjiāoqiáo (名) overpass; flyover

【立即】lìjí (立刻 lìkè) (副) at once; immediately; right away

【立志】lìzhì (動) be determined; make a strong determination

【立足】lìzú (動) ❶ have a place to stand on and survive: 獲得~之地 gain a footing ❷ base oneself on

【立足點】lìzúdiǎn (名) foothold; footing

【立法】lìfǎ I (動) make law II (名) law-making; legislation: ~機構 legislature

【立定】lìdìng (動) halt

【立竿見影】lì gān jiàn yǐng 〈成〉 produce immediate results

【立案】lì'àn (動) ❶ register ❷〈法〉file a case

【立時】lìshí (副) immediately

【立國】lìguó (動) found a state

【立場】lìchǎng (名) stand; position

【立意】lìyì I (動) make up one's mind II (名) idea; approach: ~不凡 show originality in one's approach

【立誓】lìshì (動) vow; take a pledge

【立論】lìlùn (動) make a point; advance an argument

【立憲】lìxiàn (名) constitutionalism: 君主~ constitutional monarchy

【立錐之地】lì zhuī zhī dì 〈成〉 a small piece of land: 貧無~ too poor to own a small piece of land; have no room to swing a cat in

【立櫃】lìguì (名) wardrobe

【立體】lìtǐ (形) three-dimensional; stereoscopic

【立體電影】lìtǐ diànyǐng (名) three-dimensional (3D) film; cinerama

【立體聲】lìtǐshēng (名) stereophony

站

站 zhàn I (動) ❶ stand; be on one's feet: 讓我們並肩~在一起。Let us stand side by side. ❷ stop; halt: 快車這裏不~。The express does not stop here. II (名) ❶ station; stop: 汽車~ bus stop ❷ service centre; service station: 醫療~ medical centre / 加油~ petrol station; gas station

【站住】zhànzhù (動) ❶ stop; halt ❷ keep one's feet: 他累得幾乎站不住。He was so exhausted that he could hardly stand on his feet. ❸ stand one's ground; consolidate one's position ❹ hold water; be tenable: 他的解釋站不住。His explanation does not hold water.

【站崗】zhàngǎng (動) keep guard; stand sentry

【站隊】zhànduì (動) line up; stand in line

【站臺】zhàntái (名) platform (in a railway station)

【站臺票】zhàntáipiào (名) platform ticket

【站櫃臺】zhàn guìtái (動) serve as a shop assistant; serve behind a counter

章

章 zhāng (名) ❶ chapter; section: 第三~ the third chapter / 樂~ movement (of a symphony, etc.) ❷ regulations; constitution: 簡章 general regulations / 憲~ charter ❸ order: 雜亂無~ in utter disorder ❹ seal; stamp: 公~ official seal ❺ badge; medal: 袖~ armband / 獎~ medal ❻ (Zhāng) a surname

【章法】zhāngfǎ (名) ❶ art of composition ❷ methodical ways (of doing sth.)

【章魚】zhāngyú (名) octopus

【章程】zhāngchéng (名) rules; regulations; constitution

【章節】zhāngjié (名) chapters and sections

竟 jìng Ⅰ (動) finish; complete; fulfil: 未～之志 an unfulfilled aspiration Ⅱ (介) all through; throughout: ～日 all day long Ⅲ (副) ❶ finally; eventually ❷ unexpectedly; surprisingly ❸ impudently: 他一張口罵人。He had the impudence to swear at me.

【竟自】jìngzì (副) unexpectedly; surprisingly

【竟敢】jìnggǎn (動) dare; have the insolence to: 他一不服從上級命令。He had the audacity to defy orders from above.

【竟然】jìngrán (副) ❶ surprisingly ❷ impudently; impertinently

童 tóng (名) ❶ child: 報～ newsboy ❷ (Tóng) a surname

【童工】tónggōng (名) ❶ child labourer ❷ child labour

【童年】tóngnián (名) childhood

【童話】tónghuà (名) fairy tale

竣 jùn (動) complete; finish

【竣工】jùngōng (動) (of construction, project, etc.) be completed: 提前～ be finished ahead of schedule

豎 shù Ⅰ (形) vertical; perpendicular: ～井 (vertical) shaft Ⅱ (動) stand erect; set upright Ⅲ (名) vertical stroke in a Chinese character

【豎立】shùlì (動) stand (erect): 那裏～着一塊石碑。There stands a stone tablet.

【豎起】shùqǐ (動) erect; set upright

【豎琴】shùqín (名) harp

竭 jié (動) exhaust; drain: ～澤而漁 drain the pond to catch fish; kill the goose that lays the golden eggs

【竭力】jiélì (動) spare no effort; do one's utmost

【竭誠】jiéchéng (副) whole-heartedly; in all sincerity

【竭盡】jiéjìn (動) exhaust; drain: ～挑撥離間之能事 do everything possible to sow discord

端 duān Ⅰ (名) ❶ end: 棍的兩～ the ends of a rod ❷ item; point: 舉其一～ to cite only one example Ⅱ (動) hold sth. level with both hands: ～幾杯茶來 bring in a few cups of tea Ⅲ (形) upright; decent

【端午】Duānwǔ (名) the Dragon Boat Festival (the 5th day of the 5th lunar month)

【端正】duānzhèng Ⅰ (形) upright; proper: 品行～的人 a man of moral integrity Ⅱ (動) make correct: ～學習態度 adopt a correct attitude towards study

【端倪】duānní (名) clue; inkling

【端莊】duānzhuāng (形) composed; dignified

【端量】duānliáng (動) gaze at: 把來人上下～一番 look the visitor up and down

【端詳】duānxiáng Ⅰ (動) scrutinize Ⅱ (名) detail

競 jìng（動）compete; contend; vie

【競走】jìngzǒu（名）〈體〉(heel-and-toe) walking race

【競技】jìngjì（名）athletics; games: 處於最佳～狀態 in top form

【競爭】jìngzhēng（動）compete; rival; vie

【競選】jìngxuǎn（動）stand for election; campaign for (office); run for

【競賽】jìngsài（名）race; contest

竹 部

竹 zhú（名）bamboo

【竹子】zhúzi（名）bamboo

【竹板】zhúbǎn（名）bamboo clappers

【竹帛】zhúbó（名）bamboo slips and silk (used for writing on in ancient times)

【竹刻】zhúkè（名）bamboo carving

【竹林】zhúlín（名）bamboo grove

【竹竿】zhúgān（名）bamboo pole

【竹筏】zhúfá（名）bamboo raft

【竹筍】zhúsǔn（名）bamboo shoot

【竹器】zhúqì（名）bamboo article

【竹簍】zhúlǒu（名）bamboo basket

【竹簡】zhújiǎn（名）bamboo slip

竿 gān（名）pole; rod: 釣魚～ fishing rod

笆 bā（名）basketry

笑 xiào（動）❶ laugh; smile: 誰～在最後,誰～得最好。He laughs best who laughs last. ❷ laugh at; ridicule: 人們都～他異想天開。People all laughed at his fantastic ideas.

【笑柄】xiàobǐng（名）laughing stock: 這使他成了全鎮人的～。This made him the laughing stock of the whole town.

【笑咪咪】xiàomīmī（形）smiling; all smiles; beaming

【笑容】xiàoróng（名）smile: 她滿面～。She was all smiles.

【笑逐顏開】xiào zhú yán kāi〈成〉radiant with smiles

【笑話】xiàohua Ⅰ（名）joke: 説～ tell a joke Ⅱ（動）laugh at; ridicule: 別～他。Don't make fun of him.

【笑裏藏刀】xiào lǐ cáng dāo〈成〉hide one's evil intent behind a smile

【笑嘻嘻】xiàoxīxī（形）grinning

【笑臉】xiàoliǎn（名）smiling face

笊 zhào

【笊籬】zhàolí（名）bamboo, wicker or wire strainer

笠 lì（名）broad-brimmed bamboo hat

笨 bèn（形）❶ silly; foolish; stupid; slow: 他說這些話太～了。It was stupid of him to make such remarks. ❷ cumbersome; clumsy: 粗～的工具 clumsy tool (device)

【笨手笨腳】bènshǒu bènjiǎo（形）clumsy; awkward; all thumbs

【笨拙】bènzhuō（形）clumsy; awkward

【笨重】bènzhòng（形）cumbersome; heavy: ～的家具 cumbersome furniture

【笨蛋】bèndàn（名）〈罵〉silly ass; imbecile; idiot

【笨鳥先飛】bèn niǎo xiān fēi〈成〉slow birds start flying early; those who are slow need to start early

笆 pá

【笆籬】páluo（名）shallow basket

第 dì [prefix for ordinal numbers]:
~一 the first ／ ~五課 the fifth
lesson

【第一手】dìyīshǒu（形）first-hand

【第一名】dìyīmíng（名）first place;
champion

【第一流】dìyīliú（形）first-rate; top
notch

【第三者】dìsānzhě（名）third party

笤 tiáo

【笤帚】tiáozhou（名）whisk broom

笛 dí（名）❶ flute ❷ whistle

笙 shēng（名）〈樂〉*sheng*, a reed
pipe wind instrument

符 fú I（名）❶ symbol ❷ talisman:
護身~ amulet ❸（Fú）a surname II
（動）accord with: 言行不~。One's
words do not tally with one's deeds.

【符合】fúhé（動）agree with; tally
with: ~標準 up to standard

【符號】fúhào（名）symbol; mark;
sign

笞 chī（動）beat with a whip, stick,
etc.

筐 kuāng（名）basket

【筐子】kuāngzi（名）（relatively）
small basket

等 děng I（名）grade; class: 頭~
艙 first-class cabin II（形）equal: 大
小不~ of different sizes III（動）
wait IV（助）❶ [used after a noun
or a pronoun to indicate plural num-

ber]: 我~ we ❷ [used to end an
enumeration]: 在江蘇, 浙江, 安徽
~ 三 省 in the three provinces,
namely, Jiangsu, Zhejiang and Anhui

【等外】děngwài（形）substandard

【等外品】děngwàipǐn（名）substan-
dard goods

【等同】děngtóng（動）equate; put
in the same category

【等到】děngdào（連）by the time

【等於】děngyú（動）❶ be equal to:
二加二~四。Two plus two is four.
❷ amount to

【等待】děngdài（動）wait for: ~時
機 wait for an opportune moment

【等級】děngjí（名）rank; grade

【等候】děnghòu（動）await

【等量齊觀】děng liàng qí guān〈成〉
be put on a par

【等閑】děngxián（形）commonplace;
ordinary: ~視之 treat sth. or sb.
lightly

【等號】děnghào（名）〈數〉equality
sign

【等價】děngjià（名）equal value

策 cè I（名）policy; plan; strategy:
商量對~ discuss countermeasures
II（動）prod into action; urge on:
揚鞭~馬 whip a horse on

【策反】cèfǎn（動）rouse an insurrection within the enemy ranks; instigate defection

【策動】cèdòng（動）instigate; incite

【策略】cèlüè I（名）tactics: 請求~
be tactful II（形）tactful

【策源地】cèyuándì（名）source;
cradle; base

【策劃】cèhuà（動）plot; engineer

筆 bǐ I（名）❶ pen; Chinese writing brush: 粉～ chalk / 執～ take up one's pen; write; do the actual writing ❷ stroke (of the pen, etc. in writing): 敗～ a faulty stroke in calligraphy / 一一帶過 mention in passing ❸ technique of writing, calligraphy or painting: 寫得一一好字 write in a good hand Ⅱ (量) sum: 一大～錢 a large sum of money

【筆下】bǐxià (名) ❶ style of writing: ～不錯 have a good style of writing ❷ wording and purport of an essay: ～留情 (of writing) avoid going too far in condemning sb.

【筆尖】bǐjiān (名) ❶ nib ❷ pencil point ❸ tip of the writing brush

【筆名】bǐmíng (名) pen name; pseudonym

【筆芯】bǐxīn (名) ❶ pencil lead ❷ refill (of a ball-pen)

【筆者】bǐzhě (名) this author; the (present) writer

【筆直】bǐzhí (形) ❶ perfectly straight ❷ erect; upright

【筆法】bǐfǎ (名) ❶ calligraphic style of writing or drawing

【筆底下】bǐdǐxia (名) ability to write: ～來得快 write with ease

【筆迹】bǐjì (名) one's handwriting

【筆架】bǐjià (名) pen-rest; pen-stand; rack for writing brushes

【筆記】bǐjì (名) notes: ～本 note-book

【筆套】bǐtào (名) cap (of a pen or writing brush)

【筆挺】bǐtǐng (形) ❶ erect: 站得～ stand erect ❷ (of clothing) well-pressed

【筆桿】bǐgǎn (名) pen holder; shaft of a pen or writing brush

【筆桿子】bǐgǎnzi (名) ❶ pen holder ❷ facile writer: 耍～ wield a skilful pen

【筆畫】bǐhuà (名) stroke of a Chinese character

【筆筒】bǐtǒng (名) pen container; receptacle for keeping writing brushes

【筆試】bǐshì (名) written examination

【筆誤】bǐwù (名) slip of the pen

【筆調】bǐdiào (名) literary style: 幽默的～ (of writing) humorous touch

【筆鋒】bǐfēng (名) ❶ tip of the writing brush ❷ characteristic style of writing: ～犀利 wield a sharp pen

【筆墨】bǐmò (名) ❶ pen and ink ❷ writing; literary work: 值得費些～ be worth writing about at some length

【筆墨官司】bǐ mò guān si〈成〉battle of words; written polemics

【筆頭】bǐtóu Ⅰ (名) ❶ nib; pen point; hairs of the writing brush ❷ skill of writing: ～快 wield a facile pen; write with facility Ⅱ (形) written: ～作業 written assignment

【筆錄】bǐlù Ⅰ (名) record; notes; written account Ⅱ (動) write down; put down in writing

【筆譯】bǐyì (名) written translation

筒

tǒng (名) ❶ section of thick bamboo ❷ thick tube-shaped object: 傳聲～ megaphone

答

dá
see also dā

【答理】dālǐ (動) respond: 不～ cut sb. dead

【答應】dāying (动) ❶ answer; respond ❷ promise; agree

答 dá (动) ❶ answer; respond: 不~ make no response ❷ return: 报~ repay sb.'s kindness
see also dā

【答拜】dábài (名) return visit

【答案】dá'àn (名) answer; key; solution

【答词】dácí (名) speech in reply

【答复】dáfù (动) reply

【答谢】dáxiè (动) express thanks in return for sb.'s kindness: ~信 thank-you note

【答辩】dábiàn I (动) speak in one's own defence II (名) (of an MA or a Ph.D. thesis) oral defence

筋 jīn (名) ❶ muscle ❷ tendon; sinew: 抽~ have a cramp ❸ 〈口〉veins: 额上露着青~。Veins stand out on one's forehead. ❹ anything that resembles a tendon or vein: 橡皮~ rubber band

【筋斗】jīndǒu (名) ❶ somersault: 翻~ turn a somersault ❷ fall; tumble: 栽了个~ have a fall; trip and fall; suffer a setback

【筋骨】jīngǔ (名) muscles and bones; physique

【筋疲力盡】jīn pí lì jìn 〈成〉entirely exhausted

筍 sǔn (名) bamboo shoot: ~尖 tender tip of a bamboo shoot

【筍乾】sǔngān (名) dried bamboo shoots

【筍鶏】sǔnjī (名) broiler; young chicken

筏 fá (名) raft

筷 kuài (筷子 kuàizi) (名) chopsticks

筢 pá (名) bamboo rake

【筢子】pázi (名) bamboo rake

節 jiē
see also jié

【節骨眼】jiēguyǎn (名) 〈方〉critical stage; juncture: 在這~上，我們需要的是勇氣和決心。At this juncture, what we need is courage and resolution.

節 jié I (名) ❶ parts where two sections of an object meet; joints; node ❷ section; part: 有關章~ relevant chapters and paragraphs ❸ festival; holiday: 中秋~ Mid-Autumn Festival ❹ trifling matter; item: 生活小~ trivial matters of everyday life ❺ moral integrity: 高風亮~ noble qualities; nobility of character ❻ knot; nautical mile ❼ (Jié) a surname II (动) ❶ save; use sparingly: ~水 economize on water; reduce water consumption / ~流 retrench expenditure ❷ restrict; check: ~哀 restrain one's grief ❸ abridge: ~本 abridged edition III (量) section: 第三~車廂 third carriage
see also jiē

【節日】jiérì (名) festival; holiday

【節支】jiézhī (动) cut down on expenditure

【節目】jiémù (名) items on the programme

【節外生枝】jié wài shēng zhī 〈成〉complicate an issue by raising new problems; side issues crop up

【節衣縮食】jié yī suō shí 〈成〉cut

expenses on food and clothing; lead a frugal life

【節拍】jiépāi (名) metre; rhythmic beat in music

【節制】jiézhì (動) do things with restraint or in a regular way: ~飲食 exercise moderation in eating and drinking; be on a diet

【節育】jiéyù (名) birth control

【節省】jiéshěng (動) save; use sparingly

【節食】jiéshí (動) be on a diet

【節約】jiéyuē (動) practise economy

【節奏】jiézòu (名) rhythm

【節能】jiénéng (動) save energy

【節氣】jiéqi (名) ❶ (in lunar calendar) one of the 24 periods of a year ❷ seasonal changes

【節假日】jiéjiàrì (名) holidays

【節減】jiéjiǎn (動) reduce: ~ 經費 reduce expenditure

【節儉】jiéjiǎn I (形) thrifty; economical II (名) economy and frugality

【節餘】jiéyú I (動) have a surplus of money; have enough and to spare II (名) surplus

【節操】jiécāo (名) exemplary moral behaviour; political integrity

【節錄】jiélù (名) excerpt; extract: ~發表 be published in excerpts

筲 shāo (名) pail; bucket

筵 yán (名) feast

【筵席】yánxí (名) feast; banquet

箔 bó (名) ❶ screen (made of reeds, sorghum stalks, etc.) ❷ (large, round) bamboo tray (for raising silkworms) ❸ foil; tinsel: 鋁~ aluminium foil

管 guǎn I (名) ❶ tube; pipe ❷ wind instrument ❸ (Guǎn) a surname II (動) ❶ be in charge of; manage ❷ meddle in; bother about: 這事我不能不~。I'll have to look into the matter. ❸ teach: ~孩子 teach the children to behave themselves III (介) [used in the structure "管...叫..."]: 大家~他叫"話匣子"。People call him "chatterbox". IV (量): 一~毛筆 a writing brush

【管束】guǎnshù (動) restrict; control

【管事】guǎnshì (動) ❶ be in charge ❷ be effective: 這辦法真~。The method really works.

【管制】guǎnzhì (名) ❶ control: 外匯~ foreign exchange control ❷ surveillance

【管押】guǎnyā (動) keep in custody; detain

【管弦樂】guǎnxiányuè (名) orchestral music: ~隊 orchestra

【管保】guǎnbǎo (動) guarantee; assure

【管理】guǎnlǐ (動) administer; manage; run: 行政~人員 administrative personnel

【管道】guǎndào (名) pipeline; piping

【管樂器】guǎnyuèqì (名) 〈樂〉 wind instrument

【管窺】guǎnkuī (名) partial view: ~所及 from my point of view

【管轄】guǎnxiá (動) have jurisdiction over; administer

箕 jī (名) ❶ (of a finger-print) loop ❷ see 簸箕 (bòji)

箍 gū I (動) bind round; hoop: ~

桶 bind a hoop round a bucket Ⅱ
(名) hoop; band

箋 jiān (名) ❶ letter
paper; notepaper: 便 ~ notepaper ❷ letter
annotations; notes
【箋註】jiānzhù (名) notes on classical Chinese texts

算 suàn Ⅰ (名) computation: 珠 ~
reckoning on the abacus Ⅱ (動) ❶
calculate; compute: ~ 一 ~ 成本
reckon the cost ❷ count in;
include: ~ 上司機加 20 人 twenty
people including the driver ❸ plan;
scheme: 打 ~ 去上海 plan to go to
Shanghai ❹ count as; take as: 可以
~ 得上是一個極好機會 can count
as a splendid chance ❺ suppose;
reckon: 我 ~ 你比我小兩歲。I
guess you are two years my junior.
❻ count: 這個人話說了可以不
~。This chap often goes back on his
work. ❼ [followed by 了] let it be;
forget it: ~ 了，別爭了。There,
there, no more arguing. Ⅲ (副) finally; in the end: 總 ~ 不虛此行
have not made a fruitless trip after
all
【算命】suànmìng (動) tell sb.'s fortune: ~ 先生 fortune-teller
【算計】suànjì (動) ❶ compute;
reckon ❷ plan; intend: 他 ~ 着去
桂林旅遊 He is contemplating a
sightseeing trip to Guilin. ❸
expect; think: 我 ~ 他們馬上就要
到達車站了。I suppose they'll be
arriving at the station soon. ❹ plot
against sb.: ~ 陷害無辜的人
scheme against innocent people
【算是】suànshì (副) at long last: 現
在 ~ 萬事俱備了。Everything is

ready at long last.
【算術】suànshù (名) arithmetic
【算數】suànshù (動) count: 他的話
~。He means what he says. (His
words count.)
【算賬】suànzhàng (動) ❶ do accounts ❷ make out a bill: 服務員，
~ 吧。Waiter, bring us the bill
please. ❸ settle accounts (with
sb.): 我要跟他 ~。I've a score to
settle with him.
【算盤】suànpan (名) abacus: 這是
打如意 ~。This is wishful thinking.

筝 zhēng (名) zheng, a Chinese
zither with 21 or 25 strings

篇 piān Ⅰ (名) ❶ a piece of
writing: 短 ~ 小說 short story ❷
sheet: 歌 ~ song sheet Ⅱ (量)
[used for certain kinds of writing
such as essays, novels, etc.]: 一 ~
報道 a (news) report
【篇目】piānmù (名) ❶ titles and
headings of chapters and sections in
a book ❷ table of contents
【篇章】piānzhāng (名) ❶ writings;
articles ❷ chapters and sections
【篇幅】piānfu (名) ❶ length (of a
piece of writing) ❷ space: ~ 有限。
Space is limited. (Space forbids.)

箭 jiàn (名) arrow
【箭步】jiànbù (名) quick big step;
big stride: 一個 ~ 竄過去 make a
dash for it in one big stride
【箭桿】jiàngǎn (名) arrow shaft
【箭靶子】jiànbǎzi (名) target (for
archery)
【箭樓】jiànlóu (名) watch-tower
with arrow slits, usu. built on a city
gate

【箭頭】jiàntóu (名)❶ arrowhead ❷ arrow (as a sign)

範 fàn (名)❶ model; example ❷ limits: 就～ keep within limits

【範文】fànwén (名) model essay

【範本】fànběn (名) model copybook (for calligraphy or painting)

【範例】fànlì (名) model; good example

【範圍】fànwéi (名) scope; sphere: 勢力～ sphere of influence

【範疇】fànchóu (名) category

箱 xiāng (名) box; case: 信～ mail box; post box

篆 zhuàn (名)❶ seal character: 大～ big-seal style / 小～ small-seal style ❷ seal

【篆刻】zhuànkè (名) seal cutting

【篆書】zhuànshū (名) seal character

篙 gāo (名) punt-pole

篝 gōu

【篝火】gōuhuǒ (名) bonfire; campfire

篤 dǔ (形)❶ sincere; earnest ❷ serious; critical: 病～ be terminally ill

【篤定】dǔdìng Ⅰ (副) certainly Ⅱ (形) composed

【篤信】dǔxìn (動) believe devoutly in

【篤學】dǔxué (形) diligent in study

築 zhù (動) build; construct: 修～鐵路 construct a railway

篛 ruò

【篛竹】ruòzhú (名)〈植〉indocalamus

篡 cuàn (動) usurp; seize

【篡改】cuàngǎi (動) tamper with; distort

【篡位】cuànwèi (動) usurp the throne

【篡奪】cuànduó (動) usurp

蓬 péng (名)❶ awning: 帳～ tent ❷ sail

篩 shāi Ⅰ (名) sieve; sifter; screen Ⅱ (動) sift; sieve

【篩子】shāizi (名) sieve; sifter; screen

【篩分】shāifēn (動) screen; sieve

【篩選】shāixuǎn (動) screen; sieve; carefully select

箆 bì Ⅰ (名) double-edged, fine-toothed comb (usu. made of bamboo): ～子 double-edged, fine-toothed comb Ⅱ (動) comb one's hair

簇 cù Ⅰ (動) cluster round Ⅱ (量) cluster; bunch: 一～花 a bunch of flowers

【簇新】cùxīn (形) brand-new (usu. of clothes)

【簇擁】cùyōng (動) swarm; flock round

篾 miè (名) thin bamboo strip

【篾匠】mièjiàng (名) craftsman who makes bamboo articles

【篾席】mièxí (名) bamboo-strip mat

簍 lǒu (名) basket

簧 huáng (名)❶〈樂〉reed: ～風琴 reed organ ❷ spring: 彈～spring

簪 zān (名) hairpin

【簪子】zānzi（名）hair clasp

簡 jiǎn Ⅰ（名）❶ strip of bamboo or wood used for writing or inscribing on in ancient times ❷ letter; note; written message Ⅱ（形）brief; laconic; simple: ～言之 to put it in a nutshell Ⅲ（動）simplify: 精～機構 streamline the administrative struction

【簡介】jiǎnjiè（名）synopsis; summary; brief

【簡化】jiǎnhuà（名）make simple; simplify

【簡化漢字】jiǎnhuà Hànzì（名）simplified Chinese character

【簡明】jiǎnmíng（形）concise; brief

【簡易】jiǎnyì（形）simple and easy; handy: ～讀物 simplified readings

【簡直】jiǎnzhí（形）virtually; simply; really: 我～不能相信自己的眼睛。I can hardly believe my eyes.

【簡便】jiǎnbiàn（形）simple and convenient; easy: 携帶～ easy to carry

【簡陋】jiǎnlòu（形）（of houses, facilities, etc.）simple; shabby; crude

【簡要】jiǎnyào（形）brief; summary

【簡政放權】jiǎn zhèng fàng quán（動）streamline the administration and decentralize power

【簡訊】jiǎnxùn（名）news in brief; newsflash

【簡捷】jiǎnjié（形）direct and outspoken; forthright

【簡略】jiǎnlüè（形）brief; sketchy

【簡章】jiǎnzhāng（名）general regulations

【簡單】jiǎndān（形）❶ easy to learn or understand; not complicated or complex: ～明瞭 succinct; brief and explicit ❷ casual; crude; rude;

他的態度有點～。He is a bit blunt. ❸ [often used in the negative] ordinary; common: 他可不～。He is really out of the ordinary.

【簡短】jiǎnduǎn（形）short; brief: ～的報導 a brief report

【簡報】jiǎnbào（名）bulletin

【簡稱】jiǎnchēng Ⅰ（名）abbreviated form Ⅱ（動）be called ... for short

【簡編】jiǎnbiān（名）[often used in titles of books] concise edition; outline: 中國革命史～ A Brief History of the Chinese Revolution

【簡潔】jiǎnjié（形）terse; succinct: 行文～ written in a terse style

【簡練】jiǎnliàn（形）（of writing）succinct; terse

【簡寫】jiǎnxiě Ⅰ（名）simplified form of a Chinese character Ⅱ（動）simplify a book (for beginners)

【簡歷】jiǎnlì（名）resumé; curriculum vitae

【簡樸】jiǎnpǔ（形）simple; plain; unpretentious

【簡譜】jiǎnpǔ（名）numbered musical notation

【簡體字】jiǎntǐzì（名）simplified Chinese character

簿 bù（名）book: 支票～ chequebook

【簿子】bùzi（名）notebook

【簿記】bùjì（名）bookkeeping: ～員 bookkeeper

簾 lián（名）curtain

簸 bǒ（動）winnow: 吉普車在崎嶇的道路上顛～着。The jeep was bumping along a rugged road.
see also bò

【簸揚】bǒyáng（動）winnow

【簸穀機】bǒgǔjī（名）winnower; winnowing fan

簸 bò

see also bǒ

【簸箕】bòji（名）❶ dustpan ❷ winnowing pan

簫 xiāo（名）xiao, a vertical bamboo flute

簽 qiān Ⅰ（動）sign (one's name)：～字 sign; affix one's signiture Ⅱ（名）label; sticker; marker

【簽名】qiānmíng Ⅰ（動）sign one's name; autograph Ⅱ（名）signature

【簽到】qiāndào（動）register one's attendance; sign in

【簽訂】qiāndìng（動）(conclude and) sign：～合同 sign a contract

【簽註】qiānzhù（動）write comments on a document

【簽發】qiānfā（動）sign and issue (a document, etc.)

【簽署】qiānshǔ（動）sign (an official document)

【簽證】qiānzhèng（名）visa：～申請表 visa application form ／ 入境～ entry visa ／ 出境～ exit visa ／ 過境～ transit visa

籌 chóu Ⅰ（名）chip; tally：略勝一～ be a notch above sb.; be slightly better Ⅱ（動）plan; prepare：運～ devise strategies

【籌建】chóujiàn（動）make preparations for the setting up of (a school, hospital, factory, etc.)

【籌措】chóucuò（動）raise (money)

【籌集】chóují（動）raise（money）：～資金 raise funds

【籌備】chóubèi（動）prepare and plan; make preparations for

【籌劃】chóuhuà（動）plan

【籌碼兒】chóumǎr（籌馬 chóumǎ）（名）chip; counter

籃 lán（名）❶ basket ❷〈體〉goal; basket：～板球 rebound

【籃子】lánzi（名）basket：菜～ vegetable basket; food basket

【籃球】lánqiú（名）basketball

籍 jí（名）❶ book; written work：軍事書～ military literature ❷ membership：開除學～ be expelled from school ❸ home town; native place：原～福建 hail from Fujian (Province) ❹ citizenship：美～華人 American of Chinese descent; Chinese-American ❺（Jí）a surname

【籍貫】jíguàn（名）native place; birthplace

籠 lóng（名）❶ cage：竹～ bamboo cage ／ ～中之鳥 caged bird ❷ food steamer

see also lǒng

【籠屜】lóngtì（名）steam box; food steamer

【籠頭】lóngtóu（名）bridle; headstall

籠 lǒng（動）cover; shroud

see also lóng

【籠絡】lǒngluò（動）win sb. over with petty favours：～人心 court popularity

【籠統】lǒngtǒng（副）vaguely; in general terms：～地講 generally speaking

【籠罩】lǒngzhào（動）shroud; enwrap：雲霧～山峰。The peak is enveloped in mist.

籟 lài（名）noise：萬～無聲。All is

quiet and still.

籬 lí（名）bamboo or twig fence (around a house, etc.); hedge; hedge-row: 樹~ hedge; hedge-row

【籬笆】líbā（名）bamboo or twig fence

簍 luó（名）bamboo basket

【簍筐】luókuāng（名）bamboo (or wicker) basket

籲 yù（動）appeal; plead: 呼~ appeal

米 部

米 mǐ（名）❶ (uncooked) rice ❷ shelled seed: 花生~shelled peanut ❸（Mǐ）a surname

【米色】mǐsè（名）cream-coloured

【米老鼠】mǐlǎoshǔ （名） Micky Mouse

【米制】mǐzhì（名）metric system

【米酒】mǐjiǔ（名）rice wine

【米粉】mǐfěn（名）❶ rice flour ❷ rice-flour noodles

【米黃】mǐhuáng（形）cream-coloured

【米湯】mǐtāng（名）thin rice gruel

【米飯】mǐfàn（名）(cooked) rice

【米糠】mǐkāng（名）rice bran

【米糧川】mǐliángchuān（名）bread-basket of the land; granary

籽 zǐ（名）(of vegetables and certain other plants) seed

【籽棉】zǐmián（名）unginned cotton

籼 xiān

【籼米】xiānmǐ（名）polished long-grained nonglutinous rice

【籼稻】xiāndào（名） long-grained nonglutinous rice; *indica* rice

粉 fěn（名）❶ powder: 麵~ flour / 花~ pollen / 香~ face powder ❷ pink colour

【粉身碎骨】fěn shēn suì gǔ〈成〉die in a most horrible manner (with one's bones smashed to pieces)

【粉刺】fěncì（名）acne

【粉刷】fěnshuā（動）whitewash

【粉筆】fěnbǐ（名）chalk

【粉碎】fěnsuì（動）❶ smash to smithereens ❷ shatter; destroy; crush

【粉飾】fěnshì（動）whitewash [oft. used in a figurative sense]

【粉塵】fěnchén（名）powderlike industrial waste

【粉墨登場】fěn mò dēng chǎng〈成〉〈貶〉make oneself up and go on stage; embark on a political venture

粒 lì Ⅰ（名）grain: 鹽~ grains of salt Ⅱ（量）一~種子 a seed

【粒子】lìzǐ（名）〈物〉particle: ~加速器 particle accelerator

【粒肥】lìféi（名）granulated fertilizer

粘 zhān（動）glue; stick: ~牙 stick to the teeth

【粘連】zhānlián（名）〈醫〉adhesion

【粘貼】zhāntiē（動）paste; stick: ~年畫 stick New Year pictures on the wall

粗 cū Ⅰ（形）❶ thick ❷ unrefined; coarse: ~布 coarse cloth ❸ rough; rude ❹ careless Ⅱ（副）roughly: ~通文字 be barely literate

【粗心】cūxīn（形）careless; negligent

【粗劣】cūliè（形）of inferior quality

【粗壯】cūzhuàng（形）❶（of a person）stalwart ❷（of sound）resonant

【粗枝大葉】cū zhī dà yè（形）careless; sloppy

【粗俗】cūsú（形）vulgar; coarse

【粗活】cūhuó（名）unskilled labour

【粗陋】cūlòu（形）rough and crude

【粗重】cūzhòng（形）❶ deep in sound: ～的喘息聲 heavy breathing ❷ massive: ～的家具 cumbersome furniture ❸ thick and heavy: ～的筆觸（in painting, calligraphy）strong and sturdy strokes ❹ heavy: ～的工作 strenuous work

【粗笨】cūbèn（形）❶ clumsy ❷ heavy; cumbersome

【粗略】cūlüè（形）rough: ～的估計 rough estimate

【粗淺】cūqiǎn（形）superficial; shallow

【粗疏】cūshū（形）careless; inattentive

【粗話】cūhuà（名）coarse language

【粗製濫造】cū zhì làn zào（動）produce crudely

【粗魯】cūlǔ（形）unrefined; boorish

【粗暴】cūbào（形）rude; brutal

【粗糙】cūcāo（形）❶ rough; coarse: ～的手 gnarled hands ❷ crude

【粗獷】cūguǎng（形）❶ rough ❷ bold; dashing

【粗糧】cūliáng（名）coarse food grain（e. g. maize, sorghum, etc.）

粟 sù（名）❶ millet ❷（Sù）a surname

粥 zhōu（名）gruel; porridge

粵 Yuè（名）another name for Guangdong Province

【粵劇】yuèjù（名）Guangdong opera

梁 liáng（名）fine grain

粳 jīng

【粳米】jīngmǐ（名）husked roundish-grained nonglutinous rice

【粳稻】jīngdào（名）roundish-grained nonglutinous rice; *japonica* rice

粲 càn Ⅰ（形）（of a smile）bright; beaming Ⅱ（名）smile

粽 zòng

【粽子】zòngzi（名）rice dumpling wrapped in reed leaves

粹 cuì（形）❶ pure: ～白 snow-white ❷ quintessence: 精～ the cream; the elite

精 jīng Ⅰ（形）❶ purified or selected: ～兵 crack troops ❷ perfect; best: 字句～練 precise and well-chosen words ❸ fine; accurate ❹ clever; astute ❺ good .(at); skilled: ～於針灸 be good at acupuncture Ⅱ（副）❶ down to minute details: ～讀 read carefully; intensive reading ❷ extremely: 我的衣服淋得～濕. My clothes are soaked with rain. Ⅲ（名）❶ essence: 樟腦～ spirit of camphor ❷ energy; vigour: 無～打采 listless; in low spirits ❸ sperm; semen: ～子 sperm ❹ ethereal being: 狐狸～ bewitching slut

【精力】jīnglì（名）energy; stamina: ～旺盛 be full of vigour; be in the prime of life

【精心】jīngxīn（副）with great care; painstakingly

【精巧】jīngqiǎo（形）elegant; exquisite

【精打細算】jīng dǎ xì suàn〈成〉careful planning and calculation

【精光】jīngguāng（副）with everything gone; completely: 票不到一個鐘頭就賣得～。The tickets were all sold out in less than an hour.

【精良】jīngliáng（形）excellent; fine in quality: 製作～with fine workmanship

【精壯】jīngzhuàng（形）able-bodied

【精明】jīngmíng（形）shrewd and resourceful

【精明強幹】jīng míng qiáng gàn〈成〉astute and capable

【精度】jīngdù（名）precision

【精美】jīngměi（形）choice; exquisite: ～的手工藝品 exquisite handicrafts

【精品】jīngpǐn（名）article of top-notch quality; choice article

【精英】jīngyīng（名）the best and brightest; cream; elite

【精神】jīngshén（名）❶ spirit; soul: ～狀態 state of mind ❷ gist; substance: 抓住～實質 grasp the gist

【精神】jīngshen Ⅰ（名）spirits; vitality: 打起～ invigorate oneself; rouse oneself（to do sth.）Ⅱ（形）energetic; lively

【精神分裂症】jīngshén fēnlièzhèng（名）〈醫〉schizophrenia

【精神病】jīngshénbìng（名）psychosis; mental disorder

【精神衰弱】jīngshén shuāiruò（名）〈醫〉neurosis

【精疲力竭】jīng pí lì jié〈成〉exhausted; fatigued; fagged out

【精益求精】jīng yì qiú jīng〈成〉be ever ready to improve one's skill; always endeavour to do better and better

【精悍】jīnghàn（形）❶（of a person）astute and able ❷（of writing）pithy

【精通】jīngtōng（動）be expert at; be well versed in

【精耕細作】jīng gēng xì zuò〈成〉intensive farming

【精彩】jīngcǎi（形）marvelous; superb; wonderful: ～的表演 superb performance

【精密】jīngmì（形）precise; accurate: ～儀器 precision instrument

【精細】jīngxì（形）meticulous; extremely careful

【精湛】jīngzhàn（形）excellent; consummate

【精華】jīnghuá（名）quintessence; cream

【精當】jīngdàng（形）（of words）well-chosen and appropriate to the context

【精幹】jīnggàn（形）❶（of a group）small in number but very efficient ❷（of a person）astute and capable

【精煉】jīngliàn（動）refine: 原油要送到煉油廠去～。The crude oil will be funneled to the refinery for purification.

【精裝】jīngzhuāng（名）（of books）clothbound: ～本 de luxe edition

【精製】jīngzhì（動）manufacture with special care: ～糕點 superfine pastry

【精粹】jīngcuì（名）best and brightest; cream; elite

【精練】jīngliàn（形）succinct; pithy

【精確】jīngquè (形) accurate; exact

【精銳】jīngruì (形) (of military units) crack; first-rate

【精選】jīngxuǎn Ⅰ (動) hand-pick; carefully select: ～品 choice article Ⅱ (名) 〈礦〉 ore dressing

【精緻】jīngzhì (形) exquisite; elegant

【精雕細刻】jīng diāo xì kè 〈成〉 work with meticulous care

【精簡】jīngjiǎn (動) streamline; retrench: ～機構 streamline the structure

【精闢】jīngpì (形) incisive; penetrating; in-depth; pithy

【精髓】jīngsuǐ (名) marrow; essence

【精靈】jīnglíng (名) spirit; ethereal being; goblin

【精鹽】jīngyán (名) table salt; refined salt

鄰 lín

【鄰鄰】línlín (形) (of water) clear

糊 hū (動) plaster: ～牆 plaster a wall
see also hú; hù

糊 hú Ⅰ (動) stick with paste; paste Ⅱ (名) gruel; porridge: 玉米～ maize gruel Ⅲ (形) (of food) burnt
see also hū; hù

【糊口】húkǒu (動) make a living

【糊塗】hútu (形) muddled; confused: 他越說，我越～。The more he said, the more confused I became.

糊 hù (名) paste: 芝蔴～ sesame mush
see also hū; hú

【糊弄】hùnong (動) 〈方〉 ❶ deceive; fool ❷ do a sloppy job

糖 táng Ⅰ (名) ❶ sugar: ～衣 sugarcoating ❷ candy: ～果 sweets; candy; confectionery Ⅱ (形) sugared; in syrup: ～葫蘆 stick of sugarcoated haws

【糖水】tángshuǐ (名) syrup

【糖尿病】tángniàobìng (名) diabetes

【糖精】tángjīng (名) saccharin

【糖廠】tángchǎng (名) sugar refinery

【糖醋】tángcù (形) sweet and sour: ～黃魚 yellow croaker in sweet and sour sauce

【糖漿】tángjiāng (名) syrup: 止咳～ cough mixture

糕 gāo (名) cake; pudding

【糕點】gāodiǎn (名) cake; pastry

糙 cāo (形) coarse: 皮膚粗～ rough skin

【糙米】cāomǐ (名) brown rice; unpolished rice

糜 mí Ⅰ (名) ❶ gruel ❷ (Mí) a surname Ⅱ (形) rotten; putrescent Ⅲ (動) waste

【糜費】mífèi (動) waste: 厲行節約，防止～。Practise strict economy and stop waste.

【糜爛】mílàn (形) rotten; corrupt: ～不堪 rotten to the core; extremely corrupt

糠 kāng Ⅰ (名) bran; husk Ⅱ (形) (of a radish) hollow and spongy

糟 zāo Ⅰ (名) distillers' grains Ⅱ (形) ❶ pickled with grains or pickled in wine: ～豆腐 pickled bean curd ❷ rotten; not sound: 她的情緒很～。She is in a bad mood. ❸ in a mess: 你把事情全搞～了。You have made a mess of everything.

【糟粕】zāopò（名）dross; dregs; scum

【糟糕】zāogāo（形）how terrible; too bad: ～! 票丟了。My God! I've lost my ticket.

【糟蹋】zāota（動）❶ waste; ruin; spoil: 不要～食品。Don't let any food run to waste. ❷ insult; trample: ～婦女 attack a woman sexually

糞 fèn（名）excrement; manure; night soil

【糞土】fèntǔ（名）muck; dirt; sth. absolutely worthless

【糞肥】fènféi（名）manure

【糞便】fènbiàn（名）excrement and urine

糧 liáng（名）grain; food

【糧店】liángdiàn（名）grain shop

【糧食】liángshi（名）grain; cereals: ～定量供應 food grain rationing

【糧草】liángcǎo（糧秣 liángmò）（名）army provisions

【糧倉】liángcāng（名）granary; barn

【糧票】liángpiào（名）grain coupon

【糧稅】liángshuì（名）grain tax

【糧棧】liángzhàn（名）storehouse for grain

糯 nuò（形）(of cereal) glutinous

【糯米】nuòmǐ（名）glutinous rice

糰 tuán（名）dumpling

【糰子】tuánzi（名）dumpling

糴 dí（動）buy grain

糸 部

系 xì（名）❶ system; series: 銀河～ the Milky Way system ❷ department: 數學～ department of mathematics

糾 jiū（動）❶ involve ❷ assemble: ～合 gang up; band together ❸ rectify; put right: 有錯必～。Wrongs must be righted whenever discovered.

【糾正】jiūzhèng（動）rectify; redress: ～不良傾向 check unhealthy social trends

【糾紛】jiūfēn（名）dispute; controversy: 勞資～ labour-management dispute

【糾偏】jiūpiān（動）rectify a wrong tendency in policy; correct a deviation from the right course of action

【糾集】jiūjí（糾合 jiūhé）（動）〈貶〉gang up; gather together: ～一羣歹徒 gather together a bunch of ruffians

【糾葛】jiūgé（名）entanglement; dispute

【糾察】jiūchá Ⅰ（動）maintain order at a mass rally Ⅱ（名）picket: 設置～綫 set up a picket line

【糾纏】jiūchán（動）❶ be entangled; be involved: 他跟許多名聲不好的人～在一起。He got mixed up with quite a few disreputable people. ❷ pester; badger

紅 hóng（形）❶ red ❷ successful; lucky ❸ favourite

【紅人】hóngrén（名）person in sb.'s grace; a rising star

【紅十字會】Hóngshízìhuì（名）the Red Cross

【紅外綫】hóngwàixiàn（名）〈物〉infrared ray

【紅血球】hóngxuěqiú（名）red blood cell; erythrocyte

【紅汞】hónggǒng（紅藥水 hóngyàoshuǐ）（名）〈藥〉mercurochrome

【紅利】hónglì（名）bonus; extra dividend

【紅茶】hóngchá（名）black tea

【紅暈】hóngyùn（名）blush; flush

【紅腫】hóngzhǒng（形）red and swollen

【紅領巾】hónglǐngjīn（名）❶ red scarf（worn by Young Pioneer）❷ Young Pioneer

【紅綠燈】hónglǜdēng（名）traffic light

【紅塵】hóngchén（名）this mortal world: 看破 ～ see through the vanity of human life

【紅潤】hóngrùn（形）ruddy; rosy

【紅薯】hóngshǔ（名）sweet potato

紀 Jǐ（名）a surname
see also jì

紀 jì（名）❶ record; notes: ～年 annals ❷ discipline; system of regulations: 目無法 ～ have no respect for law and discipline ❸ age; era; century: 中世 ～史 medieval history ❹〈地〉period: 第三 ～ Tertiary period
see also jǐ

【紀元】jìyuán（名）❶ beginning of an era ❷ epoch; era: 開創人類歷史的新 ～ usher in a new epoch in human history

【紀行】jìxíng（名）travel notes; travelogue

【紀念】jìniàn I（動）honour the memory of; commemorate; mark: ～法國大革命兩百週年 commemorate the bicentenary of the French Revolution II（形）commemorative: ～ 郵票 commemorative stamp III（名）souvenir; memento: 留作 ～ keep sth. as a souvenir

【紀念堂】jìniàntáng（名）memorial hall

【紀念碑】jìniànbēi（名）monument: 人民英雄 ～ the Monument to the People's Heroes

【紀要】jìyào（名）summary; outline: 新聞 ～ news in brief

【紀律】jìlǜ（名）discipline: 加强 ～ 性 enhance discipline

【紀實】jìshí（名）truth; eye-witness account: 宮廷政變 ～ a true account of a palace coup d'état

【紀檢】jìjiǎn（名）inspection of discipline

紉 rèn（動）❶ sew; stitch ❷ thread（a needle）: ～針 thread a needle

約 yāo（動）〈口〉weigh: 她～了五斤梨。She weighed out five jin of pears.
see also yuē

約 yuē I（動）❶ make an appointment; arrange: 我們～好在門口見面。We agreed to meet at the gate. ❷ invite: ～人吃飯 invite sb. to dinner ❸ restrict; confine: 制 ～ restrict II（名）appointment; pact; treaty: 踐 ～ keep an appointment / 條 ～ pact; treaty III（副）about;

approximately: ～十小時 about ten hours

see also yāo

【約旦】Yuēdàn（名）Jordan: ～人 Jordanian

【約束】yuēshù Ⅰ（動）restrain; confine Ⅱ（名）restriction; restraint

【約定】yuēdìng（動）agree to; arrange; make an appointment

【約法】yuēfǎ（名）provisional constitution

【約計】yuējì（動）be roughly estimated at; come approximately to

【約略】yuēlüè（形）general; rough: 這不過是一種～估計。This is but a rough estimate.

【約莫】yuēmo（副）about; or so: ～二十人 some twenty people

【約會】yuēhuì（名）appointment; date; rendezvous

【約請】yuēqǐng（動）invite

【約數】yuēshù（名）❶ approximate number ❷〈數〉divisor

紈 wán（名）fine silk fabric

【紈袴子弟】wán kù zǐ dì（成）dandy; playboy

紊 wěn（形）disorderly; messy: 有條不～ in good order

【紊亂】wěnluàn（名）disorder; confusion: 消化系統～ disorder of the digestive system

素 sù Ⅰ（形）❶ white (colour of mourning) ❷ plain; quiet; unadorned: 衣着樸～ be simply dressed ❸ natural; native: ～性 one's nature ❹ vegetarian: ～油 vegetable oil Ⅱ（副）usually; customarily: ～昧平生 have never had the pleasure of making sb.'s ac-

quaintance Ⅲ（名）❶ vegetable; vetetarian food: ～餐 vegetarian meal ❷ (basic) element: 稀有元～ rare element

【素材】sùcái（名）(of art and literature) source material

【素來】sùlái（副）always; customarily: 對他我們～是尊敬的。We have always held him in respect.

【素食】sùshí（名）vegetarian diet; vegetarian food

【素淨】sùjing（形）(of colour) plain but with a quiet grace

【素菜】sùcài（名）vegetable dish; vegetarian food

【素描】sùmiáo（名）❶ (in painting) sketch ❷ literary sketch

【素雅】sùyǎ（形）simple but elegant; unadorned but tasteful

【素養】sùyǎng（名）accomplishment: 有～的作家 accomplished writer

【素質】sùzhì（名）quality: 提高服務人員的～ raise the quality of the service personnel

索 suǒ Ⅰ（名）❶ large rope or chain: ～道 cableway Ⅱ（動）❶ search; look for ❷ demand; ask: ～價甚昂。The asking price is pretty high. Ⅲ（形）insipid; dull: ～然寡歡 lonely and unhappy

【索引】suǒyǐn（名）index

【索性】suǒxìng（副）just as well; simply: 我們去也是遲到，～不去好了。We would be late anyway, so we may just as well not go.

【索取】suǒqǔ（動）demand; ask for; extort: 向大自然～財富 wrest wealth from nature

【索馬里】Suǒmǎlǐ（名）Somalia: ～

人 Somali

紋 wén (名) lines; vein: 指～ fingerprint / 皺～ wrinkles

【紋理】wénlǐ (名) vein; texture

【紋路】wénlù (名) lines; grain

紡 fǎng (動) spin

【紡車】fǎngchē (名) spinning wheel

【紡紗】fǎngshā (動) spin

【紡紗工】fǎngshāgōng (名) spinner

【紡錘】fǎngchuí (名) spindle

【紡織】fǎngzhī (動) spin and weave: ～工業 textile industry

純 chún (形) ❶ pure: ～金 solid gold ❷ simple: ～屬無知. It is pure ignorance. ❸ skilful; well-versed; accomplished: 雕刻技藝～熟 well-versed in sculpture ❹ net: ～利 net profit

【純正】chúnzhèng (形) pure: 他說的是～的普通話. He speaks standard Chinese.

【純淨】chúnjìng (形) pure and clean: 溪水～。 The water of the brook is as clear as crystal.

【純真】chúnzhēn (形) pure; sincere

【純粹】chúncuì Ⅰ (形) pure Ⅱ (副) solely; purely: ～出於偶然 by sheer chance; accidentally

【純種】chúnzhǒng (名) purebred

【純熟】chúnshú (形) skilful: 她的演技～。 Her acting is superb.

【純潔】chúnjié (形) pure; chaste

【純樸】chúnpǔ (形) simple and honest

紐 niǔ (名) ❶ button ❷ link; bond

【紐扣】niǔkòu (名) button

【紐帶】niǔdài (名) link; tie: 感情的～ bonds of affection

【紐襻】niǔpàn (名) button loop

紗 shā (名) ❶ yarn: 粗紡毛～ woollen yarn ❷ gauze: 窗～ window screen

【紗巾】shājīn (名) gauze kerchief

【紗布】shābù (名) gauze

【紗窗】shāchuāng (名) screen window

【紗罩】shāzhào (名) ❶ gauze or screen cover (for food) ❷ mantle (of a lamp)

【紗線】shāxiàn (名) yarn

【紗錠】shādìng (名)〈紡〉spindle

【紗櫥】shāchú (名) screen cupboard

納 nà (動) ❶ let in; receive: 吐故納新 expel the old and take in the new ❷ accept; adopt: 採～建議 accept sb.'s suggestion ❸ pay: ～貢(of a vassal state) offer tributes ❹ sew; stitch

【納入】nàrù (動) fit into; bring into: ～計劃 incorporate into the plan

【納米比亞】Nàmǐbǐyà (名) Namibia: ～人 Namibian

【納西族】Nàxīzú (名) the Naxi (Nahsi) nationality

【納涼】nàliáng (動) refresh oneself in the cool

【納悶】nàmèn (動) feel puzzled; be bewildered

【納稅】nàshuì (動) pay taxes

【納稅人】nàshuìrén (名) tax-payer

【納賄】nàhuì (動) ❶ take bribes ❷ offer bribes

【納福】nàfú (動) lead a happy family life

【納粹】Nàcuì (名) Nazi: ～分子 Nazi

【納粹主義】Nàcuì zhǔyì（名）Nazism

紕 pī

【紕漏】pīlòu（名）careless mistake; slip

紛 fēn（形）numerous; confused

【紛至沓來】fēn zhì tà lái〈成〉come in succession

【紛紛】fēnfēn（副）in great numbers; in succession: ～進入城區 flock to urban areas

【紛紜】fēnyún（形）confused and confusing: 眾說～。Opinions differ.

【紛亂】fēnluàn（形）confused; in confusion

【紛繁】fēnfán（形）multifarious and complicated: 事務～ have a heavy load of work; be snowed under with work

【紛擾】fēnrǎo（形）in chaos or turmoil

級 jí I（名）❶ rank; level: 最高～會談 top-level talks; summit ❷ grade; form: 一年～小學生 pupils in the first grade ❸ step: 拾～而上 ascend the steps ❹〈語〉degree: 最高～ the superlative degree II（量）step; stage: 三－運載火箭 three-stage carrier rocket

【級別】jíbié（名）grade; rank

紙 zhǐ（名）paper: 打包～ brown paper

【紙上談兵】zhǐ shàng tán bīng〈成〉be an armchair strategist; indulge in empty talk

【紙板】zhǐbǎn（名）paperboard: 硬～ cardboard

【紙條】zhǐtiáo（名）slip of paper

【紙張】zhǐzhāng（名）paper

【紙牌】zhǐpái（名）playing cards

【紙煙】zhǐyān（名）cigarette

【紙幣】zhǐbì（名）paper currency; note

【紙醉金迷】zhǐ zuì jīn mí〈成〉be intoxicated by luxury and extravagance; wallow in the mire of dissipation

【紙漿】zhǐjiāng（名）paper pulp; pulp

【紙繩】zhǐshéng（名）paper string

紮 zā（動）tie; bind: 用彩帶把盒子～起來 tie the box with a coloured ribbon

see also zhā

紮 zhā（動）encamp; pitch (a tent)

see also zā

【紮營】zhāyíng（動）pitch a tent; encamp

累 léi

see also lěi; lèi

【累贅】léizhui I（動）❶ burdensome; superfluous ❷ not concise; redundant II（名）burden; nuisance; millstone round the neck

累 lěi I（動）❶ amass; accumulate: 積～資金 accumulate capital ❷ involve; implicate: ～及家人 involve one's family ❸ pile (stones, etc.) one on top of another: 危如～卵 as precarious as piled-up eggs; in an utterly precarious situation II（形）continuous; consecutive: 成年～月 throughout the years; year in, year out

see also léi; lèi

【累犯】lěifàn（名）habitual criminal; recidivist

【累年】 lěinián（副）year in, year out; for years

【累計】 lěijì Ⅰ（動）add up Ⅱ（名）(grand) total

【累進】 lěijìn（名）progression: ～所得稅 progressive income tax

【累累】 lěiléi Ⅰ（副）repeatedly: ～勸其從善 repeatedly advise sb. to do good Ⅱ（形）countless; numerous: 果實～ laden with fruit

【累積】 lěijī（動）accumulate; amass; add up

累 lèi Ⅰ（形）tired; exhausted Ⅱ（動）❶ tire; wear out: 過度勞～ over-exert oneself ❷ toil; do hard work

see also léi; lěi

絆 bàn（動）stumble; trip: 被石頭～了一下 stumble over a stone

【絆住】 bànzhù（動）hinder; hold back; tie up: 他被家務～了。She was tied down by household chores.

【絆倒】 bàndǎo（動）(cause to) trip; (cause to) stumble

【絆腳石】 bànjiǎoshí（名）stumbling block; obstacle

紺 gàn（名）dark purple

組 zǔ Ⅰ（動）organize; form: 改～內閣 reshuffle the cabinet Ⅱ（名）group: 科研小～ a scientific research group ／ 分～ split into groups Ⅲ（量）group; set: 一～數字 a set of figures

【組成】 zǔchéng（動）be composed of; consist of: 委員會由七人～。The committee consists of seven members.

【組合】 zǔhé Ⅰ（動）make up; compose: 詞組是由詞一～而成。A

phrase is made up of a group of words. Ⅱ（名）combination: ～鑽牀 combination drilling machine/ ～音響 stereo components

【組曲】 zǔqǔ（名）〈樂〉suite

【組建】 zǔjiàn（動）organize; set up (an institution, unit, etc.)

【組裝】 zǔzhuāng（動）assemble; put together the parts of a machine

【組歌】 zǔgē（名）〈樂〉suite of songs

【組閣】 zǔgé（動）form a cabinet

【組稿】 zǔgǎo（動）(of an editor) commission authors to write on a given topic

【組織】 zǔzhī Ⅰ（動）organize; form: ～聯歡晚會 organize a get-together Ⅱ（名）❶ organization: 下屬～ subordinate organization ❷ tissue: ～療法 tissue therapy

紳 shēn（名）gentry

【紳士】 shēnshì（名）gentleman; gentry

細 xì（形）❶ thin; fine; slender: ～絲 fine shred ❷ soft and thin: 她嗓子很～。She has a soft voice. ❸ minute; trifling: ～情節很～的故事 a story filled with fine descriptive details ❹ careful; detailed: ～說 tell in detail ❺ fine; delicate; exquisite: 活兒～ fine workmanship

【細小】 xìxiǎo（形）small; tiny; trivial

【細心】 xìxīn（形）careful; thoughtful

【細水長流】 xì shuǐ cháng liú〈成〉❶ practise economy to make resources last long ❷ build up little by little

【細雨】 xìyǔ（名）drizzle

【細則】xìzé（名）detailed rules and regulations

【細胞】xìbāo（名）cell

【細密】xìmì（形）❶ fine; close: 這塊地毯織得～。This rug is fine and closely woven. ❷ detailed: ～的觀察 minute observation

【細菌】xìjūn（名）germ; bacterium

【細微】xìwēi（形）slight; subtle: ～的變化 slight change; inperceptible change

【細節】xìjié（名）detail

【細嫩】xìnèn（形）delicate; tender

【細心】xìxīn（形）meticulous; careful; minute: 深入～的分析 indepth and minute analysis

【細膩】xìnì（形）❶ fine; delicate: ～的瓷質 fine china ❷ exquisite; detailed: ～的描寫 minute description

【細糧】xìliáng（名）flour or rice

紬 chù（形）inadequate: 相形見～ be cast into the shade by comparison

終 zhōng Ⅰ（名）❶ end; finish: 有始有～ carry sth. one begins through to the end ❷ death: 臨之際 when dying; when one breathes one's last Ⅱ（副）in the end; eventually: ～會成功 will succeed in the end Ⅲ（形）whole; entire: ～天之恨 lifelong regret

【終日】zhōngrì（副）all day; all day long

【終止】zhōngzhǐ（動）stop; end; terminate: 合同將自動～。The contract will be terminated automatically.

【終生】zhōngshēng（副）one's whole life: ～不忘 never forget as long as one lives

【終年】zhōngnián Ⅰ（副）all year round Ⅱ（名）age at which one dies: ～九十歲 die at the age of ninety

【終身】zhōngshēn（副）all one's life; lifelong: ～制 life tenure

【終於】zhōngyú（副）at last; finally

【終結】zhōngjié（名）end; conclusion

【終場】zhōngchǎng（名）end of a performance or show

【終端】zhōngduān（名）terminal

【終點】zhōngdiǎn（名）❶ terminal point; destination ❷〈體〉finish

【終歸】zhōngguī（終究 zhōngjiū）（副）eventually; after all; in the end: 他～會回心轉意的。He'll come round eventually.

紫 zǐ（形）purple; violet

【紫丁香】zǐdīngxiāng（名）（early）lilac

【紫外綫】zǐwàixiàn（名）〈物〉ultraviolet ray

【紫菜】zǐcài（名）〈植〉laver

【紫羅蘭】zǐluólán（名）violet

【紫藥水】zǐyàoshuǐ（名）〈藥〉gentian violet

絮 xù Ⅰ（名）wadding: 棉～ cotton wadding Ⅱ（動）wad with cotton: ～棉襖 wad a coat with cotton

【絮叨】xùdao（形）long-winded

絞 jiǎo Ⅰ（動）❶ twist; wring; mix up: 把毛巾～乾 wring the towel dry／許多事情～在一起了。Many things got entangled. ❷ hang ❸ wind; coil ❹ ream Ⅱ（量）skein: 一～毛綫 a skein of knitting wool

【絞刑】jiǎoxíng（名）execution by hanging: 處以～ send sb. to the gallows

【絞車】jiǎochē（名）winch; windlass

【絞索】jiǎosuǒ（名）hangman's noose

【絞痛】jiǎotòng（名）angina

【絞結】jiǎojié（動）entangle; tangle

【絞盡腦汁】jiǎo jìn nǎo zhī〈成〉rack one's brains

結 jiē（動）bear
see also jié

【結巴】jiēba I（動）stammer; stutter II（名）stammerer

【結實】jiēshi（形）❶ solid; durable ❷ sturdy; of a powerful build

結 jié（動）❶ tie up; make a knot: ~紮 ligate ❷ congeal; curdle ❸ combine; form: ~社 form an association ❹ end; put an end to: 了一椿產權糾紛 put an end to a dispute over property II（名）knot: 打活~ tie a slipknot
see also jiē

【結仇】jiéchóu（結怨 jiéyuàn）（動）harbour a feeling of enmity: 彼此結下仇恨 bear hatred against each other

【結石】jiéshí（名）concretion; calculus

【結冰】jiébīng（動）freeze; ice up

【結成】jiéchéng（動）form; forge: ~姐妹院校 become twin colleges

【結合】jiéhé（動）❶ link closely with; combine: ~目前條件制訂計劃 draw up plans in light of the present circumstances ❷ be united in wedlock

【結交】jiéjiāo（動）forge social relationships with; associate with

【結局】jiéjú（名）outcome; upshot: 比賽~很難預料。The outcome of the competition is anybody's guess.

【結束】jiéshù（動）conclude; finish; terminate: ~語 concluding remarks

【結尾】jiéwěi（名）ending; final phase: 故事的~ the ending of the story

【結伴】jiébàn（動）go in a group: ~遠行 travel together on a long jour-

---

統 tǒng I（名）❶ interconnection: 財貿系~ organizations in the fields of finance and commerce ❷ tube-shaped part of clothing, etc.: 長~襪 stockings II（形）all; unified; centralized: ~配 under centralized distribution

【統一】tǒngyī I（動）unify: ~戰綫 united front II（形）unified; centralized: ~招生 unified enrolment

【統考】tǒngkǎo（名）unified entrance examination to college, etc.

【統共】tǒnggòng（副）in all

【統治】tǒngzhì（動）rule; govern

【統計】tǒngjì I（名）statistics: ~表 statistical chart II（動）count; add up

【統帥】tǒngshuài（名）commander

【統率】tǒngshuài（動）command

【統統】tǒngtǒng（通通 tōngtōng）（副）all; completely; without exception

【統艙】tǒngcāng（名）steerage（passenger accommodation）

【統購統銷】tǒnggòu tǒngxiāo（名）state monopoly in purchasing and marketing farm produce

【統籌】tǒngchóu（動）make overall plans

【統籌兼顧】tǒng chóu jiān gù〈成〉do central planning with due consideration for all sectors and localities concerned

ney

【結果】jiéguǒ Ⅰ（名）result; fruit; outcome: 體格檢查的～ results of a physical checkup Ⅱ（副）as a result; at last: ～雙方達成了協議。Finally the two sides reached an agreement. Ⅲ（動）finish off; put an end to (sb.'s life)

【結拜】jiébài（動）be tied in a vow of brotherhood or sisterhood: ～爲姐妹 become sworn sisters

【結核】jiéhé（名）tuberculosis: 肺～ pulmonary tuberculosis

【結婚】jiéhūn（動）marry; get married

【結彩】jiécǎi（動）festoon: 門前結～ festoon the entrance with ribbons and strips of coloured paper

【結晶】jiéjīng Ⅰ（動）crystallize Ⅱ（名）crystal; crystallization; fruit; quintessence

【結盟】jiéméng（動）align; ally: 不～運動 non-aligned movement

【結業】jiéyè（動）conclude one's studies (in a short-term course)

【結算】jiésuàn（動）settle accounts; balance accounts

【結構】jiégòu（名）structure; organization: 混凝土～ concrete structure / 文章的～ structure or organization of an essay

【結論】jiélùn（名）conclusion: 過早下～ jump to conclusions

【結髮夫妻】jié fà fū qī〈成〉 husband and wife of the first marriage

【結餘】jiéyú（名）surplus; balance

【結親】jiéqīn（動）❶ marry; get married ❷ (of two families) become related through marriage

【結識】jiéshí（動）get acquainted with; get to know

【結黨營私】jié dǎng yíng sī〈成〉gang up to pursue selfish ends

絨 róng（名）❶ fine hair; down: 貉～ racoon dog fur / 鴨～被 eiderdown quilt ❷ cloth with a soft nap: 棉～ cotton velvet

【絨毛】róngmáo（名）fine hair; down

【絨布】róngbù（名）flannelette; cotton flannel

【絨衣】róngyī（名）sweat shirt

【絨綫】róngxiàn（名）❶ floss for embroidery ❷ knitting wool

【絨褲】róngkù（名）sweat pants

【絨繡】róngxiù（名）〈工美〉woollen needlepoint tapestry; woollen embroidery: ～掛毯 woollen needlepoint tapestry

絕 jué Ⅰ（動）sever; break off: 和外界隔～ be secluded from the outside world Ⅱ（形）❶ exhausted; at an end: 斬盡殺～ exterminate ❷ desperate; despairing: ～處達生 luckily get out of a desperate situation; have a narrow escape ❸ superb; fabulous: ～藝 consummate art or skill Ⅲ（副）❶ extremely; by far: ～大部分人 the great majority of people ❷ [placed before a negative expression] absolutely; ever: ～不失信 never go back on one's word ❸ leave no leeway: 把事做～ leave no room for manoeuvre

【絕口】juékǒu（動）❶ [used only after 不] stop talking; cease mentioning: 對這幅畫讚不～ praise the painting profusely; speak in lavish praise of the painting ❷ keep one's mouth shut; avoid the mention of:

～不提 never breathe a word about it

【絕交】 juéjiāo（動）(of friends or states) sever relations

【絕技】 juéjì（名）unrivalled craftsmanship; marvellous feat; stunt

【絕妙】 juémiào（形）magnificent; superb; ingenious

【絕招】 juézhāo（名）unique feat; stunt: 有 ～ have some trick up one's sleeve

【絕育】 juéyù（名）〈醫〉sterilization

【絕版】 juébǎn（形）out of print

【絕迹】 juéjì（動）disappear; be extinct

【絕食】 juéshí（動）be on a hunger strike

【絕後】 juéhòu（形）❶ without offspring ❷ unlikely to be repeated; unique: 空前～ without either precedent or a possible recurrence

【絕症】 juézhèng（名）fatal disease; hopeless case

【絕頂】 juédǐng（副）utterly; exceedingly: ～ 聰明 exceedingly intelligent

【絕望】 juéwàng（動）be in despair

【絕密】 juémì（形）top-secret; strictly confidential

【絕無僅有】 jué wú jǐn yǒu〈成〉unique; extremely rare

【絕路】 juélù（名）blind alley; dead end

【絕種】 juézhǒng（動）(of a species) be extinct

【絕對】 juéduì Ⅰ（形）absolute; unconditional: ～ 信任 absolute trust Ⅱ（副）absolutely; to the letter: ～ 信守合同 carry out the contract to the letter

【絕境】 juéjìng（名）impasse; deadlock

【絕緣】 juéyuán Ⅰ（動）be isolated; be cut off Ⅱ（名）〈物〉insulation

給 gěi Ⅰ（動）❶ give; assign: ～他一個機會。Give him a chance. ❷ let; allow Ⅱ（介）❶ for; to: 他～大家辦了許多事。He has done a lot for all of us. ／ ～父母寫信 write (a letter) to his parents ❷ [used in a passive voice]: 窗户～風吹開了。The window was blown open by the wind.

see also jǐ

【給以】 gěiyǐ（動）give; grant

給 jǐ（動）supply; provide: 補～綫 supply line ／ 配～ ration ／ 自～自足 self-sufficient

see also gěi

【給予】 jǐyǔ（動）give; afford: ～ 獎勵 give awards ／ ～ 幫助 give sb. a hand; render assistance

【給養】 jǐyǎng（名）provisions (for the armed forces)

絇 xuàn（形）gorgeous; colourful

【絢麗】 xuànlì（形）brilliant; gorgeous: ～多姿 gorgeous and lovely

【絢爛】 xuànlàn（形）splendid

絳 jiàng（形）deep purplish-red; crimson

【絳紫】 jiàngzǐ（形）dark reddish purple

絡 lào

see also luò

【絡子】 làozi（名）❶ small net for holding a folding fan, etc. ❷ spool for winding yarn

絡 luò Ⅰ（名）❶ net ❷ sth. that is

like a net; network: 血管網~ the blood vessel network Ⅱ（動）❶ wrap up with a net ❷ twine: ~綫 reel thread in
see also lào

【絡腮鬍子】luòsāi húzi（名）whiskers

【絡繹不絕】luòyì bùjué（形）in a continuous stream: 人們~地走進禮堂。People streamed into the auditorium.

絲 sī（名）❶ silk ❷ fine thread of any kind ❸ tiny bit; slight trace: 一~風也沒有。There isn't even a light puff of wind.

【絲瓜】sīguā（名）〈植〉towel gourd; dishcloth gourd

【絲毫】sīháo（副）[used mostly in negative sentences] in the slightest degree: ~沒有改變 have not changed a bit

【絲絨】sīróng（名）velvet

【絲綿】sīmián（名）silk floss

【絲綢】sīchóu（名）silk（cloth）: ~之路 Silk Road; Silk Route

【絲綫】sīxiàn（名）silk thread; silk yarn

【絲織品】sīzhīpǐn（名）silk fabric; silk knit goods

綁 bǎng（動）bind; tie up: 捆~ truss up

【綁架】bǎngjià（動）kidnap

【綁票】bǎngpiào（動）kidnap（for ransom or for other purposes）

【綁腿】bǎngtuǐ（名）puttee

經 jīng Ⅰ（名）❶〈紡〉warp; lengthwise yarn: ~紗 warp ❷〈地〉longitude ❸〈中醫〉channel（of energy circulation）❹ Chinese

classics: 名不見~傳 a mere nonentity ❺ menstruation: ~期 menstrual period; period Ⅱ（動）❶ go through; pass by: 流~中原 flow across the Central Plains ❷ manage; administer; run: ~商 go into business ❸ sustain; endure: ~不起聲色誘惑 cannot resist the temptations of sensual pleasure Ⅲ（介）after; through: ~小組討論做出決定 make a decision through panel discussion Ⅳ（形）regular; normal
see also jìng

【經久】jīngjiǔ（形）❶ prolonged; lasting: ~不息的掌聲 prolonged applause ❷ durable: ~耐穿 stand wear; be durable

【經手】jīngshǒu（動）handle; conduct: ~救濟款 handle relief funds

【經心】jīngxīn（形）careful; conscientious

【經由】jīngyóu（介）via; by way of

【經年累月】jīng nián lěi yuè〈成〉for months and years on end

【經受】jīngshòu（動）experience; suffer

【經典】jīngdiǎn Ⅰ（名）❶ classics ❷ scripture; sutra Ⅱ（形）classical

【經度】jīngdù（名）longitude; LONG

【經紀人】jīngjìrén（名）broker; agent

【經常】jīngcháng Ⅰ（形）everyday; regular Ⅱ（副）regularly; often

【經理】jīnglǐ Ⅰ（動）manage; deal with: ~進出口貿易 handle import and export Ⅱ（名）manager; managing director

【經過】jīngguò Ⅰ（動）pass by; go through Ⅱ（介）through; after: ~各有關方面協商,問題解決了。

The problem was solved through consultations with all parties concerned. Ⅲ（名）course（of an event）：詳述事件～ recount the incident from beginning to end

【經絡】jīngluò（名）〈中醫〉channels（for the circulation of vital energy in the body, along which acupuncture points are located）

【經費】jīngfèi（名）fund; expenditure

【經管】jīngguǎn（動）take charge of; administer

【經銷】jīngxiāo（經 售 jīngshòu）（動）deal in; sell

【經歷】jīnglì Ⅰ（動）undergo; experience：千 辛 萬 苦 encounter countless hardship Ⅱ（名）experience：個人～ personal experience

【經營】jīngyíng（動）manage; operate

【經濟】jīngjì Ⅰ（名）❶ economy：搞活～ enliven the economy ❷（of an individual or household）financial condition Ⅱ（形）❶ economic：～特區 special economic zone ／ ～學 economics ❷ significant for economy：～作物 industrial crop; cash crop ❸ economical：～大方的禮品 inexpensive but presentable gift

【經濟指標】jīngjì zhǐbiāo（名）〈經〉economic indicator; economic norm

【經濟核算】jīngjì hésuàn（名）〈經〉economic accounting; business accounting

【經濟旅行】jīngjì lǚxíng（名）budget travel

【經濟艙】jīngjìcāng（名）〈民航〉coach class; economy class; tourist class

【經驗】jīngyàn（名）experience：沒

有～ without experience

經 jīng（名）〈紡〉warp
see also jìng

絹 juàn（名）thin, stiff silk

【絹花】juànhuā（名）〈工美〉silk flower

【絹畫】juànhuà（名）painting on silk

綏 suí

【綏靖】suíjìng（動）pacify; appease

緊 jǐn Ⅰ（形）❶ tight; tense：繃得太～ be stretched too tight ❷ firm; fast：他～～握住我的手。He firmly grasped my hand. ❸ close：～鄰 next-door or close neighbour ❹ urgent; imperative：加～施工 step up the construction ❺ hard up：手頭～ be short of money ❻ strict; rigid：他對小孩管得很～。He is very strict with his children. Ⅱ（動）tighten：～一～螺絲釘 tighten the screw Ⅲ（副）closely：在後面～跟 follow sb. closely

【緊迫】jǐnpò（形）pressing; imminent

【緊俏】jǐnqiào（形）（of commodities）in short supply but in great demand; hard to come by

【緊要】jǐnyào（形）crucial; important：～時刻 crucial moment

【緊急】jǐnjí（形）urgent; emergent; critical：如果發生～情況 in the event of emergency

【緊急出口】jǐnjí chūkǒu（名）emergency exit

【緊急着陸】jǐnjí zhuólù（名）emergency landing

【緊急樓梯】jǐnjí lóutī（名）emergency staircase

【緊缺】jǐnquē（形）in short supply

【緊密】jǐnmì I（副）closely II（形）thick and fast: 雪片～。Snowflakes fell thick and fast.

【緊張】jǐnzhāng（形）❶ nervous ❷ tense ❸ in short supply

【緊湊】jǐncòu（形）compact; terse

【緊縮】jǐnsuō（動）cut down; curtail; retrench: ～開支 retrench the expenditure

綜 zōng（動）put together

【綜合】zōnghé I（動）synthesize; sum up II（形）synthetical; comprehensive: ～大學 comprehensive university

【綜合症】zōnghézhèng（名）syndrome

【綜述】zōngshù（動）summarize; sum up

綻 zhàn（動）split; burst: 破～ a burst seam

綾 líng（名）damask silk

【綾羅綢緞】língluó chóuduàn（名）silks and satins; costly dresses

緒 xù（名）❶ thread ❷ order in sequence: 一切就～。Everything is in order. ❸ mood: 心～不佳 be in a bad mood

【緒論】xùlùn（緒言 xùyán）（名）introduction

綺 qǐ I（名）figured silk fabric II（形）beautiful

【綺麗】qǐlì（形）beautiful: 風景～。The scenery is beautiful.

線 xiàn I（名）❶ thread; wire: 尼龍～ nylon thread ❷ line; route: 運輸～ transportation route ❸ boundary; brink: 貧困～ poverty

line II（形）made of cotton: ～襪子 cotton socks III（量）一～希望 a gleam of hope

【線索】xiànsuǒ（名）clue

【線條】xiàntiáo（名）〈美術〉line

【線圈】xiànquān（名）〈電〉coil

【線路】xiànlù（名）❶ line; route ❷〈電〉circuit

【線裝書】xiànzhuāng shū（名）thread-bound book

【線繩】xiànshéng（名）cotton rope

綴 zhuì（動）❶ sew; stitch: ～扣子 sew a button on (a coat, etc.) ❷ embellish; decorate: 點～ set off; embellish

綽 chāo（動）grab; take up: ～起工具就幹 grab a tool and start to work right away
see also chuò

綽 chuò（形）ample; spacious
see also chāo

【綽號】chuòhào（名）nickname

【綽綽有餘】chuò chuò yǒu yú〈成〉more than sufficient; enough and to spare

網 wǎng I（名）❶ net: 落～ (of a criminal) be captured ❷ network: 電視～ television network II（動）❶ net: ～着兩條武昌魚 net two bluntsnout breams ❷ cover as with a net

【網球】wǎngqiú（名）❶ tennis: 草地～ lawn tennis ❷ tennis ball

【網兜】wǎngdōu（名）string bag

【網絡】wǎngluò（名）〈電〉network

【網點】wǎngdiǎn（名）shops of a sales or service network

【網羅】wǎngluó I（名）net for

catching fish or birds; trap Ⅱ(動) enlist the services of

綱 gāng (名) key link; guiding principle: 提 ～ 挈領 concentrate on the main points

【綱目】gāngmù (名) detailed outline

【綱要】gāngyào (名) outline

【綱領】gānglǐng (名) programme; guiding principle; main headings

緋 fēi (形) red: ～ 紅的晚霞 red evening clouds

綸 lún (名) synthetic fibre: 滌 ～ polyester fibre

綢 chóu (名) silk

【綢緞】chóuduàn (名) silks and satins

綹 liǔ (量): 一 ～ 頭髮 a tuft of hair / 一 ～ 毛綫 a skein of knitting wool

維 wéi (動)❶ link; hold together: ～ 繫人心 maintain popular morale ❷ safeguard; uphold

【維生素】wéishēngsù (名) vitamin

【維妙維肖】wéi miào wéi xiào 〈成〉 lifelike: 這是一幅 ～ 的畫像。This portrait is true to life.

【維吾爾族】Wéiwú'ěrzú (名) Uygur (Uighur) nationality (in northwest China)

【維持】wéichí (動) maintain; keep: ～ 治安 maintain public order

【維修】wéixiū (動) maintain; service: ～ 手冊 maintenance manual

【維新】wéixīn (名) reform; reformation

【維護】wéihù (動) safeguard; protect: ～ 和平共處五項原則 uphold the Five Principles of Peaceful Coexistence

綿 mián Ⅰ(名) silk floss Ⅱ(形)❶ soft: 軟 ～ ～ 的聲音 soft voice ❷ continuous

【綿亙】miángèn (動) stretch in a connected line

【綿羊】miányáng (名) sheep

【綿延】miányán (動) extend far; stretch long: 山脈 ～ 數國。The mountains stretch across several countries.

【綿紙】miánzhǐ (名) tissue paper

【綿裏藏針】mián lǐ cáng zhēn 〈成〉 a kindly face masks a stony heart

【綿薄】miánbó (名)〈謙〉my meagre strength; limited power: 竭盡 ～ do what is in one's power (to help)

綠 lù see also lǜ

【綠林】lùlín (名) band of outlaws: ～ 好漢 outlaws in the forest; heroes in the greenwood

綠 lǜ (形) green see also lù

【綠化】lǜhuà (動) afforest; cover with vegetation: ～ 這一地區 plant trees in this district; surround this district with greenery

【綠地】lǜdì (名) space reserved for greenery

【綠豆】lǜdòu (名) mung bean

【綠豆芽】lǜdòuyá (名) mung bean sprouts

【綠肥】lǜféi (名) green manure

【綠油油】lǜyōuyōu (形) green and

lustrous: 一片～的稻田 a stretch of green paddy fields

【绿洲】lǜzhōu (名) oasis

【绿茶】lǜchá (名) green tea

【绿灯】lǜdēng (名) ❶ green (traffic) light ❷ permission; consent: 爲這些人開～ give the green light to those people

【绿寶石】lǜbǎoshí (名) emerald

缔 dì (动) ❶ form; conclude ❷ restrain: 取～ ban

【缔交】dìjiāo (动) ❶ forge ties of friendship ❷ establish diplomatic relations

【缔约】dìyuē (动) conclude a treaty

【缔约国】dìyuēguó (名) signatory states

【缔造】dìzào (动) found; create: ～者 founder

【缔结】dìjiē (动) conclude: ～和约 conclude a peace treaty

编 biān Ⅰ (动) ❶ weave; plait; braid: ～辮子 plait the hair ❷ organize; arrange: ～成四组 divide into four groups ❸ edit; compile: ～雜誌 edit a magazine ❹ compose; write: ～兒歌 write a nursery rhyme ❺ fabricate; cook up: ～瞎話 fabricate a lie Ⅱ (名) ❶ part of a book; book: 續～ sequel (to a book) ❷ volume: 上(中, 下)～ Part Ⅰ (Ⅱ, Ⅲ); Volume Ⅰ (Ⅱ, Ⅲ)

【编入】biānrù (动) ❶ enrol; include: ～第一组 be put in the first group ❷ classify: ～甲類 be classified under category A

【编目】biānmù Ⅰ (动) compile a catalogue; catalogue Ⅱ (名) catalogue; list

【编年史】biānniánshǐ (名) chronicle; annals

【编者】biānzhě (名) editor; compiler: ～的話 editor's note; compiler's note

【编制】biānzhì (名) structure of an organization and quota of its staff members: 超過～ overstaffed

【编造】biānzào (动) ❶ make; compile; draw up: ～名册 compile a register (of names) ❷ fabricate; concoct; cook up; make up: ～罪名 frame up a case

【编排】biānpái (动) ❶ arrange (in order); lay out ❷ write and rehearse Ⅱ (名) ❶ writing and directing of a play ❷ (of a magazine) layout

【编组】biānzǔ (动) ❶ organize into groups ❷ marshall railway carriages or wagons into a train

【编著】biānzhù (动) compile; write

【编队】biānduì Ⅰ (动) organize into teams; form into columns Ⅱ (名) formation: 混合～ composite formation

【编号】biānhào Ⅰ (动) number: 給箱子～ number the suitcases Ⅱ (名) serial number

【编製】biānzhì (动) ❶ weave; plait; braid ❷ work out; draw up: ～報表 work out reports and charts of statistics

【编导】biāndǎo Ⅰ (动) write and direct (a play, film, etc.) Ⅱ (名) playwright- (scenarist-, choreographer-) director

【编剧】biānjù Ⅰ (动) write a play or scenario Ⅱ (名) playwright; scenarist; script writer

【编寫】biānxiě (动) ❶ compose;

write ❷ compile

【編審】biānshěn Ⅰ(動) edit Ⅱ(名) senior editor

【編輯】biānjí Ⅰ(動) edit; compile: ～電視節目 edit a television programme Ⅱ(名) editor; compiler: 助理～ assistant editor

【編輯部】biānjíbù(名) editorial department: ～人員 editorial staff

【編織】biānzhī(動) knit; plait; braid; crochet

【編譯】biānyì(動) compile and translate

【編鐘】biānzhōng(名) ancient Chinese chime with 12 bells

【編纂】biānzuǎn(動) compile; edit

練 liàn Ⅰ(動) practise; exercise: ～鋼琴 practise on the piano Ⅱ(形) experienced; trained Ⅲ(名)(Liàn) a surname

【練功】liàngōng(動) do regular exercises (in gymnastics, martial arts etc.)

【練兵】liànbīng(動) ❶ drill troops ❷ train intensively

【練武】liànwǔ(動) practise martial arts

【練習】liànxí Ⅰ(動) practise Ⅱ(名) practice; exercise: ～本 exercise book

緬 miǎn(形) far away; remote

【緬甸】Miǎndiàn(名) Burma: ～人 Burmese / ～語 Burmese (language)

【緬懷】miǎnhuái(動) recall; cherish the memory of: ～故友 cherish the memory of a deceased friend / ～童年歲月 recall one's childhood

絨 jiān(動) seal up (often inscribed after the sender's name on the envelope): 上海王～ from Wang, Shanghai

【緘口】jiānkǒu(動) keep one's mouth shut; keep silent

【緘默】jiānmò(動) remain silent: ～不言 be reticent

【緘藏】jiāncáng(動) keep to oneself

緯 wěi(名) ❶ weft: ～紗 woof; weft (yarn) ❷ latitude: 北(南)～ north (south) latitude

【緯度】wěidù(名)〈地〉 latitude

【緯綫】wěixiàn(名) ❶〈地〉 parallel ❷〈紡〉 weft

緝 jī(動) seize; catch: 通～逃犯 issue a public notice for the capture of a wanted fugitive

【緝私】jīsī(動) detect smuggling activities; bring smugglers to justice

【緝毒】jīdú(名) drug law enforcement

【緝拿】jīná(緝捕 jībǔ)(動) arrest; bring to justice

【緝獲】jīhuò(動) place a criminal under arrest

緩 huǎn Ⅰ(形) slow; unhurried Ⅱ(動) ❶ delay; postpone; put off: ～辦 defer (an action, consideration, etc.) ❷ recuperate; revive: 昏過去又～過來 go off in a faint and then come to

【緩刑】huǎnxíng(名)〈法〉 suspended sentence; probation

【緩兵之計】huǎn bīng zhī jì〈成〉 stalling (delaying) tactics

【緩和】huǎnhé Ⅰ(動) relax; mitigate; alleviate Ⅱ(名) détente; relaxation

【緩急】huǎnjí(名) greater or lesser

urgency: 區分輕重～ distinguish between what's urgent and what's not

【緩期】huǎnqī（動）postpone a deadline; suspend

【緩慢】huǎnmàn（形）slow

【緩衝】huǎnchōng（名）cushion; buffer

緞 duàn（名）satin

緣 yuán（名）❶ cause; reason ❷ predestination; fate; luck ❸ edge; fringe: 邊～ edge; brink ❹ relationship: 血～ blood relationship

【緣分】yuánfèn（名）predestined lot; fate; luck

【緣由】yuányóu（名）reason; cause

【緣故】yuángù（名）cause; reason

縈 yíng（動）〈書〉entangle; ravel

【縈迴】yínghuí（動）return to one's mind time and again

【縈繞】yíngrào（動）linger; hover: 昔日情景，～於心。Scenes of the old days still linger in my mind.

【縈懷】yínghuái（動）（of sth.）take up one's thoughts

縣 xiàn（名）county

縞 gǎo（名）❶ white silk ❷ white

縊 yì（動）hang; strangle: 自～ hang（strangle）oneself

縛 fù（動）tie up; bind fast: 作繭自～ be caught in one's own trap

縝 zhěn

【縝密】zhěnmì（形）careful; meticulous: ～的安排 careful arrangement

緻 zhì（形）fine; delicate: 細～ meticulous

縐 zhòu（名）crape; crepe

【縐布】zhòubù（名）cotton crepe; crepe

【縐紙】zhòuzhǐ（名）crepe paper

縫 féng（動）sew; stitch
see also fèng

【縫合】fénghé（動）sew up

【縫紉】féngrèn（名）needlework

【縫紉機】féngrènjī（名）sewing machine

【縫補】féngbǔ（動）sew and mend

縫 fèng（名）seam
see also féng

繁 fán（形）❶ complicated ❷ numerous: 事～體弱 be overworked and in poor health

【繁文縟節】fán wén rù jié〈成〉elaborate but often superfluous formalities; red tape

【繁忙】fánmáng（形）busy: 工作～ be snowed under with work

【繁育】fányù（動）breed

【繁衍】fányǎn（動）multiply

【繁茂】fánmào（形）lush; exuberant

【繁重】fánzhòng（形）heavy; arduous

【繁殖】fánzhí（動）reproduce; breed

【繁華】fánhuá（形）bustling; prosperous: ～地區 the downtown area

【繁榮】fánróng Ⅰ（形）prosperous; flourishing Ⅱ（動）make prosperous

【繁雜】fánzá（形）multifarious; numerous and varied

【繁體字】fántǐzì〈書〉complex form of a Chinese character

縮 suō（動）❶ contract; shrink ❷

withdraw: 畏～不前 flinch; recoil

【縮小】 suōxiǎo（動）reduce; diminish; contract

【縮水】 suōshuǐ（動）（of cloth）shrink after washing

【縮手縮腳】 suō shǒu suō jiǎo〈成〉timid; gingerly: 他做事總是～的。He is always overcautious in handling matters.

【縮減】 suōjiǎn（動）reduce; curtail: ～開支 retrench the expenditure

【縮短】 suōduǎn（動）shorten: ～他的中東之行 cut short his visit to the Middle East

【縮微】 suōwēi（動）make a microfilm of: ～膠片 microfilm; microfiche

【縮寫】 suōxiě Ⅰ（動）❶ abbreviate ❷ abridge: ～本 abridged version Ⅱ（名）abbreviation

【縮影】 suōyǐng（名）epitome; microcosm

縴 qiàn（名）towline

【縴夫】 qiànfū（名）(boat) tracker

績 jī（名）achievement; deed; contribution: 豐功偉～ spectacular achievements, signal contributions

縹 piāo

【縹緲】 piāomiǎo（形）faintly visible: 如霧仙～ like the visionary figures of immortals

繆 Miào（名）a surname

縷 lǚ Ⅰ（名）thread Ⅱ（量）wisp: ～～炊煙 wisps of smoke curling up from village chimneys

【縷述】 lǚshù（動）make a detailed statement

繃 bēng（動）❶ tighten; pull tight: 弦～斷了。The string was pulled so tight that it snapped. ❷ spring or bounce suddenly ❸（of clothes）be taut ❹ baste; sew with loose stitches; pin
see also běng; bèng

【繃帶】 bēngdài（名）bandage

【繃緊】 bēngjǐn（動）tighten; tauten

繃 běng（動）〈口〉pull (a long face): ～着臉 pull a long face; keep a straight face
see also bēng; bèng

繃 bèng（動）crack; fracture; split open
see also bēng; běng

【繃直】 bèngzhí（形）〈口〉perfectly straight

總 zǒng Ⅰ（動）assemble; sum up; gather: ～其成 do the summing up Ⅱ（形）❶ general; overall; total: ～產值 total output value ❷ chief; main; general: ～動員 general mobilization ❷ chief; main; general: ～則 general principles / ～服務臺 front desk; reception desk Ⅲ（副）❶ always; invariably: 他～不肯聽別人的。He would never listen to others. ❷ after all; anyway: 這件事～是要辦的。We have got to do it one way or another.

【總之】 zǒngzhī（副）in short; in a word

【總支】 zǒngzhī（名）general (Party or Youth League) branch

【總共】 zǒnggòng（副）altogether; in all; in total

【總而言之】 zǒng ér yán zhī〈成〉in a word; to sum up

【總和】zǒnghé（名）sum; sum total

【總計】zǒngjì（動）amount to; total; sum up to

【總則】zǒngzé（名）general rules; general principles

【總指揮】zǒngzhǐhuī（名）❶ commander in chief ❷ general director

【總務】zǒngwù（名）general affairs

【總得】zǒngděi（動）have to; must: 你～親自去一趟。You've got to go there yourself.

【總理】zǒnglǐ（名）premier; prime minister

【總統】zǒngtǒng（名）president

【總結】zǒngjié Ⅰ（動）sum up; summarize: ～經驗教訓 sum up one's experience and lessons Ⅱ（名）summary

【總督】zǒngdū（名）governor-general; governor

【總裝】zǒngzhuāng（名）assembly

【總稱】zǒngchēng（名）general name; general term

【總管】zǒngguǎn（名）manager

【總算】zǒngsuàn（副）❶ at last; finally: 他的病～好了。He has finally recovered. ❷ all things considered; at least; anyway: 我們～沒有白費勁。At least our efforts were not in vain.

【總領事】zǒnglǐngshì（名）consul general

【總數】zǒngshù（名）sum;（sum）total

【總機】zǒngjī（名）switchboard;（telephone）exchange

【總額】zǒng'é（名）total amount; total

【總歸】zǒngguī（副）after all; anyway: 他～還年輕，經驗不足。After all, he is still young and inexperi-

enced.

【總體】zǒngtǐ（名）totality; entirety: ～規劃 overall planning

縧 tāo（名）silk braid or ribbon: 花～子 lace

縱 zòng Ⅰ（形）vertical; lengthwise Ⅱ（動）❶ set free; release: 欲擒故～ release in order to capture ❷ indulge; let oneself go: ～目遠望 look as far as one can see / ～慾 indulge in carnal pleasures ❸ jump; leap: ～身越過柵欄 jump over the fence Ⅲ（連）〈書〉even if; though

【縱火】zònghuǒ（動）set on fire; commit arson

【縱使】zòngshǐ（連）even if; even though

【縱虎歸山】zòng hǔ guī shān（成）let the enemy escape and thus keep alive the source of trouble

【縱容】zòngróng（動）indulge; pamper; spoil: 不應該～孩子。It's not right to pamper（or spoil）one's children.

【縱酒】zòngjiǔ Ⅰ（動）indulge in drinking Ⅱ（名）alcoholism

【縱深】zòngshēn（名）depth: 向～發展 develop in depth

【縱情】zòngqíng（副）heartily; to one's heart's content: ～歌唱 sing heartily

【縱然】zòngrán（連）even if: ～失敗，我們也要試一試。Even if we may fail, we should have a try.

【縱隊】zòngduì（名）column; file

【縱橫】zònghéng（形）vertical and horizontal; lengthwise and crosswise: ～交錯 crisscross

【縱斷面】zòngduànmiàn（名）vertical section

繅 sāo (動) reel silk from cocoons; reel

【繅絲】 sāosī (名) silk reeling; filature

【繅絲廠】 sāosīchǎng (名) reeling mill; filature

織 zhī (動) weave; knit: ～ 布 weave cotton cloth / ～ 襪子 knit stockings

【織物】 zhīwù (名) fabric

【織針】 zhīzhēn (名) knitting needle

【織錦】 zhījǐn (名) ❶ brocade ❷ picture-weaving in silk

【織機】 zhījī (名) loom

繕 shàn (動) ❶ repair; mend; fix ❷ copy: ～ 寫 copy; make a fair copy of

繞 rào (動) ❶ wind; coil: 把毛綫 ～ 成一圈 wind wool into a ball ❷ make a detour: ～ 遠 make a long detour ❸ move round; circle: 鳥～ 着樹飛。 The birds are circling over the tree. ❹ confuse; baffle: 一時～ 住了, 這道題沒有算出來。 I was baffled for a moment, and failed to work out the problem.

【繞口令】 ràokǒulìng (名) a language game with tongue twisters

【繞圈子】 ràoquānzi (動) ❶ go in circles ❷ talk in a roundabout way; beat about the bush

【繞道】 ràodào (動) make a detour

【繞嘴】 ràozuǐ (動) (of a word, etc.) be difficult to articulate; be a bit of a mouthful

【繞彎子】 rào wānzi (動) fail to come straight to the point

繚 liáo (動) ❶ ravel; entangle ❷ sew; stitch

【繚亂】 liáoluàn (形) puzzled; dazzled

【繚繞】 liáorào (動) (of smoke) coil up; (of song) linger

繫 jì (動) tie; fasten; fix: ～着圍脖兒 wear a scarf / ～在浮筒上的汽艇 motorboat moored to a buoy
see also xì

【繫泊】 jìbó (動) moor

繫 xì (動) ❶ tie; fasten: ～牛 lasso a cow ❷ feel concerned
see also jì

繭 jiǎn (名) ❶ cocoon: 作～自縛 spin a cocoon around oneself; get enmeshed in a web of one's own spinning ❷ callus

繮 jiāng (名) rope or strap for controlling a draught animal; reins: 脱～之馬 a runaway horse

【繮繩】 jiāngshéng (名) reins; halter

繡 xiù I (動) embroider II (名) embroidery

【繡花】 xiùhuā (動) embroider

【繡花枕頭】 xiùhuā zhěntou (名) ❶ pillow with an embroidered case ❷ worthless person with falsely impressive looks; outwardly attractive but worthless person

【繡像】 xiùxiàng (名) tapestry portrait; embroidered portrait

繩 shéng I (名) ❶ rope; string: 尼龍～ nylon cord ❷ rule of conduct: 準～ criterion; guideline ❸ (Shéng) a surname II (動) restrain; punish: ～之以法 punish sb. according to law; restrain sb. by enforcing the law

【繩子】 shéngzi (名) rope; string

繪 huì (動) paint; draw

【繪畫】 huìhuà (名) drawing; painting

【繪製】 huìzhì (動) draw: ～ 藍圖 draw a blueprint

【繪聲繪色】 huìshēng huìsè (形) (of writing) vivid; graphic

繳 jiǎo (動) ❶ hand in; deliver; pay: ～學費 pay tuition ❷ take by force; capture; seize

【繳械】 jiǎoxiè (動) ❶ disarm; deprive of weapons ❷ lay down one's arms

【繳獲】 jiǎohuò (動) seize from the enemy

辮 biàn (名) plait; braid; queue: 草帽 ～ plaited straw (for making hats)

【辮子】 biànzi (名) ❶ plait; braid: 梳 ～ plait one's hair ❷ sth. that one gets hold of as evidence against one's opponent: 抓 ～ take advantage of sb.'s minor failing to attack him

纂 zuǎn (動) edit; compile: 編 ～ compile

繽 bīn

【繽紛】 bīnfēn (形) in wild confusion; in rich variety: 五彩 ～ colourful; in a riot of colour

繼 jì I (動) go on; follow; take over: 相 ～ 出現 appear one after another; occur in succession II (副) then; soon afterwards

【繼父】 jìfù (名) stepfather

【繼母】 jìmǔ (名) stepmother

【繼任】 jìrèn (動) succeed sb. as: ～ 駐美大使 succeed sb. as Ambassador to the United States

【繼而】 jì'ér (副) then; soon after: 他先失去了知覺，～停止了呼吸。 He lost consciousness, and then stopped breathing.

【繼承】 jìchéng (動) ❶ inherit; be heir to ❷ take over; carry on: ～ 文化傳統 carry on the cultural tradition

【繼承人】 jìchéngrén (名) heir; successor: 合法 ～ legitimate heir

【繼往開來】 jì wǎng kāi lái (成) carry forward the cause initiated by the predecessors and open up new vistas for the future

【繼續】 jìxù (動) continue; keep on; extend: 把實驗 ～ 下去 go on with the experiment

纏 chán (動) ❶ wind: 傷口 ～ 着繃帶。 The wound is bandaged. ❷ bother; pester: 胡攪蠻 ～ pester sb. by talking unreasonably ❸〈方〉 handle; deal with: 難 ～ hard to deal with

【纏手】 chánshǒu (形) hard to

【纏綿】 chánmián (形) ❶ (of illness, sentiment, etc.) lingering: ～病榻 be laid up with a lingering illness ❷ touching: 歌聲柔和 ～ gentle and charming voice ❸ sentimental tenderly attached to each other

【纏繞】 chánrǎo (動) ❶ wind ❷ worry; harass

續 xù (動) ❶ continue: 後 ～ 行動 follow-up action ❷ add: 再往鍋裏 ～ 點水 ladle a little more water into the cooker

【續弦】xùxián（動）(of a widower)
remarry

【續訂】xùdìng（動）renew one's sub-
scription

【續借】xùjiè（動）renew: 書～一月
renew the book for another month

【續假】xùjià（動）extend one's
leave: ～一週 extend one's leave
for another week; ask for a week's
extension of one's leave

【續集】xùjí（名）(of a book) continuation; sequel

【續編】xùbiān（名）sequel

纓 yīng（名）❶ tassel ❷ ribbon

纖 xiān（形）fine; tiny

【纖小】xiānxiǎo（形）fine; small

【纖巧】xiānqiǎo（形）delicate; exquisite

【纖柔】xiānróu（形）fine and tender;
thin and soft

【纖弱】xiānruò（形）slender and delicate

【纖細】xiānxì（形）thin; fine: 筆畫
～ delicate brushstroke

【纖維】xiānwéi（名）fibre; staple

【纖維板】xiānwéibǎn（名）fibre-
board

纔 cái（副）❶ just; just now: 他～
來。He has just arrived. ❷ only; as
late as: 大風到半夜～停。The gale
did not subside until midnight. ❸
[used to indicate a prerequisite]
only: 只有努力～能成功。Only by
working hard can you succeed. ❹
[used together with 就] as soon as:
他一回學院就到實驗室去了。He
went to the lab as soon as he came
back to the campus. ❺ [used to indicate a change] not until; then and

only then: 直到火撲滅了我～離
開。I did not leave until the fire was
put out. ❻ [used to indicate sth.
that is surprisingly small in size or
low in frequency, etc.] only; no
more than: 他們一家～三口人。
There are only three people in his
family. ❼ [used for emphasis] indeed; just: 我們玩得～好呢。We
enjoyed ourselves very much indeed.

纜 lǎn Ⅰ（名）❶ tow-rope or cable
(for mooring a ship) ❷ thick rope
or cable: 海底電～(submarine) cable Ⅱ（動）tie (a ship) with a rope

【纜車】lǎnchē（名）cable car; cable
railway; cable transporter: ～終點
站 cable terminal

【纜繩】lǎnshéng（名）thick rope;
cable

缶 部

缸 gāng（名）vat; jar; crock: 茶～
tea mug

缺 quē Ⅰ（動）be short of; lack: ～
現錢 be short of cash／～貨 be out
of stock; be in short supply Ⅱ（名）
vacancy: 頂～ fill a vacancy; act as
a stopgap

【缺口】quēkǒu（名）breach; gap;
opening

【缺少】quēshǎo（動）lack; be short
of

【缺斤短兩】quē jīn duǎn liǎng（成）
short weight: ～進行詐騙 give
people short measure

【缺乏】quēfá（動）lack; be short of: ~責任心 lack a sense of responsibility

【缺席】quēxí（動）be absent from (a meeting, etc.)

【缺陷】quēxiàn（名）defect; flaw

【缺勤】quēqín Ⅰ（動）be absent from one's work Ⅱ（名）absence from work

【缺損】quēsǔn（形）flawed or damaged

【缺德】quēdé（形）mean; . wicked; low

【缺點】quēdiǎn（名）shortcoming; defect

【缺額】quē'é（名）vacancy

磬 qìng（動）use up

【磬竹難書】qìng zhú nán shū〈成〉(of crimes) too numerous to enumerate

罌 yīng

【罌粟】yīngsù（名）〈植〉opium poppy

罐 guàn（名）canister; tin: 一~沙丁魚 a tin of sardines

【罐車】guànchē（名）tank car; tank truck; tanker

【罐頭】guàntou（名）tin; can: ~水果 canned fruit

网 部

罕 hǎn（副）rarely; scldom

【罕見】hǎnjiàn（形）of rare occurrence; rare

罔 wǎng Ⅰ（副）not: 對朋友的勸告œ若~聞 not heed the advice of one's friends Ⅱ（動）deceive; cheat: 欺~ hoodwink

署 shǔ Ⅰ（名）governnment bureau; government office Ⅱ（動）❶ assign; dispose; deploy: 部~新的任務 assign new tasks ❷ affix one's signature to

【署名】shǔmíng（動）put one's signature to (a letter, document, article, etc.)

置 zhì（動）❶ place; put: ~之案頭 put it on the desk / 淡然~之 dismiss sth. with an air of indifference ❷ set up; install: 設~一個專門機構 set up a special organization ❸ buy; purchase: 添~一些新的儀器 procure some new instruments

【置之不理】zhì zhī bù lǐ〈成〉pay no attention to; close one's eyes to; ignore; disregard

【置之度外】zhì zhī dù wài〈成〉not take into consideration; ignore; set aside: 個人安危~ with no thought for one's personal safety

【置身事外】zhì shēn shì wài〈成〉sit on the sidelines

【置信】zhìxìn（動）[used mostly in the negative] believe: 不可~ should not give credence to; incredible

【置若罔聞】zhì ruò wǎng wén〈成〉turn a deaf ear to; ignore completely

【置疑】zhìyí（動）[used mostly in the negative] doubt: 不容~ undoubtedly

【置辦】zhìbàn（動）buy; purchase: ~醫療器械 purchase medical appliances

罩 zhào Ⅰ（動）cover; wrap; cloak:

把菜～起來 put a cover over the dishes Ⅱ（名）❶ cover; shade: 紗～ gauze covering／燈～ lampshade ❷ bamboo basket for catching fish

【罩衫】zhàoshān（名）overall; dust-coat; smock

罪 zuì（名）❶ guilt; crime: 犯～ commit a crime／認～ admit one's guilt ❷ fault; blame: 你不應歸～於別人。You should not pin the blame on others. ❸ suffering; hardship: 受過不少～ have undergone a good deal of hardship

【罪大惡極】zuì dà è jí〈成〉have committed most atrocious crimes

【罪犯】zuìfàn（名）criminal; convict

【罪名】zuìmíng（名）charge; accusation

【罪行】zuìxíng（名）crime; offence

【罪狀】zuìzhuàng（名）facts about a crime; criminal charges

【罪惡】zuì'è（名）crime; evil

【罪過】zuìguo（名）fault; offence; sin

【罪魁】zuìkuí（名）arch-criminal

【罪證】zuìzhèng（名）evidence of a crime

【罪孽】zuìniè（名）sin; iniquity: ～深重 sink deep in iniquity

罰 fá（動）punish; penalize

【罰球】fáqiú（名）〈籃〉penalty shot／〈足球〉penalty kick

【罰款】fákuǎn（罰金 fájīn）（名）fine

罵 mà（動）curse; scold

【罵名】màmíng（名）evil repute: ～千載 leave an ill name to posterity

【罵架】màjià（動）quarrel; bicker

【罵街】màjiē（動）shout abuse in public

【罵罵咧咧】màmà liēliē（動）be foul-mouthed; use strong（offensive）language

罷 bà（動）❶ stop; cease: 欲～不能 cannot stop now that one has started; unable to extricate oneself from an embarrassing situation ❷ dismiss; discharge; fire

【罷了】bàle（助）[used at the end of a sentence] only; just; that's all: 我不過開開玩笑～。I was only joking.

【罷了】bàliǎo（動）[used to express tolerance]: 他不來也就～。It's all right if he doesn't want to come.

【罷工】bàgōng Ⅰ（動）strike; go on strike Ⅱ（名）strike; walkout: 靜坐～ sit-down strike

【罷手】bàshǒu（動）stop; give up; cease doing sth.: 決不～ will not stop halfway no matter what happens

【罷市】bàshì Ⅰ（名）shopkeepers' strike Ⅱ（動）（of shopkeepers）go on strike

【罷休】bàxiū（動）give up; have done with; let the matter drop

【罷免】bàmiǎn（動）recall; dismiss from office

【罷官】bàguān（動）be relieved of official duties

【罷教】bàjiào Ⅰ（名）teachers' strike Ⅱ（動）（of teachers）go on strike

【罷課】bàkè Ⅰ（名）students' strike; suspension of classes Ⅱ（動）（of students）go on strike; boycott classes

【罷黜】bàchù（動）❶ be relieved of one's post ❷ ban; reject

懼 lí（動）suffer from（a disaster or

disease)

【羅難】línàn（動）❶ be killed in a disaster ❷ be murdered

羅 luó
see also luó

【羅嗦】luōsuo（形）❶ long-winded; verbose; wordy: 説話～ a long-winded speaker ❷ troublesome: 這事可真～。This is a real nuisance.

羅 luó Ⅰ（動）❶ catch (birds) with a net ❷ gather; collect ❸ display ❹ sieve: 把麵再一一遍 sift the flour once more Ⅱ（名）❶ net (for catching birds); snare ❷（Luó）a surname
see also luō

【羅列】luóliè（動）enumerate; list: 僅僅～現象是不行的。It won't do to merely list the phenomena.

【羅致】luózhì（動）collect; enlist: ～人才 recruit people of talent; scout for talent

【羅馬尼亞】Luómǎníyà（名）Romania: ～人 Romanian ／～語 Romanian (language)

【羅馬數字】Luómǎ shùzì（名）Roman numerals

【羅圈腿】luóquāntuǐ（名）bowlegs; bandy legs: 這孩子是個～。The boy is bowlegged.

【羅漢】luóhàn（名）〈宗〉arhat

【羅網】luówǎng（名）net; trap: 佈下～ spread an escape-proof net

【羅盤】luópán（名）compass

【羅鍋】luóguō（名）hunchback

【羅織】luózhī（動）frame sb. up: ～誣陷 make a false charge against sb.

羈 jī Ⅰ（名）bridle; halter Ⅱ（動）❶ restrain; restrict: ～押 detain; put under arrest ❷ stay or live (away from home）; detained by business: ～旅異邦 long sojourn in a foreign country

【羈留】jīliú（動）❶ stay away from one's hometown or reside abroad ❷ detain; be in custody

【羈絆】jībàn（名）fetters; yoke: 爲家務～ be tied down by domestic affairs

羊 部

羊 yáng（名）sheep; goat

【羊毛】yángmáo（名）sheep's wool; fleece: 純～ pure wool

【羊毛衫】yángmáoshān（名）woollen sweater

【羊皮】yángpí（名）sheep-skin

【羊肉】yángròu（名）mutton: ～串 shish kebab

【羊角風】yángjiǎofēng（名）epilepsy

【羊羔】yánggāo（名）lamb

【羊倌】yángguān（名）shepherd

【羊圈】yángjuàn（名）sheep-fold; sheep pen

【羊絨衫】yángróngshān（名）cashmere sweater

【羊腸小道】yángcháng xiǎodào（名）zigzag footpath; winding mountain path

羌 qiāng

【羌族】Qiāngzú（名）the Qiang (Chiang) nationality

美 měi Ⅰ（形）❶ good-looking; beautiful ❷ good; satisfactory ❸ complacent: 心裏～滋滋的 feel self-contented Ⅱ（名）（Měi）short

for America

【美人计】měirénjì（名）sextrap

【美工】měigōng（名）❶ art designing ❷ art designer

【美女】měinǚ（美人 měirén）（名）beautiful woman; beauty

【美元】měiyuán（名）U. S. dollar; buck; greenback

【美化】měihuà（动）beautify; prettify: ～校园 beautify the campus

【美中不足】měi zhōng bù zú〈成〉a flaw that mars perfection; a fly in the ointment

【美不胜收】měi bù shèng shōu〈成〉cannot take in such an array of beautiful things in an instant

【美好】měihǎo（形）good; fine; happy: ～的景色 beautiful landscape ／～生活 happy life

【美名】měimíng（名）good reputation

【美妙】měimiào（形）beautiful; wonderful

【美言】měiyán（动）put in a good word for sb.

【美金】měijīn（名）U.S. dollar

【美味】měiwèi（名）delicious food; delicacy

【美育】měiyù（名）aesthetic education

【美洲】Měizhōu（名）the Americas: 中～ Central America

【美差】měichāi（名）easy task; cushy job

【美食餐厅】měishí cāntīng（名）gourmet restaurant

【美酒】měijiǔ（名）good wine

【美容】měiróng（动）(of women) take beauty treatments for the face, hair, etc.

【美容厅】měiróngtīng（美容院 měi-róngyuàn）（名）beauty parlour

【美术】měishù（名）fine arts: ～馆 art gallery ／～家 artist

【美国】Měiguó（名）the United States; America: ～人 American

【美景】měijǐng（名）beautiful scenery

【美感】měigǎn（名）sense of beauty

【美满】měimǎn（形）happy; satisfactory: ～的婚姻 happy marriage

【美梦】měimèng（名）fond dream; sweet dream

【美称】měichēng（名）good name

【美德】měidé（名）virtue; morality

【美学】měixué（名）aesthetics

【美丽】měilì（形）beautiful; fair

【美观】měiguān（形）nice to look at; beautiful: 设计～ with a beautiful design

羔 gāo（名）lamb

【羔羊】gāoyáng（名）❶ lamb ❷ weakling

羞 xiū Ⅰ（形）❶ shy; timid: 别怕～。Don't be shy. ❷ ashamed: 与那些人共事 feel it beneath one's dignity to work alongside those people Ⅱ（名）shame; disgrace

【羞怯】xiūqiè（形）timid; shy

【羞辱】xiūrǔ Ⅰ（名）shame; humiliation Ⅱ（动）humiliate: 蒙受～ be put to shame; suffer humiliation

【羞耻】xiūchǐ（名）shame: 不知～ have no sense of shame

【羞答答】xiūdādā（形）shy; coy; bashful

【羞愧】xiūkuì（形）ashamed; bashful: 感到很～ feel rather ashamed of oneself

【羞惭】xiūcán（动）feel ashamed

【羞澀】 xiūsè （動）feel shy and embarrassed

着 zhāo （名）❶ a move (in chess) ❷ trick; move: 我没～了。I'm at my wits' end. ／ 這是冒險的一～。This is a risky move.
see also zháo; zhe; zhuó

着 zháo （動）❶ touch: ～地 touch the ground／ 不～邊際 have no bearing on the subject; be wide of the mark ❷ feel; catch: ～急 feel anxious ／ ～涼 catch cold ❸ burn: 大火～了三天了。The fire has been burning for three days. ❹ fall asleep: 她很快就睡～了。He soon fell asleep. ❺ [used after a verb to indicate accomplishment or result]: 他說～了。What he said proved to be true.
see also zhāo; zhe; zhuó

【着火】 zháohuǒ （動）catch fire
【着忙】 zháománg （動）be in a hurry
【着迷】 zháomí （動）be fascinated; be spellbound
【着慌】 zháohuāng （動）get nervous; fall into a panic
【着魔】 zháomó （動）be bewitched

着 zhe （助）❶ [used to indicate an action in progress or a static state]: 他正等～你呢。He is waiting for you. ／桌子上放～一本書。There's a book on the desk. ❷ [used to stress the tone in an imperative sentence]: 慢～點。Slow down. ❸ [used after a verb to form a preposition]: 照～ according to／ 爲～ in order to
see also zhāo; zháo; zhuó

着 zhuó·（動）❶ wear (clothes): 穿

～ clothing ❷ touch; contact: 不～邊際 have no bearing on the subject ❸ apply; use: ～筆 set pen to paper; begin to write or paint ❹ send: ～人去取 send sb. for sth.
see also zhāo; zháo; zhe

【着力】 zhuólì （動）exert oneself; apply oneself to: 能做到的一定～幫助 will do whatever one can to help

【着手】 zhuóshǒu （動）set about; get down to: ～進行工作 get down to one's work

【着色】 zhuósè （動）apply colour

【着重】 zhuózhòng （副）emphatically; forcefully: 他在文章裏一指出這一點。He stressed that point in his essay.

【着眼】 zhuóyǎn （動）see from the angle of: 從大處～,從小處着手。Keep the ultimate goal in mind while doing the spadework.

【着陸】 zhuólù （of an airplane) land; touch down

【着落】 zhuóluò （名）❶ whereabouts: 誰都不知道她的～。Nobody knows her whereabouts. ❷ assured source: 他的學費至今還没～。He hasn't yet got enough to pay the tuition.

【着想】 zhuóxiǎng （動）consider the interests of: 爲孩子們～ have the interests of the children at heart

【着實】 zhuóshí （副）❶ really; indeed: 他～能幹。He is really capable. ❷ severely: 我～批評了他。I severely criticized him.

羚 líng

【羚羊】 língyáng （名）antelope

羡 xiàn

【羨慕】xiànmù（動）admire; envy

羥

qiǎng

【羥基】qiǎngjī （名） hydroxyl (group)

義

yì I（名）❶ justice; righteousness: 深明大～ have a strong sense of justice ❷ meaning: 兩詞同～. The two words are synonyms. II（形）❶ just; righteous ❷ adopted; adoptive: ～子 adopted son

【義士】yìshì（名）righteous man; champion of a just cause

【義不容辭】yì bù róng cí〈成〉have a bounden duty; be duty-bound

【義正詞嚴】yì zhèng cí yán〈成〉speak solemnly and on just grounds

【義氣】yìqì（名）personal loyalty; faithfulness: 對朋友講～ be faithful to one's friends

【義務】yìwù I（名）duty; obligation II（形）❶ voluntary: 盡～ offer voluntary service ❷ compulsory: ～教育 compulsory education

【義無反顧】yì wú fǎn gù 〈成〉 be duty-bound to advance unflinchingly

【義演】yìyǎn（名）benefit performance

【義賣】yìmài（名）charity sale; sale for a good cause

【義憤】yìfèn（名）righteous indignation

【義憤填膺】yì fèn tián yīng〈成〉boil with noble indignation

羣

qún I（名）crowd; group; multitude: 合～ sociable; gregarious / 牛～ herd of cattle II（量）group; flock; herd: 一～旅客 a group of tourists / 一～流氓 a horde of hooligans

【羣氓】qúnméng（名）〈書〉mob

【羣架】qúnjià（名）gang fight; free-for-all

【羣島】qúndǎo（名）archipelago

【羣情】qúnqíng（名）public sentiment; popular feeling: ～激憤. Popular feeling runs high.

【羣婚】qúnhūn（名）group marriage; communal marriage

【羣衆】qúnzhòng（名）the masses; the public

【羣策羣力】qún cè qún lì〈成〉make use of collective wisdom and act in unison

【羣落】qúnluò（名）❶〈生〉community ❷〈建〉architectural complex

【羣魔亂舞】qún mó luàn wǔ〈成〉rogues of all kinds running wild

羹

gēng（名）thick soup

【羹匙】gēngchí（名）soup spoon; tablespoon

羶

shān（名）smell of mutton

羽 部

羽

yǔ（名）feather; plume

【羽毛】yǔmáo（名）feather; plume

【羽毛未豐】yǔ máo wèi fēng〈成〉young and inexperienced: 他～。He is a fledgling.

【羽毛扇】yǔmáoshàn（名）feather fan

【羽毛球】yǔmáoqiú（名）❶ badminton ❷ shuttlecock

【羽紗】yǔshā（名）camlet

【羽絨】yǔróng（名）eiderdown: ～衣 eiderdown outwear

翅 chì (名) ❶ wing ❷ fin
【翅膀】chìbǎng (名) wing

翁 wēng (名) ❶ old man ❷ (Wēng) a surname

翌 yì (形)〈書〉next: ～日 the next day

習 xí I (動) ❶ practise; review: 實～ practice ❷ be used to; be good at II (名) ❶ habit; custom: 固～ deeprooted habit ❷ (Xí) a surname
【習以為常】xí yǐ wéi cháng〈成〉grow accustomed to sth.; tolerate sth. as a matter of course
【習用】xíyòng (動) commonly use
【習字】xízì (動) practise calligraphy
【習作】xízuò I (動) do exercises in writing II (名) exercise in writing or drawing
【習性】xíxìng (名) habit; characteristic: 北極熊的～ the habits of the polar bear
【習俗】xísú (名) common practice; custom
【習氣】xíqì (名) bad habit; bad practice; unhealthy trend
【習語】xíyǔ (名) idiom
【習慣】xíguàn I (名) habit; custom: 風俗～ local customs and practices II (動) get used to: ～新環境 get used to the new environment
【習慣勢力】xíguàn shìlì (名) force of habit
【習題】xítí (名) exercise: 幾何～ exercises in geometry

翎 líng (名) plume; feather

翔 xiáng (動) circle in the air; fly:

滑～ glide

翠 cuì (形) green
【翠微】cuìwēi (名) ❶ verdure of a hill ❷ green hill
【翠綠】cuìlǜ (名) emerald

翡 fěi
【翡翠】fěicuì (名) jadeite

翟 Zhái (名) a surname

翩 piān
【翩翩】piānpiān I (副) gracefully; (dance) lightly II (形) (of one's bearing) graceful and elegant: 風度～ have a graceful bearing

翦 Jiǎn (名) a surname

翰 hàn (名) ❶ writing brush ❷ writing
【翰墨】hànmò (名) ❶ writing or painting brush and ink ❷ writing, calligraphy or painting

翱 áo (動) take wing
【翱翔】áoxiáng (動) soar; hover; wheel: 在空中～ soar in the sky

翼 yì (名) wing
【翼側】yìcè (名) flank
【翼翼】yìyì (副) cautiously: 小心～ with great caution

翹 qiáo (動) ❶ raise (one's head) ❷ warp: 這張唱片～了。The disc has warped.
see also qiào
【翹望】qiáowàng (動) ❶ raise one's head and look ❷ eagerly look forward to

翹 qiào (動) raise; hold up
see also qiáo

【翹尾巴】qiàowěiba（動）be cocky; get stuck-up: 別一有成績就～。Don't get cocky when you've achieved something.

翻 fān（動）❶ turn over ❷ reverse; overthrow ❸ cross; climb over ❹ translate ❺ multiply: ～兩番 quadruple

【翻天覆地】fān tiān fù dì〈成〉shake the world: ～的變化 earth-shaking change

【翻印】fānyìn（動）reprint

【翻地】fāndì（動）plough

【翻身】fānshēn（動）❶ turn over ❷ rise; be freed: ～奴隸 liberated slaves

【翻版】fānbǎn（名）reproduction; duplication

【翻來覆去】fān lái fù qù Ⅰ（動）toss about Ⅱ（副）over and over again

【翻胃】fānwèi（動）upset one's stomach

【翻修】fānxiū Ⅰ（動）rebuild; repair Ⅱ（名）repair; face-life

【翻悔】fānhuǐ（動）go back on one's word

【翻案】fān'àn（動）overturn the verdict

【翻然】fānrán（翻然 fānrán）（副）quickly and completely: ～醒悟 be suddenly awake to one's error

【翻新】fānxīn（動）revamp; renovate

【翻跟頭】fān gēntou（動）turn a somersault

【翻滾】fāngǔn（動）roll; boil: 白浪～。The sea is seething.

【翻閱】fānyuè（動）browse; thumb through

【翻臉】fānliǎn（動）fall out（with sb.）

【翻譯】fānyì Ⅰ（動）translate; interpret Ⅱ（名）translator; interpreter

【翻騰】fānteng（動）be turbulent

耀 yào Ⅰ（動）shine Ⅱ（名）honour

【耀武揚威】yào wǔ yáng wēi〈成〉make a show of one's strength; bluff and bluster

【耀眼】yàoyǎn（形）dazzling: ～的燈光 dazzling lights

老 部

老 lǎo Ⅰ（形）❶ old; advanced in years: ～太太 old lady ❷ old; of long standing: ～搭檔 old partner; old workmate ／ ～主顧 regular patron ❸ outdated: ～腦筋 old way of thinking ❹ original; former: ～脾氣 the same old temper ／ ～樣子沒有變 look exactly the same as before ❺ tough（as opposed to tender）: 芹菜長得太～了。The celery has overgrown. ❻ overdone in cooking: 牛肉炒～了。The beef is overfried. ❼〈口〉youngest: ～妹子 the youngest sister Ⅱ（副）❶ for a long time; for ages: ～半天 quite a while ／ ～說個沒完 speak interminably ❷ always: ～是遲到 be always late ❸ very: ～晚纔回家 come back home very late Ⅲ（名）❶ the aged: 男女～少 men and women, old and young ❷ [used before one's surname to indicate familiarity]: ～張 Lao Zhang ❸ [used to denote seniority among brothers and sisters]: 這是～二。This is the second child. ❹ (Lǎo) a surname

【老一套】lǎoyítào (名) same old stuff; outmoded methods

【老九】lǎojiǔ (臭老九 chòulǎojiǔ) (名) fellow No. 9 — derogatory nickname for Chinese intellectuals

【老人家】lǎorenjia (名) 〈敬〉[respectful form of address for an old person]❷ your parent

【老大】lǎodà I (名) ❶ eldest child of a family ❷ 〈方〉 head sailor; master of a sailing crew II (副) very much: 心裏～不願意 extremely reluctant

【老大娘】lǎodàniang (名)〈敬〉[often used to address an unfamiliar old woman] granny; auntie

【老大爺】lǎodàye (名)〈敬〉[often used to address an unfamiliar old man] grandpa; uncle

【老大難】lǎo dà nán (形) (of a problem) long-standing, big and thorny

【老手】lǎoshǒu (名) old hand

【老化】lǎohuà I (動) ❶ become old ❷ become obsolete II (名) ageing: 人口～ ageing of the population / ～現象 ageing trend

【老毛病】lǎomáobìng (名) ❶ old ailment; inveterate disease ❷ old weakness

【老天爺】lǎotiānyé (名) God; heaven

【老旦】lǎodàn (名) role of the old famale in traditional Chinese opera

【老本】lǎoběn (名) capital (investment): 連～都賠了進去 lose every penny one has invested

【老叼】lǎodiāo (名)〈口〉hoist; crane

【老兄】lǎoxiōng (名)[used among

men as an intimate form of address] old chap

【老生】lǎoshēng (名) role of the old man in traditional Chinese opera

【老生常談】lǎo shēng cháng tán〈成〉shopworn idea; banality

【老成】lǎochéng (形) experienced; mellow: ～持重 experienced and prudent

【老朽】lǎoxiǔ (形) senile and decrepit

【老年】lǎonián (名) old age: ～公民 senior citizen

【老好人】lǎohǎorén (名) good-natured person; person who offends nobody

【老奸巨滑】lǎo jiān jù huá〈成〉extremely cunning; a crafty old scoundrel

【老百姓】lǎobǎixìng (名)〈口〉❶ common people (as opposed to officials) ❷ civilian(s) (as opposed to the military)

【老弟】lǎodì (名)[intimate form of address for a man younger than oneself] brother

【老伴兒】lǎobànr (名)〈口〉(of an aged married couple) wife; husband; old mate

【老底】lǎodǐ (名) sb.'s past (usu. kept secret)

【老虎】lǎohǔ (名) ❶ tiger ❷ embezzler; grafter: 打～ punish embezzlers

【老百子】lǎobǎizi (名) sleeky old bird

【老姑娘】lǎogūniang (名) spinster; old maid

【老狐狸】lǎohúli (名) old wily fox; cunning person

【老花鏡】lǎohuājìng (名) presbyopic

glasses

【老家】lǎojiā (名) hometown; native place

【老师】lǎoshī (名) teacher

【老羞成怒】lǎo xiū chéng nù〈成〉be shamed into a rage

【老马识途】lǎo mǎ shí tú〈成〉an experienced man always knows where to go and what to do

【老将】lǎojiàng (名) ❶ old general ❷ veteran ❸ seasoned fighter

【老婆】lǎopo (名)〈口〉wife: 讨～ (of a man) get married

【老掉牙】lǎodiàoyá (形) completely obsolete

【老眼光】lǎoyǎnguāng (名) fixed views: 你不能用～去看她。You shouldn't judge her with fixed views.

【老乡】lǎoxiāng (名) ❶ fellow-townsman; fellow-provincial ❷ [used as a friendly form of address for a man from the countryside] my good neighbour

【老路】lǎolù (名) beaten track; usual way

【老鼠】lǎoshǔ (名) mouse; rat

【老话】lǎohuà (名) ❶ old saying ❷ remarks about things in the past

【老爷】lǎoye (名) ❶ [old form of address for officials] master; my lord ❷ [formerly used by servants to address the master of the family] master ❸〈方〉(maternal) grandpa

【老干部】lǎo gànbù (名) veteran cadre

【老汉】lǎohàn (名) ❶ old man; old fellow ❷ [used by an old man to refer to himself]～我 I the old man

【老实】lǎoshi (形) ❶ frank; honest: ～告诉你 to be frank with you

❷ behaving well; silent and unobtrusive ❸〈婉〉simple-minded: ～人 a person who can be easily taken in; an honest person

【老调】lǎodiào (名) old tune: ～重弹 harp on the same string; repeat what one has said many times

【老挝】Lǎowō (名) the Laos: ～人 Laotian

【老练】lǎoliàn (形) experienced, cautious and resourceful: 在政治斗争中很～ be shrewd or skillful in political struggle or in fighting

【老头儿】lǎotóur (名)〈口〉old man; old fellow

【老迈】lǎomài (形) ageing: ～多病 ageing and ailing

【老板】lǎobǎn (名) boss; owner of a business enterprise

【老龄】lǎolíng (名) old-age group

【老鹰】lǎoyīng (名) eagle; hawk

考

【考】kǎo Ⅰ (动) ❶ give (take) an examination, test or quiz: 高考没～取 fail in the college (university) entrance examinations ❷ check; examine: 口～ examine orally ❸ study; do research on: ～据 textual research Ⅱ (名) one's deceased father: 如丧～妣 as if one had just lost one's parents

【考分】kǎofēn (名) examination mark; examination results

【考古】kǎogǔ Ⅰ (动) engage in archaeological work Ⅱ (名) archaeology: ～学家 archaeologist

【考生】kǎoshēng (名) examinee

【考究】kǎojiu Ⅰ (动) ❶ study carefully ❷ be particular about: 不必～衣着 There is no need to be fastidious about one's dress. Ⅱ (形) perfect; exquisite; elegant

【考卷】kǎojuàn（名）exam paper: 批
阅～ mark exam papers

【考取】kǎoqǔ（动）be admitted to a
school (after an examination)

【考查】kǎochá（动）check and appraise by a certain standard: ～他們
的成績 assess their achievements

【考核】kǎohé（动）check up on;
make an assessment of: 年終～制
度 year-end checkup system

【考場】kǎochǎng（名）examination
hall (room)

【考評】kǎopíng（动）check and rate

【考勤】kǎoqín（动）check on work
attendance: 月～表 monthly work-
attendance record

【考試】kǎoshì（名）examination: ～
(不)及格 pass (fail) an examination

【考察】kǎochá（动）❶ make an on-
the-spot inspecton or investigation:
～邊遠地區的教育問題 investigate
the problems of education in remote
areas ❷ study; examine carefully

【考慮】kǎolǜ（动）think over before
making a decision; consider; weigh:
他的建議值得～。His suggestion is
worth considering.

【考驗】kǎoyàn Ⅰ（动）test; put to
the test: ～一個人的品質 put a
person's moral integrity to the test Ⅱ
（名）test: 經得起時間的～ can
stand the test of time

者 zhě（助）［used after an
adjective, verb, etc. to indicate a
person or a thing］學～ scholar/
弱－ the weak/前－ the former/
新聞工作～ journalist / 種族主義
～ racist

而 部

而 ér Ⅰ（连）❶ and; as well as: 戰
～勝之 fight to win ❷［used to
connect an adverbial and a verb］侃
侃～談 talk with ease and assurance
Ⅱ（介）to: 從上～下 from top to
bottom

【而已】éryǐ（助）merely; nothing
but: 這不過是白日做夢～。This is
nothing but daydreaming.

【而今】érjīn（副）now; at present

【而且】érqiě（连）❶ furthermore;
but also ❷ and

【而後】érhòu（副）then

耐 nài（动）be able to bear;
endure; last: 這種布很～穿。This
kind of cloth stands hard wear.

【耐力】nàilì（名）endurance; stamina

【耐人尋味】nài rén xún wèi〈成〉be
pregnant with meaning; give much
food for thought

【耐久】nàijiǔ（形）durable; lasting

【耐心】nàixīn（形）patient: 對人～
be patient with others

【耐火】nàihuǒ（形）fire-resistant;
refractory

【耐火磚】nàihuǒzhuān（名）refracto-
ry brick; fire brick

【耐用】nàiyòng（形）durable: ～品
durable goods; durables

【耐性】nàixìng（名）patience; endurance

【耐寒】nàihán（形）cold-resistant

【耐勞】nàiláo（动）be able to endure
hardships

【耐烦】nàifán（形）patient: 不 ~
impatient

【耐酸】nàisuān（形）acid-resisting;
acidproof

【耐热】nàirè（形）heat-resisting;
heatproof

【耐磨】nàimó（形）wear-resisting;
wearproof

耍 shuǎ（动）❶ play; amuse oneself ❷ play with (a knife, monkey,
etc.) in a circus: ~ 坛子 juggle
with jars ❸〈贬〉display; carry out
by dishonest means: ~ 态度 get
tough with sb.; vent one's spleen on
sb.

【耍弄】shuǎnòng（动）❶ deceive:
~ 人 make a fool of sb. ❷〈贬〉re-
sort to: ~ 一切不正当手段 use all
dishonest means

【耍花招】shuǎ huāzhāo（动）❶
play petty tricks ❷ resort to a
sleight of hand

【耍威风】shuǎ wēifēng（动）lord it
over

【耍流氓】shuǎ liúmáng（动）behave
like a hooligan; behave shamelessly
(esp. towards a woman)

【耍笔杆子】shuǎ bǐgǎnzi（动）wield
a facile pen with no practical knowledge of reality

【耍脾气】shǎ píqi（动）get into a
temper

【耍滑】shuǎhuá（耍 滑 头 shuǎ
huátóu）〈口〉shirk work or responsibility with an excuse; cheat

【耍赖】shuǎlài（耍无赖 shuǎ wúlài）
（动）act like a scoundrel

【耍嘴皮子】shuǎ zuǐpízi（动）❶
talk glibly; brag ❷ pay lip service

耒 部

耕 gēng（动）plough; till

【耕田】gēngtián（动）plough the
fields

【耕地】gēngdì Ⅰ（动）plough Ⅱ（名）
farmland

【耕作】gēngzuò（名）farming; cultivation

【耕具】gēngjù（名）farm tools

【耕耘】gēngyún（名）ploughing and
weeding; cultivation

【耕畜】gēngchù（名）farm animal

【耕种】gēngzhòng（动）plough and
sow; cultivate

耘 yún（动）weed: ~ 锄 hoe

耙 bà Ⅰ（名）harrow: 钉 齿 ~
spike-tooth harrow Ⅱ（动）draw
harrow over (field): ~ 地 harrow a
field
see also pá

【耙子】bàzi（名）harrow

耙 pá Ⅰ（名）rake; harrow Ⅱ（动）
rake; harrow: ~ 地 harrow (up) a field
see also bà

【耙子】pázi（名）rake; harrow

耗 hào Ⅰ（动）❶ consume; cost ❷
delay; stall: ~ 时间 stall for time Ⅱ
（名）message of misfortune: 噩 ~
announcement of sb.'s death

【耗子】hàozi（名）〈方〉mouse; rat

【耗费】hàofèi（动）consume; ex-
pend

【耗损】hàosǔn Ⅰ（动）waste; consume Ⅱ（名）consumption: 招致财

力的～ incur a financial loss

【耗竭】hàojié (名) exhaust; drain

耠 huō (動) hoe

【耠子】huōzi (名) a hoeing implement

耢 pǎng (動) hoe

耩 jiǎng (動) sow with a drill

耳 部

耳 ěr I (名) ear II (形) ear-shaped

【耳目】ěrmù (名) ❶ what one sees and hears; information ❷ informer: 爲人～ serve sb. as a spy

【耳目一新】ěr mù yī xīn 〈成〉 find that everything has taken on a new look

【耳目閉塞】ěr mù bì sè 〈成〉ill-informed; be ignorant of what's going on in the outside world

【耳朵】ěrduo (名) ear

【耳光】ěrguāng (名) slap in the face; box on the ear

【耳房】ěrfáng (名) side room

【耳背】ěrbèi (形) hard of hearing

【耳挖子】ěrwāzi (名) earpick

【耳針】ěrzhēn (名) ear-acupuncture: ～療法 ear-acupuncture therapy

【耳語】ěryǔ (名) whisper

【耳鳴】ěrmíng (名)〈醫〉 ringing in the ear

【耳鼻喉科】ěr bí hóu kē (名) E. N. T. department; otolaryngology: ～醫生 otolaryngologist

【耳聞】ěrwén (動) hear about

【耳機】ěrjī (名) earphone

【耳環】ěrhuán (名) earring

【耳邊風】ěrbiānfēng (名) advice falling on deaf ears

耶 yē

【耶和華】Yēhéhuá (名) Jehovah

【耶穌】Yēsū (名) Jesus

【耶穌教】Yēsūjiào (名) Protestantism

耷 dā (名) big ear

【耷拉】dāla (動) droop

耽 dān (動) stay; delay

【耽誤】dānwù (動) hold up; delay: ～不少時間 waste a lot of time

【耽擱】dānge (動) ❶ stay; stop off: 在北京～兩天 stop off in Beijing for two days ❷ delay: 不能再～ cannot afford any further delay

耿 gěng I (形) honest and just; upright II (名) (Gěng) a surname

【耿直】gěngzhí (形) honest and frank; upright

【耿耿】gěnggěng (形) ❶ disturbed; troubled: ～不寐 be too perturbed to fall asleep ❷ devoted; faithful ❸ bright: ～星河欲曙天。The Milky Way still shines at daybreak.

聆 líng (動) listen

【聆聽】língtīng (動) listen respectfully

聊 liáo I (副) merely; slightly: ～以解嘲 just to relieve embarrassment II (動) chat

【聊天】liáotiān (動) chat: 一邊喝茶，一邊～ chat over a cup of tea

【聊且】liáoqiě (副) for the time being

【聊勝於無】liáo shèng yú wú 〈成〉 a

little is better than none

【聊賴】liáolài（名）[usu. used in such negative combinations as "無~", "百無~"] sth. to live for; sth. to fall back upon: 百無 ~ be infinitely bored; languish in boredom

聒 guō（動）(of noise) irritate

【聒耳】guō'ěr（動）grate on one's ears

【聒噪】guōzào（形）noisy; clamorous

聖 shèng Ⅰ（名）saint; sage Ⅱ（形）
❶ holy: ~ 城 Holy City ❷ imperial: ~ 旨 imperial edict

【聖人】shèngrén（名）Sage; man of great virtue and wisdom

【聖母】Shèngmǔ（名）〈宗〉Virgin Mary; Madonna

【聖地】shèngdì（名）❶〈宗〉Holy Land ❷ shrine; sacred place

【聖多美和普林西比】Shèngduōměi hé Pǔlínxībǐ（名）São Tomé and Principe

【聖馬力諾】Shèngmǎlìnuò（名）San Marino: ~ 人 San Marinese

【聖經】Shèngjīng（名）The (Holy) Bible

【聖誕】shèngdàn（名）birthday of Jesus Christ: ~ 老人 Santa Claus / ~ 樹 Christmas tree

【聖誕節】Shèngdànjié（名）Christmas Day

【聖賢】shèngxián（名）sages and men of virtue

聘 pìn（動）❶ engage; employ: 他爲技術顧問 engage him as technical adviser ❷ betroth

【聘用】pìnyòng（動）appoint; hire

【聘任】pìnrèn（動）appoint

【聘書】pìnshū（名）letter of appointment; contract

【聘請】pìnqǐng（動）engage; hire

【聘禮】pìnlǐ（名）betrothal presents

聚 jù（動）gather; congregate: 全家團 ~ family reunion

【聚合】jùhé Ⅰ（動）gather together; assemble Ⅱ（名）〈化〉polymerization

【聚光燈】jùguāngdēng（名）spotlight

【聚居】jùjū（動）(of an ethnic group, etc.) inhabit; live in a compact community

【聚衆鬧事】jù zhòng nào shì（動）gang up with unruly elements and kick up a row

【聚集】jùjí（動）gather; congregate

【聚會】jùhuì Ⅰ（動）have a get-together Ⅱ（名）get-together; party

【聚精會神】jù jīng huì shén（成）be all attention; give all one's attention to; concentrate on: 他 ~ 地研究案情。He studied the case with full concentration.

【聚積】jùjī（動）accumulate; amass

【聚餐】jùcān（動）dine together to celebrate an occasion

【聚寶盆】jùbǎopén（名）magic treasure bowl; land rich in natural resources; land of plenty

【聚攏】jùlǒng（動）assemble; congregate

【聚變】jùbiàn（名）〈物〉fusion

聞 wén Ⅰ（動）❶ hear: 所見所 ~ what one sees and hears; one's impressions ❷ smell: 這菜 ~ 起來挺香。The dish smells delicious. Ⅱ（名）❶ news; story: 傳 ~ hearsay

❷ (Wén) a surname III (形) famous; renowned: 她變得默默無~了。She has drifted into obscurity.

【聞名】wénmíng (形) well-known; famous: ~於世 well known all over the world

【聞所未聞】wén suǒ wèi wén (形) unheard-of; never heard of before

【聞風而動】wén fēng ér dòng〈成〉take immediate action at the news; make a quick response

【聞風喪膽】wén fēng sòng dǎn〈成〉be panic-stricken (in face of danger)

聲 shēng I (名) ❶ sound; noise ❷ tone: 四~ the four tones (of a Chinese character) ❸ reputation; fame: 名~不好 have a bad reputation II (動) make a sound; speak out; declare: ~言 profess III (量) (of cries, salvoes, etc.): 連~道謝 thank (sb.) again and again

【聲名】shēngmíng (名) reputation: ~狼藉 be notorious

【聲色】shēngsè (名) voice and countenance (of a person): ~俱厲 look severe and speak sternly

【聲波】shēngbō (名)〈物〉sound wave

【聲明】shēngmíng I (動) state; declare II (名) statement; declaration: 發表~ make a statement

【聲威】shēngwēi (名) fame and influence; prestige

【聲音】shēngyīn (名) sound; voice; noise

【聲浪】shēnglàng (名) clamour; roar; outcry

【聲納】shēngnà (名)〈物〉sonar

【聲討】shēngtǎo (動) denounce; condemn publicly

【聲帶】shēngdài (名) ❶〈生理〉vocal cord(s) ❷〈電影〉sound track

【聲望】shēngwàng (名) fame; prestige

【聲張】shēngzhāng (動) disclose; make known

【聲援】shēngyuán (動) publicly express support for; voice solidarity with

【聲勢】shēngshì (名) momentum; impact: ~浩大 be great in strength and momentum/ 造~ build up a momentum

【聲像】shēngxiàng (形) audio-video: ~器材 audio-video equipment

【聲稱】shēngchēng (動) claim; assert

【聲調】shēngdiào (名) ❶ tone; voice: 以嚴屬的~ in a harsh voice ❷〈語〉tone of a Chinese character

【聲價】shēngjià (名) fame and position; reputation

【聲樂】shēngyuè (名)〈樂〉vocal music: ~家 vocalist

【聲嘶力竭】shēng sī lì jié〈成〉get exhausted and hoarse from shouting; shout oneself hoarse

【聲學】shēngxué (名) acoustics

【聲譽】shēngyù (名) reputation; renown: 享有國際~ enjoy international fame

【聲辯】shēngbiàn (動) defend; justify: 無法~ unable to defend one's position

【聲響】shēngxiǎng (名) noise; sound

聰 cōng (形) (of hearing) sensitive: 耳~ be able to hear clearly

【聰明】cōngming (形) intelligent;

bright

聯 lián I (動) unite; join II (名) first or second line of a couplet; couplet

【聯大】 liándà (名)(short for 聯合國大會 liánhéguó dàhuì) the UN General Assembly

【聯名】 liánmíng (形) joint; jointly signed; ~抗議 lodge a joint protest

【聯合】 liánhé I (動) unite; ally II (形) joint; combined; ~舉辦 be under the joint auspices of

【聯合王國】 Liánhé wáng guó (名) the United Kingdom

【聯合公報】 liánhé gōngbào (名) joint communiqué

【聯合收割機】 liánhé shōugējī (名) combine(d) harvester

【聯合政府】 liánhé zhèngfǔ (名) coalition government

【聯合國】 Liánhéguó (名) the United Nations

【聯合會】 liánhéhuì (名) federation; union

【聯防】 liánfáng (名) joint defence

【聯邦】 liánbāng (名) federation; commonwealth

【聯軍】 liánjūn (名) allied forces

【聯姻】 liányīn (名) be related by marriage

【聯席會議】 liánxí huìyì (名) joint meeting

【聯結】 liánjié (動) bind; link

【聯運】 liányùn (名) through transport

【聯絡】 liánluò I (動) make contact with II (名) contact; liaison: 失去 ~ lose contact with / ~官員 liaison officer

【聯絡處】 liánluòchù (名) liaison office

【聯號商店】 liánhào shāngdiàn (連鎖店 liánsuǒdiàn) (名) chain store

【聯盟】 liánméng (名) union; alliance

【聯想】 liánxiǎng I (名) (of ideas) association II (動) associate one thing with another

【聯誼會】 liányìhuì (名) association; fraternity

【聯播】 liánbō (名) hookup; broadcast over a radio or television network

【聯賽】 liánsài (名) league matches; tournament

【聯繫】 liánxì (動) get in touch with; relate

【聯歡】 liánhuān (動) have a get-together; have a party

【聯歡晚會】 liánhuān wǎnhuì (名) evening party; evening; soiree; gala night

聳 sǒng (動) ❶ tower; rise high ❷ astonish; arouse the attention of: ~人聽聞 create a sensation

【聳入雲霄】 sǒng rù yún xiāo 〈成〉 tower into the clouds

【聳立】 sǒnglì (動) tower; rise high; soar: 羣山~。The tall mountains soar into the skies.

【聳肩】 sǒngjiān (動) shrug (one's shoulders)

職 zhí (名) ❶ duty: 失~ neglect one's duty ❷ post; position; office: 身居要~ hold an important post

【職工】 zhígōng (名) staff and workers

【職位】 zhíwèi (名) position; post

【職員】 zhíyuán (名) office worker; staff member

【職能】zhínéng（名）function

【職務】zhíwù（名）post; job

【職責】zhízé（名）duty; responsibility

【職業】zhíyè（名）occupation; profession: ～學校 vocational school

【職稱】zhíchēng（名）professional title

【職權】zhíquán（名）authority of office: 濫用～ abuse one's office or power

聶 Niè（名）a surname

聾 lóng（形）deaf

【聾子】lóngzi（名）deaf person

【聾啞人】lóngyǎrén（名）deaf-mute

聽 tīng Ⅰ（動）❶ hear; listen to: ～收音機 listen in to a radio ❷ be receptive; listen（to）: 他不～我的。He wouldn't listen to me. ❸ let: ～之任之 allow sth. to go unchecked ❹ administer: ～政 hold court Ⅱ（量）tin; can: 三～咖啡 three tins of coffee

【聽力】tīnglì（名）❶ hearing ❷ aural comprehension

【聽天由命】tīng tiān yóu mìng〈成〉be resigned to one's fate; trust to luck

【聽見】tīngjian（動）hear: 聽不見 can't hear/ 聽得見 can hear

【聽取】tīngqǔ（動）listen to

【聽其自然】tīng qí zì rán〈成〉allow things to take their natural course

【聽信】tīngxìn（動）believe: ～傳謠 give credence to hearsay

【聽信兒】tīngxìnr（動）wait for information: 再也聽不到他的信兒。He was never heard of again.

【聽候】tīnghòu（動）wait for（a decision, etc.）

【聽起來】tīngqǐlai（動）sound: ～挺熟悉 sound rather familiar

【聽從】tīngcóng（動）obey; accept（advice）

【聽眾】tīngzhòng（名）audience

【聽筒】tīngtǒng（名）telephone receiver

【聽話】tīnghuà（動）be obedient

【聽話兒】tīnghuàr（動）〈口〉wait for an answer: 明天～ will give a reply tomorrow

【聽說】tīngshuō（動）hear about; it is said that: ～他出國了。It's said that he has gone abroad.

【聽課】tīngkè（動）❶ attend a lecture ❷ sit in on a class

【聽憑】tīngpíng（動）let sb. do as he pleases: ～裁決 abide by sb.'s decision

【聽講】tīngjiǎng（動）attend a talk or lecture

【聽覺】tīngjué（名）sense of hearing

聿 部

肆 sì Ⅰ（數）[the elaborate form of the numeral 四, used on cheques, banknotes, etc.] four Ⅱ（副）wantonly; recklessly: 大～誣蔑 wantonly vilify

【肆虐】sìnüè（動）wreak havoc: 洪水～。The floods are wreaking havoc.

【肆無忌憚】sì wú jì dàn〈成〉unbridled; impertinent

【肆意】sìyì（副）wantonly; dissolutely: ～誹謗 wantonly slander

肅 sù (形) ❶ respectful: ～ 立 stand in solemn silence; stand in awe ❷ awe-inspiring; serious: 氣 氛嚴 ～ awe-inspiring atmosphere

【肅清】sùqīng (動) eliminate; get rid of; wipe out: ～封建主義餘毒 eliminate the pernicious influence of feudalism

【肅貪】sùtān (動) stamp out corruption

【肅靜】sùjìng (形) solemn and silent

【肅穆】sùmù (形) in respectful silence

肄 yì (動) study

【肄業】yìyè (動) study in a school: 大學～ study at college for some time

肇 zhào (動) start; cause; create

【肇事】zhàoshì (動) cause trouble; create an accident: ～者 the one responsible for an accident; the trouble-maker

肉 部

肉 ròu (名) ❶ meat; flesh: 五花 ～ streaky pork / 聽裝～ canned meat ❷ pulp; flesh (of fruit): 桂圓 ～ dried longan pulp

【肉丁】ròudīng (名) diced meat

【肉丸子】ròuwánzi (名) meatball

【肉牛】ròuniú (菜牛 càiniú) (名) beef cattle

【肉末】ròumò (肉糜 ròumí) (名) minced meat

bouillon

【肉店】ròudiàn (名) butcher's (shop)

【肉食】ròushí Ⅰ (名) meat (food) Ⅱ (形) carnivorous: ～動物 carnivorous animal

【肉桂】ròuguì (名) 〈植〉 Chinese cassia tree; Chinese cinnamon

【肉眼】ròuyǎn (名) naked eye: ～可 以看見。It can be seen with the naked eye

【肉排】ròupái (名) steak

【肉麻】ròumá (形) disgusting; sickening; fulsome

【肉絲】ròusī (名) shredded meat

【肉湯】ròutāng (名) broth

【肉搏】ròubó (動) engage in a hand-to-hand fight: ～戰 bayonet fighting

【肉餅】ròubǐng (名) meat pie; mince pie

【肉瘤】ròuliú (名) 〈醫〉 sarcoma

【肉慾】ròuyù (名) carnal desire; lust

【肉餡】ròuxiàn (名) meat stuffing; chopped meat

【肉鬆】ròusōng (名) dried meat floss

【肉鷄】ròujī (名) meat chicken

【肉體】ròutǐ (名) human body

肋 lèi (名) ❶ rib; costa ❷ side of the chest

【肋木】lèimù (名) 〈體〉 stall bars

【肋骨】lèigǔ (名) rib

肌 jī (名) muscle

【肌肉】jīròu (名) muscle; flesh

【肌腱】jījiàn (名) tendon; sinew

【肌膚】jīfū (名) human skin

【肌體】jītǐ (名) ❶ human body: ～ 的抵抗力 resistance (to disease) of the body ❷ organism

肖 xiào（動）resemble; be like: 維
妙維～ be strikingly true to life
【肖像】xiàoxiàng（名）portrait

肝 gān（名）liver
【肝火】gānhuǒ（名）irascibility: 動
～ vent one's spleen
【肝炎】gānyán（名）〈醫〉hepatitis
【肝腦塗地】gān nǎo tú dì〈成〉die a
tragic death; lay down one's life
【肝癌】gān'ái（名）〈醫〉liver cancer
【肝膽相照】gān dǎn xiāng zhào〈成〉
treat each other with all sincerity
【肝臟】gānzàng（名）liver

肚 dǔ（名）tripe
see also dù

肚 dù（名）belly: ～臍 navel
see also dǔ

肛 gāng（名）anus
【肛門】gāngmén（名）anus

肘 zhǒu（名）elbow
【肘子】zhǒuzi（名）❶ upper part of
a leg of pork ❷ elbow

育 yù Ⅰ（動）❶ give birth to: 計劃
生 ～ family planning ❷ rear;
breed: ～苗 grow seedlings Ⅱ（名）
education: 智 ～ intellectual education
【育秧】yùyāng（動）〈農〉raise rice
seedlings
【育種】yùzhǒng（動）〈農〉breeding

肩 jiān Ⅰ（名）shoulder: ～ 並 ～
shoulder to shoulder; side by side Ⅱ
（動）shoulder; take upon; assume
(responsibility)
【肩負】jiānfù（動）carry on the
shoulder; shoulder; assume（re-

sponsibility）: ～着掃盲的任務 be
entrusted with the task of wiping
out illiteracy
【肩胛骨】jiānjiǎgǔ（名）scapula
【肩章】jiānzhāng（名） epaulette;
shoulder-strap
【肩膀】jiānbǎng（名）shoulder

肯 kěn（動）agree; be ready to: 他
～幫助人。He is always ready to
help people.
【肯尼亞】Kěnníyà（名）Kenya: ～
人 Kenyan
【肯定】kěndìng Ⅰ（動）afffirm; consider (as) correct: 我們～他的觀
點。We consider his views correct.
Ⅱ（形）positive; definite: ～的答
復 definite answer; answer in the
affirmative Ⅲ（副）surely; definitely

朊 ruǎn（名）protein

肢 zhī（名）limb: 上～ upper limbs
【肢體】zhītǐ（名）❶ limbs ❷ limbs
and trunk

肺 fèi（名）lung
【肺炎】fèiyán（名）pneumonia
【肺活量】fèihuóliàng（名）vital capacity
【肺結核】fèijiéhé（名）(pulmonary)
tuberculosis; TB
【肺腑】fèifǔ（名）bottom of one's
heart: ～之言 the words from the
bottom of one's heart
【肺癌】fèi'ái（名）lung cancer

肫 zhūn（名）gizzard (of a fowl):
鷄～ chicken gizzard

肥 féi Ⅰ（形）❶ fat ❷ fertile; rich
❸ loose; large: ～大的衣服 big-

sized garment Ⅱ (名) fertilizer Ⅲ (动) fatten; fertilize

【肥力】féilì (名)(soil) fertility

【肥大】féidà (形) fat; plump

【肥沃】féiwò (形) fertile; rich

【肥皂】féizào (名) soap

【肥壮】féizhuàng (形) stout and strong

【肥胖】féipàng (形) fat; obese

【肥料】féiliào (名) fertilizer

【肥硕】féishuò (形) big and sturdy

股 gǔ Ⅰ (名)❶ thigh ❷ (of an organization) section ❸ share; portion Ⅱ (量): 一～土匪 a gang of bandits

【股本】gǔběn (名) capital stock

【股份】gǔfèn (名) share; stock: ～公司 joint-stock company

【股份制】gǔfènzhì (名) shareholding system

【股金】gǔjīn (名) share capital

【股东】gǔdōng (名) shareholder; stockholder

【股息】gǔxī (名) dividend

【股票】gǔpiào (名) share certificate; share; stock: ～經紀人 stockbroker / ～市場 stock market

胡 hú Ⅰ (副) recklessly; wantonly Ⅱ (名) (Hú) a surname

【胡扯】húchě (名) talk nonsense

【胡作非爲】hú zuò fēi wéi〈成〉act wantonly; run riot

【胡來】húlái (动) act haphazardly or wantonly

【胡思亂想】hú sī luàn xiǎng〈成〉give free rein to one's imagination

【胡琴】húqín (名) huqin (two-stringed Chinese fiddle)

【胡話】húhuà (名) ravings; rigmarole

【胡亂】húluàn (副)❶ carelessly; casually ❷ at will; without reason

【胡說八道】hú shuō bā dào (动) talk downright nonsense

【胡鬧】húnào (动) act or behave unreasonably; make a scene

【胡謅】húzhōu (名) tall story; pure fabrication

【胡蘿蔔】húluóbo (名) carrot

【胡攪】hújiǎo (名)❶ disturbance ❷ quibble; sophistry

背 bēi (动)❶ carry on the back ❷ bear; shoulder (a load, burden, etc.)

see also bèi

【背包】bēibāo (名) knapsack; field pack; package carried on the back

【背包袱】bēibāofu (动) have a load on one's mind

【背負】bēifù (动) carry on the back; bear; shoulder (a load, responsibility)

【背黑鍋】bēi hēiguō (动)〈口〉bear the blame for others; be a scapegoat; have one's reputation tarnished for no fault of one's own

【背債】bēizhài (动) run into debt; be in debt

背 bèi Ⅰ (名)❶ back (of the body) ❷ back (of an object): 手～ back of a hand Ⅱ (动)❶ hide; avoid: 你不應該～着我們说這些不負責任的話。You shouldn't have made such irresponsible comments behind our backs. ❷ go against; violate: ～棄前言 go back upon one's word ❸ recite from memory Ⅲ (形)❶ secluded or out-of-the-way: ～街小巷 back streets and small lanes ❷ somewhat deaf: 耳朵～ be hard of hearing Ⅳ (介) with the back towards: ~着燈光 (sit or stand) with one's back to the lamplight see also bēi

【背心】 bèixīn (名) waistcoat; vest: 毛~ sleeveless woollen sweater

【背水一戰】 bèi shuǐ yī zhàn 〈成〉 put up a desperate fight by cutting off one's own retreat; succeed or die in the attempt

【背井離鄉】 bèi jǐng lí xiāng 〈成〉 leave one's native place (often to make a living); be away from home

【背光】 bèiguāng (動) be against the light

【背地裏】 bèidìli (副) secretly; behind sb.'s back

【背後】 bèihòu Ⅰ (名) rear (of): 山~ behind the hills Ⅱ (副) not to sb.'s face: ~議論人 gossip about sb. behind his back

【背風】 bèifēng (形) leeward

【背約】 bèiyuē (動) break a promise; go back on one's word; violate an agreement

【背信棄義】 bèi xìn qì yì 〈成〉 act without faith or in defiance of justice; be perfidious

【背面】 bèimiàn (名) reverse side

【背叛】 bèipàn (動) betray; forsake

【背時】 bèishí (形) ❶ behind the times ❷ unlucky

【背書】 bèishū Ⅰ (動) recite a lesson Ⅱ (名) endorsement (on a cheque)

【背部】 bèibù (名) back (of the body, house, etc.)

【背景】 bèijǐng (名) background; backdrop; setting: 時代~ historical setting

【背棄】 bèiqì (動) betray; desert; abandon: ~諾言 break one's promise

【背道而馳】 bèi dào ér chí 〈成〉 act counter to; be diametrically opposed to

【背誦】 bèisòng (動) recite from memory

【背影】 bèiyǐng (名) (a person's) back seen from a distance

【背離】 bèilí (動) depart from; deviate from

胃 wèi (名) stomach

【胃口】 wèikǒu (名) appetite: ~欠佳 lack appetite; have a jaded appetite

【胃病】 wèibìng (名) stomach trouble

【胃液】 wèiyè (名) gastric juice

【胃潰瘍】 wèikuìyáng (名) gastric ulcer

【胃癌】 wèi'ái (名) stomach cancer

胖 pàng (形) fat; plump: 肥~ fat

【胖子】 pàngzi (名) fat person; fatty

【胖頭魚】 pàngtóuyú (名) bighead; variegated carp

胚 pēi (名) 〈生〉 embryo

【胚乳】 pēirǔ (名) 〈植〉 endosperm

【胚胎】 pēitāi (名) 〈生〉 embryo: ~學 embryology

【胚珠】 pēizhū (名) 〈植〉 ovule

胗 zhēn (名) gizzard: 鴨~ duck's gizzard

胞 bāo Ⅰ (名) ❶ placenta and fetal membrane; afterbirth: 雙~胎 twin ❷ compatriot: 同~ fellow countryman Ⅱ (形) born of the same parents: ~姐 full (blood) sister

胎 tāi Ⅰ (名) ❶ foetus ❷ padding; wadding ❸ tyre: 防滑輪~ nonskid tyre Ⅱ (量) birth: 懷了第二~ be

pregnant for the second time / 一～生了五頭豬仔 give birth to five piglets at a litter

【胎位】tāiwèi (名)〈醫〉position of a foetus

【胎兒】tāi'ér (名) foetus

脊 jǐ (名) ❶ backbone ❷ ridge see also jí

【脊梁】jǐliang (名) back (of the human body)

【脊梁骨】jǐlianggǔ (名) backbone; spine

脊 jí (名) ❶ backbone; spine: 背～ back of the human body ❷ ridge see also jǐ

【脊背】jíbèi (名) back of the human body

【脊椎】jízhuī (名) vertebra

【脊髓】jísuǐ (名) spinal cord

脅 xié Ⅰ (名) upper part of the side of the human body Ⅱ (動) intimidate; coerce

【脅迫】xiépò (動) coerce; compel; force

【脅從】xiécóng (名) accomplice under duress

胈 mī (名)〈化〉amidine

胰 yí (名)〈生理〉pancreas

【胰子】yízi (名) ❶〈方〉soap ❷〈口〉pancreas (of pigs, sheep, etc.)

【胰島素】yídǎosù (名)〈藥〉insulin

胯 kuà (名) crotch

胭 yān

【胭脂】yānzhi (名) rouge

脂 zhī (名) ❶ fat; grease ❷

rouge: ～粉 rouge and powder; cosmetics

【脂肪】zhīfáng (名) fat

胮 sà (名)〈化〉osazone

脆 cuì (形) ❶ fragile; brittle; crisp: 黃瓜絲很～。The shredded cucumber is crisp. ❷ clear: 清～的聲音 a ringing voice

【脆弱】cuìruò (形) frail; fragile

胸 xiōng (名) ❶ chest; breast: ～悶 suffer from the constriction of the chest ❷ mind; heart: ～中裝着全國人民 have the well-being of the whole nation at heart

【胸口】xiōngkǒu (名) pit of the stomach; chest

【胸中有數】xiōng zhōng yǒu shù〈成〉have a firm grasp of the situation and know how to act

【胸有成竹】xiōng yǒu chéng zhú〈成〉have a well-prepared overall plan in mind; have a preconceived idea; have complete confidence

【胸部】xiōngbù (名) chest; thorax

【胸脯】xiōngpú (名) chest

【胸無大志】xiōng wú dà zhì〈成〉devoid of ambition

【胸無點墨】xiōng wú diǎn mò〈成〉haven't a jot of learning; uneducated; ignorant

【胸像】xiōngxiàng (名) bust

【胸膛】xiōngtáng (名) chest

【胸襟】xiōngjīn (名) mind; breadth of mind

【胸懷】xiōnghuái Ⅰ (名) mind; heart: ～開闊 be broad-minded Ⅱ (動) have at heart: ～大志 cherish ambitious aspirations

胳 gā

see also gē; gé

【胳肢窝】gāzhiwō（名）armpit

胳 gē

see also gā; gé

【胳膊】gēbo（名）arm

【胳膊肘】gēbozhǒu（名）elbow

胳 gé

see also gā; gē

【胳肢】gézhi（动）tickle sb.

脈 mài（名）❶ arteries and veins ❷ pulse ❸ vein（in a leaf, an insect wing, or of mineral, etc.）

see also mò

【脈絡】màiluò（名）❶ arteries and veins ❷ sequence of ideas: ～分明 的文章 a well-organized article

【脈搏】màibó（名）pulse: 数～ count one's pulses

【脈衝】màichōng（名）pulse: ～信 號 pulse signal

脈 mò

see also mài

【脈脈】mòmò（形）loving; affectionate: 含情～ full of tender affection

能 néng I（名）❶ ability; skill: 技 ～ technical ability; skill ❷〈物〉 energy: 電～ electrical energy II （形）able; capable: ～手 expert; dab III（动）can; be able to: 你～來 嗎？Can you come?

【能人】néngrén（名）able person; strongman

【能力】nénglì（名）ability; capability

【能上能下】néng shàng néng xià〈成〉 be able to work either at a higher or lower level

【能見度】néngjiàndù（名）visibility

【能者多勞】néng zhě duō láo〈成〉 able people should do more work; there're always numerous claims on an able person

【能屈能伸】néng qū néng shēn〈成〉 able to stoop or stand as the occasion arises

【能耐】néngnai（名）〈口〉skill; ability: 他没有什麼～。He has not much ability to speak of.

【能耗】nénghào（名）energy consumption

【能夠】nénggòu（动）can; be able to

【能量】néngliàng（名）❶〈物〉energy ❷（of a person）capabilities: 他這個人～很大。He has the ability to make people go around with him.

【能幹】nénggàn（形）able; capable

【能源】néngyuán（名）energy; energy source: ～危機 energy crisis

【能說會道】néng shuō huì dào〈成〉 have a ready tongue; be a glib talker

脱 tuō I（动）❶（of skin, hair, etc.）come off; lose: ～髮 trichomadesis; going bald ❷ take off: ～帽 take off（raise）one's hat（to pay respects）❸ get away from; be free from: 如：～繮之馬 like a runaway horse; running out of control ❹ miss out（words）II（名）〔Tuō〕 a surname

【脱口而出】tuō kǒu ér chū〈成〉say sth. without thinking; blurt out

【脱手】tuōshǒu（动）❶ slip off the hand ❷ sell

【脱水】tuōshuǐ（动）❶〈醫〉loss of body fluids ❷〈化〉dehydration; dewatering

【脱身】tuōshēn（动）get away: 人

家拉住我，不得～。I was button-holed and couldn't get away.

【脱轨】tuōguǐ (动) derail

【脱粒】tuōlì (动)〈农〉thresh; shell: ～機 thresher

【脱产】tuōchǎn (动) be released from work: ～進修 be released from work for a study course

【脱贫】tuōpín (动) shake off poverty

【脱钩】tuōgōu (动) be disconnected; get unhooked

【脱落】tuōluò (动) come off; lose (one's hair, etc.): 牆皮～。The plaster on the wall is peeling off.

【脱节】tuōjié (动) be dislocated; be separated (divorced) from

【脱销】tuōxiāo (动) be out of stock; be sold out

【脱险】tuōxiǎn (动) be out of danger

【脱离】tuōlí (动) break with; break free from; be divorced from: ～現實 be divorced from reality

【脱党】tuōdǎng (动) leave a political party; give up one's party membership

脖 bó (名) neck: 圍～兒 scarf; muffler

【脖子】bózi (名) neck

脯 fǔ (名) ❶ dried meat ❷ preserved fruit: 桃～ preserved peaches

see also pú

脯 pú (名) chest; breast: 胸～ chest

see also fú

胫 jìng (名)〈生理〉shin; shank: ～骨 shin bone; shank; tibia

脲 niào (名)〈化〉urea; carbamide

腐 fǔ (形) rotten; stale

【腐化】fǔhuà (形) corrupt

【腐朽】fǔxiǔ (形) decadent; rotten

【腐乳】fǔrǔ (名) fermented bean curd

【腐败】fǔbài Ⅰ (形) ❶ rotten ❷ corrupt Ⅱ (名) corruption

【腐殖質】fǔzhízhì (名) humus

【腐蚀】fǔshí (动) corrode; corrupt

【腐蚀劑】fǔshíjì (名)〈化〉corrosive agent

【腐爛】fǔlàn (名) rot; decay

肾 shèn (名) kidney: ～結石 kidney stone; renal calculus

【肾臟】shènzàng (名) kidney

腚 dìng (名)〈方〉buttocks

腔 qiāng (名) ❶ cavity: 腹～ abdominal cavity ❷ tune; pitch: 花～ coloratura ❸ accent: 講話帶有外國～ speak with a foreign accent

【腔調】qiāngdiào (名) ❶ tune: 唱不同的～ sing a different tune ❷ accent

腕 wàn (名) wrist

【腕子】wànzi (名) wrist

腋 yè (名) armpit

【腋毛】yèmáo (名) armpit hair

【腋臭】yèchòu (名) underarm odour

【腋窝】yèwō (名) armpit

腈 jīng (名)〈化〉nitrile

【腈綸】jīnglún (名) acrylic fibres

脹 zhàng (动) ❶ expand: 金屬受熱膨～。Metals expand with heat. ❷ swell; be bloated: 肚子發～ feel bloated

腌 ā
【腌臢】āza（形）〈方〉filthy; dirty

腓 féi（名）calf (of the leg)
【腓骨】féigǔ（名）〈生理〉fibula

腴 yú（形）❶ fat; plump: 豐 ～ plump ❷ fertile: 膏～之地 fertile land

脾 pí（名）spleen
【脾胃】píwèi（名）taste: 迎合某人 ～ cater for sb.'s taste
【脾氣】píqì（名）temper; disposition: ～變化無常 have an uncertain temper / 對某人大發～ vent one's spleen on sb.

腰 yāo（名）❶ waist ❷ middle; halfway: 爬到半山～ climb halfway up a mountain
【腰子】yāozi（名）〈口〉kidney
【腰包】yāobāo（名）purse; wallet
【腰身】yāoshēn（名）waist; waist measurement: 褲子的～ waist of the trousers
【腰部】yāobù（名）waist
【腰帶】yāodài（名）belt; girdle
【腰桿子】yāogǎnzi（名）back: ～不硬 have no powerful backing
【腰痛】yāotòng（名）pain in the back; backache
【腰圍】yāowéi（名）waistline; waist

腱 jiàn（名）tendon
【腱鞘炎】jiànqiàoyán（名）tenosynovitis

腿 tuǐ（名）❶ leg: 飛毛～ the swift-footed / 褲～ legs of a pair of trousers ❷ leg-shaped support: 凳子～ legs of a stool

【腿腳】tuǐjiǎo（名）ability to move around: ～不方便 have difficulty moving around

腸 cháng（名）intestines: 好心～ a kind heart
【腸斷】chángduàn（形）heartbroken; brokenhearted

腮 sāi（名）cheek
【腮腺】sāixiàn（名）〈生理〉parotid gland
【腮腺炎】sāixiànyán（名）parotitis; mumps
【腮幫子】sāibāngzi（名）〈口〉cheek

腥 xīng（名）❶ fish; meat ❷ unpleasant smell of fish or mutton etc.
【腥風血雨】xīng fēng xuè yǔ（成）blood bath; reign of terror
【腥氣】xīngqi（名）fishy; unpleasant smell

腭 è（名）〈生理〉palate: 軟(硬)～ soft (hard) palate

腳 jiǎo（名）❶ foot ❷ base; bottom support: 高～杯 goblet
【腳力】jiǎolì（名）strength of one's legs: 他個子高，～不錯。He is lanky and has wiry legs.
【腳手架】jiǎoshǒujià（名）scaffolding
【腳本】jiǎoběn（名）scenario; script
【腳印】jiǎoyìn（名）footprint
【腳步】jiǎobù（名）❶ footstep ❷ pace
【腳氣】jiǎoqì（名）〈醫〉beriberi
【腳註】jiǎozhù（名）footnote; note
【腳腕子】jiǎowànzi（腳脖子 jiǎobózi）（名）ankle
【腳跟】jiǎogēn（名）heel

【腳踏兩隻船】 jiǎo tà liǎng zhī chuán 〈成〉 sit on the fence; hedge one's bets; have a foot in either camp

【腳踏實地】 jiǎo tà shí dì 〈成〉 be practical and conscientious; down-to-earth

【腳鐐】 jiǎoliào (名) fetters; shackles

腫 zhǒng (動) swell: 他的踝關節 ～了。His ankle is swollen.

【腫瘤】 zhǒngliú (名) tumour: 惡性 ～ malignant tumour

腹 fù (名) belly; abdomen; stomach

【腹地】 fùdì (名) hinterland

【腹背受敵】 fù bèi shòu dí 〈成〉 be exposed to enemy attacks from front and rear

【腹腔】 fùqiāng (名)〈生理〉 abdominal cavity

【腹痛】 fùtòng (名) abdominal pain

【腹稿】 fùgǎo (名) mental draft: 打～ work out a mental draft

【腹瀉】 fùxiè (名) diarrhoea

腺 xiàn (名) gland

腦 nǎo (名) brain: 電～ electronic brain; computer

【腦力勞動】 nǎolì láodòng (名) mental labour

【腦子】 nǎozi (名)❶ brain ❷ mental ability; brains; mind: 他沒有～。He has no brains.

【腦炎】 nǎoyán (名) encephalitis

【腦海】 nǎohǎi (名) brain; mind: 一個念頭忽然閃過他的～。A sudden idea flashed across his mind.

【腦袋】 nǎodai (名)〈口〉 head

【腦筋】 nǎojīn (名)❶ mental faculty; brains; mind: 費～ tax one's

brains ❷ way of thinking; ideas: 老～ old-fashioned chap

【腦溢血】 nǎoyìxuè (名) cerebral haemorrhage

【腦滿腸肥】 nǎo mǎn cháng féi 〈成〉 (of rich people) heavy-jowled and pot-bellied

【腦膜】 nǎomó (名)〈生理〉 meninx

【腦膜炎】 nǎomóyán (名) meningitis

膏 gāo (名)❶ fat; grease; oil ❷ paste; cream; ointment: 梨～ pear syrup (for relieving coughs) ❸ plaster
see also gào

【膏腴】 gāoyú (形)〈書〉 fertile; rich

【膏藥】 gāoyào (名) plaster (for medical use)

膏 gào (動) lubricate
see also gāo

脊 lǚ

【膂力】 lǚlì (名) (physical) strength

膀 bǎng (名)❶ shoulder; arm: 肩～ shoulder ❷ wing (of a bird): 翅～ wing
see also pāng; páng

【膀子】 bǎngzi (名)❶ upper arm; arm: 光着～ naked to the waist ❷ wing: 雞～ chicken wing

【膀臂】 bǎngbì (名)❶ arm ❷ capable assistant; one's right-hand man

【膀闊腰圓】 bǎng kuò yāo yuán (形) broad-shouldered and of sturdy build

膀 pāng (形) dropsical
see also bǎng; páng

膀 páng
see also bǎng; pāng

【膀胱】 pángguāng (名) (urinary)

bladder

【膀胱炎】pángguāngyán（名）cystitis

髈

髈 bó（名）arm

see also bo

髈

髈 bo（名）arm：胳～ arm

see also bó

膈

膈 gé

【膈膜】gémó（名）diaphragm

膚

膚 fū（名）skin

【膚色】fūsè（名）colour of skin

【膚淺】fūqiǎn（形）skin-deep; shallow; superficial

膘

膘 biāo（名）(of an animal) fat：長～ put on flesh; fatten up

膜

膜 mó（名）membrane; film

【膜拜】móbài（動）worship; prostrate oneself

膝

膝 xī（名）knee

【膝蓋】xīgài（名）knee

【膝關節】xīguānjié（名）knee joint

膠

膠 jiāo Ⅰ（名）❶ glue; gum：萬能～ all-purpose adhesive ❷ rubber：～輪 rubber tyre Ⅱ（形）sticky; adhesive Ⅲ（動）stick as with glue：～合板 plywood; veneer board

【膠水】jiāoshuǐ（名）glue; mucilage

【膠片】jiāopiàn（名）film

【膠布】jiāobù（名）❶ adhesive plaster ❷ rubberized fabric

【膠印】jiāoyìn（名）offset printing

【膠泥】jiāoní（名）❶ clay ❷ plasticine; modelling material

【膠卷】jiāojuǎn（名）roll film; film

【膠着】jiāozhuó（形）stalemated; deadlocked：處於～狀態 reach an

impasse (or a deadlock)

【膠鞋】jiāoxié（名）❶ rubber shoe; galosh ❷ sneaker; rubber-soled shoe

【膠囊】jiāonáng（名）capsule

膛

膛 táng（名）❶ chest：開～ cut the chest open; disembowel ❷ bore; chamber：把子彈推上～ load a gun

膳

膳 shàn（名）meals; board：午～ lunch

【膳食】shànshí（名）meals; food

【膳宿】shànsù（名）board and lodging

【膳費】shànfèi（名）fee for regular meals; board expenses

膩

膩 nì（形）❶ (of food) greasy; oily：這菜太～。The dish is too rich. ❷ bored; tired of：～透了 be bored stiff

【膩煩】nìfán（動）❶ get bored; be sick of ❷ loathe; dislike：我最～這種人。I am fed up with such people.

膨

膨 péng（動）expand

【膨脹】péngzhàng（動）expand; inflate; swell：熱使氣體～。Heat causes the expansion of gases. / 通貨～ inflation

【膨體紗】péngtǐshā（名）〈紡〉bulk yarn

膺

膺 yīng Ⅰ（名）〈書〉breast：義憤填～ be fired with righteous indignation Ⅱ（動）bear; receive：榮～模範工作者稱號 be awarded the title of model worker

臀

臀 tún（名）buttock

【臀部】túnbù（名）buttocks

臂 bì (名) arm: 助一~之力 lend a hand

【臂章】bìzhāng (名) ❶ armband; arm badge ❷ shoulder emblem

【臂膊】bìbó (名) (upper) arm

臆 yì Ⅰ (名) chest Ⅱ (副) subjectively

【臆造】yìzào (動) fabricate; make up

【臆測】yìcè (動) surmise; guess

【臆說】yìshuō (名) assumption

【臆斷】yìduàn (動) assume: 殊難~ be difficult to conjecture

臃 yōng

【臃腫】yōngzhǒng (形) ❶ fat and clumsy; corpulent ❷ (of an organization) overstaffed

膈 gú (名) distension

【膈脹】gúzhàng (名) 〈中醫〉 tympanites; distension of abdomen

臊 sāo (形) smell of urine; body odour; offensive smell
see also sào

臊 sào (形) ashamed; bashful
see also são

膿 nóng (名) pus

【膿包】nóngbāo (名) ❶ 〈醫〉 pustule ❷ good-for-nothing

【膿腫】nóngzhǒng (名) 〈醫〉 abscess

【膿瘡】nóngchuāng (名) running sore

臉 liǎn (名) face; cheek: 丟~ lose face / 拉長~ pull a long face

【臉皮】liǎnpí (名) face: ~ 厚 shameless / ~薄 shy

【臉色】liǎnsè (名) ❶ complexion ❷ look; facial expression: ~陰沉 wear a sullen look

【臉紅】liǎnhóng (動) blush; flush

【臉盆】liǎnpén (名) wash-basin

【臉盆架】liǎnpénjià (名) wash-stand

【臉蛋】liǎndàn (名) face; cheeks

【臉譜】liǎnpǔ (名) (of male characters in traditional Chinese operas) facial design; facial makeup

膾 kuài

【膾炙人口】kuài zhì rén kǒu 〈成〉 (of writings, etc.) be immensely popular; enjoy universal admiration

膽 dǎn (名) ❶ gallbladder ❷ boldness; courage ❸ inner container: 暖瓶 ~ inner flask

【膽小】dǎnxiǎo (形) timorous: ~ 如鼠 be chicken-hearted

【膽大】dǎndà (形) daring; bold

【膽大包天】dǎn dà bāo tiān (形) extremely audacious

【膽大妄爲】dǎn dà wàng wéi (動) act recklessly

【膽怯】dǎnqiè (形) timid; shy

【膽固醇】dǎngùchún (名) 〈生化〉 cholesterol

【膽敢】dǎngǎn (動) dare; venture

【膽略】dǎnlüè (名) courage and tactical skill

【膽量】dǎnliàng (名) courage

【膽寒】dǎnhán (形) panic-stricken; horrified

【膽戰心驚】dǎn zhàn xīn jīng 〈成〉 shiver with fear

【膽識】dǎnshí (名) courage and vision

臍 qí (名) 〈生理〉 navel; umbilicus

【臍風】qífēng (名) 〈中醫〉 umbilical tetanus

【臍帶】qídài (名)〈生理〉umbilical cord

臘 là (名)❶ the 12th month of the lunar year: ～八粥 porridge of mixed cereals, beans, nuts, and dried fruits ❷ (of meat, fish, etc.) salted and dried: ～味 cured meat, fish, etc.

【臘肉】làròu (名) cured meat; bacon
【臘梅】làméi (名)〈植〉wintersweet
【臘腸】làcháng (名) sausage

臟 zàng (名) internal organs of the body; viscera: 肝～ liver / 心～ heart

臣 部

臣 chén (名) official under a feudal sovereign; subject

【臣民】chénmín (名) subject (of a sovereign)
【臣服】chénfú (動) acknowledge allegiance to (a sovereign or state)

臥 wò (動) lie; crouch

【臥車】wòchē (名)❶ sleeping car; sleeper ❷ car; automobile
【臥床】wòchuáng (動) lie in bed; stay in bed: ～不起 be bedridden
【臥具】wòjù (名) bedding
【臥室】wòshì (臥房 wòfáng)(名) bedroom
【臥倒】wòdǎo (動) lie down
【臥病】wòbìng (動) be laid up
【臥舖】wòpù (名) sleeping berth; sleeper: ～票 (sleeping) berth ticket

【臥薪嘗膽】wò xīn cháng dǎn (成) temper oneself in hardships so as to keep alive one's determination to stage a comeback

臧 Zāng (名) a surname

臨 lín Ⅰ (動)❶ arrive; be present: 身～其境 be on the scene ❷ face; encounter: ～河的陽臺 a balcony overlooking the river Ⅱ (形) right before; on the brink of: ～死 breathe one's last; on one's deathbed
【臨了】línliǎo (副)〈口〉in the end; at last: ～我們決定再開會。In the end, we decided to hold another meeting.
【臨危】línwēi (動)❶ be seriously ill ❷ face death; face grave danger: ～不懼 be fearless in the face of danger
【臨別】línbié (動) at parting; part: ～贈言 parting advice / 這張照片是我們～晚會的留念。This photo is a memento of our farewell party.
【臨近】línjìn (形) near: ～午夜 approaching midnight / ～火車站 close to the railway station
【臨牀】línchuáng (形) clinical
【臨到】líndào (動)❶ be about to: ～飛機起飛,他還沒有到。He didn't show up when the plane was about to take off. ❷ befall: 要是這事～他頭上,他會有辦法。He would find a solution if it should happen to him.
【臨界】línjiè (形) critical: ～狀態 critical state
【臨時】línshí (形)❶ at the last moment ❷ temporary; for the time being
【臨時代辦】línshí dàibàn (名)

charge d'affaires ad interim

【臨時政府】línshí zhèngfǔ〈名〉provisional government

【臨陣脫逃】lín zhèn tuō táo〈成〉disappear before battle; run away in the heat of a battle

【臨陣磨槍】lín zhèn mó qiāng〈成〉make no preparation until the last moment

【臨產】línchǎn（臨盆 línpén）〈副〉just before giving birth

【臨終】línzhōng〈形〉dying; just before one's death

【臨渴掘井】lín kě jué jǐng〈成〉begin to dig a well only when one gets thirsty; do nothing till the eleventh hour

【臨淵羨魚】lín yuān xiàn yú〈成〉indulge in wishful thinking without making any effort to achieve one's goal

【臨摹】línmó〈動〉copy (a model of calligraphy or painting)

【臨頭】líntóu〈動〉befall; be imminent: 大難～。Calamity is approaching.

自 部

自 zì Ⅰ（代）oneself; one's own: 獨 ～ by oneself／～給～足 self-sufficiency Ⅱ（副）certainly; naturally: 其中～有道理。There must be a reason for it. Ⅲ（介）from; since: ～那時起 since then／～始至終 from first to last; from start to finish

【自力更生】zì lì gēng shēng〈成〉rely on one's own efforts; self-reliance

【自大】zìdà（形）swollen-headed; conceited

【自己】zìjǐ Ⅰ（代）oneself: 我要～處理這個問題。I'll attend to it myself. Ⅱ（形）closely related; own: 咱們是～人。You're among friends.

【自以為是】zì yǐ wéi shì〈成〉count oneself invariably correct and remain intransigent

【自白】zìbái Ⅰ（名）written statement making clear one's position and views; self-exculpation Ⅱ（動）vindicate oneself

【自立】zìlì〈動〉stand on one's own feet; be independent

【自主】zìzhǔ〈動〉be one's own master; act independently

【自由】zìyóu Ⅰ（名）freedom; liberty Ⅱ（形）free; unchecked: ～市場 free market／～貿易 free trade／～港 free port

【自由化】zìyóuhuà〈名〉liberalization

【自在】zìzài〈形〉comfortable; at ease: 不～ ill at ease

【自如】zìrú〈副〉freely; with ease; at home: 運用～ wield skilfully

【自行】zìxíng〈副〉❶ by oneself: ～處理 act as one sees fit ❷ of oneself; of one's own accord

【自行車】zìxíngchē〈名〉bike; bicycle

【自決】zìjué〈名〉self-determination

【自私】zìsī〈形〉selfish; egoistic

【自我】zìwǒ〈代〉oneself; self: ～克制 self-control／～批評 self-criticism

【自助】zìzhù〈名〉self-service: ～午餐 a buffet lunch

【自身】zìshēn（名）self; oneself

【自言自语】zì yán zì yǔ〈成〉murmur to oneself; think aloud

【自作自受】zì zuò zì shòu〈成〉be stewed in one's own juice

【自作聪明】zì zuò cōng míng〈成〉imagine oneself clever and offer uncalled-for advice or act on one's own

【自吹自擂】zì chuī zì léi〈成〉blow one's own horn; praise oneself in glowing terms

【自投罗网】zì tóu luó wǎng〈成〉walk right into a trap; rise to the bait

【自告奋勇】zì gào fèn yǒng〈成〉volunteer to undertake a difficult task

【自拔】zìbá（动）extricate oneself (from sth.)

【自供】zìgòng（动）confess

【自居】zìjū（动）pretend to be; pose as: 以专家～ pose as an expert

【自治】zìzhì（名）autonomy; self-government: ～区 autonomous region

【自制】zìzhì（名）self-control; self-restraint

【自知之明】zì zhī zhī míng〈成〉knowledge of one's limitations; self-knowledge

【自来水】zìláishuǐ（名）running water; tap water

【自来水笔】zìláishuǐbǐ（名）fountain pen

【自命不凡】zì mìng bù fán〈成〉regard oneself as being out of the ordinary or above the ordinary run

【自取灭亡】zì qǔ miè wáng〈成〉court destruction

【自卑】zìbēi（动）feel inferior; have a sense of inferiority: ～感 inferiority complex

【自首】zìshǒu（动）(of a criminal) give oneself up (to the police, etc.)

【自信】zìxìn Ⅰ（形）self-confident; confident Ⅱ（名）confidence

【自修】zìxiū（动）❶ (of a student) prepare or review one's lessons ❷ study on one's own; teach oneself: ～英语 teach oneself English

【自重】zìzhòng（动）be careful in speech and behaviour; behave with dignity

【自封】zìfēng（动）proclaim oneself: ～的明星 a self-styled "star"

【自负】zìfù（形）conceited

【自负盈亏】zì fù yíng kuī（动）(of an enterprise) assume sole economic responsibility for itself

【自食其力】zì shí qí lì〈成〉earn one's own living; stand on one's own feet; live on one's toil

【自食其果】zì shí qí guǒ〈成〉eat the bitter fruit of one's own doing; reap what one has sown

【自相矛盾】zì xiāng máo dùn〈成〉contradict oneself; contradictory

【自相残杀】zì xiāng cán shā〈成〉(of persons or factions within a group, party, etc.) carry out mutual killings; engage in an internecine strife

【自杀】zìshā Ⅰ（动）commit suicide Ⅱ（名）suicide

【自流】zìliú（动）❶ (of water) flow automatically ❷ (of a thing) take its natural course; be left to drift along

【自留地】zìliúdì（名）private plot

【自高自大】zì gāo zì dà〈成〉conceited; self-important

【自讨苦吃】zì tǎo kǔ chī〈成〉ask

for trouble; court trouble

【自從】zìcóng〈介〉since; from

【自理】zìlǐ〈動〉be at one's own expense; have to do the job oneself: 住宿～pay for one's own accommodation

【自得】zìdé〈形〉pleased with oneself; complacent

【自動】zìdòng〈形〉❶ voluntary; of one's own accord ❷ automatic: ～控制 automatic control / ～售賣機 coin-operated vending machines; vendor

【自動化】zìdònghuà〈名〉automation

【自發】zìfā〈形〉spontaneous

【自費】zìfèi〈副〉at one's own expense

【自尊】zìzūn〈名〉self-respect

【自然】zìrán Ⅰ〈名〉nature: 征服～subdue nature Ⅱ〈形〉❶ natural: ～形態 natural form ❷ natural; at ease: 她面對話筒，態度極其～。She looked completely at ease before the microphone. Ⅲ〈副〉❶ in the course of events: 聽其～ let things take their own course ❷ naturally; of course: 以後你～會明白的。You'll eventually understand it.

【自然主義】zìrán zhǔyì〈名〉naturalism

【自然界】zìránjiè〈名〉nature; natural world

【自強不息】zì qiáng bù xī〈成〉strive resolutely to improve oneself

【自欺欺人】zì qī qī rén〈成〉deceive people with a palpable falsehood; deceive oneself as well as others

【自愛】zì'ài〈名〉self-respect

【自新】zìxīn〈動〉turn over a new leaf; start afresh

【自誇】zìkuā〈動〉brag; boast

【自傳】zìzhuàn〈名〉autobiography

【自圓其說】zì yuán qí shuō〈成〉justify one's statement

【自稱】zìchēng〈動〉claim to be: ～知名人士 claim to be a well-known public figure

【自豪】zìháo〈動〉be proud of oneself

【自滿】zìmǎn〈形〉complacent; self-satisfied

【自鳴得意】zì míng dé yì〈成〉be self-satisfied; be ostensibly pleased with oneself

【自餒】zìněi〈動〉be diffident; lose heart

【自暴自棄】zì bào zì qì〈成〉give oneself up as hopeless

【自衛】zìwèi〈名〉self-defence

【自薦】zìjiàn〈動〉suggest oneself as a candidate for a vacant position

【自轉】zìzhuàn〈名〉〈天〉rotation

【自願】zìyuàn〈形〉voluntary; of one's own free

【自覺】zìjué Ⅰ〈動〉be conscious of; be aware of: ～理虧 be conscious that one is in the wrong Ⅱ〈副〉consciously: ～執行大會的決議 consciously carry out the decision of the meeting

【自覺自願】zì jué zì yuàn〈成〉of one's own free will; willingly: ～地要求調到邊遠地區去 ask of one's own free will for a transfer to some remote area

臭 chòu Ⅰ〈形〉❶ smelly; stinking ❷ disgusting: 擺～架子 put on lousy airs Ⅱ〈副〉severely; mercilessly: 把他～罵一頓 give him a good scolding

【臭名遠揚】chòu míng yuǎn yáng (臭名昭著 chòu míng zhāo zhù)〈成〉notorious

【臭味相投】chòu wèi xiāng tóu〈口〉be birds of a feather; be two of a kind

【臭烘烘】chòuhōnghōng（形）stinking

【臭氣】chòuqì（名）foul smell; stench

【臭氧】chòuyǎng（名）〈化〉ozone: ~層 ozone layer

【臭蟲】chòuchóng（名）bedbug

至 部

至 zhì Ⅰ（介）to; until: ~今晚八點 until eight o'clock this evening Ⅱ（副）extremely: 高興之~ feel extremely happy; be beside oneself with joy

【至今】zhìjīn（副）up to now; so far: 他的態度~未改。His attitude has so far not changed.

【至少】zhìshǎo（副）at（the）least: ~你該先告訴我。You should have at least told me beforehand.

【至交】zhìjiāo（名）best friend: 多年~ close friends of long standing

【至多】zhìduō（副）at（the）most; no more than: ~二十人 no more than twenty people

【至於】zhìyú（連）as to; as for: 這個問題，我在下一章還將談到。As for this problem, I'll take it up again in the next chapter.

【至高無上】zhì gāo wú shàng〈成〉highest; supreme: ~的權力

supreme power

【至誠】zhìchéng（形）sincere; honest

【至遲】zhìchí（副）at（the）latest: 她~明早回電話。She'll call back tomorrow morning at the latest.

致 zhì Ⅰ（動）❶ send; extend (respects, congratulations, etc.): ~以親切的問候 convey one's warm regards ❷ devote: ~力於科學研究 devote oneself to scientific research ❸ incur; result in: 招~重大損失 incur heavy losses Ⅱ（名）interest; appeal: 興~勃勃 full of zest

【致力】zhìlì（動）devote oneself to

【致冷】zhìlěng（名）refrigeration

【致命】zhìmìng（形）fatal; mortal: ~的弱點 fatal weakness

【致使】zhìshǐ（動）cause; result in: ~三人死亡 result in three deaths

【致富】zhìfù（動）become rich: 脫貧~ shake off poverty and got rich

【致敬】zhìjìng（動）salute; pay one's respects to

【致意】zhìyì（動）send one's regards to; extend one's greetings to

【致謝】zhìxiè（動）extend one's thanks to

【致癌物質】zhìái wùzhì（名）carcinogen; carcinogenic substance

【致辭】zhìcí（動）deliver a speech; address

臺 tái Ⅰ（名）❶ platform; stage; podium ❷ support; base: 蠟~ candlestick; candelabrum ❸ anything in the shape of a platform or terrace: ~秤 platform scale ❹（radio or TV）station; transmitter ❺ special telephone service: 報時~（tele-

phone) time inquiry service ❻
(Tái) short for Taiwan Province ❼
(Tái) a surname Ⅱ (量) ❶ (of theatrical performances): 會唱三～戲 have a repertory of three operas ❷ (of machines, etc.): 一～拖拉機 a tractor

【臺胞】táibāo (名) compatriot in Taiwan

【臺柱子】táizhùzi (名) pillar; mainstay; core

【臺座】táizuò (名) pedestal

【臺詞】táicí (名) actor's lines

【臺階】táijiē (名) ❶ flight of steps: 上～ go up the steps ❷ way to free oneself from an awkward position: 找個一下 find an excuse to get away with good grace

【臺灣】Táiwān (名) Taiwan (Province)

臻 zhēn (動) attain (a high level): 日～完美 make steady improvements towards perfection

臼 部

臼 jiù (名) ❶ motar ❷ anything in the shape of a motar ❸ joint (of bones): 脫～ dislocation (of joints)

【臼齒】jiùchǐ (名) molar; molar tooth

舀 yǎo (動) ladle

舂 chōng (動) pound with a pestle: ～米 husk rice with a pestle

與 yǔ Ⅰ (連) and; together with: 理論～實踐 theory and practice /

～父母同住 live together with one's parents Ⅱ (動) give; offer: 交 ～本人 deliver to the person concerned Ⅲ (介) with; against: ～此 無關 have nothing to do with it see also yù

【與人爲善】yǔ rén wéi shàn 〈成〉 cherish good intentions towards; be well-intentioned

【與日俱增】yǔ rì jù zēng 〈成〉 increase every day; grow with each passing day

【與世長辭】yǔ shì cháng cí 〈成〉 pass away

【與世無爭】yǔ shì wú zhēng 〈成〉 stand aloof from worldly strife; be indifferent to the world; be far from the madding crowd

【與世隔絕】yǔ shì gé jué 〈成〉 shut off oneself from society

【與其】yǔqí (連) [often used together with 不如, 寧可, or 毋寧] would rather...than...; more...than...: ～說是感到不安, 不如說是鬆了一 口氣 feel relieved rather than worried

【與眾不同】yǔ zhòng bù tóng 〈成〉 be different from ordinary people; be out of the ordinary

與 yù (動) take part in; participate in
see also yǔ

【與會】yùhuì (動) attend a meeting: ～者 participant (in a conference or meeting)

舅 jiù (名) ❶ uncle; mother's brother ❷ brother-in-law; wife's brother: 小～子 wife's younger brother

【舅父】jiùfù (名) uncle; mother's

brother

【舅母】jiùmǔ（名）aunt; wife of mother's brother

【舅妈】jiùmā（名）〈口〉auntie; wife of mother's brother

【舅舅】jiùjiu（名）〈口〉uncle; mother's brother

興 xīng（動）❶ give currency to ❷ be prevalent; be in vogue: 這一套現在不～了。This practice is no longer in vogue. ❸ prosper; rise: 振～國家 rejuvenate one's country ❹ start

see also xìng

【興旺】xīngwàng（名）prosperity or decadence: 國家～, 匹夫有責。Every individual must hold himself responsible for the prosperity or decadence of his country.

【興妖作怪】xīng yāo zuò guài〈成〉create disturbances

【興利除弊】xīng lì chú bì〈成〉start what is good to us and eliminate what is harmful

【興旺】xīngwàng（形）flourishing; thriving: 我們的國家日益～。Our country is becoming more and more prosperous with each passing day.

【興修】xīngxiū（動）begin to build; start to construct: ～鐵路 build railways

【興建】xīngjiàn（動）build

【興風作浪】xīng fēng zuò làng〈成〉stir up disorder; make trouble

【興起】xīngqǐ（動）rise; emerge

【興盛】xīngshèng（形）prosperous; thriving

【興隆】xīnglóng（形）flourishing; prosperous: 買賣～。Business is thriving.

【興奮】xīngfèn（形）excited: 感到～ feel excited / 令人～的事件 an exciting event; an inspiring event

【興辦】xīngbàn（動）establish; set up

興 xìng（名）interest; excitement

see also xīng

【興致】xìngzhì（名）desire; inclination: 我既沒有時間, 也沒有～去做。I have neither time nor inclination to do it.

【興致勃勃】xìng zhì bó bó〈成〉in high spirits; in an ebullient mood

【興高采烈】xìng gāo cǎi liè〈成〉be buoyant with joy

【興會】xìnghuì（名）inspiration: 我乘一時～寫成了這篇文章。I had an inspiration and improvised the essay.

【興趣】xìngqù（名）interest: 產生～ develop an interest

【興衝衝】xìngchōngchōng（副）excitedly; happily: ～地跑進禮堂 rush into the auditorium excitedly

【興頭】xìngtóu（名）enthusiasm; interest: 正在～上 when one's zest is the keenest

舉 jǔ I（動）❶ raise; hold up: ～着一束鮮花 hold a bouquet of fresh flowers ❷ start; undertake: ～兵進攻 move troops to start an offensive ❸ elect; nominate; recommend: ～薦 recommend (sb.) for a post ❹ cite; adduce: 列～事實說明觀點 cite instances to prove one's point II（動）act; move: 一～一動都十分小心 be very cautious in making a move III（形）entire: ～家 the whole family

【舉手】jǔshǒu（動）put up one's

hand(s): ~之勞 sth. requiring little effort

【舉止】jǔzhǐ (名) behaviour; conduct; deportment; manner: ~落落大方 act with grace and ease; behave with gentleness and dignity

【舉世】jǔshì (副) all over the world: ~震驚 shock the whole world

【舉目無親】jǔ mù wú qīn 〈成〉 have neither friends nor relatives in a strange land

【舉行】jǔxíng (動) hold; stage; conduct: ~記者招待會 give a press conference

【舉足輕重】jǔ zú qīng zhòng 〈成〉 occupy a position of great influence

【舉杯】jǔbēi (動) raise one's glass (to drink a toast)

【舉例】jǔlì (動) give an example: ~來說 for example

【舉重】jǔzhòng (名) 〈體〉 weight lifting

【舉動】jǔdòng (名) act; move; behaviour: 這種~是很不明智的。 This is a very unwise move.

【舉國】jǔguó (名) the whole nation

【舉報】jǔbào (動) report (an offence) to the authorities

【舉棋不定】jǔ qí bù dìng 〈成〉 be indecisive in making a move

【舉辦】jǔbàn (動) conduct; run; sponsor: ~義務演出 give a benefit performance

舊 jiù I (形) ❶ past; outdated; old: ~友 old friend ❷ worn; used; second-hand: ~ 書 second-hand books ❸ former: ~地重遊 a place revisited II (名) old friendship; old acquaintance: 懷 ~ miss one's old friends

【舊式】jiùshì (形) old-type; old-fashioned

【舊址】jiùzhǐ (名) former site; site (of a former establishment, building, etc.)

【舊居】jiùjū (名) former residence; former home

【舊約】jiùyuē (名) 〈宗〉 the Old Testament

【舊時】jiùshí (名) old times

【舊都】jiùdū (名) former capital

【舊詩】jiùshī (名) classical (Chinese) poetry

【舊曆】jiùlì (名) the lunar calendar: ~ 年 the lunar New Year; the Spring Festival

舌 部

舌 shé (名) ❶ tongue ❷ sth. shaped like a tongue: 帽~ peak of one's cap

【舌尖】shéjiān (名) tip of the tongue

【舌苔】shétāi (名) 〈中醫〉 coating on the tongue; fur: ~厚 a furred tongue

【舌敝唇焦】shé bì chún jiāo 〈成〉 keep talking till the tongue becomes weary and the lips dry

【舌戰】shézhàn (動) have a battle of words; argue vehemently

【舌頭】shétou (名) tongue

舍 shè (名) house; shed: 宿~ dormitory; hostel / 豬~ pig house

舐 shì (動) lick; pass the tongue over

舒 shū Ⅰ (動) unfold; relax; feel at ease: ～筋活絡 stimulate blood circulation and relax muscles and joints Ⅱ (形) relaxed; leisurely Ⅲ (名) (Shū) a surname

【舒服】shūfu Ⅰ (形) comfortable: 你坐那兒～嗎? Are you comfortable sitting there? Ⅱ (動) be well: 他有點不～。He is a bit under the weather.

【舒坦】shūtan (形) free from worry; comfortable

【舒展】shūzhan (形) ❶ unfold; become smooth ❷ stretch; limber up: ～四肢躺在海灘上曬太陽 lie stretched on the beach sunbathing

【舒暢】shūchàng (形) in a happy mood; free from worry

【舒適】shūshì (形) cosy; comfortable; easy

【舒鬆】shūsōng (形) relaxed and comfortable

舔 tiǎn (動) lick

舖 pù (名) ❶ shop; store: 雜貨～ grocery ❷ plank bed

【舖子】pùzi (名) shop; store

【舖位】pùwèi (名) bunk; berth

【舖板】pùbǎn (名) bed board

舛 部

舛 chuǎn (名) error; mishap

【舛誤】chuǎnwù (名) mistake; mishap

舞 wǔ Ⅰ (名) dance: 交誼～ ballroom dancing Ⅱ (動) dance with sth. held in one's hands; brandish

【舞女】wǔnǚ (名) dance hostess; taxi-dancer

【舞文弄墨】wǔ wén nòng mò 〈成〉 ❶ indulge in rhetoric; juggle with words ❷ distort a case by deliberately misinterpreting the law

【舞曲】wǔqǔ (名) dance music

【舞池】wǔchí (名) dance floor

【舞伴】wǔbàn (名) dance partner

【舞弄】wǔnòng (動) wave; brandish

【舞場】wǔchǎng (名) dance hall; ballroom

【舞會】wǔhuì (名) dance; ball

【舞臺】wǔtái (名) stage; arena: 旋轉～ revolving stage / 政治～ political arena

【舞弊】wǔbì (動) engage in fraudulent practice: 考試～ (caught) cheating in the exam

【舞劇】wǔjù (名) dance drama

【舞蹈】wǔdǎo (名) dance

【舞廳】wǔtīng (名) dance hall

舟 部

舟 zhōu (名) 〈書〉 boat: 逆水行～ sail against the current

舢 shān (名)

【舢板】shānbǎn (名) sampan

舫 fǎng (名) boat: 遊～ pleasure boat

航 háng (名) ❶ boat; ship ❷ navigation (by water or air): 民～ civil aviation

【航天】hángtiān (名) space-flight;

～飛機 space shuttle

【航向】hángxiàng（名）course (of a ship or a plane)

【航行】hángxíng（動）navigate by water or by air

【航空】hángkōng（名）aviation

【航空公司】hángkōng gōngsī（名）airline

【航空母艦】hángkōng mǔjiàn（名）aircraft carrier

【航空信】hángkōngxìn（名）air letter; air mail

【航海】hánghǎi（名）navigation：～家 navigator

【航班】hángbān（名）scheduled flight：～號 flight number

【航運】hángyùn（名）shipping

【航程】hángchéng（名）passage; voyage

【航道】hángdào（名）course; channel; lane

【航路】hánglù（名）air or water route

【航綫】hángxiàn（名）line; route

【航標】hángbiāo（名）navigation mark

般 bān（名）kind; type; way：百～抵賴 try every means to deny / 雷鳴～的掌聲 thunderous applause

舵 duò（名）rudder; helm：方向～ steering wheel

【舵手】duòshǒu（名）helmsman

舷 xián（名）ship's side：～窗 porthole

【舷梯】xiántī（名）❶ gangway (ladder); accommodation ladder ❷ ramp

舸 gě（名）barge

船 chuán（名）boat; ship

【船長】chuánzhǎng（名）captain

【船員】chuányuán（名）(ship's) crew; seaman

【船隻】chuánzhī（名）vessels; ships：往來～ shipping traffic

【船舶】chuánbó（名）vessels; shipping

【船期】chuánqī（名）sailing date：～表 sailing schedule

【船塢】chuánwù（名）dock; dockyard

【船艙】chuáncāng（名）cabin

舶 bó（名）ocean-going ship：各式船～ boats and ships of all types

【舶來品】bóláipǐn（名）goods of foreign make; imported goods

艄 shāo（名）❶ stern ❷ rudder; helm

【艄公】shāogōng（名）❶ helmsman ❷ boatman

艇 tǐng（名）light vessel; boat：橡皮～ pneumatic boat

艘 sōu（量）(of boats or ships)：一～遊艇 a pleasure boat

艙 cāng（名）❶ cabin; hold：獨立～面上 stand alone on the deck ❷〈宇航〉module

【艙位】cāngwèi（名）berth; seat in a cabin

艦 jiàn（名）warship; naval vessel

【艦長】jiànzhǎng（名）captain (of a warship)

【艦隊】jiànduì（名）fleet

【艦艇】jiàntǐng（名）general term for naval ships and boats

艮 部

良 liáng Ⅰ(形) good Ⅱ(副) very: 用心～苦 give much thought to the matter; go to great pains Ⅲ(名) (Liáng) a surname

【良久】liángjiǔ (副) a long while

【良心】liángxīn (名) conscience

【良好】liánghǎo (形) good; fine: 講文明的～習慣 civilized behaviour; good manners

【良辰美景】liáng chén měi jǐng 〈成〉 good weather and beautiful scenery

【良性】liángxìng (形) benign: ～腫瘤 benign tumour

【良師益友】liángshī yìyǒu (名) good teacher and helpful friend; mentor

【良莠不齊】liáng yǒu bù qí 〈成〉 good and bad people are intermingled

【良港】liánggǎng (名) good harbour

【良種】liángzhǒng (名) fine breed; improved strain

【良機】liángjī (名) good opportunity; opportune moment

【良藥苦口】liáng yào kǔ kǒu 〈成〉 good medicine tastes bitter; good advice often sounds unpleasant

艱 jiān (形) difficult; hard

【艱巨】jiānjù (形) extremely difficult; arduous

【艱辛】jiānxīn (名) hardship: 歷盡～，方有今日。We have gone through numerous hardships to achieve what we have today.

【艱苦】jiānkǔ (形) hard; arduous

【艱苦樸素】jiān kǔ pǔ sù 〈成〉 hard work and plain living

【艱深】jiānshēn (形) (of writing) difficult to understand; abstruse

【艱險】jiānxiǎn (名) difficulties and dangers: 不畏～ fear neither hardship nor danger

【艱澀】jiānsè (形) (of writing) involved and obscure

【艱難】jiānnán (形) hard; arduous

【艱難險阻】jiān nán xiǎn zǔ 〈成〉 hardships and formidable obstacles

色 部

色 sè (名) ❶ colour: 綠～ green (colour) ❷ facial expression: 面有慍～ wear an angry look ❸ scene; scenery: 夜～ dusk ❹ kind; variety: 花～齊全 have a rich assortment (of goods) ❺ quality (of precious metals, goods, etc.): 足～ of standard purity ❻ feminine charm; lust; sex
see also shǎi

【色拉】sèlā (名) salad: ～調(味拌)料 salad dressing

【色盲】sèmáng (名) 〈醫〉 achromatopsia; colour blindness

【色素】sèsù (名) 〈生〉 pigment

【色紙】sèzhǐ (名) coloured paper

【色情】sèqíng (形) pornographic; sensual: ～電影 sex films / ～文學 pornographic literature

【色彩】sècǎi (名) colour; hue; flavour: 絢麗的～ gorgeous hue / 宗教～ religious colour

【色調】sèdiào (名) tone; hue; tinge

【色厲內荏】sè lì nèi rěn 〈成〉 a bully in appearance but a coward at heart

【色泽】sèzé (名) colour and lustre

色 shǎi (名)〈口〉colour: 掉～ (of cloth) lose colour; fade
see also sè

艳 yàn (形) gorgeous; resplendent

【艳史】yànshǐ (名) love story

【艳阳天】yànyángtiān (名) bright spring day

【艳丽】yànlì (形) bright-coloured; flowery

艸 部

艾 ài I (名) ❶〈植〉Chinese mugwort (*Artemisia argyi*); moxa ❷ (Ài) a surname II (动) stop: 方兴未～ be burgeoning; be under way

【艾绒】àiróng (名)〈中医〉moxa punk

【艾滋病】àizībìng (名)〈医〉AIDS (Acquired Immune Deficiency Syndrome)

芒 máng (名) awn

【芒刺在背】máng cì zài bèi〈成〉be on pins and needles

【芒果】mángguǒ (名) mango

芋 yù (名)〈植〉❶ taro ❷ tuber crops

【芋艿】yùnǎi (名)〈植〉taro

【芋头】yùtou (名)〈植〉❶ taro ❷〈方〉sweet potato

芍 sháo

【芍药】sháoyào (名)〈植〉Chinese herbaceous peony

芳 fāng (名) ❶ fragrance ❷ good reputation: 留～千古。One's name will go down in history.

【芳香】fāngxiāng (形) fragrant: ～剂 aromatic

【芳菲】fāngfēi (名) ❶ flowers and herbs ❷ fragrance

芯 xīn (名) rush pith
see also xìn

芯 xìn (名) ❶ core ❷ wick
see also xīn

【芯子】xìnzi (名) fuse; wick

芙 fú

【芙蓉】fúróng (名)〈植〉❶ lotus ❷ hibiscus

荒 yán
see also yuán

【荽荽】yánsui (名) coriander

荒 yuán
see also yán

【荒花】yuánhuā (名) lilac daphne

芸 yún

【芸豆】yúndòu (名) kidney bean

【芸芸众生】yúnyún zhòngshēng (名)〈宗〉all living beings

芽 yá (名) bud; sprout: 豆～ bean sprouts

芭 bā (名) certain fragrant herb

【芭蕉】bājiāo (名) plantain; banana

【芭蕉扇】bājiāoshàn (名) palm-leaf fan

【芭蕾】bālěi (芭蕾舞 bālěiwǔ) (名) ballet: ～女演员 ballerina

芮 Ruì (名) a surname

芬 fēn （名）fragrance

【芬蘭】Fēnlán （名）Finland： ～人
Finn ／ ～語 Finnish (language)

芥 jiè （名）❶ mustard ❷ trifle;
worthless thing: 視如草 ～ consider
as unworthy of notice； regard as
worthless； treat like dirt

【芥子氣】jièzǐqì （名）mustard gas

【芥末】jièmo （名）mustard (powder)

花 huā Ⅰ（名）❶ flower； blossom；
bloom ❷ anything resembling a
flower: 雪 ～ snowflakes ❸ fireworks: 禮 ～ fireworks display ❹
wound: 掛 ～ get wounded in battle
❺ pattern: 紅地黑 ～ black patterns on a red background ❻ (Huā)
a surname Ⅱ（形）❶ multicoloured;
coloured； variegated: ～衣服 garments of printed cotton； clothing in
gay colours ❷ (of eyes) blurred;
dim ❸ tricky; tricky Ⅲ（動）
spend; expend: ～時間 be time-
consuming

【花天酒地】huā tiān jiǔ dì 〈成〉live
a life of dissipation

【花白】huābái （形）(of hair) grey;
grizzled

【花甲】huājiǎ （名）a cycle of sixty
years: 年逾～ over sixty years old

【花生】huāshēng （名）peanut

【花卉】huāhuì （名）❶ flowers and
plants ❷ traditional Chinese painting of flowers and plants

【花朵】huāduǒ （名）flower; bloom;
blossom

【花名冊】huāmíngcè （名）register
(of names); roster

【花色】huāsè （名）❶ design and
colour ❷ (of merchandise) variety

【花匠】huājiàng （名）gardener

【花束】huāshù （名）bouquet； bunch
of flowers

【花言巧語】huā yán qiǎo yǔ 〈成〉
insincere fine words

【花房】huāfáng （名）greenhouse

【花招】huāzhāo （名）❶ eye-catching movement in martial arts ❷
trick; game

【花花公子】huāhuā gōngzǐ （名）
dandy; coxcomb; playboy

【花花世界】huāhuā shìjiè （名）
world of sensual pleasures

【花花綠綠】huāhuā lǜlǜ （形）colour-
ful

【花枝招展】huā zhī zhāo zhǎn 〈成〉
(of a woman) be gorgeously dressed

【花盆】huāpén （名）flowerpot

【花茶】huāchá （名）scented tea: 茉
莉～ jasmine tea

【花圃】huāpǔ （名）flower garden

【花哨】huāshao （形）❶ (of dress)
garish; gaudy ❷ ornate: 他的文章
風格太～。His style of writing is
too ornate.

【花紋】huāwén （名）decorative pattern

【花展】huāzhǎn （名）flower show

【花圈】huāquān （名）(floral) wreath

【花崗巖】huāgāngyán （名）granite

【花費】huāfèi Ⅰ（動）spend； expend;
cost Ⅱ（名）expenditure

【花腔】huāqiāng （名）❶〈樂〉col-
oratura ❷ insincere fine-sounding
words; unctuous phraseology

【花絮】huāxù （名）titbits； (of
news) sidelights

【花園】huāyuán （名）garden

【花團錦簇】huā tuán jǐn cù 〈成〉
colourful and gorgeous spectacle

【花樣】huāyàng （名）❶ pattern

trick

【花銷】huāxiāo（名）expense; cost

【花壇】huātán（名）flower bed; flower terrace

【花環】huāhuán（名）garland

【花蕾】huālěi（名）(flower) bud

【花邊】huābiān（名）❶ decorative border; floral border ❷ lace ❸ fancy border in printing

【花瓣】huābàn（名）petal

【花籃】huālán（名）flower basket

芹 qín

【芹菜】qíncài（名）celery

芻 chú（名）hay; fodder: 反～動物 ruminant animal

【芻議】chúyì（名）〈謙〉my humble opinion

范 Fàn（名）a surname

苧 zhù

【苧麻】zhùmá（名）〈植〉ramie

茉 mò

【茉莉】mòlì（名）jasmine

【茉莉花茶】mòlì huāchá（名）jasmine tea

苣 qǔ

【苣藚菜】qǔmǎicài（名）endive

苛 kē（形）very harsh; severe: ～責 criticize sb. harshly; excoriate sb.

【苛求】kēqiú（動）be over-critical; demanding

【苛刻】kēkè（形）harsh; severe: 我們不能接受這樣～的條件。We cannot accept such harsh terms.

【苛政】kēzhèng（名）tyranny; tyrannical rule

【苛捐雜稅】kē juān zá shuì〈成〉exorbitant taxes and excessive levies

苯 běn（名）〈化〉benzene: ～中毒 benzene poisoning

苦 kǔ I（形）bitter II（名）misery; pain; hardship: 吃～耐勞 work hard under severe circumstances III（副）❶ patiently; wholeheartedly; strongly: ～勸 strongly advise ❷〈方〉(of sth. much too wornout, etc.) too much: 這雙鞋穿得太～, 不能修理了。This pair of shoes is much too worn out for repair. IV（動）❶ cause suffering to (sb.): 這就～了她的父母了。This caused a lot of trouble to her parents. ❷ suffer from: ～於不大懂得技術 suffer from inadequate knowledge of technical know-how

【苦工】kǔgōng（名）hard manual labour

【苦口婆心】kǔ kǒu pó xīn〈成〉advise sb. most earnestly and with the best of intentions

【苦水】kǔshuǐ（名）❶ water which contains certain chemical elements and tastes bitter ❷ bitter liquid secreted from the stomach on account of illness ❸ misery; suffering; grievances

【苦心】kǔxīn I（名）painstaking effort II（副）painstakingly

【苦心孤詣】kǔ xīn gū yì〈成〉take great pains to attain one's goal

【苦功】kǔgōng（名）painstaking efforts; assiduous work: 下～ make painstaking efforts

【苦瓜】kǔguā（名）❶〈植〉balsam pear ❷ bitter gourd; *Memordica charantta*

【苦肉计】 kǔròujì〈成〉ruse of inflicting a serious injury on oneself to win the enemy's confidence and consequently bring about his ruin

【苦果】 kǔguǒ〈名〉bitter fruit

【苦苦】 kǔkǔ〈副〉painstakingly; earnestly: ~哀求 entreat piteously

【苦思冥想】 kǔ sī míng xiǎng (冥思苦索 míng sī kǔ suǒ)〈成〉think long and hard

【苦衷】 kǔzhōng〈名〉difficulty arising from one's own embarrassing situation: 我知道他的~。I understand the difficulty he is in.

【苦笑】 kǔxiào〈动〉force a smile; smile wryly

【苦处】 kǔchu〈名〉suffering; difficulty: 她有她的~。She has her own difficulties.

【苦闷】 kǔmèn I〈形〉bored; depressed II〈名〉boredom

【苦恼】 kǔnǎo〈形〉distressed; vexed

【苦痛】 kǔtòng (痛苦 tòngkǔ)〈名〉suffering; misery; agony: 单相思带来的~ pangs of unrequited love

【苦干】 kǔgàn〈动〉work with a will: 埋头~ work hard and quietly

【苦尽甘来】 kǔ jìn gān lái〈成〉after suffering comes happiness

【苦头】 kǔtou〈名〉hardship; misfortune: 他吃过~。He has learnt a hard lesson.

【苦难】 kǔnàn〈名〉suffering; tribulation; hardships

若

若 ruò I〈连〉if: 天气~有变化,比赛可能延期举行。In case of any change in weather, the match might be postponed. II〈动〉seem; like: ~有~无 be faintly discernible

【若干】 ruògān〈数〉a certain number: ~年前 several years ago

【若即若离】 ruò jí ruò lí〈成〉keep sb. at a respectful distance; be neither close nor distant

【若非】 ruòfēi〈连〉if not: ~你的帮助,我们决不会成功的。We wouldn't have succeeded without your help.

【若是】 ruòshì〈连〉if: 我~你,决不会那麽说。If I were you, I'd never have said so.

【若无其事】 ruò wú qí shì〈成〉appear very calm as if nothing had happened

茂

茂 mào〈形〉luxuriant; exuberant

【茂密】 màomì〈形〉thick; dense: 绿叶~的树林 green wood thick with foliage

【茂盛】 màoshèng〈形〉luxuriant; thriving

茅

茅 máo〈名〉❶ cogongrass ❷ (Máo) a surname

【茅坑】 máokēng〈名〉〈口〉latrine pit

【茅舍】 máoshè (茅屋 máowū)〈名〉thatched cottage; (straw) hut

【茅房】 máofáng (茅厕 máocè)〈名〉〈口〉latrine

【茅草】 máocǎo〈名〉cogongrass; thatch

【茅草棚】 máocǎopéng〈名〉thatched shed

【茅塞顿开】 máo sè dùn kāi〈成〉be suddenly enlightened

【茅台酒】 máotáijiǔ〈名〉Maotai (spirit)

茄

茄 jiā
see also qié

【茄克】 jiākè〈名〉jacket

茄 qié (名) eggplant
see also jiā

【茄子】 qiézi (名) eggplant

苫 shān (名) straw mat
see also shàn

【苫布】 shānbù (名) tarpaulin

苫 shàn (動) cover (with a straw mat, tarpaulin, etc.): 用席把貨車 ~上 cover up the lorry with mats
see also shān

【苫蓋】 shàngài (動) cover; overspread

苜 mù

【苜蓿】 mùxu (名) lucerne; alfalfa

苗 miáo (名) ❶ seedling; young plant: 小樹~ sapling ❷ vaccine ❸ (Miáo) a surname

【苗子】 miáozi (名) ❶ young plant ❷ young person who has the potential of becoming a worthy successor: 他是棵好~。 He is a promising young man.

【苗牀】 miáochuáng (名) seedbed

【苗圃】 miáopǔ (名) nursery (of young plants)

【苗條】 miáotiao (形) slender; slim

【苗族】 Miáozú (名) the Miao nationality

【苗頭】 miáotou (名) sign; indication of a tendency; straw in the wind

英 yīng (名) ❶ hero; outstanding person: ~雄 hero ❷ (Yīng) a surname

【英寸】 yīngcùn (名) inch

【英文】 yīngwén (名) English (language)

【英尺】 yīngchǐ (名) foot

【英名】 yīngmíng (名) celebrated name

【英里】 yīnglǐ (名) mile

【英明】 yīngmíng (形) wise; brilliant

【英兩】 yīngliǎng (名) ounce

【英勇】 yīngyǒng (形) heroic; valiant; brave

【英姿】 yīngzī (名) heroic bearing

【英俊】 yīngjùn (形) ❶ brilliant; outstanding: ~有爲 brilliant and capable ❷ handsome

【英畝】 yīngmǔ (名) acre

【英國】 Yīngguó (名) Britain; England: ~人 the British

【英語】 yīngyǔ (名) English (language)

【英鎊】 yīngbàng (名) pound sterling

苘 qíng (名) piemarker

【苘蔴】 qíngmá (名) piemarker

茁 zhuó

【茁壯】 zhuózhuàng (形) sturdy; healthy and strong: ~活潑的孩子 vivacious children

苞 bāo (名) bud: 花~ bud

【苞米】 bāomǐ (名) 〈方〉 maize; corn

苟 gǒu (形) ❶ temporary ❷ careless; negligent: 一絲不~ tolerate not the slightest inaccuracy; be scrupulous about every detail

【苟且】 gǒuqiě (動) muddle along: ~偷安 seek temporary security by compromising oneself

【苟全】 gǒuquán (動) stay away from danger in troubled times

【苟安】 gǒu'ān (動) seek temporary peace and comfort

【苟同】 gǒutóng (動) agree readily

【苟延殘喘】gǒu yán cán chuǎn〈成〉be at one's last gasp

苔 tái（名）〈植〉moss

茫 máng（形）❶ boundless ❷ ignorant

【茫昧】mángmèi（形）vague; unclear

【茫茫】mángmáng（形）immense; vast: ~大海 boundless sea

【茫然】mángrán（形）at a loss; ignorant: 我對事情始終~不知。I am completely in the dark about the matter. / 神情~ look bewildered

【茫無頭緒】máng wú tóu xù〈成〉be all at sea; be entirely at a loss

芰 jiāo

【芰白】jiāobái（名）wild rice stem

荒 huāng Ⅰ（名）❶ famine; crop failure ❷ wasteland ❸ shortage; scarcity: 煤~ coal shortage Ⅱ（形）❶ desolate; deserted: ~山 barren hill ❷ incorrect; absurd Ⅲ（動）lie waste

【荒地】huāngdì（名）wasteland; uncultivated land

【荒年】huāngnián（名）famine year; lean year

【荒唐】huāngtáng（形）❶ absurd; fantastic ❷ profligate

【荒原】huāngyuán（名）wasteland

【荒涼】huāngliáng（形）desolate; sparsely populated

【荒野】huāngyě（名）wilderness

【荒淫】huāngyín（形）debauched; dissolute

【荒疏】huāngshū（形）rusty; out of practice

【荒無人煙】huāng wú rén yān〈成〉desolate and uninhabited

【荒誕】huāngdàn（形）fantastic; absurd

【荒廢】huāngfèi（動）❶ lie waste; leave uncultivated ❷ neglect; be out of practice: ~學業 neglect one's studies ❸ waste: ~時間 waste time

【荒蕪】huāngwú（形）uncultivated; desolate

【荒謬】huāngmiù（形）absurd; preposterous

荆 jīng（名）❶ chaste tree; brambles ❷（Jīng）a surname

【荆條】jīngtiáo（名）twig of the chaste tree

【荆棘】jīngjí（名）thorns; thorny undergrowth

茸 róng Ⅰ（形）fine and soft; downy Ⅱ（名）young pilose antler

茜 qiàn Ⅰ（名）〈植〉madder Ⅱ（形）alizarin red

茬 chá Ⅰ（名）❶ stubble: 稻~兒 rice stubble ❷ short and hard hair or beard Ⅱ（量）crop: 一年種三~兒 grow three crops a year

【茬口】chákǒu（名）order of crops for rotation: 選好~ proper arrangement for rotation of crops

荔 lì

【荔枝】lìzhī（名）litchi

草 cǎo Ⅰ（名）❶ grass; weed ❷ straw: 稻~ rice straw ❸（in Chinese calligraphy）cursive style of writing Ⅱ（形）❶ careless; hasty; slipshod: 寫字潦~ write in a sloppy hand ❷〈口〉(often of domestic

animals) female Ⅲ (动) draft: 起~
计划 draw up a plan

【草木皆兵】cǎo mù jiē bīng〈成〉be
panic-stricken as if surrounded by
the enemy on all sides; every bush
is a soldier

【草包】cǎobāo (名) ❶ straw bag
❷ duffer; blockhead; idiot

【草地】cǎodì (名) meadow; lawn:
勿踏~。Keep off the grass.

【草坪】cǎopíng (名) lawn

【草垛】cǎoduò (名) haystack; hay-
rick

【草屋】cǎowū (名) thatched cottage

【草原】cǎoyuán (名) prairie; grassland

【草草】cǎocǎo (副) carelessly;
hastily: ~过目 glance through

【草料】cǎoliào (名) hay; forage;
fodder

【草案】cǎo'àn (名)(of a document,
plan, etc.) draft

【草书】cǎoshū (名)(in Chinese calligraphy) cursive style of writing;
running hand

【草莓】cǎoméi (名) strawberry

【草率】cǎoshuài (副) perfunctorily;
carelessly

【草菅人命】cǎo jiān rén mìng〈成〉
treat human life like dirt; trifle with
human lives

【草帽】cǎomào (名) straw hat

【草席】cǎoxí (名) straw mat

【草图】cǎotú (名) sketch; draft;
rough map

【草鞋】cǎoxié (名) straw sandal

【草稿】cǎogǎo (名) draft: 起個~
make a draft

【草拟】cǎonǐ (动) draft; draw up:
~文件 draft a document

【草药】cǎoyào (名) medicinal

herbs; herbal medicine

茵
yīn (名) mattress: 绿草如~。
The ground is beautifully covered
with a stretch of green grass.

茴
huí

【茴香】huíxiāng (名)〈植〉fennel

茶
chá (名) ❶ tea plant ❷ tea: 茉
莉花~ jasmine tea ❸ name for
certain beverage or liquid food: 杏
仁~ almond paste

【茶几兒】chájīr (名) teapoy

【茶杯】chábēi (名) teacup; cup

【茶花】cháhuā (名) camellia

【茶具】chájù (名) tea set

【茶座】cházuò (名) ❶ tea saloon ❷
seat in the teahouse

【茶湯】chátāng (名)(sorghum) millet paste

【茶壺】cháhú (名) teapot

【茶葉】cháyè (名) tea; tea leaves

【茶話會】cháhuàhuì (名) tea party

【茶館】cháguǎn (名) teahouse

【茶點】chádiǎn (名) refreshments;
tea and cookies

荀
Xún (名) a surname

荏
rěn

【荏苒】rěnrǎn (动)〈书〉(of time)
slip by

荸
bí

【荸荠】bíqi (名) water chestnut

莽
mǎng Ⅰ (名) rank grass; grass Ⅱ
(形) rash; impulsive

【莽原】mǎngyuán (名) wilderness;
vast grassland

【莽莽】mǎngmǎng (形) ❶ luxuriant
❷ boundless

【莽苍】 mǎngcāng Ⅰ (名) open country Ⅱ (形) hazy; misty

【莽汉】 mǎnghàn (名) boorish fellow

【莽撞】 mǎngzhuàng (形) rash; imprudent

荚 jiá (名) pod; legume

茎 jīng (名) stem; stalk

莫 mò Ⅰ (动) don't: ～ 哭。Don't cry. Ⅱ (副) not: 变幻～测 change unpredictably Ⅲ (名) (Mò) a surname

【莫大】 mòdà (形) most; greatest: ～的荣誉 the highest honour

【莫不】 mòbù (副) no...not...; invariably: 大家～为此消息感到惊奇。Every one of us was surprised at the news.

【莫名其妙】 mò míng qí miào 〈成〉 be puzzled; be puzzling; be unaccountable: 我觉得有些～。I felt perplexed. / 真是～! This is inconceivable indeed!

【莫非】 mòfēi (副) perhaps; probably: ～ 他就是那个百万富翁? Could he be that very millionaire?

【莫逆之交】 mò nì zhī jiāo 〈成〉 close associates; bosom friends

【莫桑比克】 Mòsāngbǐkè (名) Mosambique: ～人 Mosambican

【莫测】 mòcè (形) unfathomable; impossible to understand: 高深～ too profound to understand

【莫须有】 mòxūyǒu (形) groundless; made-up: 這是～的事。This is sheer nonsense.

苋 xiàn

【苋菜】 xiàncài (名) three-coloured amaranth

莊 zhuāng (名) ❶ village: 山～ mountain village ❷ place of business: 布～ drapery store / 飯～ restaurant ❸ (Zhuāng) a surname

【莊戶】 zhuānghù (名) peasant household

【莊重】 zhuāngzhòng (形) solemn; grave

【莊園】 zhuāngyuán (名) manor

【莊稼】 zhuāngjia (名) crops

【莊嚴】 zhuāngyán (形) solemn; dignified; imposing

茶 tú

【茶毒生靈】 tú dú shēng líng 〈成〉 plunge the people into the abyss of misery; cause suffering to the people

莠 yǒu (名) ❶ green bristlegrass ❷ bad people: ～良不齊。The bad people are mingled with the good people.

莓 méi (名) berries: 黑～ blackberry

荷 hé (名) lotus
see also hè

【荷包】 hébāo (名) small bag; pouch

【荷花】 héhuā (名) lotus

【荷爾蒙】 hé'ěrméng (名) hormone

【荷蘭】 Hélán (名) the Netherlands (Holland): ～人 Dutchman / ～語 Dutch

荷 hè Ⅰ (动) carry on one's shoulder or back Ⅱ (名) burden; responsibility Ⅲ (套) [often used in letter-writing] grateful; obliged: 爲～ (it) would be highly appreciated
see also hé

【荷載】hèzài（名）load

莜 yóu

【莜麥】yóumài（名）〈植〉naked oats

萍 píng（名）duckweed

【萍水相逢】píng shuǐ xiāng féng〈成〉(of strangers) meet by chance; meet casually

菝 bō

【菠菜】bōcài（名）spinach
【菠蘿】bōluó（名）pineapple

菩 pú

【菩提】pútí（名）〈宗〉bodhi; enlightenment
【菩提樹】pútíshù（名）pipal; bo tree
【菩薩】púsà（名）❶ Bodhisattva ❷ Buddhist image ❸ kind-hearted person

菁 jīng

【菁華】jīnghuá（名）quintessence; cream; elite

華 huá I（名）❶ China: ～東 east China ❷ elite: 英～ the cream II（形）❶ flashy; extravagant: 樸實無～ plain and simple ❷ (of hair) grey
see also huà

【華而不實】huá ér bù shí〈成〉of the showy type; flashy and superficial
【華夏】huáxià（名）an ancient name for China
【華貴】huáguì（形）luxurious; sumptuous; costly
【華裔】huáyì（名）foreign citizen of Chinese descent
【華僑】huáqiáo（名）overseas Chinese

【華麗】huálì（形）magnificent; gorgeous

華 Huà（名）a surname
see also huá

菱 líng

【菱形】língxíng（名）rhombus
【菱角】língjiao（名）water caltrop

著 zhù I（形）marked; notable: 顯～成效 produce a marked effect II（動）write: 合～ write in collaboration with sb.; coauthor III（名）book; work: 巨～ monumental work

【著名】zhùmíng（形）famous; well-known; celebrated
【著作】zhùzuò（名）work; writings
【著稱】zhùchēng（動）be celebrated for: 杭州以西湖～於世。Hangzhou is well known throughout the world for the West Lake.

其 qí（名）beanstalk: 豆～ beanstalk

萊 lái

【萊索托】Láisuǒtuō（名）Lesotho: ～人 Lesothian
【萊塞】láisài（名）〈物〉laser

萘 nài（名）〈化〉naphthalene

萌 méng（名）sprout; bud

【萌芽】méngyá（名）bud; shoot
【萌動】méngdòng（動）❶ sprout ❷ start up: 春意～。There is a savour of spring in the air.
【萌發】méngfā（動）sprout; germinate

菌 jūn（名）❶ fungus ❷ bacterium
see also jùn

菌 jūn (名) mushroom
see also jūn

菲 fēi (形) fragrant: 芳～ fragrant
see also fěi

【菲律賓】Fēilǜbīn (名) the Philippines: ～人 Filipino

菲 fěi
see also fēi

【菲薄】fěibó I (形)〈謙〉 meagre; humble; poor: ～的禮物 a small gift II (動) look down upon; despise: 妄自～ improperly belittle oneself

菜 cài (名) ❶ vegetable; greens ❷ rape: ～油 rape oil ❸ non-staple food; dish: 買～ buy groceries; buy food

【菜刀】càidāo (名) kitchen knife
【菜牛】càiniú (名) beef cattle
【菜豆】càidòu (名) kidney bean
【菜花】càihuā (名) ❶ cauliflower ❷ rape flower
【菜籽】càizǐ (名) ❶ vegetable seed ❷ rapeseed; colza
【菜場】càichǎng (名) (short for 菜市場 càishìchǎng) food market
【菜單】càidān (名) menu
【菜圃】càiyuán (菜圃子 càiyuánzi) (名) vegetable garden; kitchen garden
【菜肴】càiyáo (名) dishes (usu. meat dishes)
【菜譜】càipǔ (名) recipe
【菜籃】càilán (菜籃子 càilánzi) (名) grocery basket; food basket

萎 wēi (動) decline; go down; fall
see also wěi

萎 wěi (動) wither; wilt
see also wēi

【萎縮】wěisuō (動) ❶ wilt; wither ❷〈經〉 decline; shrink

菊 jú (名) chrysanthemum: 雛～ Bellis perennis
【菊花】júhuā (名) chrysanthemum

萄 táo (名) grape

菇 gū (名) mushroom

落 là (動) ❶ be missing; omit: 這裏有一句話～了。A phrase is missing here. ❷ leave behind: 我把書包～在操場上了。I left my satchel in the playground. ❸ fall behind: 一下很遠 be left far behind
see also lào; luò

落 lào (動) drop; come down: ～價了。The prices have dropped.
see also là; luò

【落枕】làozhěn (名)〈中醫〉 stiff neck

落 luò I (動) ❶ fall; drop: 樹葉～了。The leaves have fallen. ❷ decline; subside: ～到這般可恥的下場 come to such a disgraceful end ❸ fall behind: 在後面 lag behind ❹ fall on; rest with: 他的目光～在老人臉上。His eyes fell on the old man's face. II (名) settlement: 羣～ community
see also là; lào

【落戶】luòhù (動) settle down
【落日】luòrì (名) setting sun
【落井下石】luò jǐng xià shí〈成〉 hit sb. when he is down; take advantage of sb.'s adversity to harm him
【落水狗】luòshuǐgǒu (名) drowning

【落伍】luòwǔ（動）lag behind; drop out of society

【落成】luòchéng（動）be completed: 新的火車站已經～。The new railway station has been completed.

【落地】luòdì（動）❶ fall on the ground ❷ (of a baby) be born

【落地窗】luòdìchuāng（名） French window

【落地電扇】luòdì diànshàn （名） electric fan with adjustable stand

【落地燈】luòdìdēng（名）floor lamp

【落空】luòkōng（動）come to nothing; fail: 計劃～。The plan went up in smoke.

【落泊】luòbó（形）down and out; destitute and frustrated

【落花生】luòhuāshēng（名）peanut

【落花流水】luò huā liú shuǐ〈成〉be thoroughly defeated: 他們的籃球隊被打得～。Their basketball team suffered a crushing defeat.

【落後】luòhòu Ⅰ（動）lag behind Ⅱ（形）backward: 貧窮～ poor and backward

【落荒而逃】luò huāng ér táo〈成〉flee in panic; be scurrying for one's life

【落得】luòde（動）end in: ～身敗名裂 end up in total ruin of one's reputation and career

【落款】luòkuǎn（動） write the names of the sender and the recipient on a painting, gift, letter, etc.; inscribe (a present)

【落筆】luòbǐ（動）set pen to paper; start writing or drawing

【落湯雞】luòtāngjī（名）（figurative use) like a chicken which has fallen into hot water; like a drowned rat:

他淋得渾身隻～。He got soaked in the pouring rain.

【落葉松】luòyèsōng（名）larch

【落落大方】luò luò dà fang〈成〉behave gently; be gentle and self-assured

【落落寡合】luò luò guǎ hé〈成〉be sentimental and fond of solitude; hold oneself aloof

【落腳】luòjiǎo（動）stay; stop over: 在小客棧～ put up at an inn

【落實】luòshí（動）❶ carry out; implement: ～任務 assign a task to sb.; fulfil a mission ❷ confirm; make sure: ～日期 confirm the date

【落網】luòwǎng（動）be captured: 劫機犯已經～。The hijackers have been caught.

【落選】luòxuǎn（動）be defeated in an election; be voted out of office

【落潮】luòcháo（動）ebb tide

【落難】luònàn（動）meet with adversity; fall into misfortune

蒂 dì（名）base of a flower or fruit

葷 hūn（形）(of a dish) of meat or fish

【葷油】hūnyóu（名）animal fat; lard

【葷菜】hūncài（名）meat dish

葫 hú

【葫蘆】húlu（名）bottle gourd; calabash

葉 yè（名）❶ leaf ❷ part of a historical period: 十八世紀末～ the late 18th century ❸（Yè）a surname

【葉子】yèzi（名）leaf

【葉公好龍】Yè Gōng hào lóng〈成〉like Lord Ye who professed fondness for dragons; one fears what one claims to love

【葉落歸根】yè luò guī gēn 〈成〉 a person living away from home returns eventually to his native land

【葉綠素】yèlǜsù (名)〈生化〉chlorophyll

葬 zàng I (動) bury; inter II (名) burial: 火～ cremation

【葬身】zàngshēn (動) be buried: ～於熊熊大火之中 be burned to death in a big fire

【葬送】zàngsòng (動) ruin: ～了自己的前程 ruin one's own future

【葬禮】zànglǐ (名) funeral ceremony; funeral

葦 wěi (名) reed

【葦子】wěizi (名) reed

【葦蓆】wěixí (名) reed mat

葵 kuí (名) herbaceous plants having big flowers: 種向日～ plant sunflowers

【葵花】kuíhuā (名) sunflower

【葵花子兒】kuíhuāzǐr (名) sunflower seeds

【葵扇】kuíshàn (名) fan made from a palm leaf

萬 wàn I (數) ten thousand II (名)(Wàn) a surname III (副) extremely; absolutely: ～～不可能 absolutely impossible

【萬一】wànyī I (連) if by any chance; just in case: 你還是帶雨傘去好, 以防～嘛。You had better take your umbrella along with you, just in case. II (名) eventuality; contingency

【萬千】wànqiān (形) of great variety; innumerable: 氣象～ a majes-

tic spectacle revealing itself in its infinite facets

【萬丈】wànzhàng (形) very high or very deep; boundless: 光芒～ with dazzling brilliance; splendid; magnificent

【萬分】wànfēn (副) very much; utterly; highly: ～感激 extremely grateful

【萬水千山】wàn shuǐ qiān shān 〈成〉 a journey across innumerable mountains and rivers; a long, arduous journey

【萬不得已】wàn bù dé yǐ 〈成〉 if the worst comes to the worst

【萬世】wànshì (副) for all ages; from generation to generation; through all eternity

【萬古長青】wàn gǔ cháng qīng 〈成〉 be evergreen; remain eternally green

【萬全】wànquán (形) surefire; very sound: ～之計 an absolutely safe measure

【萬有引力】wànyǒu yǐnlì (名)〈物〉universal gravitation

【萬里長城】Wànlǐ Chángchéng (名) (for short 長城 Chángchéng) the Great Wall

【萬事】wànshì (名) all things: ～大吉。All is well.

【萬狀】wànzhuàng (副) extremely: 危險～ fraught with danger

【萬幸】wànxìng (形) most fortunate: 他沒有捲進這場風波, 實屬～。It was most fortunate of him not to get involved in the trouble.

【萬金油】wànjīnyóu (名) ❶ balm for alleviating headaches and other minor complaints ❷ Jack of all trades but master of none

【萬花筒】wànhuātǒng（名）kaleido-scope

【萬能】wànnéng（形）❶ omnipotent; almighty ❷ all-purpose: ～膠 universal gum／～鑰匙 master key

【萬惡】wàn'è Ⅰ（形）fiendish; diabolical; extremely evil Ⅱ（名）all the evils: ～之源 the root of all evil

【萬衆】wànzhòng（名）multitude of people: ～歡呼. Millions of people cheered.

【萬無一失】wàn wú yī shī〈成〉the chances of anything going wrong are absolutely slim; be absolutely safe

【萬萬】wànwàn Ⅰ（副）［used in a negative statement］absolutely; (not) in any way: 這件事～幹不得. One should by all means refrain from such an action. Ⅱ（數）hundred million

【萬歲】wànsuì〈套〉long live: 友誼～! Long live (our) friendship!

【萬壽無疆】wàn shòu wú jiāng〈成〉(wish sb.) a long, long life

【萬難】wànnán Ⅰ（形）extremely difficult; quite impossible: ～接受 find it absolutely impossible to accept Ⅱ（名）all difficulties

【萬靈藥】wànlíngyào（名）panacea; cure-all; wonder drug

萼 è（名）〈植〉calyx

萵 wō

【萵苣】wōjù（名）lettuce

【萵筍】wōsǔn（名）asparagus lettuce

葛 Gě（名）a surname

董 dǒng Ⅰ（動）supervise; direct Ⅱ（名）(Dǒng) a surname

【董事】dǒngshì（名）director: ～長

chairman of the board of directors

葡 pú

【葡萄】pútáo（名）grape: ～乾 raisin

【葡萄牙】Pútáoyá（名）Portugal: ～人 Portuguese／～語 Portuguese (language)

【葡萄胎】pútáotāi（名）〈醫〉hydatidiform mole; vesicular mole

【葡萄糖】pútáotáng（名）glucose

葱 cōng（名）❶ onion; scallion: 大～ Chinese scallion／洋～ onion ❷ grassy green: 鬱鬱～～ lush and green

【葱花】cōnghuā（名）chopped scallion

【葱綠】cōnglǜ（形）❶ pale grassy green ❷ verdant

【葱蘢】cōnglóng（形）woody; verdant

【葱鬱】cōngyù（形）lush and green

葆 bǎo Ⅰ（動）preserve; keep: 永～青春 be perennially alive with youth and vigour Ⅱ（名）luxuriant growth

蒲 pú（名）❶ cattail ❷ (Pú) a surname

【蒲公英】púgōngyīng（名）dandelion

【蒲包】púbāo（名）cattail bag; rush bag

【蒲式耳】púshì'ěr（名）bushel

【蒲扇】púshàn（名）cattail leaf fan

【蒲蓆】púxí（名）cattail mat

【蒲團】pútuán（名）hassock

莅 lì（動）〈敬〉arrive

【莅會】lìhuì（動）be present at a meeting

【莅臨】lìlín（動）be present: 敬請～

request your gracious presence

蓑 suō
【蓑衣】suōyī（名）rain cape made of straw or palm bark

蒺 jí
【蒺藜】jílí（名）pucture vine; thorn

蓆 xí（名）mat: 竹～ bamboo mat
【蓆子】xízi（名）mat

蓄 xù（動）❶ save up; store: 缸裏水已～滿。The vat is full to the brim with water. ❷ grow (a beard, etc.): ～長髮 wear one's hair long ❸ entertain; harbour: ～志 have a long-cherished wish
【蓄水】xùshuǐ（動）store water: ～池 reservoir
【蓄洪】xùhóng（動）store floodwater
【蓄意】xùyì（副）deliberately; wilfully: ～攻擊 deliberately attack; make a premeditated attack
【蓄電池】xùdiànchí（名） storage battery; accumulator
【蓄積】xùjī（動）store up; accumulate
【蓄謀】xùmóu（動）harbour evil intent; plot: ～殺人 plot to assassinate sb.; premeditated murder

蒙 mēng I（動）❶ cheat; fool: 欺上～下 cheat the superiors and hoodwink the subordinates ❷ make a wild guess: 瞎～沒好處。It's no use making wild guesses. II（形）unconscious: 頭發～ feel dizzy
see also méng; měng
【蒙蒙亮】mēngmēngliàng（動）day breaks: 天～ at the crack of dawn
【蒙頭轉向】mēng tóu zhuàn xiàng〈成〉be completely at a loss; be utterly confused; lose one's bearings
【蒙騙】mēngpiàn（動）cheat; hoodwink

蒙 méng I（形）ignorant; unenlightened II（動）❶ cover; enshroud: 用圍巾～住頭 cover one's head with a kerchief ❷ receive: ～你指教, 不勝感激。I am very grateful for your advice.
see also mēng; měng
【蒙太奇】méngtàiqí（名）〈電影〉montage
【蒙在鼓裏】méng zài gǔli〈成〉be kept in the dark; be all at sea
【蒙受】méngshòu（動）suffer: ～不白之冤 suffer an unrighted injustice
【蒙哄】ménghǒng（動）hoax; swindle
【蒙昧】méngmèi（形）❶ uncivilized; illiterate ❷ ignorant
【蒙昧主義】méngmèi zhǔyì（名）obscurantism
【蒙混】ménghùn（動）mislead; deceive
【蒙混過關】ménghùn guòguān〈成〉muddle through
【蒙蔽】méngbì（動）deceive; dupe; hoodwink: ～大眾 hoodwink the public
【蒙難】méngnàn（動）fall into the enemy's trap

蒙 měng
see also mēng; méng
【蒙古】Měnggǔ（名）Mongolia: ～人 Mongolian ／ ～語 Mongol (language)
【蒙古包】měnggǔbāo（名）yurt
【蒙古族】Měnggǔzú（名）the Mongol nationality
【蒙鑲】měngxiāng（名）〈工美〉in-

laid Mongolian ware

蒜 suàn（名）garlic: 一頭大～ a bulb of garlic / 兩瓣～ two cloves of garlic

【蒜苗】suànmiáo（名）garlic bolt

【蒜黃】suànhuáng（名）blanched garlic leaves

蓮 lián（名）〈植〉lotus

【蓮子】liánzǐ（名）lotus seed

【蓮花】liánhuā（名）lotus flower

【蓮蓬】liánpéng（名）lotus seedpool

【蓮蓬頭】liánpéngtóu（名）shower nozzle

蓋 gài I（名）❶ lid; cover ❷（Gài）a surname II（動）❶ cover; conceal: ～着雪 be covered with snow ❷ build ❸ set (one's seal to): ～章 affix a seal to (a document, receipt, formal letter, etc.) ❹ excel

【蓋世】gàishì（形）peerless; unsurpassed: ～無雙 matchless in the world

【蓋世太保】Gàishìtàibǎo（名）Gestapo

【蓋棺論定】gài guān lùn dìng（成）we can pass final judgment on a person when the last nail has been driven into his coffin

蒸 zhēng（動）❶ evaporate ❷ steam: 清～鷄 steamed chicken

【蒸汽】zhēngqì（名）steam: ～機 steam engine / ～浴室 sauna; massage parlor

【蒸氣】zhēngqì（名）vapour

【蒸發】zhēngfā（動）evaporate

【蒸蒸日上】zhēng zhēng rì shàng〈成〉achieve ever greater prosperity; thriving

【蒸鍋】zhēngguō（名）steamer

【蒸餾】zhēngliú（名）distillation: ～水 distilled water

【蒸籠】zhēnglóng（名）food steamer

蒼 cāng（形）❶ blue or dark green ❷ grey

【蒼天】cāngtiān（名）❶ blue sky ❷ heaven; sky

【蒼白】cāngbái（形）pale; pallid

【蒼老】cānglǎo（形）（of appearance）aged; aging; senile

【蒼勁】cāngjìng（形）❶ sturdy ❷（of brush strokes in Chinese calligraphy and painting）bold and vigorous

【蒼茫】cāngmáng（形）❶ vast: ～大海 the boundless ocean ❷ wide and dim: 暮色～ gathering shades of dusk

【蒼涼】cāngliáng（形）bleak; desolate

【蒼蒼】cāngcāng（形）❶ hoary; grey ❷ dark green; prosperous: 鬱鬱～ luxuriant ❸ vast and hazy

【蒼翠】cāngcuì（形）verdant

【蒼蠅】cāngying（名）fly

剷 kuǎi（名）❶ wool grass ❷（Kuǎi）a surname

蓬 péng I（名）bitter fleabane II（形）fluffy; unkempt

【蓬勃】péngbó（形）thriving; vigorous: ～發展 develop briskly

【蓬頭垢面】péng tóu gòu miàn〈成〉be unkempt

【蓬鬆】péngsōng（形）（of hair, etc.）fluffy

蓓 bèi

【蓓蕾】bèilěi（名）(flower) bud

蓖 bì

【蓖麻】bìmá（名）castor-oil plant:
~子 castor bean

蔗 zhè（名）sugarcane

【蔗糖】zhètáng（名）❶ 〈化〉su-
crose ❷ cane sugar

蔫 niān I（動）wither; droop: 花兒
缺水~了。The flowers are droop-
ing for want of water. II（形）
listless; in low spirits

蔚 wèi

【蔚為大觀】wèi wéi dà guān〈成〉
present a grand view; be spectacular

【蔚然成風】wèi rán chéng fēng〈成〉
become a prevailing trend

【蔚藍】wèilán（形）sky blue; azure

蔭 yīn（名）shade
see also yìn

【蔭蔽】yīnbì（動）be shaded or hidden by foliage

蔭 yìn（形）shady; sheltered from
bright sunlight; moist and cool
see also yīn

【蔭涼】yìnliáng（形）shady and cool:
裏面~得很。It is very cool inside.

蔓 màn（名）

【蔓生植物】mànshēng zhíwù（名）
trailing plant

【蔓延】mànyán（動）creep; spread:
瓜藤~。The melon vine sprawled
all over the place. / 阻止火勢~。
Stop the fire from spreading.

【蔓草】màncǎo（名）creeping weed

蔑 miè（動）❶ despise; look down
upon ❷ slander: 誣~ defame;

slander

【蔑視】mièshì（動）despise; disdain

蔣 Jiǎng（名）a surname

蔡 Cài（名）a surname

蕩 dàng I（動）❶ swing; wave: ~
船 row a boat ❷ wash; rinse: ~除
sweep away ❸ roam; loaf: 遊~
wander about II（形）dissolute III
（名）shallow lake

【蕩產】dàngchǎn（動）dissipate
one's fortune

【蕩婦】dàngfù（名）loose woman;
slut

【蕩然無存】dàng rán wú cún〈成〉
all gone; nothing left

【蕩滌】dàngdí（動）wash away;
clean up

【蕩漾】dàngyàng（動）ripple

【蕩蕩】dàngdàng（形）❶ vast;
great ❷ spacious

蕊 ruǐ（名）stamen or pistil

蕨 jué（名）〈植〉brake; fern: ~類
植物 pteridophyte

蕁 qián

【蕁麻】qiánmá（名）〈植〉nettle

【蕁麻疹】qiánmázhěn（名）〈醫〉net-
tle rash; urticaria

蔬 shū（名）vegetable

【蔬菜】shūcài（名）vegetable

蔽 bì（動）❶ cover; shelter: ~風
雨 shelter from wind and rain ❷
sum up: 一言以~之 in one word

蕪 wú（形）❶ overgrown with
weeds ❷ messy; mixed; in disorder

【蕪詞】wúcí（名）superfluous words

【蕉雜】wúzá（形）disorderly；（of writing）poorly-organized

蕎 qiáo
【蕎麥】qiáomài（名）buckwheat

蕉 jiāo
（名）certain broadleaf plants：美人～canna

薄 báo
Ⅰ（形）❶ thin：～冰 thin ice ❷ weak；light：～霧 thin mist ❸ poor；infertile：土地瘠～ barren land Ⅱ（副）coldly：待他不～ treat him kindly；do well by him

see also báo；bó

【薄片】báopiàn（名）slice；flake
【薄板】báobǎn（名）sheet：鋁～ sheet aluminium
【薄脆】báocuì（名）crisp fritter
【薄餅】báobǐng（名）thin pancake

薄 bó
Ⅰ（形）❶ slight；light；thin：如履～冰 as though treading on thin ice ❷ mean；unkind：待人刻～ treat people meanly ❸ frivolous：輕～ frivolous behaviour Ⅱ（動）❶ despise；slight：厚此～彼 treat one person favourably while slighting another ❷ approach；near：～暮 dusk；twilight Ⅲ（名）（Bó）a surname

see also báo；bò

【薄片】bópiàn（名）thin slice；thin section
【薄技】bójì（名）〈謙〉my slight skill
【薄利多銷】bó lì duō xiāo（成）smaller profit but better sale
【薄命】bómìng（形）（usu. said of a woman）ill-fated；ill-starred；born under an unlucky star
【薄弱】bóruò（形）weak；feeble；frail：兵力～ insufficient military strength
【薄弱環節】bóruò huánjié（名）vulnerable point；Achilles' heel；weak link
【薄情】bóqíng（形）fickle
【薄膜】bómó（名）membrane；film：金屬～ metal film
【薄霧】bówù（名）thin mist；haze

薄 bò
see also báo；bó

【薄荷】bòhe（名）〈植〉peppermint；mint：～糖 peppermint sweets（candy）

薪 xīn
（名）❶ firewood ❷ salary
【薪水】xīnshuǐ（名）salary；wages
【薪金】xīnjīn（名）salary；pay

薦 jiàn
Ⅰ（動）recommend：自～ recommend oneself（for a job）；offer one's service Ⅱ（名）❶ grass；straw ❷ straw mat
【薦舉】jiànjǔ（動）recommend（sb. for an office）

蕾 lěi
（名）flower bud
【蕾鈴】lěilíng（名）cotton bud and boll

薑 jiāng
（名）ginger：生～ ginger

薔 qiáng
【薔薇】qiángwēi（名）〈植〉rose

蕭 xiāo
Ⅰ（形）bleak；slack Ⅱ（名）（Xiāo）a surname
【蕭條】xiāotiáo Ⅰ（形）bleak；slack Ⅱ（名）〈經〉depression
【蕭瑟】xiāosè Ⅰ（動）rustle in the air：秋風～ the rustling autumn wind Ⅱ（形）bleak；desolate

薯 shǔ
（名）potato；yam：烤白～

baked sweet potato

薈 huì (名) luxuriant growth (of vegetation)

【薈萃】huìcuì (動) (of distinguished people or exquisite objects) gather together; assemble: 人才～a galaxy of talent

薛 Xuē (名) a surname

薺 jì

【薺菜】jìcài (名) shepherd's purse

藉 jiè (動) utilize; exploit: ～此機會 avail oneself of the opportunity

藍 lán I (形) blue: 蔚～的天空 azure sky II (名) ❶〈植〉indigo plant ❷ (Lán) a surname

【藍本】lánběn (名) original version of a book

【藍田人】Lántiánrén (名)　〈考古〉Lantian Man

【藍圖】lántú (名) blueprint; plan; scheme

【藍領工人】lánlǐng gōngrén (名) blue-collar worker

藏 cáng (動) ❶ hide ❷ store; lay aside: 收～古玩 collect curios
see also zàng

【藏身】cángshēn (動) ❶ hide oneself ❷ take shelter

【藏書】cángshū (名) collection of books

【藏匿】cángnì (動) hide; conceal

【藏躲】cángduǒ (動) go into hiding

藏 zàng (名) ❶ storing place; depository ❷ Buddhist or Taoist scriptures ❸ (Zàng) short for Xizang (Tibet)
see also cáng

【藏青】zàngqīng (形) dark blue

【藏族】Zàngzú (名) the Zang (Tibetan) nationality

薩 Sà (名) a surname

【薩克號】sàkèhào (名)〈樂〉saxhorn

【薩克管】sàkèguǎn (名)〈樂〉saxophone

【薩其馬】sàqímǎ (名) candied fritter

【薩爾瓦多】Sà'ěrwǎduō (名) El Salvador: ～人 Salvadoran

【薩摩亞】Sàmóyà (名) Samoa: ～人 Samoan / ～語 Samoan (language)

藐 miǎo I (形) little; tiny; insignificant II (動) belittle; slight

【藐小】miǎoxiǎo (形) tiny; negligible

【藐視】miǎoshì (動) look down upon; despise

藩 fān (名) ❶ fence: ～籬 hedge ❷ (of a feudal dynasty) vassal state

藕 ǒu (名) lotus root

【藕粉】ǒufěn (名) lotus root starch

【藕斷絲連】ǒu duàn sī lián〈成〉have not completely severed relations with sb.

藝 yì (名) ❶ skill: 棋～ skill in chess ❷ art

【藝人】yìrén (名) ❶ actor; artist ❷ artisan; handicraftsman

【藝名】yìmíng (名) stage name

【藝苑】yìyuàn (名) world of art and literature

【藝術】yìshù (名) art: ～界 art circles / ～家 artist

藤 téng（名）❶ cane; rattan ❷ vine: 葡萄～ grapevine

【藤椅】téngyǐ（名）cane chair

【藤蘿】téngluó（名）〈植〉Chinese wisteria

藥 yào Ⅰ（名）medicine; drug Ⅱ（動）❶ kill with poison; poison

【藥丸】yàowán（名）pill

【藥方】yàofāng（名）prescription

【藥水】yàoshuǐ（名）liquid medicine: 咳嗽～ cough mixture

【藥片】yàopiàn（名）tablet

【藥皂】yàozào（名）medicated soap

【藥材】yàocái（名）herbal medicine; crude drugs

【藥房】yàofáng（名）❶ dispensary ❷ pharmacy; chemist's; drugstore

【藥物】yàowù（名）drugs; medicines

【藥品】yàopǐn（名）medicine

【藥酒】yàojiǔ（名）medicinal liquor

【藥粉】yàofěn（名）medicinal powder

【藥棉】yàomián（名）absorbent cotton

【藥膏】yàogāo（名）ointment

【藥廠】yàochǎng（名）pharmaceutical factory

【藥箱】yàoxiāng（名）medical kit

【藥舖】yàopù（名）herbal medicine shop

【藥罐子】yàoguànzi（名）❶ pot for decocting herbal medicine ❷ sickly person

藻 zǎo（名）❶ algae ❷ aquatic plants

【藻類植物】zǎolèi zhíwù（名）algae

藹 ǎi（形）kindly; amiable: 和～可親 amiable

蘑 mó

【蘑菇】mógu Ⅰ（名）mushroom Ⅱ（動）❶ pester: 別跟他～了。Don't keep pestering him. ❷ dawdle; waste time

【蘑菇雲】móguyún（名）mushroom cloud

蘆 lú（名）reed

【蘆筍】lúsǔn（名）asparagus

【蘆葦】lúwěi（名）reed

蘋 píng

【蘋果】píngguǒ（名）apple

【蘋果汁】píngguǒzhī（名）apple juice

【蘋果酒】píngguǒjiǔ（名）cider; apple jack

【蘋果醬】píngguǒjiàng（名）apple jam

蘇 sū Ⅰ（動）regain consciousness Ⅱ（名）（Sū）❶ short for Jiangsu Province ❷（short for 蘇維埃 Sūwéiʼāi）Soviet ❸ a surname

【蘇丹】sūdān（名）❶ Sultan ❷（Sūdān）the Sudan: ～人 Sudanese

【蘇打】sūdá（名）soda: ～水 soda water

【蘇醒】sūxǐng（動）regain consciousness; come to

【蘇聯】Sūlián（名）the former Soviet Union（now Commonwealth of Independent States）

【蘇繡】sūxiù（名）Suzhou embroidery

蘊 yùn（動）accumulate; contain

【蘊藏】yùncáng（動）contain; hold in store: 該地～着豐富的石油。The place is rich in oil deposits.

蘭 lán（名）orchid
【蘭花】lánhuā（名）orchid

蘸 zhàn（動）dip in（liquid, powder or paste）：用麵包～湯 dip pieces of bread into the soup

蘿 luó（名）trailing plants
【蘿蔔】luóbo（名）radish; turnip
【蘿蔔乾】luóbogān（名）❶ dried radish ❷ pickled radish

虍　部

虎 hǔ Ⅰ（名）tiger Ⅱ（形）brave; valiant; daring
【虎口】hǔkǒu（名）❶ tiger's mouth; jaws of death：～餘生 narrow escape from the jaws of death ❷ part of the hand between the thumb and the index finger
【虎穴】hǔxué（名）tiger's den; danger：不入～,焉得虎子？How can you capture the cubs without entering the lions' den?（Nothing venture, nothing have.）
【虎視眈眈】hǔ shì dān dān〈成〉glare covetously
【虎鉗】hǔqián（名）vice
【虎頭蛇尾】hǔ tóu shé wěi〈成〉the vigorous spirit displayed at the start slacks off towards the end

虐 nüè（形）brutal; tyrannical
【虐待】nüèdài（動）ill-treat; maltreat
【虐政】nüèzhèng（名）tyrannical government; tyranny
【虐殺】nüèshā（動）butcher

虔 qián（形）pious; sincere
【虔誠】qiánchéng（形）pious; devout

虛 xū（形）❶ empty; void：座無～席（of a lecture hall, etc.）packed to full capacity; a full house ❷ waste; to no avail：～度光陰 idle away one's time ❸ false：弄～作假 practise fraud ❹ weak：身子～ in poor health ❺ timid; diffident：心中發～ lack self-confidence
【虛幻】xūhuàn（形）illusory; visionary：～的奇境 visionary wonderland
【虛心】xūxīn（形）modest; openminded：～接受批評 be open-minded in one's response to criticism
【虛汗】xūhàn（名）abnormal sweating due to general debility
【虛名】xūmíng（名）undeserved reputation
【虛有其表】xū yǒu qí biǎo〈成〉look good but lack real substance; fair without, foul within
【虛度】xūdù（動）waste（one's time）
【虛胖】xūpàng（形）fat; puffy
【虛弱】xūruò（形）weak; feeble：～的老人 a senile person/ 國力～ weak in national strength
【虛假】xūjiǎ（形）false; unreal：～的話 hypocritical remark
【虛掩】xūyǎn（動）（of doors）be left unlocked or unbolted
【虛脫】xūtuō（名）〈醫〉collapse; prostration
【虛設】xūshè（形）nominal; in name only：形同～ as good as nominal; exist only in name
【虛情假意】xū qíng jiǎ yì〈成〉pretence of friendship; hypocritical

show of affection; a mere sham

【虛張聲勢】xū zhāng shēng shì〈成〉put on a display of might; put on a good bluff; bluff and bluster

【虛報】xūbào（動）give a false report of

【虛詞】xūcí（名）〈語〉function word

【虛無】xūwú（名）nihility; nothingness: ～縹緲 imaginary and visionary

【虛無主義】xūwú zhǔyì（名）nihilism

【虛誇】xūkuā（動）exagerate; boast; overstate

【虛歲】xūsuì（名）nominal age

【虛榮】xūróng（名）vain glory; vanity: 愛～ be vain /～心 vanity

【虛構】xūgòu（動）fabricate; make up: ～的故事 a cooked-up story; a fictitious story

【虛偽】xūwěi（名）hypocrisy: ～至極 be stewed deep in hypocrisy

【虛實】xūshí（名）true condition; actual situation: 打聽～ try to get a clear picture of the actual situation

【虛擬】xūnǐ（形）❶ invented; fictitious: ～的情節 fictive story ❷〈語〉subjunctive mood: ～語氣 the subjunctive mood

【虛驚】xūjīng（名）false alarm

處 chǔ（動）❶ get along with: 難以相～ difficult to get along with ❷ be in a certain position: 處在不利的情況中 be at a disadvantage ❸ handle; manage; tackle ❹ punish: ～以三年徒刑 be sentenced to 3 years' imprisonment

see also chù

【處女】chǔnǚ（名）virgin: ～航 maiden voyage /～地 virgin soil

【處方】chǔfāng（名）〈醫〉prescription

【處分】chǔfèn（名）penalty; punishment; disciplinary measure

【處心積慮】chǔ xīn jī lǜ〈成〉try by every conceivable means (to achieve an evil end)

【處世】chǔshì（動）get along with people in society: ～哲學 philosophy of life

【處死】chǔsǐ（動）execute; put to death

【處決】chǔjué（動）execute; put to death

【處於】chǔyú（動）be in (a certain state): ～危急時刻 be at a critical juncture

【處理】chǔlǐ（動）❶ handle; tackle; deal with: ～糾紛 settle a dispute ❷ sell (goods) at a reduced price; dispose of

【處置】chǔzhì（動）handle; tackle; settle: ～失當 mishandle matters

【處境】chǔjìng（名）(usu. unfavourable) condition; situation: ～困難 be in a difficult situation

【處罰】chǔfá（動）punish; penalize

處 chù Ⅰ（名）❶ place: 問訊～ information desk ❷ point; part: 林中深～ in the depth of a forest ❸ department; division; section: ～長 director of a department Ⅱ（量）(of places; mistakes in writing, etc.): 三～錯誤 three errors

see also chǔ

【處處】chùchù（副）everywhere; in every way

號 háo（動）cry with a howl; yell

see also hào

【號叫】háojiào（動）howl

【號啕】háotáo（動）wail: ～大哭 cry one's heart out

號 hào（名）❶ name: 牌～ trade-mark ❷ mark; sign; signal: 記～ mark; sign / 驚嘆～ exclamation mark ❸ number: 編～ serial number ❹ trumpet or bugle ❺〈舊〉business house: 分～ branch shop see also háo

【號令】hàolìng（名）order; verbal command

【號外】hàowài（名）extra（of a newspaper）

【號召】hàozhào（名）call; appeal

【號角】hàojiǎo（名）❶ bugle; horn ❷ bugle call; clarion

【號脈】hàomài（動）feel or take sb.'s pulse

【號稱】hàochēng（動）❶ be known as ❷ appear to be

【號碼】hàomǎ（名）number

虞 yú I（名）❶ prediction; anticipation: 以防不～ prepare against the time of need ❷ anxiety; worry: 衣食無～ have no worries about one's clothing or food ❸（Yú）a surname II（動）cheat; deceive: 爾～我詐 cheat and intrigue against one another

【虞美人】yúměirén（名）〈植〉corn poppy

虜 lǔ I（名）captive II（動）capture; take prisoner

【虜獲】lǔhuò（動）capture（men or weapons）

虧 kuī I（名）loss; deficit: 吃眼前～ suffer immediate loss II（動）❶ suffer losses: ～本生意 losing business ❷ be deficient in; be short of:

自知理～ know that one is in the wrong ❸ be unfair to（sb.）: 別～了人家。You mustn't be unfair to anybody. III（副）❶ fortunately: 多～他幫忙。Luckily I had his timely help. ❷［used in reproachful irony］: ～他幹得出來! He had the cheek to act like this! IV（形）（of the moon）waning

【虧心】kuīxīn（動）have a guilty conscience; be conscience-stricken: 做～事 do what is contrary to one's sense of justice

【虧本】kuīběn（動）lose money in business; lose one's capital: ～生意 a losing proposition

【虧空】kuīkong I（動）fail to make both ends meet and thus run into debt II（名）debt; deficit; loss of money that has been incurred

【虧待】kuīdài（動）treat sb. unfairly or with the least thoughtfulness

【虧耗】kuīhào（名）loss incurred in the course of transportation or during storage

【虧產】kuīchǎn（動）fail to reach the output quota

【虧得】kuīde（副）❶ fortunately; thanks to: ～你幫助我, 纔渡過難關。I owe it to you that I have tided over the difficulties. ❷［used in reproachful irony］fancy: 這麼熱天還穿毛衣, 真～你! Fancy your wearing a sweater in this warm weather!

【虧損】kuīsǔn（名）❶ loss; deficit ❷ physical weakness caused by lack of nutrition or illness

【虧蝕】kuīshí I（名）eclipse of the sun or moon II（動）lose（money）in business

虫 部

虱 shī (名) louse

【虱子】shīzi (名) louse

虻 méng (名) horsefly; gadfly

虹 hóng (名) rainbow
see also jiàng

【虹膜】hóngmó (名)〈生理〉iris

虹 jiàng (名)〈口〉rainbow
see also hóng

虼 gè

【虼蚤】gèzao (名)〈口〉flea

蚤 zǎo (名) flea

蚊 wén (名) mosquito

【蚊子】wénzi (名) mosquito

【蚊香】wénxiāng (名) mosquito coil incense

【蚊帐】wénzhàng (名) mosquito net

蚜 yá

【蚜虫】yáchóng (名) aphid; aphis

蚋 ruì (名) buffalo gnat; blackfly

蚍 pí

【蚍蜉】pífú (名) big ant

【蚍蜉撼大樹】pí fú hàn dà shù〈成〉an ant trying to topple a giant tree; be ludicrously ignorant of one's strength

蚌 bàng (名) clam; freshwater mussel

【蚌殼】bàngké (名) ❶ clam ❷ shell

蛋 dàn (名) ❶ egg: ～白 egg white / ～黄 yolk ❷ egg-shaped thing

【蛋白質】dànbáizhì (名) protein

【蛋糕】dàngāo (名) cake

蛇 shé (名) snake; serpent

蛀 zhù (動)(of moth, etc.) eat into: 這件毛衣被蛀～了。The sweater is moth-eaten.

【蛀蟲】zhùchóng (名) moth; borer

蚶 hān (名)〈動〉blood clam

蛆 qū (名) maggot

蚰 yóu

【蚰蜒】yóuyán (名) common house centipede

蚱 zhà

【蚱蜢】zhàměng (名) grasshopper

蚯 qiū

【蚯蚓】qiūyǐn (名) earthworm

蛟 jiāo (名) flood dragon

【蛟龍】jiāolóng (名) flood dragon, a mythological creature capable of invoking strong winds and heavy rains

蛙 wā (名) frog

【蛙泳】wāyǒng (名) breaststroke

蛭 zhì (名) leech

蛐 qū

【蛐蛐兒】qūqur (名)〈方〉cricket

蛔 huí

【蛔蟲】huíchóng (名) roundworm; ascarid

蛤 gé (名) clam

see also há

蛤 há

see also gé

【蛤蟆】háma（名）❶ frog ❷ toad

蛛 zhū（名）spider

【蛛絲馬跡】zhū sī mǎ jì〈成〉clues; spoors; traces: 總有一些人們沒有注意到的～。There must be some clues which have escaped people's notice.

【蛛網】zhūwǎng（名）cobweb; spiderweb

蜇 zhē（動）sting: 被蝎子～了 be stung by a scorpion

see also zhé

蜇 zhé（名）jellyfish

see also zhē

蜃 shèn（名）clam: ～景 mirage

蜕 tuì（動）slough

【蜕化】tuìhuà（動）degenerate; degrade

【蜕變】tuìbiàn（動）（people or things）undergo a fundamental change

蛹 yǒng（名）pupa

蜈 wú

【蜈蚣】wúgōng（名）centipede

蜉 fú

【蜉蝣】fúyóu（名）antlike insect; mayfly

蛾 é（名）moth

蜂 fēng（名）bee; wasp: 養～場 apiary

【蜂王】fēngwáng（名）queen bee

【蜂房】fēngfáng（名）beehive

【蜂蜜】fēngmì（名）honey

【蜂窩】fēngwō（名）honeycomb

【蜂擁】fēngyōng（動）swarm; crowd in from all directions

蜀 Shǔ（名）another name for Sichuan Province

蜜 mì Ⅰ（名）honey Ⅱ（形）sweet

【蜜月】mìyuè（名）honeymoon: 度～ be on one's honeymoon / ～旅行 honeymooner

【蜜柑】mìgān（名）mandarin; orange

【蜜棗】mìzǎo（名）candied date; glazed jujube

【蜜蜂】mìfēng（名）honeybee; bee

【蜜橘】mìjú（名）tangerine

【蜜餞】mìjiàn（名）candied fruit; sweetmeats; preserves

蜿 wān

【蜿蜒】wānyán（動）（of a river, mountain range, road, etc.）meander; zigzag

蜣 qiāng

【蜣螂】qiāngláng（名）dung beetle

蜻 qīng

【蜻蜓】qīngtíng（名）dragonfly

【蜻蜓點水】qīng tíng diǎn shuǐ〈成〉do only superficial work without going into it deeply

蜥 xī

【蜥蜴】xīyì（名）lizard

蜘 zhī

【蜘蛛】zhīzhū（名）spider: ～網 cobweb

蜚 fēi

【蜚語】fēiyǔ（名）unfounded rumours; groundless allegations

【蜚聲】fēishēng（動）become famous: ～藝苑 enjoy high prestige in art and literary circles

蝕 shí I（動）❶ lose ❷ erode II（名）eclipse: 月～ lunar eclipse

【蝕本】shíběn（動）suffer loss in business: ～買賣 unprofitable deal

蝙 biān

【蝙蝠】biānfú（名）bat

蝴 hú

【蝴蝶】húdié（名）butterfly

蝶 dié（名）butterfly

【蝶泳】diéyǒng（名）(in swimming) butterfly stroke

蝦 xiā（名）shrimp; prawn

【蝦仁】xiārén（名）shrimp meat; shelled fresh shrimp

【蝦皮】xiāpí（名）dried small shrimp

【蝦米】xiāmi（名）dried shelled shrimp

【蝦醬】xiājiàng（名）shrimp paste

蝎 xiē（名）scorpion

【蝎子】xiēzi（名）scorpion

蝸 wō（名）snail

【蝸牛】wōniú（名）snail

【蝸輪】wōlún（名）〈機〉worm gear; worm wheel

蝮 fù

【蝮蛇】fùshé（名）Pallas pit viper

蝌 kē

【蝌蚪】kēdǒu（名）tadpole

蝗 huáng（名）locust

【蝗蟲】huángchóng（名）locust

螢 yíng（名）firefly; glowworm

【螢火蟲】yínghuǒchóng（名）firefly; glowworm

【螢石】yíngshí（名）〈礦〉fluorite; fluorspar

融 róng（動）❶ melt; thaw ❷ blend; fuse

【融化】rónghuà（動）melt; thaw

【融合】rónghé（動）blend; fuse; amalgamate

【融洽】róngqià（形）on friendly terms; in harmony: 關係～ get on well with one another

【融解】róngjiě（動）melt; thaw

【融會貫通】róng huì guàn tōng〈成〉achieve perfect understanding by a comprehensive study; comprehend thoroughly

螃 páng

【螃蟹】pángxiè（名）crab

螟 míng

【螟蛾】míng'é（名）snout moth

【螟蟲】míngchóng（名）snout moth's larva

螞 mǎ

see also mà

【螞蟥】mǎhuáng（名）leech

【螞蟻】mǎyǐ（名）ant

螞 mà

see also mǎ

【螞蚱】màzha（名）〈方〉locust; grasshopper

蟄 zhé（動）hibernate

【蟄伏】zhéfú（名）〈動〉dormancy; hibernation

【蟄居】zhéjū（名）live in seclusion

蟑 zhāng
【蟑螂】zhānglāng（名）cock-roach; roach

蟒 mǎng（名）boa; python
【蟒蛇】mǎngshé（名）boa; python

螨 mǎn（名）〈動〉mite

螳 táng（名）〈動〉mantis
【螳螂】tánglāng（名）〈動〉mantis

螻 lóu（名）mole cricket
【螻蛄】lóugū（名）mole cricket
【螻蟻】lóuyǐ（名）mole crickets and ants; tiny creatures; nobodies

螺 luó（名）snail; spiral shell
【螺母】luómǔ（螺帽 luómào）（名）〈機〉（screw）nut
【螺釘】luódīng（螺絲釘 luósīdīng）（名）screw
【螺紋】luówén（名）❶ whorl; spiral (in fingerprint) ❷〈機〉thread of a screw
【螺旋】luóxuán（名）spiral: 物價～上升 price spiral
【螺旋槳】luóxuánjiǎng（名）〈機〉propeller
【螺絲】luósī（名）screw
【螺絲刀】luósīdāo（名）screwdriver
【螺鈿】luódiàn（名）〈工美〉mother-of-pearl inlay
【螺號】luóhào（名）shell trumpet

蟈 guō
【蟈蟈】guōguo（名）katydid; long-horned grasshopper

蟋 xī
【蟋蟀】xīshuài（名）cricket

蟯 náo
【蟯蟲】náochóng（名）pinworm
【蟯蟲病】náochóngbìng（名）enterobiasis

蟬 chán（名）cicada
【蟬聯】chánlián（動）continue to hold (office or title)：～冠軍 win the championship again (and again)

蟲 chóng（名）insect; worm: 魚～ water flea (used as fish feed)
【蟲害】chónghài（名）insect pest

蟠 pán（動）curl; twist
【蟠桃】pántáo（名）flat peach

蟻 yǐ（名）ant
【蟻巢】yǐcháo（名）ant nest

蟶 chēng（蟶子 chēngzi）（名）razor clam

蠅 yíng（名）fly
【蠅拍】yíngpāi（名）fly swatter
【蠅頭】yíngtóu（形）tiny: ～小楷 very small characters (in handwriting)

蟾 chán（名）toad
【蟾宮】chángōng（名）moon
【蟾蜍】chánchú（名）toad

蟹 xiè（名）crab

蠔 háo（名）oyster
【蠔油】háoyóu（名）oyster sauce

蠐 qí
【蠐螬】qícáo（名）grub

蠑 róng
【蠑螈】róngyuán（名）salamander; newt

蠕 rú（動）wriggle

【蠕動】rúdòng（動）wriggle

【蠕蟲】rúchóng（名）worm; helminth

蠢 chǔn（形）stupid; foolish: ~ 人 fool; blockhead

【蠢材】chǔncái（蠢貨 chǔnhuò）（名）〈罵〉idiot; dumbbell; silly ass

【蠢笨】chǔnbèn（形）clumsy; awkward

【蠢蠢欲動】chǔn chǔn yù dòng〈成〉〈貶〉scheme or be ready to take action

蠟 là（名）❶ wax ❷ candle ❸ polish: 上光 ~ wax polish

【蠟人】làrén（名）waxwork; wax figure

【蠟果】làguǒ（名）〈工美〉wax fruit

【蠟染】làrǎn（名）〈紡〉wax printing: ~ 布 wax-stencilled material

【蠟紙】làzhǐ（名）❶ wax paper ❷ stencil: 刻 ~ cut stencil

【蠟黃】làhuáng（形）❶（esp. of human skin）sickly; pale; yellowish ❷ wax yellow

【蠟筆】làbǐ（名）crayon

【蠟燭】làzhú（名）candle: 點 ~ light a candle

蠱 gǔ（名）most poisonous insect

【蠱惑人心】gǔ huò rén xīn〈成〉misguide people by demagogy

蠹 dù Ⅰ（名）moth Ⅱ（動）be moth-eaten

【蠹蟲】dùchóng（名）❶ moth ❷ person doing great harm to the collective from the inside

蠶 cán（名）silkworm: 柞 ~ tussah silkworm

【蠶豆】cándòu（名）broad bean

【蠶食】cánshí（動）nibble at

【蠶絲】cánsī（名）natural silk

【蠶繭】cánjiǎn（名）silkworm cocoon

蠻 mán Ⅰ（形）rude; unreasoning; ferocious Ⅱ（副）very; pretty: 今天天氣~不錯。It's a very nice day.

【蠻不講理】mán bù jiǎng lǐ〈成〉very unfriendly and unreasonable; unreasonable and unaccommodating

【蠻幹】mángàn（動）act recklessly regardless of the consequences

【蠻橫】mánhèng（形）savage in behaviour

【蠻纏】mánchán（動）pester; harass: 胡攪 ~ pester sb. with unreasonable requests

蠼 qú

【蠼螋】qúsōu（名）earwig

血 部

血 xiě（名）〈口〉blood
see also xuè

【血淋淋】xiělínlín（形）bloody

血 xuè（名）blood
see also xiě

【血口噴人】xuè kǒu pēn rén〈成〉make slanderous attacks on sb.

【血汗】xuèhàn（名）sweat and toil; sweat on the brow

【血肉】xuèròu（名）flesh and blood: ~ 相連 be intimately related like flesh and blood

【血色】xuèsè（名）colour; complexion: 面無～ look pale; have a pallid complexion

【血沉】xuèchén（名）〈醫〉erythrocyte sedimentation rate

【血吸蟲】xuèxīchóng（名）blood fluke: ～病 snail fever; schistosomiasis

【血泊】xuèpō（名）pool of blood

【血洗】xuèxǐ（名）bloodbath

【血型】xuèxíng（名）blood group; blood type

【血迹】xuèjī（名）bloodstain

【血案】xuè'àn（名）murder case

【血氣】xuèqì（名）❶ energy; vigour: ～方剛 full of vim and vigour ❷ upright moral passion: 有～的青年 young people full of courage and uprightness

【血庫】xuèkù（名）blood bank

【血海深仇】xuè hǎi shēn chóu〈成〉deep and intense hatred

【血淚】xuèlèi（名）blood and tears; tragic experience

【血液】xuèyè（名）blood

【血統】xuètǒng（名）blood relationship; blood lineage: 有中國～的美籍學者 American scholar of Chinese descent

【血腥】xuèxīng（形）bloody; sanguinary; cruel: ～鎮壓 bloody suppression

【血債】xuèzhài（名）debt of blood

【血管】xuèguǎn（名）blood vessel

【血緣】xuèyuán（名）blood relationship; consanguinity

【血戰】xuèzhàn（名）bloody battle

【血壓】xuèyā（名）blood pressure

【血壓計】xuèyājì（名）sphygmomanometer

衆 zhòng Ⅰ（形）many; numerous:

～人拾柴火焰高。Fire fed by many burns brighter.（Work shared by many becomes lighter.）Ⅱ（名）crowd; multitude: 公～ the public

【衆人】zhòngrén（名）everybody

【衆口難調】zhòng kǒu nán tiáo〈成〉it is difficult to please everyone

【衆矢之的】zhòng shǐ zhī dì〈成〉target of public condemnation

【衆目睽睽】zhòng mù kuí kuí〈成〉the gaze of the public is scrutinizing: ～之下 in the public eye

【衆多】zhòngduō（形）numerous

【衆志成城】zhòng zhì chéng chéng〈成〉unity of will is a citadel of strength

【衆所周知】zhòng suǒ zhōu zhī〈成〉as is known to all

【衆叛親離】zhòng pàn qīn lí〈成〉be opposed by the public and forsaken by one's trusted followers

【衆望】zhòngwàng（名）people's expectations: ～所歸 enjoy popular confidence

【衆說紛紜】zhòng shuō fēn yún〈成〉different people have different views; opinions differ

行　部

行 háng（名）❶ line; row: 第三頁第四～ line 4 on page 3 ❷ business firm; store ❸ trade; profession: 同～ colleague ❹ order of seniority among brothers and sisters
see also xíng

【行列】hángliè（名）ranks

【行家】hángjia（名）expert; connoisseur

【行情】hángqíng（行市 hángshì）（名）❶ commodity prices ❷ quotations (on the foreign exchange market)

【行業】hángyè（名）trade; profession

【行話】hánghuà（名）jargon

【行會】hánghuì（名）guild

行 xíng（動）❶ walk; go: 步～ go on foot／～車 drive ❷ prevail: 風～一時 become the fashion of the day; be very much in vogue for a time ❸ do; perform: 見機～事 do as one sees fit; act at one's own discretion ❹ be all right: 這個計劃能～。This plan will work.／問他準～。He is the right person to approach. ❺ be capable: 你真～！How wonderful you are!
see also háng

【行人】xíngrén（名）pedestrian

【行乞】xíngqǐ（動）go begging; beg

【行文】xíngwén（動）compose a piece of writing: ～晦澀，殊不易懂。The writing couched in obscure terms is difficult to understand.

【行方便】xíngfāngbian（動）make things easy for sb.; stretch a point for sb.

【行不通】xíngbùtōng（動）won't do; be infeasible

【行刑】xíngxíng（動）carry out a death sentence; execute

【行兇】xíngxiōng（動）resort to violence

【行好】xínghǎo（動）take pity on sb. and pardon him for his fault

【行走】xíngzǒu（動）go; walk

【行李】xíngli（名）luggage; baggage: ～寄存處 checkroom

【行劫】xíngjié（動）commit robbery; rob

【行刺】xíngcì（動）assassinate

【行使】xíngshǐ（動）exercise; use: ～否決權 exercise the veto

【行事】xíngshì（動）act: 按規定～ act according to regulations

【行政】xíngzhèng（名）administration

【行屍走肉】xíng shī zǒu ròu〈成〉walking corpse; worthless person

【行星】xíngxīng（名）planet

【行軍】xíngjūn（名）(of troops) march

【行軍牀】xíngjūnchuáng（名）camp bed

【行時】xíngshí（動）❶ be in fashion ❷ be in the ascendent

【行書】xíngshū（名）running hand (in Chinese calligraphy)

【行徑】xíngjìng（名）act; behaviour; conduct: 卑鄙的～ ignominious act

【行商】xíngshāng Ⅰ（動）do business Ⅱ（名）itinerant trader; pedlar

【行動】xíngdòng Ⅰ（動）❶ move; get about: ～不便 walk with difficulty ❷ act: 立即～ act promptly Ⅱ（名）action; move; operation

【行進】xíngjìn（動）march on; move forward

【行得通】xíngdetōng（動）will do; be workable: 這個計劃～。This plan is feasible.

【行將就木】xíng jiāng jiù mù〈成〉have one foot in the grave

【行程】xíngchéng（名）distance of travel; journey

【行善】xíngshàn（動）do good works; give charities

【行期】xíngqī（名）date of departure

【行爲】xíngwéi（名）conduct; behaviour

【行裝】xíngzhuāng（名）outfit for a journey: 打點～ pack up one's things

【行賄】xínghuì（動）offer a bribe; bribe

【行經】xíngjīng（動）go by; pass through: 汽車深夜～居民區。The car passed through a residential area at midnight.

【行踪】xíngzōng（名）whereabouts

【行銷】xíngxiāo（動）sell

【行駛】xíngshǐ（動）（of a vehicle, ship, etc.）go; run

【行樂】xínglè（動）make merry; enjoy oneself in game or any other form of recreation

【行頭】xíngtou（名）stage costumes and properties

【行營】xíngyíng（名）field headquarters

【行禮】xínglǐ（動）salute

【行醫】xíngyī（動）practise medicine; practise as a physician

【行騙】xíngpiàn（動）cheat; deceive

【行竊】xíngqiè（動）steal

衍 yǎn

【衍變】yǎnbiàn（動）evolve; develop

術 shù（名）❶ art; skill; feat: 技～水平 technical competence ❷ method; tactics; strategy: 玩弄權～ play politics

【術語】shùyǔ（名）technical term; terminology

街 jiē（名）street

【街坊】jiēfang（名）〈口〉neighbours: 我們是～。We are neighbours.

【街道】jiēdào（名）❶ street; avenue ❷ neighbourhood: ～診療所 neighbourhood clinic

【街談巷議】jiē tán xiàng yì〈成〉idle chat; tittle-tattle: 成了～的話題 become the talk of the town

【街頭】jiētóu（副）in the street: 流落～ become homeless

【街頭巷尾】jiē tóu xiàng wěi〈成〉every street and alley; everywhere in the streets

衙 yá

【衙內】yánèi（名）son of an influential official

【衙門】yámen（名）〈舊〉yamen; government office

衚 hú

【衚衕】hútòng（名）lane; alley

衛 wèi（動）defend; protect

【衛士】wèishì（名）guard; bodyguard

【衛生】wèishēng（名）sanitation; hygiene ～間 toilet / ～巾 sanitary towel

【衛戍】wèishù（名）garrison: ～區 garrison command

【衛兵】wèibīng（名）guard; sentinel

【衛星】wèixīng（名）❶ satellite; moon ❷ artificial satellite: 間諜～ spy satellite

【衛隊】wèiduì（名）team of bodyguards

衝 chōng I（動）❶ charge; dash: 俯～（of aircraft）dive ❷ conflict II（名）thoroughfare; hub: 要～ hub
see also chòng

【衝天】chōngtiān（形）vigorous;

powerful: 怨氣～ be deeply resentful

【衝突】chōngtū Ⅰ(名) conflict: 邊界～ border conflicts Ⅱ(動) clash; contradict: 開會與歷史課～。The meeting clashes with the history class.

【衝破】chōngpò (動) break through

【衝動】chōngdòng Ⅰ(名) impulse Ⅱ(動) get excited

【衝散】chōngsàn (動) break up; disperse

【衝撞】chōngzhuàng (動) ❶ collide ❷ offend: 不是有意～他 not mean to offend him

【衝衝】chōngchōng (副) excitedly: 怒氣～ in a towering rage

【衝鋒】chōngfēng (動) charge

【衝擊】chōngjī Ⅰ(動) ❶ (of water) swash; lash ❷ charge; assault Ⅱ(名) impact

衝 chòng Ⅰ(副) forcefully; with vigour and drive: 傷口的血流得很～。Blood is gushing from the wound. Ⅱ(形) (of smell) strong; pungent: 酒味特別～ (of liquor) have a very strong flavour Ⅲ(介)〈口〉 towards: ～南 face south see also chōng

【衝牀】chòngchuáng (名) 〈機〉 punch; punch press

衡 héng Ⅰ(名) weighing apparatus Ⅱ(動) weigh; measure; judge: 權～利弊 weigh the pros and cons

【衡量】héngliáng (動) weigh; measure; judge: ～得失 weigh up the gains and losses

衣 部

衣 yī (名) ❶ clothing; clothes: 冬～ winter clothes ❷ coating; covering: 花生～ membrane of peanuts

【衣夾】yījiā (名) clothes peg

【衣刷】yīshuā (名) clothes brush

【衣物】yīwù (名) one's clothes and other personal belongings

【衣服】yīfu (名) clothing; clothes; garment

【衣衫襤褸】yī shān lán lǚ〈成〉 be in rags; be poorly dressed

【衣架】yījià (名) ❶ (coat) hanger ❷ clothes stand; clothes tree

【衣冠】yīguān (名) hat and gown; dress

【衣冠楚楚】yī guān chǔ chǔ〈成〉 well-dressed

【衣食住行】yīshí zhùxíng (名) clothing, food, housing and transport

【衣料】yīliào (名) dress material

【衣着】yīzhuó (名) dress; apparel

【衣帽間】yīmàojiān (名) cloakroom; checkroom

【衣鉢】yībō (名) mantle; heritage: 繼承～ take over sb.'s mantle

【衣裳】yīshang (名)〈口〉 clothes; clothing

【衣領】yīlǐng (名) collar

【衣箱】yīxiāng (名) trunk; suitcase

【衣櫥】yīchú (名) wardrobe

【衣櫃】yīguì (名) wardrobe

衩 chà (名) slit in the sides of a garment: 開～ make a side slit

衫 shān（名）jacket; gown; shirt: 長～ long gown/襯～ shirt

表 biǎo Ⅰ（名）❶ surface; exterior; outside: 他是～裏一致的。He always means what he says. ❷ model;（good）example: 爲人師～ be a paragon of virtue and learning ❸ form; table; list; schedule: 價目～ price list ❹ meter; gauge: 計程～ taxi-meter ❺ relatives of one's mother or father's sister: ～哥 cousin ❻ memo to the monarch Ⅱ（動）show; express; demonstrate: 深～謝意 express one's profound gratitude

【表白】biǎobái（動）express or vindicate（one's own real feelings, intentions, etc.）

【表皮】biǎopí（名）〈生〉epidermis; cuticle

【表示】biǎoshì（動）show; indicate: ～同意(反對) agree (disagree)

【表册】biǎocè（名）lists, tables, charts, etc. bound in book form

【表決】biǎojué（動）vote; decide by votes: 舉手～ vote by a show of hands

【表決權】biǎojuéquán（名）right to vote

【表明】biǎomíng（動）make clear; indicate: ～態度 defind one's position

【表述】biǎoshù Ⅰ（動）give expression to Ⅱ（名）wording

【表面】biǎomiàn（名）surface; appearance

【表面上】biǎomiànshàng Ⅰ（形）superficial; ostensible; seeming: ～的動機 ostensible motive Ⅱ（副）ostensibly; superficially; outwardly:

從～看來 on the surface; apparently

【表面文章】biǎomiàn wénzhāng（名）a matter of formality; mere formalities

【表面現象】biǎomiàn xiànxiàng（名）superficial phenomenon

【表格】biǎogé（名）form; table

【表情】biǎoqíng（名）expression; look: 不自然 look unnatural

【表率】biǎoshuài（名）（good）example; model: 起～作用 set a good example for

【表現】biǎoxiàn Ⅰ（名）expression; manifestation: ～手法 technique of expression Ⅱ（動）❶ show; express; display ❷ behave: ～好 behave（conduct oneself）well ❸ show off: 好～ be fond of showing off

【表現形式】biǎoxiàn xíngshì（名）form of expression; manifestation

【表達】biǎodá（動）express; voice; convey

【表揚】biǎoyáng（動）praise（in public）; cite; commend: 值得～ be praise-worthy

【表裏不一】biǎo lǐ bù yī〈成〉fail to act and think in the same way

【表裏如一】biǎo lǐ rú yī〈成〉think and behave in one and the same way

【表態】biǎotài（動）clarify one's position; take a clear-cut stand

【表語】biǎoyǔ（名）〈語〉predicative

【表彰】biǎozhāng（動）commend; cite; honour: ～傑出的科學家 commend outstanding scientists

【表演】biǎoyǎn Ⅰ（動）❶ perform: ～體操 put on a gymnastic show ❷ demonstrate（skills, techniques, etc.）Ⅱ（名）performance

【表演賽】biǎoyǎnsài（名）exhibition match

【表層】biǎocéng（名）surface layer; top layer

【表親】biǎoqīn（名）relative of one's mother or father's sister

衷 zhōng（名）heart; inner feelings: 言不由～ speak unctuously

【衷心】zhōngxīn（形）heartfelt; wholehearted; from the bottom of one's heart: ～欽佩 sincerely admire

衰 shuāi（動）decline; weaken: 盛～ rise and fall／年老力～ be old and weak; be aging and ailing

【衰亡】shuāiwáng Ⅰ（動）decline and fall: 羅馬帝國的～ the decline and fall of the Roman Empire Ⅱ（動）wither away

【衰老】shuāilǎo（形）senile

【衰退】shuāituì（動）deteriorate; wane; recede: 經濟～ economic recession

【衰弱】shuāiruò（動）become weak: 他是一位身體～的老人。He is aged and weak (aging and ailing).

【衰敗】shuāibài（動）decline; decay

【衰落】shuāiluò（動）decline: 一種文明的～ the decline of a civilization

【衰竭】shuāijié（名）〈醫〉exhaustion: 心力～ heart failure

衹 zhǐ（副）only; merely: 手術用了兩個鐘頭。The operation took only two hours.

【衹不過】zhǐbùguò（副）only; just; merely: 我～是想幫幫忙。I was just trying to help.

【衹有】zhǐyǒu（連）only; alone: ～

他知道事情內幕。He alone knows the inside story.

【衹是】zhǐshì Ⅰ（副）❶ merely; only; just: 我們～一面之交。We have only met once. ❷ simply: 這～時間問題。It's simply a matter of time. Ⅱ（連）but; however: 我很想和你一起去，～沒時間。I'd like very much to go with you, only I don't have the time.

【衹要】zhǐyào（連）so long as: ～不下雨，我們就去野餐。We'll go on a picnic, provided it does not rain.

【衹得】zhǐdé（衹好 zhǐhǎo）（動）have to; have no alternative but to: 由於健康不佳，他～放棄計劃。He had to give up his plan on account of ill health.

【衹管】zhǐguǎn（副）by all means: 有什麼看法你～說。Say what's in your mind by all means.

【衹顧】zhǐgù（動）be absorbed in: 他～看書，半天沒有說話。He was so absorbed in his book that he didn't say a single word for a long while.

袁 Yuán（名）a surname

衾 qīn（名）quilt

被 bèi Ⅰ（名）❶ quilt; comforter: 毛巾～ cotton terry blanket ❷ cover: 保護植～ preserve the vegetation Ⅱ（動）(a passive marker) ❶ [used before a verb to form a passive phrase equivalent in function to the English past participle, but often with a connotation of undesirableness]: ～佔領的領土 the occupied territory ❷ [used in a passive construction as an equivalent for the English verb "be", positioned after the subject and with the agent that is to follow often omitted]：那棵樹～（大風）刮倒了。The tree was blown down (by a gale).

【被子】bèizi（名）quilt

【被告】bèigào（名）〈法〉defendant; the accused：～席 dock (in a law court)

【被俘】bèifú（動）be captured; be taken prisoner

【被面】bèimiàn（名）face layer of a quilt

【被套】bèitào（名）❶ quilt cover ❷ bed sack ❸ (cotton) wadding for a quilt

【被害人】bèihàirén（名）〈法〉victim; injured party

【被動】bèidòng（動）passive

【被動語態】bèidòng yǔtài（名）passive voice

【被單】bèidān（名）sheet (for the bed)

【被裹】bèilǐ（名）lining of a quilt

【被選舉權】bèi xuǎnjǔquán（名）right to be elected; right to stand for election

【被褥】bèirù（名）bedding; bedding and mattress; bedclothes

【被難】bèinàn（動）be killed (in an accident, incident or natural disaster)

祖 tǎn（動）❶ expose part of one's body above the waist or strip oneself to the waist ❷ shield; protect：不偏～任何一方 be partial to none of the parties involved

【袒護】tǎnhù（動）shield

袖 xiù（名）sleeve

【袖子】xiùzi（名）sleeve

【袖口】xiùkǒu（名）cuff (of a sleeve)

【袖手旁觀】xiù shǒu páng guān〈成〉sit on the sidelines and watch with folded arms; sit back and watch

【袖珍】xiùzhēn（形）pocket-size：～地圖冊 pocket atlas

【袖章】xiùzhāng（名）armband

【袖標】xiùbiāo（名）armband

袍 páo（名）robe; gown：旗～ Chinese gown (for woman)

袋 dài I（名）bag; sack II（量）：一～大米 a sack of rice

【袋鼠】dàishǔ（名）kangaroo

裁 cái I（動）❶ cut (paper, fabric, etc.)：～衣服 cut out a garment ❷ reduce; dismiss：～員 reduce staff ❸ judge; decide：專制獨～ autocratic dictatorship ❹ check; sanction：法律制～ legal sanction II（名）form：文章體～ form and style of writing

【裁決】cáijué I（動）consider and decide II（名）ruling; verdict

【裁判】cáipàn I（動）pass judgment II（名）❶〈法〉judgment ❷〈體〉judge; referee

【裁併】cáibìng（動）cut down and merge (government organizations so as to make them work more efficiently)

【裁定】cáidìng（名）ruling; adjudication

【裁軍】cáijūn（名）disarmament

【裁剪】cáijiǎn（動）cut out：～一條裙子 cut out a skirt

【裁減】cáijiǎn（動）reduce; cut down：～軍備 arms reduction

【裁縫】cáifeng（名）tailor

裂 liè（動）crack; splinter

【裂口】lièkǒu（名）gap; chink

【裂紋】lièwén（名）tiny crack

【裂痕】lièhén（名）crack; rift: 消除兩國之間的～ heal the rift between the two countries

【裂開】lièkāi（動）split

【裂縫】lièfèng（名）cleft; crevice

【裂變】lièbiàn（名）fission

裏 lǐ Ⅰ（名）lining: 大衣～兒 the lining of an overcoat Ⅱ（介）inside; in: 花園～ in a garden Ⅲ [added as a suffix to 這,那,哪 to indicate location]: 這～ here/ 哪～ where

【裏子】lǐzi（名）lining

【裏手】lǐshǒu（名）expert; dab hand

【裏脊】lǐji（名）tender-loin

【裏間】lǐjiān（裏屋 lǐwū）（名）inner room

【裏裏外外】lǐlǐwàiwài（副）inside and outside; within and without

【裏頭】lǐtou（介）in; inside

【裏應外合】lǐ yìng wài hé〈成〉a coordinated blow; launch an attack from outside in coordination with an attack from within

【裏邊】lǐbian（裏面 lǐmiàn）（介）in; inside: ～有什麼? What's in there?

裔 yì（名）descendants; posterity: 華～美國人 Chinese-American

裕 yù（形）ample; plentiful: 富～ affluent; well-to-do

【裕固族】Yùgùzú（名）the Yugur (Yuku) nationality

補 bǔ Ⅰ（動）❶ mend; repair; restore to good condition ❷ fill; replenish; supplement: ～空缺 fill up a vacancy ❸ nourish: ～～身體 tone up the body Ⅱ（名）help; bene-

fit: 於事無～ not help matters

【補牙】bǔyá（名）have a tooth filled

【補充】bǔchōng Ⅰ（動）replenish; supplement; add: ～裝備 replenish equipment Ⅱ（形）additional; complementary: ～材料 supplementary material

【補考】bǔkǎo（名）make-up examination: ～數學 have a make-up exam in mathematics

【補血】bǔxuè（動）help the growth of red blood cells: ～藥 haematic tonic; blood tonic

【補足】bǔzú（動）make up a deficiency; fill a gap; replenish: ～經費 replenish the funds

【補助】bǔzhù Ⅰ（名）subsidy; allowance; grant-in-aid: 生活～ living allowance Ⅱ（動）subsidize; help finance

【補品】bǔpǐn（名）tonic

【補釘】bǔdīng（名）patch

【補缺】bǔquē（動）fill up a vacancy

【補益】bǔyì（名）help; good; benefit: 大有～ be of great help

【補習】bǔxí（動）take supplementary lessons: ～學校 continuation school

【補救】bǔjiù（動）remedy: 無法～ beyond remedy

【補給】bǔjǐ（名）〈軍〉supply; provisions

【補過】bǔguò（動）make up for a mistake; remedy a fault

【補發】bǔfā（動）resupply（sth. lost）; reissue; pay retroactively

【補貼】bǔtiē（名）subsidy; allowance: 出口～ export subsidy

【補養】bǔyǎng（動）take tonics or nourishing food

【補語】bǔyǔ（名）〈語〉complement: 賓語～ objective complement

【補綴】bǔzhuì（動）❶ mend; patch; darn（clothes）❷ write a patchwork article

【補漏洞】bǔlòudòng（動）plug a hole （or leak）; remedy inadequacies

【補選】bǔxuǎn Ⅰ（名）by-election Ⅱ （動）hold a by-election for

【補遺】bǔyí（名）addendum; supplement

【補償】bǔcháng（動）compensate; recoup; recompense; ～損失 make good a loss

【補償貿易】bǔcháng màoyì（名）compensation trade

【補繳】bǔjiǎo（補付 bǔfù）（動）pay arrears; make a deferred payment

【補藥】bǔyào（名）tonic; restorative

裙

qún（名）skirt

【裙子】qúnzi（名）skirt

【裙帶關係】qúndài guānxì（名）social connections forged through one's female relatives

裘

qiú（名）❶ fur coat ❷（Qiú）a surname

裝

zhuāng Ⅰ（動）❶ dress up; play the role of: ～點 decorate / 他～一個鄉村醫生。He masqueraded as a village doctor. ❸ pretend; feign: ～瘋 feign madness / ～出一副恭恭敬敬的樣子 assume a deferential manner ❸ load; fill; hold: 給油箱～滿汽油 fill up the tank with petrol / 把照相機～上膠卷 load a film into a camera ❹ install; fit: ～電話 install a telephone; have a telephone installed Ⅱ（名）clothing; outfit: 冬～ winter clothes

【裝甲】zhuāngjiǎ（形）armoured: ～兵 armoured troops

【裝束】zhuāngshù（名）dress; attire

【裝扮】zhuāngbàn（動）❶ dress up; deck out ❷ disguise

【裝門面】zhuāng ménmiàn（動）maintain an outward show; preserve appearances

【裝卸】zhuāngxiè（動）❶ load and unload: ～工 loader ❷ assemble and disassemble

【裝修】zhuāngxiū（動）fit up（a house, etc.）

【裝訂】zhuāngdìng Ⅰ（動）bind a book, etc. Ⅱ（名）binding

【裝料】zhuāngliào（動）feed（a machine）

【裝配】zhuāngpèi（動）assemble

【裝貨】zhuānghuò（動）load（cargo）

【裝假】zhuāngjiǎ（動）put up a false appearance; try to give a false impression

【裝備】zhuāngbèi Ⅰ（動）equip; furnish Ⅱ（名）equipment; installation

【裝腔作勢】zhuāng qiāng zuò shì（成）behave in an affected manner

【裝飾】zhuāngshì Ⅰ（動）decorate; embellish Ⅱ（名）decoration

【裝載】zhuāngzài（動）load

【裝置】zhuāngzhì Ⅰ（動）install; fit Ⅱ（名）installation; device: 安全～ safety device

【裝裱】zhuāngbiǎo（動）mount（a painting, etc.）

【裝蒜】zhuāngsuàn（動）〈口〉pretend not to know; feign ignorance

【裝樣子】zhuāng yàngzi（動）do sth. for appearance's sake

【裝模作樣】zhuāng mó zuò yàng（成）give oneself airs; pretence

【裝璜】zhuānghuáng（名）package; decoration

【裝殮】zhuāngliàn（動）dress and lay

a corpse in a coffin

【裝聾作啞】 zhuāng lóng zuò yǎ〈成〉 play the deaf; pretend to be ignorant of everything

裊 niǎo（形）slender and delicate

【裊娜】 niǎonuó（形） slender and graceful

【裊裊】 niǎoniǎo（動）❶ (of smoke) curl upwards ❷ sway in the wind: 楊柳～。The willow branches are swaying in the breeze. ❸ (of music) linger: 餘音～。The sound lingers long in one's ears.

裹 guǒ（動）❶ bind; wrap ❷ kidnap

【裹足不前】 guǒ zú bù qián〈成〉 be reluctant to advance; hesitate to go further

【裹脅】 guǒxié（動）force sb. to do evil; coerce

裱 biǎo（動）mount; paste up: ～一張國畫 have a traditional Chinese painting mounted

【裱糊】 biǎohú（動）paper (a wall, etc.); paste paper on: ～房間 paper a room

褂 guà（名）gown; jacket

褹 duō（動）mend: 補～ patch up (worn-out clothes)

裸 luǒ（形）naked; unclothed

【裸綫】 luǒxiàn（名）〈電〉bare wire

【裸露】 luǒlù（形）uncovered; exposed

【裸體】 luǒtǐ（名）nude; naked: ～人像 nude human figure; nude

褹 bì（名）advantage; benefit

【褹益】 bìyì（名）benefit; advantage;

help: 毫無～ of no help; of no avail

裴 Péi（名）a surname

製 zhì（動）make; manufacture: ～圖 make charts

【製片人】 zhìpiànrén （名）〈電影〉 producer

【製冷】 zhìlěng（名）refrigeration

【製表】 zhìbiǎo（名）tabulation

【製版】 zhìbǎn（名）〈印〉plate making

【製革】 zhìgé（動） process hides; tan: ～廠 tannery

【製品】 zhìpǐn（名）products: 木～ wood products

【製造】 zhìzào（動）❶ make; manufacture: ～產品 manufacture a product ❷ create; fabricate: ～事端 provoke incidents

【製劑】 zhìjì（名）〈藥〉preparation

【製糖】 zhìtáng（動） refine sugar: ～廠 sugar refinery

【製藥】 zhìyào（名）pharmacy

褒 bāo（動）commend; praise

【褒貶】 bāobiǎn（動）pass laudatory or censorious judgment on; evaluate; appraise

【褒貶】 bāobian（動）criticize; speak ill of

【褒義】 bāoyì（名） complimentary connotation

【褒獎】 bāojiǎng（動）honour; extol; commend and award

褊 biǎn（形）narrow; cramped

【褊狹】 biǎnxiá（形）narrow-minded; narrow

褪 tuì（動）❶ take off (clothes); shed (feathers) ❷ (of colour) fade

褙 bèi（動）stick one piece of cloth (paper) on top of another: 裱～ mount (a piece of Chinese painting or calligraphy)

褐 hè Ⅰ（名）coarse cloth or clothing Ⅱ（形）brown
【褐煤】hèméi（名）brown coal; lignite

複 fù（形）repeated; complex
【複本】fùběn（名）duplicate
【複句】fùjù（語）compound or complex sentence
【複合】fùhé（形）compound; complex
【複印】fùyìn（動）〈印〉photocopy; duplicate; xerox: ～機 duplicator
【複述】fùshù（動）retell
【複習】fùxí（名）review: ～大綱 outline for review
【複製】fùzhì（動）duplicate; copy
【複製品】fùzhìpǐn（名）replica; reproduction
【複數】fùshù（名）〈語〉plural number
【複寫】fùxiě（動）duplicate; make a carbon copy
【複寫紙】fùxiězhǐ（名）carbon paper
【複雜】fùzá（形）complex; complicated

褲 kù（名）trousers; pants; slacks: 牛仔～ jeans / 女用襪～ panty hose
【褲子】kùzi（名）trousers; pants; jeans
【褲衩】kùchǎ（名）underpants

褥 rù（名）cotton-padded mattress
【褥子】rùzi（名）cotton-padded mattress

【褥單】rùdān（名）bed sheet
【褥瘡】rùchuāng（名）〈醫〉bedsore; decubitus

褫 chǐ（動）deprive; strip
【褫奪】chǐduó（動）deprive

褻 xiè
【褻瀆】xièdú（動）blaspheme; profane

襄 xiāng（動）〈書〉assist; help
【襄理】xiānglǐ（名）assistant manager

褶 zhě（名）pleat; crease: 褲子上的～兒 the creases in one's trousers
【褶皺】zhězhòu（名）❶〈地〉fold ❷ wrinkle (in the skin)

襁 qiǎng
【襁褓】qiǎngbǎo（名）❶ swaddling clothes ❷ infancy: ～之中 in one's infancy

襟 jīn（名）❶ front part of a garment ❷ brothers-in-law (whose wives are sisters): 他們是連～。 They are brothers-in-law.
【襟懷】jīnhuái（名）mental attitude; heart: ～坦白 frankhearted

襠 dāng（名）(of trousers) crotch

襖 ǎo（名）Chinese-style coat or jacket: 夾～ lined jacket

襤 lán
【襤褸】lánlǚ（形）(of clothes) ragged; tattered; worn-out: 衣衫～ be in rags

襪 wà（襪子 wàzi）（名）sock; stocking
【襪帶】wàdài（名）suspenders;

garter

襲 xí（動）❶ attack; assail: 空～ make an air raid ❷ follow: 承～舊習慣 follow the old habits

【襲用】xíyòng（動）continue to use; take over; follow

【襲取】xíqǔ（動）❶ seize by surprise ❷ follow; take over: 後人～這個故事，寫成了戲。Somebody later wrote a play on the basis of the story.

【襲擊】xíjī（動）make a surprise attack on; raid; hit

襯 chèn Ⅰ（動）❶ line: ～着絨布 be lined with flannelette ❷ set off: 陪～ serve as a contrast; set off Ⅱ（名）lining

【襯托】chèntuō（動）set off; serve as a foil to

【襯衣】chènyī（名）❶ underclothes ❷ shirt

【襯衫】chènshān（名）shirt

【襯褲】chènkù（名）underpants

襻 pàn Ⅰ（名）❶ button loop ❷ sth. resembling a button loop Ⅱ（動）fasten with a thread, string, etc.

西 部

西 xī（名）west

【西方】xīfāng（名）❶ west ❷ the West

【西天】xītiān（名）〈宗〉❶ Western paradise ❷ the nether world: 送他上～ send him to hell

【西瓜】xīguā（名）water-melon

【西半球】xībànqiú（名）western hemisphere

【西西】xīxī（名）cc; c. c.（cubic centimetre）

【西服】xīfú（名）Western-style clothes

【西洋】xīyáng（名）the West

【西洋參】xīyángshēn（名）American ginseng

【西洋鏡】xīyángjìng（名）❶ peep show ❷ trickery; trick

【西紅柿】xīhóngshì（名）tomato: ～醬 tomato paste; ketchup

【西班牙】xībānyá（名）Spain: ～人 Spaniard / ～語 Spanish（language）

【西經】xījīng（名）west longitude

【西葫蘆】xīhúlú（名）summer squash

【西餐】xīcān（名）European-style food; Western food

【西醫】xīyī（名）❶ doctor trained in Western medicine ❷ Western medicine

【西藏】xīzàng（名）Xizang（Tibet）; the Xizang（Tibet）Autonomous Region

【西藥】xīyào（名）Western medicine

要 yāo（動）❶ ask; demand ❷ coerce; compel
see also yào

【要求】yāoqiú Ⅰ（動）ask; demand; require: ～轉學 ask for a transfer to another school Ⅱ（名）demand; request: 合乎～ meet the requirements

【要挾】yāoxié（動）coerce; threaten

要 yào Ⅰ（形）important; essential: ～義 main idea Ⅱ（動）❶ want; need: 錶～修一下。The watch needs repairing. / 他～私下和我談談。He would like to have a word with me in private. ❷ ask; require; let: 他～我唱支歌。He asked me to sing a song. ❸ must; should: 我們～努力工作。We must work hard. ❹ shall; will; be going to: 他就～到了。He is arriving. ❺ need; take: 叫他改變決定～費很多唇舌。It will take much persuading to talk him out of his decision. III（連）if; in case: ～有問題的話，請馬上告訴我。Please let me know promptly if any problem crops up.

see also yāo

【要人】 yàorén（名）VIP

【要不】 yàobù（連）or; otherwise: 我必須馬上走,～就會挨雨淋了。I have to leave this very moment, otherwise I'll be caught in the rain.

【要不是】 yàobushì（連）but for; without: ～你及時幫忙,我們不會成功。We could not have succeeded without your timely help.

【要不得】 yàobude（動）cannot be allowed; be intolerable: 粗心大意～。It won't do to be careless.

【要犯】 yàofàn（名）important criminal

【要地】 yàodì（名）strategic point

【要好】 yàohǎo（動）be friends with: 他當時跟我很～。He was friends with me then.

【要旨】 yàozhǐ（名）main idea; gist

【要命】 yàomìng I（動）〈口〉cause the loss of life: ～的活兒 a killing job II（副）extremely; terribly: 窮得～ penniless; broke

【要是】 yàoshì（連）if: ～沒有空,我會給你去電話的。I will give you a call if I am busy.

【要面子】 yàomiànzi（動）be anxious

to save face

【要害】 yàohài（名）vital part; main point: 抓住～ grasp the key points

【要素】 yàosù（名）key element

【要道】 yàodào（名）important route

【要飯】 yàofàn（動）beg: 挨門挨戶～ beg from door to door

【要強】 yàoqiáng（動）be eager to be among the best; refuse to fall behind

【要塞】 yàosài（名）fort; stronghold

【要隘】 yào'ài（名）strategic pass

【要領】 yàolǐng（名）main points; essentials

【要麽】 yàome（連）either...or: 你～把這件事幹到底,～洗手不幹。Either you see the matter through or you wash your hands of it.

【要聞】 yàowén（名）important news

【要緊】 yàojǐn I（形）important; urgent: ～的事 important matters II（動）matter; be serious: 今天下不下雨都不～。It doesn't matter whether it will rain today.

【要價】 yàojià（動）ask a price; charge: 你～多少? How much do you ask?

【要點】 yàodiǎn（名）main idea; gist

【要職】 yàozhí（名）important post

覃 Qín（名）a surname

see also Tán

覃 Tán（名）a surname

see also Qín

覆 fù（動）❶ cover ❷ overturn; capsize

【覆亡】 fùwáng（名）fall（of a nation）

【覆水難收】 fù shuǐ nán shōu〈成〉what is done cannot be undone

【覆没】fùmò（動）❶ capsize and sink ❷ be completely wiped out

【覆滅】fùmiè（動）be utterly destroyed

【覆蓋】fùgài（動）cover

【覆轍】fùzhé（名）the track where the cart was once overturned: 重蹈～ follow the same disastrous route; adopt the same measure that caused disaster

見 部

見 jiàn Ⅰ（動）❶ see: 由此可～ thus one can see; from this we can come to the conclusion ❷ come into contact with; come across; meet: ～光 be exposed to light ❸ show signs of; appear ❹ pay a short visit to; call on ❺ refer to; vide: 參～附錄 See Appendix Ⅱ（助）[used before a verb]: ～教 enlighten me with your advice Ⅲ（名）idea; opinion: 門户之～ sectarian bias

【見方】jiànfāng〈口〉square: 兩米～ two square metres

【見仁見智】jiàn rén jiàn zhì〈成〉different people have different views

【見不得】jiànbude（動）should not be exposed to

【見不得人】jiànbuderén（形）scandalous; shameful: 這是～的事。This is a scandal.

【見外】jiànwài（動）consider sb. as an outsider; behave as if one were a stranger: Please make yourself at hime. Don't behave like a stranger.

【見世面】jiàn shìmiàn（動）see the world; be seasoned in worldly affairs

【見地】jiàndì（名）insight; discernment; judgment: 顏有～ have good judgment

【見好】jiànhǎo（動）(of a patient's condition) improve; get better; be on the mend

【見好就收】jiàn hǎo jiù shōu〈成〉stop when one has achieved satisfactory results; know when best to leave off

【見多識廣】jiàn duō shí guǎng〈成〉have extensive knowledge and experience

【見長】jiàncháng（動）be good at; excel in

【見長】jiànzhǎng（動）grow taller than ever

【見怪】jiànguài（動）be angry; be displeased: 不要～。Please don't take offence.

【見所未見】jiàn suǒ wèi jiàn〈成〉never seen before

【見面】jiànmiàn（動）meet

【見風轉舵】jiàn fēng zhuǎn duò（見風使舵 jiàn fēng shǐ duò）〈成〉trim one's sails; switch (one's stand) with the change of situation

【見效】jiànxiào（動）take effect; become effective

【見鬼】jiànguǐ Ⅰ（形）absurd; ridiculous; fantastic: 秋天下雪，真是～了。Snowing in autumn! It's fantastic, isn't it? Ⅱ（動）go to hell; go to the devil: 讓這個謊言～去吧! To hell with the lie!

【見笑】jiànxiào（動）laugh at (me): 我還不會用筷子, 請別～。Don't laugh at me. I can't manage the chopsticks yet.

【見習】jiànxí（動）work on probation

【見得】jiàndé（動）[used in negative or interrogative sentences]：不～好 not necessarily good /怎麼～這對我們有好處? How do you know it is of benefit to us?

【見異思遷】jiàn yì sī qiān〈成〉be inconsistent; change one's mind whenever sth. new turns up

【見報】jiànbào（動）be reported in the press; be published in the newspapers

【見解】jiànjiě（名）view; opinion; idea：～正確 a correct idea

【見義勇爲】jiàn yì yǒng wéi〈成〉ready to take up cudgels for a just cause

【見聞】jiànwén（名）❶ knowledge and experience ❷ information ❸ impressions

【見機】jiànjī（副）according to circumstances; at one's discretion：～而作 act as the occasion arises

【見樹不見林】jiàn shù bù jiàn lín〈成〉cannot see the wood for the trees

【見縫插針】jiàn fèng chā zhēn〈成〉stick in a pin whenever there is room; make the most of every bit of time or space

【見識】jiànshí Ⅰ（動）broaden one's horizons; gain experience Ⅱ（名）knowledge and experience

【見證】jiànzhèng（名）❶ witness ❷ evidence

【見證人】jiànzhèngrén（名）eyewitness

視

視 shì（動）❶ look：對這種弊端，不能～而不見。We cannot turn a blind eye to this kind of abuse. ❷ regard; consider：～同路人 look upon sb. as a stranger ❸ watch;

observe：監～ keep watch on

【視力】shìlì（名）vision; sight：～衰退 failing eyesight

【視死如歸】shì sǐ rú guī〈成〉look upon death as nothing; face death bravely

【視野】shìyě（名）field of vision

【視線】shìxiàn（名）line of vision：轉移～ divert one's attention

【視察】shìchá Ⅰ（動）inspect Ⅱ（名）inspection; inspection tour

【視覺】shìjué（名）vision; optical sensation：～靈敏 be keen of sight

【視聽】shìtīng Ⅰ（名）what one sees and hears; impression：以正～ correct the wrong impression made on the public Ⅱ（形）audio-visual

規

規 guī Ⅰ（名）❶ compasses; dividers：圓～ compasses ❷ rule; regulation：革除陋～ abolish undesirable regulations Ⅱ（動）❶ plan; map out ❷ admonish; advise

【規定】guīdìng Ⅰ（動）fix; stipulate; provide：～加班費 make provision for overtime emolument Ⅱ（名）rule; stipulation

【規則】guīzé Ⅰ（名）rule; regulation：行路安全～ road safety rules Ⅱ（形）regular

【規律】guīlǜ（名）law; rule：自然～ law of nature

【規格】guīgé（名）specifications：合乎～ up to standard

【規矩】guīju Ⅰ（名）rule; custom; regular practice Ⅱ（形）well-behaved; law-abiding

【規章】guīzhāng（名）rule; regulation

【規程】guīchéng（名）rule; regulation

【規劃】guīhuà（名）planning; programme

【規模】guīmó（名）scale; dimension

【規範】guīfàn（名）standard; norm: ～化 standardization

【規避】guībì（動）evade; elude; avoid

【規勸】guīquàn（動）admonish; advise

覓 mì（動）look for; seek: ～路出 森林 try to find one's way out of the forest

親 qīn I（形）❶ closest relative; next of kin: ～叔叔 paternal uncle / ～姐妹 full sisters ❷ close or intimate: ～如手足 be as close as brothers II（名）parent: 父～ father ❷ related by blood or marriage: ～友 relatives and friends ❸ marriage; match: 定～ betrothal III（動）kiss: ～她的手 kiss her on the hand IV（副）in person; by oneself
see also qìng

【親人】qīnrén（名）❶ member of one's own family ❷ one's beloved one

【親口】qīnkǒu（副）(say sth.) personally: 他～說的就是如此。This is exactly what he said.

【親手】qīnshǒu（副）with one's own hands; personally: 媽媽～織的毛 衣 a sweater knitted by mother herself

【親王】qīnwáng（名）prince

【親切】qīnqiè（形）kind; warmhearted: ～的語言 kind words

【親本】qīnběn（名）〈生〉parent

【親生】qīnshēng（形）one's own (children; parents)

【親自】qīnzì（副）personally; in person: 他會～過問這件事。He will personally attend to the matter.

【親近】qīnjìn I（形）intimate; close: 他倆很～。The two are close friends. II（動）get along with: 此 人冷漠不易～。He is rather cold and hard to approach.

【親身】qīnshēn（副）personally: 這 是我們路上～經歷的事。This is what we actually saw on the journey.

【親事】qīnshì（名）marriage; matrimony

【親呢】qīnnì（形）very intimate; affectionate

【親信】qīnxìn（名）trusted follower; henchman

【親眷】qīnjuàn（名）one's relatives; one's family members

【親戚】qīngqi（名）relative

【親密】qīnmì（形）close; intimate

【親眼】qīnyǎn（副）with one's own eyes: 這是她～所見。This is what she saw with her own eyes.

【親善】qīnshàn（形）close and friendly

【親筆】qīnbǐ I（形）in one's own hand II（名）(of calligraphy) one's handwriting

【親痛仇快】qīn tòng chóu kuài〈成〉grieve one's friends and delight one's enemies

【親愛】qīn'ài（形）dear; beloved

【親熱】qīnrè（形）intimate; affectionate; warm-hearted

【親屬】qīnshǔ（名）relatives; kinsfolk

親 qìng
see also qīn

【親家】qīngjia（名）❶ families related by marriage ❷ parents of one's daughter-in-law or son-in-law

覬 jì

【覬覦】jìyú（動）covet; cast covetous glances at

覷 qù（動）look; gaze: 冷眼相 ~ eye each other coldly; give one a cold stare

覲 jìn（動）❶ have an audience with (a monarch) ❷ go on a pilgrimage

覺 jiào（名）sleep; nap: 睡午 ~ take an afternoon nap
see also jué

覺 jué I（動）❶ feel; sense: 你感 ~ 怎樣? How do you feel now? ❷ wake (up); become awake II（名）sense: 嗅 ~ 很靈 have a keen sense of smell
see also jiào

【覺悟】juéwù I（名）consciousness; awareness: 政治 ~ political awareness II（動）become aware of; come to see: ~ 到時代變了 come to realize that times have changed

【覺得】juéde（動）❶ feel: ~ 很高興 feel very happy ❷ think; find: 我 ~ 他有點不對頭。I feel something is wrong with him.

【覺察】juéchá（動）detect; discover

【覺醒】juéxǐng I（動）awaken: ~ 了的人民 awakened people II（名）awakening

覽 lǎn（動）see; read: 遊 ~ go sightseeing/ 展 ~ exhibition / 閱 ~ 室 reading room

觀 guān I（動）watch; observe II（名）❶ spectacle; view: 壯 ~ a grand view ❷ outlook; concept: 人生 ~ outlook on life
see also guàn

【觀光】guānguāng I（動）go sightseeing II（名）sightseeing trip

【觀念】guānniàn（名）concept; idea; sense: 道德 ~ moral sense

【觀看】guānkàn（動）watch; view: ~ 電視連續劇 watch a T.V. series (serial)

【觀望】guānwàng（動）look on with folded arms; wait and see: ~ 態度 wait-and-see attitude

【觀眾】guānzhòng（名）audience; spectators; viewers

【觀測】guāncè（動）observe; watch: ~ 站 observatory

【觀感】guāngǎn（名）impressions

【觀察】guānchá（動）observe; examine

【觀賞】guānshǎng（動）view and admire: ~ 長江三峽 enjoy the sight of the Three Gorges of the Yangtze River

【觀摩】guānmó（動）watch each other's performances and exchange experience

【觀點】guāndiǎn（名）standpoint; viewpoint: 歷史 ~ historical perspective

【觀瞻】guānzhān（名）sight; view; the appearance of a place and the impressions it leaves: 有礙 ~ be repugnant to the eye; offend the eye

觀 guàn（名）Taoist temple
see also guān

角 部

角 jiǎo I (名) ❶ horn ❷ sth. horn-shaped: 一對~ a pair of antennae (feelers) ❸ corner: 眼~ corners of one's eyes ❹ bugle: 吹號~ blow a horn ❺〈數〉angle: 三~形 triangle ❻ jiao, a denomination of money in China (1/10) of a yuan or 10 fen) II (量) quarter
see also jué

【角度】jiǎodù (名) ❶〈數〉degree of an angle; angle ❷ viewpoint; angle: 從各個~觀察 viewed from various angles

【角球】jiǎoqiú (名)〈體〉corner (kick)

【角落】jiǎoluò (名) ❶ corner ❷ secluded place; nook

角 jué I (名) ❶ role; part: 主~ leading role ❷ (in traditional Chinese opera) type of role ❸ actor; actress II (動) vie; contend: 口~ quarrel; bicker
see also jiǎo

【角力】juélì (動) have a contest in strength; wrestle

【角色】juésè (名) ❶ role; part: 扮演哈姆雷特的~ play (the part of) Hamlet ❷ (in traditional Chinese opera) types of role

【角逐】juézhú (動) compete (often by resorting to force); struggle for supremacy

【角門】juédòu (動) wrestle; grapple

解 jiě I (動) ❶ separate; sever: 老的組織瓦~了。The old organization disintegrated. ❷ undo; unfasten: ~繩結 untie the knot ❸ assuage; relieve: ~乏 relieve fatigue ❹ explain: 註~這部古書不易。It's no easy task to annotate this classical writing. ❺ understand: 通俗易~的書 a popular book which is easy to understand II (名)〈數〉solution
see also jiè; xiè

【解手】jiěshǒu (動) relieve oneself; go to the lavatory

【解決】jiějué (動) ❶ settle; work out (a solution): ~矛盾 solve a contradiction ❷ annihilate; wipe out; finish off

【解放】jiěfàng (動) liberate; free: ~思想 emancipate one's mind

【解放軍】jiěfàngjūn (名) ❶ (short for 中國人民解放軍 Zhōngguó Rénmín Jiěfàngjūn) the Chinese People's Liberation Army (PLA) ❷ PLA man

【解恨】jiěhèn (動) relieve the feeling of hatred

【解剖】jiěpōu (動) dissect; anatomize

【解氣】jiěqì (動) give vent to one's anger; work off one's anger; vent one's spleen

【解凍】jiědòng (動) ❶ thaw ❷ lift the freeze on (funds, assets, etc.)

【解除】jiěchú (動) remove; lift; annul: ~疑慮 remove sb.'s doubts / ~合同 terminate a contract

【解救】jiějiù (動) rescue; give relief to

【解脫】jiětuō (動) extricate; relieve

【解答】jiědá (動) explain; work out (a sum)

【解散】jiěsàn（动）❶ (of assembled people) dismiss; disperse ❷ (of an organization, etc.) dissolve

【解围】jiěwéi（动）❶ break the enemy siege (to rescue the besieged) ❷ relieve sb. from a difficult or embarrassing situation

【解开】jiěkāi（动）untie; unfasten; unbutton: ～鞋带 undo shoelaces

【解聘】jiěpìn（动）dismiss; lay off

【解说】jiěshuō（动）explain orally; comment

【解雇】jiěgù（动）discharge; dismiss; give sb. the sack

【解职】jiězhí（动）remove from office

【解释】jiěshì（动）explain; account for: ～误会 clarify a misunderstanding

【解体】jiětǐ（动）disintegrate; break up

【解馋】jiěchán（动）satisfy a craving for delicious food

解 jiè（动）send under escort: 押～出境 deport under escort
see also jiě; xiè

解 Xiè（名）a surname
see also jiě; jiè

触 chù（动）❶ touch: ～礁 (of a ship, etc.) run into rocks or reefs ❷ hurt sb.'s feelings: ～犯上级 offend one's superior

【触犯】chùfàn（动）offend; go against: ～校规 violate school regulations

【触目惊心】chù mù jīng xīn〈成〉startling; shocking

【触角】chùjiǎo（名）〈动〉antenna; feeler

【触怒】chùnù（动）make angry; enrage; infuriate

【触动】chùdòng（动）❶ touch (sth.) ❷ move (sb.); stir up one's feelings: ～了他的心事 touch a responsive cord in his heart

【触发】chùfā（动）touch off; trigger: 一场农民起义 touch off a peasant uprising

【触媒】chùméi（名）〈化〉catalyst; catalytic agent

【触景生情】chù jǐng shēng qíng〈成〉the scene touches a responsive chord in one's heart

【触电】chùdiàn（动）get an electric shock

言 部

言 yán Ⅰ（名）❶ word; speech: 违心之～ words said against one's own conscience ❷ Chinese character: 洋洋万～ run to thousands of words Ⅱ（动）say; speak: 直～ speak straightforwardly; make straightforward remarks

【言之无物】yán zhī wú wù〈成〉be just empty verbiage; (of speech or writing) have no substance

【言不由衷】yán bù yóu zhōng〈成〉speak unctuously; say one thing and mean another

【言外之意】yán wài zhī yì〈成〉implication; hidden meaning: ～,他是大才小用了。The implication is he is wasting his talent at a petty job.

【言行】yánxíng（名）words and deeds: ～一致 match one's words with one's deeds

【言而有信】yán ér yǒu xìn〈成〉always keep one's promise

【言而無信】yán ér wú xìn〈成〉never make good one's promise

【言和】yánhé（動）bury the hatchet; patch up a quarrel

【言過其實】yán guò qí shí〈成〉overstate; exaggerate: 此人言過其實，不可重用。As he is prone to exaggerate, he is not to be entrusted with important tasks.

【言路】yánlù（名）avenues through which public opinion is channelled to the leadership: 廣開～ provide ample opportunity for the public to put forward their views

【言傳身教】yán chuán shēn jiào〈成〉teach both by precept and by example

【言語】yányǔ（名）spoken language; speech

【言語】yányu（動）〈口〉speak; say: 要幫忙就～一聲。Don't hesitate to tell us if you need help.

【言論】yánlùn（名）opinions; views; comments

【言談】yántán（名）how one speaks and what one speaks about: ～得體 speak appropriately

【言歸正傳】yán guī zhèng zhuàn〈成〉to come back to the story; to hark back to the subject

【言歸於好】yán guī yú hǎo〈成〉become friends again after a quarrel; be reconciled

【言簡意賅】yán jiǎn yì gāi〈成〉concise and comprehensive

【言辭】yáncí（名）words: ～誇張 in exaggerated terms

【言聽計從】yán tīng jì cóng〈成〉act readily on sb.'s advice

計 jì Ⅰ（動）calculate; compute; reckon: 數以百～ by the hundred; hundreds of Ⅱ（名）❶ idea; scheme; stratagem; trap: 頓生一～ hit upon an idea ❷ meter; gauge: 氣壓～ barometer

【計件工資】jìjiàn gōngzī（名）piece rate: ～制 piecework system

【計時工資】jìshí gōngzī（名）time wage

【計量】jìliàng（動）measure; estimate: 不可～ incalculable ／～單位 unit of measurement

【計策】jìcè（名）stratagem; ruse; trap

【計程表】jìchéngbiǎo（名）taximeter

【計較】jìjiào（動）❶ argue ❷ care about; take to heart: 他那些話是隨便說的，不要～。Don't take to heart those casual remarks of his. ❸ think over: 日後再做～。Let's think it over later.

【計劃】jìhuà Ⅰ（名）plan; scheme; project: 訂工作～ draw up a work plan Ⅱ（動）plan; devise; map out: ～生育 family planning

【計算】jìsuàn Ⅰ（動）count; calculate; reckon: ～生產成本 calculate the cost of production ／～票數 count the votes Ⅱ（名）consideration; calculation; planning: 凡事都得有個～。You should have a plan for everything.

【計算器】jìsuànqì（名）calculator

【計算機】jìsuànjī（名）computer

【計謀】jìmóu（名）stratagem; plot; trick

【計議】jìyì（動）consider; deliberate; discuss: 此事亟待～。There is an urgent need to deliberate the question.

訂 dìng (動)❶ subscribe to; book: ~雜誌 subscribe to a magazine / 在旅館~房間 book a hotel room ❷ draw up: ~條約 conclude a treaty ❸ revise; 修~計劃 revise a plan ❹ bind up

【訂戶】dìnghù (名) subscriber

【訂立】dìnglì (動) conclude (a treaty; contract, etc.)

【訂正】dìngzhèng (動) correct

【訂書】dìngshū (動) staple together: ~釘 staple

【訂書機】dìngshūjī (名) stapling-machine; stapler

【訂婚】dìnghūn (動) be engaged to

【訂貨】dìnghuò (動) order goods

【訂閱】dìngyuè (動) subscribe to

【訂購】dìnggòu (動) order (goods)

訃 fù (名) obituary

【訃告】fùgào (名) obituary notice; obituary

討 tǎo (動)❶ conduct a punitive expedition against: ~伐 send armed forces on a punitive expedition ❷ condemn: 聲~ denounce ❸ ask for; seek: ~飯 beg for food / ~債 press for the payment of a debt ❹ incur; court: 自~苦吃 ask for trouble ❺ discuss: 商~對策 discuss what countermeasures to take; discuss countermeasures to be taken ❻ marry (a woman): ~老婆(媳婦) take a wife

【討好】tǎohǎo (動)❶ curry favour with: ~雙方 try to please both sides ❷ [often used in negative sentences] get positive results: 不~的工作 thankless job

【討厭】tǎoyàn Ⅰ (動) dislike; detest Ⅱ (形)❶ disagreeable; annoying ❷ troublesome; nasty

【討論】tǎolùn (動) discuss; deliberate: ~會 discussion; seminar; symposium

【討價還價】tǎo jià huán jià〈成〉 haggle: ~ 的籌碼 bargaining counter

【討饒】tǎoráo (動) beg for mercy

訌 hòng (名) discord: 内~ internal strife

記 jì Ⅰ (動)❶ keep in mind; remember: ~仇 nurse hatred ❷ record; score up; put down in writing: ~日記 keep a diary Ⅱ (名)❶ notes; written account: ~要 summary ❷ mark; sign: 胎~ birthmark Ⅲ (量) slap (in the face): 給他一~耳光 give him a box on the ear

【記分】jìfēn (動) keep the score; register points (in games, school-work, etc.): ~牌 scoreboard

【記功】jìgōng (動) cite (sb.) for distinguished service; record one's merit

【記名】jìmíng (形) bearing the name of the holder: 無~投票 secret ballot / ~支票 bearer cheque

【記住】jìzhù (動) bear in mind; commit to memory; learn by heart: ~這些區別 keep these distinctions in mind

【記取】jìqǔ (動) keep in mind; take to heart: 我們會永遠~這次慘痛的教訓。We will always remember this bitter lesson.

【記述】jìshù (動) narrate in written form; give a written account of

【記性】jìxìng（名）(the faculty of) memory: 没～ have a short memory

【記者】jìzhě（名）journalist; reporter; correspondent: ～招待會 press conference

【記叙文】jìxùwén（名）narrative; narration

【記起】jìqǐ（動）recall; recollect: 我怎麼也記不起他的名字。I simply cannot recall his name.

【記得】jìde（動）remember; recall: 您不～了? Can't you recall it?

【記過】jìguò（動）record a demerit: 已經一兩次 have two demerits recorded on one's personal file

【記號】jìhao（名）mark; sign: 用紅筆做～ make a mark with a red pencil

【記載】jìzǎi I（動）put down in writing; record (in written form): 忠實地～事實 faithfully record the facts II（名）written account; record

【記賬】jìzhàng（動）❶ keep accounts ❷ charge to an account

【記憶】jìyì（動）recollect; recall; remember: 有驚人的～力 have a remarkable memory II（名）memory; recollection: ～猶新 be still fresh in one's memory

【記錄】jìlù I（動）make a record of; take notes: 小組討論時我做～。 I'll take notes at the group discussion. II（名）❶ notes; minutes of a meeting ❷ [used in sports, etc.] record: 刷新跳高的全國～ set a new national record in high jump

【記錄片】jìlùpiàn（名）documentary (film)

訕 shàn I（動）mock; ridicule II（形）embarrassed; awkward: 發～

feel embarrassed

【訕笑】shànxiào（動）sneer at; mock; ridicule

訊 xùn I（動）ask; question II（名）message; news; news bulletin; news release

【訊問】xùnwèn（動）❶ make inquiries about: ～原委 inquire about the details ❷ interrogate: ～案情 conduct an interrogation into a legal case

訖 qì（形）settled; completed: 付～ paid

訓 xùn I（動）teach; lecture; reprove: 挨一頓～ get a dressing-down II（名）❶ exhortation: 遺～ behest of a deceased person ❷ training: 軍～ military training

【訓斥】xùnchì（動）reprimand; reproach; scold

【訓詞】xùncí（名）instructions

【訓練】xùnliàn（動）train; drill

訪 fǎng（動）visit

【訪問】fǎngwèn（動）visit: 國事～ state visit

訝 yà（動）be astonished

訣 jué I（名）❶ formula in rhyme: 乘法口～ multiplication table in rhyme ❷ knack: 成功的妙～ golden key to success II（動）part: 永～ part never to meet again

【訣別】juébié（名）farewell

【訣竅】juéqiào（名）knack; trick of the trade: 懂得其中～ know the ropes

訟 sòng（動）❶ debate in court: 民事訴～ civil lawsuit ❷ argue;

debate: 爭～ dispute

許 xǔ I (動) ❶ allow; permit: 這裏不一停車。No parking (is permitted here.) ❷ promise: 他～過要幫忙。He promised to help. II (副) perhaps; maybe: 他沒參加會議，～是不知道。He didn't attend the meeting; maybe he didn't know about it at all. III (名) (Xǔ) a surname

【許久】xǔjiǔ (副) for a long time; for long

【許可】xǔkě (動) permit; allow: 如果條件～ if conditions permit / 若是天氣～ weather permitting

【許可證】xǔkězhèng (名) permit; licence

【許多】xǔduō (形) many; much; numerous

【許配】xǔpèi (動) betroth one's daughter to sb. (in an arranged match): 她女兒已～人家了。Her daughter is already engaged.

【許諾】xǔnuò (動) promise: 做出～ make a promise; promise

【許願】xǔyuàn (動) ❶ burn incense vowing to a god that one will heartily thank him if one's wish is granted ❷ promise sb. a favour

設 shè (動) ❶ set up; establish: 這家公司在城裏～了兩個分公司。The company has two branches in town. ❷ display; arrange: 陳～ display / ～宴招待 give a dinner party in honour of sb. ❸ plan; work out: ～法 manage; try ❹ 〈數〉suppose: ～X＝3 Given: X＝3

【設立】shèlì (動) set up; establish

【設防】shèfáng (動) build defences

【設身處地】shè shēn chǔ dì〈成〉put oneself in another's position; imagine yourself facing the same difficulty

【設施】shèshī (名) installation; facilities

【設計】shèjì (動) design; plan

【設備】shèbèi (名) equipment; installation

【設置】shèzhì (動) ❶ set up; establish: ～新課程 offer new courses ❷ install; fix: 在會場裝～了耳機和擴音器 have earphones and microphones installed in the meeting place

【設想】shèxiǎng (動) ❶ imagine; assume: ～一種新方案 conceive a new plan ❷ give thought to: 處處為孩子們～ give every thought to the needs of the children

訛 é I (名) error: 以～傳～ pass on wrong information from one to another II (動) blackmail

【訛詐】ézhà (動) blackmail; extort

【訛傳】échuán (名) unfounded rumour

註 zhù I (動) ❶ annotate; add explanatory notes to: 評～ make comments and annotations ❷ record; register II (名) notes; annotations

【註冊】zhùcè (動) register

【註音】zhùyīn (名) 〈語〉phonetic notation

【註腳】zhùjiǎo (名) footnote

【註解】zhùjiě I (動) annotate; explain with notes II (名) note; annotation

【註銷】zhùxiāo (動) cancel sth. that has been registered; write off

【註釋】zhùshì (名) note; annotation

評 píng（動）❶ comment; review ❷ evaluate; appraise

【評比】píngbǐ（動）compare and appraise

【評分】píngfēn（動）mark; grade

【評介】píngjiè（動）review (a literary work)

【評判】píngpàn（動）judge; decide

【評定】píngdìng（動）assess; appraise: 民主～ democratic appraisal

【評級】píngjí（動）fix the ranks or grades of employees according to their abilities and experiences

【評書】píngshū（名）professional story-telling

【評理】pínglǐ（動）pass judgment on the rights and wrongs of matters

【評註】píngzhù（名）notes and commentary

【評傳】píngzhuàn（名）critical biography

【評語】píngyǔ（名）comment; remark

【評價】píngjià（動）appraise

【評論】pínglùn Ⅰ（動）comment on Ⅱ（名）commentary

【評論員】pínglùnyuán（名）commentator

【評論家】pínglùnjiā（名）critic; reviewer

【評選】píngxuǎn（動）choose by consulting the public: ～本年度十大流行歌曲 choose ten top hits of pop music for the current year

【評頭論足】píng tóu lùn zú（成）❶ make flippant remarks about a woman's appearance ❷ be fault-finding

【評斷】píngduàn（動）judge; arbitrate

【評議】píngyì（動）discuss and decide

詞 cí（名）❶（語）word: 用字遣～ choice of words ❷ speech; address: 祝酒～ toast ❸ ci, a genre of classical Chinese poetry

【詞不達意】cí bù dá yì（成）one's words do not convey the real meaning

【詞句】cíjù（名）words and sentences; expressions

【詞序】cíxù（名）〈語〉word order; syntax

【詞典】cídiǎn（名）dictionary

【詞組】cízǔ（名）〈語〉phrase

【詞源】cíyuán（名）etymology

【詞匯】cíhuì（名）vocabulary

【詞義】cíyì（名）〈語〉meaning of a word

【詞語】cíyǔ（名）words and expressions

【詞綴】cízhuì（名）〈語〉affix

【詞類】cílèi（名）〈語〉part of speech

詔 zhào

【詔書】zhàoshū（名）imperial edict

詛 zǔ

【詛咒】zǔzhòu（動）curse; swear; abuse

診 zhěn（動）examine (a patient); diagnose: 會～ consultation of doctors

【診所】zhěnsuǒ（名）clinic

【診室】zhěnshì（名）consulting room

【診脈】zhěnmài（動）feel the pulse

【診療】zhěnliáo（動）give diagnosis and medical treatment

【診斷】zhěnduàn Ⅰ（動）diagnose Ⅱ

（名）diagnosis

詐 zhà（動）❶ pretend; feign ❷ cheat; deceive; swindle: ～財 swindle money out of a person

【詐死】zhàsǐ（動）sham death

【詐降】zhàxiáng（動）pretend surrender

【詐唬】zhàhǔ（動）bluff; swagger

【詐騙】zhàpiàn（動）swindle; defraud

詆 dǐ（動）speak ill of

【詆毀】dǐhuǐ（動）vilify; slander

訴 sù（動）❶ tell; recount; express: ～苦 pour out one's grievances ❷ charge; accuse: 勝（敗）～ win (lose) a lawsuit ❸ appeal to; resort to: ～諸武力 appeal to force

【訴訟】sùsòng（名）〈法〉lawsuit: 刑事～ criminal suit

【訴說】sùshuō（動）tell (with emotion); recount

詫 chà（動）be surprised: 驚～萬分 be utterly surprised

【詫異】chàyì（動）be astonished

該 gāi I（動）❶ should; ought to: 這是他一做的事。This is part of his duty. ❷ be one's turn: 今晚誰值班了？Who is to be on duty tonight? ❸ owe: ～人錢 owe sb. money II（代）this; that; the above-mentioned: ～員 this person III（副）[used for emphasis]: 要是他能來～多好啊！If only he could come!

【該死】gāisǐ〈口〉[used to express disgust or anger]: ～！我又要遲到了。Damn it! I'll be late again.

【該賬】gāizhàng（動）be in debt

詳 xiáng I（形）detailed; minute: 不厭其～ go into minute details II（動）❶ be (clearly) known: 內容不～。The content is unknown. ❷ explain in detail; elaborate: 餘再～。The rest will be explained in detail later.

【詳情】xiángqíng（名）details; particulars: 不知～ not be clear about the details

【詳細】xiángxì（形）detailed; minute

【詳盡】xiángjìn（形）detailed; complete

誆 kuāng（動）dupe; cheat

【誆騙】kuāngpiàn（動）cheat; hoax

試 shì I（動）try; test; experiment: ～穿 try on (a suit, etc.) II（名）examination; try: ～一～ have a try／面～ interview

【試用】shìyòng（動）❶ try out ❷ be on probation: ～三個月 be on probation for three months／～期 probationary period

【試行】shìxíng（動）try out; do sth. on a trial basis

【試車】shìchē（名）〈機〉trial run

【試表】shìbiǎo（動）〈口〉take sb.'s temperature

【試卷】shìjuàn（名）examination paper

【試金石】shìjīnshí（名）touchstone

【試飛】shìfēi（名）flight test; test flight

【試紙】shìzhǐ（名）〈化〉test paper

【試探】shìtàn（動）sound out; probe: 讓我們～他一下。Let us sound him out.／～性的 of an exploratory nature

【試問】shìwèn (動) [used in a rhetorical question] (we) may well ask: ~ 誰對這個事件負責? We might as well ask who is responsible for the incident?

【試場】shìchǎng (名) examination hall; examination room

【試想】shìxiǎng (動) just imagine

【試管】shìguǎn (名) test tube: ~ 兒 test-tube baby

【試製】shìzhì (動) trial-produce

【試圖】shìtú (動) try; attempt; endeavour

【試銷】shìxiāo (名) trial sale

【試題】shìtí (名) exam question: 出 ~ set an exam paper

【試驗】shìyàn (名) test; experiment: 地下核 ~ underground nuclear test

詩 shī (名) poem; poetry: 抒情 ~ lyric; 史 ~ epic

【詩人】shīrén (名) poet

【詩句】shījù (名) line of a poem

【詩集】shījí (名) collected poems

【詩意】shīyì (名) poetic flavour

【詩歌】shīgē (名) poetry; verse

【詩篇】shīpiān (名) ❶ poem; poetry ❷ moving story: 壯麗的 ~ magnificent story

【詩壇】shītán (名) poetry circles

【詩興】shīxìng (名) poetic urge; poetic inspiration

詰 jié (動) interrogate: 盤 ~ cross-examine

【詰問】jiéwèn (動) interrogate

詼 huī

【詼諧】huīxié (形) humorous; jocular

誇 kuā (動) ❶ exaggerate; over-state: 浮 ~ 風 trend of boasting and exaggeration ❷ praise; extol

【誇大】kuādà (動) exaggerate

【誇口】kuākǒu (動) speak boastfully

【誇張】kuāzhāng (動) exaggerate: ~法 hyperbole

【誇誇其談】kuā kuā qí tán 〈成〉 speak boastfully; shoot off one's mouth

【誇獎】kuājiǎng (動) praise; commend

【誇耀】kuāyào (動) boast about (one's own ability, achievement, influence, etc.); show off

誠 chéng I (形) honest; sincere II (副) really; indeed: ~非明智之舉 not a wise move indeed

【誠心】chéngxīn (名) sincerity: ~ 誠意 in real earnest; in all sincerity; bona fides

【誠意】chéngyì (名) good faith; sincerity

【誠實】chéngshí (形) honest

【誠摯】chéngzhì (形) earnest; sincere

【誠樸】chéngpǔ (形) simple and honest

【誠懇】chéngkěn I (形) sincere II (副) sincerely

詣 yì (名) attainments: 藝術造 ~ artistic attainments

詮 quán

【詮釋】quánshì (名) annotation; explanatory notes; annotated notes

誅 zhū (動) 〈書〉 ❶ put (a criminal) to death: 罪不容 ~。 Even a death sentence is not severe enough for the crime. ❷ condemn; denounce: 口～筆伐 denounce by tongue and pen

話 huà Ⅰ(名)word; remark Ⅱ(動)talk about; say: ～舊 talk about the old days

【話別】huàbié (動)say goodbye; bid farewell

【話柄】huàbǐng (名)butt for ridicule; laughing stock

【話務員】huàwùyuán (名)(telephone)operator

【話筒】huàtǒng (名)❶ microphone ❷ telephone transmitter ❸ megaphone

【話鋒】huàfēng (名)course of the conversation

【話劇】huàjù (名)modern drama; stage play

【話題】huàtí (名)topic of the conversation

詭 guǐ (形)❶ tricky; sly ❷ odd; strange: ～異 odd; extraordinary

【詭計】guǐjì (名)cunning ploy; schemes: ～多端 have plenty of tricks up one's sleeve

【詭秘】guǐmì (形)surreptitious; secretive: 行踪～ secretive in one's movements

【詭詐】guǐzhà (形)crafty

【詭稱】guǐchēng (動)falsely allege; pretend

【詭譎】guǐjué (形)❶ erratic ❷ eccentric

【詭辯】guǐbiàn (名)sophistry; quibble: ～術 sophistry

詢 xún (動)ask

【詢問】xúnwèn (動)ask; inquire

詬 gòu Ⅰ(名)humiliation Ⅱ(動)abuse

【詬病】gòubìng (動)denounce; condemn

詹 Zhān (名)a surname

說 shuì (動)attempt to persuade: ～客 lobbyist

see also shuō

說 shuō Ⅰ(動)❶ speak; say: 他没有細～。He didn't go into detail. ❷ explain; expound: 把問題～清楚 explain the problem clearly ❸ scold; criticize: 挨～ get a scolding Ⅱ(名)doctrine; school of thought: 衆～紛紜。Opinions differ.

see also shuì

【說大話】shuō dàhuà (動)boast; brag

【說不上】shuō bu shàng (動)〈口〉❶ cannot tell for sure: 我也～究竟是怎麼回事。I don't know what is really the matter. ❷ be not worth mentioning; be irrelevant: 你這些話都～。What you said is quite irrelevant.

【說不好】shuō bu hǎo (動)〈口〉I don't know; I'm not sure

【說不定】shuō bu dìng (副)maybe; perhaps

【說不來】shuō bu lái (動)〈口〉not get on very well: 他跟誰都～。He does not get along with anybody.

【說不過去】shuō bu guò qù (動)〈口〉cannot be justified; be unacceptable

【說好】shuōhǎo (動)come to an agreement or understanding

【說合】shuōhe (動)❶ bring two or more parties together ❷ talk over

❸ mediate

【説死】 shuōsǐ（動）make it definite: 我們～明天下午五時開會。Let's make it absolutely certain that the meeting is to be held at 5 o'clock tomorrow afternoon.

【説妥】 shuōtuǒ（動）reach agreement

【説定】 shuōdìng（說 好 shuōhǎo）（動）agree; settle: 我們～第二天晚上再見面。We agreed to meet again the next evening.

【説法】 shuōfǎ（名）❶ wording: 有另外一種～ have another way of saying it ❷ statement; version

【説服】 shuōfú（動）convince; persuade: 需要做一些～工作 require some persuading

【説明】 shuōmíng Ⅰ（動）❶ explain; clarify: ～自己立場 clarify one's own position ❷ prove; testify: 這～他的話是對的。This testifies to the truth of his remark. Ⅱ（名）explanation; caption: 圖片附有簡單～。Attached to the pictures are brief explanations.

【説明書】 shuōmíngshū（名）manual; synopsis; specification

【説到底】 shuō dàodǐ（副）in the last analysis

【説來話長】 shuō lái huà cháng〈口〉it's a long story

【説穿】 shuōchuān（說 破 shuōpò）（動）expose; lay bare: 他的心事被老趙一句話～了。In one word Lao Zhao pinpointed what was on his mind.

【説書】 shuōshū（名）story-telling

【説理】 shuōlǐ（動）argue: 對他這樣的人～没用。You can't reason with a person like him.

【説教】 shuōjiào（動）❶ preach ❷ speak like a boring moralist

【説情】 shuōqíng（動）plead on sb.'s behalf; intercede for sb.

【説得來】 shuō de lái（動）〈口〉on friendly terms with; be chummy with: 他跟我還～。He is pretty chummy with me.

【説得過去】 shuō de guò qù（動）〈口〉be passable; pass muster

【説閑話】 shuō xiánhuà（動）gossip

【説話】 shuōhuà Ⅰ（動）❶ speak; say: 學～ learn to speak ❷ chat; talk ❸ criticize: 你最好早點來，省得別人～。You had better come early lest other people should criticize you. Ⅱ（副）〈口〉in no time; at once: 他一就來。He will be around in a minute.

【説謊】 shuōhuǎng（動）lie; tell a lie

誠 jiè Ⅰ（動）warn（against）; exhort; 訓～ admonish Ⅱ（名）commandment: 十～ the Ten Commandments

誌 zhì Ⅰ（名）❶ records; annals: 日～ daily record ❷ mark; sign: 友誼日益增長的標～ sign of growing friendship Ⅱ（動）record; keep in mind

誣 wū（形）false: 言之不～。What one says is perfectly true.

【誣告】 wūgào（動）falsely accuse

【誣陷】 wūxiàn Ⅰ（動）frame: ～好人 frame up innocent people Ⅱ（名）frame-up

【誣賴】 wūlài（動）falsely incriminate

【誣衊】 wūmiè（動）slander; blacken; defame

語 yǔ Ⅰ（名）language; words: 外

~ foreign language / 三言兩~説不完 cannot say it in just a few words Ⅱ (動) speak; say: 自言自~ think aloud

【語文】 yǔwén (名) ❶ language ❷ (short for 語言文學 yǔyán wénxué) language and literature

【語句】 yǔjù (名) sentence

【語系】 yǔxì (名) language family

【語序】 yǔxù (名) 〈語〉 word order

【語言】 yǔyán (名) language

【語言學】 yǔyánxué (名) linguistics

【語法】 yǔfǎ (名) grammar

【語音】 yǔyīn (名) pronunciation

【語音學】 yǔyīnxué (名) phonetics

【語重心長】 yǔ zhòng xīn cháng 〈成〉 speak in all earnestness

【語病】 yǔbìng (名) faulty wording or construction

【語氣】 yǔqì (名) ❶ tone ❷ 〈語〉 mood: 虛擬 ~ subjunctive mood

【語族】 yǔzú (名) linguistic subfamily

【語域】 yǔyù (名) 〈語〉 register

【語詞】 yǔcí (名) words and phrases

【語無倫次】 yǔ wú lún cì 〈成〉 speak incoherently; stammer out disconnected remarks

【語感】 yǔgǎn (名) feel for the language

【語彙】 yǔhuì (名) vocabulary

【語義學】 yǔyìxué (名) semantics

【語源學】 yǔyuánxué (名) etymology

【語境】 yǔjìng (名) linguistic context

【語態】 yǔtài (名) 〈語〉 voice: 主動 ~ active voice

【語調】 yǔdiào (名) 〈語〉 intonation

【語錄】 yǔlù (名) quotation

誦 sòng (動) ❶ read aloud; chant (scripture, etc.): 朗~課文 read a text aloud ❷ recite

認 rèn (動) ❶ recognize; distinguish; identify: 你還~得我嗎? Do you still recognize me? ❷ admit; acknowledge: ~錯 admit one's mistake

【認可】 rènkě (動) approve; grant: 點頭 ~ nod approval

【認生】 rènshēng (名) (of a child) be shy with strangers

【認定】 rèndìng (動) maintain; hold; be convinced

【認命】 rènmìng (名) regard one's misfortunes as predestined; accept one's fate

【認真】 rènzhēn Ⅰ (形) serious; conscientious Ⅱ take sth. seriously: 這是椿小事,爲什麼那麼 ~ 呢? This is a trifling matter. Why take it so seriously?

【認清】 rènqīng (動) see clearly; recognize: ~ 是非 distinguish between right and wrong

【認爲】 rènwéi (動) think; consider; regard

【認罪】 rènzuì (動) plead guilty: 不 ~ plead 'not guilty'; refuse to admit one's fault

【認領】 rènlǐng (動) identify and claim (one's lost child or property)

【認賬】 rènzhàng (動) admit what one has said or done

【認輸】 rènshū (動) admit defeat: 不 ~ refuse to accept defeat

【認購】 rèngòu (動) offer to purchase; subscribe: ~ 股票 subscribe for shares

【認識】 rènshi Ⅰ (動) ❶ know or recognize sb. ❷ realize; comprehend: 充分~到形勢的嚴重性 fully recognize the gravity of the situation Ⅱ (名) understanding; cognition; knowledge

误 wù Ⅰ (名) mistake: 无~ without fail Ⅱ (动) ❶ miss: ~了火车 miss one's train ❷ harm: ~人~己 do harm to others as well as to oneself Ⅲ (副) by mistake; unintentionally: 我~拿了别人的书。I took somebody's book by mistake.

【误工】wùgōng Ⅰ (动) delay one's work Ⅱ (名) loss of working time

【误事】wùshì (动) cause delay in a matter; ruin a matter by delay

【误差】wùchā (名) error

【误杀】wùshā (名)〈法〉manslaughter

【误伤】wùshāng (动) injure or wound sb. by accident

【误会】wùhuì Ⅰ (动) misunderstand Ⅱ (名) misunderstanding: 造成~ give rise to misunderstanding

【误解】wùjiě Ⅰ (动) misunderstand; misinterpret: 你似乎~了他的意图。It seems you misinterpret his intentions. Ⅱ (名) misunderstanding: 避免~ avoid misunderstanding

【误点】wùdiǎn (动) be late; be overdue: 航班~了。The flight is overdue.

海 huì (动) teach: 教~ instruct

【海人不倦】huì rén bù juàn〈成〉be tireless in teaching; do teaching work with the greatest patience and enthusiasm

【海淫海盗】huì yín huì dào〈成〉give currency to stories of sex and violence

诱 yòu (动) ❶ induce; teach: 循循

善~ good at guiding other people methodically in their studies ❷ lure; entice: ~降 lure into surrender

【诱拐】yòuguǎi (动) abduct; kidnap

【诱奸】yòujiān (动) seduce

【诱惑】yòuhuò (动) ❶ lure; tempt; seduce ❷ attract; fascinate

【诱饵】yòu'ěr (名) bait

【诱导】yòudǎo (动) induce; guide

【诱骗】yòupiàn (动) lure and swindle; inveigle

诞 dàn Ⅰ (名) birth: 圣~ the anniversary of the birth of Jesus Christ; Christmas Ⅱ (形) absurd

【诞生】dànshēng (动) be born

【诞辰】dànchén (名) birthday

诳 kuáng

【诳语】kuángyǔ (名) lie; untruth

誓 shì Ⅰ (动) vow; pledge: ~不罢休 vow never to stop until the matter is settled Ⅱ (名) oath; pledge: 宣~就职 take the oath of office

【誓不两立】shì bù liǎng lì〈成〉vow to fight to the end with one's rival

【誓死】shìsǐ (动) pledge to do sth. even at the cost of one's life: ~不二 pledge unswerving loyalty

【誓师】shìshī (动) ❶ (of an army) pledge resolution before going to battle ❷ pledge resolution before embarking upon a major undertaking

【誓词】shìcí (誓言 shìyán) (名) oath; pledge; vow

谊 yì (名) friendship

谆 zhūn

【谆谆】zhūnzhūn (副) sincerely and untiringly: ~教导 tireless instruction

諒 liàng (動) ❶ forgive; condone ❷ think; suppose: ～他不會來。I don't think he'll come.

【諒解】liàngjiě (動) understand

談 tán I (動) talk; discuss: ～家常 engage in small talk; chitchat II (名) ❶ talk; conversation: 奇～怪 論 absurd argument ❷ (Tán) a surname

【談心】tánxīn (名) have a heart-to-heart talk

【談天】tántiān (動) chat; have a chat

【談不上】tán bu shàng (談不到 tán bu dào) (動) be out of the question

【談不來】tán bu lái (動) not get along (well)

【談吐】tántǔ (名) manner and style of conversation: 他～文雅。His language is refined and his manner urbane.

【談判】tánpàn (動) negotiate; talk: ～桌 negotiating table

【談何容易】tán hé róng yì〈成〉it's not at all that easy

【談笑風生】tán xiào fēng shēng〈成〉brim with good humour

【談得來】tán de lái (動) get along well

【談話】tánhuà (名) ❶ conversation; talk ❷ statement (usu. of a political nature): 向新聞界發表～ make a statement to the press

【談論】tánlùn (動) discuss; talk about: ～世界上正在發生的重要 變化 dwell on the significant changes now taking place in the world

請 qǐng (動) ❶ ask; request: ～人 幫忙 ask a favour of sb. ❷ invite; send for: 我們～他吃飯。We invited him to dinner. ❸ [used as a polite form of request] please: ～來兩 杯威士忌酒。Two whiskies, please.

【請勿】qǐngwù (動) please don't: ～ 打擾。Do not disturb. / ～踐踏草 地。Keep off the grass. / ～亂扔紙 屑雜物。No littering, please.

【請示】qǐngshì (動) ask for instructions

【請安】qǐng'ān (動) pay one's respects to; inquire after and send best wishes to

【請求】qǐngqiú I (動) ask; request II (名) request

【請客】qǐngkè (動) invite sb. to dinner; entertain guests

【請柬】qǐngjiǎn (請帖 qǐngtiě) (名) invitation (card)

【請便】qǐngbiàn (動) please yourself; do as you like

【請假】qǐngjià (動) ask for leave: ～ 兩天 ask for two days' leave

【請教】qǐngjiào (動) seek advice; consult

【請問】qǐngwèn〈敬〉[used to introduce a question] please; may I ask...: ～這件上衣多少錢? Excuse me, could you tell me how much his coat is?

【請罪】qǐngzuì (動) ask for punishment for the error one has committed; make apologies

【請調】qǐngdiào (動) ask for a transfer

【請願】qǐngyuàn (動) present a petition

【諸願書】qīngyuànshū（名）petition

諸 zhū（形）many; various

【諸如】zhūrú（副）such as: ～此類的問題尚待解決。Problems such as this remain to be solved.

【諸位】zhūwèi（代）[polite form of address for a group of people]: 歡迎～光臨敝校。Welcome to our school, everybody!

【諸葛】Zhūgé（名）a surname

課 kè Ⅰ（名）❶ course; subject: 選修～ elective course ❷ class; period: 上午上四節 have four periods in the morning ❸ lesson: 第三～ Lesson Three Ⅱ（動）levy (tax)

【課本】kèběn（名）textbook

【課外】kèwài（形）extracurricular; after class: ～作業 homework

【課堂】kètáng（名）classroom

【課稅】kèshuì（動）levy taxes

【課程表】kèchéngbiǎo（名）school timetable

【課間操】kèjiāncāo（名）setting-up exercises during the break

【課題】kètí（名）❶ subject for research or discussion ❷ vital issues requiring immediate attention

誹 fěi（動）slander

【誹謗】fěibàng（動）slander; calumniate

論 lùn Ⅰ（動）❶ discuss; analyze and explain: 辯～ debate ❷ treat; regard: 以 違法 ～ regard as a breach of law ❸ determine Ⅱ（副）in terms of; according to: ～票房價值,這部片子大獲成功。In box-office terms, the film is a huge success. Ⅲ（名）❶ view; commentary

❷ theory: 相對 ～ the theory of relativity

【論文】lùnwén（名）paper; thesis; dissertation: 學期～ term paper / 博士 ～ doctoral dissertation

【論功行賞】lùn gōng xíng shǎng（成）confer rewards commensurate with one's merit

【論件計酬】lùnjiàn jìchóu（動）pay by the piece

【論述】lùnshù（動）state and analyse; discuss: ～該文的優缺點 discuss the merits and inadequacies of the essay

【論爭】lùnzhēng（名）argument; debate; contention

【論處】lùnchǔ（動）punish: 依法～ punish according to law

【論理】lùnlǐ Ⅰ（副）as things go; it is common sense that...: ～他不該瞎說。Indeed, he should not have made irresponsible remarks. Ⅱ（名）logic

【論著】lùnzhù（名）research report; (academic) work

【論罪】lùnzuì（動）decide on the nature of the guilt

【論資排輩】lùn zī pái bèi（成）give top priority to seniority

【論調】lùndiào（名）view: 荒謬的～ absurd argument

【論據】lùnjù（名）argument: 他有強有力的～為自己辯護。He has a strong case.

【論壇】lùntán（名）forum; tribune

【論戰】lùnzhàn（名）polemics; debate

【論點】lùndiǎn（名）argument: 令人信服的～ a convincing argument

【論斷】lùnduàn（名）judgment; thesis; conclusion

【論證】lùnzhèng（動）prove by argument; prove: ~該項工程的可行性 prove the feasibility of the project

諉 wěi（動）shirk: 互相推~ shift responsibility onto each other

調 diào I（動）transfer: ~職 transfer to another post II（名）❶〈樂〉melody; tune: 走~ out of tune ❷〈語〉tone; intonation: 升（降）~ rising (falling) tone ❸ accent
see also tiáo

【調子】diàozi（名）❶ tune ❷ mode ❸（of speech or writing）tone; note: 低~的聲明 a low-key statement

【調令】diàolìng（名）transfer order

【調兵遣將】diào bīng qiǎn jiàng〈成〉dispatch troops; muster troops

【調虎離山】diào hǔ lí shān〈成〉lure the tiger away from the mountains; entice the enemy to leave his base

【調查】diàochá（動）investigate; survey

【調度】diàodù I（動）❶ dispatch ❷ arrange; manage II（名）dispatch

【調配】diàopèi（動）allot; deploy

【調動】diàodòng（動）❶ transfer; move ❷ bring into play; mobilize

【調換】diàohuàn（動）swap; replace

【調集】diàojí（動）assemble; concentrate: 在邊境~大軍 concentrate massive forces on the frontier

【調遣】diàoqiǎn（動）dispatch; send

【調撥】diàobō（動）allocate; appropriate

調 tiáo（動）❶ mix; blend: ~配

顏色 mix colours ❷ adjust well; suit wonderfully ❸ mediate ❹ tease
see also diào

【調皮】tiáopí（形）❶ naughty; mischievous ❷ intractable; tricky

【調和】tiáohe（動）❶ be in harmony ❷ mediate ❸〔often used in negative sentences〕compromise: 沒有~的可能。There is no possibility of compromise.

【調味】tiáowèi（動）season (food); flavour

【調料】tiáoliào（名）seasoning; condiment

【調唆】tiáosuo（動）incite; abet

【調控】tiáokòng（動）regulate and keep under control

【調情】tiáoqíng（動）flirt

【調節】tiáojié（動）regulate: ~稅 regulatory business tax

【調解】tiáojiě（調處 tiáochǔ; 調停 tiáotíng）（動）mediate: ~鄰里糾紛 mediate a dispute between neighbours

【調資】tiáozī（動）raise wages

【調養】tiáoyǎng（調理 tiáolǐ）（動）recuperate; nurse oneself back to health

【調價】tiáojià（名）price adjustment

【調整】tiáozhěng（動）readjust; regulate; modify

【調劑】tiáojì（動）adjust; redistribute

【調戲】tiáoxì（動）harass (a woman)

【調羹】tiáogēng（羹匙 gēngchí）（名）spoon

諂 chǎn（動）flatter; toady

【諂媚】chǎnmèi（動）flatter; curry favour with

誰 shuí（or shéi）（代）❶ who:

打電話來? Who called? ❷ whom, who: 你說～呢? Who are you talking about? ❸ [used in negative sentences] nobody: ～也沒想到事情會到這個地步。Nobody expected that things would come to this. ❹ somebody; anybody: 這件事～都能幹。Anybody can do it.

諛 yú (動) 〈書〉 flatter: 阿～奉承 flatter and toady

諦 dì I (副) carefully; attentively II (名) meaning: 真～ truth
【諦聽】dìtīng (動) be all attention; listen attentively

諳 ān (動) be skilled in: 素～針灸之術 be skilled in acupuncture and moxibustion
【諳練】ānliàn (形) skilled; proficient; experienced

諺 yàn (名) proverb
【諺語】yànyǔ (名) proverb; saying

諢 hùn (名) joke: 打～ be joking; be cracking jokes
【諢名】hùnmíng (名) nickname

諞 piǎn (動) 〈方〉 show off: ～能 make a display of one's abilities

謎 mí (名) ❶ riddle: 燈～ lantern riddles ❷ mystery; puzzle
【謎底】mídǐ (名) ❶ answer to a riddle ❷ truth
【謎語】míyǔ (名) riddle

諫 jiàn (動) remonstrate; admonish

諾 nuò (名) ❶ promise: 軍事承～ military commitment ❷ yes: 唯唯～～的人 yes man

【諾言】nuòyán (名) promise: 違背～ break one's promise

諜 dié (名) ❶ espionage ❷ secret agent: 間～ spy
【諜報】diébào (名) intelligence

謀 móu I (名) stratagem; resourcefulness: 多～善斷 resourceful and decisive II (動) ❶ plan; work for; seek: 爲世界～和平 work for world peace ❷ consult; discuss
【謀士】móushì (名) counsellor to politicians in ancient China; adviser
【謀反】móufǎn (動) conspire against the government; plot treason
【謀生】móushēng (動) make a living
【謀求】móuqiú (動) seek; work for: ～和解 try to bring about a reconciliation; attempt a peaceful settlement
【謀利】móulì (動) seek profit
【謀事】móushì (動) ❶ make a plan ❷ hunt for a job
【謀取】móuqǔ (動) try to obtain; seek: ～私利 seek private gains
【謀害】móuhài (動) plot to assassinate; try to frame up sb.
【謀殺】móushā (動) murder; assassinate
【謀略】móulüè (名) resourcefulness: 他很有～。He is full of resources.
【謀劃】móuhuà (動) plan; scheme

諱 huì I (動) avoid as taboo: 直言不～ speak freely and frankly II (名) taboo
【諱言】huìyán (動) be afraid or reluctant to speak up: 無庸～ needless to say
【諱疾忌醫】huì jí jì yī 〈成〉 cover up one's shortcomings to avoid criticism

【諱莫如深】huì mò rú shēn〈成〉take great pains to guard a secret

謂 wèi（動）❶ say ❷ call; name; mean: 何～未來派? What is meant by futurism?

【謂語】wèiyǔ（名）〈語〉predicate

諧 xié（形）❶ in harmony; in concordance ❷ humorous: 詼～ humorous; jocular

【諧和】xiéhé（形）harmonious

【諧音】xiéyīn（形）homophonic; homonymic

【諧謔】xiéxuè（動）banter: 相互～exchange banter

諷 fěng（動）satirize; exhort

【諷刺】fěngcì Ⅰ（動）satirize Ⅱ（名）sarcasm

【諷喻】fěngyù（名）parable

謗 bàng（動）slander; libel; vilify

謙 qiān（形）modest

【謙卑】qiānbēi（形）humble; meek

【謙恭】qiāngōng（形）modest and courteous

【謙虛】qiānxū（形）modest

【謙遜】qiānxùn（形）modest and unassuming

【謙讓】qiānràng（動）politely decline an offer

講 jiǎng Ⅰ（動）❶ speak; say: 請～慢點。Please speak more slowly. ❷ explain; illustrate: 這篇文章是～經濟改革的。This article deals with economic reform. ❸ consult; negotiate: 不～價錢 without bargaining ❹ attend to; emphasize: ～環境衛生 pay attention to environmental hygiene Ⅱ（介）with regard

to: ～戲劇, 他要學的還多着呢。As regards drama, he's got a lot to learn yet. Ⅲ（名）lecture; talk

【講求】jiǎngqiú（動）stress (a particular aspect of work, writing, etc.): ～內容, 不～形式 stress the substance, not the form

【講究】jiǎngjiu Ⅰ（動）lay stress: ～實效 stress practical results Ⅱ（名）sth. worthy of serious attention: 漢語聲調大有～。The tonal patterns in Chinese pronunciation merits meticulous study. Ⅲ（形）exquisite; tasteful: 他衣着很～。He is immaculately dressed.

【講和】jiǎnghé（動）make peace; come to terms

【講明】jiǎngmíng（動）state in explicit terms; clarify; define: 你必須向我～事情的經過。You have to tell me exactly what has happened.

【講述】jiǎngshù（動）recount; narrate: ～自己的經歷 give an account of one's own experience

【講座】jiǎngzuò（名）lecture; series of lectures

【講師】jiǎngshī（名）university lecturer

【講理】jiǎnglǐ（動）❶ reason with: 我要跟他～去。I'll have it out with him. ❷ be reasonable: 他是～的。He is amenable to reason.

【講情】jiǎngqíng（動）plead for sb.; intervene on sb.'s behalf

【講授】jiǎngshòu（動）teach; lecture ～英國文學 lecture in English literature

【講排場】jiǎng páichang（動）go in for pomp; put up a grandiose facade

【講義】jiǎngyì（名）lecture notes

【講話】jiǎnghuà Ⅰ（動）speak; talk;

speak out: 善於～ good at making speeches Ⅱ (名) ❶ speech; address ❷ [often used as part of a book title] a type of popular writing: 《普通生物學～》 Introduction to General Biology

【講解】jiǎngjiě (動) explain; make explanations (as a guide at an exhibition)

【講臺】jiǎngtái (名) lecture platform

【講演】jiǎngyǎn (名) speech; address; lecture: 登臺～ mount the platform to deliver a lecture

【講稿】jiǎnggǎo (名) notes; script

【講課】jiǎngkè (動) give lectures

【講學】jiǎngxué (動) give lectures: 出國～ go on a lecture tour abroad

【講壇】jiǎngtán (名) ❶ rostrum ❷ forum

謊 huǎng Ⅰ (名) lie; falsehood: 扯 ～ tell a lie Ⅱ (形) false; untrue

【謊言】huǎngyán (名) falsehood; lie

【謊話】huǎnghuà (名) lie

謠 yáo (名) ❶ ballad; folk song; rhyme ❷ rumour: 傳～ spread a rumour

【謠言】yáoyán (名) groundless allegation; rumour; cooked-up story: 毫無根據的～ absolutely unfounded rumours

【謠傳】yáochuán (名) rumour: ～談判陷入僵局。Rumour has it that the negotiations have come to a deadlock.

謅 zhōu (動) fabricate (tales, etc.); make up: 胡～ talk rubbish

謝 xiè Ⅰ (動) ❶ thank: 請代我～～他。Thank him on my behalf. ❷

make an apology: ～罪 apologize for one's fault ❸ decline: 辭～ decline with thanks ❹ (of flowers, leaves) wither Ⅱ (名) (Xiè) a surname

【謝絕】xièjué (動) decline politely: ～參觀. Not open to visitors.

【謝意】xièyì (名) gratitude; thanks

【謝幕】xièmù (動) take a curtain call

【謝謝】xièxie (動) thank you; thanks

謄 téng (動) transcribe; copy

【謄清】téngqīng (動) make a fair copy

【謄寫】téngxiě (動) copy out

謫 zhé (動) (in feudal times) demote a senior official and exile him to a remote place

謳 ōu (動) sing

【謳歌】ōugē (動) ❶ sing ❷ sing the praises of; extol

謹 jǐn Ⅰ (形) very cautious; prudent Ⅱ (副) sincerely; earnestly; respectfully: ～上 [used at the end of a letter to one's parent, superior, etc.] yours ever; yours respectfully

【謹小慎微】jǐn xiǎo shèn wēi 〈成〉 overcautious in small matters; punctilious

【謹防】jǐnfáng (動) beware of: ～假冒 Beware of fakes (fake goods).

【謹慎】jǐnshèn (形) cautious; discreet: 他處理這個問題很～。He was very cautious in handling this case.

謬 miù (形) wrong; false: 荒～ absurd

【謬誤】miùwù (名) error; falsehood

【謬種】miùzhǒng (名) fallacy; ab-

surd theory
【謬論】miùlùn (名) fallacy; nonsense

謾 mán (動) deceive
see also màn

謾 mán (形) rude; impolite
see also màn
【謾罵】mànmà (動) abuse; vilify

識 shí I (動) know; recognize: 素不相～ have never made sb.'s acquaintance II (名) understanding; knowledge: 學～ learning
【識大體】shí dàtǐ (動) have the overall interests in mind: ～，顧大局 bear the public interests in mind and give consideration to the overall situation
【識字】shízì (動) learn to read; be literate: 不～ be illiterate
【識別】shíbié (動) distinguish; identify (as different): ～真偽 distinguish between truth and falsehood
【識相】shíxiàng (識趣 shíqù) (動) act with proper restraint; be tactful
【識破】shípò (動) see through; discover; uncover: ～他的本來面目 see through his true features
【識時務者爲俊傑】shí shí wù zhě wéi jùn jié〈成〉he who understands the trends of the times is a great man; the wise man bows to the inevitable
【識貨】shíhuò (動) be able to judge the quality of a commodity; know the true worth of a person

譜 pǔ I (名) ❶ table; chart: 光～ spectrum ❷ manual; guide: 畫～ a book of model paintings or drawings ❸ music score: 五綫～ staff; stave ❹ sth. to go by: 做事有～兒 know exactly what one is about II (動) set

to music; compose
【譜曲】pǔqǔ (動) set a song to music
【譜號】pǔhào (名)〈樂〉clef
【譜寫】pǔxiě (動) compose (music)

譚 Tán (名) a surname

證 zhèng I (動) prove; verify: 論～ expound and prove II (名) evidence; certificate: 人～ testimony of a witness / 身份～ identity card / 學生～ student card
【證人】zhèngrén (名) witness
【證件】zhèngjiàn (名) credentials; testimonial papers
【證明】zhèngmíng I (動) prove; testify; bear testimony to: 完全～他是無辜 bear unmistakable testimony to his innocence II (名) certificate; proof
【證券】zhèngquàn (名) negotiable securities; certificate: ～交易所 stock exchange
【證書】zhèngshū (名) certificate; credentials: 畢業～ diploma
【證章】zhèngzhāng (名) badge
【證詞】zhèngcí (名) testimony
【證實】zhèngshí (動) confirm; verify: 這一消息尚待～。This news has yet to be verified.
【證據】zhèngjù (名) evidence; testimony; proof

譏 jī (動) ridicule; satirize; deride: 反唇相～ answer back with a sneer
【譏笑】jīxiào (動) laugh at; ridicule
【譏誚】jīqiào (動) speak of sb. ironically; taunt
【譏諷】jīfěng (動) speak of sb. with veiled but biting sarcasm; hold sb. to ridicule

議 yì I (動) discuss; deliberate: 把

计划～一～。Let's have an exchange of views about the plan. Ⅱ（名）view; opinion

【议和】yìhé（动）negotiate peace

【议事】yìshì（名）discussion

【议长】yìzhǎng（名）speaker; president

【议定书】yìdìngshū（名）protocol

【议员】yìyuán（名）member of a legislative assembly; member of parliament; congressman

【议院】yìyuàn（名）legislative assembly: 上～ the upper chamber / 下～ the lower chamber

【议案】yì'àn（名）proposal; motion; bill

【议程】yìchéng（名）agenda

【议会】yìhuì（名）parliament; congress; assembly

【议价】yìjià Ⅰ（动）negotiate a price Ⅱ（名）negotiated price

【议论】yìlùn（动）talk about; discuss; make comments

【议论文】yìlùnwén（名）(of writing) argumentation; argument

【议题】yìtí（名）topic for discussion

谴 qiǎn

【谴责】qiǎnzé（动）denounce; censure

译 yì（动）translate; interpret

【译文】yìwén（名）translated text; translation

【译本】yìběn（名）translation

【译名】yìmíng（名）translated name; translated term

【译者】yìzhě（名）translator

【译音】yìyīn（名）transliteration

【译员】yìyuán（名）interpreter

【译电】yìdiàn（动）❶ encode; enci-

pher ❷ decode; decipher

【译制】yìzhì（动）〈电影〉dub: ～片 dubbed film

谵 zhān

【谵妄】zhānwàng（名）〈医〉delirium

【谵语】zhānyǔ（名）ravings; delirious speech

警 jǐng Ⅰ（名）❶（short for 警察 jǐngchá）police: 交通～ traffic policeman ❷（short for 警报 jǐngbào）alarm（signal）Ⅱ（动）❶ guard against; alert ❷ admonish; alarm Ⅲ（形）alert; vigilant

【警句】jǐngjù（名）epigram

【警告】jǐnggào Ⅰ（动）warn（sb. of the need to rectify his mistakes）; give a warning to Ⅱ（名）warning; alarm

【警戒】jǐngjiè（动）❶ warn; caution ❷ keep watch; guard（against）

【警惕】jǐngtì Ⅰ（动）guard against; be on the alert against Ⅱ（名）vigilance

【警报】jǐngbào（名）alarm（signal）: 飓风～ typhoon warning

【警备】jǐngbèi（动）garrison; guard: ～森严 be heavily guarded

【警铃】jǐnglíng（名）alarm bell

【警察】jǐngchá（名）police; policeman: 武装～ armed police /～岗亭 police box; police stand

【警卫】jǐngwèi（名）guard

【警醒】jǐngxǐng（形）(of a sleeper) light

【警钟】jǐngzhōng（名）alarm bell: 敲～ sound the alarm (for sb.)

【警觉】jǐngjué（名）vigilance

譬 pì（动）take an example

【譬如】pìrú（副）for example; for instance

【譬喻】pìyù（名）figure of speech; analogy

譽 yù Ⅰ（名）reputation; fame: 沽名釣～ angle for fame and compliments Ⅱ（動）praise; eulogize: 稱～ praise

護 hù（動）❶ protect; guard Ⅱ be partial to; shield: ～短 cover up sb.'s defects

【護士】hùshì（名）nurse: ～長 head nurse／實習～ student nurse

【護身符】hùshēnfú（名）talisman

【護送】hùsòng（動）escort; convoy

【護城河】hùchénghé（名）city moat

【護航】hùháng（動）escort; convoy: ～艦 convoy ship

【護理】hùlǐ（動）nurse

【護照】hùzhào（名）passport

【護膝】hùxī（名）〈體〉kneepad; kneecap

讀 dú（動）❶ read; read aloud ❷ attend school: ～完小學 finish primary school

【讀本】dúběn（名）textbook; reader

【讀者】dúzhě（名）reader

【讀物】dúwù（名）reading material: 科普～ popular science reader

【讀音】dúyīn（名）pronunciation

【讀書】dúshū（動）❶ read ❷ study: ～用功 study hard; work hard

變 biàn Ⅰ（動）❶ change; alter; transform: ～冷 get cold ❷ become; turn into ❸ transform; change; alter: 改～主意 change one's mind Ⅱ（名）❶ change: 巨～

radical change; great change ❷ unexpected turn of events: 政～ coup d'état

【變天】biàntiān（名）❶ change of weather (usu. from fine to bad): 快～了。I smell a change in the weather. ❷ restoration of reactionary rule

【變心】biànxīn（動）transfer one's affection to another person; change in love; transfer one's allegiance: 永不～ remain for ever loyal

【變化】biànhuà Ⅰ（動）change; alter; vary Ⅱ（名）alteration; variation; transformation

【變化多端】biànhuà duō duān（形）capricious; changeful

【變化無常】biàn huà wú cháng〈成〉changeable; capricious; constantly changing

【變幻】biànhuàn（動）change unexpectedly; fluctuate: 風雲～ fast-changing situation

【變幻莫測】biàn huàn mò cè〈成〉unpredictable; changeable

【變本加厲】biàn běn jiā lì〈成〉intensify; step up; worsen

【變成】biànchéng（變為 biànwéi）（動）become; turn into; change to

【變色】biànsè（動）❶ change colour; discolour ❷ turn angry

【變色龍】biànsèlóng（名）chameleon

【變更】biàngēng（動）change; alter: ～旅行計劃 modify the itinerary of one's journey

【變形】biànxíng（動）❶ be deformed; be out of shape ❷ change shape; warp

【變法】biànfǎ（名）〈史〉constitutional reform

【變卦】biànguà（動）〈貶〉(suddenly) change one's mind; backpedal on

【變革】biàngé Ⅰ (動) change; transform Ⅱ (名) change; reform

【變故】biàngù (名) accident; unforeseen event; mishap

【變相】biànxiàng (形) in disguised form; in another form: ～敲詐 disguised blackmail

【變奏】biànzòu (名)〈樂〉variation

【變速】biànsù Ⅰ (動) change speed; shift gears Ⅱ (名)〈機〉speed change; gearshift: ～器 gearshift

【變通】biàntōng (動) make adjustments; stretch a point: ～辦法 expedient or flexible measures

【變動】biàndòng Ⅰ (動) change; alter; reshuffle: ～計劃 change the plan Ⅱ (名) change; alteration: 做了些～ make some alterations

【變換】biànhuàn (動) vary; change; alternate

【變節】biànjié Ⅰ (動) defect; betray one's country; turn one's coat: ～分子 defector; turncoat Ⅱ (名) defection; betrayal

【變亂】biànluàn (名) turmoil; turbulence; upheaval

【變電站】biàndiànzhàn (名)〈transformer〉substation

【變種】biànzhǒng (名)❶〈生〉variety; mutation ❷〈貶〉variant

【變態】biàntài Ⅰ (形) abnormal Ⅱ (名)〈生〉metamorphosis

【變態反應】biàntài fǎnyìng (名)〈醫〉allergy

【變遷】biànqiān (名) vicissitude; change; evolution: 四季的～ the change of the seasons

【變賣】biànmài (動) sell off (one's possessions) for cash

【變質】biànzhì (動) go bad; spoil;

degenerate

【變臉】biànliǎn (動) show an unpleasant countenance; assume a hostile attitude

【變戲法】biàn xìfǎ (動) juggle; conjure; perform magic tricks: ～的人 juggler; magician; conjurer

【變壓器】biànyāqì (名)〈電〉transformer

讓

讓 ràng Ⅰ (動)❶ give way; yield: 讓～ decline out of modesty ❷ cede; transfer: 轉～高技術 transfer high technology ❸ let; allow: 他不～孩子們今晚去看戲。He doesn't want his children to go to the theatre tonight. ❹ invite; offer: 把客人～進來。Usher the guests in Ⅱ (介) [used in a passive sentence to introduce the agent] by: 他一車撞了。He was knocked down by a car.

【讓出】ràngchū (動) give up; offer: ～兩間房子給客人住 vacate two rooms for visitors

【讓步】ràngbù (動) make a concession; yield

【讓位】ràngwèi (動)❶ resign one's position of authority in favour of sb. else ❷ vacate a seat

【讓座】ràngzuò (動)❶ give up one's seat to sb. ❷ ask the guests to take their seats (at a dinner table)

【讓路】rànglù (動) make way for sb. or sth.

讕

讕 lán

【讕言】lányán (名) slander; fabrication: 純屬～。It's a slander, pure and simple.

讒

讒 chán (動) slander

【讒言】chányán（名）calumny; malicious talk to sow discord

【讒害】chánhài（動）vilify and persecute; frame sb. up

谷 部

谷 gǔ（名）❶ valley; gorge; canyon ❷（Gǔ）a surname

豁 huò I（名）slit; crack: ～口 opening; breach II（動）give up; sacrifice: ～出去了 determined to take any risks
see also huō

豁 huō
see also huò

【豁免】huòmiǎn（動）exempt: ～權 immunity

【豁亮】huòliàng（形）spacious and bright

【豁達】huòdá（形）broadminded

【豁然開朗】huò rán kāi lǎng〈成〉feel enlightened all of a sudden; suddenly see the truth

豆 部

豆 dòu（名）❶ bean: 蠶～ broad beans / 大～ soybeans / 青～ green beans ❷ bean-shaped thing: 花生～ peanut ❸（Dòu）a surname

【豆豉】dòuchǐ（名）fermented soybean

【豆腐】dòufu（名）bean curd: ～乾 dried bean curd / ～乳 fermented bean curd

【豆製品】dòuzhìpǐn（名）bean products

豇 jiāng

【豇豆】jiāngdòu（名）cowpea

豈 qǐ（副）[used to form a rhetorical question]: 這樣～不更好? Wouldn't that be better?

【豈有此理】qǐ yǒu cǐ lǐ（形）absurd; preposterous: 真是～! That's the height of absurdity!

【豈能】qǐnéng（副）how could; how is it possible: 你～這麼說? How could you say such things?

【豈敢】qǐgǎn〈套〉that is more than I deserve; I wish I could deserve your compliments

豌 wān

【豌豆】wāndòu（名）pea

【豌豆黃】wāndòuhuáng（名）pea flour cake

豐 fēng I（形）❶ plentiful; rich ❷ big; great II（名）（Fēng）a surname

【豐功偉績】fēng gōng wěi jī〈成〉noble contributions

【豐年】fēngnián（名）year of good harvest

【豐收】fēngshōu（名）bumper harvest

【豐茂】fēngmào（形）growing in profusion; exuberant

【豐盈】fēngyíng（形）❶ plump ❷ ample

【豐厚】fēnghòu（形）generous

【豐盛】fēngshèng（形）rich; plentiful

【豐產】fēngchǎn（名）high yield

【豐富】fēngfù（形）rich; abundant

【豐富多采】fēng fù duō cǎi（形）rich and colourful

【豐裕】fēngyù（形）affluent

【豐碑】fēngbēi（名）great achievements; immortal masterpiece

【豐滿】fēngmǎn（形）❶ plentiful ❷ plump; full: ～的麥穗 plump ears of wheat

【豐碩】fēngshuò（形）sizable and in abundance; splendid

豕 部

象 xiàng（名）❶ elephant ❷ appearance; shape: 印～ impression / 萬～更新。Everything has taken on a new look.

【象牙】xiàngyá（名）elephant's tusk; ivory: ～雕刻 ivory carving

【象牙海岸】Xiàngyá Hǎi'àn（名）the Ivory Coast

【象形】xiàngxíng（名）pictograph: ～文字 pictograph; hieroglyph

【象棋】xiàngqí（名）(Chinese) chess

【象徵】xiàngzhēng Ⅰ（動）symbolize Ⅱ（名）symbol; emblem: 雪是純潔的～。Snow is a symbol of purity.

【象聲詞】xiàngshēngcí（名）〈語〉onomatopoeia

豢 huàn

【豢養】huànyǎng（動）feed; groom; raise

豪 háo Ⅰ（名）person of outstanding ability: 文～ a titan in the literary world Ⅱ（形）❶ uninhibited; unrestrained ❷ tyrannical; despotic

【豪言壯語】háo yán zhuàng yǔ（成）brave words; heroic pledge

【豪放】háofàng（形）unconventional

【豪門】háomén（名）rich and powerful family

【豪氣】háoqì（名）heroism; heroic spirit

【豪情】háoqíng（名）lofty and heroic spirit; noble aspirations

【豪爽】háoshuǎng（形）straight-forward; outspoken

【豪強】háoqiáng Ⅰ（名）bully who has powerful backing Ⅱ（形）tyrannical

【豪華】háohuá（形）sumptuous; luxurious: ～版 de luxe edition／～飯店 luxury hotel

【豪傑】háojié（名）hero; person of exceptional talent and ability

【豪邁】háomài（形）heroic

【豪興】háoxìng（名）in high spirits

豬 zhū（名）pig

【豬皮】zhūpí（名）pigskin

【豬肉】zhūròu（名）pork

【豬肝】zhūgān（名）pork liver

【豬油】zhūyóu（名）lard

【豬苗】zhūmiáo（名）piglet; pigling

【豬食】zhūshí（名）pigfeed; swill

【豬倌】zhūguān（名）swineherd

【豬排】zhūpái（名）pork chops

【豬圈】zhūjuàn（名）pigsty; pigpen

【豬鬃】zhūzōng（名）(hog) bristles

【豬獾】zhūhuān（名）sand badger

豫 Yù（名）another name for Henan Province

【豫劇】yùjù（名）Henan opera

豸部

豺 chái （名）jackal

【豺狼】cháiláng （名）jackals and wolves; cruel and evil persons

豹 bào （名）leopard; panther

【豹子】bàozi （名）leopard; panther

貂 diāo （名）marten: 水～ mink

貉 hé （名）racoon dog

貌 mào （名）appearance; look: 其～不揚 look repulsive

【貌不驚人】mào bù jīng rén〈成〉look plain

【貌似】màosì （動）seem; appear: ～公允 pretend to play fair ／～有理 be fair and reasonable on the surface

【貌合神離】mào hé shén lí〈成〉friendly in outward manner but divided at heart

貓 māo （名）cat
see also máo

【貓哭老鼠】māo kū lǎo shǔ〈成〉a case of the cat weeping over the death of the mouse; shed crocodile tears

【貓頭鷹】māotóuyīng （名）owl

貓 máo
see also māo

【貓腰】máoyāo〈方〉arch one's back

貝部

貝 bèi （名）❶ shellfish: 珍珠～ pearl shell ❷ cowrie (used as money in early stages of civilization) ❸ (Bèi) a surname

【貝母】bèimǔ （名）〈中藥〉bulb of fritillary (*Fritillaria thunbergii*)

【貝殼】bèiké （名）shell

【貝寧】Bèiníng （名）Benin: ～人 Beninian

【貝雕】bèidiāo （名）shell carving; shell work: ～畫 shell mosaic

【貝類】bèilèi （名）molluscs; shellfish

負 fù Ⅰ（動）❶ carry; bear: 擔～責任 shoulder responsibility ❷ suffer: ～傷 be wounded ❸ depend on: ～險固守 take advantage of one's strategic position to put up a stubborn resistance ❹ enjoy: 久～盛名 enjoy a high reputation of long standing ❺ betray ❻ owe ❼ lose; be beaten Ⅱ（形）minus; negative: ～二 minus two

【負心】fùxīn （動）be faithless

【負疚】fùjiù （動）feel guilty

【負約】fùyuē （動）break a promise

【負荷】fùhè （名）〈電〉load

【負責】fùzé Ⅰ（動）assume responsibility: ～這項工程 be in charge of the project Ⅱ（形）conscientious

【負責人】fùzérén （名）person in charge

【負極】fùjí （名）〈電〉negative pole

【負隅頑抗】fù yú wán kàng〈成〉〈貶〉make a desperate resistance

like a cornered beast

【負號】 fùhào（名）negative sign

【負數】 fùshù（名）〈數〉negative number

【負擔】 fùdān（名）burden; load: 減輕～ lighten the burden

貞 zhēn（形）❶ faithful; loyal: 堅～不屈 faithful and unyielding ❷ (of women) chaste

【貞節】 zhēnjié（名）chastity

【貞潔】 zhēnjié（形）chaste; pure

【貞操】 zhēncāo（名）❶ loyalty; moral integrity ❷ chastity

貢 gòng（名）❶ tribute: 進～ pay tribute (to the emperor) ❷（Gòng）a surname

【貢品】 gòngpǐn（名）tribute articles

【貢稅】 gòngshuì（名）tribute and taxes

【貢獻】 gòngxiàn Ⅰ（動）contribute; devote Ⅱ（名）contribution

財 cái（名）wealth; money

【財力】 cáilì（名）financial resources

【財主】 cáizhu（名）rich man

【財物】 cáiwù（名）property; effects: 公共～ public property

【財政】 cáizhèng（名）finance: ～部 Ministry of Finance; the Exchequer; the Treasury Department

【財迷】 cáimí（名）money-grubber

【財神】 cáishén（名）God of Wealth

【財務】 cáiwù（名）financial affairs

【財產】 cáichǎn（名）property

【財富】 cáifù（名）wealth; riches

【財貿】 cáimào（名）finance and trade

【財源】 cáiyuán（名）source of revenue; financial resources

【財團】 cáituán（名）financial group:

國際～ consortium

【財寶】 cáibǎo（名）treasure; money and valuables

責 zé Ⅰ（名）duty; responsibility: 負～ be responsible for Ⅱ（動）❶ demand; require: 嚴～己 be strict with oneself ❷ blame; censure; reproach: 譴～ condemn; denounce ❸ question closely

【責令】 zélìng（動）order; instruct: ～他們在四十八小時内離境 demand that they leave the country within 48 hours

【責成】 zéchéng（動）entrust; enjoin: 問題已～專人解決。We've entrusted someone with the task of working out a solution.

【責任】 zérèn（名）❶ duty; responsibility ❷ responsibility for a mistake; blame

【責任制】 zérènzhì（名）system of job responsibility: 聯產承包～ output-related system of contracted responsibilities

【責任感】 zérèngǎn（名）sense of responsibility

【責怪】 zéguài（動）blame

【責問】 zéwèn（動）call sb. to account; take sb. to task

【責備】 zébèi（動）reproach; blame

【責罰】 zéfá（動）punish

【責罵】 zémà（動）scold; chide

【責難】 zénàn（動）rebuke; censure

貶 biǎn（動）❶ demote; dismiss; banish from court ❷ reduce in price; degrade in rank ❸ censure; condemn

【貶低】 biǎndī（動）belittle; disparage; play down

【貶值】 biǎnzhí Ⅰ（動）〈經〉depreci-

ate; devalue Ⅱ (名) 〈經〉 deval-
uation; depreciation

【貶義】biǎnyì (名) derogatory sense

【貶義詞】biǎnyìcí (名) derogatory
term

【貶謫】biǎnzhé (動) (said of an official) degrade in rank; banish from
court and send into exile

販 fàn Ⅰ (動) peddle Ⅱ (名) pedlar

【販子】fànzi (名) dealer; vendor

【販運】fànyùn (動) buy goods in one
place for sale in another

【販賣】fànmài (動) trade in: ～毒
品 traffic in drugs

貫 guàn Ⅰ (動) ❶ pass through ❷
link up; join together Ⅱ (名)
(Guàn) a surname

【貫注】guànzhù (動) concentrate
on; focus one's attention on: 全神
～ be preoccupied with

【貫串】guànchuàn (貫串 guànchuàn)
(動) run through; penetrate

【貫通】guàntōng (動) ❶ understand
thoroughly ❷ (of highways) link up

【貫徹】guànchè (動) carry through;
implement

貪 tān Ⅰ (形) venal; corrupt: ～贓
枉法 take bribes and bend the law;
pervert justice for a bribe Ⅱ (動) ❶
desire insatiably; crave: ～ 杯 be
too fond of drinking ❷ covet; long:
～便宜 desire to get things on the
cheap; seek petty advantages

【貪心】tānxīn (形) greedy; avari-
cious

【貪生怕死】tān shēng pà sǐ 〈成〉
cling to life and fear death; save
one's skin and choose to live in ignominy

【貪污】tānwū Ⅰ (動) embezzle Ⅱ
(名) corruption: ～盜竊 graft and
embezzlement

【貪佔】tānzhàn (動) embezzle: ～
公款 embezzle public funds

【貪官污吏】tān guān wū lì 〈成〉
corrupt officials

【貪圖】tāntú (動) covet; hanker after: ～享樂 seek pleasure; be plea-
sure-loving

【貪嘴】tānzuǐ (形) gluttonous; vora-
cious

貧 pín (形) ❶ poor; poverty-
stricken ❷ deficient; lacking: ～油
poor in oil resources

【貧乏】pínfá (形) poor; insufficient:
內容～ (of article, book, etc.)
lacking in substance

【貧民】pínmín (名) the poor; the
destitute; pauper

【貧民窟】pínmínkū (名) slum

【貧血】pínxuè (名) 〈醫〉 anaemia

【貧困】pínkùn (形) poor; destitute

【貧苦】pínkǔ (貧窮 pínqióng) (形)
poor; needy

【貧寒】pínhán (形) poor; impoverished

【貧瘠】pínjí (形) (of land) barren;
bare

【貧嘴】pínzuǐ (形) garrulous

【貧礦】pínkuàng (名) lean ore

貨 huò (名) ❶ currency; money:
通～ current money; currency ❷
goods; commodity

【貨色】huòsè (名) ❶ goods ❷
stuff; junk; rubbish

【貨車】huòchē (名) ❶ goods train;
freight train ❷ goods wagon;
freight car ❸ lorry; truck

【貨物】huòwù（名）goods; merchandise

【貨真價實】huò zhēn jià shí〈成〉quality goods at a reasonable price Ⅱ（形）〈貶）out-and-out: ～的偽君子 a perfect hypocrite

【貨船】huòchuán（名）cargo ship; freighter

【貨單】huòdān（名）manifest; waybill; shipping list

【貨款】huòkuǎn（名）payment for goods

【貨運】huòyùn（名）freight transport

【貨棧】huòzhàn（名）warehouse

【貨源】huòyuán（名）source of goods; supply of goods

【貨樣】huòyàng（名）sample goods; sample

【貨幣】huòbì（名）currency; money: ～貶值 depreciation of currency

【貨艙】huòcāng（名）（cargo）hold

【貨攤】huòtān（名）stall; stand

貳 èr（數）two（the elaborate form of the numeral 二, used on cheques, banknotes, etc.）

賁 bēn

【賁門】bēnmén（名）〈生理〉cardia

費 fèi Ⅰ（名）fee; charge: 學～ tuition / 軍～ military expenditure Ⅱ（動）cost; spend: 白～唇舌 waste one's breath

【費力】fèilì（費勁 fèijìn）（形）laborious; strenuous

【費心】fèixīn（動）take the trouble

【費用】fèiyòng（名）cost; expenses: 日常～ running expenses

【費事】fèishì（動）have some trouble: 事情這樣辦也不～。I won't have much trouble getting my work done this way.

【費神】fèishén（動）〈套〉trouble: 請～照看一下我的行李。Would you please keep an eye on my luggage for a while?

【費解】fèijiě（形）difficult to understand

【費盡心機】fèi jìn xīn jī〈成〉stint no effort; leave no stone unturned

【費錢】fèiqián（形）expensive

賀 hè Ⅰ（動）congratulate Ⅱ（名）（Hè）a surname

【賀年】hènián（動）extend New Year greetings; pay a New Year call

【賀年片】hèniánpiàn（名）New Year card

【賀信】hèxìn（名）letter of congratulation

【賀詞】hècí（名）speech or message of congratulation; congratulations

【賀喜】hèxǐ（動）extend congratulations to sb.（on a happy occasion）

【賀電】hèdiàn（名）congratulatory telegram; message of congratulation

【賀禮】hèlǐ（名）gift（given on a festive or any other occasion worth celebrating）

貯 zhù（動）store up; lay up; reserve

【貯存】zhùcún（動）store; stockpile

【貯運】zhùyùn（動）store and transport

【貯藏】zhùcáng（動）store up; hoard

貼 tiē Ⅰ（動）❶ glue; stick: 把宣傳畫～在牆上 paste up a poster on the wall ❷ keep close: 緊～欄杆站著 lean close against the railings ❸ subsidize Ⅱ（名）subsidy: 生活補～ living allowance

【貼心】tiēxīn（形）intimate; chummy

【貼近】tiējìn（動）keep or press close to: 耳朵一牆壁就能聽到 can hear it by pressing one's ear to the wall

【貼身】tiēshēn（形）next to the skin: ～小褂（Chinese-style）undershirt

【貼金】tiējīn（動）❶ gild; coat with gold ❷ beautify

【貼現】tiēxiàn（動）〈銀行〉discount (on a promissory note): ～率 discount rate

【貼補】tiēbǔ（動）subsidize; give financial assistance（usu. to one's relative or close friend）

【貼邊】tiēbiān（名）hem（of a garment）

貽 yí（動）❶ give ❷ leave behind

【貽人口實】yí rén kǒu shí〈成〉afford occasion for idle gossip

【貽害】yíhài（動）cause trouble: ～無窮 be a source of endless trouble

【貽笑大方】yí xiào dà fāng〈成〉make oneself a butt for ridicule before experts

【貽誤】yíwù（動）affect adversely: ～後學 mislead future scholars

貴 guì Ⅰ（形）❶ expensive; costly; dear ❷ precious; valuable ❸ of high rank; noble ❹〈敬〉your: ～校 your school Ⅱ（名）(Guì) short for Guizhou (Province)

【貴州】Guìzhōu（名）Guizhou (Province)

【貴重】guìzhòng（形）valuable; precious: ～物品 valuables

【貴族】guìzú（名）noble; aristocrat; the nobility

貴賓 guìbīn（名）guest of honour; distinguished guest

買 mǎi（動）buy; purchase: ～東西 make a purchase

【買方】mǎifāng（名）buyer

【買方市場】mǎifāng shìchǎng（名）buyer's market

【買主】mǎizhǔ（名）buyer; customer

【買好】mǎihǎo（動）play up to sb.

【買空賣空】mǎikōng màikōng（動）buy and sell on margin; speculate

【買通】mǎitōng（動）bribe; buy off: ～看守 bribe the jailer

【買賬】mǎizhàng（動）[oft. used in the negative] acknowledge the superiority of; show respect for: 他老愛發號施令,但他的下級有時不～ He was in the habit of bossing others about, but his subordinates sometimes simply refused to obey.

【買賣】mǎimai（名）business; trade: 做～ go into business / ～成交 make a deal

【買賣人】mǎimairén（名）businessman; merchant

【買辦】mǎibàn（名）comprador

【買關節】mǎi guānjié（動）bribe; grease the palm of

貸 dài（動）❶ borrow; lend: ～款 grant a loan ❷ shirk (responsibility): 責無旁～ be dutybound ❸ pardon: 嚴懲不～ punish severely; punish without mercy

貿 mào Ⅰ（名）trade: 外～ foreign trade Ⅱ（副）rashly

【貿易】màoyì（名）trade: 對外～ foreign trade / 國內～ domestic trade

【貿易中心】màoyì zhōngxīn（名）

trade centre

【貿易伙伴】màoyì huǒbàn （名）
trade partner

【貿易保護主義】màoyì bǎohù zhǔyì
（名）trade protectionism

【貿易差額】màoyì chā'é （名） fa-
vourable balance of trade

【貿易風】màoyìfēng （名）〈氣〉
trade wind

【貿易貨棧】màoyì huòzhàn （名）
trade warehouse

【貿易港】màoyìgǎng （名） trading
port

【貿易額】màoyì'é （名） volume of
trade

【貿然】màorán （副） thoughtlessly;
rashly: ～行事 act rashly

資 zī I（名）❶ money; capital;
fund: ～財 capital and goods /投～
investment ❷ qualifications; record
of service: ～深學者 senior scholar
II（動）provide; supply: 以～參考
for your reference

【資方】zīfāng （名）those representing capital; capital

【資本】zīběn （名）capital: 金融～
financial capital/ ～家 capitalist

【資本主義】zīběn zhǔyì （名）capi-
talism

【資助】zīzhù （名）financial aid; pe-
cuniary aid

【資金】zījīn （名）fund; capital: 預
算外～ non-budgeted funds / 流動
～ floating capital

【資料】zīliào （名）❶ data; information; material ❷ means: 生產～
means of production

【資格】zīgé （名）qualifications; status: 申請人～ qualifications required of an applicant; one's status

as an applicant

【資產】zīchǎn （名）assets; property;
capital

【資產階級】zīchǎn jiējí （名）bour-
geoisie

【資源】zīyuán （名）resources: 經濟
～ economic resources

【資歷】zīlì （名）qualifications and
record of service; one's credentials

買 gǔ I（名）tradesman; merchant
II（動）engage in trade; buy
see also Jiǎ

賈 Jiǎ （名）a surname
see also gǔ

賊 zéi I（名）❶ thief ❷ traitor:
民～ traitor to the people／工～
scab; blackleg II（形）❶ wicked;
furtive: ～心 evil intentions ❷
cunning; crafty

【賊喊捉賊】zéi hǎn zhuō zéi〈成〉a
thief crying "Stop thief!"

【賊頭賊腦】zéi tóu zéi nǎo〈成〉act
furtively

賄 huì （名）bribe: 行～ offer a
bribe

【賄賂】huìlù （名）bribe; bribery

【賄選】huìxuǎn （名）election through
bribery

賃 lìn （動）rent; lease: ～了一輛
車 hire a car

賓 bīn （名）guest; visitor

【賓至如歸】bīn zhì rú guī〈成〉（of a
hotel, etc.）where visitors feel happy and comfortable; a home from
home

【賓客】bīnkè （名）guest; visitor

【賓語】bīnyǔ （名）〈語〉object

【賓館】bīnguǎn（名）guesthouse

賑 zhèn

【賑災】zhènzāi（動）relieve the people in stricken areas

【賑濟】zhènjì（動）relieve; aid: ～難民 give relief to the refugees

賒 shē（動）buy or sell on credit

【賒賬】shēzhàng（動）buy or sell on credit

【賒購】shēgòu（動）buy on credit

賣 mài（動）❶ sell: 書全～光了。All books were sold out. ❷ betray: ～友 betray one's friend ❸ try one's best; make an effort: 他工作很～力氣。He is very energetic in his work. ❹ show; show off

【賣大號】màidàhào（動）(of a retail store) sell retail goods (usu. those in short supply) wholesale to pedlars

【賣方】màifāng（名）seller

【賣方市場】màifāng shìchǎng（名）seller's market

【賣功】màigōng（名）boast of one's merits

【賣好】màihǎo（動）curry favour with

【賣呆】màidāi（動）❶ be dumbfounded ❷ watch the fun

【賣弄】màinòng（動）show off: ～他的技巧 show off his skill

【賣身】màishēn（動）〈舊〉sell oneself or one's wife or child to a rich family: ～契 a contract which states such a deal

【賣身投靠】màishēn tóukào（動）seek the patronage of the rich and powerful by compromising one's honour; sell oneself for support

【賣命】màimìng（動）❶ work for all

one is worth for sb. ❷ risk one's life: 不願爲非正義戰爭～ refuse to serve as cannon fodder in an unjust war

【賣狗皮膏藥】mài gǒu pí gāo yào〈成〉sell quack medicine; fob off fake or shoddy stuff on sb.

【賣俏】màiqiào（動）flirt; behave like a coquette

【賣勁】màijìn（動）stint no effort in doing sth.

【賣座】màizuò（動）draw large audiences: 這部電影很～。This film is a box-office success.

【賣唱】màichàng（動）make a living by singing

【賣淫】màiyín Ⅰ（動）become a prostitute Ⅱ（名）prostitution

【賣國】màiguó（動）betray one's country

【賣國賊】màiguózéi（名）traitor (to one's country)

【賣價】màijià（名）selling price; price

【賣嘴】màizuǐ（動）❶ boast ❷ pay lip service

【賣藝】màiyì（動）make a living by giving performances

【賣關子】mài guānzi（動）keep the listener in suspense

賢 xián Ⅰ（形）able and virtuous; worthy Ⅱ（名）able and virtuous person

【賢良】xiánliáng（形）talented and virtuous

【賢明】xiánmíng（形）capable and far-sighted

【賢妻良母】xián qī liáng mǔ〈成〉a good wife and loving mother

【賢達】xiándá（名）prominent public

figure

【賢惠】xiánhuì (形) (of a woman) virtuous and kind

賞

shǎng Ⅰ (名) reward; award: 論功行 ~ confer rewards on people according to their deserts Ⅱ (動) admire; appreciate: 鑒 ~ appraise and appreciate

【賞心悅目】shǎng xīn yuè mù (成) (of scenery) be pleasant to both the eye and the mind

【賞光】shǎngguāng 〈套〉[used to request acceptance of an invitation]: 務請 ~ request the honour of your presence

【賞金】shǎngjīn (名) money reward

【賞罰】shǎngfá (名) rewards and punishments

【賞賜】shǎngcì (動) bestow a reward

【賞識】shǎngshí (動) appreciate; value

賠

péi (動) compensate for loss; pay for damage

【賠不是】péi búshì (動) apologize

【賠本】péiběn (動) suffer losses in business (transactions)

【賠笑】péixiào (動) smile apologetically; force a smile to please sb.

【賠款】péikuǎn (名) indemnity: 戰爭 ~ war indemnity

【賠罪】péizuì (動) apologize

【賠償】péicháng (動) compensate; pay an indemnity: ~ 損耗 pay for the loss

【賠禮】péilǐ (動) make an apology

賦

fù Ⅰ (動) ❶ bestow; endow ❷ compose (a poem) Ⅱ (名) a form of classical Chinese literature (a mixture of verse and prose)

【賦予】fùyǔ (動) endow; give

【賦性】fùxìng (名) inborn nature

【賦稅】fùshuì (名) taxes; levies

【賦閑】fùxián (形) (of an official, etc.) out of employment; out of office

賬

zhàng (名) ❶ account: 流水 ~ day-to-day account / 結 ~ settle accounts ❷ debt: 欠 ~ be in debt

【賬戶】zhànghù (名) account

【賬目】zhàngmù (名) accounts

【賬單】zhàngdān (名) bill; check

【賬簿】zhàngbù (名) account book

賭

dǔ (動) ❶ gamble ❷ bet

【賭咒】dǔzhòu (動) swear

【賭注】dǔzhù (名) stake

【賭氣】dǔqì (動) act resentfully

【賭博】dǔbó (動) gamble

【賭場】dǔchǎng (名) gambling house (den)

賤

jiàn Ⅰ (形) ❶ cheap; worthless ❷ humble; low; lowly: 貧 ~ poor and humble ❸ mean; base; ignoble Ⅱ (代) 〈謙〉my: ~ 內 my wife

【賤骨頭】jiàngǔtou (名) 〈貶〉wretch

賜

cì (動) give; award

【賜教】cìjiào (動) 〈敬〉give advice: 不吝 ~ 教 feel free to make suggestions

質

zhì Ⅰ (名) ❶ nature; character: 實 ~ essence ❷ matter; substance: 鐵 ~ 的器具 iron implements ❸ quality: 保 ~ 保量 guarantee both quality and quantity ❹ pledge: 人 ~ hostage Ⅱ (動) question

【質子】zhìzǐ (名) proton

【質地】zhìdì（名）quality; texture

【質問】zhìwèn（動）question; interrogate

【質量】zhìliàng（名）❶ quality ❷〈物〉mass

【質感】zhìgǎn（名）feel (of the texture)

【質疑】zhìyí（動）raise doubts

【質樸】zhìpǔ（形）sincere and honest; unaffected: ～無華 (of a style) simple and free from affectation

【質點】zhìdiǎn（名）〈物〉particle

【質變】zhìbiàn（名）qualitative change

賴 lài Ⅰ（動）❶ depend on: 可信～的人 a dependable person ❷ hang on (at a place); refuse to leave ❸ refuse to admit; deny ❹ falsely accuse (sb.): 誣～好人 incriminate innocent people ❺〈口〉blame: 你出岔兒可別～我。Don't lay the blame at my door if you get into trouble. Ⅱ（形）no good: 這主意真不～! What a brilliant idea it is! Ⅲ（名）(Lài) a surname

【賴皮】làipí（形）〈口〉shameless: 別跟我要～。Don't play the fool with me.

【賴債】làizhài（動）repudiate one's debt

【賴賬】làizhàng（動）❶ repudiate a debt ❷ go back on one's word; break one's promise

賽 sài Ⅰ（名）match; competition; contest: 排球～ volleyball match Ⅱ（動）be comparable to; compare favourably with; surpass: 一個～一個 each surpassed by the next

【賽車】sàichē（名）❶ cycle racing; motorcycle race; automobile race ❷ racing bicycle

【賽馬】sàimǎ（名）horse race

【賽船】sàichuán（名）boatrace; regatta

【賽跑】sàipǎo（名）race

【賽過】sàiguò（動）surpass; overtake: 技術上～別人 surpass others in skill

賺 zhuàn（動）make (money)

購 gòu（動）buy; purchase

【購買】gòumǎi（動）buy: ～力 purchasing power

【購置】gòuzhì（動）purchase

【購銷】gòuxiāo（名）purchase and sale

贅 zhuì（形）superfluous; redundant

【贅言】zhuìyán（名）verbosity; superfluous comments

【贅述】zhuìshù（動）make superfluous remarks: 無庸～ no need to go into detail

【贅疣】zhuìyóu（名）❶ wart ❷ superfluity

贋 yàn（形）counterfeit; fake

【贋本】yànběn（名）spurious edition; spurious copy

【贋品】yànpǐn（名）counterfeit; fake

贈 zèng（動）give as a present; present as a gift: ～款 grant

【贈言】zèngyán（名）parting advice

【贈券】zèngquàn（名）complimentary ticket

【贈送】zèngsòng（動）give as a present; present as a gift: 向兒童～圖書 donate books for children

【贈品】zèngpǐn（名）gift; donation; offering; sales aid

【贈閱】zèngyuè（動）(of a book, periodical, etc.) be given free by the publisher

贊 zàn（動）❶ support; assist ❷ praise; commend

【贊比亞】Zànbǐyà（名）Zambia: ～人 Zambian

【贊不絕口】zàn bù jué kǒu〈成〉praise lavishly

【贊成】zànchéng（動）approve of; agree with: 我完全～你的抉擇。I fully agree with the choice you have made.

【贊同】zàntóng（動）approve of; endorse

【贊助】zànzhù（動）support; assist: 這厢展覽會得到當地華僑的～。The exhibition had the help and support of the overseas Chinese there.

【贊美】zànměi（動）praise; admire

【贊美詩】zànměishī（名）〈宗〉hymn

【贊許】zànxǔ（動）approve of; commend

【贊揚】zànyáng（動）praise; speak highly of: 這種一心爲公的精神值得～。This spirit of selflessness deserves commendation. / 熱烈～兩國人民之間的友誼 pay warm tribute to the friendship between the two peoples

【贊頌】zànsòng（動）extol; eulogize

【贊歌】zàngē（名）song of praise

【贊嘆】zàntàn（動）admire; marvel at: 遊客對這裏美麗的景色～不已。The tourists are full of admiration for the beautiful scenery.

【贊賞】zànshǎng（動）appreciate; admire: ～他高貴的品質 admire his nobility of character; admire him for his moral integrity

贏 yíng（動）❶ win: 以 15:5～了這場比賽 win the match with a score of 15-5 ❷ gain (profit)

【贏利】yínglì（名）profit; gain

【贏得】yíngdé（動）win; gain: ～很大榮譽 win great honour / ～羣眾支持 gain popular support

【贏餘】yíngyú（名）surplus; profit: 略有～ with a small favourable balance

贍 shàn（動）support financially; provide for: ～養親屬 provide for one's family dependents

贓 zāng（名）❶ stolen goods; booty; spoils: 分～ share the spoils ❷ bribe: 貪～枉法 take bribes and twist the law

【贓物】zāngwù（名）❶ stolen goods; spoils: 吐～ disgorge stolen goods ❷ bribe

贖 shú（動）❶ redeem; buy back: ～價 ransom price ❷ atone for; expiate: 以～前愆 atone for one's past offence

【贖身】shúshēn（動）(of slaves, prostitutes) redeem (or ransom) oneself; buy back one's freedom

【贖金】shújīn（名）ransom (money)

【贖買】shúmǎi（動）buy out; redeem

【贖罪】shúzuì（動）atone for one's crime: 立功～ perform meritorious services to atone for one's crime

贛 Gàn（名）another name for Jiangxi Province

赤 部

赤 chì (形) ❶ red; crimson ❷ loyal ❸ bare; empty

【赤字】chìzì (名) deficit: 預算～ budgetary deficit

【赤金】chìjīn (名) pure gold

【赤道】chìdào (名) equator

【赤道幾内亞】Chìdào Jǐnèiyà (名) Equatorial Guinea: ～人 Equatorial Guinean

【赤誠】chìchéng (名) absolute sincerity

【赤裸裸】chìluǒluǒ (形) ❶ nude; naked ❷ undisguised: ～的詭詐 naked blackmail

【赤膊】chìbó (形) bare to the waist

赦 shè (動) cancel or refrain from exerting a penalty

【赦免】shèmiǎn (動) pardon; remit a punishment

【赦罪】shèzuì (動) absolve sb. from guilt or sin

赫 hè I (形) conspicuous; magnificent II (名) ❶ hertz: 千～ kilohertz ❷ (Hè) a surname

【赫哲族】Hèzhézú (名) the Hezhen nationality

【赫然】hèrán (副) ❶ to one's surprise ❷ terribly: ～而怒 terribly angry

【赫赫】hèhè (形) outstanding; illustrious: ～有名 distinguished

赭 zhě (形) reddish brown; burnt ochre

【赭石】zhěshí (名)〈礦〉ochre

走 部

走 zǒu (動) ❶ walk; go: 他～在我們前邊。He is walking ahead of us./ 孩子剛會～。The child has just learnt to walk. ❷ move: ～了一個棋子 move a piece; make a move (in a board game)/我的錶又不～了。My watch has stopped again. ❸ leave; depart: 他早就～了。He left long ago. ❹ go and pay a visit to: ～親戚 visit one's relative ❺ leak; let out: ～漏消息 leak out the news ❻ depart from the original: ～色 lose colour; fade

【走火】zǒuhuǒ (動) (of firearms) discharge accidentally

【走失】zǒushī (動) be lost; be missing

【走向】zǒuxiàng (動) head for; move towards

【走私】zǒusī (動) smuggle

【走投無路】zǒu tóu wú lù〈成〉be caught in a dilemma

【走味】zǒuwèi (動) lose flavour

【走卒】zǒuzú (名) pawn; lackey

【走狗】zǒugǒu (名) lackey; flunkey

【走後門】zǒuhòumén (動) get in by the back door; have back-door dealings

【走神兒】zǒushénr (動) be absentminded; be in a trance

【走馬看花】zǒu mǎ kàn huā〈成〉go and admire flowers on horseback; make a superficial observation

【走動】zǒudòng (動) ❶ walk about;

stretch one's legs: 課後出來～～。
Come out to stretch your legs after
class. ❷ visit each other: 這兩家
是鄰居，但不常來。The two fami-
lies are next-door neighbours, but
they seldom visit each other.

【走訪】zǒufǎng（動）have an interview with; pay a visit to

【走着瞧】zǒuzheqiáo（動）wait and
see: 採取～的態度 adopt a wait-
and-see attitude

【走運】zǒuyùn（動）have good luck

【走廊】zǒuláng（名）corridor; passageway

【走過場】zǒuguòchǎng（動）do sth.
perfunctorily; go through the motions

【走路】zǒulù（動）walk; go on foot

【走樣】zǒuyàng（動）lose the original shape; deviate from the original
style

【走調兒】zǒudiàor（動）(of singing,
etc.) be out of tune

【走嘴】zǒuzuǐ（動）make a slip of
the tongue

【走鋼絲】zǒugāngsī（動）❶ tight-
rope walking; wire-walking; rope-
dancing ❷ run a great risk

【走題】zǒutí（動）digress from the
subject; stray from the point

【走獸】zǒushòu（名）beast

【走讀】zǒudú（動）attend a day
school: ～生 nonresident student;
day student

赴 fù（動）❶ attend ❷ devote oneself to: 全力以～ go all out

【赴任】fùrèn（動）be on the way to
one's post

【赴宴】fùyàn（動）attend a banquet

【赴湯蹈火】fù tāng dǎo huǒ〈成〉go
through fire and water

【赴難】fùnàn（動）rush to the aid of
the homeland

趄 jiū

【趄趄】jiūjiū（形）valiant; formidable: ～武夫 valiant warriors

起 qǐ Ⅰ（動）❶ rise; get up ❷ begin; start: 從現在～ starting from
now ❸ grow; come about: ～變化
undergo changes ❹ build; set up:
白手～家 build up from nothing ❺
extract; remove: ～圖釘 pull out a
thumbtack ❻ draft; work out Ⅱ
（量）case; instance: 一～火警 a
case of fire alarm Ⅲ（副）[used after a verb to indicate the upward direction or beginning of an action]:
打～鼓 beat the drum Ⅳ [used after
a verb together with "得" or "不"
to mean "can" or "cannot afford /
stand"]: 瞧不～ look down upon
(sb.) /花得～這筆錢 can afford
the expense

【起子】qǐzi（名）❶ bottle opener ❷
baking powder ❸ screwdriver

【起立】qǐlì（動）stand up; rise to
one's feet

【起用】qǐyòng（動）promote or assign sb. to an important position

【起名】qǐmíng（動）give a name;
name

【起色】qǐsè（名）improvement: 經
濟況有了～ show improvement
in the economic situation

【起先】qǐxiān（副）at first; in the
beginning

【起因】qǐyīn（名）cause; origin

【起伏】qǐfú（動）rise and fall; wave

【起死回生】qǐ sǐ huí shēng〈成〉re-
store the dying to life

【起初】qǐchū（副）at first; in the beginning

【起步】qǐbù（動）start; begin

【起身】qǐshēn（動）❶ get out of bed ❷ start off on a journey

【起牀】qǐchuáng（動）get out of bed; get up

【起泡】qǐpào（動）blister; bubble

【起居】qǐjū（名）daily life

【起來】qǐlái Ⅰ（動）rise; get up Ⅱ（副）❶ [used after a verb] up; upwards: 把手擧～。Put up your hand. ❷ [used to indicate the beginning of an action or process]: 他大聲唸～。He started to read aloud. ❸ [used to indicate successful fulfilment]: 去年實驗室建立～了。The lab was set up last year. ／想不～了 cannot recall ❹ [used after a verb to introduce a pertaining impression or judgment]: 聽～不錯 It sounds nice.

【起哄】qǐhòng（動）❶ stir up trouble ❷ jeer; boo and hoot

【起飛】qǐfēi（動）(of aircraft) take off Ⅱ（名）〈經〉takeoff: 經濟～ economic takeoff

【起勁】qǐjìn（副）vigorously; enthusiastically

【起重車】qǐzhòngchē（名）derrick car

【起重機】qǐzhòngjī（名）hoist; crane

【起草】qǐcǎo（動）draft; draw up: ～委員會 drafting committee

【起動】qǐdòng（動）start; set in motion

【起動機】qǐdòngjī（名）starter

【起筆】qǐbǐ（名）first stroke of a Chinese character

【起程】qǐchéng（動）start off on a journey; set out

【起訴】qǐsù（動）start a lawsuit against; sue

【起運】qǐyùn（動）start shipment

【起源】qǐyuán Ⅰ（名）origin Ⅱ（動）originate; arise from

【起義】qǐyì（名）uprising; insurrection

【起誓】qǐshì（動）take an oath; vow

【起碼】qǐmǎ Ⅰ（形）minimum; elementary: ～的條件 minimum conditions Ⅱ（副）at least: 你～可以試一試嘛! You can at least have a try.

【起頭】qǐtóu Ⅰ（動）start; initiate: 這事由他～的. It was he who started all this. Ⅱ（名）beginning: 這事從～就很順利. It has been a success from the outset. Ⅲ（副）at first; in the beginning

【起縐】qǐzhòu（動）wrinkle; crease

【起點】qǐdiǎn（名）starting point

【起錨】qǐmáo（動）weigh anchor

越 yuè（動）❶ cross over; climb over ❷ overstep; bypass

【越冬】yuèdōng（動）(of plants, insects, etc.) survive the winter

【越位】yuèwèi（名）〈體〉offside

【越軌】yuèguǐ（動）transgress: 這是一種～行爲. This is an act of transgression.

【越南】Yuènán（名）Vietnam: ～人 Vietnamese ／ ～語 Vietnamese (language)

【越俎代庖】yuè zǔ dài páo（成）overstep one's powers to meddle in other's affairs

【越級】yuèjí（動）bypass the immediate superior leadership levels

【越野】yuèyě（形）cross-country:

~賽跑 cross-country race

【越…越…】yuè…yuè… (副) the more…, the more: ~快~好。The quicker, the better. / 天氣~來~暖和。It's getting warmer and warmer.

【越發】yuèfā (副) all the more; even more: 過了中秋,天氣~涼快了。The weather became still cooler after mid-autumn.

【越過】yuèguò (動) cross over; surmount: ~一片大草原 cross over an expanse of grasslands/ ~重重障礙 surmount numerous obstacles

【越境】yuèjìng (動) cross the border illegally

【越獄】yuèyù (動) escape from prison

【越劇】yuèjù (名) Shaoxing opera

【越權】yuèquán (動) overstep one's authority

超 chāo I (動) ❶ exceed; overtake ❷ go beyond II (形) [used as a prefix] super-; ultra-; extra-

【超人】chāorén I (名) superman II (形) superhuman: ~的毅力 superhuman stamina

【超支】chāozhī (動) overspend; overdraw

【超出】chāochū (動) exceed; transcend; overstep: ~人的忍耐程度 exceed human endurance; be beyond endurance

【超車】chāochē (動) overtake another vehicle: 不準~。No overtaking. (traffic sign)

【超重】chāozhòng (名) overload; overweight: 這輛車~了。The car is overloaded.

【超音速】chāoyīnsù I (名) super-sonic speed II (形) trans-sonic; supersonic

【超速】chāosù (動) exceed the speed limit

【超級】chāojí (形) super-: ~市場 supermarket / ~明星 superstar / ~大國 superpower

【超產】chāochǎn (動) overfulfil the output quota: ~部分 the above-quota part

【超脫】chāotuō I (動) stand aloof; detach oneself: ~現實 detach oneself from reality II (形) unconventional

【超假】chāojià (動) overstay one's leave

【超然】chāorán (形) detached; aloof: 採取~的態度 keep aloof

【超過】chāoguò (動) surpass; outstrip

【超越】chāoyuè (動) transcend; surmount: ~障礙 surmount an obstacle

【超短裙】chāoduǎnqún (名) miniskirt

【超載】chāozài (名) 〈交〉overload

【超導】chāodǎo (名) 〈物〉superconduction

【超聲波】chāoshēngbō (名) supersonic wave

【超額】chāo'é (動) exceed a quota: ~完成任務 overfulfil one's work quota

趁 chèn I (動) avail oneself of II (副) while

【趁早】chènzǎo (副) promptly; before it is too late: ~下決心。Make your decision while there is still time (before it is too late).

【趁便】chènbiàn (動) at the opportune moment

【趁熱打鐵】chèn rè dǎ tiě〈成〉
strike while the iron is hot

【趁機】chènjī〈動〉take the opportunity

趂 liè

【趂趄】lièqie〈動〉stagger: 他打了
個～，摔倒了。He stumbled and
fell.

趙 Zhào〈名〉a surname

趕 gǎn

Ⅰ〈動〉❶ catch up with: ～
上班上同學 catch up with the rest
of the class ❷ rush for: ～火車 try
to catch the train / ～任務 hurry
through one's work to meet a deadline ❸ drive: ～驢 drive a donkey
❹ happen to: 正～上下雨。It happened to be raining. Ⅱ〈介〉until:
～明兒再說。Put it off until tomorrow.

【趕巧】gǎnqiǎo〈副〉by chance

【趕忙】gǎnmáng〈動〉hasten; hurry: ～告訴他 tell him without delay

【趕快】gǎnkuài〈副〉quickly; at
once: ～回去 hurry back

【趕時髦】gǎnshímáo〈動〉follow the
fashion

【趕集】gǎnjí〈動〉go to a village fair

【趕路】gǎnlù〈動〉hurry on one's
way

【趕緊】gǎnjǐn〈動〉make haste; hurry up

趣 qù

Ⅰ〈名〉❶ interest; delight ❷
aspiration; bent: 志～ aspiration;
inclination Ⅱ〈形〉interesting: ～聞
interesting news

【趣味】qùwèi〈名〉❶ interest; delight ❷ taste; liking: ～高雅的人

people of taste

趟 tàng〈量〉(of trips): 每星期回
一～家 go back home once a week

趨 qū

〈動〉❶ tend to; lean
towards: 意見～於一致 gradually
come to a consensus of opinion ❷
hasten; hurry

【趨向】qūxiàng Ⅰ〈動〉tend to; incline to: 形勢～緊張。The situation
is becoming tense. Ⅱ〈名〉trend;
tendency

【趨奉】qūfèng〈動〉toady to; fawn
on

【趨炎附勢】qū yán fù shì〈成〉play
the sycophant to the powerful

【趨勢】qūshì〈名〉trend; tendency

足　部

足 zú

Ⅰ〈名〉foot Ⅱ〈形〉enough;
full; plenty: 勁頭十～ be full of
drive / 雨水充～ have plenty of
rainfall

【足以】zúyǐ〈形〉enough or sufficient to (do sth.): 這些事實～說
明他可貴的品質。These facts are
enough to prove his sterling
qualities.

【足迹】zújī〈名〉footprint; footmark

【足夠】zúgòu〈形〉enough; sufficient: 有～的時間總結經驗 have
sufficint time to sum up one's experience

【足球】zúqiú〈名〉football; soccer

【足智多謀】zú zhì duō móu〈成〉be
able and resourceful

趴 pā〈動〉❶ lie prone: ～在地上

lie prone on the floor ❷ bend over: ～在窗臺上 lean over the windowsill

趾 zhǐ (名) toe

【趾甲】zhǐjiǎ (名) toenail

【趾高氣揚】zhǐ gāo qì yáng (成) be bloated with pride; give oneself airs and swagger about

距 jù I (名) distance; spacing: 南北之間的差～ the gap between the North and the South II (動) be away from: 相～甚遠 be poles apart

【距離】jùlí I (名) distance; spacing: 從這裏到廣播電臺還有一定～。 The broadcasting station is some distance from here. II (動) be apart from; be away from: ～市中心不遠 not far from the city centre

跋 bá I (動) trudge over mountains II (名) postscript

【跋涉】báshè (動) trudge; trek: 跋山涉水 make a long and arduous journey across mountains and rivers

【跋扈】báhù (形) bossy; domineering; recalcitrant: 飛揚～ arrogant and domineering

跛 bǒ (形) lame; crippled

【跛子】bǒzi (名) cripple; lame person

【跛腳】bǒjiǎo (形) crippled

跌 diē (動) ❶ fall: 從自行車上～下來 fall off a bicycle ❷ drop

【跌倒】diēdǎo (動) trip and fall

【跌撞撞】diē diē zhuàng zhuàng (動) stumble along

【跌跤】diējiāo (動) ❶ stumble and fall ❷ suffer a setback

【跌落】diēluò (動) fall; drop

【跌價】diējià (動) fall in price

跑 pǎo I (動) ❶ run: 賽～ race ❷ escape; flee: 別讓他～掉。Do not let him get way with it. ❸ leak: ～水了。It's leaking water. ❹ run about doing sth.; run errands: ～買賣 be a travelling salesman II (副) away; off

【跑步】pǎobù (動) run; jog

【跑車】pǎochē (名) racing bike

【跑堂的】pǎotángde (名) waiter (in a restaurant)

【跑道】pǎodào (名) ❶ 〈航空〉 runway ❷ 〈體〉track

【跑腿兒】pǎotuǐr (動) run errands; do odd jobs

【跑鞋】pǎoxié (名) running (track) shoe; spike

【跑錶】pǎobiǎo (名) stopwatch

【跑龍套】pǎo lóngtào (動) play an insignificant role

跨 kuà (動) ❶ take a (big) step forward or sideways ❷ straddle; stand or sit astride: 河上～着一座鐵索橋。A chain bridge spans the river. ❸ cut across the bounds of: ～年度 go beyond the year

【跨國公司】kuàguó gōngsī (名) transnational corporation

【跨越】kuàyuè (動) ❶ go beyond the limits of space or time ❷ surmount

【跨綫橋】kuàxiànqiáo (名) flyover; overpass

【跨欄賽跑】kuàlán sàipǎo (名)〈體〉hurdle race

跟 gēn I (名) heel II (動) follow III (連) and: 我～我的妻子 my wife and I IV (介) to; towards: ～他講

明白 make it clear to him

【跟前】gēnqián（副）nearby; in front of

【跟踪】gēnzōng（動）trail; shadow

【跟隨】gēnsuí（動）follow; accompany

【跟頭】gēntou（名）❶ fall: 摔～ have a fall ❷ somersault

路 lù（名）❶ road; way: 問～ ask the way ❷ journey; distance: 三公里～ (a distance of) three kilometres / ～還很遠 have yet a long way to go ❸ way; means: 活～ way out ❹ route; line: 五一無軌電車 No. 5 trolleybus ❺ sort; kind: 那一～人 that sort of people / ～貨色 trash of the same sort; birds of the same feather ❻（Lù）a surname

【路人】lùrén（名）passerby; the man in the street: ～皆知 known to everybody

【路上】lùshang（副）❶ on the road: ～車很多。There is much traffic on the road. ❷ on the way; on one's journey: ～多加小心。Take good care of yourself on the journey.

【路子】lùzi（名）means; method: ～對 the right approach

【路口】lùkǒu（名）crossing; intersection: 十字～ at the crossroads

【路不拾遺】lù bù shí yí〈成〉no one pockets anything left on the road; good morals prevail in society

【路劫】lùjié（名）mugging; highway robbery

【路面】lùmiàn（名）road surface

【路徑】lùjìng（名）❶ route; way ❷ means; method: 成功的～ way to success

【路途】lùtú（名）❶ road ❷ journey

【路基】lùjī（名）roadbed

【路程】lùchéng（名）journey; distance

【路費】lùfèi（名）travel expenses

【路過】lùguò（動）pass by; pass through: ～商店 pass by a shop / 我回家途中～南京。I passed through Nanjing on my way home.

【路綫】lùxiàn（名）❶ route; itinerary: 安排旅遊～ fix one's itinerary ❷ line of policy

【路障】lùzhàng（名）roadblock; barricade

【路標】lùbiāo（名）road sign

【路燈】lùdēng（名）street light

踩 duò（動）stamp: ～腳 stamp (one's foot)

跪 guì（動）kneel; go down on one's knees

跳 tiào（動）❶ jump; skip ❷ beat; move up and down ❸ drop; skip over

【跳水】tiàoshuǐ（名）〈體〉diving

【跳皮筋】tiào píjīn（跳猴皮筋兒 tiào hóupíjīnr）（動）skip and dance over a chain of rubber bands

【跳板】tiàobǎn（名）❶ gangplank ❷ springboard

【跳蚤】tiàozao（名）flea: ～市場 flea market

【跳高】tiàogāo（名）〈體〉high jump

【跳馬】tiàomǎ（名）❶ vaulting horse ❷ horse-vaulting

【跳動】tiàodòng（動）beat; move up and down

【跳棋】tiàoqí（名）❶ Chinese checkers ❷ halma

【跳傘】tiàosǎn Ⅰ（動）parachute Ⅱ（名）〈體〉parachute jumping

【跳遠】tiàoyuǎn（名）〈體〉long jump; broad jump

【跳舞】tiàowǔ（動）dance

【跳槽】tiàocáo（動）give up one job in favour of another

【跳繩】tiàoshéng（名）rope skipping

【跳躍】tiàoyuè（動）jump; leap

跟 liàng

【踉蹌】liàngqiàng（動）stagger

踪 zōng（名）footprint; trace: 失～ disappear; be missing

【踪迹】zōngjì（名）trace; track

【踪影】zōngyǐng（名）trace; sign

跕 diǎn（動）tiptoe

蹺 quán（動）curl up; huddle up

【蹺伏】quánfú（動）huddle up

【蹺曲】quánqū（動）curl; coil

踐 jiàn（動）❶ trample ❷ carry out; practise

【踐約】jiànyuē（動）fulfil an appointment; keep a promise

【踐踏】jiàntà（動）trample on: 請勿～草地。Keep off the grass.

踞 jù（動）❶ crouch; squat ❷〈貶〉illegally or forcibly occupy: 盤～在邊區的匪徒 bandits entrenched in the border regions

蹓 tāng（動）❶ ford; wade: ～水過河 wade across（a river）❷ hoe: ～地 hoe

踝 huái（名）ankle

踢 tī（動）❶ kick ❷〈足球〉play: ～後衛 play fullback

【踢皮球】tī píqiú（動）❶ kick a rubber ball ❷ pass the buck

【踢踏舞】tītàwǔ（名）tap dance

踏 tā

see also tà

【踏實】tāshi（形）❶（of one's attitude towards work or study）down-to-earth; dependable: 他學習～。He is serious-minded and methodical in his studies. ❷ at ease; assured; confident

踏 tà（動）❶ tread; walk on: 請勿～草地。Keep off the lawn. ❷ go to the spot（for a survey）: ～勘 survey; make an on-the-spot survey

see also tā

【踏步】tàbù（動）〈軍〉〈體〉mark time

【踏青】tàqīng（動）go on an outing to the countryside in spring

踩 cǎi（動）tread; trample: ～油門 step on the gas

【踩水】cǎishuǐ（動）〈體〉tread water

踟 chí

【踟躕】chíchú（動）hesitate: ～不前 hesitate to go forward

踒 wō（動）sprain（one's ankle or wrist）; strain: ～了腳脖子 sprain one's ankle

蹄 tí（名）hoof

躇 duó（動）walk slowly: ～來～去 walk to and fro

蹉 cuō

【蹉跌】cuōdiē（動）❶ trip and fall ❷ commit a serious error

【蹉跎】cuōtuó（動）waste time: ～歲月 idle away one's time

蹂 róu
【蹂躪】róulìn (動) tread on; ravage:
～百姓 tread the people underfoot;
ride roughshod over the people

踊 yǒng (動) leap; jump
【踊躍】yǒngyuè Ⅰ (動) leap; jump Ⅱ
(形) eager; enthusiastic: 發言～
rise to speak one after another

踹 chuài (動) ❶ kick: 用腳一～
give a kick at sth. ❷ tread; stamp
【踹踏】chuàità (動) trample; tread

踵 zhǒng (名) heel: 接～而至
tread on the heels of

蹇 jiǎn (形) not smooth-going: ～
滯 unlucky and unhappy

蹈 dǎo (動) ❶ stamp; tread: 赴湯
～火 go through water and fire; risk
one's life ❷ skip: 手舞足～ dance
with joy
【蹈襲】dǎoxí (動) follow suit

蹊 qī
see also xī
【蹊蹺】qīqiāo (形) odd; fishy; dubious

蹊 xī (名) path; footpath
see also qī
【蹊徑】xījìng (名) path; method;
way

蹒 pán
【蹒跚】pánshān (動) hobble; stagger

蹦 bèng (動) jump; spring; hop:
歡～亂跳 dance with joy
【蹦躂】bèngda (動) hop: ～不了幾
天 won't last long; will soon die

【蹦蹦跳跳】bèngbèng tiàotiào (動)
frolic; frisk about

蹩 bié (動) 〈方〉 sprain (one's ankle or wrist)
【蹩腳】biéjiǎo (形) shoddy; poor;
inferior: ～貨 inferior stuff

蹴 cù (動) ❶ kick ❷ tread: 一～
而就 accomplish at one stroke

蹲 dūn (動) ❶ squat ❷ stay

蹭 cèng (動) ❶ scrape; rub: ～破
了手指頭 scrape one's finger ❷
dilly-dally; loiter: 磨磨～～ dawdle

蹺 qiāo Ⅰ (動) ❶ lift up (a leg);
raise (a finger): ～着大拇指叫好
raise one's thumb and shout 'bravo'
❷ be on tiptoe Ⅱ (形) lame
【蹺蹺板】qiāoqiāobǎn (名) seesaw

蹶 jué (名) fall; setback: 從此一～
不振 have never recovered from the
mishap ever since
see also juě

蹶 juě
see also jué
【蹶子】juězi (名) (of horses, don-
keys, etc.) kick of the hind legs:
尥～ kick with the hind legs

蹼 pǔ (名) web (of the feet of
ducks, frogs, etc.)
【蹼足】pǔzú (名) webfoot
【蹼趾】pǔzhǐ (名) webbed toe

躁 zào (形) rash; impetuous: 煩～
irritable; fretful
【躁動】zàodòng (動) be restless

躊 chóu
【躊躇】chóuchú Ⅰ (動) hesitate; wa-

ver: ~不决 hesitating; irresolute Ⅱ (形) complacent; smug: ~满志 be enormously proud of one's success

躍 yuè〈動〉leap; jump: 不勝雀~ cannot but jump with joy

【躍進】yuèjìn〈動〉make progress by leaps and bounds; leap forward

【躍躍欲試】yuè yuè yù shì〈成〉be very eager for a try

竄 cuàn〈動〉jump up

躡

躡

【躡手躡脚】niè shǒu niè jiǎo〈成〉walk quietly; tiptoe

身 部

身 shēn Ⅰ（名）❶ body ❷ main part of a structure; body: 打字機的機~ the body of a typewriter ❸ life: 喪~ lose one's life ❹ oneself: ~不由主 unable to act of one's own will ❺ one's moral character or conduct ❻ pregnancy: 有了~子 be pregnant Ⅱ（量）(of clothing) suit: 做一~西服 have a suit of Western clothes

【身上】shēnshàng（副）❶ on one's body; physically: ~穿着皮大衣 wear a fur coat ❷ (have sth.) on one; with one: ~錢不多 haven't got much money on one

【身子】shēnzi（名）❶ body ❷ pregnancy

【身心】shēnxīn（名）body and mind: ~受到摧殘 be injured both physically and mentally

【身手】shēnshǒu（名）skill: 大顯~ show great skill

【身分】shēnfèn（名）❶ position; capacity: 他以大會主席~，宣布大會休會。In his capacity as chairman, he declared the meeting adjourned. ❷ dignity: 你這樣做有失~。It was beneath your dignity to act like this.

【身分證】shēnfènzhèng（名）identity card; ID card

【身世】shēnshì（名）one's life story; one's life experience

【身孕】shēnyùn（名）pregnancy

【身材】shēncái（身個 shēngè）（名）stature; figure

【身長】shēncháng（名）❶ height (of a person) ❷ length of a garment from shoulder to hemline)

【身段】shēnduàn（名）❶ (woman's) figure ❷ (dancer's) posture

【身高】shēngāo（名）height (of a person)

【身教】shēnjiào（動）teach by one's own example: ~重於言教。Example is better than precept.

【身敗名裂】shēn bài míng liè〈成〉bring discredit and ruin upon oneself

【身强力壯】shēn qiáng lì zhuàng〈成〉(of a person) strong and robust

【身經百戰】shēn jīng bǎi zhàn〈成〉have been tested in a hundred battles; be a seasoned fighter

【身價】shēnjià（名）one's social status: ~百倍 receive a tremendous boost in one's social status

【身臨其境】shēn lín qí jìng〈成〉be on the scene

【身邊】shēnbiān（副）❶ by one's side: 坐在他的~ sit by his side ❷ (have sth.) on one; with one: 他~總有一些零錢。He always has some loose change with him.

【身軀】shēnqū（名）body; build

【身體】shēntǐ（名）❶ body ❷ health: 保重～ take good care of oneself

【身體力行】shēn tǐ lì xíng〈成〉practise what one preaches

躬 gōng Ⅰ（副）personally Ⅱ（動）bow

躲 duǒ（動）hide; dodge

【躲躲閃閃】duǒduǒ shǎnshǎn（動）be evasive; speak equivocally

【躲避】duǒbì（動）avoid

【躲藏】duǒcáng（動）hide oneself; conceal

躺 tǎng（動）lie; recline: ～倒不幹 pretend to be ill and refuse to work

【躺椅】tǎngyǐ（名）deck chair

軀 qū（名）human body

【軀殼】qūqiào（名）body; outer form

【軀幹】qūgàn（名）〈生理〉trunk; torso

【軀體】qūtǐ（名）body

車 部

車 chē Ⅰ（名）❶ vehicle: 小汽～ car ❷ rotating machine: 風～ windmill ❸ machine: 開（停）～ start (stop) the machine ❹（Chē）a surname Ⅱ（動）❶ lathe; turn: ～光 smooth sth. on a lathe ❷ lift water by waterwheel
see also jú

【車水馬龍】chē shuǐ mǎ lóng〈成〉continuous stream of vehicles; a long line of passing traffic

【車次】chēcì（名）train (coach) number

【車把式】chēbǎshì（名）carter

【車牀】chēchuáng（名）lathe

【車庫】chēkù（名）garage

【車站】chēzhàn（名）❶ railway station ❷ bus stop

【車票】chēpiào（名）train (bus) ticket

【車廂】chēxiāng（名）railway carriage

【車費】chēfèi（名）fare

【車間】chējiān（名）workshop

【車軲轆】chēgūlu（名）〈口〉wheel (of a vehicle)

【車禍】chēhuò（名）traffic accident

【車輛】chēliàng（名）vehicle

【車輪】chēlún（名）wheel (of a vehicle)

車 jú（名）❶（in Chinese chess）chariot: 捨～馬保將帥 give up a chariot to save the marshal; make minor sacrifices to safeguard major interests ❷（in chess）castle; rook
see also chē

軋 yà（動）roll; run over
see also zhá

【軋花】yàhuā（動）gin cotton

【軋傷】yàshāng（動）run over and injure

軋 zhá（動）roll (steel)
see also yà

【軋鋼】zhágāng（名）steel rolling

【軋鋼廠】zhágāngchǎng（名）steel rolling mill

【軍】jūn（名）❶ armed forces: 海～ the navy／陸～ the army／空～ the air force ❷ army（usu. consisting of two or three divisions）

【軍人】jūnrén（名）serviceman; soldier

【軍工】jūngōng（名）（short for 軍事工業 jūnshì gōngyè）war industry

【軍心】jūnxīn（名）troop morale; morale

【軍火】jūnhuǒ（名）munitions; ordnance; ammunition

【軍令】jūnlìng（名）military order: ～如山倒。Military orders admit of no delay. ／～狀 a pledge to carry out a military order; a pledge to fulfil an assignment

【軍民】jūnmín（名）the military and the civilians

【軍用】jūnyòng（形）military; for military use: ～品 military supplies

【軍法】jūnfǎ（名）military law: ～審判 court-martial

【軍事】jūnshì（形）military: ～科學 military science／～機關 military establishment

【軍官】jūnguān（名）officer: 陸軍～ army officer

【軍紀】jūnjì（名）military discipline

【軍師】jūnshī（名）❶〈舊〉military strategist ❷ mentor; mastermind

【軍區】jūnqū（名）military area command

【軍國主義】jūnguó zhǔyì（名）militarism

【軍備】jūnbèi（名）armaments: 裁減～ disarmament

【軍隊】jūnduì（名）armed forces; troops

【軍費】jūnfèi（名）military expenditure; military spending

【軍援】jūnyuán（名）military assistance

【軍裝】jūnzhuāng（軍服 jūnfú）（名）military uniform

【軍種】jūnzhǒng（名）（armed）services

【軍閥】jūnfá（名）warlord

【軍管】jūnguǎn Ⅰ（名）（short for 軍事管制 jūnshì guǎnzhì）military control Ⅱ（動）put under military control

【軍銜】jūnxián（名）military rank

【軍樂】jūnyuè（名）martial music: ～隊 military band

【軍醫】jūnyī（名）army surgeon; medical officer

【軍艦】jūnjiàn（名）warship; naval vessel; war vessel

【軍屬】jūnshǔ（名）soldier's dependants; serviceman's family

【軍體】jūntǐ（名）military sports

【軌】guǐ（名）❶ rail; track: 無～電車 trolley-bus ❷ order; path; rule: 走上正～ be just on the right path

【軌道】guǐdào（名）❶ track ❷ orbit: 地球～ the orbit of the earth ❸ course; path

【軌範】guǐfàn（名）criterion of human conduct

【軒】xuān

【軒昂】xuān'áng（形）impressive-looking

【軒然巨波】xuān rán jù bō〈成〉uproar; disturbance; storm: 在基層引起～ cause an uproar at the grass roots level

【輗】è（名）yoke

【軟】ruǎn（形）❶ soft; flexible: ～語

【軟軟】soft-spoken words ❷ weak; feeble: ～骨頭 weak-kneed person ❸ easily moved or influenced: 耳朵～ be easily swayed by a different opinion

【軟化】ruǎnhuà（動）soften

【軟水】ruǎnshuǐ（名）soft water

【軟木】ruǎnmù（名）cork: ～畫 cork patchwork

【軟片】ruǎnpiàn（名）(a roll of) film

【軟件】ruǎnjiàn（名）〈計算機〉software

【軟和】ruǎnhuo（形）〈口〉soft: 這條被很～。The quilt is very soft.

【軟臥】ruǎnwò（名）soft berth (in a sleeper)

【軟食】ruǎnshí（名）soft food; soft diet

【軟席】ruǎnxí（名）soft seat or berth

【軟弱】ruǎnruò（形）weak; feeble: 病後感到～無力 feel very weak after illness / 生性～ be weak by nature

【軟骨】ruǎngǔ（名）〈生理〉cartilage

【軟硬兼施】ruǎn yìng jiān shī〈成〉adopt boh coercive and conciliatory measures

【軟腭】ruǎn'è（名）〈生理〉soft palate

【軟禁】ruǎnjìn（動）put sb. under house arrest

【軟場塌】ruǎntātā（形）❶ weak; feeble ❷ meek; docile

【軟膏】ruǎngāo（名）paste; ointment

【軟緞】ruǎnduàn（名）soft satin

【軟體動物】ruǎntǐ dòngwù（名）mollusc

【軟癱】ruǎntān（動）collapse from physical exhaustion

軲 gū

【軲轆】gūlu（名）〈口〉wheel

軸 zhóu I（名）❶ axis; axle: ～座 axle seat ❷ scroll; reel: 把綫繞在～上 wind thread on a reel /畫～ roller for a scroll of Chinese painting II（量）：一～綫 a reel of thread

【軸心】zhóuxīn（名）axis; axle centre

【軸承】zhóuchéng（名）〈機〉bearing

【軸綫】zhóuxiàn（名）❶〈機〉axis ❷ reel (spool) thread

軼 yì

【軼事】yìshì（名）anecdote

載 zǎi I（名）year: 三年五～ in a few years II（動）record; write down: 轉～ reprint /～入人類史冊 go down in the annals of human history

see also zài

載 zài（動）carry; be loaded with: 滿～木材的列車 a train fully loaded with timber

see also zǎi

【載波】zàibō（名）carrier wave; carrier

【載重】zàizhòng（名）load; carrying capacity

【載荷】zàihè（名）load

【載貨】zàihuò（動）carry cargo

【載運】zàiyùn（動）transport; carry

【載歌載舞】zài gē zài wǔ〈成〉singing and dancing in jubilation

【載體】zàitǐ（名）〈化〉carrier

較 jiào I（介）than; as compared with: ～前困難 more difficult than before II（副）relatively; comparatively: ～有説服力 relatively convincing; fairly persuasive

【較比】jiàobǐ（副）〈方〉comparatively; quite

【較量】jiàoliàng（動）have a trial of strength (with); contest (with)

輔 fǔ（動）compliment; aid: 相～而行 work in cooperation

【輔助】fǔzhù Ⅰ（動）assist Ⅱ（形）auxiliary; supplementary

【輔音】fǔyīn（名）〈語〉consonant

【輔導】fǔdǎo（動）coach; give tutorials to

輒 zhé（副）always; often: 動～發怒 get angry easily; be irascible

輕 qīng Ⅰ（形）❶ light in weight: 這箱子很～。The suitcase is quite light. ❷ small in number, degree, etc.: ～傷 minor injury/他的工作很～。His workload is light. Ⅱ（副）❶ softly; gently: ～～地拍了他肩膀一下 pat him gently on the shoulder ❷ thoughtlessly; rashly: ～舉妄動 act thoughtlessly Ⅲ（動）slight; belittle: 決不能～敵。One can never underestimate one's adversary.

【輕工業】qīnggōngyè（名）light industry

【輕手輕腳】qīng shǒu qīng jiǎo（副）quietly

【輕巧】qīngqiǎo（形）❶ light and ingenious: 一架～的照相機 a handy camera ❷ agile; dexterous ❸ easy; simple: 世界上沒有什麼事像你想的那樣～。Nothing on earth is as simple as you imagine.

【輕生】qīngshēng（動）commit suicide

【輕而易舉】qīng ér yì jǔ〈成〉easy to accomplish

【輕快】qīngkuài（形）❶ springy; brisk ❷ cheerful; happy and gay

【輕車熟路】qīng chē shú lù〈成〉a case of an experienced man doing an easy and familiar job

【輕佻】qīngtiāo（形）flirtatious; coquettish

【輕易】qīngyì（副）❶ easily and by simple means: 市場上～買不到 not easily available in the market ❷ rashly; on the spur of moment: 不要～作出判斷。Don't make any hasty judgment.

【輕放】qīngfàng（動）put down gently: 小心～。Handle with care.

【輕於鴻毛】qīng yú hóng máo〈成〉as light as a feather; insignificant

【輕便】qīngbiàn（形）light; portable

【輕活】qīnghuó（名）light work; easy job

【輕柔】qīngróu（形）soft; gentle

【輕信】qīngxìn（動）be credulous: 不要～謠言。Give no credence to rumours.

【輕型】qīngxíng（形）light; light-duty

【輕盈】qīngyíng（形）lithe; limber

【輕重】qīngzhòng（名）❶ weight ❷ extent of seriousness; relative importance: 我們說的話無足～。What we say carries little weight. ❸ (of speech or action) propriety: 做事有～ act with propriety

【輕重倒置】qīng zhòng dào zhì〈成〉put the unimportant before the important

【輕音樂】qīngyīnyuè（名）light music

【輕浮】qīngfú（形）frivolous; flighty

【輕紗】qīngshā（名）fine gauze

【輕率】qīngshuài（形）(of speech or

action) rash; casual

【輕視】qīngshì〔動〕despise; slight

【輕量級】qīngliàngjí〔名〕〔體〕light-weight

【輕描淡寫】qīng miáo dàn xiě〈成〉mention sth. casually, leaving out of account what is essential

【輕裝】qīngzhuāng〔副〕with a light pack: ～就道 travel light

【輕微】qīngwēi〔形〕slight; light

【輕賤】qīngjiàn〔形〕mean; base

【輕蔑】qīngmiè〔形〕contemptuous; disdainful: 以非常～的目光盯着他 look at him with infinite scorn

【輕機槍】qīngjīqiāng〔名〕light machine gun

【輕薄】qīngbó〔形〕frivolous; flirtatious

【輕聲】qīngshēng Ⅰ〔副〕in a soft voice Ⅱ〔名〕〈語〉(in Chinese pronunciation) light tone, unstressed syllable pronounced without its original pitch

【輕鬆】qīngsōng〔形〕relaxed; light

【輕飄飄】qīngpiāopiāo〔形〕❶ drifting slowly ❷ buoyant ❸ light-hearted

輛 liàng〔量〕[of vehicles]: 兩～電車 two trolley-buses

輟 chuò〔動〕stop; suspend

【輟學】chuòxué〔動〕drop out of school; discontinue one's studies

輪 lún Ⅰ〔名〕❶ wheel ❷ steamboat: 貨～ freighter Ⅱ〔動〕take turns: ～着開車 take turns driving Ⅲ〔量〕❶ (of the sun or moon): 一～紅日 a red sun ❷ round: 第一～網球賽 the first round of tennis tournament

【輪子】lúnzi〔名〕wheel

【輪休】lúnxiū〔名〕stagger holidays; take holidays by turns

【輪胎】lúntāi〔名〕tyre

【輪流】lúnliú〔動〕take turns: ～看護病人 take turns to attend to the patient

【輪班】lúnbān〔副〕in turn; in shifts: ～工作 work in shifts

【輪船】lúnchuán〔名〕steamship

【輪渡】lúndù〔名〕(steam) ferry

【輪番】lúnfān Ⅰ〔動〕take turns Ⅱ〔副〕by turns

【輪換】lúnhuàn〔動〕rotate; do sth. by turns

【輪椅】lúnyǐ〔名〕wheelchair

【輪廓】lúnkuò〔名〕❶ contour; outline ❷ general picture: 對局勢有了個～ have a general picture of the situation

輝 huī

【輝映】huīyìng〔動〕shine; reflect

【輝煌】huīhuáng〔形〕magnificent; brilliant; splendid

輩 bèi〔名〕❶ generation: 同～人 person of the same generation ❷ (said of people) kind; group; like: 我～ we; people like us ❸ lifetime: 受了半～子的苦 suffered (hardships) for half of one's lifetime

【輩子】bèizi〔名〕lifetime: 一～ one's whole life; all one's life

【輩分】bèifen〔名〕(order of) seniority (in family descent): 論～ by seniority in the family line; according to the family tree

【輩出】bèichū〔動〕emerge in large numbers

輻 fú〔名〕spoke

【輻射】fúshè〈物〉Ⅰ(動) radiate Ⅱ (名) radiation

輯 jí Ⅰ(動) compile; edit Ⅱ(名) part; volume; book: 特～ special issue (of a periodical, etc.)

【輯要】jíyào(名) abstract; brief; synopsis

【輯錄】jílù Ⅰ(動) compile Ⅱ(名) compendium

輸 shū(動)❶ transport; transmit: ～油管 petroleum pipeline ❷ be beaten; lose: ～錢 lose money in gambling; ～了第一局 lose the first game

【輸入】shūrù Ⅰ(動) import Ⅱ(名) ❶ import ❷〈電〉input

【輸出】shūchū Ⅰ(動) export Ⅱ(名) ❶ export ❷〈電〉output

【輸血】shūxuè Ⅰ(名) blood transfusion Ⅱ(動) ❶ transfuse blood ❷ bolster; shore up

【輸送】shūsòng(動) convey; transport; send

【輸氧】shūyǎng(名)〈醫〉oxygen therapy

【輸理】shūlǐ(動) be in the wrong; be defeated in argument

【輸液】shūyè(動)〈醫〉put on a drip

【輸電】shūdiàn(動) transmit electricity: 高壓～ hightension power transmission

轄 xiá Ⅰ(名) linchpin Ⅱ(動) govern; administrate: 直～市 municipality directly under the Central Government

【轄制】xiázhì(動) control; rule

【轄區】xiáqū(名) area under one's jurisdiction

轅 yuán(名) shafts of a cart or carriage

輾 zhǎn

【輾轉】zhǎnzhuǎn(動) ❶ toss and turn (in bed) ❷ pass through many hands or places

輿 yú(形) public; popular

【輿情】yúqíng(名) public sentiment; popular feelings

【輿論】yúlùn(名) public opinion: ～工具 mass media

轆 lù

【轆轆】lùlù(象) rumble: 大車發出 笨重的～聲 the heavy, rumbling noise of a moving cart

【轆轤】lùlu(名) windlass; winch

轉 zhuǎn(動) ❶ turn; change: 向 右～ turn right ❷ transfer; pass on: 那封信已經～給他了。The letter has been forwarded to him./ ～到另外一個系 transfer to another department
see also zhuàn

【轉入】zhuǎnrù(動) switch to: ～反 攻 switch over to the counteroffensive

【轉口】zhuǎnkǒu(名) transit: ～貿 易 transit trade

【轉化】zhuǎnhuà(動) change; turn: 禍可以～爲福。A misfortune may turn into a blessing.

【轉手】zhuǎnshǒu(動) ❶ pass sth. on to another ❷ sell the goods obtained from one side to another; resell

【轉引】zhuǎnyǐn(動) quote from a secondary source

【轉交】zhuǎnjiāo(動) pass on; forward

【轉向】zhuǎnxiàng (動) change the direction or orientation

【轉危爲安】zhuǎn wēi wéi ān 〈成〉 pass from danger to safety; turn danger into safety

【轉身】zhuǎnshēn (動) (of a person) turn round

【轉車】zhuǎnchē (動) change trains or buses

【轉告】zhuǎngào (動) pass on (a message): 我們明天下午三時開會,請～其他人。We'll meet at three o'clock tomorrow afternoon. Please pass on my message to the others.

【轉折】zhuǎnzhé (名) turn in the course of events: ～點 turning point

【轉念】zhuǎnniàn (動) think again; on second thoughts

【轉述】zhuǎnshù (動) report; retell

【轉送】zhuǎnsòng (動) ❶ pass on ❷ make a present of sth. which one has received from another as a gift

【轉租】zhuǎnzū (動) sublet; sublease

【轉動】zhuǎndòng (動) turn; move

【轉眼】zhuǎnyǎn (副) in the twinkling of an eye

【轉移】zhuǎnyí Ⅰ (動) ❶ transfer; shift: ～視綫 divert one's attention / ～立場 shift one's position ❷ change; transform: ～社會風氣 change the social trends Ⅱ (名) 〈醫〉 metastasis: 癌～ metastasis of cancer

【轉達】zhuǎndá (動) convey; pass on: 請向他～我的謝意。Please convey to him my gratitude.

【轉換】zhuǎnhuàn (動) transform; change

【轉業】zhuǎnyè (動) (of an army-man) be demobilized and transferred to civilian work

【轉載】zhuǎnzǎi (動) reprint (an article that has been published elsewhere)

【轉嫁】zhuǎnjià (動) shift; transfer: 把責任～給別人 shift the responsibility on to others

【轉播】zhuǎnbō (動) (of radio or TV broadcast) relay

【轉賬】zhuǎnzhàng (動) transfer accounts

【轉機】zhuǎnjī (名) turn for the better; favourable change: 經濟有了～。The economy took a favourable turn.

【轉學】zhuǎnxué (動) (of a student) transfer to another school: ～生 transfer student

【轉戰】zhuǎnzhàn (動) fight from one region to another

【轉瞬】zhuǎnshùn (副) in the twinkling of an eye; in an instant

【轉彎子】zhuǎnwānzi (動) ❶ make a turn; turn a corner ❷ timely read just one's position and thinking to the change of circumstances

【轉彎抹角】zhuǎn wān mò jiǎo 〈成〉 beat about the bush

【轉變】zhuǎnbiàn Ⅰ (名) change: 態度～ change of attitude Ⅱ (動) change

【轉讓】zhuǎnràng (動) ❶ transfer the ownership of sth. to another ❷ transfer to another the right or privilege one is entitled to: 這項權利不能～。This right is intransferable.

轉 zhuàn Ⅰ (動) turn; revolve; spin: 繞軸而～ rotate on an axis/

月球繞着地球～。The moon turns round the earth. Ⅱ(量) revolution: 每分鐘四百～ 400 revolutions per minute

see also zhuǎn

【轉向】zhuànxiàng (動) lose one's orientation: 暈頭～ lose one's bearings

【轉門】zhuànmén (名) revolving door

【轉速】zhuànsù (名) rotational speed

【轉動】zhuàndòng (動) turn; rotate; revolve

【轉椅】zhuànyǐ (名) swivel chair; revolving chair

【轉數】zhuànshù (名)〈機〉revolution

【轉盤】zhuànpán (名) ❶〈機〉turntable ❷〈雜技〉disc-spinning

【轉輪手槍】zhuànlún shǒuqiāng (名) revolver

【轉爐】zhuànlú (名)〈冶〉converter

轍 zhé (名) track of a wheel; rut: 如出一～ as if following the same pattern

轎 jiào (名) sedan (chair)

【轎子】jiàozi (名) sedan (chair)

【轎車】jiàochē (名) car; bus: 大～ coach

轟 hōng Ⅰ(動) ❶ bombard; explode ❷ drive off: ～他出去。Show him the door. Ⅱ(象) bang; boom

【轟炸】hōngzhà (動) bomb: ～機 bomber

【轟動】hōngdòng (動) create a sensation: ～一時 make a great stir

【轟隆】hōnglōng (象) rumble; roll

【轟鳴】hōngmíng (動) roar; thunder

【轟擊】hōngjī (動) shell; bombard

【轟轟烈烈】hōng hōng liè liè〈成〉vigorously and magnificently

彎 pèi (名) bridle

辛 部

辛 xīn Ⅰ(形) ❶ hot (in flavour); pungent ❷ hard-working; laborious: 歷盡千～萬苦 undergo untold hardships ❸ sad; bitter Ⅱ(名) (Xīn) a surname

【辛迪加】xīndíjiā (名) syndicate

【辛苦】xīnkǔ Ⅰ(形) hard; laborious; exhausting Ⅱ(動) cause trouble to; go through hardship: 她辛辛苦苦收集了大量資料。She went to great pains to collect a wealth of relevant materials.

【辛勞】xīnláo (形) toiling; painstaking

【辛勤】xīnqín (形) hardworking; industrious; diligent

【辛辣】xīnlà (形) ❶ hot (in flavour) ❷ biting (in criticism)

【辛酸】xīnsuān (形) sad; bitter

辜 gū (名) ❶ guilt; crime ❷ (Gū) a surnmae

【辜負】gūfù (動) fail to live up to; let down

辟 bì Ⅰ(名) sovereign; monarch: 復～ restore a monarch, etc. Ⅱ(動) ward off

【辟邪】bìxié (動) ward off evils

辣 là Ⅰ(形) ❶ peppery; pungent; hot ❷ ruthless; merciless: 陰險毒～ sinister and ruthless Ⅱ(動) (of peppery smell) burn; bite; sting (mouth, nose or eyes)

【辣手】làshǒu Ⅰ (名) ruthless means Ⅱ (形) ❶ merciless ❷ thorny; hard to resolve: ～的問題 a thorny problem

【辣椒】làjiāo (名) 〈植〉 cayenne; chilli; pepper

辨 biàn (動) ❶ differentiate; distinguish: 分～真偽 distinguish truth from falsehood ❷ identify; recognize

【辨別】biànbié (動) differentiate; discriminate: ～是非 differentiate between right and wrong

【辨別力】biànbiélì (名) discerning power; ability to see things as they are

【辨明】biànmíng (動) ❶ make a clear distinction between ❷ identify clearly

【辨認】biànrèn (動) identify; make out: ～筆迹 identify sb.'s handwriting

辦 bàn (動) ❶ attend to; handle; do; tackle: ～手續 go through the formalities ❷ set up; organize ❸ run; manage: 民～學校 a community-run school ❹ get sth. ready; arrange; prepare: ～貨 purchase goods ❺ punish; penalize; bring to justice

【辦公】bàngōng (動) do office work; attend to business: ～時間 office hours

【辦公室】bàngōngshì (名) office

【辦公桌】bàngōngzhuō (名) desk; bureau

【辦法】bànfǎ (名) way to handle matters or solve problems

【辦事】bànshì (動) handle (manage, conduct) things: ～麻利 handle affairs with competence

【辦事員】bànshìyuán (名) clerk; office worker

【辦事處】bànshìchù (名) office (building)

【辦案】bàn'àn (動) (of a judge or official) handle a case

【辦理】bànlǐ (動) manage; handle; take charge of: ～公務 handle official business

【辦報】bànbào (動) run or operate a newspaper

【辦學】bànxué (動) run a school

辭 cí Ⅰ (名) ❶ diction; phraseology: 措～得當 appropriate wording ❷ a type of classical Chinese literary writing Ⅱ (動) ❶ say goodbye: ～歲 ring out the old year ❷ decline: ～去職務 resign (one's position) ❸ dismiss: 把保姆～了 dismiss one's maid ❹ shirk; dodge: 不～辛苦 make light of difficulty; despite the strain or hardship

【辭令】cílìng (名) polite expressions used in social intercourse: 外交～ diplomatic language

【辭行】cíxíng (動) bid farewell (to one's friends and relatives) on the eve of a long journey

【辭別】cíbié (動) bid farewell to

【辭呈】cíchéng (名) (written) resignation

【辭典】cídiǎn (名) dictionary

【辭退】cítuì (動) dismiss; fire; sack

【辭謝】cíxiè (動) decline politely

【辭職】cízhí Ⅰ (動) resign Ⅱ (名) resignation

【辭藻】cízǎo (名) ornate diction;

florid language

辯 biàn (動) argue; debate: ～個
水落石出 argue the matter out

【辯才】biàncái (名) eloquence

【辯白】biànbái (動) ❶ defend oneself verbally ❷ justify oneself: 她力
圖爲自己的行爲～。 She made a
vigorous attempt to justify her behaviour.

【辯解】biànjiě (動) try to justify;
make excuses for

【辯駁】biànbó (動) refute; argue a-
gainst: 不可～的事實 indisputable
(irrefutable) fact

【辯論】biànlùn I (動) argue; debate
II (名) debate; argument

【辯證】biànzhèng (形) dialectical:
～地看問題 approach a problem
from a dialectical point of view

【辯證法】biànzhèngfǎ (名) dialec-
tic(s): 唯物～ materialist dialectics

【辯護】biànhù (動) defend; plead;
爲他～ speak in his defence; plead
for him

【辯護人】biànhùrén (名) defender;
defence counsel; advocate

【辯護士】biànhùshì (名) apologist

辰 部

辰 chén (名) ❶ celestial bodies;
stars ❷ one of the 12 two-hour periods into which the day was divided
in ancient China, each being given
the name of one of the 12 Earthly
Branches: 時～ such a two-hour period ❸ fifth of the 12 Earthly
Branches ❹ day; time: 良～ a fine

day

【辰光】chénguāng (名)〈方〉 time:
～不早了。 It is rather late now.

辱 rǔ I (名) disgrace; indignity: 含
垢忍～ have to put up with all sorts
of indignities II (動) bring disgrace
to; humiliate

【辱沒】rǔmò (動) disgrace; bring
shame upon; be unworthy of

【辱罵】rǔmà (動) swear at; shout
abuse at; insult

農 nóng (名) ❶ farmer; peasant ❷
agriculture; farming

【農夫】nóngfū (名) farmer

【農戶】nónghù (名) a farmer's family; a farming household

【農田】nóngtián (名) farmland

【農民】nóngmín (名) farmer; peasant

【農奴】nóngnú (名) serf: ～制 serf-
dom

【農忙】nóngmáng (名) busy farming
work: ～季節 busy season for farm
work

【農村】nóngcūn (名) countryside;
country; rural area

【農作物】nóngzuòwù (名) crops

【農具】nóngjù (名) farm tools

【農活】nónghuó (名) farm work

【農時】nóngshí (名) farming season:
不違～ not miss the farming season

【農產品】nóngchǎnpǐn (名) farm
produce

【農場】nóngchǎng (名) farm

【農閑】nóngxián (名) slack season
for farm work

【農貿市場】nóngmào shìchǎng (名)
country fair; market for farm produce

【農業】nóngyè (名) agriculture; farming: ～國 agricultural country

【農機】nóngjī (名) agricultural machinery; farm machinery

【農曆】nónglì (名) traditional Chinese calendar; lunar calendar

【農藥】nóngyào (名) agricultural chemicals; insecticide

【農藝師】nóngyìshī (名) agronomist

辵 部

迂 yū (形) ❶ circuitous; winding ❷ pedantic; impractical

【迂迴】yūhuí Ⅰ (形) tortuous; devious; roundabout Ⅱ (動)〈軍〉outflank

【迂腐】yūfǔ (形) pedantic

【迂闊】yūkuò (形) impractical

迅 xùn (形) swift; rapid

【迅即】xùnjí (副) immediately; at once: ～返校 return to college at once

【迅疾】xùnjí (形) swift; fast

【迅速】xùnsù (副) rapidly; speedily: ～採取行動 take immediate action

【迅猛】xùnměng (形) swift and violent

【迅雷不及掩耳】xùn léi bù jí yǎn ěr〈成〉the events move so fast that they take one quite unprepared; come all of a sudden at lightning speed and catch people off guard

迄 qì (副) up to; till

【迄今】qìjīn (副) up to now; so far

迎 yíng (動) ❶ meet; greet: ～新會 a welcoming party (for newcomers) ❷ move towards: ～面碰見某人 come across sb; run into sb.

【迎刃而解】yíng rèn ér jiě〈成〉(of a problem) be easily resolved

【迎合】yínghé (動) cater to: ～大眾口味 cater to the popular taste

【迎春】yíngchūn (名)〈植〉winter jasmine

【迎風】yíngfēng (動) face the wind: 坐在這裏正～,特別涼爽。One gets the breeze sitting here. It's really cool.

【迎候】yínghòu (動) meet sb. at a specified place: 派人去機場～ send somebody to meet sb. at the airport

【迎接】yíngjiē (動) meet; welcome

【迎頭痛擊】yíng tóu tòng jī〈成〉deal head-on blows

【迎頭趕上】yíng tóu gǎn shàng〈成〉try hard to catch up with the advanced

近 jìn (形) ❶ recent; latest: ～況 recent developments; things at present ❷ near; close; immediate: ～便 close at hand ❸ intimate; close: 他是我的～鄰。He is a close neighbour of mine. ❹ approximating; close to: 價值～千元 cost or be worth nearly 1,000 yuan

【近日】jìnrì (副) ❶ in recent days ❷ within a few days

【近水樓臺】jìn shuǐ lóu tái〈成〉(short for 近水樓臺先得月 jìn shuǐ lóu tái xiān dé yuè) the pavilion along the waterside catches the first moonbeams; be in a favourable position to get special advantages

【近代】jìndài (名) modern times

【近乎】jìnhu (副) nearly; approximately: ～减绝的物种 species on the verge of extinction

【近似】jìnsì（形）similar; approximate

【近因】jìnyīn（名）immediate cause

【近来】jìnlái（副）recently; of late

【近郊】jìnjiāo（名）outskirts（of a city）; suburbs

【近旁】jìnpáng（副）nearby; close by

【近海】jìnhǎi Ⅰ（名）coastal waters Ⅱ（形）inshore: ～油田 offshore oilfields

【近视】jìnshì（名）myopia; shortsightedness: ～眼 near-sighted

【近道】jìndào（近路 jìnlù）（名）shortcut

【近期】jìnqī Ⅰ（副）in the near future Ⅱ（形）short-term

返 fǎn（动）return: 日内～京 return to Beijing in a few days

【返工】fǎngōng（动）（have sth. shoddy）done over again

【返老还童】fǎn lǎo huán tóng〈成〉become rejuvenated; regain youthful vigour

【返祖现象】fǎnzǔ xiànxiàng（名）〈生〉atavism

【返航】fǎnháng（动）go（come）on a return voyage of flight; return from a voyage or flight

【返潮】fǎncháo（动）get damp; become moist

述 shù（动）state; relate; recount: 上～各项 all the above-mentioned items

【述评】shùpíng（名）review; commentary

【述说】shùshuō（动）recount; narrate; relate

【述职】shùzhí（动）report in person on the performance of one's official duties

迢 tiáo（形）far; remote

【迢迢】tiáotiáo（形）（of distance covered）long; far: 从非洲千里～来到这里 come here all the way from Africa

迪 dí（动）guide; inspire: 启～ enlighten

迥 jiǒng（形）utterly different

【迥然不同】jiǒng rán bù tóng〈成〉altogether different; be a far cry from

迭 dié Ⅰ（动）change; alternate Ⅱ（副）repeatedly: ～次 again and again

【迭起】diéqǐ（动）occur frequently

迫 pǎi
see also pò

【迫击炮】pǎijī pào（名）mortar

迫 pò Ⅰ（动）❶ compel; force: 被～关闭 be forced to close down ❷ approach; draw near Ⅱ（形）urgent; pressing
see also pǎi

【迫不及待】pò bù jí dài〈成〉lose no time: ～地对别人进行恶毒攻击 lose no time in launching a venomous attack on others

【迫不得已】pò bù dé yǐ〈成〉cannot help it: ～进行冒险 cannot but take risks; be compelled to take risky steps

【迫切】pòqiè（形）urgent; pressing

【迫在眉睫】pò zài méi jié〈成〉very urgent; imminent: 此事～。

This is a matter of great urgency.

【迫近】pòjìn (动) approach; draw near: 假期～了。The vacation is drawing near.

【迫使】pòshǐ (动) force; compel: ～敌人退却 force the enemy to retreat

【迫降】pòjiàng (名) forced landing

【迫害】pòhài (动) persecute

迹 jì (名) ❶ trace; mark ❷ remains; vestige: 遗～ historical remains ❸ act; deed: 英雄事～ heroic deeds

【迹象】jìxiàng (名) indication; sign: 一切～表明問題遠没有解决。There is every indication that the problem is far from solved.

送 sòng (动) ❶ deliver; carry to: ～报纸信件 deliver newspapers and letters ❷ present sth. as a gift ❸ see (sb.) off; escort: ～往迎来 see off departing guests and welcome new arrivals

【送人情】sòng rénqíng (动) do sb. a good turn to win his favour

【送死】sòngsǐ (动)〈口〉court death

【送交】sòngjiāo (动) deliver to; hand over to

【送行】sòngxíng (动) ❶ see off ❷ hold a send-off party

【送命】sòngmìng (动) be killed

【送客】sòngkè (动) see a visitor out

【送信儿】sòngxìnr (动)〈口〉send word: 去送个信儿 go and pass on a message

【送货】sònghuò (动) deliver goods: ～费 drop-off charge

【送终】sòngzhōng (动) ❶ wait upon a dying senior person ❷ hold a funeral for a deceased senior person

【送葬】sòngzàng (动) join a funeral procession; attend a burial

【送还】sònghuán (动) return; give back

【送礼】sònglǐ (动) give a present

进 bèng (动) burst forth; gush; spurt

【迸发】bèngfā (动) break forth; gush; spurt: ～出雷鸣般的掌声 burst into thunderous applause

【迸裂】bèngliè (动) split; burst apart

迷 mí I (动) ❶ be lost: 他～了方向。He got lost. ❷ be mad about; be addicted to: 對足球着了～ be mad about football II (名) fan; fiend

【迷人】mírén (形) charming; enchanting

【迷信】míxìn (名) superstition; blind faith: 個人～ personality cult

【迷宫】mígōng (名) maze; labyrinth

【迷航】míháng (动) (of a ship, plane, etc.) get lost; lose one's course; lose one's bearings

【迷茫】mímáng (形) ❶ vast and hazy: 傍晚的大海一片～。At dusk the sea is covered with mist stretching into infinity. ❷ confused; stupefied

【迷途】mítú I (动) lose one's way; go astray II (名) wrong path

【迷途知返】mí tú zhī fǎn〈成〉mend one's ways when one realizes one's error

【迷惘】míwǎng (动) be at sea; be perplexed

【迷惑】míhuò (动) confuse; bewilder

【迷路】mílù (动) get lost; lose one's way

【迷夢】mímèng (名) illusion; shadowy dream

【迷魂陣】míhúnzhèn （名） trap; maze

【迷魂湯】míhúntāng （名）magic potion; honeyed words; flattery

【迷醉】mízuì （動） be intoxicated (with); be fascinated (by)

【迷糊】míhu （形）❶ confused; befogged; muddle-headed: 可真把他弄～了。He got utterly confused. ❷ blurred; dimmed: 淚水～了她的雙眼。Her eyes were dimmed with tears.

【迷離】mílí （形）misted: ～恍惚 blurred and baffled

【迷戀】míliàn （動） be infatuated with; be enamoured of

逆 nì Ⅰ（形）contrary; counter; reverse Ⅱ（動）counter; go against: ～歷史潮流 go against the tide of history Ⅲ（名）traitor: 叛～ rebel

【逆水】nìshuǐ （副）against the current: 如～行舟。It is like rowing a boat against the tide.

【逆行】nìxíng （動）(of vehicles) go against the traffic

【逆耳】nì'ěr （動）be unpleasant to the ear: 忠言～。Good advice often offends the ear.

【逆定理】nìdìnglǐ （名）〈數〉 converse theorem

【逆來順受】nì lái shùn shòu 〈成〉endure adversity meekly

【逆差】nìchā （名）deficit; unfavorable balance: 貿易～ trade deficit

【逆風】nìfēng Ⅰ（副） against the wind Ⅱ（名）contrary wind; adverse wind

【逆料】nìliào （動）predict: 局勢如何，仍難～。It is still difficult to forecast what the situation will be like.

【逆流】nìliú （名）adverse current; counter current

【逆境】nìjìng （名） adverse circumstances

【逆轉】nìzhuǎn （動） worsen; reverse: 不可～的 irreversible

退 tuì （動）❶ move backwards: 請稍往後～。Please step back a little bit. ❷ repulse; remove: 把膠卷從相機裏～出來 remove the film from the camera ❸ quit; leave: ～黨 withdraw from a political party/ ～學 leave school/ ～居二綫 resign from office to take up an honorary position ❹ recede; descend: ～潮 ebb (tide) ❺ return: ～款 refund/ ～房間 book out; check out ❻ cancel; invalidate: ～親(婚) break off an engagement

【退一步說】tuì yí bù shuō （副）even if the case is not so; even so

【退化】tuìhuà （動）degenerate; degrade

【退出】tuìchū （動）quit (an organization); walk out (of a meeting); withdraw from (a competition, etc.)

【退回】tuìhuí （動）❶ send back ❷ turn back; go back

【退休】tuìxiū （動）retire

【退色】tuìshǎi （動）fade

【退役】tuìyì (退伍 tuìwǔ)（動）be released from military service; be demobilized

【退兵】tuìbīng （動） ❶ retreat; withdraw troops ❷ repulse; drive back the enemy

【退步】tuìbù Ⅰ（動）fall behind; do

worse than before Ⅱ（名）leeway; room for manoeuvre

【退却】tuìquè（动）❶ retreat ❷ shrink back

【退席】tuìxí（动）❶ walk out (of a meeting, banquet, etc.) ❷ leave (a meeting, banquet)

【退票】tuìpiào（动）return a ticket; get a refund for a ticket

【退换】tuìhuàn（动）replace (a purchase)

【退路】tuìlù（名）❶ leeway; space for manoeuvre ❷ route of retreat

【退赔】tuìpéi（动）return what is illegally taken or pay compensation for it

【退烧】tuìshāo（动）❶ allay a fever: ～药 anti-pyretic ❷ (of a fever) be gone

【退还】tuìhuán（动）return; give back

【退缩】tuìsuō（动）recoil; flinch

【退职】tuìzhí（动）quit one's job: ～金 severance pay

【退让】tuìràng（动）concede; yield: 做些～ make some concessions

【退赃】tuìzāng（动）disgorge (one's booty)

追 zhuī Ⅰ（动）❶ chase; pursue: 努力～上同班同學 try to catch up with the rest of the class ❷ seek; pursue: ～名逐利 go after fame and wealth ❸ trace; investigate: ～根問底 get to the bottom of the matter ❹ recall; reminisce: ～懷往事 recall the past Ⅱ（副）posthumously

【追加】zhuījiā（动）add to (the original amount): ～費用 make an additional allocation for expenses

【追回】zhuīhuí（动）recover (stolen property)

【追究】zhuījiū（动）look into; investigate: ～責任 try to ascertain exactly where the responsibility lies

【追求】zhuīqiú（动）❶ seek; pursue: ～享樂 seek ease and comfort; pursue sensual pleasure ❷ woo; court

【追查】zhuīchá（动）investigate: ～事故 investigate an accident

【追思】zhuīsī（动）recollect; recall

【追悔】zhuīhuǐ（动）repent; chew the bitter cud of remorse

【追捕】zhuībǔ（动）pursue and capture

【追逐】zhuīzhú（动）❶ chase; pursue ❷ seek

【追悼】zhuīdào（动）mourn sb.'s death: ～會 funeral

【追問】zhuīwèn（动）question closely; cross-examine

【追尋】zhuīxún（动）search for; track down: ～失踪人員 search for the missing personnel

【追溯】zhuīsù（动）trace back to: 可以～到戰爭年代 can be traced back to the war years

【追認】zhuīrèn（动）be recognized posthumously: ～人民英雄 be posthumously honoured as People's Hero

【追趕】zhuīgǎn（动）pursue; run after: ～逃敵 be in pursuit of the fleeing enemy troops

【追踪】zhuīzōng（动）track; trace

【追隨】zhuīsuí（动）follow; go after: ～潮流 swim with the tide

【追憶】zhuīyì（动）recall; look back

【追擊】zhuījī（动）pursue and attack

逃 táo（动）❶ flee; escape: 死裏

~生 escape by the skin of one's teeth; have a narrow escape ❷ evade; dodge: ~荒 flee from a famine-stricken area

【逃亡】táowáng (動) flee one's homeland; be a fugitive

【逃犯】táofàn (名) runaway convict

【逃兵】táobīng (名) (army) deserter

【逃走】táozǒu (動) escape; take flight

【逃命】táomìng (動) flee for one's life

【逃脫】táotuō (動) escape; evade: 企圖~事故的責任 attempt to shirk responsibility for an accident

【逃稅】táoshuì Ⅰ (動) evade a tax Ⅱ (名) tax evasion

【逃跑】táopǎo (動) run away from a dangerous situation to save one's skin; take flight; flee

【逃避】táobì (動) escape; evade: ~關稅 evade customs duty

【逃學】táoxué (動) play truant; cut class

【逃難】táonàn (動) flee one's native place because of war or natural disaster

這 zhè Ⅰ (代) this: ~人我見過。 I've met this man before. Ⅱ (副) now: 他~就回來。 He'll be back in no time.

【這次】zhècì (形) this time; present: ~座談會 the present forum

【這兒】zhèr (代) here: 告訴他馬上到~來。 Tell him to come here at once.

【這些】zhèxiē (代) these

【這個】zhège (代) this one; this:

~年輕人 this young man / ~更好一些。 This one is better.

【這裏】zhèlǐ (副) here

【這麼】zhème (代) so; such; like this: ~冷的天 such a cold day / ~說是真的。 So it is true.

【這樣】zhèyàng (代) so; such; like this: ~的事情 things like this

【這邊】zhèbiān (副) this side; here: 走~。 Come this way.

逗 dòu (動) ❶ stop; stay ❷ tease; tantalize: ~孩子玩 tease the children playfully

【逗留】dòuliú (動) stay: ~一宿 make an overnight stop

【逗號】dòuhào (名) comma

【逗趣】dòuqù (動) make remarks jesting

連 lián Ⅰ (動) ❶ join; link: 兩市有鐵路相~。 The two cities are linked by a railway. ❷ include: 這個委員會~主席共五人。 The committee consists of five people, including the chairman. Ⅱ (名) ❶ (of army) company ❷ (Lián) a surname Ⅲ (副) ❶ in succession; repeatedly: 時裝表演一個一個的。 Fashion shows came in quick succession. ❷ [used for emphasis] even: 他~信封都沒打開，別說看信了。 He didn't even open the letter, let alone read it.

【連日】liánrì (副) for days; day in and day out

【連天】liántiān (副) ❶ for days on end: ~連夜 day and night ❷ constantly: 叫苦~ complain endlessly ❸ as if merging with the sky: 水~。 The water seems to meet the sky.

【连亘】 liángèn（形）continuous: 山脈～ range after range of mountains

【连忙】 liánmáng（副）at once; hurriedly

【连年】 liánnián（副）in successive years; year after year

【连任】 liánrèn（动）be reelected; be reappointed

【连同】 liántóng（副）together with; coupled with

【连衣裙】 liányīqún（名）（woman's）dress

【连字號】 liánzìhào（名）hyphen

【连夜】 liányè（副）the same night: 村民們～開會。The villagers held a meeting on that very night.

【连长】 liánzhǎng（名）company commander

【连帶】 liándài（形）related: 有～關係 be related to each other

【连接】 liánjiē（动）link; connect

【连累】 liánlěi（动）implicate; get sb. into trouble

【连貫】 liánguàn Ⅰ（形）coherent; consistent Ⅱ（动）link: ～南北的運河 a canal that links up north and south

【连陰天】 liányīntiān（名）successive cloudy days

【连詞】 liáncí（名）〈語〉conjunction

【连隊】 liánduì（名）（of army）company

【连載】 liánzǎi（动）publish in instalments: ～小説 serial（story）

【连緻】 liánzhuì（动）join: 這些情節～在一起就有趣了。These details when pieced together are very interesting.

【连綿】 liánmián（形）continuous; successive: 小山～ unending ranges of hills

【连篇】 liánpiān（副）❶ page after page ❷ throughout the pages: 廢話～ page after page of sheer nonsense

【連篇累牘】 lián piān lěi dú〈成〉（of writing）voluminous

【連環】 liánhuán（名）chain of rings; things related to one another

【連環畫】 liánhuánhuà（名）picture-story book; comic strip

【連鍋端】 liánguōduān（动）〈口〉be removed or wiped out for good and all

【連鎖】 liánsuǒ（形）interlocking; continuous

【連鎖反應】 liánsuǒ fǎnyìng（名）chain reaction

【連襟】 liánjīn（名）（relation between）the husbands of sisters: 他是我的～。he is my brother-in-law.

【連續】 liánxù（副）continuously; consecutively: ～講了三個小時 speak for three hours on end

【速】 sù Ⅰ（名）speed; velocity: 超音～ supersonic Ⅱ（形）fast; quick; speedy: 局勢迅～起了變化。The situation is changing fast.

【速成】 sùchéng（形）（of a training or educational programme）short-term; quick; crash: 開辦英語～班 run a crash course in English

【速度】 sùdù（名）❶〈物〉velocity; speed: 加～ acceleration ❷ speed; pace; tempo: ～限制 speed limit/～計 speedometer

【速記】 sùjì（名）shorthand; stenography

【速效】 sùxiào（形）quick-acting; producing prompt results

【速凍】 sùdòng（动）quick-freeze: ～豌豆 quick-frozen fresh peas

【速溶咖啡】sùróng kāfēi（名）instant coffee

【速写】sùxiě（名）❶（in painting）sketch ❷ literary sketch

逝 shì（动）❶ pass; elapse: 随着时间的流～ with the passage of time ❷ die; pass away

【逝世】shìshì（动）pass away; die

逐 zhú I（动）❶ drive away; expel: 被～出境 be expelled from a country; be deported ❷ chase; compete: 角～ contend/ 追～残敌 pursue the remnant troops of the enemy II（副）one by one: ～日 day by day / 一项解说 explain item by item

【逐年】zhúnián（副）year by year

【逐字逐句】zhú zì zhú jù〈成〉word for word; word by word; verbatim: ～解释 explain word by word

【逐步】zhúbù（副）step by step; gradually: ～进行 proceed step by step

【逐个】zhúgè（副）one by one: 问题～处理 tackle problems one by one

【逐渐】zhújiàn（副）gradually

通 tōng I（动）❶ clear obstructions by poking: ～一下炉子 give the fire a poke ❷（of a road）lead to: 这条路一往机场 This road leads to the airport. ❸ channel; intercourse; have contact with: ～敌 collude with the enemy secretly ❹ tell; inform ❺ understand; be proficient in: 不～人情 not understand what is natural in human relationships/ ～晓五种语言 be well versed in five languages II（副）❶ through: 我打不～到上海的电话。

I can't get through to Shanghai. ❷ coherently: 文章写得不～。The essay is crude and full of error. ❸ effectively: 这个办法可能行得～。Maybe this plan will work. III（形）❶ general; common: ～史 comprehensive（general）history ❷ whole: ～夜 all night long IV（名）❶ expert; old hand: 中国～ China hand ❷（Tōng）a surname see also tòng

【通力合作】tōng lì hé zuò〈成〉work in concert

【通天】tōngtiān（形）❶ extremely high; exceptional ❷ having direct access to the highest authorities

【通心粉】tōngxīnfěn（名）macaroni

【通令】tōnglìng I（名）circular order II（动）issue a circular order

【通用】tōngyòng（形）❶ in general use: ～月票 Go-As-You-Please; monthly ticket for all urban and suburban bus and trolley services/ ～信用卡 all-purpose credit card ❷（of some Chinese characters）interchangeable

【通共】tōnggòng（副）altogether; in all

【通行】tōngxíng（动）（of pedestrians, vehicles, etc.）pass through: 禁止～。Closed to traffic.（No thoroughfare.）/ ～证 pass; laissez-passer/ ～费 toll II（形）current; in common use

【通车】tōngchē（动）❶（of a railway or highway）be open to traffic ❷ have transport service

【通告】tōnggào I（名）announcement; circular II（动）give a public notice

【通身】tōngshēn（副）all over the

body: ～白毛的貓 cat with an all-white coat of hair

【通明】tōngmíng（形）well lit; brilliantly illuminated

【通知】tōngzhī I（動）notify: 沒有他。He has not been informed. II（名）notice; circular: ～書 notification

【通風】tōngfēng（動）❶ ventilate: 開窗～ open the window to let in fresh air/～設備 ventilation ❷ be well ventilated: 不～ be ill ventilated ❸ leak information (to a rival party): 給他～報信 give him secret information

【通紅】tōnghóng（形）flaming red

【通姦】tōngjiān（動）commit adultery

【通俗】tōngsú（形）popular: ～歌曲 pop song

【通信】tōngxìn（動）correspond; communicate by correspondence: ～處 mailing address/～員 messenger

【通病】tōngbìng（名）common fault

【通航】tōngháng（動）be open to navigation or air traffic; there is navigation or air service at a place

【通氣】tōngqì（動）❶ ventilate: ～孔 ventilation hole; orifice ❷ keep each other informed

【通通】tōngtōng（統統 tǒngtǒng）（副）all; completely; without exception: 你要的東西～弄到了。Everything you want has been secured.

【通宵】tōngxiāo（通夜 tōngyè）（副）all night

【通訊】tōngxùn（名）❶ communication: 衛星～ communication by satellite ❷ press report; news dispatch: 新華～社 Xinhua News Agency /～員 reporter/～錄 address book

【通常】tōngcháng（副）generally; usually; as a rule

【通婚】tōnghūn（動）intermarry; become connected by marriage

【通貨】tōnghuò（名）〈經〉currency; money: 硬～ hard currency/～膨脹 inflation

【通票】tōngpiào（名）through ticket

【通商】tōngshāng（動）(as between states) trade; have commercial relations

【通情達理】tōng qíng dá lǐ II（成）be understanding and sensible

【通郵】tōngyóu（動）be accessible through postal communication; have postal communication

【通報】tōngbào I（動）❶ circulate a notice ❷ inform; notify II（名）❶ circular ❷（scientific）bulletin or journal

【通道】tōngdào（通路 tōnglù）（名）thoroughfare; passage-way

【通過】tōngguò I（動）❶ pass; go through: ～兩條封鎖綫 run two blockades / (of a passing vehicle) 一慢二看三～ slow down, look around and then go ahead ❷ adopt; pass (a bill, resolution, etc.) ❸ secure the permission or approval of: 在羣眾中通不過 fail to get public consent II（介）by; through: ～談判達成協議 reach an agreement through negotiation

【通順】tōngshùn（形）(of writing) coherent; logical; smooth

【通電】tōngdiàn I（動）❶ have electricity supply: 這個村去年通的電。This village began to have electricity supply last year. ❷ electrify;

become live ❸ issue an open telegram Ⅱ (名) circular (open) telegram

【通話】tōnghuà (動) ❶ talk over the telephone: ～費 call rate ❷ converse

【通牒】tōngdié (名) diplomatic note: 發出最後～ deliver an ultimatum

【通暢】tōngchàng (形) ❶ unobstructed: 保持道路～ keep the road clear/ 大便不～ unable to empty the bowels effectively ❷ (of writing) easy and fluent; readable

【通稱】tōngchēng Ⅰ (動) be commonly known as Ⅱ (名) general term; commonly accepted name

【通緝】tōngjī (動) list as wanted; issue a circular order for the arrest of (a criminal)

【通盤】tōngpán (形) overall; all-round: ～籌劃 overall planning

【通融】tōngróng (動) stretch (rules, regulations, etc.) to accommodate sb.; be flexible: 這事可不～。It's difficult to make an exception of this case.

通 tòng (量) (of actions): 挨了一～兒說 be given a dressing down
see also tōng

逍 xiāo

【逍遙】xiāoyáo (形) carefree

【逍遙法外】xiāo yáo fǎ wài〈成〉go scot-free; be at large

逞 chěng (動) ❶ display; flaunt ❷ indulge: ～性子 be wilful ❸〈貶〉succeed in one's evil enterprise: 如果陰謀得逞～ should the evil design materialize

【逞兇】chěngxiōng (動) commit atrocities

【逞能】chěngnéng (動) show off (one's ability)

【逞强】chěngqiáng (動) flaunt one's physical or intellectual superiority

途 tú (名) way; route; course: 中～退場 leave in the middle of a performance or a meeting

【途徑】tújìng (名) way: 通過外交～ through diplomatic channels

【途經】tújīng (副) by way of: 香港回國 go home via Hongkong

造 zào (動) ❶ make; build: ～船工業 shipbuilding industry ❷ invent; cook up: ～謠 start rumours ❸ train: 就人才 train qualified personnel ❹ go to; reach: ～訪 pay a visit

【造反】zàofǎn (動) rise in rebellion; revolt (against)

【造化】zàohuà (名) ❶ good luck ❷ Mother Nature; Creator

【造册】zàocè (動) compile a register

【造成】zàochéng (動) create; generate; produce: ～假象 create a false impression

【造作】zàozuò (形) affected; artificial

【造表】zàobiǎo (動) draw up a form or list

【造林】zàolín (名) afforestation

【造物主】zàowùzhǔ (名)〈宗〉the Creator

【造型】zàoxíng (名) mould-making; modelling: ～藝術 plastic arts

【造紙】zàozhǐ (名) paper-making

【造紙廠】zàozhǐchǎng (名) paper mill

【造船廠】zàochuánchǎng（名）ship-yard

【造詣】zàoyì（名）attainment; accomplishment: 一個頗有～的學者 an accomplished scholar

【造福】zàofú（動）bring benefit to; benefit: ～於民 work for the welfare of the people

【造影】zàoyǐng（名）〈醫〉radiography

【造價】zàojià（名）production cost; construction cost

【造孽】zàoniè（動）do evil（with the implication that retribution will come sooner or later）

透 tòu Ⅰ（動）❶ penetrate; pierce: ～過鏡片的光綫 rays of light coming through the lens ❷ tip off; inform secretly: 給人～個信兒 tip sb. off about sth. Ⅱ（副）thoroughly; completely: 煩～了 be bored stiff; be fed up

【透支】tòuzhī（動）〈經〉overdraw

【透雨】tòuyǔ（名）soaking rain: 下了一場～ have a saturating rain

【透明】tòumíng（形）transparent; limpid: 水是無色～的液體。Water is a colourless transparent liquid.

【透明度】tòumíngdù（名）clearness in policy; transparency

【透風】tòufēng（動）❶ let in air: 不～的屋子 an airtight room ❷ leak a secret: 她不會給人～的。She won't leak out anything.

【透亮】tòuliang（形）❶ bright; clear: 這房子朝南，早晨出太陽就～。The room has a southern exposure and is very light when the sun comes out in the morning. ❷ clear: 一堂課下來，我心裏就～了。The

lecture enlightened me.

【透氣】tòuqì（動）❶ let in air ❷ breathe smoothly: 我憋得透不過氣來。I'm stifling.

【透頂】tòudǐng（副）〈貶〉exceedingly: 糊塗～ absolutely muddle-headed

【透視】tòushì（名）❶ perspective: ～圖 perspective drawing ❷〈醫〉fluoros-copy

【透徹】tòuchè（形）thorough; penetrating: ～的瞭解 thorough understanding / ～的分析 penetrating analysis

【透露】tòulù（動）divulge; disclose: 據該報～ as revealed by the newspaper

逢 féng（動）encounter

【逢凶化吉】féng xiōng huà jí〈成〉turn a misfortune into a blessing

【逢迎】féngyíng（動）cringe; flatter; fawn

【逢集】féngjí（名）market day

【逢場作戲】féng chǎng zuò xì〈成〉join in the fun when the occasion requires

逛 guàng（動）stroll; take a walk: ～公園 take a stroll in the park

【逛蕩】guàngdang（動）loaf about; dawdle

逵 kuí（名）road

逮 dǎi（動）catch: ～小偷 catch a pickpocket or thief
see also dài

逮 dǎi（動）reach: 力所不～ beyond one's ability
see also dài

【逮捕】dàibǔ（動）arrest

透 wēi

【逶迤】wēiyí (形) (of a road, river, mountain range etc.) wind its way; winding

逸 yì I (動) run away; flee II (名) ease; leisure: 勞 ~ work and leisure

【逸事】yìshì (名) anecdote

進 jìn I (動) ❶ move onwards: 大踏步前 ~ make big strides forward ❷ enter; make way into: ~ 門 enter a house (room) ❸ take; receive: ~ 賬 income ❹ eat; drink: 共 ~ 午餐 have luncheon with; lunch together ❺ present; offer: ~ 貢 pay tribute (to a suzerain or monarch) II (介) [used after a verb] into; in: 走 ~ 大廳 go into a big hall

【進一步】jìn yī bù (副) further: ~ 改善工作條件 further improve the working conditions

【進入】jìnrù (動) enter; move into

【進口】jìnkǒu I (動) ❶ import: ~ 報關 customs entry / ~ 許可證 import licence; import authorization ❷ sail into a port II (名) entrance

【進化】jìnhuà (名) evolution

【進去】jìnqu (動) go in; get in

【進去】jìnqu (副) [used after a verb to indicate inward movement, away from the speaker] in: 擠 ~ squeeze in; push one's way in

【進犯】jìnfàn (動) invade (a country)

【進出】jìnchū I (動) come (or go) in and out II (名) turnover (in business)

【進出口】jìnchūkǒu (名) ❶ import and export ❷ entrances and exits; exit

【進行】jìnxíng (動) ❶ carry out; perform: ~ 談判 hold negotiations ❷ be under way; progress: 試驗在順利 ~。The experiment is going on smoothly. ❸ be on the march: ~ 曲 march

【進而】jìn'ér (動) proceed to; and then: 掌握了英文之後，他 ~ 攻讀法語。After mastering English, he proceeded to study French.

【進步】jìnbù I (動) progress; advance II (形) (politically) progressive

【進攻】jìngōng (動) launch an offensive; attack

【進來】jìnlai (動) come in

【進來】jìnlai (副) [used after a verb to indicate inward movement] in: 溜 ~ sneak in

【進取】jìnqǔ (動) be enterprising; be up-and-coming

【進度】jìndù (名) ❶ (rate of) progress ❷ schedule; planned progress

【進軍】jìnjūn (動) (of an army or a large number of persons) march

【進修】jìnxiū (動) go in for advanced studies; join a training course

【進退兩難】jìn tuì liǎng nán 〈成〉 be caught in a dilemma

【進展】jìnzhǎn I (動) make headway: ~ 極其緩慢。The progress has been very slow. II (名) progress; improvement: 取得一些 ~ make some headway

【進程】jìnchéng (名) course; process: 人類進步的 ~ course of human progress

【進發】jìnfā (動) head (for); march (to)

【進餐禮儀】jìncān lǐyí （名） table manners

遊 yóu （動） ❶ go sightseeing; tour; travel: 旅～ go on a tour ❷ roam; rove: ～牧民族 a nomad tribe ❸ make friends: 交～ make friends

【遊人】yóurén （名） visitor; tourist

【遊手好閑】yóu shǒu hào xián 〈成〉 loaf around doing nothing

【遊民】yóumín （名） vagrant; vagabond

【遊行】yóuxíng （名） parade; demonstration

【遊伴】yóubàn （名） travel companion; fellow traveller

【遊玩】yóuwán （動） ❶ play; amuse (oneself) ❷ go sight-seeing

【遊客】yóukè （名） tourist; traveller

【遊記】yóujì （名） travel notes; travels

【遊逛】yóuguàng （動） stroll about; saunter

【遊船】yóuchuán （名） pleasure-boat; yacht

【遊艇】yóutǐng （名） pleasure-boat; yacht

【遊樂場】yóulèchǎng （名） amusement grounds; amusement park

【遊戲】yóuxì （名） game

【遊覽】yóulǎn （動） go sightseeing; visit; tour

運 yùn Ⅰ （動）❶ carry; transport: 空～郵件 air mail ❷ use; apply: ～筆直書 set pen to paper Ⅱ （名） ❶ motion; movement ❷ fortune; luck: 時～接連而來 have a run of bad luck

【運用】yùnyòng （動） apply; utilize; put to use: 這條定律可以普遍～。 This theory is universally applicable.

【運行】yùnxíng （動） (of celestial bodies, vehicles, vessels, etc.) move; revolve; circulate

【運河】yùnhé （名） canal

【運送】yùnsòng （動） transport; convey

【運氣】yùnqi （名） fortune; luck: 他～好。 He has got good luck.

【運動】yùndòng （名） ❶ motion; movement ❷ sports; exercise: ～使人強壯。 Exercise makes one strong. ❸ social movement; campaign: 勞工～ labour movement/掃盲～ anti-illiteracy campaign

【運動員】yùndòngyuán （名） athlete; sportsman

【運動場】yùndòngchǎng （名） sports ground; playground

【運動會】yùndònghuì （名） athletic meeting; sports meet

【運費】yùnfèi （名） transportation expenses; freight; carriage: ～待收 freight to be collected

【運載】yùnzài （動） carry; deliver: ～工具 means of delivery / ～火箭 carrier rocket

【運算】yùnsuàn （名）〈數〉 operation

【運輸】yùnshū （名） transport: ～工具 means of transport

【運輸機】yùnshūjī （名） 〈航空〉 airfreighter; transport plane; packplane

【運轉】yùnzhuàn （動） ❶ revolve; rotate ❷ work; operate

【運籌帷幄】yùn chóu wéi wò 〈成〉 work out strategic plans at the headquarters

【運籌學】yùnchóuxué （名） operational research

遍 biàn Ⅰ （副） everywhere; all

over; throughout: 走～全國 travel all over the land Ⅱ（量）time: 一～又一～ time and again; over and over again

【遍天下】biàn tiānxià（副）all over the world

【遍地】biàndì（副）everywhere; all around; far and wide

【遍佈】biànbù（動）spread all over; be found everywhere: ～全市 all over the city

【遍體鱗傷】biàn tǐ lín shāng〈成〉be covered all over with cuts and bruises; be beaten black and blue

道 dào Ⅰ（名）❶ road; course; path ❷ reason; principle: 頭頭是～ pursue a topic with apparent logic ❸ way; method: 處世之～ way of getting along in the world ❹ doctrine: 孔孟之～ teachings of Confucius and Mencius ❺ Taoism Ⅱ（動）say; speak: 一語～破 reveal by one illuminating remark what is precisely the truth Ⅲ（量）一～題 a question / 五～菜的一頓飯 a five-course dinner

【道士】dàoshi（名）Taoist priest

【道地】dàodì（形）genuine: ～的中國地毯 genuine Chinese rugs

【道具】dàojù（名）〈劇〉stage properties

【道理】dàolǐ（名）❶ reason; sense: 講～ reason things out ❷ principle; truth

【道教】dàojiào（名）〈宗〉Taoism

【道賀】dàohè（動）congratulate

【道路】dàolù（名）road; path; way

【道義】dàoyì（名）moral righteousness: 由於～的原因 on moral grounds

【道歉】dàoqiàn（動）apologize

【道貌岸然】dào mào àn rán〈成〉pose as a man of great dignity; sanctimonious

【道德】dàodé（名）morality; ethics: 職業～ professional ethics

【道謝】dàoxiè（動）extend one's thanks

【道聽途説】dào tīng tú shuō（名）hearsay; rumour

遂 suì Ⅰ（動）❶ satisfy; content ❷ succeed; accomplish: 未～政變 aborted coup d'état Ⅱ（副）thereupon

【遂心】suìxīn（遂意 suìyì）（形）smooth and satisfactory; gratifying

【遂願】suìyuàn（動）fulfil one's wish

達 dá Ⅰ（動）❶ extend; arrive: 直～列車 through train ❷ comprehend: 通情～理 amenable to reason ❸ reach; realize ❹ inform; express: 傳～ pass on a message; relay (a report, etc.) Ⅱ（名）（Dá）a surname

【達旦】dádàn（副）until daybreak

【達成】dáchéng（動）reach; realize: ～協議 reach agreement

【達到】dádào（動）achieve

【達官顯貴】dáguān xiǎnguì（名）dignitaries; VIPs

【達意】dáyì（形）(of language) convey the meaning

【達斡爾族】Dáwò'ěrzú（名）the Daur nationality

【達觀】dáguān（形）optimistic: 他很～。He takes things philosophically.

逼 bī（動）❶ force; compel; coerce: 威～利誘 combine (alternate) threats with inducements ❷ extort; press for ❸ press on towards; close in on

【逼人】bīrén (形) pressing: 時間 ~. Time presses.

【逼上梁山】bī shàng Liáng Shān 〈成〉 be driven to extremities; be forced to take desperate; be driven to revolt action

【逼死】bīsǐ (动) ❶ harass sb. to death ❷ be driven to extremities

【逼近】bījìn (动) close in on; press on towards

【逼迫】bīpò (动) pressurize; compel

【逼供】bīgòng (动) extort a confession

【逼真】bīzhēn Ⅰ (形) lifelike; true to life; vivid Ⅱ (副) clearly: 看得 ~ see clearly

【逼债】bīzhài (动) exact the payment of a debt; demand quick payment of a debt; dun

違 wéi (动)❶ violate; go against: ~意 violate the constitution; be unconstitutional ❷ be absent from: 自~教範 since I ceased to attend your instruction

【違反】wéifǎn (动) violate; go against: ~紀律 a breach of discipline

【違心】wéixīn (形) insincere; against one's conscience: 做了~的事 do something against one's conscience

【違抗】wéikàng (动) disobey; disregard: ~上級命令 defy orders from above

【違法】wéifǎ (动) refuse to obey the law; act against the law

【違約】wéiyuē (动) ❶ violate a treaty; fail to honour a contract ❷

go back on one's word; break an appointment

【違背】wéibèi (动) violate; run counter to; go against: ~我的意願 be against my will

【違章】wéizhāng (动) violate rules and regulations: ~停車 parking against traffic regulations

【違禁】wéijìn (动) violate a ban: ~品 contraband goods

遐 xiá (形)❶ far ❷ long; lasting

【遐想】xiáxiǎng (动) be sunk in reverie; fall into a reverie

【遐邇】xiá'ěr (形) 〈书〉 far and near: 名聞~. One's name spreads far and wide.

過 guò Ⅰ (动)❶ exceed Ⅱ (名) (Guō) a surname
see also guò

過 guò Ⅰ (动) ❶ pass; cross ❷ go through (a process): ~秤 be weighed (on a scale) ❸ exceed; go beyond: ~半數 more than half the number Ⅱ (名) error; fault: 改~ mend one's ways Ⅲ (助) [used after a verb to indicate experience or completed action]: 吃~虧 have suffered for it
see also guō

【過分】guòfèn (形) excessive; going too far: ~敏感 oversensitive

【過火】guòhuǒ (动) go too far; overact

【過戶】guòhù (动) 〈法〉 transfer ownership

【過不去】guòbuqù (动) ❶ cannot get across ❷ create difficulties for; find fault with: 他不會和你~。 He won't be too hard on you. ❸ feel sorry: 给你添了很多麻烦,我心裏真~。I'm sorry to have put you to so much trouble.

【過去】guòqù Ⅰ(形) past; former; previous: ~的事就讓它一吧。Let bygones be bygones. Ⅱ(動) cross; pass by

【過目】guòmù (動) look over: ~不忘 have a very retentive memory

【過失】guòshī (名) fault; error; mistake

【過年】guònián (動) spend the New Year holiday

【過來】guòlái (動) come over; come up

【過往】guòwǎng (動) come and go: ~車輛 passing vehicles

【過夜】guòyè (動) put up for the night; stay overnight

【過於】guòyú (副) too; unduly; excessively: ~自信 overconfident; cocksure

【過河拆橋】guò hé chāi qiáo〈成〉drop a friend whose service is no longer needed

【過後】guòhòu (副) afterwards; later

【過活】guòhuó (動) make a living

【過度】guòdù (副) excessively; unusually: ~緊張 unusually nervous

【過時】guòshí (形) out-of-date; out-of-fashion; obsolete

【過問】guòwèn (動) concern oneself with: 親自~ attend to the matter personally

【過敏】guòmǐn Ⅰ(名)〈醫〉allergy Ⅱ(形) allergic

【過得去】guòdeqù (動) ❶ be able to get through ❷ be passable: 生活還~。We can manage to get by. ❸ feel at ease

【過眼雲煙】guò yǎn yún yān〈成〉disappear like dissolving mists

【過場】guòchǎng Ⅰ(名)(of drama) interlude Ⅱ(動) cross the stage: 走~ go through a mere formality

【過程】guòchéng (名) course; process

【過道】guòdào (名) passage-way; corridor; aisle

【過渡】guòdù Ⅰ(動) pass over Ⅱ(名) transition

【過期】guòqī (動) expire; be overdue: ~雜誌 back number of a magazine

【過剩】guòshèng (形) surplus; excessive: 生産~ overproduction

【過硬】guòyìng (形) able to stand the stiffest test: ~本領 superb skill

【過猶不及】guò yóu bù jí〈成〉overshooting the mark is as undesirable as falling short of the target

【過節】guòjié (動) spend a festival

【過路】guòlù (動) pass by on one's way

【過意不去】guò yì bù qù (動) feel sorry for: 你沒有必要覺得~。You don't have to feel apologetic about it.

【過獎】guòjiǎng (名) lavish praise; undeserved praise

【過境】guòjìng (動) pass in transit: ~簽證 transit visa

【過磅】guòbàng (動) weigh (on the scales)

【過錯】guòcuò (名) fault; mistake

【過頭】guòtóu (副) beyond the limit: 他把事情做一了。He has overstepped the limits.

【過謙】guòqiān (形) too modest

【過濾】guòlù (動) filter: ~嘴香煙 filter-tipped cigarette

【過關】guòguān (動) pass the acid test; fulfil the requirement

【過繼】guòjì (動) adopt (a relative's son as one's own)

【過癮】guòyǐn (動) satisfy an urge; find sth. extremely satisfying

遏 è (動) control; restrain: 歪風難~。Unhealthy trends are difficult to restrain.

【遏止】èzhǐ (動) hold back: 不可~的歷史洪流 irresistible historical tide

【遏制】èzhì (動) restrain; contain

遇 yù I (動) ❶ meet; 相~ meet each other ❷ treat: 禮~ give sb. a courteous reception; treat sb. with courtesy II (名) chance; opportunity: 機~ opportunity

【遇見】yùjiàn (動) meet; encounter

【遇到】yùdào (動) meet (with); encounter; run into

【遇害】yùhài (動) be murdered; be assassinated

【遇救】yùjiù (動) be rescued

【遇險】yùxiǎn (動) be in danger; be faced with danger

【遇難】yùnàn (動) ❶ be killed in an accident ❷ be murdered

逾 yú (動) exceed; go beyond

【逾期】yúqī (動) exceed the time limit: ~不還圖書 fail to return books to the library in good time

【逾越】yúyuè (動) exceed; go beyond: ~界限 exceed the bounds

遁 dùn (動) flee; escape

【遁詞】dùncí (名) subterfuge; excuse

遠 yuǎn (形) far; distant; remote: 在不~的將來 in the not too distant future / 深~的 far-reaching / ~離家鄉 far away from one's hometown

【遠大】yuǎndà (形) broad; long-range; lofty: 目光~ have foresight

【遠方】yuǎnfāng (名) distant place

【遠古】yuǎngǔ (名) remote ages

【遠見】yuǎnjiàn (名) far-sightedness; foresight

【遠近】yuǎnjìn I (副) far and near; far and wide II (名) distance: 我們都要去, 不計~。We would all like to go and not mind the distance.

【遠足】yuǎnzú (名) excursion; hike; outing

【遠走高飛】yuǎn zǒu gāo fēi 〈成〉soar into distant skies; go far away

【遠房】yuǎnfáng (形) remotely related: ~親戚 a distant relative

【遠東】Yuǎndōng (名) Far East

【遠征】yuǎnzhēng (名) expedition

【遠洋】yuǎnyáng (名) ocean: ~船 ocean-going vessel; ocean liner

【遠郊】yuǎnjiāo (名) outer suburbs; outlying districts

【遠祖】yuǎnzǔ (名) remote ancestor

【遠視】yuǎnshì (名) long sight; far-sightedness

【遠道】yuǎndào (名) a long way: 從英國~而來 come all the way from England

【遠程】yuǎnchéng (形) long-range; long-distance: ~轟炸機 long-distance bomber / ~飛行 long-haul flight

【遠期】yuǎnqī (形) forward: ~合同 long-term forward contract

【遠景】yuǎnjǐng (名) prospect; long-range perspective

【遠慮】yuǎnlǜ (名) foresight; long view: 人無~, 必有近憂。Those

who lack foresight are close to danger.

【遠親】 yuǎnqīn (名) distant relative

遜 xùn (形) ❶ modest; humble ❷ inferior

【遜色】 xùnsè (形) inferior: 毫無～ be in no way inferior

遣 qiǎn (動) ❶ send; dispatch: 派～代表團 send a delegation ❷ expel; discharge: ～悶 divert oneself

【遣返】 qiǎnfǎn (動) send back; repatriate: ～難民 repatriate refugees

【遣送】 qiǎnsòng (動) send back (those people who do not answer to the requirements of residence): ～出境 deport

【遣散】 qiǎnsàn (動) disband and send back

遙 yáo (形) remote; far

【遙相呼應】 yáo xiāng hū yìng〈成〉 echo each other over a distance; coordinate each other's effort despite the distance

【遙控】 yáokòng (名) remote control; telecontrol

【遙望】 yáowàng (動) look into the distance; look afar

【遙測】 yáocè (名) telemetering

【遙遠】 yáoyuǎn (形) faraway; remote

【遙遙】 yáoyáo (副) far away: ～無期 relegated to a distant future／～領先 be far ahead; lead by a long chalk

【遙感】 yáogǎn (名) romote sensing

遛 liù (動) stroll; walk

【遛大街】 liùdàjiē (動) go window-shopping

【遛馬】 liùmǎ (動) walk a horse

【遛彎兒】 liùwānr (動) go for a walk

遞 dì (動) ❶ pass; hand; send: 把鹽～給我。Pass me the salt. ❷ follow in succession

【遞交】 dìjiāo (動) present; hand over

【遞送】 dìsòng (動) deliver

【遞補】 dìbǔ (動) fill vacancies according to the established system of priority

【遞增】 dìzēng (動) increase progressively

適 shì (形) ❶ fit; suitable; appropriate: ～於課堂討論的問題 problem suitable for classroom discussion ❷ just right ❸ comfortable; cosy: 安～的生活 a life of ease and comfort

【適口】 shìkǒu (形) palatable; agreeable in taste

【適中】 shìzhōng (形) ❶ moderate; not excessive: 大小～ of the right size ❷ (of a place) well situated

【適用】 shìyòng (形) suitable for use; applicable

【適可而止】 shì kě ér zhǐ〈成〉know when to stop; enough is enough

【適合】 shìhé (動) suit; be just right for: 這塊地一種蔬菜。This plot of land is fit for growing vegetables.

【適宜】 shìyí (形) suitable; proper

【適者生存】 shì zhě shēng cún〈成〉survival of the fittest

【適度】 shìdù (形) moderate; not excessive

【適時】 shìshí (副) at the right time; at the opportune moment

【適得其反】shì dé qí fǎn〈成〉turn out to be the opposite of what one desires

【適量】shìliàng（形）of the right amount

【適當】shìdàng（形）appropriate; fitting and proper

【適意】shìyì（形）enjoyable; pleasant; comfortable: ～的旅行 enjoyable trip

【適銷】shìxiāo（動）sell well; sell like hot cakes

【適應】shìyìng（動）adapt; suit: 不太～這裏的氣候 be not quite used to the climate here

【適齡】shìlíng（形）of the right age: 鼓勵～青年參加俱樂部 encourage young people of the right age to join the club

遮 zhē（動）hide from view; screen: 掛個草簾子～～陽光 put up a straw curtain to keep out the sunshine／～人耳目 deceive the public

【遮羞】zhēxiū（動）❶ cover up one's private parts ❷ cover up sth. shameful with falsely pleasant words

【遮羞布】zhēxiūbù（名）fig leaf

【遮掩】zhēyǎn（動）❶ cover; envelop ❷ conceal; cover up

【遮蓋】zhēgài（動）❶ cover; 大雪～了原野。The heavy snow covered the boundless fields. ❷ conceal; cover up: 謊言～不了事實。Lies cannot cover up facts.

【遮蔽】zhēbì（動）hide from view; block

【遮擋】zhēdǎng（動）shelter from; keep out

【遮醜】zhēchǒu（動）cover up one's defect

遨 áo（動）stroll; saunter

【遨遊】áoyóu（動）roam; wander: ～太空 travel in space

遭 zāo Ⅰ（動）meet with (disaster, misfortune, etc.); suffer: ～人暗算 fall prey to a sinister plot Ⅱ（量）❶ round: 上那裏去了一～ make a trip to the place ❷ time; turn: 我們在那裏見面還是頭一～。We met there for the first time.

【遭劫】zāojié（動）be caught in a disaster

【遭到】zāodào（動）meet with; encounter; suffer: ～迫害 be persecuted／～屠殺 be massacred

【遭受】zāoshòu（動）suffer; be subjected to: ～嚴厲的批評 be subjected to severe criticism; be severely criticized／～失敗 suffer defeat

【遭殃】zāoyāng（動）suffer: 他們一定會～的。They are bound to suffer.

【遭遇】zāoyù Ⅰ（動）meet by accident; encounter: 中途～敵人 encounter the enemy midway Ⅱ（名）(bitter) experience; suffering: 不幸的～ unhappy experience

遵 zūn（動）abide by; obey; observe: 難以～命 find it difficult to comply with your wishes

【遵守】zūnshǒu（動）abide by; observe: ～規章 observe the rules／～時間 be punctual

【遵從】zūncóng（動）obey; comply with

【遵循】zūnxún（動）follow; adhere to; act in accordance with

【遵照】zūnzhào（動）obey; follow; conform to: ～你的指示 act in conformity with your instructions

遴 lín（動）choose carefully

【遴選】línxuǎn（動）select; choose

遷 qiān（動）❶ move (to another place) ❷ change: 變～ vicissitude

【遷併】qiānbìng（動）move and merge (with)

【遷居】qiānjū（動）move (house)

【遷怒】qiānnù（動）vent one's spleen on sb. who is not to blame

【遷移】qiānyí（動）move; migrate

【遷就】qiānjiù（動）accommodate oneself to; give in to

遼 liáo Ⅰ（形）far Ⅱ（名）(Liáo) short for Liaoning (Provinse)

【遼遠】liáoyuǎn（形）faraway; remote

【遼寧】Liáoníng（名）Liaoning (Province)

【遼闊】liáokuò（形）vast

遲 chí Ⅰ（形）❶ late: 姍姍來～ be slow in coming; be late ❷ tardy Ⅱ（名）(Chí) a surname

【遲早】chízǎo（副）sooner or later

【遲延】chíyán（動）delay; postpone

【遲到】chídào（形）late: ～半個小時 be half an hour late

【遲鈍】chídùn（形）slow; stupid: 頭腦～ slow of understanding

【遲疑】chíyí（動）hesitate: ～不決 be unable to make up one's mind; hesitate to make a decisive move Ⅱ（名）hesitation

【遲緩】chíhuǎn（形）sluggish; slow: 行動～ be slow in action

【遲遲】chíchí（形）slow; tardy: ～不作答 be tardy in replying

選 xuǎn Ⅰ（動）❶ choose; select: ～幾件紀念品 choose a few souvenirs ❷ elect: 當～爲市長 be elected mayor Ⅱ（名）selection: 文～ selected works

【選手】xuǎnshǒu（名）athlete or player selected to take part in a contest: 種子～ seeded player

【選民】xuǎnmín（名）voter; elector

【選拔】xuǎnbá（動）select; choose: ～人才 select talented people

【選派】xuǎnpài（動）select; detail: ～優秀學者參加研討會 select outstanding scholars to participate in the seminar

【選修】xuǎnxiū（動）take as an optional course: ～經濟學 take economics as an optional course

【選修課】xuǎnxiūkè（名）optional course or subject; elective course

【選票】xuǎnpiào（名）vote; ballot

【選區】xuǎnqū（名）electoral district; constituency

【選集】xuǎnjí（名）selected works; anthology

【選舉】xuǎnjǔ Ⅰ（動）elect; vote: ～權 the right to vote Ⅱ（名）election

【選擇】xuǎnzé Ⅰ（動）choose Ⅱ（名）choice; alternative; option: 面臨兩種～ be confronted with two alternatives

【選購】xuǎngòu（動）select and buy

【選題】xuǎntí（名）selected topic; assigned topic

【選讀】xuǎndú（名）selected readings

遺 yí（動）❶ lose ❷ omit; miss: 補～ addendum ❸ leave behind; keep back: 暴露無～ be thoroughly exposed

【遺失】yíshī（動）lose

【遺言】yíyán（名）words of the deceased：臨終～ one's last words

【遺忘】yíwàng（動）forget

【遺址】yízhǐ（名）ruins; relics

【遺志】yízhì（名）unfulfilled wish; behest

【遺物】yíwù（名）things left behind by the deceased

【遺孤】yígū（名）orphan

【遺迹】yíjī（名）historical remains

【遺容】yíróng（名）❶ remains（of the deceased）❷ portrait（of the deceased）

【遺留】yíliú（動）leave over; hand down：過去～下來的問題 questions left over from the past

【遺臭萬年】yí chòu wàn nián〈成〉be an object of ever-lasting shame

【遺產】yíchǎn（名）legacy; heritage

【遺著】yízhù（名）posthumous work

【遺棄】yíqì（動）desert; abandon：有被～的感覺 feel abandoned

【遺傳】yíchuán（名）heredity; inheritance：～工程 genetic engineering

【遺腹子】yífùzǐ（名）posthumous child

【遺像】yíxiàng（名）portrait of the deceased

【遺漏】yílòu（動）miss; leave out

【遺精】yíjīng（名）〈醫〉（seminal）emission

【遺稿】yígǎo（名）posthumous manuscript

【遺憾】yíhàn（名）regret; pity：不無～ not without a touch of regret

【遺骸】yíhái（名）sb.'s remains

【遺贈】yízèng（動）bequeath

【遺願】yíyuàn（名）unfulfilled wish of the deceased; last wish

【遺孀】yíshuāng（名）widow

【遺體】yítǐ（名）sb.'s remains：向～告別 pay last tribute to sb.'s remains

【遺囑】yízhǔ（名）will; dying words

【邁】mài Ⅰ（動）step forward：～過小溝 jump over a ditch Ⅱ（形）old in years; aged：年～體衰 aging and ailing; senile Ⅲ（量）mile：這輛汽車的最高速度爲每小時八十一。The top speed of the car is 80 miles per hour.

【邁步】màibù（動）make a step forward; stride ahead

【邁進】màijìn（動）stride forward; march forward in big strides

【避】bì（動）❶ hide oneself ❷ avoid; evade; dodge; keep away from：逃～現實 escape from reality ❸ prevent

【避不作答】bì bù zuò dá〈成〉decline to answer; parry a question

【避孕】bìyùn（名）contraception; birth control：～工具 contraceptive device

【避而不見】bì ér bù jiàn〈成〉refuse to see sb.; give sb. a wide berth

【避而不談】bì ér bù tán〈成〉avoid mentioning the matter

【避免】bìmiǎn（動）avoid; avert：～了一場災難 avert a disaster

【避雨】bìyǔ（動）take shelter from rain

【避風港】bìfēnggǎng（名）haven; harbour; refuge

【避風頭】bìfēngtou（動）dodge the brunt; lie low; hide from trouble

【避重就輕】bì zhòng jiù qīng〈成〉

hold forth on minor issues but avoid major ones

【避開】bìkāi (動) avoid; shun; keep away: ～暗礁 steer clear of a hidden reef

【避暑】bìshǔ (動) go away for one's summer holidays: ～勝地 summer resort

【避嫌】bìxián (動) avoid giving rise to suspicion; prevent any possible misunderstanding

【避雷針】bìléizhēn (名) lightning rod; lightning conductor

【避實就虛】bì shí jiù xū (成) ❶ stay clear of the enemy's main force and strike at his weak points ❷ dwell on generalities while avoiding crucial issues

【避諱】bìhuì I (動) avoid; dodge; taboo II (名) taboo

【避難】bìnàn (動) take refuge: 尋求政治～ seek political asylum

【避難所】bìnànsuǒ (名) sanctuary; asylum; haven

遽 jù (副) in haste; abruptly

【遽然】jùrán (副) abruptly; all of a sudden

還 hái (副) ❶ still; yet: 我～得告訴他。I have yet to let him know. ❷ also; too: 我～有一句話要說。I have one more word to say. ❸ even more; still more ❹ even ❺ tolerably; fairly: 身體～好 be fairly well ❻ [used to emphasize a rhetorical question]: 你 ～ 没 吃 夠? Haven't you had enough? (Are you still hungry?)
see also huán

【還是】háishì (副) ❶ still; nevertheless; all the same ❷ had better:

你～别管閑事。You had better mind your own business.

還 huán (動) ❶ return: ～鄉 return to one's native place ❷ give back; return: ～錢 pay back the borrowed money
see also hái

【還手】huánshǒu (動) strike back

【還俗】huánsú (動) (of Buddhist or Taoist priests) resume secular life; secularize

【還原】huányuán (動) return to the original condition or shape

【還債】huánzhài (動) repay a debt

【還價】huánjià (動) counter-offer; counter-bid: 討價 ～ bargain; haggle

【還嘴】huánzuǐ (動) 〈口〉 retort

【還擊】huánjī (動) fight back; counterattack

【還禮】huánlǐ (動) return a salute

邀 yāo (動) ❶ invite; request: 應 ～ on invitation ❷ seek

【邀功】yāogōng (動) take credit for another's achievements

【邀集】yāojí (動) invite (a considerable number of) people to come together

【邀請】yāoqǐng (動) invite: 我們已～她出席這次會議。We have invited her to attend this conference.

【邀請信】yāoqǐngxìn (名) (letter of) invitation

【邀請賽】yāoqǐngsài (名) invitational tournament

邂 xiè

【邂逅】xièhòu (動) 〈書〉 meet by chance

邈 miǎo (形) faraway

邊 biān Ⅰ（名）❶（in geometry）line of an angle or side of a shape ❷ edge; side：路～ roadside ❸ floral border (as an ornament)：鑲花～兒 trim with lace ❹ frontier; boundary; border：保衛～疆 safeguard the frontier ❺ limit; bound：不沾～ irrelevant ❻（Biān）a surname Ⅱ（副）(suffix in certain adverbials of place)：東（西，南，北）～ in the east (west, south, north)

【邊卡】biānqiǎ（名）border checkpost

【邊防】biānfáng（名）frontier defence

【邊門】biānmén（名）side door

【邊沿】biānyán（名）edge; border

【邊界】biānjiè（名）border; boundary：～衝突 border conflict

【邊界綫】biānjièxiàn（名）boundary line

【邊區】biānqū（名）border area

【邊陲】biānchuí（名）frontier; border area

【邊遠】biānyuǎn（形）remote; distant; outlying：～地區 outlying district; remote region

【邊際】biānjì Ⅰ（名）bound; limit：漫無～（of sea, etc.）boundless; (of a talk, etc.) rambling; discursive; straying far from the subject Ⅱ（形）marginal：～利潤 marginal profits

【邊境】biānjìng（名）frontier; border

【邊綫】biānxiàn（名）〈體〉sideline;〈棒、壘球〉foul line

【邊寨】biānzhài（名）stockaded village in a frontier region

【邊緣】biānyuán（名）❶ outskirts; edge; verge; brink：～政策 policy of brinkmanship ❷ borderline; margin：～科學 interdisciplinary science

【邊緣戰爭】biānyuán zhànzhēng（名）peripheral war

【邊…邊…】biān…biān…［used before two verbs respectively to indicate simultaneous actions］：～唱～跳 sing while dancing; sing and dance

【邊疆】biānjiāng（名）frontier; border area; borderland

邋 lā

【邋遢】lāta（形）〈口〉sloppy; unkempt：邋裏～ slovenly

邏 luó（動）patrol

【邏輯】luóji（名）logic：～結論 logical conclusion／不合～ illogical

【邏輯學】luójixué（名）logic：～家 logician

邑 部

邢 Xíng（名）a surname

邪 xié（形）evil; perverse; heretical：歪風～氣 perverse trends; unhealthy social trends

【邪念】xiéniàn（名）wicked idea

【邪門歪道】xié mén wāi dào〈成〉crooked means; vile practices

【邪道】xiédào（名）evil ways

【邪惡】xié'è（形）evil; wicked; villainous

【邪說】xiéshuō（名）heresy; heretical idea

那 nà I (代) that: ～個人 that man / 一事好辦。That's easily done. II (副) then: 你不是學生，～是幹什麼的? If you aren't a student, what are you then?

【那兒】 nàr (副) there; in that place

【那些】 nàxiē (代) those

【那個】 nàge I (代) that: ～梨比這個大。That pear is bigger than this one. II (副) ❶ [used before a verb or an adjective to imply a touch of cynicism]: 看他～機靈樣。He is that smart, you see! ❷ [used to avoid a direct statement]: 他幹的事也太～了。What he did is a bit too …, well, you know what I mean.

【那時】 nàshí (副) at that time; then

【那裏】 nàli (副) there: 他住在～。He lives there.

【那麼】 nàme I (副) ❶ so; like that: 來了～多人。So many people came. / 你怎能一說～話! How can you talk like that! ❷ then; in that case: 大家都來了，～咱們都擺擺自己觀點。Now that everybody is here, let's all air our views. II (形) about; or so: 他走了有～七八天了。He's been away for about a week.

【那樣】 nàyàng (副) so; that way; like that: 他哥哥不像他～聰明。His brother is not so clever as he. / 什麼事把你氣成～? What makes you so angry?

【那邊】 nàbiān (副) there; over there

邦 bāng (名) country; nation; state: 友～ friendly country

【邦交】 bāngjiāo (名) diplomatic relations: ～正常化 normalization of diplomatic relations

【邦聯】 bānglián (名) confederation

邵 Shào (名) a surname

邱 Qiū (名) a surname

邸 dǐ (名) residence of a high official: 官～ official residence

邰 Tái (名) a surname

郊 jiāo (名) suburbs: 西～ west suburbs

【郊區】 jiāoqū (名) suburbs; suburban area; outlying district

【郊遊】 jiāoyóu (名) outing; excursion

郎 láng (名) ❶ (a form of address for men): 兒～ young man / 伴～ best man / 情～ lover ❷ 〈舊〉 [used by a woman to address her husband or lover] my darling ❸ ancient official title ❹ (Láng) a surname

【郎才女貌】 láng cái nǚ mào (成) a man of talent and a woman of beauty; a well-matched pair

【郎中】 lángzhōng (名) 〈方〉 practitioner of traditional Chinese medicine

【郎姆酒】 lángmǔjiǔ (名) rum

郁 yù I (形) strongly fragrant II (名) (Yù) a surname

郝 Hǎo (名) a surname

郡 jùn (名) ❶ prefecture (in ancient China) ❷ county (in England and Wales)

郗 Xī (名) a surname

郜 Gào（名）a surname

部 bù Ⅰ（名）❶ part; section: 局~ 與整體的關係 the correlation between the part and the whole ❷ ministry; department: 門診~ outpatient department; clinic ❸ headquarters（of armed forces at and above the company level）: 營~ battalion headquarters Ⅱ（量）（of books, films, vehicles, machines, etc.）: 一~轎車 a car

【部下】bùxià（名）❶ troops under a commander ❷ subordinate

【部分】bùfen Ⅰ（名）part; portion: 大~ most; a great part of Ⅱ（形）partial: ~癱瘓 partial paralysis Ⅲ（副）partially; partly: ~自給 partially self-sufficient

【部件】bùjiàn（名）part; component

【部位】bùwèi（名）❶ location ❷ part（of the body, a machine, etc.）

【部長】bùzhǎng（名）minister; director; head of a department

【部門】bùmén（名）branch; sector; department: 金融~ financial department

【部首】bùshǒu（名）〈語〉radical（of a Chinese character）

【部隊】bùduì（名）❶ armed forces ❷ unit; troops

【部落】bùluò（名）tribe

【部署】bùshǔ Ⅰ（動）deploy; arrange Ⅱ（名）deployment; disposition; arrangement

【部屬】bùshǔ Ⅰ（名）subordinate Ⅱ（形）affiliated to a ministry: ~研究所 research institute under a ministry

郭 guō（名）❶ outer wall of a city

❷（Guō）a surname

都 dōu（副）❶ all ❷ even: 連小孩 ~搬得動。Even a child can move it. ❸ already: 他~七十了。He is already seventy.
see also dū

都 dū（名）❶ big city ❷ capital ❸（Dū）a surname
see also dōu

【都城】dūchéng（名）capital city

【都會】dūhuì（都市 dūshì）（名）metropolis

郵 yóu Ⅰ（動）post; mail Ⅱ（形）postal; mail: ~筒 pillar box

【郵包】yóubāo（名）(postal) parcel

【郵件】yóujiàn（名）postal matter; post; mail

【郵局】yóujú（名）post office

【郵政】yóuzhèng（名）postal service: ~編號 postcode; zip code

【郵寄】yóujì（動）send by post; post

【郵票】yóupiào（名）postage stamp; stamp

【郵袋】yóudài（名）mailbag; postbag

【郵費】yóufèi（名）postage

【郵資】yóuzī（名）postage

【郵匯】yóuhuì（動）remit by post

【郵電】yóudiàn（名）post and telecommunications

【郵遞員】yóudìyuán（名）postman; mailman

【郵箱】yóuxiāng（名）postbox; mailbox

【郵購】yóugòu（名）mailorder

【郵戳】yóuchuō（名）postmark

鄂 È（名）another name for Hubei Province

【鄂倫春族】Èlúnchūnzú（名）the Oroqen nationality

【鄂溫克族】Èwēnkèzú（名）the E-wenki nationality

鄉 xiāng（名）❶ countryside ❷ native place

【鄉下】xiāngxia（名）〈口〉village; country: ～人 country folk

【鄉土】xiāngtǔ Ⅰ（名）native land; home village Ⅱ（形）local

【鄉巴佬】xiāngbālǎo（名）〈貶〉bumpkin; country cousin

【鄉村】xiāngcūn（名）village; countryside

【鄉長】xiāngzhǎng（名）township head

【鄉思】xiāngsī（名）home-sickness; sentimental feeling for one's native place

【鄉音】xiāngyīn（名）accent of one's native place; local accent

【鄉親】xiāngqīn（名）❶ fellow villager; fellow townsman ❷ folks

【鄉鎮】xiāngzhèn（名）❶ small towns ❷ villages and towns

【鄉鎮企業】xiāngzhèn qǐyè（名）town and township enterprises

鄒 Zōu（名）a surname

鄔 Wū（名）a surname

鄙 bǐ Ⅰ（形）mean and vulgar; contemptible; despicable: 粗 ～ uncouth; coarse and vulgar Ⅱ（動）despise; scorn; disdain

【鄙人】bǐrén（代）〈謙〉my humble self; your humble servant

【鄙夷】bǐyí（動）disdain; scorn

【鄙俗】bǐsú（形）philistine; vulgar; low

【鄙視】bǐshì（動）despise; scorn;

look down upon

【鄙棄】bǐqì（動）loathe; disdain

【鄙薄】bǐbó（動）despise; slight; loathe

鄭 Zhèng（名）a surname

【鄭重】zhèngzhòng（形）serious; earnest: ～其事 in real earnest

鄰 lín Ⅰ（名）neighbour Ⅱ（形）neighbouring; adjacent

【鄰近】línjìn（形）near; in the vicinity of

【鄰里】línlǐ（名）neighbourhood; neighbours

【鄰邦】línbāng（名）neighbour country

【鄰居】línjū（名）neighbour

【鄰接】línjiē（動）border on; be contiguous to

鄧 Dèng（名）a surname

鄺 Kuàng（名）a surname

酈 Lì（名）a surname

酉 部

酋 qiú（名）❶ chief of a tribe ❷ chieftain

【酋長】qiúzhǎng（名）❶ chief of a tribe ❷ sheik(h); emir

【酋長國】qiúzhǎngguó（名）sheikhdom; emirate

酊 dīng（名）tincture

酒 jiǔ（名）alcoholic drink; wine; liquor: 白葡萄～ white wine

【酒色之徒】jiǔ sè zhī tú（成）man

fond of wine and women; libertine

【酒肉朋友】jiǔ ròu péng yǒu〈成〉companions on drinking sprees; fair-weather friend

【酒吧】jiǔbā(酒吧间 jiǔbājiān)(名) pub (public house); bar

【酒店】jiǔdiàn(名) pub; wineshop

【酒席】jiǔxí(名) feast; banquet

【酒家】jiǔjiā(名)❶ wineshop ❷ restaurant

【酒鬼】jiǔguǐ(酒徒 jiǔtú)(名) drunkard; tippler

【酒壶】jiǔhú(名) wine pot; flagon

【酒量】jiǔliàng(名) one's capacity for liquor: 他～大。He has enormous capacity for drinking.

【酒会】jiǔhuì(名) cocktail party

【酒窝】jiǔwō(名) dimple

【酒精】jiǔjīng(名) alcohol

【酒厂】jiǔchǎng(名) brewery; winery

【酒囊饭袋】jiǔ náng fàn dài〈成〉good only for eating, drinking and merrymaking; good-for-nothing

配 pèi(动)❶（of people）pair; join in marriage;（of animals）mate ❷ compound; blend ❸ apportion; allocate: 定量分～ ration（allocation）❹ have sth. replaced: ～了一副新眼镜 have got a new pair of spectacles ❺ match: 这条领带和你的上衣不相～。The tie does not match your coat. ❻ deserve; be worthy of: 她不～"模范教师"这个称号。She is unworthy of the title of "model teacher".

【配方】pèifāng Ⅰ(动) make up a prescription Ⅱ(名) formula

【配合】pèihé(动) cooperate; coordinate

【配件】pèijiàn(名) accessory; part

【配角】pèijué(名) minor role

【配音】pèiyīn(动) dub（a film）: ～演员 dubbing actor／这部电影有英文～。This film has been dubbed into English.

【配套】pèitào(动) make up a complete set; serialize

【配偶】pèi'ǒu(名) spouse

【配给】pèijǐ(名) ration; allocation

【配备】pèibèi Ⅰ(动) furnish; allocate; equip: ～家具的房子 a furnished house Ⅱ(名) equipment; outfit

【配置】pèizhì(动) dispose; deploy

【配种】pèizhǒng(名) breeding; mating

【配製】pèizhì(动) make up; prepare

【配乐】pèiyuè(动) dub in background music

酌 zhuó(动)❶ drink（wine）: 自斟自～ drink all alone ❷ consider; deliberate: ～情处理 act at one's discretion

【酌量】zhuóliàng(动) consider; deliberate; make an estimate of: ～情况予以帮助 make a general estimate of the situation and give whatever help is needed

酗 xù

【酗酒】xùjiǔ(动) drink excessively

酚 fēn(名)〈化〉phenol: ～酞 phenolphthalein

酣 hān(副) heartily

【酣饮】hānyǐn(动) drink one's fill

【酣畅】hānchàng(形) merry（with drinking）; sound（sleep）

【酣睡】hānshuì（动）sleep soundly

【酣戰】hānzhàn（动）fight a fierce battle

酥 sū Ⅰ（形）❶ crisp ❷ (of a person's limbs and trunk) weak and numb：～麻 limp and numb Ⅱ（名）shortbread; shortcake：花生～ peanut shortbread

【酥油】sūyóu（名）butter

【酥脆】sūcuì（形）(of food) crisp

【酥軟】sūruǎn（形）limp; soft; feeble

【酥糖】sūtáng（名）crunchy candy

酬 chóu Ⅰ（名）❶ remuneration; reward：同工同～ equal pay for equal work ❷ friendly exchange：忙於應～ be busy with social intercourse Ⅱ（动）❶ reward; requite ❷ fulfil; realize：壯志未～身先死 died before one's aspirations were fulfilled

【酬金】chóujīn（名）remuneration; monetary reward

【酬勞】chóuláo Ⅰ（动）recompense or reward (sb. for his trouble) Ⅱ（名）such a recompense or reward

【酬報】chóubào（动）requite; repay sb.'s kindness

【酬謝】chóuxiè（动）present sb. with a gift as an expression of appreciation

酯 zhǐ（名）〈化〉ester

酩 mǐng

【酩酊】mǐngdǐng（形）in a drunken state：～大醉 be dead drunk

酪 lào（名）❶ junket; cheese：奶～ cheese ❷ fruit jelly ❸ jam; sweet paste made from crushed nuts：杏仁～ almond paste

酵 jiào（动）ferment

【酵母】jiàomǔ（名）yeast

酷 kù Ⅰ（形）brutal; cruel; ruthless：嚴～的現實 harsh reality Ⅱ（副）extremely：～愛文學 be very fond of literature

【酷刑】kùxíng（名）savage torture

【酷暑】kùshǔ（名）sweltering summer; dog days

【酷熱】kùrè（形）terribly hot

酶 méi（名）enzyme; ferment

酸 suān Ⅰ（名）〈化〉acid Ⅱ（形）❶ sour; tart; aciduous：～澀 sour and puckery ❷ sad; anguished：辛～的往事 poignant memories ❸ aching; painful：～ tingle with pain ❹ pedantic; priggish：窮～ impoverished pedantic (scholar)

【酸奶】suānnǎi（名）yoghurt; sour milk

【酸性】suānxìng（名）〈化〉acidity

【酸雨】suānyǔ（名）acid rain

【酸甜苦辣】suān tián kǔ là〈成〉life's joys and sorrows; the sweets and bitters of life; vicissitudes of life

【酸軟】suānruǎn（形）aching and weak

【酸梅湯】suānméitāng（名）sweet-sour plum juice

【酸痛】suāntòng（酸疼 suānténg）（动）ache; feel painful：我全身～。I'm aching all over.

【酸菜】suāncài（名）pickled Chinese cabbage; pickled vegetable

【酸溜溜】suānliūliū（形）❶ sour ❷ painful; aching ❸ sad ❹ jealous ❺ pedantic

【酸辣湯】suānlàtāng（名）vinegar-pepper soup; sour and hot soup

醇 chún I（名）❶ mellow wine ❷ alcohol: 甲～ methyl alcohol II（形）pure; mellow: ～酒 mellow wine

【醇厚】chúnhòu（形）(of taste or smell) mellow; full-flavoured

醉 zuì（形）❶ drunk; intoxicated: 他昨晚喝得爛～。He got dead drunk last night. ❷ (of certain food) liquor-saturated: ～棗 liquor-saturated dates

【醉心】zuìxīn（動）be bent on; be absorbed in: ～於學術研究 be entirely absorbed in academic research

【醉生夢死】zuì shēng mèng sǐ〈成〉dream away one's life; live an aimless life; be on the batter

【醉鬼】zuìguǐ（名）drunkard; sot

【醉意】zuìyì（名）tipsiness: 他已有幾分～。He is somewhat tipsy.

【醉漢】zuìhàn（名）drunken man; drunkard

【醉醺醺】zuìxūnxūn（形）drunk; intoxicated

醋 cù（名）❶ vinegar ❷ jealousy: 吃～ be jealous

醃 yān（動）pickle; preserve in salt: ～魚 salted fish

【醃肉】yānròu（名）salted meat; bacon

【醃菜】yāncài（名）pickles; salted vegetables

醚 mí（名）〈化〉ether

醒 xǐng（動）❶ wake (up): 我七點鐘～了。I woke up at seven. / 把他叫～。Wake him up. ❷ come

to; sober up

【醒目】xǐngmù（形）eye-catching; easily seen; conspicuous

【醒悟】xǐngwù（名）awakening

【醒酒】xǐngjiǔ（動）sober up; get rid of a hangover

醜 chǒu（形）❶ ugly: ～八怪 person with a hideous face ❷ odious; shameful

【醜化】chǒuhuà（動）vilify

【醜陋】chǒulòu（形）ugly

【醜惡】chǒu'è（形）ugly; hideous; repulsive

【醜態】chǒutài（名）hideous features: ～百出 cut a sorry figure

【醜聞】chǒuwén（名）scandal

【醜劇】chǒujù（名）farce

醛 quán（名）〈化〉aldehyde

醞

【醞釀】yùnniàng（動）❶ brew; ferment ❷ deliberate on: 與別人～學習計劃 have a preliminary discussion with sb. about study plans

醫 yī I（動）treat; cure: 就～ seek medical advice II（名）❶ doctor; physician: 中～ doctor of traditional Chinese medicine ❷ medicine; medical science

【醫士】yīshì（名）medical practitioner

【醫生】yīshēng（名）doctor; physician

【醫治】yīzhì（動）treat; cure

【醫科】yīkē（名）medicine

【醫院】yīyuàn（名）hospital

【醫務】yīwù（名）medical matters: ～所 clinic

【醫師】yīshī（名）doctor

【醫術】yīshù（名）medical skill

【醫道】yīdào（名）skill of a doctor

【醫德】yīdé（名）ethics of the medical profession

【醫學】yīxué（名）medical science: ～院 medical college

【醫療】yīliáo（名）medical treatment: 公費～ public health service; free medical care

【醫藥】yīyào（名）medicine: ～費 medical expenses

【醫囑】yīzhǔ（名）doctor's advice; doctor's orders

醬 jiàng Ⅰ（名）❶ thick paste made from fermented soya-beans, wheat flour, etc. ❷ any pastelike substance; sauce; jam: 豆瓣辣～ thick broad bean chilli sauce Ⅱ（形）cooked or pickled in soy sauce: ～牛肉 braised beef seasoned with soy sauce

【醬豆腐】jiàngdòufu（名）fermented bean curd

【醬油】jiàngyóu（名）soy sauce

【醬菜】jiàngcài（名）vegetables pickled in soy sauce

【醬園】jiàngyuán（名）shop selling sauce, pickles, etc.

醺 xūn（形）drunk: 醉～～ blind drunk

釀 niàng（動）❶ make by fermentation: 這酒是用米～的。The wine is made from rice. ❷（of bees）make（honey）❸ grow; gradually become

【釀成】niàngchéng（動）bring on; develop: ～大患 develop into a disaster

【釀酒】niàngjiǔ（動）make wine: ～

廠 winery; brewery

【釀造】niàngzào（動）make（wine, vinegar, etc.）; brew（beer, etc.）

釁 xìn（名）dispute; quarrel: 挑～ 行爲 provocative act

釅 yàn（形）thick; strong

【釅茶】yànchá（名）strong tea

采 部

釉 yòu（名）glaze: ～陶 glazed pottery

釋 shì（動）❶ explain; interpret: 註～ annotate ❷ dispel; remove: 疑團盡～。All doubts are dispelled. ❸ put aside; lay down: 愛不～手 like sth. too much to let go of it ❹ set free: 保～ be released on bail

【釋迦牟尼】Shìjiāmóuní（名）Sakyamuni, founder of Buddhism

【釋放】shìfàng（動）❶ set free; release: 從監獄～出來 be released from prison ❷〈物〉release: ～出 原子能 release nuclear energy

【釋義】shìyì（名）lexical or textual analysis

里 部

里 lǐ（名）❶ lǐ a Chinese unit of length（1/2 kilometre）❷ hometown: 故～ native place ❸ neighbours: 鄰～ neighbourhood ❹（Lǐ）a surname

【里弄】 lǐlòng（名）lanes; neighbourhood

【里程】 lǐchéng（名）❶ mileage ❷ course (of development)

【里程表】 lǐchéngbiǎo（名）odometer

【里程碑】 lǐchéngbēi（名）milestone

重 chóng Ⅰ（副）again: ～建家园 rebuild one's homeland Ⅱ（名）layer; range; ring: 双～领导 dual leadership
see also zhòng

【重申】 chóngshēn（动）reiterate; reassert

【重返】 chóngfǎn（动）return

【重版】 chóngbǎn（动）be reprinted

【重洋】 chóngyáng（名）seas and oceans: 远涉～ travel across the oceans

【重奏】 chóngzòu（名）〈乐〉ensemble: 弦乐五～ string quintet

【重重】 chóngchóng（形）ring upon ring; numerous: 克服～障碍 surmount one obstacle after another

【重逢】 chóng féng（动）have a reunion: 久别～ meet again after a long separation

【重孙】 chóngsūn（名）great-grandson

【重唱】 chóngchàng（名）music composition for two or more voices: 二～ duet

【重复】 chóngfù（动）repeat; duplicate: 不会～这种错误 will not repeat this kind of mistake

【重阳】 Chóngyáng（名）Double Ninth Festival (the ninth day of the ninth lunar month)

【重叠】 chóngdié（形）overlapping: 机构～ overlapping administrative organizations

【重新】 chóngxīn（动）again: ～安排 rearrange

【重演】 chóngyǎn（动）❶ restage ❷ repeat: 故伎～ play the same old trick

【重弹老调】 chóng tán lǎo diào〈成〉harp on the same familiar string

【重整旗鼓】 chóng zhěng qí gǔ〈成〉rally one's forces (after a defeat)

【重蹈覆辙】 chóng dǎo fù zhé〈成〉follow the track of the overturned cart; repeat the same mistake

重 zhòng Ⅰ（形）❶ weighty; heavy: ～负 heavy load ❷ deep; serious: ～罚 severe punishment ❸ important: 江南～镇 strategic place south of the Yangtze ❹ discreet: 老成持～ experienced and prudent Ⅱ（名）weight: 超～ overweight Ⅲ（动）attach weight to: ～友谊 set store by friendship
see also chóng

【重力】 zhònglì（名）〈物〉gravity; gravitational force

【重大】 zhòngdà（形）great; major; significant: ～历史事件 a major historical event

【重工业】 zhònggōngyè（名）heavy industry

【重水】 zhòngshuǐ（名）heavy water

【重心】 zhòngxīn（名）❶〈物〉centre of gravity ❷ core; focus; crux

【重用】 zhòngyòng（动）place sb. in a responsible position: ～亲信 plant one's trusted followers in key positions

【重任】 zhòngrèn（名）important task: 肩负～ shoulder heavy responsibility

【重托】 zhòngtuō（名）great trust:

受人民～ entrusted by the people

【重兵】zhòngbīng（名）massive forces：～把守 heavily guarded

【重武器】zhòngwǔqì（名）heavy weapon

【重金屬】zhòngjīnshǔ（名）heavy metal

【重活】zhònghuó（名）heavy work

【重型】zhòngxíng（形）heavy-duty; heavy

【重要】zhòngyào（形）important; significant

【重音】zhòngyīn（名）〈語〉stress; accent

【重視】zhòngshì（動）attach weight to; set store by：～外國語的學習 pay great attention to the study of foreign languages

【重量】zhòngliàng（名）weight

【重量級】zhòngliàngjí（名）〈體〉heavyweight

【重點】zhòngdiǎn（名）focal point; emphasis：～工程 key project

【重讀】zhòngdú（名）〈語〉stress

野

野 yě I（名）open country; field：曠～ open field II（形）❶ rude; rough：粗～無禮 rude and barbarous ❷ wild; undomesticated：～果 wild fruit ❸ unbridled; unruly：性子～ be wild by nature ❹ not in power：下～ relinquish power

【野心】yěxīn（名）wild ambition; careerism

【野心家】yěxīnjiā（名）careerist

【野生】yěshēng（形）uncultivated; wild：～動物 wild animal; wildlife

【野史】yěshǐ（名）unofficial history

【野外】yěwài（名）open field

【野味】yěwèi（名）game (as food)

【野草】yěcǎo（名）weeds

【野菜】yěcài（名）edible wild herbs

【野豬】yězhū（名）wild boar

【野戰】yězhàn（名）〈軍〉field operations：～軍 field army

【野餐】yěcān（名）picnic

【野營】yěyíng（動）camp：～車 camper; recreational vehicle ／ ～地 camping site

【野獸】yěshòu（名）wild animal; beast

【野雞】yějī（名）❶ pheasant ❷ 〈口〉street girl; whore

【野蠻】yěmán（形）❶ savage; uncivilized ❷ brutal; barbarous：～鎮壓 bloody crackdown

量

量 liáng（動）❶ measure：～血壓 take sb.'s blood pressure ❷ estimate

see also liàng

【量角器】liángjiǎoqì（名）protractor

【量杯】liángbēi（名）measuring glass

【量具】liángjù（名）measuring tool

【量度】liángdù（名）measurement

量

量 liàng I（動）measure; estimate II（名）❶ capacity：膽～過人 have matchless courage ❷ quantity：重質不量～ attach more importance to quality than quantity

see also liáng

【量力】liànglì（動）measure one's own ability：～而行 do whatever is within one's ability; never go beyond one's depth

【量入爲出】liàng rù wéi chū〈成〉make ends meet; never live beyond one's means

【量子】liàngzǐ（名）〈物〉quantum：～力學 quantum mechanics

【量才錄用】liàng cái lù yòng（動）give sb. a job suited to his abilities

【量詞】liàngcí（名）〈語〉measure word; classifier

【量變】liàngbiàn（名）quantitative change

【量體裁衣】liàng tǐ cái yī〈成〉suit one's action to actual circumstances

釐 lí（名）❶ li, a unit of length (1/3 millimetre)❷ li, a unit of area (0.666 square metre)❸ li, a unit of weight (0.05 gram)❹ li, 1/1000 yuan ❺ li, a unit of monthly interest rate (0.1%)❻ li, a unit of annual interest rate (1%)❼ fraction

【釐米】límǐ（名）centimetre

金 部

金 jīn Ⅰ（名）❶ gold (Au)：～子 gold ❷ metals (usu. referring to gold, silver, copper, iron, tin, etc.)❸ money：救濟～ relief fund ❹（Jīn）a surname Ⅱ（形）❶ golden; colour of gold ❷ precious：～貴 invaluable

【金不換】jīnbuhuàn（形）more valuable than gold; priceless

【金字塔】jīnzìtǎ（名）pyramid

【金剛】jīngāng（名）〈宗〉Buddha's warrior guard：四大～ Four Warrior Guards

【金剛鑽】jīngāngzuàn（金剛石 jīngāngshí）（名）diamond

【金魚】jīnyú（名）goldfish

【金黃】jīnhuáng（形）golden; golden yellow

【金牌】jīnpái（名）〈體〉gold medal：～獲得者 gold medalist

【金箔】jīnbó（名）gold leaf

【金碧輝煌】jīn bì huī huáng〈成〉(of architecture) splendid; magnificent

【金幣】jīnbì（名）gold coin

【金錢】jīnqián（名）money

【金融】jīnróng（名）finance

【金橘】jīnjú（名）kumquat

【金縷玉衣】jīn lǚ yù yī（名）royal garment made of jade pieces sewn up with gold thread

【金額】jīn'é（名）sum (amount) of money

【金蟬脫殼】jīn chán tuō qiào〈成〉make one's escape from a predicament by artifice

【金屬】jīnshǔ（名）metal：稀有～ rare metal

針 zhēn（名）❶ needle：縫紉～ sewing needle ❷ stitch：在褲子上縫了幾～ put a few stitches in the trousers ❸ anything like a needle：秒～ second hand (of a clock or watch) / 飾～ brooch ❹ acupuncture ❺ injection：打一～葡萄糖 give an injection of glucose

【針灸】zhēnjiǔ（名）acupuncture and moxibustion

【針刺麻醉】zhēncì mázuì（名）acupuncture anaesthesia

【針眼】zhēnyǎn（名）❶ eye of a needle ❷ pinprick

【針線】zhēnxiàn（名）needlework; sewing：～包 sewing kit

【針對】zhēnduì（動）be directed at; be aimed at：我的話不是～你的。My remarks were not directed at you.

【針鋒相對】zhēn fēng xiāng duì〈成〉tit for tat; measure for measure

【針劑】zhēnjì（名）injection

【针织】 zhēnzhī (名) knitting: ～品 knit goods; knit-wear; hosiery

钉 dīng I (名) nail; tack II (动) ❶ follow closely ❷ urge; inquire: ～ 着他要注意身體。Remind him to take good care of himself.
see also dìng

【钉子】 dīngzi (名) ❶ nail ❷ obstacle: 碰歉～ meet with polite refusal

【钉梢】 dīngshāo (动) tail sb.

【钉鞋】 dīngxié (名) spiked shoe

钉 dìng (动) ❶ nail ❷ sew
see also dīng

钌 liǎo (名) 〈化〉 ruthenium (Ru)
see also liào

钌 liào
see also liǎo

【钌铞】 liàodiào (名) hasp and staple

釜 fǔ (名) cauldron

【釜底抽薪】 fǔ dǐ chōu xīn 〈成〉 solve a problem by taking radical measures

【釜底游鱼】 fǔ dǐ yóu yú 〈成〉 a person whose fate is as good as sealed

钗 chāi (名) hairpin

钎 qiān (名) drill rod; borer

【钎头】 qiāntóu (名) bit

钓 diào (动) ❶ fish with hook and line ❷ angle for (fame and wealth)

【钓具】 diàojù (名) fishing tackle

【钓竿】 diàogān (名) fishing rod

【钓鱼】 diàoyú (动) go fishing

【钓钩】 diàogōu (名) fish-hook

【钓饵】 diào'ěr (名) bait

钏 chuàn (名) bracelet

钐 shān (名) 〈化〉 samarium (Sm)

钕 nǚ (名) 〈化〉 neodymium (Nd)

钙 gài (名) 〈化〉 calcium (Ca): ～ 片 calcium tablet

【钙化】 gàihuà I (动) calcify II (名) 〈医〉 calcification

钝 dùn (形) ❶ dull; blunt ❷ dull-witted

钮 niǔ (名) ❶ button; knob ❷ (Niǔ) a surname

钞 chāo (名) paper money; 美～ American dollar

【钞票】 chāopiào (名) banknote

钠 nà (名) 〈化〉 sodium (Na)

钧 jūn I (名) ancient unit of weight, equal to 15 kilograms: 雷 霆萬～之力 with the tremendous force of a thunderbolt II (代) 〈敬〉 you; your: ～安 Best regards [used at the end of a letter to one's superior or elder]

钩 gōu I (名) ❶ hook: 秤～ steelyard hook ❷ hook stroke (in Chinese characters) II (动) ❶ hang with a hook; hook ❷ sew with large stitches

【钩针】 gōuzhēn (名) crochet hook

【钩虫】 gōuchóng (名) hookworm

钳 qián I (名) pincers; pliers II (动) grip; clamp

【钳子】 qiánzi (名) pincers; pliers; forceps

【钳工】 qiángōng (名) fitter

【钳制】 qiánzhì (动) contain; pin down

鉢 bō（名）❶ earthen bowl ❷ alms bowl (of a Buddhist monk)

鈸 bó（名）〈樂〉cymbals

鈮 ní（名）〈化〉niobium (Nb)

鉬 mù（名）〈化〉molybdenum (Mo)

鉀 jiǎ（名）〈化〉potassium (K)：高錳酸～ potassium permanganate

【鉀肥】jiǎféi（名）potash fertilizer

鈾 yóu（名）〈化〉uranium (U)

鈴 líng（名）❶ bell ❷ bell-shaped thing：棉～ cotton boll

【鈴鐺】língdang（名）small bell; hand bell

鉋 bào Ⅰ（名）plane; planing machine Ⅱ（動）plane sth. (down)

【鉋子】bàozi（名）plane (as used by a carpenter)

【鉋冰】bàobīng（名）frappé; a drink with shaved ice

【鉋牀】bàochuáng（名）lathe for planing; planer

鉛 qiān（名）lead (Pb)

【鉛印】qiānyìn（名）typographic printing; stereotype

【鉛字】qiānzì（名）(printing) type

【鉛版】qiānbǎn（名）〈印〉stereotype

【鉛球】qiānqiú（名）〈體〉shot; shot put

【鉛筆】qiānbǐ（名）pencil：～盒 pencil-case

鉚 mǎo（名）〈機〉riveting

【鉚工】mǎogōng（名）riveter

【鉚釘】mǎodīng（名）rivet

【鉚接】mǎojiē（動）rivet

【鉚槍】mǎoqiāng（名）riveting gun

銨 ǎn（名）ammonium

鉸 jiǎo（動）❶〈口〉cut with scissors ❷ ream

銥 yī（名）〈化〉iridium (Ir)

【銥金筆】yījīnbǐ（名）iridium-point pen

銬 kào Ⅰ（名）handcuffs：手～腳鐐 handcuffs and shackles Ⅱ（動）handcuff

銪 yóu（名）〈化〉europium (Eu)

銀 yín（名）silver (Ag)

【銀子】yínzi（名）silver

【銀白】yínbái（形）silvery white

【銀耳】yín'ěr（名）white fungus

【銀行】yínháng（名）bank：～家 banker／～匯票 bank draft; bank bill

【銀河】yínhé（名）Milky Way

【銀根】yíngēn（名）money market; money：～緊。Money is tight.

【銀針】yínzhēn（名）acupuncture needle

【銀婚】yínhūn（名）silver wedding

【銀牌】yínpái（名）silver medal

【銀圓】yínyuán（名）silver dollar

【銀幕】yínmù（名）(motion-picture) screen

【銀幣】yínbì（名）silver coin

【銀器】yínqì（名）silverware

銅 tóng（名）copper; brass; bronze

【銅匠】tóngjiang（名）coppersmith

【銅臭】tóngchòu（名）stink of money; avarice

【銅像】tóngxiàng（名）bronze statue

【銅管樂隊】tóngguǎn yuèduì（名）brass band

【銅器】tóngqì（名）copper（bronze, brass）ware

銦 yīn（名）〈化〉indium（In）

銑 xǐ（動）mill

【銑工】xǐgōng（名）miller

銘 míng Ⅰ（動）engrave; inscribe: 永～於心 be for ever engraved in one's mind Ⅱ（名）inscription: 墓誌～ inscription on a tombstone

【銘文】míngwén（名）inscription; epigraph

【銘刻】míngkè（動）❶ inscribe ❷ be for ever engraved（in one's mind, memory, etc.）

【銘記】míngjì（動）always remember

鉈 sè（名）〈化〉cesium（Cs）

銣 rú（名）〈化〉rubidium（Rb）

銜 xián Ⅰ（動）hold in the mouth Ⅱ（名）rank; title: 少將～ rank of major general

【銜恨】xiánhèn（動）harbour enmity for

【銜接】xiánjiē（動）link; join

鋬 pàn（名）handle（of a utensil）

鋅 xīn（名）〈化〉zinc（Zn）

鋃 láng

【鋃鐺】lángdāng Ⅰ（名）iron chains; fetters; shackles: ～入獄 go to prison in handcuffs Ⅱ（象）clanging sound

銳 ruì Ⅰ（形）sharp; keen: 感覺敏～ have keen senses / 鋒～ sharp Ⅱ（名）vigour; dash: ～不可當 be ir-

resistible Ⅲ（副）rapidly: ～減 decrease rapidly

【銳角】ruìjiǎo（名）〈數〉acute angle

【銳利】ruìlì（形）sharp; keen: 目光～ have sharp eyes

【銳氣】ruìqì（名）dash; drive: 缺乏～ lack drive

鋪 pū（動）❶ spread; unfold: ～開被褥 spread out the bedding ❷ pave; lay

【鋪天蓋地】pū tiān gài dì（成）on a gigantic scale and at an overpowering pace: 大風雪～而來。A blizzard is coming on with tremendous force.

【鋪牀】pūchuáng（動）make the bed

【鋪軌】pūguǐ（動）lay a railway track

【鋪敘】pūxù（動）（of writing）describe in detail

【鋪張】pūzhāng（名）extravagance: 批評有關部門～浪費 criticize the departments concerned for extravagance and waste

【鋪設】pūshè（動）lay: ～鐵路 build a railway

【鋪路】pūlù（動）pave the way（for sth.）

【鋪蓋】pūgài（名）bedding; bedroll

銅 jū（動）mend（pottery or porcelain）with cramps

【銅子】jūzi（名）cramp used in mending pottery or porcelain

銷 xiāo Ⅰ（動）❶ cancel ❷ sell: 供～ supply and marketing ❸ expend: 開～ expenditure ❹ melt（metal）Ⅱ（名）pin: 插～ bolt（for a door）; window, etc.）

【銷售】xiāoshòu（動）sell; market: 年～量 annual sales

【銷假】xiāojià（動）report back after

leave of absence

【銷毀】xiāohuǐ (動)　destroy by burning or melting

【銷路】xiāolù (動)sale; market: 這種東西沒有～。There is no market for such goods.

【銷魂】xiāohún (動)feel transported

【銷聲匿迹】xiāo shēng nì jì〈成〉cease to make public appearances; lie low

鋰 lǐ (名)〈化〉lithium (Li)

鋤 chú I (名)hoe II (動)❶ hoe ❷ eradicate; wipe out

【鋤頭】chútou (名)hoe

鋇 bèi (名)〈化〉barium (Ba)

【鋇餐】bèicān (名)〈醫〉barium meal

鋁 lǚ (名)aluminium (Al)

【鋁合金】lǚhéjīn (名)aluminium alloy

鋌 tǐng

【鋌而走險】tǐng ér zǒu xiǎn〈成〉make a desperate move

銹 xiù I (名)rust; 防～ rust-free II (動)become rusty; rust: 螺絲～住了。The screw has rusted in.

鋒 fēng (名)❶ cutting edge; sharp point ❷ forefront of an army

【鋒利】fēnglì (形)sharp; incisive

【鋒芒】fēngmáng (名)❶ spearhead ❷ talent; superficial brilliance

【鋒芒畢露】fēng máng bì lù〈成〉make an undisguised show of one's ability

錠 dìng I (名)❶〈紡〉spindle ❷ ingot; ingot-shaped tablet II (量):

一～墨 a stick of Chinese ink

錶 biǎo (名)watch: 對～ set the watch

【錶帶】biǎodài (名)watch strap

【錶鏈】biǎoliàn (名)watch chain

鍺 zhě (名)〈化〉germanium (Ge)

錯 cuò I (名)fault; mistake: 知～就改。Correct your mistake when you find it. II (形)❶ wrong; mistaken: 答～了 give a wrong answer ❷ interlocked ❸ bad: 戲不～。The opera is not bad. III (動)stagger: ～開辦工時間 stagger the office hours

【錯別字】cuòbiézì (名)　wrongly-written character; misspelt word

【錯怪】cuòguài (動)wrongly blame a person

【錯過】cuòguò (動)miss: ～最後一趟進城的班車 miss the last bus to town

【錯亂】cuòluàn (形)in disorder; abnormal; deranged

【錯落】cuòluò (形)straggly: 村舍～ straggly cottages

【錯誤】cuòwù I (名)mistake; fault II (形)wrong; erroneous: ～觀點 erroneous views

【錯綜複雜】cuòzōng fùzá (形)highly complicated

【錯覺】cuòjué (名)illusion; misconception

錢 qián I (名)❶ coin ❷ money ❸ fund; sum: 一筆～ a sum of money ❹ (Qián) a surname ❺ (量) [a unit of weight] 1 qian (= 5g)

【錢包】qiánbāo (名)wallet; purse

【錢財】qiáncái (名)money; wealth

【錢幣】qiánbì（名）coin

鋅 bēn Ⅰ（名）adze Ⅱ（動）cut with an adze

【锛子】bēnzi（名）adze

鋸 jù Ⅰ（名）saw：～條 saw blade Ⅱ（動）saw：～牀 sawing machine

【鋸末】jùmò（名）sawdust

【鋸齒】jùchǐ（名）sawtooth

錳 měng（名）〈化〉manganese（Mn）

【錳結核】měngjiéhé（名）〈礦〉manganese nodule

【錳鋼】měnggāng（名）manganese steel

鋼 gāng（名）steel：合金～ alloy steel

【鋼印】gāngyìn（名）❶ steel seal ❷ embossed stamp

【鋼材】gāngcái（名）steels

【鋼坯】gāngpī（名）〈冶〉steel billet

【鋼盔】gāngkuī（名）steel helmet

【鋼筆】gāngbǐ（名）fountain pen

【鋼筋】gāngjīn（名）reinforcing bar：～混凝土 reinforced concrete

【鋼琴】gāngqín（名）piano：～家 pianist

【鋼絲】gāngsī（名）steel wire

【鋼絲牀】gāngsīchuáng（名）spring bed

【鋼管】gāngguǎn（名）steel tube

【鋼精】gāngjīng（名）aluminium：～鍋 aluminium pot（pan, boiler, etc.）

【鋼錠】gāngdìng（名）steel ingot

【鋼鐵】gāngtiě（名）iron and steel

鍆 mén（名）〈化〉mendelevium（Md）

錫 xī（名）〈化〉tin（Sn）

【錫匠】xījiàng（名）tinsmith

【錫伯族】Xībózú（名）Xibe nationality

【錫金】Xījīn（名）Sikkim

【錫紙】xīzhǐ（名）silver paper；tinfoil

【錫箔】xībó（名）tinfoil paper

【錫礦】xīkuàng（名）❶ tin ore ❷ tin mine

錚 zhēng

【錚錚】zhēngzhēng（象）clank；clang

錘 chuí Ⅰ（名）hammer：鐵～ iron hammer Ⅱ（動）hammer

【錘煉】chuíliàn（動）temper：千錘百煉 be thoroughly tempered

錐 zhuī（名）❶ awl：改～ screwdriver ❷〈數〉cone

【錐子】zhuīzi（名）awl

【錐形】zhuīxíng（名）〈機〉taper；cone

【錐面】zhuīmiàn（名）〈數〉cone

錦 jǐn Ⅰ（名）brocade Ⅱ（形）splendid；beautiful

【錦上添花】jǐn shàng tiān huā〈成〉embroider flowers on a piece of brocade；add charm to a thing of beauty；make a happy event even happier

【錦旗】jǐnqí（名）silk banner（often embroidered with words of praise, offered as award or gift）

【錦標】jǐnbiāo（名）prize；title：～賽 championships；tournament

【錦緞】jǐnduàn（名）brocade

【錦繡】jǐnxiù（形）brilliant；splendid：～前程 bright future

鍁 xiān（名）shovel

錄 lù I（動）❶ write down; record: 照～不誤 record word for word ❷ tape-record: 把歌～下來 have a song recorded ❸ employ II（名）written record

【錄用】lùyòng（動）employ

【錄供】lùgòng（動）put sb.'s confession on record

【錄取】lùqǔ（動）enrol; admit: ～新生 enrol new students / ～通知書 admission notice

【錄音】lùyīn（名）audio or sound recording: 放～ play the recording

【錄音帶】lùyīndài（名）tape; audiotape

【錄音機】lùyīnjī（名）tape-recorder

【錄像】lùxiàng（名）video: 放～ show a video

【錄像帶】lùxiàngdài（名）video cassette; video tape

【錄像機】lùxiàngjī（名）video recorder

【錄製】lùzhì（動）make gramophone records, audiotapes or video tapes

鍍 dù（動）plate: ～銀匙 a silver-plated spoon

【鍍金】dùjīn（動）❶ gild ❷ gain a veneer of culture of learning（such as trying to get a foreign degree）; join a training course or do physical labour as a stepping-stone to promotion

鎂 měi（名）〈化〉magnesium（Mg）

【鎂光燈】měiguāngdēng（名）flash lamp; magnesium torch

鍥 qiè（動）carve; engrave

【鍥而不捨】qiè ér bù shě〈成〉work（at sth.）without letup; keep at it

錯 nuò（名）〈化〉nobelium（No）

錨 máo（名）anchor: 拋（起）～ cast（weigh）anchor

【錨地】máodì（名）anchorage

【錨泊】máobó（動）anchor

鍵 jiàn（名）key（of a piano, typewriter, computer, etc.）

【鍵盤】jiànpán（名）keyboard

鎇 méi（名）〈化〉americium（Am）

鍘 zhá I（名）hand hay cutter; fodder chopper II（動）cut or chop with a hay cutter

【鍘刀】zhádāo（名）hand hay cutter; fodder chopper

鍋 guō（名）❶ pot; pan; boiler; cauldron: 沙～ earthenware pot ❷ bowl（of a tobacco pipe, etc.）

【鍋巴】guōbā（名）rice crust

【鍋爐】guōlú（名）boiler: ～房 boiler room

鍾 zhōng（動）concentrate（one's affections, etc.）

【鍾情】zhōngqíng（動）be deeply in love with; have deep affection for

【鍾愛】zhōng'ài（動）love dearly; cherish

鍬 qiāo（名）spade; shovel

鍛 duàn（動）forge

【鍛工】duàngōng（名）forger

【鍛煉】duànliàn（動）❶ forge ❷ do physical exercises ❸ temper; steel

鎊 bàng（名）pound sterling

鎬 gǎo（名）pick; pickaxe

鏈 liàn（名）chain

【鏈式反應】liànshì fǎnyìng （名）chain reaction

【鏈條】liàntiáo（名）chain

【鏈盒】liànhé（名）chain cover (of a bicycle)

【鏈球】liànqiú（名）〈體〉hammer

【鏈霉素】liànméisù（名）〈藥〉streptomycin

鎮 zhèn Ⅰ（動）❶ suppress; keep down ❷ guard; garrison ❸ cool with cold water or ice: 冰～汽水 iced soda water Ⅱ（形）calm; composed Ⅲ（名）❶ garrison post: 重～ place of strategic importance ❷ town: 集～ market town

【鎮守】zhènshǒu（動）guard; garrison

【鎮定】zhèndìng（鎮 靜 zhènjìng）（形）calm; composed

【鎮紙】zhènzhǐ（名）paperweight

【鎮痛】zhèntòng（動）relieve pain

【鎮壓】zhènyā（動）suppress; put down; quell; crack down (on)

鎖 suǒ Ⅰ（名）lock Ⅱ（動）❶ lock up: 把箱子～上 lock the suitcase ❷ seal up; close: 閉關～國 close one's country to the outside world

【鎖匠】suǒjiàng（名）locksmith

【鎖骨】suǒgǔ（名）〈生理〉clavicle; collarbone

【鎖鏈】suǒliàn（名）❶ chain ❷ shackles; fetters

鎧 kǎi

【鎧甲】kǎijiǎ（名）(suit of) armour

錞 ná（名）〈化〉neptunium (Np)

鎳 niè（名）〈化〉nickel (Ni)

鎢 wū（名）tungsten; wolfram (W)

【鎢絲】wūsī（名）tungsten filament

鎦 liú（名）gold-plating
see also liù

鎦 liù
see also liú

【鎦子】liùzi（名）〈方〉ring

鏖 áo（動）fight fiercely

【鏖戰】áozhàn（動）be locked in bitter fighting

錾 zàn Ⅰ（動）engrave; carve: 在金上～花樣 engrave designs on gold Ⅱ（名）engraving tool; chisel

【錾刀】zàndāo（名）(engraver's) burin; graver

【錾子】zànzi（名）chisel

鏡 jìng（名）❶ mirror; looking glass ❷ lens; glasses: 變色～ sunsensitive glasses

【鏡子】jìngzi（名）❶ looking glass; mirror ❷〈口〉spectacles

【鏡框】jìngkuàng（名）❶ frame of a mirror ❷ gallery frame; picture frame ❸ spectacles frame

【鏡臺】jìngtái（名）dressing table

【鏡頭】jìngtóu（名）❶ camera lens ❷（photographic）shot; (cinematic) scene

鏟 chǎn Ⅰ（名）shovel; spade: 機～ mechanical shovel Ⅱ（動）shovel: 把土堆～平 level the mound with a shovel

【鏟子】chǎnzi（名）shovel; spade

【鏟車】chǎnchē（名）〈機〉forklift

【鏟除】chǎnchú（動）uproot; eradicate：～雜草 weed

鏺 xuān（動）peel; lathe：～蘿蔔 peel a turnip

鏢 biāo（名）dartlike weapon (made of iron)：保～ bodyguard

鏗 kēng（象）clanging sound
【鏗鏘】kēngqiāng（象）clang; clatter

鏜 táng（動）〈機〉bore：～牀 borer; boring lathe

鏤 lòu（動）engrave; carve
【鏤花】lòuhuā（名）ornamental engraving
【鏤刻】lòukè（動）engrave
【鏤空】lòukōng（動）hollow out

鏝 màn（名）trowel
【鏝刀】màndāo（名）trowel
【鏝板】mànbǎn（名）patter

鏘 qiāng（象）clang; gong

鐘 zhōng（名）❶ bell：警～ warning bell; tocsin ❷ clock：電子～ electronic clock ❸ time as measured in hours and minutes：十點～ ten o'clock／五分～ five minutes
【鐘樓】zhōnglóu（名）❶ bell tower ❷ clock tower
【鐘頭】zhōngtóu（名）〈口〉hour
【鐘錶】zhōngbiǎo（名）clocks and watches; time-piece
【鐘點】zhōngdiǎn（名）time; hour
【鐘擺】zhōngbǎi（名）pendulum

鏵 huá（名）plough-share

鐐 liào（名）fetters
【鐐銬】liàokào（名）shackles

鏹 qiāng
【鏹水】qiāngshuǐ（名）strong acid

鐮 lián（名）sickle
【鐮刀】liándāo（名）sickle

鐵 tiě Ⅰ（名）❶ iron：～板 iron plate ❷ arms：手無寸～ barehanded; unarmed ❸（Tiě）a surname Ⅱ（形）❶ hard; strong：～脚板 tough feet ❷ irrefutable; ironclad：～證 conclusive evidence Ⅲ（動）❶ look grim：～着臉 pull a long face ❷ firmly make up (one's mind)：～了心 be firmly determined
【鐵人】tiěrén（鐵漢子 tiěhànzi）（名）iron man; physically and mentally tough person
【鐵水】tiěshuǐ（名）molten iron
【鐵皮】tiěpí（名）iron sheet：白～煙筒 tinplate stovepipe
【鐵匠】tiějiang（名）blacksmith
【鐵青】tiěqīng（形）(of one's complexion) ashen; livid：氣得臉色～ livid with rage
【鐵砂】tiěshā（鐵礦砂 tiěkuàngshā）（名）iron sand
【鐵軌】tiěguǐ（名）rail
【鐵索】tiěsuǒ（名）cable; iron chain
【鐵腕】tiěwàn（名）iron arm：～人物 strongman
【鐵窗】tiěchuāng（名）❶ window with iron grating ❷ prison：～生活 life behind bars
【鐵絲】tiěsī（名）iron wire：～網 wire netting; barbed wire entanglements
【鐵畫】tiěhuà（名）〈工美〉iron picture
【鐵道】tiědào（名）railway
【鐵飯碗】tiěfànwǎn（名）iron rice

bowl; permanent employment; secure job

【鐵路】tiělù（名）railway; railroad: ~車輛 rolling stock / ~道口 railway crossing; level crossing

【鐵餅】tiěbǐng（名）〈體〉❶ discus ❷ discus throw

【鐵銹】tiěxiù（名）(iron) rust

【鐵器】tiěqì（名）ironware

【鐵鍬】tiěxiān（名）shovel; spade

【鐵鏈】tiěliàn（名）iron chain

【鐵礦】tiěkuàng（名）iron mine; iron ore

鐺 chēng（名）shallow, flat pan
see also dāng

鐺 dāng（象）clank
see also chēng

鐲 zhuó（名）bracelet

鐫 juān（動）carve; engrave

【鐫刻】juānkè（動）carve; engrave

鑒 jiàn Ⅰ（名）❶ ancient bronze mirror ❷ instructive example; warning; lesson: 借~ draw lessons from ❸ history; past events: 年~ yearbook Ⅱ（動）❶ reflect ❷ scrutinize Ⅲ〈套〉[old use in Chinese letter-writing] for your perusal

【鑒戒】jiànjiè（名）warning; lesson

【鑒別】jiànbié（動）make judgment on; differentiate: ~真偽 discern the fake from the genuine; distinguish between truth and falsehood

【鑒定】jiàndìng Ⅰ（名）appraisal (of a person's contribution, achievement, strong and weak points, etc.) Ⅱ（動）appraise; evaluate

【鑒於】jiànyú（介）in view of; considering

【鑒賞】jiànshǎng（動）judge (as a connoisseur); appreciate

鑄 zhù（動）cast: ~鐵 cast iron

【鑄工】zhùgōng（名）foundry worker

【鑄件】zhùjiàn（名）〈冶〉casting

【鑄造】zhùzào（動）cast; found

鑣 biāo（名）mouthpiece of a bridle: 分道揚~ part company; go different ways

鐒 lǔ（名）〈化〉lutetium (Lu)

鑲 xiāng（動）❶ mount; inlay; set: 在金戒指上~寶石 mount gems in a gold ring ❷ rim; edge: 給手帕~上花邊 edge a handkerchief with lace

【鑲牙】xiāngyá（動）have a denture made

【鑲板】xiāngbǎn（名）〈建〉panel

【鑲嵌】xiāngqiàn（動）inlay; set; mount

鑰 yào
see also yuè

【鑰匙】yàoshi（名）key

鑰 yuè（名）key
see also yào

鑹 cuān（名）ice pick

鑷 niè

【鑷子】nièzi（名）tweezers

鑼 luó（名）gong: 敲~打鼓慶新年 beat drums and strike gongs to celebrate the New Year

【鑼鼓】luógǔ（名）❶ gong and drum ❷ traditional Chinese percussion instruments

鑽 zuān（動）❶ drill; bore: 在鐵板上～個孔 drill a hole in the iron plate ❷ go through; make one's way into: 設法～過鐵絲網 manage to pass through the barbed-wire entanglements ❸ make a serious study of: ～業務 devote oneself to professional study
see also zuàn

【鑽牛角尖】zuān niú jiǎo jiān〈成〉split hairs

【鑽空子】zuān kòngzi（動）take advantage of loopholes

【鑽研】zuānyán（動）make a serious study of; go in for（a subject or skill）

【鑽探】zuāntàn（動）drill for exploratory purposes

【鑽營】zuānyíng（動）toady to sb. in power for personal advantages

鑽 zuàn（名）❶ drill; auger: 臺～ bench drill ❷ diamond; jewel: 十七～的手錶 a 17-jewel watch
see also zuān

【鑽井】zuànjǐng（名）well drilling

【鑽石】zuànshí（名）diamond

【鑽牀】zuànchuáng（名）〈機〉drilling machine; driller

【鑽塔】zuàntǎ（名）〈礦〉derrick; boring tower

【鑽頭】zuàntóu（名）bit（of a drill）

【鑽機】zuànjī（名）〈石油〉（drilling）rig

鑿 záo Ⅰ（名）chisel Ⅱ（動）chisel; dig: ～井防旱 dig wells to provide against a drought / ～個眼兒 bore a small hole
see also zuò

【鑿子】záozi（名）chisel

鑿 zuò Ⅰ（形）certain; irrefutable: 證據確～。The evidence is conclusive. Ⅱ（名）mortise
see also záo

長 部

長 cháng Ⅰ（形）❶ long: 拉～了臉 pull a long face ❷ lasting: ～存 last for ever Ⅱ（名）❶ length: 身～ length（of a garment）❷ merit; strong point: 揚～避短 make amends for one's weaknesses by exploiting one's strengths Ⅲ（動）be good at: ～於攝影 be a good photographer
see also zhǎng

【長久】chángjiǔ（形）lasting; for long

【長江】Chángjiāng（名）the Changjiang（Yangtze）River

【長年】chángnián（形）all the year round; year in, year out: ～在外 have been away from home for years

【長此以往】cháng cǐ yǐ wǎng〈成〉if things should go on like this

【長足】chángzú（形）rapid: ～的進步 marked progress

【長征】chángzhēng（名）❶ expedition ❷（Changzheng）the Long March

【長波】chángbō（名）long wave

【長城】Chángchéng（名）❶ the Great Wall ❷（chángchéng）impregnable bulwark

【長度】chángdù（名）length

【長眠】chángmián（名）〈婉〉death; eternal sleep

【長途】chángtú（形）long-distance: 打～電話 make a trunk call

【長處】chángchu（名）forte; merit; strength

【長短】chángduǎn（名）❶ length ❷ mishap (exp. one which may endanger one's life): 萬一有個～ should sth. untoward happen ❸ strengths and weaknesses; merit and demerit: 背地裏說人～ criticize a person behind his back

【長跑】chángpǎo（名）long-distance running

【長期】chángqī（形）long-term: ～共存, 互相監督 long-term coexistence and mutual supervision

【長遠】chángyuǎn（形）long-term; long-range: ～打算 long-term planning

【長嘆】chángtàn（動）heave a deep sigh

【長壽】chángshòu（名）longevity; long life

【長篇小說】chángpiān xiǎoshuō（名）novel

【長篇大論】cháng piān dà lùn〈成〉an eloquent speech or a lengthy article

長 zhǎng Ⅰ（動）❶（begin to）grow; develop: 鍋～銹了。The pan is getting rusty. / 小孩頭髮～長了。The baby's hair has grown longer. ❷ gain; increase: ～志氣 strengthen the morale Ⅱ（形）❶ older; elder; senior: 他比她年一一歲。He is one year her senior. ❷ eldest; oldest: ～子 eldest son Ⅲ（名）chief; head: 組～ group leader / 部～ minister

see also cháng

【長大】zhǎngdà（動）grow up; be brought up

【長者】zhǎngzhě（名）❶ one's senior ❷ venerable elder

【長相】zhǎngxiàng（名）looks; appearance: ～平平 be plain in appearance

【長孫】zhǎngsūn（名）eldest grandson

【長進】zhǎngjìn（動）make progress

【長勢】zhǎngshì（名）condition of the crops: 今年莊稼～良好。The crops are growing well this year.

【長輩】zhǎngbèi（名）elder; senior

門　部

門 mén Ⅰ（名）❶ door; gate: 機艙～ entrance hatch ❷ switch; valve: 水～ water valve ❸ family: 滿～老小 the whole family ❹（religious）sect; school: 佛一弟子 Buddhist disciples ❺ knack; key: 摸着點～兒 be picking up the rudiments of a subject Ⅱ（量）: 一～科學 a science / 一一高級英語課 an advanced English course

【門口】ménkǒu（名）entrance

【門巴族】Ménbāzú（名）the Moinba (Monba) nationality

【門戶】ménhù（名）❶ door; gate ❷ gateway; passageway ❸ faction: ～之見 sectarian views (of rival schools of thought)

【門牙】ményá（名）front tooth

【門生】ménshēng（名）disciple; student

【門市部】ménshìbù（名）retail department; salesroom; shop

【鬥外漢】ménwàihàn（名）layman; novice

【鬥可羅雀】mén kě luó què〈成〉there are vary few callers; scarcely any visitors turn up

【鬥把】ménbà（名）door knob

【鬥房】ménfáng（名）❶ gate house; janitor's room ❷ gatekeeper; janitor

【鬥面】ménmiàn（名）❶ shop front ❷ facade; veneer; appearance: 他總想保持富有的～。He always tried to maintain a facade of wealth. ／講～ keep up appearances

【鬥面話】ménmiànhuà（名）lip service

【鬥閂】ménshuān（名）door bolt

【鬥框】ménkuàng（名）door-frame

【鬥徒】méntú（名）disciple; follower

【鬥庭若市】mén tíng ruò shì〈成〉have an endless stream of visitors

【鬥崗】méngǎng（名）gate sentry

【鬥將】ménjiàng（名）goalkeeper

【鬥第】méndì（名）family status

【鬥票】ménpiào（名）admission ticket

【鬥道】méndào（名）❶ ways and means: 工業增產有很多～。There are ways and means to increase industrial production. ❷ social connections

【鬥廊】ménláng（名）porch

【鬥診】ménzhěn（名）outpatient service: ～時間 consulting hours

【鬥診部】ménzhěnbù（名）outpatient department

【鬥牌】ménpái（名）house number; address plate (put up over the front door)

【鬥鈴】ménlíng（名）doorbell

【鬥路】ménlu（名）❶ trick; knack;

know-how ❷ social connections: 那時候沒有～什麼事也辦不成。In those days you could do nothing without the right social connections.

【鬥當戶對】mén dāng hù duì〈成〉be well-matched for marriage in family background

【鬥衛】ménwèi（名）entrance guard

【鬥樓】ménlóu（名）arch over a gateway

【鬥聯】ménlián（名）couplet on the door

【鬥類】ménlèi（名）category; class

【鬥檻】ménkǎn（名）❶ threshold ❷ knack of doing things: 他～精不會上當。He is too shrewd to be taken in.

【鬥鏡】ménjìng（名）peephole

【鬥簾】ménlián（名）door curtain

【鬥警】ménjǐng（名）entrance guard

【鬥廳】méntīng（名）entrance hall; foyer; lobby

閂 shuān Ⅰ（名）bolt; latch Ⅱ（動）fasten with a bolt or latch: ～上鬥 bolt the door

閃 shǎn（動）❶ flash; sparkle: 山後～出一條小路來。There appeared a path behind the mountain. ❷ dodge; duck: ～開 quickly get out of the way ❸ strain; sprain: ～了腰 strain one's back

【閃失】shǎnshī（名）accident; mishap

【閃光】shǎnguāng（動）flash; gleam

【閃光燈】shǎnguāngdēng（名）〈攝〉photoflash

【閃念】shǎnniàn（名）brainwave

【閃閃】shǎnshǎn（動）sparkle; glitter; twinkle: ～發光的鑽石 sparkling diamonds

【閃現】shǎnxiàn（名）flash; appear

【閃電】shǎndiàn（名）lightning

【閃鋅礦】shǎnxīnkuàng（名）〈礦〉(zinc) blende; sphalerite

【閃避】shǎnbì（動）dodge quickly; evade

【閃擊戰】shǎnjīzhàn（名）blitzkrieg; blitz

【閃爍】shǎnshuò（動）❶ twinkle; flicker; glint：～的星星 twinkling stars ❷ evade; dodge：～其詞 talk evasively

【閃耀】shǎnyào（動）shine; scintillate; sparkle

閉 bì（動）❶ shut; close; conclude：關～大門 close the gate ❷ obstruct; block up：封～瓶口 seal up the bottle

【閉門造車】bì mén zào chē〈成〉evolve a plan in isolation from objective reality

【閉門羹】bìméngēng（名）act of denying admittance：吃～ be refused admittance

【閉氣】bìqì（動）hold one's breath

【閉塞】bìsè Ⅰ（動）block; obstruct Ⅱ（形）secluded from the outside world; ill-informed：耳目～ uninformed

【閉會】bìhuì（動）(of a meeting) close; adjourn; not be in session

【閉路電視】bìlù diànshì（名）closed-circuit television

【閉幕】bìmù（動）❶ (of a meeting, etc.) conclude; close ❷ (of a show, etc.) the curtain falls; lower the curtain

【閉幕式】bìmùshì（名）closing ceremony

【閉幕詞】bìmùcí（名）closing speech

【閉嘴】bìzuǐ（動）shut up; hold your tongue

【閉關自守】bì guān zì shǒu〈成〉follow the policy of closing down the country to the outside world

【閉關鎖國】bì guān suǒ guó〈成〉isolate the country from the international community

閏 rùn（形）〈天〉intercalary

【閏日】rùnrì（名）leap day

【閏月】rùnyuè（名）leap month

【閏年】rùnnián（名）leap year

開 kāi Ⅰ（動）❶ open：～門 open the door ❷ open up; make accessible or available：～路 open a way; blaze a trail ❸ (of a connection) separate; come loose：(衣服)～綫了 (of clothes) come unsewn ❹ (of rivers) thaw ❺ lift (a ban, blockade, etc.)：～齋 resume a meat diet after a fast; break one's fast ❻ set in motion; operate：大客車～走了。The coach has left. / 把電視機打～ turn on the TV ❼ (of troops) set out; move：～赴前綫 start for the front ❽ set up; open：～了一家飯店 open a restaurant ❾ begin：明年～春 at the beginning of next spring ❿ run; hold (a meeting, etc.)：～展覽會 give an exhibition ⓫ make a list; write out; write：～病假條 write a certificate for sick leave ⓬ pay (salary, fare, etc.)：～工資 pay wages ⓭ boil：鍋～了。The water is boiling. ⓮〈口〉eat up Ⅱ（名）❶ percentage; ratio：你我房租四六一。You pay 40 per cent of the rent and I 60 per cent. ❷ k (karat)：24～金 24K gold ❸ [used after numbers to indicate the size of a piece of paper or a book: 8 ～本 octavo ❹〈Kǎi〉a surname Ⅲ（副）❶ [used after a verb to indicate extension or expansion]: 人羣散～了。The crowd dispersed. ❷ [used after a verb to indicate continuous action]: 村裏人對這件事議論～了。This incident has become the talk of the villagers. ❸ [used after a verb to indicate partition] up: 切～蛋糕 cut the cake ❹ away; off: 躲～ get out of the way; dodge ❺ [used after a verb to indicate capacity]: 車間太小，機器擺不～。The workshop is too small to house the machines.

【開刀】kāidāo（動）❶〈口〉perform or undergo an operation ❷ punish sb. as a warning to others

【開工】kāigōng（動）❶（of factories, etc.）begin operation ❷（of construction projects）start

【開口】kāikǒu（動）❶ open one's mouth; begin to speak; speak out ❷ sharpen the edge of a new blade)

【開戶】kāihù（動）open a bank account

【開火】kāihuǒ（動）open fire

【開心】kāixīn（動）❶ feel happy ❷ make fun of; tease; jeer

【開支】kāizhī Ⅰ（動）pay（expenses）Ⅱ（名）spending; expenditure

【開水】kāishuǐ（名）boiled water

【開天闢地】kāi tiān pì dì〈成〉since the creation of the universe; from the very outset

【開外】kāiwài（副）upwards of; over; beyond: 他九十～了。He is over 90.

【開列】kāiliè（動）make a list; list: ～名單 draw up a list of names

【開車】kāichē（動）❶ drive a car, truck, train, etc. ❷ set a machine in motion

【開花】kāihuā（動）❶ blossom: ～結果 blossom and bear fruit; bear positive results ❷（of a bullet, etc.）burst

【開卷】kāijuàn（動）open a book; do some reading: ～考試 open-book examination

【開例】kāilì（動）set a precedent

【開明】kāimíng（形）enlightened; liberal

【開始】kāishǐ Ⅰ（動）❶ begin; commence ❷ set about Ⅱ（名）initial period; outset

【開往】kāiwǎng（動）（of a coach, train, ship, etc.）head for; be bound for

【開放】kāifàng（動）❶ bloom; be in flower ❷ liberalize; lift a ban ❸（of airports, roads, etc.）be open for public use ❹（of parks, libraries, etc.）be open to the public ❺（of state policy）open to the outside world

【開放大學】kāifàng dàxué（名）open university

【開夜車】kāiyèchē（動）work far into the night; burn the midnight oil

【開玩笑】kāi wánxiào（動）〈口〉crack a joke; jest ❷ trifle with

【開架】kāijià（形）open-shelf

【開胃】kāiwèi（動）whet the appetite

【開胃菜】kāiwèicài（名）appetizer

【開朗】kāilǎng（形）❶（of place）spacious and bright ❷（of mentality, mind, character, etc.）cheerful; optimistic 胸懷～ be frank and straightforward

【開除】kāichú（動）expel; dismiss

【開航】kāiháng（動）❶（of waterways, airlines, etc.）open up a new air or sea route ❷ set sail; sail

【開庭】kāitíng（動）〈法〉hold a court session; call the court to order

【開通】kāitōng（動）remove obstructions（blocking a path, etc.）

【開通】kāitong（形）liberal; open-minded

【開展】kāizhǎn Ⅰ（動）launch; carry out Ⅱ（名）development; unfolding Ⅲ（形）open-minded; forward-looking

【開倒車】kāi dàochē（動）❶ back a car, etc. ❷ turn the clock back; retrograde

【開採】kāicǎi（動）mine; extract

【開船】kāichuán（動）set sail; navigate a ship

【開動】kāidòng（動）❶ set in motion ❷（of troops, etc.）set out on a march

【開票】kāipiào（動）❶ have a ballot box opened and ballots counted ❷ make out invoice

【開設】kāishè（動）❶ set up（a shop, factory, hospital, etc.）❷ offer（a course in college, etc.）: 學院～了三門文學課程。The college offers three courses in literature.

【開脫】kāituō（動）exculpate; absolve sb. from（blame, guilt, etc.）

【開張】kāizhāng Ⅰ（動）begin a business Ⅱ（名）the first business transaction in a day

【開場】kāichǎng（動）（of a show or other public activities）open; begin:～白 prologue（of a play, etc.）; introductory remarks

【開創】kāichuàng（動）initiate; in-

augurate

【開發】kāifā（動）develop, exploit or tap（natural resources）

【開飯】kāifàn（動）serve a meal

【開腔】kāiqiāng（動）open one's mouth: 大家還沒有說話，他先～了。He started to speak ahead of all others.

【開業】kāiyè（動）❶（of a shop, enterprise, clinic, etc.）begin business ❷ set up a practice（as a lawyer, doctor, etc.）

【開禁】kāijìn（動）lift a ban; relax restrictions（on）

【開會】kāihuì（動）hold a meeting; attend a meeting

【開誠佈公】kāi chéng bù gōng〈成〉frank and sincere

【開幕】kāimù（動）❶（of a show, etc.）the curtain rises ❷（of a conference, exhibition, etc.）open:～式 opening ceremony

【開端】kāiduān（名）start; beginning; opening

【開槍】kāiqiāng（動）fire（a rifle, pistol, etc.）; open fire

【開演】kāiyǎn（動）（of a play, film, etc.）begin; start

【開標】kāibiāo（動）open sealed tenders

【開導】kāidǎo（動）enlighten; give verbal guidance to; talk sb. around

【開課】kāikè（動）❶ school begins ❷（of a teacher）give a course: 去年她開三門課。Last year she offered three courses.

【開銷】kāixiāo Ⅰ（動）pay（expenses）Ⅱ（名）expenses: 旅費～ travel expenses

【開墾】kāikěn（動）reclaim（wasteland）

【开办】kāibàn（动）set up; open（a factory, school, business, hospital, etc.）

【开学】kāixué（动）school（term）begins

【开战】kāizhàn（开仗 kāizhàng）（动）go to war

【开头儿】kāitóur（开头 kāitóu）I（动）begin; start II（副）at the beginning; at first III（名）beginning; outset

【开赛】kāisài（动）（of a match, game, etc.）begin; start

【开阔】kāikuò I（形）❶（of area or space）spacious; wide ❷（of mind）open; broad II（动）broaden; enlarge

【开裆裤】kāidāngkù（名）split pants（for small children）

【开关】kāiguān（名）switch; on-off button: 定时～ clock switch

【开矿】kāikuàng（动）open up a mine; mine; exploit mineral resources

【开辟】kāipì（动）❶ open up: ～科研新领域 open up a new area for scientific research ❷ develop: ～边疆 develop border regions

閑 xián I（形）idle; not in use: 他今天～着。He is free today. / 這個工廠已經～了兩年了。This factory was not in operation for two years. II（名）leisure; free time

【闲人】xiánrén（名）❶ person not engaged in any type of work; idler ❷ person not concerned: ～免进。No admittance except on business.

【闲工夫】xiángōngfu（名）spare time

【闲心】xiánxīn（名）leisurely mood

【闲在】xiánzài（形）idle and leisurely

【闲言碎语】xián yán suì yǔ（名）❶ digression ❷ scandal; gossip

【闲空】xiánkòng（名）free time

【闲事】xiánshì（名）other people's business: 管～ interfere in other people's affairs

【闲书】xiánshū（名）light reading

【闲逛】xiánguàng（动）take a stroll

【闲气】xiánqì（名）anger over trifles

【闲聊】xiánliáo（名）chat; chitchat

【闲情逸致】xián qíng yì zhì（名）leisurely and carefree mood

【闲散】xiánsǎn（形）❶ leisurely and carefree ❷ idle: ～人员 personnel kept idle

【闲置】xiánzhì（动）lie idle; be unused

【闲话】xiánhuà（名）❶ idle talk ❷ complaint; gossip

【闲暇】xiánxiá（名）leisure

【闲谈】xiántán（动）chat

【闲钱】xiánqián（名）spare money

【闲杂人员】xiánzá rényuán（名）❶ people without fixed duties ❷ loafers; idlers

間 jiān I（介）between; among; amongst: 师生之～的關係 teacher-student relationship II（副）during a certain period of time; in a certain place: 晚～新聞 evening news III（名）room: 衛生～ toilet IV（量）smallest unit of a house: 一～书房 a study

see also jiàn

【間不容髪】jiàn bù róng fà（成）（of a situation）be in imminent danger: 當時局勢～。The situation was critical.

【間架】jiānjià（名）❶ frame (structure) of a house ❷ form (of a Chinese character) ❸ structure (of an essay)

間 jiàn Ⅰ（名）space in between; gap; interval: 團結無～ united as one Ⅱ（動）❶ separate; part: 多雲～晴 cloudy with occasional sunshine ❷ drive a wedge between: 挑撥離～ sow discord; foment dissension
see also jiān

【間作】jiànzuò Ⅰ（名）intercropping Ⅱ（動）intercrop

【間或】jiànhuò（副）occasionally; once in a while

【間苗】jiànmiáo（動）thin out seedlings

【間接】jiànjiē（形）indirect

【間歇】jiànxiē（名）intermittence; interval

【間隔】jiàngé（名）gap in time or space: ～均勻 evenly spaced

【間隔號】jiàngéhào（名）separation dot

【間隙】jiànxì（名）gap; interval

【間諜】jiàndié（名）secret agent; spy

【間雜】jiànzá（動）be mingled with; be mixed with

【間斷】jiànduàn Ⅰ（名）interruption; disconnection Ⅱ（動）be interrupted

閘 zhá（名）❶ flood gate; sluice gate ❷ brake: 捏～ apply the brake ❸ switch

【閘門】zhámén（名）❶ sluice gate ❷ lock gate

【閘盒】zháhé（名）fuse box

閡 hé（動）separate; cut off: 隔～

estrangement; misunderstanding

閨 guī（名）boudoir: ～房 boudoir

【閨女】guīnǚ（名）❶ girl; maiden ❷〈方〉daughter

閩 Mǐn（名）another name for Fujian Province

閣 gé（名）❶ tower ❷ boudoir ❸ (of government) cabinet

【閣下】géxià〈敬〉Your (His, Her) Excellency

【閣樓】gélóu（名）attic; garret

閥 fá（名）❶ powerful person, family or group: 軍～ warlord ❷ valve

閱 yuè（動）❶ read: 批～ read through a document and make comments ❷ experience; go through ❸ inspect; review

【閱兵】yuèbīng（動）review troops

【閱歷】yuèlì（名）experience: ～深 have seen much of the world

【閱覽】yuèlǎn（動）read: ～室 reading roon

【閱讀】yuèdú（動）read

閹 yān（動）castrate

【閹割】yāngē（動）❶ castrate; spay ❷ emasculate; strip sth. of its essence: 措詞的改動～公報的精神。The communique was emasculated by this change of wording.

閻 Yán（名）a surname

【閻王】Yánwang（名）❶ King of Hades ❷ person of the most vicious type

【閻王債】yánwangzhài（名）usurious loan

【闔羅】Yánluó (名) Yana

闊 kuò (形) ❶ vast; extensive ❷ rich: ~少 son of a rich family; fop

【闊別】kuòbié (形) long separated: 見到~多年的老友 meet an old friend that one has not seen for years

【闊步】kuòbù (動) take big steps; stride ahead

【闊佬】kuòlǎo (名) rich man

【闊氣】kuòqi (形) extravagant: 大擺~ make an ostentatious show of one's wealth

闌 lán (形) late; near the end: 歲~ at the end of the year

【闌干】lángān Ⅰ (動) crisscross: 星斗~。The sky is crisscrossed with stars. Ⅱ (名) railing; banisters

【闌尾】lánwěi (名) 〈生理〉appendix: ~炎 appendicitis

闋 què (名) ❶ watchtower at the palace gate ❷ imperial palace

闖 chuǎng (動) ❶ dash; storm: ~進去 burst in ❷ (name) break through: ~出一條新路 break a new path; blaze a new trail

【闖勁】chuǎngjìn (名) pioneering spirit

【闖將】chuǎngjiàng (名) pathbreaker

【闖禍】chuǎnghuò (動) get into serious trouble; cause disaster

【闖關】chuǎngguān (動) fight one's way through a difficult pass; make a breakthrough

闔 hé Ⅰ (形) entire; whole: ~城 the whole town Ⅱ (動) shut; close

關 guān Ⅰ (動) ❶ shut; close ❷

concern; involve Ⅱ (名) ❶ pass: ~口 strategic pass ❷ barrier; critical juncture ❸ customs (house) ❹ (Guān) a surname

【關心】guānxīn Ⅰ (動) concern; care for Ⅱ (名) concern

【關切】guānqiè (動) have great concern for; feel deeply concerned about

【關押】guānyā (動) be under arrest; take into custody

【關於】guānyú (介) about; on; concerning: ~國際形勢的講話 a talk on international affairs

【關門】guānmén (動) ❶ close; shut down ❷ leave no room for further discussion

【關注】guānzhù (動) pay close attention to; follow: ~事態發展 follow closely the development of events

【關係】guānxì Ⅰ (名) relations; relationship Ⅱ (動) concern

【關閉】guānbì (動) ❶ close; shut ❷ (of a shop or factory) close down; shut down

【關稅】guānshuì (名) customs duty; tariff

【關節】guānjié (名) 〈生理〉joint: ~炎 arthritis

【關照】guānzhào (動) ❶ look after; keep an eye on ❷ inform; notify

【關頭】guāntóu (名) juncture; moment: 緊要~ critical juncture

【關鍵】guānjiàn (名) key; crux

【關聯】guānlián (動) be related

【關懷】guānhuái (動) be concerned about; show solicitude for

闡 chǎn (動) explain; expound

【闡明】chǎnmíng (動) clarify; expound

【闡述】chǎnshù（動）expound; elaborate

闢 pì Ⅰ（動）❶ open up ❷ refute; remove Ⅱ（形）penetration; thorough: 精～ penetrating and precise; pithy

【闢謠】pìyáo（動）spike a rumour

阜 部

阜 fù Ⅰ（名）mound Ⅱ（形）rich; plentiful

阡 qiān（名）footpath between fields (running north and south)

【阡陌】qiānmò（名）crisscross paths between fields

防 fáng Ⅰ（動）prepare against Ⅱ（名）❶ defence: 邊～部隊 frontier guards ❷ dyke; embankment

【防火】fánghuǒ Ⅰ（名）fire protection Ⅱ（形）fireproof

【防水】fángshuǐ（形）waterproof

【防止】fángzhǐ（動）prevent

【防不勝防】fáng bù shèng fáng〈成〉very difficult to put up any effective defence

【防守】fángshǒu（動）defend

【防治】fángzhì（動）prevent and cure (disease)

【防空】fángkōng（名）air defence

【防空洞】fángkōngdòng（名）air-raid shelter; dugout

【防毒】fángdú（名）gas defence: ～面具 gas mask

【防疫】fángyì（名）epidemic prevention

【防洪】fánghóng（防汛 fángxùn）（名）flood control

【防風林】fángfēnglín（名）windbreak

【防凍】fángdòng（名）frostbite prevention

【防務】fángwù（名）defence

【防區】fángqū（名）defence area

【防患未然】fáng huàn wèi rán〈成〉provide against rainy days

【防備】fángbèi（動）guard against: ～敵人的突然襲擊 guard against the enemy's surprise attack

【防暑】fángshǔ（名）heatstroke prevention

【防塵】fángchén（形）dustproof

【防磁】fángcí（形）〈物〉antimagnetic

【防腐】fángfǔ（形）antiseptic: ～劑 preservative

【防綫】fángxiàn（名）defence line

【防銹】fángxiù（形）antirust

【防潮】fángcháo（形）dampproof

【防彈】fángdàn（形）bulletproof

【防範】fángfàn（動）take precautions against

【防衛】fángwèi（動）defend

【防震】fángzhèn Ⅰ（名）precautions against earthquakes Ⅱ（形）shockproof

【防禦】fángyù（名）defence: ～戰 defensive warfare

【防護】fánghù（動）protect

阱 jǐng（名）trap

阮 Ruǎn（名）a surname

陀 tuó

【陀螺】tuóluó（名）top: 抽～ whip a top

阿

阿 ā (助) [used before a pet name, a surname, a title of family or some other relationships]: ～妹 younger sister

see also ē

【阿斗】Ā Dǒu (名) good-for-nothing; weakling

【阿司匹林】āsīpǐlín (名) 〈藥〉 aspirin

【阿門】āmén (嘆) amen

【阿拉伯】Ālābó (形) Arab; Arabian

【阿拉伯語】Ālābó yǔ (名) Arabic

【阿拉伯膠】Ālābó jiāo (名) gum arabic

【阿拉伯數字】Ālābó shùzì (名) Arabic numerals

【阿拉伯聯合酋長國】Ālābó Liánhé Qiúzhǎngguó (名) United Arab Emirates

【阿飛】āfēi (名) hooligan (often a youngster in bizarre clothes)

【阿訇】āhōng (名) imam

【阿姨】āyí (名) ❶ auntie; child's address for a woman of its parents' generation ❷ maid-servant; maid

【阿根廷】Āgēntíng (名) Argentina: ～人 Argentine; Argentinean

【阿曼】Āmàn (名) Oman: ～人 Omani

【阿富汗】Āfùhàn (名) Afghanistan: ～人 Afghan

【阿爾巴尼亞】Ā'ěrbāníyà (名) Albania: ～人 Albanian

【阿爾及利亞】Ā'ěrjílìyà (名) Algeria: ～人 Algerian

阿

阿 ē (動) pander to; cater for

see also ā

【阿膠】ējiāo (名) 〈中藥〉 donkey-hide gelatin (a hematic tonic)

【阿諛】ēyú (動) flatter: ～奉迎 toady and flatter

阻

阻 zǔ (動) block; obstruct; impede: 交通受～。The traffic was held up.

【阻力】zǔlì (名) resistance; obstruction: 克服～ conquer resistance

【阻止】zǔzhǐ (動) stop; prevent; obstruct: ～侵略軍向前推進 prevent the invading army from pushing ahead

【阻塞】zǔsè I (動) block; obstruct: 河道被淤泥～。The river is blocked up with silt. II (名) jam; congestion: 交通～ traffic jam

【阻撓】zǔnáo (動) obstruct; hinder; thwart: ～爭取和平解決的努力 hinder all efforts to seek a peaceful solution

【阻擋】zǔdǎng (動) stop; block; obstruct: ～敵人前進 check the enemy's advance

【阻擊】zǔjī (動) 〈軍〉 block; check: ～戰 blocking action

【阻撓】zǔnáo (動) block

【阻礙】zǔ'ài (動) hinder; impede; hamper: ～社會發展 hamper the development of society

【阻攔】zǔlán (動) stop; obstruct

附

附 fù I (形) ❶ additional ❷ close to; near II (動) depend on; sponge on; adhere to

【附上】fùshàng (動) enclose herewith: 隨信～近照一張。I enclose herewith a recent picture of mine.

【附加】fùjiā I (動) add; attach II (形) additional; extra: ～工資 extra pay

【附加稅】fùjiāshuì (名) surtax

【附件】fùjiàn (名) ❶ appended document ❷ accessory

【附近】fùjìn (形) nearby: ~的學校 nearby schools / 在北京 ~ in the vicinity of Beijing

【附言】fùyán (名) postscript (p. s.)

【附和】fùhè (動) echo; parrot: 隨聲 ~ echo others readily

【附着】fùzhuó (動) adhere to; stick to

【附帶】fùdài Ⅰ (形) supplementary; attached: ~ 聲明 supplementary statement Ⅱ (副) by the way; incidentally

【附設】fùshè (動) be attached to: 這個醫學院 ~ 一所醫院。This medical institute has a teaching hospital.

【附庸】fùyōng (名) vassal; dependency

【附註】fùzhù (名) notes; remarks

【附會】fùhuì (動) make a far-fetched interpretation

【附錄】fùlù (名) appendix

【附議】fùyì (動) second a motion

【附屬】fùshǔ (形) affiliated; subsidiary: ~ 中學 affiliated middle school

【附屬國】fùshǔguó (名) dependency; vassal state

陋 lòu (形) ❶ ugly ❷ vulgar; vile ❸ limited; little

【陋俗】lòusú (陋習 lòuxí) (名) bad customs

【陋規】lòuguī (名) bad practice

陌 mò (名) path between fields (running east and west); road

【陌生】mòshēng (形) strange; unfamiliar

【陌生人】mòshēngrén (名) stranger

【陌路】mòlù (名)〈書〉 stranger: 宛同 ~ as if one were a complete stranger

限 xiàn Ⅰ (動) set a limit; confine; restrict: 只 ~ 内部傳閱 be restricted to internal circulation / 資源有 ~。The resources are limited. Ⅱ (名) limit

【限令】xiànlìng (動) order sb. to do sth. within a time limit: ~三日完成任務 order that the work be finished within three days

【限定】xiàndìng (動) limit: 我 ~ 每天只吸五支煙。I limit myself to five cigarettes a day.

【限於】xiànyú (動) be limited to: 僅 ~ 一般性討論 be limited to a general discussion

【限制】xiànzhì Ⅰ (動) restrict; limit Ⅱ (名) restriction

【限度】xiàndù (名) limit

【限量】xiànliàng (動) set a limit: ~ 購買 restrict the quantity of purchase

【限期】xiànqī Ⅰ (動) set a time limit: ~歸還 return sth. within a specified period of time Ⅱ (名) deadline; time limit

【限額】xiàn'é (名) quota; limit; ceiling: 僱員人數 ~ quota of employees

降 jiàng (動) ❶ fall; drop; decline ❷ reduce; bring down: ~價出售 sell at a reduced price
see also xiáng

【降半旗】jiàng bànqí (動) fly at half-mast

【降低】jiàngdī (動) reduce; bring down: ~成本 reduce the cost

【降級】jiàngjí (動) ❶ demote ❷ (of

a student) be sent to a lower grade to study

【降温】jiàngwēn Ⅰ(动) lower the temperature Ⅱ(名) drop in temperature

【降落】jiàngluò(动) descend; touch down; land

【降落伞】jiàngluòsǎn(名) parachute

【降临】jiànglín(动) fall; befall: 大祸~。Disaster has befallen.

降 xiáng(动) ❶ surrender: 宁死不~ rather die than surrender ❷ subdue; put under control
see also jiàng

【降伏】xiángfú(动) subdue; tame

【降服】xiángfú(动) surrender; submit

院 yuàn(名)❶ courtyard; yard ❷ a designation for certain government offices and public places: 学~ college; institute/ 法~ law court / 戏~ theatre

【院士】yuànshì(名) academician

【院子】yuànzi(名) courtyard; yard

陣 zhèn Ⅰ(名)❶ battle formation; troops in battle array: 严~以待 remain in combat-readiness ❷ position; front: 攻占敌~ overrun the enemy's positions ❸ a period of time: 这一~我很忙。I'm rather busy these days. Ⅱ(量): 一~~笑声 roars of laughter ❸ 一~雨 a passing shower; a fall of rain

【阵亡】zhènwáng(动) be killed in action

【阵地】zhèndì(名) position; front: 防御~ defensive positions

【阵风】zhènfēng(名) gust

【阵容】zhènróng(名)❶ battle array ❷ lineup: ~整齐 an orderly lineup/ 我系教员~强大。Our department has a highly competent staff.

【阵痛】zhèntòng(名)〈医〉labour pains

【阵势】zhènshì(名)❶ battle array ❷ situation; circumstances

【阵脚】zhènjiǎo(名)❶ front line ❷ position; situation: 压住~ keep the situation under control; take the matter in hand / 乱了~ be thrown into confusion

【阵线】zhènxiàn(名) front; alignment

【阵营】zhènyíng(名) camp

陡 dǒu Ⅰ(形) steep; precipitous Ⅱ(副) suddenly

【陡峻】dǒujùn(形) high and steep

【陡峭】dǒuqiào(形) craggy

【陡然】dǒurán(副) suddenly

陝 Shǎn(名) short for Shaanxi Province

【陕西】Shǎnxī(名) Shaanxi (Province)

陛 bì(名) flight of steps leading to a palace hall

【陛下】bìxià(名) Your Majesty (Majesties); His Majesty; Her Majesty; Their Majesties

除 chú Ⅰ(动)❶ remove; rid: ~名 remove one's name from the register ❷〈数〉divide Ⅱ(介)❶ except; with the exception of ❷ besides; in addition to

【除了】chúle(介)❶ except ❷ besides

【除夕】chúxī(名) New Year's Eve

【除外】chúwài〈介〉excluding; except

【除法】chúfǎ（名）〈数〉division

【除非】chúfēi Ⅰ（连）[often used in conjunction with 纔，否则，不然，etc. to introduce a required condition] only if; only when; unless: ～請我，我纔去。I won't go unless invited. Ⅱ（介）[used in conjunction with 誰等 etc. to indicate the only choice] except: ～他，誰也不認識那位廠長。He alone, and nobody else, knows the factory director.

【除根】chúgēn（动）❶ root out; eradicate ❷（of disease）be cured once and for all

【除草】chúcǎo（动）weed

陪 péi（动）❶ accompany; keep sb. company: ～某人去車站 accompany sb. to the railway station ❷ assist: ～祭 assist in officiating at funeral rites

【陪同】péitóng（动）accompany; be in the company of

【陪伴】péibàn（动）keep sb. company

【陪客】péikè（名）ordinary guest（as distinct from the guest of honour）

【陪嫁】péijià（名）dowry

【陪葬】péizàng（动）be buried with the dead

【陪审】péishěn（动）serve on a jury

【陪审团】péishěntuán（名）jury

【陪衬】péichèn（动）set off; serve as a foil to

陈 chén Ⅰ（动）❶ display; put on show ❷ state: 慷慨～詞 vehemently present one's views Ⅱ（形）old; stale Ⅲ（名）(Chén) a surname

【陈列】chénliè（动）display; exhibit: ～櫃 showcase

【陈述】chénshù（动）state; recount

【陈酒】chénjiǔ（名）old wine

【陈规】chénguī（名）outmoded practice; outworn conventions

【陈货】chénhuò（名）old stock

【陈设】chénshè Ⅰ（动）furnish Ⅱ（名）furnishings

【陈诉】chénsù（动）state（one's grievances

【陈词滥调】chén cí làn diào〈成〉clichés; hackneyed expressions

【陈腐】chénfǔ（形）stale; outworn

【陈旧】chénjiù（形）obsolete; outmoded; out of date

陆 liù（数）[the elaborate form of the numeral 六, used on cheques, banknotes, etc.] six
see also lù

陆 lù（名）❶ land ❷（Lù) a surname
see also liù

【陆地】lùdì（名）land

【陆军】lùjūn（名）army; ground force

【陆基导弹】lùjī dǎodàn（名）land-based missile

【陆运】lùyùn（名）land transportation

【陆路】lùlù（名）land route

【陆战队】lùzhànduì（名）marines

【陆续】lùxù（副）successively; one after another: 新建工廠～投産。New factories have gone into operation one after another.

陵 líng（名）❶ hill ❷ tomb

【陵园】língyuán（名）graveyard; cemetery

【陵墓】língmù (名) mausoleum; tomb

陰 yīn Ⅰ (名) ❶ (in Chinese philosophy, medicine, etc.) *yin*, the feminine or negative principle in nature ❷ moon ❸ shade; shady place: 山的～面 the north side of a mountain ❹ private parts (esp. of the female) Ⅱ (形) ❶ cloudy; overcast ❷ hidden; covert; sinister ❸〈物〉negative

【陰天】yīntiān (名) cloudy day; overcast day

【陰冷】yīnlěng (形) raw; gloomy and cold

【陰私】yīnsī (名) unmentionable secret

【陰沉】yīnchén (形) cloudy; dull; gloomy

【陰性】yīnxìng (形) negative

【陰雨】yīnyǔ (形) overcast and rainy

【陰涼】yīnliáng Ⅰ (形) shady and cool Ⅱ (名) cool place; shade

【陰部】yīnbù (名)〈生理〉private parts

【陰莖】yīnjìng (名) penis

【陰極】yīnjí (名) 〈物〉 negative pole; negative electrode

【陰間】yīnjiān (名) nether world

【陰道】yīndào (名)〈生理〉vagina

【陰森】yīnsēn (形) grisly; ghastly

【陰雲】yīnyún (名) dark cloud

【陰陽怪氣】yīn yáng guài qì (形) cynical; eccentric; enigmatic

【陰暗】yīn'àn (形) dark; gloomy: ～的地窖 dark cellar

【陰電】yīndiàn (名) negative electricity

【陰溝】yīngōu (名) sewer; drain; gutter

【陰魂】yīnhún (名) soul; spirit

【陰影】yīnyǐng (名) shadow

【陰曆】yīnlì (名) lunar calendar

【陰謀】yīnmóu (名) conspiracy; plot

【陰險】yīnxiǎn (形) wily; insidious

【陰錯陽差】yīn cuò yáng chā〈成〉errors arising from a curious coincidence

【陰鬱】yīnyù (形) depressed; sad

陲 chuí (名) frontier: 邊～ border region

陶 táo Ⅰ (名) ❶ pottery; ceramics: 黑～ black pottery ❷ (Táo) a surname Ⅱ (動) educate; cultivate; nurture: 薰～ influence imperceptibly Ⅲ (形) joyful; contented

【陶冶】táoyě (動) exert an imperceptible (or subtle) influence on (one's character, temperament, etc.); mould: ～高尚的情操 cultivate noble sentiments

【陶俑】táoyǒng (名) pottery figurine

【陶瓷】táocí (名) pottery and porcelain: ～藝術 ceramic art

【陶陶】táotáo (形) happy and contented: 樂～ feel exceedingly happy

【陶然】táorán (形) happy and relaxed

【陶醉】táozuì (動) be intoxicated: ～在大自然的懷抱裏 revel in the bosom of Mother Nature

【陶器】táoqì (名) earthen-ware; pottery; ceramics

陷 xiàn Ⅰ (名) trap Ⅱ (動) ❶ sink; get stuck: ～進苦難的深淵 be plunged into the abyss of misery ❷ make a false charge against: 誣～好人 frame up an innocent person

【陷入】xiànrù（動）sink into; be bogged down in: ～絕境 land oneself in an impasse

【陷阱】xiànjǐng（名）pitfall; trap

【陷害】xiànhài（動）frame

【陷落】xiànluò（動）❶ cave in; subside ❷（of a city, etc.）fall; be captured

隊 duì（名）❶ line（of people）: 站～ stand in a line / 排～ queue up ❷ team; group: 排球～ volleyball team

【隊伍】duìwu（名）❶ ranks; contingent ❷ troops

【隊長】duìzhǎng（名）team leader; captain

【隊員】duìyuán（名）team member

隋 Suí（名）a surname

陽 yáng I（名）❶（in Chinese philosophy, medicine, etc.）*yang*, the masculine or positive principle in nature ❷ sun ❸ south of a mountain; north of a river II（形）❶ open; overt ❷〈物〉positive

【陽光】yángguāng（名）sunshine; sunlight

【陽性】yángxìng（名）❶〈物〉positive ❷〈語〉masculine gender

【陽奉陰違】yáng fèng yīn wéi〈成〉comply in public but refuse to obey in private; feign compliance while acting in opposition

【陽春白雪】yáng chūn bái xuě〈成〉highbrow art and literature

【陽極】yángjí（名）〈物〉positive pole; anode

【陽間】yángjiān（名）this world

【陽傘】yángsǎn（名）parasol; sunshade

【陽溝】yánggōu（名）open drain

【陽痿】yángwěi（名）〈醫〉impotence

【陽臺】yángtái（名）balcony

【陽曆】yánglì（名）Gregorian calendar

階 jiē（名）❶ steps; stairs: 登上臺～ go up a flight of steps ❷ rank: ～官 official rank

【階下囚】jiēxiàqiú（名）person in the dock; prisoner at the bar; prisoner

【階段】jiēduàn（名）stage; phase; period

【階級】jiējí（名）（social）class

【階梯】jiētī（名）flight of stairs; （social）ladder

【階層】jiēcéng（名）stratum; social rank

隆 lóng I（形）❶ grand ❷ prosperous; flourishing ❸ deep; profound II（動）rise; swell III（名）（Lóng）a surname

【隆冬】lóngdōng（名）the depth of winter; the coldest days in winter

【隆重】lóngzhòng I（形）grand; solemn: ～的葬禮 stately funeral II（副）solemnly; ceremoniously: ～開幕 be ceremoniously inaugurated

【隆起】lóngqǐ（動）rise; bulge

【隆情厚誼】lóng qíng hòu yì〈成〉profound kindness and friendship

【隆隆】lónglóng（象）boom; rumble: 坦克～駛過。The tanks lumbered past.

隍 huáng（名）dry moat outside a city wall

隘 ài I（形）narrow: 心胸狹～

narrow-minded Ⅱ（名）place of strategic importance: 關～ strategic pass

【隘口】àikǒu（名）(mountain) pass

【隘路】àilù（名）narrow strategic path; defile

隔 gé（動）❶ separate; partition ❷ be at a distance from; be at an interval of: ～行寫 write in every other line / ～時～數年 after (an interval of) several years

【隔岸觀火】gé àn guān huǒ〈成〉look at sb.'s misfortune with folded arms

【隔音】géyīn（名）sound insulation

【隔音室】géyīnshì（名）sound-proof room

【隔絕】géjué（動）isolate; cut off

【隔靴搔癢】gé xuē sāo yǎng〈成〉(of speech or writing) fail to get to the root of the matter

【隔閡】géhé（名）misunderstanding; estrangement

【隔膜】gémó Ⅰ（形）unfamiliar Ⅱ（名）lack of mutual understanding

【隔壁】gébì（名）next door

【隔牆有耳】gé qiáng yǒu ěr〈成〉walls have ears

【隔斷】géduàn（動）sever; cut off

【隔離】gélí（動）isolate; segregate: ～病人 isolate a patient

隕 yǔn（動）fall from the sky or outer space

【隕石】yǔnshí（名）〈天〉aerolite; stony meteorite

【隕星】yǔnxīng（名）〈天〉meteorite

【隕落】yǔnluò（動）(of a meteorite, etc.) drop from the sky or outer space

隗 Kuí（名）a surname

障 zhàng Ⅰ（動）hinder; obstruct Ⅱ（名）barrier; obstruction: 風～ windbreak

【障礙】zhàng'ài（名）obstacle; barrier; hindrance

隙 xì（名）❶ crack; cleft: 門～ a crack between the door and its frame ❷ loophole; opportunity: 乘～反對 grasp the opportunity to raise objections ❸ discord; rift: 仇～ hatred

【隙地】xìdì（名）unoccupied place

際 jì Ⅰ（名）❶ border; margin; edge: 一望無～的草原 boundless expanse of grassland ❷ occasion; moment: 值此工程落成之～ on the occasion of the completion of the project ❸ one's lot or circumstance: ～遇 chance Ⅱ（介）❶ a-mong; inter-: 人～關係 interpersonal relationships ❷ in: 浮現腦～ flash across one's mind ❸ on the occasion of: ～此佳節 on this festive occasion

隧 suì

【隧道】suìdào（名）tunnel

隨 suí Ⅰ（動）❶ follow; ensue ❷ comply with: 入鄉～俗. When in Rome, do as the Romans do. ❸ as one wishes: ～他去. Let him do as he likes. It's up to you. ❹〈方〉resemble: 他～他的祖父. He takes after his grandpa. Ⅱ（副）along with: ～風轉舵 trim one's sails

【隨口】suíkǒu（動）blurt out: ～答應 comply thoughtlessly with sb.'s request

【隨大溜】suí dàliù（隨大流 suí dàliú）（動）follow the herd

【隨手】suíshǒu（副）conveniently; with no extra trouble; immediately: ～關門。Close the door behind you.

【隨心所欲】suí xīn suǒ yù〈成〉do as one pleases

【隨叫隨到】suí jiào suí dào（動）〈口〉at someone's beck and call

【隨同】suítóng（動）accompany; escort

【隨地】suídì（副）everywhere; anywhere: 這種人隨時～都可以碰到。You can come across such people at any time and at any place.

【隨行人員】suíxíng rényuán（名）entourage; party

【隨行就市】suíháng jiùshì（動）（of commodity prices）fluctuate according to market conditions

【隨身】suíshēn（副）（carry）on one's person;（take）along with one: ～行李 accompanying baggage

【隨和】suíhe（形）amiable; agreeable; bland

【隨波逐流】suí bō zhú liú〈成〉drift with the tide

【隨後】suíhòu（副）[often followed by 就] soon afterwards; later: 他～就來。He'll be here in a minute.

【隨便】suíbiàn（副）❶ casually; randomly; haphazardly: 這是～説的。It was a casual remark. ❷ carelessly; thoughtlessly: ～答應 commit oneself without thinking ❸ as one pleases: 大家可以～一些。Make yourself at home.（Don't stand on ceremony.）/ 請您～挑。You can choose whatever you like. ❹ unruly: ～打人 attack people

without provocation

【隨風倒】suífēngdǎo（動）〈口〉be easily swayed by the prevailing wind; bend with the wind

【隨時】suíshí（副）❶ at any time: 您可以～打電話來。You can call me at any time. ❷ when the occasion arises

【隨員】suíyuán（名）❶ entourage; party ❷〈外交〉（junior）attaché

【隨着】suízhe（介）along with; with: ～局勢變化而變化 change with the change of the situation

【隨處】suíchù（副）everywhere; anywhere: 這些情況～可以打聽到。This kind of information can be obtained anywhere.

【隨從】suícóng I（動）accompany（one's superior）: 他～工廠經理到北京。He accompanied the factory manager to Beijing. II（名）attendant; entourage

【隨筆】suíbǐ（名）jottings; random notes

【隨意】suíyì（副）at will; as one pleases: 請～用菜。Please help yourself.

【隨機應變】suí jī yìng biàn〈成〉seize the opportunity in changing circumstances and act flexibly

【隨聲附和】suí shēng fù hè〈成〉echo others' opinions

險 xiǎn I（名）❶ danger; peril ❷ place which is difficult of access; narrow pass: 據～死守 rely on a natural barrier to make a last-ditch stand II（形）❶ dangerous; risky ❷ vicious; insidious ❸（副）almost; nearly: ～遭大難 escape disaster by the skin of one's teeth

【險些】xiǎnxiē（副）nearly; narrowly: ~喪命 nearly lose one's life; have a narrow escape

【險阻】xiǎnzǔ Ⅰ (形) (of a road) steep and difficult Ⅱ (名) barrier: 艱難~ barriers and difficulties

【險要】xiǎnyào (形) steep and important strategically

【險症】xiǎnzhèng (名) dangerous illness

【險峰】xiǎnfēng (名) steep mountain; precipitous peak

【險峻】xiǎnjùn (形) steep; precipitous

【險象環生】xiǎn xiàng huán shēng 〈成〉 signs of danger appear on all sides

【險詐】xiǎnzhà (形) treacherous; vicious and cunning

【險勝】xiǎnshèng (動) win by a hair's breadth

【險惡】xiǎn'è (形) ❶ dangerous; hazardous: 形勢~。The situation is fraught with danger. ❷ vicious; evil: 心地~奸詐 sly and sinister

隱 yǐn Ⅰ (動) hide; conceal: ~而不見 be hidden from view Ⅱ (形) hidden; latent; lurking: ~情 hidden thoughts or feelings; unrevealed truth

【隱士】yǐnshì (名) recluse; hermit

【隱私】yǐnsī (名) private matters; one's secrets

【隱約】yǐnyuē (形) unclear; indistinct; faint: ~可辨 faintly discernible

【隱患】yǐnhuàn (名) hidden danger: 消除~ remove the hidden danger

【隱晦】yǐnhuì (形) obscure; vague: ~詩詞 obscure poems

【隱痛】yǐntòng (名) unhappy experi-

ence; trauma

【隱喻】yǐnyù (名)〈語〉 metaphor

【隱憂】yǐnyōu (名) hidden trouble; secret worry

【隱蔽】yǐnbì (動) hide; take cover

【隱瞞】yǐnmán (動) conceal; hold back; hide the truth

【隱諱】yǐnhuì (動) cover up: ~其事 cover up the story

【隱藏】yǐncáng (動) hide; conceal

隴 Lǒng (名) another name for Gansu (Province)

隸 部

隸 lì Ⅰ (動) be subordinate to; be affiliated with Ⅱ (名) person in a subordinate position; servant

【隸書】lìshū (名) lìshu (a style of Chinese calligraphy)

【隸屬】lìshǔ (動) be subordinate to; be under

隹 部

隻 zhī (量): 兩~鳥 two birds / 一~手套 a glove / 一~皮包 a briefcase

【隻言片語】zhī yán piàn yǔ 〈成〉 some words quoted out of context

【隻身】zhīshēn (副) alone; by oneself: ~趕赴災區 rush to the stricken area alone

雀 què (名) sparrow

【雀斑】 quèbān （名）freckle

【雀躍】 quèyuè （动）leap with joy

雅 yǎ （形）elegant; graceful: 情趣高～ have a cultivated taste

【雅俗共赏】 yǎ sú gòng shǎng 〈成〉cater to both refined and popular tastes; appeal both to highbrows and lowbrows

【雅致】 yǎzhì （形）refined; tasteful: 装饰～的房间 room furnished with good taste

【雅座】 yǎzuò （名）better-furnished small room in a restaurant

【雅兴】 yǎxìng （名）poetic mood; inclination: 不知你是否有去看花展的～。I wonder if you have any inclination to visit the flower show.

【雅观】 yǎguān （形）（often used in negative sentences）graceful （in manner or dress）: 那座楼很不～。That building is an eyesore.

雁 yàn （名）wild goose

雄 xióng （形）❶ male: ～蜂 drone ❷ powerful; mighty: 百萬～師 a mighty army; a million strong

【雄才大略】 xióng cái dà lüè 〈成〉（man）of supreme wisdom and bold vision

【雄心】 xióngxīn （名）great ambition: ～壮志 lofty aspirations

【雄壮】 xióngzhuàng （形）mighty; majestic: ～的國歌 the majestic national anthem

【雄姿】 xióngzī （名）august appearance

【雄厚】 xiónghòu （形）rich; strong; plentiful: 技术力量～ have a strong technical force

【雄健】 xióngjiàn （形）strong; vigorous: 笔力～ with vigorous strokes in brushwork

【雄伟】 xióngwěi （形）grand; magnificent

【雄图】 xióngtú （名）ambitious plan

【雄關】 xióngguān （名）impregnable pass

【雄鸡】 xióngjī （名）cock; rooster

【雄辩】 xióngbiàn Ⅰ（名）eloquence Ⅱ（形）eloquent; convincing

集 jí Ⅰ（动）gather; assemble; collect: 工人～居的地方 a district inhabited mostly by working people Ⅱ（名）❶ anthology; collection （of writings, photographs, etc.）: 地圖～ atlas ❷ volume; part: 上（中、下）～ Part （Volume）Ⅰ（Ⅱ, Ⅲ）❸ fair; market

【集子】 jízi （名）collection of essays or other writings; collected works; anthology

【集中】 jízhōng （动）concentrate; centralize; focus: ～精力 concentrate one's effort / ～注意力 focus one's attention

【集中营】 jízhōngyíng （名）concentration camp

【集市】 jíshì （名）country fair; market

【集合】 jíhé （动）gather together; assemble; call together: 在廣場～ assemble at the square

【集成電路】 jíchéng diànlù （名）integrated circuit

【集思廣益】 jí sī guǎng yì 〈成〉pool the ideas of the public; pool collective wisdom

【集訓】 jíxùn （动）assemble for training

【集結】 jíjié Ⅰ（动）mass; assemble Ⅱ

（名）buildup：兵力 ～ military buildup

【集郵】jíyóu（名）philately; stamp-collecting

【集散地】jísàndì（名）centre for collecting local goods to be shipped out; distributing point

【集會】jíhuì（名）gathering; rally

【集資】jízī（動）raise funds

【集團】jítuán（名）bloc; group

【集鎮】jízhèn（名）town

【集權】jíquán（名）centralization of power

【集體】jítǐ Ⅰ（名）collective; group Ⅱ（形）collective：～所有制 collective ownership

雍 yōng（名）❶ harmony ❷（Yōng）a surname

【雍容】yōngróng（形）of quiet elegance; dignified and poised

雉 zhì（名）pheasant

雋 juàn Ⅰ（形）of absorbing interest：～永（of a remark, poem, etc.）meaningful; thought-provoking Ⅱ（名）（Juàn）a surname

雌 cí（形）female

【雌雄】cíxióng（名）❶ male and female ❷ victory or defeat：決一～ fight it out

雕 diāo Ⅰ（名）vulture Ⅱ（動）carve; sculpture

【雕花】diāohuā（名）carving

【雕刻】diāokè（動）carve; engrave

【雕砌】diāoqì（名）rhetorical flourishes; liking for a florid style：喜愛～like flowery language; be fond of an ornate style

【雕琢】diāozhuó（動）❶ chisel ❷ polish; embellish

【雕塑】diāosù（名）sculpture：～家 sculptor

【雕像】diāoxiàng（名）statue

【雕漆】diāoqī（名）carved lacquer-ware

【雕蟲小技】diāo chóng xiǎo jì〈成〉（usually said of literary writing）an insignificant skill

雖 suī（連）though; even if

【雖然】suīrán（連）although; though

【雖說】suīshuō（連）〈口〉although; though

雜 zá Ⅰ（形）miscellaneous; mixed; assorted：～亂 disorderly; in confusion Ⅱ（動）mix; mingle：把兩種配料摻～在一起 mix the two ingredients

【雜文】záwén（名）essay

【雜交】zájiāo（動）〈生〉hybridize; crossbreed：～優勢 hybrid vigour

【雜色】zásè（形）variegated; multicoloured

【雜技】zájì（名）acrobatics

【雜念】zániàn（名）selfish considerations; distracting thoughts

【雜拌】zábàn（名）❶ assorted preserved fruits ❷ mixture; miscellany

【雜耍】záshuǎ（名）variety show

【雜品】zápǐn（名）sundry goods; groceries

【雜音】záyīn（名）❶ noise ❷〈醫〉murmur

【雜草】zácǎo（名）weeds

【雜貨】záhuò（名）sundry goods; groceries：～店 grocery

【雜費】záfèi（名）miscellaneous expenses

【雜牌】zápái（名）inferior brand

【雜亂無章】zá luàn wú zhāng〈成〉be in utter disorder

【雜種】zázhòng（名）❶〈生〉hybrid; crossbreed ❷ bastard

【雜誌】zázhì（名）magazine

【雜質】zázhì（名）impurity

【雜燴】záhuì（名）❶ stew（of meat, vegetables etc.）; hotchpotch; chowder ❷ miscellany; medley

【雜糧】záliáng（名）food grains other than rice and wheat

雛 chú（形）（of bird）young: ～鳥 nestling

【雛形】chúxíng（名）❶ embryonic form ❷ microcosm; miniature

雙 shuāng Ⅰ（形）❶ two; both: ～方 both parties ❷ even: ～號（of seats, tickets, etc.）even-numbered ❸ double; twofold: ～層公共汽車 double-decker（bus）Ⅱ（量）pair: 一～長統襪 a pair of stockings Ⅲ（名）(Shuāng) a surname

【雙人牀】shuāngrénchuáng（名）double bed

【雙人房】shuāngrénfáng（名）double (-bedded) room

【雙手】shuāngshǒu（名）both hands: 舉～贊成 be all for（sth.）

【雙月刊】shuāngyuèkān（名）bimonthly

【雙打】shuāngdǎ（名）〈體〉doubles: 混合～ mixed doubles

【雙百方針】shuāngbǎi fāngzhēn（名）Party policy for art and literature: let a hundred flowers blossom and a hundred schools of thought contend

【雙重】shuāngchóng（形）double; dual: ～身分 dual capacity

【雙軌】shuāngguǐ（名）double track:

價格～制 two-tier price system / 外匯～制 two-tiered currency system

【雙胞胎】shuāngbāotāi（名）twins

【雙面繡】shuāngmiànxiù（名）double-faced embroidery

【雙眼皮】shuāngyǎnpí（名）double-fold eyelids

【雙槓】shuānggàng（名）〈體〉parallel bars

【雙邊】shuāngbiān（形）bilateral: ～協定 bilateral agreement

【雙職工】shuāngzhígōng（名）working couple

【雙關語】shuāngguānyǔ（名）pun

【雙體船】shuāngtǐchuán（名）catamaran; twinhull

離 lí Ⅰ（動）leave; part with: 我～家多年。I've been away from home for many years. Ⅱ（介）❶ off: ～市中心不遠 not far from the city centre ❷ without; short of: 他看書～不開放大鏡。He can't read without a magnifying glass.

【離子】lízǐ（名）〈物〉ion

【離任】lírèn（動）leave one's post

【離休】líxiū（動）retire on full pay or on full perks

【離別】líbié（動）part（for quite a long time）

【離店】lídiàn（動）check out: ～時限 checkout time / ～手續 checkout procedure

【離奇】líqí（形）fantastic; bizarre

【離岸價格】lí'àn jiàgé（名）〈經〉free on board (FOB)

【離婚】líhūn（動）divorce: 辦理～ go through the legal formalities of a divorce

【離散】lísàn（形）dispersed: 家人

~。The family is broken up.

【離開】líkāi（動）depart from; deviate from

【離間】líjiàn（動）sow discord or dissent; alienate sb. from sb. else

【離境】líjìng Ⅰ（動）leave a country Ⅱ（名）exit: ~ 口岸 port of exit / ~ 稅 exit tax

【離題】lítí（動）digress; stray from the point: 別~。Keep to the point.

【離職】lízhí（動）❶ leave one's post: ~ 休養 leave one's post to take a rest ❷ quit one's job

【離職金】lízhíjīn（名）severance pay

【離譜】lípǔ（動）be off the beam; be out of place; go against accepted conventions

難 nán Ⅰ（形）❶ hard; difficult: ~ 掌握 difficult to grasp / ~ 消化 hard to digest ❷ bad; unpleasant: ~ 聞 smell bad Ⅱ（動）puzzle sb.: 這個問題把她~住了。This question puzzles her. Ⅲ（名）difficulty; trouble; problem: 住房~ housing problem

see also nàn

【難以】nányǐ（形）difficult to manage: ~ 處理 hard to deal with

【難色】nánsè（名）reluctance: 面有 ~ show hesitation

【難言之隱】nán yán zhī yǐn〈成〉sth. one finds hard to bring up

【難免】nánmiǎn（形）hard to avoid; cannot help: 他初次上臺講話，~ 有點緊張。He can hardly help feeling nervous speaking in public for the first time.

【難忘】nánwàng（形）unforgettable; memorable

【難怪】nánguài Ⅰ（連）little wonder;

她得了頭獎，~ 這麼高興。She won first prize. No wonder she was so happy. Ⅱ（形）understandable; not to blame: ~ 他不喜歡這個電影。It's understandable that he does not like this film.

【難受】nánshòu（形）❶ unwell; uncomfortable ❷ dejected; unhappy

【難度】nándù（名）degree of difficulty

【難看】nánkàn（形）❶ ugly ❷ unhealthy; pallid ❸ disgraceful; shameful

【難保】nánbǎo（動）cannot be sure: ~ 他不說出去。You can't be sure that he won't leak it out.

【難能可貴】nán néng kě guì〈成〉difficult to achieve and thus worthy of praise

【難產】nánchǎn Ⅰ（名）〈醫〉（of childbirth）difficult labour; dystocia Ⅱ（形）（of a writing, plan, etc.）hard to materialize; slow in coming out

【難處】nánchǔ（動）be difficult to get along with

【難處】nánchù（名）difficulty

【難得】nándé Ⅰ（形）hard to get; rare: 一本 ~ 的書 a rare book to come by Ⅱ（副）seldom; rarely: 她 ~ 出去。She seldom goes out.

【難道】nándào（副）[used to pose an emphatic rhetorical question]: ~ 你不相信我? Don't you believe me?

【難過】nánguò Ⅰ（動）have a hard time Ⅱ（形）sad; distressed

【難堪】nánkān（形）❶ unbearable; embarrassing ❷ embarrassed: 她犯了這麼大錯誤，覺得 ~。She felt embarrassed, as she had make such a bad mistake.

【難爲情】nánwéiqíng（形）shy; embarrassed

【難解難分】nán jiě nán fēn〈成〉❶ be locked together in a fight; be deeply involved in a dispute ❷ reluctant to part with each other

【難說】nánshuō（動）it's hard to say

【難題】nántí（名）knotty problem

【難關】nánguān（名）difficulty; difficult situation: 技術～ technical difficulty

【難聽】nántīng（形）❶ unpleasant to the ear ❷（of language, behaviour）offensive; repulsive

難 nàn（名）disaster; calamity see also nán

【難友】nànyǒu（名）mates in an accident, prison cell, etc.

【難民】nànmín（名）refugee: ～營 refugee camp

【難兄難弟】nànxiōng nàndì（名）fellow sufferers; two of a kind

雨 部

雨 yǔ（名）rain: ～過天晴 after rain comes sunshine; good times come after bad

【雨水】yǔshuǐ（名）rainwater; rain

【雨布】yǔbù（名）waterproof cloth

【雨衣】yǔyī（名）raincoat

【雨季】yǔjì（名）rainy season; wet season

【雨具】yǔjù（名）rain gear（i.e., umbrella, raincoat, etc.）

【雨披】yǔpī（名）plastic rain cape

【雨後春筍】yǔ hòu chūn sǔn〈成〉spring up like mushrooms

【雨量】yǔliàng（名）〈氣〉rainfall

【雨帽】yǔmào（名）rain cap

【雨棚】yǔpéng（名）〈建〉canopy

【雨傘】yǔsǎn（名）umbrella

【雨鞋】yǔxié（名）rubber boot; galosh

【雨點】yǔdiǎn（名）raindrop

【雨露】yǔlù（名）❶ rain and dew ❷ bounty; favour

雪 xuě Ⅰ（名）snow Ⅱ（動）clear; avenge: 報仇～恨 avenge oneself on（a person or group）; take revenge on

【雪人】xuěrén（名）snowman

【雪山】xuěshān（名）snow-covered mountain

【雪片】xuěpiàn（名）snowflake: 求職申請如～飛來。Applications for the job poured in.

【雪中送炭】xuě zhōng sòng tàn〈成〉provide what is urgently needed; offer timely help

【雪白】xuěbái（形）snowwhite

【雪松】xuěsōng（名）cedar

【雪花】xuěhuā（名）snowflake

【雪花膏】xuěhuāgāo（名）vanishing cream

【雪茄】xuějiā（名）cigar

【雪亮】xuěliàng（形）❶ shiny: ～的匕首 a gleaming dagger ❷ clear; sharp: ～的眼睛 sharp eyes

【雪冤】xuěyuān（動）right a wrong

【雪球】xuěqiú（名）snowball

【雪崩】xuěbēng（名）snowslide

【雪橇】xuěqiāo（名）sled; sledge

【雪糕】xuěgāo（名）ice cream

雲 yún（名）❶ cloud ❷（Yún）short for Yunnan Province ❸（Yún）a surname

【雲母】yúnmǔ（名）〈礦〉mica

【雲杉】yúnshān（名）〈植〉dragon spruce

【雲南】Yúnnán（名）Yunnan（Province）

【雲消霧散】yún xiāo wù sàn〈成〉vanish like mist; melt into thin air

【雲彩】yúncai（名）〈口〉cloud

【雲雀】yúnquè（名）〈動〉skylark

【雲梯】yúntī（名）scaling ladder

【雲集】yúnjí（動）come in large crowds

【雲圖】yúntú（名）〈氣〉cloud atlas; cloud chart

【雲層】yúncéng（名）cloud layer

【雲霞】yúnxiá（名）rosy clouds

【雲霧】yúnwù（名）cloud and mist; mist

【電】diàn Ⅰ（名）❶ electricity ❷ telegram Ⅱ（動）give or get an electric shock

【電力】diànlì（名）electric power

【電子】diànzǐ（名）electron

【電工】diàngōng（名）electrician

【電文】diànwén（名）(of telegram) text

【電化教學】diànhuà jiàoxué（動）teach with audio-visual aids

【電池】diànchí（名）battery

【電冰箱】diànbīngxiāng（名）refrigerator; fridge

【電車】diànchē（名）tram

【電表】diànbiǎo（名）electric meter

【電波】diànbō（名）electric wave

【電阻】diànzǔ（名）(electric) resistance

【電信】diànxìn（名）telecommunications

【電流】diànliú（名）electric current

【電氣】diànqì（名）electric: ～化 electrification

【電容】diànróng（名）electric capacity

【電扇】diànshàn（名）electric fan

【電訊】diànxùn（名）❶ telegraphic dispatch: ～稿 news bulletin ❷ telecommunications

【電動】diàndòng（形）power-driven

【電焊】diànhàn（名）electric welding: ～工 welder / ～條 welding rod

【電梯】diàntī（名）lift; elevator

【電唱機】diànchàngjī（名）gramophone; record player

【電視】diànshì（名）television: ～劇 teleplay; TV play / ～連續劇 TV series; TV serial / ～播放 televise / 閉路～ closed-circuit television

【電視機】diànshìjī（名）television set

【電報】diànbào（名）telegram; cable

【電場】diànchǎng（名）electric field

【電費】diànfèi（名）charges for electricity

【電筒】diàntǒng（名）electric torch; flashlight

【電極】diànjí（名）electrode

【電鈕】diànniǔ（名）push button

【電椅】diànyǐ（名）electric chair

【電匯】diànhuì（名）telegraphic transfer（TT）; telegraphic money order

【電傳】diànchuán（名）telex

【電鈴】diànlíng（名）electric bell

【電路】diànlù（名）circuit

【電腦】diànnǎo（名）computer

【電源】diànyuán（名）power source

【電話】diànhuà（名）telephone: 長途～ long-distance call / 市內～ local call

【電話分機】diànhuà fēnjī（名）（telephone）extension

【電話簿】diànhuàbù（名）telephone directory

【電臺】diàntái（名）❶ transceiver; transmitter-receiver ❷ radio station

【電綫】diànxiàn（名）electric wire: ～杆（electric wire）pole

【電網】diànwǎng（名）electrified wire netting

【電碼】diànmǎ（名）（telegraphic）code

【電影】diànyǐng（名）film; movie

【電影院】diànyǐngyuàn（名）cinema; movie house

【電機】diànjī（名）generator; electromotor

【電器】diànqì（名）electrical appliances

【電燈】diàndēng（名）electric light

【電療】diànliáo（名）〈醫〉electrotherapy

【電鍍】diàndù（動）electroplate

【電壓】diànyā（名）voltage

【電爐】diànlú（名）electric stove; electric heater

【電纜】diànlǎn（名）cable

雷 léi（名）❶ thunder ❷〈軍〉mine: 埋地～ lay（land）mines ❸（Léi）a surname

【雷同】léitóng（形）❶ parroting others' views ❷ identical by chance

【雷雨】léiyǔ（名）thunder and rain; thunderstorm

【雷陣雨】léizhènyǔ（名）thunder shower; passing shower

【雷達】léidá（名）radar: ～交通控制 radar approach control; RAPCON / ～顯示器 radarscope

【雷電】léidiàn（名）thunder and lightning

【雷管】léiguǎn（名）primer; detonator

【雷厲風行】léi lì fēng xíng〈成〉resolutely and promptly

【雷霆】léitíng（名）❶ thunderclap: 以～萬鈞之勢 with tremendous force and momentum ❷ rage: 大發～ fly into a fury

【雷擊】léijī（動）be struck by lightning

【雷聲】léishēng（名）thunder; thunderbolt: ～大，雨點小 loud thunder, but only tiny raindrops; talk big but do little

零 líng Ⅰ（數）zero: 電話號碼三～九 telephone number 309 / 一一三路電車 No. 103 trolleybus Ⅱ（名）❶ naught; nothing: 光說不幹等於～。All talk and no work accomplishes nothing. ❷ fragment; part Ⅲ（動）（of flowers, leaves, etc）wither and fall

【零工】línggōng（名）odd job

【零用】língyòng Ⅰ（動）spend occasionally and in small sums Ⅱ（名）pocket money

【零件】língjiàn（名）spare parts

【零花】línghuā（名）pocket money

【零度】língdù（名）（of temperature）zero degree

【零食】língshí（名）tuck; snacks

【零星】língxīng（形）❶ scrappy; fragmentary: ～的消息 bits of information ❷ sporadic; occasional: ～的戰鬥 sporadic fighting

【零活】línghuó（名）odd chores: 抽空做家裏的～ find time to do household chores

【零售】língshòu（動）retail

【零散】língsǎn（形）scattered; found here and there: 海灘上～地躺着幾個人。A few people lay here and there on the beach.

【零落】língluò（形）❶ withered; decayed: 整個建築物已經～了。The whole building has fallen into decay. ❷ scattered; sporadic

【零碎】língsuì Ⅰ（形）fragmentary Ⅱ（名）odds and ends; scraps

【零零散散】línglíng sǎnsǎn（形）sparse; scattered here and there: 電影院裏的人坐着幾個人。There's only a sparse audience in the cinema.

【零敲碎打】líng qiāo suì dǎ（副）piecemeal; off and on

【零錢】língqián（名）❶ small change: 五分～ five fen in change ❷ pocket money

【零頭】língtóu（名）odd; remnant

【零頭布】língtóubù（名）remnant of cloth: 賣～ a remnant sale

【零點】língdiǎn（名）midnight

雹 báo（名）hail

【雹子】báozi（名）hail; hailstone

【雹災】báozāi（名）disaster caused by hailstorm

需 xū Ⅰ（動）need: 所～的一切 all that is needed Ⅱ（名）necessaries

【需求】xūqiú（名）requirement; demand: ～大於供應。Demand exceeds supply.

【需要】xūyào Ⅰ（動）need; want: ～支持 call for support／～進一步改善 to be further improved; require further improvement Ⅱ（名）demand; need: 生活的第一～ the first need of life

震 zhèn（動）❶ shake; shock; quake: 玻璃被～得粉碎。The glass was shattered by the shock.／地～ earthquake ❷ be shocked; be astounded

【震耳欲聾】zhèn ěr yù lóng〈成〉deafening; ear-splitting

【震波】zhènbō（名）〈地〉earthquake wave

【震怒】zhènnù（動）be furious; be exasperated

【震動】zhèndòng（動）shake; shock; quake: 這件事～了全世界。The event shook the world.

【震撼】zhènhàn（動）shake; stir: ～世界的大事 earth-shaking event

【震盪】zhèndàng（動）shake; rock

【震顫】zhènchàn（動）shiver; tremble

【震驚】zhènjīng（動）shock; stun; astonish: 這個消息使我感到～。I was shocked by the news.

霄 xiāo（名）clouds; sky: 高入雲～ tower into the clouds; soar into the skies

霆 tíng（名）thunderbolt

霉 méi（動）mould; mildew: 麵包發～了。The breed has gone mouldy.

【霉天】méitiān（名）rainy season

【霉菌】méijūn（名）mould

【霉爛】méilàn（動）rot: 這樣的天氣，白菜很快就要～了。The cabbages will rot soon in such weather.

霎 shà（名）a split second: ～時 in the twinkling of an eye

霖 lín（名）heavy rain that continues

for days: 秋～ continuous autumn rain

【霖雨】línyǔ（名）heavy rain that goes on and on

霏 fēi（副）continuously: 淫雨～～. It has been raining for days on end.

霍 huò Ⅰ（副）suddenly; quickly Ⅱ（名）(Huò) a surname

【霍然】huòrán Ⅰ（副）suddenly Ⅱ（動）(of a patient) be quickly restored to health

【霍亂】huòluàn（名）〈醫〉cholera

霓 ní（名）〈氣〉secondary rainbow

【霓虹燈】níhóngdēng（名）neon light

霜 shuāng Ⅰ（名）❶ frost ❷ white powder: 砒～（white）arsenic Ⅱ（形）hoary: 兩鬢～白 greying at the temples

【霜凍】shuāngdòng（名）frost

霞 xiá（名）rosy clouds which appear at daybreak or sunset

【霞光】xiáguāng（名）golden sunlight; bright sunshine

霧 wù（名）fog; mist

【霧氣】wùqì（名）fog; mist

【霧濛濛】wùméngméng（形）misty

霸 bà Ⅰ（名）❶ tyrant; despot: 惡～ local tyrant ❷ chief of feudal princes; overlord ❸ hegemony; hegemonic power: 永不稱～ never seek hegemony Ⅱ（動）dominate; lord it over

【霸王】bàwáng（名）overlord; autocrat; despot

【霸主】bàzhǔ（名）❶ suzerain ❷ overlord: 海上～ maritime overlord

【霸佔】bàzhàn（動）seize by force

【霸道】bàdào（名）❶ tyranny; despotism ❷ high-handedness: 橫行～ ride roughshod over

【霸權】bàquán（名）hegemony; supremacy: ～主義 hegemonism

霹 pī

【霹靂】pīlì（名）thunderbolt: 晴天～ a bolt from the blue

【霹靂舞】pīlìwǔ（名）break dance

露 lòu（動）〈口〉show see also lù

【露一手】lòu yī shǒu（動）show off; show one's special skill

【露怯】lòuqiè（動）〈口〉make stupid mistakes for want of knowledge; make an ass of oneself

【露底】lòudǐ（動）unwittingly reveal the truth of the matter

【露面】lòumiàn（動）appear in public: 他好久沒有～. He has not made public appearances for a long time.

【露馬腳】lòu mǎjiǎo（動）show the cloven hoof; betray oneself

【露餡兒】lòuxiànr（動）let the cat out of the bag; give oneself away

【露臉】lòuliǎn（動）win credit; come off with flying colours: ～的事 sth. that brings credit

露 lù Ⅰ（名）❶ dew ❷ fruit juice; syrup: 玫瑰～ rose-flavoured juice Ⅱ（動）show: 他臉上一出笑容。A smile dawned on lis face.
see also lòu

【露水】lùshuǐ（名）dew

【露天】lùtiān（動）open-air: 在～工作 work in the open

【露天開採】lùtiān kāicǎi（名）open-cast mining; strip mining

【露天煤礦】lùtiān méikuàng（名）open-cut coal mine

【露骨】lùgǔ（形）barefaced; undisguised

【露酒】lùjiǔ（名）alcoholic drink flavoured with fruit juice; wine

【露宿】lùsù（動）sleep in the open

【露頭角】lù tóujiǎo（動）(begin to) show one's talent: 初 ～ begin to distinguish oneself

【露營】lùyíng（動）encamp; go camping

霭 ǎi（名）mist; haze: 暮～沉沉。Dusk is falling.

靈 líng（形）❶ effective: 這種藥治肝炎很～。This medicine is effective against hepatitis. ❷ clever; acute: 眼睛很～ have a keen eye-sight / 腦子～ be quick-witted ❸ supernatural

【靈丹妙藥】líng dān miào yào〈成〉panacea; elixir

【靈巧】língqiǎo（形）dexterous; agile

【靈光】língguāng（名）halo

【靈車】língchē（名）hearse

【靈芝】língzhī（名）glossy ganoderma

【靈柩】língchuáng（名）bier

【靈便】língbian（形）❶ nimble ❷ handy

【靈活】línghuó（形）❶ agile; nimble ❷ flexible

【靈柩】língjiù（名）coffin（with a corpse inside）

【靈通】língtōng（形）well-informed: 消息～人士 well-informed sources

【靈敏】língmǐn（形）quick; sharp; keen: 嗅覺～ be sharp-nosed; have a keen sense of smell

【靈堂】língtáng（名）mourning hall

【靈感】línggǎn（名）inspiration

【靈魂】línghún（名）soul; spirit

【靈機】língjī（名）sudden idea: ～一動 have a brainwave

【靈驗】língyàn（形）❶ effective: 藥到病除，非常～。The medicine can effect an immediate cure. ❷ true; correct: 他的預言果然～。His prediction came true.

青 部

青 qīng Ⅰ（形）❶ black: ～絲 black hair (of a woman) ❷ blue or green: ～草 green grass ❸ young Ⅱ（名）❶ green grass; young crops: 放～ graze the cattle ❷（Qīng）short for Qinghai Province

【青工】qīnggōng（名）young worker

【青天】qīngtiān（名）❶ blue sky ❷ just judge; upright official

【青少年】qīngshàonián（名）teen-agers; juvenile: ～犯罪 juvenile delinquency

【青出於藍】qīng chū yú lán〈成〉the pupil excels the master

【青衣】qīngyī（名）role of a serious young or middle-aged woman in Chinese opera (usu. dressed in blue)

【青年】qīngnián（名）youth; young people

【青光眼】qīngguāngyǎn（名）〈醫〉glaucoma

【青豆】qīngdòu（名）green soya

bean

【青果】qīngguǒ（名）Chinese olive

【青松】qīngsōng（名）pine

【青花瓷】qīnghuācí（名）blue and white porcelain

【青苗】qīngmiáo（名）shoots of food crops

【青苔】qīngtái（名）moss

【青春】qīngchūn（名）youth; youthfulness

【青春期】qīngchūnqī（名）puberty; adolescence

【青红皂白】qīng hóng zào bái〈成〉the rights and wrongs of a matter: 他不问～，把那孩子痛骂了一顿。He gave the child a dressing-down without thinking twice about it.

【青面獠牙】qīng miàn liáo yá〈成〉be hideous in appearance

【青瓷】qīngcí（名）celadon（ware）

【青海】Qīnghǎi（名）Qinghai（Province）

【青鱼】qīngyú（名）black carp

【青梅竹马】qīng méi zhú mǎ〈成〉childhood playmates

【青菜】qīngcài（名）❶ green vegetables ❷ Chinese green cabbage

【青椒】qīngjiāo（名）green pepper

【青蛙】qīngwā（名）frog

【青筋】qīngjīn（名）blue veins

【青黄不接】qīng huáng bù jiē〈成〉temporary shortage of grain before the harvest

【青云直上】qīng yún zhí shàng〈成〉rise rapidly in one's professional career; be a rising star

【青睐】qīnglài（名）favour: 他似乎得到顶头上司的～。He seems to enjoy the favour of his immediate superior.

【青饲料】qīngsìliào（名）green fodder; green-feed

【青翠】qīngcuì（形）lustrous and green

【青蒜】qīngsuàn（名）garlic sprouts

【青铜】qīngtóng（名）bronze

【青霉素】qīngméisù（名）〈药〉penicillin

靖 jìng Ⅰ（形）peaceful; tranquil Ⅱ（动）pacify; appease: 绥～政策 appeasement policy

靓 liàng（形）〈方〉pretty; charming

【靓女】liàngnǚ（名）pretty girl

靛 diàn（名）❶ indigo ❷ blue dye

静 jìng（形）❶ silent; quiet: ～寂无声 be quiet and still ❷ tranquil; calm; peaceful: 心境平～ be calm, feel unperturbed ❸ still; motionless: ～物画 still life（painting）

【静止】jìngzhǐ（形）static; stationary; motionless

【静坐】jìngzuò（动）sit still: ～示威 sit-in demonstration

【静脉】jìngmài（名）〈生理〉vein: ～注射 intravenous injection

【静悄悄】jìngqiāoqiāo（形）noiseless; quiet

【静电】jìngdiàn（名）〈物〉static electricity

【静电复印】jìngdiàn fùyìn（动）xerox

【静养】jìngyǎng（动）have a good rest; recuperate

【静默】jìngmò（动）❶ become quiet: 會場上又是一陣～。A silence fell on the meeting room again. ❷ mourn in silence: ～三分鐘 observe three minutes' silence

非 部

非 fēi I（名）error; wrong: 明辨是～ distinguish between right and wrong II（形）no; non-: ～鐵金屬 non-ferrous metals III（動）reproach; criticize

【非凡】fēifán（形）outstanding; exceptional: ～的才能 outstanding talent

【非正式】fēizhèngshì（形）informal; unofficial

【非正義】fēizhèngyì（形）unjust

【非同小可】fēi tóng xiǎo kě（成）be a matter of no small importance

【非但】fēidàn（連）not only

【非法】fēifǎ（形）illegal; unlawful

【非常】fēicháng I（副）very; extremely: ～美麗 very beautiful II（形）unusual; extraordinary: ～會議 extraordinary session

【非得】fēiděi（動）must; have to

【非暴力】fēibàolì（名）non-violence

【非難】fēinàn（動）censure; blame: 無可～ be by no means blameworthy

【非議】fēiyì（動）〔often used in negative or interrogative sentences〕censure; reproach: 無可～ be indisputably correct

靠 kào I（動）❶ rest against; lean on: ～墊（～枕）back cushion ❷ come close to ❸ rely on: 學習全～自己的努力。Learning depends solely on one's own effort. ❹ have faith in: 據可～方面消息 according to reliable sources II（介）near; a-

long: ～海的小鎮 a small town by the sea

【靠山】kàoshān（名）patron; backer

【靠不住】kào bu zhù（形）unreliable; not trustworthy

【靠右行駛】kàoyòu xíngshǐ（動）keep right

【靠近】kàojìn I（動）come near; approach II（介）near; close to: ～拐角有一所郵局。There is a post office round the corner.

【靠得住】kào de zhù（形）reliable; trusty

【靠邊】kàobiān（動）keep to the side: ～走 keep to the side of the road

【靠邊站】kàobiānzhàn（動）stand aside: 你什麼也不懂，還是～吧。You know nothing, so step aside.

【靠攏】kàolǒng（動）draw near: 船快～碼頭了。The ship is docking.

靡 mǐ（形）blown off by a strong wind: 風～全國 become all the rage nationwide

【靡靡】mǐmǐ（形）catering to low tastes: ～之音 cheap sentimental music

面 部

面 miàn I（名）❶ face: 他滿～愁容。He looked worried. ❷ surface; face: 湖～上 on the lake ❸ aspect; side: 三～環山 surrounded by mountains on three sides ❹ range; extent: 擴大知識～ widen one's scope of knowledge II（動）face: ～壁（in Buddhism）sit facing the wall in meditation Ⅲ（副）personally; face to face: ～商 personally take up the matter with sb. Ⅳ（量）：一～红旗 a red flag

【面子】miànzi（名）❶ outer part; outside: 被～ the facing of a quilt ❷ face; reputation: 极力保全～ try one's best to save face

【面巾纸】miànjīnzhǐ（名）face tissue; kleenex

【面孔】miànkǒng（名）face

【面不改色】miàn bù gǎi sè〈成〉remain unperturbed; not betray a trace of fear

【面生】miànshēng（动）look unfamiliar

【面目】miànmù（名）❶ face; look; appearance: ～狰狞 be sinister in appearance; have ugly features ❷ face; self-respect

【面目一新】miàn mù yī xīn〈成〉sense of assume a new look; undergo a radical change

【面色】miànsè（名）look; complexion: ～难看 put on an ugly expression

【面向】miànxiàng（动）❶ look on: ～大海 face the sea ❷ cater to; serve: ～少年儿童 cater for children

【面如土色】miàn rú tǔ sè〈成〉look pale with horror

【面具】miànjù（名）mask: 氧气～ oxygen mask

【面洽】miànqià（动）talk the matter over in person

【面前】miànqián（副）in the face of; before: 我们～有两大任务。Two important tasks confront us.

【面红耳赤】miàn hóng ěr chì〈成〉blush; flush

【面面相觑】miàn miàn xiāng qù〈成〉look at one another helplessly

【面面俱到】miàn miàn jù dào〈成〉consider a problem down to small details: 很难做到～。It would be difficult to take every small factor into account.

【面容】miànróng（名）face; facial features: ～和善 look benign / ～严肃 have a stern face

【面纱】miànshā（名）veil

【面值】miànzhí（名）❶ par value; face value ❷ denomination

【面授机宜】miàn shòu jī yí〈成〉give instructions in person

【面黄肌瘦】miàn huáng jī shòu（形）sallow and skinny

【面试】miànshì（名）oral exam; interview

【面罩】miànzhào（名）face mask

【面对】miànduì（动）face: ～这种严重的威胁 be faced with this grave threat / ～强敌 be confronted with a formidable enemy (opponent, adversary)

【面对面】miànduìmiàn（形）face-to-face; vis-à-vis: ～的接触 face-to-face contact

【面貌】miànmào（名）❶ face; features ❷ look; appearance: 农村的～起了很大的变化。The face of the countryside has undergone a great change.

【面熟】miànshú（动）look familiar

【面谈】miàntán（动）talk face to face with sb.; have an interview with sb.

【面积】miànjī（名）area: 农场～为 80 平方公里。The farm is 80 square kilometres in area.

【面颊】miànjiá（名）cheek

【面謝】miànxiè（動）extend one's thanks in person

【面臨】miànlín（動）be faced (confronted) with：～種種困難 be confronted with all kinds of difficulties

【面額】miàn'é（名）denomination：小～紙幣 notes of small denominations／100 元～的鈔票 100-*yuan* banknote

【面龐】miànpáng（名）facial contours；face

靦 miǎn

【靦覥】miǎntiǎn（形）shy；timid

革 部

革 gé I（名）❶ leather；hide：皮～ leather；hide ❷（Gé）a surname II（動）❶ change；transform：變～社會制度 change the social system ❷ remove from office；dismiss

【革命】gémìng（名）revolution：～家 revolutionary

【革除】géchú（動）❶ get rid of；abolish；eliminate：～陋習 abolish bad habits and customs ❷ dismiss；expel：～公職 dismiss from public employment

【革新】géxīn I（名）innovation II（動）reform；innovate

【革職】gézhí（動）dismiss；remove from office；sack

靶 bǎ（名）target：打～ do target practice

【靶子】bǎzi（名）target

【靶心】bǎxīn（名）bull's eye

【靶場】bǎchǎng（名）shooting range

靴 xuē（名）boot

靳 Jìn（名）a surname

鞏 gǒng I（動）consolidate II（名）（Gǒng）a surname

【鞏固】gǒnggù I（形）solid；stable：基礎～ have a solid foundation II（動）consolidate；strengthen：～地位 consolidate one's position

鞍 ān（名）saddle：馬～ saddle

【鞍馬】ānmǎ（名）❶ pommelled horse；vaulting horse ❷ saddle and horse：～生活 life at the front

鞋 xié（名）shoe

【鞋匠】xiéjiàng（名）shoe-maker；cobbler

【鞋底】xiédǐ（名）sole (of a shoe)

【鞋刷】xiéshuā（名）shoe brush

【鞋油】xiéyóu（名）shoe polish

【鞋帶】xiédài（名）shoelace；shoe-string

【鞋跟】xiégēn（名）heel (of a shoe)

【鞋墊】xiédiàn（名）shoepad；insole

鞘 qiào（名）sheath；scabbard see also shāo

鞘 shāo（名）whiplash see also qiào

鞠 jū I（動）raise；rear：～育 bring up (children) II（名）（Jū）a surname

【鞠躬】jūgōng I（動）bow II（名）bow：在肖像前三～ make three bows before the portrait

【鞠躬盡瘁】jū gōng jìn cuì〈成〉do one's duty to the best of one's ability：～，死而後已 remain loyal and devoted to the last；give one's best, give one's all, till one's heart ceases to beat

鞣 róu（動）tan: ～料 tanning material

鞦 qiū

【鞦韆】qiūqiān（名）swing

鞭 biān Ⅰ（名）❶ whip; lash: 皮～ leather whip ❷ thing that resembles a whip: ～毛蟲 flagellate ❸ braid of small firecrackers: 一掛～ a string of firecrackers ❹ iron staff (an ancient Chinese weapon) Ⅱ（動）whip; lash; flog: 快馬加～ spur on the steed; at top speed

【鞭子】biānzi（名）whip

【鞭打】biāndǎ（動）flog; lash

【鞭長莫及】biān cháng mò jí（成）too far away to be brought under control

【鞭炮】biānpào（名）❶ firecracker ❷ string of small firecrackers

【鞭策】biāncè Ⅰ（動）spur on; stimulate; give an impetus to: ～他不斷進取 urge him to make steady progress Ⅱ（名）stimulation; encouragement

韋 部

韋 Wéi（名）a surname

韌 rèn（形）resilient; wiry

【韌性】rènxìng（名）resilience

【韌帶】rèndài（名）〈生理〉ligament

韓 Hán（名）a surname

韜 tāo Ⅰ（名）❶ sheath; bow case

❷ art of war: ～略 military strategy Ⅱ（動）conceal; hide

【韜光養晦】tāo guǎng yǎng huì〈成〉hide one's talent and live in obscurity

韭 部

韭 jiǔ（名）leek; Chinese chives

【韭菜】jiǔcài（名）leek; Chinese chives

音 部

音 yīn（名）❶ sound; voice: 説話帶鼻～ speak with a nasal twang ❷ news: 佳～ good news

【音色】yīnsè（名）tone colour; timbre

【音信】yīnxìn（名）news; tidings; message: ～全無 have not heard from sb.'s ever since

【音速】yīnsù（名）velocity of sound

【音素】yīnsù（名）〈語〉phoneme

【音容笑貌】yīn róng xiào mào（名）sb.'s voice and appearance

【音符】yīnfú（名）〈樂〉note

【音階】yīnjiē（名）〈樂〉scale

【音量】yīnliàng（名）volume（of sound）

【音節】yīnjié（名）syllable

【音像】yīnxiàng（名）❶ sound recording and videotaping ❷ sound and video equipment

【音標】yīnbiāo（名）phonetic symbol

【音調】yīndiào（名）tone

【音箱】yīnxiāng（名）speaker systems

【音質】yīnzhì（名）❶ tone quality ❷ acoustic fidelity

【音樂】yīnyuè（名）music: ～家 musician／～廳 concert hall

【音樂會】yīnyuèhuì（名）concert

【音譯】yīnyì（名）transliteration

【音響】yīnxiǎng（名）sound: ～效果 sound effect; acoustics／～組合 stereo

韻 yùn（名）❶ rhyme: ～文 rhymed prose or poetry ❷ charm: 風～ grace or charm

【韻母】yùnmǔ（名）〈語〉simple or compound vowel (of a Chinese syllable)

【韻味】yùnwèi（名）sophisticated appeal

【韻律】yùnlǜ（名）❶ metre (in verse) ❷ rhyme scheme

【韻腳】yùnjiǎo（名）rhyming word at the end of a line of verse; rhyme

響 xiǎng Ⅰ（名）sound; noise: 聽不見～兒了。No more sound could be heard. Ⅱ（動）❶ echo; resound ❷ sound; make a sound: 門鈴～了。The doorbell rang.／一聲不～ keep silent Ⅲ（形）noisy; loud: 再唸～些。Read louder.

【響尾蛇】xiǎngwěishé（名）rattlesnake

【響亮】xiǎngliàng（形）resounding; loud and clear

【響動】xiǎngdòng（名）sound of movement

【響徹雲霄】xiǎng chè yún xiāo〈成〉resound across the skies

【響應】xiǎngyìng（動）respond; answer: ～號召 answer the call

【響聲】xiǎngshēng（名）sound; noise

頁 部

頁 yè（名）page; leaf

【頁碼】yèmǎ（名）page number

【頁邊】yèbiān（名）margin (on a page)

頂 dǐng Ⅰ（名）top; peak Ⅱ（動）❶ carry on the head ❷ resist ～風暴 brave a storm ❸ replace: ～替 take sb's place ❹ equal; be as good as ❺ withstand: 他一個人～得住。He can cope with it alone. Ⅲ（副）most: ～小的女兒 the youngest daughter Ⅳ（量）一～帽子 a cap

【頂天立地】dǐng tiān lì dì〈成〉be absolutely honest and aboveboard; be dauntless

【頂多】dǐngduō（副）at most

【頂住】dǐngzhù（動）withstand

【頂呱呱】dǐngguāguā（形）excellent; first-rate

【頂事】dǐngshì（頂用 dǐngyòng）（形）useful; helpful

【頂峰】dǐngfēng（名）peak; summit

【頂樑柱】dǐngliángzhù（名）pillar backbone

【頂撞】dǐngzhuàng（動）answer back to (one's boss or elder) or repudiate (his ideas) rudely

【頂嘴】dǐngzuǐ（動）talk back

【頂頭上司】dǐng tóu shàng si（名）one's immediate superior; one's direct boss

【頂點】dǐngdiǎn（名）summit; peak; apex: 達到事業的～ reach the apex

of one's career

頃 qǐng Ⅰ (量) *qing,* unit of area (= 6.667 hectares) Ⅱ (名) a short while: ～刻 in an instant

項 xiàng Ⅰ (名) ❶ nape (of the neck) ❷ item: 事～ item; matter ❸ sum (of money): 用～ expenditures ❹ (Xiàng) a surname Ⅱ (量) [of items]: 一～工程 a project / 一～任務 a task

【項目】 xiàngmù (名) item

【項鏈】 xiàngliàn (名) necklace

順 shùn Ⅰ (介) along; in the same direction as: ～着這條路一直往前走 go straight on along this road Ⅱ (動) ❶ put in good order: 把卡片都～過來 arrange all the cards in order ❷ submit (to); be obedient: 咱們得～着他一點。We must humour him. / 一我者昌, 逆我者亡。Those who submit will prosper while those who resist shall perish. ❸ make use of an available opportunity: ～手牽羊 lead away a goat off hand; walk off with sth. Ⅲ (形) ❶ pleasant; agreeable ❷ in sequence

【順口】 shùnkǒu (動) ❶ (of writing) read smoothly: 這篇文章很～。This essay reads well. ❷ speak or sing off-handedly

【順口溜】 shùnkǒuliū (名) doggerel; jingle

【順心】 shùnxīn (形) satisfactory; gratifying

【順手】 shùnshǒu (副) ❶ without a hitch; smoothly: 最初談判不大～。The negotiations were not very smooth at the initial stage. ❷ (get sth. done) simply by stretching one's hand: 他一從池塘裏撈起一顆菱角來。He stretched his hand and picked up a water caltrop from the pond. ❸ do sth. else conveniently or without extra trouble while going about one's own business: 你去商店～給我捎本筆記本來。Please get me a notebook since you are going to the shop.

【順水推舟】 shùn shuǐ tuī zhōu 〈成〉 act in accordance with the trend of things; follow the natural course of events

【順耳】 shùn'ěr (形) pleasant to the ear

【順次】 shùncì (副) in sequence; in order: ～排列 arrange in order

【順利】 shùnlì (副) smoothly; without a hitch: 進展～ make headway

【順序】 shùnxù Ⅰ (名) order Ⅱ (副) in sequence; in order: ～前進 proceed in proper order; march in file

【順延】 shùnyán (動) postpone till the next opportunity

【順便】 shùnbiàn (順帶 shùndài) (副) in passing; at one's convenience: ～問一句, 你給他打過電話了嗎? By the way, have you called him?

【順差】 shùnchā (名) surplus: 貿易～ favourable balance of trade

【順風】 shùnfēng Ⅰ (名) tail wind; fair wind Ⅱ (動) have a favourable wind; sail with the wind: 祝您一路～ wish you a pleasant journey; bon voyage

【順風轉舵】 shùn fēng zhuǎn duò (隨風轉舵 suí fēng zhuǎn duò) 〈成〉 (貶) trim one's sails; chop round with the wind

【順眼】 shùnyǎn (形) pleasant to the

eye: 那座房子真不～。That building is really an eyesore.

【順從】shùncóng（動）submit to; obey: 作為下級，我只好～。As a subordinate, I have to obey.

【順當】shùndàng（副）without a hitch; smoothly: 這件事進行得很～。The matter has been going on smoothly.

【順路】shùnlù（順__兒 shùndàor）I（副）on one's way: 去書店途中，他～去了郵局。He stopped at the post office on his way to the bookstore. II（名）direct route: 這條走不～。We are not taking a direct route.

【順暢】shùnchàng（形）smooth; unobstructed: 儘管大雪紛飛，水運仍然～。Despite the heavy snow, water transport was unaffected.

【順應】shùnyìng（動）be adapted to; act in harmony with: ～民心 act in conformity with the popular feeling

須 xū（動）must; have to: 務～抓緊時間複習功課 must lose no time in going over one's lessons

【須知】xūzhī I（名）musts; dos and don'ts: 參觀～ notice to visitors II（動）must be known: ～自然資源是有限的。It should be kept in mind that natural resources are not inexhaustible.

【須要】xūyào（動）must; have to; need: 要人尊重，～謙虛 need to be modest to command respect

頑 wán（形）❶ stupid and ignorant; refractory ❷ obstinate; stubborn: ～抗 stubborn resistance ❸ naughty: ～童 urchin

【頑皮】wánpí（形）naughty; mischievous

【頑固】wángù（形）stubborn; hopelessly obstinate: ～派 the diehards

【頑強】wánqiáng（形）tenacious of purpose

頓 dùn I（動）❶ pause ❷ settle; arrange: 安～下來 settle in II（副）suddenly; abruptly: ～悟 be suddenly enlightened III（形）tired: 困～ dog-tired IV（量）三～飯 three regular meals

【頓足】dùnzú（動）stamp one's foot

【頓時】dùnshí（副）immediately

【頓號】dùnhào（名）a punctuation mark in Chinese（、）for a short pause, used to set off items in a series

預 yù I（副）in advance; beforehand: ～定 fix in advance; schedule II（動）participate; have a hand in: 干～ intervene; interfere

【預支】yùzhī（動）advance（payment）

【預付】yùfù（動）prepay; pay in advance: ～款 advance payment

【預示】yùshì（動）betoken; presage; forebode

【預先】yùxiān（副）in advance; beforehand

【預兆】yùzhào（名）omen; sign

【預扣】yùkòu（動）withhold

【預見】yùjiàn I（動）foresee; predict II（名）foresight; prevision

【預防】yùfáng（動）prevent; provide against: ～勝於治療。Prevention is better than cure.

【預言】yùyán I（動）prophesy; foretell II（名）prophecy

【預告】yùgào I（動）notify beforehand; herald II（名）advance notice

【預計】yùjì（動）reckon in advance;

estimate: ～到達時間 estimated time of arrival

【預訂】yùdìng（動）subscribe; book; reserve

【預科】yùkē（名）preparatory course (in a college)：醫～ pre-medical (course)

【預約】yùyuē（動）make an appointment

【預展】yùzhǎn（動）(of an exhibition) preview

【預料】yùliào（動）expect; predict; anticipate

【預售】yùshòu（名）advance sale：～券 advance sales ticket

【預習】yùxí（動）(of students) prepare lessons before class; preview

【預產期】yùchǎnqī（名）〈醫〉expected date of childbirth

【預報】yùbào（動）forecast：天氣～ weather forecast

【預備】yùbèi（動）prepare; get ready：～乘客 stand-by passenger

【預測】yùcè（動）forecast; predict

【預期】yùqī（動）expect; anticipate

【預感】yùgǎn（名）premonition; presentiment

【預想】yùxiǎng（動）anticipate; expect：結果比～的要好。The outcome is better than expected.

【預算】yùsuàn（名）budget

【預演】yùyǎn（動）(of a performance or film) preview

【預製】yùzhì（動）prefabricate：～部件 prefabricated parts

【預選】yùxuǎn（名）preliminary election

【預謀】yùmóu（動）premeditate：～殺人 premeditated murder

【預賽】yùsài（名）〈體〉preliminary contest

頒 bān（動）❶ promulgate ❷ confer (a prize, medal, etc.) ❸ distribute

【頒行】bānxíng（動）issue (a decree, etc.) for enforcement

【頒佈】bānbù（動）promulgate; issue; decree：～大赦令 decree an ammesty

【頒發】bānfā（動）❶ issue; promulgate ❷ award; bestow：～獎狀 award a certificate of merit

頌 sòng I（動）extol; acclaim; laud II（名）ode; eulogy

【頌詞】sòngcí（名）eulogy; complimentary address

【頌揚】sòngyáng（動）laud; eulogize

【頌歌】sònggē（名）ode; song of praise

頎 qí

【頎長】qícháng（形）(of a person) tall

頗 pō（副）rather; considerably：～久 for quite a long time

領 lǐng I（名）❶ neck ❷ collar：小圓～ small round collar ❸ main point; outline：不得要～ miss the point; fail to see what it is all about II（動）❶ lead; usher：～人入座 usher sb. to his seat ❷ possess; have jurisdiction over ❸ receive; take：～工資 draw one's salary; get one's pay ❹ understand ❺ adopt (a child) III（量）：一～蓆 a mat

【領子】lǐngzi（名）collar

【領巾】lǐngjīn（名）scarf：紅～ red scarf

【領口】lǐngkǒu（名）❶ collarband;

neckband ❷ meeting place of the two ends of a collar

【領土】 lǐngtǔ（名）territory: ～主權 territorial sovereignty

【領水】 lǐngshuǐ（名）❶ territorial waters ❷ inland waters

【領地】 lǐngdì（名）❶ manor ❷ territory

【領先】 lǐngxiān（動）lead: 在馬拉松中～ lead in the marathon / ～三米 have a lead of three metres over sb.

【領空】 lǐngkōng（名）territorial airspace

【領取】 lǐngqǔ（動）receive as due: ～獎金 receive a bonus

【領事】 lǐngshì（名）consul: 總～ consul-general

【領事館】 lǐngshìguǎn（名）consulate

【領班】 lǐngbān（名）foreman; overseer

【領海】 lǐnghǎi（名）territorial sea

【領航】 lǐngháng（動）navigate; pilot: ～員 navigator

【領悟】 lǐngwù（動）comprehend

【領袖】 lǐngxiù（名）leader

【領域】 lǐngyù（名）❶ field; realm: 藝術～ realm of art ❷ territorial domain

【領教】 lǐngjiào（動）❶〈套〉[used to indicate approval or appreciation]: thank; be obliged to: 您的意見對極了，～。Thank you very much for your sound advice. ❷〈敬〉seek your wise counsel: 這件事想向您～。I hope I may have the benefit of your advice. / 不敢～。I beg to disagree.

【領章】 lǐngzhāng（名）collar insignia

【領唱】 lǐngchàng（名）leading singer

【領帶】 lǐngdài（名）necktie; tie

【領略】 lǐnglüè（動）understand; appreciate: ～美好風光 enjoy the beautiful scenery

【領情】 lǐngqíng（動）be obliged to sb. for his kindness

【領港】 lǐnggǎng Ⅰ（動）pilot (a ship in or out of a harbour) Ⅱ（名）pilot

【領隊】 lǐngduì Ⅰ（動）lead a team Ⅱ（名）leader; head

【領結】 lǐngjié（名）bowtie

【領會】 lǐnghuì（動）understand: ～本書要點 grasp the essential points of the book

【領銜】 lǐngxián（動）head the list of signatures

【領導】 lǐngdǎo Ⅰ（動）lead Ⅱ（名）leader; leadership

【領頭】 lǐngtóu（動）take the lead: ～鬧事 be the ringleader of a row

頦

頦 kē（名）chin: 下巴～兒 chin

頜

頜 hé（名）〈書〉jaw: 上(下)～ the upper (lower) jaw

頭

頭 tóu Ⅰ（名）❶ head: 昏～昏腦 muddleheaded ❷ hair; hairstyle: 剪平～ have a close crop ❸ top: 城～ top of the city wall ❹ beginning; end: 沒個～ endless / 到～來 in the end ❺ short remaining part: 煙～ cigarette stub; cigarette end ❻ chief; leader: 辦公室的～兒 head of the office ❼ side: 兩～不是人 offend both sides Ⅱ（形）❶ first: ～一回 for the first time ❷ leading: ～馬 lead horse ❸ previous: ～天早上 the previous morning Ⅲ（量）❶（of domestic animals): 兩～豬 two pigs ❷（of garlic) bulb

see also tou

【頭子】tóuzi（名）chief; ringleader

【頭巾】tóujīn（名）scarf; kerchief; turban (for Muslims)

【頭目】tóumù（名）head of a gang; chieftain

【頭皮】tóupí（名）❶ scalp: 硬着～接受任務 pluck up one's courage to accept the assignment ❷ dandruff

【頭角】tóujiǎo（名）brilliance; talent: 初露～ (of a young person) begin to show one's ability or talent

【頭昏】tóuhūn（動）feel dizzy (giddy)

【頭版】tóubǎn（名）front page (of a newspaper): ～頭條消息 top-line front-page news

【頭面人物】tóumiàn rénwù（名）big shot; public figure; dignitary; top brass

【頭疼】tóuténg（頭痛 tóutòng）（動）have a headache

【頭頂】tóudǐng（名）crown of the head

【頭等】tóuděng（形）first-class; first-rate; topnotch: ～艙 first-class or saloon cabin

【頭裏】tóuli（副）〈口〉❶ in front; ahead: 數學這一門她總是走在～。She is always ahead of others in maths. ❷ in advance; at the very beginning: 咱們把話說在～,我是不贊成這個計劃的。Let's make this clear in advance that I am not for the plan.

【頭號】tóuhào（形）No.1; size one; top grade

【頭腦】tóunǎo（名）❶ thought; mind: ～發熱 be swayed by momentary enthusiasm; be overenthusiastic / ～簡單 be simple-minded ❷ main threads: 摸不着～ be ab-

solutely uncertain how the matter stands; cannot understand ❸〈口〉chief; chieftain

【頭銜】tóuxián（名）official or academic title

【頭緒】tóuxù（名）main threads: 事情還沒有～ haven't got things into shape yet

【頭髮】tóufa（名）hair (on the human head): 做～ have one's hair dressed

【頭頭兒】tóutour（名）〈口〉chief or head of an organization; boss

頭 tou [suffix for a noun, verb or adjective]: 舌～ tongue / 沒看～ not worth seeing
see also tóu

頰 jiá（名）cheek

頸 jǐng（名）neck

【頸項】jǐngxiàng（名）neck

【頸椎】jǐngzhuī（名）〈生理〉cervical vertebra

頻 pín Ⅰ（形）frequently; time and again: 經濟戰線捷報～傳。News of success has been pouring in from the economic front. Ⅱ（名）frequency: 調～ frequency modulation

【頻率】pínlǜ（名）〈物〉frequency

【頻道】píndào（名）frequency channel; channel

【頻頻】pínpín（副）repeatedly; time and again: ～點頭 repeatedly nod approval

【頻繁】pínfán（形）frequent: 他們接觸～。They have frequent contacts.

領 hàn Ⅰ（名）chin Ⅱ（動）nod

頹 tuí（形）❶ ruined; decayed: ～

垣斷壁 a dilapidated building with crumbling walls ❷ declining; decadent ❸ dejected; depressed

【頹唐】tuítáng（形）dejected; listless; languid

【頹喪】tuísàng（形）dejected; disheartened; downcast

【頹勢】tuíshì（名）declining trend

【頹廢】tuífèi（形）dejected; decadent

顆 kē（量）（of grains, pearls, beans, stars, etc.）: 拔了兩～牙 have two teeth pulled out

【顆粒】kēlì（名）❶ particle; granule: 生産～肥料 produce granulated fertilizer ❷ grain: 顆～歸倉 every grain to the granary

額 é（名）❶ forehead ❷ quota

【額外】éwài（形）extra; additional: ～工作 extra work

【額定】édìng（形）specified（number or amount）

顏 yán（名）❶ face; facial expression: 容～憔悴 look haggard ❷ colour ❸（Yán）a surname

【顏色】yánsè（名）❶ colour: 暗淡的～ dull colour ❷ facial expression: 給他點～看看 teach him how to behave; teach him a lesson

【顏面】yánmiàn（名）face

【顏料】yánliào（名）pigment; dyestuff

題 tí I（名）❶ topic; subject; theme II（動）inscribe; write: ～名 give one's autograph; sign

【題目】tímù（名）❶ title; topic ❷ question（in an exercise or examination）

【題字】tízì I（動）inscribe a few words to commemorate a certain occasion II（名）inscription

【題材】tícái（名）subject matter; theme

【題詞】tící I（動）write a short paragraph for encouragement or commemoration II（名）❶ inscription for such purposes ❷ foreword

顎 è（名）jaw

類 lèi I（名）kind; sort: 分～ classify; categorize / 這一～人 this kind of person II（動）resemble; be like

【類人猿】lèirényuán（名）anthropoid（ape）

【類比】lèibǐ（名）〈邏〉analogy

【類似】lèisì（形）similar; alike

【類別】lèibié（名）category; class; division

【類型】lèixíng（名）type; class

【類推】lèituī（動）analogize; infer: 依此～ the rest may be inferred; and so on and so forth

顛 diān I（名）❶ top; peak: 塔～ spire ❷ beginning: ～末 from start to finish II（動）❶ fall; topple ❷ jolt

【顛三倒四】diān sān dǎo sì〈成〉incoherent; confused and confusing

【顛沛】diānpèi（動）suffer hardship or setback: ～流離 wander miserably from place to place

【顛倒】diāndǎo（動）turn upside down: ～是非 confuse right and wrong

【顛倒黑白】diān dǎo hēi bái〈成〉confuse black and white; stand truth on its head

【顛撲不破】diān pū bù pò〈成〉ir-
refutable; indisputable

【顛覆】diānfù（動）❶ overturn ❷
subvert

【顛簸】diānbǒ（動）jolt; bump: 汽
車~而行。The car bumped along.

願 yuàn Ⅰ（名）wish; hope; desire:
夙~ long-cherished wish Ⅱ（動）be
willing: 自～退出比賽 withdraw
from a competition of one's own will

【願望】yuànwàng（名）wish; desire;
aspiration

【願意】yuànyì（動）❶ be willing; be
ready: ～效勞 be willing to offer
one's services ❷ wish; like; hope:
我不～麻煩你。I don't want to put
you to any bother.

顧 gù Ⅰ（動）❶ look round; look:
回～ look back ❷ visit; call on ❸
attend to; take into account Ⅱ（名）
(Gù) a surname

【顧及】gùjí（動）attend to; take into
consideration: 很難～這些零碎
事 cannot afford to attend to these trifling matters

【顧全】gùquán（動）show consideration for: ～大局 have the overall
public interest at heart

【顧此失彼】gù cǐ shī bǐ〈成〉cannot
attend to one thing without losing
sight of the other

【顧名思義】gù míng sī yì〈成〉as
the name suggests; judging by the
title

【顧忌】gùjì（名）scruple

【顧客】gùkè（名）customer; client

【顧問】gùwèn（名）adviser; consultant

【顧慮】gùlǜ（名）misgiving; worry:
有～ not without some misgivings

顫 chàn（動）tremble; quiver
see also zhàn

【顫抖】chàndǒu（動）shiver; shake

【顫悠】chànyou（形）shaking; flickering

【顫動】chàndòng（動）quiver; vibrate; shake

顫 zhàn（動）shiver; tremble
see also chàn

【顫慄】zhànlì（動）tremble; shiver

顯 xiǎn Ⅰ（形）obvious; apparent;
conspicuous Ⅱ（動）show; display

【顯示】xiǎnshì（動）show; demonstrate: ～威力 display one's
strength

【顯而易見】xiǎn ér yì jiàn（副）ob-
viously; clearly; evidently

【顯身手】xiǎnshēnshǒu（動）display
one's abilities

【顯明】xiǎnmíng（形）obvious; clear

【顯要】xiǎnyào Ⅰ（形）powerful; influential Ⅱ（名）dignitary; VIP

【顯得】xiǎnde（動）look; seem: 他
～很疲乏。He looks very tired.

【顯現】xiǎnxiàn（動）appear; manifest oneself

【顯眼】xiǎnyǎn（形）conspicuous;
showy: 我討厭坐在～的地方。I
hate to sit in a conspicuous place.

【顯然】xiǎnrán（副）evidently; apparently: ～是你的錯。Obviously,
it's your fault.

【顯著】xiǎnzhù（形）marked; outstanding; remarkable

【顯像管】xiǎnxiàngguǎn（名）〈電子〉
kinescope; cathode-ray tube

【顯微鏡】xiǎnwēijìng（名）micro-
scope

【顯赫】xiǎnhè（形）❶ celebrated;

illustrious: 名聲 ~ enjoy a very high reputation ❷ mighty; powerful

【顯影】xiǎnyǐng（動）develop（a film）

【顯露】xiǎnlù（動）show; become visible

顰

顰 pín（動）bend one's brows

顱

顱 lú（名）skull; cranium

【顱骨】lúgǔ（名）skull

顳

顳 niè

【顳骨】niè</gǔ（名）〈生理〉temporal bone

【顳顬】nièrú（名）〈生理〉temple

顴

顴 quán（名）cheekbone

【顴骨】quángǔ（名）cheekbone

風 部

風 fēng I（名）❶ wind ❷ scene; view ❸ trend; convention; practice: 不正之 ~ unhealthy trend ❹ style: 學 ~ style of study ❺ information; news: 吹 ~ briefing ❻（Fēng）a surname II（形）unfounded; groundless: ~ 言 ~ 語 groundless rumours; gossip

【風力】fēnglì（名）wind force; wind power

【風口】fēngkǒu（名）draught

【風口浪尖】fēng kǒu làng jiān〈成〉in the teeth of the storm

【風土人情】fēngtǔ rénqíng（名）natural surroundings and customs of a locality

【風化】fēnghuà（名）custom and cultivated behaviour: 事關 ~ a matter of social morals

【風水】fēngshui（名）geomancy

【風帆】fēngfān（名）sail

【風光】fēngguāng（名）scenery

【風行】fēngxíng（動）prevail; come into fashion: ~ 全國 be popular all over the country

【風衣】fēngyī（名）wind-cheater; breaker; wind-proof clothing

【風向】fēngxiàng（名）wind direction

【風向標】fēngxiàngbiāo（名）wind vane

【風車】fēngchē（名）wind mill

【風沙】fēngshā（名）wind and sand; dust storm

【風災】fēngzāi（名）windstorm; cyclone disaster

【風吹草動】fēng chuī cǎo dòng〈成〉the slightest sign of disturbance

【風波】fēngbō（名）trouble; disturbance; storm: 政治 ~ political disturbance

【風采】fēngcǎi（名）charisma

【風尚】fēngshàng（名）prevailing social custom; established social practice

【風味】fēngwèi（名）relish: 地方 ~ local flavour

【風雨】fēngyǔ（名）storm; hardships

【風雨同舟】fēng yǔ tóng zhōu〈成〉stand together to brave any storm; be in the same boat

【風雨無阻】fēng yǔ wú zǔ〈成〉in all weathers; rain or shine

【風雨飄搖】fēng yǔ piāo yáo〈成〉tottering on the brink of collapse; tottering

【風度】fēngdù（名）manners; bearing

【風俗】fēngsú（名）social custom

【風姿】fēngzī（名）charming manner

【風速】fēngsù（名）wind velocity

【風格】fēnggé（名）style

【風骨】fēnggǔ（名）❶ unyielding spirit ❷ vigorous style

【風流】fēngliú（形）endowed with great charm and talent：～人物 talented men who scorn social conventions; a romantic person

【風氣】fēngqì（名）social trends

【風疹】fēngzhěn（名）〈醫〉nettle rash

【風扇】fēngshàn（名）electric fan

【風浪】fēnglàng（名）storm：杯中～ storm in a teacup

【風馬牛不相及】fēng mǎ niú bù xiāng jí〈成〉be absolutely irrelevant

【風起雲涌】fēng qǐ yún yǒng〈成〉surging forward with tremendous force

【風乾】fēnggān（動）airdry

【風涼話】fēngliánghuà（名）sarcastic remarks：事後說～ speak with biting sarcasm after the event

【風情】fēngqíng（名）coquetry：賣弄～ flirt with sb.

【風發】fēngfā（形）vigorous; energetic：意氣～ daring and enthusiastic

【風寒】fēnghán（名）cold：受～ catch a cold or chill

【風帽】fēngmào（名）hood

【風琴】fēngqín（名）organ

【風華】fēnghuá（名）youth and talent：～正茂 in the flower of youth

【風雲】fēngyún（名）winds and clouds：～突變 drastic change in the (political) situation

【風雲人物】fēngyún rénwù（名）man of the hour

【風景】fēngjǐng（名）scenery; landscape：～奇觀 scenic wonders

【風景區】fēngjǐngqū（名）scenic spot

【風景畫】fēngjǐnghuà（名）landscape (painting)

【風雅】fēngyǎ（形）refined; gentle

【風傳】fēngchuán（名）hearsay; rumour

【風馳電掣】fēng chí diàn chè〈成〉at lightning speed

【風塵】fēngchén（名）tiring long journey：～僕僕 be travel-worn

【風聞】fēngwén（動）hear of; learn by hearsay

【風貌】fēngmào（名）style and features

【風箏】fēngzheng（名）kite

【風暴】fēngbào（名）storm

【風潮】fēngcháo（名）mass agitation

【風趣】fēngqù（名）wit and humour

【風箱】fēngxiāng（名）bellows

【風調雨順】fēng tiáo yǔ shùn〈成〉favourable weather conditions

【風險】fēngxiǎn（名）risk：承擔～ take risks

【風頭】fēngtou（名）❶ trend of events; development of events：避避～ lie low ❷ publicity：愛出～ crave publicity; like to be in the limelight

【風燭殘年】fēng zhú cán nián〈成〉a candle in the wind

【風霜】fēngshuāng（名）hardships：飽經～ have suffered numerous hardships

【風聲】fēngshēng（名）news; rumour：～漸緊。Tensions are building up.

【風聲鶴唳】fēng shēng hè lì〈成〉feel panic-stricken for fear of enemy encirclement; any sound in nature is taken for the enemy's movement

【風濕症】 fēngshīzhèng（名）〈醫〉 rheumatism

【風鏡】 fēngjìng（名）goggles

【風靡一時】 fēng mǐ yī shí〈成〉be in vogue; be all the rage

【風韻】 fēngyùn（名）charm（of a woman）

颯 sà

【颯爽】 sàshuǎng（形）〈書〉valiant; valorous: ～英姿 valiant and heroic bearing

【颯颯】 sàsà（象）sough; rustle: 樹葉～作響。The leaves are rustling.

颱 tái

【颱風】 táifēng（名）〈氣〉typhoon: ～警報 typhoon warning

颶 jù

【颶風】 jùfēng（名）〈氣〉hurricane

飘 piāo（動）flutter; waft: 花香沿着走廊一過來。The fragrance of the flowers wafted along the corridor.

【飄帶】 piāodài（名）streamer; ribbon

【飄揚】 piāoyáng（動）wave; flutter: 國旗迎風～。The national flag fluttered in the breeze.

【飄搖】 piāoyáo（動）❶ flutter ❷ (of a regime) be unstable: 風雨～ tottering

【飄零】 piāolíng（形）❶ (of flowers or leaves) withered and fallen ❷ (of people) set adrift; homeless

【飄蕩】 piāodàng（動）drift; flutter; float

【飄飄然】 piāopiāorán（形）as if treading on air; smug

飆 biāo（名）violent windstorm; hurricane

飛　部

飛 fēi Ⅰ（動）fly; hover Ⅱ（副）swiftly Ⅲ（形）unexpected: ～災 unexpected misfortunes

【飛毛腿】 fēimáotuǐ（名）fast runner

【飛行】 fēixíng Ⅰ（動）fly: ～員 pilot; aviator Ⅱ（名）flight

【飛地】 fēidì（名）enclave

【飛快】 fēikuài（副）fast; at lightning speed

【飛船】 fēichuán（名）airship: 宇宙～ spacecraft

【飛翔】 fēixiáng（動）(of birds, aircraft, etc.) fly in the air

【飛揚】 fēiyáng（動）fly up; float in the air

【飛揚跋扈】 fēi yáng bá hù〈成〉be haughty and insolent; act like an overlord

【飛短流長】 fēi duǎn liú cháng〈成〉spread malicious stories about sb.

【飛黃騰達】 fēi huáng téng dá〈成〉have a steep rise to power; rise spectacularly

【飛馳】 fēichí（動）run at top speed: ～而過 race past; speed past

【飛蛾投火】 fēi é tóu huǒ〈成〉court one's own destruction like a moth flying to the fire

【飛禽】 fēiqín（名）birds: ～走獸 birds and beasts

【飛漲】 fēizhǎng（動）soar; skyrocket: 物價～。Prices are soaring.

【飛舞】 fēiwǔ（動）flutter: 雪花～。

Snowflakes dance in the air.

【飛機】fēijī（名）aeroplane

【飛機場】fēijīchǎng（名） airport; airfield

【飛濺】fēijiàn（動）splash

【飛躍】fēiyuè（動）leap

食 部

食 shí I（動）eat：～慾不振 lose one's appetite II（名）❶ food; meal：素～ vegetarian diet ❷ feed ❸ eclipse：日全～ total solar eclipse III（形）edible：～糖 sugar

【食用】shíyòng（形）edible：～菌 edible mushrooms

【食言】shíyán（動）go back on one's word

【食物】shíwù（名）food; edibles：～中毒 food poisoning

【食油】shíyóu（名）edible oil

【食指】shízhǐ（名）index finger

【食品】shípǐn（名）food; foodstuff; grocery：副～商店 grocery

【食宿】shísù（名） board and lodging：～自理 pay for one's own board and lodging

【食堂】shítáng（名）❶ mess hall; canteen; dining room ❷ restaurant

【食道】shídào（名）esophagus; gullet

【食糧】shíliáng（名）cereals; grain; food

【食譜】shípǔ（名）cookbook; recipes

【食鹽】shíyán（名） kitchen salt; table salt

飢 jī I（形）hungry; starving II（名）hunger

【飢不擇食】jī bù zé shí〈成〉nobody will be choosy when in dire need of food

【飢民】jīmín（名）victims of famine; famine refugees

【飢寒交迫】jī hán jiāo pò〈成〉 be hungry and cold; be starving and freezing

【飢腸轆轆】jī cháng lù lu〈成〉one's stomach is rumbling

【飢餓】jī'è（名）starvation：忍飢挨餓 be famished

飭 chì（動）put in order：整～紀律 enhance discipline

飲 yǐn I（動）❶ drink ❷ nurse (a feeling); suffer (an injustice)：～恨 suffer a gross injustice; nurse a grievance II（名）drink：冷～ cold drinks
see also yìn

【飲水思源】yǐn shuǐ sī yuán〈成〉 remember with gratitude the source of one's happiness

【飲用水】yǐnyòngshuǐ（名）drinking water

【飲泣】yǐnqì（動）〈書〉choke down tears

【飲食】yǐnshí（名）food and drink; diet

【飲料】yǐnliào（名）drink; beverage

【飲鴆止渴】yǐn zhèn zhǐ kě〈成〉 quench thirst with poison; seek a temporary relief which might bring deadly consequences

飲 yìn（動）give (animals) water to drink：馬已經～過了。The horse has been watered.
see also yǐn

飯 fàn（名）❶ cooked rice ❷ meal

【飯店】fàndiàn（名）❶ restaurant ❷ hotel

【飯桶】fàntǒng（名）❶ rice bucket ❷ worthless person

【飯盒】fànhé（名）lunch-box

【飯量】fànliàng（名）appetite

【飯菜】fàncài（名）food

【飯碗】fànwǎn（名）❶ rice bowl ❷ job: 鐵~ iron rice bowl; permanent employment

【飯館】fànguǎn（名）restaurant

【飯廳】fàntīng（名）dining hall; mess hall

飼 sì（動）raise (animals)

【飼草】sìcǎo（名）forage grass

【飼料】sìliào（名）fodder; feed; forage: 鷄~ chicken feed

【飼養】sìyǎng（動）raise (animals): 家禽~場 poultry farm

飾 shì Ⅰ（名）ornament; embellishment: 首~盒 jewel case Ⅱ（動）❶ adorn; decorate ❷ gloss over: 掩~ conceal ❸ play the part of: ~羅米歐 play (the role of) Romeo

【飾物】shìwù（名）adornment; ornament

飽 bǎo Ⅰ（形）full; having eaten one's fill: 溫~ have enough to eat; be moderately well-off Ⅱ（副）fully; to the full: 一餐一頓 enjoy a meal to the full Ⅲ（動）fill; glut; satisfy: 中~私囊 line one's pockets

【飽和】bǎohé Ⅰ（形）saturated: ~溶液 saturated solution Ⅱ（名）saturation: ~點 saturation point

【飽受】bǎoshòu（動）endure to the fullest extent

【飽嗝兒】bǎogér（名）belch: 打~ belch

【飽經風霜】bǎo jīng fēng shuāng〈成〉weather-beaten; seasoned; have gone through thick and thin: ~的臉 weather-beaten face

【飽滿】bǎomǎn（形）full; plump: 精神~ vigorous; full of energy

【飽嘗】bǎocháng（動）suffer enough from

飴 yí（名）maltose

養 yǎng（動）❶ give birth to ❷ provide for; support: ~家 support one's family ❸ raise; grow: ~鴿子 keep pigeons / ~花 grow flowers ❹ rest; convalesce ❺ cultivate; develop; foster: 從小~成節約的習慣 develop a frugal habit from childhood

【養分】yǎngfèn（名）nutrient

【養生】yǎngshēng（動）keep oneself in good health: ~之道 the way to keep fit

【養老】yǎnglǎo（動）❶ provide for the aged ❷ spend one's remaining years in retirement

【養老金】yǎnglǎojīn（名）old-age pension

【養育】yǎngyù（動）bring up; rear

【養虎遺患】yǎng hǔ yí huàn〈成〉to rear a tiger is to court disaster; tolerance of evil leads to calamity

【養活】yǎnghuo（動）support; provide for: ~一家老小 provide for the whole family

【養神】yǎngshén（動）keep mental repose

【養病】yǎngbìng（動）convalesce: 他在鄉下~。He is convalescing in the countryside.

【養料】yǎngliào（名）nutriment

【養魚】yǎngyú（動）breed fish: ~

場 fish farm

【養殖】yǎngzhí〈動〉breed; cultivate: ～蘑菇 cultivate mushrooms

【養尊處優】yǎng zūn chù yōu〈成〉live in lordly comfort; live like a lord

【養蜂】yǎngfēng〈名〉beekeeping: ～場 apiary

【養路】yǎnglù〈動〉maintain a road; maintain a railway: ～費 road toll

【養精蓄銳】yǎng jīng xù ruì〈成〉conserve energy and build up strength

【養豬】yǎngzhū〈動〉raise pigs: ～場 pig farm

【養護】yǎnghù〈動〉keep in good repair; maintain

餃 jiǎo〈名〉half-moon-shaped dumpling

【餃子】jiǎozi〈名〉*jiaozi;* dumpling (usu. with meat and vegetable stuffing); ravioli: ～皮 dumpling wrapper

餅 bǐng〈名〉❶ cake; pastry: 燒～ sesame-seed cake ❷ round and flat object: 豆～ soya-bean residue cake

【餅乾】bǐnggān〈名〉cracker; biscuit; 蘇打～ soda cracker

餌 ěr〈名〉bait

餐 cān Ⅰ〈動〉eat: 飽～一頓 eat one's fill Ⅱ〈名〉meal; food: 快～ fast food; snack Ⅲ〈量〉meal: 一日三～ three meals a day

【餐巾】cānjīn〈名〉(table) napkin

【餐車】cānchē〈名〉diner; dining car

【餐具】cānjù〈名〉tableware; dinner set; mess kit

【餐券】cānquàn〈名〉meal ticket; meal coupon

【餐廳】cāntīng〈名〉dining hall; restaurant

餒 něi〈形〉disheartened: 氣～ be dejected; lose heart

餘 yú〈形〉❶ surplus; spare: ～糧 surplus grain ❷ odd; over: 十一人 more than ten people

【餘存】yúcún〈名〉remainder; balance

【餘地】yúdì〈名〉leeway; margin; room (for a purpose): 給人留有～ leave sb. room for manoeuvre; allow sb. leeway

【餘年】yúnián〈名〉remaining years of one's life

【餘波】yúbō〈名〉repercussions

【餘味】yúwèi〈名〉aftertaste

【餘毒】yúdú〈名〉remnant harmful influence

【餘音】yúyīn〈名〉lingering sound: ～繚繞，不絕於耳。The song has stopped, but the voice remains in the ears of the hearer.

【餘勇可買】yú yǒng kě gǔ〈成〉still have strength left and to spare

【餘悸】yújì〈名〉lingering fear

【餘暇】yúxiá〈名〉spare time; leisure

【餘熱】yúrè〈名〉❶ residual heat ❷ (of a retired person) remnant enthusiasm for work; remaining usefulness

【餘數】yúshù〈名〉〈數〉remainder

【餘震】yúzhèn〈名〉〈地〉earth tremors; aftershock

【餘興】yúxìng〈名〉❶ lingering interest ❷ entertainment (after a meeting or a dinner party)

【餘額】yú'é（名）❶ vacancy ❷ remaining sum; balance

【餘燼】yújìn（名）ashes; embers

餓 è I（形）hungry II（動）starve

館 guǎn（名）❶ accommodation for guests or tourists: 旅～ hotel ❷ official building for diplomatic or consular personnel: 使～ embassy ❸ (of service trades) shop: 理髮～ barbershop ❹ cultural establishments: 天文～ planetarium / 圖書～ library

饯 jiàn I（動）give a farewell dinner II（名）sweetmeats: 蜜～ candied fruits

【饯行】jiànxíng（動）hold a farewell dinner party for sb.

餛 hún

【餛飩】húntún（名）wonton; soup dumplings

餚 yáo（名）meat and fish dishes; dishes

餡 xiàn（名）filling; stuffing: ～餅 pie; tart

餿 sōu（形）(of food) sour or bad: 出～主意 give bad advice

餾 liù（動）heat up in a steamer: ～米飯 heat up the cold cooked rice

饈 xiū（名）nice food; delicacy

饃 mó（名）〈方〉steamed bread

饅 mán

【饅頭】mántou（名）steamed bread

饒 ráo I（形）rich; affluent; abundant: 礦產富～ abound in minerals II（動）have mercy on; forgive: 不能輕～了他。He should not be let off lightly. III（名）(Ráo) a surname

【饒舌】ráoshé（形）talkative; loquacious

【饒命】ráomìng（動）spare sb.'s life

【饒恕】ráoshù（動）forgive; pardon; absolve

饋 kuì（動）present (a gift)

【饋贈】kuìzèng（動）present (gifts)

饑 jī（名）famine; crop failure

【饑荒】jīhuang I（名）famine: 鬧～ be famine-stricken II（形）be hard up; be in debt: 拉～ run into debt

【饑饉】jījǐn（名）famine

饞 chán（形）❶ gluttonous; greedy ❷ covetous: 眼～ be covetous; be envious

【饞涎欲滴】chán xián yù dī〈成〉mouth watering with greed; covet

【饞嘴】chánzuǐ（形）gluttonous

首 部

首 shǒu I（名）❶ head ❷ leader; head: 國家元～ head of state II（形）first: ～任駐華大使 the first ambassador accredited to China III（動）lodge a charge against: 投案自～ surrender oneself to the police; give oneself up IV（量）(of songs, poems, etc.): 唱～歌 sing a song

【首次】shǒucì（副）(for) the first time

【首先】shǒuxiān（副）❶ first; first and foremost：～踢進一球 be the first to kick a goal ❷ first of all; to begin with

【首位】shǒuwèi（名）first place; first priority：放在～ be placed in the first place

【首長】shǒuzhǎng（名）senior officer; senior official

【首府】shǒufǔ（名）❶ provincial capital ❷ capital of an autonomous region or prefecture ❸ capital of a colony

【首屈一指】shǒu qū yī zhǐ〈成〉be of the highest order; be second to none

【首相】shǒuxiàng（名）prime minister; premier

【首要】shǒuyào（形）of cardinal importance; chief; principal：～任務 a task of cardinal importance

【首倡】shǒuchàng（動）initiate; pioneer; be the first to advocate

【首航】shǒuháng（動）maiden voyage; first flight

【首席】shǒuxí Ⅰ（名）seat of honour Ⅱ（形）chief：～法官 chief justice

【首都】shǒudū（名）（national）capital

【首創】shǒuchuàng（動）originate; initiate; begin：～精神 initiative

【首富】shǒufù（名）richest family （in an area）

【首惡】shǒu'è（名）chief culprit; archcriminal

【首腦】shǒunǎo（名）head：～會議 summit

【首飾】shǒushì（名）women's jewelry; trinkets

【首領】shǒulǐng（名）leader; chieftain

香 部

香 xiāng Ⅰ（形）❶ fragrant; scented：鳥語花～。Birds chirp and flowers are pleasantly fragrant. ❷ delicious; appetizing：這菜真～。The dish smells delicious. ❸ popular; welcome：這些貨物在農村很吃～。These goods are most popular in the countryside. Ⅱ（副）❶（eat）with relish ❷（sleep）soundly Ⅲ（名）❶ perfume or spice：檀～ sandalwood ❷ incense; joss stick：盤～ incense coil

【香水】xiāngshuǐ（名）scent; perfume

【香瓜】xiāngguā（名）musk-melon

【香皂】xiāngzào（名）toilet soap

【香味】xiāngwèi（名）scent; fragrance

【香油】xiāngyóu（名）sesame oil

【香客】xiāngkè（名）pilgrim

【香料】xiāngliào（名）❶ perfume ❷ spice

【香草】xiāngcǎo（名）❶ vanilla ❷ sweet grass

【香脂】xiāngzhī（名）❶ face cream ❷ balm; balsam

【香粉】xiāngfěn（名）face powder

【香甜】xiāngtián Ⅰ（形）fragrant and sweet; delicious Ⅱ（副）（sleep）soundly

【香港】Xiānggǎng（名）Hong Kong

【香菇】xiānggū（名）mushroom

【香菜】xiāngcài（名）coriander

【香煙】xiāngyān（名）cigarette

【香腸】xiāngcháng（名）sausage

【香椿】xiāngchūn（名）〈植〉Chinese toon

【香精】xiāngjīng（名）essence：～油 essential oil

【香噴噴】xiāngpēnpēn（形）❶ sweet-smelling ❷ savoury; appetizing

【香蕉】xiāngjiāo（名）banana

【香鼬】xiāngyòu（名）alpine weasel

【香檳酒】xiāngbīnjiǔ（名）champagne; fizz

【香爐】xiānglú（名）incence burner

馥 fù（名）fragrance

【馥郁】fùyù（名）strong fragrance

馬 部

馬 mǎ（名）❶ horse ❷（Mǎ）a surname

【馬刀】mǎdāo（名）sabre

【馬力】mǎlì（名）horsepower

【馬上】mǎshàng（副）at once; immediately：客人～就到。The guests will arrive in a minute. / 我們吃過晚飯後～就去機場。We'll start for the airport immediately after dinner.

【馬大哈】mǎdàhā Ⅰ（形）careless Ⅱ（名）careless person; scatterbrain

【馬口鐵】mǎkǒutiě（名）tinplate; galvanized iron

【馬扎】mǎzhá（名）folding stool

【馬不停蹄】mǎ bù tíng tí〈成〉nonstop：～地趕到村莊 rush nonstop to the village

【馬甲】mǎjiǎ（名）vest

【馬列主義】Mǎlièzhǔyì（名）Marxism-Leninism

【馬耳他】Mǎ'ěrtā（名）Malta：～人 Maltese / ～語 Maltese（language）

【馬車】mǎchē（名）❶ carriage ❷ cart

【馬里】Mǎlǐ（名）Mali：～人 Malian

【馬克思主義】Mǎkèsī zhǔyì（名）Marxism

【馬具】mǎjù（名）harness

【馬虎】mǎhu（形）careless：工作～ be careless in one's work

【馬到成功】mǎ dào chéng gōng〈成〉gain instant success

【馬來西亞】Mǎláixīyà（名）Malaysia：～人 Malaysian

【馬來語】Mǎláiyǔ（名）Malay（language）

【馬拉松】mǎlāsōng（名）marathon

【馬拉維】Mǎlāwéi（名）Malavi：～人 Malavian

【馬前卒】mǎqiánzú（名）cat's-paw; pawn

【馬後炮】mǎhòupào（名）belated message; belated counsel

【馬革裹屍】mǎ gé guǒ shī〈成〉fall in battle

【馬海毛】mǎhǎimáo（名）〈紡〉mohair yarn

【馬馬虎虎】mǎmǎ hūhū（形）❶ careless; sloppy：不能～ permit no carelessness ❷ so-so; after a fashion：他網球打得～。He plays tennis after a fashion.

【馬腳】mǎjiǎo（名）loophole; cloven foot：他一張口說話立刻露出了～。He betrayed himself as soon as he opened his month.

【馬球】mǎqiú（名）polo

【馬術】mǎshù（名）❶ horsemanship ❷ equestrian sports

【馬桶】mǎtǒng（名） night-stool;

commode

【馬厩】mǎjiù（名）stable

【馬隊】mǎduì（名）❶ caravan ❷ cavalry

【馬掌】mǎzhǎng（名）horseshoe

【馬達】mǎdá（名）motor

【馬達加斯加】Mǎdájiāsījiā（名）Madagascar：～人 Madagascan

【馬路】mǎlù（名）road; pavement; street

【馬靴】mǎxuē（名）riding boot

【馬蜂】mǎfēng（名）wasp; hornet

【馬蜂窩】mǎfēngwō（名）hornet's nest：捅～ stir up a hornet's nest; invite a great deal of trouble

【馬鈴薯】mǎlíngshǔ（名）potato

【馬褂】mǎguà（名）mandarin jacket

【馬爾代夫】Mǎ'ěrdàifū（名）Maldives：～人 Maldivian

【馬椿】mǎzhuāng（名）hitching post

【馬槽】mǎcáo（名）manger

【馬鞍】mǎ'ān（名）saddle

【馬鞍形】mǎ'ānxíng（形）U-shaped

【馬褲】mǎkù（名）riding breeches

【馬褲呢】mǎkùní（名）whipcord

【馬燈】mǎdēng（名）barn lantern; lantern

【馬頭琴】mǎtóuqín（名）〈樂〉*matouqin*, 4-stringed instrument of the Mongol nationality

【馬蹄】mǎtí（名）horse's hoof

【馬蹄錶】mǎtíbiǎo（名）round or hoof-shaped desk clock; usu. an alarm clock

【馬蹄鐵】mǎtítiě（名）❶ horseshoe ❷ U-shaped magnet

【馬幫】mǎbāng（名）caravan

【馬戲】mǎxì（名）circus

【馬戲團】mǎxìtuán（名）circus

【馬賽克】mǎsàikè（名）〈建〉mosaic

【馬糞紙】mǎfènzhǐ（名）strawboard

【馬鬃】mǎzōng（名）horse mane

【馬鞭】mǎbiān（名）horsewhip

【馬鐙】mǎdèng（名）stirrup

【馬騾】mǎluó（名）mule

馮 Féng（名）a surname

馭 yù（動）drive (a carriage)

馱 duò（名）load or pack carried on the back of a draught animal
see also tuó

馱 tuó（動）carry on the back
see also duò

馳 chí（動）gallop; ride fast：飛～ speed along

【馳名】chímíng（動）be famous：～天下 be known throughout the world

【馳騁】chíchěng（動）gallop

馴 xún（動）tame; subdue; domesticate

【馴化】xúnhuà（動）tame

【馴服】xúnfú Ⅰ（動）tame; control：～老虎 tame a tiger／～咆哮的河流 harness (control) a roaring river Ⅱ（形）docile and obedient

【馴鹿】xúnlù（名）reindeer

【馴養】xúnyǎng（動）domesticate

駁 bó Ⅰ（動）refute; rebut; disprove：無可辯～的事實 irrefutable fact Ⅱ（名）barge; lighter：油～ oil barge Ⅲ（形）mottled; motley：斑～陸離 of different hues or colours

【駁斥】bóchì（動）refute; contradict; denounce：～謬論 refute a fallacy Ⅱ（名）refutation

【駁回】bóhuí（動）reject; turn

down: ～賠償的要求 reject a demand for compensation

【駁倒】bódǎo（動）confute; defeat sb. in debate; refute sb. by argument

【駁船】bóchuán（名）barge; lighter

【駁運】bóyùn（動）transport（by lighter）

駝 tuó I（名）camel II（形）hunchbacked

【駝背】tuóbèi I（名）hunchback II（形）hunchbacked

【駝峰】tuófēng（名）hump（of a camel）

【駝絨】tuóróng（名）❶ camel hair ❷ camel hair cloth

駐 zhù（動）stay; be stationed: ～京某部 an army unit stationed in Beijing / ～華大使 ambassador to China

【駐守】zhùshǒu（動）garrison

【駐地】zhùdì（名）❶ station; encampment ❷ seat

【駐防】zhùfáng（動）be on garrison duty

【駐軍】zhùjūn（名）garrison（troops）

【駐紮】zhùzhá（動）（of troops）be stationed

駛 shǐ（動）❶（of a vehicle, horse, etc.）speed ❷ sail（a ship）; drive（a vehicle）; pilot（a plane）: 駕～員 driver; pilot

駟 sì

【駟馬】sìmǎ（名）team of four horses: 一言既出，～難追。What is said cannot be unsaid.

駒 jū（名）❶ colt ❷ foal

駙 fù

【駙馬】fùmǎ（名）〈舊〉emperor's son-in-law

駕 jià I（動）❶ put a harness on ❷ drive（a vehicle）: ～機 pilot a plane II〈敬〉respectful reference to a person: 大～ your good self

【駕馭】jiàyù（動）❶ drive（horse, cart, etc.）; harness ❷ harness; tame; control

【駕輕就熟】jià qīng jiù shú〈成〉be on familiar grounds; drive a light carriage on a familiar road

【駕駛】jiàshǐ（動）drive（a vehicle）; pilot（a plane）: 無人～飛機 pilotless aircraft

【駕駛室】jiàshǐshì（名）driver's cabin; wheel house

【駕駛員】jiàshǐyuán（名）driver（of vehicle）; pilot（of an aircraft）

【駕駛執照】jiàshǐ zhízhào（名）driving licence

【駕臨】jiàlín（名）〈敬〉your gracious presence: 敬請～ respectfully request your gracious presence

駭 hài（動）be shocked

【駭人聽聞】hài rén tīng wén（形）shocking; horrifying

【駭怪】hàiguài（動）be astonished; be taken by surprise

【駭然】hàirán（形）panic-stricken

駱 Luò（名）a surname

【駱駝】luòtuo（名）camel

騁 chěng（動）gallop; dash about

駿 jùn（名）steed

【駿馬】jùnmǎ（名）steed

騎 qí（動）ride（an animal, bicycle,

etc.）：～自行車 ride a bicycle; cycle

【騎士】qíshì（名）knight; cavalier

【騎兵】qíbīng（名）cavalryman; cavalry

【騎虎難下】qí hǔ nán xià〈成〉one has got a tiger by the tail that one can't let go; be caught in a dilemma

【騎術】qíshù（名）horsemanship; equestrian art

【騎牆】qíqiáng（動）sit on the fence

騙 piàn（動）deceive; cheat; delude: 我們受～買下了那幅畫。We were deceived into buying the painting.

【騙子】piànzi（名）swindler; trickster

【騙局】piànjú（名）fraud; deception: 精心策劃的 ～ a cleverly planned swindle

【騙取】piànqǔ（動）cheat sb. out of sth.：～同情 gain sympathy by falsehood / ～人們對他的信任 hoodwink people into believing him

騸 shàn（動）castrate; spay

騷 sāo Ⅰ（動）disturb; upset Ⅱ（形）coquettish; flirtatious

【騷動】sāodòng Ⅰ（名）commotion; turmoil Ⅱ（動）be in a tumult; become disorderly

【騷亂】sāoluàn（名）disturbance; chaos; commotion

【騷擾】sāorǎo（名）harass; molest

騰 téng（動）❶ gallop; leap: 奔～ 向前 surge forward ❷ soar; shoot up: 物價～貴 soaring prices ❸ vacate; make room: ～出房間 vacate a room / ～出時間 set time aside

❹ [used after certain verbs to indicate repetition]: 我們還得再折～一遍。We'll have to do it all over again.

【騰飛】téngfēi Ⅰ（動）soar; shoot up Ⅱ（名）leap; upsurge: 經濟～ economic upsurge; economic takeoff

【騰騰】téngténg（形）steaming; seething; vivacious: 包子剛出籠，熱氣～。The buns are just off the steamers and still steaming. ／工廠裏熱氣～。The factory is a beehive of activity.

驅 qū（動）❶ drive (a horse, car, etc.): ～車越過草原 drive across the grasslands ❷ expel; drive away: ～邪 exorcise ❸ run quickly: 長～直入 (of an army) drive straight on

【驅使】qūshǐ（動）❶ order about ❷ prompt; impel: 為良心所～ obey the dictates of one's conscience

【驅除】qūchú（動）drive away; expel

【驅逐】qūzhú（動）drive out; oust

【驅逐艦】qūzhújiàn（名）〈軍〉destroyer

【驅動】qūdòng（名）〈機〉drive: 四輪～ four-wheel drive

【驅散】qūsàn（動）disperse; scatter

【驅蟲藥】qūchóngyào（名）anthelmintic; vermifuge

驟 luó（名）mule

【騾子】luózi（名）mule

驀 mò（副）suddenly: ～然 all of a sudden

驍 xiāo

【驍勇】xiāoyǒng（形）valiant; brave

驕 jiāo（形）❶ arrogant; haughty;

cocky: ～必敗。Pride goes before a fall. ❷ fierce; severe: ～陽 scorching sun

【驕奢淫逸】jiāo shē yín yì〈成〉lead a life of luxury and dissipation

【驕傲】jiāo'ào Ⅰ(形)❶ conceited; haughty; overbearing ❷ proud: 感到～ feel proud Ⅱ(名)pride: 青年一代人的～ the pride of the younger generation

【驕橫】jiāohèng(形)arrogant and imperious: ～跋扈 arrogant and overbearing

【驕縱】jiāozòng(形)arrogant and unrestrained

驛 yì(名)post

【驛站】yìzhàn(名)post

【驛道】yìdào(名)post road

驗 yàn(動)❶ examine; test; check: ～身份證 check sb.'s ID card ❷ prove effective

【驗收】yànshōu(動)check and accept: ～貨物 check the goods on delivery

【驗血】yànxiě(名)blood test

【驗光】yànguāng(名)optometry

【驗屍】yànshī(名)postmortem; autopsy

【驗證】yànzhèng(動)verify

驚 jīng(動)❶ be startled; start: 大爲震～ give sb. a big surprise ❷ alert; disturb: 一場虛～ a false alarm ❸ shy; stampede: 雷聲把馬羣～。With the rumble of the thunder, the horses broke into a stampede.

【驚人】jīngrén(形)amazing; shocking: ～的能力 amazing ability / 這種浪費是～的。This kind of waste

is shocking.

【驚弓之鳥】jīng gōng zhī niǎo〈成〉panic-stricken person

【驚天動地】jīng tiān dòng dì〈成〉shaking the world; earth-shaking

【驚心動魄】jīng xīn dòng pò〈成〉soul-stirring; breathtaking

【驚叫】jīngjiào(動)cry out in panic; scream

【驚呼】jīnghū(動)cry out in panic

【驚奇】jīngqí(動)wonder; marvel; be surprised: 我對你的充沛精力很～。I marvel at your energy.

【驚恐】jīngkǒng(形)scared; seized with panic

【驚訝】jīngyà(形)surprised; amazed

【驚異】jīngyì(形)surprised; filled with wonder

【驚動】jīngdòng(動)❶ disturb; bother: 沒有必要～他嘛。There is no need to bother him anyway. ❷ alarm; alert

【驚悉】jīngxī(動)be shocked to learn

【驚喜】jīngxǐ(動)be pleasantly surprised: 又驚又喜 be filled with a feeling of surprise and joy

【驚愕】jīng'è(形)stunned; struck dumb

【驚慌】jīnghuāng(驚惶 jīnghuáng)panicky

【驚慌失措】jīng huāng shī cuò〈成〉seized with panic; scared out of one's wits

【驚嘆】jīngtàn(動)exclaim in surprise or admiration: 我們對她的才能～不止。We have infinite admiration for her talent.

【驚疑】jīngyí(形)surprised and puzzled

【驚魂未定】jīng hún wèi dìng〈成〉
not yet recovered from a shock

【驚醒】jīngxǐng（動）❶ wake up
with a start ❷ rouse sb. suddenly
from sleep

【驚醒】jīngxǐng（副）(sleep) lightly

【驚險】jīngxiǎn（形）breathtaking;
hair-raising

【驚嚇】jīngxià（動）frighten; terrify

【驚濤駭浪】jīng tāo hài làng〈成〉
terrifying waves; storm and stress

【驚擾】jīngrǎo（動）alarm; disturb:
我們不能半夜裏～人家。We can-
not disturb them at midnight.

驟 zhòu Ⅰ（動）(of a horse) trot Ⅱ
（形）sudden; abrupt: 狂風～起。
There was a gale suddenly blowing
up. / 局勢～變。There was a sudden change in the situation.

【驟然】zhòurán（副）suddenly; abruptly: 天氣～冷起來了。It sud-
denly became cold.

驢 lǘ（名）donkey

驥 jì（名）fine horse; steed

骨　部

骨 gū
see also gú; gǔ

【骨朵】gūduo（名）〈口〉flower bud

【骨碌】gūlu（動）roll: 從牀上一～
爬起來 roll out of bed

骨 gú
see also gū; gǔ

【骨頭】gútou（名）❶ bone ❷ (of a
person) character: 硬～ a person of

iron will

骨 gǔ（名）❶ bone ❷ skeleton;
framework ❸ (of a person) character; spirit: ～氣 moral courage
see also gū; gú

【骨灰】gǔhuī（名）ashes（of the
dead）

【骨肉】gǔròu（名）flesh and blood;
kindred: ～團聚 family reunion

【骨折】gǔzhé（名）〈醫〉fracture

【骨架】gǔjià（名）skeleton; framework

【骨科】gǔkē（名）〈醫〉department
of orthopaedics: ～醫生 ortho-
paedist

【骨牌】gǔpái（名）dominoes

【骨幹】gǔgàn（名）backbone; mainstay: ～分子 core member

【骨骼】gǔgé（名）〈生理〉skeleton

【骨髓】gǔsuǐ（名）〈生理〉marrow

骯 āng

【骯髒】āngzāng（形）dirty; filthy

骷 kū

【骷髏】kūlóu（名）❶ human skull ❷
human skeleton

骸 hái（名）❶ bones of the body;
skeleton ❷ body

【骸骨】háigǔ（名）human bones;
skeleton

骼 gé（名）bone: 骨～ skeleton

髂 qià

【髂骨】qiàgǔ（名）〈生理〉ilium

髓 suǐ（名）〈生理〉marrow: 脊～
spinal cord

髒 zāng（形）dirty; filthy: 你把襯
衫弄～了。You've soiled your shirt.

【髒話】zānghuà (名) obscene word; swearword

髑 dú

【髑髏】dúlóu (名)〈書〉skull of a dead person

體 tǐ

I (名) ❶ body: 量～裁衣 take sb.'s measurement and cut out the garment ❷ substance: 實～ entity ❸ form; type: ～裁 type or form of literature ❹ system of organization II (動) experience personally: ～察民情 (said of a ruler) feel the public mood

【體力】tǐlì (名) bodily strength: ～勞動 physical labour; manual work

【體系】tǐxì (名) system; setup; structure: 思想～ ideological system

【體形】tǐxíng (名) build; form of the body: 她的～變了。She has lost her figure.

【體制】tǐzhì (名) system; structure: 政治～改革 political restructuring

【體育】tǐyù (名) physical culture; physical education

【體育場】tǐyùchǎng (名) stadium

【體育館】tǐyùguǎn (名) gymnasium; indoor stadium

【體面】tǐmiàn I (名) face; pride: 有傷～ hurt one's pride II (形) ❶ honourable; respectable ❷〈口〉respectable

【體重】tǐzhòng (名) weight (of a person): 她～五十公斤。She weighs fifty kilograms.

【體格】tǐgé (名) physique; constitution: ～檢查 medical examination

【體現】tǐxiàn (動) embody; reflect: ～基本的民主原則 reflect the spirit of fundamental democratic principles

【體貼】tǐtiē (形) thoughtful; considerate

【體統】tǐtǒng (名) decorum; propriety: 不成～ most indecorous

【體溫】tǐwēn (名) (body) temperature: 量～ take one's temperature / ～計 (clinical) thermometer

【體會】tǐhuì I (動) realize; appreciate through firsthand experience: ～到團結就是力量 have come to realize that unity is strength II (名) appreciation; understanding

【體罰】tǐfá (名) corporal punishment

【體諒】tǐliàng (動) show understanding for; be sympathetic: ～他的難處 make allowances for his difficulties

【體魄】tǐpò (名) constitution and vigour

【體質】tǐzhì (名) constitution; physical make-up

【體積】tǐjī (名) volume; space occupied by an object

【體操】tǐcāo (名) gymnastics; physical exercise

【體驗】tǐyàn (動) learn through personal experience

高 部

高 gāo

I (形) ❶ tall; high ❷ senior in grade, class or rank: ～幹 high-ranking official; senior cadre II〈敬〉superior: ～見 your opinion III (名) (Gāo) a surname

【高大】gāodà (形) ❶ tall and sturdy ❷ lofty; noble: ～形象 noble

image

【高山族】Gāoshānzú〈名〉the Gao-shan nationality

【高中】gāozhōng〈名〉(short for 高级中學 gāojí zhōngxué) senior middle school

【高手】gāoshǒu〈名〉master; master player

【高亢】gāokàng〈形〉sonorous

【高不可攀】gāo bù kě pān〈成〉too high to reach; inaccessible; high and mighty

【高地】gāodì〈名〉highland

【高血壓】gāoxuèyā〈名〉〈醫〉hypertension; high blood pressure

【高低】gāodī〈名〉❶ height ❷ higher or lower level: 難分～ difficult to say which side is superior ❸ sense of propriety: 不知～ not hnow what is proper

【高妙】gāomiào〈形〉ingenious; superb

【高技術】gāojìshù〈形〉high-tech: ～工業 high-tech industry

【高利貸】gāolìdài〈名〉usury; high-interest loans: ～者 usurer

【高呼】gāohū〈動〉shout fervently

【高空】gāokōng〈名〉high altitude

【高昂】gāo'áng〈形〉❶ high; lofty: 鬥志～ have high morale ❷ expensive; costly

【高尚】gāoshàng〈形〉❶ noble; lofty: 品質～ noble-minded ❷ in good taste

【高明】gāomíng Ⅰ〈形〉wise; clever Ⅱ〈名〉mastermind

【高官厚祿】gāo guān hòu lù〈成〉a high position with a handsome salary to match

【高枕無憂】gāo zhěn wú yōu〈成〉feel relaxed and carefree

【高度】gāodù Ⅰ〈名〉height; altitude Ⅱ〈副〉highly ～評價 speak of (sb. or sth.) in glowing terms

【高級】gāojí〈形〉❶ senior; high-ranking: ～講師 senior lecturer ❷ high-grade; of high quality

【高速】gāosù〈名〉high speed: ～公路 expressway; superhighway

【高原】gāoyuán〈名〉plateau; highland

【高峻】gāojùn〈形〉high and steep; precipitous

【高峰】gāofēng〈名〉peak; summit

【高峰時間】gāofēng shíjiān〈名〉rush hours; peak hours

【高高在上】gāo gāo zài shàng〈成〉be far removed from the public

【高射炮】gāoshèpào〈名〉anti-air-craft gun

【高深】gāoshēn〈形〉advanced; recondite; profound

【高產】gāochǎn〈名〉high yield

【高視闊步】gāo shì kuò bù〈成〉walk about with a swagger

【高蛋白】gāodànbái〈形〉high-pro-tein

【高超】gāochāo〈形〉superb; excellent

【高強】gāoqiáng〈形〉highly skilful

【高貴】gāoguì〈形〉❶ noble; lofty ❷ privileged

【高等】gāoděng〈形〉higher: ～院校 institutions of higher learning

【高等教育】gāoděng jiàoyù〈名〉higher education

【高帽子】gāomàozi〈名〉❶ dunce cap ❷ flattery: 戴～ make flatter-ing remarks

【高梁】gāoliang〈名〉 *kaoliang*; sorghum

【高溫】gāowēn〈名〉high temperature

【高傲】 gāo'ào (形) haughty; arrogant

【高矮】 gāo'ǎi (名) height: ~ 不一 of different heights

【高跟鞋】 gāogēnxié (名) high-heeled shoe

【高僧】 gāosēng (名) monk versed in Buddhist Scripture; eminent monk

【高涨】 gāozhǎng (动) rise; soar

【高寿】 gāoshòu Ⅰ (名) longevity Ⅱ 〈敬〉 age: 老大爺 ~ 啦? Grandpa, how old are you?

【高爾夫球】 gāo'ěrfūqiú (名) ❶ golf: ~ 場 golf course ❷ golf ball

【高潮】 gāocháo (名) ❶ high tide ❷ climax

【高談闊論】 gāo tán kuò lùn 〈成〉 hold forth at great length

【高調】 gāodiào (名) high-sounding words

【高價】 gāojià (名) high price

【高樓大廈】 gāolóu dàshà (名) tall buildings and large mansions; high-rise building

【高頻】 gāopín (名) 〈電〉 high frequency

【高燒】 gāoshāo (名) high fever: 發 ~ run a high fever

【高興】 gāoxìng (形) happy; glad; delighted

【高壓】 gāoyā (名) ❶ 〈物〉〈氣〉 high pressure ❷ 〈電〉 high voltage

【高聳】 gāosǒng (动) stand tall and erect; tower

【高檔】 gāodàng (形) high-grade; expensive: ~ 商品 high-grade commodity

【高瞻遠矚】 gāo zhān yuǎn zhǔ 〈成〉 farseeing; farsighted

【高攀】 gāopān (动) (of friendship or marriage) forge ties of kinship with a family of higher status

【高蹺】 gāoqiāo (名) stilts

【高爐】 gāolú (名) blast furnace

【高齡】 gāolíng (名) advanced age

髟 部

髮 fà (名) hair

【髮卡】 fàqiǎ (名) hairpin

【髮油】 fàyóu (名) hair oil

【髮指】 fàzhǐ (动) bristle with anger

【髮型】 fàxíng (名) hair style; hairdo

【髮蠟】 fàlà (名) pomade

髯 rán (名) whiskers; beard

髻 jì (名) hair worn in a bun or coil on the top or at the back of the head

髭 zī (名) moustache

鬃 zōng (名) hair on the neck of a pig, horse, etc.: 豬 ~ (pig's) bristles

鬈 quán (形) curly; wavy

【鬈曲】 quánqū (形) crimpy; curly; crisp

鬆 sōng Ⅰ (形) ❶ loose; not tight: 腰帶 ~ 了 waistband getting slack ❷ fluffy; puffy: ~ 餅 puff; muffin ❸ better off: 手頭還不 ~ still quite hard up Ⅱ (动) ❶ loosen; slacken: ~ 腦筋 relax one's mind ❷ unfasten; untie Ⅲ (名) dried meat floss: 魚 ~ dried fish floss

【鬆口】sōngkǒu (動) soften one's tone; become less severe: 他本來矢口否認與此事有什麼牽涉，但後來～了。Originally he absolutely denied any involvement in the affair but later he relented.

【鬆手】sōngshǒu let go

【鬆弛】sōngchí (形) ❶ limp; flaccid ❷ (of discipline, etc.) lax; slackening

【鬆快】sōngkuai Ⅰ(形) ❶ roomy; less crowded ❷ relaxed Ⅱ(動) relax

【鬆勁】sōngjìn (鬆氣 sōngqì) (動) slacken; relax one's efforts

【鬆脆】sōngcuì (形) crisp

【鬆動】sōngdòng (形) ❶ become less crowded: 廣場上人羣已有～。The square is less crowded. ❷ be a little better off: 他手頭～一些了。He is not so hard up as before. ❸ (of one's position, stance, etc.) be more flexible ❹ loose: 螺釘有點～。The screw is loose.

【鬆軟】sōngruǎn (形) spongy; soft; puffy

【鬆散】sōngsǎn (形) ❶ loose: 文章各節鬆得～。The parts of the essay do not hang together. ❷ slack; negligent

【鬆閑】sōngxián (形) unoccupied and relaxed

【鬆綁】sōngbǎng (動) ❶ untie (a person) ❷ give more freedom (to a state-run enterprise, etc.)

【鬆緊】sōngjǐn Ⅰ(名) degree of elasticity Ⅱ(形) elastic: ～帶 elastic ribbon

【鬆懈】sōngxiè (形) inattentive; slack

【鬆糕】sōnggāo (名) sponge cake

【鬆鬆垮垮】sōngsōng kuǎkuǎ (鬆垮垮 sōngkuǎ) (動) 〈口〉be slack and undisciplined: 組織上～ organizationally lax

鬍

鬍 hú (名) moustache; whiskers; beard

【鬍鬚】húxū (鬍子 húzi) (名) beard; moustache; whiskers

鬚 xū (名) beard; moustache

【鬚髮】xūfà (名) beard and hair

鬢 bìn (名) ❶ temple ❷ hair on the temples: 兩～蒼蒼 greying temples ❸ hair: ～雲～ woman's hairdo

【鬢角】bìnjiǎo (名) region or hair just below the temple (in front of the ear)

【鬢髮】bìnfà (名) hair on the temples: ～皆白 hoary-haired

鬥 部

鬥 dòu (動) ❶ fight; struggle: 戰天～地 battle the elements ❷ contest; rival ❸ put together: 把意見～一～。Let's put our heads together.

【鬥牛】dòuniú (名) bullfight: ～士 bullfighter

【鬥志】dòuzhì (名) morale

【鬥爭】dòuzhēng (動) ❶ fight; struggle ❷ accuse; criticize ❸ strive for

【鬥嘴】dòuzuǐ (動) squabble

鬧 nào Ⅰ(形) noisy Ⅱ(動) ❶ make a noise; stir up trouble: 和人

~翻了 fall out with sb. / ~待遇 demand higher wages ❷ suffer from; be troubled by: ~病 fall ill / ~鬼 (of a haunted house) be troubled by apparitions ❸ give vent (to one's anger, resentment, etc.): ~情绪 be cross and disgruntled ❹ go in for; undertake: ~工潮 (of workers) go on strike and hold demonstrations

【闹市】nàoshì (名) busy streets; downtown area

【闹肚子】nào dùzi (动) 〈口〉 suffer from diarrhoea; have loose bowels

【闹事】nàoshì (动) cause trouble; create disturbances

【闹革命】nào gémìng (动) make revolution

【闹哄哄】nàohōnghōng (形) noisy; uproarious; boisterous

【闹笑话】nào xiàohuà (动) make a fool of oneself; make a laughing stock of oneself

【闹着玩儿】nàozhe wánr (动) joke; do sth. for fun

【闹脾气】nào píqì (动) get into a temper

【闹乱子】nào luànzi (动) stir up trouble; start a riot

【闹意见】nào yìjiàn (动) be at odds with each other

【闹剧】nàojù (名) farce

【闹别扭】nào bièniu (动) be at loggerheads with sb.

【闹钟】nàozhōng (名) alarm clock

阄 jiū (名) lot: 抓~ draw lots

鬯 部

鬱 yù (形) ❶ luxuriant; exuberant ❷ depressed; dismal: 抑~ gloomy

【鬱血】yùxuè (名) 〈醫〉 stagnation of the blood; venous stasis

【鬱金香】yùjīnxiāng (名) 〈植〉 tulip

【鬱悶】yùmèn (形) gloomy; depressed

【鬱積】yùjī (形) pent-up; smouldering

【鬱鬱葱葱】yùyù cōngcōng (形) green and lush

鬼 部

鬼 guǐ I (名) ❶ ghost; spirit; phantom ❷ 〈罵〉: 吸血~ vampire / 小氣~ miser / 酒~ drunkard ❸ sinister plot; dirty trick: 這裏面有~。There's something fishy about it. / 一把戲 dirty trick; wicked game II (形) ❶ damnable; wretched: ~地方 God-for-saken place ❷ 〈口〉 clever; smart: 小~ little devil

【鬼怪】guǐguài (名) monsters; demons

【鬼斧神工】guǐ fǔ shén gōng 〈成〉 superb craftsmanship

【鬼使神差】guǐ shǐ shén chāi 〈成〉 by a strange coincidence

【鬼胎】guǐtāi (名) sinister design: 心懷~ harbour evil intentions

【鬼哭狼嗥】guǐ kū láng háo 〈成〉

set up loud and dreadful cries

【鬼鬼祟祟】guǐ guǐ suì suì〔形〕sneaking or skulking around

【鬼混】guǐhùn〔動〕drift along aimlessly; fool around

【鬼蜮】guǐyù〔名〕(sea) monster: ～伎倆 devilish devices

【鬼魂】guǐhún〔名〕ghost; spirit; apparition

【鬼臉】guǐliǎn〔名〕wry face; grimace: 做～ make faces

魂

hún〔名〕❶ soul ❷ mood; spirit: 神～顛倒 be infatuated

【魂不附體】hún bù fù tǐ〔成〕be frightened out of one's senses

【魂飛魄散】hún fēi pò sàn〔成〕not dare to say one's soul is one's own; be terribly scared

【魂魄】húnpò〔名〕soul

魁

kuí I〔名〕number one man; number one position: 奪～ contend for the championship; win first prize II〔形〕tall and robust

【魁首】kuíshǒu〔名〕person who occupies the leading position among his contemporaries: 文章～ literary giant

【魁梧】kuíwú〔形〕tall and robust; stalwart

魄

pò〔名〕❶ soul: 驚心動～ soul-stirring ❷ vitality; spirit

【魄力】pòlì〔名〕boldness and resolution: 有～的人 a man of courage and resolution

魅

mèi〔名〕ghost; demon

【魅力】mèilì〔名〕charm; attraction: 富有特殊～ have peculiar charms

魏

Wèi〔名〕a surname

魍

wǎng

【魍魎】wǎngliǎng〔名〕monsters; demons

魔

mó I〔名〕devil; evil spirit II〔形〕magic

【魔方】mófāng〔名〕Rubic's Cube

【魔爪】mózhǎo〔名〕devil's claws; tentacles: 匪幫的～ the tentacles of the bandit gang

【魔王】mówáng〔名〕❶ King Devil ❷ cruel and vicious person; devil

【魔杖】mózhàng〔名〕magic wand

【魔法】mófǎ〔名〕magic; wizardry

【魔怪】móguài〔名〕demon; monster

【魔鬼】móguǐ〔名〕devil; Satan

【魔術】móshù〔名〕magic; conjuring: ～師 magician

【魔掌】mózhǎng〔名〕evil hands; clutches: 落入～ fall into the clutches of an evildoer

魚 部

魚

yú〔名〕fish

【魚叉】yúchā〔名〕fish spear; harpoon; fish fork

【魚子】yúzǐ〔名〕roe: ～醬 caviare

【魚丸】yúwán〔名〕fish ball

【魚目混珠】yú mù hùn zhū〔成〕palm off the fake as the genuine

【魚汛】yúxùn〔名〕fishing season

【魚米之鄉】yú mǐ zhī xiāng〔成〕a land of plenty

【魚卵】yúluǎn〔名〕(fish) roe

【魚肚】yúdǔ〔名〕fish maw

【魚肝油】yúgānyóu〔名〕codliver oil

【魚刺】yúcì (名) fishbone

【魚苗】yúmiáo (名) fry

【魚竿】yúgān (名) fishing rod

【魚翅】yúchì (名) shark's fin

【魚秧】yúyāng (名) fingerling

【魚貫】yúguàn (副) in single file; one by one: ～而入 file in

【魚鉤】yúgōu (名) fishhook

【魚雷】yúléi (名)〈軍〉torpedo

【魚群】yúqún (名) shoal of fish

【魚漂】yúpiāo (名) cork on a fishing line; float

【魚網】yúwǎng (名) fishnet; fishing net

【魚餌】yú'ěr (名)(fish) bait

【魚龍混雜】yú lóng hùn zá〈成〉good and bad people are mingled

【魚蟲】yúchóng (名) water flea

【魚鱗】yúlín (名) fish scale

【魚鷹】yúyīng (名) fish hawk

魷 yóu

【魷魚】yóuyú (名) squid

魯 lǔ I (形) ❶ foolish; slow-witted ❷ rude; rash II (名) (Lǔ) ❶ another name for Shandong (Province) ❷ a surname

【魯莽】lǔmǎng (形) rash; thoughtless and rude

魟 píng (名) left-eyed flounder

鲅 bà

【鲅魚】bàyú (名) Spanish mackerel

鮎 nián (名) catfish

鮑 Bào (名) a surname

【鮑魚】bàoyú (名) abalone

鮣 yìn (名) remora; shark sucker

鮮 xiān (形) ❶ fresh: ～魚 fresh fish ❷ bright-coloured; bright: 襯衫顏色太～。The shirt is garish. ❸ delicious

【鮮血】xiānxuè (名) blood

【鮮明】xiānmíng (形) ❶ (of colour) bright ❷ distinct; clear: ～的態度 a clear-cut stance

【鮮花】xiānhuā (名) (fresh) flower

【鮮果汁】xiānguǒzhī (名) fruit squash

【鮮紅】xiānhóng (形) bright red; scarlet

【鮮美】xiānměi (形) delicious; tasty

【鮮艷】xiānyàn (形) gaily coloured

鮭 guī (名) salmon

鯊 shā (名) shark

【鯊魚】shāyú (名) shark

鯽 jì

【鯽魚】jìyú (名) crucian carp

鯉 lǐ (名) carp

【鯉魚】lǐyú (名) carp

鯨 jīng (名) whale

【鯨吞】jīngtūn (動) gobble up (like a whale)

【鯨魚】jīngyú (名) whale

鱀 qí (名)

【鱀鰍】qíqiū (名) dorado; dolphinfish

鯢 ní (名) salamander

鯔 zī (名) mullet

鳊 biān

【鳊魚】biānyú (名) (fresh-water) bream

鰈 dié (名) flatfish

鰓 sāi （名）gill; branchia

鳑 páng
【鳑鲏】pángpí（名）bitterling

鰱 lián （名）silver carp
【鰱魚】liányú（名）silver carp

鰭 qí （名）fin

鰣 shí
【鰣魚】shíyú（名） hilsa herring; shad

鰥 guān（名）man without a wife; widower
【鰥寡孤獨】guān guǎ gū dú〈成〉widowers, widows, orphans and the childless

鱅 yōng
【鱅魚】yōngyú（名）variegated carp; bighead

鱈 xuě
【鱈魚】xuěyú（名）cod

鰾 biào （名）〈動〉 air bladder; swim bladder

鰻 mán （名）eel
【鰻鱺】mánlí（名）eel

鱉 biē （名）soft-shelled turtle: 甕中之～ like a turtle in a jar; trapped

鱔 shàn （名）eel; finless eel

鱒 zūn （名）trout

鱗 lín （名）scale of fish: 刮魚～ scrape the scales off the fish
【鱗爪】línzhǎo（名）scraps; fragments

【鱗片】línpiàn （名）scale（of fish, etc.）

【鱗次櫛比】lín cì zhì bǐ（形）（of buildings, etc.）in a compact mass: 市内房屋～。The houses appear in a compact mass in the urban area.

鱖 guì （名）mandarin fish

鱘 xún （名）sturgeon

鱷 è （名）crocodile
【鱷魚】èyú（名）crocodile; alligator

鱸 lú （名）perch

鳥 部

鳥 niǎo （名）bird
【鳥瞰】niǎokàn（動）have a bird's-eye view
【鳥嘴】niǎozuǐ（名）beak; bill
【鳥籠】niǎolóng（名）birdcage

鳩 jiū（名）〈動〉turtledove

凫 fú Ⅰ（名）wild duck Ⅱ（動）swim

鳴 míng （動）❶ cry; chirrup; sing: 鳥～樹上。Birds are chirruping in the trees. ❷ ring; sound: 汽笛長～。The steam whistle blew ceaselessly. ❸ express; voice: 百家爭～。A hundred schools of thought contend.
【鳴冤叫屈】míng yuān jiào qū（動）voice one's complaints and grievances
【鳴笛】míngdí（動）blow a whistle; whistle; sound a siren
【鳴號】mínghào（動）blow a trumpet

【鳴槍】 míngqiāng（動）fire a shot

【鳴謝】 míngxiè（動）express one's thanks

【鳴禮炮】 mínglǐpào（動）fire a salute

鳳 Fèng（名）a surname

【鳳毛麟角】 fèng máo lín jiǎo〈成〉(of persons or things) extremely rare and invaluable

【鳳尾魚】 fèngwěiyú（名）anchovy

【鳳凰】 fènghuáng（名）phoenix

鴉 yā（名）crow

【鴉片】 yāpiàn（名）opium

【鴉雀無聲】 yā què wú shēng〈成〉be extremely quiet: 他走後～。Silence reigned after he left.

鴇 bǎo（名）❶ bustard（bird）❷ procuress

【鴇母】 bǎomǔ（名）bawd; procuress

鴨 yā（名）duck: 烤～ roast duck

【鴨舌帽】 yāshémào（名）peaked cap

【鴨蛋】 yādàn（名）duck's egg

【鴨梨】 yālí（名）pear

【鴨絨】 yāróng（名）duck's down; eider down

鴛 yuān

【鴛鴦】 yuānyāng（名）❶ mandarin duck ❷ lovebirds;（affectionate）couple: ～樓 apartment house for newlyweds

鴕 tuó

【鴕鳥】 tuóniǎo（名）ostrich

鴻 hóng Ⅰ（名）❶ swan; goose ❷ letter Ⅱ（形）great; grand

【鴻毛】 hóngmáo（名）❶ goose feather ❷ sth. of very small significance

【鴻溝】 hónggōu（名）wide gap; chasm

【鴻鵠】 hónghú（名）❶ swan ❷ person who cherishes lofty ideals

鴿 gē（名）pigeon; dove: 信～ carrier pigeon

【鴿子】 gēzi（名）pigeon; dove

【鴿派】 gēpài（名）(of politics) the doves; advocates of peace

鵠 gǔ（名）target; bull's-eye
see also hú

鵠 hú（名）swan
see also gǔ

鵝 é（名）goose

【鵝毛】 émáo（名）goose feather

【鵝卵石】 éluǎnshí（名）cobble

【鵝絨】 éróng（名）goose down

鵲 què（名）magpie

【鵲鴝】 quèqú（名）magpie robin

鵪 ān

【鵪鶉】 ānchun（名）quail

鵬 péng（名）roc

【鵬程萬里】 péng chéng wàn lǐ〈成〉have a bright future

鶚 è（名）osprey; fish hawk

鶯 yīng（名）warbler; oriole

鶴 hè（名）crane

【鶴立雞羣】 hè lì jī qún〈成〉stand head and shoulders above others

【鶴嘴鋤】 hèzuǐchú（名）pick; pick-axe

鷄 jī（名）chicken: 公～ rooster; 母～ hen / 肉～ meat chicken

【鷄犬不寧】jī quǎn bù níng〈成〉
cause great confusion: 鬧得～ turn
everything upside down in the house
or neighbourhood

【鷄毛蒜皮】jī máo suàn pí〈成〉tri-
fles; trivialities: ～的事 trifling
matter

【鷄尾酒】jīwěijiǔ（名）cocktail: ～
會 cocktail party

【鷄冠】jīguān（名）cockcomb

【鷄飛蛋打】jī fēi dàn dǎ〈成〉end
up losing everything; all is lost

【鷄眼】jīyǎn（名）corn; hardening of
the shin on the foot, esp. near the
toes

【鷄蛋】jīdàn（名）(hen's) egg

【鷄蛋碰石頭】jī dàn pèng shí tou
〈成〉(like) an egg striking a rock;
suicidal attack

【鷄蛋裏挑骨頭】jī dàn li tiāo gú tou
〈成〉pick holes in something perfectly sound

鷓 zhè

【鷓鴣】zhègū（名）〈動〉partridge

鷗 ōu（名）gull: 海～ seagull

鷲 jiù（名）vulture

鷸 yù（名）sandpiper; snipe

鷹 yīng（名）eagle; hawk

【鷹犬】yīngquǎn（名）(like) falcons
and hounds (in hunting); cat's paw;
flunkey

鸚 yīng

【鸚鵡】yīngwǔ（名）parrot

【鸚鵡學舌】yīng wǔ xué shé〈成〉
parrot what someone else has said

鸛 guàn（名）stork

鹵 部

鹵 lǔ I（名）❶ bittern ❷ thick
gravy II（動）stew in soy sauce: ～
鴨 pot-stewed duck

【鹵水】lǔshuǐ（名）❶ bittern ❷
brine

【鹵味】lǔwèi（名）pot-stewed fowl,
meat, etc. served cold

鹹 xián（形）salty; salted

【鹹水】xiánshuǐ（名）salt water

【鹹肉】xiánròu（名）salted meat;
bacon

【鹹魚】xiányú（名）salted fish

【鹹菜】xiáncài（名）salted vegetables; pickles

鹽 yán（名）salt

【鹽水】yánshuǐ（名）salt solution;
brine

【鹽鹵】yánlǔ（名）bittern

【鹽酸】yánsuān（名）〈化〉hydro-
chloric acid

【鹽鹼地】yánjiǎndì（名）saline and
alkaline land

鹼 jiǎn（名）❶ alkali ❷ soda

【鹼性】jiǎnxìng（名）alkalinity; ba-
sicity

鹿 部

鹿 lù（名）deer

【鹿角】lùjiǎo（名）deerhorn; antler

【鹿茸】lùróng（名） newly-sprouted

antler of a stag

【鹿砦】lùzhài（鹿寨 lùzhài）（名）a-
batis

麂 jǐ（名）muntjac; *Moschus chi-
nensis*

【麂皮】jǐpí（名）chamois

麋 mí（名）elk

【麋羚】mílíng（名）hartebeest

【麋鹿】mílù（名）*mi-lu*; David's
deer

麒 qí

【麒麟】qílín（名）*kylin*;（Chinese）
unicorn

麗 lì（形）beautiful

麝 shè（名）❶ musk deer ❷ musk

【麝牛】shèniú（名）musk ox

【麝香】shèxiāng（名）musk

麥 部

麥 mài（名）❶ wheat: 種 ~ raise
wheat ❷（Mài）a surname

【麥子】màizi（名）wheat

【麥片】màipiàn（名）oatmeal: ~ 粥
oatmeal porridge

【麥收】màishōu（名）wheat harvest:
~ 季節 wheat harvest season

【麥克風】màikèfēng（名）micro-
phone; mike

【麥乳精】màirǔjīng（名）malted milk

【麥芽】màiyá（名）malt: ~ 糖 malt
sugar; maltose

【麥苗】màimiáo（名）wheat seedling

【麥茬】màichá（名）wheat stubble

【麥浪】màilàng（名）billowing wheat

【麥稈畫】màigǎnhuà（名）〈工美〉
wheat straw patchwork

【麥精】màijīng（名）malt extract

【麥秸】màijiē（名）wheat straw

【麥麩】màifū（名）wheat bran

【麥穗】màisuì（名）ear of wheat

麩 fū（名）wheat bran

麴 qū（名）leaven; yeast

麵 miàn（名）❶ flour: 豆 ~ bean
flour / 玉米 ~ corn flour ❷
noodles: 方便 ~ instant noodles ❸
powder

【麵人兒】miànrénr（名）dough figurine

【麵包】miànbāo（名）bread

【麵包房】miànbāofáng（名）bakery

【麵食】miànshí（名）wheaten food;
food made of wheat（flour-bread,
noodles etc.）

【麵粉】miànfěn（名）wheat flour;
flour

【麵條】miàntiáo（名）noodles

【麵筋】miànjin（名）gluten

【麵團】miàntuán（名）dough

【麵糊】miànhù（名）paste

麻 部

麻 má（形）❶ coarse; rough: ~ 面
牆可以吸音。Rough wall surface is
sound-absorbing. ❷ numb; tin-
gling: 我的腳凍 ~ 了。My feet
grew numb with cold.

【麻子】mázi（名）❶ pockmarks ❷
person with a pockmarked face

【麻木】mámù（形）❶ numb ❷ apathetic

【麻木不仁】má mù bù rén〈成〉apathetic: ～的卑劣小人 an unfeeling wretch

【麻利】máli（形）deft; quick and neat: 幹活～work dexterously; work with efficiency

【麻花】máhuā（名）fried dough twist

【麻風】máfēng（名）〈醫〉leprosy

【麻疹】mázhěn（名）〈醫〉measles

【麻雀】máquè（名）sparrow

【麻將】májiàng（名）mahjong: 打～play mahjong / ～牌 mahjong pieces

【麻痺】mábì Ⅰ（名）〈醫〉paralysis Ⅱ（動）benumb; dope: 用甜言蜜語～人們 lull people's vigilance with honeyed words

【麻痺大意】má bì dà yì（形）careless; inattentive; off one's guard: 決不能～must never lose one's vigilance

【麻煩】máfan Ⅰ（形）troublesome: 咳嗽很～，不容易好。Coughing is a nuisance very hard to shake off. Ⅱ（動）bother; give sb. trouble: 對不起，～你了。Sorry to have troubled you!

【麻醉】mázuì Ⅰ（名）〈醫〉anaesthesia; narcosis: 針刺～acupuncture anaesthesia Ⅱ（動）poison: 用黄色書刊～青年 poison young people with pornography

【麻臉】máliǎn（名）pockmarked face

【麻藥】máyào（名）anaesthetic

麼 me [used as a suffix]: 那～in that way; like that; then / 什～what / 這字怎～寫? Do you know how to write this character?

黄 部

黄 huáng Ⅰ（形）❶ yellow; sallow ❷ pornographic Ⅱ（名）❶ pornography: 掃～anti-porn campaign ❷（Huáng）a surname

【黄土】huángtǔ（名）loess

【黄牛】huángniú（名）ox

【黄瓜】huángguā（名）cucumber

【黄色】huángsè（形）❶ yellow ❷ obscene; pornographic: ～小説 pornographic novel

【黄豆】huángdòu（名）soya bean; soybean

【黄昏】huánghūn（名）dusk

【黄金】huángjīn（名）gold: ～儲備 gold reserve

【黄油】huángyóu（名）❶ butter ❷ lubricating grease

【黄河】Huánghé（名）the Huanghe (Yellow) River

【黄花魚】huánghuāyú（名）yellow croaker

【黄疸】huángdǎn（名）〈醫〉jaundice

【黄酒】huángjiǔ（名）yellow rice wine

【黄魚】huángyú（名）yellow croaker

【黄道吉日】huángdào jírì（名）auspicious date; lucky day

【黄粱夢】huángliángmèng（名）idle dream of worldly success; pipe dream

【黄蜂】huángfēng（名）wasp

【黄鼠狼】huángshǔláng（名）yellow weasel

【黄銅】huángtóng（名）brass

【黄種】huángzhǒng（名）the yellow

race

【黄热病】huángrèbìng（名） yellow fever

【黄历】huánglì（名）almanac

黍 部

黍 shǔ（名）broomcorn millet; *Panicum miliaceum*

黎 Ⅰ（名） ❶ multitude; throng; crowd ❷（Lí）a surname

【黎巴嫩】Líbānèn（名）Lebanon：～人 Lebanese

【黎明】límíng（名）daybreak; dawn

【黎族】Lízú（名）the Li nationality

黏 nián（形）glutinous; sticky

【黏土】niántǔ（名）clay

【黏合】niánhé（动）〈化〉bind; adhere：～剂 binder; adhesive

【黏性】niánxìng（名）stickiness; viscosity

【黏度】niándù（名）〈化〉viscosity

【黏液】niányè（名）〈生理〉mucus

【黏稠】niánchóu（形）sticky; viscous; gluey

【黏胶】niánjiāo（名）〈化〉viscose

【黏膜】niánmó（名）〈生理〉mucous membrane; mucosa

【黏虫】niánchóng（名）armyworm

黑 部

黑 hēi Ⅰ（形） ❶ black; dark ❷ secret; illegal：～交易 shady deal ❸

wicked; sinister Ⅱ（名）（Hēi）short for Heilongjiang Province

【黑人】hēirén（名）black people; black

【黑手党】Hēishǒudǎng（名）Mafia

【黑白】hēibái（形）black and white; right and wrong：～电视 black-and-white television / 混淆～ confuse right and wrong

【黑市】hēishì（名）black market

【黑名单】hēimíngdān（名）blacklist

【黑板】hēibǎn（名）blackboard：～擦 blackboard eraser

【黑麦】hēimài（名）rye

【黑货】hēihuò（名）smuggled goods; contraband

【黑貂】hēidiāo（名）sable：～皮 sable fur

【黑猩猩】hēixīngxing（名）chimpanzee

【黑暗】hēi'àn（形） ❶ dark ❷ decadent

【黑话】hēihuà（名）argot; thieves' cant

【黑幕】hēimù（名）inside story (of a plot)

【黑漆漆】hēiqīqī（形）pitch-dark

【黑龙江】Hēilóngjiāng（名） ❶ Heilongjiang（Province） ❷ Heilongjiang River

【黑压压】hēiyāyā（形）a dark mass of：～的一片人 a dark mass of human peoples

【黑体字】hēitǐzì（名）〈印〉boldface type

默 mò Ⅰ（形）silent; quiet Ⅱ（动）write from memory：～出整篇课文 write down the whole text from memory

【默哀】mò'āi（动）stand in silent

tribute

【默契】mòqì (名) tacit understanding; implicit agreement

【默許】mòxǔ Ⅰ (動) tacitly assent Ⅱ (名) tacit consent

【默然】mòrán (形) silent: ～相對 look at each other in silence

【默認】mòrèn Ⅰ (動) agree without saying so Ⅱ (名) tacit agreement; acquiescence

【默寫】mòxiě (動) write from memory

【默默】mòmò (形) quiet; speechless: ～地坐着 sit speechlessly

【默默無聞】mò mò wú wén (動) remain unknown; live in obscurity

【默禱】mòdǎo (動) pray in silence

【默讀】mòdú (動) read silently

黔 Qián (名) another name for Guizhou Province

【黔驢技窮】Qián lǘ jì qióng (成) be at the end of one's tether; the game's up

點 diǎn Ⅰ (名) ❶ drop; spot: 墨～ ink stains ❷ point: 起～ starting point ❸ time: 幾～了? What time is it? ❹ dot stroke in Chinese characters Ⅱ (動) ❶ put a dot to ❷ count; check: ～數 check the number ❸ light; kindle: ～煙 light a cigarette ❹ order; choose: ～菜 order dishes Ⅲ (量) a bit; a little: 喝～牛奶 have some milk

【點子】diǎnzi (名) ❶ drop; speck ❷ idea: 出～ offer advice ❸ key point

【點火】diǎnhuǒ (動) ❶ light; kindle ❷ stir up trouble; foment discord

【點心】diǎnxin (名) refreshments; snack

【點名】diǎnmíng (名) make a roll call: ～册 roll book

【點染】diǎnrǎn (動) embellish; polish

【點破】diǎnpò (動) point out

【點綴】diǎnzhui (動) adorn; decorate

【點燃】diǎnrán (動) light; ignite

【點頭】diǎntóu (動) nod: 同他有～之交 have a nodding acquaintance with him

【點頭哈腰】diǎntóu hāyāo (動) bow and scrape

黜 chù (動) dismiss; remove sb. from office

【黜免】chùmiǎn (動) dismiss from office; remove from office

黝 yǒu (形) black; dark: 皮膚～黑 dark-skinned

點 xiá (形) 〈書〉clever and cunning

黢 qū (形) dark; black

【黢黑】qūhēi (形) pitch-dark

黨 dǎng Ⅰ (名) ❶ political party: 執政～ the ruling party ❷ group; clique: 結～營私 band together for personal gains ❸ (Dǎng) a surname Ⅱ (動) favour; be partial to

【黨羽】dǎngyǔ (名) henchman

【黨同伐異】dǎng tóng fá yì (成) gang up with those who share the same views and attack those who do not; engage in factional strife

【黨委】dǎngwěi (名) party committee

【黨性】dǎngxìng (名) party spirit

【黨紀】dǎngjì (名) party discipline

【黨風】dǎngfēng (名) work style of

a party

【黨派】dǎngpài（名）political parties; factions

【黨徒】dǎngtú（名）member of a clique

【黨員】dǎngyuán（名）party member

【黨章】dǎngzhāng（名）party constitution

【黨報】dǎngbào（名）party newspaper; party organ

【黨綱】dǎnggāng（名）party programme; party platform

【黨魁】dǎngkuí（名）party boss

【黨籍】dǎngjí（名）party membership

黯 àn（形）gloomy; dim

【黯然】ànrán Ⅰ（形）dim; faint Ⅱ（副）unhappily: ～淚下 shed tears in sadness

黷 dú（動）❶ act recklessly ❷ blacken; tarnish

【黷武】dúwǔ（動）wantonly engage in military aggression

黿 部

黿 yuán

【黿魚】yuányú（名）soft-shelled turtle

鼎 部

鼎 dǐng（名）ancient cooking vessel; tripod

【鼎立】dǐnglì（名）tripartite equilibrium

【鼎足之勢】dǐng zú zhī shì〈成〉a situation of tripartite confrontation

【鼎沸】dǐngfèi（形）❶ noisy and confused: 人聲～。There is a scene of noise and confusion. ❷（of situation）unstable; seething with unrest

【鼎盛】dǐngshèng（名）period of great prosperity

【鼎鼎大名】dǐngdǐng dàmíng（形）celebrated; renowned

鼓 部

鼓 gǔ Ⅰ（名）drum Ⅱ（動）❶ beat; strike; sound ❷ blow with bellows ❸ rouse; summon: ～足幹勁 go all out ❹ swell; bulge

【鼓吹】gǔchuī（動）advocate; preach

【鼓風爐】gǔfēnglú（名）〈冶〉blast furnace

【鼓動】gǔdòng（動）agitate; arouse; incite

【鼓掌】gǔzhǎng（動）clap one's hands; applaud

【鼓舞】gǔwǔ（動）inspire; rouse; hearten: 歡欣～ be exultant

【鼓樓】gǔlóu（名）drum-tower

【鼓膜】gǔmó（名）〈生理〉eardrum; tympanic membrane

【鼓噪】gǔzào（動）clamour; create an uproar

【鼓勵】gǔlì（動）encourage; urge

鼠 部

鼠 shǔ (名) mouse; rat

【鼠目寸光】shǔ mù cùn guāng〈成〉a mouse sees only an inch; be short-sighted

【鼠疫】shǔyì (名) black death; plague

【鼠輩】shǔbèi (名) ignoble creatures

【鼠竄】shǔcuàn (動) run away like a frightened rat; scamper off

鼬 yòu (名)〈動〉weasel: 黃 ~ yellow weasel

【鼬獾】yòuhuān (名) ferret badger

鼹 yǎn

【鼹鼠】yǎnshǔ (名) mole

鼷 xī

【鼷鼠】xīshǔ (名) house mouse

鼻 部

鼻 bí (名) nose; snout: 嗤之以 ~ sneer at

【鼻子】bízi (名) nose; snout

【鼻孔】bíkǒng (名) nostril: 一 ~ 出 氣, parrot each other's words

【鼻兒】bír (名)〈方〉❶ eye; hole in an article or utensil for a string, etc. to pass through ❷〈口〉whistle: 打響 ~ (of a horse, mule, etc.) snort

【鼻青臉腫】bíqīng liǎnzhǒng (形) with one's face badly bruised; beaten black and blue

【鼻音】bíyīn (名)〈語〉nasal sound: ~ 很重 speak with a nasal twang

【鼻祖】bízǔ (名) founder; originator; father

【鼻涕】bítì (名) nasal mucus: 擤 ~ blow one's nose

【鼻息】bíxī (名) breath: ~ 粗 breathe heavily

【鼻煙】bíyān (名) snuff: ~ 壺 snuff bottle

【鼻竇】bídòu (名)〈生理〉nasal sinus: ~ 炎 nasosinusitis

鼾 hān (名) snore

齊 部

齊 qí I (形) ❶ neat; in good order: 把椅子放 ~ put the chairs in order ❷ alike; similar: 心 ~ be of one mind ❸ simultaneous; together: ~ 頭並進 keep pace with one another ❹ all ready; complete: 菜來 ~ 了。The last course has been served. ❺ to or at the level of: 河水 ~ 腰深。The river is waist-deep. II (名) (Qí) a surname

【齊心協力】qí xīn xié lì〈成〉work in concert (with)

【齊名】qímíng (動) (of two persons) be equally celebrated for their achievements: 唐代詩人中, 李白與杜甫 ~。Of the Tang poets, Li Bai and Du Fu enjoyed equal fame.

【齊全】qíquán (形) (of stock, etc.) complete; available in a great variety

【齊備】qíbèi (形) all ready; complete

【齊聲】qíshēng（副）in chorus; in unison

齎 zhāi（名）❶ room or building: 書～ study ❷ vegetarian diet adopted for religious reasons: 吃～ be on a vegetarian diet ❸ fast

【齋戒】zhāijiè（名）fast

齏 jī（形）fine: ～粉 fine powder; bits

齒　部

齒 chǐ（名）❶ tooth: 齲～ decayed tooth ❷ anything resembling the tooth in shape: 鋸～ sawtooth

【齒輪】chǐlún（名）gear

【齒齦】chǐyín（名）〈生理〉gum

齟 jǔ

【齟齬】jǔyǔ（名）squabble; dispute; disagreement: 雙方發生～ fall out with each other

齡 líng（名）❶ age ❷ length（of time）: 工～ years of service

鮑 bāo

【鮑牙】bāoyá（名）bucktooth

鮋 chū（量）（of traditional Chinese operas）: 一～戲 an opera

齦 yín（名）〈生理〉gum

齷 wò

【齷齪】wòchuò（形）filthy; foul

齲 qū

【齲齒】qǔchǐ（名）❶ dental caries

❷ decayed tooth

龍　部

龍 lóng Ⅰ（名）❶ dragon ❷（Lóng）a surname Ⅱ（形）imperial

【龍王】lóngwáng（名）the Dragon King（God of the Sea in Chinese mythology）

【龍井】lóngjǐng（名）longjing tea; Dragon Well tea

【龍爭虎鬥】lóng zhēng hǔ dòu（成）battle of the Titans

【龍卷風】lóngjuǎnfēng（名）tornado; cyclone

【龍飛鳳舞】lóng fēi fèng wǔ（成）（of calligraphy）lively and vigorous strokes

【龍骨】lónggǔ（名）keel

【龍套】lóngtào（名）minor role; walk-on part: 跑～ play a minor role in a performance; do a trivial job

【龍船】lóngchuán（龍舟 lóngzhōu）（名）dragon boat

【龍眼】lóngyǎn（名）longan

【龍蝦】lóngxiā（名）lobster

【龍潭虎穴】lóng tán hǔ xué（成）dangerous place; lion's lair

【龍燈】lóngdēng（名）dragon lantern

【龍頭】lóngtóu（名）❶ tap; faucet ❷ lead; a person or thing that plays the leading or pioneering role

【龍鍾】lóngzhōng（名）doddery; senility

龐 páng Ⅰ（形）❶ enormous ❷ multifarious Ⅱ（名）❶ face: 面～ face ❷（Páng）a surname

【龐大】pángdà（形）enormous; gigantic: 機構~ an unwieldy organization / 開支~ an enormous expenditure / ~的正規軍 a massive regular army

【龐然大物】pángrán dàwù（名）colossal creature; sth. cumbersome

【龐雜】pángzá（形）numerous and disorderly

龔 Gōng（名）a surname

龕 kān（名）niche

龜 部

龜 guī（名）tortoise
see also jūn

龜 jūn
see also guī

【龜裂】jūnliè（動）❶（of a parched field) be full of cracks ❷（of skin) chap

附錄（Appendices）

漢語拼音方案

Scheme for the Chinese Phonetic Alphabet

一　字母表

字母:	Aa	Bb	Cc	Dd	Ee	Ff	Gg
名稱:	ㄚ	ㄅㄝ	ㄘㄝ	ㄉㄝ	ㄜ	ㄝㄈ	ㄍㄝ

	Hh	Ii	Jj	Kk	Ll	Mm	Nn
	ㄏㄚ	ㄧ	ㄐㄧㄝ	ㄎㄝ	ㄝㄌ	ㄝㄇ	ㄋㄝ

	Oo	Pp	Qq	Rr	Ss	Tt	
	ㄛ	ㄆㄝ	ㄑㄧㄡ	ㄚㄦ	ㄝㄙ	ㄊㄝ	

	Uu	Vv	Ww	Xx	Yy	Zz
	ㄨ	ㄪㄝ	ㄨㄚ	ㄒㄧ	ㄧㄚ	ㄗㄝ

v 只用來拼寫外來語、少數民族語言和方言。

字母的手寫體依照拉丁字母的一般書寫習慣。

二　聲母表

b	p	m	f		d	t	n	l
ㄅ玻	ㄆ坡	ㄇ摸	ㄈ佛		ㄉ得	ㄊ特	ㄋ訥	ㄌ勒

g	k	h			j	q	x
ㄍ哥	ㄎ科	ㄏ喝			ㄐ基	ㄑ欺	ㄒ希

zh	ch	sh	r		z	c	s
ㄓ知	ㄔ蚩	ㄕ詩	ㄖ日		ㄗ資	ㄘ雌	ㄙ思

在給漢字註音的時候，爲了使拼式簡短，zh ch sh 可以省作 ẑ ĉ ŝ。

三　韻母表

	i 丨　衣	u ㄨ　烏	ü ㄩ　迂
a ㄚ　啊	ia 丨ㄚ　呀	ua ㄨㄚ　蛙	
o ㄛ　喔		uo ㄨㄛ　窩	
e ㄜ　鵝	ie 丨ㄝ　耶		üe ㄩㄝ　約
ai ㄞ　哀		uai ㄨㄞ　歪	
ei ㄟ　欸		uei ㄨㄟ　威	
ao ㄠ　熬	iao 丨ㄠ　腰		
ou ㄡ　歐	iou 丨ㄡ　憂		
an ㄢ　安	ian 丨ㄢ　煙	uan ㄨㄢ　彎	üan ㄩㄢ　冤
en ㄣ　恩	in 丨ㄣ　因	uen ㄨㄣ　溫	ün ㄩㄣ　暈
ang ㄤ　昂	iang 丨ㄤ　央	uang ㄨㄤ　汪	
eng ㄥ　亨的韻母	ing 丨ㄥ　英	ueng ㄨㄥ　翁	
ong (ㄨㄥ)轟的韻母	iong ㄩㄥ　雍		

(1) "知、蚩、詩、日、資、雌、思"等七個音節的韻母用 i，即：知、蚩、詩、日、資、雌、思等字拼作 zhi, chi, shi, ri, zi, ci, si。

(2) 韻母儿寫成 er，用做韻尾的時候寫成 r。例如："兒童"拼作 ertong，"花兒"拼作 huar。

(3) 韻母ㄝ單用的時候寫成 ê。

(4) i 行的韻母，前面沒有聲母的時候，寫成：yi(衣)，ya(呀)，ye(耶)，

yao(腰), you(憂), yan(煙), yin(因), yang(央), ying(英), yong(雍)。

u 行的韻母,前面沒有聲母的時候,寫成:wu(烏), wa(蛙), wo(窩), wai(歪), wei(威), wan(彎), wen(溫), wang(汪), weng(翁)。

ü 行的韻母,前面沒有聲母的時候,寫成:yu(迂), yue(約), yuan(冤), yun(暈);ü 上兩點省略。

ü 行的韻母跟聲母 j, q, x 拼的時候,寫成:ju(居), qu(區), xu(虛),ü 上兩點也省略;但是跟聲母 n, l 拼的時候,仍然寫成:nü(女), lü(呂)。

(5) iou, uei, uen 前面加聲母的時候,寫成:iu, ui, un。例如 niu(牛), gui(歸), lun(論)。

(6) 在給漢字註音的時候,爲了使拼式簡短,ng 可以省作 ŋ。

四　聲調符號

<table>
<tr><td>陰平</td><td>陽平</td><td>上聲</td><td>去聲</td></tr>
<tr><td>-</td><td>ˊ</td><td>ˇ</td><td>ˋ</td></tr>
</table>

聲調符號標在音節的主要母音上,輕聲不標。例如:

媽 mā	麻 má	馬 mǎ	罵 mà	嗎 ma
(陰平)	(陽平)	(上聲)	(去聲)	(輕聲)

五　隔音符號

a, o, e 開頭的音節連接在其他音節後面的時候,如果音節的界限發生混淆,用隔音符號(')隔開,例如:pi'ao(皮襖)。

漢語拼音聲母韻母和
國際音標對照表

Consonants and Vowels of the Chinese Phonetic Alphabet and Their Corresponding International Phonetic Symbols

漢語拼音	國際音標	漢語拼音	國際音標
b	[p]	s	[s]
p	[pʻ]	zh	[tʂ]
m	[m]	ch	[tʂʻ]
f	[f]	sh	[ʂ]
d	[t]	r	[ʐ]
t	[tʻ]		
n	[n]	y	[j]
l	[l]	w	[w]
g	[k]		
k	[kʻ]	a	[a]
h	[x]	o	[o]
j	[tɕ]	e	[ə]
q	[tɕʻ]	i	[i]
x	[ɕ]	u	[u]
z	[ts]	ü	[y]
c	[tsʻ]	-i	[ɿ][ʅ]*

---

* [ɿ]用於 z c s 後，[ʅ]用於 zh ch sh r 後。

漢語拼音	國際音標	漢語拼音	國際音標
ê	[ɛ]	ian	[ian]
er	[ɚ]	in	[in]
		iang	[iaŋ]
ai	[ai]	ing	[iŋ]
ei	[ei]	iong	[yŋ]
ao	[au]	ua	[ua]
ou	[əu]	uo	[uə]
an	[an]	uai	[uai]
en	[ən]	ui, uei	[uei]
ang	[aŋ]	uan	[uan]
eng	[əŋ]	un, uen	[uən]
ong	[uŋ]	ueng	[uəŋ]
ia	[ia]	uang	[uaŋ]
ie	[iɛ]	üe	[yɛ]
iao	[iau]	üan	[yan]
iu, iou	[iəu]	ün	[yn]

中國歷史年代簡表

A Brief Chinese Chronology

夏 Xia Dynasty		約前 21 世紀 – 約前 16 世紀
商 Shang Dynasty		約前 16 世紀 – 約前 11 世紀
周 Zhou Dynasty	西 周 Western Zhou Dynasty	約前 11 世紀 – 前 771
	東 周 Eastern Zhou Dynasty	前 770 – 前 256
	春 秋 Spring and Autumn Period	前 770 – 前 476
	戰 國 Warring States	前 475 – 前 221
秦 Qin Dynasty		前 221 – 前 206
漢 Han Dynasty	西 漢 Western Han	前 206 – 公元 24
	東 漢 Eastern Han	25 – 220
三 國 Three Kingdoms	魏 Wei	220 – 265
	蜀 漢 Shu Han	221 – 263
	吳 Wu	222 – 280
西 晉 Western Jin Dynasty		265 – 316

東晉 Eastern Jin Dynasty			317 – 420
南北朝 Northern and Southern Dynasties	南朝 Southern Dynasties	宋 Song	420 – 479
		齊 Qi	479 – 502
		梁 Liang	502 – 557
		陳 Chen	557 – 589
	北朝 Northern Dynasties	北魏 Northern Wei	386 – 534
		東魏 Eastern Wei	534 – 550
		北齊 Northern Qi	550 – 577
		西魏 Western Wei	535 – 556
		北周 Northern Zhou	557 – 581
隋 Sui Dynasty			581 – 618
唐 Tang Dynasty			618 – 907
五代 Five Dynasties	後梁 Later Liang		907 – 923
	後唐 Later Tang		923 – 936
	後晉 Later Jin		936 – 946
	後漢 Later Han		947 – 950
	後周 Later Zhou		951 – 960

宋 Song Dynasty	北宋 Northern Song Dynasty	960 – 1127
	南宋 Southern Song Dynasty	1127 – 1279
遼 Liao Dynasty		916 – 1125
金 Jin Dynasty		1115 – 1234
元 Yuan Dynasty		1271 – 1368
明 Ming Dynasty		1368 – 1644
清 Qing Dynasty		1644 – 1911
中華民國 Republic of China		1912 – 1949
中華人民共和國 People's Republic of China		1949 成立

中國各省、自治區、直轄市的名稱、簡稱及其人民政府所在地

Names and Abbreviations of China's Provinces, Autonomous Regions and Municipalities Directly under the Central Government and Their Seats of the People's Government

名　稱 Name	簡稱 Abbreviation	人民政府所在地 Seat of the People's Government
北京市 Beijing Shi	京 Jing	北京市 Beijing Shi
上海市 Shanghai Shi	滬 Hu	上海市 Shanghai Shi
天津市 Tianjin Shi	津 Jin	天津市 Tianjin Shi
河北省 Hebei Sheng	冀 Ji	石家莊市 Shijiazhuang Shi
山西省 Shanxi Sheng	晉 Jin	太原市 Taiyuan Shi
內蒙古自治區 Nei Menggu Zizhiqu	內蒙古 Nei Menggu	呼和浩特市 Huhehaote Shi
遼寧省 Liaoning Sheng	遼 Liao	瀋陽市 Shenyang Shi
吉林省 Jilin Sheng	吉 Ji	長春市 Changchun Shi
黑龍江省 Heilongjiang Sheng	黑 Hei	哈爾濱市 Harbin Shi
山東省 Shandong Sheng	魯 Lu	濟南市 Ji'nan Shi
河南省 Henan Sheng	豫 Yu	鄭州市 Zhengzhou Shi
江蘇省 Jiangsu Sheng	蘇 Su	南京市 Nanjing Shi

安徽省 Anhui Sheng	皖 Wan	合肥市 Hefei Shi
浙江省 Zhejiang Sheng	浙 Zhe	杭州市 Hangzhou Shi
江西省 Jiangxi Sheng	贛 Gan	南昌市 Nanchang Shi
福建省 Fujian Sheng	閩 Min	福州市 Fuzhou Shi
臺灣省 Taiwan Sheng	臺 Tai	
湖北省 Hubei Sheng	鄂 E	武漢市 Wuhan Shi
湖南省 Hunan Sheng	湘 Xiang	長沙市 Changsha Shi
廣東省 Guangdong Sheng	粵 Yue	廣州市 Guangzhou Shi
廣西壯族自治區 Guangxi Zhuangzu Zizhiqu	桂 Gui	南寧市 Nanning Shi
甘肅省 Gansu Sheng	甘 Gan 隴 Long	蘭州市 Lanzhou Shi
青海省 Qinghai Sheng	青 Qing	西寧市 Xining Shi
寧夏回族自治區 Ningxia Huizu Zizhiqu	寧 Ning	銀川市 Yinchuan Shi
陝西省 Shaanxi Sheng	陝 Shaan	西安市 Xi'an Shi
新疆維吾爾自治區 Xinjiang Weiwuer Zizhiqu	新 Xin	烏魯木齊市 Wulumuqi Shi
四川省 Sichuan Sheng	川 Chuan 蜀 Shu	成都市 Chengdu Shi
貴州省 Guizhou Sheng	貴 Gui 黔 Qian	貴陽市 Guiyang Shi
雲南省 Yunnan Sheng	雲 Yun 滇 Dian	昆明市 Kunming Shi
西藏自治區 Xizang Zizhiqu	藏 Zang	拉薩市 Lasa Shi
海南省 Hainan Sheng	瓊 Qiong	海口市 Haikou Shi

十二生肖

Chinese Zodiac

Each Chinese year is popularly known by one of the following 12 animals of the Chinese Zodiac:

鼠(子)	Rat	1924, 1936, 1948, 1960, 1972, 1984, 1996, 2008, 2020
牛(丑)	Ox	1925, 1937, 1949, 1961, 1973, 1985, 1997, 2009, 2021
虎(寅)	Tiger	1926, 1938, 1950, 1962, 1974, 1986, 1998, 2010, 2022
兔(卯)	Rabbit	1927, 1939, 1951, 1963, 1975, 1987, 1999, 2011, 2023
龍(辰)	Dragon	1928, 1940, 1952, 1964, 1976, 1988, 2000, 2012, 2024
蛇(巳)	Serpent	1929, 1941, 1953, 1965, 1977, 1989, 2001, 2013, 2025
馬(午)	Horse	1930, 1942, 1954, 1966, 1978, 1990, 2002, 2014, 2026
羊(未)	Sheep	1931, 1943, 1955, 1967, 1979, 1991, 2003, 2015, 2027
猴(申)	Monkey	1932, 1944, 1956, 1968, 1980, 1992, 2004, 2016, 2028
鷄(酉)	Rooster	1933, 1945, 1957, 1969, 1981, 1993, 2005, 2017, 2029
狗(戌)	Dog	1934, 1946, 1958, 1970, 1982, 1994, 2006, 2018, 2030
豬(亥)	Boar	1935, 1947, 1959, 1971, 1983, 1995, 2007, 2019, 2031

國際時間計算表

International Time Calculator

國家　　　　country		標準時間
澳大利亞（悉尼、墨爾本） AUSTRALIA (Sydney, Melbourne)		+ 10
緬甸 BURMA		+ 6.30
加拿大 CANADA	東部時間 Eastern Time 太平洋標準時間 Pacific Time	− 5 − 8
中國 CHINA		+ 8
丹麥 DENMARK		+ 1
埃塞俄比亞 ETHIOPIA		+ 3
法國 FRANCE		+ 1
德國 GERMANY		+ 1
伊朗 IRAN		+ 3.30
伊拉克 IRAQ		+ 3
意大利 ITALY		+ 1
日本 JAPAN		+ 9
朝鮮民主主義人民共和國 DEMOCRATIC PEOPLE'S REPUBLIC OF KOREA		+ 9
科威特 KUWAIT		+ 3
巴基斯坦 PAKISTAN		+ 5
菲律賓 PHILIPPINES		+ 8
羅馬尼亞 ROMANIA		+ 2
新加坡 SINGAPORE		+ 8
瑞典 SWEDEN		+ 1

瑞士 SWITZERLAND	+ 1
泰國 THAILAND	+ 7
土耳其 TURKEY	+ 2
阿拉伯聯合酋長國 UNITED ARAB EMIRATES	+ 4
英國 UNITED KINGDOM	格林威治 標準時間
美國 U.S.A 東部時間 Eastern Time 太平洋標準時間 Pacific Time	− 5 − 8
俄羅斯(莫斯科) RUSSIA(MOSCOW)	+ 3

本表所列各國標準時間是格林威治標準時間差,快(+)或慢(−)幾小時和
幾分鐘。

Standard Clock Time is shown in hours and minutes fast(+) or slow(−) of
Greenwich Mean Time (G. M. T.)